jp Biz-Je

By Brian G

24th edition

ISBN 0 9517166 1 1

30 colour photos

Published and Distributed by:

**BUCHair (U.K.), Ltd.
P.O. Box 89
Reigate, Surrey RH2 7FG**

**Phone: (0737) 76 28 30
Telefax: (0737) 76 28 73**

Correct through January 1991
Printed in Great Britain

Copyright © by BUCHair (U.K.), Ltd. 1991

No part of this publication may be reproduced, stored in a retrieval system, or transmitted, in any form or by any means, electronic, mechanical, photocopying, recording and/or otherwise, without the prior written permission of the publishers.

Acknowledgements

My sincere thanks are due to the following for their invaluable help: Falcon Jet Corp., Dassault International, British Aerospace PLC., Bombardier Inc., IATS Inc., Aviation Research Co., Dan Willink-American Register Quarterly, Air Britain Digest, Aviation Letter, A. Heumann for Swiss allocations, P. Gerhardt for West German data, F. Løvenvig for Danish update, W. Bigsworth for Australian information, Pierre Parvaud for French allocations, P. Thompson for G2B retrofit dates, P. Longley, D. Milne, J. Rose, D. Day, D. Oldfield, J. Birch and to the many other enthusiasts and companies who provided little but essential data.

Where to get the products of BUCHair (U.K.) Ltd. and Bucher Publications?

If you cannot get your **jp Biz-Jet** or **jp airline-fleets** international at your local bookstore or if you need information about publication dates or prices, please contact the following organizations in, or nearest to, your country:

Australia:	Danmark:	BR Deutschland:	Finland:	France:
Mr. James L. Bell BUCHER PUBLICATIONS (Australia) P.O. Box 70 Riddell, Victoria 3431	NYBODER BOGHANDEL ApS 114 Store Kongensgade DK-1264 Copenhagen K Phone: 33 32 33 20 Telefax: 33 32 33 62	BUCHER PUBLIKATIONEN Postfach 44 CH-8058 Zürich-Flughafen Schweiz Postcheckkonto: Ffm 3010 21-604 Telefon: 0041 1 810 03 11 Telefax: 0041 1 810 85 45	AKATEEMINEN KIRJA- KAUPPA Keskuskatu 1 SF-00101 Helsinki Phone: (90) 121 41 Telefax: (90) 121 44 41	LA MAISON DU LIVRE 75, Boulevard Malesherbes F-75008 Paris Phone: (1) 45 22 74 16 Telefax: (1) 42 93 81 23

Great Britain (mailorder):	Great Britain (pick-up):	Ireland:	Israel:	Italy:
BUCHair (U.K.), Ltd. P.O. Box 89 Reigate, Surrey RH2 7FG Phone: (0737) 24 14 64 Telefax: (0737) 76 28 73	BUCHair (U.K.), Ltd. 28 Station Road, Room 4 Redhill, Surrey RH1 1PD Phone: (0737) 24 14 64 Telefax: (0737) 76 28 73	IRISH AIR LETTER Mr. Paul Cunniffe 25 Phoenix Ave./Pecks Lane Castleknock Dublin 15	HAKHEN AGENCIES, Ltd. 44 Derech Petah-Tikva P.O. Box 36125 Tel Aviv 61361 Phone: (03) 37 59 85 Telefax: (03) 37 68 07	LA BANCARELLA AERONAUTICA Corso Peschiera, 146 I-10138 Torino Phone: (011) 37 79 08 Telefax: (011) 37 79 08

Japan:	Netherlands:	North America:	Norway:	Österreich:
NISHIYAMA YOSHO Co. Ltd. Takin Bldg. 3F 4-7-11, Ginza, Chuo-ku Tokyo 104 Phone: (03) 562-0820 Telefax: (03) 562-0828	BOEKHANDEL VENSTRA B.V. Binnenhof 50 Postbus 77 NL-1180 AB Amstelveen Phone: (020) 41 98 80	World Transport Press, Inc. 1224 N.W. 72nd Avenue P.O. Box 521238 Miami, FL 33152-1238 Phone: (800) 875-6711 Telefax: (305) 599-1995	NARVESEN, A/S P.O. Box 6125 - Etterstad N-0602 Oslo 6 Phone: (02) 68 40 20 Telefax: (02) 68 53 47	BUCHER PUBLIKATIONEN Postfach 44 CH-8058 Zürich-Flughafen Schweiz Telefon: 050 1 810 03 11 Telefax: 050 1 810 85 45

Portugal:	Schweiz und Liechtenstein (Bestellungen):	Schweiz und Liechtenstein (Abholer):	South Africa:	Spain:
MR. PAULO NUNO MARQUES MENGO Apartado 413 P-2405 Leiria Codex	BUCHER PUBLIKATIONEN Postfach 44 CH-8058 Zürich-Flughafen Postcheckkonto: Zürich 80-30353-6 Telefon: (01) 810 03 11 Telefax: (01) 810 85 45	BUCHairSHOP BUCHER PUBLIKATIONEN Kanalstrasse 17, 2. Stock CH-8152 Glattbrugg Telefon: (01) 810 03 11 Telefax: (01) 810 85 45	THE AVIATION SHOP Mr. Karel Zayman P.O. Box 316 Melville 2109	LA AERTOTECA LIBRERIA MIGUEL CREUS C/Congost, 11 E-08024 Barcelona Phone: (93) 210 54 07 Telefax: (93) 210 59 92

Sweden:
ESSELTE BOKHANDEL Gamla Brogatan 26 Box 62 SE-101 20 Stockholm Phone: (08) 23 79 90 Telefax: (08) 24 25 43

The front cover and frontispiece illustrations were provided by British Aerospace PLC and International Jet Aviations Services of Denver, Colorado.

Introduction

"The state of business aviation is not bad, but uncertainties about the economy may affect the industry, and rising interest rates could trigger a serious recession."

(NBAA, Washington, DC)

British Aerospace has introduced the 125/700-2 giving a range of 2700 nm upgraded EFIS avionics, new interior, custom paint and airframe/avionics warranties. The 125/800 has now sold over 200 units worldwide. The 4150 nm range, 33" fuselage stretch BAe 1000, powered by PW305 turbofans, is now in flight test and certification is expected in 1991. Initial orders exceed 20 units.

Production of Cessna's Citation SII and III have ceased at 160 and 200 units respectively. They will be replaced in 1991 by the VI, an economy version of the II, and the VII in 1992, which features enhanced performance with more powerful versions of the Garrett TFE731 engine. Orders for the lightweight FJ44 powered 525 Citationjet exceed 100, and deliveries of the II and V have reached 675 and 100 respectively. Unveiled at this year's NBAA was the Citation X, "the fastest business jet in history", powered by twin Allison GMA3007 engines. First flight is anticipated early 1993.

Bombardier Inc. acquired Learjet Corp. in 1990, and, in addition to the current 31 and 35 models, will be introducing an enhanced 31A version, and a stretched re-engined PW305 Series 60 as a replacement for the Learjet 55. On the larger side Canadair Challenger sales now stand over 230 worldwide.

Top of the range Gulfstream 4 continues to outspace its French rival with 150 now delivered. Gulfstream Aerospace and the Soviet Sukhoi Design Bureau have reaffirmed their plan to build a supersonic business jet, should the market assessment show enough potential. First American Aviation are offering G-2/G-3 retrofits replacing the Spey with Tay engines.

Dassault's Falcon 900 has almost reached a 100 sales. The Falcon 50 progresses well with 212 units sold. Considerable competition exists for the Falcon 20 retrofit programme. Garrett claims 60 sales for its TFE731-5AR, whilst Volpar and Flight Safety Group are just entering with the PW305 programmes. Dassault's next project is the Falcon 2000 8-10 passenger, large cabin, cruise at M.8/M.85 and 41 000 ft, powered by advanced GE/Garrett CFE738 turbofans.

The Astra SP has made considerable inroads into the mid-sized market with good sales in North and Latin America. First flight of the Swearingen-Jaffe FJ44 powered SJ30 light twin is anticipated by year end. Beech Aircraft, winner of the TTTS programme with its Beechjet (Jayhawk), has commenced 400A deliveries with strong sales, especially in Europe.

This 24th edition maintains the same format as previous years, even with the new publishers. Production lists are an excellent reference source for sales and marketing.

February 1991   *Brian Gates*

Dear Reader

jp Biz-Jet 1991 is the 24th edition of the original annual directory of bizjets. It is the first time, that this book is being produced by BUCH**air** (U.K.) Ltd. As a sister company of **Bucher Publications**, **Zurich-Airport**, Switzerland, who has been producing the world's famous original-fleetlist-reference-yearbook **jp airline-fleets** international since 1966, we had a very successful start-up year.

In order to fulfill the needs of several customers, we had to look for a database of all bizjets available, and since Brian Gates is unquestionably the leading authority on this subject, it was only logical for us to approach him and ask him to join our fast growing ship. After not having produced a «**Biz-Jet 1990**», Brian was left with a lot of changes of the data, but was not able to release them to you – his customers!

BUCH**air** (U.K.) Ltd. will make sure that the **jp Biz-Jet** will be published regularly in the future at about the same time of the year.

Due to the fact, that time was very short this first year of publication through BUCH**air** (U.K.) Ltd., there have not been made many changes to the general layout and the way of printing.

We also did not want to change the well established appearance of the book, as thousands of readers were used to it. But it is our intention to bring the «look», the «layout» and the «printing quality» to the standard of the **jp airline-fleets** international, while keeping about the current size.

BUCH**air** (U.K.) Ltd. is also specialized in developing computer software for the processing of the data provided by **Bucher Publications**, **Zurich-Airport**, for the **jp airline-fleets** international and by **Brian Gates** for the **jp Biz-Jet**. The data are also available electronically either as BUCH**air**DATA without any software or as BUCH**air**DATABASE with software working on IBM MS-DOS compatible computers.

The possibilities of such a database are tremendous and very fast becoming the essential tool of the World's leading aircraft brokers, dealers, insurers, manufacturers, maintenance companies, airport operators and government-agencies etc.

BUCH**air** (U.K.) Ltd. is also the general-sales-agency handling wholesale and retail business in Great Britain for all the products of **Bucher Publications**, **Zurich-Airport**, Switzerland; calendars of the Japanese publishers **Tsubasa Publishing**, Tokyo, as well as the products of **World Transport Press, Inc.**, Miami, Florida, such as the quarter colour magazine «**Airliners**» and the monthly official update magazine to the **jp airline-fleets** international – the «**Airliners Monthly News**».

If you have any suggestions or changes to the **jp Biz-Jet 1991**, please do not hesitate to let us know.

The next issue – **jp Biz-Jet 1992** – will be published in early spring 1992 and we hope, that you will again be among our readers.

BUCH**air** (U.K.) Ltd.

February 1991   Ronald P. Harman   F. E. Bucher

The following is a list of civilian and military 'Executive Jets' operating throughout the world. Each aircraft is listed by registration, type, serial/constructors number, owner/operator and previous identity.

Civil operated

Monaco

3A-MGR	Falcon 20F	473	Prince Rainier of Monaco, Nice.	F-GEJR/F-WRQT

Swaziland

3D-AAC	Gulfstream 3	354	Peak Timber Sales (Pty) Ltd. Piggs Peak.	
3D-ACB	Falcon 10	21	Falcon Air Ltd/Rembrandt Tobacco, Capetown, RSA.	(HB-VDT)/F-WJMK
3D-ACT	Citation	550-0237	Peak Timber Sales (Pty) Ltd. Piggs Peak.	N6804M
3D-ADH	Learjet	35A-475	Lonrho, Rand, Johannesburg, RSA.	N3797K/N10873
3D-ADH	Citation	500-0667	Premier Milling, Rand, RSA.	ZS-LHP/N2649D
3D-ADR	Falcon 100	202	Falcon Air Ltd/Rembrandt Tobacco, Capetown, RSA.	F-GDSA/F-WZGD
3D-AEZ	Learjet	25B-160	Schwartz Jeweller Swaziland P/L. Lanseria, RSA.	ZS-MTD/Z-WKY/VP-WKY/ZS-MTD
3D-ART	Falcon 10	61	W/o 3 Oct 86.	F-BFDG/(F-BIPF)/F-WZGD/D-CBMB/F-WPUV
3D-AVL	BAe 125/800B	8025	Anglovaal Group, Lanseria, RSA.	

Israel

4X-...	Astra-1125	003	IAI third prototype, static and fatigue test airframe.	
4X-COA	Jet Commander	71	IAI, Tel Aviv. (Avionics Development Aircraft).	/N721GB/N150HR/N150CT N150CM/N150OM
4X-COJ	Jet Commodore	29	w/o 21 Jan 70.	N615J
4X-WIA	Astra-1125	002	Israel Aircraft Industries, Tel Aviv.	
4X-WIN	Astra-1125	001	wfu 31 Aug 86.	

Libya

5A-DAD	Learjet	23-075	W/o 5 Jun 67.	
5A-DAG	Falcon 20C	143	Libyan Arab Airlines, Benghazi.	F-WMKH
5A-DAJ	JetStar-8	5136	LAA/Government of Libya, Tripoli.	/LAAF001/N5500L
5A-DAK	B 707-3L5C	21228	Government of Libya, Tripoli.	
5A-DAR	JetStar 2	5221	W/o 16 Jan 83.	N5547L
5A-DCK	Corvette	38	Government of Libya, Tripoli. (Air Ambulance).	(F-ODIF)
5A-DCM	Falcon 50	68	Government of Libya, Tripoli.	F-WZHQ
5A-DCO	Falcon 20	190	Directorate of Civil Aviation, Tripoli.	5A-DAH/LAAF002/F-WNGN
5A-DDR	Gulfstream 2	240	Government of Libya, Tripoli.	
5A-DDS	Gulfstream 2	242	Government of Libya, Tripoli.	

Cyprus

5B-CGP	JetStar-731	16/5128	Athenian Jet Aviation/Athens Tanker Manufacturers,	/N26S/N7973S
5B-CHE	Jetstar-731	18/5114	Lenassi Leasing, Athens.	N26GL/N111GU/N94K/N930M/N930MT/N7959S
5B-CHX	Challenger	1028	Seatankers USA Corp. Limassol.	N600ST/HB-VHC/C-GLXM

Tanzania

5H-CCM	F-28-3000	11137	Government of Tanzania, Dar es Salaam. 'Uhuru na Umoja'	PH-ZBS/PH-EXS
5H-SMZ	HS 125/700B	7172	Government of Zanzibar.	G-5-568/5H-SMZ/G-BKFS/5H-SMZ

Nigeria

5N-AER	HS 125/1B-522	25099	Wfu. Located Zaria-Nigeria.	(N121AC)/(N2246)/HB-VAU
5N-AGN	F-28-1000	11049	Federal Military Government, Lagos.	PH-EXG/PH-EXD
5N-AGV	Gulfstream 2	177	Federal Military Government, Lagos.	N17587
5N-AGZ	BAe 125/800B	8143	Central Bank, Lagos.	/5N-NPF/G-5-656
5N-ALH	HS 125/1B	25089	Aero Contractors (Nigeria) Ltd. Lagos.	OO-SKJ/G-ATPB
5N-AMF	HFB 320	1028	W/o 25 Jul 77.	D-CASU
5N-AMR	Citation	550-0045	Ashaka Cement Co Ltd.	N4CR/N4CH/N3284M

Regis-	Type	c/n	Owner / Operator	Previous
tration			Page 5	identity

Registration	Type	c/n	Owner / Operator	Previous identity
5N-AMX	HS 125/700B	7115	Jaguar Aviation/RCN, Lagos.	G-BMIH/(G-5-502)/HZ-DA
5N-AMY	HS 125/F403B	25227	Chief M K O Abiola/RCN, Lagos.	G-MKOA/G-AYF
5N-AOC	Learjet	25D-322	AIC Co. Ltd. Lagos.	
5N-AOG	HS 125/3B-RA	25143	OGI Cargo Co.	G-AVXK/D-CHTH/G-AVXK/G-5-1
5N-AOL	HS 125/600B	6050	Okada Air, Lagos.	G-BLOI/5N-ANG/G-5-1
5N-APN	Citation	500-0286	Nigerian Police Force, Lagos.	N286CC/N5286
5N-ASQ	Learjet	25D-344	W/o 22 Jul 83.	N37943/N3798
5N-ASZ	HS 125/1B	25063	Wfu. Broken up at Southampton-UK 11/86.	G-ONPN/G-BAXG/HB-VA
5N-AVJ	HS 125/700B	7118	Aero Contractors/S I O Properties Ltd. Ikoyi, Lagos.	//(G-BIHZ
5N-AVK	HS 125/700B	7160	Federal Ministry of Aviation (CAFU), Lagos.	/G-5-1
5N-AVL	Citation	501-0317	Civil Aviation Flying Unit.	N2626
5N-AVM	Citation	501-0233	Civil Aviation Flying Unit.	N2626
5N-AVV	HS 125/3B	25138	Intercontinental Airlines Ltd. Lagos.	I-BOGI/HB-VBN/G-AVVA/G-5-1
5N-AVZ	HS 125/3B-RA	25113	Intercontinental Airlines Ltd. Lagos. (status ?).	G-AVDX/(G-5-13
5N-AWB	HS 125/1B	25025	Chagoury & Chagoury Construction. (wfu ?).	(F-OCGK)/F-BOHU/HB-VAR/D-COM
5N-AWD	HS 125/1	25008	Panatrade Ltd. Lagos. (located Luton-UK).	G-ASS
5N-AWJ	Citation	550-0228	Soc Lasies/Jet Fleet (Nigeria) Ltd.	(N702BC)//N6802
5N-AWS	HS 125/600B	6042	W/o 31 Dec 86.	G-BKBU/G-BBRO/5N-AWS/(G-5-505
5N-AXO	HS 125/700B	7196	Government of Nigeria, Lagos.	/G-5-1
5N-AXP	HS 125/700B	7203	W/o 31 Dec 85.	/G-5-1
5N-AYA	Citation	550-0632		N1257
5N-AYK	HS 125/600B	6060	Aero Contractors/Yakamata Air Services, Kano.	G-BFIC/HZ-MF1/G-5-1
5N-FGN	B 727-2N5	22825	Federal Military Government, Lagos.	5N-AG
5N-FGO	Falcon 900	52	Federal Government of Nigeria, Lagos.	F-WWF
5N-FGP	Gulfstream 4	1126	Federal Government of Nigeria, Lagos.	N426G
5N-NPC	BAe 125/800B	8109	Aero Contractors/Nigerian Petroleum Co. Lagos.	G-5-58

Mauritania

5T-RIM	Caravelle 6R	91	Government of Islamic Republic of Mauritania. (wfu ?).	5T-MAL/5T-CJ OY-SBV/PH-TVZ/OY-SBV/N1006
5T-UPR	Gulfstream 2	175	Government of Islamic Republic of Mauretania, Nouakchott.	/HZ-AFG/N1758

Togo

5V-TAA	Gulfstream 2	149	W/o 26 Dec 74.	N17586/N896G
5V-TAF	DC-8-55F	45692	Government of Togo, Lome.	F-RAFB/(F-BOLI)/N801S
5V-TAG	B 707-312B	19739	Government of Togo, Lome.	N600CS/9V-BB

Uganda

5X-UPF	Gulfstream 2	133	Government of Uganda, Entebbe.	N88906/N1758

Senegal

6V-AAR	Caravelle 3	5	Wfu 1 Aug 85. Located Dakar-Senegal.	6V-ACP/F-BHR
6V-AEF	B 727-2M1	21091	Government of Senegal, Dakar.	N40104/(PK-PJP)/N8284
6V-AFL	Gulfstream 2	136	Monair S.A. Celigny, Switzerland/Mbaye Djilly, Dakar.	N207GA/3D-AAC/ZS-JI N65M/N874G

Yemen

7O-ADC	BAe 125/800B	8037	Shaher Traders, Sana'a. 'Anisa IV'.	4W-ACN/G-5-501/G-5-1

Malawi

7Q-YTL	Citation	501-0200	Limbe Leaf Tobacco Co.	/N6783

Algeria

7T-VCW	HS 125/700B	7163	E.N. pour l'Exploitation Meteorlogique et Aeronautique.	/G-5-1
7T-VHB	Gulfstream 2	230	W/o 3 May 82.	N1758
7T-VRE	Falcon 20C	156	W/o 30 May 81.	F-WMK

Barbados

8P-LAD	Gulfstream 2	210	Augusto Lopez/Avianca, Bogota, Colombia.	/G-IIRR/HB-IEY

Malta

9H-ABO	Sabre-65	465-22	Aliserio/Euro Cereal Co Ltd. Turin, Italy.	N678AM/N996W

Zambia

9J-ADU	Citation	500-0153	Mines Air Service/Nchanga Consolidated Copper Mines, Lusaka.	
9J-AEJ	Citation	500-0353	Mines Air Service Ltd. Lusaka.	(N5359J)
9J-RON	Challenger 601	3057	Roan Air/Mines Air Services, Lusaka.	/N19J/C-G...

Kuwait

9K-AEG	Gulfstream 3	408	Kuwait Airways Corp.	
9K-AEH	Gulfstream 3	419	Kuwait Airways Corp.	
9K-AGA	HS 125/700B	7184	Kuwait Airways Corp.	/G-5-12
9K-AGB	HS 125/700B	7187	Kuwait Airways Corp.	/G-5-14

Malaysia

9M-...	Gulfstream 4	1106	Government of Johore. (maybe 9M-ISJ)	N17608
9M-ATM	Falcon 100	216	Hornbill Skyways, Kuching.	VH-JDW/N100H/N276FJ/F-WZGZ
9M-HLG	HS 125/400B	25257	Hornbill Skyways, Kuching, Sarawak.	G-BATA/G-5-19
9M-JMF	Citation	550-0610	Ranlod Aviation Services,	N1242B
9M-SSL	HS 125/700B	7112	Malaysian Helicopter Services, Kuala Lumpur.	(9M-SSS)/G-5-553/G-BNBO G-5-536/D-CMVW

Zaire

9Q-...	Falcon 20D	193	MIBA, Zaire.	N400DB/N37JF/N930L/N4383F/F-WMKG
9Q-CBS	Challenger 601-3A	5061	SCIBE Airlift, Kinshasa.	C-FHHD/C-G...
9Q-CFW	HS 125/600B	6031	Gecamines, Lumbumbashi.	G-5-14
9Q-CGK	Falcon 50	177	ALG Aeroleasing/Gecamines, Kinshasa.	F-WPXF
9Q-RDZ	B 727-30	18934	Government of Republic of Zaire, Kinshasa. 'Ville de Lisala'	VR-CHS/JY-AHS JY-HMH/N62119/D-ABI

Rwanda

9XR-CH	Caravelle 3	209	Government of Rwanda, Kigali.	F-BUFM/YU-AJE/F-BRUJ/LN-KLN
9XR-NN	Falcon 50	6	Government of Rwanda, Kigali.	N815CA/N1871R/N50FB/F-WZHB

Botswana

A2-AGM	Citation	...	Executive Charter P/L.	

Oman

A40-AA	Gulfstream 2TT	183	Sultan H.M. Qaboos bin Said, Seeb. (r/c Oman 3).	N17581
A40-AB	VC 10/1103	820	wfu 7/87,	G-ASIX
A40-CF	B 727-30	18369	Inspector General of Police, Oman.	D-ABIN
A40-HA	Gulfstream 2	214	Sultan H.M. Qaboos bin Said, Seeb. (r/c Oman 4).	G-BSAL/N17582
A40-HMQ	DC-8-73CF	46149	Sultan H.M. Qaboos bin Said, Seeb. (r/c Oman 2).	A40-AA/N803WA/(N6167A)
A40-SC	Citation	550-0486	Oman Aviation Services Co. Jibroo, Muscat.	(N1253Y)
A40-SO	B 747SP-27	21785	Government of Oman, Seeb. (r/c Oman 1).	N351AS/N603BN

United Arab Emirates

A6-...	Falcon 900	86	Government of UAE.	F-W...
A6-...	Falcon 900	84	Government of UAE.	F-WWFD
A6-AAA	B 737-2P6	21613	Government of UAE, Abu Dhabi.	(A6-HHK))/(A40-BI)

Regis-	Type	c/n	Owner / Operator	Previous
tration				identity

Registration	Type	c/n	Owner / Operator	Previous identity
A6-AUH	Falcon 900	...	Government of UAE.	
A6-CKZ	Gulfstream 3	317	Government of Dubai, UAE.	N344GA/C-GKRL
A6-DPA	B 707-330C	20123	Government of UAE.	D-ABUJ
A6-ESH	B 737-2W8	22628	Government of Sharjah.	N180RN
A6-HEH	Gulfstream 3	356	Government of Dubai, UAE.	
A6-HEM	Falcon 20F	344	Dubai Air Wing, UAE.	F-WRQP
A6-HHH	Gulfstream 4	1011	Government of Dubai, UAE.	N17581
A6-HHS	Gulfstream 3	376	Government of Abu Dhabi, UAE.	N17582
A6-HPZ	B 707-3L6B	21049	Sheikh Zayed, Abu Dhabi.	(A6-HHP)/N62393/9M-TDM/N62393
A6-HRM	B 707-3L6C	21096	Ruler of Dubai. (r/c Falcon One).	G-CDHW/9M-TMS/N48055
A6-PFD	Airbus A300C4-620	374	Government of UAE, Abu Dhabi.	F-WWAJ
A6-SHK	BAe 146 Statesman	E1091	Government of UAE, Abu Dhabi.	G-BOMA/G-5-091
A6-SHZ	Airbus A300B4-620	354	Government of UAE, Abu Dhabi.	F-ODRM/(A6-XAI)/F-WZYA
A6-SMR	B 747SP-31	21961	Government of UAE, Dubai.	N58201
A6-UAE	Falcon 900	...	Government of UAE.	
A6-ZKM	Falcon 900	47	Government of Abu Dhabi.	F-WWFA
A6-ZSN	B 747SP-31	23610	Government of UAE.	N60659

Qatar

Registration	Type	c/n	Owner / Operator	Previous identity
A7-...	Falcon 900	91	Qatari Government, Doha.	F-W...
A7-...	Falcon 900	94	Qatari Government, Doha.	F-W...
A7-AAA	B 707-3P1C	21334	Ruler of Qatar, Doha. (r/c Amiri One).	
A7-AAB	B 727-2P1	21595	Qatari Government, Doha. (r/c Amiri Two).	
A7-AAC	B 707-336C	20375	Ruler of Qatar, Doha. (r/c Amiri Three).	G-AXGX

Bahrain

Registration	Type	c/n	Owner / Operator	Previous identity
A9C-BA	B 727-2M7	21824	Government of Bahrain. (r/c Bahraini One).'Al Bahrain'	N740RW
A9C-BB	Gulfstream 3	393	Government of Bahrain.	N17587
A9C-BG	Gulfstream 2TT	202	Government of Bahrain. (r/c Bahraini Two).	N17586

Canada

Registration	Type	c/n	Owner / Operator	Previous identity
C-FAAL	Challenger 601	3005	ALCAN Aluminium Ltd. Montreal.	/C-G...
C-FAAU	BAe 125/800A	8099	ALCAN Aluminium Ltd. Montreal.	N537BA/G-5-565
C-FADL	Citation	500-0067	Air Dorval Ltee. Montreal.	N5301J/XB-DBA/N3PC/N567CC
C-FALI	Citation	S550-0142	Irving Oil Transport Ltd. St John.	N542CC/(N1295M)
C-FANL	HS 125/731	25042	J L Levesque Stables Ltd. Montreal.	
C-FAWW	Westwind-1124	313	Bowes Publishers Ltd. Edmonton.	N146J/4X-CRG
C-FBCL	Citation	500-0042	Voyageur Airways Ltd. Hornell Heights, Ontario.	N542CC
C-FBCM	Citation	500-0071	South West Air Ltd. Windsor, Ontario.	N571CC
C-FBEL	Challenger 601	3028	Execaire/Bell Canada Enterprises, Montreal, PQ.	C-GLXB
C-FBFP	Learjet	35-038	Appeal Enterprises/Canada Jet Charters Ltd. Richmond.	//VH-ELJ/(VH-UDC)
C-FBSS	Falcon 10	87	Dow Chemical Canada Inc. Clearwater.	N682D/N662D/(N200AF)/N167FJ/F-WPXK
C-FCEH	Falcon 200	507	Central Trust Co/159887 Canada Ltd. Moncton, NB.	N200FJ/N220FJ/F-WPUV
C-FCFL	HS 125/400A	NA741	W/o 9 Dec 77.	G-AXTT
C-FCFP	Citation	500-0125	536031 Ontario Ltd (Air One), Mississauga.	
C-FCHJ	Citation	500-0091	Starline Aviation Ltd. Mississauga.	/N50PR/(PT-LAW)/N76RE/N591CC
C-FCLJ	Learjet	55-118	Canada Jet Charters Ltd. Vancouver, BC.	
C-FCPW	Citation Eagle	500-0002	West Wind Aviation Inc. Saskatoon.	N8202Q/(N502CC)
C-FDJQ	Citation	500-0018	Aero 1 Prop-Jet Inc. Sault Ste Marie.	/N222MS/N978EE/(N58AN)/N5QZ/N5Q/N5B N518CC
C-FDTF	JetStar-6	5088	Cx C- 19 Sep 86 to ?	/N9244R
C-FDTX	JetStar-6	5018	Wfu 8/86. Located Rockcliffe Museum-Ottawa.	N9287R
C-FDYL	Citation	550-0341	Sobeys Stores Ltd. Stellarton, NS.	N182U/C-GJAP/N68032
C-FEMA	Citation	S550-0040	Manitoba Emergency Aero-Medical Services, Winnipeg.	(N1269D)
C-FETB	B 720-023B	18024	Canadian Pratt & Whitney Aircraft, Longueuil, PQ.	OD-AFQ/N7538A
C-FEXB	HS 125/700A	NA0306	Execaire Inc. Montreal.	N270MH/N700DD/G-5-17/(G-5-13)
C-FEYG	Jet Commander	81	W/o 26 May 78.	CF-KBI/N6617V
C-FFTM	BAe 125/800A	NA0437	Execaire/Canadian Pacific Forest Products, Montreal.	/G-BPXW/G-5-636
C-FGGH	Westwind-1124	431	Chartright Air Inc. Weston.	N431AM/4X-CUN
C-FHDM	Learjet	35A-410	Hayes-Dana Inc. St. Catherines, Ont.	/N1210M/N12109

Registration	Type	c/n	Owner / Operator	Previous identity
C-FHLL	HS 125/1A	25034	Wfu. Accident 4/83. Wing fitted to s/n 25027.	
C-FHPM	Gulfstream 2	104	American Barrick Resources Corp. Mississauga, Ontario.	/N858W/N856W/N856GA
C-FHSS	HS 125/600A	6003	FHSS Enterprises Inc. Unionville.	N80BH
C-FIGD	Falcon 20C	109	National Research Council of Canada, Ottawa.	/117506/20506/F-WNGM
C-FIMO	Citation	650-0065	Imperial Oil Ltd. Toronto.	N500E/(N1314T)
C-FIPG	HS 125/700A	NA0294	Interhome Energy Inc. Edmonton.	G-BIMY
C-FJES	Falcon 900	55	Execaire/J E Seagram, Montreal.	N439FJ/F-WWFO
C-FLDM	Citation	500-0261	Syncrude Canada Ltd. Fort McMurray.	N41JP/C-FLDM/N40GS/N68616
C-FLPC	Challenger 601-3A	5006	Canadian Pacific Ltd. Montreal.	C-G...
C-FLTL	Citation	650-0007	Odessey Aviation Ltd. Mississauga.	/N929DS/N657CC/(N3Q)/(N13047)
C-FMAN	Citation	500-0086	Toronto Airways Ltd. Markham, Ont.	N503GP/N586CC
C-FMFL	Falcon 50	96	McCain Foods Ltd. Florenceville, N.B.	/N4AC/F-WZHE
C-FMKF	HS 125/3A-RA	NA710	Mackenzie Financial Corp. Toronto, Ont.	N500YB/C-GKCO/N226G/N228G/N223G G-AWMW/N1259K
C-FMPP	Citation	550-0411	Royal Canadian Mounted Police Air Services, Ottawa.	N200YM/N1216N
C-FMWW	Westwind-Two	380	Miller Western Industries Ltd. Edmonton, Alberta.	N380DA/N50DW/4X-CUM
C-FNCG	Gulfstream 2	208	Sugra Ltd/Norcan Energy, Toronto.	/N62CB/N808GA
C-FNER	HS 125/731	NA714	Toronto Dominion Bank/Execaire Aviation, Montreal.	G-AWPD
C-FONX	Falcon 20D	225	Purolator Courier/Soundair Corp. Mississauga, Ont.	N102AD/(N30AD)/N338DB N332FE/N37WT/N25MJ/OH-FFJ/F-BOFH/TR-LRU/TR-KHA/F-WZXD
C-FPCP	BAe 125/800A	8095	Pancanadian Petroleum Ltd. Calgary.	(N500LL)/N200LS/N534BA/G-5-561
C-FPEL	Citation	550-0042	Air Dorval Ltee. Montreal.	N66AT/N57MB/N666RC/(N3283M)
C-FPQG	HS 125/1A	25036	Government of Quebec, Quebec City.	
C-FREE	Falcon 100	224	Perimeter Inland Airlines, Winnipeg.	N128FJ/F-WZGH
C-FROC	Gulfstream 2	134	Ranger Oil (Canada) Ltd. Calgary.	/N806CC
C-FROX	Learjet	25C-070	Ranger Oil (Canada) Ltd. Calgary.	N255GL
C-FROY	Westwind-1124	429	Royal Plastics Ltd. Weston, Ont.	4X-CUK
C-FRPP	BAe 125/800A	NA0414	Execaire/Repap Enterprises Corp. Montreal.	/G-BOTX/N559BA/G-5-593
C-FSDH	HS 125/731	NA724	Kruger Organization/Ledair Ltd. Montreal.	
C-FSEN	HS 125/1A	25027	Government of Quebec. (Air Ambulance).	
C-FSIP	Challenger 600S	1048	Intera Technologies Ltd. Calgary.	N601LS/N600LS/N500LS/N600TT/N29687 C-GLXK
C-FTAM	HS 125/731	25108	Samuel & Sons, Toronto.	N31B/N901TG/N901TC/N1025C/G-ATUY
C-FTEN	Falcon 10	45	Noranda Mines Ltd. Toronto.	N110CG/N120HC/N131FJ/F-WJML
C-FTLA	BAe 125/800A	8015	Husky Oil Operations-Nova Alberta Corp. Calgary.	G-BLPC/G-5-17
C-FTXT	Learjet	25-057	Harvard Developments Ltd. Regina.	
C-FURG	Challenger 601	3063	Government of Quebec, Quebec City. (Air Ambulance).	C-GLYH
C-FWCE	HS 125/700A	NA0344	Westcoast Energy Inc. Vancouver, BC.	N502S/N1C/N710BT/G-5-16
C-FWSC	Falcon 900	75	Windlass Corp. Boston, Ma.	N458FJ/F-WWFC
C-GABX	HS 125/700A	NA0233	Execaire/Nova an Alberta Corp. Calgary.	/G-BFZI
C-GAWH	BAe 125/800A	8087	IMASCO Ltd. Montreal.	/N800TR/N529BA/G-5-552
C-GAZU	JetStar 2	5222	Cathton Holdings Ltd. Edmonton.	N509J/(N509TF)/N509T/N5548L
C-GBCA	Citation	550-0590	Government of British Columbia, Victoria.	(N1302A)
C-GBCB	Citation	550-0051	Government of British Columbia, Victoria.	C-GJAP/N1958E
C-GBCC	Challenger 600S	1005	B C Government Air Services Branch, Sidney, BC.	//N600CL/C-GBDH-X
C-GBCE	Citation	550-0591	Government of British Columbia, Victoria.	(N1302C)
C-GBCK	Citation	500-0204	Government of British Columbia, Victoria.	
C-GBDX	JetStar 2	5219	Bumper Development Corp. Calgary.	N21VB//N107G/N5545L
C-GBFL	Falcon 20F	239	Fletcher Challenge Canada Ltd. Vancouver, B.C.	N1OMT/N4417F/F-WPXM
C-GBFP	Learjet	25B-167	North American Airlines Ltd. Edmonton, Alberta.	
C-GBNE	Citation	500-0378	Province of Manitoba, Winnipeg.	N3156M
C-GBRM	HS 125/700A	NA0266	Gulf Canada Resources/Petro Canada Exploration Ltd. Calgary.	/G-BHMP/G-5-11
C-GBRW	Learjet	36-001	Canadian Pratt & Whitney Aircraft, Longueuil, PQ.	N26GL
C-GBTB	Citation Eagle	501-0138	Beach Industries/Russell Beach, Smith Falls, Ont.	8P-BAB/8P-BAR/(N26509)
C-GBWA	Learjet	24D-261	North American Airlines Ltd. Edmonton, AB.	D-COOL/D-IDAT
C-GBWL	Learjet	35-049	Brooker Wheaton Aviation Ltd. Edmonton.	/N3759C/JY-AEV
C-GCFG	Challenger 601	3022	Govt of Canada, DoT Aircraft Services Directorate, Ottawa.	/C-G...
C-GCFI	Challenger 601	3020	Govt of Canada, DoT Aircraft Services Directorate, Ottawa.	/C-G...
C-GCFP	Citation	650-0145	Canadian Forest Products Ltd. Vancouver, BC.	N1325Z
C-GCGR-X	Challenger	1001	W/o 3 Apr 80.	
C-GCGT	Challenger 601	3991	Bombardier Inc. Montreal. (-X suffix for test flights).	/
C-GCIB	BAe 125/800A	8048	Canadian Imperial Bank of Commerce, Toronto.	(N125BA)/G-BMMO/G-5-16
C-GCJD	Learjet	25B-096	Canada Jet Charters Ltd. Vancouver.	N405RS/N48FN/N742Z/N742E

Registration	Type	c/n	Owner / Operator	Previous identity
C-GCLQ	Citation	500-0348	Bombardier Inc. Montreal.	/N301HC/N300HC/(N5348J)
C-GDDC	Citation	551-0046	Pal Air Ltd/Champs Foods Ltd. Winnipeg.	N6804Y
C-GDDM	Citation	501-0101	247756 Alberta Ltd. Calgary.	N3170M
C-GDJH	Learjet	35A-353	Canada Jet Charters Ltd. Vancouver.	/N3819G
C-GDLR	Citation	550-0062	Interhome Energy Inc. Calgary.	//(N77SF)/(N26615)
C-GDPD	Citation	550-0071	AMOCO Petroleum Canada Ltd. Calgary.	/N4308G
C-GDPF	Citation	550-0112	AMOCO Petroleum Canada Ltd. Calgary.	(C-GDPE)/(N26656)
C-GDUC	Westwind-1124	357	Dupont Canada Inc. Montreal.	(N357W)/4X-CUK
C-GDUP	HS 125/600A	6020	Dupont of Canada Inc.	N334JR/N125CU/N29BH
C-GDWS	Citation Eagle	500-0303	Capital Aviation Services Ltd. Gloucester.	N19U/N19M/(N5303J)
C-GEEN	Learjet	24-087	High Line Drilling International Inc. Edmonton.	D-IKAB/N7VS/CF-UYT/N407V
C-GENJ	Citation	500-0196	Capital Aviation services Ltd. Gloucester.	/N74FC
C-GERC	Citation	S550-0037	ESSO Resources Canada Ltd. Calgary.	(N12616)
C-GERL	Citation	S550-0056	ESSO Resources Canada Ltd. Calgary.	(N1271B)
C-GESO	Westwind-1124	298	ESSO Resources Canada Ltd. Calgary.	N610JA/4X-CQR
C-GESZ	Citation	500-0022	The Craig Evan Corp (Flightexec), London.	N800JD/N522JD/N522CC
C-GFEE	Citation	501-0169	Voyageur Airways Ltd. Hornell Heights, Ontario.	D-IBWG/N2617U
C-GFJB	Learjet	24D-260	Cx C- 12/89 to ?	N60GL
C-GGFW	Citation	550-0276	British Columbia Telephone Ltd. Vancouver. 'Telco Two'	N68649
C-GHYD	Citation	550-0063	Government of B.C. Victoria, B.C.	(N26616)
C-GIAC	Citation	500-0076	Lignum Ltd. Vancouver.	N810SG/N810SC/N576CC
C-GIAD	Citation	500-0185	Innotech Aviation Ltd. Montreal.	N500AZ/N500WP/N500JB/N22FH/N22EH
C-GIOH	Challenger 601-3A	5034	Imperial Oil Ltd. Mississauga, Ontario.	C-G...
C-GIRE	Learjet	35-004	536031 Ontario Ltd (Air One), Toronto.	//N74MJ/N74MB/N74MP
C-GJBJ	HS 125/700A	NA0335	Sears Canada Inc. Toronto.	N702E/N710BX/G-5-18
C-GJEM	Citation Eagle	500-0011	Execaire Inc. Montreal.	/N20FM/N18UR/N13UR//N227H/N511CC
C-GJLK	Westwind-1124	278	Canadian Pacific Forest Products Ltd. Thunder Bay.	N505BC/4X-CNX
C-GJLQ	Citation	500-0058	Air Niagara Express Inc. Etobicoke.	N46RB/N11WQ/N11WC/N558CC
C-GJPG	Challenger 600S	1043	Jim Pattison Industries Ltd. Richmond, BC.	/N229GC/C-GLWX
C-GKCI	HS 125/700A	NA0248	Irving Oil Transport Ltd. Saint John.	G-BGSR/G-5-13
C-GKLB	BAe 125/800A	NA0406	Nova Corp of Alberta, Calgary.	/G-BNZW/G-5-577
C-GKPM	HS 125/700A	NA0239	American Barrick Resources, Toronto.	//N33BK/G-BGBL/G-5-17
C-GLCR	Citation	S550-0140	Luscar Ltd. Edmonton.	(N1295G)
C-GLMK	Citation	551-0143	Northwest International Airways Ltd. NWT. (was 550-0100).	//N140DA/C-FKHD N2S/N801G/(N801L)/N2664T
C-GMAT	Citation	500-0231	Skycraft/General Motors Air Transport, Oshawa, Ont.	/N2TN/N99TD/(N5231J)
C-GMAV	Citation	S550-0067		N550FS/(N1272V)
C-GMEA	HS 125/3A-RA	NA702	Metro Jet Inc. Mississauga.	//N813PR/(N13MJ)/CF-KCI/CF-AAG/G-AVJD
C-GMGB	Citation	S550-0149	Magna International Inc. Markham, Ont.	N149QS
C-GMLC	Citation	500-0305	Capital Aviation Services/Mike Loeb Ltd. Ottawa.	N805BB/N305BB/(N5305J)
C-GMOL	BAe 125/800A	NA0443	Molson Companies Ltd. Toronto.	/G-BRCZ/G-5-639
C-GMSM	Citation	550-0603	Canadian Forest Products Ltd. Richmond, BC.	N603CJ
C-GMTR	BAe 125/800A	NA0435	Alberta Energy Co Ltd.	N800BA/N589BA/G-5-632
C-GMTT	Westwind-1124	288	Alberta Energy Corp. Calgary.	N1124Q/4X-CQH
C-GMTV	Citation	S550-0015	Alberta Energy Co Ltd. Calgary.	(N1258U)
C-GNPT	Learjet	35A-626	Northwood Pulp & Timber Ltd. Prince George, BC.	N711NF/N35AJ/N7261R/N39398
C-GNSA	Citation	500-0160	Brooker Wheaton Aviation Ltd. Edmonton.	N59TS/N146JC/(N146BE)/N146BF
C-GNTL	Falcon 20F	257	Northern Telecom Ltd. Toronto.	N300CC/N781W/N4425F/F-WMKH
C-GNTY	Falcon 20F	330	Northern Telecom Ltd. Ottawa.	N300AL/N4460F/F-WNGM
C-GOCM	Citation	500-0154	Millardair Ltd. Toronto.	
C-GPAW	Citation	550-0004	Canadian Pratt & Whitney Aircraft, Longueuil, P.Q.	N98786
C-GPCO	Citation	500-0317	Ainsworth Lumber Ltd. Kamloops, BC.	N37489/D-ICCA/N5317J
C-GPFC	Westwind-Two	328	PFC Aviation Inc. Edmonton.	/N819JA/N816JA/4X-CRV
C-GPGD	Challenger 601	3039	P G Desmarais/Power Corp of Canada, Montreal.	/C-GLYH
C-GPTR	Citation	550-0078	Ptarmigan Airways Ltd. Yellowknife, NT.	N78GA/N71FM/N31KW/(N2662B)
C-GPUN	Learjet	35-058	Canada Jet Charters Ltd. Vancouver.	/
C-GRBC	Challenger 601	3041	Royal Bank of Canada, Mississauga, Ontario.	C-GLWV
C-GRDP	Westwind-1124	188	McCain Foods, Florenceville, N.B.	N1124G/4X-CKL
C-GRDT	Falcon 10	6	Capital Aviation Services Ltd. Gloucester.	N139DD/N10AG/(N110FJ)/N600BT N102FJ/F-WJML
C-GRHC	Citation	550-0046	Chevron Canada Resources Ltd. Calgary.	(N3292M)
C-GRIO	Citation	550-0133	Air Niagara Express Inc. Etobicoke.	G-BHBH/N2634Y
C-GRIS	Falcon 10	2	Skycharter Ltd. Toronto.	N103JM/N10F/F-WJMM

Registration	Type	c/n	Owner / Operator	Previous identity
C-GRQA	Citation	500-0374	Voyageur Airways Ltd. Hornell Heights, Ontario.	N3141M
C-GRSD	Falcon 20C	157	Innotech Aviation/Dept of Mines & Technical Surveys, Ottawa.	/C-GRSD-X 117508//N166RS/N4463F/F-WJMM
C-GSAS	Learjet	25B-109	Skycharter Ltd. Toronto.	N333HP/N888DH
C-GSBR	Gulfstream 3	307	Steven Roman/Denison Mines Ltd. Toronto.	/N17584
C-GSCL	HS 125/700A	NA0222	Shell Canada Ltd. Calgary.	//G-BFSI
C-GSCR	Citation	550-0328	Shell Canada Ltd. Calgary.	N550MD/G-BJIL/N67988
C-GSCX	Citation	550-0348	Shell Canada Ltd. Calgary.	N550CA/I-VIKI/N381CC
C-GSFA	Citation	550-0075	Time Air Inc. Lethbridge, Alberta.	/N58BH/N55BH/N3314M
C-GSKA	Falcon 20C	9	Skycharter Ltd. Toronto.	N3668/N366G/N809F/F-WMKI
C-GSKC	Falcon 20C	29	Skycharter Ltd. Toronto.	N368L/N368G/N849F/F-WMKI
C-GSKL	Learjet	25B-179	Skycharter Ltd. Toronto.	C-GBQC/N659HX
C-GSKN	Falcon 20C	65	Skycharter Ltd. Toronto.	N5052U/N1U/N777WL/N777WJ/N393F/N383RF/N890F F-WNGM
C-GSKQ	Falcon 20C	40	Skycharter Ltd. Toronto.	N65LE/N65LC/N854WC/N354WC/N354H/N19BC/CF-BFM
C-GSKS	Falcon 20C	34	Skycharter Ltd. Toronto.	N3690/N369G/N808F/F-WMKJ
C-GSKV	HS 125/3A-RA	NA704	Skycharter Ltd. Toronto.	N888WK/(N90WP)/N14GQ/N14GD/N208H/N55G/N75C/G-AVOK G-5-12
C-GSLL	Citation Eagle	501-0030	Ajex Aviation Ltd. Calgary.	N100CJ/N301MG/N301MC/N36890
C-GSTR	Citation	501-0241	Scepter Manufacturing Ltd. Toronto.	N207G/N174CB/(N2624L)
C-GSUN	Citation	501-0100	Suncor Inc. Calgary.	(N26MW)/N41ST/N485CC/(N3207M)
C-GSWS	Learjet	25D-370	Sunwest Charters Ltd. Calgary.	N223TG/N220TG/N610JB/N610JR/N72600
C-GTAK	Falcon 20D	197	Soundair Corp. Toronto.	N399SW/N4387F/F-WPXF
C-GTCI	Citation	550-0585	Toyota Canada Ltd. Scarborough, Ontario.	N1301K
C-GTCP	Falcon 900	29	Trans Canada Pipelines, Toronto,	N421FJ/F-WWFA
C-GTDN	HS 125/700A	NA0304	Execaire/Tele-Direct Ltee. Montreal.	N707DS//N700BB/G-5-17
C-GTDO	Citation	S550-0080	Tim Donut Ltd. Calgary.	
C-GTPL	Falcon 50	137	Trans Canada Pipelines, Toronto.	(N119FJ)/N50FJ/N127FJ/F-WZHC
C-GTVO	Falcon 10	137	Fraser Co. Ltd. Edmundston, N.B.	/N837F/N200FJ/F-WZGI
C-GTXV	Challenger	1046	Petro-Canada Inc. Calgary.	C-GLXD
C-GUUU	Citation	550-0423	LID Brokerage & Realty Co (1977) Ltd. Saskatoon.	N45MC/N12171
C-GVCA	Learjet	35-043	414660 Alberta Ltd/Business Flights, Edmonton.	/
C-GVER	Citation	500-0369	West Wind Aviation Inc. Saskatoon.	N3132M
C-GVVA	Learjet	35-002	Echo Bay Mines Ltd. Edmonton.	/N35SC/N352GL
C-GVVT	Citation	501-0087	Sky Service FBO Inc. Dorval, Quebec.	N501SE/(N3183M)
C-GWCR	Citation	550-0191	Weldwood of Canada Ltd. Vancouver.	N88707
C-GWFG	Learjet	24D-256	West Fraser Air Ltd. Vancouver, BC.	N703J/HB-VCW
C-GXFZ	Citation	500-0032	W/o 26 Sep 84.	(N5364U)/N536V/N532CC
C-GXYN	HS 125/700A	NA0281	AMOCO Canada Petroleum Co Ltd. Calgary.	/N533/N125AN/G-5-18
C-GYPH	BAe 125/800B	8007	Power Financial Corp. Montreal.	/C-GKRL/G-5-554/G-GAEL/G-5-20/G-GAEL
C-GYPJ	Falcon 50	162	Petro Canada Inc. Calgary.	N90R/N145FJ/F-WZHB
CF-BRL	Sabre-40A	282-107	W/o 27 Feb 74.	N7584N/N4ONR
CF-CFL	HS 125/400A	NA725	W/o 11 Nov 69.	

Bahamas

Registration	Type	c/n	Owner / Operator	Previous identity
C6-BER	Falcon 50	20	Petroclor Services Inc. New York.	/N50FR/F-WZHK
C6-BET	HS 125/700B	7054	Norwest Aviation, Nassau.	
C6-BEV	MS 760 Paris-2	111	Petrocolor Services Inc. New York.	I-FINR

Mozambique

Registration	Type	c/n	Owner / Operator	Previous identity
C9-TAC	HS 125/700B	7175	Empresa Nacional de Transporte e Trabalho Aereo, Maputo.	(C9-TTA)

Chile

Registration	Type	c/n	Owner / Operator	Previous identity
CC-ECE	Citation	650-0033	CORFO=Corporacion de Fomento, Santiago.	(N1309A)
CC-ECL	Citation	650-0131	CORFO-Corporacion de Fomento, Santiago.	(N1323R)
CC-ECN	Citation	550-0104	Aeroservicio Ltda. Santiago.	N2633N

Morocco

Registration	Type	c/n	Owner / Operator	Previous identity
CN-ANV	Citation V	560-0025	Government of Morocco,	(N12285)

CN-ANW	Citation V	560-0039	Government of Morocco.	
CN-TNA	Falcon 100	212	Office of National Aluminium,	F-WZGU

Portugal

CS-ATD	Falcon 20C	30	UNIMAT/Avialgarve Air Taxi, Lisbon.	N407PC/N368EJ/YV-126CP/(JY-AEK)/N368EJ N804F/F-WMKF
CS-ATE	Falcon 20C	94	Avialgarve Air Taxi, Lisbon.	F-ODSK/I-ATMO/F-WNGO
CS-ATF	Falcon 20C	112	Avialgarve Air Taxi, Lisbon. 'Carloto'	N200CX/N830MF/N2989/N991F/F-WJMJ

Federal Republic of Germany

D-....	Citation V	560-0042	Adolf Wurth GmbH. Kunzelsau.	N42CV/(N26648)
D-ADAM	VFW 614	G17	DFVLR, Braunschweig. (status ?).	D-BABP
D-BFAR	Falcon 50	16	Dornier Reparaturwerft GmbH. Munich.	D-BIRD/(N50FM)/F-WZHH
D-BFFB	Falcon 50	65	F & F Burda GmbH. Baden Baden.	/N65HS/N90FJ/N50FJ/F-WZHT
D-C...	Learjet	35A-415		N415DJ/N19GL/N125AX
D-CADA	HS 125/700B	7007	Aero-Dienst GmbH. Nuremberg.	//HB-VFA
D-CAEP	Learjet	55-059	Flugzeugleasing GmbH/Ratioflug GmbH. Frankfurt. (now 55C ?).	/(N211BY)
D-CALL	Falcon 20F	392	Dr. F Flick, Dusseldorf.	F-WRQT
D-CAPO	Learjet	35A-159	Phoenix Air GmbH. Munich.	/(N135CK)/N93CK/N93C
D-CARA	HFB 320	1021	Wfu. Cx D- register 3 Jul 84. Broken up for spares.	
D-CARE	HFB 320	1022	Wfu Apr 72. Located at Luftwaffe Museum Uetersen-Hamburg.	
D-CARL	Learjet	35A-387	Aero Dienst GmbH. Nuremberg.	/
D-CARP	Learjet	55-050	Aero Dienst GmbH. Nuremberg.	/
D-CART	Learjet	35A-354	Bavaria Flug KG. Munich.	N1450B
D-CASY	HFB 320	1029	W/o 29 Jun 72.	
D-CATY	Learjet	35A-114	Aviation Leasing KG. Dusseldorf.	/N851L/N18G/D-CONA/N3807G
D-CAVE	Learjet	35A-423	AVIA Luftreederei GmbH/Air Traffic GmbH. Dusseldorf.	(N335GA)/N200TC
D-CBAG	Falcon 10	91	Bertelsmann AG. Paderborn.	F-WJMJ
D-CBBE	Westwind-1124	154	LHI Leasing KG/RFB, Lubeck.	N919JH/(D-CBBE)/4X-CJA
D-CBMW	BAe 125/800B	8155	BMW GmbH. Munich.	N800BM/G-5-628
D-CBNA	Falcon 20C	63	Ortwin Naske/Naske-Air, Braunschweig.	PH-LPS/F-WMKI
D-CBUR	Falcon 10	98	Burda GmbH. Offenburg.	F-WPXG
D-CBUS	Citation	S550-0027	Erwin Gruber, Munich.	N1260K
D-CCAA	Learjet	35A-315	Deutsche Rettungsflugwacht, Stuttgart.	/N662AA/N927GL
D-CCAY	Learjet	35A-112	Quelle-Flug GmbH. Nuremberg.	3810G
D-CCCA	Learjet	35A-160	Maschinenfabrik E Mollers GmbH. Paderborn.	
D-CCDB	Falcon 20F	381	Daimler Benz AG. Stuttgart.	(I-LAFA)/F-WRQS
D-CCHB	Learjet	35A-089	Bauhaus GmbH. Mannheim.	N3547F
D-CCMB	Falcon 20F-5	377	Daimler Benz AG. Stuttgart.	F-WRQZ
D-CCPD	Learjet	36-004	Aviation Lsg KG/Mini-Trans Transportbetriebe GmbH. Munich.	(D-CCAC)/N1918W
D-CDFA	Learjet	36-006	W/o 26 Mar 80.	D-CAFO/HB-VEA/(I-CRYS)
D-CDPD	Learjet	25B-177	W/o 18 May 83.	N74SW/N11PH
D-CDRB	Diamond 1	A053SA	Aviation Leasing KG/EVEX Flug GmbH. Dusseldorf.	N353DM
D-CDWN	Learjet	35A-175	Diehl Werke KG/Aero Dienst GmbH. Nuremberg.	
D-CELL	Falcon 20D	201	Transalpina Flugzeughalter GmbH. Munich.	F-WLCY
D-CEVW	BAe 125/800B	8067	Volkswagenwerk AG. Braunschweig.	G-5-525
D-CFAN	BAe 125/800B	8094	Haeger & Schmidt GmbH/Thyssen, Dusseldorf.	G-5-576
D-CFCF	HS 125/F400B	25248	Wolfgang Bornheim, Koeln.	
D-CFOX	Learjet	36A-031	Commerz u Industrie Leasing/Fuchs KG. Munster-Osnabruck.	N20UG/N20UC
D-CFPD	Learjet	24E-345	Peter K Wichmann, Dusseldorf.	N500RR/N500RP
D-CFSK	HS 125/600B	6053	Federal Govt/Gemeinsame Flugvermessungstelle, Lechfeld.	
D-CFTG	Learjet	35A-204	FTG Air Service KG. Cologne-Bonn.	/(N277AM)//N7PE/N99ME/N87MJ/D-COSY N1466B
D-CFVG	Learjet	24B/A-223	Diskont u Kredit AG/FVG GmbH. Munich.	D-IFVG/D-IOGA/D-COGA
D-CFVW	BAe 125/800B	8073	Volkswagenwerk AG. Braunschweig.	G-5-532
D-CGFD	Learjet	35A-139	Gesellschaft fuer Flugzieldarstellung mbh. Hohn AFB.	/N15SC
D-CGFE	Learjet	36A-062	Gesellschaft fuer Flugzieldarstellung mbH. Hohn AFB.	
D-CGFF	Learjet	36A-063	Gesellschaft fuer Flugzieldarstellung mbH. Hohn AFB.	N1048X
D-CGFV	Diamond 1A	A051SA	GFV Gmbh/EVEX Flug GmbH. Dusseldorf.	(N35P)/N550HS/N351DM
D-CGPD	Learjet	35A-202	Peter Dreidoppel/Air Traffic GmbH. Dusseldorf.	//N499G/VH-MIQ
D-CGVW	BAe 125/800B	8076	Volkswagenwerk AG. Braunschweig.	G-5-535

Regis-tration	Type	c/n	Owner / Operator	Previous identity

Registration	Type	c/n	Owner / Operator	Previous identity
D-CHEF	Learjet	25D-260	Helmut Gaertner/FVG GmbH. Munich.	(D-CHBM)/N39413
D-CHFB	HFB 320	V1	W/o 12 May 65.	
D-CHJH	Citation	S550-0131	WAT Leasing GmbH/Hema Charterflug GmbH. Paderborn.	N12934
D-CHPD	Learjet	35A-309	Peter Dreidoppel/Air Traffic GmbH. Dusseldorf.	N100MN//N8216Z/OE-GAR HB-VGT
D-CHVB	Citation	550-0629	Viessmann Werke KG. Allendorf.	N1256T
D-CIAO	Citation	S550-0135	V Bondarenko/Interdean International Spedition, Munich.	OE-GPD
D-CIEL	Falcon 10	155	Hertie Stiftung, Frankfurt.	(N220FJ)/F-WZGC
D-CIRO	HFB 320	1044	W/o 18 Dec 70.	
D-CIRS	Learjet	35A-091	Aviation Leasing KG/MTM Aviation GmbH. Munich.	N8GA/C-GBLF/VH-TLJ
D-CITY	Learjet	35A-177	Helmut Idzkowiak, Ahlen.	//N174CP/N77CQ/N77CP/N1461B
D-CJET	HS 125/F600B	6027	European Private Charter GmbH. Luftverkehrs KG. Dusseldorf.	G-5-585/D-CJET
D-CLAN	Learjet	35A-397	Private Jet Charter KG. Dusseldorf.	N33PT
D-CLOU	HFB 320	V2	Wfu Sep 70. Located at Deutsches Museum-Munich.	
D-CLOU	Citation	S550-0121	LHI Leasing KG/MBB GmbH. Munich.	(N12925)
D-CLUB	Learjet	55-034	Ratioflug GmbH. Frankfurt.	N84DJ/D-CARX/N3795Y
D-CLUE	Citation	650-0174	EFS Flug-Service KG. Dusseldorf.	N674CC/(N1782E)
D-CMAD	Learjet	55C-143	Gustav und Grete Schickedanz KG. Fuerth.	/N10871
D-CMAX	Falcon 20D	158	Grundig AG. Nuremberg.	F-WMKJ
D-CMET	Falcon 20E	329	DFVLR, Oberpfaffenhofen.	F-WRQV
D-CMIR	BAe 125/800B	8110	Miro Flug KG/Aero Dienst GmbH. Nuremberg.	G-5-584
D-CMMM	Learjet	24D-328	Franz Gausepohl, Munster-Osnabruck.	D-IMMM
D-CMTM	Learjet	55-042	Aviation Leasing KG/MTM Aviation GmbH. Munich.	/N160TL/N3796U
D-CNCI	Citation V	560-0061	Nixdorf Computer KG. Paderborn.	N2701J
D-COCO	Learjet	35A-466	DS Flugdienst KG. Nuremberg.	/N600WJ/(N700WJ)/N39SA/VH-WFP
D-COME	Falcon 10	67	H Bauer Verlag, Hamburg.	N151FJ/F-WLCU
D-COSA	HFB 320	1056	M-B-B GmbH. Munich.	
D-I...	Citation V	560-0031	Eschmann Air,	N1229F
D-IADD	Citation	551-0481	Juergen Sauer/Aerostar Aircraft Charter GmbH. Nuremberg.	N550MW/N1253D
D-IAEC	Citation	501-0203	W/o 31 May 87.	N67830
D-IANE	Citation	501-0106	Kuri-Flugdienst KG. Friedrichshafen.	OE-FYF/(N123YF)/(N2649J)
D-IANO	Citation	501-0121	UVW Leasing GmbH. Ettlingen/Renta-Jet GmbH-Stuttgart.	HB-VID/D-IANO/N26506
D-IATC	Citation	500-0116	EFS-Flug Service GmbH. Dusseldorf.	EC-CJH/N116CC
D-ICAB	Citation	551-0180	Verkehrsfliegerschule Hanover GmbH. (was 550-0136).	N852WR///N8520J (D-CACS)
D-ICCC	Citation	500-0269	EFS Flug Service GmbH. Dusseldorf.	(D-IKUC)/N5269J
D-ICTA	Citation	551-0051	Preussag AG. Hanover.	(D-IHAT)/N6863C
D-ICUR	Citation	550-0379	E Kubon/Kuri-Flugdienst KG. (was 551-0029).	N500ER/N551PL/N168CB/N26369
D-IEXC	Citation	500-0036	Loeser Jets & Props GmbH. Egelsbach.	/SE-DEU/OY-DVL/N536CC
D-IFAI	Citation	500-0100	Axtmann & Schloegel/Flight Ambulance Service KG. Nuremberg.	OE-FNP/HB-VDC OE-FNL/D-ICPW/HB-VDC/N69566
D-IGGK	Citation	501-0143	Metimex Metal Trading & Services GmbH. Dusseldorf.	N26523
D-IGRC	Citation	551-0163	G Paetzold, Frankfurt.	N80BS/N27457
D-IHAQ	Learjet	23-007	W/o 12 Dec 65.	N826L
D-IHLZ	Learjet	24B-225	W/o 18 Jun 73.	N618R
D-IJHM	Citation	551-0033	W/o 19 May 82.	N88692
D-ILAN	Citation	551-0614	Leistritz AG. Nuremberg.	
D-IMRX	Citation	501-0688	Rena Informationstechnik GmbH. Deisenhofen.	
D-IMTM	Citation	551-0009	Heinrich Then/Then Air KG. Coburg.	N1959E

Angola

D2-ECB	Gulfstream 3	474	LAA/Government of Angola, Luanda.	N311GA

Spain

EC-...	Falcon 900	97		F-W...
EC-...	Falcon 900	93	Bank of Santander,	F-W...
EC-551	Falcon 20C	128	DHL/Air Truck, Madrid.	/C-GNAA/YN-BZH/5A-DAF/F-WMKJ
EC-CGG	Citation	500-0108	W/o 22 Nov 74.	N108CC
EC-CKR	Learjet	25B-184	Eurojet/MAC Aviation SRL. Zaragoza.	
EC-DFA	Learjet	35A-196	W/o 13 Aug 80.	HB-VFU
EC-DOH	Citation	551-0039	Explotaciones Aereas y Navegacion S.A. Madrid.	ECT-023/N6860Y

Registration	Type	c/n	Owner / Operator	Previous identity
EC-DQC	Corvette	24	Uni-Air International, Toulouse.	F-BVPI
EC-DQE	Corvette	26	Teire S.A. Madrid.	F-GDAY/PH-JSB/F-ODFQ/N618AC/F-WNGV
EC-DQG	Corvette	27	Dominguez Toledo S.A. Malaga.	F-BVPH
EC-EAC	HS 125/600B	6005	Alfa Jet Charter SA. Madrid.	/G-CYII/G-BART
EC-EAP	Citation	650-0125	Gestair, Madrid.	N13222
EC-EAS	Citation	650-0122	Gestair, Madrid.	(N1322K)
EC-EAV	HS 125/600A	6032	Aeronaves La Dorada S.A. Madrid.	N332TA/C-GLBD/N38BH/N4BR/G-DBOW
EC-EBR	Citation	500-0089	NAYSA Aerotaxis, Las Palmas.	//N589CC
EC-ECB	Falcon 20DC	210	W/o 30 Sep 87.	N66VG/N29FE/N4397F/F-WNGL
EC-EDC	Falcon 20C	6	DHL/Audeli Air Express, Zaragoza.	N750SS/N497/N65311/C-GOQG/N21DT/N21JM N20JM/N805F/F-BMKH/F-WMKH
EC-EDL	Falcon 20DC	220	DHL/Audeli Air, Zaragoza.	OO-STF/N36VG/N24FE/N4404F/F-WPUU
EC-EDN	Citation	501-0010	Instituto Carto Grafico de Catelonia, Barcelona.	VH-POZ/(N500MD)/N7WF EP-PBC/N7WF/N36859
EC-EDO	Falcon 20DC	50	DHL/Air Truck, Madrid. 'Pelicano II'	N56VG/(N145FE)/N6FE/N6565A/N804F N879F/F-WNGO
EC-EEU	Falcon 20DC	218	DHL/Audeli Air, Zaragoza.	N86VG/OO-STE/N86VG/N36FE/N4372F/F-WMKJ
EC-EFI	Falcon 20D	189	w/o 11 Oct 87.	N444BF/N47JE/N47JF/N950L/N4380F/F-WPUU
EC-EFR	Falcon 20D	183	TAHIS-Transportes Aereos Hispanos S.A. Madrid.	N2979/N4377F/F-WLCY
EC-EGL	HS 125/600A	6023	Alfa Jet Charter SA. Madrid.	EC-121/N514V/N35BH
EC-EGM	Falcon 20DC	204	DHL/Air Truck, Madrid. 'Pelicano III'	EC-113/N120FS/N26FE/N4392F/F-WMKI
EC-EGS	HS 125/600A	6034	Alfa Jet/Euravia S.A. Barcelona.	EC-115/N600SB/N600FL/N90BL/N90B/N39BH
EC-EGT	HS 125/1A-522	25080	Catalonia S.A. Barcelona. (wfu ?).	N23KL/C-GLEO/EI-BGW/G-BDYE/3D-AAB VQ-ZIL
EC-EGY	Learjet	25D-373	MAC Aviation SRL. Zaragoza.	N29EW
EC-EHC	Falcon 20DC	46	DHL/Audeli Air Express, Zaragoza.	N46WG/(N144FE)/N7FE/N23555/CF-ESO/F-WMKG (N144FE)
EC-EHD	Falcon 20C	55	Alfa Jet Charter S.A. Madrid.	HB-VBS/VR-BCJ/F-WNGO
EC-EHF	HS 125/600A	6011	Euravia S.A. Barcelona. 'Marta'	N81D/N42622/VR-BGS/N555GB/N555CB/N6001H N24BH
EC-EIV	Falcon 20DC	221	DHL/Air Truck, Madrid. 'Pelicano IV'	EC-165//N300NL/N25FE/N4406F/F-WPUV
EC-EKK	Falcon 20C	106	DHL/Audeli Air Express, Madrid.	/N31V/N9300M/F-GBPG/N987F/F-WJMM
EC-ELK	BAe 125/800B	8022	Alfa Jet Charter SA. Madrid.	EC-193/HZ-KSA/G-5-569/G-JJCB/G-5-16
EC-EOQ	HS 125/600B	6012	Alfa Jet Charter SA. Madrid.	EC-272/G-BAYT/G-BNDX/G-BAYT/5N-ALX/G-BAYT G-5-17
EC-EQP	Falcon 20C	149	Alfa Jet Charter SA. Madrid.	EC-263/N568Q/N1818S/N4359F/F-WNGO
EC-EQX	Citation	650-0119	Gestair, Madrid.	/N100WH/HB-VIN/VR-BJS/(N13217)
EC-ERJ	HS 125/600A	6063	Aeronaves la Dorada, Madrid.	EC-349/N484W/G-5-17/G-BSPH/A6-RAK/G-5-13
EC-ERX	HS 125/600B	6062	North Atlantic Airways, Alicante.	EC-319/G-TMAS/G-MFEU/G-5-15
EC-ETI	HS 125/700B	7040	Gestair/Services de Aerotransportes Especiales SA. Madrid.	/EC-375/G-OWEB HZ-RC1

Ireland

Registration	Type	c/n	Owner / Operator	Previous identity
EI-BJL	Citation	551-0084	Helicopter Maintenance/Carrow More Ltd. Castlebar.	/G-BJHH/(N3237M)
EI-BUY	Citation	551-0555	Tool & Mould Steel (Ireland) Ltd. Koln-Bonn.	(EI-BUN)/N1297Z
EI-BYM	Citation	500-0179	Leoni Aviation, Shannon.	(N997S)/N427DM/N111KR/N111KR/N444J
EI-BYN	Citation	550-0171	GPA Group Ltd. Shannon.	N333CG/(N984H)/N934H/N43D/(C-GDPE)/(N88797)
EI-CAH	Gulfstream 4	1129	Ardelis/Arklow P/L. Johannesburg-RSA.	N17585
EI-LJG	Challenger 601-3A	5023	Larry Goodman/Ven Air, Dublin.	/N608CC/C-GLYO
EI-SNN	Citation	650-0183	Westair/GPA Group, Shannon.	N2614Y

Liberia

Registration	Type	c/n	Owner / Operator	Previous identity
EL-OSZ	Caravelle 3	254	Sheikh Onama Siraj Zahran/Atlantic Aviation, Monrovia.	EL-AAG/SU-BBV CN-CCT
EL-SKD	B 707-351C	18586	Government of Liberia, Monrovia.	N351SR//N651TF/VR-CAO/VR-HGO/N353US
EL-VDY	Falcon 20E	245	Government of Liberia, Monrovia.	/HB-VDY/HB-VDP/F-BUIX/SX-ABA/F-WLCS

Iran

Registration	Type	c/n	Owner / Operator	Previous identity
EP-AGA	B 737-286	21317	Islamic Republic of Iran, Teheran.	
EP-AGX	Falcon 20E	283	W/o 21 Nov 74.	F-WRQS

Page 14

Registration	Type	c/n	Owner / Operator	Previous identity
EP-AGY	Falcon 20E	286	Islamic Republic of Iran, Teheran.	F-WRQU
EP-AKC	Falcon 20E	301	National Iranian Oil Co. Teheran.	F-WNGL
EP-FIC	Falcon 20E	334	Civil Aviation Organization, Teheran.	F-WRQU
EP-FID	Falcon 20E	338	Civil Aviation Organization, Teheran.	F-WMKG
EP-FIE	Falcon 20E	251	Iran Asseman Airlines/Civil Aviation Organization, Tehera.	EP-VAP/F-WRQR
EP-FIG	Falcon 20E	318	Civil Aviation Organization, Teheran.	EP-VSP/(EP-VAS)/F-WRQT
EP-PLN	B 727-30	18363	Islamic Republic of Iran, Teheran.	EP-SHP/N16768/D-ABIF
EP-SEA	Falcon 20E	367	Atomic Energy Organization, Teheran.	F-WRQR

France

Registration	Type	c/n	Owner / Operator	Previous identity
F-BIHY	Falcon 20-5	141	Ste. Jas Hennessy & Cie. Cognac.	F-BPIO/F-WMKF
F-BINR	Falcon 50	2	Regourd/Europe Falcon Service, Le Bourget.	/F-RAFJ/F-BINR/F-WINR
F-BJET	MS 760 Paris-1A	39	Euralair/Assoc Les Amis des Grands Constructeurs, Paris.	F-WJAA
F-BJLH	Falcon 10	1	SLIBAIL/Leadair Unijet, Paris-Le Bourget.	F-WJLH/PH-ILT/F-BSQU/F-WSQU
F-BKMF	HS 125/1	25007	W/o 5 Jun 66.	HB-VAH/G-ASTY/(G-ASSH)
F-BLKL	MS 760 Paris-3	01	Euralair International, Paris.	F-WLKL
F-BMSS	Falcon 20F	2	IGN=Institut Geographique National, Creil.	F-WMSS
F-BRNL	Learjet	24B-183	W/o 18 Dec 85.	OY-AGZ/N676LJ
F-BSIM	HS 125/3B	25130	BAIL EQUIPEMENT/Ste Joelle, Paris-Le Bourget.	TR-LXO/F-BSIM/HB-VAZ/G-AVRD G-5-14
F-BSQN	Falcon 10	03	Wfu. CoA expiry 4/81.	F-WSQN
F-BSRL	Learjet	24B-210	W/o 10 Jun 85.	ZS-LLG
F-BSTM	AC 680V-TU	1540-6	Ste. Turbomeca, Pau.	F-WSTM/G-AWXK/N6300
F-BSTR	Falcon 20F	246	Shell-Gabon/Regourd Aviation, Paris.	F-WJMK
F-BSYF	Falcon 20C	25	IGN=Institut Geographique National, Creil.	HB-VCO/F-BOON/F-WNGN
F-BTCY	Falcon 20C	13	Europe Falcon Service, Paris.	D-CILL/F-BOEF/TR-LOL/F-BOEF/F-WMKH
F-BTEL	Citation	550-0190	Euralair/Havas/Ste Tournees C Barret/Avenir Publicite/SEGI.	N98715
F-BTML	Falcon 20C	67	Air Service Nantes, Nantes.	F-BOOA/F-WJMN
F-BTTU	Corvette	37	W/o 31 Jul 90.	
F-BTYV	Learjet	24B-206	PARNAVIS BAIL/Air Entreprise, Paris-Le Bourget.	HB-VBY
F-BUQN	Corvette	3	S.N.I.A.S., Toulouse-Blagnac.	F-WUQN
F-BUQP	Corvette	4	BNP Bail/Uni-Air International, Paris.	F-WUQP
F-BUUL	Citation	500-0136	Ste Locanorm/Guiraudie et Auffeve, Toulouse.'Chateau Donzac'	
F-BUUV	Learjet	24B-195	DB Finances SA/Aie Entreprise, Paris-Le Bourget.	N272GL/N202BT
F-BVEC	Learjet	24D-271	SLIBAIL/C G Aviation, Valence.	HB-VDK/N3818G
F-BVPA	Corvette	5	SOFINABAIL/S.A.R.L. Mavina, Paris-Le Bourget.	
F-BVPB	Corvette	6	S.F.A.C.T., St. Yan.	F-OGJL/F-BVPB/F-WUQR
F-BVPG	Corvette	25	DB Finances SA/Aie Entreprise, Paris-Le Bourget.	F-OBZV/F-BVPG/F-WNGU
F-BVPK	Corvette	7	S.F.A.C.T., St. Yan.	N611AC/F-OBZR
F-BVPN	Falcon 20E	311	Manufacture Francaise PNEUS Michelin, Clermont Ferrand.	F-WRQS
F-BVPR	Falcon 10	5	AMD-BA/Europe Falcon Service, Le Bourget.	F-WVPR/F-BVPR/F-WLCT
F-BVPS	Corvette	14	DB Finances SA/Air Entreprise, Paris-Le Bourget.	
F-BVPT	Corvette	16	S.F.A.C.T., St. Yan.	
F-BXAS	AC 690A-TU	11240	Ste. Turbomeca, Pau.	F-WXAS
F-BXPT	Learjet	23-014	BNP Bail/Darta/SARL Aerojet Prive, Paris-Le Bourget.	(HB-VEL)/JY-AEG N426EJ/N814L
F-BXQL	MS 760 Paris-2B	105	Euralair International, Paris.	N760Q/PH-MSU/F-BJZT
F-BYAL	Learjet	25C-084	Euralair/Ste Material Aeronautique/Air Provence, Marselles.	N200SF/N200QM (C-GWUZ)/N2000M
F-BYCV	Falcon 10	93	Natiolocation/DB Aviation, Paris-Le Bourget.	F-WNGN
F-BYFB	HS 125/700B	7166	Ste. Bouyghes/Groupement International de Commerce, Paris.	/G-5-18
F-G...	Citation	550-0415	Darta, Paris-Le Bourget.	N1949M/N1949B/OH-CUT/D-CNCI/N12164
F-GAMA	Learjet	23-023	Bail Equip/Transair, Paris. (damaged and stored at LBG).	HB-VEL/JY-AEH N429EJ
F-GAPC	Falcon 20C	184	EFS/UCINA-Interjet, Paris-Le Bourget.	D-COMF/F-BTMF/F-WRQQ
F-GAPY	Learjet	23-027	Wfu.	(N108TW)/F-GAPY/HB-VES/JY-AEI/N430EJ
F-GBMB	Learjet	35-018	P Fabre/Cie Interagra/Uni-Air, Toulouse-Blagnac.	D-CORA
F-GBMH	Falcon 10	103	Aero France/B.A.I.I/Global Assistance et Transport, Paris.	F-WPXL
F-GBRF	Falcon 10	38	Ste. Roquette Freres, Merville-Callonne.	N20EE/N20ET/N20ES/N127FJ/F-WJMM
F-GBTC	Falcon 10	124	W/o 15 Jan 86.	F-WPUY
F-GBTI	Falcon 10	24	Technal/Ste Bail Equipement/Jetair, Toulouse-Blagnac.	N1924V/N116FJ/F-WJML
F-GBTL	Citation	550-0073	Ste. Euralair, Paris-Le Bourget.	N4621G

Regis- tration	Type	c/n	Owner / Operator	Previous identity

Registration	Type	c/n	Owner / Operator	Previous identity
F-GBTM	Falcon 20GF	397	AMD-BA/Europe Falcon Service, Paris.	F-WBTM/F-GBTM/F-WRQP
F-GDAE	Learjet	24-105	Wfu.	TR-LYB/N111EJ/N111EK/N425NJ
F-GDAV	Learjet	23-017	W/o 30 Jan 89.	F-GBTA/N30BP/N32SD/N658L/N233R
F-GDCP	Learjet	35A-071	BNP Bail/Uni Air International, Toulouse.	/F-WDCP/JY-AFD
F-GDHR	Learjet	55-070	W/o 5 Feb 87.	
F-GDLR	Falcon 10	121	SANOFI/Ste Chaussures Andre/Leadair, Paris.	HB-VFT/(HB-VFS)/F-WPUU
F-GDLU	Falcon 20E	314	Leadair Jet Services, Paris-Le Bourget.	D-COTT/F-WNGL
F-GDRN	Falcon 10	152	Regourd Aviation, Paris-Le Bourget.	N8463/JA8463/N8463/N216FJ/F-WZGY
F-GECI	Learjet	24B-219	Yves St Laurent Couture, Paris.	N100KK/N711CE/N658AT
F-GECR	HS 125/3B	25128	Slibail/Alain Afflelou, Paris-Le Bourget.	G-AVOI
F-GEDB	Falcon 100	197	EFS/Kadan Trading Inc. Panama.	F-WZGC
F-GEFB	Citation	550-0182	Soder Bail/Transvol/Miriardair, Paris-Le Bourget.	N78TF/F-GCSZ/(F-BKFB) N88830
F-GEFS	Falcon 20F	486	Europe Falcon Service, Paris.	F-WLCV
F-GELA	Falcon 10	16	Ste Turbomeca, Pau.	N48TT/N110FJ/F-WLCT
F-GELE	Falcon 10	69	Europe Falcon Service, Paris.	N3RC/N43CC/N153FJ/F-WJML
F-GELS	Falcon 100	208	Natio Equipement/Lyon Air/S.A. SOFOMAT, St Etienne.	F-W...
F-GELT	Falcon 100	211	Natio Equipement/Lyon Air/S.A. SOFOMAT, St Etienne.	F-WZGT
F-GEPL	Citation	500-0164	Ste. Euralair, Paris-Le Bourget.	N4209K/D-IHSV/N164CC
F-GEPQ	Corvette	19	BNP Bail/Ste Uni-Air, Toulouse.	F-SEBH/(F-GDRC)/TZ-PBF/F-BVPL/F-OCJL F-BVPL
F-GEQF	Corvette	15	LOCAMIC/Wallisair, Paris-Le Bourget.	N17AJ/SE-DEN/F-GDUB/OO-MRE/OO-MRA SE-DEN/F-WIFA
F-GERO	Falcon 10	179	Ste Francaise de Transport Aerien/Ste Rallye & Cie, Brest.	(F-GGRA)/I-DJMA F-WZGL
F-GESZ	Citation	500-0476	Soloma + Camebail/Transvol-Miriardair, Cannes.	N408MW/N408MM/N305M/N2991A
F-GFBG	Falcon 10	157	Cora/Revillon/G.I.E-Air BG, Paris.	N80GP/N101EF/(N900AR)/N222FJ/F-WZGF
F-GFDH	Corvette	13	SNIAS Helicopters, Marseilles.	N601AN/F-BVPD
F-GFEJ	Corvette	10	SNIAS, Paris-Le Bourget.	N600AN/F-BVPO
F-GFFP	Falcon 10	160	SLIBAIL/Ste Pinault Location de Material, Paris.	N31TM/N223HS/N225FJ F-WZGK
F-GFGB	Falcon 10	177	Cora/Revillon/G.I.E-Air BG, Paris.	N533CS/N243FJ/F-WZGJ
F-GFHG	Falcon 10	126	Natiolocation/DB Aviation, Paris-Le Bourget.	HB-VIX/(F-GFHH)/I-CHIC/F-WNGM
F-GFHH	Falcon 10	113	Natiolocation/D B Aviation, Paris-Le Bourget.	HB-VIW/(F-GFHG)/I-CHOC (I-SHOP)/F-WPXE
F-GFJL	Citation	550-0470	G.I.E. ELIS, Paris-Le Bourget.	N10RU/N1251Z
F-GFMD	Falcon 10	136	Aero France, Paris-Le Bourget.	I-MUDE/F-WZGH/F-WZGS
F-GFMP	HS 125/3B	25125	SLIBAIL/Ste. SDIF, Paris-Le Bourget.	G-AVAI/LN-NPA/G-AVAI
F-GFMZ	Learjet	25B-182	Air Corse, Ajaccio.	//N4300L/C-GLBT
F-GFPF	Falcon 10	68	Aero France/Maxitel, Paris-Le Bourget.	N80MP/N91DH/N11DH/N7NL/N7NP/N152FJ F-WLCV
F-GFPO	Citation	550-0092	Transair France/Regourd Aviation, Paris-Le Bourget.	/N89Q///N89B/(N26643)
F-GFUN	Falcon 20C	162	Ste Elymar II, Paris-Le Bourget.	(F-GFLL)/OO-DOK/F-ODOK/HB-VED/D-CBBT OO-WTB/F-WNGO
F-GGAL	Citation	650-0117	Euralair/S.P.F.D. Holding, Paris-Le Bourget,	N1321N
F-GGBL	Falcon 20F	379	Euralair/L'Oreal, Paris-Le Bourget.	N33AH/(N33AJ)/(N37AH)/N130F/F-WMKF
F-GGCP	Falcon 50	9	Ste Sporto/Aero France, Paris-Le Bourget.	(N100WJ)/VR-CBR/XA-LOH/I-SAFP F-WZHD
F-GGGA	Citation	550-0586	BNP Bail/Ste Locanorm/Guiraudie et Auffeve, Le Bourget.	N1301N
F-GGGT	Citation	550-0611	Pan Europeenne Air Service/MTS Helicopteres, Annecy.	(N1242K)
F-GGKE	Falcon 20C	118	Air Service Nantes, Nantes.	N512T/N996F/F-WMKG
F-GGMM	Falcon 20E	300	BNP Bail/Uni-Air, Toulouse. 'Ville de Toulouse'	(F-GEJX)/(F-GIBT)/I-EDIF F-WRQP
F-GGPG	Learjet	24D-327	Materiel Aeronautique/Air Provence, Marseilles.	N327EJ
F-GGRH	Falcon 900	5	Natiolocation/DB Aviation/Air Enterprise, Paris-Le Bourget.	VH-BGF/N404FJ F-WWFB
F-GGVB	Falcon 50	11	SLIBAIL/Leadair Unijet, Paris-Le Bourget.	N5739/N501NC/N50FH/F-WZHE
F-GGVR	Falcon 10	138	Esquel Industries/Darta, Paris-Le Bourget.	(N942M)/N100BG/N30TH/N203FJ F-WZGJ
F-GHAE	Learjet	35A-413	Air Entreprise, Troyes.	/N2637Z/HB-VHE
F-GHAQ	Falcon 50	149	FIBIVIAT/Elf Acqitaine/Regourd Aviation, Paris-Le Bourget.	N1904W/N135FJ F-WZHJ
F-GHBT	Falcon 20C	160	Sofal/SNC E D (Elie Dalan) Aviation, Paris.	I-DKET/F-WMKG

Registration	Type	c/n	Owner / Operator	Previous identity
F-GHCR	Falcon 20F	313	G.I.E. Moet Hennessy Services, Paris-Le Bourget.	I-PERF/N560R/N56CC/N744CC N220FJ/N4449F/F-WMKJ
F-GHDT	Falcon 20-5	176	Europe Falcon Service, Paris-Le Bourget.	F-WGTM/I-SNAM/F-WMKG
F-GHDX	Falcon 10	140	Ste West Reefer Line/Doux, Quimper.	N88WL/N70WC/N205FJ/F-WZGL
F-GHDZ	Falcon 10	17	Leadair Unijet, Paris-Le Bourget.	N33HL/N27DA/N29966/VH-FFB/OH-FFB/F-WLCS
F-GHEA	Falcon 900	33	Natio Location/FIBAVIAT/Elf Acquitaine, Paris-Le Bourget.	/N298W/N424FJ F-WWFC
F-GHER	Falcon 10	88	Regourd Aviation, Paris-Le Bourget.	F-GKCD/N3600X/N169FJ/F-WPXL
F-GHFB	Falcon 10	169	Ste Bouyghes/Groupement International de Commerce, Paris.	N725P/VH-DJT N235FJ/F-WZGV
F-GHFO	Falcon 10	33	Leadair Jet Service, Paris-Le Bourget.	N900UC/(N246N)/N881P/N123FJ/F-WJMJ
F-GHFP	Falcon 20C	119	BNP Bail/Pierre Ossona, Paris.	I-SNAV/F-WJMK
F-GHFQ	Falcon 20E	279	Air Excel/LOCAMIC-Ste Ascar, Paris-Le Bourget.	(F-GHPO)/F-GHFQ/I-FKET F-WMKJ
F-GHHG	HS 125/700B	7055	Locafrance Equipment/COGIA, Paris-Le Bourget.	F-WZIG/G-BOXI/N876JC/HZ-RC2 G-5-16
F-GHLN	Falcon 20E	255	Leadair Unijet, Paris-Le Bourget.	/VH-MIQ/VH-HIF/N2724K/HB-VDZ/RJAF-122 F-WRQP
F-GHLT	Falcon 10	92	Natio Location/DB-Dominique Bouillon Aviation, Le Bourget.	(N58B)/N1PB (N61BP)/N172FJ/F-WNGM
F-GHMD	Falcon 20F	345	Ste Aigle-Azur, Pointoise.	N678BM/N4463F/F-WMKI
F-GHMP	Learjet	35-048	Concorde Equipement/Michel Pinseau, Paris-Le Bourget.	/N64MH/N233R
F-GHPA	Falcon 20C	170	EFS/Paltor Enterprises, Panama.	I-EKET/F-WPUV
F-GHPB	Falcon 100	215	BNP Bail/Lyon Air, Lyon-Bron.	F-W...
F-GHPL	Falcon 10	147	Korreda-Bermuda/Euralair, Paris-Le Bourget.	N12TX/N212FJ/F-WZGS
F-GHRV	Falcon 10	48	Caisse Centrale des Banques Populaire/Ste Jet Cop, Chailley.	F-WGTF/N333SR N720ME/N720ML/N133FJ/F-WJMM
F-GHSG	Falcon 20C	77	BNP Bail/Transvol-Miriadair, Cannes.	/F-WGTF/F-GHDN/(F-GJBR)/I-RIED/F-WNGO
F-GHSK	Falcon 100	218	CALIF/Lyon-Air, Lyon-Bron.	F-W...
F-GHTD	Falcon 900	96	Dassault Aviation, Paris-Le Bourget.	F-WWFF
F-GHVK	Falcon 10	146	Air Vendee Investissments,	/N211FJ/F-WZGR
F-GHVR	Falcon 20F	262	FIBIVIAT/Elf Acquitaine/Regourd Aviation, Paris-Le Bourget.	C-GTLU/N501AS VH-WLH/N750ME/N720ML/N4427F/F-WJMK
F-GICB	Falcon 20D	171	BNP Bail/CAA Avn/Transports Aeriens Mediterranneens, Cannes.	(F-GHRE)/ N900JL/N570L/N4371F/F-WMKG
F-GICF	Falcon 20-5	120	BAAI Leasing/Aero France/Ciments Francais, Paris-LBG	(F-GKAF)/N205FJ N410US/N4340F/F-WMKI
F-GICN	Falcon 50	210	CGE=Compagnie Generale d'Electricite, Paris-Le Bourget.	F-W...
F-GIDC	Falcon 50	116	DB Aviation/Air Entreprise, Paris-Le Bourget.	N69R/N781B/N112FJ/F-WZHD
F-GIDE	Falcon 900	1	Europe Falcon Service, Paris-Le Bourget.	/F-WIDE
F-GIFL	Falcon 100	217	Euralair/Pechiney, Paris-Le Bourget.	N100WG/N100FJ/N277FJ/F-WZGA
F-GIFP	Falcon 20F	259	BNP Bail/Pierre Fabre SA. Toulouse.	/SE-DHK/N45WN/N45WH//N212H/N4418F F-WLCT
F-GILM	Corvette	32	Mariette Gillon/Wallisair, Paris-Le Bourget.	EC-DUF/OY-ARA/SE-DED/OY-ARA F-BTTQ/F-WNGR
F-GIPH	Falcon 100	194	Regourd Aviation, Paris-Le Bourget.	N61FC/N100FJ/N260FJ/F-WZGZ
F-GIQP	Falcon 10	43	BNP Bail/Air Ingenierie Finance, Paris-Le Bourget.	(F-GHFI)///N510CP N1515P/N135FJ/F-WJMN
F-GIVR	Falcon 900	62	Natio Location/DB Aviation, Paris-Le Bourget.	/F-WWFJ
F-GJAP	Corvette	31	Locamic/ATA-Alain Taieb, Paris-Le Bourget.	EC-DYE/F-WZSB/N602AN/F-BTTK F-WNGZ
F-GJAS	Corvette	8	CECICO Enterprises/S.N.C. Evasion, Paris-Le Bourget.	6V-AEA/F-WPTT
F-GJCC	Falcon 20C	72	Claude Cambou/Locavion, Cannes.	N725P/VH-DWA/N99KT/N1270F/HB-VAW/F-WNGO
F-GJDB	Falcon 20C	76	Natiolocation/DB Aviation, Paris-Le Bourget.	F-GGFO/N776DS/N937GC/N970F F-WMKF
F-GJDE	HS 125/3B	25131	Ste Conquest, Cannes.	3A-MDB/F-GFDB/I-RASO/G-FOUR/F-BPMC/G-AVRE
F-GJFB	Falcon 10	166	Ste Bouyghes/Groupement International de Commerce, Paris.	N94MC/N232FJ F-WZGS
F-GJHG	Falcon 10	181	Locafrance/COGIA, Toulon.	(N151JC)/N151GS/N87GT/N247FJ/F-WZGC
F-GJHK	Falcon 10	108	Leadair/Ste Transdis/Gondrand Freres, Paris-Le Bourget.	(F-GFJK)/N88LD N91DH/N11DH/N246FJ/F-BIPC/F-WZGF/HZ-AKI/F-WPUZ
F-GJJL	Falcon 10	118	Locamic/GIE NRS Promotion/Air Affaires, Paris-Le Bourget.	I-DNOR/N848MP HZ-AO2/HZ-NOT/HZ-AMA/F-WPXI

Page 17

Registration	Type	c/n	Owner / Operator	Previous identity
F-GJJS	Falcon 20F	264	BNP Bail/Setton Management SA. Toulouse-Blagnac.	(N86BL)//N773V/N777V N373KC/N4428F/F-WJMN
F-GJLA	Falcon 20C	133	BNP Bail/Lease Air International, Lyon-Bron.	VR-BKR/N894F/N4349F/F-WNGO
F-GJLB	Corvette	39	BNP Bail/Ste HELIPART/Uni-Air, Paris-Le Bourget.	TL-RCA/TL-SMI/F-OBYG F-WNGY
F-GJLL	Falcon 10	22	SLIBAIL/Leadair Unijet, Paris-Le Bourget.	N48JC/N44JC/N114FJ/F-WLCX
F-GJMA	Falcon 10	116	France Leasing International-Nantes/Lease Air, Lyon-Bron.	N525RC/N925JG N4DS/N189FJ/F-WNGL
F-GJPM	Falcon 900	66	BFCE BAIL/Michelin, Clermont Ferrand.	F-WWFE
F-GJPR	Falcon 20C	5	Air Provence, Marseilles.	N747W/N804F/F-WMKI
F-GJRN	Falcon 10	163	Lease Air, Lyon.	N163F/N151WC/N227FJ/F-WZGP
F-GJSF	Falcon 20F	299	Ste Aigle Azur, Pointoise.	N585UC/N90CN/N456SR/N21FJ/(N734S)/F-WMKI
F-GJXX	Citation V	560-0070	J C Decaux, Toussus.	
F-GKAE	Falcon 100	213	Natiolocation/DB Aviation, Paris-Le Bourget.	ZK-MAZ/N274FJ/F-WZGV
F-GKAL	Falcon 20F	455	Soc Au Petit Paris/Beghin Say/Chargeurs S.A/Euralair, Paris.	F-WRQS
F-GKAR	Falcon 50	204	Lyon Air, Lyon-Bron.	F-WWHD
F-GKBC	Falcon 10	99	Sofinabail/Michelet International/Darta, Paris-Le Bourget.	N67JW/N500GM N656PC/N10TJ/N176FJ/F-WPXH
F-GKBZ	Falcon 50	185	GIE Air BG, Paris-Le Bourget.	/N238Y/N23SY/C-GDCO/N184FJ/F-WWHE
F-GKCC	Falcon 100	201	Heli-Union/Promodes, Paris-Le Bourget.	(F-GKPZ)/N30TH/JA8494/N8494/N266FJ F-WZGH
F-GKCJ	Beechjet 400A	RK-14	CEGID, Lyon-Bron.	
F-GKDB	Falcon 20E	271	Natiolocation/DB Aviation, Paris-Le Bourget.	F-GHPO/7T-VRP/F-WNGN
F-GKDR	Falcon 50	86	FIBIVIAT/Elf Acquitaine/Regourd Aviation, Paris-Le Bourget.	N238U/N94FJ F-WPXD
F-GKGA	Corvette	11	Gallic Aviation & Marine, Paris-Le Bourget.	F-WFPD/EI-BNY/(F-BIFU)/N613AC F-BTTS/TR-LWY/F-ODKS/F-BTTV
F-GKGB	Corvette	30	Gallic Aviation, Paris-Le Bourget.	/EC-DUE/OO-MRC/TR-LAH/OO-MRC/F-BTTP F-WNGQ
F-GKGL	Citation V	560-0058	Ste Euralair, Paris-Le Bourget.	N2686Y
F-GKHL	Citation V	560-0059	Ste Euralair, Paris-Le Bourget.	N2687L
F-GKID	Citation	500-0319	Sinair, Grenoble.	N9MA/D-ICUW/N22LH/N5319J/HZ-NCI/N5319J
F-GKIR	Citation	500-0361	Montlaur Distribution SA. Montpellier. (was 501-0265).	/N90EB/N5361J C-GOIL/N5361J/F-WIKPW/N5361J
F-GKIS	Falcon 20E	307	Ste Kis France SA/Ste Sporto/Aero-France, Paris-Le Bourget.	OE-GLL/I-GCAL HB-VDV/F-WRQT
F-GKJB	Corvette	20	Ste Uni-Air, Paris-Le Bourget.	TR-LZT/F-BTTN/N616AC/F-WNGS
F-GKJL	Citation V	560-0093	Ste Euralair, Paris-Le Bourget.	
F-GKLV	Falcon 10	41	Slibail/Intl CPU/Nova Finance, Paris-Le Bourget.	N53DB/N50DM/N1HM/N129FJ F-WLCS
F-GKME	Falcon 20F	256	Natiolocation/Pret pour Impression, Paris.	C-GNTZ/N3RC/N4416F/F-WNGL
F-GKPB	Falcon 100	207	Heli-Union/Pechelbronn/Air Entreprise, Paris-Le Bourget.	N711MT/N271FJ F-W...
F-GKPP	MS 760 Paris 2	98	Patrick Pierron, Nice.	3A-MPP/HB-VEP/F-BOHN/D-INGA
F-GKTV	Falcon 50	111	Euralair/Elf Acquitaine, Paris-Le Bourget.	//N297W/F-WZHZ
F-GLIM	Citation V	560-0156	L G Services/Limagrain, Clermont Ferrand.	
F-GLJA	Citation	500-0264	Euralair/SARL Ligier Jet Air, Vichy-Charmeil.	/N205FM/N5264J
F-GMJS	Falcon 10	80	Euralair/Chargeurs SA/Air Affaires International, Paris.	N48R/(N913CB) N161FJ/F-WPXD
F-GPAK	Gulfstream 4	1061	H R H Prince Karim Aga Khan, Paris.	/N457GA
F-GPLT	Citation	550-0033	SOLOMA/Pitchairmer/Air Affaires, Paris-Le Bourget.	N46DA/N755CM/N59MJ TR-LYE/(N3252M)
F-GPSA	Falcon 50	123	Ste Gefco & Cie/Air Gefco, Paris.	/N211EF/VH-SFJ/(F-GDSC)/F-WZHH
F-ODSR	Corvette	35	BNP Bail/Global Aerofinance, Ivato, Malagasy.	YV-01CP/YV-589CP/F-GDAZ PH-JSC
F-ODUT	Citation	550-0050	Sofinabail/Wanair SRL. Papeete, Tahiti.	N250CF/D-CJJJ/N362DJ/N102FC (N3298M)
F-OGSI	Falcon 200	511	BASF AG. Ludwigshafen.	F-WWGR
F-OHES	Falcon 200	514	GIE Sofia/Isotimpex, Sofia, Bulgaria.	(F-GJIS)/F-WWGP
F-WAMD	Falcon 30	01	Wfu. Project shelved 1975. Wings to Falcon 20-486 F-GEFS.	
F-WDFJ	Falcon 20G	362	AMD-BA., Bordeaux. (20G prototype).	F-WATF/F-WZAS
F-WFAL	Falcon 10	01	W/o 31 Oct 72.	
F-WLKB	Falcon 20	01	Wfu. Located Musee de l'Air, Paris-Le Bourget.	F-BLKB/F-WLKB

Registration	Type	c/n	Owner / Operator	Previous identity
F-WMSH	Falcon 20C	1	Wfu. Donated to Rene Lemaire for Bordeaux-Merignac museum.	F-ZACV/F-WMSH F-BMSH/F-WMSH
F-WNDB	Falcon 50	1	AMD-BA., Istres-Le Tube.	F-BNDB/F-BAMD/F-WAMD
F-WRSN	Corvette	01	W/o 23 Mar 71.	
F-WZIH	HFB 320	1024	Musee de l'Air, Paris-Le Bourget. (back to 16+07 ?).	16+07/D-9536/(YA+111) (CA+111)/D-CARO

Great Britain

Registration	Type	c/n	Owner / Operator	Previous identity
G-....	Beechjet 400A	RK-7		
G-....	Beechjet 400A	RK-9		
G-ARVF	VC 10-1101	808	Wfu Apr 83. Located Hermeskeil collection Nr Trier-W Germany	
G-ARYA	HS 125/1	25001	Wfu. Completely dismantled at Kelsterton College-Wales 1985.	
G-ARYB	HS 125/1	25002	Wfu. Located Module training section Hatfield.	
G-ARYC	HS 125/1	25003	Wfu. Located Mosquito Museum-Hatfield.	
G-ASNU	HS 125/1	25005	Flintgrange Ltd/National People's Party of Nigeria, Lagos.	D-COMA/(D-CFKG) G-ASNU
G-ASSM	HS 125/1-522	25010	Wfu. Located at Wroughton for Science Museum.	5N-AMK/G-ASSM
G-ATPD	HS 125/1B-522	25085	Group 4 International Airborne Services Ltd. Heathrow.	5N-AGU/G-ATPD
G-ATPE	HS 125/1B-522	25092	Cx UK 14 Mar 90 as Wfu.	
G-AVGW	HS 125/3B	25120	W/o 23 Dec 67.	
G-AWXO	HS 125/400B	25178	Merchant Enterprises Ltd. Jersey, C.I.	
G-AXDM	HS 125/400B	25194	GEC Ferranti Defence Systems Ltd. Edinburgh.	
G-AXPS	HS 125/3B	25135	W/o 20 Jul 70.	HB-VAY/G-5-14
G-AYRR	HS 125/403B	25247	Grosvenor Estates, Chester.	(G-5-672)/9Q-CCF/G-AYRR
G-AZCH	HS 125/3B-RA	25154	Wfu. Central fuselage in use at Luton as a mobile display.	EP-AHK
G-BAZB	HS 125/400B	25252	Short Brothers Harland Ltd. Belfast, N.I.	XX505/G-5-17
G-BBRT	HS 125/400B	6036	Wfu. Fuselage used in paint spraying trials, Chester.	
G-BCUX	HS 125/600B	6043	W/o 20 Nov 75.	
G-BCXF	HS 125/600B	6054	Beecham International Aviation Ltd. London.	9K-AED/G-BCXF/G-5-17
G-BEJM	BAC 1-11/423ET	118	Ford Motor Co. Stansted.	VC92-2111/G-16-2
G-BEJW	BAC 1-11/423ET	154	Ford Motor Co. Stansted.	VC92-2110
G-BETV	HS 125/600B	6035	Rolls Royce Ltd. Filton.	F-BKMC
G-BFAN	HS 125/F600B	25258	British Aerospace Aircraft Group, Hatfield.	G-AZHS/(G-5-14)
G-BFAR	Citation	500-0368	Club Air (Europe) Ltd. Maidstone.	A6-SMH/G-BFAR/ZS-LPH/G-BFAR/N36912
G-BFMC	BAC 1-11/414EG	160	Ford Motor Co. Stansted.	D-ANNO/G-16-6
G-BFRM	Citation	550-0027	Marshalls of Cambridge (Engineering) Ltd.	N527CC/N3245M
G-BFVI	HS 125/700B	7037	Marine & Avn Mgmt Intl/Bristow Helicopters Ltd. Redhill.	/G-5-18
G-BGOP	Falcon 20F	406	Falcon Jet Centre/Nissan (UK) Ltd. London.	F-WMKF
G-BGTU	BAC 1-11/409AY	108	Turbo Union Ltd. Filton.	YS-01C/TI-1056C
G-BGYR	HS 125/F600B	6045	British Aerospace Aircraft Group, Warton.	G-5-11/EC-CQT/G-5-18
G-BHLF	HS 125/700B	7091	GEC-Marconi/Magec Aviation Ltd. Luton.	
G-BHSU	HS 125/700B	7103	Shell Aircraft Ltd. London.	/G-5-12
G-BHSV	HS 125/700B	7107	Shell Aircraft Ltd. London.	
G-BHSW	HS 125/700B	7109	Shell Aircraft Ltd. London.	
G-BHTJ	HS 125/700B	7097	British Aerospace PLC. Hatfield.	/G-BRDI/G-HHOI/(G-BHTJ)
G-BHTT	Citation	500-0404	Eurojet/Paycount Ltd. London.	N2614H
G-BJDJ	HS 125/700B	7142	Consolidated Contractors International, London.	/G-5-12
G-BJIR	Citation	550-0296	Gator Aviation Ltd. Jersey.	N6888C
G-BKSR	Citation	550-0469	Moseley Group (PSV) Ltd. Loughborough.	N1251V
G-BLDH	BAC 1-11/492GM	262	McAlpine Aviation Ltd/Instone, London.	
G-BLHD	BAC 1-11/492GM	260	McAlpine Aviation Ltd/Instone, London.	G-16-25
G-BLSM	HS 125/700B	7208	Dravidian Air Services Ltd. London.	G-5-19/(G-BLMJ)/(N710BR)
G-BLTP	HS 125/700B	7210	Dravidian Air Services Ltd. London.	G-5-18/(G-BLMK)/(N710BQ)
G-BNEH	BAe 125/800B	8078	High Speed Flight Ltd.	/G-5-544
G-BNFW	HS 125/700B	7100	British Aerospace PLC. Filton.	G-5-549/D-CLVW/(G-5-19)
G-BNSC	Citation	550-0559	IDS Aircraft Ltd. London.	N1298H
G-BOCB	HS 125/1B-522	25106	Wfu.	G-OMCA/G-DJMJ/G-AWUF/5N-ALY/G-AWUF/HZ-BIN
G-BPCP	Citation	500-0403	W/o 1 Oct 80.	N1710E
G-BRBZ	Beechjet 400	RJ-60	Bass PLC.	N1560T
G-BRUC	BAe 146-100	E1009	British Aerospace PLC. Hatfield.	TZ-ADT
G-BRXR	HS 125/403B	25217	Osprey Aviation Ltd. Dunsfold. (status ?).	G-5-651/9Q-CHD/G-AXYJ
G-BSUL	BAe 125/800B	8186	British Aerospace PLC. Hatfield.	G-5-683

Registration	Type	c/n	Owner / Operator	Previous identity
G-BSVL	Citation V	560-0077	P & G S Thomas, Cardiff.	N2745R
G-BSZP	Beechjet 400	RJ-56	Air Hanson Aircraft Sales Ltd. Farnborough.	/N1556W
G-BTAB	BAe 125/800B	8088	Abbey Investment Co. London.	/G-BOOA/(ZK-RHP)/G-5-563
G-CCCL	Citation	500-0354	Corporate Jet Services/Colt Car Co Ltd. Staverton.	N51GA//G-BEIZ/(N5363J)
G-CITI	Citation	501-0084	Messenger Group PLC. Warrington.	(N11JC)/(N463CJ)/N3160M
G-CJET	Learjet	35A-365	Interflight (CI) Ltd. Gatwick.	/G-SEBE/G-ZIPS/(N4564S)/G-ZONE
G-CZAR	Citation V	560-0046	N M Jagger, Jersey, C.I.	(N26656)
G-DBAL	HS 125/3B	25117	RCR International Ltd. Eastleigh.	G-BSAA/5N-AKT/5N-AET
G-DBII	Citation V	560-0032	Artix Ltd. Peterlee, Co. Durham.	N1229M
G-DJLW	HS 125/3B-RA	25140	Source International Ltd. Andover.	/G-AVVB/G-5-17
G-DNVT	Gulfstream 4	1078	Shell Aircraft Ltd. London.	N17589
G-EJET	Citation	550-0154	Euro-Jet/European Jet Ltd. Belfast, N.I.	/G-DJBE/(N8887N)
G-ELOT	Citation	550-0601	Elliots Brick Ltd. Leeds.	(N1303M)
G-ELRA	BAe 1000	9003	British Aerospace PLC. Hatfield.	G-5-6..
G-EXLR	BAe 1000	8151	British Aerospace PLC. Hatfield.	
G-EXPM	BAC 1-11/217EA	124	European Aviation Ltd.	A12-124
G-FANN	HS 125/600B	6019	Macavia International Ltd. London.	HZ-AA1/G-BARR
G-FASL	BAe 125/800B	8149	Fisons PLC. East Midlands.	G-5-635
G-FBMB	Challenger 601-3A	5041	Challenger Aviation Ltd/M Bouyghes, Paris.	/C-FETZ/C-G...
G-FFLT	HS 125/600B	6057	Albion Aviation Management Ltd. Gatwick.	HZ-KA2/G-5-17
G-FIVE	HS 125/1	25004	Wfu. Wings used in rebuild of s/n 25008.	G-ASEC
G-FRAA	Falcon 20EW	385	F R Aviation Ltd. Hurn.	N118R/N139F/F-WJMJ
G-FRAB	Falcon 20EW	356	F R Aviation Ltd. Hurn.	N27RX//N27R/N4468F/F-WMKG
G-FRAC	Falcon 20EW	254	F R Aviation Ltd. Hurn.	C-FYPB/N4423F/F-WNGO
G-FRAD	Falcon 20EW	304	F R Aviation Ltd. Hurn.	G-BCYF/F-WRQP
G-FRAE	Falcon 20EW	280	F R Aviation Ltd. Hurn.	N910FR/I-EDIS/F-WPXK
G-FRAF	Falcon 20EW	295	F R Aviation Ltd. Hurn.	N911FR/I-EDIM/F-WRQQ
G-FRAH	Falcon 20EW	223	F R Aviation, Bournemouth.	N900FR/(N904FR)/N22FE/N4407F/F-WPUX
G-FRAI	Falcon 20EW	270	F R Aviation, Bournemouth.	N901FR/(N907FR)/N37FE/N4435F/F-WPUZ
G-FRAS	Falcon 20EW	82	FR Aviation Ltd. Hurn.	117501/20501/F-WJMM
G-FRAT	Falcon 20EW	87	FR Aviation Ltd. Hurn.	117502/20502/F-WJMJ
G-FRAU	Falcon 20EW	97	FR Aviation Ltd. Hurn.	117504/20504/F-WJMJ
G-FRAV	Falcon 20EW	103	FR Aviation Ltd. Hurn.	/117505/20505/F-WMKH
G-FRAW	Falcon 20EW	114	FR Aviation Ltd. Hurn.	/117507/20507/F-WJMM
G-GAUL	Citation	550-0127	Chauffair/The WCRS Group PLC. London.	N550TJ/(N29TG)/N29TC/N2631N
G-GAYL	Learjet	35A-429	Northern Executive Aviation Ltd. Manchester.	//G-ZING
G-GEIL	BAe 125/800B	8021	Heron Management Services Ltd. Luton.	
G-GJCB	BAe 125/800B	8079	J C Bamford (Excavators) Ltd. East Midlands. 'Exporter 9'	G-5-542
G-HYGA	BAe 125/800B	8034	Helpfactor Ltd. London.	//G-5-12
G-ICED	Citation	501-0230	Iceland Frozen Foods PLC. Manchester.	N5RL/N653F/N2616G
G-JEAN	Citation	500-0339	Foster Associates Ltd. Hatfield.	N300EC/N707US//G-JEAN/(N5339J)
G-JETA	Citation	550-0094	IDS Aircraft Ltd. London.	(N26630)
G-JETB	Citation	550-0288	IDS Aircraft Ltd. London.	G-MAMA/G-JETB/N4564P/G-JETB/N6865C
G-JETC	Citation	550-0282	Nelson Leasing & Finance Ltd. Southend.	N68644
G-JETE	Citation	500-0198	IDS Aircraft Ltd. London.	/G-BCKM
G-JETI	BAe 125/800B	8056	Jet One/Yeates of Leicester/Magec Aviation, Luton.	/G-5-509
G-JETL	Learjet	35A-656	Cameron Hall Developments Ltd. Hatfield.	/N3810G
G-JJSG	Learjet	35A-324	John Jefferson Smurfit Group, St Louis, Mo-USA.	/
G-JSAX	HS 125/3B-RA	25157	Wfu. Broken up at Southampton Apr 86.	G-GGAE/VR-BGD/D-CAMB
G-KASS	HS 125/F3B	25127	Thurston Aviation/Eroten Ltd. London.	G-5-623/G-AVPE
G-KROO	BAC 1-11/217EA	125	European Aviation Ltd.	A12-125
G-LEAR	Learjet	35A-265	Northern Executive Aviation Ltd. Manchester.	(G-ZEST)/N1462B
G-LJET	Learjet	35A-643	Tiger Aviation Ltd. Woking.	/N39418
G-LORI	HS 125/403B	25246	Re-Enforce Trading Co. Ltd. London. (status ?).	G-AYOJ/9Q-COH/G-AYOJ (G-5-15)
G-MARS	Beechjet 400	RJ-36	Havilland Air Ltd. Guernsey, Channel Islands.	N3236Q/G-RSRS/N3236Q/G-RSRS N3236Q
G-MHIH	HS 125/700B	7139	Queens Moat Houses PLC. Southend.	//G-BKAA/(G-GAIL)/G-5-18
G-MTLE	Citation	501-0170	Talan Ltd. Norwich.	/G-GENE/N501HP/(N6778Y)
G-NEVL	Learjet	35A-662	Atlantic Learjet Sales Ltd. Cranfield.	
G-OBEL	Citation	500-0220	Aviation Beauport/Gator Aviation Ltd. Jersey, C.I.	G-BOGA/N932HA/N93WD N5220J
G-OBOB	HS 125/3B	25069	W/o 30 Jan 89.	G-BAXL/VH-ECF

Page 20

Registration	Type	c/n	Owner / Operator	Previous identity
G-OCBA	HS 125/3B	25132	CB Group Ltd/CB Helicopters, London.	/G-MRFB/G-AZVS/OY-DKP
G-OCCC	BAe 125/800B	8013	Consolidated Contractors International. (based Athens).	//G-5-14
G-OHEA	HS 125/3B-RA	25144	Rogers Aviation/Hatfield Executive Aviation, Hatfield.	G-AVRG/G-5-12
G-OKSP	Citation	500-0364	Osiwel Ltd. Leavesden.	N20WP/(N221JB)/N221AC/HB-VFF/N36892
G-OMCL	Citation	550-0413	Quantel Ltd. Biggin Hill.	N12160
G-OMGA	HS 125/600B	6024	S H Services Ltd/Magec Aviation Ltd. Luton.	G-BSHL/G-BBMD/N50GD/G-BBMD
G-OMGB	HS 125/600B	6039	Magec Aviation Ltd. Luton.	/EC-EAO/G-BKBM/N410AW/(N61TF)/G-BKBM/G-BCCL
G-OMGC	HS 125/600B	6056	Magec Aviation Ltd. Luton.	G-BKCD/5N-ARN/G-BKCD/G-BDOA/G-5-13
G-OPFC	BAe 1000	8159	British Aerospace PLC. Hatfield.	
G-OPOL	HS 125/F3B-RA	25171	Launchroy/Magec Aviation Ltd. Luton.	(N171AV)/G-BXPU/G-AXPU/G-IBIS/G-AXPU HB-VBT/G-5-19
G-ORCE	Citation	550-0343	Oracle Corp. London.	A6-SMS/N56FB/N20GT/N721US/G-MINE/(N1214D)
G-OSMC	Citation	550-0122	SMC Aviation Ltd. London.	C-FCEL/N70GM//N135CC/N2746E
G-OSNB	Citation	550-0569	Scottish & Newcastle Breweries PLC. Edinburgh.	G-JFRS/N1299P
G-OTMC	Beechjet 400	RJ-50	Donnington Aviation/Tarmac PLC. East Midlands.	N1550Y
G-OXEC	Citation	500-0093	Streamline/I F Aviation Ltd. East Midlands.	N611SW/OO-FBY/PH-CTB/N593CC
G-PBWH	BAe 125/800B	8182	Freedom Trust SA/Lynton Aviation Ltd.	G-5-676
G-PNNY	Citation	500-0165	Merline Marine Aviation (Jersey) Ltd. Jersey, C.I.	//N19MQ/N19M
G-POSN	BAe 125/800B	8120	P & O Containers (Assets) Ltd. Hatfield.	G-5-606
G-PRMC	HS 125/700B	7031	RMC Group Services Ltd. Biggin Hill.	/G-BFSP
G-RAFF	Learjet	35A-504	Graff Aviation Ltd. London.	N8568B
G-SSOZ	Citation	550-0597	Arrows Aviation Co Ltd. Manchester.	N13027
G-TACE	HS 125/403B	25223	Lynx Aviation Ltd. Cranfield. (wfu ?).	G-AYIZ/F-BSSL/PJ-SLB/G-AYIZ
G-TEFH	Citation	500-0176	Birmingham Aviation Ltd. Elmdon.	/G-BCII
G-THCL	Citation	550-0563	Tower House Consultants Ltd. St Clement, Jersey, C.I.	N1298P
G-TOMI	HS 125/600B	6030	Falcon Jet Centre Ltd. Heathrow.	G-BBEP/5N-ARD/G-BBEP/G-BJOY/G-BBEP
G-TOMY	Diamond 1A	A090XA	Lynton Aviation Ltd. Kidlington.	/N312DM
G-TPHK	BAe 125/800B	8130	Tiphook PLC. London.	G-FDSL/G-5-620
G-TSAM	BAe 125/800B	8028	British Aerospace PLC. Hatfield.	//G-5-12
G-UESS	Citation	500-0326	W/o 8 Dec 83.	N45LC/N5326J
G-UKCA	HS 125/700B	7214	Magec Aviation/Civil Aviation Authority, London.	/HZ-SJP/G-5-17
G-VIPS	Learjet	35A-614	Executive Air Charter, Biggin Hill.	/G-SOVN/HB-VJC//G-PJET/N3815G
G-VJAY	HS 125/F400B	25254	Jensen & Nicholson (Singapore) Pte Ltd. 'Sidhartha'	G-5-624/G-AYLG/3D-AVL G-AYLG
G-WBPR	BAe 125/800	8085	Trust House Forte Airport Services Ltd. London.	G-5-551
G-XMAF	Gulfstream 3	407	Fayair (Jersey) Ltd. C.I.	N17603
G-XRMC	BAe 125/800B	8180	RMC Group Services Ltd. Biggin Hill.	G-5-675
G-YUGO	HS 125/1B-522	25094	Burtonwood Developments Ltd. Birmingham.	G-ATWH/HZ-BO1/G-ATWH

Switzerland & Liechtenstein

Registration	Type	c/n	Owner / Operator	Previous identity
HB-IAB	Falcon 900	9	GFTA Trendanalysen, Basle.	(PH-ILC)/F-WWFJ
HB-IAC	Falcon 900	26	ALG Aeroleasing SA. Geneva.	F-WWFM
HB-IAD	Falcon 900	35	ALG Aeroleasing S.A/Industrie Leasing Zurich S.A. Lausanne.	F-WWFC
HB-IAE	Falcon 50	150	IBM (Schweiz), Zurich.	N136FJ/F-WZHC
HB-IAF	Falcon 900	30	Pan Ocean Oil Co/ALG Aeroleasing S.A. Geneva.	F-WWFL
HB-IAG	Falcon 900	174	ALG Aeroleasing S.A. Geneva.	F-WPXE
HB-IAK	Falcon 900	15	Sofijet SA-Fribourg/Gatair S.A. Geneva.	/F-WWFM
HB-IAL	Falcon 50	63	Lubis SA-Lugano/Gofir SA. Agno.	//N841F/N78FJ/F-WZHF
HB-IAM	Falcon 50	164	IBM (Schweiz), Zurich.	N164FJ/F-WZHD
HB-IEC	Falcon 50	134	ALG Aeroleasing S.A. Geneva.	F-WPXK
HB-IEE	B 757-23A	24527	Petrolair Systems SA. Geneva.	HB-IHU
HB-IEF	DC 9-14	45702	Industrie Leasing Zurich SA/ALG Aeroleasing SA. Geneva.	HB-IAA/N99YA/N15NP I-SARJ/N3307L
HB-IEH	B 737-2V6	22431	Petrolair Systems, Athens.	N57008
HB-IEP	Falcon 50	67	ALG Aeroleasing SA/Koci S.A. Geneva.	//N76FJ/F-WZHG
HB-IER	Falcon 50	57	Socavia AG/Giesecke und Devrient, Munich.	F-WZHC
HB-IES	Falcon 50	61	Logarcheo Anstalt Vaduz, Geneva.	F-WZHI
HB-IFA	DC-9-15	45731	ALG Aeroleasing SA. Geneva.	N120NE/N2H/N901B/N60FM/N8500/HB-IFA
HB-IKS	Challenger 601-3A	5042	Air Charter AG/Kraus & Naimer, Vienna.	C-FEUV/C-G...
HB-IKT	Challenger 601-3A	5003	Belugair SA/Ortigest SA. Neuchatel.	/N778XX/C-GDHP/C-G...
HB-ILH	Challenger 600S	1025	C Hirshman/Jet Aviation, Zurich.	N111J/N111G/N2636M/C-GLXF
HB-ILK	Challenger 601	3033	Impala Air/Trimjet Ltd. Zurich.	N601TJ/C-GLXQ

Registration	Type	c/n	Owner / Operator	Previous identity
HB-ILM	Challenger 601	3024	Vad Air, Mezzovico-Lugano.	N711SD/N711ST/C-GLYA
HB-IMX	Gulfstream 3	335	JABJ/Bright Star Estab. Vaduz.	/
HB-IMY	Gulfstream 4	1084	Sit Set AG. Geneva.	(N448GA)/N1761S
HB-ITN	Gulfstream 3	367	Helmut Horten/Interjet AG/Private Jet Services, Basle	/N17588/(N910A)
HB-ITT	Gulfstream 4	1064	Compagnie NOGA SA. Geneva.	N439GA
HB-ITV	Gulfstream 2B	139	Allway Estab. Geneva.	/HZ-PET/N18N/N880GA
HB-ITW	Gulfstream 2	192	Minute Maid SA. Zurich.	N677RW/N678RW/N811GA
HB-ITZ	Gulfstream 4	1083	Lonrho Ltd/Lonair SA. Zug.	N1761Q
HB-PAA	MS 760 Paris	69	cx Swiss register 25 Jun 84 to ?	J-4117/HB-PAA
HB-VAM	Learjet	23-044	W/o 28 Aug 72.	N22B
HB-VAP	Falcon 20C	37	W/o 1 Oct 67.	(N7922)/(N11WA)/F-WMKF
HB-VBM	Falcon 20C	136	Jetcom S.A. Geneva.	F-GCGU/9K-ACQ/HB-VBM/F-WMKJ
HB-VCG	Falcon 20D	231	W/o 20 Feb 72.	F-WPXE
HB-VDX	Falcon 10	56	ALAG-Alpine Luft, Zurich.	F-WPUY
HB-VEG	Falcon 10	70	Starjet Establishment for Aviation, Vaduz.	F-WJMM
HB-VEM	Learjet	35A-068	Swiss Air Force, Dubendorf.	/
HB-VEV	Falcon 20E	317	Jet Aviation Business Jets, Zurich.	N88FE/N92K/N99E/N31CM/N4452F/F-WMKG
HB-VFB	Learjet	35A-145	Swiss Air Force, Dubendorf.	N39394
HB-VFO	Learjet	35A-184	W/o 6 Dec 82.	N1462B
HB-VFS	Learjet	36A-042	Executive Jet Aviation, Geneva.	N39391
HB-VFW	Challenger 600S	1049	Swiss Air Ambulance, Zurich. 'Fritz Bühler'	N2720B/C-GLXM
HB-VGA	Challenger 600S	1029	Air Charter AG/Kraus & Naimer, Vienna.	C-GLX.
HB-VGF	HS 125/700B	7062	Scintilla/Robert Bosch, Stuttgart.	/G-5-16
HB-VGG	HS 125/700B	7070	Scintilla/Robert Bosch, Stuttgart.	
HB-VGP	Citation	550-0189	Jet Aviation Business Jets. Zurich.	/D-CCAT/N98601
HB-VGR	Citation	550-0080	Jet Aviation Business Jets, Zurich.	G-BFLY/(N26624)
HB-VGS	Citation	550-0183	Jet Aviation Business Jets, Zurich.	(XC-DUF)/N98630
HB-VGZ	Learjet	55-024	R Schwarz Beteiligungen AG. Hilterfingen.	N224DJ/HB-VGZ
HB-VHH	Citation	S550-0028	JABJ/Cranex AG. Zurich.	(N1260L)
HB-VHI	Citation	500-0344	Aero geneva Executive SA. Geneva.	(N632SQ)/N632SC/(N5344J)
HB-VHL	Learjet	55-054	Transair (Suisse) S.A. Geneva.	
HB-VHR	Learjet	35A-501	Jet Air Service AG. Zurich.	
HB-VHU	BAe 125/800B	8152	Rabbit-Air AG. Zurich.	G-5-626
HB-VHV	BAe 125/800B	8153	Rabbit-Air AG. Zurich.	G-5-627
HB-VHW	Citation	650-0060	Sky Jet AG. Zurich.	N1313Q
HB-VHY	Falcon 20F	429	Republic New York Corp/ALG Aeroleasing SA. Geneva.	VR-BHL/F-WMKF
HB-VIA	Diamond 1A	A087SA	Sirius AG. Zurich.	N487DM
HB-VIB	Learjet	55-009	Argos Jet Estab. Geneva.	/N55SJ/N42ES
HB-VIC	Citation	501-0098	Swissphone Components/Gruezi Air Services Ltd. Wollerau.	(N144AB)/N144AR
HB-VIF	Learjet	36A-057	ALG Aeroleasing SA. Singapore.	N44RD/N3161M
HB-VII	Learjet	35A-503	Fidinam Fudiciara S.A. Lugano.	/N8567A
HB-VIK	BAe 125/800B	8091	Swiss Air Ambulance, Zurich.	G-5-560
HB-VIL	BAe 125/800B	8097	Swiss Air Ambulance, Zurich.	G-5-567
HB-VIM	Learjet	31-018	General Beverage (Managem) SA. Geneva.	N40144
HB-VIO	Citation	551-0205	Skywork Corp AG. Berne. (was 550-0161)	N342DA//N3951Z/XA-KIQ/N999AU/N88732
HB-VIR	Citation	551-0339	Speed Air/R Schwarz Beteiligungen AG. Berne. (was 550-0299).	/N538M/N6888L
HB-VIS	Citation	550-0447	Jean Pierre Magnin/Air City SA. Geneva.	(N447CJ)/N12482/(N1248K)
HB-VIT	Citation	550-0197	Starways S.A. Lugano.	N44FC/(N30F)/N6798Z
HB-VIU	Citation	550-0465	Albagno SA/Sunshine Aviation S.A. Lugano.	N68JW/N206TC/N1251H
HB-VIY	Citation	650-0040	Industrie Leasing AG-Zurich/Execair SA. Lugano.	VR-BJY/N82TC
HB-VIZ	Citation	550-0188	High Line AG. Zurich.	/VH-SWL/N98675
HB-VJB	Citation	501-0067	Speed-Air/Rudolf Schwarz Beteiligungen AG. Hilterfingen.	D-IGMB/SE-DEO
HB-VJF	Sabre-65	465-59	Starways S.A. Lugano.	N2959A N65AN
HB-VJH	Citation	550-0207	Unilabs Holdings SA. Geneva.	N1823C/N60BB/N163CB/(N95CC)/N6800C
HB-VJI	Learjet	31-011	ALG Aeroleasing SA. Geneva.	N3803G
HB-VJJ	Learjet	35A-649	Executive Jet Aviation SA. Geneva.	N10870
HB-VJK	Learjet	35A-651	ALG Aeroleasing SA. Geneva.	
HB-VJL	Learjet	35A-653	ALG Aeroleasing SA. Geneva.	
HB-VJR	Citation	500-0343	Servair Private Charter AG. Zurich.	N91D/C-FRHL/N525AC/(N5343J)
HB-VJS	Falcon 20F	383	ALG Aeroleasing SA. Geneva.	5N-AYO/D-CONU/F-WRQR
HB-VJT	Citation	650-0076	Jetag AG. Zurich.	N876SC/N376SC/N1315V

Registration	Type	c/n	Owner / Operator	Previous identity
HB-VJV	Falcon 20D-5	237	ALG Aeroleasing SA. Geneva.	VR-BKH/VR-CBT/N4227Y/D-CITY/(D-CALM)/(D-CHCH)/F-WPXF
HB-VJW	Falcon 20D-5	175	ALG Aeroleasing SA. Geneva.	N116BK/N688MC//N4246R/I-CAIB/F-GBMS/F-ODHA D-COFG/F-BUFG/N866MM/N4373F/F-WMKF
HB-VJX	Falcon 20E	293	ALG Aeroleasing SA. Geneva.	HZ-PL1/N2613/N2615/N4442F/F-WMKJ
HB-VJY	BAe 125/800B	8176	JABJ/Tricom Inc. Lugano.	G-5-652
HB-VJZ	Citation V	560-0055	Belugair SA. Neuchatel.	N2681F
HB-VKA	Citation	S550-0137	Zimex Aviation Ltd. Zurich.	D-CNCA/(N12945)
HB-VKD	Citation	501-0221	Elie Weber, Geneva.	N389JP/N217RR/N643MC/(N26228)

Dominican Republic

Registration	Type	c/n	Owner / Operator	Previous identity
HI-500CT	Citation	550-0220	Coturisca C.A. Santo Domingo.	HI-500SP/HI-500/N288CC/N275CC/N95CC/N6802S
HI-527SP	Citation	501-0012	C.A. de Inversiones Immobiliares, Santo Domingo.	HI-527/N8PJ/N8P/N99GC N99XY/N999RB/N190K/N36858
HI-581SP	Citation	501-0172	Santo Domingo Motors Co CA. Santo Domingo.	/N907KH/(N6782P)

Colombia

Registration	Type	c/n	Owner / Operator	Previous identity
HK-2150	Westwind-1124	181	Helicol-Avianca, Bogota.	HK-2150X/4X-CKE
HK-2485X	Westwind-Two	239	Helicol-Avianca, Bogota.	4X-CMK
HK-2624P	Learjet	25D-339	Carlos Edwardo Restrepo, Bogota.	HK-2624X/N3798D
HK-3121	Learjet	35A-439	Astral Ltd. Bogota.	/HK-3121X/N439ME
HK-3265	Learjet	24D-297	Aeroejecutivos S.A. Bogota.	(N317MR)/N716US/XA-ACC/N297EJ
HK-3400X	Citation	550-0363	Aerovias del Valle y Occidente,	N444CC/(N777NJ)/N1214S

South Korea

Registration	Type	c/n	Owner / Operator	Previous identity
HL7226	Citation	500-0294	Korean Air Lines, Seoul.	N5294J
HL7234	Falcon 20F	370	Korean Air Lines, Seoul.	N1038F/F-WMKG
HL7277	Citation	500-0327	Korean Ministry of Transport, Seoul.	N5327J
HL7386	Falcon 50	179	Korean Airlines, Seoul.	N180FJ/F-WZHP

Honduras

Registration	Type	c/n	Owner / Operator	Previous identity
HR-CEF	Westwind-	...		

China

Registration	Type	c/n	Owner / Operator	Previous identity
B-4005	Challenger 601	3046	Government of People's Republic of China, Beijing.	C-GDBX/C-GLXH
B-4006	Challenger 601	3047	Government of People's Republic of China, Beijing.	C-GBZQ/C-GLXM
B-4007	Challenger 601	3052	Government of People's Republic of China, Beijing.	C-GDCQ
B-4010	Challenger 601-3A	5024	Government of Peoples Republic of China, Beijing.	C-FCDF/C-GLYH
B-4011	Challenger 601-3A	5025	Government of Peoples Republic of China, Beijing.	C-FCGS/C-GLWR
B-4101	Citation	S550-0049	Airborne Remote Sensing Centre,	N1270K
B-4102	Citation	S550-0050	Chinese National Aero-Technical Import Corp.	N1270S
HY-984	Learjet	36A-053	Geological survey for Chinese Governemnt.	N39418
HY-985	Learjet	36A-034	Geological survey for Chinese Government.	N763R
HY-986	Learjet	35A-601	Poly Technologies Inc.	
HY-987	Learjet	35A-602	Poly Technologies Inc.	
HY-988	Learjet	35A-603	Poly Technologies Inc.	

Saudi Arabia

Registration	Type	c/n	Owner / Operator	Previous identity
HZ-...	Challenger 601-3A	5079		C-GLWV
HZ-AB1	BAC 1-11/414EG	158	Abdul Aziz Al-Ibrahim.	HZ-AMH/HZ-MF1/D-AISY
HZ-AB2	Falcon 900	61	Sheikh Abdul Aziz Ibrahim/Al Anwae Aviation,	VR-CSA/F-WWFB
HZ-ADC	Gulfstream 4	1037	Raytheon Middle East Systems, Jeddah.	VR-BKE/N17588
HZ-AF.	Gulfstream 4	1038	Saudia Special Flight Services, Jeddah.	/N438GA/N17603
HZ-AFH	Gulfstream 2	171	Saudia Special Flight Services, Jeddah.	N17586
HZ-AFI	Gulfstream 2TT	201	Saudia Special Flight Services, Jeddah.	N17585
HZ-AFJ	Gulfstream 2TT	203	Saudia Special Flight Services, Jeddah.	N17587
HZ-AFK	Gulfstream 2TT	239	Saudia Special Flight Services, Jeddah.	N17582

Registration	Type	c/n	Owner / Operator	Previous identity
HZ-AFL	Gulfstream 3	311	Saudia Special Flight Services, Jeddah.	N17585
HZ-AFM	Gulfstream 3	324	Saudia Special Flight Services, Jeddah.	
HZ-AFN	Gulfstream 3	364	Saudia Special Flight Services, Jeddah.	N1761D
HZ-AFP	Citation	550-0472	Saudia Special Flight Services, Jeddah.	N12511
HZ-AFQ	Citation	550-0473	Saudia Special Flight Services, Jeddah.	N12513
HZ-AFR	Gulfstream 3	410	Saudia Special Flight Services, Jeddah.	/N350GA
HZ-AFT	Falcon 900	21	Saudia Special Flight Services, Jeddah.	(HZ-R4A)/F-WWFJ
HZ-AFU	Gulfstream 4	1031	Saudia Special Flight Services, Jeddah.	/N434GA
HZ-AFV	Gulfstream 4	1035	Saudia Special Flight Services, Jeddah.	/N435GA
HZ-AMB	BAC 1-11/401AK	069	Sheikh Abdul M Baroom/AMC Aviation, Jeddah.	VR-CAM/3D-LLG/N5029
HZ-BL1	BAC 1-11/401AK	080	Sheikh bin Laden/AMC Aviation, Jeddah.	HZ-MFA/N9OTF/N22RB/N10HM/N5038
HZ-BL2	BAe 125/800A	NA0419	Bin Laden Organization,	/N564BA/G-5-597
HZ-DA4	HS 125/700B	7124	Dallah AVCO.	
HZ-DAT	B 707-123B	17644	Dallah AVCO.	N7517A
HZ-DC2	Falcon 20F	363	Sheikh Al Khereiji.	F-WRQV
HZ-DG1	B 727-51	19124	Dallah AVCO,	N604NA/N478US
HZ-FMA	HS 125/1B	25105	Saudi Arabian Carpets, Jeddah.	G-AYRY/D-CKCF/(D-CKOW)
HZ-FNA	JetStar-8	5056	Saudi FAL Group,	HZ-FK1/HZ-FNA/N300AG/N105GH/N105G/N9223R
HZ-GP5	Learjet	25XR-199	W/o 11 Jan 82.	HZ-RI1/HB-VEI
HZ-HE4	B 727-29C	19987	Al Anwae Aviation/Sheikh Hassan Enany.	N444SA/N696WA/OO-STE
HZ-HM1A	B 747-3G1	23070	Saudi Royal Family.	N1784B
HZ-HM1B	B 747SP-68	21652	Saudi Royal Family.	HZ-HM1/N1780B
HZ-HM2	B 707-368C	21081	Saudi Royal Family.	HZ-HM1
HZ-HM3	B 707-368C	21368	Saudi Royal Family.	HZ-ACK
HZ-HM4	B 737-268	22050	Saudi Royal Family.	HZ-AGT
HZ-HR2	Gulfstream 3	346	Saudi Oger Ltd. Riyadh.	HZ-RH2/N17581
HZ-HR3	B 727-2Y4	22968	Saudi Oger Ltd/Rafic Hariri, Riyadh.	HZ-RH3
HZ-HR4	Gulfstream 3	415	Saudi Oger Ltd. Riyadh.	N17582
HZ-KA3	Falcon 20C	174	Sheikh Kamal Adham, Jeddah.	F-WSHT/HB-VER/TL-KAZ/TL-AAY/F-WNGL
HZ-KA4	B 720-047B	18453	Sheikh Kamal Adham, Jeddah.	N93147
HZ-KA5	HS 125/600B	6049	Sheikh Kamal Adham, Jeddah.	G-BCXL/ZS-JHL/G-BCXL
HZ-MA1	JetStar-8	5105	Sheikh Ashmawi/Saudi Arabian Markets, Jeddah.	/N17005/N7005/N2277T/N277T
HZ-MAA	BAC 1-11/401AK	060	AMC Aviation/National Commercial Bank, Jeddah.	HZ-NB3/HZ-GP2/HZ-GRP/N102GP N111NA/N5020
HZ-MAJ	BAC 1-11/401AK	088	Jarallah Corp.	HZ-NIR/N5042
HZ-MAL	Gulfstream 3	379	Dallah AVCO/Mawarid Ltd/Saudi International Trading Estab.	/N17586
HZ-MNC	Gulfstream 4	1076	Mouawad S.A.	N17586
HZ-MS1	Learjet	35A-467	Saudi Armed Forces Medical Services, Riyadh.	N3796Q
HZ-MS11	DC 8-72	46084	Saudi Armed Forces Medical Services, Riyadh.	N2547R/6Y-JII/N8972U
HZ-MS3	Gulfstream 3	385	Saudi Armed Forces Medical Services, Riyadh.	N1761K
HZ-MS4	Gulfstream 2	103	Saudi Armed Forces Medical Services, Riyadh.	N833GA/P2-PNG/P2-PNF/N833GA G-BDMF/N801GA/N855GA
HZ-MSD	Gulfstream 2	256	Saudi Armed Forces Medical Services, Riyadh.	/N17581
HZ-NB2	BAC 1-11/401AK	064	AMC/National Commercial Bank, Jeddah.	N5024
HZ-ND1	Gulfstream 2TT	216	NADCO=National Development Co. Dhahran.	N200RG/N63SD/HB-IEZ
HZ-NR1	Sabre-75A	380-71	Rashid Engineering, Riyadh.	
HZ-OFC	BAe 125/800B	8050	Olayan Finance Co. Al Khobar.	G-5-503
HZ-PCA	Gulfstream 3	179	Presidency of Civil Aviation, Jeddah.	HZ-CAD/N17588
HZ-RC3	Gulfstream 3	331	Royal Commission for Jubail & Yanbu, Riyadh.	N17LB/N307GA
HZ-SAA	Challenger	1074	Arab Wings, Riyadh.	N10FE/N1FE/N317FE/C-GLYK
HZ-SAB	Falcon 50	73	SABIC=Saudi Arabian Basic Industries Corp. Riyadh.	F-WPXE
HZ-SJP	BAe 125/800B	8068	Jouanou & Parskevaides Saudi Arabia Ltd. Riyadh.	G-5-653/HZ-SJP/G-5-539
HZ-SM3	Falcon 50	165	M M A Edrees/Saudi Arabian Monetary Agency/ARABASCO, Riyadh.	F-WZHF
HZ-TAS	B 707-321B	18338	Prince Turki Faisal Bandar. (wfu ?).	N98WS/N111MF/N763W/N763PA
HZ-TFA	B 727-21	19006	Rifaat Al Assad/Pinecroft Ltd. Paris.	N2CC/N324AS/N324PA
HZ-TNA	JetStar-731	26/5120	Prince Turki bin Nasser, Jeddah.	/N40DC/N7965S
HZ-WBT	B 727-95	19252	Khalid bin Al Waleed Foundation, 'KR-2'	N740EV
HZ-ZTC	Citation V	560-0036	Omega Holding/Zahid Tractor & H.M. Co Ltd.	N107CR/N107CF
SA-R-7	DH Comet 4C	6461	W/o 20 Mar 63.	

Italy

Registration	Type	c/n	Owner / Operator	Previous identity
I-....	Falcon 900	89	Soc. CAI, Rome.	F-W...
I-ACCG	Falcon 20F	474	Soc. Air Capitol S.p.A. Rome.	(I-ACPL)/F-GFFS/F-WMKF
I-ACIF	Beechjet 400	RJ-28	Fortune Aviation/Soc Air Capitol, Rome.	N31428
I-ACTL	Falcon 20F	427	Soc. Air Capitol S.p.a. (status ?).	5N-AYN/F-WRQV
I-ADAG	Falcon 50	131	Soc. Fiat, Turin.	/HZ-BB2/F-WPXD
I-AEAL	Citation	500-0053	Soc. Italfly, Rovereto-Trento.	HB-VGO/I-KUNA/N90WJ/I-CITY/N553CC
I-AGEB	Learjet	35A-243	Soc. Eurojet Italia, Milan.	N81863/HZ-ABM/N3812G
I-AGEN	Learjet	35A-491	Soc. Eurojet Italia, Milan.	N485/N241AG/N491HS/N8563N
I-AGER	Learjet	55-045	Soc. Eurojet Italia S.p.A. Milan.	(N49PD)/N49PE/N90583/EC-DSI/VR-BHV EC-DSI/HB-VHK
I-AGSM	Citation	551-0419	Soc. SIAI Marchetti S.p.A. Milan.	(N1OPX)/N200RN/N200RT/N1217P
I-AIFA	Learjet	36A-021	W/o 10 Dec 79.	N3524F
I-AIRV	Citation	501-0102	Soc. Air Vallee S.p.A. Aosta.	(N223RE)/N486CC/(N2646X)
I-ALBS	Citation	500-0023	Alitaxi SRL. Milan.	N900JD/N523JD/N523CC
I-ALGU	Diamond 1A	A067SA	ALITAXI SRL. Milan.	N123VJ/N367DM
I-ALKA	Citation	550-0351	Soc. Aliadriatica, Pescara.	N99KW/
I-ALKB	Citation	550-0352	Soc. Aliadriatica, Pescara.	(N72B)/N140V/(N140DV)/(N1214J)
I-ALPG	Citation	551-0355	Ithifly S.p.a/ALPI Eagles, Thiene (VI).	N551AS/N5451G
I-ALPM	Learjet	35A-133	Soc. Ithifly S.p.A. Venezia.	/N58RW/N35NB/N728GL
I-ALPR	Learjet	55-078	Soc. ALPI Eagles, Thiene (VI).	N56TG/N55GV/(N55GJ)
I-ALPT	Learjet	35A-198	Ithifly S.p.a/ALPI Eagles, Thiene (VI).	/N25FS
I-ALSE	Beechjet 400	RJ-10	Soc. Aliserio, Bergamo. (was A1010SA Diamond 2).	N410BA/N499DM
I-ALSI	Beechjet 400	RJ-31	Soc. Aliserio SRL. Milan.	N5450M/N545GM
I-ALSO	Beechjet 400	RJ-34	Soc. Aliserio, Bergamo.	N3134T
I-AMAW	Citation	500-0095	Executive Air Centre/Soc. Ital Trade Act, Roma-Urbe.	/N500KP/N4249A YV-15CP//(N578WB)/N2200R/N595CC
I-AMCT	Citation	500-0114	New Aviation Service/Soc. Romaleasing, Rome.	/(G-BNZP)//N899N/N999JB (N614CC)
I-AMCU	Citation	500-0109	Soc. Aviomar, Roma-Urbe.	/G-RAVY////N44SA
I-AMME	Learjet	24D-310	W/o 6 Feb 76.	HB-VDU
I-ASAZ	Citation	550-0432	Soc. Benetton/Benair S.p.A. Treviso.	N432CC/(N12191)
I-ATSA	Citation	650-0161	Aerotaxi Sud S.p.A. Naples.	N161CC/(N1312K)
I-ATSB	Citation V	560-0033	Aerotaxi Sud S.p.A. Naples.	N1229N
I-ATSC	Citation	...	Aerotaxi Sud SpA. Naples.	
I-ATSE	Citation	550-0649	Aerotaxi Sud SpA. Naples.	
I-ATSE	Citation	550-0659	Aerotaxi Sud SpA. Naples.	
I-AUNY	Citation	501-0213	Panair Compagnia Aereo Mediterranea SRL. Rome.	N6785D
I-AVGM	Citation	550-0492	A A A V Aerea Radiomisure, Rome.	(N1254G)
I-AVJD	Learjet	25D-214	Soc. Avioriprese, Capodichino-Napoli.	N90BR/N3UW/N3OW
I-AVJE	Learjet	25D-254	Soc. Avioriprese, Capodichino-Napoli.	N973
I-AVRM	Citation	550-0491	A A A V Aerea Radiomisure, Rome.	(N1254D)
I-AVVM	Citation	S550-0062	A A A V Aerea Radiomisure, Rome.	N12715
I-BAEL	Falcon 20F	426	Soc. Alba Serv Aerotrasporti, Milan.	N416RM/N555PT/N123WH/N427F/F-WJMK
I-BEAU	Falcon 900	23	Soc. SARAS, Milan.	F-WWFK
I-BETV	Falcon 50	104	Soc. Olimpias S.p.A. Milan.	N13195
I-BEWW	Challenger 601-3A	5020	Soc. Benetton S.p.A. Veneto-Treviso.	C-FBKR/C-GLYA
I-BLSM	Challenger 600S	1076	Soc. ITALNOLI S.p.A. Milan.	/N7SP/N8000/C-GLXK
I-BMFE	Learjet	25C-146	Cie Generale Ripresa Aerea, Parma.	N6KJ//N9HN/C-GRQX/N9HN/N9HM/N146LJ
I-CAFB	Falcon 50	138	Soc. Fiat, Turin.	N941CC/N75G/F-WPXD
I-CAFC	Falcon 50	145	Soc. Fiat/Soc. Servizi Gestionali-SEGEST, Turin.	/A6-ZKM/F-GEXE/F-WPXE
I-CAFD	Falcon 50	183	Soc. Fiat, Turin.	F-WWHF
I-CAFE	Falcon 50	190	Soc. Fiat, Turin.	F-WHHG
I-CALC	Falcon 10	127	Soc. Calcestruzzi S.p.a. Ravenna.	F-GCTT/F-WNGG
I-CEFI	Citation	S550-0047	Soc. Salumificio Cesare Fiorucci S.p.A. Roma-Urbe.	/N12695
I-CIGA	Citation	550-0217	Soc. CIGA Hotels Aviation, Venice.	N340DA/N66DN/N66DD/N88DD/N6804L
I-CIGB	Citation	501-0163	Soc. CIGA Hotels Aviation, Venice.	(I-AGIK)/N1354G
I-CIPA	Citation	501-0166	Soc. Kelemata S.p.a. Turin.	/N476X/N2614C
I-CIST	Citation	650-0085	Soc. CISET-Cia Italiana Servizi Tecnici S.p.a. Brescia.	/N650DA/JA8249 N1317G
I-CMUT	Falcon 20F	389	Soc. Aer Marche S.p.A. Ancona.	F-WRQV
I-CNEF	Falcon 200	506	Soc. CAI, Rome.	F-WPUZ

Registration	Type	c/n	Owner / Operator	Previous identity
I-COTO	Learjet	25D-285	Wfu. Broken up at Paris-Le Bourget 10/86.	/N422G/N666KK/N6666K/(N28RW) N6666R
I-CREM	Falcon 10	161	Soc. Interjet SRL, Castelvetro di Modena.	N50SL/N30CN/N230FJ/F-WZGM
I-CSGA	Falcon 50	203	Soc. Ferruzzi-Consorzio Servizi di Gruppo, Forli-Ravenna.	F-WWHA
I-CSGB	Falcon 50	208	Soc. Ferruzzi-Consorzio Servizi di Gruppo, Forli-Ravenna.	F-WWHP
I-DEAF	Citation	550-0255	Soc. SIBA Brescia, Milan.	N6861L
I-DECI	Citation	501-0118	Soc. Frifly, Ronchi dei Legionari.	N2649Z
I-DEGF	Falcon 50	176	Soc. Sirio SRL/Star, Monza.	/N95GC//N157SP/VH-PDJ/N178FJ/F-WZHN
I-DENR	Falcon 50	125	Soc. Norfin S.p.A/De Nora, Ciampino.	N711KT/N118FJ/F-WZHB
I-DIDY	Citation	501-0249	303 Aviation/Sc . United Leasing Nord, Roma.	G-OHLA/N133DM/ZS-LOW/N4263X RP-C237/N2650M
I-DLON	Learjet	35A-346	Soc. Nauta SRL. Venezia.	/N35AJ/C-GMGA/N3803G
I-DOCA	Diamond 1A	A059SA	Soc. SNA-Navigazione Aerea S.p.a. Palermo.	N344DM
I-DUMA	Citation	500-0263	Aerotop-Roma/Soc. Romaleasing, Roma.	(N90WA)///N819H/(N126KP)/N126KR N5263J
I-DVAL	Citation	501-0238	Soc. Delta Air, Rome.	N238JS//N2626A
I-EAMM	Learjet	35A-634	Soc. Dragomar S.p.a. Rome.	
I-EDIK	Falcon 50	132	Soc. Orion S.p.a. Milan.	/F-WPXF
I-EJIB	Learjet	35A-331	Soc. Executive Jet Italiana SRL. Milan.	/HB-VGU/N10870
I-EJIC	Falcon 10	89	Soc. Executive Jet Italiana SRL. Milan.	HB-VIG/3X-GCI/I-CAIC/F-WPXM/D-CADB F-WZGF
I-EJID	Learjet	35A-222	Soc. Executive Jet Italiana SRL. Milan.	HB-VFZ
I-ERDN	Falcon 50	48	Soc. Eridania Zuccherifici Nazionali S.p.a.	/HB-IET/F-WZHK
I-FBCK	Citation	500-0178	Soc. CAT-Cia Aviazione Turistuca SRL. Urbe-Rome.	/D-IKFJ
I-FBCT	Citation	550-0081	Panair Compagnia Aereo Mediterranea SRL. Rome.	/N26626
I-FFLY	Learjet	35A-325	Soc. Frifly, Ronchi dei Legionari.	/D-CARO
I-FICV	Falcon 900	54	Soc. CAI, Rome.	F-WWFC
I-FIMI	Learjet	35A-090	Soc. Recordati Industria Chimica e Farmacia, Milan.	//HB-VEY
I-FIPE	Falcon 20F	368	Intercon/Soc Fimair S.p.A. Milan-Linate.	N83D/VH-NCF/N800CF/N200DE/N800CF N1036F/F-WMKI
I-FIPP	Challenger 601-3A	5069	Soc. Fimair S.p.A. Milan.	/C-FIGR/C-G...
I-FLYA	Citation	501-0099	Eurofly Service S.p.a. Turin.	N3170A
I-FLYB	Citation	500-0392	Eurofly Service S.p.a. Turin/Locafit S.p.a. Turin.	N26461
I-FLYC	Learjet	35A-298	Eurofly Service S.p.a. Turin/Olivetti Leasing, Turin.	
I-FLYD	Citation	550-0393	Soc. CENU=Cementi Nuoresi, Turin.	N12GK/N6862D
I-FLYF	Falcon 20F	428	Soc. Olivetti Computers S.p.a. Firenze.	/N98R/N426F/F-WMKI
I-FLYG	Learjet	35A-593	Eurofly Service S.p.a. Turin.	/N32B
I-FLYH	Learjet	35A-498	Eurofly Service S.p.a. Turin.	/N8564P
I-FLYK	Falcon 20E	241	Eurofly Service S.p.A. Turin.	HZ-PL7/HZ-HE4/N48AD/SE-DCO/F-WRQP
I-FLYL	Astra-1125	036	Eurofly Service S.p.A. Turin.	4X-C..
I-FOMN	Citation	501-0111	Soc. UNIVEX-Universal Import Export, Milan.	N777FE/(N333RB)/N140WC/N2649D
I-FRAB	Diamond 1	A052SA	Diamond Jet/Soc. Eliadamello SpA. Milan.	HB-VHT/N352DM
I-FREU	Learjet	24D-279	Soc. Pozzo S.p.a. Ronchi dei Legionari.	N3DZ/N3DU/VH-SBC/N849GL
I-FTAL	Beechjet 400	RJ-42	Soc. Fruttital/Riviera Air Service, Albenga.	/N400PL/N31542
I-GAMB	Citation	551-0056	Soc Gambogi Costruzione S.p.a.	/(N312CC)/N6864X
I-GCFA	Beechjet 400A	RJ-44	Fincomid Air/Soc. Eliadamello S.p.A. Milan.	N3144A/HB-VJE/N3144A
I-GENC	Diamond 1	A065SA	Casillo Grani/Soc. Romaleasing, Foggia.	OY-CDK/N165GA/N65JN/N361DM
I-GIAZ	Falcon 20E	252	Soc. Ithifly/ALPI EAGLES, Thiene (VI).	F-WRQP
I-GIRL	Diamond 1A	A012SA	Soc. Fincomid Air, Milan.	N107T/N7RC/N82CT/N308DM
I-GJMA	Citation	501-0148	Soc. Desio e Brianza Leasing, Turin.	N500DL/N700ER/N167CB/(OO-ECT)/N1758E
I-ITPR	Falcon 10	115	Soc. LOCAT, Turin/Consorzio Alital, Roma.	F-GGAR/N420JD/N211SR/(N511SR) N511S/N188FJ/F-WPXH
I-JESA	Citation	551-0133	CGA-Compagnia Generale Aeronautica S.p.A. Genova.	/N222TG/G-JRCT/N2663N
I-JUST	Citation	501-0214	Soc. Olimpias, Peretola (Firenze).	N567L/N6887R
I-KALI	Learjet	35A-249	Soc. Gitanair, Bologna.	N107JM
I-KELM	Learjet	35A-406	Soc. Kelemata S.p.a. Turin.	/N35Q/N764G
I-KESO	Citation	550-0398	Soc. Gitanair, Bologna.	N101DD/VH-BRX/N6889T
I-KILO	Learjet	55-007	Soc. Gitanair, Bologna.	/N41ES
I-KIWI	Citation	550-0433	Soc. CIGA Hotels Aviation, Venice.	N1219D
I-KODE	Citation	501-0218	Soc. Grosso e Speier S.p.a. Milan.	N1958E
I-KODM	Learjet	35A-620	Codemi/Soc. Locafit, Rome.	
I-KUSS	Learjet	35A-237	Soc. Gitanair S.p.a. Bologna.	N78MN/N843GL
I-KWYJ	Citation	501-0040	Soc. Recchi Impresa Construzione Generale, Turin.	/N85FS/N87258

Registration	Type	c/n	Owner / Operator	Previous identity
I-LAWN	Citation	501-0208	Soc. Delta Aerotaxi SRL. Campi Bisenzio (FI).	N54MJ/N6784P
I-LCJG	Falcon 10	53	Soc. Air Dolomiti, Trento.	/N891CQ/(N890E)/N125EM/N810US/N8100E/N139FJ F-WLCS
I-LCJT	Falcon 10	96	Soc Air Dolomiti S.p.A/Leali S.p.a. Orio Al Serio (BG).	OE-GLG/XA-SAR N174FJ/F-WNGD
I-LEAR	Learjet	25D-207	Soc. Prelloyd, Portoferraio-Livorno.	(I-GIAN)/N3513F
I-LIAB	Falcon 20C	172	Soc. ALI=Aero Leasing Italiana, Rome.	F-BRHB/F-WNGM
I-LIAC	Falcon 20D	234	Soc. ALI=Aero Leasing Italiana, Rome.	D-COLL/(D-CIBM)/F-WLCU
I-LIAD	Learjet	35A-111	Soc. ALI=Aero Leasing Italiana, Rome.	/OE-GMA/(I-SIDU)/(HB-VFE)/N3815G
I-LOOK	Learjet	55-021	Soc. SNA-Navigazione Area, Florence.	/EI-BSA/N700TG/N3794B
I-LPHZ	Challenger 600S	1069	Filippo Fochi SpA. Bologna.	/N816PD//N203G/C-GLXM
I-LUBE	Falcon 10	7	Soc. Executive Jet Italiana SRL. Milan.	HB-VDE/F-BXAG/VR-BFF/F-WJMN
I-LUBI	Gulfstream 4	1123	Silvio Berlusconi/Soc. Alba, Milan.	N457GA
I-LXAG	Falcon 50	159	Soc. Luxottica S.p.a. Tessera-Venezia.	/LX-NUR/F-WZHC
I-MADU	Gulfstream 3	448	Daclama Co Ltd/Silvio Berlusconi/Soc. Alba, Milan.	/N255SB/N117JJ/N339GA
I-MAFU	Falcon 200	501	Soc. CAI, Rome.	F-WZZD
I-MCSA	Learjet	35A-099	W/o 22 Feb 78.	HB-VFC/N40146
I-MESK	Citation	551-0003	Industrie Grafiche Meschi/Soc. TAM Leasing S.p.a. Milan.	N72RC/N4445N YV-205CP/N3237M
I-MMAE	Learjet	35A-116	Soc. Fortune Aviation SRL. Rome.	/
I-MOCO	Learjet	35A-445	E A S-Executive Aviation Services, Vicenza.	/HB-VHG/N3802G
I-MPIZ	Beechjet 400	RJ-25	Soc. Impresa Pizzarotti & C. Milan.	N3025T
I-MRDV	Challenger 600S	1078	Soc. Delta Aerotaxi SRL. Milan.	I-MRDV//N600CF/N600DL/C-GLYO
I-MTDE	Falcon 900	43	Feruzzi/Soc. Immobiliare Genova, Forli-Ravenna.	F-WWFF
I-MTNT	Citation	550-0105	Soc. Mistral Air, Rome.	D-CNCP/N116CC/N26649
I-NICK	Sabre-40	282-25	Univex SRL. Genoa.	//N40SJ/I-SNAK/HB-VAK/N6379C
I-NIKJ	Learjet	35-055	EBM Group, Roma-Urbe.	//N70WW/D-CONO
I-NLAE	Falcon 20C	134	Grup-Air, Bergamo/Soc. Finprogetti S.p.a. Milan.	N897D/N897DM/N895F/N4350F F-WMKH
I-NNUS	Challenger 601-3A	5044	SIBA Aviation, Milan.	C-FBBY/C-G...
I-NORT	Citation	500-0320	Eurofly/Soc. Locat, Turin.	N341CC/N299WV/N341CC/N320CC/(N5320J)
I-NYCE	Citation V	560-0053	Soc. Delta Aerotaxi SRL. Florence.	N53CV/N2680X
I-OMEP	Citation	501-0091	Soc. TAM Leasing SpA. Roma-Urbe.	/(JA8361)/N39BE/N33BE/(N55BE)/(N887DM) N3194M
I-OTEL	Citation	501-0048	Soc. CIGA Hotels Aviation, Venice.	(I-DAEP)/N414CC/N87510
I-PALP	Citation	501-0182	Soc. Air Vallee SpA. Aosta.	N360DJ/N6780J
I-PAPE	Citation	501-0256	Soc. Panavio, Milan.	D-ILLL//N2631N
I-PATY	Sabre-60	306-133	Soc. Interfly SRL. Reggio Emilia.	N700WS/N9NP/N6NE/N2151J
I-PEGA	Citation	500-0081	Soc. Icaro, Forli.	HB-VDA/N5B/N581CC
I-PIAI	PD 808	503	W/o 18 Jun 68.	
I-PIAL	PD 808	504	Soc. Rinaldo Piaggio, Genoa.	
I-PLLL	Citation	500-0230	Panair Compagnia Aerea Mediterranea SRL. Ciampino.	/HB-VEH/N230CC/N5230J
I-PNCA	Citation	550-0235	Panair Compagnia Aereo Mediterranea SRL. Ciampino-Roma.	///N67SG/(N6803T)
I-POLE	Falcon 50	180	Soc. Gitanair, Milan.	F-WWHC
I-PTCT	Challenger	1082	Eli-Air SRL. Reggio Emilia.	N600ST/N3854B/C-GLXB
I-RACE	HS 125/1	25006	Soc. Cadabo, Milan.	HB-VAG
I-REAL	Falcon 20E	267	Rusconi Editore S.p.a. Milan.	F-WRQZ
I-RELT	Sabre-40A	282-133	Soc. Elettronica, Rome.	N41MP/N65740
I-ROST	Citation	500-0381	Soc. Gretair SRL. Udine.	N445CC/N3104M
I-RYVA	Learjet	35A-391	Soc. ICIPA, Milan-Malpensa.	N89AT/N813RR/N444BF/N3793D
I-SAFR	Falcon 50	29	Soc. Fiat Aviazione, Turin.	F-WZHB
I-SALV	Citation	550-0561	Mistral Air/Salvagnini Transferica, Sarego, Vicenza.	(I-TNTP)/N1298K
I-SAME	Falcon 50	37	Soc. CAI, Rome.	(I-CAIK)/F-WZHM
I-SAMI	Beechjet 400	RJ-35	Aero Taxi Milano/Soc. Primo Leasing, Siena.	/N85TT
I-SELM	Diamond 1A	A064SA	Graziano Transmissioni/Soc. LOCAT, Turin.	N246GA//N364DM
I-SFRA	Falcon 10	130	Soc. Fermar/Feruzzi, Forli-Ravenna.	F-WZGB
I-SHIP	Falcon 10	110	Soc. Parmalat, Collecchio-Parma.	N901MH/N90MH/N184FJ/F-WNGO
I-SIMD	Learjet	25B-193	ALPI Eagles/Soc. Instituto Trivento del Leasing, Rome.	HB-VIE/I-KISS HB-VEF
I-SNAB	Falcon 50	169	Soc. Naz. Metanodotti, Milan.	F-WPXD
I-SNAC	Falcon 50	30	Soc. Naz. Metanodotti, Milan.	F-WZHD
I-SNAF	HS 125/3B	25145	Wfu.	G-AVXL/LN-NPC/G-AVXL/(G-5-20)
I-SNAG	Falcon 20E	240	Soc. Naz. Metanodotti, Milan.	F-WLCX

Registration	Type	c/n	Owner / Operator	Previous identity
I-SNAP	MS 760 Paris	99	W/o 27 Oct 62.	
I-SNAX	Falcon 900	69	Soc. Naz. Metanodotti, Milan.	F-WWFD
I-SOBE	Falcon 200	487	Soc. CAI, Rome.	(F-GDSD)/F-WDSD/N206FJ/F-WZZB
I-SREG	Falcon 20F	442	Soc. Sirio SRL/STAR, Monza.	N203TA/VH-FJZ/N446F/F-WJML
I-STAP	Beechjet 400	RJ-18	Transfly/Sergio Tacchini/Soc. LOCAFIT, Brescia.	N3130T
I-TALG	Citation	S550-0122	ALI/Soc. Fime Leasing, Naples.	N12929
I-TFLY	Falcon 10	188	Soc Italfly SRL. Roma-Urbe.	HB-VJM/D-CLLL/N64F/N188DH/N253FJ/F-WZGS
I-TNTR	Citation	550-0466	Soc. Mistral Air, Rome.	N1251K/HI-420/N1251K
I-TOIO	Citation	501-0252	Soc. Jolly Hotels, Rome.	N574CC/N825HL/N2628Z
I-UUNY	Citation	500-0358	Panair Compagnia Aereo Mediterranea SRL. Ciampino-Roma.	SE-DEP/N82MJ (EP-PAQ)/N36870
I-VEPA	Falcon 20C	100	Soc. Servizi Trasporti SRL. Milan-Linate.	N200FT/N605RP/N983F/F-WJMN
I-VIGI	Diamond 1	A013SA	Aironjet/Avioline, Cagliari-Sardinia.	/N81HH
I-VIKY	Learjet	55-073	Perini/Soc Romaleasing, Rome.	HB-VHN
I-ZAMP	Citation	S550-0133	Gretair/Leaseindustria Industrie Italiano, Venezia-Tessera.	N7047K/G-VKRS
I-ZOOM	Learjet	35A-135	Soc. Perini Fabio, Pisa.	/N11AK/N719US/D-CDAX/N22MJ/(OO-LFX)

Djibouti

Registration	Type	c/n	Owner / Operator	Previous identity
J2-KBA	Falcon 50	71	Government of Djibouti,	/YI-ALB/F-WZHF

Japan

Registration	Type	c/n	Owner / Operator	Previous identity
JA8246	Diamond 1A	A092SA	W/o 23 Jul 86.	
JA8247	Citation	500-0259	Ito Gumi, Sapporo.	N410ND/N5259J
JA8248	Diamond 1	002	Mitsubishi Heavy Industries, Nagoya.	JQ8003/N81DM/JQ8002
JA8284	Citation	501-0228	Nippon Aerotech Co/Kaigai Bussan Kaisha Ltd.	N501CM/(N999CB)/N2612N
JA8298	Diamond 1A	A074SA	Syowa Koku, Nanki Shirahama.	N22WJ/N374DM
JA8367	Citation	650-0177	Kozeni Housing, Hanamaki.	N1930E
JA8378	Citation	650-0178	Nozaki Sanyo, Kikai.	N178CC/N95CC/N1958E
JA8431	Gulfstream 2	141	JCAB=Japanese Civil Aviation Board, Tokyo.	N17584
JA8438	Citation	500-0321	Asahi Shimbun Publishing Co. Tokyo.	N5321J
JA8474	Citation	500-0415	Asahi Shimbun Publishing Co. Tokyo.	N2072A
JA8493	Citation	501-0324	San-Kei Press Ltd. Haneda.	N2651J
JA8570	Falcon 900	53	Japanese Maritime Safety Agency,	N438FJ/F-WWFN
JA8571	Falcon 900	56	Japanese Maritime Safety Agency,	N440FJ/F-WWFB
JA8575	Falcon 50	196	Sony Corp. Tokyo.	N8575J/N285FJ/F-WWHD

Jordan

Registration	Type	c/n	Owner / Operator	Previous identity
JY-ADP	B 707-3D3C	20495	Government of Jordan, Amman.	
JY-AEW	Learjet	35-052	W/o 28 Apr 77.	
JY-AFC	Learjet	36A-020	W/o 21 Sep 77.	
JY-AFH	Sabre-75A	380-57	Arab Wings, Amman.	HZ-RBH/N75A/N80RS/N2147J
JY-AFP	Sabre-75A	380-62	Arab Wings, Amman.	
JY-HKJ	TriStar	1247	Governmant of Jordan, Amman.	N64854

Norway

Registration	Type	c/n	Owner / Operator	Previous identity
LN-AAA	Falcon 20CC	73	Wfu. Parted out by The Memphis Group 1/89.	LX-AAA/(OO-ADA)/(OO-RJX)/9Q-CKZ VH-BIZ/(F-BHRB)/VH-BIZ/F-WJML
LN-AAB	Falcon 20C	12	Wfu /89 as parted out at Memphis, Tn.	N51SF/N221B/N803F/F-WMKI
LN-AAC	Falcon 20F	281	Norsk Hydro A/S-Air Express A/S. Oslo.	N20CG/D-CORF/F-WRQR
LN-AAD	Citation	550-0373	Air Express A/S. Oslo. 'Petter' (was 551-0018).	N556CC/N666AJ/N455DM N2663F
LN-AAE	Citation	551-0245	W/o 15 Nov 89.	//N224CC/N67988
LN-AAI	Citation	551-0109	P C G Sundt/Air Express A/S. Oslo. (was 550-0074)	LN-NAT//(N86JM)/N48ND N4754G
LN-AFC	Citation	501-0262	SeaTeam Finans A/s-SVS Shipping A/S. Oslo.	N9712T/YV-79CP/(YV-O-SID-3) N36898
LN-AFG	Citation	551-0223	Ascor Flyservice A/S. Oslo. (was 550-0177).	///N550LP/(N200MR)/N98468
LN-FOE	Falcon 20C	62	W/o 12 Dec 73.	(N17401)/F-BOLX/F-WMKJ

Registration	Type	c/n	Owner / Operator	Previous identity
LN-HAT	Citation	500-0331	Norsk Luftambulanse/Valdresfly A/S. Lommedalen.	/N40AC/N96RE/N86RE/N331CC (N5331J)
LN-NEA	Citation	550-0123	Norsk Luftambulanse,	/SE-DEV/N81TF/N36CJ/(CC-CGX)/N2746F

Argentina

Registration	Type	c/n	Owner / Operator	Previous identity
LQ-MRM	Citation	500-0386	Argentine Federal Police, Buenos Aires.	LV-PAX/N3173M
LV-AIT	Learjet	35A-408	Direccion de Aeronautica, Tierra del Fuego.	LV-POG/N3798P/(N33VG)
LV-ALF	Learjet	35A-371	Cia Loma Negra S.A.	LV-P..
LV-ALW	HS 125/700B	7133	W/o 11 Apr 85.	LV-PMM/G-5-14
LV-APL	Citation	551-0361	TIA S.A/Citi Bank NA. Buenos Aires. (was 550-0330).	LV-PNB/N6799C
LV-AXZ	HS 125/400B	25251	Alparamis S.A.	5-T-30-0653
LV-JTZ	Learjet	24D-234	National Bank of Livoro,	LV-PRA
LV-JXA	Learjet	24D-240	Aeromaster S.R.L. Buenos Aires.	LV-PRB
LV-LOG	Learjet	36-005	Bunge y Born, Buenos Aires.	
LV-LRC	Learjet	24D-316	Province of Tierra del Fuega.	
LV-LZR	Citation	500-0332	Arbol Solo, Buenos Aires.	LV-PUY/N5332J
LV-MBP	Learjet	25D-229	Banco de Intercambio Regional S.A. Buenos Aires.	N39415
LV-MGB	Citation	500-0372	Massalin Particulares, Buenos Aires.	LV-PZI/N36943
LV-MMR	Citation	500-0375	Automotores y Servicios S.A. Buenos Aires.	LV-PAT/N3147M
LV-MMV	Learjet	25D-259	W/o 23 Sep 89.	LV-PAW
LV-MST	Learjet	25D-245	SALTA Gobernacion Provinciade, Buenos Aires.	LV-PAF/N39398
LV-OAS	Learjet	35A-271	Ledesma, Buenos Aires.	N1088A
LV-OEL	Learjet	25D-307	Sarmiento Newspapers, Buenos Aires.	LV-PEU
LV-OFV	Learjet	35A-312	Estab. Modelo Terrabusi SACI, Buenos Aires.	LV-PHX
LV-ONN	Learjet	35A-355	Dahm Automotores S.A.C.I.I.F. Buenos Aires.	LV-PJZ/N1468B
LV-TDF	Learjet	35A-478	w/o 15 May 84.	N3815G

Luxembourg

Registration	Type	c/n	Owner / Operator	Previous identity
LX-AER	Falcon 900	11	Tabamark S.A. Luxembourg.	F-WWFK
LX-MAM	BAC 1-11/488GH	259	Sheikh M Al Midani.	HZ-MAM
LX-MMM	B 727-2K5	21853	Al Tas Heel Littigara Ltd/Sheikh Midani, Saudi Arabia.	LX-MJM/D-AHLV N8290V
LX-RVR	Falcon 50	107	Rupint Aviation/Rembrandt Tobacco, Capetown, RSA.	ZS-LJM/F-WPXK

United States of America

Registration	Type	c/n	Owner / Operator	Previous identity
N.....	Falcon 20C	78	Hunter Aviation Inc. Annapolis, Md.	/VH-JSX/A11-078/F-WNGM
N.....	Falcon 20C	85	Hunter Aviation Inc. Annapolis, Md.	/VH-JSY/A11-085/F-WMKH
N.....	HS 125/700B	7046	Continental Aviation Sales, Rolling Meadows, Il.	/VH-LRH/VH-JCC/G-BKJV 4W-ACE
N1	Gulfstream 4	1071	FAA, Washington, DC.	N410GA
N1AH	Learjet	35A-398	AGH Aviation/U.S. Financial Corp. Dallas, Tx.	N3797A
N1AP	Citation	650-0082	Arnold Palmer, Charlotte, NC.	N651AP/(N13162)
N1BG	BAe 125/800A	8011	Brown Group Inc. Chesterfield, Mo.	N800VV/G-5-20/(G-5-18)
N1BL	JetStar-731	38/5029	B L Yachts Inc. Eaton Park, Fl.	//N340/N3EK/N3E
N1BX	Falcon 50	47	Baxter Healthcare Corp. McGaw Park, Il.	N23AQ/N23AC/N150WC/N65FJ/F-WZHP
N1C	Gulfstream 3	388	Sears Roebuck & Co. Chicago, Il.	N902C/N309GA
N1CA	Learjet	35A-657	C A Leasing, St Louis, Mo.	
N1CC	Sabre-65	465-6	Carlson Companies Inc. Minneapolis, Mn.	N65SR/N65NC
N1CF	Sabre-65	465-3	Intermet Corp. Atlanta, Ga.	N170CC//N170JL/N6K/N65RS
N1DC	Learjet	35A-246	Dallas Cowboys/Ark Air Flight Inc. Little Rock, Ar.	/N555GB/N50PL/N50PH
N1EC	Jet Commander	51	Cheque Jet Inc. Lafayette, La.	/N18JL/N93JR/N21BC/N69WW/N303LA/SE-DCK N618JC
N1ED	Learjet	35A-392	Edward J DeBartolo Corp. Youngstown, Oh.	N931GL
N1EM	JetStar-6	5077	W/o 25 Mar 76.	N1924V/N9236R
N1FE	Challenger	1055	Federal Express Corp. Memphis, Tn.	N2707T/C-GLYE
N1GC	Citation	S550-0109	First National Leasing Corp. Milwauke, Wi.	N509CC/N1291P
N1HA	Citation	501-0072	Kenridge Co. Dover, De.	N3110M
N1HF	Falcon 20F	289	Harbison-Fischer Mfg Co. Crowley, Tx.	N54JJ/N54J/N20FJ/N4439F/F-WMKG
N1HP	Learjet	35-039	Helmerich & Payne Inc. Tulsa, Ok.	
N1JB	Citation	501-0188	Morgan Massey, Richmond, Va.	/N6778C

Page 29

Registration	Type	c/n	Owner / Operator	Previous identity
N1JN	Gulfstream 2B	154	Jack Nicklaus/Air Bear Inc. N Palm Beach, Fl.	/N1625
N1JR	Learjet	25B-188	W/o 28 Jul 84.	A40-AJ/G-BCSE
N1JS	Westwind-1124	249	John Scantlin, Klamath Falls, Or. (status ?).	4X-CMU
N1JU	Jet Commander	13	Wfu.	XA-SFS/(N404PC)/N1JU/N12CJ/N50VF/N450RA
N1JX	Sabre-60	306-61	Technographics International, Fitchberg, Ma.	N1JN/N76GT/(N1VC)/N961R/N965R
N1KT	Westwind-1124	230	McDonald Group Inc. Birmingham, Al.	N102U/XC-HCP/4X-CMB/N4995N/4X-CMB
N1MC	Citation V	560-0014	Marathon Corp. Birmingham, Al.	N1217S
N1MX	Citation	501-0158	Manitowoc Co Inc. Manitowoc, Wi.	N2611Y
N1NA	Gulfstream 3	309	NASA, Washington, DC.	//N18LB
N1NR	Sabre-75A	380-70	Rockwell International Corp. Pittsburgh, Pa.	N101ME/(N15ME)/(N13ME)
N1PB	Falcon 100	198	Baldwin & Baldwin Inc. Marshall, Tx.	N100RB/N5738/N551NC/N263FJ/F-WZGF
N1PG	Gulfstream 3	334	Procter & Gamble Co. Cincinnati, Oh.	
N1PN	Sabre-60	306-58	Great Planes Sales Inc. Tulsa, Ok.	/N1MN/N80ER/N80E/N7578N
N1PR	Falcon 50	40	Astrojet/Paragon Ranch Inc. Broomfield, Co.	N50GF/N90005/9K-AEF/F-WZHG
N1R	B 720-023B	18022	Wfu. To USAF for KC-135E spares 4/83.	N7536A
N1RW	Learjet	25B-135	Randolph Williams/LRW Aircraft Sales Inc. McLean, Va.	N7600K/G-BBEE
N1S	Gulfstream 3	391	Sun Co Inc. Dallas, Tx.	N29S/N349GA
N1SF	Gulfstream 4	1060	Samuel Fly/Gulf States Toyota Inc. Houston, Tx.	N427GA
N1SV	Citation	550-0150	Vierson & Cochran Drilling Co. Okmulgee, Ok.	N2668A
N1TM	Gulfstream 4	1087	Toyota Motor Credit Corp. Torrance, Ca.	N310SL/(N94SL)/N463GA
N1U	Learjet	24XR-274	Northwest Jet Sales & Leasing, Bend, Or.	N3871J
N1UA	Citation	550-0162	University of Alabama, Tuscaloosa, Al.	N550KP/VH-UOH/N2745T
N1UL	Citation	S550-0057	O E Company, Shaker Heights, Oh.	N1271D
N1UP	Citation	650-0024	The Upjohn Co. Kalamazoo, Mi.	
N1VA	Citation	S550-0143	EJA/Commonwealth of Virginia, Richmond, Va.(1500th Citation)N143QS/(N1295N)
N1VU	Citation	501-0146	Karl Edmark III, Carefree, Az.	//N61CD/N54MH/N545CC/(N1782E)
N1WP	Gulfstream 4	1030	Wm Pennington/WNP Aviation Inc. Wilmington, De.	(N811JK)/N430GA
N1WS	Westwind-1124	252	Jahawar Lal Tandon, Simi Valley, Ca.	(N9WW)/4X-CMX
N1ZC	Citation	650-0031	Bexar Equipment Co. San Antonio, Tx.	/N631CC
N2	Citation	550-0006	FAA-Dept of Transportation, Washington DC.	N98820
N2AV	Westwind-Two	322	Ali Air Inc/Squitieri Inc. Gainesville, Fl.	4X-CRP
N2BT	Citation	501-0054	Pierce Lathing Co. Fresno, Ca.	N98563
N2CA	Citation	551-0024	W/o 18 Dec 82.	N26628
N2DD	Learjet	24E-335	R S Dupont Assocs. Wilmington, De.	N87JL/N721GL
N2FE	Challenger	1075	Federal Express Corp. Memphis, Tn.	N600CP/C-GLXO
N2FU	Falcon 20F	412	Motor Racing Development Corp. Biggin Hill-UK.	N85VE//N85V/N409F/F-WMKI
N2G	HS 125/731	NA709	Gencorp Inc. Fairlawn, Oh.	N55G/N208H/G-AWMV/G-5-16
N2HP	HS 125/700A	NA0328	Helmerich & Payne Inc. Tulsa, Ok.	N710BG/G-5-16
N2HW	Falcon 200	488	Howmet Airplane Co. Greenwich, Ct.	N123CC/N682JB/HB-VHS/F-WZZF
N2JR	Gulfstream 2B	131	Budget Jet Inc. Oneida, Tn.	/N759A/9M-ATT/N17582
N2KH	Citation	550-0570	GTE South Inc. Durham, NC.	(N1299P)
N2KW	HS 125/700A	NA0341	Kellwood Co/Tri W Corp. St. Louis, Mo.	N710BV/G-5-19
N2MG	BAe 125/800A	8092	Media General Inc. Richmond, Va.	N532BA/G-5-558
N2PK	Gulfstream 2	206	Listowel Inc. NYC.	/
N2PW	Learjet	25D-363	Western Wings Aircraft Sales Co. Oakland, Or.	N91MT/N85654/N39416
N2SG	BAe 125/800A	8090	Hanson Industries/HM Holdings Inc. Newark, De.	/N531BA/G-5-556
N2SN	Learjet	23-072	Azza Corp. NYC.	N31S/N4VS/N331JR/N331WR
N2TE	MS 760 Paris	5	Jose Garza, Beverly Hills, Ca.	N2NC/N760H
N2TF	Falcon 200	490	Friedkin Intl/Gulf States Toyota Inc. Houston, Tx.	N806F/N14EN/N204FJ F-WPUY
N2UP	Citation	650-0010	The Upjohn Co. Kalamazoo, Mi.	(N1305N)
N2WU	Jet Commander	72	Fair Sky Corp. NYC.	//VR-CAU/N2WU/I-LECO/N7KR/N777WJ/N757AL
N2YY	Learjet	24-143	Sunco Aircraft Inc. Seminole, Fl.	N900BD/N49AJ/N778GA/N145JN/N592GA
N3AS	Learjet	28-001	Arizona Bank, Phoenix, Az.	/N128MA/N9KH/N9RS
N3AV	Westwind-Two	361	Avjet Corp. Burbank, Ca.	N610HC/N6053C/4X-CUO
N3BL	Learjet	23-003	Freedom Leasing Inc. Warren, Oh.	(N10MC)/N2008/N200Y/N803L
N3BM	Sabre-65	465-51	Morris Communications Corp. Augusta, Ga.	
N3BY	Falcon 100	193	TCBY Enterprises Inc. Little Rock, Ar.	N259FJ/F-WZGY
N3D	Citation	S550-0038	A B Wharton III, Vernon, Tx.	
N3FE	Challenger 601-3A	5054	Federal Express Corp. Memphis, Tn.	N619FE/C-G...
N3GT	Citation	550-0345	General Telephone Co. Fort Wayne, In.	N312DC/N6804Y
N3HB	Challenger 600S	1059	Hamilton Oil Corp. Denver, Co.	//N227GL/N227G/C-GLXY
N3JL	Challenger 600S	1080	John Lupton/Great Western Coca Cola Bottling, Chattanooga.	/N800CC/C-GLWX

Page 30

Registration	Type	c/n	Owner / Operator	Previous identity
N3M	Gulfstream 4	1021	3M Co. St Paul, Mn. (r/c Mining One).	N412GA
N3MB	Citation	550-0367	Miglin Beitler Developments Inc. Chicago, Il.	N17LV/N17LK/N95CC/(N1216A)
N3MF	HS 125/1A-522	25093	Wfu. Used in repair of s/n 25271.	N306L/N77D/G-ATSN
N3NP	Learjet	36A-048	William Bricker Jr. NYC.	N24PT/N3NP/N2FU/(N14FU)/N3999B/HB-VHF
N3PC	Astra-1125	037	Trinity Broadcasting, Pembroke Park, Fl.	4X-C..
N3PG	Gulfstream 3	336	Procter & Gamble Co. Cincinnati, Oh.	
N3RA	Learjet	35A-138	National Co-operative Refinery, McPherson, Ks.	/N31FB/N7735A
N3TJ	Learjet	24D-236	Indian River Aviation Inc. Melbourne, Fl.	/N55DD/N25ZW/N48JW/N26VM
N3VF	Westwind-Two	324	V F Corp. Reading, Pa.	4X-CRR
N3VG	Learjet	35A-305	Flight International Inc. Jacksonville, Fl.	
N3ZA	Learjet	23-024	Cx USA 6/81 as wfu.	N3ZA/N803JA/N488J/N21U/N202Y/(N702RK)
N4	Citation	500-0084	FAA. Seattle, Wa.	N25/N2/N10/N584CC
N4AC	Falcon 10	184	AMCA International, Charlotte, NC.	N346P/N250FJ/F-WZGP/N346P
N4AZ	McDonnell 220	1	Greco Air Inc. El Paso, Tx.	N220N/N119M
N4CP	Falcon 50	187	Pfizer Inc. Trenton, NJ.	N279FJ/F-WWHG
N4CR	HS 125/1A-522	25109	Henig Furs Aviation Services Inc. Montgomery, Al..	N201H/G-ATUZ
N4EG	Citation	650-0139	Edward S Gordon Co. NYC.	(N13242)
N4EM	Astra-1125SP	050		4X-C..
N4GB	Learjet	35A-228	Gene O Bicknell/National Pizza Co. Pittsburgh, Ks.	//N101PG
N4J	Learjet	35A-110	McCrae Aviation Services Inc. Wilmington, De.	/(N12EP)
N4KH	Citation	500-0062	Southeast Aviation Inc. Columbia, SC.	/N4CH/N526CC
N4LG	Sabre-60	306-9	Loe Lamar, Jackson, Ms.	/N5071L/N32UT/N1298/N958R/N998R/N4717N
N4LK	Citation	500-0140	San Francisco Coupon Clearing, San Francisco, Ca.	/N2FA/N135JW/XA-EKO N977EE/(N777SC)/N111AT/N300PX/N140CC
N4M	Sabre-65	465-18	Midcon Corp/Natural Gas Pipeline Co. Chicago, Il.	
N4MB	Sabre-65	465-17	Mellon Bank NA. Pittsburgh, Pa.	N905K/N2537E
N4NR	Gulfstream 2B	255	Rockwell International Corp. Pittsburgh, Pa.	/N442A
N4PG	Challenger 601-3A	5052	Procter & Gamble Co. Cincinnati, Oh.	C-G...
N4SP	Gulfstream 2	20	Saral Publications Inc. Opa Locka, Fl.	//N755S/N2PG
N4SX	JetStar-8	5081	cx USA 8/87 to ? Parted out ?	/N4SP/N200AL/N200A
N4TL	Citation V	560-0048	Amory Garment Co. Amory, Ms.	N2667X
N4UP	Gulfstream 4	088	Upjohn Co. Kalamazoo, Mi.	N464GA
N4VF	Citation	550-0053	H D Lee Inc. Shawnee Mission, Ks.	(N3300M)
N4WG	Westwind-1124	200	J & L Land Co. Ketchum, Ok.	N1124X/4X-CKX
N5BK	Gulfstream 4	1025	Howard Keck Sr/Galway Bay Corp. Van Nuys, Ca.	N419GA
N5C	BAe 125/800A	8083	Union Pacific Resources, Fort Worth, Tx.	/(N800HS)/N526BA/G-5-546
N5D	Learjet	23-095	H & H Enterprises inc. Las Vegas, NV 89102.	N974D/N366EJ
N5DL	Falcon 50	7	Regal Quad Inc. Cincinnati, Oh.	N26LB/N8516Z/HZ-AO3/HZ-AKI/F-WZHA
N5EJ	Diamond 1A	A033SA	sale, 329 Williams St. Bristol, VA 24201.	N223S/N520TT/N312DM
N5ES	Falcon 10	174	E Systems Inc. Greenville, Tx.	N240FJ/F-WZGE
N5FG	Citation	500-0224	First South Development & Investment, Greensboro, NC.	//N3ZD/N77RE (N224CC)
N5G	BAe 125/800A	8053	Gencorp/Diversitech General Inc. Akron, Oh.	/N361BA/G-5-11
N5JR	Jet Commander	49	Jacob Bowman, Anderson, SC.	N430C
N5LL	Learjet	25B-183	Connie Kalitta Services Inc. Lakeview, Or.	N66JD
N5NC	Learjet	25D-372	Noland Co. Newport News, Va.	N72606
N5PG	Challenger 601-3A	5053	Procter & Gamble Co. Cincinnati, Oh.	C-G...
N5QY	Learjet	23-028	Air Ambulance Network One Inc. Wilmington, De.	(N500YY)/(N56PR)/N5DM N818LJ
N5RD	Gulfstream 2	142	RDC Marine Inc. Houston, Tx.	N60CC/N882GA
N5SJ	Gulfstream 2	52	Personal Way Aviation Inc. Dallas, Tx.	(N52NE)//N5SJ/N38KM/N69SF/C-FFNM
N5TM	Challenger 601-3A	5076	Toyota Motor Credit Corp. Torrance, Ca.	C-G...
N5TR	Citation	500-0288	Boyce & Sons, Manteca, Ca.	(N81TR)/N5TR/N9013S/OY-ASD/D-IDWN/N288CC (N5288J)
N5VF	Falcon 50	163	Vanity Fair/VF Corp. Wyomissing, Pa.	N185FJ/N50FJ/N146FJ/F-WZHA
N5VG	Learjet	31-014	Airsupport Services Corp. Miami, Fl.	N1468B
N5VP	Citation	501-0046	Sunday Unlimited, El Monte, Ca. .	N405CC/N36916
N5YP	Citation	501-0083	Flint Engineering & Construction Co. Tulsa, Ok.	N462CC/N3158M
N5ZZ	Citation	500-0155	Zeff Management Inc. Detroit, Mi.	N920W/(N655CC)
N6BX	Gulfstream 3	392	Baxter Healthcare Corp. Waukegan, Il.	/N30AH
N6CD	Citation	500-0151	Warner Investment Co. Long Beach, Ca.	N151CC
N6EL	Citation	551-0378	American Aviation Financial Corp. Reno, Nv. (was 550-0342).	N115VH/(N43D) N4581Y/G-BJVP/N6804L

Page 31

Registration	Type	c/n	Owner / Operator	Previous identity
N6ES	JetStar-6	5023	United CCM Corp. San Antonio, Tx. (status ?)	N2ES/N20PY/N723ST/N879RA N979RA/N767Z/N1107Z/N711Z/I-SNAL/N9221R (N1229A)
N6FE	Citation V	560-0028	FEDEX, Memphis, Tn.	
N6HF	Citation	550-0260	HCF Realty Inc. St Clair Shores, Mi.	N8CF/N82JJ/N32JJ/N67986
N6JL	JetStar-731	24/5037	Pine Ridge Aviation Inc. Sulphur, La.	N10DR/N9OTC/(N71UF)/N11UF/N6OCH N6OCN/N3060/N519L/N2600/N9211R
N6JW	Gulfstream 2	138	Walter Industries Inc. Tampa, Fl.	
N6LL	Learjet	25D-256	Connie Kalitta Services Inc. Lakeview, Or.	
N6NF	Learjet	25-021	Alabama Avn & Technical College Foundation, Blackwell Field.	N4OSN/N4OSW N1LL/N1JR/N111LL/N942GA/N4OSN
N6NR	Sabre-65	465-29	Rockwell International Corp. Pontiac, Mi.	
N6PC	Gulfstream 2B	775	Paramount Communications Inc. Van Nuys, Ca.	N723J/N13GW/N804GA
N6Q	Citation	550-0043	Command Charter Corp. Houston, Tx.	/N3285M
N6SG	Challenger 601-3A	5046	HM Industries Inc. Newark, NJ.	C-G...
N6SP	Sabre-80A	380-9	Almar Corp. Showell, Md.	N510BB/N5108
N6SS	HS 125/1A-522	25100	Rainbow Air Corp. Naperville, Il.	N44TQ/N44TG/N104/N7SZ/N952B/N125J/G-ATNT N44TQ
N6TM	BAe 125/800A	8026	Torchmark/Globe Life-Accident Insurance, Oklahoma City, Ok.	N800HS/G-5-18
N6UB	HS 125/700A	NA0215	Fuqua National Corp. Atlanta, Ga.	/N6JB/N125GP/N54555/G-BFLF
N6VG	Falcon 10	62	Deverian Airways Inc. Hollywood-Burbank, Ca.	N12LB/N146FJ/F-WJMM
N6WU	Citation	550-0187	El Dorado Aviation Inc. San Jose, Ca.	N143DA/N303X/N98432
N6YY	Learjet	36A-023	Dulles Equities Inc. Vienna, Va.	N767RA//(N64FN)/N187MZ/N1871P/N1871R
N7CC	Citation	550-0029	Quorum Sales Inc. Denver, Co.	/N202PB/N718VA/N502AL/G-JEEN/(N3247M)
N7DJ	Westwind-1124	265	DJ Aircraft Inc. Wilmington, De.	N167J/4X-CNK
N7ES	HFB 320	1045	Don Haynes Aviation Inc. Fort Lauderdale, Fl.	N4ZA/N894HJ/N5602/D-CIRU
N7FE	Citation V	560-0063	FEDEX, Memphis, Tn.	
N7GF	Learjet	23-016	George F Vernon, Fullerton, Ca.	N7CF/N500K
N7GP	Learjet	23-082	Guillermo Portillo, El Paso, Tx.	(N700NP)/N805JA/N280C
N7NE	Citation	501-0261	Northern Engraving Corp. Sparta, Wi. (was 500-0351).	N52CC/N5352J
N7NR	Sabre-65	465-44	Rockwell International Corp. El Segundo, Ca.	
N7PQ	Gulfstream 2	62	O Gara Aviation Co. Las Vegas, Nv.	/N7PG/N3ZQ/N1PG/N372GM/N372CM/N834GA
N7PW	Diamond 1	A027SA	Poulan Weed Eater, Shreveport, La.	N27TJ/N800RD//N237CC/N319DM
N7SZ	JetStar-8	5124	Ben C Tisdale, Anchorage, Ak.	/N46F/N7969S
N7US	Learjet	55B-128	U S Aviation Underwriters Inc. NYC.	N255BL/N1087T
N7WC	HS 125/400A	NA768	Woodford Holding Co. Versailles, Ky.	N11FX/XA-DIN/N69KA/N125BH/N65BH G-5-20
N7YP	Citation	550-0164	Pacific Capital Inc. Reston, Va.	/N164CC
N8AD	Citation	551-0065	Metropolitan Leasing Co. Charlotte, NC.	//N6888Z
N8AF	Sabre-40	282-24	Sabre Investments Ltd. Wilmington, De.	N4ODW/N360Q/N720J/N6378C
N8BG	Learjet	24F-348	William J Mayo II, Denver, Co.	(N10GM)/N4RU/N4RT/N725GL
N8DE	Citation	500-0166	D M Emerson Jr. Seattle, Wa.	(N29MW)/N313JL//N500WR
N8EH	Citation	501-0294	Harvey Sales Inc. Dallas, Tx. (was 500-0391).	/N38TM/N2LN/N3205M
N8FE	Falcon 20DC	199	Wfu Aug 83. Located Paul E Gerber facilty, Md.	N4388F/F-WMKH
N8GE	Jet Commander	63	Cherry Air Inc. Dallas, Tx.	N8GA/N9DM/N15G/N7784/N6546V
N8JG	Citation	500-0074	Teton Development Corp. Covina, Ca.	N574W/N574CC
N8LA	Learjet	35A-124	Lucas Aerospace, Jamestown, ND.	N35WG/N1500E
N8MQ	Learjet	25B-085	New Creations Inc. Columbus, Oh.	N8MA
N8NR	Sabre-60	306-141	Rockwell International Corp. Pittsburgh, Pa.	(N8NF)/(N89N)/N8NR
N8PQ	Gulfstream 2	21	O Gara Aviation Co. Las Vegas, Nv.	/N8PG/N7ZX/N3PG/N4PG
N8RA	Jet Commander	104	Wfu. Broken up for spares at Fort Lauderdale 1984.	N87B/N4674E
N8TG	Citation	500-0253	Mid Coast Jet Service Inc. Watsonville, Ca.	N722US/YV-07P/YV-19P/YV-T-MMM N5253J
N9BF	Gulfstream 2TT	46	Boston Group Services Inc. Hanscom Field, Ma.	N721CP/N9272K/C-GSLK/N111RF N40CC/N806CC
N9BX	Falcon 50	45	Baxter Healthcare Corp. Waukegan, Il.	//N731F/N63FJ/F-WZHE
N9CH	Learjet	35A-282	Hurd Distributing Co. El Paso, Tx.	/N80GD/N80CD//N504Y
N9CN	Learjet	35-016	State Development Board, Columbia, SC.	N5867/N136GL
N9DM	Falcon 20C	18	Sternair Inc. Dallas, Tx. (N210RS)/N9DM/N777JF/D-COLO/N803LC/N803F/N840F	F-WNGM
N9EE	Learjet	35A-193	E & E Partnership, Bellevue, Wa.	/N2743T/VH-SBJ/N620J/VH-SBJ/(YV-131CP) N1465B
N9FE	Falcon 20DC	84	Wfu 1986. Exhibited at FEDEX Corporate HQ. Memphis, Tn.	(N150FE)/N1FE N530L/N975F/F-WJMK

Registration	Type	c/n	Owner / Operator	Previous identity
N9GN	Sabre-75A	380-2	Sierra Aviation Inc. Houston, Tx.	N380SR/N19PC/N2440C/N2440G/N8445N
N9GT	Citation	S550-0159	GTE North Inc. Westfield, In.	N289CC/N50GT/(N2646X)
N9KH	Citation	S550-0082	GTE South Inc. Durham, NC.	/N97TJ/N1274D
N9LD	Learjet	24F-336	Great Plains Resources Inc. Melstone, Mt.	N162J/I-DDAE/N3818G
N9NE	Citation	501-0180	Northern Engraving Corp. Sparta, Wi.	N593DS/N695CC/(N593CC)/(N6781T)
N9PG	Gulfstream 2	251	Procter & Gamble Co. Hangar 4, Lunken Airport, Oh.	/N944H
N9TK	Citation	501-0064	Westair Leasing Corp. La Jolla, Ca.	(N33KW)/N2768A
N9V	Citation	500-0150	Calvary Chapel Outreach Fellowship, Santa Ana, Ca.	(N78MC)/N501JG/OE-FAU N5LG/VH-WRM/N5B/N150CC
N9VF	Citation	550-0646	Cessna Finance Corp. Wichita, Ks.	
N9VQ	Westwind-1123	162	Phoenix Commodities Inc. Tyler, Tx.	/N9VC/N234RC/N78LB/N1123S/4X-CJL
N9X	Falcon 50	14	NYNEX Corp. White Plains, NY.	N283U/N233U/N50FL/F-WZHG
N10AH	Falcon 10	139	Foster Poultry Farms, Livingston, Ca.	(N110J)/(N610J)/(N810J)/N10AH/N204FJ F-WZGK
N10AQ	Learjet	35A-069	HPH Aviation Inc. Englewood, Co.	/N1CA//N591D/N103GL
N10AT	Falcon 50	194	Quaker Oats Co. Wheeling, Il.	N284FJ/F-WWHM
N10AZ	Learjet	35A-080	Anschutz Corp. Denver, Co.	N23HB/N109GL
N10BD	Learjet	35A-506	Daniels Holdings Inc. Denver, Co.	N317BG
N10C	HS 125/700A	NA0235	Dennis O'Connor, Victoria, Tx.	N700GB/G-5-18
N10CF	Citation	550-0202	Gaines Motor Lines Inc. Hickory, NC.	N590RB/N6799Y
N10CP	Learjet	55-029	Miami Leasing Aviation Co. Miami, Fl.	/D-CLIP/N4CP
N10CR	Learjet	55-057	National Cash Register Corp. Dayton, Oh.	
N10DG	Citation	500-0120	B & B Air Charter Inc. Zanesville, Oh.	////N120CC/(N620CC)
N10DR	JetStar-731	54/5139	World Equipment Leasing Corp. Syracuse, Tn.	N991F/N991/N5503L
N10EA	Jet Commander	39	Wfu 15 May 82. Located at Copenhagen.	N16FP/N1BC/N80TF/N66TS/N666JD/N550NM N6505V
N10EG	Citation	550-0055	EG&G/United States Dept. of Energy, Las Vegas, Nv.	(N1466K)/N2JZ/N55CC (N3308M)
N10F	Falcon 10	12	DB Aviation Inc. Houston, Tx.	N3100X/N107FJ/F-WJML
N10FG	Westwind-1124	318	Sheet Metal Transportation Co. Washington, DC.	N298A/N298W/4X-CRL
N10FN	Learjet	36-015	Flight International Inc. Jacksonville, Fl.	/N14CF
N10GE	Citation	501-0022	W/o 21 May 85.	/(N800WC)/N110H/N11DH/N385CC/N36884
N10JK	Citation	550-0175	Continental Aviation Sales Inc. Rolling Meadows, Il.	/
N10JP	Citation	500-0080	Paco Aire Inc. Louisville, Ky.	/N767PC/N222KW/N59019/C-GJAP/N419K/N50CC N580CC
N10JV	Jet Commander	96	Robert E Holberg, Houston, Tx.	(N2ES)/N10JV/N10JP/N1QH/N1QL/N7EC/N59CT N56WH/N56S
N10LB	Gulfstream 4	1008	Great American Insurance Co. Cincinnati, Oh.	N10LQ/N26LB
N10LN	HS 125/3A-RA	25156	Deltex Leasing Inc. Davis, Ca.	N522M/G-AVZJ
N10LR	Citation	551-0122	DJL Properties Inc. Baker, Or. (was 550-0059).	(N2662F)
N10M	Sabre-75	370-2	B & B Resources Inc. Fayetteville, Ar.	N80K/N8NR/N75NR/N7585N
N10MB	Westwind-1123	157	Atlantic Aviation Corp. Wilmington, De. (wfu ?).	(N820RT)//N10MB/N1123Q 4X-CJG
N10MZ	Astra-1125	028	M Zuckerman/U S News & World Resort,	/4X-CU.
N10NC	Falcon 10	172	Hayward Enterprises Inc. High Point, NC.	N172CP/YV-99CP/N238FJ/F-WZGZ
N10PW	HS 125/700A	NA0273	Keystone Foods Corp. Bryn Mawr, Pa.	G-5-20
N10ST	Citation	650-0113	System Services Inc. New Orleans, La.	N1321C
N10TC	Citation	650-0008	Overnight Transportation Co. Richmond, Va.	N618CC/(N13049)
N10TN	HS 125/700A	7085	Coca Cola Bottling of Western Carolinas, Asheville, NC.	/RP-C1714/G-BHIO G-5-15
N10TX	Falcon 10	9	TXI Aviation/Pegasus Ltd. Dallas, Tx.	N103FJ/F-WJMM
N10UH	Citation	500-0304	University of Alabama, Birmingham, Al.	N70U/N5253E/N5253A/N304CC/N5304J
N10WE	Falcon 10	159	Werner Aire Inc/Werner Enterprises Inc. McMinnville, Or.	N224BP/N224RP N224FJ/F-WZGJ
N10WF	BAe 125/800A	8030	Rough Creek Aviation Co. Portland, Or.	N6GG/N600TH/G-5-14
N10XY	B 727-76	19254	Occidental Petroleum Corp. Los Angeles, Ca.	N8043B/VH-TJD
N10YJ	Falcon 10	57	Jones Intercable/International Aviation Ltd. Englewood, Co.	(N50YJ)/N50TB N142V/N142FJ/F-WJMJ
N11A	Citation	500-0111	Duncan Aircraft Sales, Venice, Fl.	N111CC
N11AM	Learjet	35A-340	International Association of Machinists, Washington, DC.	
N11AN	Gulfstream 4	1108	GECC, Atlanta, Ga.	N114AN/N410GA/N17584
N11AQ	Sabre-60	306-18	TW Air Inc. Ashland, Ky.	(N60RL)/N36HH/N18HH/N339GW/N908R/N4728N
N11AZ	Challenger 600S	1032	Priester Aviation Inc. Chicago, Il.	/N200CN/N455SR/C-GLXU

Registration	Type	c/n	Owner / Operator	Previous identity
N11FH	Citation	550-0012	Aircraft Trading Center, Jupiter, Fl.	C-GHOL/N513CC/N3208M
N11HJ	Citation	500-0034	Hamlin Jet, Hatfield-UK.	(N111FS)/N500DN//N980EE//N25HC/N581CC/N534CC
N11KA	Citation	500-0119	sale, Box 877, Greeneville, TN 37743.	N111SU/N619CC
N11MC	Learjet	25B-125	Pacific Western Aviation Inc. Irvine, Ca.	N97AC/N94AT/N89AT/(N85AT)/N9AT N4MR
N11NZ	Citation	650-0143	IEPL Aviation Inc/Wellesley Resources Ltd. Wellington, NZ.	N143WR/N1325X
N11QM	Learjet	23-091	Cx USA 12/89 to ?	N110M/N430J/N430JA
N11SS	Citation	550-0437	Smith Services Inc. Birmingham, Al.	N437CF/N235KK/N1219Z
N11TC	Falcon 20C	146	Teledyne Industries Inc. Mobile, Al.	N777EG/N964M/N4357F/F-WJMN
N11TS	HS 125/700A	NA0336	Aircraft Operations Inc/NTS Corp. Louisville, Ky.	/(N477RW)/N677RW/N710BA G-5-17
N11UE	JetStar-6	5038	Fischer's Restaurant, Belleville, Il.	(N44KF)//N11UE/N11UF/N22CH/N341N N341NS/N9212R
N11UF	Gulfstream 2	8	UFCW International, Washington, DC.	N225CC/N5UD/N504TF/PJ-ARI/N777GG N400SA/(N820GA)/HB-IMV/N400SA/N400SJ/N18N/N833GA
N11UL	Sabre-60	306-103	Universal Leaf Tobacco Co. Richmond, Va.	N65794
N11WF	Diamond 1A	A075SA	Flowers Industries Inc. Thomasville, Ga.	(N13WF)/N375DM
N12AM	Citation	500-0235	Gutmann Leather Co. Chicago, Il.	N235CC/N5235J
N12DE	Citation	501-0081	Copeland Corp. Sidney, Oh.	N3146M
N12FN	Learjet	36-016	Flight International Inc. Jacksonville, Fl.	N616DJ/F-GBGD/JY-AET/HB-VEE
N12MB	Falcon 10	112	Wing Corp. Hobby-Houston, Tx.	N12XX/N186FJ/F-WPXD
N12MK	Learjet	24B-192	W/o 6 Jan 77.	N1919W
N12RN	Citation	501-0219	Island Aircraft Assocs Inc. Dallas, Tx.	N501BW/N58BT/N625J/N625CH/N678DG N25CJ/N1772E
N12RP	Learjet	35A-278	Stevens Aviation Inc. Greer, SC.	N17GL/N300ES/EC-DJC/ECT-028/HB-VGL/N1476B
N12TV	Citation	551-0026	Photo Electronics Corp. West Palm Beach, Fl. (was 550-0377).	//N551R (N26648)
N12U	Gulfstream 4	1112	United Technologies Corp. Hartford, Ct.	/N12UT/N417GA
N12WF	Diamond 1A	A083SA	Flowers Industries Inc. Thomasville, Ga.	N383DM
N13BK	Falcon 10	94	Steen Aviation Inc. Charlotte, NC.	N54RS/N171FJ/F-WNGO
N13BT	Citation	501-0078	Vivat Inc. Wilmington, De.	(N777BT)/(N3127M)
N13FE	DC-9-14	45706	Funk Exploration, Oklahoma City, Ok.	N5NE/I-SARV/N3311L
N13FN	Learjet	36-045	Flight International Inc. Jacksonville, Fl.	/N900MD
N13HJ	Citation	500-0182	Hamlin Jet, Hatfield-UK.	//C-FNOC/N525GA/D-IABC
N13JE	Learjet	36-013	Flying A Ltd. San Antonio, Tx.	/N3PC/N3280E/SE-DDH/(N852WC)/N352WC
N13MJ	Learjet	24D-314	W/o 6 Nov 82.	N501MH
N13RC	Citation	501-0059	Richard Cree Sr. Dallas, Tx.	N431CC/N2079A
N13SN	Learjet	23-009	Connie Kalitta Services Inc. Lakeview, Or.	N5BL/N425EJ
N13ST	Citation	501-0285	Shuttleworth Inc. Huntington, In. (was 500-0366).	N100BX/N2887A
N13VG	Learjet	35A-386	Corporate Aviation Services Inc. Tulsa, Ok.	/
N14CG	Falcon 50	100	Beta Aircraft Corp. NYC.	/N102FJ/F-WZHN
N14DM	Diamond 1	A017SA	Raleigh Jet Enterprises, Los Angeles, Ca.	
N14FG	Falcon 20D	177	Alaskan Daisy Corp. Indianapolis, In.	N6701/N4374F/F-WMKI
N14FN	Learjet	25C-126	Flight International Inc. Jacksonville, Fl.	///(N162AC)/N114CC/N12WK
N14GD	HS 125/F600A	6068	Gordon Gund, Princeton, NJ.	N90WP/(G-5-16)/N90WP/N33RP/G-BDZR/(G-5-20)
N14JD	Sabre-75A	380-56	Soho Air Inc. New Orleans, La.	JY-AFL/N2146J
N14LT	Gulfstream 2TT	246	SME Aircraft Leasing Co. Raleigh, NC.	//HB-IEZ/N17587
N14PT	Learjet	25XR-139	Tilcorp Inc. San Antonio, Tx.	/N12MH/N225AC/N618R
N14T	Citation	500-0143	K B Graphics Inc. NYC.	/N14JZ/N3W/XB-CXF/XC-GUQ/N143CC
N14TX	Learjet	36A-033	TXI Aviation/LB-4 Inc. Dallas, Tx.	N762L
N14U	Falcon 10	90	U S West/Mountain States T & T Co. Denver, Co.	N170FJ/F-WNGD
N15AW	Citation	500-0139	A W Alloys Inc. Wilmington, De. (UK based ?).	N3771U/OE-FDP/(N5353J)
N15CC	Sabre-65	465-42	Golden Horseshoe Aviation Inc. Charlotte, NC.	N41TC/N415CS/N2561E
N15CQ	Citation	500-0101	Earl T Smith, Amarillo, Tx.	N15CC//N6JU/N6JL/N1HM/N12MB/N101CD/N601CC
N15EA	Citation	551-0450	David Wyman/Seattle Citation Group, Wa.	N1249K
N15EH	Learjet	35A-126	Sinclair Marketing Inc. Sinclair, Wy.	N744GL
N15ER	Learjet	25D-267	E W Richardson, Albuquerque, NM.	
N15FN	Learjet	36A-038	Flight International Inc. Jacksonville, Fl.	/N304E
N15H	Sabre-60	306-60	John S Howell III, Fort Worth, Tx.	//N555RR/N31BC/N115L/N947R
N15M	Learjet	25TF-036	Barken International Inc. Salt Lake City, Ut.	N15CC/N741ED/N741E/N956J N956GA
N15NY	Citation	501-0110	W/o 2 Aug 79.	(N26481)
N15PR	Citation	501-0077	Central Control Co. Dallas, Tx.	(N3124M)

Registration	Type	c/n	Owner / Operator	Previous identity
N15QS	Citation	650-0015	EJA/III Corp. Port Jefferson, NY.	/N369G/N83CT/(N1306F)
N15SP	Citation	550-0566	Sealed Power Corp. Muskegon, Mi.	(N1299B)
N15TM	Falcon 10	114	Torchmark/Liberty National Life Insurance, Birmingham, Al.	N807F/N100YM N200YM/N187FJ/F-WPXF
N15TT	Citation	650-0192	Cleo J Thompson, Ozona, Tx.	N2622C
N15TV	Citation	551-0459	711 Air Corp. Teterboro, NJ.	N15TW//N12500
N15TW	Learjet	35A-106	W/o 8 Dec 85.	/N101BG
N15TW	Astra-1125	029	World Publishing Co. Tulsa, Ok.	/N79AD/4X-CU.
N15TX	Falcon 10	13	TXI=Texas Instruments Aviation Inc. Dallas, Tx.	N777SN/N10JZ/N72EU/N210FJ N734S/N108FJ/F-WLCS
N15UC	Gulfstream 2	176	The United Co. Blountville, Tn.	/N176SB/N176P/N806GA
N15VF	Citation	650-0012	H D Lee Co. Shawnee Mission, Ks.	N1305V
N15WH	Learjet	35A-085	River City Investments Inc. San Antonio, Tx.	//
N16AJ	Citation	650-0075	Concord Jet Service Inc. Troutdale, Or.	//N1315T
N16AZ	JetStar-8	5156	David Topokh, El Paso, Tx.	/XB-DBT/N70TP/9K-ACO/N5520L
N16BJ	Learjet	35A-165	AMR Combs Florida Inc. Fort Lauderdale, Fl.	/VH-HOF/A40-CA/N40144
N16CP	Falcon 50	153	Pfizer Inc. W Trenton, NJ.	N5OFJ/N138FJ/F-WZHE
N16FN	Learjet	35-030	Flight International Inc. Jacksonville, Fl.	N816M
N16GS	HS 125/700A	NA0332	Weber-Stephen Products Co. Palatine, Il.	N400QH/N400CH/N710BC/G-5-11
N16GT	Learjet	25D-230	General Telephone Co. San Angelo, Tx.	
N16HC	Learjet	24-126	Smith Air Inc. Jonesboro, Ga.	(N345SF)/N332FP/N352WR/N653LJ
N16MK	Jet Commander	84	Jesse Yohanan, Burlingame, Ca.	N600ER/N600TP/N600TD/N312S
N16NK	Gulfstream 2B	156	Castor Trading Co. Coral Gables, Fl.	//N7000G/N400SJ/N806GA
N16NL	Citation	501-0043	O'Neal Steel Inc. Birmingham, Al.	N10NL/N98510
N16NM	Citation V	560-0084	Nigel Mansell Services Ltd. Port Erin, Isle of Man.	(N2747U)
N16R	Falcon 50	141	R J Reynolds Tobacco Co. Winston Salem, NC.	//N129FJ/F-W...
N16SK	Jet Commander	101	Cx USA 5/88 to Norway as instructional airframe.	N16MA/N16A/N5JC/N45JF N100KY/N899S
N16VG	Citation	501-0157	Gordon Rosenburg, San Ardo, Ca.	(N88BR)/N2052A
N16WJ	Learjet	24-133	General Financial Services Inc. Hockessin, De.	N46WB/N555PV/N40JE/N40JF N660LJ
N17AH	Learjet	25D-316	United States Financial Corp. Dallas, Tx.	(N782JR)/N1AH/N3793X
N17AN	Citation	650-0054	AON Aviation Inc. Chicago, Il.	/(N26RG)/N1183/N1103/(N1312D)
N17CN	Challenger 601	3027	CNG Transmission Corp. Bridgeport, WV.	N5402X/C-GLWZ
N17FL	Citation	550-0627	Lyne Martha Steed, Dallas, Tx.	(N1256N)
N17FN	Learjet	24B-220	Flight International Inc. Jacksonville, Fl.	/N248J/N292BC
N17GL	Learjet	55-099	E D S Corp. Dallas, Tx.	N2992/(N5599)
N17JT	Falcon 20D	179	Jack Tar Village Management Corp. Dallas, Tx.	N12MF/N12LB/N10LB/N4375F F-WNGO
N17LJ	Learjet	36-017	Texas Instruments Inc. Dallas, Tx.	N1010A
N17LK	Citation V	560-0037	Leber Katz Partners Inc. NYC.	
N17MK	BAC 1-11/410AQ	054	Executive Air Leasing Inc. Burbank, Ca.	N17VK/N8007U/N77QS/N77QS/N77CS N3939V/G-ASYE/N4111X/HZ-AMK
N17ND	Gulfstream 2	63	James A Morse/Jetaway Air, Muskegon, Mi.	/N149JW/N239P/N238U/N835GA
N17SL	HS 125/1A-522	25082	Wiley Sanders Truck Lines Inc. Troy, Al.	N1MY/N125CA/N2125/N909B/G-ATNM
N17TE	Citation	650-0011	Turner Enterprises Inc. Atlanta, Ga.	N91LA/(N90LA)//(C-GWPA)/N1305U
N17TJ	Diamond 1	A023SA	Tyler Jet Aircraft Sales Inc. Tyler, Tx.	/N79GA/OY-BPC/SE-DDW/OY-BPC N314DM
N17UC	Westwind-1124	283	United Co. Blountville, Tn.	(N70WW)/N666JM/N483A/4X-CQC
N17VC	Learjet	31-017	Airsupport Services Corp. Miami, Fl.	N4289U
N18AK	Learjet	25B-092	Ed Unicume Inc. Spokane, Wa.	N258G/N9671A/N1ED
N18BA	Diamond 1	A036SA	Laminated Papers/Aviation Materials Inc. Memphis, Tn.	N326DM
N18BH	JetStar-731	5/5099	Bob L Hope, N Hollywood, Ca.	N62KK/N62K/N323P/N277NS//N594KR/N533EJ/N9255R
N18CA	Jet Commander	5	Wfu. Cx USA register 7 Oct 86.	C-GKFT/N18CA/N334RK/N364G
N18CG	Learjet	55-104	Corning Enterprises Inc. NYC.	
N18FN	Learjet	35A-105	Flight International Inc. Jacksonville, Fl.	N612KC/N102GP/N102GH/(N720GH)
N18GW	Westwind-1124	187	Denison Jet Sales Corp. Sarasota, Fl.	(N715GW)/(N943CL)/N18GW/N1124N 4X-CKK
N18HC	Citation	501-0223	Dillon Companies Inc. Hutchinson, Ks.	(N26HA)/N18HC/N1959E
N18HH	B 727-30	18936	Helmsley Spear Inc/Geni Aircraft Corp. Georgetown, De.	N5073L/N33UT/N16764 D-ABIV
N18JN	Diamond-Two	A1006SA	Luxair Inc. Linville, NC.	N106DM
N18MX	Falcon 10	117	Harbor Land Co. Dallas, Tx.	N923DS/N23DS/N190FJ/F-WPXG

Registration	Type	c/n	Owner / Operator	Previous identity
N18RA	Learjet	25D-280	Allan Rothman, Lititz, Pa.	/N18TA/N280LA
N18T	Diamond 1A	A061SA	Addison Products Co. Addison, Mi.	N348DM
N18TF	Sabre-75A	380-15	Tudor Investment Corp. Ronkonkoma, NY.	N15PN/N1841F/N1841D/N80NR/(N338K) N65766
N18TM	Gulfstream 3	351	Waverly Aviation Ltd. Teterboro, NJ.	N836MF/N308AF//N888MC
N18WE	Learjet	35A-377	Bandag Inc. Muscatine, Ia.	N10WF/N933GL/(N711EV)
N18X	Sabre-60	306-137	Great Planes Sales Inc. Tulsa, Ok.	N650C/N60SL/N2506E
N18ZD	Learjet	55-122	Philip Crosby/Sun Bank National Assoc. Orlando, Fl.	N8568P
N19AF	Citation	S550-0026	Lithibar Matik Inc. Holland, Mi. .	
N19EE	Westwind-1123	172	Cx USA 5/89 to ?	XB-AER/N1123H/4X-CJV
N19FN	Learjet	25-034	Flight International Inc. Jacksonville, Fl.	N17AR/N3UC///(N1UT)/N6GC N242WT/N954FA/N954GA
N19GB	Citation	501-0682	Gart Aviation Inc. Araphoe County Airport, Co.	N3951/N2617B
N19HF	Challenger 600S	1081	Hershey Foods Corp. Hershey, Pa.	C-GLWZ
N19J	Citation	501-0037	Carpenter Technology Corp. Reading, Pa.	N10J/N36922
N19LH	Learjet	35A-279	Orion Aircraft Sales Inc. Burbank, Ca.	/
N19LT	Learjet	31-019	Lider Taxi Aereo Ltda. Belo Horizonte, Brazil.	/
N19MX	Falcon 20F-5	339	Maxus Energy Corp. Dallas, Tx.	N22FS/(N402NC)/N131DB/(N200GX)/N200GN N100GN/N200GN/N4461F/F-WMKH
N19R	Diamond 1A	A043SA	Delaware Aviation, Muncie, In.	N322DM
N19UC	Westwind-1124	232	United Co. Blountville, Tx.	N1124Q/4X-CMD
N20AE	Falcon 20F	258	Double Wharf Co. East Haven, Ct.	N544X/N20JM/N4426F/F-WNGM
N20AP	JetStar-731	59/5054	API Supply Inc. New Brighton, Mn.	/N7600/N7600J/N9220R
N20CN	Citation	550-0285	CNG=Consolidated Natural Gas Corp. Bridgeport, WV.	N6863T
N20CR	Learjet	55-097	NCR Corp. Dayton, Oh.	N40CR/N8566Q
N20CV	Beechjet 400	RJ-20		I-ONDO/N3120Y
N20DH	Westwind-1124	383	Hughes & Hughes Oil & Gas, Beeville, Tx.	N82HH/(N301PC)/4X-CUO
N20DK	Learjet	25B-198	Farrell & Co. Pittsburgh, Pa.	
N20DL	Learjet	25D-263	Petrolift Aviation Service, Durham, NC.	N14VC/N40162
N20EP	Learjet	23-008	Grover Harben III, Gainesville, Ga.	N20BD/N20S/N1203/N825LJ
N20ES	Sabre-40A	282-124	National Wholesale Co Inc. Lexington, NC.	/N40JE/N2006/N200E/N193AT
N20FM	Falcon 20F	321	First Mississippi Corp. Jackson, Ms.	/N24CCA/N702SC/N2525/N4454F/F-WMKJ
N20FX	Gulfstream 2	120	Twentieth Century Fox Film Co. Los Angeles, Ca.	N677V/N777V/N901BM/N825GA
N20G	Challenger 600S	1085	Goodyear Tire & Rubber Co. Akron, Oh.	C-GLXQ
N20GB	JetStar 2	5202	Bet-Jet Inc. Falls Church, Va.	N333KN/N717X/N717/N5528L
N20GX	Sabre-60	306-59	Loral Systems/Goodyear Aerospace Corp. Litchfield Park, Az.	N20G/N945R
N20M	Learjet	23-094	W/o 15 Dec 72.	N417LJ
N20MW	Citation	650-0052	Hidro Gas Juarez S.A/Highland Aviation Inc. El Paso, Tx.	
N20NY	Falcon 20C	61	Air Force Systems Command, Bedford, Ma.	/N299NW/N887F/F-WMKI
N20PL	Falcon 20C	83	Cal Aviation Inc. Charlotte, NC.	/N68JK/N55ME/N1TC/N12WP/N22JW/N80506 N805CC/N974F/F-WJMJ
N20RD	Citation	650-0142	Executive Car & Trucking Leasing, West Palm Beach, Fl.	/N142CC/N1325L
N20RM	Citation	501-0025	LDDS Communications Inc. Jackson, Ms.	////N21BS/N389CC/N36888
N20TA	Learjet	23-062	Connie Kalitta Services Inc. Lakeview, Or.	N670MF
N20TX	Falcon 20F-5	296	TXI=Texas Industries/R J W Inc/Rolin Venture, Dallas, Tx.	N19TX/(N711FJ) N297CK/N214JP/N4960S/J5-GAS/D2-EBB/HB-VDB/F-WRQP
N20WP	Falcon 10	23	Corporate Charter Inc. New Knoxville, Oh.	N91MH/N310FJ/N73B/N115FJ/F-WLCY
N20XY	Gulfstream 4	1080	Occidental Petroleum Corp. Bakersfield, Ca.	N447GA
N21AK	Jet Commander	59	Barron Thomas Aviation Inc. Las Vegas, NM.	N59JC/N6538V
N21AM	Gulfstream 2	110	Hughes Aircraft Co/Joseph A Dupont, Phoenix, Az.	//N200PB/N200GN/N5000G N814GA
N21CC	Citation	500-0099	Retina Associates of Connecticut, NYC.	N599CC
N21DA	Citation	550-0082	Passenger Car Assocs/Enterprise Airlines, Cincinnati, Oh.	///G-BMCL/N26627
N21EG	Citation	S550-0087	Kola Air Inc. Wilmington, De.	N1274Z
N21NC	Falcon 20C	161	Noel Carr/UMC Inc. Annapolis, Md.	N93FH/N19BD/N93CD/N4365F/F-WMKF
N21VB	Learjet	55-026	V B Aviation Inc. Englewood, Co.	/N55HD/N8565H
N22	Gulfstream 4	1042	Gulfstream Aerospace Corp. Savannah, Ga.	//N400GA/N17608
N22BG	Westwind-Two	410	Mercury Aviation, Wynnewood, Pa.	(N410EL)/N1124Z/4X-CUO
N22BM	Learjet	36A-032	Aircraft Trading Center, Jupiter, Fl.	/N745GL/N40146
N22EH	Citation	S550-0074	Ernest W Hahn, Rancho Santa Fe, Ca.	/N550LC/N1273J
N22FM	Citation	550-0461	Federal Mogul Corp. Southfield, Mi.	N12507
N22FM	Citation	500-0229	W/o 26 Apr 83.	
N22G	Learjet	55-105	Goodyear Tire & Rubber Co. Akron, Oh.	N55GK

Registration	Type	c/n	Owner / Operator	Previous identity
N22GA	Citation	550-0031	LB Industries Inc. Boise, Id.	/RP-C296/RP-C550/N3250M
N22HC	Falcon 20C	14	Jet Fleet Corp. Dallas, Tx.	//N22DL//CF-DML/N804F/F-WMKJ
N22KH	HS 125/700A	NA0232	Carlsbad Aviation Inc. Carlsbad, Ca.	N22EH/N500ZB/(N300LD)/N900CC/G-BFYV (G-5-15)
N22LP	Citation V	560-0083	Peterson Industries Inc. Decatur, Ar.	(N2747R)
N22MB	Citation	500-0337	Banque SAGA, Paris-Le Bourget.	/N873D/N5337J
N22MS	Learjet	35A-209	Evergreen International Aviation, McMinnville, Or.	N711DS/N339W/N399W
N22NJ	Learjet	25C-097	WER Aviation Corp. Fort Lauderdale, Fl. 'Jackie'	I-SFER/(OY-ASK)/I-SFER HB-VCS
N22RB	JetStar-8	5093	Cx USA 10/90 to ?	//N76EB/N5000B/N5000C/N711Z/N9249R
N22RD	Jet Commander	99	N22RD Inc/David L Perry & Assoc. Corpus Christi, Tx.	N22RT/N922CP/N922CR N4661E
N22RG	Citation	550-0639	Riversville Aircraft Corp. Greenwich, Ct.	N1259B
N22SF	Learjet	35A-168	State Farm Mutual Auto Insurance Co. Bloomington, Il.	
N22T	Falcon 50	53	TAB Services Inc. Fort Worth, Tx.	(N50SJ)/N45SJ/(N77SW)/N150JT/F-WZHS
N22TP	Citation	501-0014	Tango Corp. Baker, Or.	N36860
N22UL	Citation	S550-0039	Universal Leaf Tobacco Inc. Richmond, Va.	
N23A	Gulfstream 2	153	Maguire Cushman Aviation, Van Nuys, Ca.	(N602CM)//N23A/N881GA
N23AC	Gulfstream 4	1047	Alberto Culver/Sally Beauty Co Inc. Wilmington, De.	/N461GA
N23AJ	Learjet	23-053	Wfu.	F-BTQK/HB-VBC/N361EJ
N23BX	Sabre-65	465-61	Corporate Property Investors, NYC.	
N23CJ	HS 125/3A-RA	25152	Air Laurel Inc/Telephone Electronics Corp. Bay Springs, Ms.	N50MJ/N28686 XA-IIT/N123RZ/N45793/CF-QNS/G-AVTZ
N23DB	Learjet	25B-086	B&J Leasing Inc. Franklin, Tn.	N28BP/N123DM
N23FE	JetStar-8	5142	Aureus Aviation Inc. Detroit, Mi.	N39LG/N86TP/N91UJ/N91LJ/N86TP/N90658 HZ-SH3/N20SH/N1UP/N5113H/N5506L
N23FN	Learjet	25-040	Flight International Inc. Jacksonville, Fl.	(N98RH)//N9CZ/N41AJ/C-GOSL (N2273G)/F-BSUR/HB-VBI/N687LJ
N23G	Learjet	55-012	Goodyear Tire & Rubber Co. Akron, Oh.	N55GH
N23M	Gulfstream 4	1022	3M Co. St Paul, Mn.	(N63M)
N23PL	Falcon 20C	139	Warm Air Inc. Cincinnati, Oh.	/N1868N/N1868M/N926LR/N334JR/N4353F/F-WNGM
N23SB	Challenger 601-3A	5074	U S Tobacco Co. Greenwich, Ct.	C-G...
N23SJ	Westwind-1124	289	Richardson Carbon & Gas Co. Fort Worth, Tx.	N45SJ/N711CJ/4X-CQI
N23SK	HS 125/700A	NA0216	Canadair Challenger Inc. Windsor, Ct.	/N23SB/N800CB/N72505/G-BFFH
N23ST	MS 760 Paris	50	Stonewall Transport Inc. Albuquerque, NM.	N42BL//N111ER/N6068/CF-MAJ CN-MAJ
N23SY	Gulfstream 4	1086	Daikyo (North Queensland) P/L. Cairns.	/N888MC/N460GA
N23TJ	Learjet	23-033	Wfu.	N60DH/XA-GAM/XA-LGM/N453JT/N453LJ/N158MJ
N23VG	Learjet	35A-379	Flight International Inc. Jacksonville, Fl.	
N23W	Gulfstream 2	116	Conair Travel Corp. Stamford, Ct.	(N410LR)//N23W/N20XY/9M-ARR/N821GA
N23Y	Westwind-1123	155	Triad Aviation Corp. Corpus Christi, Tx.	4X-CJE
N24AJ	Learjet	24-151	Koehler Investment Properties, Elizabeth, NJ.	N50JF/N664GL/N664CL/N111HJ N153H
N24BA	Learjet	24A-100	Jetflite Inc. Fort Lauderdale, Fl.	N361AA/N424NJ/N989SA/N144X/CF-BCJ N427LJ
N24BS	Learjet	25XR-022	Connie Kalitta Services Inc. Lakeview, Or.	N131MS/(N93JH)/N99CQ/N1ZC N925WP/N943GA
N24CK	Learjet	55-004	Combined Aviation Co. Phoenix, Az.	/N24JK/N50L/N90E
N24DB	Westwind-1124	294	Grand Air Charter Inc. Durham, NC.	(N73GB)//N24DB/D-CBBA/4X-CQN
N24DS	Westwind-1124	258	Duncan Aircraft Sales, Venice, Fl.	//N29AP/N1857W//N1OMR/4X-CND
N24E	Citation	550-0651	Commonwealth Leasing Corp. Richmond, Va.	
N24FN	Learjet	25-045	Flight Internationl Inc. Jacksonville, Fl.	N123EL/N33CJ/N815J/CF-DWW N963GA
N24G	Learjet	55-062	Goodyear Tire & Rubber Co. Akron, Oh.	N62GL
N24JK	Challenger 600S	1070	Central Investment/Prudential Insurance Co, Newark, NJ.	N70DJ/HZ-MF1 N3237S/C-GLXO
N24KF	Learjet	24-161	Sierra American Corp. Wilmington, De.	N24KT/N224KT/N649G
N24KT	Citation	650-0132	Jostens Inc. Minneapolis, Mn.	/N1323V
N24KW	Learjet	25D-297	Sam Aldabbagh, Las Vegas, Nv.	N297EJ/N36NW/N297EJ
N24LW	Learjet	24-136	Laura W Woodford, Fort Worth, Tx.	N954S/N222RB/N664LJ
N24SA	Learjet	23-025	Cx USA 6/89 as wfu.	N508M/N50DM/N37DM/N3JL/N5DM/N60QG/N600G
N24SB	BAe 125/800A	8049	UST Corp/United States Tobacco Co. Greenwich, Ct.	/N800EX/N825AA/G-5-19
N24SR	Westwind-Two	332	Burlington Northern Railroad, Fort Worth, Tx.	4X-CRZ

Registration	Type	c/n	Owner / Operator	Previous identity
N24VH	Westwind-1124	391	Four Twenty One Leasing Corp. Jefferson City, Mo.	N24WW/4X-CUG
N24VM	Learjet	24-051	Cx USA 8/88 as wfu.	N70JC/N990TM/(N69LL)/N100MJ/N1500G/N1500B
N24XR	Learjet	24XR-150	Cx USA 8/90 to ?	N211BL/N211HJ/N596HF/N596GA/N3807G
N25AM	Learjet	25D-321	Alex Matway/Interair Services Inc. Clearwater, Fl.	/
N25BF	Gulfstream 2	114	Fortson Oil Co. Fort Worth, Tx.	N100PM/N818GA
N25BR	Beechjet 400	RJ-57	BR Air Inc. Birmingham, Al.	
N25BX	Sabre-75A	380-47	Air N25BX Inc. Southfield, Mi.	N25BH/N2126J
N25CP	Falcon 20C	121	W C Cox & Co. Tucson, Az.	N1199M/N813P/N813PA/N242LB/N4341F/F-WJMJ
N25DB	Falcon 20C	91	Delta Bravo Inc. Dayton, Oh.	(N900DB)//N115TW/N979F/F-WMKJ
N25DD	Citation	501-0085	Wellons Inc. Sherwood, Or.	N34AA/N475CC/N3189M
N25EC	Learjet	25-026	M & M Executive Aircraft Holdings Ltd. New York, NY.	/N281R/N283R/C-GMAP N7ZA/N4005S
N25FM	Learjet	25-063	Procedures Inc. Santa Monica, Ca.	N24LT/N5DM//N68PJ//N680J/N184J/C-GPDZ N919S
N25FN	Learjet	25-015	Flight International Inc. Jacksonville, Fl.	/N708TR/N713US/CF-HMV/N858GM
N25GW	Learjet	24D-258	Echelon Services Inc. Mobile, Al.	N25VZ//N75KV
N25HA	Learjet	25XR-141	Hill Aircraft & Leasing Inc. Atlanta, Ga.	N94RS/N424JP/N424JR/N52L
N25HS	Citation	501-0222	Charles Maund Oldsmobile, Tx.	N6781R
N25JD	Learjet	25B-114	Scope Leasing Inc. Columbus, Oh.	N77PK/N45HB/(C-GLRE)/N47HC
N25MD	Learjet	25-054	Bullet Jet Charter Inc. St Charles, Il.	N509G/N500JW/N12373/OY-AKL
N25MJ	HS 125/731	NA705	Medjet International Inc. Birmingham, Al.	(N60AM)/N770DA/N822CC/N7440C N744CC/N9040/N688CC/N9040/N7055/G-AVOL
N25NY	Learjet	25D-304	Advantage Aviation Inc. Newark, NJ.	
N25PM	HS 125/3A	25114	Michigan Air Charter/Robert S Day, Rialto, Ca.	N78RZ/N44KG/N44K/N425K G-ATYK
N25RE	Learjet	25B-163	Suncoast Air Charter, Clearwater, Fl.	N59SG/N333AW/C-FBEA/N70606/N173LP SE-DFC/N173LR
N25S	Falcon 20F	453	Oryx Energy Co. Dallas, Tx.	N460F/F-WJMK
N25TA	Learjet	25B-196	W/o 11 Apr 80.	N711WD
N25TK	Learjet	25B-100	REN Aviation Inc. Henderson, NC.	(N59AC)///N741F/N741E/N262E/N262JE
N25TX	Falcon 20C	24	TXI Aviation Inc. Dallas, Tx.	N20YA//N703SC/N60SN/N60SM/N738RH/N2255Q N30JM/N297AR/N845F/F-WNGM
N25TZ	Learjet	25D-364	Tomas Zaragoza Ltd. El Paso, Tx.	N8565Y/N10873
N25W	Beechjet 400	RJ-15	Watkins Associated Industries Inc. Charlotte, NC.	N3115B
N25WZ	JetStar 2	5204	WPW Aviation Inc. Orlando, Fl.	/N167R//N500PR/N59AC/N19ES/N5530L
N26AT	Learjet	25B-130	Air Transport Inc/Co-Motion Inc/NKL Inc. El Paso, Tx.	N25PL/N111BL
N26CT	Citation	550-0319	Morrison Inc. Mobile, Al.	N26SC/N8BX/N6890G
N26ES	Falcon 10	171	Econair Corp. Plandome, NY.	N30TB/N237FJ/F-WZGY
N26FN	Learjet	25B-134	Flight International Inc. Jacksonville, Fl.	/N712JA/N15BH/N52GL
N26GB	Learjet	35A-131	Fayez Sarofin & Co. Houston, Tx.	N3812G
N26H	HS 125/700A	NA0325	Halliburton Co. Dallas, Tx.	N700HA/G-5-20
N26L	Gulfstream 2B	165	ABCO Aviation Inc. Wilmington, De.	//VR-BHR/N788C/N7000C/N810GA
N26LA	Falcon 20F	274	Guess Inc. Los Angeles, Ca.	N256M/N121WT/N370WT/N4433F/F-WJMM
N26LB	Falcon 900	51	26LB Associates, Cincinnati, Oh.	N59LB/N437FJ/F-WWFM
N26LC	Learjet	31-006	Cappelli Development Corp. Dover, De.	
N26SC	Sabre-40A	282-104	Swiss Colony Inc. Monroe, Wi.	N100KS/N99XR/N78BC/N40CH
N26SD	Citation	650-0099	SD Aviation Inc/Square D Co. Palatine, Il.	(N555EW)/N1319B
N26T	Westwind-1124	293	B E & K Inc. Birmingham, Al.	/N26TV/4X-CQM
N26WP	Gulfstream 2	24	Weyerhaeuser Co. Seattle, Wa.	(N98G)/N4S/N536CS
N27AC	Falcon 10	151	AMCA Intl Corp. Charlotte, NC.	N4581R/OE-GAG/N26CP/N217FJ/F-WZGX
N27AT	Westwind-1123	176	Aero Taxi Inc. Lester, Pa.	//N661MP/C-FNRW/N661MP/C-GJCD/N1123T/4X-CJZ
N27B	Citation	S550-0036	Cessna Finance Corp. Wichita, Ks.	N36HR/N36H/N95CC
N27BD	Jet Commander	53	CPA Ventures Inc. Tulsa, Ok.	N925HB/N103F
N27BJ	Learjet	24B-227	Pacific Northwest Aviation Inc. Spokane, Wa.	/N28AT/N4576T/N43W/N10CB N90797/XA-TIP
N27BL	Learjet	35A-163	New Creations Inc. Columbus, Oh.	/YV-173CP
N27CD	Gulfstream 4	1136	Schering Plough Corp. Madison, NJ.	N401GA
N27FN	Learjet	25-062	Flight International Inc. Jacksonville, Fl.	N86MJ/HZ-GP4/N303JJ/N105BJ N4981/OY-AKZ
N27HF	Learjet	35A-251	Arcadia Aviation Ltd. Asheville, NC.	/N27NB
N27KG	Sabre-40	282-77	Keith D Graham, Abilene, Tx.	N96CM/N189AR/N608AR/N608S/N2244B
N27MD	Jet Commander	102	Mason Dixon Lines Inc. Kingsport, Tn. (wfu ?).	

Registration	Type	c/n	Owner / Operator	Previous identity
N27MH	Citation	550-0153	Perfect Landing of Delaware Inc. Hockessin, De.	/N50HE/N50HS/N278A/N27BA (N88842)
N27R	Falcon 20E	303	W/o 12 Nov 76.	N4445F/F-WMKH
N27RC	JetStar-731	44/5086	Seagull Aircraft Corp. NYC. (N65JW)/N27RC/N711AG/HZ-FBT/N60UJ/N60OJ/N27RL	N27R
N27SD	Citation	S550-0052	Respond Transportation Inc. Wilmington, De. (N552CF)/N4TU/N4TL/N12703	
N27SF	Citation	500-0064	Seneca Flight Operations/S S Pierce Co. Dundee, NY.	N564CC
N27SL	Gulfstream 2	84	Wiley Sanders Truck Lines Inc. Troy, Al.	N5101T/N5101
N27TS	Citation Eagle	501-0147	Eagle SP 147 Inc. Wilmington, De.	N392DA/CP-2105/N254TW//N1728E
N27TT	Learjet	35A-122	United Executive Jet/Thomas Tureen, Portland, Me.	OE-GMP/D-CCHS/N3810G
N27U	Citation	550-0322	Charter 27 Inc. Issaqua, Wa.	N612CC/N7FD/(N6890E)
N27WW	Citation V	560-0074	Sabre Resources Inc. Dallas, Tx.	N2727F
N28C	Falcon 20F	404	Edwin Cox, Athens, Tx.	N404F/F-WJMK
N28FN	Learjet	25-005	Corporate Aviation Services Inc. Tulsa, Ok. /N707TR/(N707TP)/N777RA/N1969W	N646GA
N28GC	Citation	501-0074	Venture Aviation/S & K Aviation, Dover, De.	//N717RB/N888DS/YV-232CP N3118M
N28GP	HS 125/700A	NA0296	Genuine Parts Co. Atlanta, Ga.	N31AS/N490MP/G-5-15
N28JG	Citation	501-0194	W W Williams & Geupel Construction Co. Columbus, Oh.	//N6781L
N28LA	Learjet	25XR-029	Chipola Aviation Inc. Marianna, Fl.	//N280LC
N28R	Gulfstream 3	490	R J Reynolds Tobacco Co. Winston Salem, NC.	/N332GA
N28S	Citation	550-0200	Sun Pipe Line Co. Tulsa, Ok.	N287/N28S//N34SS/(G-BHVA)/N67989
N28ST	Learjet	23-013	w/o 31 Jul 87.	N37BL/N888DS/N201BA/N613W
N29	DC-9-15	45732	FAA, Oklahoma City, Ok.	N119/HB-IFB
N29AC	Citation	501-0226	AMCA International Corp. Hanover, NH.	(N2615D)
N29AF	DC-9-15F	45826	U.S. Dept. of Energy, Albuquerque, NM.	CF-TON/N8901
N29AU	Citation	S550-0019	Associated Aviation Underwriters, Short Hills, NJ.	N519CJ/N15TT
N29CL	Westwind-1124	197	Colonial Life & Accident Insurance, Columbia, SC.	N29GH/N214CC/4X-CKU
N29CR	HS 125/731	25098	Bertea Aviation Inc. Corvallis, Or. /N926LR/N45SL/N11AR/N57G/N666SC/N10121	G-ATNS
N29FN	Learjet	25-018	Flight International Inc. Patrick Henry Airport, Va. (N23FN)/N15MJ/N117CH N99ES/N32PC/N77SA/N323WA/N861GA	
N29GP	HS 125/700A	NA0250	Genuine Parts Co. Atlanta, Ga.	N130BE/G-5-15
N29LB	Jet Commander	61	W/o 19 Dec 80.	N29LP/N999FB/N100NR/N51CH/N666DC/N1196Z
N29PC	Westwind-1124	263	Pittway Corp. Northbrook, Il.	4X-CNI
N29RP	HS 125/700B	7088	Jimbar Inc. Fort Lauderdale, Fl.	//G-5-531/HZ-DA2
N29X	Citation	S550-0096	W/o 5 Mar 89.	/N95CC/(N1275N)
N30AB	Westwind-1124	235	A M Biedenharn Jr. Boerne, Tx.	N65A/(N24PP)/N1124E/4X-CMG
N30AJ	Astra-1125SP	047		4X-C..
N30AN	Westwind-1123	173	Rush Aircraft Sales Inc. Las Vegas, Nv.	N30JM/N680K/N1123Q/4X-CJW
N30AV	HFB 320	1055	American Aircraft Sales International Inc. Sarasota, Fl.	N87950/N11NT N897HJ/D-CORY
N30BE	Sabre-40	282-14	Wfu.	(N30PN)/N31BQ/N31BC/N2009/N6368C
N30CC	Sabre-60A	306-81	Carrier Corp. Syracuse, NY.	N6ND/N6NR
N30EM	Learjet	24E-338	Cx USA 12/89 to ?	N30LM/N729GL
N30F	BAe 125/800A	8035	Firestone Tire & Rubber, Akron, Oh.	N816AA/G-5-20
N30FJ	Citation	551-0022	Big South Oil Co. Brigham City, Ut.	/N313BT/N26640
N30GL	Gulfstream 3	395	E D S Administration Corp. Dallas, Tx.	PK-PJA/N1761Q
N30GL	Learjet	55-076	E D S Corp. Dallas, Tx.	/N2855/(N155JC)
N30GR	Citation	550-0656	Oil & Gas Rental Services Inc. Morgan City, La.	
N30JD	Citation	550-0205	Deere & Co. Moline, Il.	(N88727)
N30LJ	Learjet	31-024	Cx USA 11/90 to ?	
N30MR	Westwind-1124	225	Mike Rutherford. Buda, Tx.	N1124U/4X-CLW
N30NS	Westwind-1124	329	Accounting & Management Services Inc. Oklahoma City, Ok.	4X-CRW
N30PA	Learjet	35A-245	World Jet Inc. Fort Lauderdale, Fl.	/N1526L/N2WL
N30PC	Citation V	560-0090		
N30PD	Westwind-Two	347	John F Bridges, Washington, DC.	N347WW/4X-CTO
N30PR	Gulfstream 2	35	Rutherford Oil Co. Houston, Tx.	/N830TL/N1004T
N30RE	Citation	501-0109	Roseburg Lumber Co. Roseburg, Or.	N30RL/(N2647Y)
N30RL	Citation	550-0653	Roseburg Lumber Co. Roseburg, Or.	N36854
N30SA	Citation	550-0308	U S Bancorp Leasing & Financial, Portland, Or.	3D-AVH/N68891
N30SB	Citation	500-0272	Eastern Air Center Inc. Norwood, Ma.	//N505GP/N5272J
N30W	Learjet	35A-488	Thomas Worrell Jr Newspapers, Charlottesville, Va.	N848GL/N8563G

Registration	Type	c/n	Owner / Operator	Previous identity
N30W	Sabre-40	282-5	W/o 21 Dec 67.	
N30YM	Westwind-1124	213	NOY Aviation Inc. Miami, Fl.	N580GV/N530GV/N555J/N213WW/4X-CLK
N31AA	Learjet	25-041	U S Jet Sales Inc. Sarasota, Fl.	(N25RE)/N31AA/N205SA/N205SC/N960GA
N31BG	Learjet	24D-301	M E Coutches, Hayward, Ca.	(N87MJ)/N111TT/N137GL
N31CG	Learjet	31-003	Chrysler Capital/Builders Transport Inc. Phoenix, Az.	
N31CK	Learjet	23-079	Connie Kalitta Services Inc. Ypsilanti, Mi. (wfu ?).	N240AQ/N240AG
N31DA	Citation	550-0253	Eichlay Holdings Inc. Pittsburgh, Pa. (was 551-0308)	N18ND/N23ND/N68621
N31DA	Citation	551-0010	Duncan Aircraft Sales, Venice, Fl.	/YV-137CP/N3291M
N31DP	Learjet	35-062	Innovation Data Processing Inc. Little Falls, NJ.	N310BA/N701US/TL-ABD ZS-LII/N217CS
N31F	BAe 125/800A	8036	Firestone Tire & Rubber, Akron, Oh.	N817AA/G-5-18
N31FN	Learjet	35-033	Flight International, Jacksonville, Fl.	//N2297B/HZ-KA1/N7KA
N31LB	Learjet	24B-211	Jabil Circuit Co. St Petersburg, Fl.	N222AP/N30EH/N388P
N31LJ	Learjet	31-020	Learjet Inc. Wichita, Ks.	N4290G
N31LT	Falcon 20C	69	Imperial Oil Co. Tampa, Fl.	N176BN/N176NP/N893F/F-WMKF
N31RC	Citation	501-0093	Cessna Aircraft Co. Wichita, Ks.	/N88CF/N3163M
N31SJ	Falcon 10	72	St. John Knits Inc. Carlsbad, Ca.	N10TB/N154FJ/F-WLCX
N31SK	Learjet	24-118	W/o 27 Mar 87.	N1919W/N1008S/N100GS/N452LJ
N31TJ	HS 125/400A	NA731	Tyler Jet Aircraft Sales Inc. Tyler, Tx.	/N300LD/N700CC/N65LT/G-AXJG
N31TR	B 727-212RE	21948	Triangle Aircraft Services Co. West Palm Beach, Fl.	VR-COJ/N310AS/9V-SGJ
N31V	Falcon 50	59	Anheuser Busch Companies Inc. St Louis, Mo.	/N31DM/N75FJ/F-WZHB
N31VT	HS 125/400A	NA726	Village Transport Corp. Wilmington, De.	N731G/N60BD/N60B/N949CW/N111MB G-AXDR
N31WH	Challenger 601-3A	5014	Whitman Corp. Chicago, Il.	N21CX/C-GLXY
N31WS	Learjet	35-027	Denveraire Inc. Weston, Ct.	
N31WT	Learjet	24XR-283	Kallista Inc. Hillsboro, Or.	N20GT/N51JT/D-IEGO/SE-DFA
N32B	Falcon 900	59	Black & Decker Corp. Baltimore, Md.	N442FJ/F-WWFD
N32BC	Challenger 600S	1053	Brunswick Corp. Skokie, Il.	/N4424P/HB-VHO/C-GLYA
N32CA	Learjet	24-132	Condor Aviation Co. Midland, Tx.	N238R/N233R/N658LJ
N32DD	Citation	500-0043	Tyler Turbine Sales Inc. Tyler, Tx.	//N5072E/PT-KXZ/N5072E/N5072L/N34UT N104UA/N543CC
N32FN	Learjet	35A-067	Air Stewart Inc. Sarasota, Fl.	(N66FN)/N888DJ/N118K
N32HM	Learjet	35A-187	Southaire Inc. Memphis, Tn.	/N755GL
N32JJ	Citation	650-0170	ADM Milling Co. Wilmington, De..	N170CC/N95CC/N1414V
N32KB	HS 125/731	NA773	Rochester Aviation Inc. Rochester, NY.	C-FPPN/N70BH
N32KC	Learjet	35A-189	Executive Fliteways Inc. Ronkonkoma, NY.	(N32FN)/N35KC/N32FN/N32TC (N189TC)/N39292/VH-AJV/N3811G
N32KR	JetStar 2	5220	Knight-Ridder Inc. Miami, Fl.	N5546L
N32MJ	Citation	501-0058	Fairfield Communities Inc. Little Rock, Ar.	N36GC/N444AG/N44MC/N2627A
N32PA	Learjet	36A-025	Phoenix Air Group Inc. Cartersville, Ga.	N800BL/(N98A)/N500MJ/C-GVVB OE-GLP/N774AB/N730GL
N32W	Citation	500-0105	Marlin Air Inc. Detroit, Mi.	N105JJ/N105CC
N32WE	Westwind-1123	164	International Executive Aircraft Corp. NYC.	N9114S/D-CAAS/4X-CJN
N33BC	Citation	650-0047	Brunswick Bowling & Billiards, Muskegon, Mi.	N650CN/(N1109)/N1102
N33CX	Citation	501-0079	G P Aeronautics Inc. Encino, Ca.	N555EW/N3144M
N33D	Falcon 20C	166	Dow Chemical Corp. Midland, Tx.	N4368F/F-WLCS
N33EK	Citation	550-0281	King Radio Corp. Glenbrook, Nv.	N31RK/N6864Z
N33GG	Falcon 50	97	George Gund III, San Francisco, Ca.	C-FSCL/(N101FJ)/F-WZHL
N33GK	Citation	550-0250	Gold Kist Inc. Atlanta, Ga.	/N9LR/N68599
N33GL	Learjet	55-082	Electronic Data Systems, Dallas, Tx.	N1075X
N33HC	Citation	501-0104	Chicago Aero Sales Inc. Sugar Grove, Il.	/N29CA/N81CC/N312GK/(N2647Z)
N33JW	Sabre-60	306-92	Newman Racing, Santa Monica, Ca.	N74AB/N328JS/N711S/N65775
N33L	Falcon 20D-5	202	Dow Chemical Corp. Midland, Mi.	N814PA/N4391F/F-WNGM
N33M	Gulfstream 4	1056	3M Co. St Paul, Mn.	N436GA
N33MK	Westwind-Two	374	Chase Manhattan Service Corp. NYC.	N248H/N56AG/N18SF/4X-CUL
N33PF	Learjet	25-028	Network Air Medical Systems Inc. Rockford, Il.	N277LE/N263GL/N592KR
N33RH	Citation	550-0079	RWH Investments Inc. Carollton, Tx.	N789SS/N26DA/N930BS/(N26222)
N33SJ	JetStar-731	55/5087	Craig Aviation Inc. Delmar, Ca.	N75MG/N31WG//N31LJ/N800J/N41N/N9243R
N33TP	Falcon 20C	27	Aero Systems Inc. Billings, Mt.	N677SW/N847F/F-WMKJ
N33TR	Sabre-60	306-54	Trinity Industries Inc. Dallas, Tx.	(N100EU)/N38JM/N1020P/N370VS/N7574N
N33TW	Sabre-40	282-61	Word Industries Inc. Tulsa, Ok.	(N60WL)/N2568S/XA-EGC/XA-RGC/N231A/N550LL N550L
N33UT	Sabreliner CT-39A	276-34	University of Tennessee, Tullahoma, Tn.	62-4481

Registration	Type	c/n	Owner / Operator	Previous identity
N33WB	Learjet	35A-376	National Guardian Security Services, Greenwich, Ct.	/N77FK/N458JA
N33WW	Citation	501-0065	W R J Inc. Bloomfield Hill, Mi.	N2888A
N34AM	Sabre-40	282-31	Sabre Investment Ltd. Wilmington, De.	N577VM/N700R/N800Y/N23G
N34CD	Challenger 601	3030	Schering Realty Corp. Morristown, NJ.	/N611CL/C-GLXH
N34CW	Learjet	25D-277	Winn Exploration, Eagle Pass, Tx.	N20MJ
N34FN	Learjet	35A-254	Flight International Inc. Jacksonville, Fl.	/N666CC
N34GB	Learjet	55-114	Konfara Co. Ann Arbor, Mi.	N72608
N34NW	Jet Commander	117	Intercontinental Industries, Las Vegas, Nv.	N54WC/N220KP/N400HC/N200BP N237JF
N34RE	HS 125/700A	7022	Raleigh Jet Enterprises, Los Angeles, Ca.	/G-5-17/F-GASL/(G-5-11)
N34SW	Jet Commander	97	D & S Realty Co. Northport, NY.	//N3082B/N3032/N96B/N4644E
N34TC	Learjet	35A-199	Lindsey Leasing Inc. St Joseph, Mi.	N30DH/(N9HV)/N9HM/N40144
N34TR	JetStar 2	5236	Rollins Properties Inc. Wilmington, De.	N2JR//N531M/N4056M
N34W	Sabre-40	282-47	W/o 4 Jan 74.	N740R
N34WP	Citation	550-0111	Weyerhaeuser Co. Hot Springs, Ar.	N3R/N26652
N34WR	JetStar 2	5207	Orkin Extermination Inc. Atlanta, Ga.	/N176BN/N5533L
N35AH	Learjet	35A-316	Atlas Hotels Inc. San Diego, Ca.	N1507/N1503/N39398
N35AK	Learjet	35A-314	World Jet inc. Fort Lauderdale, Fl.	/(N118GM)/N35AK
N35AS	Learjet	35A-605	ASCO Inc. Englewood, Co.	/N185HA
N35AW	Learjet	35A-233	Arkansas Wings Inc. Wilmington, De.	/N35SL
N35BG	Learjet	35A-402	Louise L Gund, Berkeley, Ca.	/N7AB/N610JR/N3402
N35BP	Citation	551-0296	Price Express Group Inc. Sarasota, Fl. (was 550-0246).	/N68ME/(N396DA) N69ME//N78TC/N72TC/N6861E
N35CC	Sabre-40	282-79	Crown Controls Corp. New Bremen, Oh.	N701NC/N797R/N2248C
N35D	Westwind-1123	156	Rowe Inc. Springfield, Va.	N566MP/(N666MP)/N40BG/N40AS/N1123H/4X-CJF
N35DL	Learjet	35A-348	Panoramic Flight Svc/Cameron-Henkind Corp. Scarsdale, NY.	/N35TL/N500MJ N600BE/N3798B/(N17ND)
N35ED	Learjet	35A-215	E H Darby & Co. Sheffield, Al.	/N80GD/N80CD/N2951P/VH-UPB
N35FP	Challenger 601	3048	Crown American Corp. Johnstown, Pa.	C-GLXO
N35GC	Learjet	35A-266	DLS Enterprises Inc. Houston, Tx.	/N922GL/SE-DDI/N39404
N35HC	Citation	550-0151	Skyflight Services Inc. Portland, Or.	/(N98528)
N35KT	Learjet	35A-590	K T Developments One Inc. Biggin Hill-UK.	/N35GA
N35LD	Citation	501-0297	Consolidated Stores Intl Corp. Columbus, Oh. (was 500-0394).	/N32DA/VH-SWC (N2648Y)
N35LH	Westwind-Two	413	Liberty Homes Inc. Goshen, In.	N413WW/4X-CJS
N35MH	Learjet	35A-258	Marriott Corp. Washington, DC.	N28BG/(N1700)
N35MR	Learjet	35-057	Erie Airways Inc. Erie, Pa.	/N57GL/C-GHOO/N57GL/N551MD
N35MV	Learjet	35A-416	Duncan Aviation Inc. Lincoln, Ne.	/N306M
N35NP	Learjet	35A-492	Heitman Holdings Ltd. Dover, De.	/N8566B
N35NX	Learjet	35A-328	Amerada Hess Corp. Wilmington, De.	/N35NY/N1502/N3807G
N35PD	Learjet	35A-606	Lear Flite Inc. Portland, Or.	/N1735J
N35RZ	Falcon 20F	359	Ray Enterprises Inc. Annapolis, Md.	N647JP/N64769/HZ-A01/HZ-TAG/(N64769) F-WRQR
N35SE	Learjet	35A-191	Heitman Holdings Ltd. Dover, De.	N35NP/N75TF/HB-VFX/(YV-15CP)/N3810G
N35SM	Learjet	35A-419	State of Mississippi, Jackson, Ms.	/N53JM/N25EL/N935GL
N35TL	Citation	501-0232	Reno Investment Inc. San Carlos, Ca.	//N853KB/N2616C
N35WB	Learjet	35A-350	Wagner & Brown, Midland, Tx.	/(N88NE)
N35WR	Learjet	35A-234	LOR Inc/Rollins Inc. Atlanta, Ga.	
N36CC	Learjet	25XR-079	Chipatchi Inc. Rancho Murieta, Ca.	N50DH/OE-GLA/D-CCAT
N36CE	Citation	550-0036	Clark Transportation Co. Bethesda, Md.	(N54DA)//N5Q/N58AN/(N3262M)
N36FD	Citation	501-0209	Heli-Service Inc. Conroe, Tx.	N111DT/N501CR//N56MJ/N6784X
N36FN	Learjet	35A-119	Flight International Inc. Jacksonville, Fl.	(N64DH)/N36FN/N93MJ/OY-ASO N93MJ/D-CHER/HB-VFG
N36H	Citation V	560-0035	Halstead Industries Inc. Greensboro, NC.	N1229Z
N36MJ	Learjet	36A-036	Apple Computers/ACM Aviation Inc. San Jose, Ca.	N610GE/N1426B
N36MK	HS 125/1A	25073	W/o 28 Dec 70.	N372GM/N372CM/G-ATLI
N36NP	HS 125/700A	NA0225	Tracey Leasing Corp. Herndon, Va.	/G-5-16
N36PD	Learjet	36A-022	P Dussmann Inc. Wichita, Ks.	N38WC/N761A
N36PJ	Learjet	36A-030	A L 1 Aircraft Corp. Hialeah, Fl.	N360LS/N74TP/N71TP
N36SJ	Citation	500-0306	A T Massey Coal/Royalty Smokeless Coal Co. Richmond, Va.	N36CJ/N5306J
N36SK	Learjet	36A-047	Stanley Kurzet Trustee, Coos Bay, Or.	N14CN/N2972Q/G-ZEIZ
N37BE	Westwind-1124	396	Baldor Electric Co. Fort Smith, Ar.	8P-BAR/4X-CUR

Registration	Type	c/n	Owner / Operator	Previous identity
N37BL	Learjet	23-069	Flight International, Williamsburg Airport, Va.	N37BL//////N6GJ/N9AJ/N814LJ
N37BM	Citation	550-0307	Irvin Industries Inc. Rochester Hills, Mi.	N6860R
N37CB	Learjet	24-127	Pacific Northwest Aviation Inc. Spokane, Wa.	//N127LJ/(N127HG)/N111LJ/N654LD/N654JC/N654LJ
N37CD	Citation	650-0037	Cessna Finance Corp. Wichita, Ks.	/N411BB
N37FN	Learjet	35A-263	Flight International Inc. Patrick Henry Airport, Va.	/N4577Q/D-CCAD
N37GB	Learjet	25-053	Charter Leasing Corp. Irvine, Ca.	/N37MB/N974M/N974GA
N37GF	Sabre-75	370-4	Gary Hall & F/W Oil Interests, Houston, Tx.	N75UA/N75U/N7587N
N37HE	Gulfstream 3	466	Hercules Inc. Wilmington, De.	N325GA
N37P	HS 125/700A	NA0210	British Aerospace Inc. Washington, DC.	/G-BFFL/G-5-18
N37SJ	Jet Commander	38	John H Dean, Fort Worth, Tx.	N106CJ/N1776F/(N200WN)/N217AL/N217PM/N901JL
N37TA	Learjet	35-034	RLO Aviation Inc. Peoria, Il.	/
N37WH	Gulfstream 2	180	Huizenga Holdings/WACO Services Inc. Fort Lauderdale, Fl.	/N359K/N329K/N859GA
N37WP	Citation	550-0210	Weyerhaeuser Co. Seattle, Wa.	N3PC/(N177CM)/N762PF/N68018
N38B	Beech 200	BB-1	Wfu. Project shelved 1978.	
N38BG	JetStar 2	5208	Konfara Co. Scottsdale, Az.	(N29TC)/N123CC///N322CS/N5534L
N38D	Learjet	55-068	Mar Flite Ltd Corp. Portland, Or.	
N38DJ	Learjet	25B-191	Delmarva Jet Inc. Georgetown, De.	N78BT/N1DD
N38DM	Learjet	23-036	Cx USA 7/89 to ?	N111WM/N210PC/N477K
N38FN	Learjet	35A-247	Flight International Inc. Jacksonville, Fl.	/N110JD/YV-265CP
N38GL	Gulfstream 2B	16	Hill Air Corp. Dallas, Tx.	/N711MT/N697A/N890A
N38N	Gulfstream 2	41	Gulfstream Aerospace Corp. Savannah, Ga.	
N38PS	Learjet	35A-206	Palace Station Inc. Las Vegas, Nv.	/N123CC/N189TC//HB-VGH/(N66HM)/N760GL
N38SM	Citation	500-0001	Apollo Aviation Inc. Spring, Tx.	N20SM/N502CC/(N510CC)
N38TT	Citation	551-0311	Litton Systems Inc. Beverly Hills, Ca. (was 550-0268)	N500FX/N500EX/N298CJ/N68625
N38WP	Citation	650-0032	Weyerhaeuser Co. Seattle, Wa.	N54WC
N39CB	Sabre-60	306-116	Hi-Acres Services Inc. Orlando, Fl.	N44WD/N605RG/N2119J
N39DK	Learjet	35A-480	David Kemenash, Milmay, NJ.	/(N484)/N35CK/N8563A/(VH-ALH)/N3819G
N39DM	Learjet	35-040	W/o 5 Mar 86.	/C-GGYV
N39E	Learjet	55-018	TRANSCO, Houston, Tx.	
N39FA	Citation	550-0139	First Aero Sales Corp. Fort Lauderdale, Fl.	PT-LJA//N222MJ/ZS-KOO/N2646Y
N39FN	Learjet	35-006	Flight International Inc. Newport News, Va.	N39DM/N356P
N39J	Citation	500-0207	AMR Combs Memphis Inc. Memphis, Tn.	N929A/N92BA
N39JN	Westwind-1124	261	DBN Investments Inc. Dover, De.	/N87GS/N249E/N167C/4X-CNG
N39KM	Learjet	24B-198	Skyway Air Inc. Las Vegas, Nv.	N21XB/N21XL/N111GW/N66RP
N39MB	Learjet	35A-216	Richard Black, Moose, Wy.	N24MJ/D-CATE
N39N	Gulfstream 3	403	Union Carbide Corp. NYC.	N39NA/N347GA
N39Q	JetStar-8	5126	Wfu as spares 1983.	N39E/N20S/N955HL/N955H/N7971S
N39TH	Falcon 100	199	Sony Corp. NYC.	(N1CN)/N330MC/N264FJ/F-WZGG
N39WP	Citation	650-0039	Weyerhaeuser Inc. Seattle, Wa.	/N81TC
N40	B 727-25QC	19854	FAA, Oklahoma City, Ok.	N8171G
N40AJ	Astra-1125	031	U S Bancorp Leasing & Financial, Portland, Or.	4X-CU.
N40AS	Falcon 50	171	Allied-Signal Inc. Morristown, NJ.	N171FJ/F-WZHJ
N40AW	Citation	501-0190	INB National Bank, Indianapolis, In.	N393DA/N333MS/N584CC/(N6780M)
N40BC	Learjet	25B-128	W/o 6 Jul 79.	N1MX/N67PC
N40BD	Learjet	35A-140	Newcastle Corp. Wichita Falls, Tx.	/N72TP/N888BL/N742GL
N40BP	Sabre-40	282-40	Drug Enforcement Agency, Addison, Tx.	N715MR/N738R/N6395C
N40CH	Gulfstream 3	377	Wayfarer Ketch/Chase Manhattan Bank, NYC.	N342GA
N40CN	Falcon 50	92	Champion International Corp. Stamford, Ct.	/N85A/N97FJ/F-WZHZ
N40DK	Learjet	35A-171	Corporate Jets Inc. Pittsburgh, Pa.	(N48DK)/N455RM/N196DT/N1968T/N1968A/N823J/C-GNSA/N747GL
N40F	Falcon 50	82	Walter Fuller Aircraft Sales, Addison, Tx.	(N767W)/RP-C754/N293BC/N88FJ/F-WZHG
N40GC	Diamond 1A	A005SA	Galaxy Air Services Inc. Wilmington, De.	N15AR///N450TJ//N304DM/JQ8005
N40HP	Citation	500-0104	Rocky Mountain Sunshine Inc. Denver, Co.	C-GPJW/N200KQ/N200KC/(N604CC)
N40JW	Sabre-40A	282-122	Patsie C Campana, Lorain, Oh.	
N40LB	Learjet	25-009	W/o 25 Sep 73.	9Q-CHC/N670LJ/N843GA
N40LB	Sabre-40	282-36	Commercial Aviation Enterprises Inc. Boca Raton, Fl.	N200MP/N88JM/N59KQ/N59K/N22BN/N1903W/N6391C/
N40MP	Westwind-Two	334	Petrie Stores Corp. Secaucus, NJ.	(N45MP)/4X-CTB

Page 42

Registration	Type	c/n	Owner / Operator	Previous identity
N40MT	Citation	550-0215	McNeilus Truck & Manufacturing Co. Dodge Center, Mn.	(N240MC)/(N400MT) N500WP/N68003
N40N	Gulfstream 4	1122	Union Carbide Corp. Wilmington, De.	
N40NS	Sabre-40A	282-126	Hughes Aircraft Co. Van Nuys, Ca.	
N40PC	HS 125/600A	6010	W/o 28 Apr 77.	N23BH
N40PH	Citation	650-0201		
N40PK	Learjet	35A-260	Porta Kamp Manufacturing Co. Inc. Houston, Tx.	
N40SH	DC-9-15	45775	Seattle Seahawks Inc. Kirkland, Wa.	/N9KR/N241TC/N1061T
N40TA	Sabre-40	282-94	Telford Aviation Inc. Waterville, Me.	///N147CF/N6TE/N216R/N16R/N4703N
N40TH	Falcon 50	85	Sony Aviation Inc. Teterboro, NJ.	N50FJ/N90FJ/F-WZHO
N40UA	Jet Commander	40	Rabie & Sindoni, Stanton, Ca. (wfu ?)	N40AJ/N40JC/N913HB
N40Y	HS 125/731	NA756	Boston Group Services Inc. Foxboro, Ma.	C-GFCD/N100MT/N7NP/N701Z/N51BH
N40YA	Sabre-40	282-20	Auto Wax Co Inc. Dallas, Tx.	/N3298D/N265R/N6374C
N41	Jet Commander-C	143	FAA, Oklahoma City, Ok.	N81/4X-CPJ/N9043N
N41BH	Citation	551-0567	Ty-Tex Exploration Inc. Tyler, Tx.	N321F/(N1299H)
N41CD	Falcon 20C	88	Jet Fleet/Normandy Inc/Irving G Deal, Dallas, Tx.	N665B/N665P/N130B/N977F F-WNGN
N41FL	Jet Commander	41	Glasair Inc. Tucson, Az.	//N187G/N6510V
N41FN	Learjet	35A-137	Flight International Inc. Jacksonville, Fl.	//EC-DEB/HB-VFL/N3819G
N41GS	Sabre-40	282-16	Pan Aviation Inc. Miami Beach, Fl. (wfu ?)	N40GP/N227S/N227SW/N6370C
N41H	Learjet	25D-217	L J Associates, Blairesville, Pa.	
N41JP	Citation	501-0090	Petrolift Aviation Services Inc. Charlotte, NC.	N3165M/XC-CIR/N3165M
N41PC	Falcon 20C	19	AGL Inc. Pontiac, Mi.	(N41PD)/N500PX/N500PC/N841F/F-WNGN
N41PJ	Learjet	35-041	Northeast Jet Co Inc. Allentown, Pa.	N711BH/N202BD/N202BT
N41RC	Gulfstream 2	29	Yorke Air Co. Jacksonville, Fl.	//N919G/N930BS/N869GA
N41ST	Citation	650-0063	Sterling Inc. Akron, Oh.	//N13138
N41TC	Learjet	24E-346	B & C Aviation Company Inc. Nashville, Tn.	/N61SF
N41TH	Falcon 50	201	Sony Corp. Teterboro, NJ.	N289FJ/F-WWHA
N41WH	Westwind-1124	268	Whitman Corp. Chicago, Il.	N200HR/N21CX/N606AB/N821H/(N13HH)/4X-CNN
N41ZP	Learjet	25D-279	LMH Aviation Inc. Overland Park, Ks.	
N42	Convair 880	55	FAA, Oklahoma City, Ok.	N112
N42	Jet Commander-C	142	FAA, Oklahoma City, Ok.	N82/4X-CPI/N9042N
N42BL	HS 125/400A	NA769	B L Yachts Inc. Eaton Park, Fl.	N125PP/N972D/N872D/N66BH
N42BM	Citation	550-0101	Moran Foods Inc. Wilmington, De.	/N91MJ/(N2664U)
N42CM	Westwind-1124	189	Garney Companies Inc. Kansas City, Mo.	N200DL/N926DS/N26DS/4X-CKM
N42EH	Falcon 10	28	Scintag, Sunnyvale, Ca.	N500DS/N813AV/N130B/N119FJ/F-WJML
N42FJ	Falcon 900	42	Brierly Investments, Wellington, New Zealand.	N900FJ/N431FJ/F-WWFJ
N42G	Falcon 10	20	Philip R Palm, Great Falls, Mt.	N113FJ/F-WLCV
N42HP	Learjet	35A-507	Aero Service Co. Southgate, Mi.	N35HP/N35GJ
N42KR	JetStar 2	5225	Knight Ridder Inc. Miami, Fl.	N990CH//N746UT/N4021N
N42LC	Gulfstream 2	178	Loral Properties Inc. NYC.	/(N128AD)/N104ME/N390F/N819GA
N42PG	Learjet	24D-247	Avex Inc. Sanford, Fl.	/N23AM/D-ICAP/HB-VCN
N42QB	Jet Commander	6	Wfu.	N420P/CF-ULG/N5418
N43	Jet Commander-A	131	FAA, Oklahoma City, Ok.	N83/4X-CPR/N5039E
N43BE	Falcon 50	49	Beatrice Companies, Chicago, Il.	/N43ES/N66FJ/F-WZHL
N43CF	Sabre-40	282-59	George W Mathews Jr. Atlanta, Ga.	N40SE/N465S/XA-ESR/N17LT/N2SN/N48WP N48WS/N7509V
N43CT	Learjet	23-039	California Type Ratings Inc. Zephyr Cove, Nv.	/N9JJ/N30SC/N15SC/N800JA N43B
N43EL	Learjet	35A-121	George Shinn Sports Inc. Charlotte, NC.	//(D-CFVG)/N43EL
N43FE	Learjet	35A-573	Hop a Jet Inc. Fort Lauderdale, Fl.	G-ZEAL/N10872
N43FN	Learjet	24D-305	Flight International Inc. Newport News, Va.	N43DM/N305EJ/N98DK/N305EJ
N43H	Learjet	35A-426	Wingspan Inc. Wichita, Ks.	/N43W/D-CARD
N43JG	Sabre-60	306-79	J L G Industries Inc. McConnelsburg, Pa.	(N7682V)/N768DV/N4NE/N4NR
N43LJ	Learjet	36A-043	Texas Instruments Inc. Dallas, Tx.	N1010G
N43M	Gulfstream 4	1057	3M Co. St Paul, Mn.	N437GA
N43R	Gulfstream 2	18	Rockwell International Corp. Pittsburgh, Pa.	/N205M/N838GA
N43SA	Citation	550-0086	U S Customs Service, Washington, DC.	/(N93CW)//N414GC/N2663G
N43TC	Citation	650-0036	Town & Country Food Markets Inc. Wichita, Ks.	/N36CD/N20RD/(N700RD)/N700CS
N43TR	Learjet	35A-645	Three Rivers Aluminum Co.	
N43VS	Citation	S550-0069	V S Flights Inc. San Juan, PR.	(N12720)
N43W	Sabre-40	282-15	H L Brown Jr. Midland, Tx.	/N21PF/N40SE/(N19MS)/N32BQ/N32BC/N1062/N106G N6369C

Registration	Type	c/n	Owner / Operator	Previous identity
N43ZP	Learjet	24-157	Joda Partnership, Highland Park, Il.	N124WL/N94HC/N191DA/N1919G/N1919W/N640GA
N44	Jet Commander-A	130	W/o 2 Nov 88.	N84/4X-CPD/N5038E
N44AS	Citation	550-0047	United Leasing & Holding Corp. Dover, De.	//N66VM/OB-M-1171/(N66VM)/N3313M
N44CJ	Learjet	24-146	W/o 1 Oct 81.	N235Z/N672LJ
N44CP	Learjet	24B-185	Rasmark Jet Charter Inc. El Paso, Tx.	N754M
N44EL	Learjet	55-123	Lynn Insurance/U S Epperson Underwriting Co. Boca Raton, Fl.	
N44FE	Learjet	25D-215	Hop a Jet Inc. Fort Lauderdale, Fl.	
N44FM	Citation	501-0156	Procedures Inc. Santa Monica, Ca.	N123FG/N26517
N44GA	Learjet	24-129	W/o 30 Jan 84.	C-GSAX/N44GA/D-IFUM/N656LJ
N44GT	Citation	S550-0099	General Telephone Company of the NW. Everett, Wa.	N1290G
N44HC	Citation Eagle	500-0295	CJ Enterprises Inc. Conway, Ar.	N2274B/EP-KIA/EP-PA0/N5295J
N44HG	Learjet	35A-180	H S Geneen/HSG Aviation Inc. NYC.	/N35CX/N222BK/N222BE/N3819G
N44JC	Falcon 20F	471	John L Cox, Midland, Tx.	N478F/F-WJMK
N44LC	Citation	501-0176	Lowes Companies Inc. North Wilkesboro, NC.	N6779L
N44LF	Citation	550-0277	Inter American Flight Co Inc. W Lebanon, NH.	/(N550MT)/N44LF/N6864B
N44LJ	Learjet	36A-044	Texas Instruments Inc. Dallas, Tx.	N1010H
N44M	Citation	650-0050	Corporate Jets/A W Mathieson-Mellon Bank, Pittsburgh, Pa.	(N1311K)
N44MD	B 727-44	19318	Davis Oil Co. Los Angeles, Ca.	N727EC/N727MB/N2689E/ZS-SBF/ZS-EKW
N44MK	Falcon 50	44	Morrison Knudsen Co. Boise, Id.	N50LT/N150JP/N62FJ/F-WZHA
N44MW	Learjet	35-044	Westwind Partners/Carlton Financial Inc. Las Vegas, Nv.	(N44VW)/N44MW/N38TA
N44NT	Falcon 20F	319	Northern Telecom Aviation Inc. Nashville, Tn.	N730V/N4453F/F-WMKF
N44PA	Learjet	25B-144	Jet Monterey Inc. N Canton, Oh.	N10NT
N44PR	Westwind-1123	169	N44PR Inc. Corpus Christi, Tx.	N1100D/N1500C/N1123D/4X-CJS
N44PW	HS 125/3A	25123	American Multicapital/Pratt & Wheeler Invs. Palo Pinto, Tx.	N46TG/N77CD/N77C/N706M/N700M/G-AVAG
N44QG	Learjet	28-003	Quad/Graphics Inc. Englewood, Co.	N555JK/N42ZP/N157CB
N44ZP	Citation	550-0192	Southtrust Corp. Birmingham, Al.	/N88716
N45	Jet Commander-C	144	FAA, Oklahoma City, Ok.	(N40)/N80/4X-CPK/N9044N
N45AW	Learjet	35A-078	A/M Transport Inc. Cincinnati, Oh.	/N121EL/N440JB/N711SD/N711SW/N95BH/N95BA
N45BA	Citation V	560-0067	Ann S Bowers, Austin, Tx.	N2722F
N45BE	Falcon 50	75	Georgetown Interstate Aviation/Beatrice Co. Ontario, Ca.	/N45ES/N95FJ/F-WZHH
N45ED	Learjet	24-104	E H Darby & Co. Sheffield, Al.	N924ED/N433LJ
N45ES	Learjet	25D-295	SES Properties Inc. Dover, De.	(N298GS)/N295DJ/OE-GHL/ZS-LUD/N137K/N229AP
N45GA	Citation	550-0314	Marc Fruchter Aviation Inc. Wernersville, Pa.	N39KY/N39K/N395CC/(N1214Z)
N45GP	Citation	S550-0110	Gate Asphalt Co. Jacksonville, Fl.	N1291V
N45KK	Learjet	35A-592	K K Amini, San Antonio, Tx.	/N925GL
N45MK	Citation	501-0193	Moki Corp. Alpine, NJ.	N39300/XA-LIM/N164CB/N6778T
N45RC	Citation V	560-0071A	Rent-A-Center Inc. Wichita, Ks.	N2728N
N45SJ	Falcon 900	37	Sid Richardson Carbon & Gasoline, Fort Worth, Tx.	N427FJ/F-WWFN
N45Y	BAe 125/800A	NA0427	Manville Sales Corp. Denver, Co.	/N581BA/G-5-613
N45ZP	Learjet	25D-238	Southtrust Corp. Birmingham, Al.	/N40SW/N39416
N46A	Citation	550-0424	Bell Telephone Co. Philadelphia, Pa.	N18CC/N12173
N46F	Challenger 601-3A	5055	Hunt Oil Co. Dallas, Tx.	N601HC/C-G...
N46MK	Citation	550-0410	Merillat Industries Inc. Adrian, Mi.	(N258P)/N1216K
N46MT	Citation	550-0553	Manchester Tank & Equipment Co. Lynwood, Ca.	N553CC
N46RD	Citation	500-0244	Richard Donaldson, Hockessin, De.	(N91BS)///N91LS//N400BH/N244WJ/SE-DDM/(N5244J)
N46SC	Citation	501-0137	Salem Carpet Mills Inc. Winston Salem, NC.	N26503
N46TE	Gulfstream 2	243	W/o 19 Jan 90.	N119RC/N119R
N46UF	Astra-1125	015	Unifi Inc. Greensboro, NC.	N887PC/4X-CUP
N46WC	HS 125/700A	NA0334	Weldbend Corp. Chicago, Il.	N93GC/N702M/N710BY/G-5-18
N47A	Gulfstream 2	71	B R Leasing Inc. Seattle, Wa.	N48JK/N907SW/N711SW/N4CQ/N4CP
N47BA	Learjet	35-060	Breed Equipment Corp. Wilmington, De.	/N64MR/N64MP
N47CF	Citation	501-0227	Business Investment Properties, Billings, Mt.	N374GS/N2614H
N47CG	BAe 125/800A	8169	Tigervest Leasing Inc. Miami, Fl.	G-5-644
N47CM	Citation	650-0153	Carolina Mills Inc. Maiden, NC.	N653CC/N95CC/N1326K
N47DC	Westwind-1123	163	B & P Aviation Inc. Indianapolis, In.	N4444U/N1123T/4X-CJM
N47DK	Learjet	25B-154	Fred Shaulis/Corporate Jets Inc. West Mifflin, Pa.	N30DK/N100K

Page 44

Regis-tration	Type	c/n	Owner / Operator	Previous identity
N47EC	Gulfstream 2	231	Eastman Chemical Co. Kingsport, Tn.	/N205K//N18RN/VR-BHD/VR-CAG/N1102 N808GA
N47HW	HS 125/600A	6014	F H Walsh Oil, Fort Worth, Tx.	N5SJ/N922GR/N922CR/N26BH
N47JR	Learjet	35-007	Flight International Inc. Jacksonville, Fl.	(N65FN)//N47JR/N75DH/D-CONI
N47LP	Westwind-1124	411	High Valley Air Service Inc. Colorado Springs, Co.	N96WW/4X-...
N47MJ	Citation	S550-0010	Inexcal Inc. Wilmington, De.	N49MJ/N651CC
N47TJ	Diamond 1	A047SA	St Joe Air Charter Inc. St Joe, Mo..	N76LE/N138RC/N347DM
N47UC	JetStar-731	14/5123	Union Camp Corp. Wayne, NJ.	/N441A/N559GP/N1844S/N7968S
N47WU	HS 125/600A	6047	Umphrey Swearingen Eddins, Hope, Ar.	N47EX/XA-JEQ/N600TT/N400NE/N400NW N4203Y/(C-GBNS)/N44BH/G-5-16
N48AJ	Learjet	24-172	New Creations Inc. Columbus, Oh.	N234WR
N48BA	Learjet	24-152	Sky Way Enterprises Inc. Belleville, Mi.	N9LM/N98DK/N21U/N597GA/N3807G
N48CC	Gulfstream 2	181	Centex Service Co. Dallas, Tx.	N924DS/N24DS/N860GA
N48CG	Sabre-40	282-75	Cx USA 16 Dec 83 as wfu.	(N48CE)/N48CG/N2241C
N48DA	Citation	500-0297	Nutmeg Aviation Inc. Princeton, NC.	YV-62CP/(N818CD)/N5297J
N48FJ	Citation	501-0152	G M Hock Construction Inc. Durham, NC.	N40FJ/N501ED/N501FM/N547CC/(N1847E)
N48FU	Falcon 200	495	Ventura Air Services/Fantasy Unlimited, Garden City, NY.	N522C/VH-BGL N210FJ/(N290BC)/F-WZZE
N48GL	Falcon 50	168	Hunter Air Corp. Dallas, Tx.	/N711SC/N167FJ/F-WZHH
N48L	Learjet	24A-107	Royal Air Freight Inc. Waterford, Mi.	
N48MG	Sabre-60	306-53	Jet Source International Imnc. Waterville, Me.	N624FA/N963WA/N963WL/N99AA N957R/N7573N
N48MJ	Learjet	35A-448	Jervis Webb Co. Farmington Hills, Mi.	
N48R	Falcon 50	160	R J Reynolds Tobacco Co. Winston Salem, NC.	//N143FJ/F-WZHI
N48SD	Westwind-Two	399	Consolidated Aircraft Leasing, Wilmington, De.	N78WW/4X-CUF
N48SR	Beechjet 400	RJ-39	Susan S Root (Trustee), Daytona Beach, Fl.	/N3239K
N48TT	Citation	650-0105	Cleo J Thompson, Ozona, Tx.	N15TT/N655CC/(N1320B)
N48UC	JetStar-731	31/5125	Union Camp Corp. Wayne, NJ.	/N47UC/N7970S
N48WS	Sabre-60A	306-124	Whiteco Industries Inc. Merrillville, In.	N60RS/N65NR/N2133J
N48Y	BAe 125/800A	8009	Manville Sales Corp. Denver, Co.	N45Y/N408AL/N400AL/G-5-15/(G-5-12)
N49BE	Learjet	35A-192	CWW Inc. Denver, Co.	N49PE/N225QC/N225CC/N4995A
N49DM	Learjet	24D-238	Flight International Inc. Jacksonville, Fl.	N472EJ/N262GL
N49EA	Citation	500-0017	American Avionics Inc. Seattle, Wa.	N49E/N508PB/N500PB/(N317AB)/N517CC
N49MJ	Citation V	560-0026	Melvin L Joseph Construction Co. Georgetown, De.	/N560LC/(N12286)
N49MP	Citation	501-0135	Moorman Pontiac Inc. Dayton, Oh.	N711GL/N77TW/N2650Y
N49MW	Astra-1125	019	Pinole Point Steele Co. Larkspur, Ca.	N30AJ/4X-CUE
N49RJ	Sabre-40	282-69	Duncan Aircraft Sales. Venice, Fl.	N777VZ/N777V/N43NR/N1MN/N125NL/N256MA N125N/N2236B
N49TJ	Citation	550-0049	Cincinnati Contractors Aviation, Cincinnati, Oh.	/N999WA/G-HOTL///N66LB N1AP/N3296M
N49UC	JetStar-731	47/5110	Duncan Aviation Inc. Lincoln, Ne.	//N788S/N2601/N2600/N7955S
N49UR	Challenger 601-3A	5016	Kingson Corp. Longmont, Co.	/N604CC/C-GLXQ
N49WC	Citation	501-0103	Alltel Corp. Little Rock, Ar.	(N2647U)
N50AJ	Astra-1125SP	044	Astra Jet Corp. Princeton, NJ.	4X-C..
N50AM	Citation	500-0041	G B Boots Smith Corp. Laurel, Ms.	N50AS/N541AG/N541CC
N50AS	HS 125/1A-522	25083	sale, 1125 Guibal Avenue, Gilroy, CA 95020. (wfu ?).	N538/N533/N437T/N435T N16777/G-ATOW
N50B	Learjet	25D-224	CSX Beckett/Ernst & Whinney, Cleveland, Oh.	
N50BA	Learjet	24-043	Cx USA as N43AC on USCAR 8/89. Wfu.	(N43AC)/N50BA/N24MW/N39T/N368MJ
N50BF	Falcon 50	106	Canadair Challenger Inc. Windsor, Ct.	/N96FJ/F-WZHT
N50CD	Sabre-40	282-42	Police Aviation Department, Detroit, Mi.	N500RK/N40EL/(N61FC)/N904KB/N904K N727R/N6397C
N50CR	Sabre-50	287-1	Rockwell International Corp. Cedar Rapids, Ia.	N287NA
N50DD	Learjet	55-066	The Deerpath Group, Wheeling, Il.	/(N550DD)/N237R
N50DG	Sabre-60	306-19	Sabre Investments Ltd. Chesterfield, Mo.	//N80000U/N918R/N4729N
N50DR	Westwind-1124	266	Intersouth Inc. Dover, De.	/N24KE/N24KT/4X-CNL
N50DS	Citation	S550-0031	First Southeast Aviation Corp. Lake Geneva, Wi.	/N531CC
N50DT	Learjet	25-042	Sarasota Jet Center Inc. Sarasota, Fl.	(N429TJ)/N958DM/N958GA
N50EC	JetStar-731	56/5033	Altex Equipment Corp. Dallas, Tx.	//N25WA/XB-FIS/N200CG/N200CC/N100AC N100CC/N33EA/N16200/N1620
N50FC	HS 125/F400A	25253	East Bay Air Inc. Rocky Mount, NC.	N50EB/N3338/N731HS/G-BROD/OY-APM/G-5-18
N50FJ	Falcon 50	197	Falcon Jet Corp. Teterboro, NJ.	N286FJ/F-WWHA
N50FN	Learjet	35A-070	Flight International Inc. Jacksonville, Fl.	N503RP/N3GL/D-CITA

Registration	Type	c/n	Owner / Operator	Previous identity
N50HH	HS 125/1A-522	25022	W/o 2 Aug 86.	N100GB/N505PA/CF-SDA/G-ASZO
N50HS	HS 125/700A	NA0269	Johnston Coca Cola Bottling, Chatanooga, Tn.	N70SK/N89PP/N125Y/G-5-15
N50JP	Jet Commander	69	sale, 12 Hartwell Ave. Lexington, MA 02173.	N10SN/N89B
N50JR	HS 125/700A	NA0311	Occidental Chemical Corp. Dallas, Tx.	(N620CC)/N50JR/N91Y/G-5-15
N50LB	Jet Commander	93	Hampton Aviation Corp. Allentown, Pa.	(N999RA)//N50LB/N221CF/N619JC
N50M	Westwind-1124	327	Multimedia Inc. Greenville, SC.	4X-CRU
N50MJ	Learjet	35A-164	Falcon Aircraft Conversions Inc. San Antonio, Tx.	/N248HM/N1473B
N50MK	Falcon 50	98	Morrison Knudsen Co. Boise, Id.	N39461/VR-CBO/F-WPXF
N50MM	Citation	500-0118	Royal Jet Inc. San Diego, Ca.	//N972GW/(N1OBF)//N972JD/N221CC/N220CC (N618CC)
N50MT	Learjet	35A-118	Automotive Management Service, Daytona Beach, Fl.	/N118MA/HB-VFK/N39391
N50MW	Falcon 200	503	Barry Wood/M P S Inc. Omaha, Ne.	N300HA/N218FJ/F-WPUY
N50NE	HS 125/731	NA757	Banc One Corp. Columbus, Oh.	/N499SC/N999RW/(N44BH)/N154/N10C/N125BH/N52BH
N50PH	Learjet	35A-497	Pace Setter Corp. Omaha, Nb.	/N8565N
N50PJ	Learjet	23-076	Jetway Aviation Inc. Fort Lauderdale, Fl.	N12GP/N801JA/N1966W
N50PM	BAe 125/800A	NA0451	Philip Morris Inc. Richmond, Va.	N613BA/G-5-666
N50SF	Learjet	36-010	Bechtel Investments Inc. San Francisco, Ca.	
N50SK	Westwind-Two	309	W/o 4 Apr 86.	N240S/4X-CRC
N50TC	Falcon 50	115	O Sullivan Industries Inc. Lamar, Mo.	/N777MJ/N111FJ/F-WZHC
N50TE	Falcon 10	86	Torrey Leasing Co/Scarabair, La Jolla, Ca.	N411WW/N410WW/N166FJ/F-WPXJ
N50TG	Falcon 50	117	Tulsa Aircraft Charter Corp. Charlotte, NC.	/HB-ITH/F-WPXI
N50TX	Sabre-40	282-23	Compson of Florida, Boca Raton, Fl.	(N265AC)//N301HA/N80QM/N800M/N8400B N282NA/N6377C
N50UD	JetStar-6	5019	Wfu.	N50UD/N5UD/(N70TP)/N105GN/N105GM/N9288R
N50US	Citation	501-0132	Gulf Coast Marine, Wilmington, De.	N2651G
N50VG	Falcon 50	104	Volvo AB/VFNA Jet Leasing Inc. Washington, DC.	F-WWHK/F-GFGQ/N90AE/N105FJ F-WZHR
N50XX	Westwind-Two	412	Automobile Accessories Inc. Oklahoma City, Ok.	N412SC/N412W/4X-CUP
N50XY	Gulfstream 3	412	Occidental International Exploration, Bakersfield, Ca.	/N20XY/N354GA
N51BL	Learjet	25D-269	B L Yachts Inc. Eaton Park, Il.	N269MD/N109SJ
N51BP	Falcon 10	51	IBP=Iowa Beef Processors Inc. Sioux City, Ia.	N137FJ/F-WJML
N51CA	Learjet	25-030	W/o 30 Mar 83.	N45DM/N380LC/N48HM/N30PS/N745W/N999MK/N999M/N951GA
N51DB	Learjet	25XR-246	W/o 24 Oct 86.	N40162
N51DT	Learjet	25D-367	Thompson International Inc. Henderson, Ky.	N7262A
N51FN	Learjet	35-059	Flight International Inc. Jacksonville, Fl. (status ?).	/N221Z
N51LC	Learjet	35A-302	LAICO Inc/Corporate Wings, Cleveland, Oh.	N631CW/N41ST/N78QA/N780A/N717RS
N51MN	Sabre-40	282-51	Media News Group Inc. Sugarland, Tx.	/N225LS/N227LS/N108X/N108G/N733R
N51PD	Westwind-1124	297	Wesces Inc. Atlanta, Ga.	/N76TG/D-CBBC/4X-CQQ
N51V	HS 125/1A-522	25070	M&G Electronics Corp. Virginia Beach, Va.	N84W/N2148R/N214JR/N520M/G-ATKN
N51WP	Citation	501-0133	Weber Plywood & Lumber Co. Tustin, Ca.	(N955WP)/N2651J
N52	Sabre-75A	380-10	FAA, Oklahoma City, Ok.	
N52AN	Citation	500-0030	Aviation Resources Inc. Portsmouth, NH.	N530CC
N52CT	Learjet	55B-131	Coyne Textiles/Textron Financial Corp. Fort Worth, Tx.	N7260K
N52DC	Falcon 50	51	Dow Chemical, Freeland, Mi.	/N70FJ/F-WZHR
N52FC	Westwind-1124	379	Foremost Aviation Inc. Concord, NH.	4X-CUJ
N52LC	HS 125/700A	NA0293	Lone Star Industries Inc. Stamford, Ct.	N520M/N80G/N700BA/G-5-11
N52RF	Citation	550-0021	U S Dept of Commerce/Federal Airways Corp. Potomac, Md.	N900LJ/(N171CB)/ N296AB/N98871
N52SM	Westwind-1124	397	Service Merchandise Inc. Nashville, Tn.	4X-CUN
N52TC	Citation	500-0324	Thomas F Harter, Naperville, Il.	N324C/(N5324J)
N52WS	Citation	500-0110	Ozark Aviation Inc. St James, Mo.	/N154G/N500AB/(N610CC)
N53	Sabre-75A	380-14	FAA, Oklahoma City, Ok.	
N53CC	Citation	550-0400	Cx USA 7/90 as w/o 1 Oct 89.	//N888EB/N350CC/N5492G
N53FN	Learjet	35-053	Flight International Inc. Jacksonville, Fl.	/N1976L
N53M	Gulfstream 4	1089	3M Co. St Paul, Mn.	N465GA
N53SF	Astra-1125	034	53rd Street Advertising Inc. Hillsboro., Or.	4X-CUJ
N53TC	Learjet	25D-305	Palumbo Aircraft Sales Inc. Uniontown, Oh.	N88JA
N53WF	Citation	551-0017	Northstar Air Express Inc. Missoula, Mt.	/(N33FW)/N1UH/N2052A
N53WW	Westwind-1124	393	Rotary Forms Press Inc. Hillsboro, Oh.	4X-CUK
N54AM	Citation	S550-0085	Cessna Finance Corp. Wichita, Ks.	(N285CF)/N54AM/N683CF/N683MB/N1274P
N54BE	Diamond 1A	A063SA	Lease Air Inc. Youngstown, Oh.	/N363DM
N54CC	Citation	550-0083	Cherne Contracting Corp. Minneapolis, Mn.	N98718
N54DC	Falcon 900	22	Dow Chemical Co. Freeland, Mi.	N416FJ/F-WWFD

Page 46

Registration	Type	c/n	Owner / Operator	Previous identity
N54DS	Citation	501-0027	Richard F Schaden PC. Birmingham, NC.	/N10EH/N350CC/N5350J
N54FN	Learjet	25C-083	Flight International Inc. Jacksonville, Fl.	/N200MH/N200Y/N31CS
N54GL	Learjet	35A-597	Electronic Data Systems, Bethesda, Md.	N8567R
N54HU	Learjet	25B-124	Coast Operations (US) Inc. Boca Raton, Fl.	N54H/N15CU/N15CC//N59BP/N39JE N44MJ
N54J	Gulfstream 2	193	W W Grainger Inc. Wheeling, Il.	/N26LT/N26L/N808GA
N54JC	Learjet	24E-340	24E 340 Inc. Tucson, Az.	C-FHFP/N10FU
N54PR	Challenger 601	3054	Quantum Inc. Carson City, Nv.	/VH-MZL/N605CL/C-G...
N54SB	Gulfstream 4	1063	United States Tobacco Co. White Plains, NY.	/N17584
N54TS	Citation	501-0643	Peter L Sturdivant Inc. Ketchum, Id. (was 500-0293).	N54CM/N8RF/(N5293J)
N54V	Falcon 10	35	Jonathan Corp. Norfolk, Va.	N125FJ/F-WLCV
N54YR	Falcon 50	158	Phifer Wire Products Inc. Tuscaloosa, Al.	N142FJ/F-WZHH
N55AR	Challenger 600S	1044	AAR Corp. Chicago, Il.	N205MM/N541MM/C-GLWZ
N55AS	Learjet	55-072	Boise Cascade/Albertsons Inc. Portland, Or.	N58AS
N55BH	Citation	650-0041	Gilbert Imported Hardwoods Inc. Gilbert, WV.	
N55BP	Falcon 50	207	800 BP Corp. Portland, Or.	N292FJ/F-WWHC
N55CJ	Learjet	36-003	B&K Transportation Inc. Portland, Or.	/N36TA/N363GL
N55CR	Sabre-75	370-9	Executive Aircraft Consulting, Newton, Ks.	N8NB/N8NR/N7592N
N55DG	Learjet	55-102	Enterprise Leasing Co. Charlotte, NC.	
N55F	Learjet	35A-147	New Creations Inc. Columbus, Oh.	N717W/N499G/HZ-KTC/N717W
N55FN	Learjet	25-050	Flight International Inc. Jacksonville, Fl.	/N27MJ/D-CONE/N44EE/N44EL
N55GH	Learjet	55-075	Western Aviation Corp. Miami, Fl.	N55GM/N675M//N8563Z
N55GJ	Learjet	55-088	Express One International Inc. Dallas, Tx.	/
N55GY	Learjet	55-110	Huber Hunt & Nichols Inc. Indianapolis, In.	
N55H	Citation	501-0162	Allied Signal Inc. Detroit, Mi.	N455H/N1959E
N55HF	Citation	650-0126	James T Hudson, Rogers, Ar.	(N1323A)
N55HK	Learjet	55-040	Hekro Air Inc. Wichita, Ks.	/N426EM/HZ-AM2/HZ-AMII/N3802G
N55HL	Learjet	55-046	San Francisco Aviation Co. Salinas, Ca.	N3HB/(N13HB)/N23HB
N55JM	Diamond 1	A026SA	Jerry Morton, Oklahoma City, Ok.	N5UE
N55KS	Learjet	55-051	Kelly-Springfield Tire Co. Cumberland, Md.	N22GH/N22G/N734
N55LK	Learjet	55-120	Fort Howard Paper Co. Green Bay, Wi.	(N486)/N55LK/N72629
N55LS	Citation	550-0616	LSI Lighting Systems Inc. Cincinnati, Oh.	(N1253K)
N55MJ	Learjet	25D-296	Lawrence Corp. Wilmington, De.	N55DD/N712SJ/N712RW
N55NC	JetStar-6	5060	cx USA 7/88 as parted out.	//N31F/N9225R
N55NJ	Learjet	24-162	Duncan Aircraft Sales, Venice, Fl. (w/o ?).	M835AG/N835AC/N919K/N91MK N338DS/N841GA
N55NT	Falcon 50	87	Northern Telecom Inc. Nashville, Tn.	N283K/N91FJ/F-WZHS
N55PD	Learjet	25B-105	James Markel & Assocs Inc. San Rafael, Ca.	N7AT/N905WJ///N234RB//N713Q N711WE/N1RA/N1BR
N55RG	Gulfstream 2	1	R W Galvin/Motorola Inc. Wheeling, Il.	/N801GA
N55RT	Learjet	55-095	Townsend Engineering Co. Des Moines, Ia.	N8565Z
N55SC	Citation	650-0148	Scharbauer Cattle Co. Midland, Tx.	(N1326A)
N55SK	Citation	500-0315	Skyline Corp. Elkhart, In.	N5315J
N55SL	Learjet	25XR-219	Sutherland Lumber Southwest Inc. Kansas City, Mo.	
N55SN	Falcon 50	189	Sonat Services Inc. Birmingham, Al.	N50WG/N281FJ/F-WWHB
N55TH	Falcon 20C	17	Tollman Hotels/SD Travel Inc. Mahwah, NJ.	N5CE/N5C/N5450/N545C/N802F F-WMKF
N55VC	Learjet	55B-130	R T Vanderbilt Co. Norwalk, Ct.	
N55WG	Citation	501-0231	Super Shops Inc. Newport Beach, Ca.	(N29HE)/N55WG/N6783C
N55WH	Citation	501-0056	Cheyenne Leasing & Material, Danville, Il.	(N501SF)/N426CC/N98688
N55WL	Citation	550-0140	Emery Air Charter/Lane Air Inc. Northbrook, Il.	N2646Z
N55ZM	Sabre-60	306-84	Zimair Corp. Miami, Fl.	/N383TS//N8025X/PT-KOU/N65762
N56	Sabre-75A	380-20	FAA, Oklahoma City, Ok.	
N56AG	Astra-1125SP	043	Atlanta Gas Light Co. Atlanta, Ga.	4X-C..
N56B	BAC 1-11/401AK	055	NPC Leasing Corp. Miami Beach, Fl.	N1JR/N111NA/N5015
N56DR	Learjet	24D-311	Intersouth Inc. Dover, De.	N50DR/N19FM/N19HM/N5TD/N5TR/N66LW
N56GH	Learjet	24XR-233	Phoenix Air Group Inc. Cartersville, Ga.	N124TS/N500RW/N23SQ/N23SG/N78AF D-IGSO/N253GL
N56GT	Citation	550-0137	General Telephone Co. of NW, Everett, Wa.	N2638A
N56LW	Gulfstream 3	302	Newsflight Inc. NYC.	N2610/N62GG/N302GA
N56LW	Citation	501-0314	R D D Leasing Inc. Elgin, Il.	N56MC/N6887M
N56MC	Diamond 1A	A069SA	PDG Air Inc. Jacksonville, Fl.	N355DM
N56MM	Learjet	24F-332	Northeastern Aviation Corp. Wilmington, De.	N13KL

Registration	Type	c/n	Owner / Operator	Previous identity
N56RD	Learjet	24XR-286	RDC Marine Inc. Houston, Tx.	N86GC/N59GL
N56RN	Sabre-60A	306-122	Reserve National Insurance Co. Oklahoma City, Ok.	N168H/N2131J
N57B	Learjet	55-020	General Telephone Co of SW, San Angelo, Tx.	/N20DL/N720M
N57BC	Citation	550-0478	Island Air, Ronaldsway, Isle of Man.	N4FE/N1252N
N57BJ	Gulfstream 3	327	TEA Executive Jet Services, Melsbroek, Belgium.	(N72PS)/N70PS
N57DC	Falcon 50	119	NEMLC Leasing Corp. Boston, Ma.	N83FC/N114FJ/F-WZHN
N57EL	Falcon 50	205	Enterprise Leasing Co. Charleston, SC.	/N291FJ/F-WWHD
N57FF	BAe 125/800A	8033	Ore Ida Foods Inc. Boise, Id.	/N157H/G-5-19
N57FL	Learjet	24XR-243	Flight Operations Inc. Cleveland, Oh.	//N56WS/N83RG/(N85DH)/N2909W/HB-VCI
N57MC	Citation	501-0229	Massman Construction, Kansas City, Mo.	N636CC/(N2615L)
N57MK	Citation	550-0124	Klein Tools Inc. Skokie, Il.	N4557W/LN-VIP/N2746U
N57PM	Learjet	55-025	Philip Morris Management Corp. Teterboro, NJ.	(N58PM)/N236R
N57TA	Learjet	55-010	W/o 13 Nov 81.	
N58	Sabre-75A	380-24	FAA, Oklahoma City, Ok.	
N58BL	Learjet	24D-268	B L Yachts Inc. Eaton Park, Fl.	(N66FN)/N92TC/N123CC/N111WW/N53GL
N58BT	HS 125/731	25023	Robert Lee Turley, Greensboro, NC.	/N125BM/(N125BW)/N338/N1125/G-ASZP
N58CG	Learjet	55-124	Corning Enterprises Inc. Corning, NY.	
N58CM	Sabre-65	465-70	CMCA Inc/Charter Medical Corp. Macon, Ga.	N15EN/N15AK
N58CP	Learjet	25B-133	Central Parking System, Nashville, Tn.	N51MJ/N10RZ/N10RE
N58CW	Learjet	35-015	Worthington Ford Inc. Anchorage, Ak.	/N58FF/N57FF/N291BC
N58FN	Learjet	24B-184	Flight International Inc. Newport News, Va.	N58DM/N28DL/N78BH/N36RS/N84J D-IMWZ/N950GA
N58GL	Learjet	35A-599	Hill Air Corp. Dallas, Tx.	/N40144
N58JF	Gulfstream 2	65	Sterling Jet/Richmor Aviation Inc. Hudson, NY.	N500PC/N1JG/N720E/N837GA
N58JM	Sabre-60A	306-24	Jaco Aircraft inc. Clinton, Ar.	/N300TB/N5419/N958R/N4734N
N58M	Learjet	55-077	United Omaha Life Insurance Co. Omaha, Nb.	N8563M/N3812G
N58MM	Learjet	35A-261	Malecki Music Inc, Grand Rapids, Mi.	N63DH/N35FN/N35SJ/XA-ELU/N900RD
N58PM	Learjet	55-085	Kraft Inc. Glenview, Il.	/N238R
N58RD	B 707-441	18694	Cx USA 7/89 to ?	PP-VJJ
N58RW	Citation	650-0006	REW Air Inc. Irving, Tx.	(N306QS)/N44HS/N656CC
N59CC	Citation	551-0431	Crain Communications Inc. Detroit, Mi.	N900TN/N218H/N21EH/N1218N
N59CD	JetStar-731	32/5155	Dame/Greenbrook Leasing, San Ramon, Ca.	N79AE//N10PN/N55NE/N4248Z/XA-FES N711Z/N5519L
N59CF	Falcon 50	209	Compass Foods Inc. Montvale, NJ.	N293FJ/F-WWHE
N59CL	Citation	500-0173	S W M Co. Bassett, Va.	N77CP
N59DF	Citation V	560-0098		
N59EC	Citation	S550-0034	Imperial Eagle Corp. Amlin, Oh.	N34CJ/OE-GAP
N59FN	Learjet	35A-205	Flight International Inc. Newport News, Va.	/N59DM/N80SM/N39418
N59GL	Learjet	35A-604	Electronic Data Systems, Heathrow-UK.	
N59JG	Learjet	24B-221	Lee Way Company Inc. Flint, Mi.	(N570JG)/N570P/N977GA
N59JM	Sabre-60	306-135	Jet Management Group Inc. Syracuse International Airport, NY	/N64CM/N9NT N9NR/N2535E
N59JR	Gulfstream 2	190	Fightertown Inc. Houston, Tx.	N59JR/N59CD/N7WQ/N1WP/N900WJ//N169B/N159B N130K
N59K	Sabre-60	306-82	B100 Inc. Birmingham, Al.	N60SL/N65759
N59MA	Citation	501-0050	Skip Bush, Strang, Ok.	/N750LA///N880CM/N20SP/N36901
N59PM	Falcon 50	178	Philip Morris Management Corp. Teterboro, NJ.	N239R/N179FJ/F-WZHO
N59RD	B 707-441	17905	Cx USA 7/89 to ?	PP-VJA/N5090K
N59TJ	Diamond 1	A004SA	Western New Mexico Telephone Co. Silver City, NM.	(N40BK)/N302DM/JQ8004
N60	Sabre-75A	380-28	FAA, Oklahoma City, Ok.	
N60AF	Sabre-60	306-140	American Family Corp. Columbus, Ga.	N636MC/N636
N60AJ	Astra-1125SP	042	Ellen Tracy Inc. Lyndhurst, NJ.	4X-C..
N60B	Diamond 1A	A045SA	Lease Air Inc. Youngstown, Oh.	N154GA/N99FF/N334DM/N335DM
N60BC	JetStar-8	5116	sale, Box 10056, St Louis, MO 63145.	//N3HB/N222QA//N7961S
N60CC	Citation	550-0034	Unitech Electronics/Carrier Corp. Syracuse, NY.	/N697A/N771A/N3258M
N60CE	Sabre-65	465-5	Celeron Corp. Houston, Tx.	N52GG/N55KS/N24G
N60CN	Falcon 50	79	Champion International Corp. Stamford, Ct.	N86FJ/F-WZHE
N60CR	Sabre-60	306-7	C R Anthony Co. Oklahoma City, Ok.	/N60GH/N30PY/N531NC/N63NC/N523N/N4715N
N60CT	Gulfstream 3	454	Continental Telephone, Atlanta, Ga.	/N334GA
N60DE	Sabre-60	306-25	Dwabel Ltd Partnership, Baton Rouge, La.	N60DL/(N613E)/N47MM/N212F/N210F N4735N
N60DK	Learjet	35A-394	Scott Brothers Aviation Corp. Wilmington, De.	N94MJ/N816JA/N1466K
N60E	Learjet	55-106	TRANSCO, Houston, Tx.	

Registration	Type	c/n	Owner / Operator	Previous identity
N60EE	JetStar-8	5160	Invesco Enterprises Inc. Memphis, Tn. (wfu ?)	/C-FRBC/N5524L
N60EL	Sabre-60	306-13	Gilbert Aviation Inc. Greenville, SC.	(N256MT)/N33BQ/N33BC/N555SL/N60Y N4723N
N60EW	Citation	501-0319	Jet Star Inc. Wilmington, De.	/N124KC
N60FC	Challenger 601-3A	5062	Emery/First National Bank of Chicago, Chicago, Il.	C-G...
N60FM	B 727-27	19535	Forbes Magazine, Butler-Hangar 12, Newark, NJ.	N7294
N60FN	Learjet	24E-339	Flight International Inc. Jacksonville, Fl.	N690/N851CC/N15MJ
N60GG	Challenger 601-3A	5007	Henley Group, Manchester, NH.	/C-G...
N60GL	Citation	550-0574	Transnational Motors Inc. Grand Rapids, Mi.	N12998
N60GT	MS 760 Paris-1A	8	J E Thompson, St Cloud, Fl.	G-APRU/G-36-2/F-WJAC
N60HC	Sabre-60	306-21	Hintam International Inc. Laredo, Tx.	(N8LC)/N442A/N948R/N4731N
N60HU	HS 125/1A-522	25103	Midlantic Jet Charters Inc. Pleasantville, NJ.	N601UU/N210M/N533/G-ATUV
N60JC	Sabre-60	306-51	Chapel Hill Leasing & Sales, Kent, Oh.	N141JA/C-GDCC/N928R/N7531N
N60JD	Citation	550-0195	John Deere & Co. Moline, Il.	N68032
N60JM	JetStar 2	5213	Jet Management/WHA Aircraft Inc. Syracuse, NY.	N501J/N501T/N5539L
N60JN	Sabre-60	306-14	Telford Aviation, Waterville, Me.	N43GB/N1JN/(N60AG)/N24GB/N24G/N4724N
N60JP	Westwind-1124	320	Prewitt Leasing Inc. Bedford, Tx.	4X-CRN
N60LT	Learjet	55-060	Airsupport Services Corp. Miami, Fl.	N8YY/N86AJ//N53JL/N60MJ
N60MB	Falcon 10	15	W/o 3 Apr 77.	N109FJ/F-WJMM
N60MP	Citation	500-0325	SDH International Inc. Miami, Fl.	/N50TR/N25CJ/(N5325J)
N60MS	Challenger 601	3051	Melvin Simon & Assocs Inc. Indianapolis, In.	/N445AC/C-G...
N60PM	BAe 125/800A	NA0453	Philip Morris Inc. Richmond, Va.	N615BA/G-5-670
N60PR	Citation	501-0160	Bedford Properties, Portland, Or.	(N58BD)/N1951E
N60RV	Westwind-1124	250	Winnebago RV Inc. Wilmington, De.	N29995/C-GFAO/N250WW/4X-CMV
N60S	Citation V	560-0066	TCO Insurance Services, Solvang, Ca.	
N60SL	Falcon 10	189	O'Sullivan Corp. Winchester, Va.	N605T/N254FJ/F-WZGT
N60TM	Sabre-60	306-72	Torchmark/Liberty Natl Life Insurance Co. Birmingham, Al.	N6TM/N550SL N231A/N231CA
N61BP	Falcon 10	102	IBP Inc/Iowa Beef Processors Inc. Sioux City, Ia.	N178FJ/F-WPXK
N61CT	BAe 125/800A	NA0408	Contel Management Co. Atlanta, Ga.	/N553BA/G-5-579
N61DF	Sabre-60	306-131	Cintas Corp. Cincinnati, Oh.	N35DL/N5DL/N2149J
N61EW	Learjet	25B-161	Corporate Aviation Services Inc. Tulsa, Ok.	N4VC
N61FN	Learjet	24B-224	Flight International Inc. Newport News, Va.	N61DM/(N722DM)/N102PA/C-GPCL N30DH/N99606/D-IOGE
N61HA	Citation	550-0312	First Union Transportation, Charlotte, NC.	N58H/N6889E
N61MD	Sabre-60	306-3	Tyler Turbine Sales Inc. Tyler, Tx.	N925Z/N1001G/N177A
N61MS	HS 125/731	NA765	Melvin Simon & Assoc Inc..Indianapolis, In.	N708BW/N700BW/N125PA/N62BH
N61RH	Sabre-40	282-27	Enstrom West Corp. Palos Verdes Es. Ca.	N111EA/N129GB/N129GP/N720R/N6381C
N61RS	Westwind-Two	384	Stark Aviation Ltd. Fort Dodge, Ia.	N48WW/4X-CUB
N61SB	HS 125/600A	6002	Avionics International Inc. Orlando, Fl.	N915JT/N631SQ/N631SC/N79BH (N92BH)
N61TS	Learjet	23-029	Wfu.	N66AS/N1BU/N715BC/N7000K
N62	Sabre-75A	380-31	FAA, Oklahoma City, Ok.	
N62B	Learjet	55-091	Bruce S Gillis, Los Angeles, Ca.	N91PR/N991CH/N91CH/N8566F
N62BL	Challenger	1062	Brooke Aviation Inc. Greensboro, NC.	N4FE/M31-01/C-GBTT/C-GLWV
N62CF	Sabre-60	306-62	Integrated Financial Services inc. Kansas City, Mo.	//N32BC/N905P/N905R N7090/N66NR/N967R
N62DK	Learjet	35A-231	Donald Koll Co-Trustee, Newport Beach, Ca.	N911DB/(N712DM)/(N10AB)
N62FN	Learjet	24B-194	Flight International Inc. Newport News, Va.	N62DM/N851BA/N77LS/N952GA
N62HA	Citation	550-0203	First Union Transportation, Charlotte, NC.	N12JA/N67990
N62K	Gulfstream 2	93	Cook International Inc. Palm Beach, Fl.	/N215GA/TJ-AAK/N8785R/N885GA
N62MS	Challenger 601	3050	Melvin Simon & Assocs Inc. Indianapolis, In.	/(N9680N)/N9680Z/C-GLXS
N62TC	HS 125/731	NA763	Thiokol Corp. Brigham City, Ut.	N125MT/N55B/N246N/N46B/(N68BW)/N246N (N91BH)/N58BH/(G-5-15)
N62WA	Citation	550-0583	Muscatine Corp. Muscatine, Ia.	N1301B
N62WH	BAC 1-11/401AK	078	Southern Aircraft Services Inc. Coral Gables, Fl.	HZ-TA1/N800PW/(N800MC) N9WP/N5036
N62WL	HS 125/700A	NA0289	Flightcraft Inc. Portland, Or.	/N62WH/N125CG/N125AJ/G-5-17
N62WM	Learjet	35A-596	Waste Management Inc. Wilmington, De.	N72612
N63CC	Citation	550-0489	Hughes Aircraft/Cessna Finance Corp. Wichita, Ks.	N12539
N63LE	Learjet	35A-250	Land's End Yacht Stores Inc. Dodgeville, Wi.	//(N87RS)/N3250
N63PM	Falcon 20F	355	Philip Morris Management Corp. NYC.	N550M/N344G/N27AC/N20FJ/N4467F/F-WMKF
N63TM	Citation	550-0457	F T Stent, Stone Mountian, Ga.	N457CF/N220CC/N1250L

Page 49

Registration	Type	c/n	Owner / Operator	Previous identity
N64	Sabre-75A	380-35	Cx USA 8/88 as w/o 9/86.	
N64BE	Falcon 900	45	Beatrice Companies, Chicago, Il.	N433FJ/F-WWFB
N64BH	Challenger 601-3A	5027	Laguna Niguel Properties, Orange County, Ca.	N244BH/C-G...
N64CA	Citation	550-0030	Huron Pointe Marina Inc. Mt Clemens, Mi.	G-MSLY/G-FERY/G-DJBI/(N3249M)
N64CE	Learjet	24B-205	Royal Air Freight Inc. Waterford, Mi.	(N721J)/N64CE/N64CF/N974JD
N64CF	Learjet	35A-461	CF Industries Inc. Chicago, Il.	
N64GL	Challenger	1064	Brooke Aviation Inc. Greensboro, NC.	N14FE/M31-02/C-GBUB/C-G...
N64HB	Learjet	24-149	Parmley Aviation Services Inc. Council Bluffs, Ia.	/N300LB/N300HH/N2945C N294BC
N64MA	Sabre-40	282-44	Finalco, Boca Raton, Fl.	N600JS/N44NP/N1QC/N1DC/N4567/N6399C
N64MP	Learjet	35A-490	Boone T Pickens Jr/Mesa Petroleum Co. Amarillo, Tx.	
N64MQ	Sabre-65	465-73	Concorde Aviation Inc. E Alton, Il.	N64MC
N64PM	Citation	550-0467	Philip Morris Management Corp. NYC.	N1883/N1251N
N64RT	Citation	501-0191	Rubaiyat Trading Co. Birmingham, Al.	/N98ME/N6780Y
N64TF	Citation	550-0064	Carlisle Air Inc. Newport, Ky.	(N336CP)/YV-36CP/N26617
N64VM	Diamond-Two	A1001SA	Verco Manufacturing/Nektor Industries Inc. Portland, Or.	
N64WH	Learjet	25B-102	Space Coast Jet Service Inc. Rockledge, Fl.	N52AJ/N962/N52AJ/N311CC/N999ML N999M/N267GL
N64WM	Learjet	55-022	Waste Management Inc. Wilmington, De.	
N65	Sabre-75A	380-37	FAA, Oklahoma City, Ok.	
N65AF	Sabre-65	465-62	American Family Corp. Columbus, Oh.	N56NW
N65AH	Sabre-65	465-68	Allied Automotive, Romulus, Mi.	
N65AK	Sabre-65	465-35	North Pacific Enterprises Inc. Kirkland, Wa.	N2590E
N65AM	Sabre-65	465-58	Allied Signal/King-Bendix, Olathe, Ks.	
N65AR	Sabre-65	465-67	Concord Aviation Inc. Antwerp, Belgium.	
N65B	Falcon 50	10	Borden Inc. Morristown, NJ.	N50FG/F-WZHD
N65DD	Sabre-65	465-26	Central Soya, Fort Wayne, In.	N2548E/N465SL
N65DW	HS 125/400A	NA737	Blue Fire Development Inc. Wilmington, De.	N65EC/N2500W/G-AXOE
N65FC	HS 125/1A	25091	Bill Walker & Assoc Inc. McKinnon Airport, Ga.	//N90RG/N20RG/N1230G/G-ATNE
N65FF	Sabre-65	465-46	Frederick P Furth, Healdsburg, Ca.	N79CD/N20UC
N65L	Sabre-65	465-76	Acopian Technical Co. Easton, Pa.	
N65LC	HS 125/700A	NA0342	Liebert Corp. Columbus, Oh.	(N67LC)/N518S/N710BU/G-5-17
N65R	Sabre-65	306-114	Winn Dixie Stores Inc. Jacksonville, Fl.	N60TF/N65R/N2109J
N65RC	Sabre-65	465-19	Robertshaw Controls, Richmond, Va.	
N65SA	Citation	550-0108	Sacramento Aviation Inc. Sacramento, Ca.	/N4EK/N4TL/(N2665F)
N65ST	Gulfstream 2	5	Petersen Publishing Co. Los Angeles, Ca.	/N100PJ/N100P
N65TC	Sabre-65	465-30	Thornton Corp. Los Angeles, Ca.	N89MM//N25ZC
N65TF	Citation	550-0155	Warehouse Management Inc. Cincinnati, Oh.	(N298CP)/YV-298CP/(YV-209CP) N6566C
N65TL	Sabre-65	465-56	Ziegler Inc/Trent Leasing Co. Minneapolis, Mn.	N265JS/N544PH
N65TS	Sabre-65	465-34	Tutor-Saliba Corp. Sylmar, Ca.	N80FH/N112KM/N50DG
N65Y	Learjet	55-121	Bielfeldt Lauritsen & Hagemeyer, Peoria, Il.	N8568J
N66AG	Citation	501-0136	Publishers Air Service, Dover, De.	N66AT/(N26502)
N66AM	HS 125/731	25087	O'Gara Aviation Co. Las Vegas, Wa.	C-FALC/G-ATOX
N66CC	Citation	500-0066	Hehr International Co. Van Nuys, Ca.	N566CC
N66CF	Falcon 10	65	Stevedoring Services of America, Seattle, Wa.	(F-GJMA)/N21DB/XB-BAK/N149FJ F-WJMJ
N66DD	Gulfstream 3	483	Duchossois Enterprises/D-Aire Inc. Advance, NC.	N309GA
N66ES	Citation	550-0032	Starwood Air Service Inc. Englewood, Co.	/N55BP//N810SG/N810SC/N3251M
N66FE	Learjet	35A-383	Clay Lacy Aviation Inc. Van Nuys, Ca.	/
N66GE	Sabre-60	306-99	Grey Eagle Distributors Inc. Chesterfield, Mo.	N16PN/N905R/N65789
N66HA	HS 125/3A	25126	W/o 13 Aug 89.	/N510X/G-AVDL/G-5-11
N66HH	Falcon 10	176	Herbert Dow, Midland, Mi.	N179AG/HK-2968/HK-2968X/N242FJ/F-WZGI
N66JE	Westwind-1124	326	Professional Jet/NJE Aircraft Corp. Newark, De.	(N88JE)/4X-CRT
N66LE	Citation Eagle	500-0170	Longley Supply Co/Wright Chemical Corp. Wilmington, NC.	/N818R/N90237 N60MS
N66LJ	Learjet	35A-401	Carrier Research Inc. Naples, Fl.	/
N66LN	Learjet	35A-500	L & N Equities Inc. Dallas, Tx.	/N8566X
N66LX	Westwind-Two	375	Summit Aviation Inc. Dallas, Tx.	N79AP/N79AD/4X-CUF
N66MF	Challenger 600S	1036	Maxair Inc. Pontiac, Mi.	/N88AT/N80AT/C-GBOQ/C-GLYC
N66MP	JetStar-6	5015	Wfu.	//N9046F/N505T/N103KC/N172L/NASA4
N66MS	Citation	551-0053	Modern Supply Co. Ponca City, Ok.	(N6890C)
N66NJ	Learjet	25-039	National Jets Inc. Fort Lauderdale, Fl.	N17JF/N959RE/N959GA

Registration	Type	c/n	Owner / Operator	Previous identity
N66NT	Falcon 20F	349	Northern Telecom Inc. Nashville, Tn.	N273K/N4465F/F-WMKG
N66TR	Falcon 10	29	Trinity Industries Inc. Rocky Mount, NC.	N999F/N332J/N66MF/N234U/N120FJ
N66WB	Falcon 20D	242	WRBC Leasing Inc. Greenwich, Ct.	///N911TR/N2622M/(N320FJ)/N800CF/N4418F F-WPUZ
N66WM	Learjet	55C-145	Waste Management Inc. Oak Brook, Il.	
N67BK	Sabre-40A	282-135	Beckley Flying Service Inc. Mt Hope, WV.	/N2006/N200E/N820JR/N55PP/N7778L N777SL/N4GV
N67HB	Learjet	25B-189	Watersoft Inc. Saxonburg, Pa.	N888DF/N352SC/N111SZ/N111SF
N67JR	Falcon 20F	247	John Roth, Brisbane, Ca.	N730S/VH-FAX/N730S/N4419F/F-WPXE
N67KM	Sabre-75A	380-7	W/o 14 Jun 75.	
N67MA	Citation	500-0277	Zahara Enterprises Inc. Fort Wayne, In.	N67MP/N277CC/(N5277J)
N67MP	Citation	550-0444	Somerset Acres Inc. Fort Wayne, In.	(N1248G)
N67PA	Learjet	35A-208	JP Foodservice Inc. Hanover, Md.	//(N39DJ)/N39DK///(N691NS)/N40TA/N40149
N67PR	Gulfstream 2	67	Rental Fleet Leasing Inc. Montgomery, Al.	/N400JD/N10HR/EL-WRT/N711S N839GA
N67SF	Citation	500-0184	Seneca Flight Operations, Penn Yann, NY.	N71RC/N77RC
N67WB	Falcon 900	24	Finevest Services Leasing Corp. White Plains, NY.	/N901B/N417FJ/F-WWFE
N67WM	Learjet	55B-132	Waste Management Inc. Wilmington, De.	
N68AA	Sabre-40	282-38	Aero Air Inc. Hillsboro, Or.	//N100FS/N299LR/N2997/N6393C
N68BC	Falcon 20C	155	John M Rogers, Brandon, Ms.	N404R/N212C/(N205SE)/N205SC/N500Y/N4362F F-WJMK
N68CB	Citation	500-0270	Cracker Barrel Old Country Store, Lebanon, Tn.	/N72BC/N712N/N712J/N5270J
N68EA	Citation	501-0068	Executive Air Services Ltd. N Canton, Oh.	N50GT/N9GT/N438CC/N2841A
N68FN	Learjet	24-101	Flight International Inc. Newport News, Va.	N68DM/N473/N473EJ/N15PL/N316MF N316M
N68HC	Citation V	560-0016	Hospital Corp of America, Nashville, Tn.	N12173
N68KM	Sabre-75A	380-23	Kerr McGee Corp. Oklahoma City, Ok.	N65776
N68LU	Learjet	24-163	Lewis University, Romeoville, Il. (wfu ?).	N65WM/N77AE/N65339/N1AP/N701AP
N68MA	Sabre-60	306-23	Healthsouth Rehabilitation Co. Birmingham, Al.	/N77AT/N15RF/CF-BLT/N908R N4733N
N68MJ	Learjet	35A-607	Jervis B Webb Co. Farmington Hills, Mi.	/PT-LIJ/N72614
N68PL	Diamond 1A	A077SA	Pay Less Drug Stores Northwest Inc. Wilsonville, Or.	N377DM
N68SK	Citation	650-0156	Safety-Kleen/S-K Transportation Co. Wilmington, De.	/N13267
N68WW	Westwind-1124	386	N Hassid/GECC, Wilton, Ct.	(VH-JPL)/4X-CUE
N69BH	Learjet	35A-276	Dorothy Josephs, Hayward, Ca.	/N613RR/N44LJ
N69EC	Falcon 10	109	Altex Equipment Corp. Dallas, Tx.	C6-BEN/N77NR/N183FJ/F-WNGD
N69FF	Gulfstream 3	320	Lease Plan USA Inc. Atlanta, Ga.	/N873E
N69GP	Gulfstream 4	1033	Interfly Inc. Los Angeles, Ca.	(HB-IMY)
N69GT	Jet Commander	44	W/o 11 Jun 85.	N273LF/N273LP/N700CB/N700C/N200M
N69KB	Learjet	23-042	Wfu.	N701RZ/N1ZA/N2932C/N293BC
N69KM	Sabre-75A	380-30	Kerr McGee Corp. Oklahoma City, Ok.	N65793
N69LD	Citation	650-0080	McKee Baking Co. Collegedale, Tn.	/N1316E
N69ME	JetStar-731	17/5076	Dolphin Oil Ltd. Eugene, Or.	//N3EK/N3E//N100C/N9235R
N69MT	JetStar-8	5107	J Edward Connelly Assoc Inc. Pittsburgh, Pa.	/N7788/YV-187CP/N7788//N337US N118K
N69PS	Learjet	35-014	Powerplant Specialists Inc. Costa Mesa, Ca.	/N98VA/(N72TB)/N73TP/N71TP
N69X	MS 760 Paris	90	RPJ Energy Fund Management Inc. Burnsville, Mn.	N454HC/D-INGE
N70AA	Citation	501-0212	Orcas Aircraft Leasing, Eastsound, Wa.	/N67GM/N6785L
N70AR	HS 125/700A	NA0326	Aristech Chemical Corp. Pittsburgh, Pa.	//N522M/G-5-11
N70BC	Sabre-40A	282-132	F C Leasing/Bryce Corp. Memphis, Tn.	N28TP/N9252N
N70CE	Learjet	25B-142	Lear Group Inc. Burbank, Ca.	/N42HC/(N142HC)/N515WH
N70EW	Falcon 900	25	East West Air Inc. Teterboro, NJ.	N418FJ/F-WWFF
N70FC	HS 125/700A	NA0339	Emery/First National Chicago Association, Il.	/G-5-18
N70FL	Falcon 50	144	Falcon Jet Corp. Teterboro, NJ.	//N133FJ/F-WZHL
N70HB	HS 125/1A-522	25043	Bill Walker & Assocs Inc. St Simons Island, Ga.	//N300R/N3007/N1230V/N125J G-ATGA
N70HC	Sabre-75	370-8	Howell Petroleum Corp. Houston, Tx. (status ?)	N3TE/N7591N
N70JF	Learjet	25D-278	Jet Fleet Corp. Dallas, Tx.	
N70KM	Sabre-75A	380-52	Kerr-McGee Corp. Oklahoma City, Ok.	N177NQ/N177NC/N75A/N2136J
N70LY	HS 125/400A	NA760	Olympic Trading & Transport, Roswell, NM.	/N731X/N55BH/G-5-12
N70MD	Falcon 20D	153	J Ray McDermott & Co. New Orleans, La.	N4361F/F-WLCT
N70NE	BAe 125/800A	NA0407	Banc One Corp. Columbus, Oh.	N552BA/G-5-578

Registration	Type	c/n	Owner / Operator	Previous identity
N70PM	HS 125/700A	NA0303	Philip Morris Management Corp. Milwaukee, Wi.	(N80PM)/N125P/G-5-14
N70PS	Gulfstream 4	1058	American International Aviation, Wilmington, De.	N458GA
N70SK	BAe 125/800A	8006	Johnston Coca-Cola Bottling Co. Chattanooga, Tn.	/N800S/N800WW/G-5-17
N70TG	Citation V	560-0069	Texas Gas Transmission Corp. Owensboro, Ky.	
N70TH	Falcon 200	509	Sony Corp. NYC.	JA8270/(N8495B)/N222FJ/F-WPUX
N70TJ	Learjet	24B-199	Yelvington Transport Inc. Daytona Beach, Fl.	N444HC/N855W/N333CR
N70U	Falcon 20F	399	Anheuser-Busch Companies, St Louis, Mo.	N70NF/N70NE/N881G/N184F/F-WMKI
N71A	Learjet	35A-352	Aeromet Inc. Tulsa, Ok.	N600G/N30GD/YV-326CP
N71CC	Sabre-60A	306-71	Air Moose Inc. Austin, Tx.	N1028Y/N370M/N31BM
N71CE	Learjet	25B-136	Lear Group Inc. Burbank, Ca.	N221TC/N180YA/N920US/N920CC
N71CP	Falcon 20C	89	Hanlin Group/LCP=Linden Chemicals & Plastics, Edison, NJ.	N345BM/N978F F-WMKG
N71DM	Learjet	25C-129	Flight International, Jacksonville, Fl.	N551WC
N71EM	Citation	S550-0006	Cessna Aircraft Co. Wichita, Ks.	N71FM/N101EC/(N1256N)
N71GH	Diamond 1A	A071SA	Excel Air Inc. Jacksonville, Fl.	N70GA/N371DM
N71HS	Learjet	35A-287	Hi-Stat Manufacturing Co. Lexington, Oh.	N17EM
N71JC	Learjet	31-008	North American Plastics Inc. Aberdeen, Ms.	
N71L	Citation	501-0242	Lindair Inc. Sarasota, Fl.	N500BK/N40PL/N2623B
N71LJ	Learjet	23-071	McComas Properties Inc. Medford, Or.	/N1001A
N71M	Challenger 600S	1077	Sundstrand Corp. Rockford, Il.	/N152SM/C-GBZK/(N778XX)/N994TA/C-GLXM
N71NK	Citation V	560-0040	Flint Ink Corp. Detroit, Mi.	
N71NP	BAe 125/800A	8041	Nationwide Mutual Insurance Co. Columbus, Oh.	N819AA/G-5-18
N71RP	Gulfstream 2B	199	General Transportation Corp. NYC.	N74RP/N75RP/N75WC/N829GA
N71TP	Learjet	55-032	Tesoro Petroleum Corp. San Antonio, Tx.	(N72TP)/N75TP
N72BB	Falcon 20C	59	KCM Co. Midland, Tx.	N202TA/N227CC/N227GC/N710MT/N710MW/N263MW N971F/F-WNGO
N72CT	Citation V	560-0072	Cessna Aircraft Corp. Wichita, Ks.	N572CV/N2726J/(N91FA)/N72FE
N72DA	Learjet	35A-098	Duncan Aviation Inc. Lincoln, Nb.	(N998DJ)/N44UC/N21GL/N20CR
N72FP	Learjet	24-137	Murray Aviation Inc. Ypsilanti, Mi.	/N77RY/N73HG/N907CS
N72HB	Westwind-1124	254	Original Honey Baked Ham Co. Atlanta, Ga.	N112AB/N888R/N600TD/4X-CMZ
N72HC	HS 125/731	NA780	Harsco Corp. Camp Hill, Pa.	N78BH
N72K	BAe 125/800A	NA0429	Key Bank NA/Key Corp. Scotia, NY.	/N583BA/G-5-615
N72LT	Westwind-1123	180	Furnival Machinery Co. Hatfield, Pa.	//(N180JS)///N1019K/HP-1A/4X-CKD
N72NP	BAe 125/800A	8044	Nationwide Mutual Insurance Co. Columbus, Oh.	N821AA/G-5-12
N72PS	Falcon 900	18	American International Aviation Corp. Teterboro, NJ.	N413FJ/F-WWFA
N72RK	Gulfstream 3	306	Reebok International Inc. Stoughton, Ma.	/N777SW/N306GA
N72TQ	Jet Commander	4	Jack Ormes, Los Angeles, Ca.	N72TC/N77TC/N77F
N73B	Falcon 10	79	The Kroger Co. Cincinnati, Oh.	N160FJ/F-BPXB/F-WPXB
N73DJ	Learjet	25D-273	Duncan Aviation Inc. Lincoln, Ne.	/N321AS
N73FW	Citation	501-0150	Admiral Beverage Corp. Worland, Wy.	N95MJ/N2616G
N73GP	Learjet	55B-127	Gerber Products Co. Fremont, Mi.	/HZ-AM2
N73HB	Citation	500-0256	Original Honey Baked Ham Co. Atlanta, Ga.	N456GB/N73TF/N83TF/SE-DDN/N256CC
N73HP	Sabre-40A	282-120	Rocky Creek Leasing Inc. Dublin, Oh.	
N73LP	Gulfstream 2B	119	Louisiana Pacific Corp. Hillsboro, Or.	N720G/(N875E)/N60HJ/N2991Q/C-FHBX N825GA/TU-VAF/N824GA
N73PS	Learjet	24B-186	Milam International Inc. Englewood, Co.	N7300K/N18G/N1SS/N100AJ/N266P
N73RP	Gulfstream 3	491	General Transportation Corp. NYC.	N337GA
N73WC	Citation	500-0338	Pioneer Private Aviation Inc. Minneapolis, Mn.	N97LA/N92LA/N3300M/N8499B HB-VEX/(N868D)/N5338J
N74A	Gulfstream 2B	36	Aviation Assets Inc. Portland, Or.	N901KB/N901K/(N211GA)/N5400G/N26LA/N26L
N74AG	JetStar-731	23/5072	Pima Enterprises Inc. Oklahoma City, Ok.	///N500Z/N9233R
N74B	HS 125/700A	NA0209	Borden Inc. Columbus, Oh.	N586JR/N453EP/N60MS/N120GA/N46901/G-BFDW/G-5-17
N74FS	Falcon 900	85	F S Air Inc. Houston, Tx.	N461FJ/F-WWFC
N74G	Citation	550-0035	Entex Inc. Houston, Tx.	(N50GG)/N74G/N333X/N50XX/N8417B/N3278M
N74GL	Learjet	55-074	Electronic Data Systems Corp. Dallas, Tx.	N5574
N74JA	Challenger 600S	1060	Josephine Abercrombie Interests, Houston, Tx.	N22AZ//N29984/C-GLYK
N74JL	Learjet	35A-396	Orea Corp. NYC.	N5FF/VR-CBU/N5139W/N938GL/N2000M
N74JM	Westwind-Two	299	Marcus Management/Flight Svcs Group, Stratford, Ct.	N922CK/N922CR/4X-CQS
N74KV	Citation	550-0298	Rickety Air Inc. Raleigh, NC.	N68873
N74NP	BAe 125/800A	NA0440	Nationwide Mutual Insurance Co. Columbus, Oh.	/N593BA/G-5-643
N74PC	BAe 125/800A	NA0439	PNC Financial Corp. Pittsburgh, Pa.	N592BA/G-5-641
N74RP	Gulfstream 4	1040	General Transportation Corp. Dover, De.	N423GA
N74RY	Learjet	55-063	Aviation Sales Co. Miami, Fl.	N1744P/N8563P

Registration	Type	c/n	Owner / Operator	Previous identity
N74SP	Citation	550-0485	Delaware State Police, (was 551-0485).	N474SP///N1253P
N74TC	Citation	550-0067	Robert Hughes/Austin Citation Partners Inc. Austin, Tx.	/N81TC/N2663B
N75BC	Westwind-1124	426	Ball Corp. Muncie, In.	N426WW/4X-CUF
N75BS	Sabre-75A	380-12	Northwest Jet Center Inc. Houston, Tx.	(N4WJ)/N120YB/D-CLAN/N75SL/D-CLAN HB-VEC/N335K/N65758
N75CC	Gulfstream 2	117	Crown Controls Corp. New Bremen, Oh.	N888SW/N580RA/N822GA
N75CS	BAe 125/800A	8066	CSX Corp. Richmond, Va.	/N369BA/G-5-521
N75CV	Citation V	560-0075		(N2745L)
N75F	Citation	550-0337	Consumers Power/KJL Ltd. Sparks, Nv.	N727C/N6802S
N75G	Sabre-65	465-71	Consumers Power/KJL Ltd. Jackson, Mi.	N728C
N75GP	Learjet	55B-129	Gerber Products Co. Fremont, Mi.	/
N75GW	Citation	500-0257	Mercury Aviation Co/Great Gibraltar 11 Corp. Cleveland, Oh.	N75FN//N75MN N5257J
N75HL	Sabre-75A	380-36	The Kenridge Co. Dover, De.	JY-AFM/N75A/N2105J
N75KV	Learjet	35A-285	Conaero Inc. Wilmington, De.	//N777RA
N75LM	Learjet	25D-233	Manderson & Assocs Inc. Atlanta, Ga.	N55LJ
N75MG	Gulfstream 2	247	MG-75 Inc. Troy, Mi.	N73MG/C-GTEP/N888MC/N828GA
N75NP	BAe 125/800A	NA0441	Nationwide Mutual Insurance Co. Columbus, Oh.	/N594BA/G-5-645
N75PX	Citation	500-0248	Com Corp Aviation Inc. Cleveland, Oh.	/(N70PB)//N75PX/(N5248J)
N75RD	Citation	650-0134	Air Operations Co. Wilmington, De.	(N1323Y)
N75RP	Gulfstream 4	1073	General Transportation Co. Dover, De.	
N75RS	Sabre-75A	380-63	Randall Stores, Mitchell, SD.	
N75SE	Sabre-75A	380-4	Air Siesta Inc. McAllen, Tx.	/N510AA/N5105
N75TD	Learjet	36A-028	Phoenix Air Group Inc. Cartersville, Ga.	N731GA
N75TG	Citation	551-0031	Al Johnson Construction Co. Minneapolis, Mn.	YV-301CP/N6565C/(N98749)
N75TJ	HS 125/400A	NA722	Tyler Jet Aircraft Sales Inc. Tyler, Tx.	N75QS/N75CS/N1393/G-AXDO
N75W	Falcon 50	152	Consumers Power Co. Jackson, Mi.	/N1841F/N137FJ/F-WZHD
N75Z	Citation	550-0214	Hughes Supply Inc. Orlando, Fl.	N44WF/N13BJ/N6800S
N76D	Citation	650-0110	Dayton Hudson Corp. Minneapolis, Mn.	(N1320X)
N76JY	Citation	501-0676	Palo Alto Town & Country Village, Ca.	N676CC/N1958E
N76LE	Diamond 1A	A076SA	Lesson Electric Corp. Grafton, Wi.	/N376DM
N76MB	Falcon 20C	80	Consolidated Minerals Inc. Leesburg, Fl.	N356JB/N356WC/N356WB/N115K/N972F F-WMKI
N77A	Sabre-65	465-1	AMP Inc. Harrisburg, Pa. (was 306-136).	N65RS/N465S/N2501E
N77AP	Sabre-40	282-37	W/o 7 Nov 77.	N265W/N6392C
N77AT	Sabre-40A	282-109	Alban Tractor Co. Baltimore, Md.	N93AC//N700CF/N4NP
N77C	JetStar 2	5232	Trenton Foods/Parn Aviation Corp. Dover, De.	N90QP/N90CP/N4046M
N77CP	Falcon 50	143	Pfizer Inc. Trenton, NJ.	N130FJ/F-WZHI
N77CS	BAe 125/800A	8065	CSX Corp. Richmond, Va.	/N368BA/G-5-520
N77D	JetStar-731	60/5097	Mine Safety Appliances Co. Pittsburgh, Pa.	/N306L/N300L/N9253R
N77FD	Citation	501-0250	Mark Eden Inc. Pebble Beach, Ca.	
N77FK	Gulfstream 3	363	K Services Inc. NYC.	//N83AL
N77FV	Jet Commander	26	Wfu.	N10MC/N614JC
N77GA	Diamond-Two	A1005SA	TIC Aviation Inc. Dallas, Tx.	
N77GJ	Citation	501-0119	Bob Jones University, Greenville, SC.	N53RC/N35TM/N35AA/(N26486)
N77HH	Jet Commander	103	H & R Ltd. Ardmore, Ok.	N13AD/N10HV/N487G/N136K/N1121S
N77HW	JetStar-6	5080	Delta Omni Corp. Corona, Ca.	//N914P//N914X
N77KW	Learjet	25B-076	Keith Wood Agency Inc. Fort Worth, Tx.	/N222MQ/N222MC/N831WM/N711CA/N160J D-CCWK/HB-VCL
N77LB	Learjet	24-135	Aviation One Insurance/Speedbird Inc. Mason, Oh.	/N85W
N77LP	Learjet	35A-321	Jet East Inc. Dallas, Tx.	/(N19LM)/N14TX
N77MR	Learjet	24E-351	Federal Truck Driving School Inc. Indianapolis, In.	N81WT/N31WT/N19MJ
N77ND	Citation	550-0005	University of N. Dakota, Grand Forks, ND.	OE-GKP/N98817
N77NJ	Learjet	25-033	National Jets Inc. Fort Lauderdale, Fl.	YV-88CP/N768MS/N143J//HB-VBP
N77NT	Jet Commander	7	Consignment Aircraft Sales Inc. San Antonio, Tx.	N77KT/(N711VK)/N30RJ N22CH/N1173Z/N112JC
N77QM	Falcon 20C	75	QMS Inc. Mobile, Al.	N800DC/N2568/N256MA/N100V/N969F/F-WNGL
N77RC	Citation	550-0130	Mason C Rudd Enterprises, Louisville, Ky.	(N88845)
N77RS	Learjet	25C-094	W/o 4 Dec 78.	N97J/VR-BFV/SX-CBM
N77ST	Jet Commander	108	Corporate Skyways Inc. Omaha, Ne.	N12JX/N12JA/N1WP/N1121Z
N77TC	Sabre-65	465-10	Timken Co. Canton, Oh.	N65SL
N77TE	Falcon 50	110	Temple Inland Forest Products, Diboll, Tx.	//VR-BJA/5N-ARE/F-WPXG
N77VJ	Learjet	23-041	Smithair Inc. Jonesboro, Ga.	C-GDDB/N666MP/N205RJ

Registration	Type	c/n	Owner / Operator	Previous identity
N77VK	HS 125/731	25051	Wfu. Parted out and cx USA register 1/87.	C6-BEY/N125HD/N9300C/N9300 G-ATGU
N77W	BAe 125/800A	NA0434	AMP Inc. Harrisburg, Pa.	N588BA/G-5-625
N77WD	Citation	550-0180	Phaethon Flyers Inc. Aiken, SC.	//N320V/N88825
N78AB	Citation	501-0070	Mantoor Inc. Wilmington, De.	(N444CW)/N3062A
N78AM	Citation V	560-0056	Alice Manufacturing Co. Easley, SC.	N2682F
N78CS	Citation	550-0172	CSX Transportation Inc. Jacksonville, Fl.	N88JJ/N72MM/(N28MM)/N88795
N78D	Citation	650-0116	Dayton Hudson Corp. Minneapolis, Mn.	(N1321L)
N78GA	Citation	550-0087	Kinnarps-Sweden. (551-0132 ?).	C-GTBR/(C-FCFP)/N2663J
N78GJ	Westwind-1124	310	Applied Industrial Materials, Deerfield, Il.	D-CBBD/4X-CRD
N78JR	Falcon 20C	70	Wfu 20 Mar 89.	(N400NL)/N78JR/(N647SA)/N647JP/N966F/F-WMKH
N78MC	Learjet	35A-117	Gerard Aircraft Sales & Leasing, Wilmington, De.	//N3155B
N78MD	Falcon 10	18	McDermott International Aviation Inc. Singapore.	N111FJ/F-WJMJ
N78PH	Citation	550-0025	Parker Hannifin Corp. Cleveland, Oh.	/N664J/N664JB/N9014S/EP-KIC/N3239M
N78RP	Gulfstream 3	328	General Transportation Corp. NYC.	/N75RP/N309GA
N79AD	Challenger 601-3A	5063	Arthur DeMoss Foundation, Philadelphia, Pa.	/N612CC/C-GLXS
N79AE	HS 125/1A	25031	American European Sales & Leasing, Marietta, Ga.	/N43WJ//N1923M/G-ATBB
N79B	HS 125/400A	NA751	Borden Inc. Columbus, Oh.	/N125GH/N75RN/N75RD/N120GB/N120GA/G-BCLR/N640M N47BH
N79BP	Falcon 10	178	Borden Inc/Creamette Co. Minneapolis, Mn.	N10QD/N244FJ/F-WZGK
N79DD	Citation	500-0254	W/o 24 Sep 90.	///N29991/C-GJTX/N26PA/N5254J
N79HA	Falcon 10	128	EAF/Houston Astros, Teterboro, NJ.	N1871R/N197FJ/F-WNGO
N79HC	HS 125/700A	NA0246	Harsco Corp. Camp Hill, Pa.	N130BB/G-5-20
N79PB	Falcon 10	47	Heather Hill Sportswear Co Inc. Hockessin, De.	N90LA/N91LA/N101GZ/N3914L YV-101CP/YV-221CP/PJ-AYA/YV-07CP/N132FJ/F-WLCY
N79PM	Falcon 200	510	Principal Mutual Life Insurance Co. Des Moines, Ia.	N223FJ/F-WPUY
N79RS	Learjet	24XR-280	Stern Air, Portland, Or.	D-ICHS
N79SF	Learjet	36A-041	Phoenix Air Group Inc. Marietta, Ga.	
N79SL	DC-9-15F	47011	U.S. Department of Energy, Albuquerque, NM.	N60AF/CF-TOP/N8903
N80AS	Learjet	35A-446	UCLA Medical Center, Los Angeles, Ca.	//N37962
N80AT	Gulfstream 4	1151	Taubman Air Inc. Bloomfield Hills, Mi.	N375GA
N80AW	Citation	550-0186	Atwood Vacuum Machine/Continental Leasing Co. Rockford, Il.	YV-187CP//N80AW N98418
N80BT	Learjet	35A-343	Northrop Corp. Los Angeles, Ca.	N135MB
N80CD	Learjet	35A-477	Baron Leasing Inc Trustee, Charlotte, NC.	/N82GL/N3797B
N80CN	Falcon 50	105	Champion International Corp. Stamford, Ct.	N106FJ/F-WZHS
N80DH	Learjet	24B-191	Cx USA 3/89 as Wfu.	(N44TL)/N44LJ/N855W
N80F	Falcon 900	6	Anheuser-Busch Companies Inc. Wilmington, De.	/N405FJ/F-WWFD
N80GM	Citation	550-0147	Cargill Leasing Corp. Minnetonka, Mn.	/(N155JK)/N98682
N80J	Gulfstream 3	441	USX Corp. Pittsburgh, Pa.	N306GA
N80K	HS 125/700A	NA0298	USX Corp. Pittsburgh, Pa.	N125G/G-5-17
N80KA	HS 125/700A	7001	Polestar Corp. Rowayton, Ct.	/N101XS/N101SK/N700SV/(N4555E)/G-BEFZ/VR-HIM G-BEFZ
N80L	Gulfstream 3	406	USX Corp. Pittsburgh, Pa,	N356GA
N80MF	Citation	501-0154	Cessna Aircraft Co. Wichita, Ks.	N2613C
N80PM	HS 125/700A	NA0300	Philip Morris Management Corp. Milwaukee, Wi.	N70PM/G-5-20
N80R	Sabre-65	465-53	Winn-Dixie Stores Inc. Jacksonville, Fl.	N76NX
N80SF	Citation	501-0189	Kenneth Padgett Sr. Vero Beach, Fl.	(N500SS)/N80SF/N6780C
N81CC	Citation	550-0089	J F Wilbur Jr Inc. Fayetteville, NC.	N43RW/(N444WJ)/(N44JX)/N88MJ/(N26623)
N81CH	Learjet	55-036	Facilities Management Installation, Louisville, Ky.	/N76AW/N81CH/N555GL N3803G
N81EB	Citation	501-0003	Thomas Mueller, Fort Smith, Ar.	N781L/N55CJ/N5355J
N81HH	HS 125/700A	7189	Horsehead Industries Inc. NYC.	/N94B/N700BA/G-OSAM/(G-OBSM)/G-BKHK
N81KA	HS 125/700A	NA0227	Crusader Aviation/Keystone Aviation Service Inc. Oxford, Ct.	/N10CZ/G-5-19
N81MC	Learjet	24F-344	W/o 10 Nov 84.	
N81P	Falcon 10	31	Pilot Oil Corp. Knoxville, Tn.	N50TC/N27C/N2MP/N122FJ/F-WLCU
N81R	Falcon 50	148	R J Reynolds Tobacco Co. Winston Salem, NC.	//N134FJ/F-WZHB
N81RR	HS 125/731	NA727	Geneva International Ltd. Arlington, Va.	N114B/N814M/G-AXDS
N81SH	Citation	S550-0146	Conair Inc. Franklin, Pa.	N1296B/(G-JBCA)
N82A	Gulfstream 3	342	Prudential Insurance Co of America, Newark, NJ.	/N91LJ/N441A
N82AT	Citation	500-0312	AMR Combs Memphis Inc. Memphis, Tn.	//N33MQ/(N233ME)/N33ME/N5312J
N82CR	Sabre-65	465-49	Rockwell International Corp. Cedar Rapids, Ia.	/N500RR/N455LB/N455SF
N82LS	Citation	501-0681	Les Schwab Warehouse Center Inc. Prineville, Or.	N2616G

Registration	Type	c/n	Owner / Operator	Previous identity
N82MD	Falcon 10	77	McDermott Inc. Dubai, UAE.	N158FJ/F-WNGN
N82ML	Sabre-40	282-83	Duncan Aircraft Sales, Venice, Fl.	N160TC/N232T/N642LR/N726R
N82R	Sabre-40A	282-131	Viqui Aviation Inc. Miami, Fl.	/N3QM/N3BM/N9251N
N82RP	Falcon 50	18	Rich Products Inc. Lake Worth, Fl.	N1102A/N720M/N187S/N50FN/F-WZHJ
N83CP	Learjet	35A-274	Capital Holding Corp. Louisville, Ky.	N274JH/N274JS/N1087Y
N83CT	Westwind-1124	321	Century Service Group Inc. Monroe, La.	N1124N/N900WW/4X-CRO
N83EA	Learjet	25D-240	Sparkomatic Corp. Milford, Pa.	N78GL
N83FJ	Falcon 50	74	Anheuser-Busch Inc. St. Louis, Mo.	F-WZHA
N83FN	Learjet	36-007	Flight International Inc. Newport News, Va.	N83DM/VR-BHB/SX-AHF/N226CC N138GL
N83HC	Learjet	24B-193	Combs Aviation Corp. Peyton, Co.	N83H/N140CA/N33RE/N500RE/N500RP/N31TC D-IOGI
N83MD	Falcon 10	78	McDermott Inc. New Orleans, La.	N159FJ/F-WLCT
N83MP	Falcon 50	103	Boone T Pickens Jr/Mesa Petroleum Co. Amarillo, Tx.	N104FJ/F-WZHQ
N83ND	Citation	501-0178	University of North Dakota, Grand Forks, ND.	N4246A/LV-PML/N67799
N83TF	Sabre-65	465-43	BCTD/American Federation of Labour, Washington, DC.	N228LS/N950CS
N84A	Gulfstream 2	122	Burlington Northern Railroad, Fort Worth, Tx.	/N61SM/N4290X/N429JX/N832GA
N84BA	BAe 125/800A	8047	Bell Atlantic/Tri-Continental Leasing Corp. Paramus, NJ.	/N824AA/G-5-11
N84CF	Citation	501-0254	Carlton Forge Works, Paramount, Ca.	N2629Z
N84EA	Citation	550-0484	Executive Air Services/Roger Deville, Wilmington, De.	N1253N
N84EB	Citation	550-0488	Elkhart Brass Manufacturing Co. Elkhart, In.	N12536
N84FN	Learjet	36-002	Flight International Inc. Newport News, Va.	N84DM/N3239A/D-CELA/N18AT YV-89CP/YV-161P/YV-TASG/D-CMAR/N362GL
N84G	Citation	650-0045	Executive Jet Sales Inc. Columbus, Oh.	/
N84GA	Diamond 1A	A070SA	Tracinda Corp. Beverly Hills, Ca.	/OY-BPI/D-CNEX/N370DM
N84GC	Citation	550-0493	Burcliff Sales Inc. Franklin, NC.	/N84AW/(N258P)/N1254P
N84GP	Peregrine	551	Gulfstream Aerospace Corp. Bethany, Ok.	N9881S/(N550GA)
N84HP	Falcon 50	56	Hewlett-Packard Co. San Jose, Ca.	N112FJ/F-WDFE/F-GDFE/F-WZHR
N84LA	Westwind-1124	378	World Jet/Air Travel Inc. Ronkonkoma, NY.	4X-CUI
N84LP	Sabre-60	306-8	Duncan Aircraft Sales Inc. Venice, Fl.	N361DA/N73GR/N73G/N4716N
N84PH	Westwind-1124	314	Minterne Corp. NYC.	N2454M/VH-IWW/4X-CRH
N84V	Falcon 20E	302	Jet East/Evlin Corp. Dallas, Tx.	OE-GDP/D-COMM/F-WRQP
N84WW	Westwind-1124	401	Fire-Lite Alarms Inc. New Haven, Ct.	4X-CUQ
N85	Sabre-40	282-97	W/o 14 Jan 76.	N4706N
N85AW	Citation	650-0084	Management Financial Services, Duluth, Ga.	/N13168
N85CA	Learjet	35A-421	ConAgra Inc. Omaha, Ne.	/N44MJ
N85CC	JetStar-8	5102	Grand Associates Inc. New Bremen, Oh.	/N7500/N75CC/N500ZB/N326K/N9235R
N85D	Falcon 900	28	Castle Aviation Inc. Van Nuys, Ca.	N420FJ/F-WWFI
N85DB	Falcon 20C	52	Banner Group Inc. Lake Forest, Il.	N72ET/N881F/F-WNGN
N85EQ	Gulfstream 2	28	Equitable Bancorporation, Baltimore, Md.	N120EA/C-GCFB/N7004T/N700ST N695ST
N85HP	Sabre-60	306-126	Hewlett Packard Co. Palo Alto, Ca.	N1CH/N7NF/N7NR/N60SL/N2141J
N85JM	Falcon 10	85	Ben Franklin Properties Inc. Washington, Fl.	N165FJ/F-WPXI
N85LB	Falcon 200	494	Willhead Aviation Inc/Williams Engineering-UK.	N209FJ/F-WZZD
N85MG	Citation	550-0024	Enterprise/Cincinnati Contractors Aviation, Cincinnati, Oh.	/N533M/N3276M
N85MP	Citation	S550-0016	McClaskey Aviation/Red Lion Inns, Portland, Or.	(N99VC)/(N1259B)
N85PM	Learjet	35A-595	Green Bay Packaging Inc. Green Bay, Wi.	/
N85SV	Learjet	35A-427	Silicon Valley Express Inc. San Jose, Ca.	/OE-GNP
N86	Sabre-40	282-86	FAA, Oklahoma City, Ok.	N2255C
N86AK	Falcon 50	52	Air Ketchum/Helen Dow Whiting, Sun Valley, Id.	/N18G/JY-HAH/F-BMER/F-WZHV
N86BE	Learjet	35A-194	Burbank Jet Ltd. Chelmsford, Ma.	N86BL/N91W
N86BL	Learjet	35A-422	Bruce Leven, Redmond, Wa.	/YV-434CP
N86CC	Learjet	24-115	Wm. Mayo/M & N Co. Denver, Co. (wfu ?).	N591DL/N591D/N458LJ/N449LJ
N86CE	Gulfstream 2	109	Coca Cola Enterprises Inc. Atlanta, Ga. 'The Enterprise'	N882W/N679RW N811GA
N86CP	Sabre-60	306-76	Duty Free Aviation Inc. Glen Burnie, Md.	N82MW/N333NC/N333PC/N67NR
N86HP	Sabre-60	306-48	Hewlett Packard Co. San Jose, Ca.	N75HP/N60AG/N284U/N234U/N938R/N7519N
N86MT	Citation	501-0088	Windway Capital Corp. Sheboygan, Wi.	N22TY/N22TS/N31MT/N473CC/(N3181A)
N86PC	Learjet	35A-108	Samuel Primack/PC Air Charter Inc. Englewood, Co.	(N86PQ)/N86PC/F-GCLE D-COCO
N86QS	Citation	S550-0086	Robert Beckley/B & B Equipment & Supply Co.	N900RB/N586CC/(N1274X)
N86SG	Citation	550-0350	Seymour Grubman, Beverly Hills, Ca.	

Registration	Type	c/n	Owner / Operator	Previous identity
N86SH	Sabre-80A	380-32	Southern Holdings Inc. New Orleans, La.	N66ED/N66ES/N64MQ/N64MC/N75RS N2100J
N86SK	Gulfstream 2	85	James Lenane, Livermore, Ca.	N510G/N5102
N87	Sabre-40	282-87	FAA, Frankfurt, West Germany.	N2256B
N87AC	Gulfstream 3	427	Casden Co. Burbank, Ca.	N42MD/N44MD/N327GA
N87AG	HS 125/700A	NA0247	Beneto Inc. W Sacramento, Ca.	/(N530TE)/N530TL/N30PR/N130BC/G-5-11
N87AT	Learjet	35A-096	Midlantic Aircraft Sales, King of Prussia, Pa.	/(N11JV)//N214LS
N87CM	Sabre-40	282-21	Centurion Investments/Intermark Capital Co. St Louis, Mo.	N168D/N168H N6375C
N87CR	Sabre-40A	282-137	Collins Radio Group, Cedar Rapids, Ia.	N9NR/N53WC/N5512A/N5511A/N65763
N87DC	HS 125/731	25214	Cable Holdings Aviation Corp. Glenville, Ct.	N569CS/N369CS/N12AE/N12BN N731HS/G-5-20/G-AXTU/G-AXTU/N40PC/N60PC/N60QA
N87DG	Jet Commander	14	TTM Inc/Sid John Aircraft, Oklahoma City, Ok.	N87DC/N121BN/N350M
N87DL	Jet Commander-B	126	Free Wind Corp/Rade Air, Buenos Aires.	N87DC//N113MR/N315SA/N4983E/4X-COM
N87EC	BAe 125/800A	8052	Ethyl Corp. Richmond, Va.	N360BA/G-5-20
N87FL	Citation	501-0258	Flying Lion Inc. Nashville, Tn.	N900RD/N900RB/N664CC
N87HP	Gulfstream 3	338	Hewlett Packard Co. San Jose, Ca.	N372GM/N372CM/N862GA
N87NS	Westwind-1124	432	Wilmington Trust Co. Wilmington, De.	4X-CUH
N87PT	Citation	550-0174	TPT Aviation, Gastonia, NC.	/(N666WW/N201CC/(N98510)
N87SF	Citation	550-0096	Michel Thielen, Fresno, Ca.	N30UC/N550EW/N26632
N88	Sabre-40	282-88	FAA, Frankfurt, West Germany.	N2237C
N88AE	Gulfstream 3	398	American Express Co. Stewart International Airport, NY.	/N315GA
N88B	Learjet	24-015	Louise Timken, Canton, Oh.	
N88BF	Sabre-65	465-60	Bassett Furniture Industries, Bassett, Va.	/N2580E
N88BY	Learjet	25B-168	Dickerson Associates, W Columbia, SC.	///N88BT/N72TP
N88CH	Convair 880	58	Ligon Air, Ligonier, In.	VR-HGF/JA8022
N88CR	Diamond 1A	A089SA	Romana Citation Inc. High Point, NC.	N89SC/N100EA/N483DM
N88DD	Citation	650-0058	DD66 Corp. Elmhurst, Il.	/
N88G	Citation	S550-0017	Burlington Industries Inc. Greensboro, NC.	(N188G)/(N1259G)/N88G/N1259G (N47LP)
N88GA	Gulfstream 4	1085	Armour & Co/Greyhound Corp. Phoenix, Az.	N449GA
N88HA	Challenger 601-3A	5072	C Itoh Aviation Inc. El Segundo, Ca.	N609K/C-G...
N88HF	Citation	550-0615	Hudson Foods Inc. Rogers, Ar.	N12522
N88JF	Learjet	24A-110	Cx USA 6/89 as wfu.	N35JF/N362AA/N1969H/N388R
N88JJ	Citation	650-0169	Agri-Empire, San Jacinto, Ca.	N169CC
N88JM	JetStar-731	1/5011	Duncan Aviation Inc. Lincoln, Nb. (wfu ?).	/N159B/N10461/C-GKRS//N731A PK-PJH/9V-BEE/PK-PJS/T17845/N9282R
N88MF	Diamond 1A	A066SA	Murphy Farms Inc. Rose Hill, NC.	(N66FG)/(N185GA)/N1TX/N366DM
N88ML	Citation	550-0196	Marathon Le Tourneau Co. Longview, Tx.	N800EC/N1212H/N68DS/N6798Y
N88MM	Citation	501-0689	Richard McMahan, Carlsbad, Ca.	N689CC//N46MT
N88MR	HS 125/1A	25013	Wfu. Cx USA register 6/86.	N4646S/N7125J/N2426/N125J/G-ASSJ
N88NB	BAC 1-11/201AC	005	Cx USA 8/89 to ?	N97KR/N3756F/VR-CAQ/XB-MUO/TP-0201/XB-MUO/N734EB/G-ASJA
N88NE	Learjet	35A-227	General Service Operations Inc. Cleveland, Oh.	N25RF/N211BY
N88NJ	Learjet	25-008	New Creations Inc. Pontiac, Mi.	N645L//N1976S/N744W/VP-BDM/N744W/N648GA
N88NT	Falcon 20F	416	Northern Telecom, Nashville, Tn.	N416F/N415F/F-WLCT
N88PV	Westwind-1124	264	Phoenix Ventures Inc. Dallas, Tx.	///(N125NY)/(XA-MAR)/N351C/4X-CNJ
N88RD	Learjet	24B-196	B W Spradling Sr. Newton, Ks.	/N573LR/N573LP/N173LP/N99E/N99ES/N1125E N99SC
N88TB	Citation	501-0002	Gateway Aviation Inc. Carlsbad, Ca.	(N501WK)/N501WJ/N39301/XA-LUN/N165CB OE-FPO/N5253J
N88WG	Challenger 601-3A	5068	Kwoya (Hawaii) Inc. Honolulu, Hi.	N609CC/C-G...
N88ZL	B 707-330B	18928	Lowa Ltd. Boston, Ma.	N5381X/D-ABUF
N89	Sabre-40	282-89	FAA, Oklahoma City, Ok.	N2276C
N89AB	Gulfstream 3	349	Nike Inc. Beaverton, Or.	N89AE
N89AE	Gulfstream 3	496	National Express Co Inc. Newburgh, NY.	N21NY/N310SL/N372GA
N89AM	Westwind-Two	389	Atherton & Murphy Investment Co. Tulsa, Ok.	N812G/N100WP/N812G/N812M/N49WW 4X-CUF/(N612M)
N89BM	Citation V	560-0017	Emerald Holding Co. Pittsburgh, Pa.	(N1218P)
N89D	Citation	550-0056	Aviation Enterprises Inc. Wilmington, De.	/N444FJ/N752RT/N5342J
N89EM	Diamond 1A	A055SA	Electromatic Products Inc. Farmington Hills, Mi.	/N877T/N877S
N89FC	Falcon 50	184	Fleming Companies Inc. Oklahoma City, Ok.	N50FJ/N183FJ/F-WWHD
N89HB	HS 125/1A-522	25097	Bill Walker & Assocs Inc. St Simons Island, Ga.	//N21MF/N12KW/N125V/LN-NPE G-ATSP

Registration	Type	c/n	Owner / Operator	Previous identity
N89K	BAe 125/800A	NA0403	Crawford Fitting Co. Cleveland, Oh.	N540BA/G-5-573
N89KM	Beechjet 400	RJ-62	K Mart Corp. Troy, MI.	
N89LS	Citation	550-0623	Les Schwab Warehouse Center Inc. Prineville, Or.	(N1255L)
N89MR	Jet Commander	9	Barron Thomas Aviation Inc. Allen, Tx.	(N98KK)/N66EW/N9BY/C-FWUL/N459JD
N89SR	HS 125/731	NA778	R S Aircraft/Rifkin & Assoc. Denver, Co.	N450JD /N67EC/N2694C/C-GCEO/N733K/N555CB N75BH
N89TC	Learjet	35-026	N A Degerstrom Inc. Spokane, Wa.	/N54754/D-CBRK/D-CDHS
N89TD	Citation	S550-0076	Teledyne Industries Inc. Latrobe, Pa.	C-GQMH/N95CC
N89UH	Westwind-Two	353	U S Bancorp Leasing & Financial, Portland, Or.	/N86UR/N90CH/N379JR/4X-CTU
N89XL	Westwind-1123	171	X L Air 89 Inc/Xcel Laboratories Inc. Elmhurst, Il.	/N223PA/C-GJLL/4X-CJU
N90AE	Gulfstream 4	1068	National Express Co. NYC.	N95AE/N17585
N90AH	Learjet	35-036	AWH Corp. Winston Salem, NC.	/N76GP/N76GL/N134GL
N90AM	Sabre-75A	380-25	Electric Prunes Inc. NYC.	N50PM
N90CF	Citation	501-0184	Peter Karagines/Orange County Food Service Co. Anaheim, Ca.	N67786
N90CP	Gulfstream 2TT	224	Chesebrough Ponds Inc/Hudson Finance Inc. NYC.	N631SC/N810GA/N17584
N90EC	Sabre-60	306-73	Carrier Corp-Elliot Co. Flight Dept. Latrobe, Pa.	N601MG/N7NR
N90EW	Falcon 900	27	East West Air Inc/Aviation Methods, San Francisco, Ca.	N419FJ/F-WWFH
N90GM	Sabre-75A	380-27	Kidde Industries Inc. Shady Grove, Pa.	N6NG/N6NR/N10CN/N8NB/N8NR/N65787
N90HH	Gulfstream 2	78	O Gara Aviation Co. Las Vegas, Wa.	/C-FIOT/PH-FJP/N17585
N90HM	Westwind-1123	170	Sharp Concepts Inc. Germantown, Tn.	N150HR/N112RC/N1123W/4X-CJT
N90J	Learjet	24-060	Sunward Corp. Littleton, Co.	N899WF
N90JD	Citation	550-0315	Deere & Co. Moline, Il.	N6889Z
N90JJ	Citation	550-0571	B A Leasing Corp. San Francisco, Ca.	(N1299T)
N90KC	Westwind-Two	339	Teterboro Intercoastal Leasing, Teterboro, NJ.	N74AG/N782PC/N333CG (XC-HDA)/4X-CTG
N90LC	Gulfstream 3	360	Lockheed-California Co. Burbank, Ca.	N90LC/N341GA
N90MD	Gulfstream 2	241	McDermott Inc. New Orleans, La.	/(N801GA)/(N60TA)/N830GA
N90ME	JetStar-6	5057	cx USA 2/87 as parted out.	/N90U/N1007
N90MF	Citation V	560-0060	Mclean-Fogg/Caledonia Leasing Partnership, Mundelein, Il.	(N2689B)
N90MT	Citation	501-0116	Timothy Mellon, Amherst, NH.	/N7QJ/N7CJ/N500XX/(N26496)
N90N	Sabre-75A	380-72	Midcon Corp/Natural Gas Pipeline Co. Houston, Tx.	N380N/HZ-SOG
N90PG	Citation V	560-0002	Procter & Gamble Cellulose Co. Memphis, Tn.	N562CV/N1209T
N90SF	Gulfstream 3	366	SFP Properties Inc. Chicago, Il.	N2SP
N90TH	Falcon 900	63	Sony Corp. NYC.	N445FJ/F-WWFF
N90U	Astra-1125	030	Zurich Holding Co of America, Overland Park, Ks.	N50AJ/4X-CU.
N90UC	Challenger	1023	Union Camp Corp. Morristown, NJ.	N680M/N630M/C-GLXB
N90WA	Learjet	31-028		
N90WJ	Gulfstream 3	340	JP Aviation Inc. Charlotte, NC.	N99WJ/F-GDHK/(F-WDHK)
N90WP	HS 125/731	25032	Walter Probst, Fort Wayne, In..	N65MK/G-ATBC
N90Z	Citation	550-0336	International Paper Co. Mobile, Al.	N6830Z
N91AE	Gulfstream 4	1053	National Express Co Inc. NYC.	N26SL/N47SL
N91AP	Citation	501-0117	Euroflite Inc. Dover, De.	LV-MZG/LV-PDW/N26493
N91B	Citation	550-0194	CSX Beckett/Scott Fetzer Co. Lakewood, Oh.	N88723
N91CR	Gulfstream 3	405	Facilities Management Installation, Louisville, Ky.	/N91CH/N4ON/N40NB N348GA
N91CV	Falcon 20C	48	Allegheny & Western Energy, Charleston, WV.	N910Y/N878F/F-WMKG
N91D	Citation	650-0151	Jack Prewitt & Assocs. Bedford, Tx.	/G-MLEE/N1326G
N91FD	Astra-1125SP	045	Air Dayco Corp. Miami, Fl.	4X-C..
N91LA	Gulfstream 2B	198	Leucadia Aviation Inc. Salt Lake City, Ut.	N3652/N365G/N825GA
N91LS	Falcon 20C	107	LESEA-Lester Sumral Evangelistic Assoc. South Bend, In.	N330PC/N155NK N965BC/N988F/F-WMKJ
N91ME	Citation	S550-0132	Montgomery Elevator Co. Moline, Il.	N533CC/(N1294D)
N91TH	Falcon 900	60	Sony Aviation Leasing Corp. Teterboro, NJ.	N900FJ/N443FJ/F-WWFG
N92B	Citation Eagle	500-0212	Lease Air Inc. Youngstown, Oh.	/N223MC/N223AS/N223LB/N222LB/N1LB
N92BD	Citation	550-0588	Dillard Department Stores, Little Rock, Ar.	N255CC/N1301V
N92CC	Citation	501-0026	Skylane Farms Inc. Woodburn, Or.	N36891
N92DF	Learjet	24XR-117	Garr Aero Inc. Stillwater, Ok.	N90DH/HZ-SMB/N16MJ/F-BRAL/N288VM
N92EB	Westwind-1124	381	WWI Inc. Tulsa, Ok.	N928G/N928GV/N929GV/N501U/VH-KNJ/4X-CUW
N92GS	B 720-047B	18452	Pan Aviation Inc. Miami, Fl. (status ?).	N93146
N92LA	Gulfstream 2B	125	Leucadia Aviation Inc. Salt Lake City, Ut.	N3643/N364G/N367G/N870GA
N92ME	Citation	S550-0044	Montgomery Elevator Co. Moline, Il.	
N92NE	Learjet	35A-092	Martin Aviation Inc. Santa Ana, Ca.	//N46931/C-GPFC/N424JR/N722GL

Registration	Type	c/n	Owner / Operator	Previous identity
N92QS	Citation	S550-0092	EJA/Todd Pipe & Supply, Hawthorn, Ca.	N1275A
N92RW	Beechjet 400	RJ-4	Indiana Beechcraft Inc. Indianapolis, In. (was A1004SA).	(N401TJ)/N92RW /N504DM
N92SM	Citation	500-0124	Eight One Alpha Inc. Dallas, Tx.	N8FC//N303PC/N300HQ/N300HC/N124CC
N92WW	Westwind-Two	392	GECC, Wilton, Ct.	4X-CUA
N93BD	Citation	550-0454	Dillard Department Stores Inc. Little Rock, Ar.	N12490
N93BE	Jet Commander	27	Wfu.	N93B
N93BR	Learjet	24D-231	Jet Components Inc. Houston, Tx.	N37DH/N693LJ/I-CART/HB-VBU
N93CP	Falcon 20C	7	New England Air Transport Inc. Hamilton, NY.	N110CE/N12GH/N20GH/N777FA CF-GWI/N740L/N607S/N807F/F-WMKK/N12GH
N93CR	HS 125/700A	NA0283	BDA/U S Service Ltd. Wilmington, De.	//N220FL/(N90BN)/N90B/N125AS/G-5-20
N93DK	Citation	650-0112	Beatrice Foods/FPC Holding Inc III, Oak Brook, Il.	N60BE/N1321A
N93JM	JetStar 2	5201	DGM Group Inc. Lauderhill, Fl. (status ?).	//N711DZ/N711Z/N5527L
N93LA	Gulfstream 2	164	AIC Leasing Services Inc. Norwalk, Ct.	A6-HHZ/9K-ACX/N17582
N93QQ	Gulfstream 2	7	Gulfstream Aerospace Corp. Savannah, Ga.	/N9300/CF-HOG
N93QS	Citation	S550-0093	Cessna Aircraft Co. Wichita, Ks.	N33DS/N593CC/N1275B
N93RM	Jet Commander	74	Acutus Industries Inc. Pontiac, Mi.	N300DH/N47DM/N535D
N93RS	Falcon 20C	81	Sternair Inc. Dallas, Tx.	N747T/N661J/N661JB/N799G/N973F/F-WNGN
N93SC	Jet Commander	90	Cherry Air Inc. Dallas, Tx.	N1121E/N188WP
N94BD	BAe 125/800A	8004	Dillard Department Stores Inc. Little Rock, Ar.	(N98DD)/N94BD/N800EE G-BLGZ/G-5-15
N94DE	Citation	500-0094	Goldfeder Aircraft Inc. Wilmington, De. (UK based).	N594CC
N94MF	Citation	550-0368	Ward Equipment Co. Cockeysville, Md.	N94ME/(N12155)
N94PK	Learjet	25C-181	Super 8 Administration Inc. Aberdeen, SD.	/VH-TNN
N94WA	Jet Commander	94	EWC Electronics Inc. Oklahoma City, Ok.	N1424/N1424Z/N1424
N95AB	Learjet	24B-213	PFC FAC of New York Inc. Chicago, Il.	N103TC/N43KC/N999RA/N886WC/N986WC N555MH
N95AE	BAe 125/800A	NA0447	IDS Aircraft Services Corp. Minneapolis, Mn.	/N599BA/G-5-648
N95AP	Learjet	35A-471	Tarkenton Investments Inc. Atlanta, Ga.	///VH-BQR
N95B	Jet Commander	19	Cx USA 5/88 to Norway for instructional airframe.	
N95CC	Citation	650-0193	Cessna Aircraft Co. Wichita, Ks.	N2622Z
N95CP	Westwind-1124	201	MML Transportation Inc. Dallas, Tx.	(N85EA)/N85EQ/N58WW/N56AG/N1124N N1124Q/4X-CKY
N95DA	Learjet	24XR-267	Lowell Dunn Co. Hialeah, Fl.	HB-VCY/VR-BHC/N124GA/N78AE/N46023/HB-VCY
N95GS	JetStar-6	5014	Garabet Soghanalian, Miami Beach, Fl. (wfu ?).	//N54BW/N9MD/N158CG/N58CG
N95RC	Sabre-60	306-129	Juan Rodriguez, Akron, Oh.	/N749UP/N711ST/N2144J
N95SC	Learjet	55C-137	Sea Containers Assoc Inc. NYC. (based UK).	N39413
N95TC	Learjet	35-020	W/o 20 Dec 84.	//XA-BUK
N95TJ	Sabre-75A	380-38	Tyler Jet Aircraft Sales Inc. Tyler, Tx.	HZ-AFN/N3RN/N85031/D-CAVW/N2102J
N95WW	Westwind-Two	395	Great Planes Sales Inc. Tulsa, Ok.	/4X-CUC
N96AA	Learjet	24A-139	Ajax Aircraft Leasing Inc. Dover, De.	//N481EZ/N42AJ/N52JH/N590GA
N96AC	Learjet	35A-224	Colpay Inc. White Plains, NY.	/
N96AE	Gulfstream 4	1024	National Express Co. NYC.	N412GA/N130B
N96AL	Westwind-Two	385	Cx USA 1/90 to ?	4X-CUC
N96B	B 727-30	18365	Bank One Indianapolis NA. Indianapolis, In.	G-BMZU/HZ-TA1/N16767/D-ABIH
N96BB	JetStar-6	5049	Glenn Cunningham, East Freetown, Ma.	/N96B///N1230R/N9216R
N96CE	Falcon 50	139	United States Fidelity & Guarantee Co. Baltimore, Md.	/N128FJ/F-WZHD
N96CP	Sabre-60	306-64	Syracuse Executive Air Service, Syracuse, NY.	(N500RK)/N1024G/N370L/N21BM N8357N
N96FN	Learjet	35A-186	Flight International Inc. Newport News, Va.	N96DM/(N317JD)/N96DM/N590 N753GL
N96G	Citation	500-0200	Reading Pretzel Machinery Corp. Robesonia, Pa.	/N250AA/N200MW/N520CC
N96GS	JetStar-731	27/5068	W/o 6 Jan 90.	//N9231R
N96JJ	Citation V	560-0096		
N96LB	Falcon 900	10	Edward J DeBartolo Corp. Youngstown, Oh.	N26LB/(N910FJ)/N900FJ/N407FJ F-WWFF
N96PC	Astra-1125	004	P C Air Charter Inc. Englewood, Co.	4X-CUA
N96PM	Falcon 900	36	U S F & G Finance Co. Baltimore, Md.	N426FJ/F-WWFE
N96RE	Sabre-65	465-52	Reliance Electrical Co. Cleveland, Oh.	N500E
N96RS	Learjet	25XR-175	Sternair Inc. Dallas, Tx.	N462BA/N462B
N96RT	Falcon 20C	159	Rock Tenn Converting Co. Norcross, Ga.	/N96WC/N411CC/N5RC/N4364F/F-WMKJ
N96TD	Citation	550-0596	Teledyne Indutries Inc. Fort Wayne, In.	(N13026)
N97	B 727-30	18360	FAA, Oklahoma City, Ok.	N77/N68649/D-ABIB/N68649

Page 58

Registration	Type	c/n	Owner / Operator	Previous identity
N97D	Learjet	35A-417	Sacramento Aviation Inc. Sacramento, Ca.	///D-CONO/(N117RJ)/N117FJ/N934GL
N97DM	Learjet	24D-253	W/o 5 Mar 86.	N417JD/N97DM/(N30FL)/N711DB/N30FL/N999U/N123VW
N97FN	Learjet	25-003	Flight International Inc. Newport News, Va.	N97DM/N4PN/N11JC/N594GA
N97J	Learjet	55-039	General Telephone Co of SW, San Angelo, Tx.	/N770JM/N39418
N97MJ	Learjet	23-093	Jeti Inc. Alexandria, Va.	N101AD/N101AR/N486G/N38JD/N12TA/N416LJ/N3350 N416LJ
N97QS	Citation	S550-0097	EJA/Daily Variety Ltd. NYC. (status ?)	N1290B
N97RS	Learjet	25XR-162	Sternair Inc. Dallas, Tx.	N663JB/N661MP/N62ZS
N97S	Citation	550-0238	Patton Aviation Corp. New Castle, De.	N67999
N97SK	Citation	500-0316	McClean Aviation Inc. Fairfax, Va.	N398RP/N5316J
N97SM	Westwind-Two	307	Seattle Baseball Management Co. Indianapolis, In.	/N925Z/N825JL/(N301HC) N300HC/N1124K/YV-388CP/4X-CRA
N98BE	Citation	550-0060	Enterprise/Cincinnati Contractors Aviation, Cincinnati, Oh.	/N75KR/(N550KR) N26610
N98KT	Caravelle 6R	102	sale, 10535 Vestone Way, Los Angles, CA 90077. (status?).	N2296N/N555SL PH-TRU/N1017U
N98LB	Sabre-60	306-97	Commercial Aviation Inc. Kerrville, Tx.	N707DB/N85DB/N344K/N3WQ/I-FBCA N65785
N98MB	Citation	500-0054	Victory Inc. Traverse City, Mi.	/N54SK/N554CC
N98MD	Learjet	35A-086	Valkyrie Helicopter Corp. Bellevue, Wa.	/N26DA/N435M
N98Q	Citation	500-0040	Helicopters Inc. St Louis, Mo.	/N600WM/N2170J/OY-ARP/D-IKAN/N714US/JA8422 N540CC
N98QS	Citation	S550-0098	EJA/Enduro Plumbing Inc. Columbus, Oh.	(N1290E)
N98RS	Learjet	25XR-148	Sternair Inc. Dallas, Tx.	N336WR/N58GL
N98WW	Westwind-1124	398	Atlantic Jet Charter/Allen Gold, Dallas, Tx.	4X-CUO
N99AA	Learjet	24D-308	Texas Biz-Jet Inc. Fort Worth, Tx.	N308EJ
N99BC	Citation	500-0187	Morrison Leasing Inc. Anthony, Ks.	N345KC/N99MC/(N75KC)//N20VP//N187MW (TI-ACB)/(HB-VDR)/N187CC
N99FN	Learjet	35A-652	Flight International Inc. Jacksonville, Fl.	N6307H
N99GA	Gulfstream 3	421	Greyhound Armour & Co. Phoenix, Az.	/N318GA
N99GM	Gulfstream 4	1006	Bucephalus Enterprises Inc. Saltaire Fire Isl. NY.	
N99GS	Jet Commander	31	Stanley Shaw, Dallas, Tx.	N399D
N99HB	MS 760 Paris-2B	102	Bodmer Financing Co. Wilmington, De.	HB-VEU///N760E/PH-MSR/F-BJZQ
N99KR	HS 125/3A-R	25149	Northrop University, Inglewood, Ca.	N99GC/N99SC/N1125E/G-AVRJ
N99MC	Citation	500-0190	Morrison Leasing Inc. Anthony, Ks.	//N99BC/N190CC
N99MR	JetStar-731	7/5112	HSN Aviation Inc. Wilmington, De.	////N910G/N7957S
N99NJ	Learjet	25XR-220	National Jets Inc. Fort Lauderdale, Fl.	N220NJ/(N25WL)/(N419BL)/N220HS
N99RS	Learjet	36A-039	Tudor Corp. Wilmington, De.	N25PK/N4998Z/C-GSRN/N217CS
N99S	Sabre-65	465-64	W/o 11 Jan 83.	
N99TC	Learjet	23-098	Wfu.	N711AE/N711/N2DD/N11111/N112T
N99W	Jet Commander	46	Space Coast Jet Service Inc. Cocoa Beach, Fl.	N202ST/N200GT/N200RM/N200BP N1500C
N99WA	Falcon 10	150	Wheels Avn Inc/Wings of Africa, Botswana.	N212NC/N212N/N215FJ/F-WZGV
N99WJ	Gulfstream 4	1139	JP Aviation Inc. Charlotte, NC.	
N99WR	Citation V	560-0019	Maha Inc. Naples, Fl.	(N1219D)
N99XZ	Learjet	25C-087	Robert E Hibbert, Milwaukie, Or.	N777LF/N723LF
N100A	Gulfstream 4	1072	Exxon Corp. Dallas, Tx.	N17586
N100AC	Citation	550-0364	Kloeckner Pentaplast of America, Charlottesville, Va.	N12157
N100AR	Gulfstream 4	1100	ARCO-Atlantic Richfield Co. Burbank, Ca.	
N100BC	Westwind-1124	438	Ball Corp. Muncie, In.	N438AM/4X-CUJ
N100CE	Sabre-60	306-128	Metz Baking Co. Sioux City, Ia.	N80CR/N2143J
N100CJ	Citation	550-0167	Airway Inc. Columbus, Oh.	/N88737
N100CK	Falcon 100	222	Cheaspeake Corp. Sandston, Va.	N125FJ/F-WZGF
N100CT	Falcon 100	203	Searay Inc. Wichita, Ks.	VR-CLA/N267FJ/F-WZGJ
N100DL	Learjet	24B-201	T S P Development Corp. Chattanooga, Tn.	C-GTFA/D-CDDD/D-IDDD/N273GL N3871J
N100EA	Learjet	24-019	Extraordinary Air Jet Services Inc. Carson City, Nv.	N654DN/N889JF/HB-VAI N464LJ
N100EJ	Sabre-75A	380-1	Everest Flight Operations, Roseville, Mn.	N30GB/N87Y/N6K/N7593N
N100EP	Learjet	35A-150	W/o 11 May 87.	/
N100FG	Sabre-40A	282-99	Barry Wehmiller Group Inc. St Louis, Mo.	N400GM//N22CH/N78TC/N7594N
N100FL	Sabre-60	306-46	State of Florida, Tallahassee, Fl.	N3600X/N4764N
N100GN	Gulfstream 4	1007	Gannett Inc. Arlington, Va.	N420GA

Registration	Type	c/n	Owner / Operator	Previous identity
N100GP	Learjet	35-064	Pal Waukee Aviation Inc. Wheeling, Il.	/N291BC/N290BC
N100GX	Gulfstream 3	321	Glaxo Aviation Inc. Raleigh, NC.	N321GA/N94GC//N3ORP
N100HB	Citation	550-0058	G Heileman Brewing Co Inc. La Crosse, Wi.	N71CJ/N5348J
N100HE	HS 125/731	NA749	National City Corp. Wilmington, De.	N100HF/N583CM/N119CC/N81T/N45BH/G-AXYH
N100HG	Challenger 601	3055	Management Financial Services Inc. Duluth, Ga.	/C-G...
N100JJ	Citation	500-0192	Eagle Aviation Inc. West Columbia, SC.	//N220S/N508S/N4TK
N100K	Learjet	35A-170	Fred Shaulis, Friedens, Pa.	
N100KK	Learjet	35A-420	Kohler Co. Kohler, Wi.	N35PT/N35RT
N100KT	Challenger 601-3A	5066	TNS Mills Inc. Blacksburg, SC.	N506TN/C-G...
N100LL	Jet Commander	79	Lincoln Log Homes Inc. Kannapolis, NC.	/N454SR
N100LR	HS 125/700A	NA0320	Lars Aviation Inc. Cleveland, Oh.	/N300HB/N300LS/N500LS/N710BN/G-5-17
N100MK	Learjet	25-019	W/o 21 Oct 78.	N88FP/N88EP/N591KR
N100NR	Learjet	25D-356	Kenwood Aviation Services Inc. Dover, De.	N78DT
N100PM	Gulfstream 4	1144	Philip Morris Management Corp. Teterboro, NJ.	N415GA
N100QR	HS 125/600A	6055	Q & R Charter Inc. Palm Beach, Fl.	N777SA/N94BF/N94B/G-BDOP/G-5-19
N100RA	Learjet	24-180	Tri-City Hospital Inc. Green Castle, Mo.	///N802JA/N556RB
N100RC	Jet Commander	60	W/o 14 Nov 70.	N6545V
N100RS	Diamond 1A	A029SA	Southern Michigan News Co. Jackson, Mi.	N89TJ/N10TE/N1UT/N321DM
N100SC	Citation	550-0093	100SC Partners, Chattanooga, Tn.	N888HW/N888RF/N210MJ/N95CC/(N108CT) N2664F
N100SQ	Learjet	24-113	Brandis Aircraft, Springfield, Il. (status ?).	N204Y/(N402Y)/N438LJ
N100SR	Westwind-1124	267	Steven Rayman, Big Rock, Il.	N297A/N297W/4X-CNM
N100T	Learjet	35A-074	TCC Inc. Dallas, Tx.	/N666JR/N530J/N5000B
N100TA	Learjet	23-045	W/o 6 May 82.	N711MR/N242F
N100TM	Sabre-75A	380-60	Mike Pinson Aircraft sales, Harker Heights, TX.	//N4260K/D-CBVW/N2521E
N100TR	Jet Commander	76	Enviromental Equipment Corp. San Leandro, Ca.	N1000R/N100DG/CF-VVX/N1121C
N100UB	Falcon 10	42	UMB=University Medical Building Corp. Milwaukee, Wi.	(N9147F)/N18X/N126FJ F-WLCU
N100VQ	Learjet	24-140	American Jets International Inc. Tampa, Fl.	N100VC/N252M/N593KR/N663LJ N663L/N663LJ
N100WC	Challenger 601	3023	Frito-Lay Inc. Dallas, Tx.	/N778YY/C-G...
N100WG	Falcon 10	120	Gilliam & Co. Charleston, SC.	N369V//N359V/N20ES/N192FJ/F-WPXM
N100WM	Jet Commander	73	Surburban Air Freight Inc. Crete Municipal, Nb.	N100W/N98S/N98SA
N100WN	Learjet	25D-288	New Creations, Columbus, Oh.	(N40BC)/N100WN/N40BC/N61WT/N31WT
N100WP	Citation V	560-0073	Arawak Air Inc. Newport Beach, Ca.	
N100X	Learjet	23-035	Great Planes Sales Corp. Tulsa, Ok.	/(N10QX)/N100X
N101AD	HS 125/731	NA777	AFM Corp/Ames Department Stores Inc. Wilmington, De.	N125MD/N125FM/N228GC N571GH/N571CH/N74BH
N101AJ	Learjet	36-008	Duncan Aviation Inc. Lincoln, Ne.	(N43A)/N101AJ/(N701AR)/N101AR/N84MJ VR-BJO/VR-BJD/N20JA
N101AR	Learjet	35A-610	AMCA/Aircraft Services Corp. Dunwoody, Ga.	
N101AW	JetStar-8	5103	DEA Brokerage Inc. Livingston, NJ. .	//N176AN/N176BN/N672M/N23M
N101BU	Jet Commander	32	Baylor University/Paul Piper, Waco, Tx.	N32JC/N92BT/N92B
N101BX	Citation	550-0157	Gantt Aviation Inc. Georgetown, Tx.	/N550K/N6799T
N101CV	Citation V	560-0101		
N101DB	Learjet	23-070	Kenneth Fischer, Belleville, Il.	N111CT/N197GL/N1976L/CF-ARE
N101HB	Citation	500-0203	Richard E Weston, San Francisco, Ca.	N101HF/(N724CC)/N95DR
N101HC	Citation	501-0033	Port East Transfer Inc. Baltimore, Md.	/N517BA/(N715DG)/N300PB/(N400GB) N36908
N101HF	HS 125/700A	7013	Hardees Food System Inc. Rocky Mount, NC.	/N75ST/N219JA//G-CBBI
N101HG	Citation	500-0213	Cincinnati Contractors Aviation, Cincinnati, Oh.	N100UH/N100UF/N73WC N741JB/N355H/N62HB
N101HS	Westwind-1124	193	Beckair Co Inc/Goshen Sash & Door Co Inc. New Paris, In.	//N60AL/4X-CKQ
N101KK	Citation	550-0209	Kohler Co. Kohler, Wi.	/N121C/N67997
N101LB	Jet Commander	8	Robert Mace, Globe, NC.	/N749MC/N31CF//N157JF/N749MP
N101MU	Gulfstream 4	1107	Century Industries Inc. Honolulu, Hi.	(JA8366)/N17581
N101PK	Challenger 601-3A	5005	Kalikow Real Estate Corp. Teterboro, NJ.	N613CL/C-G...
N101PP	Learjet	23-085	W/o 4 Jun 84.	N385J/N825LJ
N101QS	Citation	S550-0101	EJA/Great Western Leasing Corp. Reno, Nv.	(N1290Y)
N101SK	Challenger 601-3A	5058	Charles E Smith Management Inc. Washington, DC.	N404SK/C-G...
N101ST	Challenger 600S	1033	EJA, Columbus, Oh.	N101SK/N600YY/VR-CKK/N2642F/C-GLXW
N101SV	Westwind-1124	246	Super Valu Stores Inc. Minneapolis, Mn.	4X-CMR

Page 60

Registration	Type	c/n	Owner / Operator	Previous identity
N101TF	Falcon 10	144	National Textile Corp/NTC Aviation Inc. Wilmington, De.	(N79FJ)/N1TC N208FJ/F-WZGP
N101VS	Learjet	24B-218	Advanced Technology Center, Buffalo, NY.	N682LJ
N101ZE	Falcon 20DC	108	Zephyr Express, Burbank, Ca. N26VG/(N147FE)/N4FE/N5CA/D-CBAT/F-WNGO	
N102AD	Citation	500-0280	Turbine Air Mgmt/Ames Department Stores Inc. Rocky Hill, Ct.//N100HP/N280CC (N5280J)	
N102BW	Westwind-1123	165	TCB Air Inc. Detroit, Mi.	C-GWSH/4X-CJO/N1123R
N102C	Learjet	24E-343	Kempthorne Inc. Canton, Oh.	///N102B
N102CJ	Jet Commander	78	Lynwell Corp. Miami, Fl.	/N866DH/N1121E
N102HF	Citation	500-0275	Original Honey Baked Ham Co. Atlanta, Ga.	/N352WG/N352WC/(N38MM)/N40MM N600SR/(N275CC)
N102MU	Gulfstream 4	1145		
N102ST	Learjet	55-069	Westinghouse Communities Inc. Coral Springs, Fl.	/N551UT
N102VS	Learjet	25B-180	Arvin Calspan Corp. Buffalo, NY. N266BS/VH-LJB/N95BS/C-FEWB/N95BS/VH-BLJ	
N102ZE	Falcon 20C	126	Zephyr Express, Burbank, Ca.	/N10VG/N1047T/PH-BAG/HB-VBL/F-WMKH
N103AD	Diamond-Two	A1002SA	Joseph Spruit, Grand Rapids, Mi.	
N103BW	Jet Commander	82	First American Bank Ltd. Valdosta, Ga.	C-GPDH/N4NK/N82JC/N9932/N927S
N103C	Learjet	55-087	Adolph Coors Co. Golden, Co.	N8564Z
N103CF	Learjet	35A-318	Eagle Jet Inc. Allegheny County Airport, Pa.	/N444WB
N103CL	Learjet	35A-273	Adolph Coors Co. Vero Beach, Ca.	N103C/N35FH
N103F	HFB 320	1023	Cyngo International Corp. St Petersburg, Fl.	N320AF/N1320U/D-CARI
N103GC	Gulfstream 3	455	Ansett Industries Leasing Inc. Sun Valley, Id.	/N1SF/N335GA
N103JW	Learjet	24E-341	MW Media Inc/53rd Street Advertising, Hillsboro, Or.	/N3PW//N22NM/N22BM
N103M	Citation	551-0038	A T Massey Coal Co Inc. Richmond, Va.	N550DA/D-IBPF/N6801Z
N103MM	Falcon 10	106	McKenzie Methane Corp. Houston, Tx. N913VS/N902PC/N730PV/N1OFJ/N1JN/N181FJ F-WPUX/(N918PC)	
N103PJ	Falcon 10	148	Hydro Mill Co. Chatsworth, Ca.	N213FJ/F-WZGT
N103QS	Citation	S550-0103	EJA/Maxinkuchee Air Service Inc. Columbus, Oh.	N12900
N103RB	Learjet	24-106	R B Aviation Co. Tulsa, Ok.	/N7ORL/N100GP/N969J/N888NS
N104AR	Gulfstream 3	461	AMCA/Tower Resources Inc. Louisville, Ky.	/N323GA
N104CF	Citation	501-0149	CIT Leasing Corp. NYC.	(N1772E)
N104CJ	Jet Commander	33	Rameshar Verma, Bhopal (MP), India.	//N151CR/N1180Z
N104MC	Learjet	24D-323	Smith Management Corp. Salt Lake City, Ut.	/N744JC/N61AW
N104RS	Westwind-1124	273	Owners Jet Services Ltd. Las Vegas, Nv.	(N566PG)/N104RS/4X-CNS
N105BG	Citation	S550-0105	Barnes Group Inc. Bristol, Ct.	(N12907)
N105CF	Citation	501-0153	Eagle Aviation Inc. W Columbia, SC.	/(N1930E)
N105CV	Citation V	560-0105		
N105DM	Sabre-60	306-27	Intergalaxia Inc. McAllen, Tx.	N888WL/N11AL/I-SNAD/N978R/N4737N
N105EJ	Falcon 50	31	Eli Jacobs/Orioles Aviation Inc. Baltimore, Md	N145WF/N145W//N211CN/I-KIDO (N54FJ)/F-WZHC
N105GA	Learjet	24A-116	Joseph Gibson 111 Aviation, Frederick, Md.	N51B/N40BP/N400EP/N8FM/N77GH N52EN/N461F
N105HS	Diamond 1A	A082SA	Price Aviation Corp. La Jolla, Ca.	N382DM
N105Y	Gulfstream 2	56	Oxy Petroleum Inc. Bakersfield, Ca.	N20XY/N10XY
N106BC	Westwind-1124	220	Brock Candy Co. Chattanooga, Tn.	N9134Q/C-GHBQ/N1124G/4X-CLR
N106CC	Citation	650-0106	GFN Aviation Services Inc. NYC.	/(N106CC/(N1320K)
N106MC	Learjet	24D-277	Smith Management Corp. Salt Lake City, Ut.	/(N181RW)/(N163ME)/N181CA N131CA
N106QS	Citation	S550-0106	EJA/Great Western Leasing Corp. Reno, Nv.	(N12909)
N106SP	Citation	550-0346	Stan Partee, Big Springs, Tx.	N550CF/
N106VC	Beechjet 400	RJ-7	Calesco/Crawford & Co. Atlanta, Ga.(was A1007SA Diamond 2).	N207BA/N507DM
N106WV	Citation	501-0089	Anthony Aiello, Wayne, Il.	N471H/(N3175M)
N106XX	Learjet	35A-183	IAL Leasing Inc. Hialeah, Fl.	/N72JM/N720M/N3802G
N107A	Gulfstream 4	1070	ARAMCO Associated Co. Houston, Tx.	N407GA
N107BJ	Beechjet 400A	RK-23		
N107CJ	Sabre-40	282-12	JBQ Aviation Corp. Miami, Fl.	N368DA//N888PM/N905M/N6366C
N107GL	Learjet	24D-324	D&S Partnership, Salt Lake City, Ut.	
N107GM	JetStar 2	5206	General Mills Inc. Minneapolis, Mn.	N5532L
N107MS	Learjet	25D-362	Country Wire Corp.	N717CW/N52CT/N25GL
N107RC	Citation	S550-0150	American Yard Products Inc. Augusta, Ga.	N150CJ/(N1297B)
N107SB	Citation	551-0191	Interedec, Richmond Hill, Ga. (was 550-0148).	(N771R)/N550CP/N222AG
N107WV	Citation	550-0428	Willamette Valley Co. Eugene, Or.	N7864J/N7004/N1218P
N108BG	Falcon 20F	403	Brenlin Group/Flyco Inc. N Canton, Oh.	/N15AT/N189F/F-WJMK

Registration	Type	c/n	Owner / Operator	Previous identity
N108DB	Citation	550-0070	Adams Group Inc. Woodland, Ca.	//N564CC/N2072A
N108GA	Learjet	25-011	Joseph Gibson 111, Gaithersburg, Md.	/C-GHMH/N167LJ/N49BA
N108KC	Falcon 10	8	Keller Companies Inc. Manchester, NH.	N88ME/N21EK/N21ET/N21ES/N104FJ F-WJMN
N108MC	Citation	500-0322	Mitchell Co/Gulf Coast Building & Supply, Mobile, Al.	N1AP/N5322J
N108MR	Falcon 10	74	M Rankin/Dresser Inds. Dallas, Tx.	N518S/N34TH/N30TH/N156FJ/F-WJMJ
N108PA	Learjet	25B-195	Duncan Aviation, Lincoln, Nb. (wfu ?).	OB-M-1004
N108QS	Citation	S550-0108	EJA, Columbus, Oh.	(N1291K)
N109AL	Citation	500-0037	Pro Driving AB. Goteborg.	////N537CC
N109DC	Citation	501-0195	Consolidated Delta Corp. NYC.	N7111H/N161CB/N67814
N109G	HS 125/700A	NA0322	Chevron Corp. San Francisco, Ca.	/G-5-20
N109HT	B 727-21	18998	HT109 Inc/Jason Cotton, Boston, Ma.	N300DK/N727S/(N1CL)/N1CC/N320AS/N320PA
N109JC	Citation	550-0099	Stroud Aviation Inc. Stroud, Ok.	N2664L
N109JM	HS 125/700A	NA0272	John H McConnell, Worthington, Oh.	/N89PP/G-5-17
N109JR	Learjet	35A-101	Ruan Cab Co. Des Moines, Ia.	N40149
N109MC	Learjet	35-054	Smith's Management Corp. Salt Lake City, Ut.	/N54PR/N53650/VR-BFX
N109NC	Falcon 200	489	CSX Beckett/Nalco Chemical Co. Oak Brook, Il.	N203FJ/F-WPUX
N109RK	Falcon 20C	66	Corporate Wings/Illuminati Equipment Corp. Cleveland, Oh.	N581SS//N401AB N891F/F-WNGL
N109TH	BAC 1-11/401AK	067	American Continental Corp. Phoenix, Az.	N102ME/N909CH/HZ-GRP/N5027
N110AB	Citation	500-0262	Florida Custom Coach, Madison, NC.	N110AF/N111MU/N44JF/N5262J
N110AF	Westwind-Two	436	American Fidelity Corp. Oklahoma City, Ok.	N436WW/N50XX/N436WW/4X-CUE
N110AN	JetStar 2	5227	J B & A Aviation Inc. Houston, Tx.	/N30Y/N23SB/N211PA/N4033M
N110BR	Gulfstream 3	301	Banner Aircraft Resales Inc. Cleveland, Oh.	(N100P)/N21NY/N100P
N110DD	JetStar-731	58/5092	Daniel Industries Inc. Houston, Tx.	N110AN/(N901H)/N372H/N9248R
N110EE	Gulfstream 3	322	Time Inc/AREPO Corp. Westchester County Airport, NY.	N110LE/N130A
N110FS	Sabre-40	282-58	Executive Aircraft Consulting Inc. Newton, Ks.	//N1101G/N7508V
N110HA	Learjet	25B-110	Imaging Services Inc. Oklahoma City, Ok.	N75CA/N63ET/N50GL
N110M	Challenger 600S	1052	Olan Mills Inc. Chattanooga, Tn.	N3330L/N3330M/C-GLXS
N110MT	Gulfstream 3	444	MTI Aviation/Morton Thiokol Inc. Wheeling, Il.	/N328GA
N110PA	Learjet	36A-040	Palumbo Aircraft Sales Inc. Uniontown, Oh.	N902WJ/HB-VFV
N110ST	Jet Commander-A	129	Stewart Title Co. Houston, Tx.	N525AW/N5032E
N110TM	Citation	650-0141	Toyota Motor Sales USA Inc. Torrance, Ca.	N1325E
N110TP	Citation	501-0155	Towner Petroleum/Gawain Assoc. W. Hartford, Ct.	/(N108CT)/N110TV/N2617B
N111AC	BAC 1-11/412EB	111	Worldwide Church of God, Pasadena, Ca.	N71MA/HZ-JAM/N90AM/N767RV/N221CN AN-BBI
N111AD	Learjet	25B-201	Arapahoe Development Inc. Englewood, Co.	N777SA/N227RW
N111AL	Sabre-80A	380-21	AGL=Aviation Group Inc. Pontiac, Mi.	N577SW/N25AT/N22NT/N75A/N711A/N65773
N111BA	Beechjet 400	RJ-11	Willamette Industries, Portland, Or. (was A1011SA).	//N114DM
N111BP	Falcon 20C	111	Iowa Beef Processors Inc. Sergeant Bluff, Ia.	N111AM/N111AC/N990F/F-WMKI
N111DC	HFB 320	1030	Donohue & Associates Inc. San Jose, Ca.	(N247GW)/D-CATE
N111G	Challenger 601	3032	GTE Service Corp. Beverly, Ma.	N7011H/(N601KR)/HZ-AKI/N779YY/C-GLXM
N111GL	Learjet	35A-084	Kay Mary Ash, Dallas, Tx.	/
N111HN	Westwind-1124	421	The Marotta Fund, Wilmington, De.	//4X-CUJ
N111JD	Learjet	23-006	U S Marshalls Service, St Louis, Mo.	N23CH/N578LJ/N505PF
N111JL	Gulfstream 4	1111	James P Lennane, Naples, Fl.	N416GA
N111KK	Learjet	35A-425	Kohler Co. Kohler, Wi.	
N111LP	BAC 1-11/401AK	068	Louisiana Pacific Corp. Hillsboro, Or.	N18HD/N18HH/N200CC/N5028/N3E/N5028
N111M	Falcon 20C	10	cx USA 8/87. (wfu ?).	N810F/F-WMKK
N111ME	Citation	500-0146	Evans Meat Co of Texas, San Angelo, Tx.	/N194AT
N111NF	Westwind-1123	168	Martinaire/Bruce Martin, Dallas, Tx.	N66SM/N973EJ/4X-CJR
N111QS	Citation	S550-0111	EJA/Todd Pipe & Supply Co. Hawthorne, Ca.	(N1291Y)
N111RB	Citation	501-0185	Nexus Holding Co. Wilmington, De.	N72787//N653DR/N2614K
N111RF	Learjet	35A-217	R C Fisher, West Palm Beach, Fl.	
N111SF	Learjet	35A-608	Michigan Sugar Co. Saginaw, Mi.	N8567Z
N111TD	Jet Commander	11	Parts & Turbines Inc. St Simons Isle, Ga.	N1172L/N1172Z
N111TT	Learjet	31-015	Tradewind Aircraft Corp. Sapello, NM.	
N111US	Learjet	35A-306	First USA Management Inc. Dallas, Tx.	/N77LN/N601MC/N66LM/N926GL
N111VP	Citation V	560-0044	Nightjar 550 Inc. Wilmington, De.	N2665S
N111VV	Learjet	31-023	Inductotherm Industries Inc. Rancocas, NJ.	
N111VW	Citation	650-0194	Volkswagen of America Inc. Troy, Mi.	N26228
N111VX	Sabre-75A	380-69	Fugate Enterprises, Wichita, Ks.	//(N111VS)/N111VW/N2542E
N111WW	Falcon 10	165	Quien Sabe Ranches/R H Fulton, Lubbock Airport, Tx.	N229FJ/F-WZGR

Registration	Type	c/n	Owner / Operator	Previous identity
N111Y	Sabre-80A	380-17	Ingram Industries Inc. Nashville, Tn.	N15RF/N70TF/5N-AMM/N339K/N65768
N111YL	Jet Commander	42	Wfu.	N111Y/N6361C/N3DL/N599KC/N6511V
N111ZN	HS 125/700A	7076	Zenith Insurance Co. Woodland Hills, Ca.	/XA-LML/G-5-571/G-BMWW/G-5-524 MAAW-J1/7Q-YJI/G-5-17
N112CF	Sabre-65	465-16	Intermet Corp. Atlanta, Ga.	/N65SR/N700QG/N7000G/N31BC
N112CP	Citation	500-0183	Command Air Inc. Wilmington, De..	/N1880S//(N721CC)//N1VC/(VH-FRM)
N112CT	Learjet	25B-090	Certain-teed Products Corp. Valley Forge, Pa.	N265GL
N112DJ	Learjet	24-112	American Aircraft Sales International Inc. Sarasota, Fl.	//////N10CP N2200T/CF-ECB/N447LJ
N112K	BAe 125/800A	8042	Wells Fargo Co/Kaiserair Inc. Oakland, Ca.	N20S/N820AA/G-5-11
N112M	HS 125/731	NA736	FFL Partners, Claremont, Ca.	N30PP/N30PR/G-AXOD
N112MC	JetStar 2	5231	Smith Food & Drug Centers Inc. Salt Lake City, Ut.	N988MW//N196KC/N4043M
N112ML	Sabre-40A	282-136	Patrick Industries/Marvin Lung Inc. Elkhart, In.	/N211SF/N44PH
N112QS	Citation	S550-0112	EJA/K K Associates, Columbus, Oh.	(N12910)
N112WC	Citation	501-0092	Worsley Leasing Inc. Wilmington, NC.	///(HB-VGD)/N3197M
N113	B 727-30	18935	U .S. Marshall's Office, Oklahoma City, Ok.	N18G/VR-CBA/N833N/N90557 D-ABIT
N113EV	Gulfstream 2	135	Air Transport Inc. NYC.	N83M
N113KH	JetStar-8	5152	Al Fasco Inc. Goddard, Ks.	N500JD/N5516L
N113LB	Learjet	35A-457	Superior Industries International Inc. Van Nuys, Ca.	N874JD/N974JD/N900P
N113SH	Citation	500-0285	Canary Aircraft Sales Inc. Ft Smith, Ar.	//N86SS//N2U/(N285CC)/N5285J
N113T	Sabre-60	306-113	United Technologies Cortran Inc. Mattydale, NY.	N2626M/N712MR/N2108J
N114EL	Citation	550-0292	AFM Corp. Westfield, Ma.	N6887X
N114GB	Learjet	23-022	Skywatchers Assoc Inc. Las Vegas, Nv.	/N456SC/N88TC/N103TC/N400CS/N428EJ
N114HH	Jet Commander	106	Textile Chemical & Rubber Co. Dixville Notch, NH.	/N88AD///N40AB/N3711H N4690E
N114M	BAC 1-11/422EQ	119	W A Moncrief Jnr/Montex Drilling, Fort Worth, Tx.	N18814/PP-SRT
N114WL	Westwind-Two	338	Panda Leasing Co. Medina, Wa.	/N850WW/N350PM/N338W/4X-CTF
N115BP	Westwind-Two	417	Blandin Paper Co. Grand Rapids, Mn.	N700WE/(N417GW)/N417EL/4X-CUE
N115CR	Sabre-60	306-43	Capital Resource Corp. Skaneateles, NY.	/N1OUM/N60AH/N6NE/N6NP/N6NR/N5420 N4757N
N115DX	JetStar-8	5111	Starflite Jets Inc. Passaic, NJ.	N115MR/N11SX/N5111H/N7956S
N116DA	Learjet	55-116	T A C Holdings Inc. Bryan, Tx.	N85GL
N116EL	Learjet	35A-173	Duncan Aviation Inc. Lincoln, Ne.	(N83DM)/N116EL/N100GU/(HZ-NCI)/N750GL HZ-MIB/N750GL
N116K	Citation	550-0149	Kaiserair Inc. Oakland, Ca.	
N116KX	Jet Commander	87	Mock Electronics Inc. Decatur, Al.	N430DC/N430PC/N400PC/N920GP/N920G
N116MA	Learjet	36A-029	Mantab Aircraft Sales Inc. Hollywood, Fl.	N16MA/HB-VFD/(N79JS)
N117DF	B 737-39A	23800	Duke Farms Inc. Hillsborough, NJ.	VR-CCD
N117EL	Learjet	35A-486	Chrysler/CIT Leasing Corp. Park Ridge, Il.	//N821PC
N117EM	HS 125/600A	6046	Intermedics Inc. Angleton, Tx.	N402HR/(N401HR)/N91HR/N43BH
N117FJ	Gulfstream 2	229	PAB Aviation/First Jersey Securities Inc. NYC.	//N702H/N821GA
N117GM	Jet Commander	118	TTM Inc. Oklahoma City, Ok.	N312S/N438/(N712GM)
N117GS	Citation	550-0626	Gold Strike Aviation Inc. Boulder City, Nv.	(N1256G)
N117JJ	Gulfstream 2	163	Gavilan Corp. Miami, Fl. 'El Condor'	N117JA/N117JJ/PJ-ABA/(YV-60CP)/N17581
N117JW	Westwind-Two	352	James D Wolfensohn Inc. Wilmington, De.	N15BN/4X-CTT
N117K	Learjet	24D-272	Koch Industries Inc. Wichita, Ks.	N51GL
N117RB	Learjet	35A-154	Ramsbar Inc. Houston, Tx.	/N650NL
N117WC	Learjet	55-030	Western Conference of Teamsters, Hillsboro, Or.	N959WC/N986WC
N118AF	Westwind-1123	177	Seawinds Leasing Corp. Singer Island, FL.	(N114ED)//N118AF/N777CJ/N11WC N1123U/4X-CKA
N118B	JetStar 2	5211	Four Star International Inc. Las Vegas, Nv.	N821MD//N56PR/(N500YY)/N500T N5537L
N118CD	Citation	650-0118	Cessna Aircraft Co. Wichita, Ks.	/N6000J/(N13210)
N118DA	Learjet	35A-081	New Creations Inc. Pontiac, Mi.	N3523F/JY-AFF/N3523F
N118GA	Diamond 1	A018SA	Southern Bag Corp Ltd. Yazoo City, Ms.	N138DM/C-GRDS/N900LH
N118MA	Learjet	35A-144	Enterprise Aviation Inc. Houston, Tx.	/OY-CCT/(N84DJ)/N35KC/N705US/D-CCAP N39398
N118R	Gulfstream 4	1066	R J Reynolds Tobacco Co. Winston Salem, NC.	/N443GA
N119AC	Jet Commander	119	Lion Enterprises Inc. Wilmington, De.	C-FFBC
N119BA	Learjet	23-084	PLG II Inc. Salt Lkae City, Ut.	N101JR/N788DR
N119CP	Learjet	35A-366	Florence Wings Inc. Houston, Tx.	(N94AA)/N49AT//N411LC
N119GA	BAC 1-11/401AK	072	SS Aviation Inc. Portland, Or.	N310EL/N5030

Registration	Type	c/n	Owner / Operator	Previous identity
N119MA	Learjet	24B-200	McMoy & Assocs Inc. Dallas, Tx.	N246CM/N721JA/(N24NP)/N721J
N119MH	Diamond 1A	A057SA	Export Packaging Co Inc. Moline, Il.	N342DM
N119RC	Gulfstream 4	1077	Jack Prewitt & Assocs Inc. Bedford, Tx.	N119RC/N119R/N445GA
N120AF	Falcon 20DC	16	Ameriflight Inc. Burbank, Ca.	N122CA/N10FE/N354H/N807F/F-WNGL
N120AR	JetStar-8	5089	Monair Inc. El Paso, Tx.	/(N85DL)//N120AR/N324K/N9245R
N120BJ	Astra-1125	026	Inland Container Corp. Indianapolis, In.	4X-CU.
N120CG	Falcon 20F	384	Inland Container Corp. Indianapolis, In.	N384JK/OO-PSD/F-WRQU
N120HC	Citation	550-0577	Inland Container Corp. Indianapolis, In.	N100CX/N557CC/(N1300J)
N120JC	Sabre-60	306-42	Southwestern Jet Charter Inc. St. Louis, Mo.	N6OEL/N58CG/N8OL/N915R/N4755N
N120MB	Learjet	35A-307	Milton Bradley Co. East Longmeadow, RI.	(N119HB)/N120MB
N120MH	HS 125/700A	NA0319	Hanna Mining Co. Cleveland, Oh.	(N168H)/N710BP/G-5-15
N120S	Westwind-1124	226	Jet East Inc. Dallas, Tx.	N124MB/(N10BY)/N100BC/N300LS/N500LS/4X-CLX
N120TA	BAC 1-11/520FN	236	TigerAir Inc. Los Angeles, Ca. (status ?).	PP-SDS/G-16-15
N120YB	HS 125/700A	NA0282	Bemis Co Inc. Minneapolis, Mn.	/N1982G/N125AP/G-5-19
N121AG	Citation	650-0121	Cablevision Industries Corp. Liberty, NY.	N1322D/D-CATP/(1322D)
N121AJ	Jet Commander	57	American Jet Industries Inc. Burbank, Ca. (wfu ?).	N770WL/N6544V
N121AT	Citation	650-0158	Alltel Corp. Little Rock, Ar.	N658CJ/N1327B
N121C	Citation	550-0354	Digital Equipment Corp. Galway, Ireland.	/N121CG
N121CG	Citation	S550-0123	Columbia Gas Systems, Columbus, Oh.	N1293A
N121CP	Citation	550-0311	Cousins Properties Inc. Marietta, Ga.	N44TC/N43TE/N43TC/N6889L
N121DF	Challenger 600S	1071	Cintas Corp. Cincinnati, Oh.	N588UC/N523B/N607CL/C-GLXQ
N121EL	Learjet	25-010	New Creations Inc. Columbus, Oh.	(N82UH)/N102PS/N671WM/N846HC/N846GA
N121FJ	Falcon 100	192	w/o 15 Oct 87.	N100FJ/N258FJ/F-WZGX
N121FM	Jet Commander-B	150	Contest America Publishers Inc. Kansas City, Mo.	N173MC/N1884Z/4X-CPN N9050N
N121GW	Falcon 20C	4	W/o 18 May 78.	N116JD/N801F/F-WMKF
N121HM	Jet Commander	18	Wfu 17 Dec 78. Located at Copenhagen.	
N121JJ	Gulfstream 2	27	Liamaj Aviation Inc/Joseph D Jamail, Houston, Tx.	//N1807Z
N121JM	Gulfstream 3	332	RIM Air, San Francisco, Ca.	N65BE/N300BE/N77TG/N310GA
N121PG	Jet Commander	45	West Wind Leasing, N Canton, Oh.	N340ER/N340DR/N920R
N122AP	Citation Eagle	500-0122	Sunland Aviation Corp. Colton, Ca.	N122LM/C-FENJ/N122CC
N122CG	Citation	S550-0125	Columbia Gas Systems, Columbus, Oh.	N1293G
N122DU	Gulfstream 2	6	Jet Services Corp. Houston, Tx.	/N122DJ/N430R/N834GA
N122G	Citation	550-0110	Sheller-Globe Corp. Fort Wayne, In.	N222SG/(N2665Y)
N122MM	Citation	550-0129	Heilig Meyers Furniture Co. Richmond, Va.	N129TC/N537M/N2632Y
N122SP	Citation	551-0393	Sklar & Phillips Oil Co. Shreveport, La.	(N18CC)/N1214H
N122ST	Jet Commander-B	122	Alpha Alpha Inc. Milwaukie, Or.	///N122HL/N666BP/N122JC/N801NM/N4940E
N122WC	Learjet	25B-122	U S Bancorp Leasing & Financial, Portland, Or.	N122BS/N332LS/N23TA
N122WF	Challenger 601-3A	5021	Farley Inc. Chicago, Il.	N64F/C-GLYC
N123AC	HS 125/3A	25122	OK Aviation Inc. Monterey, Ca.	N255CB/N555CB/N12225/G-AVAF
N123CB	Learjet	24D-232	W/o 17 Apr 71.	
N123CC	Gulfstream 2	69	Circus Circus Enterprises Inc. Las Vegas, Nv.	N21066/VH-HKR/N45YP/N45Y N45JM/N33CR/N25JM/N69NG
N123CG	Learjet	25D-270	Charles C Gay, Hobe Sound, Fl.	N842GL
N123CV	Westwind-1123	178	Management Associates Inc. Oklahoma City, Ok.	N999U/N1123Z/4X-CKB
N123DG	Learjet	24F-342	Glynn Air/Dorothy Adams, Bartlesville, Ok.	N824GA/YV-178CP/N40144
N123DR	Westwind-1123	158	Europe Holdings Ltd.	N1123G/4X-CJH
N123EB	Citation	501-0020	Anderson Chemical Co. Newark, De.	N32JJ/N36873
N123FG	Sabre-60	306-90	Elmwood Land Co. Stockton, Ca.	N148JP/N13SL/N181AR/N65772
N123FH	Citation	550-0468	GTE South Inc.Durham, NC.	D-CBEL/N468CJ/(N1251P)
N123H	BAC 1-11/414EG	163	Hilton Hotels/BAC 1-11 Corp. Las Vegas, Nv.	D-AILY
N123LC	Learjet	55-027	Summit Jet Corp. Valhalla, NY.	N3796X/OE-GKN/N3796X
N123RE	Learjet	24-154	W/o 17 Oct 78.	N11AK/N7HA/N424RD/N12315/N123VW
N123RE	Falcon 20C	150	Retlaw Jet Charter, N Hollywood, Ca.	N679RE/N777XX/N8227V/(N95591)/HB-VBO F-WMKH
N123SE	Westwind-1123	182	Fenaire Corp. Toledo, Oh.	/N10122/N78BL/N18BL/N13KH/N700EC/N200HR/N1123Q 4X-CKF
N123SF	Citation	501-0201	Savannah Foods & Industries Inc. Savannah, Ga.	N130JS/N801L/N6783U
N124AR	HS 125/700A	NA0254	ARCO, Dallas, Tx.	N125TR/N125AM/(G-BHKF)/G-5-13
N124BM	HS 125/731	25101	Alesco Inc. Arlington, Tx.	/N142B/G-ATXE
N124DC	Sabre-60	306-95	Drummond Company Inc. Birmingham, Al.	N999DC/N65783
N124EZ	Learjet	24E-347	Edward Zimmer Jr/Berkeley Controls Inc. Irvine, Ca.	N724GL
N124FM	Westwind-1124	194	Aero Air Inc/Fred Meyer Inc. Portland, Or.	N343AP/N222SR/4X-CKR

Registration	Type	c/n	Owner / Operator	Previous identity
N124HL	Westwind-1124	325	H & L Air Co. New Orleans, La.	N504U/VH-WWY/4X-CRS
N124LS	Westwind-1124	354	Lincoln Service Corp. Owensboro, Ky.	N506U/N512CC/N443A/4X-CTV
N124MA	Learjet	25B-118	B & C Aviation Co Inc. Nashville, Tn.	/(N800JA)//N118SE//N601J/(D-CITO) OO-LFZ
N124PA	Westwind-1124	418	Aircraft Holdings Inc. Chattanooga, Tn.	PT-LIP/4X-CUB
N124PJ	Learjet	24-166	Air Ambulance Inc. Hayward, Ca.	/N500SB/N993KL
N124VF	Westwind-1124	174	Jack B Kelley Enterprises, Amarillo, Tx.	//N112MR/N1123X/4X-CJX
N124VS	Jet Commander	64	Glasair Inc. Tucson, Az.	/N124JB/N500GJ/N6512V
N124WK	Westwind-1124	291	Bargene Transportation Co. Tampa, Fl.	4X-CQK
N124WW	Westwind-1124	203	J Russell Flowers Inc. Greenville, Ms.	N1124G/4X-CLA
N125AC	Westwind-1124	205	Town & Country Air Inc. Miami, Fl.	/N124NY/N967A/N96BA/4X-CLC
N125AD	HS 125/1A-522	25046	Western Flight Inc. Brooklyn, Oh.	N812TT/N666AE/N125P/N4886/N48UC/G-ATGS
N125AL	HS 125/1A-522	25033	Medical Transport Inc. Salt Lake City, Ut.	//N125LC///N63BL/(N32HE) (N700AB)/(N111AX)/N111AD/N111AG/N1125G/N125G/G-ATBD
N125AR	HS 125/700A	NA0284	ARCO, Anchorage, Ak.	N826K/N326K/N125AE/G-5-11
N125AS	BAe 125/800B	8167	Aarton Senna/Cavalier Air Corp. Wilmington, De.	G-5-662
N125AW	HS 125/1A	25057	Wfu. Broken up for spares and cx USA register 4/86.	N188K/G-ATIL
N125BA	BAe 125/800A	NA0448	British Aerospace Inc. Washington, DC.	N610BA/G-5-660
N125BP	Sabre-65	465-25	Robert Pond, Eden Prairie, Mn.	N25MF/N9000F
N125BW	HS 125/700A	NA0242	Bill Walker & Associates Inc. McKinnon Airport, Ga.	/C-GPCC/N60HJ/N700UR G-5-14
N125CA	Falcon 20DC	208	W/o 29 Jun 89.	//N300JJ/VH-BRR/HB-VCA/F-WPXD
N125CG	Citation	S550-0116	Columbia Gas Systems, Columbus, Oh.	N1292K
N125CM	HS 125/400A	NA767	Latour Air Inc. New Baltimore, Mi.	N28GE/N28GP/N92BH/N64BH
N125CS	HS 125/700A	NA0212	Citizens Southern Georgia Corp. Dekalb Peachtree Airport, Ga	N662JB/N733H G-BFGU
N125DB	Learjet	25G-371	Sprite Flite Jets/RR Dawson Bridge Co. Lexington, Ky.	N72603
N125DH	HS 125/731	NA739	Outboard Marine Corp. Milwaukee, Wi.	G-AXTR
N125E	HS 125/1A-522	25110	W/o 29 Jun 83.	N3125B/G-ATZE/G-5-11
N125EA	Citation	501-0125	Eastern Alloys Inc. Maybrook, NY.	/N69EP//N96TC//N45MC/(N501DP)/N2651Y
N125EC	HS 125/731	NA754	BWG PLC/Ambrion Aviation-UK.	N125VC/N62TF/C-GVQR/C-FTEC
N125F	HS 125/3A-RA	25151	Quorum Sales Inc. Denver, Co.	G-AVTY
N125GB	Astra-1125	023	Kangra Group Ltd.	4X-CUG
N125HG	HS 125/731	25250	Glimcher Co. Columbus, Oh.	N125G/N300QC/N300CC/N24S/N20S/G-AYOK/TR-LQU G-AYOK
N125HS	HS 125/3A-RA	NA701	Mico Inc. N Mankato, Mn.	N700RG/N700RD/N700RG/N605W/N505W/N506N/N501N G-AVHB
N125JA	HS 125/600A	6021	Keystone Automotive, Exeter, Pa.	(N128JJ)/N125JJ/N125HS/G-5-11/HB-VDL C-GSTT
N125JB	BAe 125/800A	8089	Berry Investments Inc. Dayton, Oh..	N530BA/G-5-555
N125JJ	Gulfstream 2	15	Jack Kent Cooke Inc. Middleburg, Va.	//N416SH/N77SW/N375PK
N125JW	BAe 125/800B	8058	DPF Airlease Inc III, Woodcliff Lake, NJ.	//VH-NMR/ZK-EUI/G-5-510
N125LM	HS 125/731	25018	Orion Aircraft Sales Inc. Van Nuys, Ca.	C-FDOM
N125MD	HS 125/731	NA730	Mike Donahoe Aviation Co. Phoenix, Az.	N56BL//N220T/G-AXJF
N125N	Challenger 601	3044	Natural Gas/Midcon Corp. Chicago, Il.	N921K/C-GLXD
N125NE	Learjet	25D-271	W/o 21 May 80.	N183AP
N125NX	Sabre-75	370-3	Select Leasing Inc. Brookfield, Wi.	N125N/N70NR/N7586N
N125PS	Challenger 601	3058	Omni Restaurant Consulting Co. Newport Beach, Ca.	/C-G...
N125Q	Citation	650-0128	Milliken & Co. Spartanburg, SC.	N628CC/(N1323K)
N125RR	Citation	550-0125	Eagle Aviation Inc. W Columbia, SC.	N320S/N5500F/N2746Z
N125SB	BAe 125/800A	8046	McClatchy Newspapers Inc. Sacramento, Ca.	N800BA/N823AA/G-5-20
N125TB	HS 125/1A	25039	Air Georgian US Corp. Grand Rapids, Mi.	C-FSIM
N125TJ	Learjet	25D-294	Tyler Jet Aircraft Sales Inc. Tyler, Tx.	/N419GL/N27K
N126AR	HS 125/700A	NA0291	ARCO, Dallas, Tx.	N125BC/G-5-19
N126QS	Citation	S550-0126	EJA/PIR Transportation Inc. Columbus, Oh.	N1293K
N126R	Citation	500-0232	sale, 1126 Fort Worth Club Tower, TX 76102.	N500PB/N5232J
N127CF	Citation	S550-0127	Cessna Aircraft Co. Wichita, Ks.	N14UM/N1293N
N127CM	HS 125/400A	NA759	Hawkeye Aviation Inc. Highland Park, Mi.	/N810CR/N702MA/N702M/N6702/N54BH G-5-20
N127EL	Learjet	55-035	Aircraft Services Corp/AIRCOA, Denver, Co.	/N1968A/(N100GU)/N115EL
N127GT	Learjet	55-067	127 GT Corp. Dover, De.	/N120EL
N127K	Learjet	35A-447	Industrial Investment Corp. Providence, RI.	
N127MS	Sabre-75A	380-18	U S Marshalls Service, Oklahoma City, Ok.	N55

Page 65

Registration	Type	c/n	Owner / Operator	Previous identity
N127MW	HFB 320	1027	W/o 5 Oct 84.	N905MW/D-CITO/I-TALC/D-CASO
N127V	Gulfstream 2	130	El Paso Natural Gas Co. El Paso, Tx.	//N872GA
N128BJ	Learjet	24-128	Business Jet Inc. Smyrna, Tn.	N802W/(D-CJAD)/N37594/HB-VBK/N4CR/N383X N333X/N914BA/HB-VBK/N655LJ
N128CA	Learjet	35A-248	Ameriflight Inc. Burbank, Ca.	/C-GBFA/N3811G
N128CS	HS 125/700A	NA0259	Citizens & Southern Georgia Corp. Chamblee, Ga.	//N100Y/N125AH/G-5-12
N128GA	BAC 1-11/401AK	058	TABAC Inc. Washington, DC. (status?).	N128TA/N711ST/N5018
N128JS	Learjet	25-017	Air Stewart Inc. Sarasota, Fl.	/N128DM/N55WJ/N666WL/N16JP/N101WR/N720AS
N128SD	HFB 320	1035	sale, 7424 E 30th St. Tulsa, OK 74115.	PH-HFC/D-CERU
N129DM	Learjet	24B-187	B B Barr Enterprises, Dallas, Tx.	N5WJ/F-GAJD/ZS-SGH
N129K	Jet Commander	70	CCC Corp. Pearland, Tx.	N1194Z
N129KH	Sabre-60	306-44	Corporate Aviation International Inc. Pittsburgh, Pa.	(N83RH)/N60RS/N86Y N45RS/N111VW/D-CEVW/N4760N
N129ME	Learjet	24F-357	Petrolift Aviation Services Inc. Charlotte, NC.	/N288J
N130A	Falcon 50	54	Verochris Corp/Primerica, White Plains, NY.	N392U/N202DD/N204DD/(N50EF) N450X/N71FJ/F-WZHT
N130B	Gulfstream 4	1013	Thomas W May Sr. Fairmont, WV.	//N446GA
N130K	Falcon 50	70	PSI Funding Inc. NYC.	N651SB)/N130K/N230S/N81FJ/F-WZHL
N130MH	HS 125/700A	NA0238	M A Hanna Co. Cleveland, Oh.	/N33CP/N700AR/G-5-20
N130MW	HFB 320	1033	Air National Aircraft Sales, Carmel, Ca. (wfu ?).	N132MW/PH-HFB/D-CERI
N130TA	Learjet	35A-174	Templehof Airways USA Inc. Miami, Fl.	//(F-GGRG)/D-CAVI/N65DH/TR-LYC
N130YB	HS 125/700A	NA0285	Curwood Inc. Appleton, Wi.	(N14WJ)/N40CN/N125AT/G-5-13
N131BH	Sabre-40	282-18	FM Air Inc. Houston, Tx.	N15TS/N113SC/N1072/N107G/N6372C
N131EL	Citation	551-0463	GECC/Jackson Wolff, Sandusky, Oh.	N121JW/N1251B
N131MA	Learjet	24D-289	Norman Hibbard, Oakland, Ca.	/F-BRGF/(HB-VDO)
N131MS	Sabre-75A	380-22	U.S. Marshalls Service, Oklahoma City, Ok.	N132MS/N57
N131SY	Citation	501-0044	Simmonds S Corp. Mercer Island, Wa.	/(N122LG)/N944JD/N5TC/N98675
N132DB	Sabre-75A	380-48	HHM Group/Thermadyne Industries Inc. St Louis, Mo.	N27TS/N6PG/N805RG/N8NG N8NR/N2127J
N132EL	Learjet	55-061	GECC, Wilton, Ct.	N222MC/N117EL
N132MA	Learjet	24D-306	McMoy & Associates Inc. Dallas, Tx.	N98AA/N55CD/N306EJ
N132MA	Learjet	25-052	McMoy & Assocs Inc. Dallas, Tx.	/N250CC/N828QA/N8280/N232MD
N132MW	HFB 320	1032	Airborne Express Inc. Wilmington, De. (wfu ?).	N130MW/PH-HFA/D-CERE
N133LE	Citation	650-0133	Industrial Equity/Brierly Investments Ltd. Sydney.	/N633CC/N1323X
N133ME	Jet Commander	50	G W Taylor, Halfway, Mo. (wfu ?).	N612JC
N133W	Learjet	23-021	National Jets Inc. Tulsa, Ok. (status ?).	N427NJ/N427EJ
N134GB	Citation	S550-0089	Cx USA 10/90 to ?	/N12745
N134JA	Falcon 20F	463	Prince Corp/Wingspan Leasing Inc. Holland, Mi.	N471F/F-WJMJ
N134M	Citation	650-0109	Motorola Inc. Schaumburg, Il.	N20AT/N650AT/(N1320V)
N134QS	Citation	S550-0134	Nestle Enterprises Inc. Solon, Oh.	N1294M
N134RG	Diamond 1A	A037SA	Diamond 1A Inc. Hudson, NY.	N109TW/LN-SJA/OY-CCB/N327DM
N135AC	Learjet	35A-188	Aqua Air Aviation Corp/Aviation Consultants, Aspen, Co.	N343MG/N3MJ (N38FN)/N20RT/N39293/VH-AJS
N135GA	Diamond 1A	A035SA	Bullfrog of Ohio County Inc. Hartford, Ky.	HB-VHX/N300HH
N135J	Learjet	35A-097	Dana Corp. Toledo, Oh.	
N135ST	Learjet	35A-169	Southeast Toyota Distributors, Pompano Beach, Ca.	
N136JP	Learjet	35A-359	James Petropoulos/Dape Corp. Columbus, Oh.	/HB-VHB/(N127RM)
N136ST	Learjet	36A-049	Express One International Inc. Dallas, Tx.	///N661AA
N137BC	Learjet	25-024	JODA Partnership, Highland Park, Il.	N125ST/N425RD
N137GL	Learjet	25D-237	W/o 19 Jan 79.	(N28BP)
N137M	Citation	650-0163	Motorola Inc. Schaumburg, Il.	N1312T
N138F	Falcon 20F	382	First International Aviation, Miami, Fl.	HP-1A/N138F/F-WMKG
N138JB	Learjet	25B-075	Mirage Enterprises Inc. Los Angeles, Ca.	N417PJ/N241AQ/N241AG
N138M	Citation	650-0164	Motorola Inc. Schaumburg, Il.	N1312V
N138SA	Citation	500-0138	Silky Air Inc. Gainesville, Fl.	/N3056R
N138SR	B 707-138B	17697	Comtran Inc. San Antonio, Tx.	N790FA/TC-JBN/N790SA/D-ADAP/N790SA/VH-EBB
N139M	Citation	650-0149	Brunswick Bowling & Billiards, Muskegon, Mi.	/N649CC/N1326B
N140AK	HS 125/1A-522	25104	Ray L Richter, Portland, Or.	N257H/G-ATUW
N140CH	Challenger 601-3A	5047	Wayfarer Ketch, White Plains, NY.	C-G...
N140DR	Astra-1125SP	046	Donrey Inc. Las Vegas, Nv.	4X-C...
N140JS	HS 125/3A-RA	NA703	Owners Jet Services Ltd. Las Vegas, Nv.	N22GE/N2G/N612G/G-AVOJ/G-5-11
N140MM	Sabre-40	282-8	Sabre Associates Inc. Jacksonville, Fl.	/N369N/N366N/N520S/N6362C
N140RC	Learjet	23-048	Smithair Inc. Jonesboro, Ga.	N48MW/N1GW/N805LJ

Registration	Type	c/n	Owner / Operator	Previous identity
N140RF	Sabre-40A	282-67	C L Frates & Co. Oklahoma City, Ok.	N711T/N2234B
N141AB	Citation	550-0483	Allied-Signal Inc. Morris Township, NJ.	/N1253K
N141H	Sabre-40	282-60	Commercial Aviation Enterprises Inc. Boca Raton, Fl.	//N555AB/N555AE N256EA/N256EN/N256MA/N22TP/N66TP/N903G/N7510V
N141JL	HS 125/731	NA718	Jiffe Lube Intl/Kenair Inc. Dover, De.	N50SL/N16WG/(N7WG)/N900DS/N600JA N600LP/N600L/G-AWXC
N141PB	Sabre-65	465-4	Puritan Bennett Corp. Overlands Park, Ks.	N14M/N1058X
N141SM	Learjet	55-019	Kad Air Corp. Wilmington, De.	YV-41CP
N142B	Citation			
N142B	Citation	650-0190	Blount Inc. Montgomery, Al.	
N142DA	Citation	501-0004	Amerijet Leasing Inc. Portland, Or.	N86JJ/N88JJ/N5356J
N143AB	Citation	650-0120	Cathay Holdings Inc. Wilmington, De.	(N818TP)//N143AB/N13218
N143CK	Learjet	25B-143	Pacific Flights Inc. Medford, Or. (status ?).	N113RF/N111RF/(N33VF)/N96VF
N143RW	Citation	550-0316	R R Investors, Wilmington, De.	/N828B/N5428G
N144AD	Falcon 50	112	Archer Daniels Midland Co. Wilmington, De.	N107FJ/F-WZHA
N144DJ	HS 125/700A	7067	Dow Jones & Co. New York.	N360N/(N115RS)/N9113J/HZ-DA1
N144JP	Citation	500-0281	Jerry's Enterprises Inc. Minneapolis, Mn.	/N72WC//N49R/N5281J
N144LT	Learjet	55C-144	Airsupport Services Corp. Miami, Fl.	
N144SX	Challenger 601	3066	Federal Aviation/Syntex Communications Inc. Palo Alto, Ca.	N609CL/C-GLXQ
N144WB	Learjet	35A-444	Wright Bros/Standard Register Co. Vandalia, Oh.	/N444MJ/N44695/D-CARH N3818G
N144WC	Learjet	23-020	Bard Air Corp. Detroit, Mi.	/N310KR/N210GP/N2GP/N338KK/N388R
N145AJ	Jet Commander-B	145	Amerex Inc. Laredo, Tx.	/N145BW/N349DA/F-BTDA/(N17DW)/HB-VCC/N9045N
N145G	Sabre-40	282-65	Barattini Inc. Little Rock, Ar.	N2232B
N145SH	Learjet	25B-145	Valdosta Mall Inc. Duluth, Ga.	N2127E/C-GRDR/N131GL
N145ST	Gulfstream 4	1067	Southeast Toyota Distributors, Fort Lauderdale, Fl.	N446GA
N145TA	Citation	500-0145	Aviation Services Inc. Brainard, Ct.	//N145FC/N145CC
N145W	Falcon 900	40	Wetterau/Bi-GO Markets Inc. Keene, NH.	/N904M/N429FJ/F-WWFH
N146JB	Beechjet 400	RJ-46	Hangar One Inc. Atlanta, Ga.	/N1546T
N146MJ	Learjet	36A-046	Air Jet Inc. Tulsa, Ok.	N4448Y/F-BKFB
N147DA	Diamond 1	A038SA	Wolf Camera Inc. Atlanta, Ga.	N338DM
N147G	Falcon 100	214	W W Grainger Inc. West Bend, Wi.	N275FJ/F-W...
N147RP	Citation	550-0429	REP Investments Inc/Western Commander Inc. Van Nuys, Ca.	//(N7OHS)/N1218S
N147WS	Citation	500-0009	Metropolitan Air Inc. Baltimore, Md.	(N147DA)/N147DB/N147DA/N700JD/N500JD (N317AB)/N509CC
N147X	Falcon 20D	185	Morian Aviation Inc. Houston, Tx.	N3WN/I-IRIF/F-WMKF
N148DR	Citation	550-0231	Donrey Inc. Fort Smith, Ar.	N140DR/N88TB/N671B/(N221BW)/N28RF/N6860A
N148E	Jet Commander	22	W/o 41 Sep 68.	
N148JS	Citation	501-0130	Owners Jet Services Ltd. Las Vegas, Nv.	(N726BB)/N148JS/N148JB/(N2650V)
N148N	Citation	650-0147	Motorola Inc. Schaumberg, Il.	/OE-GNK/N13259
N148PE	JetStar-6	5002	Wfu.	/N81JJ/N69TP/N106GM/EP-VRP/N9202R
N149J	Learjet	25B-149	EPPS Air Service Inc. Atlanta, Ga.	EC-CIM/HB-VDI
N149PJ	Citation	500-0149	Skip Bush, Strang, Ok.	(N100FF)//N100RG/(N43TC)/N4TE/N4TL
N150AG	Learjet	23-074	Aerosmith Leasing Inc. Ypsilanti, Mi.	/N68MW/N23AN/N74MW/N23TC/D-IATD 5A-DAC
N150BG	Falcon 50	13	National Medical Enterprises Inc. Los Angeles, Ca.	/N5OFK/F-WZHF
N150F	Citation	650-0150	Dana Corp. Toledo, Oh.	(N1326D)
N150GX	Gulfstream 3	318	Gulfstream Aerospace Corp. Savannah, Ga.	/N70050/(XA-...)/(N300LF)/N300L N308GA
N150K	Falcon 50	108	Koch Industries Inc. Wichita, Ks.	N350X/N101FJ/F-WZHU
N150MS	Learjet	55-049	Martin Sprocket & Gear Inc. Arlington, Tx.	/D-CCHS/N3796C
N150TJ	Citation	501-0051	Capital Buyers Inc. W Conway, Ar.	//N422CC/N98601
N150WW	Learjet	25B-147	S S S Leasing Co. Houston, Tx.	N25KC/N55KC
N151A	Gulfstream 4	1026	International Telephone & Telegraph Co. Allentown, Pa.	
N151AE	HS 125/700A	NA0263	Aetna Life & Casualty Co. Hartford, Ct.	/N130BL/G-5-18
N151AG	Learjet	24D-298	Aero Smith Leasing Inc. Ypsilanti, Mi.	/N98AC/XA-ADD/N298EJ
N151JC	Citation	550-0477	Johnson Controls Inc. Milwaukee, Wi.	N1515P/N1252J
N151MZ	Gulfstream 3	426	R H Macy & Co/Macflight, White Plains, NY. 'The Rachel Anne'	N321GA
N151QS	Citation	S550-0151	EJA/Cimmaron Crane Co. Columbus, Oh.	(N2634E)
N151SR	Challenger	1034	Norfolk Southern Corp. Norfolk, Va.	N153SR/N2634Y/C-GLXY
N151TB	Sabre-80A	380-11	Baldwin Aircraft Corp. Raleigh, NC.	N265SR/N5109T/N5109
N151WW	Learjet	24-170	Cherry Air inc. Dallas, Tx.	N200DH
N152A	Gulfstream 4	1036	ITT Corp. Wilmington, De.	

Registration	Type	c/n	Owner / Operator	Previous identity
N152AE	HS 125/700A	NA0314	Aetna Life & Casualty Co. Hartford, Ct.	/G-5-11
N152AG	Learjet	23-068	Aero Smith Leasing Inc. Henderson, Nv.	N400PG/N9RA/N575HW/N902AB/N902AR N460F
N152JQ	Citation	550-0434	Johnston Controls Inc. Milwaukee, Wi.	N152JC/(N1515M)/N1178/N1109/(N1219G)
N153AG	Learjet	23-058	Aero Flight Service Inc. Ypsilanti, Mi.	/N7FJ/N66MP/N363EJ
N153NS	Challenger 601-3A	5056	Norfolk Southern/NW Equipment Corp. Norfolk, Va.	/N614CC/C-G...
N153RA	Gulfstream 4	1050	ITT Corp. Wilmington, De.	
N154AG	Learjet	23-034	Aero Flight Service Inc. Ypsilanti, Mi.	/N24FF/N241BN/N242WT
N154C	Gulfstream 2	253	CONOCO Inc. Allegheny County Airport, Pa.	N15TG
N154JS	HS 125/700A	NA0223	J R Simplot Co. Boise, Id.	/N853WC/N353WC/N700BA/G-BFUE/G-5-14
N155AG	Learjet	25-037	Aero Flight Service Inc. Ypsilanti, Mi.	/N28AA/N18JF/N737EF
N155AV	JetStar-731	6/5104	American Bank & Trust Co. Tulsa, Ok.	//N902KB/N902K
N155BT	Learjet	24-168	Barron Thomas Aviation Inc. Dallas, Tx.	//C-GBWB/N51CH/N109JB/N109JR
N155CA	Citation	500-0191	Express Oil & Gas of Nevada, Las Vegas, Nv.	N23WK///N448EC/N5600M
N155CS	Learjet	55-033	Central States Joint Board, Chicago, Il.	N414RF/N917S/N960E/N96CE
N155DB	Learjet	55C-141	Dal Briar, Dallas, Tx.	
N155GB	Citation	S550-0155	Comcar Services Inc. Auburndale, Fl.	N155QS/(N2638A)
N155J	Learjet	24B-182	D&H Flying Service Inc. Kenosha, Wi.	N500ZH/N500ZA/N171L/N945GA
N155JC	Learjet	55-071	Cole National Corp. Cleveland, Oh.	/(N155UT)
N155PJ	Learjet	55-041	High Flight Inc. Waco, Tx.	/N401JE
N155PL	Learjet	55B-133	Electronic Engineering Co. Miami, Fl.	
N155PT	Citation	551-0049	P J Taggares Co. Othello, Wa.	N170CC/(N88848)
N156AG	Learjet	23-065A	Aero Flight Service Inc. Henderson, Nv.	/N122M/N1GZ/(N28BR)/(N28BP)/N388Q
N156CW	Westwind-1124	204	Jayhawk Advertising Inc. Carollton, Tx.	N221MJ/4X-CLB
N157AG	Learjet	24D-252	Aero Flight Service Inc. Ypsilanti, Mi.	//N972/N711LD/N711L
N157CA	Learjet	25B-157	Connie Kalitta Services Inc. Lakeview, Or.	N2427F
N158DP	JetStar-8	5013	First City Bank, Oklahoma City, Ok. (status ?).	(N5AX)//N158DP/N8AD/N11JC HZ-MAC/N11JC/N523AC/N322K/N9284R
N158QS	Citation	S550-0158	EJA/Free Enterprises Inc. Wilmington, De.	N301QS/N158QS/(N2639Y)
N159B	Gulfstream 3	380	Carter Hawley Hale Stores, Los Angeles, Ca.	/N345GA
N159DP	Jet Commander	52	sale, 11300 Sorrento Valley Road, San Diego, CA 92121.	N159MP/N159YC N696GW/N1121G/N701AP
N159LC	Citation	501-0094	Life Care Centers of America, Cleveland, Tn.	N59CC/N103PC/N488CC/(N2646Z)
N159M	Citation	650-0130	Motorola Inc. Schaumburg, Il.	N543SC/N227BA/N227LA/(N1323Q)
N160JS	Citation	500-0250	Flightwatch Inc. N Hollywood, Ca.	C-GRJQ//N444RP/XA-JEL/N25CK/N25PA/N250C N5250J
N160S	Diamond 1A	A084SA	Shanair Inc. Visalia, Ca.	N840TJ/(N84DT)/(N484VS)/N484DM
N160VE	Citation	550-0303	Valero Management Co. San Antonio, Tx.	(N281AM)/N6851D
N160W	Sabre-40A	282-101	Westinghouse Electric Co. Baltimore, Md.	N101RR/N111XB/N1BX/N7596N
N160WC	Gulfstream 2	12	Dixie Aire/Washington Corp. Missoula, Mt.	/N121EA/N115MR/N154X/N11UM/N500R
N161CC	Citation	500-0161	Gateway Aviation Inc. Carlsbad, Ca.	C-GHEC/(C-GTEL)
N161EU	Falcon 20F-5	485	IBM Euroflight, Paris-Le Bourget.	F-WLCT
N161MM	BAe 125/800A	8061	Aircraft Associates/Goodman Realty Corp. Teterboro, NJ.	/N365BA/G-5-515
N161WC	Citation	500-0117	Washington Construction Inc. Missoula, Mt.	/N90BA/N617CC
N161WT	Falcon 20F-5	478	IBM World Trade Asia Corp. Paris-Le Bourget.	F-WJMN
N161X	Westwind-1124	234	H O Penn Machinery Co Inc. Armonk, NY.	N1124Z/HC-BGL/(N1124Z)/4X-CMF
N162DW	Citation	551-0162	Cessna Finance Corp. Wichita, Ks.	/N999BL//N131ET/LV-PHH/N2745X
N163A	Learjet	35A-073	Flight International Inc. Jacksonville, Fl.	(N64FN)//N163A/N108GL
N163DC	Jet Commander	89	Aquatic Innovations Inc. Danville, Ca.	N10BK/N1195N/N6B
N163WC	Jet Commander-B	141	Washington Construction Co. Missoula, Mt.	N177HB/N177PC/N160WC/N100CJ 4X-CPH/N9041N
N164DN	Sabre-40A	282-112	Santa Barbara Aviation Inc. Goleta, Ca.	N164DA/N74MB/N164DA/N55MT/N306PC N301PC/N6789D/N6789/N7667N
N164DW	Citation V	560-0018	Daw Forest Products, Lake Oswego, Or.	N1218Y
N164W	BAC 1-11/401AK	090	Westinghouse Defence & Electronics Center, Baltimore, Md.	G-AXCK/N5044
N165G	Gulfstream 3	414	Himont Strategic Services Inc. Wilmington, De.	/N165ST/N358GA
N165WC	Falcon 20C	140	Volpar Aircraft Corp. Van Nuys, Ca.	N314AE/N160WC/N3350M/N4350M/N4354F F-WNGN
N166CF	Citation	550-0166	Cessna Aircraft Co. Wichita, Ks.	PH-MBX/N88731
N167A	Gulfstream 2	53	Tinicum Aviation Inc. New York, NY.	/N107A
N168DB	Westwind-1124	202	Humboldt Aviation Inc. Wilmington, De.	N141LB/(N37WC)/N202DD//(N254MC) N54MC/N49968/D-CBAY/4X-CKZ
N168HC	Citation	S550-0081	HCA-Hospital Corp of America Properties, Nashville, Tn.	(N1274B)

Registration	Type	c/n	Owner / Operator	Previous identity
N168W	Sabre-40	282-33	Westinghouse Electric Corp. BWI Airport, Md.	N903KB/N903K/N737R
N169AC	Sabre-60	306-98	Truman Arnold Companies, Texarkana, Ar.	N6MK/N65786
N169B	HS 125/F600A	6061	Aircraft Trading Center Inc. Jupiter, Fl.	/N189B/N169B/N707WB/N8253A N5253A/N125HS/G-BDOB/G-5-14
N169RF	Sabre-60	306-45	Air Sabre Corp. Los Angeles, Ca.	N742K/N742R/N4763N
N170JS	Citation	501-0164	Owners Jet Services Ltd. Las Vegas, Nv.	N50DS/N750LA//N223GC/N570CC (N6778L)
N170TC	Citation	550-0619	Oshkosh Trucking Co. Oshkosh, Wi.	(N1254D)
N170VE	Learjet	55-089	Valero Energy Corp. San Antonio, Tx.	N8564X
N171CC	JetStar-8	5127	American Aviation Industries, Van Nuys, Ca. (status ?).	//N636/(N636MC) N636C/N3GR/N42GB/N42G/N7972S
N171LE	Citation	550-0324	Holiday Jet/Lee Enright, San Francisco, Ca.	/N5873C
N172AC	Jet Commander	1	Wfu.	N112AC/N610JC
N173A	Sabre-65	465-20	BOC Groupe Inc. Murray Hill, NJ.	N2544E
N173SK	Citation	501-0041	Electra Financial Corp. Van Nuys, Ca.	N50MC/N36880
N174A	BAe 125/800A	NA0445	Bank of America NT&SA. San Francisco, Ca.	N597BA/G-5-649
N174B	Falcon 10	142	Kroger Co. Cincinnati, Oh.	N5LP/N11DH/N1OHK/N207FJ/F-WZGN
N174CF	Citation	501-0174	Joseph Isabel, Amsterdam, NY.	/N702NY/N702NC/N721US/N20GT/N6779Y
N175BL	Falcon 10	168	Jet Avn of America/Liberty Mutual Insurance Co. Boston, Ma.	N234FJ/F-WZGU
N175FJ	Falcon 10	97	Marmac Corp. Parkersburg, WV.	F-WPXF
N175FS	Learjet	24A-031	Furmanski Imaging Inc. S Las Vegas, Nv.	N202BA/N777TE/N777TF/N477BL/N175FS
N175J	Citation	650-0168	Dana Commercial Credit Corp. Maumee, Oh.	/N1314H
N175ST	Challenger	1084	Southeast Toyota Distributors, Deerfield Beach, Fl.	/(N1OMZ)/N730TL/C-GLXH
N176DC	Sabre-75A	380-54	Aviation Group Inc. Pontiac, Mi.	N999M/N81GD/N350MT/N1OCN/N62NR/N6NR N2138J
N176G	Learjet	25B-088	Jaicor America Inc. West Palm Beach, Fl.	N123SF/N88GQ/N88GC
N176RS	HS 125/700A	NA0312	Carling Switch/Valley Intl Properties Inc. Wolfboro, NH.	N1896F/N1896T N700NN/G-5-18
N177CJ	Citation	550-0131	Max Pasley Inc. Sioux Falls, SD.	
N177GP	HS 125/3A	25111	PRA Development & Management, Philadelphia, Pa.	N31AS/C-GKRL/N125GC/N1041B G-ATYH
N177JC	Jet Commander	77	Harrison Haynes, Gainesville, Ga.	N121JC/N21JW/N11BK/N442WT/N523AC/N1121X
N178CP	Learjet	35-005	Epps Air Service Inc. Atlanta, Ga.	/N175J/EC-CLS/TR-LXP/EC-CLS
N178HH	Citation	550-0163	Humphrey Williams & Associates Inc. Atlanta, Ga.	N163DA/N107T/N8881N
N179T	Gulfstream 2B	86	Texas Eastern Transmission Corp. Houston, Tx.	/N880GA
N180KT	Challenger 601-3A	5004	Canadair Challenger Inc. Windsor, Ct.	/N100KT/C-GDKO
N180MC	Learjet	35A-212	International Jet Inc. Minneapolis, Mn.	/N3803G
N180PF	Citation	500-0047	Jet Lease Inc. Raleigh, NC.	N547CC
N181MA	Diamond 2	A001SA	Beech Aircraft Corp. Wichita, Ks.	JQ8001
N182K	Learjet	35A-293	Koch Industries Inc. Wichita, Ks.	
N183AJ	Citation	550-0628	Glatfelter Insurance Group, York, Pa.	(N1256P)
N183JC	Learjet	35A-363	Johnson Controls Inc. Milwaukee, Wi.	/N52MJ
N183RD	HS 125/600A	6009	Refined Metals Corp.	(N183RM)/N183RD/(N210ST)/N219ST/N3PW/N22BH
N184GP	JetStar-731	51/5064	Georgia Pacific Corp. Portland, Or.	/
N185BA	Learjet	35-025	James Markel & Assocs Inc. San Rafael, Ca.	/N510LJ/N135TX/N40TF/9K-ACT
N185MB	Westwind-Two	365	Carol Leasing/Meyer Blinder, Pompano Beach, Fl.	N793JR/4X-CUS
N185SF	Citation	S550-0029	Sovran Bank, Norfolk, Va.	
N186DS	Gulfstream 3	447	DSC Comms/Randolph Wright Trustee, Troy, Mi.	/
N186HG	Falcon 50	167	New Henley Holdings Inc. Hampton, NH.	/N166FJ/F-WZHG
N186MT	Citation	S550-0072	Maytag Co. Newton, Ia.	N1273A/(N572CC)
N186SC	Citation	500-0186	BDB Investments, Clarkdale, Ar.	/N186MW/N186CC
N187CM	Citation	650-0187	Cessna Aircraft Co. Wichita, Ks.	N2617K
N187PH	Gulfstream 2	218	Travel 17325 Inc. Wilmington, De.	N218GA/TU-VAC
N188SF	Citation	550-0159	Schwab Aviation, Hayward, Ca.	/(N45ZP/(N88721)
N188ST	Diamond 1	A040SA	Gantt Aviation Inc. Georgetown, Tx.	/N82CS
N188TC	Learjet	25D-276	Ackerley Comms/T C Aviation Inc. Portland, Or.	
N189H	Citation V	560-0004	Honeywell Inc. Phoenix, Az.	
N189K	Challenger 601-3A	5083	Crawford Fitting Co. Solon, Oh.	C-G...
N190BD	Falcon 20C	8	W E Walker Inc. Jackson, Ms.	N1500/N150CG/N1500/N806F/F-WMKJ
N190DB	Learjet	24B-190	Sylvan Kapner, Santa Ynez, Ca.	/N190SC/F-GBLA/HZ-GP4/N50TC/N9HM/N4291G
N190EB	Learjet	35A-156	Corporate Wings/Davisair Inc. Pittsburgh, Pa.	/N170L
N190K	Citation	501-0192	Robert Klabzuba, Fort Worth, Tx.	(N6781G)
N190MC	Falcon 50	26	MASCO Corp. Taylor, Mi.	N52FJ/F-WZHA

Registration	Type	c/n	Owner / Operator	Previous identity
N190MD	Sabre-60	306-142	Macklanburg Duncan Co. Oklahoma City, Ok.	N742RC/N742R/N80CR/N60RS
N190VE	Learjet	35A-301	Valero Management Co. San Antonio, Tx.	/N102BT/N102ST/N999RB/N301TP
N191CM	Citation	650-0191	Cessna Aircraft Co. Wichita, Ks.	
N191MC	Falcon 10	30	MASCO Corp. Romulus, Mi.	N3WZ/N156X/N30FJ/N294W/N121FJ/F-WLCT
N192G	Citation	500-0163	Air Austin Jet Service Inc. Tarpley, Tx.	
N192MC	Falcon 10	84	Masco Corp. Taylor, Mi.	N6PA/N526D/N8447A/JA8447/N8447A/N164FJ/F-WPXH
N192MH	Learjet	25D-239	Westheimer Aviation Inc. Houston, Tx.	
N192R	Falcon 20D	192	Reliant Airlines Inc. Ypsilanti, Mi.	N910W/N57JF/N920L/N4382F/F-WPUY
N193SS	Citation	550-0572	Spags Supply Inc. Shrewsbury, Ma.	(N12992)
N194MC	Falcon 20-5	135	MASCO Corp. Romulus, Mi.	N9999E/N40XY/N6820J/N4351F/F-WMKI
N195KC	Beechjet 400	RJ-53	Kansas City Life Insurance Co. Kansas City, Mo.	
N195MP	Falcon 20D	195	Mosinee Paper Corp. Mosinee, Wi.	/N43JK/N500GM/N191C/N186S/N200SR/N4385F F-WPXD
N196CM	Citation	650-0196		(N2624L)
N196HA	Citation	551-0050	Richard Henson, Naples, Fl. (was 550-0385).	/N1823B/N98403
N196KC	Jet Commander	68	W/o 1 Jul 68.	
N196KC	Beechjet 400	RJ-52	Kansas City Life Insurance Co. Kansas City, Mo.	
N198GH	Westwind-Two	364	Geo A Hormel & Co. Austin, Mn.	N199GH/N60DG/4X-CUR
N199AM	B 727-21	19262	First City Texas Houston NA. Houston, Tx.	(N199FS)/N727WE/N360PJ
N199BT	Learjet	25D-311	Citizens Fidelity Bank, Louisville, Ky.	N39391
N199GH	Astra-1125	027	George A Hormel & Co. Austin, Mn.	4X-C..
N199LA	JetStar-731	28/5098	Los Angeles Kings/Bruce McNall Avn. Los Angeles, CA	N417PJ/(N98MD)/ N5098G/N1967G/N9254R
N199SG	HS 125/600A	6038	Gershow Industries Inc. Dover, De.	SE-DKF/N77CU/N77C/N40BH
N199SP	Citation	500-0199	Sverdrup Corp. St. Louis, Mo.	
N200A	Gulfstream 4	1138	Exxon Corp. Dallas, Tx.	
N200BP	Gulfstream 2	115	Robert J Pond/Planes of Fame, Plymouth, Mn.	/N47JK/N457SW/N677S/N819GA
N200CC	Gulfstream 2	31	National Aircraft Sales Inc. Eagle, Co.	/N789FF/N685TA/N1621
N200CK	JetStar-6	5039	Cx USA 9/90 to ?	///N86HM/N81MR/N60QJ/N600J
N200DE	Gulfstream 3	358	Dunavant Enterprises Inc. Memphis, Tn.	N9711N/HZ-DA1/N1761B
N200G	Learjet	25-048	Green Construction Co. Oaktown, In.	N965GA
N200GF	Citation	551-0556	Golden Flake Snack Foods Inc. Birmingham, Al.	(N12979)
N200GM	Citation	500-0142	KIng Leasing Corp. Carson City, Nv.	/N650TF/VH-UCC/N142CC
N200GN	Gulfstream 3	312	Gannett Inc. Arlington, Va.	N100GN/N304GA
N200GP	Citation	550-0019	SFA of New Mexico Inc. Santa Fe, NM.	N1851D/HI-534CA/HI-534CT/HI-534 N1851D/N1851T/N3232M
N200GT	Falcon 20C	137	Allied Signal Inc. Phoenix, Az.	N777PV/N8999A/N4352F/F-BLLK/F-WLLK
N200GX	HS 125/700A	NA0224	Glaxo Inc. Raleigh, NC.	//N50TN/N50JM
N200J	Falcon 20F-5	410	Anheuser Busch Companies Inc. St Louis, Mo.	/N200CP/F-WRQT
N200KC	HS 125/731	25249	K-C Aviation Inc. Dallas, Tx.	N125KC/N107AW/N72HA/N72HT/N51993/G-AZAF G-5-16
N200KF	BAe 125/800A	8039	Kentucky Fried Chicken/KFC Natl Managemant Co. Louisville.	N400TB/N818AA G-5-19
N200LF	Jet Commander	47	cx USA 8/87 as wfu.	N222HM/N222GL/N33GL/HB-VBX/N6513V
N200LH	Citation	650-0100	De Luxe Check Printers Inc. St. Paul, Mn.	(N1319D)
N200LS	Gulfstream 2	227	Limited Stores/Northern Holding Corp. Columbus, Oh.	N18XX/N1BX/N1841L N1841D/N818GA
N200NR	Learjet	25D-328	Rail Air Leasing Inc. Cudahy, Wi.	N58DJ/OB-1313/OB-M-1313/(N12FS)/N7LC
N200PB	JetStar-731	43/5161	Bicoastal Corp. Tampa, Fl.	N1329L/N119SE/N60SM/N22ES/N5525L
N200PC	Learjet	55-058	Consolidated Airways Inc. Fort Wayne, In.	/N500BE/(N55BE)
N200PF	HS 125/731	25121	EPPS Air Service Inc. Atlanta, Ga.	N200PB/N807G/N307G/N795J/G-AVAE
N200PM	Gulfstream 4	1147	Philip Morris Management Corp. NYC.	/N419GA
N200RC	Jet Commander-B	140	W/o 25 Sep 73.	4X-CPG/N9040N
N200SA	Falcon 200	479	Source Air Corp. Charlottesville, Va.	(N60DD)/N400WT//N200LS/N200WD/N200FJ F-WPUU
N200TC	Learjet	24-134	Transcontinental Airlines Trav. Dover, De.	(N202GP)/N200GP/N215J/N282R N281R/N231R
N200WK	Falcon 20F	261	Lawrence Rockefeller, NYC.	N4368F/F-WLCU
N200Y	Learjet	36-014	Executive Express Charters Inc. Cadillac, Mi.	N900Y
N202BT	Learjet	35A-483	Big Three Industries Inc. Houston, Tx.	N8562Y
N202KH	Falcon 20C	45	Kitty Hawk Group Inc. Dallas, Tx.	N90JF/N159FC/N147X/N876F/F-WMKI
N202RB	Citation	650-0162	Jones Chemicals Inc. Le Roy, NY.	N1312Q
N202VV	Citation	500-0096	Thomas O Gara, Las Vegas, Wa.	C-GXPT/N202VV/N202VS///N222SL/N596CC

Registration	Type	c/n	Owner / Operator	Previous identity
N202WR	Learjet	35A-190	Dumont Associates Inc. Morristown, NJ.	N202VS/N32BA
N203A	Gulfstream 2	89	Midcoast Aviation Inc. St Louis, Mo.	/N100A/N882GA
N203BA	Beechjet 400	RJ-3	Bohemia Inc. Portland, Or.(was A1003SA Diamond 2).	/N508DM
N203BE	Citation	550-0134	Basin Electric Power Corp. Bismarck, ND.	HZ-ZTC/HZ-AAI/N2635D
N203CK	Learjet	24B-203	Pacific Flights Inc. Medford, Or.	N55MJ/N55LJ/(N43TL)/N3GW/N515WC
N203M	Jet Commander	120	Wfu. Destroyed/scrapped 14 Aug 84. Cx USA register 4 Jan 85.	N200M
N203R	BAe 125/800A	NA0413	Raytheon Corp. Lexington, Ma.	N558BA/G-5-591
N204A	Gulfstream 2	79	Ibister Inc. San Diego, Ca.	/N719GA/N826GA
N204C	Gulfstream 2	143	E I Dupont de Nemours & Co. New Castle, De.	/N334/N883GA
N204CA	Citation	501-0283	James M Krueger, Newport Beach, Ca. (was 500-0377).	//C-GPTC/N98749
N204GA	Gulfstream 2	74	Ugone Corp. Houston, Tx.	/(3X-GBD)/N311AC/N111AC/N845GA
N204R	HS 125/700A	NA0279	Raytheon Corp. Lexington, Ma.	N125AD/G-5-17
N204RC	Gulfstream 2	34	Air Waves Corp. Wilmington, De.	/N500JR/VR-CBM/N11SX/N130A/N230E
N205BE	Citation	550-0647		N647CC
N205BS	HS 125/700A	NA0234	Bellsouth Services Inc. Birmingham, Al.	N711YP/G-5-16
N205EL	Learjet	35A-283	Invemed Aviation Services Inc. Winston Salem, NC.	/N920C
N205PC	Citation V	560-0010	Pacificorp Trans Inc. Portland, Or.	
N205SC	Citation	550-0156	Bellsouth Services Inc. Birmingham, Al.	N205SG/(N31F)/N6567C/N98784
N205X	Falcon 10	44	Amax Inc. Indianapolis, In.	N130FJ/F-WJMJ
N206EC	Learjet	35A-487	Connecticut National Bank, Hartford, Ct.	/N206FC
N206MD	Gulfstream 2	22	Mike Donahoe Aviation Co. Phoenix, Az.	N683FM//N22FS//N145ST/N5152/N862GA
N206PC	BAe 125/800A	8038	Pacific Corp Trans/Nerco Inc. Portland, Or.	/N800TR/G-5-20
N207MJ	MS 760 Paris-2	2	McCulloch Jet Inc. Great Falls, Mt.	N1EP/N760MM/F-BOJO/EP-HIM
N207PC	HS 125/700A	7197	Pacificorp Trans Inc. Portland, Or.	G-5-17/N790Z/G-5-12
N208MM	HFB 320	1039	Nazareth Aviation Inc. Spartanburg, SC.	N205MM/N666LQ/N666LC/CF-WDU/N893HJ N118RA/D-CESO
N208N	Citation	500-0021	Eastwind Inc. Wilmington, De.	N550CC/N5B/JA8421/N521CC
N208PC	Citation V	560-0050	Pacific Trans Corp. Portland, Or.	(N26771)
N208R	Beechjet 400	RJ-14	Raytheon Co. Lexington, Ma.	N3114B
N208ST	Westwind-1124	208	SPS Financial Services Inc. Newtown, Pa.	N208MD/N961JE/(N961JD)/N961JC 4X-CLF
N209G	Citation	550-0558	Rons Inc.	(N1298G)
N210F	Citation	650-0067	Flint Aviation Inc. Tulsa, Ok.	/(N1314X)
N211CD	Learjet	25D-275	Corwin Denney, Beverly Hills, Ca.	
N211DH	Learjet	35A-253	Hagadone Newspapers Co. Coeur d'Alene, Id.	N40144
N211EF	Learjet	55-101	Evergreen Aviation Inc. Salem, Or.	N101HK/N101PK/N101HK
N211GA	Diamond 1A	A011SA	Greene County Greyhound Park, Tuscaloosa, Al.	(N77GA)/N307DM
N211JC	Learjet	25D-310	Clarence Smail Aviation, Greensburg, Pa.	N211PD/N1088C
N211MA	Citation V	560-0022	Flying Lion Inc.	(N1228Y)
N211MB	Learjet	25-059	W/o 3 Aug 80.	N425JX
N211QS	Citation	S550-0011	Pope & Talbot Inc. Columbus, Oh.	N68SK
N211VP	Citation	S550-0002	Lozier Corp. Omaha, Ne.	/N111VP/N507CJ/(N507CC)/(N1255Y)
N212AP	JetStar-8	5147	Karon Burns/KB Aviation Inc. St Louis, Mo.	///N718R/N744UT/N5511L
N212AT	Gulfstream 3	492	A T & T Resources Management, Morristown, NJ.	N339GA
N212CP	Westwind-Two	340	Cerlan Inc. Greensboro, NC.	N1124L/4X-CUA
N212CW	Jet Commander	75	Bill Walker & Assocs Inc. McKinnon Airport, Ga.	N1121R
N212H	Citation	551-0140	BAC Inc. Ketchum, Id. (was 550-0098).	/N17S/(N26635)
N212JP	Falcon 50	94	A T & T Resource Management Corp. Morristown, NJ.	N82NC/N99FJ/F-WZHC
N212K	Falcon 50	89	A T & T Resource Management Corp. NYC.	/N93FJ/F-WZHV
N212N	Falcon 50	202	AT&T Resource Management Corp. Morristown, NJ.	/N290FJ/F-WWHB
N212NE	Learjet	25D-212	Duncan Aviation Inc. Lincoln, Nb.	N911MG/N1450B
N212R	Falcon 20DC	212	Reliant Airlines Inc. Ypsilanti, Mi.	N31FF/N4399F/F-WPXG
N212T	Falcon 50	192	A T & T Resource Management Corp. Morristown, NJ.	N283FJ/F-WWHE
N212TG	Falcon 20F	273	Teterboro Aircraft Service, Teterboro, NJ.	N212TC/N212T/N4432F/F-WPUU
N213AP	JetStar-8	5122	Cx USA 3/89 as wfu.	/N1107M/N1107Z/N7967S
N213BM	Sabre-40A	282-111	Duncan Aircraft Sales, Venice, Fl.	//(N200CK)/N32654/XA-SAG/N9NR/N7662N
N213C	HS 125/700A	7213	Vulcan Materials Co. Birmingham, Al.	/G-BLEK/G-5-16
N214CA	Citation	500-0214	Idaho Forest Industries Inc. Central Point, Or.	(N371W)/N371HH/N214CC
N214GP	Gulfstream 2	3	J&H Investment Aircraft Inc. Mason City, Ia.	/N831GA
N214QS	Citation	S550-0014	Executive Jet Sales Inc. Wichita, Ks.	N32TJ/N32JJ
N215JW	Learjet	35A-223	James Wilson Jr. Montgomery, Al.	
N215SC	Westwind-1124	243	Sundstrand Data Control Inc. Redmond, Wa.	N59WK/N1124G/4X-CMO

Registration	Type	c/n	Owner / Operator	Previous identity
N216BG	Falcon 20D	196	Alcatel N.A/Celwave Transportation Inc. Claremont, NC.	N369WR/N701MG N811PA/N4386F/F-WPXE
N216FP	Falcon 900	65	Federal Paper Board Co Inc. Montvale, NJ.	N447FJ/F-WWFM
N216HE	Gulfstream 2	113	Fairways Corp. Washington, DC.	N2S/N32HC/N2S/N203GA/N60CT/N34RP/N30RP N817GA
N217AT	Learjet	24B-217	Big Sur Waterbeds Inc. Billings, Mt.	N45824/C-GDKS/N8536Y/C-GPDB/N777MQ N777MC
N217BL	Westwind-1124	284	Thomas H Lee, Boston, Ma.	N296NW//N99WH/4X-CQD
N217F	HS 125/731	NA713	Holly Farms Corp. Memphis, Tn.	G-AWPC
N217FS	Citation	550-0273	Federal Signal Corp. Oakbrook, Il.	N68637
N217RM	Sabre-60	306-94	Financial Industries Corp. Jackson, Ms.	N75JT/HZ-NCB/HZ-MA1/N65778
N217RR	Citation	650-0079	Raymond J Rutter, Irvine, Ca.	N59CD/N288CC/N290SC/N66ME/(N1316A)
N217SQ	Westwind-1124	217	Sundstrand Corp. Rockford, Il.	N217SC/N8QR/N8QP/4X-CLO
N217TL	Gulfstream 2	33	Thomas H Lee Co. Boston, Ma.	N1324/N1624
N218AC	HS 125/600A	6013	Al Copeland Enterprises Inc. Jefferson, La.	(N65GB)/N505W/N25BE/N25BH
N218DJ	Westwind-1124	218	Public Service Transit Inc. Fond du Lac, Wi.	C-GFAN/N100AK/N218WW/4X-CLP
N218NB	Learjet	25D-361	Beckair Co. Elkhart, In.	
N218R	Learjet	25D-365	ASC=American Stores Corp. Salt Lake City, Ut.	N7260C
N218SC	Westwind-1124	271	Sundstrand Corp. Rockford, Il.	N102KJ/N368S/4X-CNQ
N219EC	HS 125/F400A	25219	Central & Southwest Services, Dallas, Tx.	N128DR/(N292RC)/N292GA/N5594U G-5-12/9K-AEA/4W-ACA/G-AYEP/G-5-14
N219SC	Citation	550-0340	D & B Aviation, Midland, Tx.	N219CS/N219SC/N374FC/N6804F
N220CC	Citation	650-0140	Sacramento Aviation inc. Sacramento, Ca.	N290SC/N95CC/(N1325D)
N220M	Falcon 10	34	Olan Mills Inc. Chatanooga, Tn.	N110M/N124FJ/F-WLCS
N220MT	Citation	500-0135	Lonesome Pine Aircraft Sales Co. Wise, Va.	(N500EN)/N220MT/N111AM/N975EE N902T/N900T/N135BC/N135CC
N220RB	DC-8-21	45280	Project ORBIS Inc. Houston, Tx.	N8003U/N8038D
N220SC	Falcon 10	158	Jet Aviation/Ocean Spray Cranberries Inc. Plymouth, Ma.	N81LB/N223FJ F-WZGI
N220W	Citation	500-0025	Willett Management Corp. Longwood, Fl.	/N976EE/N745US/N70703/D-IMAN/N525CC
N221CM	Gulfstream 3	343	Admerex Inc/Mardenaire Inc. NYC.	/N400AL/N664S/N664P/N305GA
N221DT	Astra-1125	016	Heli Service Inc. Conroe, Tx.	N36FD/N716W/4X-CUQ
N221PF	Sabre-60	306-15	Sabre Investments Ltd. Wilmington, De.	N221PH/N360CH/N60BK/N101L/N4725N
N221PH	Sabre-80A	380-49	Petroleum Helicopters Inc. Lafayette, La.	N673FH//N673SH/N4PG/N4PQ/(N41B) N4PG/N2128J
N221PH	Sabre-40	282-55	cx USA 8/86 as wfu. (N221PX)/N221PH/N68HQ/N68HC/N353WC/N353WB/N2007/N7505V	
N221SG	Learjet	35A-182	Path Corp. Rehoboth Beach, De.	/N3HA/N3HB/N33HB/N1450B
N221UE	Learjet	35-042	United Engineers & Constructors Inc. Philadelphia, Pa.	
N222B	Learjet	25-047	CWW Inc. Denver, Co.	
N222BE	Learjet	35A-489	Southland Cork/Cheaspeake Leasing Co. Norfolk, Va.	
N222G	HS 125/1A-522	25064	Giant Industries Inc. Phoenix, Az.	N33BK/N125JG/N230H/G-ATXK
N222KC	Westwind-Two	434	Odin Aviation, Burbank, Ca.	(N346CP)//N330MG/4X-CUC
N222KN	JetStar-8	5118	Invesco Enterprises Inc. Memphis, Tn. (wfu ?).	/N333KN/N333QA//N7963S
N222LH	Westwind-1124	209	Lewis Hyman, Carson, Ca.	N988WH/N938WH/N662JB/N663JB/N661JB/4X-CLG
N222MC	Learjet	55-108	McCaw Communications, Seattle, Wa.	N78FK/N77FK/(N888FK)
N222MS	BAe 125/800A	NA0422	Stavola Aviation Inc. Anthony, Fl.	N125TR/N567BA/G-5-607
N222MU	Falcon 10	164	Mustang Fuel Corp. Oklahoma City, Ok.	N228FJ/F-WZGQ
N222MW	Westwind-1124	255	McWane Inc. Birmingham, Al.	4X-CNA
N222NG	HS 125/1A	25016	Nordic Air Inc. Wilmington, NC.	/N4997E/C6-BPC/C-FOPC/CF-RWA/G-ASSL
N222Q	Diamond 1	A021SA	British Motor Car Distributors Ltd. San Francisco, Ca.	
N222SL	Learjet	35A-162	Flying Best Air Inc. Wilmington, De.	/N1978L/N711HH/(HB-VFO)/N751GL
N222WA	Citation	501-0007	Unitco Air/Ralph Kiewit Jr. Sherman Oaks, Ca.	N5360J
N222WL	Citation	550-0208	White Industries Inc. Bates City, Mo. (spares).	N54RC/N6801P
N223WA	Westwind-1124	423	Texas International Gas & Oil Co. Santa Teresa, NM.	4X-CUC
N224JB	Learjet	24D-321	J B Hunt, Lowell, Ar.	N122RW/N10WF
N224KC	Citation	S550-0104	Tri-State Executive Air Inc. Winston Salem, NC.	N12903
N224N	Challenger 601	3064	Nordstrom Inc. Seattle, Wa.	N356N/N566N/C-GLYC
N225DC	Citation	500-0148	James Langley, Golden, Co.	/N410GB//N748VA/N718VA/(N100JC)
N225DS	Learjet	25-025	International Jet Aviation Services, Englewood, Co.	/N242AG/N49BB/N92V N920S/N928S/N920S
N225N	Challenger 601-3A	5036	Nordstrom Inc. Seattle, Wa.	C-G...
N225SE	Gulfstream 2	55	Chevron Corp. San Francisco, Ca.	/N225SF/N875GA
N225SF	Gulfstream 3	423	Chevron Corp. San Francisco, Ca.	N7134E/HZ-MIC/N1761D

Registration	Type	c/n	Owner / Operator	Previous identity
N226GA	Gulfstream 2	106	Gulfstream Aerospace Corp. Savannah, Ga.	/N397LE/N33M/N808GA
N226N	Citation	551-0129	James Nordstrom, Bellevue, Wa. (was 550-0084).	N156N/N808DM/N222LB/N26629
N226R	Falcon 20DC	226	Reliant Airlines Inc. Ypsilanti, Mi.	N21FE/N4409F/F-WPXI
N227CC	Challenger 600S	1004	Great Western Financial Corp. Salinas, Ca.	/N2677S/C-GXKQ/C-GXKQ-X
N227G	Gulfstream 4	1045	W R Grace & Co. Westchester County Airport, NY.	N420GA
N227GA	Gulfstream 2	76	Flight Services Group/TWA Aviation Inc. Mt Kisco, NY.	/N227G/N227GX/N227GL N227G/N711LS
N227HF	HS 125/731	25118	Hillshire Farms, Appleton, Wi.	N300KC/N731KC/N45PM/N743UT/G-ATYL
N227HP	Citation Eagle	500-0227	AMPCO Inc. Wilmington, De.	/C-GMMO/N423RD/G-BCRM/(N227CC)
N227LA	HS 125/F403A	25235	Uniair Leasing Corp. Dover, De.	N235AV/G-5-19/G-BKAJ/G-AYNR/HB-VCE/G-5-18
N227PC	Citation	550-0113	Petrolite Corp. St. Louis, Mo.	N2666A
N227R	Falcon 20DC	227	Reliant Airlines Inc. Ypsilanti, Mi.	N24EV/N14FE/N4410F/F-WMKG
N228G	Gulfstream 3	424	W R Grace & Co. Stewart International Airport, NY.	N60AC/N320GA
N228N	Westwind-1124	331	Nordstrom Stores/GECC, Seattle, Wa.	N556N/4X-CRY
N228S	Citation	500-0233	Numetrics Inc. Vanderbilt, Pa.	N223S/N233VW/N233CC/N5233J
N228SW	Learjet	25D-228	New Creations Inc. Columbus, Oh.	
N229JB	Falcon 10	71	J B Aviation/Regency Square Properties, Jacksonville, Fl.	D-CMAN/F-WJMM
N229N	Westwind-Two	427	John Hancock Leasing Corp. Boston, Ma.	N256N/N427WW/4X-CUN
N229R	Falcon 20DC	229	Reliant Airlines Inc. Willow Run Airport, Mi.	N25EV/N15FE/N4411F/F-WJMJ
N230JS	Citation	500-0107	Watson Enterprises Inc. Greenwich, Ct.	C-GWVC///N107SC/N107CC/(N607CC)
N230R	Learjet	35A-130	Dart Industries Inc. West Bend, Wi.	
N230RA	Falcon 20DC	230	Reliant Airlines Inc. Ypsilanti, Mi.	N26EV/N16FE/N4412F/F-WJMI
N231LC	Citation	501-0105	Liquid Container Corp. West Chicago, Il.	/N2648X
N231R	Learjet	35A-128	Dart Industries Inc. Orlando, Fl.	
N232CC	Citation	551-0496	CCI Corp. Wilmington, De.	(N12543)
N232HC	Gulfstream 3	373	G 1 Aviation Inc. Tampa, Fl.	N340GA
N232QS	Citation	S550-0032	Intelligent Electronics, Columbus, Oh.	N532CF/N532CC/(N1261A)
N232R	Learjet	35A-102	Global Airways Inc. Maimi, Fl.	/N1451B
N232RA	Falcon 20DC	232	W/o 15 Feb 89,	N27EV/N17FE/N4413F/F-WJMM
N232S	Astra-1125	032	Sherwin Williams Co. Cleveland, Oh.	N1125A/4X-CUN
N233CC	Learjet	35-031	CCI Corp. Tulsa, Ok.	N160AT/N77TE/N77U/N77FC
N233RS	Gulfstream 2TT	233	Straight Arrow Publishers Inc. NYC.	//N320TR/N807GA
N234CM	Learjet	24B-214	W/o 16 Dec 88.	N42NF/N214MJ/N668MC/N666CC/N192MB/N192MH
N234DB	Gulfstream 4	1000	Skybird Aviation, Van Nuys, Ca.	/N404GA
N234DT	Learjet	35A-407	Thompson Machinery Commerce Co. Lavergne, Tn.	/N3793P
N234F	Learjet	23-063	W/o 14 Nov 65.	
N234G	Jet Commander	28	Sykes Enterprises Inc. Charlotte, NC.	N77NR/N1190Z
N234MR	Learjet	24-130	Cx USA 13 Oct 87 as wfu.	N330J/N33CJ/N130J/N1871P/N1871R/N420WR/N657J N657LJ
N234ND	Learjet	25-043	Siegfried Inc/NORDAM, Tulsa, Ok.	N300PP/N808DP/N30LJ
N234SV	Learjet	25D-226	Sun Valley Jet Assocs. Las Vegas, Nv.	/N333SG
N234YP	Citation	650-0074	Yellow Pages/GTE Directories Corp. Dallas, Tx.	(N555EW)/(N1315G)
N235DH	Learjet	35A-134	DHL Airways Inc. San Francisco, Ca.	N88EP/N1473B
N235HR	Learjet	55-094	Hoffman La Roche Inc. Nutley, NJ.	
N235KC	HS 125/1A	25096	W/o 21 Nov 66.	G-ATNR
N235KK	Citation	650-0175	Kenneth Kirchman, Altamonte Springs, Fl.	N1820E/(N175J)
N235R	Learjet	23-032	W/o 23 Apr 66.	
N236BN	HS 125/700A	NA0236	Barnes Noble Corp/BDB Aircraft Charter Co Inc. Teterboro.	N64HA/N14JA N700UK/G-5-11
N236JP	Jet Commander	116	W/o 31 Oct 69.	N4743E
N236W	Westwind-1124	236	Sun Valley East West Inc. Philadelphia, Pa.	N35LH/4X-CMH
N237AF	Learjet	35A-262	Ameriflight Inc. Burbank, Ca.	/N237GA
N237SC	Citation	501-0237	Shea & Co. Atlanta, Ga.	N640BS/(N2617K)
N238RC	Learjet	35-061	Eagle Aviation Inc. W Columbia, SC.	/N4246N/N424DN
N240AC	Sabre-40	282-41	Research Triangle Timesharing, Cary, NC.	(N116AC)/(N300TK)/N57RM/N707JM N300RG/N300RC/N661P/N6396C
N240AG	Learjet	25B-197	Aerojet-General Corp. Sacramento, Ca.	N104GL
N240AR	Citation	550-0216	ARCO Pipe Line Co. Dallas, Tx.	N6801L
N240B	Learjet	35A-240	FSB/Budd Co. Troy, Mi.	
N240CC	Citation	500-0240	Falwell Fast Freight Inc. Lynchburg, Va.	N5240J
N240JS	Learjet	35A-241	Owners Jet Services Ltd. Las Vegas, Nv.	N500FD/N500GP/N42FE
N241JA	Learjet	24-131	Milam International Inc. Englewood, Co.	N11FH/N282R/N232R/N659LJ
N241LA	Citation	S550-0091	Lambda Aviation Inc. Fayetteville, NC.	N595CM/N595CC/(N12747)

Registration	Type	c/n	Owner / Operator	Previous identity
N242GM	Learjet	25D-242	George A Moore, Macon, Ga.	N102RA//N363HA/N749GL
N242LA	Citation	S550-0153	EJA/Lambda Aviation Inc. Fayetteville, NC.	N153QS/(N2637R)
N242WT	Citation	551-0066	Lawton Louisiana Inc. Lake Charles, La.	N6825X
N243AB	Citation	501-0685	S&P Aviation Services/Alton E Blakley Sr. Somerset, Ky.	N501TB/N400SR N5346C
N244A	Falcon 10	145	Archer Daniels Midland Co. Decatur Airport, Il.	N209FJ/F-WZGQ
N244JM	BAe 125/800A	NA0428	Worthington Industries/JMAC Inc. Worthington, Oh.	/N582BA/G-5-614
N245CC	Citation	550-0212	Hughes Aircraft Co. Culver City, Ca.	(N6801V)
N245TT	Challenger 601-3A	5001	WOTAN America Inc. Fort Lauderdale, Fl.	/C-GDDP
N246CM	Learjet	35A-395	Tri City Beverages Inc. Abilene, Tx.	/N30GL/N3261L/HB-VHD
N246NW	Citation	551-0345	Northwestern Public Service Co. Huron, SD. (was 550-0313).	/N393RC/N6889K
N247GA	Challenger 601-3A	5019	Orange County/Sunbird Aviation, Costa Mesa, Ca.	N915BB/N915BD/C-GLWT
N248H	Westwind-1124	214	Fleet Aircraft Leasing Inc. Providence, RI.	N24RH/N1124N/4X-CLL
N248PA	Beechjet 400	RJ-9	Indiana Beechcraft Inc. Indianapolis, In. (was s/n A1009SA).(N248PA) /N209BA N109DM
N249LJ	Learjet	25D-249	Sacramento Aviation Center Inc. Sacramento, Ca.	/(N500EF)//N211JB/N249SC/ N2OPY
N250AL	Citation	S550-0042	Luhr Brothers Inc. Columbia, Il.	
N250AS	Falcon 50	182	Albertsons Inc. Boise, Id.	N182FJ/F-WWHB
N250EC	Sabre-40A	282-110	Minnesota Jet/Mississippi Savings Bank, St Paul, Mn.	N477A/N477X/N7597N
N250JT	HS 125/1A	25053	Tyler Jet Aircraft Sales Inc. Tyler, Tx.	N254JT/N125TB/N4465N/C-FIPJ C-FIPG
N250PM	Westwind-1124	227	Pet Inc. St. Louis, Mo.	4X-CLY
N250RA	Falcon 20F	481	Rite Aid Corp. Middletown, Pa.	N502F/F-WLCS
N250SP	Citation	501-0181	Sonoco Products Co. Hartsville, SC.	N6781C
N250UA	Jet Commander-A	121	W/o 27 Apr 78.	N1121R/N250JP/N840AR/N1121X
N251AB	HS 125/400A	NA750	Chase Aircraft Finance Co. Lakeland, Fl.	/N20RG/N3933A/XB-CCM/XA-DIW N304BP/N300P/N46BH/G-AXYI
N251AF	Learjet	25-004	Aero Freight Inc. El Paso, Tx.	N47MJ/N7GJ/N1121C/N1121/N641GA
N251JA	Learjet	25B-150	Milam Intl/Intl Jet Aviation Services, Englewood, Co.	/N888RB/N714KP/N714K (N25LP)
N251JE	Sabre-65	465-2	Jacobs Engineering Group Inc. Pasadena, Ca.	N465T
N251QS	Citation	S550-0051	EJA/JI Aviation Inc. Columbus, Oh.	N1270Y
N251SP	Westwind-Two	422	Sonoco Products Co. Hartsville, SC.	N422AW/4X-COC/4X-CUI
N252BK	Learjet	25B-107	Barbara Hepner, Salt Lake City, Ut.	N25NB/N25NP/N57DM///N225CC
N252DL	Learjet	24-124	TAG Aviation Inc. Miami Springs, Fl.	/SE-DCU/OY-EGE/N462LJ
N253K	Falcon 10	10	W/o 30 Jan 80.	N105FJ/F-WJMJ
N253L	Falcon 50	19	Contran Corp. Dallas, Tx.	/N63A/N50FM/F-WZHB
N253M	Learjet	25D-253	Chattanooga Macon Express Inc. Macon, Ga.	N253J/(N202DR)/N97DK/N253EJ
N253MD	Westwind-1124	253	Annsett Industries Leasing Inc. Bellevue, Wa.	/N800WS/N800WW/N511CQ/N511CC 4X-CMY
N253QS	Citation	S550-0053	Cessna Aircraft Co. Wichita, Ks.	N75BL/N12705
N253W	Citation	550-0221	Alumax Inc. San Mateo, Ca.	N68026
N254AR	Gulfstream 2B	254	ARCO, Dallas, Tx.	/
N254CR	Gulfstream 2	184	Aviation Venture Inc. Cleveland, Oh.	N220GA/N80E/N861GA
N254JT	Learjet	24B-181	John Travolta/ATLO Inc. Dover, De.	N87CF/N44PA/N651J/N1QC/N234Q
N255DG	Diamond 1A	A056SA	Hangar One Inc. Atlanta, Ga.	//I-FRTT/N101AD//N156GA/N341DM
N255MB	Learjet	55-117	Oregon MB-35 Corp. Portland, Or.	N8567X
N255ST	Learjet	55-064	Southeast Toyota Distributors Inc. Deerfield Beach, Fl.	
N255TS	Citation	501-0016	Thomas Steel Corp. Lemont, Il.	(N38DT)/N38DA/N58BT/N38DA/N501DL/C-GHOS N517A/N36864
N256A	Falcon 20F-5	438	Bridgemark Associates, Omaha, Nb.	N263K/N442F/F-WMKI
N256M	Gulfstream 2TT	235	MAPCO Inc. Tulsa, Ok.	N16FG/N5519C/G-HADI/N17581
N256MA	Learjet	35A-235	MAPCO Inc. Tulsa, Ok.	/N600CN/N841GL
N256W	Citation	550-0026	Hersey Mountain Air Inc. Concord, NH.	/(N2231B)/N256W/N3240M
N257DJ	Learjet	35A-257	Duncan Aviation Inc. Lincoln, Ne.	//F-GCMS
N257W	Falcon 10	119	Wendy's International Inc. Dublin, Oh.	N191FJ/F-WPXK
N258G	Learjet	35A-443	258G Corp. Dover, De.	N135RJ
N258P	Citation	S550-0022	Murphy Oil USA Inc. El Dorado, Ar.	
N259HA	Learjet	35A-259	Jet Cap Inc. Chesterfield, Mo.	/N9113F/HB-VGC/N39413
N260CC	Citation	500-0260	H E Butt Grocery Co. San Antonio, Tx.	(N5260J)
N261PC	Learjet	35A-329	Park Companies, Cleveland, Oh.	/N53DM/N39412

Registration	Type	c/n	Owner / Operator	Previous identity
N261T	Sabre-60	306-125	United Technologies Cortran Inc. Rentschler Airport, Ct.	N265RW/XA-RGC N32PC/N2134J
N261WC	Learjet	25D-261	Triperoo Wings Inc. Fort Lauderdale, Fl.	N24JK/N180MC/N3802G
N261WR	Citation	S550-0119	W R Meadows Inc. Hampshire, Il.	(N12922)
N263C	Gulfstream 3	341	E I Dupont de Nemours & Co. Houston, Tx.	
N265A	Sabre-65	465-47	Armstrong World Industries, Lancaster, Pa.	
N265C	Sabre-60	306-120	Cummins Engine Co. Columbus, In.	N2124J
N265DP	Sabre-60	306-68	Dayco Products Inc. Dayton, Oh.	N2HX/N2HW/N8000
N265M	Sabre-65	465-31	Cummins Engine Co. Columbus, Oh.	N65FC/N2550E
N265U	Sabre-60	306-132	Cummins Engine Co. Columbus, In.	N60AG/N994W/N108W/N60RS/N2150J
N267GF	JetStar-731	22/5074	Bryant Air Services Inc. St Louis, Mo.	///N267P//N67B/N9234R
N267L	JetStar-6	5067	W/o 29 Mar 81.	(N267AD)/N267L/N207L/N711Z/N871D/N9234R
N268GM	Citation	500-0323	George A Mendenhall, Sunriver, Or.	N307EW/N523CC/N474L/N300PB/N5323J
N268J	Citation	550-0241	IMO Industries Inc. Lawrenceville, NJ.	N10FN/N6804Z
N268WC	Learjet	25D-268	W Coast Air Charter/R E Job Cement Contractor, Pomona, Ca.	
N269AL	Learjet	24-159	Hogan Air Inc. Middletown, Oh.	/N710TV/N66MR/N661JB/N855W/N647GA
N269CM	Citation	501-0151	Columbia Management Co. Portland, Or. (status ?).	/N269MD/(N1820E)
N269RC	Citation	500-0078	RCI DMR Inc. Los Angeles, Ca.	N110CK/N429RC/N21TV/N54531/TL-AAW/ZS-IYY N2HD/N578CC
N270A	Westwind-1124	270	Digital Equipment Corp. Maynard, Ma.	(N270WW)/4X-CNP
N270AV	HS 125/F403B	25270	Intergraph Corp. Wilmington, De.	G-BKBA/G-BBGU/G-5-13
N270HC	BAe 125/800A	8020	Manufacturers Hanover Corp. Hangar A, Westchester, NY.	/N800ZZ/G-5-14
N270LC	Westwind-1124	245	Williamson-Dickie Manufacturing, Fort Worth, Tx.	N404CB/N1124P/4X-CMQ
N270MC	HS 125/700A	NA0307	Parke Aviation Corp. NYC.	/N700GG/G-5-18
N270RA	Falcon 20F	446	Rite Aid Corp. Middletown, Pa.	N904SB/N901SB/N31WT/N454F/F-WJMN
N270SF	Citation	501-0144	Super Food Services Inc. Dayton, Oh.	N2652U
N271AC	Citation	500-0218	Givens Aircraft Sales & Leasing, Altamonte Springs, Fl.	N4AC/(N218CC)
N271CA	Citation V	560-0071	Security Pacific Equipment Leasing, San Francisco, Ca.	
N271MB	Diamond 1	A015SA	Wm J Murphy, East Moline, Il.	/N415RC//N315DM
N272BC	Diamond 1A	A046SA	Bissell Corp. Grand Rapids, Mi.	N151SP/(N146GA)/N346DM
N272JS	Gulfstream 3	489	John Jefferson Smurfit Group, Dublin.	//N328GA
N272T	Learjet	35A-349	The Flying Ws Inc. Houston, Tx.	/
N273DA	Citation	501-0273	Duncan Aircraft Sales, Venice, Fl. (was 500-0363).	N501MD///N333PE/N333PD D-IDPD/N46106/XA-HEV/(I-CCCB)/N36881
N273G	Challenger 601	3002	GTE Services Corp. Stamford, Ct.	N4449F/(N509PC)/C-GBXH
N273K	HS 125/600A	6041	KAH Inc. Virginia Beach, Va.	N888PM/N450DA/VR-CBD/G-BCJU/G-5-13
N273LR	Learjet	25-058	Consignment Aircraft Sales HQ. San Antonio, Tx.	N273LP/N2366Y
N273M	Learjet	25D-315	Pittco Inc. Memphis, Tn.	N273KH//N83TC/N3798A/N10873
N273MC	Learjet	55-119	Meredith Corp. Des Moines, Ia.	N72613
N274K	Westwind-1124	274	Oklahoma Gas & Electric Co. Oklahoma City, Ok.	N701W/N701Z/4X-CNT
N275AL	Citation	500-0333	Aeroquip Corp. Jackson, Mi.	(N5333J)
N275E	Learjet	24D-245	Steve Sandlin, Las Vegas, Nv.	JA8446/N275E/N275LE
N276AL	Citation	550-0016	Trinova Corp. Maumee, Oh.	/N3221M
N276JS	Learjet	35A-458	Fowler & Creech Investments, Jonesboro, Ar.	//
N276LE	Learjet	25B-078	Emery/Rockford Motors Inc. Rockford, Il.	N64MR/N64MP/N258GL
N277CT	HS 125/700A	NA0261	Caterpillar Inc. Peoria, Il.	/N125AL/G-5-17
N277JM	Citation	551-0035	Air Cruise/John Myers, Long Beach, Ca.	N277HM/N6860U
N277QS	Citation	S550-0077	EJA/Pinkerton Group, Columbus, Oh.	(N747GP)/N747CP/(N1273R)
N277T	Gulfstream 2	209	Trunkline Gas Co. Houston, Tx.	N806GA
N279DM	Learjet	35A-214	Monterey Airplane Co. Pebble Beach, Ca.	
N279DP	Astra-1125	020	Monterey Airplane Co. Carmel, Ca.	4X-CUS
N279DS	Astra-1125	040	Monterrey Airplane Co. Carmel, Ca.	4X-C..
N279LE	Learjet	25B-112	Rockford Motors Inc. Rockford, Il.	N173J/OY-BFC
N279SP	Learjet	35A-452	Southwestern Public Service Co. Amarillo, Tx.	/N25MJ
N279TG	Learjet	25D-265	Templehof Airways USA Inc/Berlin Air Rescue, West Germany.	N265EJ/N1462B
N280BC	Falcon 50	109	Jet Aviation/Liberty Mutual Insurance Co. Boston, Ma.	N109FJ/F-WZHV
N280JS	Citation	550-0359	Owners Jet Services Ltd. Las Vegas, Nv.	N95CT/N550WR/N67983
N280MH	Citation	550-0280	San Diego Jet Center Inc. Carlsbad, Ca.	/N6864Y
N280R	Learjet	24B-188	LJ Ventures, Chicago, Il.	N230R
N281BC	Learjet	35A-380	Jet East Inc. Dallas, Tx.	N291BC/N291BX/N82JL
N281FP	Learjet	24D-281	Valhi Inc. Dallas, Tx.	N23MJ/OY-BIZ/SE-DFB
N282AC	Learjet	24-145	International Leasing Co. Cleveland, Oh.	/(N57NB)/N57ND/N690J

Registration	Type	c/n	Owner / Operator	Previous identity
N282MC	Sabre-40R	282-52	Lost Mountain Inc. Hilton Head Island, Mt.	N303A/(N77MK)/N77MR/N4OR/N2004 N2000/N200A/N7502V
N282U	Falcon 20F	305	Universal Jet Sales Inc. Leesburg, Va.	//VR-CDB/N56SL/N16R/N4446F/F-WMKJ
N282WW	Sabre-60	306-134	Gadsden Holdings Inc. Miami, Fl.	/N323EC/N2152J
N284AM	Citation	500-0028	Los Angeles Aircraft Exchange Inc. Newport Beach, Ca.	///N103WV/N1ODG N528CC
N284RJ	Citation	501-0005	Guardian Savings & Loan Association, Huntington Beach, Ca.	/N143EP/N665JB N661AA/N5357J
N285LM	JetStar 2	5224	Laumar Corp/H B O & Co. Atlanta, Ga.	/N1924G/N4016M
N287MC	Citation	S550-0102	Maytag Corp. Newton, Ia.	N1290Z
N287W	Falcon 20D	194	Wfu 30 Jun 89.	N297W/N555RA/N100M/N4384F/F-WPUZ
N288DF	Learjet	24D-288	Exploring the Electrical Content of the Air, Teterboro, NJ.	
N288JE	Learjet	35A-288	Jet East Inc. Dallas, Tx.	N288NE/N43DD/HB-VGM/N1476B
N288QS	Citation	S550-0088	EJA, Columbus, Oh.	N825HL
N289K	Gulfstream 2	225	Crawford Fitting Co. Cleveland, Oh.	N55922/G-BGLT/N17585
N289NE	Learjet	35A-289	Martin Aviation Inc. Santa Ana, Ca.	/N289MJ/N802CC//N3JL
N290EC	BAe 125/800A	NA0444	Ethyl Corp. Richmond, Va.	N596BA/G-5-647
N290GA	Gulfstream 3	875	Gulfstream Aerospace Corp. Savannah, Ga.	N210GK/N333GU/N333GA
N290RA	Westwind-1124	390	Weaver Aero International Inc. Hesston, Ks.	(N303E)/N3RL/N57WW/4X-CUB
N291BC	Falcon 50	199	Boise Cascade Corp. Boise, Id.	N287FJ/F-WWHB
N291GA	Gulfstream 2	91	Gulfstream Aerospace Corp. Savannah, Ga.	/VR-BRM//G-OVIP/N219GA/VH-ASM G-AYMI/N17586
N292BC	Falcon 50	62	Boise Cascade Corp. Boise, Id.	N77FJ/F-WZHE
N292GA	Challenger 601	3014	Golden West Baseball Co. Anaheim, Ca.	N14PN/C-G...
N293BC	Falcon 50	135	Boise Cascade Corp. Boise, Id.	N125FJ/F-WZHA
N293K	Falcon 50	170	Kellogg Co. Battle Creek, Mi.	N169FJ/F-WZHI
N294FJ	Falcon 50	212		F-WWHH
N294NW	Learjet	25-031	Richards Aviation Inc. Memphis, Tn.	
N294W	BAe 125/800A	8014	Airtrade International Inc. Fairfield, Ct.	//N800MM/G-5-15
N295FJ	Falcon 50	213		F-WWHW
N296CF	Citation	551-0309	Cessna Finance Corp. Wichita, Ks. (was 550-0266).	/N296PH/N296CC/N68622
N296FJ	Falcon 50	214		F-WWHX
N297FJ	Falcon 50	215		F-W...
N298FJ	Falcon 50	216		F-W...
N299CT	HS 125/700A	NA0264	Caterpillar Inc. Peoria, Il.	/G-5-19
N299DB	Gulfstream 4	1137	Dun & Bradstreet Corp. NYC.	N402GA
N299FB	Gulfstream 4	1099	Fisher 299 Fox Bravo Corp. NYC.	/N489H
N299MW	Learjet	25D-299	Aircraft Trading Center Inc. Jupiter, Fl.	(N8217W)/I-KIOV/N222LW
N299RP	Citation	501-0073	Roush Bakery Products, Cedar Rapids, Ia.	/N100SV/N3117M
N299W	Falcon 50	21	Randolph Wright, Birmingham, Mi.	/9K-AEE/(9K-ACQ)/F-WZHN
N300A	Falcon 50	64	ICI Americas Inc. New Castle, De.	/N418S/N79FJ/F-WZHH
N300AA	Diamond 1A	A041SA	Flores Munoz Hockema & Reed, McAllen, Tx.	/N83AE/N45GL/(N444SL)/N330DM
N300AK	Citation	550-0612	Gerald Mansbach, Ashland, Ky.	(N1242Y)
N300BS	HS 125/700A	NA0241	Tanara Inc. Wilmington, De.	N25MK//(N64SA)/N6VC/N492CB/N700NT
N300CT	Falcon 20F	366	Airspeed Charters Inc. Raleigh, NC.	/N83V/N1020F/F-WMKG
N300DH	Diamond 1A	A010SA	David Hocker, Owensboro, Ky.	(N9FC)/N69PC/N306DM
N300DL	Gulfstream 2	57	Solar Sportsystems Inc. Buffalo, NY.	/N300DK/N770AC/N876GA
N300GA	Gulfstream 3	300	Gulfstream Aerospace Corp. Savannah, Ga.	/
N300GB	HS 125/1A-522	25074	Texas Health Ents/Jennifer Nicole Aviation Inc. Warren, Oh.	N400UW/N400NW G-ATOV
N300GN	BAe 125/800A	8057	Gannett Co Inc. Arlington, Va.	N362BA/G-5-508
N300HR	Westwind-Two	335	Hussman Corp. Chesterfield, Mo.	4X-CTC
N300HW	HS 125/1A	25021	Cristopher Crowe Productions, Pasadena, Ca.	N711WJ/N125KC/N125BT/N228GL N228G/N2504/N575DU/G-ASZN
N300JA	Learjet	24D-282	W/o 2 Dec 79.	D-INKA
N300JK	Westwind-Two	369	Westkoff Inc. Binghampton, NY.	(N54BC)//N24SB/4X-CUF
N300L	Gulfstream 4	1018	Triangle Publications, Radnor, Pa.	/N407GA
N300LH	Westwind-1124	312	Atherton Bean, Minneapolis, Mn.	N200LH/4X-CRF
N300LS	BAe 125/800A	8098	Limited Stores/Southern Holding Corp. Wilmington, De.	/N536BA/G-5-564
N300M	Gulfstream 3	417	Transair Leasing Inc. Dover, De.	N1119C/N111AC/N317GA
N300PL	Learjet	25D-247	Wfu as parted out following accident 12/83.	
N300RC	Sabre-60	306-111	Royal Crown Companies Inc. Fort Lauderdale, Fl.	N2106J
N300TS	Diamond 1	A003SA	Top Sales Co Inc. Charlotte, NC.	/N300DM/(JQ8003)

Registration	Type	c/n	Owner / Operator	Previous identity
N300WG	Learjet	25D-346	Greenleaf Corp. Saggerstown, Pa.	N3798V
N301AJ	Jet Commander	48	W/o 13 Aug 90.	/N502U/N929GV//N85MA/N486G/N8LC/N444WL/N400LR/N541M/N541SG
N301AT	HFB 320	1038	International Aviation Ltd. Southfield, Mi.	N5627/N110WS/D-CESI
N301DM	Diamond 1A	A007SA	Pennco Inc. Ashland, Ky.	
N301EC	Gulfstream 2	258	Household International, Wheeling, Il.	N823GA
N301NT	Sabre-40	282-9	Sabreliner Corp. Chesterfield, Mo.	N329SS/(N327RH)/N327JB/N620K/N620M N6363C
N301P	Diamond 1A	A030SA	W Z Inc. Norfolk, Va.	/N58TJ/N41UT/N191GS/N322DM
N301PC	Westwind-Two	377	International Aircraft Sales Inc. Fort Smith, Ar.	/4X-CUJ
N301QS	Citation V	560-0038	EJA/CIT Leasing Corp. NYC.	
N301R	Falcon 20C	3	Reliant Airlines Inc. Ypsilanti, Mi.	/N92MH/HB-VAV/VR-BCG/F-WMKG
N302A	Falcon 10	59	Great Planes Sales Inc. Tulsa, Ok.	N300A/N300GN/N144FJ/F-WJMN
N302EJ	Learjet	24D-302	W/o 14 Apr 83.	N39DM/N302EJ
N302NT	Sabre-40	282-81	Sabreliner Corp. Chesterfield, Mo.	//N1GY/N416CS/N99CR/N360N/N36065/N2250B
N302PC	Citation	S550-0130	Peabody Coal Co. St Louis, Mo.	N130CC/(N1293Z)
N303A	Sabre-65	465-32	Double WharfCorp/Andlinger & Co Inc. Tarrytown, NY.	N97RE
N303AF	Learjet	24-144	Wfu.	N700C/N9KC/N397BC/N397L/N593GA
N303AJ	Jet Commander-B	149	Aviex Jet Inc. Houston, Tx.	N343DA/(N129ME)/N666JM/N606JM/(N149BP)/(N9LP) N1121E/N700R/N78MN/N489G/N45SL/N100PC/N100MC/4X-CPM/N9049N
N303GA	Gulfstream 3	303	Airbourne Charter Inc. Burbank, Ca.	/N1761W/TU-VAF/N303GA/N300GA
N303J	Citation	550-0271	Central Coast Aviation Inc. Salinas, Ca.	/N550CA/N655EW/N555EW/(N303EC) N6863J
N303LE	JetStar-731	25/5113	Tarpon Transmission Co. Dallas, Tx.	N124RP//N505C/N7958S
N303NT	Sabre-40	282-29	Sabreliner Corp. Chesterfield, Mo.	/N170DD/N170AL/N170JL/N910E/N6383C
N303P	Diamond 1A	A034SA	Motion Industries Inc. Birmingham, Al.	/N318DM
N303PC	Westwind-1124	223	J C Pace & Co. Fort Worth, Tx.	N124TY/N1124P/4X-CLU
N304AF	Learjet	35-013	Apache Corp. Denver, Co.	/N7TJ/N1DA
N304AT	Learjet	35-045	American Transair/Betaco Inc. Indianaopolis, In.	N304TZ//N117CH/N45MJ XA-HOS/N999M/N99786/N35HB/HB-VEN/N1461B
N304LP	Learjet	24D-304	L P Aviation Inc. Indianapolis, In.	N304EJ
N304NT	Sabre-40	282-2	Sabreliner Corp. Chesterfield, Mo.	N16TA//N67WW/N57GS/N108U/N108W/N100WF N577PM/N577R
N304WW	Westwind-Two	304	Jean Vollum, Hillsboro, Or.	4X-CQX
N305AJ	Jet Commander	100	Aviex Jet Inc. Houston, Tx.	/N11WP/N4663E/N605V/N16GR
N305BB	Westwind-1124	228	Badgett Brown, Madisonville, Ky.	4X-CLZ
N305NT	Sabre-40	282-66	Sabreliner Corp. Chesterfield, Mo.	/N98CF/N54CF/N48TC/N40HC/N40NR/N737R N4943A/N355MJ/N2233B
N305PC	Citation	S550-0138	Peabody Coal Co. St Louis, Mo.	N538CC/(N1295A)
N305SC	Learjet	35A-322	Jetstream Transportation Corp. Wilmington, NC.	/
N306CW	Sabre-40A	282-108	Williams Aviation Co. Midland, Tx.	N442WP/N442WT/N7596N
N307AJ	Citation	551-0021	Beall Brothers Inc. Houston, Tx.	N107BB/N26639
N307D	Sabre-60	306-31	National Center for Atmospheric Research, Boulder, Co.	
N308AT	Citation	501-0159	American Trans Air/Betaco Inc. Indianapolis, In.	N666JJ/D-IGLU/N2652Y
N308CK	Citation	550-0106	Cincinnati Contractors Aviation, Cincinnati, Oh.	N37CR/AE-129/LQ-TFM AE-129/N2665A
N308EL	Gulfstream 2	68	Eli Lilly & Co. Indianapolis, In.	
N308WC	JetStar-6	5020	Cx USA 8/88 as wfu.	//N300CR/N371H/N9207R
N309CK	Westwind-Two	350	sale, Long Beach, Ca.	N777LU/N3838J/XA-MAK/VR-CBB/4X-CTR
N309EL	Gulfstream 2	250	Eli Lilly & Co. Indianapolis, In.	N821GA
N310AF	Citation	501-0142	Airfleet Credit Corp (USA) Inc. Miami, Fl.	/HB-VHA/N26507
N310CK	JetStar-731	35/5117	Cincinnati Contractors Aviation, Cincinnati, Oh.	N210EK//N7962S
N311AG	B 727-17	20512	Ann & Gordon Getty/Vallejo Corp/Baker Corp/Weatland Corp. Ca	N767RV/N99548 CP-1339/N99548/CF-CUR
N311EL	Gulfstream 4	1095	Eli Lilly & Co. Indianapolis, In.	N469GA
N311JK	Gulfstream 3	434	J Kroc/MacDonalds', Chicago, Il.	N811JK/N326GA
N311JS	Falcon 20F	341	Dillinger Charter Services Ltd. West Islip, NY.	N78BC/N511WR/N511WP/N66GA N20FJ/N4462F/F-WMKF
N311TT	Citation	501-0196	Geo M Martin Co. Emeryville, Ca.	/N311TP/N575SR/(N597JV)/N6782B
N312A	Falcon 50	157	American Information Technologies, Chicago, Il.	N141FJ/F-WZHG
N312AM	Falcon 100	210	American Information Technologies, Chicago, Il.	N273FJ/F-WZGR
N312AT	Falcon 100	209	American Information Technologies, Chicago, Il.	(N312AR)/N312AT/N272FJ F-WZGP
N312CF	Learjet	35A-403	KLW Aircraft Inc. Columbia, Mo.	/N312CT/N37966

Page 77

Registration	Type	c/n	Owner / Operator	Previous identity
N312CK	JetStar-731	37/5150	Sabrenel Corp. Jupiter, Fl.	//N42C/N200CG/N200CC/N516WC/N5514L
N312CT	Challenger 601-3A	5030	Centel Corp. Sugar Grove, Il.	C-G...
N312EL	Gulfstream 4	1105	Eli Lilly & Co. Indianapolis, In.	N408GA
N312K	Sabre-40A	282-105	Par Industries Inc. Medina, Oh.	N22BJ/N2QW/N2HW
N312W	Astra-1125	012	Sherwin Williams Co. Cleveland, Oh.	N25AG/N1125A/4X-CUL
N313QS	Citation	650-0013	EJA/Winston Network Inc. NYC.	(N13QS)/N119EL/(N13052)
N314AD	Westwind-Two	394	BLT Leasing Corp. NYC.	N94WW/4X-CUM
N314C	Learjet	35A-412	Carter Wallace Inc. NYC.	(N31LM)/N412GL/N6666R/N37980
N314GS	Citation	501-0322	Diamond Rug & Carpet Mills Inc. Eton, Ga.	N374GS/N2663J
N314TC	Citation	500-0216	Rosholach Inc. Wilmington, De.	//N216CC
N315JM	Westwind-1124	259	Ansett Industries Leasing Inc. Bellevue, Wa.	///N19AP//C-GSWS/N1124N 4X-CNE
N315MC	Gulfstream 4	1032	Management Corp of America/MCA Inc. Universal City, Ca.	/C-FSBR/N17585
N315MR	Citation	501-0076	Guy Mabee, Midland, Tx.	N451CJ/N3122M
N315S	Citation	501-0038	Stim Air Inc. Hillsboro, Or. 'Peggy 111'	N36923
N316CC	Citation	550-0283	Cessna Finance Corp. Wichita, Ks.	N316CF/N316H/N316CC/(N68646)
N316M	Learjet	23-061	W/o 19 Mar 66.	
N317CC	Diamond 1A	A081SA	Cozens & Cudahy Air Inc. Milwaukee, Wi.	N81TJ/N381MG/N381DM
N317SM	Citation	551-0036	Spring Mountain Enterprises Inc. Newport Beach, Ca.	N160D/N162CC/N2661P
N319AT	BAe 125/800A	8043	Allianz Technical Service Inc. Dallas, Tx.	/(D-CAZH)/G-5-12
N319BG	Westwind-1124	192	Westwind Enterprises Inc. Brentwood, Tn.	(N736US)//N71M/4X-CKP
N319MF	HS 125/F600A	6070	Texas Olefins Co. Houston, Tx.	//N322CC/G-5-15/N322CC/G-BEDT/G-5-11
N319Z	Gulfstream 3	319	Dana Corp. Toledo, Oh.	
N320DM	Diamond 1A	A028SA	Flightcraft Inc. Portland, Or.	//
N320M	Learjet	35A-320	Chesterfield Aircraft Co. Chesterfield, Mo.	N320M/N35FS/N905LD/N905LC
N320MC	HFB 320	1034	W/o 9 Mar 73.	N320J/D-CERO
N320MJ	B 707-321B	20028	W/o 20 Sep 90.	//VR-CBN/N3127K/9Y-TEZ/N891PA
N320S	Citation	S550-0090	Executive Flight Inc. La Crosse, Wi.	N777GF/N12746
N320T	Diamond 1A	A032SA	Traylor Brothers Inc. Evansville, In.	N132GA/N323DM
N320W	Jet Commander	15	Wfu.	N125K/HB-VAX/N365G
N321FM	Citation	501-0687	Fanny May Candy Shops/Coleman Foundation Inc. Chicago, Il.	
N321GL	Learjet	24-174	U S Jet Sales Inc. Sarasota, Fl.	N999JR/N661JG/N661CP/N854GA
N321SE	Citation	550-0321	AIG Aviation Inc. Atlanta, Ga.	/N5430G
N324L	Citation	501-0112	Lee Lewis, Lubbock, Tx.	N100SN/N6781Z
N325CP	Learjet	55-112	Bricair Inc. Fort Lauderdale, Fl.	YV-325CP
N325K	Sabre-40	282-63	ALT Inc. Derry, NH.	
N325PM	Citation	501-0075	Tim Blixseth, Portland, Or.	/(N325PM)/N325BC/N773LR/N773LP/N3120M
N326CB	JetStar-8	5143	sale, Rancho Cucamong, Ca.	//N620JB/C-GATU/N5878D/N5070L/N31UT/N100UA N5507L
N326EJ	Learjet	24D-326	Kokomo Aviation Inc. Kokomo, In.	(N400XB)/N326EJ
N326EW	Citation	550-0622	Leco Corp. South Bend, In.	(N1255J)
N326MM	Challenger 600S	1024	Metro Mobile Transport Inc. NYC.	/N567L/N637ML/C-GLXD
N327BC	Learjet	25D-327	Bobby Cox/Flyaway Inc. Odessa, Tx.	/(N54JC)/N52DA/N54GP
N327F	Learjet	35A-327	Barbara Fasken, Oakland, Ca.	/N135UT/N3797N
N327K	Falcon 900	3	Ford Motor Co. Dearborn, Mi.	N403FJ/F-WWFA
N328JK	Learjet	24B-212	Royal Oak Industries Inc. Atlanta, Ga.	N328TL/N291BC
N328K	Falcon 900	13	Ford Motor Co. Detroit, Mi.	N409FJ/F-WWFI
N328QS	Citation	650-0028	Executive Jet Sales, Columbus, Oh.	N148C
N329GA	Gulfstream 3	450	Gulfstream Aerospace Corp. Savannah, Ga.	/HZ-AFS/N329GA
N329J	JetStar	1001	Wfu Aug 82. Located Pacific Vocational Institute-Vancouver.	
N329K	Falcon 900	46	Ford Motor Co. Detroit, Mi.	N434FJ/F-WWFD
N330BC	Learjet	35A-432	J E R Chilton 111, Vail, Co.	N4445Y/F-GDCN
N330CC	Citation	500-0330	Interjet Inc. Addison, Tx.	(N82CF)//N330CC/(N5330J)
N330K	Falcon 900	50	Ford Motor Co. Dearborn, Mi.	N436FJ/F-WWFH
N330MC	Falcon 50	175	MCI Transcom Corp. Washington, DC.	/N334MC/N50FJ/N177FJ/F-WZHM
N330X	BAe 125/800A	8060	Texas Eastern Transmission Co. Houston, Tx.	N686CF/N364BA/G-5-511
N331DM	Diamond 1A	A042SA	Lombard Holdings Inc. NYC.	
N331DP	Learjet	23-067	W/o 18 Jan 90.	/N720UA/N703DC/N2ZA/N815LJ
N331DP	Learjet	23-059	Wfu. Parted out 6/87, N331DP transferred to 23-067.	N31DP/N364EJ
N331FP	Challenger 600S	1072	Florida Progress Corp. St Petersburg, Fl.	(N137FP)/N82A/C-GLXW
N331MC	Falcon 50	95	MCI Telecommunications/Finalco Inc. McClean, Va.	/N3950N/VR-CBL/F-WPXD
N331N	Learjet	31-022	Nibco Inc. Elkhart, In.	
N332MC	Falcon 900	78	MCI Transcon Corp. Washington, DC.	N456FJ/F-WWFH

| Regis-tration | Type | c/n | Owner / Operator | Previous identity |

Registration	Type	c/n	Owner / Operator	Previous identity
N332PC	Learjet	23-056	W/o 6 Jan 77.	N362EJ
N333AR	Gulfstream 2B	189	ARCO, Burbank, Ca.	/
N333AV	Falcon 20C	28	Cegep Edouard-Montpetit=CEM Corp. Cincinnati, Oh. C-GEAQ/N50CA/(N126JM) N280RC/YV-78CP/(JY-AEJ)/N573EJ/N10WA/N367EJ/N848F/F-WMKG	
N333AX	Gulfstream 2B	30	GECC, Danbury, Ct.	/N2607/N2601/N788S/N870GA
N333BG	Jet Commander	98	Ace Air Inc. Lafayette, La.	N301L/N482G/N101DE/N6DB/CF-WRN/N1121N
N333CG	Learjet	25D-262	Inn-Air Inc. Harvey, Il.	//N440F/N23HM
N333CJ	HS 125/3A-RA	25155	Cathryn Joy, Scottsdale, Az.	N999LF/(N411MF)/N466MP/N32F/G-AVXN/(G-5-12)
N333DP	HS 125/731	NA775	Doane Products Co. Wilmington, De.	N17HV/N7HV/N5V/N72BH
N333GA	Gulfstream 3	432	Gulfstream Aerospace Corp. Savannah, Ga.	
N333GB	BAC 1-11/401AK	076	HM Industries Inc. Newark, De.	VR-BHS/N5034
N333GM	Sabre-40	282-45	Commercial Aviation Enterprises, Boca Raton, Fl.	N255GM//N344UP/N747UP
N333M	HS 125/1A-522	25017	World Express Jet Charter/Tech Air Services, Naperville, Il.	N495G/N123JB N306MP/N3060F/N3060/G-ASSH
N333ME	HS 125/700A	NA0202	M J Aviation, San Francisco, Ca.	/N64688/G-BERP/G-5-19
N333MG	Challenger 601-3A	5035	Merv Griffin/Griffco Aviation Inc. Burbank, Ca.	/N606CC/C-G...
N333PC	HS 125/700A	NA0205	POLCO Inc. Landover, Md.	//C-GYYZ/(G-BEWV)/G-5-11
N333RL	Citation	650-0019	Russ Lyon Jr/Westcor Aviation, Scottsdale, Az.	/N30CJ/(N44BH)/(N1307D)
N333SV	Jet Commander	114	Jesus Christs Eternal Kingdom, Monroe, Ga.	N85MR/N10GR/N111ST/N448WT N442WT/4X-CPC/N4743E
N334	Westwind-Two	344	Galbreath Co. Columbus, Oh.	/4X-CTL
N334H	Citation	650-0071	Hillenbrand Industries Inc. Batesville, In.	(N1315B)
N334MD	Learjet	25D-334	Duncan Aircraft Sales, Venice, Fl.	//N57DL//N20RD
N334SP	Learjet	35A-334	Rainier Companies Inc. Seattle, Wa.	N350RB/N2815
N335EE	Learjet	35A-335	Cardal Inc. Dublin, Oh.	/N335NE/N335DJ/N15Y/N8YY/N155TD/N25MJ
N335H	Gulfstream 2TT	238	Halliburton Co. Dallas, Tx.	N831GA
N335K	Learjet	35A-381	Koch Industries Inc. Wichita, Ks.	N300CM/(N40TM)/N65DH/D-COKA
N335WJ	Falcon 20C	122	International Aviation Technical Services, Torrance, Ca.	N335WR/N779P N4342F/F-WNGL
N336MB	HS 125/731	25153	Basil Briggs Adventure Inc. Pontiac, Mi.	N731G/N30FD/N30F/G-AVXM
N336SV	Westwind-1124	336	Super Valu Stores Inc. Eden Prairie, Mn.	C-FOIL/4X-CTD/N245S
N337RE	Westwind-1124	210	Bardon Ltd. Dover, De. N59KC/N444MM/N38WW/N23AC/N662JB/N661CP/N69HM/N662JB 4X-CLH	
N338X	Learjet	24D-251	CECO Corp. Oakbrook Terrace, Il.	N333X
N339A	Gulfstream 3	339	Bank of America, Oakland, Ca.	N522SB/N302GA
N339H	Gulfstream 2	145	Halliburton Industries Corp. Duncan, Ok.	N871E/N871D/N894GA
N340DR	Westwind-1124	242	Donrey Inc. Las Vegas, Nv.	4X-CMN
N341AP	Sabre-65	465-40	Air Products & Chemicals Inc. Allentown, Pa.	
N341K	JetStar 2	5223	Kiewit Engineering Co/Midwest Aviation Inc. Omaha, Nb.	/N105G/N5549L
N341TC	B 727-22	19148	Tracinda Corp. Las Vegas, Nv.	N7084U
N342CC	Citation	550-0414	EAF/Westvaco Corp. NYC.	N12162
N342HM	Citation	650-0062	Southeastern Jet Corp. Fort Lauderdale, Fl.	N19FR/N388DA/C-GHGK/N626CC
N342K	Falcon 20C	101	Kiewit Engineering Co. Omaha, Nb.	N984F/F-WMKJ
N342QS	Citation	650-0042	Executive Jet Sales Inc. Columbus, Oh.	N142AB
N343K	Gulfstream 2B	9	Eastman Kodak Co. Rochester, NY.	//N209GA/(N115RS)/N320FE/C-FSBR
N343MG	Falcon 200	491	GPM Transport Inc. NYC. N491MB/VH-HPJ/VH-PDJ/N120FJ/N200FJ/N205FJ/F-WZZA	
N344A	Falcon 10	153	Archer Daniels Midland Co. Decatur Airport, Il.	N218FJ/F-WZGZ
N344DA	Jet Commander	12	C R Inc. Wilmington, De.	/N302AT//N711GW/N37BB/N777V/N613J/N8300
N344WC	Learjet	23-092	Bard Air Corp. Detroit, Mi.	/N105BJ/N422JR/N415LJ
N345AA	Gulfstream 2B	123	711 Air Corp. Teterboro, NJ.	/N345CP/N805CC
N345AP	Falcon 50	181	Air Products & Chemicals Inc. Allentown, Pa.	N181FJ/F-WWHA
N345DA	HS 125/3A	25116	Aerospace Trading International, Miami Lakes, Fl.	(N90SR)/N345DA//N136LK N93TC/G-ATZN
N345DM	Diamond 1A	A060SA	Venture Airways Inc. Orlando, Fl.	
N345GL	HS 125/400A	NA753	Richard Cranmer/GMA Sales Corp. West Des Moines, Ia.	/N840H/N400BH/N49BH
N345KB	Learjet	25D-345	KDC Co. Findlay, Oh.	N345EJ
N345MC	Learjet	25-046	McOCO Inc. Houston, Tx.	N33PT/N55KQ/N55KC/N964GA
N345N	Citation	501-0204	Munoco Co. El Dorado, Ar.	(N123HP)/N6784L
N345PA	Falcon 50	36	Bristol-Myers Squibb Co. NYC.	/N54FJ/F-WZHJ
N347CP	Citation	S550-0094	Princess Jet Corp-Zephyr Service, Burbank, Ca.	N594CC/(N1275D)
N347DA	Citation	501-0080	Donald L Allyn, Hanford, Ca.	N51CG//N51CC/N3145M
N347HS	Falcon 20F	347	Henry I Siegel Co Inc. NYC.	N298CK//N744CC/N4464F/F-WMKF

Registration	Type	c/n	Owner / Operator	Previous identity
N347K	Falcon 10	37	Midwest Aviation/Kiewit Engineering Co. Omaha, Ne.	N123TG/N123VV/N39515 C-GFCS/F-WJML
N347MD	Learjet	25D-347	Anthony Crane Rental, Beaumont, Tx.	/N25NM/D-CHIC/N347EJ
N348HM	Learjet	55-109	Herman Miller Inc. Zeeland, Mi.	
N348SJ	Westwind-Two	348	Anne H Bass, Fort Worth, Tx.	N348WW/4X-CTP
N349K	Falcon 50	17	Midwest Aviation Inc/Kiewit Engineering Co. Omaha, Nb.	N3456F/N4679T HB-IEB/TY-BBM/5A-DGI/F-WZHI
N349M	Jet Commander	23	Wfu.	N2100X
N349MC	Westwind-1124	224	Midland Aviation Co. Oklahoma City, Ok.	/N2756T/XA-KUG/N898SR/4X-CLV
N350AG	Learjet	25D-350	Sky Enterprises Inc. Nashville, Tn.	(N428CH)/N350AG
N350DM	Diamond 1A	A050SA	Icon International Inc. NYC.	/
N350EF	Learjet	35A-385	Executive Flight Inc. Wenatchie, Wa.	/N535MC
N350JF	Learjet	35A-219	CFS Flight Systems Inc. Coral Springs, Fl.	//N502G/VH-BJQ/N39416
N350M	Citation	501-0112	Murphy Oil USA Inc. El Dorado, Ar.	(N900LL)/N2649E
N350MD	Learjet	35A-277	Mike Donahoe Aviation Co. Phoenix, Az.	/XA-PUI/N127HC/N70CN/N723LL/N925GL
N350WB	Falcon 50	102	Wagner & Brown 11, Midland, Tx.	(N50WB)/N50BX/N103FJ/F-WZHO
N351AS	Learjet	35A-146	Albertsons Inc. Boise, Id.	N55AS
N351EF	Learjet	35A-125	Executive Flight Inc. Pangborn Memorial Airport, Wa.	N125GA/N111MZ/N777NQ N777MC/N3803G
N351GL	Learjet	35-001	Learjet Inc. Wichita, Ks. (experimental).	//N731GA
N351N	Learjet	23-054	Epps Air Service Inc. Hangar 1, Dekalb Peachtree, Ga.	N351NR/N351WC/N351WB CF-TEL
N351TC	Westwind-Two	351	Tele-Communications Inc/TCI Holdings Inc. Denver, Co.	N106WT/4X-CTS
N351WC	JetStar 2	5229	Williams Companies, Tulsa, Ok.	/N7NP/N4038M
N352MD	Learjet	24F-352	Maleco, Salem, Or.	/(N449JS)/N101US
N353CP	Falcon 20F	461	CITGO Petroleum Corp. Tulsa, Ok.	N747V/N469F/F-WMKG
N353WC	BAe 125/800A	NA0416	Williams Companies Inc. Tulsa, Ok.	/N561BA/G-5-600
N354ME	Learjet	35A-378	Bean Ball Co. Seattle, Wa.	/T-500/CX-BOI
N354WC	BAe 125/800A	NA0436	Williams Companies Inc. Tulsa, Ok.	/N590BA/G-5-633
N355CD	Sabre-60	306-85	Jet Aire Inc. Omaha, Ne.	N500RK//N217A/N65764
N355DB	Learjet	55-006	Alamo Jet Inc. Fort Myers, Fl.	N126EL/N212JP/N113EL
N355WC	BAe 125/800A	NA0450	Northwest Pipeline Corp. Salt Lake City, Ut.	N612BA/G-5-663
N355WW	Westwind-Two	355	ARMCO Inc. Middletown, Oh.	4X-CUI
N357CL	Falcon 200	484	M L Rabinowitz/U.S. West Business Resources, Los Angles, Ca.	N28U/N202FJ F-WPUV
N357H	Gulfstream 3	472	H J Heinz & Co. Pittsburgh, Pa.	/N808CC/N800CC/N806CC/N800CC/N348GA
N357MD	Diamond 1A	A091SA	Beautiful Nature Corp. Coral Gables, Fl.	/N357DM
N358LL	BAe 125/800A	8093	LPL Air Inc. Greenville, De.	N800S/N331SC/N533BA/G-5-559
N359V	Astra-1125	039	Delmarva Aircraft Inc. New Castle, De.	4X-C..
N360DA	Citation Eagle	500-0056	Richard J Ames, Burnsville, Mn.	C-GCTD//N500DB/N777JM/N556CC
N360HK	Westwind-1123	166	O K Aircraft Parts Inc. San Jose, Ca. (wfu ?).	C-GDOC/4X-CJP
N360MC	Citation	501-0036	Carrolls Aviation Inc. Warsaw, NC.	HI-493//N36CC/N406CJ/N36918
N360X	HS 125/700A	NA0230	Panhandle Eastern Pipeline Co. Kansas City, Mo.	G-5-13
N361DJ	Citation	550-0037	Sierra Citation Associates Inc. Menlo Park, Ca.	///N37HG/(N3268M)
N362CP	Citation	550-0403	Colonial Pipeline Co. Atlanta, Ga. (was 551-0058).	/N637EH/N101RL/N68027
N362DA	Sabre-40	282-90	Sabreliner Corp. Chesterfield, Mo.	//N155GM/N3831C/C-FNCG/N928R
N363BC	Learjet	24D-241	Lear Lease Corp. Wilmington, De.	N120J/HB-VCT
N364G	Gulfstream 4	1091	General Electric Co. NYC.	N467GA
N365DA	HS 125/400A	25271	Duncan Aircraft Sales, Venice, Fl.	N103CJ//N37516/EC-CMU/G-BABL/XX506 G-BABL/G-5-14
N365G	Gulfstream 4	1101	General Electric Co. White Plains, NY.	N404GA
N365N	Learjet	35A-300	ATC Air Inc. Lincoln, Ne.	/
N366AA	Learjet	25B-151	W/o 31 Aug 74.	
N366F	Gulfstream 4	1041	Figgie International, Richmond, Va.	/N433GA
N366G	Citation	650-0038	General Electric Co. Hangar E, Westchester Airport, NY.	
N367EG	Gulfstream 2	128	Gulfstream Aerospace Corp. Savannah, Ga.	N73M
N367F	Falcon 100	206	Figgie International, Cleveland, Oh.	N100FJ/N270FJ/F-W...
N367G	Citation	650-0053	General Electric Co. Hangar E, Westchester Airport, NY.	
N368BG	Learjet	35A-368	Eastern Executive Leasing Inc. High Point, NC.	//SE-DHE/N35FM
N368F	Falcon 100	220	Leco Corp. Dillon, SC.	N368F/N124FJ/F-WZGD
N368G	Citation	650-0057	General Electric Co. Hangar E, Westchester Airport, NY.	
N368MD	Westwind-Two	368	McBail Co/Ed Wes Inc. Alamo, Ca.	N28WW/4X-CUE
N368PU	Diamond 1A	A068SA	Purdue Research Foundation, W Lafayette, In.	/N368DM

Regis-tration	Type	c/n	Owner / Operator	Previous identity
N369AP	Gulfstream 2	14	Mar Flite Ltd Corp. Portland, Or.	/N217JD/N663B/N663P
N369CS	Gulfstream 2	2	Wesaire Inc. Morristown, NJ.	N801GA/N802GA
N369DA	Citation	550-0304	Harron Communication Corp. Frazer, Pa.	N208TC/N6888D
N369MJ	Learjet	25D-369	Aero Executive International, Scottsdale, Az.	N8566Z
N370GA	Gulfstream 3	494	Gulfstream Aerospace Corp. Savannah, Ga.	
N370RR	HS 125/700A	NA0213	Reynolds & Reynolds/Super Food Service Inc. Dayton, Oh.	/N370M/(G-BFGV)
N370TG	Citation	650-0070	Comdisco Aviation Inc. Rosemont, Il.	N370QS/N149C/(N1315A)
N371GA	Gulfstream 3	495	Gulfstream Aerospace Corp. Savannah, Ga.	
N372BG	Challenger 601	3034	Berwind Aviation Corp. Philadelphia, Pa.	N372BC/N374BC/C-GLXU
N372CM	Gulfstream 4	1049	Cordelia Scaife May, Pittsburgh, Pa.	N402GA
N372G	Challenger 601	3006	General Electric Co. NYC.	C-GLXY
N373G	Challenger 601	3009	General Electric Co. Cincinnati, Oh.	C-GLYO
N373LB	Gulfstream 2	13	Austin Jet Corp. Austin, Tx.	/N373LP/N2GP/5N-AMN/N98AM/N678RZ/N678RW
N373LP	Learjet	35A-220	Louisiana Pacific Corp. Hillsboro, Or.	N873LP/N220GH/N333RB/N79BH
N373LP	Gulfstream 3	310	Louisiana Pacific Corp. Hillsboro, Or.	N6513X/C-FYAG/N719A
N374G	Challenger 601	3015	General Electric Co. NYC.	C-G
N374GC	Citation	S550-0055	Graham Engineering/York Transportation & Leasing, York, Pa.	N374GS/N1271A
N375BK	Falcon 20F	236	Conaero Inc. Wilmington, De.	N375PK/C-FJES/F-WPXK/(N4416F)
N375G	Challenger 601	3019	General Electric Co. NYC.	C-G...
N375NM	Gulfstream 3	375	Arizona Executive Air Service, Burbank, Ca.	/VR-BOB/N955CP
N375PK	Challenger 600S	1018	Seagrams Distillers, London-UK.	/N198CC/N1812C/C-GLWR
N375SC	BAe 125/800A	NA0409	Steelcase Inc. Grand Rapids, Mi.	N800TR/N554BA/G-5-582
N376D	Sabre-60A	306-101	Salyer Farms Airport, Corcoran, Ca.	N68NR/N65791
N376SC	BAe 125/800A	NA0417	Steelcase Inc. Grand Rapids, Mi.	N800BA/N562BA/G-5-596
N377Q	Learjet	25D-257	1030 Corp. Durham, NC.	N377C/N700BJ
N378HC	Gulfstream 3	378	Hardesty Co/United States Aviation Co. Tulsa, Ok.	N955H/N343GA
N379XX	Gulfstream 3	394	Nexxus Products Inc. Santa Barbara, Ca. 'Jheri Reading'	N311GA/N1761P
N380AA	JetStar-8	5131	American Aviation Industries, Van Nuys, Ca.	//N212JW/N64C/N31RP/N30RP N7976S
N380CM	Diamond 1A	A080SA	Croft Metals Inc. McComb, Ms.	N380DM
N380TT	Gulfstream 3	437	Litton Industries Inc. Beverly Hills, Ca.	
N380X	HS 125/731	NA733	Panhandle Eastern Pipeline Co. Kansas City, Mo.	G-AXOB
N381AA	JetStar-731	4/5058	American Aviation Industries, Van Nuys, Ca.	/(N600DT)/N600TP/N600TT/N50AS N1500M/N100AL/N100A
N381DA	Jet Commander	118	Jack Sisemore, Angel Fire, NM.	N716BB/(N712GM)/N117GM/N438/N312S
N382AA	Fan Commander	56	Wheeler Ridge Aviation Inc. Bakersfield, Ca.	(N53AA)///N6550V
N382DA	HS 125/400A	NA744	Duncan Aircraft Sales, Venice, Fl.	//N575/N575DU/G-AXTW
N384DA	Citation	550-0048	Duncan Aircraft Sales, Lincoln, Ne.	N161BH/N534M/N3288M
N386G	Jet Commander	43	Cx USA 10/90 as wfu.	N121CS/N186G/N271E
N387PA	Astra-1125	025	Culbro Corp. NYC.	4X-CUH
N388WM	HS 125/1A	25052	Meinco Inc. Tulsa, Ok.	N812N/N812M/N816MC/N816M/G-ATIK
N389DA	HS 125/1A	25037	Duncan Aircraft Sales Inc. Venice, Fl.	//(N26WJ)//N26TL/N26T/N787X/D-CAFI G-ATFO
N389L	Citation	S550-0013	Libby Owens Ford Co. Toledo, Oh.	N277AL/(N518AS)
N391DA	HS 125/1A-522	25029	Duncan Aircraft Sales, Venice, Fl.	//N10122/G-ATAZ
N393U	Gulfstream 3	325	Unisys Corp. Mercer County Airport, Trenton, NJ.	/N89QA/N890A
N394U	Falcon 50	113	Unisys Corp. Mercer County Airport, Trenton, NJ.	/N186S/N108FJ/F-WZHB
N395SC	Citation	501-0031	Steiner Corp. Salt Lake City, Ut.	N36896
N396M	Citation	550-0362	Essex Group/United Technologies Corp. Hartford, Ct.	N12142/
N397F	Gulfstream 2	72	W/o 22 Feb 76.	
N398CC	Citation	550-0406	Rytag Inc. Pittsburgh, Pa.	(N1215A)
N399AZ	Learjet	35A-399	A Zanatti/International Airlines Holdings, Dover, De.	(N399DJ)/N540HP N37965
N399CB	Gulfstream 3	433	Citiflight Inc. NYC.	N325GA
N399CC	Gulfstream 4	1051	Citiflight Inc. New Castle, De.	N403GA
N399CF	Challenger 601-3A	5084	Citiflight Inc. New Castle, De.	C-G...
N399DM	Diamond 1A	A008SA	Marine Air Services, John Day, Or.	(N56SK)/N303DM
N399KL	Learjet	35A-362	Alabama River Pulp Co. Perdue Hill, Al.	/N888MV/N3794M
N399MJ	Diamond 1A	A039SA	Cencom Cable Assoc Inc. Chesterfield, Mo.	N139DM/C-GRDX/N328DM
N399RP	Diamond 1A	A020SA	Ring Power Corp. Jacksonville, Fl.	
N399SR	Sabre-60	306-33	Corporate Aviation International, Pittsburgh, Pa.	//N500RR/N78RR/(N660BW) N60JF/N711TW/N30TC/N3FC/XA-APD/XB-APD/N600B
N399SW	Challenger 601-3A	5009	Citiflight Inc. Teterboro, NJ.	C-G...

Registration	Type	c/n	Owner / Operator	Previous identity
N399W	Citation	650-0098	Williams Research Corp. Pontiac, Mi.	(N13189)
N399WW	Gulfstream 3	384	Canadair Challenger inc. Windsor, Ct.	/N1982C
N400A	Beechjet 400A	RK-3	Beech Aircraft Corp. Wichita, Ks.	
N400AJ	Learjet	25-038	Charter Airlines Inc. Las Vegas, Nv.	//N83GG/N444WS/N36MW/N738GL/HB-VBR EC-CKD/HB-VBR
N400CC	Gulfstream 2B	102	Wells Fargo & Co/Kaiserair, Van Nuys, Ca.	/N119CC/N210GA/N88AE/N854GA
N400CP	Jet Commander	30	W/o 21 Jan 71.	N401V
N400CT	Citation V	560-0104		N560CT
N400D	HS 125/400A	NA743	OK Aviation Inc. Monterey, Ca.	HP-1128P/HP-125JW//N125JW/XCUJH-TP108 TP-0206/XC-GOB/N9138/G-AXTV
N400DT	Citation	550-0095	Chambers Development Co. Pittsburgh, Pa.	//N26631
N400EP	Learjet	24XR-215	Charles McAdam Jr. Vero Beach, Fl.	(N57JR)/N29CA/N10EC/N201WL/N971GA
N400GA	Gulfstream 4	1001	Chrysler Financial Corp/Bill Cosby, Teterboro, NJ.	/N441GA/N17581
N400GK	Diamond 1	A019SA	DRD Aviation Inc. Purcell, Ok.	N319DM/N6PA/N9LP/N311DM
N400GN	BAe 125/800A	8059	Gannett Co Inc. Arlington, Va.	N363BA/G-5-506
N400GP	HS 125/731	NA762	Citation Builders, San Leandro, Ca.	N523M/N57BH
N400J	Gulfstream 3	493	Johnson & Johnson, West Trenton, NJ.	N322GA
N400JD	Citation	650-0035	Deere & Co. Moline, Il.	/N650MD
N400JE	Learjet	35A-120	Robert F Barber, Murfreesboro, Tn.	//(N400RV)/N400JE
N400JS	Learjet	25XR-235	Jet South/400JS Inc. Fort Myers, Fl.	N400PC
N400K	Gulfstream 3	370	Exxon Corp. Dallas, Tx.	N200A/N100A/N319GA
N400KC	HS 125/731	NA728	Kimberly Clark Corp. Neenah, Wi.	N24CH/G-AXJD
N400KV	Sabre-65	465-69	Kirke van Orsdel Inc/KVI Aviation Inc. Des Moines, Ia.	(N31BC)/N33BC
N400LH	Gulfstream 3	401	De Luxe Flight Operations, Minneapolis, Mn.	/N717/N352GA
N400LX	Citation	501-0255	Sacramento Aviation Inc. Sacramento, Ca.	G-SBEC/N707WF/N501MR/N661TW N661TV
N400M	JetStar-6	5008	W/o 27 Dec 72.	N500Z/N9281M
N400M	Gulfstream 2	132	Eckert Cold Storage Co. Manteca, Ca.	//N873GA
N400NR	Sabre-75A	380-41	JHM Leasing Corp. Pittsfield, Ma.	N400N/N33NT/N2113J
N400NW	BAe 125/800A	8012	Farley Industries/NWT Aircraft Co. Chicago, Il.	N800TT/G-5-18
N400PC	Citation	501-0055	Refreshment Services Inc. Springfield, Il.	/N552MD/N98682
N400PH	HS 125/400A	25180	W/o 5 Dec 87.	N888CR/N196KQ/N196KC/G-AWPF
N400RB	Learjet	35-011	Badgett Rogers Sr. Madisonville, Ky.	N3816G
N400RG	B 727-22	19149	EAF/Reliance Insurance Co. Philadelphia, Pa.	N7085U
N400RS	Learjet	24-138	Stern Air Inc. Dallas, Tx.	N45JF/(N106CA)/N575G/N808D/N808DP/N37P
N400TF	Westwind-1124	279	Tyson Foods Inc. Fayetteville, Ar.	N952HF/N230JK/N230TL/N885DR/N1126G 4X-CNY
N400TX	Citation	550-0408	Textron Financial Corp. Augusta, Ga.	/N1216H
N400UP	Gulfstream 4	1054	Union Pacific Aviation Co. Allentown, Pa.	N426GA
N401AC	Learjet	25B-140	Midlantic Jet Charters Inc. Cardiff, NJ.	/N68TJ//N42GX/N42G
N401AJ	Learjet	25B-171	Travel Lear Charter Service Inc. Oklahoma City, Ok.	/N888LR/N42DG///N55PT N55MF/N1DD/OY-ASP/N1DD/I-ELEN
N401DE	Jet Commander	92	Cx USA 3/89 as wfu.	N33PS/N524X/N5420
N401M	Gulfstream 2	158	BLC Corp. San Mateo, Ca.	N76QS/N76CS
N401MM	Gulfstream 4	1130	Martin Marietta Corp. Brthesda, Md.	N436GA
N401MS	Sabre-60	306-17	Jacksonville Jet Center Inc. Jacksonville, Fl.	//N13SL/N2UR/N2UP/N988R (D-COUP)/N4727N
N401SK	BAC 1-11/401AK	073	Continental Aircraft Marketing, Rancho Murieta, Ca.	//N5LC/N111FL/N5031
N401TC	Beechjet 400A	RK-21		
N402ST	Citation	550-0068	Shiloh Corp. Mansfield, Oh.	/N558CB/N558CC/N3319M
N403M	Jet Commander	132	W/o 16 Dec 69.	N200M
N403W	Westwind-1124	403	Louisiana Power & Light Co. New Orleans, La.	4X-CUH
N404BB	Learjet	35A-404	Bruce Brooks, Sacramento, Ca.	N500JS
N404CB	HS 125/700A	NA0262	Comair Inc. West Chester, Pa.	/N3234S/C-GKRS/(N130BL)/G-5-14
N404CC	Gulfstream 4	1098	Wilmar Ltd. Oakland, Ca.	N403GA
N404CE	HS 125/700A	NA0275	Bellsouth Services Inc. Atlanta, Ga.	/N664JB/N661JB/N125V/G-5-13
N404E	Citation	550-0097	Services Group of America III, Seattle, Wa.	/N404G/N26634
N404F	Falcon 900	41	WCF Corp. Detroit, Mi.	N430FJ/F-WWFI
N404G	Citation	S550-0068	P H Glatfelter Co. York, Pa.	N1272Z
N404M	Gulfstream 4	1110	Bristol Myers Squibb Co. NYC.	/N415GA
N404MA	Citation	500-0126	Squirrel UK Inc. Wilmington, De.	D-IDWH/HB-VDM/(N626CC)
N404MM	Gulfstream 3	404	Martin Marietta Corp. Bethesda, Md.	N404M/N355GA
N404R	Falcon 50	154	Bellsouth Services Inc. Atlanta, Ga.	N920K/N320K/N139FJ/F-WZHA

Registration	Type	c/n	Owner / Operator	Previous identity
N404SB	Citation	550-0426	Bellsouth Services, Atlanta, Ga.	N1218F
N404W	Westwind-Two	404	Peabody Coal Co/Westlease Aircraft Inc. NYC.	4X-CUG/4X-CJR
N405MM	Gulfstream 2	220	Martin Marietta Corp. Bethesda, Md.	N307M/N404M/N805GA
N406MM	Citation	650-0102	Martin Marietta Corp. Bethesda, Md.	(N406M)/(N1319X)
N407MM	Citation	650-0103	Martin Marietta Corp. Bethesda, Md.	(N407M)/(N13194)
N407W	Westwind-Two	407	Lorimar Charter Inc. Culver City, Ca.	
N408CC	Sabre-40	282-13	Coastal Corp/ANR Coal Co. Roanoke, Va.	N408CS/N408S/N899TG/N6367C
N408GA	Gulfstream 4	1142		
N408TR	Sabre-40	282-4	Lubrizol Corp. Ypsilanti, Mi.	N111MS/N75JD/N14M
N408W	Westwind-1124	408	American Finance Group Inc. Boston, Ma.	4X-CUB
N409AC	Citation	501-0284	Continental Aircraft Marketing, Rancho Murieta, Ca.	//N115K/N2131A
N409ER	Falcon 50	8	Ed J DeBartolo Corp. Youngstown, Oh.	N50PG/N50FE/F-WZHC
N409MA	Gulfstream 2	83	Victory Management Group/Louie J Russell III, Metairie, La.	(N48MS)/N409M N409M/N404M
N409WT	Jet Commander	3	YNR Aviation Ltd. Jefferson, SD.	N400WT/N316E/N316/N612JC
N410GA	Gulfstream 4	1143		
N410M	Gulfstream 4	1115	Bristol Myers Squibb Co. NYC.	N430GA
N410RD	Learjet	35A-647	SMI Inc. Norfolk, Va.	
N410WW	Falcon 50	76	Zeno Air Inc/Wm Wrigley Jr Co. Chicago, Il.	/N85MD/N84FJ/F-WZHB
N411BW	Diamond Two	A1008SA	Tom Benson Chevway Rental & Leasing, Metairie, La.	
N411MB	Citation	650-0195		N26233
N411SP	Learjet	24B-216	Radcliff Co. Cincinnati, Oh.	N711DB/N723LL/N212LF
N411WW	Gulfstream 2B	257	Zeno Air Inc/Wrigley Enterprises Inc. Chicago, Il.	/N872E/N822GA
N412SP	Learjet	25B-174	Jet Air Inc. Cincinnati, Oh.	N410SP/N74G
N414CB	Citation	501-0179	Robert V Jones Corp. Las Vegas, Nv. (status ?).	N589CJ/(N6781D)
N414RF	HS 125/700A	NA0244	Fisher Group Inc. Wilmington, De.	N230DP/N1183/N1103/N130BG/G-5-18
N415EL	Westwind-Two	415	Marshall Industries, El Monte, Ca.	N105BE/N415EL/4X-CUS
N415PT	BAe 125/800A	8016	Pacific Telesis Group, Oakland, Ca.	/F-GESL/G-5-18
N415SH	Gulfstream 4	1125	Eastern Aviation Inc. Honolulu, Hi.	N432GA
N416CC	Citation	550-0416	Hughes Aircraft Co. Van Nuys, Ca.	N12167
N416W	Westwind-1124	416	Maurice Connell, Naples, Fl.	4X-CUD
N417GA	Gulfstream 4	1146		
N417TF	HS 125/731	25038	Towers Financial Corp. NYC.	N301CK/N27RC//(N15UB)/N66KC/N125G/N926G/G-ATCP
N418R	Citation	501-0244	Skaggs A B/ASC Inc. Wilmington, De.	N701VF/(N711VF)/N650CJ/N2626J
N420CC	Citation	S550-0023	Laurance Rockefeller/Wayfarer Ketch, White Plains, NY.	
N420G	JetStar-6	5063	Don Larson Aviation Inc. Bloomington, Mn.	//N420A/N420L/N9228R
N420J	Falcon 20F	369	Executive Flight Management/JM Aviation Inc. Wilmington, De.	N509WP/N415JW N20SR/N1037F/F-WRQP
N420PC	Learjet	35A-132	Refreshment Services Inc. Springfield, Il.	/N431M
N420TX	Challenger 600S	1027	Textron Inc. Providence, RI.	/N420L/C-GLXK
N420W	Westwind-Two	420	Associates Commercial Corp.	4X-CUH
N421SZ	HS 125/700A	NA0301	Eagle USA Inc/Flight Service Inc. Westport, Ct.	/N744DC/N713RL//N711RL N700HB/G-5-13
N421TX	Citation	550-0213	AVCO Corp. Providence, RI.	N420P/N6802X
N422L	Falcon 200	498	Otter Corp. Kirkland, Wa.	/N422D/N200ET/N215FJ/F-WPUV
N422X	HS 125/700A	NA0253	JWP Aircraft Inc. Purchase, NY.	//(N831CJ)//N422X/G-5-19
N423D	Citation	550-0158	Fieldcrest Cannon Inc. Eden, NC.	/(N662AA)/N88738
N424DA	Citation	500-0029	Duncan Aircraft Sales, Venice, Fl.	/C-GDWN//N31ST/N529CC/N506CC
N424GA	Gulfstream 4	1004	Digital Equipment Corp. Maynard, Ma.	
N424W	Westwind-Two	424	Ingersoll Publications Co. Princeton, NJ.	4X-CUJ
N425A	Gulfstream 2	39	Meridian Oil Inc. Houston, Tx.	(N12BN)/N425A/(N124BN)/N401HR/N8000/N80Q
N425FD	HS 125/731	25079	Crown K Leasing & Sales Inc. Delray Beach, Fl.	/N425DC/N40DC/N448DC/N440DC G-ATLL
N425JF	Falcon 20C	51	Franks Petroleum Inc. Shreveport, La.	N218US/N880P/N880F/F-WMKJ
N425M	Learjet	35A-281	GEICO Corp. Washington, DC.	/N80WG
N425SP	Gulfstream 3	425	Security Pacific National Bank, Los Angeles, Ca.	//N344GA
N425WA	Westwind-Two	425	PLM International Inc. San Francisco, Ca.	4X-CUK
N426MD	Beechjet 400	RJ-26	Mike Donahoe Aviation Co. Phoenix, Az.	N388DA/(N90SR)/N88WG/N3026U
N426PS	Learjet	24-148	Phoenix Air Group Inc. Cartersville Airport, Ga.	(N47NR)/N426PS/N8482B HB-VDH/N133TW/N80CB/N406L
N427DA	HS 125/731	NA745	Duncan Aircraft Sales, Venice, Fl.	/N125AP/N125AR/N41BH/G-AXYE
N427GA	Gulfstream 4	1148		

Registration	Type	c/n	Owner / Operator	Previous identity
N428DA	JetStar-6	5048	Owners Jet Service Ltd. Las Vegas, Nv.	N500WZ/N500WN//N98MD/N98KR/N40NC N40N/N4N
N428JX	Learjet	25B-103	Wfu as parted out following accident 7/75.	
N428W	Westwind-Two	428	Sunrise Co. Palm Desert, Ca.	4X-CUO
N429DA	HS 125/1B-S522	25090	Duncan Aircraft Sales, Venice, Fl.	N102TW//G-AWYE/HB-VAT
N429GA	Gulfstream 4	1128		
N429SA	Gulfstream 3	429	United Services Automobile Association, San Antonio, Tx.	N323GA
N430MB	Sabre-40A	282-113	Leonard Fritz, Romulus, Mi.	N30AF/N40BT/N40SC/N8311N
N430SA	Gulfstream 2	92	USAA-United Services Auto Association, San Antonio, Tx.	N40SA/N994JD N114HC/N300U/N300L/N884GA
N431CB	Citation	550-0369	C R Bard Inc. Murrayhill, NJ.	N324CC/N1218Y
N431CW	Learjet	35A-431	High Energy Inc. Camden, De.	/N34FD/YV-433CP/N1088A
N432EJ	Learjet	23-028A	W/o 25 Oct 67.	N803LJ
N433WW	Westwind-Two	433	PLM International/U.S. Cement Corp.	4X-CUH
N434AN	JetStar-731	34/5050	Anstar Aviation Inc. Severna Park, Md.	HZ-THZ/N141TC/N208L/N207L
N434EJ	Learjet	23-046	W/o 9 May 70.	
N434H	Citation	650-0123	Hillenbrand Investment Advisors, Wilmington, De.	N624CC/(N1322Y)
N435GA	Gulfstream 4	1135	Earth Star Inc/Walt Disney Co. Burbank, Ca.	
N435T	Falcon 20F-5	357	Chicago Tribune, Chicago, Il.	N4469F/F-WMKI
N435U	Gulfstream 3	435	United Technologies Cortran Inc. East Hartford, Ct.	/HB-ITS/N17581
N436MP	Falcon 20F	436	Mosinee Paper Corp. Mosinee, Wi.	/N181CB/N434F/F-WJMN
N437GA	Gulfstream 4	1131	Coca Cola Co. Atlanta, Ga.	
N437WW	Westwind-Two	437	Digital Equipment Corp. Maynard, Ma.	4X-CUF
N438DM	Learjet	25D-250	CVG Aviation Inc. Cincinnati, Oh.	/N30LM
N439H	Citation	650-0005	Honeywell Inc. Phoenix, Az.	/N137S
N439WW	Westwind-Two	439	Commerce Leasing Co. Norcross, Ga.	4X-CUG
N440DM	Learjet	25D-348	CVG Aviation Inc. Cincinnati, Oh.	N37949
N440DR	B 727-77	19253	Donrey Media Group, Las Vegas, Nv.	N111EK/VR-CKL/N111EK/N110AC/VH-RMR
N440DS	Beechjet 400A	RK-8		
N440GA	Gulfstream 4	1002	Connecticut National Bank, Hartford, Ct.	
N440MC	Learjet	35A-495	McClane Company Inc. Temple, Tx.	
N440RM	JetStar-6	5016	McKay Oil Corp. Roswell, NM.	N712GW//N4258P/HZ-AFS/HZ-AFS/N20TF/N2222R N9210R
N440TX	Citation	550-0355	Textron Financial Corp. Fort Worth, Tx.	N125CJ/N122CG/(N1216Z)
N440WW	Westwind-Two	440	UB (Food Holdings) US Inc. Elmhurst, Il.	4X-CUJ
N441JT	Citation	501-0199	Moore Mill & Lumber Co. Bandon, Or.	N501MM/N6782X
N441PC	Learjet	35A-441	Allmetal Inc. Itasca, Il.	/TC-MEK/N551WC
N442DM	Learjet	35A-405	CVG Aviation Inc. Cincinnati, Oh.	/N35FS/N35AS/(N181GL)/N41MJ
N442GA	Gulfstream 4	1132	Jetstar Enterprises (USA) Inc. Wilmington, De.	
N442JT	Learjet	35A-021	Thornton Oil Corp. Louisville, Ky.	/N33TS/N91CH/N101GP
N442NE	Learjet	35A-442	W/o 26 Jul 88.	/N35BK/N3799C/N40149
N442WT	Sabre-65	465-45	Wilson Trailer Co. Sioux City, Ia.	
N444AQ	Learjet	24B-208	John Hunter/Sani-Fresh Internatioinal, San Antonio, Tx.	N444AG/N32MJ N444AG/N42HC/N72335/D-ILDE
N444FJ	Falcon 20E	284	Fletcher Jones Management Group, Las Vegas, Nv.	/N98RH//N284JJ/N132JA N4437F/F-WPXM
N444MA	Sabre-60	306-102	Minnsota Jet/Cold Spring Granite Co. Cold Spring, Mn.	N555AE/N108G/N65792
N444MK	Learjet	25D-252	Milam International Inc. Englewood, Co. 'Dream Chaser'	/N44FH/N1468B
N444MW	Citation	501-0034	McWane Inc. Birmingham, Al.	N36911
N444PE	HS 125/F600A	6001	P&E Properties Inc. NYC.	N82PP/N82RP/N711AG/G-BEWW/N711AG/N82BH/G-AZUF
N444SC	Falcon 20F	324	Southern Conference of Teamsters, Hallandale, Fl.	N4456F/F-WMKF
N444TG	Learjet	35A-469	Adrian J Scribante=AJS Leasing Co. Laurel, Mt.	N660SA
N444WC	Learjet	23-047	Baltazar A Benavides, Houston, Tx.	/N9260A/YV-15CP/YV-E-GPA/N347J/N2503L
N444WW	Learjet	25D-283	Rockwell Ditzler Assocs Inc. Pittsburgh, Pa.	/N312GK/N45826/XC-DAA/N404144
N445	Jet Commander	37	Wfu.	N723JB/N123JB/N967L
N445A	Westwind-1124	362	ARMCO Inc. Middletown, Oh.	4X-CUP
N445BL	Westwind-1124	382	PGA Tour Investments Inc. St Augustine, Fl.	/N999BL/N410NA//N900BF/4X-CUP
N446GA	Gulfstream 4	1152	3M Co. St Paul, Mn.	
N446U	Gulfstream 3	446	United Technologies Corp. E. Hartford, Ct.	N309GA
N447CC	Beechjet 400	RJ-38	Circus Circus Enterprises Inc. Las Vegas, Nv.	N147CC/N3238K
N448DC	HS 125/3A	25078	Video Tonight Inc. Tulsa, Ok.	N40DC/G-ATLK
N448GA	Gulfstream 4	1153	AREPO Corp. Westchester County Airport, NY.	
N448GG	Learjet	23-057	Jack Sharp, Prairie Village, Ks.	N448GC

Registration	Type	c/n	Owner / Operator	Previous identity
N448WG	Learjet	35A-472	CBC Sales Inc. Savoy, Il.	/N448WC/N448GC
N449ML	Challenger 601-3A	5022	WFC Air Inc. NYC.	C-GLYK
N450BM	Astra-1125	011	United States Surgical Corp. Norwalk, Ct.	N450PM/4X-CUK
N450K	Falcon 50	186	Kimball International Transit Inc. Jasper, In.	N278FJ/F-WWHH
N450KK	Learjet	35A-450	K K Associates, Columbus, Oh.	
N450PC	Diamond 1A	A024SA	Price Aviation Inc. La Jolla, Ca.	N95TJ/N320CH/N316DM
N450SC	Learjet	25B-127	Sarasota Jet Center Inc. Sarasota, Fl.	/N450/(N42BJ)/N83JM/N93CE/N93C
N451DP	Falcon 20F	249	Dad's Products Co. Meadville, Pa.	N11AK/N4421F/F-WJMM/N777JF
N452SM	BAe 125/800A	NA0424	Service Merchandise/SMC Aviation Inc. Salem, NH.	/N569BA/G-5-609
N454AC	Citation	501-0015	General Business Enterprises, Nashua, NH.	N4446P/XA-MAL/N18328/N1823B N36862
N454LJ	Learjet	24B-226	J & R Investments Inc. Wichita, Ks.	
N454RN	Learjet	24-121	W/o 26 Feb 73.	N454GL/N454LJ
N455JA	Learjet	24XR-300	W/o 20 Aug 85.	N300EJ
N455S	Westwind-1124	367	Ray Thompson, Kalispell, Mt.	N511CC/N446A/4X-CUD
N456CE	Citation	501-0224	Charles B Gillespie Jr. Midland, Tx.	N630CE/N2611Y
N456CG	Learjet	25D-343	Crisp Realty Inc. Marion, Il.	N3797L
N456FB	Citation V	560-0009	B J & R B Lewis/All Star Charter Service, Pomona, Ca.	(N12160)
N456JA	Learjet	24XR-265	W/o 24 Oct 85.	N32WL/N2WL
N456JP	Sabre-40	282-32	Turbines Inc. Terre Haute, In.	N8GA/N40WP/N40SL/N711UC/N100HC/N100Y
N456R	Citation	501-0292	Merrill Bean Chevrolet Inc. Dover, De. (was 500-0383).	YV-2295P/YV-O-MTC-2 N3180M
N456SW	Gulfstream 3	337	Sentry Insurance-A Mutual Co. Stevens Point, Wi.	
N457CA	Citation	500-0131	Grancan Inc. Coral Gables, Fl.	(N725DM)/N745DM/N1045T/D-IDAU
N457F	Falcon 20F	449	Southern Company Services Inc. Atlanta, Ga.	F-WLCT
N457H	Gulfstream 3	457	H J Heinz & Co. Pittsburgh, Pa.	N337GA
N458CC	Citation	550-0458	Rodney Robertson/Del Rio Flying Service. Del Rio, Tx.	(N458DS)/N458CC N1250P
N458HW	Citation	551-0060	Hank Williams Jr. Enterprises, Paris, Tn.	N46SD/N6805T
N458J	Learjet	25XR-106	New Creations Inc. Columbus, Oh.	N458JA/N974JD/N10FL/N10NP
N458N	Citation	550-0061	Mozark Productions, Burbank, Ca.	/N456N/(N26614)
N458SW	Falcon 20C	68	Sentry Insurance & Mutual Co. Stevens Point, Wi.	N577S/N892F/F-WMKJ
N460MC	Falcon 20C	105	Cx USA 3/89 as wfu.	N97FJ/N77GR/N243K/N986F/F-WNGL
N461GT	Gulfstream 3	411	Airmont Ltd. Sparks, Nv.	N966H/N314GA
N462FJ	Falcon 900	87	Deerport Aviation Corp. Dover, De.	F-WWFA
N463C	Citation	550-0258	Firebond Corp. Minden, La.	/N550CM/(N550DD)/N172CB/N6861S
N463LJ	Learjet	25-001	Wfu. Used in construction of s/n 25-002.	
N464CL	Learjet	24A-096	Nevada Aircraft Leasing, Las Vegas, Nv.	N1972L/N33BK/N527ER/N1967W/N421LJ
N464EC	Westwind-Two	305	TRT Aeronautical Inc. Corpus Christi, Tx.	4X-CQY
N464FJ	Falcon 900	95		F-WWFO
N465FJ	Falcon 900	98		F-WWFM
N465NW	Learjet	35A-465	Norfolk Southern Corp. Norfolk, Va.	/
N466FJ	Falcon 900	101		F-W...
N467H	Sabre-40	282-3	Hughes Aircraft Co. Culver City, Ca.	(N57QR)/N570R
N469JR	HS 125/700A	NA0321	Daniel Davis/James River Corp. NYC.	/N710BL/G-5-18
N469PW	Citation	500-0302	Kindercare, Montgomery, Al.	/N302CE/N5302J
N471SP	Challenger 600S	1083	Scott Paper Co. Philadelphia, Pa.	/N47ES/C-GLXD
N471TM	Westwind-1124	370	Aerodynamics Inc/Team Management Inc. Grand Blanc, Mi.	/N641FG/4X-CUG
N472SP	JetStar-731	3/5078	Scott Paper Co. Philadelphia, Pa.	N7105/N711Z
N474L	Citation	S550-0107	Ladish Malting Co. Milwaukee, Wi.	N1291E
N476VC	Learjet	35A-476	Corporate Funding Inc. Grand Rapids, Mi.	
N477X	Sabre-60	306-78	Dillon Companies Inc. Hutchinson, Ks.	N140JA/C-GRRS/N65752
N479CC	Citation	501-0097	Faison & Associates Inc. Charlotte, NC.	N3198M
N480CC	Citation	S550-0129	Crounse Corp. Paducah, Ky.	N87TH/N1293X
N480LR	HFB 320	1054	cx USA 1/87 as wfu.	N896HJ/D-CORU
N481DH	Jet Commander-B	139	Praegitzer Industries, Dallas, Or.	N188G/I-ARNT/N8535/4X-CPF/N5047E
N481FM	Learjet	35A-218	sale, Dover, De.	//N256TW
N482CP	Learjet	25D-331	Carl Patrick, Columbus, Ga. .	N462B/(N422B)
N482DM	Diamond 1A	A088SA	Mercantile Trust Co. St Louis, Mo.	
N482HC	Sabre-40	282-28	Northwest Jet Charter Inc. Houston, Tx.	/N40CD/N197DA/N27DA/N524AG/N524AC N6565K/N6565A/N6382C
N482SG	Learjet	35A-493	Snyder Leasing Co. Wilmington, NC.	N8564U
N482U	Learjet	5A-482	W/o 14 Feb 83.	

Registration	Type	c/n	Owner / Operator	Previous identity
N483G	Citation	550-0295	Avtex Fibers Inc/GECC, Cherry Hill, NJ.	N68876
N484KA	Citation Eagle	500-0387	Kawneer Co. Norcross, Ga.	N3206M
N485DM	Diamond 1A	A085SA	Nightingale Corp. NYC.	I-TORA//N485DM
N485S	Learjet	35A-485	Kenneth Scholz Aviation Inc. Lubbock, Tx.	
N486DM	Diamond 1A	A086SA	Florida Rock Industries Inc. Jacksonville, Fl.	
N486LM	HS 125/731	NA746	Orion Aircraft Sales Inc. Van Nuys, Ca.	C-FBNK/N42BH
N488EC	JetStar-731	48/5061	Flying Eagle Inc/Finch Air, Tortola, BVI.	N488MR/(N888WW)/N123GA/N161GS N152GS/N67GT/N47BA/N506D/N506T/N9226R
N488SB	Gulfstream 3	487	Stockwood V Inc. Morristown, NJ.	/N90005/N377GA/TC-GAP/N324GA
N490BC	Learjet	35A-364	BASF Corp. Williamsburg, Va.	/N950CS/N981TH/(N65TA)/N3794Z
N490CC	Citation	550-0490	Tanker Holding Co. Houston, Tx. (was 551-0490)	N1254C
N490ST	BAC 1-11/212AR	083	Calcutta Aircraft Leasing Inc. Bloomington, In.	N70611/VR-CBZ/N502T
N491BT	Citation	500-0102	IBT=Industrial Bearing & Transmissions, Shawnee Mission, Ks.	/N400K/N800PL (N602CC)
N491JB	Citation	650-0182	Cessna Aircraft Corp. Wichita, Ks.	N682CC/N26105
N491N	Citation	550-0329	Indium Aviation Inc. NYC.	N6800C
N492ST	Citation	550-0193	Calcutta Aircraft Leasing Inc. Bloomington, In.	N2160N/XC-FOO/(N47RP) N6802T
N494G	Citation	500-0147	Gunnell Aviation Inc. Santa Monica, Ca.	N404G
N496SW	Learjet	35A-496	Southwire Corp. Carrollton, Ga.	N856RR/N8564K
N500	HS 125/700A	NA0277	Indianapolis Motor Speedway Corp. Indianapolis, In.	N824K/N324K/N125AF G-5-16
N500AD	Citation	500-0006	Honda R & D North America Inc. Torrance, Ca.	/(N500AH)/N500AD/N506SR N506MX/N500MX/N506TF/N506CC/OE-FGP/N506CC
N500AE	Citation	550-0390	Great Northern Aircraft Inc. Wilmington, De. (was 551-0047).	/N58CG/N6805T
N500AF	Falcon 50	166	American Family Corp. Columbus, Ga.	N165FJ/F-WZHE
N500AG	Jetstar-731	29/5119	A G Spanos Construction Co. Stockton, Ca.	N508TA/N508T/N11HM/N7964S
N500AL	Gulfstream 3	416	Abbott Laboratories, Abbott Park, Il.	/N312GA
N500AX	Westwind-Two	359	AVX Corp. Mytrle Beach, SC.	N500RR/N86RR/N8JL/4X-CUM
N500BF	Learjet	23-010	Wfu.	N400BF/N29BF/N333BF/N2920C/N292BC/N805LJ
N500BL	Falcon 50	66	Brunner & Lay Inc. Asheville, NC.	(PH-SDL)/F-WZHF
N500CC	Citation	669	Citation 500 prototype. Ff 15 Sep 69. Wfu 10/76.	
N500CM	Citation	650-0111	Cargill Inc. Minneapolis, Mn.	(N13204)
N500CP	Citation	500-0087	Business Jet Partnership, Columbus, Oh.	N700RY//N85AT/(N64792)/N85AT N587CC
N500CV	Citation	500-0082	Business Jet Partnership, Columbus, Oh.	///N911JD//N103JA/N4434W/HB-VGD EC-CCY/N582CC
N500CX	Citation	500-0300	Cx USA 6/90 as w/o as OE-FAP Greece 6 Oct 84.	/OE-FAP/N5300J
N500DD	Learjet	35A-351	Uno Leasing Corp. Joliet, Il.	/N500RP
N500DE	Falcon 10	64	Diversified Energies Inc. Minneapolis, Mn.	N721DP/N100BG/N148FJ/F-WLCT
N500DL	Learjet	25-027	TAG Aviation Inc. Miami Springs, Fl.	EC-EBM/N835WB/(N835GM)/N35WB/N423RD N7000G
N500E	Gulfstream 3	372	Exxon Corp. Dallas, Tx.	N200A/N320GA
N500EF	Learjet	35A-272	Fittipaldi USA Inc. Miami, Fl.	//N272HS/N39398
N500EW	Falcon 20C	21	Corporate Aircraft Services, Aspen, Co.	(N500NU)/N370/N3444G/N843F/F-WMKI
N500EX	Learjet	35A-591	ConAgra Inc. Omaha, Ne.	//N71626
N500FC	HS 125/700A	NA0207	First City Texas Trans Inc. Houston, Tx.	/N255TT/(N255QT)/N255CT/G-BFAJ G-5-13
N500FE	Falcon 20D	163	Presidential Aircraft Sales Inc. Fort Lauderdale, Fl.	//(N500HD)/N4366F F-WNGM
N500FF	Falcon 10	58	JHD Aircraft Sales Co/Dobbs House, Memphis, Tn.	(F-GHJL)//N500FF/N458A N58AS/N76FJ/N143FJ/F-WJMM
N500FK	Citation V	560-0047	Keeley Granite-RSA/International Jet Inc. NYC.	N2666A
N500FM	Learjet	23-088	Connie Kalitta Services Inc. Lakeview, Or.	N48AS/N804JA/N11JK/N616PS N816LJ
N500GA	Citation	501-0260	Griffin Aircraft Industries, Cold Spring, Ky.	N224RP//N2613C
N500GS	Challenger 601-3A	5045	General Signal Corp. White Plains, NY.	N616CC/C-FFSO/C-G...
N500HG	Learjet	35A-238	L J Investments Inc. Wilmington, De.	N500CG/N248DA/ZS-INS/3D-ACZ/ZS-INS N8OHK/N844GL
N500J	Gulfstream 2	60	W/o 26 Sep 76.	N892GA
N500J	Westwind-Two	303	Johnson & Johnson, West Trenton, NJ.	4X-CQW
N500JA	Learjet	25-007	Malley Trading Co. Fort Lee, NJ.	N25NM/N7TJ/N551MB/N551MD
N500JJ	B 707-138B	17699	Wfu. Scrapped at Paris-Le Bourget 7/83.	G-AVZZ/VH-EBD

Regis-tration	Type	c/n	Owner / Operator	Previous identity
N500JR	Jet Commander	65	W/o 26 Sep 66.	
N500JS	Learjet	25-020	Jet South Inc. Fort Myers, Fl.	/N900CJ//N900JD/N113AK/(N90TC)/N941GA/N215Z N30TT
N500JW	Learjet	23-005	cx USA 8/87 as wfu.	N15BE/N721GB/N721HW/N994SA/N570FT/N232R
N500JW	Learjet	55-043	Golden State Foods/PHD Penske Corp. San Diego, Ca.	N785B/N5543G
N500K	Citation	501-0127	H & L Tooth Co. Montebello, Ca.	N2649H
N500KE	Westwind-1124	360	Kraco Enterprises Inc. Compton, Ca.	N816S/N816ST/N816S/4X-CUN
N500KK	Learjet	35A-211	Lincoln National Life Insurance Co. Fort Wayne, In.	/N600LC/N15MJ/D-CATY N1461B
N500LE	Citation V	560-0052	Gary C Comer, Chicago, Il.	N2680D
N500LG	Learjet	28-005	Performance Aircraft Leasing Inc. Wilmington, De.	/N8LL/(N31WT)
N500LH	Citation	501-0198	Southern Rainbow Air Inc. Miami, Fl.	N500LE/N105TW/(N602CC)/N67822
N500LJ	Citation	500-0195	Federal Airways Corp. Potomac, Md.	N440EZ/N100AQ/N100AC/N14JA
N500LS	B 727-31	20115	Limited Stores/Northwest Holding Corp. Wilmington, De.	/N505C/N505T/N7893
N500LW	Learjet	25D-232	Sierra Aircraft Leasing Inc. Columbus, Ga.	N500EW//N744LC
N500M	Astra-1125	018	Calcutta Aircraft Leasing Inc. Bloomington, In.	N1188A/4X-CUR
N500MA	HS 125/600A	6064	Mario Andretti/M A 500 Inc. Nazareth, Pa.	N666LC/N105AS/HZ-AMM/G-5-17
N500MD	Westwind-Two	300	UACC Midwest Industries, Wilmington, De.	N500M/4X-CQT
N500MF	Jet Commander	34	Air Crane Inc. W Hollywood, Fl.	TG-OMF/N500MF/(N111XL)/N130RC/N777MH N329HN/N102SY/N102SV/N1210G/N1210
N500MH	Learjet	24-158	U S Charter East Corp. Wheaton, Md.	///N500MH///N855GA//N392T/N642GA
N500MN	Gulfstream 3	460	Walt Disney Productions, Los Angeles, Ca.	N500MM/N500VS/N500LS/N322GA
N500NN	Learjet	24E-355	Haas-Foster Partnership, Lincolnshire, Il.	N7ZB/N7AB
N500NL	Sabre-75A	380-8	Norman Lively, St. Charles, Il. (rebuild ?).	N5107
N500P	Learjet	24-119	Connie Kalitta Services Inc. Lakeview, Or.	(N500PJ)/N500PP/N110W/N994SA N605GA/N453SA/N453LJ
N500PC	Challenger 601-3A	5071	Pepsico Inc. Westchester County Airport, NY.	C-G...
N500PG	JetStar-731	61/5153	Guardian Industries Corp. Northfield, Mi.	///N5517L
N500PP	Learjet	25D-208	Patrick Petroleum Co. Jackson, Mi.	N54YP/C-GZIM/N54YP/N54YR
N500R	Westwind-1124	280	NASCAR Inc. Daytona Beach, Fl.	N250RA/(N5S)/(N5BP)/N29LP/N290W/4X-CNZ
N500RP	Learjet	55-053	Hertz Penske Truck Leasing Inc. Red Bank, NJ.	N1450B/YV-374CP/N85653
N500RR	Citation	550-0638	Red Roof Inns Inc. Hilliard, Oh.	N12582
N500RW	Learjet	35A-148	W/o 24 May 88.	/N333RP/N103GP/N103GH
N500S	JetStar 2	5209	Freeport McMoRan Inc/500 Sugar Corp. Dover, De.	/N5535L
N500SK	Citation	500-0129	Richard Scruggs, Pascagoula, Ms.	N8114G/D-IMLN
N500SW	Learjet	24D-325	Performance Aircraft Leasing Inc. Wilmington, De.	//N416G/N76RV
N500TB	Challenger 601	3003	Taco Bell Corp. Santa Ana, Ca.	/N500PC/C-GLXU
N500VK	Citation	500-0202	Henry van Kesteren/VK Leasing Inc. St Petersburg, Fl.	//N500JK/N240AA N202MW
N500WD	Sabre-65	465-48	Hotel Restaurant & Employees Union, Washington, DC.	XA-MLG/N2539E
N500WH	Westwind-1124	215	Petrolift Aviation Services, Charlotte, NC.	N215DH/4X-CLM
N500WN	JetStar-8	5135	Wayne Newton, Las Vegas, Nv.	N900H/N636/N7980S
N500WW	Learjet	25B-137	Corporate Aircraft Services Inc. Aspen, Co.	N37BJ/N400
N500XY	HS 125/731	25119	Hudson Respiratory Care Inc. Temecula, Ca.	/N213H/G-AVAD/G-5-11
N500ZA	Learjet	24F-350	Onager Co. Odessa, Tx.	N741GL
N501AF	Citation	501-0139	Aviation Training Enterprises, W Chicago, Il.	/N888BH/N108JL/(N3UG)/N1LQ N526CC/N2651B
N501AL	JetStar-6	5012	Finalco Inc. Boca Raton, Fl.	N500SJ/N1012B/N10123/D-BABE/N9283R
N501AR	Citation	500-0128	Engineered Data Products Inc. Broomfield, Co.	N4OHL/N53584/D-INCC
N501AT	Citation	500-0208	Robert Montgomery, Holoidaysburg, Pa.	(N508CC)//N501AT/(N520SC)//N22JG N82JT
N501BG	Beechjet 400A	RK-5	Beechcraft West, Van Nuys, Ca.	/
N501CB	Westwind-1124	435	C T B Inc. North Milford, In.	4X-CUG
N501CC	Citation	701	Cessna Aircraft Co. Wichita, Ks. (was s/n 670).	
N501DB	Citation	501-0008	Ottesen Prop & Accessories, Phoenix, Az.	/N6HT/N362CC/N5362J
N501DD	Citation	501-0035	Dukes Deux Leasing Co. Scottsdale, Az.	/N35JF/N25MH/N112MC/N500WN/(N800M) N36915
N501EF	Citation	501-0069	Evergreen Aviation & Marine Leasing Corp. San Diego, Ca.	N2906A
N501FB	Citation	501-0023	Wings South Inc. Pine Bluff, Ar.	/N56MT/N56MC/N36885
N501FR	Citation	501-0683	Fall River Group Inc. Mequon, Wi.	N501BK
N501GK	Citation	501-0115	Alphonse Stroobants, Forest, Va.	///N501GF/N26494
N501GP	Citation	500-0026	W/o 21 Jan 81.	N526CC
N501GR	Citation	501-0018	Frank E Raper, Lake Havasu City, Az.	/N550TG/N18BG/N378CC/N36871

Registration	Type	c/n	Owner / Operator	Previous identity
N501HS	Citation	501-0096	Herbert Sutton/Southern Oregon Skyways Inc. Medford, Or.	/N660KC//(N480CC)/N660AA/N3202A
N501JC	Citation	500-0252	Stergios Rapis, Van Nuys, Ca.	/N244WJ/C-GZXA/N200WN/N10PS/N5252J
N501JP	Citation	501-0086	Patterson Capital Corp. Los Angeles, Ca.	N501CW/N32SX//N583MP/(N711AE)/N88CF/N8LG/N3195M
N501KR	Citation	501-0071	King Ranch Oil & Gas Inc. Midland, Tx.	N501SR/N3105M
N501LC	Citation	550-0146	Ida Lakin Clement, Kingsville, Tx.	(N611RR)/N580AV/N26610
N501LM	Citation	501-0325	Leonard McIntosh Enterprises, Ketchum, Id.	(D-IFGP)/N1710E
N501LS	Citation	501-0107	Moss & Rocovich PC. Roanoke, Va.	N107CC/N1UL/(N33VV)/N333BG)/N3204M
N501MB	Citation	501-0122	Mathis Brothers Furniture Co. Oklahoma City, Ok.	/(N501MD)/N501HC/N400DB/N275CQ/N275CC/(N26495)
N501MC	Citation	551-0500	Master Chemical Corp. Perrysburg, Oh.	N90RC/(N1255J)
N501MM	HS 125/700A	NA0268	Earth Star Inc. Burbank, Ca.	/(N74JE)//N74JA/XA-JIX/G-5-16
N501MS	Citation	501-0259	Shilling Corp. Naples, Fl.	/VR-BJW/N261WD/N261WR/(N261WB)/(N77111)/N1758E
N501NB	Citation	S550-0018	Indiana National Bank, Indianapolis, In.	
N501NC	Citation	501-0177	Idaho Potato Packers Corp. Blackfoot, Id.	N501DG/N22SD/(N999RB)/N6779P
N501PC	Challenger 601	3004	Pepsico Inc. White Plains, NY.	N967L/N509PC/C-GLXK
N501PS	Learjet	25B-153	W/o 26 May 77.	
N501QS	Citation V	560-0024	EJA/Stone Container Corp. Chicago, Il.	(N12284)
N501RC	Citation	501-0165	WHF Holdings Inc. Houston, Tx.	//N165NA/(N2OKW)/N557CC/N2612N
N501RF	Citation	501-0323	Robert J Fiscella, Hampton, Va.	N55HF//N2651B
N501SC	Citation	500-0314	Inland Steel Corp. Chicago, Il.	(N314CC)/N5314J
N501SP	Citation	501-0019	Corrao Charter Co. Dover, De.	(N301MC)/N36882
N501TJ	Citation	501-0013	William D Fullen, Cincinnati, Oh.	VR-BJK//(N622SS)/N36861
N501TP	Citation	501-0684	Pacific States Aviation/Deerwood Corp. San Ramon, Ca.	N3683G
N501TW	Learjet	35A-612	Tom Walkinshaw Racing Inc. Oxford-UK.	N2FU/N8568D
N502CC	Citation	501-0113	Robert L Kimball, Edensburg, Pa.	N200ES/N502CC/(N515CC)/(N2649S)
N502JC	Learjet	25D-264	Career Aviation Acadaemy, Hayward, Ca.	/N133JF/N716NC
N502MH	Learjet	25C-098	Consolidated Airways Inc. Fort Wayne, In.	N96MJ/YV-26CP/VR-BGF/N139J/VR-BEM/N7JN
N502PC	Gulfstream 2	170	Pepsico Inc. Purchase, NY.	N14PC/N991GA
N503CC	Citation	500-0003	Hugh R Sharpe Jr. Greenville, De.	
N503U	Jet Commander	83	Med Trans of Florida Inc. Tampa, Fl.	C-GHPR/N83AL/N23FF/N4550E
N504JC	Westwind-1124	277	United Jet Center Inc. Warren, Pa.	N288WW/(N2AJ)/4X-CNW
N505BC	Citation	501-0009	Beech Transportation Inc. Wayzata, Mn.	(N715JM)/N715EK/N67CC/N36850
N505EB	Beechjet 400A	RK-17		
N505EE	Learjet	35A-505	Commercial Plastics Co. Mundelein, Il.	N7259J
N505GP	Citation	550-0245	Georgia Pacific Corp. Atlanta, Ga.	/N68607
N505HG	Learjet	36-009	Hondo Oil & Gas Co. Roswell, NM.	N505RA/N15CC/N25CL/N44GL/N709J/N20000
N505JC	Citation	500-0341	United Refining Co. Warren, Pa.	N2650/(N5341J)
N505JH	Citation	501-0126	Jackson Hole Air Charter Inc. Jackson, Wy.	N505SP/N26492
N505K	Citation	500-0004	Charles Kaady, Portland, Or.	N5005//N500GE/(N500GN)/N500GS/N504CC
N506GP	Learjet	35A-109	AMR Combs, Englewood, Co.	
N506TF	Citation	501-0001	Katava Aviation/Kayne & Valeo, Los Angeles, Ca.	N51CJ/N5351J
N507GP	Citation	550-0252	Georgia Pacific Corp. Atlanta, Ga..	N6862R
N507HC	Challenger 600S	1026	Hoechst Celanese Corp. Douglas Municipal Airport, NC.	N507CC/C-GLXH
N507JC	Gulfstream 2	121	United Jet Center Inc. Warren, Pa.	/N90EA//N200P
N507U	Sabre-60	306-93	Flight Specialists Inc. North Canton, Oh.	N200CX//N182AR/N366N/N65777
N508GP	Learjet	35A-424	Georgia Pacific Corp. Atlanta, Ga.	/N2844
N508HC	Challenger 600S	1057	Hoechst Celanese Corp. Charlotte, NC.	N508CC/(VH-OZZ)/N605CL/C-GBTK/C-GLXU
N508P	Learjet	35A-390	Dana Corp. Swanton, Oh.	//N500PP
N508T	Gulfstream 2	232	Tennessee Gas Pipeline Co. Houston, Tx.	/N71WS/C-GDPB/N806GA
N509AB	Sabre-60	306-75	Allen Bradley Co. Milwauke, Wi.	N709AB/N666WL/N110G
N509GP	BAe 125/800A	8077	Georgia Pacific Corp. Atlanta, Ga.	N523BA/G-5-538
N509T	Gulfstream 2	244	Tennessee Gas Pipeline Co. Houston, Tx.	/N500T/9K-AEB/N17584
N509TC	Falcon 10	134	Pacific Northwest Bell Telephone Co. Seattle, Wa.	/N900T/N202FJ/F-WZGF
N510GP	Citation	550-0421	Georgia Pacific Corp. Atlanta, Ga.	N67HW/N1217S
N510ND	Learjet	24B-204	Tulsair Beechcraft Inc. Tulsa, Ok.	N176CP/N957E/N957GA
N510SG	Learjet	35A-268	Valley Jet Corp. Portland, Or.	N3857N/(N286CP)/YV-286CP/N10870
N510T	Gulfstream 2	248	Tennessee Gas Pipeline Co. Houston, Tx.	N501T/9K-AEC/N17589
N510US	Gulfstream 2	223	The Windsong Corp. Mt Kisco, NY.	/
N511AT	Learjet	24E-330	Beaver Aviation Service Inc. Beaver Falls, Pa.	
N511DR	Citation	550-0185	Dan River Inc. Marietta, Ga.	/N370AC///N600EZ/N815GK/N6799L

Registration	Type	c/n	Owner / Operator	Previous identity
N511GP	HS 125/700A	NA0237	Georgia Pacific Corp. Atlanta, Ga.	N697NP//N737X/G-BGBJ/G-5-19
N511WC	Citation	550-0234	Cin Jet Inc Trustee, Cincinnati, Oh.	N88798
N511WM	HS 125/731	25159	Home Depot USA Inc. Atlanta, Ga.	N4767M/C-FWOS/G-AVZL
N511WS	Citation	550-0439	B & J Jet Corp. Cincinnati, Oh.	N550RS/HK-3191X/N550RS/ZS-LHT/N1220A
N512GP	HS 125/700A	NA0329	Georgia Pacific Corp. Atlanta, Ga.	N756N/N18243/N1824T/(N277CB)/N710BF G-5-17
N512WP	Beechjet 400	RJ-16	West Point-Pepperell Inc. Columbus, Ga.	/N165F
N513GP	HS 125/700A	NA0252	Great Northern Nekoosa Corp. Atlanta, Ga.	N401GN//N900MR/N700HS/G-5-18
N513T	Falcon 20C	123	Tenneco Inc. Racine, Wi.	N4343F/F-WNGM
N514T	Falcon 20C	130	Tenneco Inc. Houston, Tx.	N4347F/F-WMKJ
N515AA	Citation	500-0085	Aronov Realty Leasing Co. Montgomery, Al.	N51MW/N585CC
N515DC	Citation Eagle	500-0112	Schatz Westair Inc. Kennewick, Wa.	N29858/C-GRJC/N3LG/VH-DRM/N512CC
N515TC	Learjet	25D-354	KOOL Radio Corp/Tom Chauncey, Phoenix, Az.	N3795U
N515VC	Citation	650-0055	Vicon Flight Inc. Livonia, Mi.	N173LR//N173LP
N515VW	Learjet	25-013	W/o 17 Apr 69.	
N516WP	Sabre-40A	282-98	Washington Water Power Co. Spokane, Wa.	N40SC/N4707N
N520RB	Citation	500-0282	Reagan Buick Inc. Omaha, Nb.	//N26WD/N282CC/(N5282J)
N520RP	Citation	S550-0115	P B & S Chemical Co. Henderson, Ky.	N505CC/(N1292B)
N520S	JetStar-731	8/5084	W/o 11 Feb 81.	/N901E/N732M/N83M/N9240R
N521JP	Learjet	25D-330	Austin Jet Corp. Austin, Tx.	(N523JP)
N521M	HS 125/3A	25129	W/o 12 Dec 72.	G-AVDM/G-5-12
N522TA	Learjet	25D-318	Terminal Airways Inc. Woodbridge, NJ.	N522JP
N523AC	BAC 1-11/203AE	015	Amway Corp. Ada, Mi.	N8LG/N5LC/N541BN/N111QA/N1541/G-ASUF
N523M	HS 125/700A	NA0333	Marathon Oil Co. Findlay, Oh.	//G-5-15
N523RB	Westwind-1123	175	RB Daniels Inc. Grand Prairie, Tx.	N51TV//N500ML/N500M/N1123R/4X-CJY
N523WC	BAe 125/800A	8086	The Cafaro Co/N523WC Inc. Youngstown, Oh.	N125BA/N528BA/G-5-550
N524AC	BAC 1-11/419EP	120	Amway Corp. Ada, Mi.	N44R/N270E
N524DW	Learjet	25B-081	Jet Charter Airlines Inc. Las Vegas, Nv.	N66TJ/HZ-BB1/HZ-AZP/HZ-MOA/N110GL N111GL
N524DW	Learjet	24-177	Connie Kalitta Services Inc. Lakeview, Or.	N555LB/N555LA/N555LB/N104MB N321Q
N524HC	Learjet	35A-358	Harbert International Inc. Birmingham, Al.	
N524M	HS 125/700A	NA0343	Marathon Oil/Cargill Leasing Corp. Minnetonka, Mn.	/G-5-15
N525ML	Westwind-1124	260	Manhattan Leasing Inc. Albuquerque, NM.	/N401BP/4X-CNF
N526AG	Citation	550-0038	Amway Corp. Ada, Mi. 'Thunderbird'	N526AC/(N3271M)
N526M	BAe 125/800A	8032	Marathon Oil Co. Findlay, Oh.	/N815AA/G-5-11
N527AC	BAe 125/800A	NA0405	Amway Corp. Ada, Mi.	N542BA/G-5-575
N527M	BAe 125/800A	8054	Marathon Oil Co. Findlay, Oh.	/G-5-15
N528AC	BAe 125/800	8070	Amway Corp. Ada, Mi.	N520BA/G-5-527
N528M	BAe 125/800A	8055	Provident Commercial Group/Marathon Oil Co. Findlay, Oh.	/G-5-504
N529AC	B 727-17	20327	Amway Corp. Ada, Mi.	N4002M/N115TA/CF-CPN
N529DM	HS 125/700A	NA0309	Trust Aviation Inc. Salem, NH.	/N700MK//N15AG/G-5-17
N530DL	Westwind-1124	287	Leprino Foods, Denver, Co.	N146BF/4X-CQG
N530G	JetStar-731	10/5096	Beta Aviation Inc. Houston, Tx.	//N9252R
N530RD	Diamond 1A	A016SA	American Property Services Inc. Sterling, Va.	N208F/N100DE/N133RC
N531CM	Citation	S550-0033	Charles Myers, Garden City, Ks.	N550ST/(G-BLSG)/(G-BLXN)
N531CW	Learjet	25D-231	Dana Commercial Credit Corp. Maumee, Oh.	/N225HW/N31MJ/N6ODK/N999ME/N999M (OO-LFW)
N531F	Citation V	560-0054	International Fertilizer & Trading, Houston, Tx.	(N26804)
N532CC	Citation	650-0167	Charlotte Pipe & Foundry Co. Charlotte, NC.	N667CC
N533P	BAe 125/800A	8075	Pacent Funding Inc. NYC.	N189B/N518BA/G-5-533
N534H	Learjet	35A-304	Hillenbrand Investment Advisors, Wilmington, De.	N112PG/N464HA
N534MW	Citation	550-0052	Atlas Leasing Inc. El Paso, Tx.	/N90MJ/OY-ASV/(OO-LFX)/N4620G
N534R	Westwind-Two	345	Rollins Properties Inc. Wilmington, De.	N534/(N533)/N1424/4X-CTM
N535CS	Gulfstream 3	464	Campbell Soup Inc. New Castle, De.	/N340GA
N535PC	Learjet	35A-291	Seanaire Inc. Midland Park, NJ.	/N7US
N540B	HS 125/700A	NA0255	Virginia Binger/Jucamcyn Theaters Corp. Minneapolis, Mn.	N125AJ/G-5-14
N540CL	Learjet	23-026	Lawrence Lavallee, Las Vegas, Nv.	N404DB/N222GH/N404AJ/N26008/F-BSTP HB-VBA/N706L
N540JB	Citation	S550-0061	New Jersey Bell Telephone Co. East Orange, NJ.	(N12712)
N540M	BAe 125/800A	NA0432	E I DuPont de Nemours & Co. Houston, Tx.	/N586BA/G-5-619
N545BF	JetStar-8	5146	Centurion Investments Inc. St Louis, Mo. (status ?).	/N499AS/N4992D/C-GWSA N80GM/N5510L

Registration	Type	c/n	Owner / Operator	Previous identity
N545GA	Citation	500-0357	State of Georgia, Atlanta, Ga.	N120RD/YV-120CP/N36854/N5368J
N545S	HS 125/731	NA719	Betman Inc. Wilmington, De.	G-AWXD
N546EX	Falcon 50	41	Bristol-Myers Squibb Co. NYC.	/N60FJ/F-WZHI
N549CC	Citation	550-0456	Cessna Aircraft Co. Wichita, Ks.	(N456CM)/N1250C
N550AS	Citation	S550-0020	Norsan Financial/A D Seenc Construction Inc.	
N550BM	Citation	550-0256	D&D Aviation Corp/Broward Marine Inc. Fort Lauderdale, Fl.	N550SM/N3300L N6861X
N550BP	Citation	550-0135	Amber Inc. San Jose, Ca.	N555BC/TF-JET/N555BC/ZS-LLO/N39142/VH-KDI/N6800J
N550CA	Citation	550-0152	Global Air Charter Inc. Nashua, NH.	/N88840/RP-C581/(N107)/N88840
N550CC	Citation	686	Citation II prototype. Ff 31 Jan 77.	
N550CD	Citation	550-0291	Chevron USA Inc. Englewood, Co.	ZP-TNB/ZP-PNB/N6887T
N550CS	Learjet	55-005	Gulfstream Flights Services Inc. Boca Raton, Fl.	N128VM/N40ES
N550DW	Citation	551-0487	The Charles Machine Works Inc. Perry, Ok.	/N444BL/(N487CC)/N12532
N550EK	Citation	550-0230	E K Fuel Co. Wilmington, De.	N141DA/N270RA/N3254G/(G-OTKI)/(N6804N)
N550FB	Citation	550-0674		
N550GT	Citation	S550-0160	Bancboston Leasing Inc. Boston, Ma.	N2646Z
N550HM	Citation	550-0044	Albert A Sparlis, Los Angeles, Ca. (was 551-0092)	///N3526M/N3286M
N550HP	Citation	550-0173	Hesco Parts Corp. Louisville, Ky.	/(N169DA)/N169JM//N286G/(N36NW)/N88822
N550J	Citation	550-0418	Justiss Oil Co. Jena, La.	N1217H
N550JR	Citation	550-0275	Bercol Corp. Miami, Fl.	N6799L
N550JS	Citation	551-0149	Enhancement of Illinois Inc. Cerillos, NM. (was 550-0107).	/N225FM/N225AD N550CB/N2665D
N550K	Jet Commander-A	127	Bohlke International Airways, St Croix, USVI.	N100SR/N20GB/N209RR/N34HD N27X/N6B
N550KC	Citation	550-0264	Carland Inc. Kansas City, Mo.	N6862L
N550L	Citation Eagle	501-0032	William H Pitt, Palm Beach, Fl.	N550T/N690MC/N377KC/N33AA/N388CJ/N36887
N550LJ	Learjet	55-015	LAS Aviation Corp. Cupertino, Ca.	N515DJ/HB-VGV
N550MT	Citation	550-0306	Gil Hodge Aviation Inc. Marietta, Ga.	N303EC/N6888X
N550MZ	Citation	550-0658		
N550RB	Citation	550-0117	Jet Service Corp. Winamac, In.	N150HE/N150HR/N575FM/N2745R
N550RG	Citation	550-0226	Duncan Aviation Inc. Lincoln, Ne.	N300JK/N29WS/N6804F
N550SA	Citation	550-0248	Security Aviation Inc/Michael O'Neill, Anchorage, Ak.	/N6804C
N550T	Citation Eagle	501-0047	Taft Broadcasting Co. Greensboro, NC.	/N1021T/HB-VFI/N87496
N550TB	Citation	S550-0012	Burlington Industries Inc. Greensboro, NC.	
N550TR	Citation	550-0170	S & H Fabricating & Engineering Inc. Kalispell, Mt.	/N550TP/N88791
N550WW	Citation	551-0584	Wasser & Winters Co. West Linn, Or. (was 550-0584).	N1301D
N551AB	Citation	550-0383	Alexander & Baldwin Inc. Honolulu, Hi. 'Imaua' (Forward).	(N98718)
N551BC	Citation	551-0012	Boyne USA Inc. Boyne Falls, Mi.	N1955E
N551DB	Learjet	55-052	Skybird Aviation Inc. Van Nuys, Ca.	N55GF/YV-292CP
N551DF	Learjet	55C-001	Learjet 55C prototype cvtd from 55-001	/N551GL
N551DP	Learjet	25D-213	Sandair Inc. Houston, Tx.	
N551HB	Learjet	55-038	First Hawaiian Bank, Honolulu, Hi.	
N551MC	Citation	550-0371	Poly-Resyn Inc. Dundee, Il.	(N26621)
N551SC	Learjet	55-008	Hal E Dickson, San Angelo, Tx.	
N551SR	Citation	550-0072	Executive Aircraft Consulting, Newton, Ks.	N969MT/(N700EA)//N36QN/N360N (N2661H)
N551TP	Westwind-Two	419	Tecumseh Products Co. Tecumseh, Mi.	N419W/4X-CUF
N552CC	Citation	551-0027	ABCM Corp. Hampton, Ia. (was s/n 550-0002).	N44GT/N552CC/N98753
N552N	HS 125/3A	25124	Gaytan Foods, Lapuente, Ca.	N125J/G-AVAJ
N552UT	Learjet	55-100	United Telecom, Hood River, Or.	
N553DJ	Learjet	55-003	Duncan Aviation Inc. Lincoln, Ne.	/N162GA/N553GP
N553M	Learjet	35A-141	Portland Glove Co. Carlton, Or.	/N66WM/N743GL
N555AJ	Citation	500-0007	W/o 19 Nov 79.	N500LF/N507CC
N555BS	JetStar-6	5051	Marlyn Bateman, Eugene, Or.	/////N310AD/N31S//N44MF/N400KC/N9217R
N555CB	HS 125/700A	NA0228	Cleveland Brothers Equipment Co. Wilmington, De.	G-5-11
N555CC	Citation	500-0039	O'Hara & Kendall/Southeastern Aircraft Leasing, Raleigh, NC.	N539CC
N555CS	Gulfstream 2B	73	Kaiser Air/Andorra Aviation, Oakland, Ca.	/N116K
N555CW	Westwind-Two	295	ARWCO Air Inc. Hanover, Pa.	N100AQ/N100AK/N295WW/4X-CQO
N555DH	Learjet	24-153	Dale Hillin/J O H Inc. Dallas, Tx.	/N878DE/(N53DE)/N159J/N1TK/N524SC
N555DM	Jet Commander	25	Jack Rudolph, W Hempstead, NY.	
N555HD	Westwind-Two	341	U S Bancorp Leasing & Financial, Portland, Or.	/N8ORE/N23AQ/N23AC/N1124P 4X-CUB
N555MX	Learjet	55C-142	Pacific Flight Services Inc. Lake Oswego, Or.	

Registration	Type	c/n	Owner / Operator	Previous identity
N555PB	JetStar-6	5047	Cx USA 10/90 as wfu.	////N409MA/N409M/N9214R
N555PT	Sabre-40	282-53	Centurion Investments Inc. St Louis, Mo.	N600BP/N67201/ZS-PTJ/(ZS-GSB) N62Q/N62K/N101T/N123MS/N999BS/N7503V
N555RB	HS 125/700A	NA0299	National Medical Care/NMC Leasing Inc. Waltham, Ma.	/N125BE/VR-BHH/N125BE G-5-19
N555SD	Learjet	25D-333	Joe Brand Inc. Laredo, Tx.	N34MJ
N555SG	JetStar-8	5090	United CCM Corp. Dallas, Tx.	/N55CJ/N10MJ/N106G/N9246R
N555SR	Falcon 10	173	Sea Ray Boats Inc. Alcoa, Tn.	N211CN/N441DM/N72BB/N239FJ/F-WZGA
N555WH	Learjet	36A-037	Rikuo Corp. Los Angeles, Ca.	RP-C5128
N555WL	Gulfstream 4	1114	Trousdale Enterprises/Wm Lyon Co. San Jose, Ca.	N444LT/N428GA
N556AT	Citation	500-0020	sale, Cooper City, Fl. (wfu ?)	C-FBAX/N520CC
N558E	Learjet	35A-100	Keith Wood Agency Inc. Fort Worth, Tx.	/N550E
N559BC	Citation	500-0059	Super Valu Stores Inc. Indianola, Ms.	N559CC
N559LC	Gulfstream 2	152	Little Ceasar Enterprises Inc. Detroit, Mi.	/N62WB/N202GA/XA-FOU/N17587
N560BL	Citation V	560-0057	B & L Properties, Fairfileld, Ca.	(N2683L)
N560CC	Citation V	550-0001	Cessna Aircraft Co. Wichita, Ks.	N5050J/(N551CC)/(N98751)
N560EL	Citation V	560-0049	Rent Air Inc. Washington, DC.	(N2672X)
N560GA	Citation	500-0217	Jennings Firearms Inc. Carson City, Nv.	N500GA/N217CC
N560GL	Citation V	560-0079	Great Lakes Chemical Corp. W Lafayettte, In.	(N2746C)
N560HC	Citation V	560-0020	Collins Brothers Corp. Las Vegas, Nv.	N520CV/N1219G
N560JR	Citation V	560-0027	Redman Investments Inc. Dallas, Tx.	(N12289)
N560MC	Jet Commander	24	Morgan Merrill/Jeti Inc. Alexandria, Va.	N360MC/N7GW/N360MC/N360M/N94B
N560W	Citation V	560-0030	Jetflight Aviation Inc. Wilmington, De.	(N1229D)
N560WH	Citation V	560-0013	W W H Inc. Las Vegas, Nv.	(N1217P)
N561B	Citation V	560-0008	J G Boswell Co. Los Angeles, Ca.	
N562CD	Citation	550-0562	sale, Miami, Fl.	D-CBAT/(N1298N)
N562R	Sabre-60	306-37	North American Royalties, Chattanooga, Tn.	//N4SE/N4S/N4750N
N564CL	Learjet	25-060	Clay Lacy, Boise, Id.	N695LJ
N564MG	JetStar-6	5021	Wfu. Parted out and cx USA register 12/86.	/C-FETN
N565A	Falcon 200	499	The Associates Bancorp. Dallas, Tx.	N213FJ/F-WZZJ
N565JS	Citation	550-0565	J B Scott, Boise, Id.	N88BM/N565CJ/N1298Y
N565TW	Citation	500-0065	Trendway Corp. Holland, Mi.	/N565CC
N566CC	Citation	550-0279	Great Lakes Gas Transmission, Detroit, Mi.	(N88838)
N566NA	Learjet	28-064	NASA, Hampton, Va.	N266GL
N566TX	Citation	550-0201	Textron Inc. Providence, RI.	N334AM/N6799E
N567DW	Sabre-40	282-35	Centurion Investments Inc. St Louis, Mo.	N341AR/N341AP/N6390C
N570R	Sabre-65	465-75	Jetco Joint Venture, Midland, Tx.	N2581E
N570RC	Citation	S550-0070	Rosewood Assets Inc. Dallas, Tx.	/N570CC/(N12722)
N571CH	HS 125/700A	NA0256	W R Grace & Co. Chemed Division, Cincinnati, Oh.	N125AK/G-5-15
N571E	HS 125/600A	6071	E I Dupont de Nemours Inc. New Castle, De.	N571DU/(N91884)/G-BEES/G-5-14
N571NC	Sabre-60	306-1	Sabre Investments Ltd. Chesterfield, Mo.	N521N/N978R/N306NA
N573CC	Citation	S550-0007	Dawn Food Products Inc. Jackson, Mi.	N51JH/(N1256P)
N573L	Citation	501-0060	Caribbean Aircraft Holding Co. West Columbia, SC.	N5737/N500ZC/N435CC N2741A
N573LP	Learjet	35A-658	Louisiana Pacific Corp. Hillsboro, Or.	N4290Y
N573LR	Learjet	35A-153	Louisiana Pacific Corp. Hillsboro, Or.	N573LP/C-GZVV
N573P	Westwind-1124	257	E I Dupont de Nemours Inc. New Castle, De.	4X-CNC
N574CF	Diamond 1A	A079SA	Central Flying Service, Little Rock, Ar.	(N574U)/N379DM
N574W	Learjet	55-011	Worthington Industries Inc. Columbus, Oh.	N411GL/N37951/(N57TA)
N575CC	Citation	500-0075	Advanced Drainage Systems Inc. Columbus, Oh.	(N600TT)/N575CC
N575SF	Gulfstream 2	221	Chevron Corp. San Francisco, Ca.	
N575W	Citation	550-0008	Holliston Aviation Inc. Woodsville, NH.	/N98840
N576CC	Citation	550-0576	Cescite Corp. Wilmington, De.	(N1300G)
N577VM	Citation	501-0057	Cleveland Newspapers Inc. Birmingham, Al.	N505BG/N500JC/N98751
N578DF	Gulfstream 2	126	San Antonio Air Inc. DC. 'Antonio Sandrita - Wings of Man'	/N581WD/N43M
N579L	Citation	550-0579	Dana Commercial Credit Corp. Swanton, Oh.	(N13001)
N580R	Citation	500-0127	Original Honey Baked Ham Co. Atlanta, Ga.	N500R/N22DN/N701AT/N701AS
N582JD	Learjet	35-024	Tap Marina Inc/Wolf Financial Group Inc. NYC.	/N24GA//N316
N583D	Gulfstream 3	471	E I DuPont de Nemours & Co. New Castle, De.	/N888WL/N347GA
N584D	Gulfstream 4	1065	E I DuPont de Nemours Inc. New Castle, De.	/N442GA
N585A	Gulfstream 2	44	E I Dupont de Nemours Inc. New Castle, De.	/N830G/N814GA
N585UC	Challenger 601-3A	5002	Utilicorp/Trans UCU Inc. Kansas City, Mo.	/N611CL/C-GDEQ/N611CL/C-GDEQ
N586RE	Citation	550-0199	U S Customs Service Office, Washington, DC.	/N67983

Registration	Type	c/n	Owner / Operator	Previous identity
N587S	Citation	650-0188	Diamond Shamrock Leasing Inc. San Antonio, Tx.	N2617P
N588CT	Citation	S550-0060	Contel Service Corp. Bakersfield, Ca.	N85AB/(N1271T)
N589UC	HS 125/700A	NA0297	Trans UCU Inc. Kansas City, Ks.	/(N78QS)/N78CS/N125BD/G-5-16
N590A	Citation V	560-0029	Alascom Inc. Anchorage, Ak.	(N1229C)
N591M	Citation V	560-0085	Modine Manufacturing Co. Racine, Wi.	(N2748F)
N592M	Citation	S550-0041	Modine Manufacturing Co. Racine, Wi.	N772M
N593DC	Falcon 10	180	Dow Corning Corp. Hangar 4, Freeland Airport, Mi.	N245FJ/F-WZGM
N593M	Citation	S550-0021	Modine Manufacturing Co. Racine, Wi.	(N1259S)
N594G	Citation	550-0482	Growmark Inc. Bloomington, Il.	N62WG/N62GC/N1253G
N595DC	Falcon 200	500	Dow Corning Corp. Hangar 4, Freeland Airport, Mi.	N214FJ/F-WPUU
N599FW	Citation	550-0599	Fegotila Ltd. NYC. (Staverton-UK based).	G-SYKS/N.....
N599SC	Citation V	560-0051	Provident Services Inc. Houston, Tx.	N2680A
N600AG	HS 125/600A	6069	Alexander H Major, NYC.	N350MH/G-BEIO
N600AS	Falcon 50	90	Allied Signal Inc. Los Angeles, Ca.	/N298W/N290W/F-WZHX
N600AT	Citation	551-0551	Alltel Corp. Little Rock, Ar.	N487LD/
N600AW	HS 125/600A	6018	American Way Casualty Corp. Southfield, Mi.	N125E/N880SC/N500GD/N28BH
N600B	Gulfstream 3	459	International Brotherhood of Teamsters, Washington, DC.	N321CA
N600BL	Gulfstream 3	482	Bausch & Lomb. Rochester. NY.	N333HK/N306GA
N600C	Learjet	55-047	Fayez Sarofim & Co. Houston, Tx.	
N600DT	Learjet	35-017	B.A.C. Inc. Ketchum, Id.	N456MS/N551CC/N119GS
N600FF	Challenger	1019	Dover Leasing Co. Los Angeles, Ca.	/N603CL/N9071M/C-GLWT
N600GH	Citation	650-0029	General Host Corp. Westchester Airport Hangar D-1, NY.	(N30CJ)
N600GM	Learjet	25D-290	Moyle Petroleum Co. Rapid City, SD.	N321RB/N221EL/XA-EIN/N221AP
N600GW	Diamond 1A	A044SA	Joe Morten & Son Inc. S Sioux City, Ne.	N606JM/N146GA/N110DK/N309DM/N334DM
N600HS	BAe 125/800A	8029	Genesee Management Inc. Rochester, NY.	/N813AA/(N600TH)/G-5-16
N600J	Westwind-Two	302	Johnson & Johnson, West Trenton, NJ.	4X-CQV
N600JC	Learjet	24D-246	Jet Charter International Ltd. Hayward, Ca.	N184AL/N61BA/(N69SF)/N50SJ N35SJ/N5SJ/N21NA/N215Z
N600JT	Learjet	25D-291	JT Inc. Southfield, Mi.	N952/N666RB/N1088D
N600K	Jet Commander-B	148	Gulf Star Air Inc. Bayou La Batre, Al.	(N22LL)/N600K/N101NK/N200DF/N200DE N8536/4X-CPL/N9048N
N600LE	Learjet	35A-149	Lands End Inc. Dodgeville, Wi.	/N273MG/N273MC/N85351/HB-VGN/OO-KJG
N600LL	Learjet	35A-438	Lincoln National Life Insurance Co. Fort Wayne, In.	(N8JA)/N17ND
N600LN	Learjet	35A-332	Lincoln National Life Insurance Co. Fort Wayne, In.	/
N600LS	BAe 125/800A	NA0411	Limited Stores/Eastern Holding Corp. Wilmington, De.	N556BA/G-5-586
N600MG	Challenger 600S	1020	Price Productions Inc. Trenton, NJ.	/N602CL/N36LB/C-GLWT
N600MK	Challenger	1050	Airtrade International Inc. Fairfield, Ct.	/C-GLXO
N600MT	Citation	500-0070	BRS Services Inc. Visalia, Ca.	N500TD/N570CC
N600PC	Learjet	25B-116	Milwaukee Jet Inc. Milwaukee, Wi.	C-FCXY
N600PM	Gulfstream 3	333	Philip Morris Management Corp. White Plains, NY.	
N600SR	Citation	500-0236	T Squared Investments Inc. Wilmington, De.	N801K/N801L/N2801L/N24PA/N236CC N5236J
N600TE	Challenger 600S	1056	Jet East/North Central Aviation Inc. Dallas, Tx.	/N600CC/N26895/C-GLYH
N600TJ	Westwind-1124	198	Status Venture Corp. San Diego, Ca.	N744JR/N800Y/4X-CKV
N600WT	Learjet	35-037	Universal Jet Inc. Corona, Ca.	/N35GQ/N58M/N100GL/N1462B
N601AG	Challenger 601	3001	Exide Corp/The Spectrum Group Inc. Los Angeles, Ca.	/N601CL/C-GBUU
N601BA	HS 125/600A	6040	Steve Blair/Bayou Helicopters Inc. Houston, Tx.	N125GS/N4224Y/C-GJCM/N41BH
N601BC	Citation	550-0091	Brunner & Lay Inc. Asheville, NC.	/N527AG/N527AC/(N2665S)
N601BF	Challenger 601-3A	5065	CIRC Service Systems Inc. Washington, DC.	C-G...
N601CV	Corvette	40	Goliat Metals Inc. Brownsville, Tx.	XB-CYI/F-ODJS/F-WNGZ
N601EG	Challenger 601-3A	5008	South Seas Helicopter Co Inc. Carlsbad, Ca.	/N601CC/C-G...
N601GL	Challenger 601	3026	Federal Express Corp. Memphis, Tn.	/N927A/N5373U/C-GLWX
N601HH	Challenger 601-3A	5018	CanadairChallenger Inc. Windsor, Ct.	C-FBHX/9Q-CBS/C-FBHX/N606CC/C-GLWV
N601HP	Challenger 601	3062	Price Aviation Corp. La Jolla, Ca.	C-GLYK
N601KR	Challenger 601-3A	5015	Rainin Instrument Co Inc. Oakland, Ca.	/C-GLXH
N601MG	Challenger 601-3A	5078	C Itoh Aviation Inc. El Segundo, Ca.	C-G...
N601RL	Challenger 601-3A	5028	Reginald Lewis/T L C Corp. Teterboro, NJ.	/N601TL/C-G...
N601S	Challenger 601	3060	Air Shamrock Inc. Burbank, Ma.	C-GLXY
N601SA	Challenger 600S	1013	Summit Aviation Corp. E Farmingdale, NY.	N2428/C-GBHZ
N601SR	Challenger 600S	1051	Executive Aircraft Consulting Inc. Newton, Ks.	///N20CX/N27341/C-GLXO
N601UT	Challenger 601	3010	United Telecom/Sharon Aviation Inc. Kansas City, Mo.	/N80CS/C-GBLX/C-GLWV
N601UU	BAe 125/800A	8005	Union Underwear Company. Bowling Green, Ky.	/N800GG/G-BLJC/G-5-15
N601WM	Challenger 601-3A	5026	Waste Management Inc. Chicago, Il.	C-G...

Registration	Type	c/n	Owner / Operator	Previous identity
N601WW	Challenger 600S	1047	Whitewind Co Ltd. White Plains, NY.	N2741Q/C-GLXH
N601Z	Challenger	1079	Bernie Eccleston/Motor Racing Development Corp. UK.	N125N/N46ES/C-GLWV
N602KB	Sabre-60A	306-109	Federated Department Stores Inc. Cincinnati, Oh.	N521NC/N64NC/N522N/N2101J
N602NC	Falcon 10	82	Newell Co. Freeport, Il.	N97MC/N168FJ/F-WPXE
N603CC	Challenger 601-3A	5067	Blue Jay Ltd/Itoh Aviation, NYC.	C-G...
N603GY	HS 125/700A	7028	Goody Products, Teterboro, NJ.	//N700TL/G-5-534//G-BFSO
N604AN	Corvette	18	Air National, Elyria, Oh. (to Spain for spares ?).	F-BTTO/N615AC/F-WNGR
N605Y	Sabre-65	465-63	Occidental Petroleum Inc. Bakersfield, Ca.	N2N
N606PT	Gulfstream 3	308	Mar Flite Ltd Corp. Portland, Or.	/N717A
N606RP	Falcon 20F	265	Ralston-Purina Co. Chesterfield, Mo.	N4429F/F-WLCX
N607RP	Falcon 20F	470	Ralston Purina Co. Chesterfield, Mo.	N477F/F-WJMJ
N607SR	Sabre-60	306-118	Charles Fry, Martinez, Ca.	N2635M/N711MR/N65NR/N2122J
N609TC	Citation	550-0609	E L Truck Rental Co. Wayne, Mi.	(N1242A)
N610CC	Falcon 20F-5	373	Occidental Chemical Corp. White Plains, NY.	N620CC)/N91Y/N922DS/N53DS N1041F/F-WMKI
N610JR	Learjet	55-125	Tele/Com Air Inc. Oak Brook, Il.	
N610LM	Learjet	25D-301	Jet East Inc. Dallas, Tx.	N416RM
N610MC	Gulfstream 2	196	May Department Stores Co. St. Louis, Mo.	N610MC/N200BE/N400J
N610R	Learjet	35A-622	Iowa Power & Light Co. Des Moines, Ia.	N7260H
N611BA	BAe 125/800A	NA0449	JF Aircraft Corp. Dearborn, Mi.	G-5-658
N611DB	Learjet	24D-318	Phoenix Air Group Inc. Cartersville, Ga.	N114JT
N611ER	Citation	550-0236	Cyclops Corp. Mansfield, Oh.	N68033
N611JC	Jet Commander	2	Wfu. Test airframe for static fatigue.	
N611MC	HS 125/700A	NA0257	May Department Stores Co. St. Louis, Mo.	N125HS/G-5-18
N611MH	Challenger 601-3A	5011	CanadairChallenger Inc. Windsor, Ct.	/JA8283/N603CC/C-GLXD
N612MC	HS 125/700A	NA0317	May Department Stores Co. St. Louis, Mo.	/N700SS/G-5-20
N613BR	Learjet	23-082A	Roever Evangelistic Assoc. Fort Worth, Tx.	N100TA/N744CF/N255ES/N823LJ
N613CK	Gulfstream 2	150	CK Aviation Inc. New York, NY. (N631CK)/N638MF/N636MF/N988H/N966H/N803GA	
N613MC	HS 125/700A	7151	May Department Stores Co. St Louis, Mo.	N161G/N161MM/G-5-12
N614BA	BAe 125/800A	NA0452	PacifiCorp Trans Inc. Portland, Or.	/G-5-669
N614HF	Gulfstream 4	1119	Uniden Jet Aviation Corp. Wilmington, De.	N407GA
N614MH	Jet Commander	95	Javier A Tostado, Los Angeles, Ca.	N95JK/N200MZ/(N3031)/N200MP/N100CA N210FE/N709Q/N7090/N6412/N5412
N614MM	Sabre-60	306-41	Coastal Aviation Management Inc. Wilmington, NC.	(N8909R)/N1909R/N173A N925R/N4754N
N615DM	Westwind-1124	196	Fairmont Aviation Inc. Fairfield, Ct.	N500WK/N505U//N250JP/N1124E/4X-CKT
N616NA	Learjet	25-035	National Aeronautics, Cleveland, Oh.	N33TR/N33GF/N683LJ
N616PA	HS 125/600A	6051	Palumbo Aircraft Sales Inc. Uniontown, Oh.	N601JJ/N601PS/N35DL/N5DL/N22DL C-GBNS/(N45BH)
N617BA	BAe 125/800A	NA0455	Fuqua National Corp. Atlanta, Ga.	/G-5-673
N617CC	Citation	501-0211	Owners Jet Services Ltd. Las Vegas, Nv.	N6785C
N617CM	Citation	550-0617	J J Gumberg Co. Pittsburgh, Pa.	(N1253Y)
N618BA	BAe 125/800A	NA0456	Norfolk Southern Corp. Norfolk, Va.	/G-5-674
N618R	Learjet	25D-360	ASC Inc. Wilmington, De.	N8563B
N619BA	BAe 125/800A	NA0457	Philip Morris Inc. Teterboro, NJ. (prob N300PM).	/G-5-675
N620JM	Learjet	35A-207	M-S Air Inc. Indianapolis, In.	N3PW/N711/N40146
N620K	Gulfstream 2B	64	Eastman Kodak Co. NYC.	/N95SV/N341NS/N950BS/N940BS/N836GA
N620M	HS 125/700A	NA0203	Olin Corp. Stamford, Ct.	G-BERV
N620S	Challenger	1031	Texasgulf Inc/Emery Air Charter, Rockford. Il.	/C-GLXS
N621JA	HS 125/700A	NA0270	Aviation Enterprises Inc. Wilmington, De.	/N621JH/C-GDAO/G-BHSK/G-5-16
N621JH	Gulfstream 3	387	Airstar Corp. Salt Lake City, Ut.	N26L
N621S	HS 125/731	NA734	S C S Investments Inc. Crystal Bay, Nv.	N621L/N111RB/N125J/G-AXOC
N621ST	HS 125/1A	25014	Wfu. Broken up for spares 3/85.	XA-JUZ/N621ST/N734AK/N125G/G-ASSK
N622AB	HS 125/700A	NA0208	Home Depot USA Inc. Atlanta, Ga.	/N700FS/N162A/N700HS/N125HS/G-BFBI/G-5-14
N622WG	Learjet	35A-611	Zarego Inc. Mesquite, NM.	
N623MW	Gulfstream 2	94	Montgomery Ward & Co. Chicago, Il.	/N202A/N200A/N886GA
N623RC	Learjet	24-173	Fisher-Thomas Inc. fort Worth, Tx.	N3GL/N102GP/N33ST/N110SQ/N872JR/N852GA
N623RM	Citation	501-0217	Smithco Leasing Inc. Camp Hill, Pa.	N1710E
N625AU	Learjet	25D-340	Union Park Pontiac & GMC, Wilmington, De.	//N980A
N625CR	Falcon 50	55	Crane Co. NYC.	N332MQ/N332MC/N1CN//N839F/N73FJ/F-WZHU
N626CC	Citation	650-0026	Damaged on production line 1984, now test airframe.	
N627L	Citation	501-0123	Lord Corp. Erie, Pa.	N513CC/N2650C
N628CH	Citation	501-0220	Coachmen Industries Inc. Elkhart, In.	N2052A

Registration	Type	c/n	Owner / Operator	Previous identity
N629P	HS 125/731	NA715	Philips Industries Inc. Dayton, Oh.	N22EH/N800QB/N800CB/N400CC/N200CC N778S/G-AWPE
N630L	Falcon 50	130	Sears Roebuck & Co. Chicago, Il.	N9314/N124FJ/F-WZHR
N630M	Challenger 601-3A	5060	Olin Corp. White Plains, NY.	N5060H/C-G...
N630N	Sabre-40	282-73	cx USA 6/85 as wfu.	N630M
N630PM	Gulfstream 2TT	236	Philip Morris Management Corp. Richmond, Va.	/N2998/N812GA
N631BA	BAe 125/800A	NA0459		/G-5-680
N631CC	Citation	550-0631		(N1257M)
N632BA	BAe 125/800A	NA0460	General Mills Restaurants Inc. Orlando, Fl.	/G-5-681
N632PB	Falcon 20D	206	Modern Welding Co. Owensboro, Ky.	N815AC/N4394F/F-WLCS
N632PE	HS 125/1A	25058	Aircraft Trading Center Inc. Jupiter, Fl.	N632PB/N470R/N215G/N9308Y/D-COMI
N633AC	Learjet	55-115	Xidex Corp. Santa Clara, Ca.	N6666K/N6666R
N633BA	BAe 125/800A	NA0461		/G-5-682
N633EE	Citation	S550-0058	A K Guthrie, Big Spring, Tx.	N1271E
N633P	Gulfstream 3	452	Aviation Methods, San Francisco, Ca.	N663P/N27R/N331GA
N633WW	Learjet	35A-654	Life Jet Services Inc. Bloomington, Il.	
N634BA	BAe 125/800A	NA0462		G-5-685
N634H	Learjet	35A-292	Hillenbrand Industries Inc. Batesville, In.	
N635AV	Gulfstream 2	168	AEAC Inc. Van Nuys, Ca.	N193CK/N26LB/N10LB/N812GA
N635BA	BAe 125/800A	NA0463		G-5-686
N636BA	BAe 125/800A	NA0464		G-5-687
N636MF	Gulfstream 4	1012	Ropa Two Corp. Teterboro, NJ.	N445GA
N636SC	Citation	500-0222	Navajo Refining Co. Dallas, Tx.	///N222CC
N639J	Westwind-Two	337	Burlington Northern Railroad, Fort Worth, Tx.	N14BN/4X-CTE
N640PM	HS 125/700A	NA0316	Philip Morris Management Corp. Madison, Wi.	N2989/N125BA/N700PP/G-5-15
N643TD	Citation	550-0438	Lynn Durham, Midland, Tx.	N437CC/(N555TD)/N12190
N645G	Learjet	35-056	Gates Corp. Denver, Co.	N106GL/(JY-AEX)
N646G	Learjet	55-016	Gates Corp. Denver, Co.	
N650	Citation	697	Citation III second prototype.	
N650AE	Citation	650-0152	Atwood Enterprises Inc. Rockford, Il.	N1326H/N4EG
N650CA	Learjet	24-050	Continental Air Transport Co. Tulsa, Ok.	N823M/N828M/N828MW
N650CC	Citation	696	Citation III prototype. Ff 30 May 79. Cx USA 11/89 as wfu.	
N650CD	Citation	650-0066	Russell Corp. Alexander City, Al.	N138V/N138M/(N1314V)
N650CM	Citation	650-0200		
N650DH	BAC 1-11/401AK	059	Dee Howard/River City Investments Inc. San Antonio, Tx.	N700JA/N100CC N5019/N112NA/N5019
N650GA	Citation	650-0198		
N650HC	Citation	650-0124	Collins Bros/Terrible Herbst Inc. Las Vegas, Nv.	//N7HV/N95CC/(N1322X)
N650J	Citation	650-0022	Hines Florida Corp. Houston, Tx.	/
N650JA	Citation	650-0073	J A Albertson Enterprises, Boise, Id.	(N1315D)
N650JC	Citation	650-0089	Jepson Assocs Inc. W Chicago, Il.	/N653CC/(N13175)
N650M	Citation	650-0044	Moebel-Mann GmbH. Baden-Baden.	(N234HM)
N650NY	Citation	650-0027	Trans Marine Management Corp. Tampa, Fl.	/N875SC/N375SC
N650PF	Gulfstream 2	118	NASA, Cleveland, Oh. (NASA 650).	(N651NA)/N650PF/N399FP/(N301FP)/N399CB N823GA
N650PM	BAe 125/800A	8081	Philip Morris Inc. White Plains, NY.	N525BA/G-5-543
N650SB	Citation	650-0018	Stockwood Inc. Morristown, NJ.	N275WN/N715BC/(N1307C)
N650TC	Citation	650-0064	City of Dayton Partnership, Vandalia, Oh.	/N801CC/(N1314H)
N650TP	Citation	650-0061	Ray-O-Vac/Banc One Equipment Finance Inc. Indianapolis, In.	/N137X/(N129TC) N137M/(N1313T)
N650WC	Citation	550-0007	CSX Beckett/Towne Management Co. Youngstown, Oh.	(N447FM)/N300PB/N98830
N650X	Falcon 50	69	Amax Inc. NYC.	N80FJ/F-WZHJ
N650Z	Citation	650-0108	Dana Commercial Credit Corp. Maumee, Oh.	/(N1302U)
N651CC	Citation	650-0001	Larken Inc. Cedar Rapids, Ia.	/N654CC/(N651AP)/N1AP/N651CC
N651CN	Citation	650-0072	Conseco Inc. Carmel, In.	/N277W/(N1315C)
N651E	Westwind-1124	406	Iowa Electric Light & Power Co. Cedar Rapids, Ia.	N406W/4X-CUA
N651GL	Sabre-65	465-36	IMC Corp. Waukegan, Il.	
N651LJ	Learjet	24A-125	Steven Lysdale, Bellevue, Wa.	
N651TC	Citation	650-0090	CTC of Dayton Partnership, Vandalia, Oh.	//N1823S/N694CC/(N1318A)
N652CN	Challenger 601-3A	5040	Conseco Inc. Indianapolis, In.	/C-G...
N654E	Falcon 20C	164	Rynes Aviation Inc. Park Ridge, Il.	//N4367F/F-WJMN
N654GC	Citation	650-0004	Executive Aircraft Consulting, Newton, Ks.	/(N654AR)
N654PC	Falcon 10	131	Prince Corp. Holland, Mi.	N196FJ/F-WZGC

Registration	Type	c/n	Owner / Operator	Previous identity
N656PS	Citation	550-0009	California Oregon Broadcasting, Medford, Or.	/N744DC/N744SW/N98853
N657CC	Citation	650-0157	Community Psychiatric Centers, Laguna Hills, Ca.	/N1327A
N657MC	Falcon 20C	148	D & D Construction & Investment, Calabasas, Ca.	//N126HC/N120HC/N4358F F-WMKG
N658CC	Citation	650-0046	Boeing Equipment Holding Co. Wichita, Ks.	
N658PC	Gulfstream 2	157	Prince Corp/Wingspan Leasing Inc. Holland, Mi.	N74JK/N940BS/N914BS/N805GA
N658TC	Learjet	25-044	W/o 18 Jan 72.	N962GA
N659HX	Learjet	25D-300	Frederick Haddad/Hecks Inc. Charleston, WV.	(N46BA)
N659WL	Gulfstream 2	204	Wingspan Leasing/Prince Corp. Holland, Mi.	N659PC/N937US/N806CC/G-CXMF N17588
N660A	Learjet	24-155	sale, 11125 Guibal Ave. Gilroy, CA 95020. (wfu ?).	N210FP/N833GA/N462BA N462B/N422U/N598GA
N660P	Falcon 20F-5	430	Phillips Petroleum Co. Bartlesville, Ok.	N428F/F-WMKG
N660RM	Sabre-60	306-91	RWR Development/Unlimited Airracing Inc. Van Nuys, Ca.	N60BP/N204G/N204R N65774
N660TC	Learjet	25D-317	Marine Shale Processors Inc. St Rose, La.	///N821LM
N660W	Jet Commander	58	Outlaw Aircraft Sales Inc. Clarksville, Tn.	N120GH/N721AS/N90B
N661GL	Falcon 10	3	International Mineral & Chemical Co. Waukegan Airport, Il.	N731FJ/N100FJ F-WJMM
N661LJ	Learjet	25-002	Wfu 7/72. AiResearch engine tests.	
N662G	Gulfstream 2	188	McWane Inc. Birmingham, Al.	/N862G/N823GA
N662P	Falcon 20F	378	Phillips Petroleum Co. Bartlesville, Ok.	(N662PP)/N107F/F-WRQT
N663CA	Learjet	35-063	Continental Air Transport Co. Tulsa, Ok.	//N828M
N664CL	Learjet	24-167	Pistol Creek Leasing/Clay Lacy, Boise, Id.	N888B/N841LC/N847GA
N664P	Falcon 50	200	Phillips Petroleum Corp. Bartlesville, Ok.	N288FJ/F-WWHE
N665P	Falcon 20F	444	Phillips Petroleum Corp. Bartlesville, Ok.	N453F/F-WJMJ
N666DA	Falcon 20C	129	George T Andros, Fresno, Ca.	N1823A/N1823F/N4346F/F-WJMM
N666ES	Citation	500-0045	Starwood Aviation Inc. Englewood, Co.	/N31MW/N11AQ/N7KH/N6VF/N4VF/N545CC
N666JT	Gulfstream 2	162	Janus Transair Corp. Bedford, NY.	N74RV/C-GTCB/N74RV/N530SW/(C-GANE)
N666K	Westwind-1124	207	John Mason/Aerojet Charter Inc. Washington, DC.	N519ME/N330PC/N6053C N1124P/4X-CLE
N666LN	Citation	S550-0005	Leon Nightingale, Reno, Nv.	(N1256G)
N666PE	Learjet	25D-359	Allen Investments Inc. Pinehurst, NC.	N666RE/N359SK/N37973
N666RE	Learjet	31-016	Allen Investments Inc. Pinehurst, NC.	N4291K
N666SA	Citation	500-0031	International Ground Support Systems, Santa Fe, NM.	/N81883/YU-BIA/N531CC
N667LC	Challenger 601-3A	5032	Loews Corp/Clinton Court Corp. Teterboro, NJ.	/N604CC/C-G...
N667P	Falcon 20F	432	Phillips Petroleum Co. Bartlesville, Ok.	N430F/F-WJMK
N668CM	Citation	550-0668		
N668JT	HS 125/731	NA721	E S Jacobs Co/Park Avenue Aviation Inc. NYC.	(N105EJ)/N668JT/N666JT/N40SK N933/N93BH/N125G/G-AWXF
N673LP	Citation	550-0179	Louisiana Pacific Corp. Hillsboro, Or.	/N60MM/N88824
N674G	Citation	550-0435	Findlay Industries Inc. Findlay, Oh.	N390DA/N20CL//N434CC/(N1219N)
N676DW	Falcon 20F	387	California Energy/Fair Green Master Trust, Columbus, Oh.	N387CE///N676DW N56CC/N162F/F-WJML
N676RW	Gulfstream 3	355	Coca Cola Co. Atlanta, Ga.	N318GA
N677RW	Gulfstream 2	191	Coca Cola Co. Atlanta, Ga.	N679RW/N680RW/N810GA
N678BC	JetStar-731	13/5109	Quadion/Minnesota Rubber Co. Minneapolis, Mn.	//N968BN/N968GN/N7945L
N678ML	Challenger 600S	1011	Berkshire Hathaway Inc. Omaha, Ne.	//N601JR/N510PS/N510PC/N42137/C-GBHS
N678RW	Gulfstream 4	1017	Coca Cola Co. Atlanta, Ga.	N405GA
N678S	Learjet	35A-342	AMR Combs Florida Inc. Fort Lauderdale, Fl.	/VH-LGH/VH-SDN/N37931/N1088D
N679BC	Citation	550-0589	Quadion Corp. Minneapolis, Mn.	(N1301Z)
N680BC	Learjet	25B-200	Chrysler Aviation Inc. Van Nuys, Ca.	N2022R
N680FM	B 727-25	18970	Freeport McMoRan Inc. New Orleans, La.	(N8221J)/N682FM/C-GQBE/N8146N
N680TT	JetStar-8	5108	Knotts Landing Catering/Jetline Inc. New Orleans, La.	N68CT/N24UG/N1207Z N7953S
N681FM	Gulfstream 3	371	Freeport McMoRan Inc. New Orleans, La.	(N8220F)/N680FM/HZ-NR3
N682B	BAe 125/800A	NA0431	E I Dupont de Nemours & Co. New Castle, De.	N585BA/G-5-618
N682D	Falcon 100	200	Dow Chemical Co. Midland, Mi.	N662D/N265FJ/F-WZGG
N682D	Citation V	560-0021	Dow Chemical Co. Freeport, Tx.	(N1228V)
N682FM	Gulfstream 3	305	Freeport McMoRan Inc. New Orleans, La.	/N235U/N305GA
N682RW	BAC 1-11/401AK	061	Detroit Red Wings Inc. Detroit, Mi.	N40AS/N5021
N683E	BAe 125/800A	NA0410	E I Dupont de Nemours & Co. New Castle, De.	/N555BA/G-5-587

Registration	Type	c/n	Owner / Operator	Previous identity
N683FM	Gulfstream 2	167	McMoRan Properties Inc. New Orleans, La.	N682FM/(N82204)/N681FM/N430DP N900SF/N204GA/VR-CBC/5V-TAC/N17583
N683MB	Citation	650-0159	Meridian Bancorp Inc. Reading, Pa.	N13113
N684C	BAe 125/800A	8063	E I Dupont de Nemours, Wilmington, De.	/N367BA/G-5-518
N684HA	Citation	500-0113	Harlan Anderson, New Canaan, Ct.	N113CC/(N613CC)
N684LA	Learjet	35A-113	Anderson Management Corp. New Canaan, Ct.	/N14M/N35RN/N35CL/N763GL
N685EM	HS 125/700A	NA0219	Brass Aviation Inc. Fairfield, NJ.	/N685FM/N372BD/N372BC/N1230A/G-BFMO
N685TA	Gulfstream 4	1003	G IV Corp/American Home Products,	N986AH/N403GA
N686FG	HS 125/700A	NA0345	General Felt Industries/21 Aviation Corp. NYC.	N686SG/N774GF/N710BS/G-5-18
N688GS	Learjet	25B-123	Scheduling Corporation of America, Oak Brook, Il.	N906SU/(N914RA)/N973JD N360AA
N688H	Gulfstream 4	1062	Henley Group Inc. Manchester, NH.	/N462GA/N17583
N688MC	Gulfstream 2	81	Delta Bravo Inc. Dayton, Oh.	/N283MM/N281GA/N44MD/N777SW
N690LJ	Learjet	23-078	W/o 30 Nov 67.	
N691RC	Gulfstream 2	43	Wham Leasing Corp. West Palm Beach, Fl.	/N33ME/N84X/F-BRUY/N17583
N692CC	Citation	650-0092	Boeing Equipment Holding Co. Wichita, Ks.	(N1318L)
N692G	Falcon 20	44	General Dynamics-Convair Division, San Diego, Ca.	N355WG/N355WC/N355WB N873F/F-WNGN
N694JC	HS 125/1A-522	25107	F & F Charter Corp. Miami, Fl.	N107BW/C-GFCL/N2426/N7125J/G-ATUX
N696HC	Citation	650-0154	Henry Crown & Co. Wheeling, Il.	N154CC/(N1326P)
N697MC	Citation	650-0097	Manor Care Aviation Inc. Silver Springs, Md.	(N1318Y)
N700AC	HS 125/700A	NA0290	Lazy Lane Farms/Perpetual Corp. Houston, Tx.	G-5-18
N700AS	Citation	551-0002	Owners Jet Services Ltd. Las Vegas, Nv.	N2OFM/YV-140CP/N3210M
N700BD	Falcon 10	81	Becton Dickinson & Co. Teterboro Airport, NJ.	N162FJ/F-WPXF
N700BW	HS 125/700A	NA0288	Borg Warner Corp. Chicago, Il.	/N125AH/G-5-16
N700CN	Gulfstream 4	1133	Copley Press Inc. La Jolla, Ca.	N443GA
N700CW	Citation	500-0205	W/o 1 Apr 83.	(N541NC)/N520N
N700DE	HS 125/700A	NA0274	Dunavant Enterprises Inc. Fresno, Ca.	/N44BB/N125TA/N125BA/(N125AB)/G-5-11
N700DK	Falcon 10	191	W/o 23 Sep 85.	N256FJ/F-WZGV
N700DW	Falcon 100	205	Durakool/Durair Inc. Elkhart, In.	N269FJ/F-WZGL
N700FA	HS 125/731	NA752	Desert Air Charters Inc. Scottsdale, Az.	N700PL/N731HS/N61MX/N61MS/N914BD N48BH
N700FC	Learjet	25B-082	United States Navy, Arlington, Va.	N654/N11AK/N15AK/N427RD/N30P/HB-VCK
N700FE	HS 125/700A	NA0278	Federated Investors Inc. Pittsburgh, Pa.	N86WC/N6GQ/N6GG//N45500/XA-KON G-5-14
N700FS	Gulfstream 2	108	Flo-Sun Aircraft Inc. High Point, NC.	/N600MB//N60GG/N11UC/N810GA
N700GD	Gulfstream 4	1104	AHP Holdings Inc. Van Nuys, Ca.	/N600ML
N700HA	HS 125/700A	NA0302	Embassy Suites Inc. Memphis, Tn.	//N700AA/G-5-19
N700HH	HS 125/700A	NA0240	Hilton Hotels Corp. Las Vegas, Nv.	N130BA/G-BFZJ
N700JC	Sabre-65	465-74	Oxley Petroleum Co. Tulsa, Ok.	
N700KC	Challenger 601-3A	5017	Kimberly-Clark Corp. Dallas, Tx.	/C-GLWX
N700LS	Gulfstream 4	1009	Limited Stores/Central Holding Corp. Wilmington, De.	N500VS/N500LS/N423GA
N700MD	Westwind-1124	212	Kal Kustom NW Inc. Salem, Or.	N900CS/N212WW/4X-CLJ
N700MK	Challenger 601	3011	Kapor Enterprises Inc. Londonderry, NH.	N899WW/N399WW/N601AG/C-GBYC/C-GLWX
N700MM	Westwind-1124	311	Great Planes Sales Inc. Tulsa, Ok.	(N788MA)/N700MM/N50XX//N700MM/4X-CRE
N700PD	HS 125/700A	NA0221	John H Harland Co. Greensboro, NC.	(N248JH)/N700PD/N465R
N700PM	Gulfstream 2B	207	Philip Morris Management Corp. Teterboro, NJ.	
N700R	Westwind-1124	222	NASCAR, Daytona Beach, Fl.	N86EF/N36EF/N294B/N294W/4X-CLT
N700RR	Citation	650-0025	National Underwriting Services Corp. Wilmington, De.	/(N277HG)/(N376HW) N200RT/N10PX
N700SB	HS 125/700A	NA0286	Steven Bochco/Air Bunky Inc. Los Angeles, Ca.	N2OFX/N125AU/G-5-14
N700SJ	Learjet	35A-082	Palumbo Aircraft Sales Inc. Uniontown, Oh.	N700GB/N285HR/N235HR
N700TF	Citation V	560-0011	Tyson Foods, Springdale, Ar.	(N1217H)
N700WM	HS 125/700B	7010	Great Planes Sales Inc. Tulsa, Ok.	//LX-MJM/HZ-MMM/(G-5-16)
N700WM	Westwind-Two	319	Miller & Miller Auctioneers, Fort Worth, Tx.	N560SH/XA-LOR/4X-CRM
N700YM	Citation	550-0126	Jetcraft Corp. Morrisville, NC.	N50HW/N82RZ/N82RP/N26863/OE-GHP/(N2747R)
N701AG	Citation	650-0077	ASC/Allied Group, Des Moines, Ia.	/N677CC/(N1315Y)
N701AS	Learjet	35A-047	New Creations Inc. Pontiac, Mi.	N13MJ/XA-ALE
N701FW	Sabre-65	465-21	Marine R Corp. Miami, Fl.	(N265CA)/N465LC/(N65HM)/N2586E
N701QS	Challenger 600S	1066	Stone Aviation, Chicago, Il.	/N721SW/N67B/C-GLXD
N701SC	Learjet	24XR-235	Midwest Corporate Aviation Inc. Wichita, Ks.	N51VL
N701Z	HS 125/F600A	6058	Zapata Corp. Houston, Tx.	N9043U/G-5-16/G-BGKN
N702BA	HS 125/700A-2	NA0243	British Aerospace Inc. Washington, DC.	/N2OSK/N2OS/N130BH/G-5-17

Registration	Type	c/n	Owner / Operator	Previous identity
N702JR	Sabre-60	306-138	John Ribeiro Builder Inc. Reno, Nv.	N700JR/N800RM/N22BX/N2508E
N702KH	Citation	551-0304	Hertel Services Inc. Kenilworth, NJ. (was 550-0262).	
N702NC	Falcon 10	55	Newell Co. Freeport, Il.	N55FJ/N141FJ/F-WPUV
N705NA	Learjet	24A-102	NASA, Moffett Field, Ca.	N365EJ/N436LJ
N706SB	Citation	S550-0139	Cessna Aircraft Co. Wichita, Ks.	N906SB/(N1295B)
N707AM	Falcon 10	26	Durakool/Jupiter Aviation Inc. Elkhart, In.	N592DC/N118FJ/F-WJMK
N707CA	Learjet	25D-342	Chicago Aero Sales Inc. Sugar Grove, Il.	I-RJVA/(N187DY)/N984JD/N820M N39391
N707EZ	JetStar-731	21/5055	Stanton Aircraft Corp. Burlingame, Ca.	N304CK/(N79MB)/(N86BP)/(N43JK) N85BP/N90ZP/N303H/N296AR/N9222R
N707FH	Sabre-40	282-74	Frank Haws/N Alabama Neurological, Huntsville, Al.	N707TG/N572R/N2241B
N707GG	Challenger 601-3A	5037	Avjet/GGS Leasing Inc. Burbank, Ca.	/(JA8360)/N608CC/C-G...
N707KS	B 707-138B	17702	Prince Bandar/First City Texas Houston NA. Houston, Tx.	/N600JJ/G-AWDG VH-EBG
N707PE	Citation	551-0452	Caribbean Cheyenne Inc. St Thomas, USVI.	N707WF/N150DM/N452CJ/(N1249T)
N707RZ	B 707-328	18375	Wfu. Broken up at Fort Lauderdale 4/85.	F-BHSU/CN-RMA/F-BHSU
N707SB	Citation	S550-0141	SBS Corporate Service Inc. St Louis, Mo.	N907SB/(N1295J)
N707SC	Learjet	24-065	Dolphin Aviation Inc. Sarasota Bradenton Airport, Fl.	N957SC///N750WJ (N750QK)/N7500K/N200DM/N2000M
N707SH	Gulfstream 2	77	Powerhouse Corp. Wilmington, De.	N7TJ/N385M/N777JS/N84MZ/N34MZ/N140CH N40CH/N100WK/N824GA
N707TE	Jet Commander-B	137	Tice Engineering & Sales Inc. Knoxville, Tn.	(N700GA)/N700BF/N5BP/N300LS N500LS/N873/N3VF/N5OVF/SE-DCZ/N5045E
N707WB	JetStar 2	5210	First Interstate Bancorp. Los Angeles, Ca.	/N400KC/N5536L
N707XX	B 707-138B	18740	TAG/Trans Oceanic Aviation, Paris-Le Bourget.	N108BN/VH-EBM
N708CT	Citation	650-0185	Centel Corp. Chicago, Il.	N2615L
N710AG	HS 125/700A	NA0338	American General Corp. Houston, Tx.	///N710BZ/G-5-15
N710AT	Learjet	35A-337	Talon Inc. Roseville, Mi.	N337WC/N80ED
N710EC	Falcon 20C	102	Edison Chouest Offshore Inc. Galliano, La.	/N53SF/N223B/N985F/F-WMKI
N710JL	Gulfstream 2	169	Lonimar Stables Inc. Phoenix, Az.	/N31SY/N39JK//HB-IEX/N17584
N710JW	Jet Commander	35	Westar Aviation Inc. Miami, Fl.	N7HL/N189G/N101GS/N100TH/N22AC/N6504V
N710K	MS 760 Paris	112	Edward G Martin, Orefield, Pa.	N7277X/N65218/F-BOJY/HB-PAC/F-EXAA
N710MB	Diamond 1A	A078SA	Merchants National Bank & Trust, Indianapolis, In.	N378DM
N711	Learjet	24B-197	Renwil Corp. Wilmington, De.	N711CN/C-FCSS/N87AC/N52GH/C-FCSS/N953GA
N711AF	Learjet	35-029	W/o 11 Aug 79.	/
N711BT	Citation	501-0240	Carnegie Construction Co. Santa Ana, Ca.	N13BK//N26232
N711CD	Learjet	35A-456	Richards Group Inc. Dallas, Tx.	/
N711CW	Learjet	24-055	Premier Jets Inc. Portland, Or.	N511WH/N2366Y/N809LJ
N711DS	Gulfstream 2	129	Delford Smith/Evergreen International Avn, McMinnville, Or.	/N1H/N871GA
N711FG	Beechjet 400	RJ-55	Unbelievable Inc. Las Vegas, Nv.	/N1555P
N711FJ	Falcon 10	149	American Electric Co. St Joseph, Mo.	(N830SR)/N711FJ/N214FJ/F-WZGU
N711GF	Citation V	560-0068	Indeck Energy Services Inc. Wheeling, Il.	(N40PL)/N2722H
N711GL	Sabre-80A	380-6	Gale Industries Inc. Daytona Beach, Fl.	N75TJ//N50GG/N5106
N711HL	Citation	501-0114	Point Zero Corp. Eugene, Or.	N485RP/N673LR/N673LP/N2649Y
N711JT	Jet Commander	91	W/o 13 Mar 75.	N73535/N1972W/N365RJ
N711MA	Learjet	35-032	Comm Scope Co. Catawba, NC.	(N711QH)/N711CH
N711MC	Gulfstream 2B	48	N & MD Investment Corp. Wilmington, De.	/N4411/N109G
N711MD	Citation	S550-0066	Marshall B Durbin Jr. Birmingham, Al.	N1272P
N711MR	Westwind-1124	191	Executive Aviation, Shreveport, La.	//N13VF/N3VF/4X-CKO
N711NR	Citation Eagle	501-0024	BCDM Corp. Dover, De.	N1CA/(N10CA)/N36886
N711NV	Citation	551-0557	Nevada Department of Transport, Carson City. (was 550-0557).	/N1298C
N711PD	Challenger 601-3A	5013	Paul L Deutz Jr/Totem Enterprises Inc. Palomar, Ca.	/C-GLXW
N711R	Learjet	35-035	ECEE Inc/Cockrell Corp. Houston, Tx.	
N711RL	Gulfstream 2	25	Polo Fashions Inc. Carlstadt, NJ.	N527K/N327K
N711SB	Gulfstream 2B	70	Kerry Packer/Consolidated Press Holdings, Sydney, Australia.	/N711SC
N711SE	Citation	500-0261	Southern Electricity Supply/Robert Merson, Meridian, Ms.	N55LF/N55HF N261CC/N5261J
N711SW	DC-9-15	45740	Golden Nugget Inc. Las Vegas, Nv.	N310MJ/N1059T
N711SX	Challenger 601	3007	Randland Cobey Holdings, Oklahoma City, Ok.	//N711SR/C-GLYE
N711TE	Citation	500-0342	Davgar Restaurants Inc. Winter Park, Fl.	N530TL/(N5342J)
N711TG	HS 125/700A	NA0324	John Sloan/Thompson Companies, Dallas, Tx.	//N710BJ/G-5-11
N711TJ	Learjet	24A-011	Riverside Air Service/Orco Aviation Inc. Riverside, Ca.	N711PJ/N50JF/ N150WL/N1966K/N233VW/N806LJ

Registration	Type	c/n	Owner / Operator	Previous identity
N711TQ	Learjet	25D-298	Jet East Inc. Dallas, Tx.	(N712CB)/N711TQ/N711TG/N923GL
N711VF	Citation	501-0236	Nayko Inc. Portland, Or.	N26227
N711VT	Learjet	25D-292	Randy Corson/Automotive Investment Group Inc. Phoenix, Az.	N92CS/N92MJ N1088C
N711WD	Learjet	25D-282	Transportation Management Inc. Rocky Mount, NC.	
N711WM	HS 125/731	25020	Barbary Coast Hotel & Casino, Las Vegas, Nv.	N365DJ/N2KN/N2KW/N959KW/N167J G-ASZM
N711WM	Citation	551-0388	w/o 6 Nov 86.	
N711Z	JetStar	1002	Wfu. Located at Andrews AFB-Md.	N329K
N711Z	Citation	550-0436	Lockheed Georgia Co. Marietta, Ga.	N1219P
N712CC	Gulfstream 4	1028	Bill Cosby, 'Camille'.	N712CW/N428GA
N712G	Citation	500-0060	JODA Partnership, Highland Park, Il.	XA-PAZ/XA-SEN/N712G/N712J/N560CC
N712J	Citation	550-0365	Eagle-Picher Industries Inc. Cincinnati, Oh.	(N12159)
N712JE	Learjet	36-012	Phoenix Air Group Inc. Cartersville, Ga.	N55GH/N222AW/N36CW/N666TB/C-GBWD N2267Z/VR-BFR/N215RL/N139GL
N712R	Learjet	24-156	Royal Cake Co. Winston Salem, NC.	N111RP/N111RF/N468DM/N599GA
N712S	Citation	S550-0035	sale, 1 East First St. Reno, NV 89431.	/
N712VS	HS 125/400A	NA712	Globe Insurance/VS Aviation Inc. Oklahoma City, Ok.	N7777B/N496G/N60JC N511WP/N1199G/N1199M/G-AWMY
N713AL	Citation	501-0187	Adalid Corp. Del Rio, Tx.	N900DL/N900DH/(N600DH)/N137GK/N23EH/N21EH/N576CC N6779D
N713DJ	Learjet	25D-355	Diamond Jet, Ypsilanti, Mi.	//N7801L/N202WM/(N830WM)
N713KM	HS 125/700A	7094	K Mart Corp. Pontiac, Mi.	N80KM/N49566/G-5-16/HB-VEK/G-OBAE
N713LJ	Learjet	25D-241	High Five Inc. McAllen, Tx.	N713RR/N712BW/N711WD/N25TB/N25TA/N432SL
N713M	Learjet	55-113	Mutual of Omaha Insurance Co. Nb.	N7262M
N713SC	Astra-1125	013	Siecor Corp. Hickory, NC.	(N413SC)/4X-CUM
N714K	Learjet	35A-230	BLC Corp. San Mateo, Ca.	/
N714S	Learjet	35A-367	General Telephone Co of Southwest, San Angelo, Tx.	
N715A	B 737-2S2C	21928	ARAMCO, Houston, Tx.	N204FE
N715JF	Learjet	25B-132	Enterprise Aviation Inc. Houston, Tx.	N54MQ/N54MC/N132GL/N202BT
N716A	B 737-2S2C	21929	ARAMCO, Houston, Tx.	N205FE
N716CB	Citation	500-0055	Cirrus Blue Inc. West Allis, Wi.	N999SF/N900MP/N900KC
N716GA	Citation	500-0210	Aircraft Management Services Corp. Roper, NC.	N210MT/N9011R/TR-LTI
N716RD	Challenger 601-3A	5048	Readers Digest Sales & Service, White Plains, NY.	N2004G/C-G...
N717EP	Learjet	25D-255	Ossian Airways 11 Inc/Philip Saunders, Rochester, NY.	N25GJ/N91MT/N91ED N1ED/N1433B
N717HB	Learjet	24XR-295	HBE Corp. Chesterfield, Mo.	
N717JB	Learjet	35A-229	Laurel Aviation Enterprises Inc. St James, NY.	/N8MA
N717JM	JetStar-6	5009	Cx USA 8/84 as wfu.	//(HB-VET)/N717/N717X/N767Z/N540G/N9206R
N717LS	Citation	S550-0054	Air Murphy Inc. Wilmington, De.	N12709
N717PC	Citation	550-0402	Pepsi Cola Bottling Co. La Crosse, Wi. (was 551-0057).	/N700LB/N6830X
N717TR	Gulfstream 3	418	Triangle Aircraft Services Co. NYC.	JY-AMN/JY-ABL/N17583
N717VL	Diamond 1A	A073SA	Cactus Aircraft Inc. Dallas, Tx.	N356DM
N717WW	Astra-1125	017	B M Aviation Inc. Miami, Fl.	4X-CUD
N718DW	Falcon 50	81	Colleen Corp. Philadelphia, Pa.	/N89FJ/F-WZHA
N718R	JetStar 2	5205	ASC Inc. Salt Lake City, Ut.	N500QC/N5000C/N5531L
N718SW	Learjet	35A-179	Dolphin Aviation Inc. Sarasota, Fl.	/D-CAPD/D-CCAR/N39412
N719AL	Falcon 10	25	American Linen Supply Co. Minneapolis, Mn.	N600GM/N60FC/N83RG/N22EH/N83RG N40N/N117FJ/F-WJMJ
N719CC	Westwind-1124	290	A & C Air Inc/World Jet, Ronkonkoma, NY.	N800JJ/4X-CQJ
N719JE	Learjet	36A-019	Phoenix Air Group Inc. Cartersville, Ga.	C-GLAL/N300DL/N300DK/N718US C-GLMK/N89MJ/N300CC
N720A	B 737-2S2C	21926	ARAMCO, Houston, Tx.	N201FE
N720C	Citation	500-0073	Berkshire Flight Group Inc. Williamstown, Ma.	(N881M)/N720C/N573CC
N720F	Gulfstream 2	66	Norden Systems Inc. Norwalk, Ct.	/N838GA
N720HC	Falcon 200	497	Harbert Corp. Birmingham, Al.	N212FJ/F-WZZA
N720ML	Citation	650-0016	Northwestern Mutual Life Insurance Co. Milwaukee, Wi.	/N1306V
N720Q	Gulfstream 2	58	W/o 24 Jun 74.	N878GA
N721CM	Learjet	35A-210	Conaero Inc. Wilmington, De.	N42HM/(N35HM)/N840GL
N721CW	Gulfstream 3	485	Caesars World Inc. Las Vegas, Nv.	N315GA
N721LH	HS 125/600A	6025	Milar Aviation Inc. San Antonio, Tx.	C-GTPC/N36BH
N721MF	B 727-2X8	22687	Wedge Aviation Inc. Houston, Tx.	N4523N
N721SW	Challenger 601-3A	5049	Golden Nugget Aviation Corp. Las Vegas, Nv.	/N721EW/C-G...

Registration	Type	c/n	Owner / Operator	Previous identity
N722CC	BAe 125/800A	8008	Crown Central Petroleum, Baltimore, Md.	/G-5-11
N722Q	MS 760 Paris	9	O'Hara & Kendall Aviation Inc. San Jose, Ca.	N300ND
N722W	Westwind-Two	306	Wheaton Industries, Millville, NJ.	(N9WW)/N555BY/YV-387CP/4X-CQZ
N723BH	Citation	650-0127	Bell Helicopter Textron Inc. Fort Worth, Tx.	N1323D
N723GL	Learjet	35A-107	W/o 12 Dec 85.	/
N723H	Learjet	55-090	IBM Corp. NYC.	
N723JW	Learjet	24-178	HPH Aviation Inc. Denver, Co.	N41BJ/N24AJ/N56LS/N56LB/N55KX/N55KS/N674LJ
N723M	Westwind-1124	237	Southeastern Aircraft, Greensboro, NC.	N39GW/4X-CMI
N723R	Westwind-1124	272	Ansett Industries Leasing Inc. Bellevue, Wa.	//N26GW/4X-CNR
N724B	HS 125/700A	NA0204	Cessna Aircraft Co. Wichita, Ks.	G-BERX/G-5-18
N724J	Learjet	55-092	IBM Corp. NYC.	
N725CC	HS 125/700A	NA0220	Central Conference of Teamsters, Chicago, Il.	N705CC/C-GPPS/G-BFMP
N725DT	B 727-23	20046	Donald Trump/Donvan Enterprises Inc. NYC.	N925DS/N2914
N725K	Learjet	55-093	IBM Corp. NYC.	
N726L	Learjet	55-098	IBM Corp. NYC.	
N727BE	B 727-30	18933	Imperial Palace Air Ltd. Las Vegas, Nv.	N129JK/VR-BHK//N727CH/N4646S D-ABIR
N727CS	Learjet	25D-313	Physicians Weight Loss Centers America, Akron, Oh.	N727AW/N37RR/N31GS N31MJ
N727GL	Learjet	35A-127	Reinholtz Aviation Inc. Madison, Wi.	/
N727HC	B 727-35	19835	Clay Lacy Aviation/A Jerold Perenchio, Van Nuys, Ca.	N900CH/N727HC/N1959
N727KS	B 727-82	20489	Kalair USA Corp. London.	N46793/CS-TBP
N727LA	B 727-21	19260	Carnival Cruise Lines/Fun Air Corp. Miami, Fl.	N727SG/N358PA
N727MC	Citation	501-0677	S C Johnson & Son Inc. Racine, Wi.	
N727NA	Citation	S550-0043	N L A Flight Inc. Birmingham, Al.	(N727AL)/N101EG
N727PJ	B 727-31	18752	Private Jet Expeditions, Wichita, Ks.	N847TW
N727RF	B 727-21	19261	Guess Jeans Inc. Las Vegas, NV.	N727DG/N359PA
N727RL	B 727-25	18253	Wfu.	EL-GOL/N8102N
N727TS	Falcon 10	76	American Maize Products, Sikorsky Airport, Ct.	F-BYCC/F-WPUU
N727WF	B 727-23	20045	Westfield Aviation, Sydney, Australia.	/N2913/(N2550)
N728A	DC-8-72	46081	ARAMCO, Houston, Tx.	N8971U
N728L	Westwind-Two	349	Kaman Corp. Fort Worth, Tx.	N723L/N65GW/N78WW/4X-CTQ
N728Q	B 707-321B	20025	Kalair USA Corp. Wilmington, De.	N886PA
N728T	Gulfstream 2	82	International Brotherhood of Teamsters, Washington, DC.	N600BT/N600B/N9040 N10LB/N711DP
N730CA	Sabre-40A	282-103	Cardinal American/BKN Corp. Clevlend, Oh.	N217E/N217TE/N217A/N9MS/N44P N7598N
N730H	HS 125/700A	NA0305	Halliburton Co. Dallas, Tx.	N73G/N700HS/G-5-11
N730TK	Gulfstream 2B	140	Pleasure Air Inc. Wilmington, De.	N189TC/VR-BJQ/N212GA/N104AR/(N101AR) N2667M/C-GTWO/N881GA
N731BW	HS 125/731	25075	Bill Walker & Associates Inc. McKinnon Airport, Ga.	N750GM/N9124N/C-FMDB N666M/G-ATLJ
N731F	Falcon 20-5	113	Allied Signal Inc. Phoenix, Az.	F-WTFF//(N731RG)/N500HK/N315PA/N333WF N100WK/N713PE/PT-FOH/PP-FOH/N993F/F-WNGL
N731MS	HS 125/731	NA758	Home Team Systems Inc. Columbus, Oh.	/N6709/N53BH/G-5-19
N731RG	Falcon 20C	168	Allied Signal Inc. Los Angeles, Ca.	/N300FJ/N108NC/N100KW/N4369F/F-WLCX
N731XL	B 727-300	24095	Elders IXL. Melbourne, Australia.	
N733A	Challenger 601	3008	HAC-Humana Inc. Louisville, Ky.	C-GLYA
N733CF	Challenger 600S	1041	C R Bard Inc. Murray Hill, NJ.	N733K/C-GLYO
N733E	Falcon 50	128	Sears Roebuck & Co. Chicago, Il.	N9313/N122FJ/F-WZHF
N733H	Citation	550-0066	JAD Inc. Louisville, Ky.	N3032/(N3031)/N26619
N733K	BAe 125/800A	NA0425	HAC Inc. Louisville, Ky.	N570BA/G-5-610
N733M	HS 125/700A	NA0265	HAC-Humana Inc. Louisville, Ky.	G-5-20
N733S	Falcon 20F	292	Shell Aviation Corp. Houston, Tx.	N4441F/F-WMKI
N734S	Falcon 20F	316	Shell Aviation Corp. Houston, Tx.	N4451F/F-WMKF
N735A	Learjet	35A-323	National Collegiate Athletic Assoc. Mission, Ks.	/
N737FN	Learjet	24-171	Erickson Jet Inc. Clearwater, Fl.	
N739R	Sabre-40	282-78	W/o 16 May 67.	
N740AC	Learjet	55-084	Auxiliary Carrier Inc. Hasbrouck Heights, NJ.	/N85643
N740F	Learjet	24B-222	Larry Siggelkow, Las Vegas, Nv.	/N740E/N692LJ
N740K	Learjet	25D-302	A OK Jets, Deerfield Beach, Fl.	N28BP/XA-KOV/N521JP
N740R	Sabre-65	465-14	TRW Inc. Lyndhurst, Oh.	N71RB/N67SC/N301MC/N651S
N740RC	Sabre-60	306-112	South Pacific Leasing Inc. Dover, De.	/N740R/N2107J

Registration	Type	c/n	Owner / Operator	Previous identity
N741C	Westwind-1124	292	Grover C Harned, Asheville, NC.	N292JC/4X-CQL
N741E	Learjet	35A-508	Eaton Corp. Cleveland, Oh.	
N741R	Sabre-65	465-24	TRW Inc. Lyndhurst, Oh.	N265PC/N65JR/N800CU/N8000U/N2545E/N65NR
N741RL	Sabre-60	306-28	Hardware Services Inc. Orlando, Fl.	N741R
N742E	Learjet	35A-630	Eaton Corp. Cleveland, Oh.	N72630/N42905
N742R	Sabre-65	465-28	TRW Inc. Lyndhurst, Oh.	N333PC/N2549E
N743R	Sabre-60	306-11	W/o 13 Apr 73.	N723R/N4721N
N744E	Learjet	35A-203	Eaton Corp. Cleveland, Oh.	
N744X	Falcon 50	58	Shamrock Aviation/Pillsbury Co. Minneapolis, Mn.	/N72FJ/F-WZHA
N745E	Learjet	35A-294	Eaton Corp. Salt Lake City, Ut.	
N745F	Learjet	23-077	W/o 30 Jul 88.	(N611CA)/N88EA/N90658/N500P/N868J/N812LJ
N746BC	HS 125/700A	NA0218	Baldwin Builders, Driggs, Id.	N546BC/N700RJ/N222RB/N37975/G-5-15/G-BGDM G-5-15
N746E	Learjet	35A-297	Eaton Corp. Milwaukee, Wi.	
N746UP	BAe 125/800A	8069	Union Pacific Railroad Co. Omaha, Ne.	N519BA/G-5-526
N747	Falcon 50	146	FMC Corp. Wheeling, Il.	N131FJ/F-WZHA
N747AN	Learjet	25D-272	Worrell Investment Co Inc. Charlottesville, Va.	N272JM/N272EJ
N747CP	Learjet	35A-502	Bretford Manufacturing Inc. Schiller Park, Il.	/N8565X
N747E	Sabre-40	282-22	Sabre Leasing Assocs/National Flight Services, Swanton, Oh.	N747/N6376C
N747GB	JetStar-8	5141	Aerospace Finance Leasing Inc. Hong Kong.	//N3982A/XB-CXO/N4436S/HZ-SH1 N4436S/N244/N12241/(N376EA)/N7967/N711Z/N5505L
N747GM	Learjet	35A-308	Aero Center Inc. Laredo, Tx.	(N7LA)/N747GM/N99MJ
N747LB	Jet Commander-B	55	Frederick Baron, Dallas, Tx.	//N11MC/4X-CON/D-CEAS/(D-CHAS)
N747UP	BAe 125/800A	8072	Union Pacific Railroad Co. Omaha, Ne.	N522BA/G-5-529
N747Y	Falcon 50	50	FMC Corp. Wheeling, Il.	N747/N67FJ/F-WZHQ
N748MN	Gulfstream 2	215	Merle Norman Cosmetics Inc. Los Angeles, Ca.	N816GA
N750AC	Gulfstream 3	422	Auxiliary Carrier/American Cyanamid, Teterboro, NJ.	N750AC/N319GA
N750CC	Sabre-65	465-37	ANR Pipeline Co. Detroit, Mi.	/N750CS
N750GM	HS 125/700A	NA0245	Norrell Corp. Atlanta, Ga.	N854WC/N354WC/N700BA/N125HS/G-5-15
N750PM	Challenger 600S	1012	Pet Inc. St Louis, Mo.	/(N78499)/N600KC/C-GBKE
N750PP	Citation	501-0686	Peter Pfendler, Petaluma, Ca.	/N6763M
N750R	Falcon 20D	187	Oral Roberts University Inc. Tulsa, Ok.	N40AC/N4379F/F-WLCV
N750SB	HFB 320	1031	sale, 7424 E 30th Hangar 30, Tulsa, OK 74115.	N300SB/D-CERA
N750WC	HS 125/731	25115	PRA Develoment & Management, Philadelphia, Pa.	N429AC/N21GN/N180ML/N111DT N317EM/N333MF/N333ME/N229P/G-ATYK
N751CC	Citation	500-0266	United States Customs Service, Washington, DC.	N5TK/N5266J
N751CR	Jet Commander	88	O'Hara & Kendall Aviation Inc. San Jose, Ca. (bu ?).	N70CS/N963WM
N752CC	Citation	550-0018	United States Customs Service, Washington, DC.	(N3225M)
N753CC	Citation	550-0109	United States Customs Service, Washington, DC.	N2665N
N753G	BAe 125/800A	NA0438	Grumman Corp. Bethpage, NY.	/N591BA/G-5-638
N754DB	Learjet	25-014	David Beggrow/New Air, Salem, Or.	N14LJ/N8CL/N127AJ/N316M/N204A/N914SB N857GA
N754G	BAe 125/800A	NA0442	Grumman Corp. Bethpage, NY.	/N595BA/G-5-646
N754GL	Learjet	35A-197	Ameriflight Inc. Burbank, Ca.	/
N754S	Falcon 50	39	Shell Aviation Corp. Houston, Tx.	N59FJ/F-WZHL
N756	Falcon 20F-5	388	Clevland Cliffs Iron Co. Cleveland, Oh.	/N731RG/F-WTFE/N920CF/N90GS/N169F F-WJMM
N756S	Gulfstream 3	348	Shell Aviation Corp. Houston, Tx.	
N757M	HS 125/700A	NA0211	McCormick & Co Inc. Hunt Valley, Md.	/N454EP/N62MS/G-BFFU/G-5-19
N757P	HS 125/600A	6022	California/Orange Enterprises, Newport Beach, Ca.	N757M/N1515P/N701A/N701Z N34BH
N758S	Citation	550-0407	Shell Aviation Corp. Houston, Tx.	(N767TR)/N600CR/(N1215S)
N760	Citation	550-0269	Union Oil Co. Los Angeles, Ca.	N74MG/N6863G
N760A	Gulfstream 3	428	IBM Credit Corp. Dutchess County Airport, NY.	N322GA
N760AC	Learjet	55-017	Auxiliary Carrier Inc. Hasbrouck Heights, NJ.	
N760AR	MS 760 Paris-2B	108	Pine Tree Jet Inc. Chapel Hill, NC.	PH-MSX/F-BJZX
N760C	Gulfstream 3	430	IBM Credit Corp. Dutchess County Airport, NY.	N324GA
N760DL	JetStar 2	5214	Ronaele Aviation/Scott Paper, Philadelphia, Pa.	/N601CM/N530M/N5540L
N760EW	Citation	650-0056	Corporate Wings/Wuliger Corp. Cleveland, Oh.	/(N273LB)/N273LP
N760FR	MS 760 Paris-1A	72	Flight Research Inc. Hattiesburg, Ms.	F-BJLV
N760G	Learjet	55-107	IBM Corp. NYC.	
N760J	MS 760 Paris	6	Don Hansen, Fort Worth, Tx. (wfu ?).	N84J
N760M	MS 760 Paris	49	W/o 3 May 69.	

Page 100

Registration	Type	c/n	Owner / Operator	Previous identity
N760NB	Citation	S550-0046	NCNB Leasing Corp. Charlotte, NC.	N553CC/(N12690)
N760PJ	MS 760 Paris-2	101	King Aircraft Sales Inc. Dallas, Tx.	(N7038Z)/F-BNRG/F-ZJNH
N760R	MS 760 Paris-2B	104	J & J Slavik Inc. Farmington Hills, Mi.	N760P/PH-MST/F-BJZS
N760S	MS 760 Paris	43	J & B Inc. Washington, DC.	N760C/N776K
N760T	MS 760 Paris-2B	103	Don Redman, Tucson, Az.	N760N/YV-163CP/N760N/PH-MSS/F-BJZR
N760U	Gulfstream 2B	75	Unocal, Burbank, Ca.	/N600CS/N100CC/N100AC/N1000/N823GA
N760X	MS 760 Paris	28	Central Pacific Mortgage Inc. Fair Oaks, Ca.	I-SNAI
N765A	Gulfstream 4	1069	ARAMCO Associated Co. Houston, Tx.	N459GA
N766NB	Citation	S550-0156	EJA/NCNB Corp. Charlotte, NC.	N156QS/(N2638U)
N767FL	Gulfstream 4	1141	Lear Siegler Management Corp. Livingstone, NJ.	N407GA
N767NY	Learjet	55C-136	General Instrument Corp. Hickory, NC.	N767AZ
N768J	Gulfstream 3	304	Aircraft Financial Services Inc. Miami, Fl.	/N600YY/HZ-NR2/N17583
N768NB	Citation	650-0180	NCNB Corp. Charlotte, NC.	(N2089A)
N769EG	Sabre-65	465-9	Kinder Care Inc. Montgomery, Al.	N769KC/N6NP
N769K	Citation	500-0228	Interfirst Bank Austin NA. Austin, Tx. (status ?).	N6365C/(N228CC)
N770AQ	Learjet	25D-209	J S Aviation Inc. Columbus, Ga.	(N770PA)/N770AC//N36SC
N770BB	Citation	550-0606	D C Smith/Mount Zion Leasing Inc. Bucyrus, Oh.	
N770JJ	Westwind-1124	296	Joda Partnership, Highland Park, Il.	/N64KT/D-CBBB/4X-CQP
N770MH	Citation	501-0011	Leland Houseman MD. San Diego, Ca.	N36JG/(N1UB)/N36842
N771CB	Learjet	25D-326	Snowy Butte Aviation Inc. Eagle Point, Or.	
N771ST	Citation	550-0017	California Hotel & Casino, Las Vegas, Nv.	/P2-RDZ//VH-MAY/N3230M
N771WW	Sabre-60	306-29	Wilkinson's Flying Service, Lexington, Ky.	N3008/N3000/N4741N
N772C	Citation	500-0180	Courtland Manufacturing Co. Appomattox, Va.	N61MJ/(PT-LAZ)/N31079/HB-VFH SE-DDO/N31079/I-AMBR/N180CC
N773FR	Citation	501-0042	Santa Barbara Jet Charter Inc. Santa Barbara, Ca.	N87185
N773LP	Citation	550-0366	Louisiana Pacific Corp. Hillsboro, Or.	/N2008/N200E/N1215G
N773M	Citation	650-0093	Marshall & Ilsley Bank, Milwaukee, Wi.	N693CC/(N1318M)
N773WB	Jet Commander	112	South Shore Holding Corp. Metairie, La.	N44WG/N4WG/N91WG/N91B
N774EC	HS 125/731	NA774	Central & South West Services, Dallas, Tx.	N70338/EI-BRG/N125DB/N18GX/N1BG N71BH
N777AN	Citation	500-0027	Private Jet Management Inc. Fort Lauderdale, Fl.	/N51B//N502GP/N527CC
N777CF	Westwind-1124	231	Reagan Air Inc. Wilmington, De.	N8514Y/HB-VFP/4X-CMC
N777EP	JetStar-6	5004	Wfu. Located at the Elvis Presley Museum-Orlando, Fl.	/N69HM//N777EP N524AC/N13304/N9204R
N777FC	Citation	500-0038	Pegasus Flight Center Inc. Fort Worth, Tx.	/N81BA/N2EL/HB-VCU/N538CC
N777FE	Citation V	560-0076	Furnas Electric Co. Batavia, Il.	(N2745M)
N777GA	HS 125/3A-RA	NA706	Laura W Woodford, Fort Worth, Tx.	(N899SA)/N999SA/N21AR/N114PC/N214TC N711SW/N21E4TC/N214JR/N7617/G-AVRH
N777GG	Citation	501-0108	Diversified Health Group Inc. Pittsburgh, Pa.	N777AJ/(N56CJ)/(N2648Z)
N777JJ	Diamond 1	A006SA	Springfield Aviation Inc. Springfield, Il.	N400TJ/C-FPAW/N325DM
N777LF	Citation	650-0034	F & A Marketing Corp. Dallas, Tx.	N34QS/N8OCC
N777MC	Learjet	55-081	Meredith Corp. Des Moines, Ia.	N85631
N777MR	Learjet	24-142	Air Response Inc. Fort Plain, NY.	N200NR/N591GA
N777NJ	Learjet	25XR-173	Wings & Water Inc. Stuart, Fl.	N780AQ/N780AC
N777PQ	HFB 320	1050	Scope Leasing Inc. Columbus, Oh.	N777PZ/N777PV/N2675W/LQ-JRH/LV-POP/D-CISU
N777SA	HS 125/731	NA748	Central Financial Services Inc. Naples, Fl.	N728KA/N143CP/N199B/N189B N144PA/N222RG/N222RB/N22DH/N44BH/G-AXYG
N777SL	Citation	500-0307	K W Plastics, Troy, Al.	N2613/N2607/N5307J
N777TX	Falcon 20F	365	Textron Inc. Providence, RI.	N1018F/F-WMKJ
N778W	Gulfstream 4	1023	Joseph E Seagram & Sons Inc. NYC.	N77SW/N415GA
N778YY	Challenger 601	3017	TAG Aviation Inc. Wilmington, De.	/HZ-SFS//N778XX/C-GBPX/C-G...
N779DD	Citation	550-0310	John T Snipes, Greenville, SC.	/N130TC/N68887
N779SW	Gulfstream 4	1014	Joseph E Seagram & Sons Inc. NYC.	N777SW/N447GA
N779XX	Challenger 601	3018	W/o 7 Feb 85.	/C-GBXW/C-G...
N780A	BAe 125/800A	8084	ALCOA, Pittsburgh, Pa.	N527BA/G-5-547
N780GT	Citation	550-0014	Gordon Trucking Inc. Sumner, Wa.	N702R/N3212M
N780PV	Jet Commander	36	Cx USA 5/88 to Norway for instructional airframe.	N730PV/N1121M
N780RH	JetStar-731	30/5095	Huffco Inc. Houston, Tx.	/N78MP/N9251R
N782JR	Learjet	35A-336	James River Corp. Richmond, Va.	N166RM/N590J/HB-VGW
N784B	Falcon 50	118	W/o 10 Nov 85.	(N183B)/N784B/N113FJ/F-WZHF
N787R	Sabre-60	306-77	Sabre Investments Ltd. Wilmington, De.	N180AR/N65751
N787WC	Citation	550-0471	Lubrizol Corp. Wickcliffe, Oh.	N797WC/N12510
N788NB	Citation	650-0155	NCNB Corp. Charlotte, NC.	N13264

Registration	Type	c/n	Owner / Operator	Previous identity
N788QC	Learjet	35A-609	Mid Ohio Aircraft Inc. Columbus, Oh.	N36NW
N789AA	Learjet	24D-309	Ajax Aircraft Leasing, Dover, De.	(N4445J)/N45AJ/N45FC/N310LJ
N789TE	Westwind-1124	241	Temple Inland Forest Products, Diboll, Tx.	4X-CMM
N790D	Citation	551-0071	Eagle Aviation Inc. W Columbia, SC. (was 550-0020).	//N79CD/N4578F/PH-HES OO-RJT/PH-HES/N3236M
N791MA	Citation	500-0309	Air Flite Inc. Long Beach, Ca.	/SE-DKM/N57LC/N1382C/N1UG/N1JN/(N1GB) N5309J
N792MA	Citation	550-0302	Maxfly Aviation Inc. Naples, Fl.	/N133BC/N441T/N329CC/N6888T
N793NA	B 707-138B	17700	Wfu. To USAF for KC-135E spares 4/84.	VP-BDE/N793SA/CF-PWW/N793SA/VH-EBE
N795MA	Citation	501-0206	Maxfly Aviation Inc. Naples, Fl.	//N501HM/N6784Y
N796MA	Falcon 10	162	CITGO Petroleum Corp. Tulsa, Ok.	N664JB/N226FJ/F-WNGN
N797CW	Citation	550-0232	U.S. Customs Service, Washington, DC.	N929DS/N6861P
N797WC	JetStar 2	5216	Land Sea Air Leasing Corp. Oregon City, Or.	/N99E/N95BA/N5542L
N799SC	HS 125/700A	NA0249	Service Corp Intl/Salvatore Air Transportation, Houston, Tx.	/N31LG/N130BD G-5-14
N800AB	Challenger	1067	Allen Bradley Co. Milwaukee, Wi.	/N50928/C-GBZE/C-GLXH
N800AR	Gulfstream 3	362	Riggs National Bank, Washington National, DC.	N408M
N800AV	Citation	500-0209	Dupage Airport Authority, West Chicago, Il.	(N919AT)/N209MW
N800BA	BAe 125/800A	NA0458	British Aerospace Inc. Washington, DC.	N630BA/G-5-679
N800BG	Gulfstream 3	488	National Medical Enterprises Inc. Santa Monica, Ca.	/(N100BG)/N700CN N325GA
N800BH	Citation	501-0039	Visalia Corp. Santa Monica, Ca.	N800DC//N403CC/N36914
N800BP	BAe 125/800A	8080	Bedford Properties/800BP Corp. Portland, Or.	/N524BA/G-5-540
N800CC	Gulfstream 4	1052	Chrysler Corp. Ypsilanti, Mi.	N419GA
N800CS	Sabre-40	282-64	Cx USA 2/90 as wfu 1986.	N9000S/N9000V
N800DA	HS 125/1A-522	25047	Square Pair Charters Inc. Farmington Hills, Mi.	N75CT/N580WS/N778SM/G-ATGT
N800DC	Falcon 20-5	74	Home Interiors & Gifts Inc. Addison, Tx.	N800PA/N800MC/N57HH/N1MB/N1851T N968F/F-WMKG
N800DL	Citation V	560-0015	Personal Way Aviation Inc. Dallas, Tx.	N12171
N800DM	Gulfstream 2	159	Personal Way Aviation Inc. Dallas, Tx.	N345UP
N800EL	Citation	550-0320	Alamo Jet Inc. Fort Myers, Fl.	N800SB/N300GM/N343CC/(N6890D)
N800FK	BAe 125/800B	8133	Keeley Granite, Lanseria, RSA.	G-5-642/G-GSAM/G-5-616
N800FL	Gulfstream 2	50	Lear Siegler Management Corp. Livingston, NJ.	/N767FL/N39NX/N39N
N800GP	Learjet	35A-158	Pal Waukee Aviation Inc. Wheeling, Il.	/N158NE/N158MJ/N835AC
N800HM	Beechjet 400	RJ-19	Health Management Associates, Naples, Fl.	N3119W
N800J	Gulfstream 3	359	Johnson & Johnson, West Trenton, NJ.	
N800JP	HS 125/F600A	6066	Jack B Piatt, Washington, Pa.	/N32RP/G-BDZH/G-5-15
N800KR	Falcon 20C	144	Genesis Air Inc. Milwaukee, Wi.	(N200WF)/N800LS/N888JR/N888L/N4356F/F-WJMJ
N800M	Sabre-65	465-41	Fitness Management Corp. Van Nuys, Ca.	N2556E
N800MA	Westwind-Two	358	Old Mountain Air Inc. Wilmington, De.	N13UR/N358CT/4X-CUL
N800MC	Gulfstream 2	61	Personal Way Aviation Inc. Dallas, Tx.	/N497TJ//N711MM/N18N
N800MN	BAe 125/800A	8074	American Flite Inc/MNC Financial Corp. Baltimore, Md.	N800MD/G-5-640 ZK-MRM/G-5-541
N800N	BAe 125/800A	8003	Navistar International Corp. Chicago, Il.	/N800BA/G-BKUW/G-5-20
N800PC	Learjet	24D-292	Milwaukee Jet Inc. Milwaukee, Wi.	(N600PC)/N426NA
N800PM	BAe 125/800A	8027	Philip Morris Management Corp. White Plains, NY.	/N812AA/G-5-12
N800RF	Learjet	25D-281	Green Forest Corp. Appleton, Wi.	N555PG/N45KB/N45KK/(N245KK)
N800RT	Gulfstream 2	47	Robert E Torray & Co. Bethesda, Md.	N800FL/N809LS/N809GA/N553MD/N35JM N803GA
N800TF	BAe 125/800A	8045	Tyson Foods Inc. Fayetteville, Ar.	N822AA/G-5-16
N800TJ	Diamond 1A	A022SA	Jaco Aircraft Inc. Clinton, Ar. (status ?).	///N322BE/N322MD/N18KE/(N816S) N313DM
N800UP	BAe 125/800A	8096	Union Pacific Aviation Co. Allentown, Pa.	N535BA/G-5-562
N800VC	BAe 125/800A	NA0415	Oakmont/Crescent Investment Co. Bend, Or.	/N560BA/G-5-594
N800W	Citation	500-0014	Carib Air Inc. Ithaca, NY.	N900W/N766FT/N514CC/N6565C
N801	JetStar-8	5138	Donald E Nama, Las Vegas, Nv.	(N801)//N31DK/N333RW/N1301P/N1301J/N5502L
N801AB	BAe 125/800A	NA0423	Alexander&Baldwin, Concord, Ca. 'Manukapu' (Treasured Bird).	/N568BA/G-5-608
N801G	BAe 125/800A	8017	Allied Signal Inc. Los Angeles, Ca.	/N800LL/G-5-16
N801L	Learjet	23-001	W/o 4 Jun 64.	
N801MS	Sabre-40	282-30	Marotta Scientific Controls/UMS Aviation Corp. Boonton, NJ.	/N709Q/N7090 N526N/N6384C
N802CC	Gulfstream 2	187	Chrysler Corp. Detroit, Mi.	/N202GA//HZ-ADC/N804GA/N17583
N802DC	BAe 125/800A	8024	Air Traffic Service Corp. Little Rock, Ar.	/N800DP/N811AA/G-5-18

Registration	Type	c/n	Owner / Operator	Previous identity
N802GA	Gulfstream 3	357	G 3 Charter Corp. Burbank, Ca.	N340/N303GA
N802JW	Learjet	35A-453	Jeld-Wen Inc. Klamath Falls, Or.	/N124MC
N802L	Learjet	23-002	Wfu. Located at Smithsonian Institute, Washington-DC.	
N802X	BAe 125/800A	NA0418	Exxon Corp. Houston, Tx.	N563BA/G-5-601
N803F	Falcon 200	492	A E Staley Manufacturing Co. Decatur, Il.	N805C/VR-BHZ/F-WPUV
N803JW	Astra-1125	038	Jeld-Wen Inc. Klamath Falls, Or.	4X-C..
N803X	BAe 125/800A	NA0420	Exxon Corp. Hangar 12, Newark, NJ.	N565BA/G-5-602
N804LJ	Learjet	23-004	Wfu. Re-certificated s/n 23-015A. Subsequently W/o 21 Oct 65	
N804LJ	Learjet	23-015A	W/o 21 Oct 65.	
N804X	BAe 125/800A	NA0421	Exxon Corp. Hangar 12, Newark, NJ.	N566BA/G-5-603
N805C	Challenger	1037	W/o 3 Jan 83.	/C-GLYE
N805F	Falcon 20C	60	W/o 5 Jul 71.	N885F/F-WMKJ
N805M	HS 125/700A	NA0292	BP Explorations, Houston, Tx.	(N256MA)/N256EN/N125AK/G-5-20
N806LJ	Learjet	23-073	A-Liner 8 Aviation, Livonia, Mi.	
N807CC	Gulfstream 2TT	212	Chrysler Corp. Ypsilanti, Mi.	/N551MD/N807GA
N808CC	HS 125/731	NA779	Commercial Aluminum Cookware, Toledo, Oh.	N408WT//N400WT/N84CP/N33CP/N88SJ N76BH
N808DS	Learjet	25D-225	DS Air Inc. N Norfolk, Va.	N222AP/9J-AED
N808EB	Sabre-75A	380-51	Lennox Industries Inc. Dallas, Tx.	(N12GP)/N711BY/N4343/N43R/N2135J
N808JA	Learjet	23-050A	Jet America International, Cambridge, Md. (status ?).	/N808LJ
N808T	Gulfstream 3	463	Gulfstream Aerospace Corp. Savannah, Ga.	N80AT/N327GA
N809F	Falcon 10	182	A E Staley Manufacturing Co. Decatur, Il.	/N111MU/N248FJ/F-WZGN
N809P	Falcon 20C	35	Heidtman Steel Products Inc. Toledo, Oh.	N809F/F-WMKG
N810BG	BAe 125/800A	8010	Basil Georges/Belchase Air Inc. Dallas, Tx.	/N84A/(G-OVIP)/(G-BLKS)/G-5-19 (G-5-14)
N810CR	HS 125/700A	NA0251	United States Shoe Corp/Chemed Corp. Cincinnati, Oh.	N396U/N514B/N130BF G-5-17
N810E	Falcon 10	60	Emerson Tool Group, Palwaukee-Wheeling, Il.	N77GT/N145FJ/F-WJML
N810GS	HS 125/700A	7061	GAP Inc. San Bruno, Ca.	N700SF/N700SS/G-OJOY/G-BGGS/G-5-19
N810M	HS 125/700A	NA0280	B P Exploration (Alaska), Anchorage, Ak.	N700K///N700CN/XA-KIS/G-5-18
N810MT	Westwind-1124	372	Biomet Inc. Warsaw, In.	N988NA/N372WW/4X-CUB
N810SC	HS 125/700A	NA0327	Southern Aircraft Services Inc. Fort Lauderdale, Fl.	//G-5-15
N811BB	Challenger 601-3A	5039	Barnett Banks Inc. Jacksonville, Fl.	C-G...
N811DF	Learjet	35A-384	Willowbrook Air Assocs. Willowbrook, Il.	///N37984
N811JK	Gulfstream 4	1140	Joan Kroc/MacDonald's Hamburgers, Chicago, Il.	N405GA
N811PD	Learjet	25B-138	TLC Air Inc. Dallas, Tx.	(N2HE)/N811PD/N711PD/N777PD/N36204/N100EP/N11BU
N812AA	Falcon 20C	57	Ajax Aircraft Leasing Inc. Dover, De.	/N711KG/N76RY/N3JJ/N677BM/N678BM N499MJ/N883F/F-WNGO
N812M	HS 125/700A	NA0258	B P America Inc. Cleveland-Hopkins Airport, Oh.	/N809M/N711CU/(N125AM) G-5-19
N813AS	Learjet	35A-167	RKM Leasing Co. Dover, De.	//N725P
N813DH	Citation	550-0184	U S Bancorp Leasing & Finance, Portland, Or.	//N80DR/N2619M
N813M	Learjet	35A-151	Old Ben Coal Co/stolen ex Wichita 13 Apr 84, cx USA 6/86.	N711L/N39399
N814AA	Falcon 20C	31	Active Aero/Ajax Aircraft Leasing Inc. Belleville, Mi.	/N34C/N806F/F-WNGM
N814CE	JetStar 2	5217	Southern California Edison Co. Ontario, Ca.	/N106G/N5543L
N814JR	Learjet	24B-202	J & R Investments Inc. Wichita, Ks.	N814HH/N123SV/N999MF/N26MJ/F-BUFN N77JN/N3816G
N814NA	JetStar-6	5003	Cx USA 12/89 to ?	NASA14/N9203R
N815A	Learjet	35A-142	Clarcor Inc. Rockford, Il.	
N815AA	Falcon 20D	205	Ajax Aircraft Leasing Inc. Dover, De.	(N426CC)/N4LH/N82A/N21W/N4393F F-WPXF
N815BC	Westwind-Two	301	L Aviation Inc. Greensboro, NC.	N815RC/N500GK/4X-CQU
N815CC	BAe 125/800A	NA0401	Chrysler Corp/NBD Transportation Co. Detroit, Mi.	N108CF/N538BA/G-5-566
N815CE	Citation	550-0204	Kaiser Steel & Southern California Edison Co. Ontario, Ca.	(N300PR)/N200JR N820/(N6801H)
N815RC	JetStar 2	5226	Continental Aviation Inc. Raleigh, NC.	/N2MK/N4026M
N816AA	Falcon 20E	290	Ajax Aircraft Leasing Inc. Dover, De.	I-TIAL//N133JA/N4440F/F-WMKH
N816LL	Citation	501-0029	Del Coronado Travel & Property Co. Coronada, Ca.	//(N411RJ)/N411WC (N411CJ)/N87253
N816M	Falcon 50	99	BP America Inc. Cleveland, Oh.	C-FMYB/(N96FJ)/F-WZHM
N816RD	JetStar 2	5218	Indianapolis Colts Inc. Indianapolis, In.	/N716RD/N5544L
N817AA	Falcon 20DC	233	Ajax Aircraft Leasing Inc. Dover, De.	I-TIAG/N76VG/N18FE/N4414F/F-WLCV
N817M	Falcon 50	24	BP America Inc. Cleveland, Oh.	N51FJ/F-WZHL

Registration	Type	c/n	Owner / Operator	Previous identity
N818	HS 125/700B	7020	ITT Automotive Inc. Pontiac, Mi.	/N125HM/(N2634B)/VR-BHE/G-EFPT/(G-BFVN)(G-BFTP)
N818CP	Falcon 20C	71	Curtis Products Co. Alpharetta, Ga.	N818SH/N33SC/N807PA/N807F/N967F/F-WNGM
N818TG	BAe 125/800A	8018	Texas Gas Transmission Corp. Owensboro, Ky.	/N800PP/G-5-12
N818TP	HS 125/F600A	6026	Jackson National Life Insurance Co. Lansing, Mi.	/N699SC/N124GS/G-5-16 N37BH
N819GA	Gulfstream 2TT	228	United Brands/Air Services Transportation Co. NYC.	(N30B)/(N700CQ)/N819GA
N819JE	Learjet	35A-077	Jet East Inc. Dallas, Tx.	N814M
N819M	HS 125/700A	NA0318	B P America Inc. Cleveland-Hopkins Airport. Oh.	/G-5-14
N819Y	Citation	550-0278	Fleetwing Aviation Inc. Wilmington, De.	(N990Y)/N6864L
N820	Citation	500-0310	RHS Carpet Mills, Morrisville, NC.	N820FJ/N1851N/N1851T/N510CC/(N5310J)
N820DY	Sabre-75A	380-40	Dixie Yarns Inc/Krystal Aviation, Chattanooga, Tn.	N920DY/N75NL/N4NB/N4NR N2112J
N820FJ	Citation	S550-0118	Fred Jones Manufacturing Co. Oklahoma City, Ok.	N600TF/N12920
N820SA	Citation	550-0289	American Aviation Financial Corp. Reno, Nv.	N820FJ/N550MD/OE-GST/D-CBAT N68629
N821AW	Learjet	25B-101	Rasmark Jet Charter Inc. El Paso, Tx.	N74JL/N600HD/N600HT/N156CB/N30AP N269AS/N575GD/N268GL
N821G	Citation	550-0604	Electric Boat Inc/General Dynamics Corp. Groton, Ct.	
N821LG	Falcon 10	170	W/o 2 Feb 86.	N236FJ/F-WZGX
N821LG	Westwind-1124	430	Seneca Livestock Co/Aaron Jones, Eugene, Or.	N430W/4X-CUM
N822LJ	Learjet	23-080	W/o 9 Dec 67.	
N823CA	Learjet	35A-600	ConAgra Inc. Omaha, Nb.	
N824CA	Gulfstream 4	1010	ConAgra Inc. Omaha, Ne.	N444TJ/N426GA
N824LJ	Learjet	23-083	Duncan Aviation Inc. Lincoln, Ne.	
N824R	Falcon 50	121	Sears Roebuck & Co. Chicago, Il.	N9311/N115FJ/F-WZHO
N825AA	Learjet	24-147	Ajax Aircraft Leasing Inc. Dover, De.	N33NJ/N444KW/N16CP/N595GA/N673LJ
N825CT	HS 125/700A	NA0229	Cooper Tire & Rubber Co. Findlay, Oh.	/N700LS/(N601UU)/N400NU/N400NW N700BB/G-5-12
N825DM	Learjet	24D-237	David Meyer, Memphis, Tn.	/N25RJ/XA-/N889WF/N353J/N32AA/N112J/N25TA/N111TT N902AR
N825PS	BAe 125/800A	NA0412	Pleuss-Stauffer/Omy Avn Inc/Cobblestone Corp. Boston, Ma.	//N557BA/G-5-589
N826GA	Gulfstream 2B	166	PPG Industries Inc. Pittsburgh, Pa.	/(N84AL)/N66AL/N515KA/N811GA
N826JP	Challenger 601-3A	5050	Portland Glove Co/Marmon Aviation, Chicago, Il.	C-G...
N827GA	Gulfstream 2	80	PPG Industries Inc. Pittsburgh, Pa.	
N828G	Citation	650-0138	General Dynamics Corp. San Diego, Ca.	(N1324R)
N830	Westwind-Two	442	Lukens Steel Co. Coatesville, Pa.	N406W/4X-C..
N830CB	Citation	S550-0004	Plastene Supply Co. Portageville, Mo.	N509CC/N1256B
N830TL	Gulfstream 2	49	CanadairChallenger Inc. Windsor, Ct.	(N830TE)/N830TL/N830TE/N830TL/N74JK N747G/N871GA
N830VL	Citation	550-0412	DSC Transportation Inc. Cupertino, Ca.	N410CC/N1216Q
N831CB	Citation	650-0160	Plastene Supply Co. Portageville, Mo.	N24UM/N95CC/N1312D
N831CW	Citation	500-0159	Kenneth Ricci, Camden, De.	//N50AC/N165BA//N36MC
N831HG	Falcon 20E	310	1M Inc. Norcross, Ga.	/N121AM/(N370ME)/N4450F/F-WMKH
N831J	Learjet	35A-166	Jet Cap Inc. Chesterfield, Mo.	/N831CJ
N831LC	HS 125/1A-522	25095	Duncan Aircraft Sales Inc. Venice, Fl.	/N25AW///N61BL/N80CC/N5001G/N1923G CF-SHZ/N125Y/G-ATSO
N831RA	Learjet	24-164	FKO Systems Inc. McAllen, Tx.	N924BW/N464J/N711L
N832MR	HS 125/731	25231	MR Interests/Maralo Inc. Houston, Tx.	(N125TJ)/N707SH/N707EZ/N125GC/G-BEME 5N-AQY/G-BEME/D-CBVW
N833JL	Citation	501-0045	J Lewis Investments, Birmingham, Al.	N833/N98468
N833NA	B 720-061	18066	W/o 1 Dec 84.	N2697V/N23/N113
N835GA	Learjet	35A-087	Parker Drilling Co. Tulsa, Ok.	/N720GL
N836GA	Learjet	36A-027	Parker Drilling Co. Tulsa, Ok.	
N841G	Citation	650-0136	General Dynamics Corp. Clayton, Mo.	(N1324D)
N843G	Citation	650-0173	General Dynamics Corp. Clayton, Mo.	(N1779E)
N844X	Falcon 50	93	Pillsbury/Shamrock Aviation, Cincinnati, Oh.	N98FJ/F-WZHB
N846YT	Learjet	25-012	True Oil Co. Casper, Wy.	/N191DA/N853DS/N853GA
N847C	Citation	S550-0003	Bellemead Development Corp. Dover, De.	N847G/(N21AG)/(N12554)
N847G	Citation	650-0101	National Gypsum Co. Charlotte, NC.	N1319M
N848C	Jet Commander	54	Cx USA 8/88 as wfu.	
N848C	Beechjet 400A	RJ-63	Crabtree Capital Corp. Wilkesboro, NC.	
N848G	Citation	S550-0152	General Dynamics Corp. San Diego, Ca.	N26369

Registration	Type	c/n	Owner / Operator	Previous identity
N848W	HS 125/600A	6044	Page Avjet Corp. Orlando, Fl.	C-GKCC/N46B/(N46BE)/N42BH/N600MB
N850CC	Sabre-65	465-38	ABCO Leasing/Coastal Corp. Houston, Tx.	N850CS
N850SC	Learjet	25-023	Sarasota Jet Center Inc. Sarasota, Fl.	(N12RA)//(N820RT)///N47AJ/(N861L) N13CR/N72CD/N577LJ
N850TJ	Diamond 1A	A054SA	Harmon Industries Inc. Blue Springs, Mo.	//N354DM
N852SC	Learjet	25-006	Sarasota Jet Center, Sarasota-Bradenton Airport, Fl.	N522SC/(N88GJ)/N88CJ N9MH/N256P
N852WC	HS 125/700A	NA0267	Northwest Pipeline/Williams Companies, Tulsa, Ok.	N352WC/N215G/N125L G-5-12
N856JB	Learjet	23-052	Sky Way Enterprises Inc. Bellesville, Mi.	N360EJ/HB-VBD/N360EJ
N856W	Gulfstream 3	484	Travelers Corp. Windsor Locks, Ct.	/N4UP/N310GA
N857W	Sabre-65	465-72	Travelers Insurance Co. Windsor Locks, Ct.	
N860E	Falcon 10	52	Emerson Electric Co. St. Louis, Mo.	N8100E/N52TJ/N342G/N138FJ/F-WLCX
N862G	Gulfstream 3	329	General Dynamics Corp. St.Louis, Mo.	N301GA
N863BD	Falcon 50	161	Becton-Dickinson/Heleasco Twenty-Four Inc. Wilmington, De.	N144FJ/F-WZHA
N864CL	Learjet	24B-229	W/o 9 Oct 84.	N551AS/N298H/N293BC
N866FP	Falcon 50	22	Falcon Jet Corp. Teterboro, NJ.	/N203BT/N50FS/F-WZHF
N866JS	Learjet	23-018	W/o 6 May 80.	N866DB/N652J/D-IKAA/N661FS/N807LJ
N869K	Citation	500-0077	Deilla Corp. Greensburg, Pa.	///N342AP/N577CC
N869KC	Sabre-65	465-33	Kinder Care Inc. Montgomery, Al.	(N869EG)/N869KC/N994
N869KM	HS 125/700A	NA0315	G D Searle & Co. Skokie, Il.	/G-5-14
N870PT	Citation	550-0349	TPT Aviation, Gastonia, NC.	/N8FD
N871D	Gulfstream 2B	245	Diamond International Aviation Corp. Ronkonkoma, NY.	/N141GS//N829GA
N873LP	Learjet	35A-659	Louisiana Pacific Corp. Hillsboro, Or.	
N873LP	Learjet	35A-104	W/o 22 Sep 85.	/N87W
N874G	Citation	650-0137	General Dynamics Corp. Fort Worth, Tx.	(N1324G)
N874RA	Gulfstream 3	361	Anadarko Petroleum Corp. Houston, Tx.	(N875E)
N876WB	Citation	500-0347	Schaefer Ambulance Service Inc. Van Nuys, Ca.	/N500XY/(N5347J)
N877C	Citation	501-0017	Norman Fink Engineering Co. Los Angeles, Ca.	N36869
N877S	Beechjet 400	RJ-17	Sparks Aviation Inc. Memphis, Tn.	N417BJ
N880A	Gulfstream 2	38	Chrysler Pentastar Aviation Inc. Ypsilanti, Mi.	//N80A
N880DP	BAC 1-11/401AK	079	Detroit Pistons/Round Ball One Corp. Northville, Mi.	N800DM/N5037
N880EP	Convair 880	38	Wfu 6 Feb 84. Located at Elvis Presley's Graceland Estate.	N8809E
N880GC	Gulfstream 4	1016	Guardian Industries Corp. Northville, Mi.	N29GY/N95AE/N427GA
N880KC	Sabre-60	306-121	CKB Petroleum Inc. Dallas, Tx.	(N15CK)//N880KC/N2130J
N880WD	Gulfstream 2	217	Guardian Industries Corp. Northville, Mi.	N81728/N88GA
N880WW	Westwind-1124	195	Trans Exec Air Service Inc. Santa Monica, Ca.	/N887PL/4X-CKS
N881CA	Citation	500-0132	Valley Bank Leasing Inc. Phoenix, Az.	N888GA/N888JD/(N10GR)/N80CC/N35LT (N632CC)
N881FC	Learjet	24-175	International Flight Center Inc. Miami, Fl.	/N28BK/N288K/N859L/N859GM
N881J	Falcon 20F-5	396	International Paper Co. NYC.	N179F/F-WMKG
N881M	Falcon 50	83	International Paper Co. NYC.	N88U/F-WZHJ
N881W	Learjet	35A-269	L R French, Midland, Tx.	
N882KB	Citation	S550-0075	F Korbel & Bros Inc. Guerneville, Ca.	N554CC/(N1273N)
N882SB	Learjet	25D-227	Cx USA 7/89 to ?	N444PB/N44BB
N886CA	Citation	500-0258	Enviromental Management Alternatives, Pittsburgh, Pa.	N66GE/(N78AM)/N80639 TI-AFB/(N5258J)
N886CS	Learjet	35-023	Comm Scope Co. Catawba, NC.	N886WC/N986WC
N886GB	HS 125/700A	NA0201	B & S Investments Inc. Lake Oswego, Or.	//N700NY/N40GT/N40WB/N700HS/G-5-20
N888AR	Falcon 20C	33	W/o 7 Aug 76.	N369EJ/N807F/F-WNGO
N888BS	Learjet	35A-409	Bank South Corp. Atlanta, Ga.	N123LC/N858TM/N50PD
N888CF	JetStar-731	52/5070	First Security Bank, Salt Lake City, Ut.	N114CL/N731AG/N177NC/N9921 C-GAZU/N9921/N992
N888DB	Learjet	25XR-073	Concrete Pipe & Products Co. Richmond, Va.	N888DB/N85FJ/N63SB/HZ-SMB/N3JX N3JL/I-TAKY/HB-VCM
N888DH	Learjet	35-010	AFG Industries Inc. Fort Worth, Tx.	/
N888DL	HFB 320	1051	Cx USA 8/90 to ?	N6ZA/N895HJ/D-CORE
N888FA	Learjet	24D-257	Foxtrot Alpha Inc. Millbury, Oh.	C-GHDP/N427JX
N888MJ	Citation	501-0446	Hanover Air Service Inc. Greensboro, NC. (was s/n 500-0097).	N63CF/N14CF N597CC
N888MW	Citation	550-0028	Acxiom Corp. Conway, Or.	/N501BL/OE-GAU/(G-BFLY)/(N3246M)
N888RW	JetStar-6	5040	Cx USA 6/88 as parted out.	/N888RW/N7SZ///N518L/N505C
N888SW	HS 125/700A	NA0295	Rapid American/View Top Corp. NYC.	N371D/N871D/G-5-13

Registration	Type	c/n	Owner / Operator	Previous identity
N888VT	B 727-76	20371	View Top Corp. NYC.	VR-BAT/VH-TJF
N889DH	BAe 125/800A	8051	Jaguar Investments Inc. Wilmington, De.	/N826AA/G-5-18
N889G	Citation	650-0023	General Dynamics Corp. Ontario, Ca.	
N890A	BAe 125/800A	8071	Aluminium Co of America, Allegheny County Airport. Pa.	N521BA/G-5-528
N890RC	HS 125/1A	25084	R H Crossland & Assocs. Hickory, NC.	/N71BL/(N745HG)/N784AE/N30EF/N154TR N453CM/N1125G/G-ATNN
N890WW	Westwind-1124	190	Stevan A Hammond, Dallas, Tx.	/N50AL/4X-CKN
N891CA	Citation	500-0168	Westward Aviation Services Inc. Garden Grove, Ca.	/N135MA/N135BK/N918A N91BA
N892CA	Citation	500-0044	Continental Aircraft Marketing, Rancho Murieta, Ca.	//N712US/N942B/N544CC
N893CA	Citation	500-0359	Continental Aircraft Marketing, Rancho Murieta, Ca.	/N300WK/N36863
N893WA	Learjet	25B-169	Air Stewart Inc. Sarasota, Fl.	/N743F/N743E/N471MM
N894CA	Falcon 10	36	California Aircraft Marketing, Rancho Murieta, Ca.	N224CC//N10UN/HB-VDD F-WJMJ
N895LD	Citation V	560-0034	Casey Co. Long Beach, Ca.	N589LD/(N1229Q)
N898CB	Citation V	560-0097		
N900AL	Gulfstream 4	1097	Abbott Laboratories/ABT Flight Inc. Waukegan, Il.	N402GA
N900BL	HS 125/700A	NA0331	Bausch & Lomb/American Finance Group, Boston, Ma.	/N700BA/G-5-12
N900BR	Gulfstream 2	111	Highland Air/Air Group Inc. Van Nuys, Ca.	/N765A/N13LB/N10LB/N815GA
N900CC	Challenger 601	3042	CIGNA Corp. Windsor Locks, Ct.	N613CL/C-GLWX
N900CL	Challenger 601-3A	5031	CIGNA Corp. Windsor Locks, Ct.	/C-G...
N900CM	Citation	650-0017	Excel Corp/Cargill Leasing Corp. Minneapolis, Mn.	/C-GHLM/N1307A
N900CR	JetStar-731	42/5036	Kenny Rogers, Beverly Hills, Ca.	N90KR/N444JH/N776JM/N41TC//N1622D/N1622
N900D	Falcon 10	141	BFI-Browning Ferris Industries Avn Svcs Inc. Houston, Tx.	(N10AH)/N206FJ F-WZGM
N900DB	Falcon 20F	327	Delta Bravo Inc. Dayton, Oh.	VH-NMN/N96L/N2H/N3H/N4458F/F-WMKI
N900DL	Learjet	24-109	Wayne C Muhler, Erie, Co.	SE-DCW/OY-RYA/HB-VAS
N900DM	Citation	501-0062	Diemakers Inc. Monroe City, Mo.	N208W/D-IBWB/N98599
N900EC	Learjet	35A-236	Jack Silberberg, Maplewood, NJ.	N4XL/N90LP/N8537B/G-ZOOM
N900EL	HS 125/731	NA747	Corporate Jets/L & M Associates, Pittsburgh, Pa.	N125EH/N43BH/G-AXYF
N900FC	Challenger 600S	1045	First City Texas Trans Inc. Houston, Tx.	/N55PG/C-GLXB
N900FJ	Falcon 900	79	Falcon Jet Corp. Teterboro, NJ.	N457FJ/F-WWFM
N900GC	Citation	500-0298	Granite Construction Co. Watsonville, Ca.	N5298J
N900HC	Falcon 900	68	Robert M Bass/Group Holdings E G Inc. Salem, Or.	N449FJ/F-WWFL
N900JA	Learjet	24-108	Malley Trading Co. Fort Lee, NJ.	/N29LA/N45811/C-GSIV/N661SS/N661BS/N661CP N745W/N1966L
N900JC	Learjet	35A-178	Jet Charter International Inc. Hayward, Ca.	/N35GG/N22CQ/N22CP/N40146
N900JD	Citation	650-0199		
N900JE	Learjet	35A-123	Jack Eckerd Corp. Clearwater, Fl.	N3802G
N900KC	HS 125/731	NA723	K C Aviation, Appleton, Wi.	N511YP/G-AXDP
N900LC	Citation	550-0040	Cessna Aircraft Co. Wichita, Ks. (was 551-0085)	/N277CJ/N220CC/(N3274M)
N900LM	Westwind-Two	373	Landmark Land Co of California, Carmel, Ca.	/N373CM/4X-CUK
N900MA	Falcon 900	67	Danaher Inc.	/N448FJ/F-WWFD
N900MC	Citation	501-0052	Wm Tillinghast, Cincinnati, Oh.	N98715
N900MJ	Falcon 900	48	ACM Aviation/Apple Computers, San Jose, Ca.	N435FJ/F-WWFG
N900MM	Citation	501-0128	Engineered Data Products Inc. Phoenix, Az.	N522CC/(N26504)
N900NA	Learjet	24A-111	AMR Combs Inc. Grand Rapids, Mi.	N44WD/N500FM/N900Y
N900NM	Challenger 601-3A	5057	Emery Air Charter, Rockford, Il.	C-GLWR
N900PA	Westwind-Two	400	Polo Aviation Inc. Wilmington, De.	N300LS/N200LS/4X-CUP
N900Q	Learjet	25-049	Majestic Leasing Co Inc. Salt Lake City, Ut.	N900P/N966GA
N900SB	Falcon 900	14	Southwestern Bell, Chesterfield, Mo.	N410FJ/F-WWFL
N900SE	Citation	551-0016	Ziegler Air Inc. Mannheim, West Germany. (was 550-0338).	N500QM/N500GM N550DW/N28968/HB-VGE/N22RJ/(N71RL)/(D-ICWB)/(N2661P)
N900SJ	Falcon 900	19	Sid R Bass Inc. Fort Worth, Tx.	N414FJ/F-WWFB
N900TJ	Citation	550-0176	Cessna Finance Corp. Wichita, Ks.	(N900TE)/N900TF/N552TF/N98563
N900TW	Citation	501-0167	White Development Co. St Louis, Mo.	N38RT//N323CB/N563CC/(N2616L)
N900VL	Gulfstream 2	99	DSC Transportation Inc. Cupertino, Ca.	N900VL/N822CA/N99GA/N851GA
N900W	Falcon 50	60	BFI-Browning Ferris Industries Aviation Inc. Houston, Tx.	/JY-HZH/F-WZHD
N900WA	Learjet	25D-248	Walbridge Aldinger Co. Livonia, Mi.	N500PP/N80BE/N80BT
N900WG	Falcon 900	83	Gilliam & Co Inc. Charleston, SC.	N460FJ/F-WWFG
N900WK	Falcon 900	57	Kellogg Co. Battle Creek, Mi.	N441FJ/F-WWFK
N901AS	Gulfstream 2B	88	I A S Inc. Shannon, Ireland.	//HB-IMZ/N2637M/N2600/N881GA
N901FH	JetStar 2	5230	Coca Cola Bottling Co. Chattanooga, Tn.	/N257H/N4042M

Registration	Type	c/n	Owner / Operator	Previous identity
N901K	Gulfstream 4	1075	Westinghouse Electric Corp. Pittsburgh, Pa.	N412GA
N901RM	Citation	550-0223	Rubbermaid Inc. Wooster, Oh.	N900BA/N6801Q
N901SB	Falcon 200	493	Southwestern Bell Telephone Co. St. Louis, Mo.	N208FJ/F-WZZC
N902	Gulfstream 2	11	Owens-Illinois General Inc. Toledo, Oh.	/N835GA
N902FR	Falcon 20EW	132	F R Aviation, Bournemouth-UK. (N23FR)/(N149FE)/N2FE/N560L/N4348F/F-WMKG	
N902K	Gulfstream 4	1113	Gateway Fleet/Westinghouse Electric Corp. West Mifflin, Pa.	/N423GA
N902RM	HS 125/700A	NA0226	Rubbermaid Inc. Wooster, Oh.	N600HC/N60TN/N60JM/G-5-17
N902SB	Falcon 200	504	Southwestern Bell Telephone Co. St. Louis, Mo.	N217FJ/F-WPUX
N903FR	Falcon 20EW	20	F R Aviation, Bournemouth-UK. (N25FR)/(N146FE)/N5FE/N367GA/N367G/N842F F-WMKJ	
N903G	Gulfstream 2	172	Owens-Illinois General Inc. Toledo, Oh.	/N804GA
N903HC	Learjet	35A-440	Hydrol Conveyor Co. Jonesboro, Ar.	N101PK/N101HK
N903K	Sabre-65	465-57	Westinghouse Electric Corp. Pittsburgh, Pa.	
N903SB	Falcon 20F	335	Southwestern Bell/SBC Corporate Services Inc. St Louis, Mo.	N901TC/N4459F F-WMKF
N904FR	Falcon 20EW	151	F R Aviation, Bournemouth-UK. (N24FR)/(N148FE)/F-WMKI/N4360F/N810F/N810PA N3FE	
N904K	Sabre-65	465-23	Westinghouse Electric Corp. Pittsburgh, Pa.	
N905FR	Falcon 20EW	213	F R Aviation, Bournemouth-UK.	N32FE/N4390F/F-WJMM
N905LC	Citation	550-0581	Special Services Corp. Greenville, SC.	(N13007)
N905SB	Falcon 20F	360	SBC Corporate Services Inc. Chesterfield, Mo.	N901YP/N1010F/F-WMKJ
N906FR	Falcon 20EW	214	F R Aviation, Bournemouth-UK.	N33FE/N4400F/F-WNGO
N907FR	Falcon 20EW	224	F R Aviation, Bournemouth-UK.	N23FE/N4408F/F-WPUY
N907M	Falcon 50	35	Bristol-Myers Squibb Co. NYC.	/N800BD/N57FJ/F-WZHF
N908FR	Falcon 20EW	207	F R Aviation, Bournemouth-UK.	N27FE/N4395F/F-WMKF
N908RF	Falcon 10	46	REFCO Group Ltd. Chicago, Il.	N815LC/N911RF/N134FJ/F-WLCT
N909FR	Falcon 20EW	209	F R Aviation, Bournemouth-UK.	N28FE/N4396F/F-WLCX
N909GA	Diamond 1A	A009SA	Rochester Aviation Inc. Rochester, NY.	N305DM
N909L	Gulfstream 2	112	Louisiana Land & Exploration Co. New Orleans, La.	/N36JK/VR-BJG/N102HS N102ML/N816GA
N909MG	Challenger 600S	1010	Huntrip Inc. Chesterfield, Mo. (status ?)	/C-GCIB
N910A	Gulfstream 3	369	AMOCO Corp. Chicago, Il.	/
N910B	Gulfstream 4	1102	AMOCO Corp. Chicago, Il.	N405GA
N910F	Citation	650-0051	AMOCO Corp. Chicago, Il.	/(N1311P)
N910G	Citation	550-0575	AMOCO Corp. Chicago, Il.	(N12999)
N910JW	Falcon 900	31	S C Johnson & Son Inc/Johnson's Wax, Racine, Wi.	N900FJ/N422FJ/F-WWFB
N910M	Citation	650-0069	AMOCO Corp. Chicago, Il.	/(N13142)
N910N	Citation	500-0158	Kansas City Aviation Center Inc. Olathe, Ks.	N910Y/N999CM
N910S	Gulfstream 2TT	234	AMOCO Corp. Chicago, Il.	/N808GA
N911BB	Citation	S550-0128	Becker Brothers Inc. Peoria, Il.	N1293V
N911DB	Gulfstream 2	100	Skybird Aviation Inc. Van Nuys, Ca.	N234DB/N400CX/N4000X/N852GA
N911EM	Learjet	25D-319	Specchio Cabelvision Co. Rantoul, Il.	N319EJ
N911GM	Citation	500-0048	Miller & Schroeder/Air Lake Lines Inc. Brooklyn Center, Mn.	//N67JR/N44BW N5500S/N11DH/N727EE/N727LE/N548CC
N911ML	Learjet	35A-256	Firstlear Leasing Inc. Wilmington, De.	/N50DD/N6GG/N712L
N911RF	Falcon 50	46	Mid Central Air/R & T Partnership, Wheeling, Il.	N908EF/N64FJ/F-WZHK
N911SP	Westwind-1124	244	Systematics Inc. Little Rock, Ar.	/N124PA/4X-CMP
N912BD	Citation	550-0580	Dillard Department Stores Inc. Little Rock, Ar.	(N13006)
N912DA	Jet Commander-B	147	Bankair Inc. W Columbia, SC. (N888MP)/N912DA/N147JK/N728MC/N720ML/N9047N	
N913MK	Falcon 20F	272	M K Aviation Inc. Dallas, Tx.	N888RF/N732S/N20FJ/N4431F/F-WMKF
N913V	Falcon 10	104	Volume Shoe Corp. Topeka, Ks.	N4557P/VR-BHJ/N90DM/N179FJ/F-WPUU
N914BD	Falcon 900	80	Dillard Department Stores Inc. Little Rock, Ar.	N459FJ/F-WWFA
N914J	Falcon 900	44	Metromedia Aircraft Co. Teterboro, NJ.	N432FJ/F-WWFA
N914X	Challenger 600S	1021	Xerox Corp. NYC.	/C-GLWX
N915US	Learjet	24B-189	Chantilly Air Inc. Silver Spring, Md.	/N711DX/N711DS/N14MJ/D-CONA/D-IKAF D-CJET
N916AN	Falcon 20C	64	Anchor Glass Container Corp. Tampa, Fl.	/N200JW/N806F/N889F/F-WMKG
N916PT	BAe 125/800A	NA0404	Pacific Telesis Group. Oakland, Ca.	N541BA/G-5-574
N917J	JetStar-731	36/5082	Wildenstein/Jetair Inc. NYC. (based Paris-Le Bourget).	//N320S
N917K	HS 125/F600A	6015	Tyler Jet Aircraft Sales Inc. Tyler, Tx.	/N600AV/G-BBCL/(D-CCEX)/G-5-11 G-BBCL/G-5-20/IAC239/G-BBCL/9K-ACZ/G-BBCL/G-BJCB/G-BBCL/G-5-19
N917MC	Learjet	31-012	Express One International Inc. Dallas, Tx.	
N917R	Gulfstream 2	17	Wildenstein/Jet Air Inc. NYC.	N305F/N91AE/N456AS/N819GA/N119K

Registration	Type	c/n	Owner / Operator	Previous identity

Registration	Type	c/n	Owner / Operator	Previous identity
N919P	BAe 125/800A	NA0433	E I DuPont de Nemours & Co. Houston, Tx.	/N587BA/G-5-621
N919TG	Gulfstream 2	160	Federal Aviation Services Corp. Dallas, Tx.	N900TP/N214GA/N801/N80J
N920DY	JetStar 2	5234	Dixie Yarns Inc. Chattanooga, Tn.	N357H/N4049M
N920E	Citation	550-0287	Bennett Holdings Inc. Las Vegas, Nv.	N67LC/N65LC/N444MM/N68648
N920G	Sabre-60	306-74	W/o 27 Dec 74.	
N920G	Falcon 20F-5	352	PAWS Inc. Albany, In.	N4466F/F-WMKF
N921FP	Learjet	55-103	W/o 6 Aug 86.	
N921ML	Falcon 20C	99	Aircraft Management/Marion Laboratories, Kansas City, Mo.	N982F/F-WJMK
N922ML	Falcon 20F	380	Aircraft Management-Kansas City Royals Baseball Team, Mo.	N9254N/N1BX/N8BX N136F/F-WMKI
N922RT	Citation	551-0398	Sagittarius Investments Inc. Reno, Nv. (was 550-0353).	N922RA/N3251H G-GAIL/(N12149)
N923ML	Gulfstream 2B	219	Marion Laboratories Inc. Kansas City, Mo.	/N307AF/VR-BJD/N84V
N924BW	Learjet	25B-158	New Creations Inc. Columbus, Oh.	/N71RB/N334LS/N85MJ/HZ-GP3/N158GL
N925CT	HS 125/731	25066	Cooper Tire & Rubber Co. Findlay, Oh.	G-ATKM
N925R	Jet Commander	80	Duncan Aircraft Sales, Venice, Fl.	N173AR/N900JL/N87B
N926JM	Jet Commander-B	146	Garwood Trust, Miami, Ok.	//N923JA/N99CK/N99CV/N9046N
N926ZT	HS 125/700A	NA0214	PHH/Hawker Associates, Hunt Valley, Md.	/N1868S/N1868M/N900KC/N34CH
N927AA	Learjet	24-169	Ajax Aircraft Leasing Inc. Dover, De.	//N127DM/(N127DN)/N9033X/D-ICAR
N929GV	Westwind-Two	356	Valassis Air Services Inc. Bloomfield Hills, Mi.	N530GV/N533/N8GA/N356WW 4X-CUJ
N929RW	Citation	500-0046	Ron Ward Construction Corp. Rocklin, Ca.	N929CA/N109BL/N109AP/N50SL/N50SK N546CC
N930GL	Learjet	35A-330	Performance Aircraft Co. FLE.(Noriega's aircraft - status ?)	////
N930SD	Gulfstream 2	97	Philadelphia Eagles Football Club, Philadelphia, Pa.	/N11AL/N66TF/I-SMEG N889GA
N930TL	F-28-1000	11016	Time Inc. NYC.	N27W/N281FH/PH-ZAL
N931CA	Citation Eagle	500-0174	Continental Aircraft Marketing, Rancho Murieta, Ca.	/N14MH/N211DB/N21NA/ N26HC
N931G	Falcon 50	126	Sears Roebuck & Co. Chicago, Il.	N9312/N119FJ/F-WZHI
N932LM	Citation	550-0267	Emissaries of Divine Light/Omni Intl. Rockville, Md.	/N68624
N933NA	Learjet	23-049	Earth Resources Laboratory, NSTL Station, Ms.	(N933N)/N701NA/NASA701
N933SH	Citation	650-0009	Shaw Industries Inc. Dalton, Ga.	N933DB/(N1305C)
N934H	Citation	650-0172	Hillenbrand Industries Inc. Batesville, In.	N672CC/(N1772E)
N935BD	Learjet	35A-094	Aircraft Management Service Corp. Roper, NC.	//N506C
N935PC	Sabre-75A	380-59	Southern Company Services Inc. Atlanta, Ga.	N80AB
N937D	Falcon 10	75	U S West/Mountain States T & T Co. Denver, Co.	N12U/N157FJ/F-WNGM
N937GL	Learjet	25G-337	McPherson Monogram Inc. Greensboro, NC.	
N937J	Falcon 10	19	Pacific Northwest Bell, Seattle, Wa.	N36JM/(N36KA)/(N30JH)/N30JM/N112FJ F-WLCU
N937M	Gulfstream 2B	42	Baudovin C Terlinden, Beverly Hills, Ca.	//N8000J
N937US	Gulfstream 4	1092	U S West Business Resources Inc. Englewood, Co.	N468GA
N938WH	Challenger	1068	Harvard Industries, Farmingdale, NJ.	/N215RL/C-GLXK
N940CC	Sabre-40	282-34	Coastal Corp/ANR Coal Co. Roanoke, Va.	N400CS/N5PQ/N5PC/N575R/N6389C
N942B	Falcon 10	105	U S West/Northwestern Bell Telephone Co. Minneapolis, Mn.	N180FJ/F-WPUV
N942C	Falcon 10	11	U S West Communications, Minneapolis, Mn.	N23ET/N23ES/N106FJ/F-WJMK
N942CC	Sabre-75A	380-64	Midwest Energy Services Co. Sioux City, Ia.	N75Y/N75NR
N943CC	Sabre-75A	380-66	The Dorsey Corp. Chattanooga, Tn.	N75L/N6PG/N6VL/N6PG/N2536E
N943JL	Westwind-1124	206	Prewitt Leasing Inc. Bedford, Tx.	N943LL/N215M/N215C/N215G/4X-CLD
N943LL	Citation	550-0442	Pioneer Teletechnologies Inc. Sergeant Bluff, Ia.	N53M/N32F/(N1220N)
N944AD	Falcon 900	17	Archer Daniels Midland Co. Wilmington, De.	N411FJ/F-WWFO
N944AF	Citation	550-0573	Sabrenel Corp. Jupiter, Fl.	C-FJOE/(N12993)
N944B	Citation	500-0318	Omega Air Inc/Principal Management, Dublin.	N518CC/N5318J
N944H	Citation	650-0083	Honeywell Inc. Minneapolis, Mn.	/N13166
N944KM	Learjet	24E-334	Kelly Moss Aviation Inc. Madison, Wi.	/N66MJ/N6KM
N944NA	Gulfstream 2	144	NASA Johnson Space Center, Houston, Tx.	/HB-ITR/N17585
N944TG	Citation	501-0267	Cardiac Systems Inc. Waxhaw, NC. (was 500-0355).	///D-IAEV/G-DJBB/N36846
N945AA	Citation	501-0066	IMP Inc. Paoli, Pa.	//C-GHRX/N501CX/N501BG/D-IHEY/(N2098A)
N945BC	Citation	501-0251	Colson & Colson Construction, Salem, Or.	/N3OBK
N945CC	Sabre-65	465-13	ANR Pipeline Co. Detroit, Mi.	(N950CS)/N13MF/N7HF
N946FP	Learjet	55-056	Frank Pasquerilla/Crown American, Cambria County Apt. Pa.	/(N854GA)/N8563E
N946FS	HS 125/3A-RA	NA700	Fred L Smith, Indian Wells, Ca.	/N725DW/N117TS//N366BR/N366MP/N338/N514VA N514V/G-AVHA/G-5-11

Registration   Type   c/n   Owner / Operator   Previous identity
Page 108

Registration	Type	c/n	Owner / Operator	Previous identity
N946JR	Sabre-60	306-10	Aero Mobile Inc. Wilmington, De.	/N125MC/N19CM/N9001V/N9000V/N30W/N4720N
N946NA	Gulfstream 2	146	NASA Johnson Space Center, Houston, Tx.	N897GA
N947NA	Gulfstream 2	147	NASA Johnson Space Center, Houston, Tx.	N898GA
N948N	Citation	501-0263	Learjet Corp. Tucson, Az. (was 500-0352).	N5354J
N950CC	BAC 1-11/401AK	086	ABCO Leasing/Coastal Corp. Houston, Tx.	N500CS/N111NA/N5040
N950F	Falcon 50	191	Russell Stover Candies Inc. Kansas City, Mo.	N282FJ/F-WWHD
N950RA	Falcon 20C	95	Reliant Airlines, Ypsilanti, Mi.	/OO-EEF/N664B/N664P/N802F/N980F/F-WNGO
N950WA	Citation V	560-0082	Woodstock Aviation Inc. Santa Rosa, Ca.	(N2746U)
N953F	Citation V	560-0005	John Sabick Tractor Co/Transfab Inc. Fenton, Mo.	
N955CC	Gulfstream 2B	54	ANR Pipeline Co. Detroit City Airport, Mi.	/C-FNOR/N123H
N955H	Gulfstream 4	1081	Honeywell Inc. Minneapolis, Mn.	
N956CC	Sabre-40	282-50	ANR Pipeline Co. Colorado Springs, Co.	N956/N757E/N6557C
N957CC	Sabre-40	282-71	Colorado Interstate Gas Co. Colorado Springs, Co.	N957/N2239B
N957TH	Falcon 20C	38	sale, 10770 Midwest Industrial Blvd. St Louis, Mo. (wfu ?).	N1107M/N842F F-WMKF
N959C	Sabre-65	465-50	American National Can Corp. Wheeling, Il.	/N129GP/N2570E
N959SA	Learjet	35A-076	Eagle Aviation Inc. West Columbia, SC.	/
N959SC	Learjet	23-045A	Bard Air Corp. Detroit, Mi.	F-BSUX/HB-VBB/N803LJ
N960AA	Learjet	35-003	Kebra Co Inc. Westwood, NJ.	N4RT/N370EC/N263GL/N931BA/N731GA
N960CC	B 707-123B	17634	First City Texas Houston NA, Houston, Tx.	N707AR/N7507A
N961JC	BAe 125/800A	8062	Cooper Industries Inc. Houston, Tx.	N366BA/G-5-516
N962J	Citation	550-0453	D & D Aviation, Grandview, Mo.	N962JC/N1249V
N962JC	Citation V	560-0006	Cooper Industries Inc. Houston, Tx.	
N963WL	Sabre-65	465-65	Corporate Air Technology/Wm Lyon Co. Newport Beach, Ca.	/(N925WL)/N65AD N29SZ/N29S
N964C	Sabre-65	465-66	National Can Co. Chicago, Il.	
N964CL	Learjet	35A-152	Clay Lacy, Van Nuys, Ca. (confiscated in Bolivia-status ?).	/N101HB
N964JC	Citation V	560-0007	Cooper Industries Inc. Houston, Tx.	
N965JC	HS 125/700A	NA0260	Cooper Industries Inc. Houston, Tx.	N202CH/N130BK/G-5-14
N966L	Falcon 20D	181	Jet Avia Inc. Waxhaw, NC.	N836UC/N4376F/F-WNGL
N967L	Challenger 601	3021	Frito-Lay Inc. Dallas, Tx.	N711SJ/N5069P/C-G...
N969F	Falcon 10	135	Arkansas Power/Central Flying Service Inc. Adams Field, Ar.	/N835F/N199FJ F-WZGG
N969MC	Citation	S550-0001	Montford of Colorado, Greeley, Co.	N95CC/(N1255L)
N969MT	Learjet	35A-459	Montford of Colorado Inc. Greeley, Co.	/N80BL/N306SP/VH-MIE
N970H	Learjet	55-055	Harris Corp. Melbourne, Fl.	N155LP
N971AS	JetStar-731	45/5007	Aerospace Finance Ltd. London-UK.	//N72CT/N110G/N9205R
N971H	Learjet	35A-095	Harris Corp. Melbourne, Fl.	
N971L	Gulfstream 4	1116	Interlease Aviation Corp. Beverly Hills, Ca.	/N431GA
N972H	Learjet	24D-322	Harris Corp. Melbourne, Fl.	N105GL/XA-DAT
N972TF	Jet Commander-B	138	Hamlin Inc. Lake Mills, Wi.	N5BA/4X-COB/N5046E
N974JD	Learjet	35A-648	Wichita Air Services Inc. Wichita, Ks.	N1045J
N975AD	Learjet	35-012	Duncan Aviation Inc. Lincoln, Ne.	N975AA/N95SC/N2242P/C-GVCB/N71LA/N711
N976BS	Learjet	25-016	Riverside Leasing Inc. Marceline, Mo.	N8FF/N83TH/N711EV/N424RD/CF-KAX N145JN
N978E	Learjet	36A-024	Neil Group Management Corp. Medford, NY.	//N38D
N978FL	Gulfstream 3	397	Hughes Aircraft Co/Top Spin Data Corp. NYC.	/N59HA/N351GA
N979C	Citation	550-0504	The Colonial Co. Montgomery, Al.	(N1255J)
N979RA	Gulfstream 2B	151	Ogden Management Services Inc. White Plains, NY.	/N804GA
N980AW	Westwind-Two	414	Morris Newspaper Corp. Savannah, Ga.	(N66MF)/N86MF/4X-CUC
N980HC	Challenger 601-3A	5070	U S Health Aviation Corp. Blue Bell, Pa.	C-G...
N980ML	Astra-1125	033	Alcram Air Inc. San Diego, Ca.	/4X-CUP
N984HF	HS 125/731	NA717	W/o 7 Nov 85.	N100HF/N162D/N162A/G-AWXB/G-5-18
N984JD	Learjet	31-001	W/o 25 Feb 90.	/N311DF
N984JD	Learjet	55C-139A	Wichita Air Services Inc. Wichita, Ks. (was s/n 55-002).	N994JD//N552GL
N985M	Citation	650-0068	Michelin Tire Corp. Greenville, SC.	/N273W/(N1314X)
N986H	HS 125/700A	NA0206	J H Snyder Co. Los Angeles, Ca.	//(N20GT)/N813H/G-BEYC/G-5-12
N986JB	Sabre-40	282-72	Sabreliner Corp. Chesterfield, Mo.	/N78GP/(N69CG)/(N880HL)/N744R
N986M	Citation	650-0048	Michelin Tire Corp. Greenville, SC.	/N98DD/N98BD
N988DB	Learjet	25B-185	Dowbrands Inc. Indianapolis, In.	/N55V/N666LP
N988H	Citation	650-0087	Honeywell Inc. Minneapolis, Mn.	(N1317Y)
N988QC	Learjet	35A-455	R D Scinto Aircraft/Flight Services Group, Fairfield, Ct.	/N455NE/N3794U
N988RS	Citation	550-0568	Estacada Lumber Co. Estacada, Or.	(N1299K)

Registration	Type	c/n	Owner / Operator	Previous identity
N989TL	Learjet	24-160	Erickson Jet Inc. Wayzata, Mn.	/N4791C/C-GTJT/N111WJ/N645G
N990AL	Citation	500-0033	North-South Leasing Inc. Gainsville, Fl.	(N130AL)/N20RF/N20RT/N58PL/N65MA N533BF/N533CC
N990L	Falcon 20C	43	W/o 8 Mar 75.	N872F/F-WMKJ
N991AS	Falcon 900	12	Allied-Signal Inc. Morristown, NJ.	/N408FJ/F-WWFH
N991BM	Citation	550-0114	N90BJ Inc. Warsaw, In.	(N900BM)/N83HF/N88HF/N55HF/(N89B)/N2745G
N991PC	Citation V	560-0043	Iowa Packing Co. Des Moines, Ia.	(N2665F)
N992	Falcon 50	77	Reynolds Metals Co. Richmond, Va.	/N366F/N85FJ/F-WZHC
N992GA	Beechjet 400	RJ-22	Transair USA, Wichita, Ks.	(VR-BLG)/N992GA/9M-ATM/N3122B
N993	Falcon 50	38	Reynolds Metals Co. Richmond, Va.	N58FJ/F-WZHK
N994JD	Gulfstream 2	37	Wichita Air Services Inc. Wichita, Ks.	N179AP/N179AR
N995PT	Falcon 20F	391	Taylor Energy Co. New Orleans, La.	N503F/VH-HPF//N876SC/N376SC/N175F F-WLCS
N997ME	Sabre-60	306-40	Metal Exchange Corp. St. Louis, Mo.	N1UT/N1UP/N711WK/N907R/N4753N
N999BL	Astra-1125	024	Brunswick Bowling & Billiards, Muskegon, Mi.	/N300JJ/4X-CUT
N999CB	Citation	500-0211	Charles Brewer Ltd. Phoenix, Az.	N990CB
N999DC	Falcon 20F	322	Drummond Company Inc. Birmingham, Al.	N1971R/N4455F/F-WMKH
N999GP	Citation	550-0331	Gary Primm Trustee, Las Vegas, Nv.	/N696A/
N999HG	Learjet	25B-178	W/o 8 Sep 77.	N999MV/N999M/N75B
N999JR	Challenger 601	3061	James River Corp. Sandston, Va.	N9708N/C-GLYO
N999LC	Westwind-Two	402	World Air Conditioning/Lonnie Christensen, Laguna Beach, Ca.	N87WW/4X-CUS
N999MS	Westwind-1124	199	Aviation Marine Enterprises Inc. Palm Beach, Fl.	N111AG/N1124P/4X-CKW
N999PJ	MS 760 Paris-2	89	Stephen Griswold, San Francisco, Ca.	F-BJLY
N999PM	Falcon 900	20	Pacific Marine Leasing Inc. Arlington, Wa.	/(N711T)/N415FJ/F-WWFC
N999RC	Citation	550-0479	Smithfield Packing Co. Smithfield, Va.	N1252P
N999SR	Challenger 600S	1042	U S Bancorp Leasing & Financial, Portland, Or.	//N770CA/C-GLWY
N999TH	Falcon 200	512	Journal Publishing Co. Albuquerque, NM.	N45WH/N224FJ/F-WPUU
N999TJ	Citation	S550-0048	Sportsmans Market Inc. Batavia, Oh.	N797TJ/N1270D
N999WS	Citation	501-0186	Weldon F Stump & Co Inc. Toledo, Oh.	/N37HW/N95EW/(N6780A)
N1000	Gulfstream 2	205	Swiflite Aircraft Corp/Oxy USA Inc. Tulsa, Ok.	/N25UG
N1000E	Sabre-40R	282-19	American Air Freight/Wolf Hoffman, Laredo, Tx.	(N40R)/N100CE/N881MD/N881MC N6373C
N1000W	Citation	S550-0079	Ash Property Inc. Dublin, Oh.	(N1273Z)
N1001L	Learjet	35A-155	Jet East Inc. Dallas, Tx.	N110KG/N760DL/N760LP
N1001U	Caravelle 6R	86	Wfu, destined for Pima Air Museum, Tucson, Az.	PT-DUW/N1001U
N1021B	Learjet	23-086	W/o 6 Nov 69.	
N1036N	Learjet	25B-121	Pal Waukee Aviation Inc. Wheeling, Il.	N500PP/N39JJ/HZ-MRP/N7GA
N1040	Gulfstream 4	1044	Cox Enterprises Inc. Atlanta, Ga.	N423GA
N1045X	Challenger 600S	1038	Xerox Corp. NYC.	N8010X/C-GLYH
N1082A	Gulfstream 4	1082	B R Leasing Inc. Seattle, Wa.	
N1087Z	Learjet	35A-660		
N1107Z	Challenger 601	3016	Richland Development Corp. Houston, Tx.	N4562Q/C-G...
N1116A	Sabre-60	306-30	Tyler Turbine Sales Inc. Tyler, Tx.	//N2440C/N2440G/N905BG/N905R/N4742N
N1121A	Jet Commander-A	123	Nashville Air Associates Inc. Gallatin, Tn.	N155VW/N5410
N1121E	Jet Commander	20	Merryman Jet Sales Inc. Oklahoma City, Ok.	///N334LP
N1121G	Jet Commander	67	Outlaw Aircraft Sales Inc. Clarksville, Tn.	N650M
N1121M	Jet Commander	111	OK Aircraft Parts Inc. Gilroy, Ca.	C-GDJW/N999CA/N344PS
N1121N	Jet Commander	110	Fred Hallmark, Warrior, Al.	////N16GH/N181SV/N101SV/4X-CPA/N4716E
N1121R	Jet Commander-A	125	Universal International Inc. Cedar Falls, Ia.	//N30LS/N1121N
N1121U	Jet Commander-A	128	Seawolf Coatings & Equipment, Stevensville, Md.	/N74XE/N74XL/N660RW
N1123H	Westwind-1123	167	ASB Inc. Albemarle, NC.	N873EJ/4X-CJQ
N1123Y	Westwind-1123	179	Windsor Gas Corp. Sonora, Tx.	4X-CKC
N1123Z	Westwind-1123	159	Silverado Airways Inc. Raleigh, NC.	(N12FH)/N1123Z/N722W/N1123E/4X-CJI
N1124G	Westwind-1124	216	Clarence L Norsworthy III, Powderhorn, Co.	/N216SC/4X-CLN
N1124K	Westwind-1124	388	Westlease Aircraft Inc/GECC, Wilton, Ct.	4X-CUH
N1124L	Westwind-Two	405	BLT Leasing Corp. NYC.	4X-CUJ
N1124N	Westwind-Two	346	Merryman Jet Sales Inc. Oklahoma City, Ok.	/N100AG/4X-CTN
N1124P	Westwind-Two	376	Marshall L Tobins Trustee, Concord, Ma.	4X-CJP/4X-CUN
N1124X	Westwind-1124	233	Gaylord Broadcasting Co. Oklahoma City, Ok.	4X-CME
N1125	BAe 125/800A	NA0402	National Intergroup Inc. Pittsburgh, Pa.	N539BA/G-5-572
N1125A	Astra-1125SP	051		4X-C..
N1125G	Westwind-1124	247	GTE Services Corp. Stamford, Ct.	4X-CMS
N1125K	Astra-1125	035	State Street Corp. Stratford, Ct.	4X-C..

Registration	Type	c/n	Owner / Operator	Previous identity
N1125M	Learjet	55-065	Miles Laboratories Inc. Elkhart, In.	//N555GL/N8565K
N1125S	Astra-1125	021	Cooper Communities Inc. Bentonville, Ar.	N1125A/4X-CUR
N1125V	Astra-1125SP	048		4X-C..
N1125Y	Astra-1125SP	049		4X-C..
N1127M	Learjet	35A-226	Miles Laboratories Inc. Elkhart, In.	
N1128B	Citation	650-0184	Florida Light & Power Co.	N95CC/N2615D
N1129M	Learjet	35A-360	Miles Laboratories/SP Statebank Leasing, San Francisco, Ca.	/N185FP
N1135K	HS 125/1A	25019	W/o 24 Feb 66.	N1125G/G-ASYX
N1151K	JetStar-731	39/5115	Rosemount Inc. Eden Prairie, MN	/N8300E/N40XY/N26TR/N933CY/N933LC/N7960S
N1159K	Gulfstream 2	101	Hillbrook Building Co. Moreland Hills, Oh.	(N237LM)/N1159K/N853GA
N1181G	Falcon 50	72	W/o 12 May 85.	/N82FJ/F-WZHM
N1188A	JetStar-6	5091	Four Star International Inc. Laredo, Tx.	/N118B/N107GH/N107G/N9247R
N1210	Sabre-60	306-4	Financial Holdings Inc. Dallas, Tx.	N178W
N1217N	Citation V	560-0012	Peer International Inc. Houston, Tx.	
N1217V	Citation V	560-0001	Slick Phillips, Greensboro, NC. (cvtd fm S550-0136?).	N560CV/N560CC
N1230B	HS 125/1A	25088	Saturn Machine & Welding Co. Sturgis, Ky.	G-ATNO
N1234X	Citation	501-0028	Taylor Industries Inc. Des Moines, Ia.	N36895
N1248K	Citation	551-0445	Roger Galland, Portland, Or.	
N1249B	Citation	550-0448	Cessna Aircraft Co. Wichita, Ks. (may still be N309AT ?).	N309AT/N964J N964JC/N1249B
N1249P	Citation	550-0451	DPF Airlease III Inc. Woodcliff Lakes, NJ.	
N1252B	Citation	550-0475	Passenger Car Assocs/Enterprise Airlines, Cincinnati, Oh.	/
N1252D	Citation	550-0476	Fuel Services Inc. Pascagoula, Ms.	
N1254X	Citation	550-0494	U.S. Customs Service/RTS Jet Inc. NYC.	
N1255K	Citation	550-0505	RTS Jet/U. S. Customs Service, Washington, DC.	
N1256Z	Citation	S550-0009	Cessna Finance Corp. Wichita, Ks.	
N1257B	Citation	550-0497	RTS Jet/U. S. Customs Service, Washington, DC.	(N12549)
N1258M	Citation	550-0636	Marand Aviation Inc. NYC.	N1258M
N1268G	Learjet	35A-661	Unicorn International (USA) Inc. Richland, Wa.	
N1271A	Challenger 601-3A	5038	Time Warner Inc. White Plains, NY.	(N602CN)/C-GBJA/C-G...
N1275H	Citation	S550-0095	Sabey Corp. Seattle, Wa.	
N1278	Citation	550-0430	Armstrong World Industries Inc. Lancaster, Pa.	N264A/N1218T
N1283M	Citation	S550-0120	Menard Inc. Eau Claire, Wi.	N12924
N1297Y	Citation	550-0554	Denair Inc. Wichita, Ks.	
N1309A	Citation	550-0641	First Aero Sales Corp. Fort Lauderdale, Fl.	
N1310C	Citation	550-0645	Cx USA 10/90 to ?	
N1401L	Citation	501-0061	Combination Leasing Inc. Albert Lea, Mn.	N34DL/N436CC/N2757A
N1454H	Gulfstream 3	350	Amerada Hess Corp. NYC.	N317GA
N1500B	Learjet	25-055	American Jet International Inc. Tampa, Fl.	
N1501	Falcon 20C	15	Mobile Telecommunications Technology, Jackson, Ms.	N151CG/N1502/N622R N806F/F-WMKK
N1515E	HS 125/1A	25035	Bill Walker & Assoc Inc. McKinnon Airport, Ga.	N1515P/G-ATCO
N1526L	Citation	650-0176	Warner Lambert Co. Morris Plains, NJ.	N1874E/N176L/N1874E
N1526M	Gulfstream 4	1118	Warner Lambert Co. Morris Plains, NJ.	N439GA
N1526R	Gulfstream 3	409	Stevens Express Leasing Inc. Washington, DC.	N1526M/N320GA/N300BK/N353GA
N1540	Gulfstream 3	314	Cox Aviation Inc. Honolulu, Hi.	/N1040
N1547B	Beechjet 400	RJ-47	Yellow Eagle Holdings Inc. Wilmington, De.	
N1549J	Beechjet 400	RJ-49	Kansas Equipment Leasing Inc. Burlington, Ks.	
N1551B	Beechjet 400A	RJ-51	will become s/n RK-1	
N1558F	Beechjet 400	RJ-58	Watt Industries Inc. Santa Monica, Ca.	
N1564B	Beechjet 400	RJ-64	Moorman Manufacturing Co. Quincy, Il.	
N1565B	Beechjet 400	RJ-65	Ogden & Sons PLC. Leeds-Bradford, UK.	
N1620	Challenger 601	3025	Texaco Inc. NYC.	C-GLWV
N1621	Westwind-1124	275	Texaco Inc. White Plains, NY.	/N1141G/4X-CNU
N1622	Challenger 601-3A	5077	Texaco Inc. Westchester County Airport, NY.	C-G...
N1623	Challenger 601	3065	Texaco Inc. NYC.	N602CC/C-GLYA
N1625	Westwind-1124	229	Texaco Inc. White Plains, NY.	N1212G/4X-CMA
N1629	Westwind-1124	363	Texaco Inc. White Plains, NY.	/N3320G/4X-CUQ
N1707Z	Gulfstream 2	213	Richland Development Corp. Houston, Tx.	
N1761D	Gulfstream 4	1154	Glaxo Aviation Inc. Raleigh, NC.	
N1761J	Gulfstream 4	1117		N1761J
N1777T	Jet Commander	62	Westar Aviation Inc. Miami, Fl.	C-GKFS/N1777T/N5415
N1812C	Challenger 601-3A	5010	Citiflight Inc. Teterboro, NJ.	(N57HK)/N57HA/C-GLXB

Registration	Type	c/n	Owner / Operator	Previous identity
N1818S	Falcon 900	39	Stephens Group Inc. Little Rock, Ar.	(N900BF)/N428FJ/F-WWFF
N1823B	Citation	550-0498	Stran Air Inc. Toledo, Oh.	/N550CJ/(N1255D)
N1823D	Gulfstream 2	59	National Jet Charter/Dwight L Stuart, Beverly Hills, Ca.	/N879GA
N1824T	Challenger 601	3029	Chemgraphics Systems Inc. Secaucus, NJ.	N5491V/C-GLXD
N1841D	Gulfstream 3	438	Dun & Bradstreet Corp. NYC.	N302GA
N1843A	Diamond 1	A025SA	Hotsy Partners Inc. Englewood, Co.	N1843S/N63GH/N317DM
N1843S	HS 125/700A	NA0308	Imperial Holly Corp/B A Leasing & Capital Corp. SFO.	/C-GYPH/N1620/N700KK G-5-19
N1846	Falcon 20C	47	W/o 13 Mar 68.	N875F/F-WNGM
N1847B	Citation	550-0335	Boatman's National Bank, St. Louis, Mo.	N6829Y
N1851T	Falcon 200	508	AFM/New York Times Co. NYC.	N219FJ/F-WPUU
N1863T	Sabre-40	282-62	cx USA 8/87 as wfu.	
N1865M	Citation	S550-0071	Milliken & Co. Spartanburg, SC.	N571CC/(N12727)
N1867W	Citation	S550-0124	M H Whittier Corp. South Pasadena, Ca.	(N1293E)
N1868M	Challenger 601-3A	5012	Metropolitan Life Insurance Co. NYC.	N107TB/C-GLXU
N1868S	Challenger 600S	1039	Metropolitan Life Insurance Co. NYC.	N1868M/N26640/C-GLYK
N1871R	Gulfstream 3	381	Ingersoll-Rand Services Co. Woodcliff Lake, NJ.	N747G/N277NS/N304GA
N1880F	Citation	550-0332	Fisher Controls International Inc. Marshalltown, Ia.	N372CC/(N6803L)
N1881Q	Falcon 20F	414	Taughannock Aviation Corp. Ithica, NY.	N412F/F-WJML
N1884	HS 125/600A	6067	Gulf States Paper Corp. Tuscaloosa, Al.	N270MQ/N270MC/(N522C)/N522X/G-BEIN
N1887S	Falcon 10	190	Stephens Inc. Little Rock, Ar.	/N255FJ/F-WZGU
N1892S	Falcon 20F	376	Real Estate Advisor Co. Chevy Chase, Md.	N2614H/N2614/N2624M/N103F/F-WRQS
N1896T	Falcon 50	127	AFM Corp/New York Times Co. NYC.	N121FJ/F-WZHD
N1900W	Gulfstream 4	1124	Whirlpool Corp. Benton Harbor, Mi.	N420GA
N1901M	Gulfstream 4	1039	Monsanto Co. St Louis, Mo.	N431GA
N1902P	Gulfstream 2	226	J C Penney Co. Dallas, Tx.	
N1902W	Beechjet 400A	RK-2	Whirlpool Corp. Benton Harbour, Mi.	
N1903G	Challenger 601-3A	5051	Gaylord Broadcasting Co. Oklahoma City, Ok.	C-G...
N1903P	BAe 125/800A	NA0430	J C Penney Co Inc. Dallas, Tx.	N584BA/G-5-617
N1903W	Falcon 50	129	Whirlpool Corp. Benton Harbor, Mi.	//N123FJ/F-WZHQ
N1909D	Sabre-40	282-57	Aero Charter/Mercy Aircraft Inc. St Louis, Mo.	N1909R/N545C/N27C/N7507V
N1909R	Sabre-65	465-54	Mike Joannes/BMA Properties Inc. Kansas City, Mo.	N600QJ/N6000J/N2579E
N1910A	BAe 125/800A	NA0454	Hallmark Cards Inc. Kansas City, Mo.	/N616BA/G-5-671
N1910H	BAe 125/800A	8023	Hallmark Cards Inc. Kansas City, Mo.	N810AA/G-5-15
N1929S	Learjet	35A-388	Cape Aviation Inc. Wilmington, De.	/
N1929Y	Gulfstream 2	19	Rokeby Farms, Washington, DC.	/N839GA
N1958N	Citation	S550-0073	Milliken & Co. Spartanburg, SC.	(N1273E)
N1963N	Learjet	23-097	Phoenix Air Group Inc. Marietta, Ga. (status ?).	N1968A/N79LS/N425SC
N1966J	Jet Commander	66	Bruton Smith, Charlotte, NC.	
N1968W	Learjet	23-089	GAR Inc. Cochranville, Pa.	N969B/N869B
N1969L	Learjet	24A-012	Dr Gene Scott Travel Inc. Los Angeles, Ca.	N1967L/N1965L
N1971R	Falcon 20F	312	Ingersoll Rand Services Co. Woodcliff Lakes, NJ.	N619MW/N2605/N4448F F-WMKH
N1972G	Learjet	24D-242	Brandis Aircraft, Taylorville, Il. (repair ?).	/N45CP/N1972G
N1983Y	Learjet	55-079	ARA Services Inc. Philadelphia, Pa.	(N2855)
N2000	Sabre-65	465-7	Oxy USA Inc/Swiflite Aircraft Corp. Tulsa, Ok.	N10580
N2000X	Citation	S550-0064	Ash Property Inc. Dublin, Oh.	(N1272G)
N2013M	Gulfstream 2	51	Monsanto Co. St. Louis, Mo.	
N2015M	HS 125/700A	NA0337	Monsanto Co. Chesterfield, Mo.	N125MT/G-5-14
N2020	HS 125/400A	NA732	Norwest Equipment Finance Inc. Minneapolis, Mn.	N109LR/N100LR/N21ES/N44CN N73JH/N500AG/G-AXOA
N2094L	Learjet	25B-095	Michael Zicka, Cincinnati, Oh.	/C-GRCO/N303SQ/N303SC/N200BC
N2120Q	Westwind-1123	107	Bernardo Serra, San Antonio, Tx. (status ?).	CA-01/N2120Q/4X-JYG/(4X-COK) 4X-COL
N2143J	B 720-047B	18451	Comtran International Inc. San Antonio, Tx.	HZ-KA1/HZ-NAA/N93145
N2200A	Sabre-75A	380-26	SOD Aviation, Oklahoma City, Ok.	N128MS/N59
N2220G	Diamond 1A	A031SA	Printpack Inc. Atlanta, Ga.	N174B
N2265Z	Sabre-75A	380-43	Norman Lively, Chicago, Il.	N6NR/N2115J
N2345M	JetStar-731	19/5075	Cidat Aviation Inc. Wilmington, De.	/N540G//N397B
N2351K	Citation	550-0594	U S Customs Service, Washington, DC.	N1302X
N2426	Falcon 10	186	Owens Corning Fiberglass Corp. Toledo, Oh.	N251FJ/F-WZGB
N2427F	Falcon 10	187	Owens Corning Fiberglass Corp. Toledo, Oh.	N252FJ/F-WZGR
N2440G	Sabre-75A	380-44	Southline Metal Products Co. Brenham, Tx.	N2116J

International Jet's Make-A-Wish Learjet
'Dream Chaser' flying terminally ill
children and young adults over Colorado.

*"Every business has something unique that
it can offer to others less fortunate.
Just look about you."*

AIRCRAFT PARTS
AVAILABLE 31,536,000 SECONDS A YEAR
Because every second counts.

AOG situations can be a serious business when your business depends on effective aircraft operations. That is why Jetborne UK offer a full 24-hour, 7 day week response - and make no additional charges!

Providing the expert professional help demanded by corporate operators, Jetborne UK hold a wide coverage of spares for the following business aircraft.

GULFSTREAM I, II, III, IV,   LEARJET - ALL SERIES
FALCON 10, 20, 50, 900   JETSTAR (JT12/731)
CITATION, 500, 550, 650   SABRELINER
CHALLENGER CL-600, 601   BEECHJET/DIAMOND

All parts carry a full warranty and are substantially discounted against manufacturers' list prices.
Parts are available on sale, exchange or loan basis.

JETBORNE U.K. LTD.

Tel: 0932 253366 Fax: 0932 253377 Telex: 8956215 SITA: LHRJBXD

ZK-MAZ   Falcon 100   Photo by: Jean-Luc Altherr

HZ-SM3   Falcon 50   Photo by: Anton Heumann

HB-IAD   Falcon 900   Photo by: Jean-Luc Altherr

OE-GCR	Falcon 20	Photo by: Anton Heumann

OO-JBB	Falcon 20-5	Photo by: Jean-Luc Altherr

HB-VEV	Falcon 20	Photo by: Anton Heumann

OO-DDD   Falcon 20   Photo by: Jean-Luc Altherr

N31TR   Boeing 727-212 (RE)   Photo by: Jean-Luc Altherr

F-GGGT   Citation 550   Photo by: Hansjörg Pfäffli

OE-FDM   Citation 501   Photo by: Anton Heumann

I-ATSB   Citation 560   Photo by: Anton Heumann

N5LC   BAC 1-11/400   Photo by: Hansjörg Pfäffli

F-GKGA   Corvette   Photo by: Pierre Parvaud

4X-CUP   Astra 1125   Photo by: Wayne Cluitt

XA-ROF   JetStar-8   Photo by: D. Milne

HB-ILM   Challenger 601   Photo by: Anton Heumann

VR-BKJ   Challenger 600   Photo by: Jean-Luc Altherr

F-GECR   HS 125-3   Photo by: Jean-Luc Altherr

VR-BKK　　　HS 125-400　　　　　　　　　　　　　　　Photo by: Hansjörg Pfäffli

Z-VEC　　　HS 125-400　　　　　　　　　　　　　　　Photo by: P. Huxford

PK-PJD　　　HS 125-600　　　　　　　　　　　　　　　Photo by: A. Marsh

VR-BMD   HS 125-700   Photo by: Hansjörg Pfäffli

N800BM   BAe 125-800   Photo by: Jean-Luc Altherr

HB-VJF   Sabreliner 65   Photo by: Hansjörg Pfäffli

5T-UPR   Gulfstream 2   Photo by: E. H. Greenman

249   Gulfstream 3   Photo by: Jean-Luc Altherr

N440GA   Gulfstream 4   Photo by: Jean-Luc Altherr

D-CDRB   Diamond   Photo by: Anton Heumann

HB-VIB   Learjet 55   Photo by: Jean-Luc Altherr

HB-VIM   Learjet 31   Photo by: Jean-Luc Altherr

Registration	Type	c/n	Owner / Operator	Previous identity
N2556R	Sabre-	...		
N2579E	Jet Commander	21	Wfu.	C-FWOA/N252R
N2600	Gulfstream 3	315	Mobil Corp. Washington, DC.	N315GA
N2601	Gulfstream 3	316	Mobil Corp. Washington, DC.	N316GA
N2604	Citation	650-0021	Mobil Corp. Fairfax, Va.	/N2624M
N2610	Gulfstream 4	1094	Mobil Oil Corp. NYC.	
N2615	Gulfstream 2B	148	Mobil Saudi Arabia Inc. Jeddah.	/N710MP/N710MR
N2617U	Citation	501-0235	CAVU Inc. Saratoga, Ca.	(N31CF)/(N13BN)/N2617U
N2624Z	Citation	501-0243	Business Properties, Irvine, Ca.	
N2627U	Citation	501-0247	W/o 12 Nov 82.	(N24CH)/N2627U
N2630	HS 125/700A	NA0323	Mobil Administrative Services, Washington, DC.	N700RR/C-GZZX/N700RR/G-5-17
N2639N	Citation	S550-0157	Life Investors/MNC Leasing Corp. Towson, Md.	
N2640	HS 125/700A	NA0310	Mobil Administrative Services=MASCO, Washington, DC.	N64GG/N700LL/G-5-20
N2649	Falcon 100	219	Mobil Administrative Services Co. Dallas, Tx.	N123FJ/F-WZGC
N2650S	Citation	501-0134	Citcon Inc. Hudson, NH.	
N2650Y	Citation	501-0253	North Park Transportation Co. Denver, Co.	
N2651	Citation	500-0401	Mobil Administrative Services, Dallas, Tx.	N2617K
N2663Y	Citation	550-0602	U S Customs Service, Washington, DC.	(N1303T)
N2721U	Learjet	25D-308	RDS Enterprises Inc. Dover, De.	XA-RMF/N23AM
N2734K	Citation	550-0595	U S Customs Service, Washington, DC.	(N13024)
N2746E	Citation V	560-0080	Nozaki America Inc. NYC.	
N2749B	Citation V	560-0087		
N2777	B 727-61	19176	United States Marshals Service, Oklahoma City, Ok.	N27/N127
N2954T	Falcon 20C	58	O K Aircraft Parts Inc. San Jose, Ca. (status ?).	HB-VDG/F-BTQZ/N600KC N884F/F-WNGL
N3000W	Citation	S550-0100	Ash Property Inc. Dublin, Oh.	(N616GB)/N3000W/(N1290N)
N3007	HS 125/600A	6007	Empire Aviation Corp. Lebanon, Mo.	N125KR/N125BH/N21BH
N3031	Westwind-1124	269	International Research & Development Corp. Mattawan, Mi.	4X-CNO
N3080	JetStar-6	5094	Pan Aviation Inc. Miami, Fl.	//N3030/N9250R
N3112K	Beechjet 400	RJ-12	Dominion Air Inc. Roanoke, Va.	N129DB/N3112B
N3113B	Beechjet 400	RJ-13	Mackair Inc/Roy McKnight, Fort Lauderdale, Fl.	
N3118M	HS 125/400A	25199	Duncan Aircraft Sales, Venice, Fl. (N905Y)/N3118M/HB-VBW/(HB-VGU)/G-AXLX HB-VBW/G-AXLX	
N3121B	Beechjet 400	RJ-21	Sara Lee Corp. Chicago, Il.	
N3123T	Beechjet 400	RJ-23	CEGID USA Inc. Baltimore, Md.	/
N3124M	Beechjet 400	RJ-24	Bunn-O-Matic Corp/Marine Bank, Springfield, Il.	
N3127R	Beechjet 400	RJ-27	Kansas Air Services Inc. Wichita, Ks.	
N3129E	Beechjet 400	RJ-29	Hubbard Leasing Inc. Mankato, Mn.	
N3130T	Beechjet 400	RJ-30	B & S Investments Inc. Lake Oswego, Or.	(N815BS)/N3130T
N3141G	Beechjet 400	RJ-41	Horton Transportation Inc. Minneapolis, Mn.	/
N3143T	Beechjet 400	RJ-43	First Financial Management Co. Atlanta, Ga.	
N3145F	Beechjet 400	RJ-45	Beech Aircraft Corp/USAF colours for TTTS programme	
N3278	Sabre-60	306-32	Rockwell International Corp. Cedar Rapids, Ia.	N4743N
N3280G	Sabre-40	282-70	United CCM Corp. San Antonio, Tx. N34LP/N17LT/N70SL/N22CH/N654E/N111AB N874AJ/N377P/N2236C	
N3444H	HS 125/700A	NA0287	Houston Industries Inc. Houston, Tx.	N299FB/N77LP/N125U/G-5-15
N3504	Sabreliner CT-39A	265-32	Wfu 7/86. Located Parks College Aviation School-St Louis, MO	USAF60-3504
N3711L	HS 125/400A	NA711	H C Aviation Co. San Antonio, Tx.	//N125J/G-AWMX
N3794W	Learjet	35A-454	Bindley Western Industries Inc. Charlotte, NC.	(N379BW)/N3794W
N3802G	Learjet	31-021		
N3833L	B 720-047B	19523	Wfu. To USAF for KC-135E spares 9/83.	5V-TAD/N3167
N3946A	B 727-191	19394	Burlington Resources Inc. Seattle, Wa.	N300BN
N3986G	Citation	550-0657	R O Davis/Pilot International, Wichita, Ks.	
N4000X	Challenger 600S	1058	Xerox Corp. NYC.	/C-GLXW
N4060K	Sabre-UTX	246-1	Wfu. Mock up until 1967, and subsequently broken up.	
N4110C	Citation	550-0090	Samedan Oil Corp. Ardmore, Ok.	N4110S/N2662Z
N4246Y	Citation	500-0290	Jeffery Kimssy, Newfoundland, NJ.	D-ICFA/N290CC/(N5290J)
N4350M	Falcon 50	142	Mead Corp. Dayton, Oh.	N132FJ/F-WZHK
N4351M	Falcon 20F	457	Mead Corp. Dayton, Oh.	N463F/F-WJMM
N4358N	Learjet	35-065	New Creations Inc. Pontiac, Mi.	N425DN
N4400E	HS 125/1A	25026	Wfu. Scapped at St Louis-Mo 4/86.	N225LL/N225K/N225KJ/G-ATAY
N4401	Learjet	35A-434	General Mills/Red Lobster Inns of America, Orlando, Fl.	/
N4402	Learjet	25B-117	General Mills Restaurant Inc. Orlando, Fl.	N170RL/N170GT/(N40AS)

Registration	Type	c/n	Owner / Operator	Previous identity
N4415M	Learjet	35A-072	JBC Aviation Inc. Wichita, Ks.	N2015M
N4447P	Learjet	25D-338	Scott Williams, Roseburg, Or.	XA-LOF
N4447T	Westwind-1124	286	Terra International Inc. Sioux City, Ia.	C-GMBH/N1124U/4X-CQF
N4503W	B 737-247	19600	Lockheed Aircraft Services, Burbank, Ca.	
N4550T	BAC 1-11/204AF	135	Southern Aircraft Services Inc. Fort Lauderdale, Fl.	HZ-MO1/N1125J
N4720T	Citation	550-0239	National Jet Charter/Dwight Stuart, Los Angeles, Ca.	8P-BAR/N6803L
N4759D	HS 125/F400A	25272	Palumbo Aircraft Sales Inc. Uniontown, Oh.	G-BAZA/G-5-15
N4875	Falcon 10	54	SONAT Services Co. Birmingham, Al.	N464AC/(XA-SAR)/N140FJ/F-WPUU
N4993H	Sabreliner T-39A	...	B K Robinson, Oklahoma City, Ok.	
N5000C	Citation	650-0002	Cargill Inc. Minneapolis, Mn.	N652CC
N5016P	Citation	501-0006	L Aviation Inc. Greensboro, NC.	(N1236P)//N121UW/N121JW/N358CC/(N5358J)
N5038	B 707-123B	17652	Wfu. To USAF for KC-135E spares 8/83.	N7525A
N5072L	Citation	501-0272	Fieldin Inc. Stamford, Ct. (was 500-0360).	///N36872
N5075L	Sabre-60A	306-16	Centurion Investments, St Louis, Mo. (status ?).	N38UT/N33UT/N105UA/N160RW N100PW/N5415/N787R/N4726N
N5094B	Jet Commander	105	Bankair Inc. West Columbia, SC.	C-GWPV/N230RC/F-BPIB/N618JC
N5103	Gulfstream 3	440	General Motors Corp. Detroit, Mi.	N304GA
N5104	Gulfstream 3	443	General Motors Corp. Detroit, Mi.	N315GA
N5105	Gulfstream 3	445	General Motors Corp. Detroit, Mi.	(N5103)/N316GA
N5109	Citation	650-0135	General Mills Inc. Minneapolis, Mn.	(N1324B)
N5114	Citation	650-0094	General Motors Corp. Detroit, Mi.	(N1318P)
N5115	Citation	650-0095	General Motors Corp. Detroit, Mi.	(N1318Q)
N5116	Citation	650-0096	General Motors Corp. Detroit, Mi.	(N1318X)
N5117H	Gulfstream 2	197	Amerada Hess Corp. Woodbridge, NJ.	N800GA
N5129K	TriStar	1250	Azur Skies/Al Anwae Aviation,	(7T-VRA)
N5253A	Gulfstream 2	222	Kiluna Aviation/CBS Inc. NYC.	N817GA
N5511A	Sabre-65	465-39	Amana Refrigeration Inc. Cedar Rapids, Ia.	N2551E
N5565	Sabre-40A	282-119	W/o 15 Jan 74.	N8341N
N5731	Falcon 900	8	Enron Corp. Houston, Tx.	/N406FJ/F-WWFE
N5732	Falcon 200	502	Enron Corp. Houston, Tx.	//N216FJ/F-WPUU
N5733	Falcon 50	156	Enron Corp. Houston, Tx.	/N140FJ/F-WZHF
N5734	Falcon 100	196	Enron Corp. Houston, Tx.	N581NC/N262FJ/F-WZGB
N5735	HS 125/700A	NA0231	American TV & Comm Corp. White Plains, NY.	//N35D/G-BFYH
N5736	Falcon 100	195	O'Neal Steel Inc. Birmingham, Al.	N561NC/N261FJ/F-WZGA
N5739	Sabre-65	465-11	Enron Corp. Houston, Tx.	N25UG/N3030/N3000
N5863	Convair 880	48	General Aviation Services, Miami, Fl. (status ?).	N58RD/N5863/TF-AVB JA8027/N8490H
N5878	MS 760 Paris-2B	106	Federal Deposit Insurance Corp. Oklahoma City, Ok.	PH-MSV/F-BJZU
N5879	MS 760 Paris-2B	107	Hyde Aircraft Inc. Kansas City, Mo.	PH-MSW/F-BJZV
N5997K	Gulfstream 2	105	Gulfstream Aerospace Corp. Savannah, Ga.	N23M/N807GA
N6001L	Citation	550-0169	U S Customs Service, Washington, DC.	/N185CC/(N88743)
N6033	HS 125/600B	6033	KLK Consulting & Management Corp. Milwaukie, Or.	G-HALK/G-PJWB/N330G HZ-YA1/G-DMAN/F-BUYP
N6516V	Citation	S550-0144	Shea Aviation, Newton, NC.	D-CNCB/(N1295P)
N6523A	Citation	550-0460	First Aero Sales Corp. Fort Lauderdale, Fl. (was 551-0460).	/PT-.../N818TB/ N818TP/N12505
N6525J	Citation	500-0308	Texas Gas Transmission Corp. Owensboro, Ky.	N70TG/N38CJ/N308CC/(N5308J)
N6617B	Learjet	36A-026	Oscar Wyatt Jr. Wilmington, De.	C-GGPF/N23G/N762GL
N6666R	Falcon 50	124	Burnett Aviation Co. Fort Worth, Tx.	N711TU/N116FJ/F-WZHA
N6789	Learjet	55-083	Thomas Watson Jr. Stowe, Vt.	N55GZ
N6800S	Citation	550-0334	Summitville Tiles Inc. Oh.	
N6862Q	Citation	550-0265	Prewitt Leasing Inc. Bedford, Tx.	/(N314MC)//N6862Q
N6887Y	Citation	550-0293	U.S. Dept. of Energy/Western Area Power Admin. Golden, Co.	
N7000C	Gulfstream 3	344	Cargill Inc. Minneapolis, Mn.	N306GA
N7000G	Citation	650-0114	Ash Property Inc. Dublin, Oh.	(N1321J)
N7005	HS 125/700A	NA0217	B F Goodrich Co. N. Canton, Oh.	N94BE/N94BD/G-BFLG
N7007Q	Citation	S550-0030	Execujet Inc/Corporate Jets Inc. Allegheny County, Pa.	(N284L)/N7007Q N7007V
N7007V	Learjet	35A-594	Mimosa Film Corp. Eugene, Or.	N72596
N7007X	HS 125/700B	7034	Tessler Aviation Leasing Corp. NYC.	/G-BFXT/G-5-14
N7008	Challenger	1054	B F Goodrich Co. N. Canton, Oh.	N8OTF/C-GLYC
N7028U	Citation	550-0262	cx USA 10/88 to 550-0304 ?	G-TIFF//G-DJHH/N6862C
N7050V	Diamond 1A	A058SA	Marvin Lumber & Cedar Co. Warroad, Mn.	VR-BKA/N384DM/N343DM

Registration	Type	c/n	Owner / Operator	Previous identity
N7110K	Citation Eagle	500-0016	U S Marshalls Service, Oklahoma City, Ok.	///N711CR/N15FS/N3JJ//N516CC
N7117	Learjet	35A-462	Business Jet Inc. Riverside, Ct.	N801K/N147K/N8562W
N7118A	Citation	S550-0065	Sun Banks Inc. Orlando, Fl.	(N1272N)
N7121K	Learjet	24D-230	John Roth, Lake Oswego, Or.	N67JR/N819GF/N482CP/N477JB/N18SD/N433JA/N433J N93CB/N93C/N329HN/N252GL
N7143N	Sabre-	...		
N7145V	JetStar-731	53/5001	U S Marshalls Service, Oklahoma City, Ok.	N11/N1/N21/N1/N9201R
N7148L	Sabre-75A	380-33	U S Marshalls Service, Oklahoma City, Ok.	N129MS/N63
N7158Q	HFB 320	1040	OK Aviation Inc. Monterey, Ca.	I-ITAL/D-CESU
N7170J	HS 125/731	NA770	Borden Inc. Columbus, Oh.	N74B///N300CF/N88GA/N67BH/G-5-11
N7200K	Learjet	23-099	Smithair Inc. Jonesboro, Ga.	
N7201U	B 720-022	17907	Wfu. Scrapped at Luton-UK 13 Jul 82.	
N7224U	B 720-022	18077		
N7261B	Learjet	25D-366	Owners Jet Services Ltd. Las Vegas, Nv.	(ZS-LRI)/N7261B
N7572N	Sabre-75	370-1	Wfu. Used as parts in other test aircraft.	
N7602	Gulfstream 2B	32	Unocal, Burbank, Ca.	/
N7638S	Jet Commander	134	Bruton Smith, Charlotte, NC.	4X-COP/5X-AAB/UAF-1/4X-FVN/N111E
N7700T	Citation	501-0248	Hutchens Industries Inc. Springfield, Mo.	N2633N
N7766Z	Gulfstream 2	174	Capital Cities ABC Inc. Westchester County Airport, NY.	/N144ST/N401M N805GA
N7775	JetStar-6	5073	Wfu. Cx USA register 12/86.	//
N7776	Gulfstream 4	1121	Dresser Industries Inc. Dallas, Tx.	N412GA
N7777B	Learjet	35A-079	Bergstrom Pioneer Auto & Truck Leasing, Neenah, Wi.	/N560KC/N660CJ/N6000J
N7782	HS 125/700A	7025	Dresser Industries, Dallas, Tx.	/N93TC/G-BFPI/VR-HIN/G-BFPI/(G-5-12)
N7784	Learjet	55-023	Addington Inc. Ashland, Ky.	//N3796B
N7788	HS 125/700A	7073	Dresser Industries, Dallas, Tx.	/G-BGTD/G-5-12
N7789	Gulfstream 2	90	Dresser Industries Inc. Dallas, Tx.	N883GA
N7842M	Falcon 20C	42	W/o 16 Jan 74.	N1503/N871F/F-WNGO
N8000U	Citation	650-0107	Ash Property Inc. Dublin, Oh.	(N1302P)
N8010X	Learjet	55-096	Xerox Corp. NYC.	(N1045X)
N8100E	Falcon 900	34	Emerson Electric Co. St Louis, Mo.	N425FJ/F-WWFD
N8200E	Falcon 10	111	Emerson Electric Co. St Louis, Mo.	/N185FJ/F-WNGO
N8216Q	Learjet	35A-370	R J Gallaher Co. Houston, Tx.	/VR-BKB/(N56PR)/N1MY/N11MY/HB-VGY
N8280	Learjet	35A-310	McDonnell-Douglas Corp. St. Louis, Mo.	(N13HQ)/N13HB/N97JL
N8281	Learjet	35A-232	McDonnell-Douglas Corp. St. Louis, Mo.	
N8300E	Falcon 50	33	Emerson Electric Co. St. Louis, Mo.	N8100E/N56FJ/F-WZHA
N8345K	Sabre-40	282-76	Aerographics, Manassas, Va. N58025/N350E/N415GS/N415CS/N124H/N787R/D-CAVW	N474VW/N2242B
N8484P	Astra-1125	014	Great Western Financial Corp. Salinas, Ca.	N400JF/N400J/4X-CUN
N8490P	Gulfstream 2B	4	Petersen Publishing Co. Van Nuys, Ca.	/HZ-MPM/VR-CAS/9K-ACY/N680RZ/N680RW N832GA
N8534	Jet Commander	113	Hamlin Inc. Lake Mills, Wi.	4X-CPB/N4732E
N8733	B 707-331B	20062	Wfu. To USAF for KC-135E spares 5/86.	
N8805	Falcon 50	3	AA & MM Co Inc. Youngstown, Oh.	N880F/N50EJ/N50FJ/F-GBIZ/F-WFJC
N8860	DC-9-15	45797	Richard Mellon Scaife, Pittsburgh, Pa.	(EC-BAX)/N8953U
N8900M	Citation	501-0675	Thompson Real Estate Investments, Marietta, Ga.	
N9000F	Falcon 50	172	Ashland Oil Inc. Worthington, Ky.	N98R/N170FJ/F-WZHK
N9023W	Jet Commander	10	Wfu.	N5BP/N600CD/N31SB/N31S
N9035Y	MS 760 Paris 1A	86	North Pacific Aircraft Development Co. Helena, Mt.	F-BJLX
N9125M	Learjet	55C-146		
N9130F	Learjet	35A-664	Learjet Inc. Wichita, Ks.	
N9166Y	Sabreliner CT-39A	265-80	North Dakota University Aerospace Dept.	61-0677
N9173L	Learjet	31-029	Learjet Inc. Wichita, Ks.	
N9300	Gulfstream 4	1020	Crown Cork & Seal, Philadelphia, Pa.	//N600CS//N408GA
N9300C	HS 125/3A-RA	25169	Crown Cork & Seal, Philadelphia, Pa.	(N9300P)/N84TF/G-AWWL/N3AL/VH-BBJ G-AWWL/G-5-17
N9353	DC-9-15RC	47154	Connie Kalitta Services Inc. Lakeview, Or.	XC-BDM/N9353/N8912
N9503Z	Sabre-40	282-10	W/o 7 Mar 73.	N525N/N6364C
N9739B	JetStar-6	5052	sale, Box 10056, St Louis, MO 63145. (for parting out ?)	C-FDTM/N66CR N300P/N9218R
N10108	Citation	500-0035	Occidental Land Research, Lake Oswego, Or.	N535CC
N10123	Gulfstream 2	107	HBD Industries Inc. Bellefontaine, Oh.	/N5113H/N809GA
N10726	Falcon 20-5	54	SONAT Services Co. Birmingham, Al.	N2005/N200P/N886F/F-WMKI

Registration	Type	c/n	Owner / Operator	Previous identity
N11827	Falcon 20C	26	Ajax Aircraft Leasing/SONAT Services Co. Birmingham, Al.	N802F/N846F F-WNGO
N12549	Citation	550-0501	RTS Jet/U.S. Customs Service, Washington, DC.	
N12576	Citation	550-0633	First Aero Sales Corp. Fort Lauderdale, Fl.	
N12659	Sabre-75A	380-16	SOD Aviation, Oklahoma City, Ok.	N126MS/N54
N13091	Citation	550-0643	Cx USA 10/90 to ?	
N21092	Sabreliner CT-39A	265-42	Blackhawk Technical College, Jamesville, Wi.	61-0639
N22265	JetStar-8	5005	OK Aircraft Parts Inc. Gilroy, Ca.	/XA-SIN/N70TP/N712RD/N716RD/N12121 N161LM
N26494	Citation	550-0605	U S Customs Service, Washington, DC.	(N13048)
N26496	Citation	550-0607	U S Customs Service, Washington, DC.	
N26621	Citation	550-0593	U S Customs Service, Washington, DC.	(N1302V)
N29019	Sabre-75	370-6	Mid Continent Systems Inc. Memphis, Tn. (status ?).	(N30EV)/N29019/XA-SGR N2TE/N7589N
N29977	HS 125/1A	25028	White Industries Inc. (accident as XA-ESQ Laredo 10 Dec 81)	XA-ESQ/N50SS N48172/C-GLFI/G-5-11
N31437	Beechjet 400	RJ-37	United Beechcraft Inc. Wichita, Ks.	LV-RCT/LV-PAM/N31437
N36886	Citation	550-0654	First Aero Sales Corp. Fort Lauderdale, Fl.	
N37971	Learjet	25D-358	Caulkins Investment Co. Denver, Co.	
N39399	Learjet	31-025	Learjet Inc. Wichita, Ks.	
N56576	Beechjet 400A	RK-6		
N67830	Citation V	560-0089		
N67848	Citation	501-0210	Imperial Transport Inc. NYC.	
N67983	Citation	551-0359	Scribner Equipment Co. Amory, Ms.	(N551SE)/N67983
N68888	Citation	550-0397	Inter-American Airways Inc. Wilmington, De.	
N70451	Citation	500-0063	Ed B Unicume, Spokane, Wa.	///SE-DDE/N563CC
N71325	Sabre-40A	282-100	Sabreliner Corp. Chesterfield, Mo.	(N302NT)/N71325/XA-LEG/N82CF/N19HF
N71460	Sabre-75A	380-5	S O D Aviation Inc. Oklahoma City, Ok.	N223LP/N125MS/N51
N71543	Sabre-75A	380-29	U.S. Marshalls Service, Oklahoma City, Ok.	N132MS/N58966/N131MS/N61
N72787	Westwind-1124	240	Sharper Image Corp. San Francisco, Ca.	N400NE/N400SJ/(N400Q)/N240WW/4X-CML
N77711	Citation V	560-0065	Par Avion Inc. Omaha, Ne.	N2721F
N90005	Gulfstream 4	1103	Siebe PLC. London.	N433GA
N90532	Learjet	24-103	Cloudquest Inc. Kansas City, Mo.	ZS-LTK/N90532/ZS-LTK/N90532/ZS-LTK/N72442 ZS-LTK/N714X/N430LJ
N91201	Learjet	31-027		
N91480	Learjet	35A-663	Learjet Inc. Wichita, Ks.	
N91669	Jet Commander	17	Av-Tec Air Inc. Tucson, Az.	C-FSUA/(HB-VAL)
N92045	HFB 320	1041	Jet Freighters International Inc. San Francisco, Ca.	//D-CIRA/16+01/D-CIRA
N92047	HFB 320	1036	Jet Freighters International, El Paso, Tx.	/N136MW/N2MK/N380EX/N891HJ D-CESA
N98386	Learjet	23-040	Cx USA 8/82 as wfu.	(N12HJ)/N98386/YV-01CP/N673WM/N433EJ
N98796	Learjet	25B-170	James R Joyce Trustee, San Francisco, Ca.	(N710EP)//N170EV/N711DS/N131G

Peru

OB-M-1195	Citation	550-0121	Southern Peru Copper Corp.	N655PC/N2746C
OB-S-1280	Citation Eagle	500-0019	ATSA=Aerotransportes S.A. Lima.	/N111QP//N256WN/(N256DT)/N11DQ/N11DH N519CC/UCSG519/N519CC
OB-T-1919	Sabre-40A	282-127	Aero Condor S.A. Lima.	N63SL/N183AR/N110PM

Lebanon

OD-PAL	Falcon 20F	395	Government of Lebanon, Beirut.	(HZ-AKI)/F-WRQX

Austria

OE-...	Learjet	35A-143	Airtaxi Bedarfsluftverkehrsges mbH. Vienna.	///N301SC
OE-BRL	BAe 146 Statesman	E1002	Government of Austria, Vienna.	G-BSTA/N720BA/G-BPNP/N801RW/G-5-005/N101RW G-SSHH/N5828B/G-5-146/G-OPSA/(G-5-17)/G-SSHH/(G-BIAE)
OE-FAN	Citation	500-0289	Avanti-Air-Bedarfsflug GmbH. Vienna.	N939KS/XA-KAH/N5591A/YV-50CP/N5289J
OE-FDM	Citation	501-0140	Dante Buzzi/Air Taxi, Klagenfurt.	N96CF/N96TD/(N99TD)/(N2651R)
OE-FFK	Citation	501-0124	W/o 26 Oct 88.	N95RE/N2650N
OE-FGN	Citation	500-0291	Tauern Air GmbH. St Salvator bei Friesach.	N291DS/ZS-J00/N5291J

Registration	Type	c/n	Owner / Operator	Previous identity
OE-FHH	Citation	501-0246	Hoedlmayr GmbH. Vienna.	N26LC/N85RS/N2627N
OE-FHP	Citation	501-0321	Interpneu Vertriebs GmbH. Vienna.	
OE-FIW	Citation	500-0398	Fluck GmbH. Schwechat-Wien.	I-GERA/(PH-JOB)/N26498
OE-FLY	Citation	501-0257	Julius Meinl AG. Vienna.	N500NW/(N992NW)/N2631V
OE-FMS	Citation	501-0239	Aircraft Innsbruck Luftfahrt GmbH. Innsbruck.	//N164CB/LV-MYN/LV-PDZ N26497
OE-FNG	Citation	500-0301	Air Salzburg Luftfahrtges mbH. Salzburg.	N747WA/N81MJ/EP-PAP/N5301J
OE-FPA	Citation	551-0552	Airlink/Porsche Konstructionen KG. Salzburg.	
OE-FPH	Citation	501-0173	Aircraft Innsbruck Luftfahrt GmbH. Innsbruck.	(N6778V)
OE-FYC	Citation	501-0207	Almeta Metallumschmelzwerke GmbH. Vienna.	(N207CF)/N968DM/N67839
OE-GAF	Learjet	35A-382	Aerzteflugambulanz GmbH. Vienna.	N382BP/N382BL
OE-GBR	Learjet	35A-088	Airtaxi Bedarfsluftverkehrsges mbH. Vienna.	N35GE/HB-VEW/N3545F
OE-GCH	Citation	550-0290	Viennair Luftfahrt GmbH/Polsterer Jets, Vienna.	VH-JBH/N6863L
OE-GCI	Citation	550-0041	Viennair Luftfahrt GmbH. Vienna.	N177HH/(N985BA)/N341AG/N8418B/N3279M
OE-GCN	Citation	650-0014	Dr. L Polsterer/Viennair Luftfahrt GmbH. Vienna.	/C-GHOO/N650CJ/(N1306B)
OE-GCR	Falcon 20D-5	191	Jet-Air Bedarfsluft GmbH. Graz.	N800CF/N200CG/N200DE/N910L/N4381F/F-WPUX
OE-GDP	Citation V	560-0023	Automobilvertiebs AG. Salzburg.	N12283
OE-GDR	Falcon 20D	203	Jet-Air Bedarfsluft GmbH. Graz.	N911WT/N20BE/N1857B/N4378F/F-WPXH
OE-GIN	Citation	550-0069	Alpen Air GmbH. Vienna.	N550CE/HZ-ALJ/HZ-AAA/3A-MWA/F-GBPL/N2069A
OE-GLF	Falcon 20E	323	LFS=Luftfahrzeug Service/Lauda Air, Vienna.	I-FCIM/HB-VEB/F-WRQS
OE-GLS	Citation	550-0270	Tyrolean Airways, Innsbruck.	N6863B
OE-GNL	Learjet	36A-055	Nikki Lauda, Vienna.	
OE-GNN	Falcon 20E	298	Alpenair GmbH. Vienna.	N98LB/N86W/N4444F/F-WMKG
OE-GNS	Citation	S550-0083	Polsterer Jets, Vienna.	N511BR/N511BB/N1274K
OE-GPA	Citation V	560-0099	Porsche Konstruktionen KG. Salzburg.	
OE-GPN	Learjet	35A-311	Alpenair GmbH. Vienna.	/N35BG/N723US/D-CDHS
OE-GRU	Falcon 20D	228	Alpenair GmbH. Vienna.	5N-AYM/HB-VEZ/C-GWSA/3D-LLG/ZS-LLG/ZS-LAL/F-WNGL
OE-GSC	Falcon 10	122	Tyrolean Jet Service/Heliair Helikopter, Innsbruck.	N312AT/N312A/N22ES N193FJ/F-WPUV
OE-GSW	Citation V	560-0088	del 17 Nov 90,	
OE-GUS	Falcon 20C	36	Alpenair GmbH. Vienna.	/N85N/N644X/N711BC/N900P/N810F/F-WMKI
OE-HCA	Falcon 100	221	Heliair, Innsbruck.	/F-W...
OE-HCL	Challenger 601	3045	Polsterer Jets, Vienna.	/N601RP/N914BB/N914BD/C-GLXH
OE-IEB	B 707-321B	18339	Flyglob Handels GmbH. Vienna. (located Tel Aviv).	N764SE/N764PA
OE-ILS	Falcon 900	58	Tyrolean Airways, Innsbruck.	F-WWFE

Finland

Registration	Type	c/n	Owner / Operator	Previous identity
OH-BAP	HS 125/700A	7212	Airwings/Planmeca OY-Kone Air OY. Helsinki.	G-5-659//G-IJET/N81CN/N81CH G-RACL/G-5-12
OH-CAR	Citation	500-0144	W/o 19 Nov 87.	N332H/(N644CC)
OH-CAT	Citation	550-0378	Jet Flite OY. Helsinki.	N3999H/YV-299CP/N2746B
OH-CIT	Citation	500-0397	Jet Flite OY. Helsinki.	N6563C/(N1958E)
OH-COC	Citation	500-0223	Finnflite OY. Vaasa.	N400SA/N444KV/N444LP/N223CC
OH-COL	Citation	500-0311	Lentotoimi OY. Tampere-Pirkkala.	/N818CD/N5311J
OH-FFA	Falcon 20C	178	Airwings OY. Helsinki.	F-WPXF
OH-FFW	Falcon 20F	243	W/o 1 Mar 72.	F-WMKH
OH-GLB	Learjet	24D-262	Air Avia OY. Helsinki.	N110PS/N38788/OH-GLB/N2GR
OH-JET	HS 125/700B	7136	Jetflite OY. Helsinki.	/G-5-545/G-BIRU
OH-JOT	BAe 125/800B	8001	Jet Flite OY-Progressor OY. Helsinki.	N785CA/ZK-TCB/G-5-557/G-UWWB/G-5-522 G-BKTF/N800BA/G-5-11
OH-KNE	Diamond 1	A014SA	Kone Elevator, Helsinki.	N339DM/(N15TW)

Belgium

Registration	Type	c/n	Owner / Operator	Previous identity
OO-DDD	Falcon 20C	11	General Technical Services International, Melsbroek.	N409PC//N4351N/N4351M N30CQ/N30CC/N220CM/N220OM/CF-SRZ/N808F/F-WMKH
OO-GBL	Learjet	35A-284	Bank Lambert/GBL-Air, Brussels.	/D-CCAX/(D-CEFL)
OO-IBI	Citation Eagle	500-0238	IBIS Investments NV. Antwerp.	N3QZ/N3Q/(N5328J)
OO-IBS	Sabre-60	306-5	IBIS Investments NV. Antwerp.	N7090/N302H/N365N
OO-JBA	Learjet	31-009	Jet Business Airlines SA. Brussels.	
OO-JBB	Falcon 20-5	116	Jet Business Airlines SA. Brussels.	HB-VJD/N994F/F-WMKJ
OO-LFA	Learjet	24D-248	Abelag Aviation, Brussels.	

Registration	Type	c/n	Owner / Operator	Previous identity
OO-LFR	Learjet	25D-320	Abelag Aviation, Brussels.	N320EJ
OO-LFT	Falcon 50	42	Abelag Aviation, Brussels.	OE-HCS/D-BDWO/N82MP/N61FJ/F-WZHE
OO-LFV	Learjet	35A-481	Abelag Aviation, Brussels.	N27NR/N729HS/HK-3122/HK-3122X/N729HS/N728MP N666KK/N6666K
OO-LFY	Learjet	35A-200	Locabel Fininvest SA/Abelag Aviation, Brussels.	D-CCAR/N3818G
OO-OOO	Falcon 20C	56	General Technical Services International, Melsbroek.	/N932S/N185S/N100SR N671SR/N882F/F-WNGM
OO-OSA	Citation	S550-0147	Bosal International NV. Antwerp.	N1296N
OO-RRR	Falcon 20C	98	General Technical Services International, Melsbroek.	N408PC/OY-AZT/TU-VAD F-WNGN
OO-TTL	Corvette	28	Publi-Air/Uni Air SA. Brussels.	F-BTTL/F-WNGX

Denmark

Registration	Type	c/n	Owner / Operator	Previous identity
OY-...	Citation	550-0443	Air Alsie A/S. Sonderborg.	N777FB/N777FE/N1220S
OY-BDS	Falcon 20C	180	Danfoss Aviation, Sonderborg.	F-WMKF
OY-BLG	Learjet	35-022	Alkair Flight Operations, Naerum.	
OY-BZT	Citation	550-0259	Midtfly A/S, Stauning.	N810JT/VH-KDP/N68617
OY-CCG	Citation	650-0003	Grundfos A/S. Bjerringbro.	/N92LA/N187CP/HZ-AAA/N653CC
OY-CCJ	Learjet	35A-468	Alkair Flight Operations, Copenhagen. 'Skydreamer'	N486LM/VH-ANI
OY-CCU	Citation	550-0115	Alkair Flight Operations, Naerum.	/SE-DDY/N127SC/N2745L
OY-CEV	Citation	500-0329	Falck Air, Odense. 'Nancy'	N4999H/XC-PPM/XC-IPP/N5329J/ZS-LOK/N5329J
OY-CGO	Citation	500-0287	Dansk Styropak A/S. Glejbjerg.	N57MB/N73LL/N287CC/(N5287J)
OY-CPK	Citation	500-0267	Aalborg Air Taxi, Aalborg.	/N626P/N1UT/N28PA/N5267J
OY-CPW	Citation	501-0120	Aage Jensen Aviation K/S. Horsens.	N487LS/N487HR/N2646Y
OY-CYD	Citation	501-0161	A B Christensen, Vejle.	///N1955E
OY-CYV	Citation	550-0440	Falck Air, Odense.	N120TC/N31FT/N31F/(N1220D)
OY-GKC	Citation	550-0085	Lego Systems, Billund.	(N2663Y)
OY-GKL	Citation	650-0043	Kirkbi A/S-Lego Systems, Billund.	(N1310B)
OY-GRC	Citation	550-0229	Greenlandair Charter, Godthab.	N550JM/N6803E
OY-JEV	Citation	550-0284	L Christiansen & Ptnrs. Roskilde.	I-ARIB/N6801R
OY-MPA	HS 125/700B	7127	Maerskair/A P Moller, Copenhagen.	/G-TJCB
OY-SBR	Corvette	23	Sterling Airways, Copenhagen.	F-BVPF
OY-SBS	Corvette	21	W/o 3 Sep 79.	F-BVPE
OY-SBT	Corvette	33	Sterling Airways, Copenhagen.	F-BTTT
OY-SUJ	Citation	500-0121	Sun-Air of Scandinavia A/S. Billund.	N939SR/N9871R//D-IANE
OY-SVL	Citation	501-0049	Eli Wallin, Vejle.	(N36WS)/N2ZC/N98586

Holland

Registration	Type	c/n	Owner / Operator	Previous identity
PH-CSA	Citation	550-0630	Cartier Europe BV. Amsterdam.	N1257K
PH-CTA	Citation	500-0088	Dynamic Air BV. Eindhoven.	G-HOLL/(OO-FAY)/PH-CTA/N588CC
PH-CTC	Citation	500-0098	Dynamic Air BV/Hetzenauer BV. Oisterwijk.	G-BNVY/(OO-FCY)/PH-CTC/N598CC
PH-CTD	Citation	500-0157	RLS, Eelde.	
PH-CTE	Citation	500-0167	RLS, Eelde.	
PH-CTF	Citation	500-0177	RLS, Eelde.	
PH-CTG	Citation	500-0234	RLD, Eelde. (Calibration).	(N5234J)
PH-ILD	Falcon 50	23	N V Philips, Eindhoven.	D-BBWK/(D-BBAD)/F-WZHG
PH-ILF	Falcon 20C	147	N V Philips, Eindhoven.	F-WLCU
PH-ILR	Falcon 50	15	N V Philips, Eindhoven.	F-WZHM
PH-ILX	Falcon 20E	266	N V Philips, Eindhoven.	F-WRQR
PH-ILY	Falcon 20E	326	N V Philips, Eindhoven.	F-WRQQ
PH-LEM	Falcon 50	28	KLM Helicopters BV. Amsterdam.	N131WT/N53FJ/F-WZHE
PH-MCX	Citation	550-0564	Martinair Holland N V. Amsterdam.	N1298C
PH-MDX	Citation	550-0634	Martinair Holland N.V. Amsterdam.	N1258B
PH-PBX	F 28-1000	11045	Dutch Royal Flight, Amsterdam.	
PH-RMA	Citation	S550-0145	Heerema Engineering Service, The Hague.	(N1295Y)
PH-WMS	Falcon 20E	285	KLM Helicopters BV. Amsterdam.	VR-CCF/PH-WMS/A4O-GA/A4O-AA/F-WRQT

Indonesia

Registration	Type	c/n	Owner / Operator	Previous identity
PK-...	Challenger 601-3A	5073	Gatari Hutama Air Services, Jakarta.	N60KR/C-G...
PK-...	HS 125/700A	NA0313	Mindo Petroleum Co. Jakarta.	N18G/XB-CXK/G-BJOW/G-5-14

Page 118

Registration	Type	c/n	Owner / Operator	Previous identity
PK-...	Gulfstream 3	431	Indonesia Air Transport/Mindo Petroleum Co. Jakarta.	/(N259B)/N25SB
PK-CAG	Falcon 20F	408	Directorate of Civil Aviation, Jakarta.	F-WRQS
PK-DJW	HS 125/3B-RA	25147	Deraya Air Taxi, Jakarta.	PK-PJR/G-5-14
PK-ERA	Beechjet 400	RJ-40		/N3240M
PK-HMG	HS 125/600B	6029	Gatari Hutama Airservices, Jakarta.	PK-PJE/(G-BBRT)
PK-PJD	HS 125/600B	6017	Pertamina Oil, Jakarta.	G-BBAS/G-5-18
PK-PJF	BAC 1-11/401AK	065	Freeport Indonesia Inc. Jakarta. N117MR/N825AQ/N825AC/N76GW/N5025/N111NA N5025
PK-PJK	F 28-4000	11192	Pertamina Oil, Jakarta.	PH-EXW
PK-PJM	F 28-4000	11178	Pertamina Oil, Jakarta.	PH-EXW
PK-PJP	BAe 146 Statesman	E2050	Pelita/President Suharto, Jakarta.	G-5-517/PK-PJP/G-5-004
PK-PJQ	B 707-3M1C	21092	Indonesian Government, Jakarta.	A-7002/PK-PJQ
PK-PJS	F 28-1000	11030	Pertamina Oil, Jakarta.	D-ABAM/PH-ZBE
PK-PJU	F 28-1000	11029	Pertamina Oil, Jakarta.	D-ABAN/PH-ZBD
PK-PJV	F 28-1000	11073	Pertamina Oil, Jakarta. (sold TAT as F-GGKC 10/87).	PH-EXT
PK-PJW	F 28-4000	11148	Pertamina Oil, Jakarta.	PH-EXT
PK-PJY	F 28-4000	11146	Pertamina Oil, Jakarta.	PH-EXN
PK-PJZ	Gulfstream 2	26	Pertamina Oil, Jakarta.	N202GA/N328K
PK-TIR	Falcon 20E	297	Indonesian Air Transport, Jakarta.	N121EU/(N370EU)/N4443F/F-WMKF
PK-TRI	Falcon 20F	173	Indonesian Air Transport, Jakarta.	N729S/N70PA/F-BLCU/F-WLCU
PK-TRJ	Citation	650-0078	Indonesian Air Transport, Jakarta.	/N652CC/(N13150)
PK-TRP	Falcon 900	71	Indonesian Air Transport, Jakarta.	/(N900BF)/N451FJ/F-WWFB
PK-WSG	Citation	550-0650		
PK-WSJ	BAe 125/800B	8106	East Indonesia Air Charter, Jakarta.	G-5-580
PK-WSO	Citation	550-0251	PTAstra International Inc. Jakarta.	N68615

Brazil

Registration	Type	c/n	Owner / Operator	Previous identity
PP-EIF	Citation	501-0680	State Government of Parana, Sao Paulo.	PT-LFR/N2614C
PP-FMX	Learjet	23-090	w/o 30 Aug 69.	
PP-SED	Sabre-40A	282-121	Taxi Aereo Marilia S.A.	N8349N
PT-...	Learjet	55-048		/N67RW//N73TP/VH-LGH/(N734)/N3796Z
PT-...	Citation	501-0678		N678CF/N3FE//N2052A
PT-...	Learjet	35A-621		N999TN/N999TH
PT-...	Challenger 601-3A	5075	Lider Taxi Aereo Ltda.	N810D/C-G...
PT-...	BAe 125/800B	8190	Mesbla	G-BTAE/G-5-684
PT-...	BAe 125/800B	8194		G-5-6..
PT-...	BAe 125/800B	8198		G-5-6..
PT-...	Citation	500-0005	Paulo Regis Silva.	/N815HC/N981EE////N501PC/N505CC
PT-...	Learjet	35A-655		N16FG
PT-...	Falcon 900	92	Lince Taxi Aereo Ltda. Sao Paulo.	N463FJ/F-WWFL
PT-...	Citation	550-0356		/N6801Z
PT-ASJ	Falcon 10	95	W/o 17 Feb 89.	N173FJ/F-WPXD
PT-CMY	Learjet	25C-108	W/o 6 Apr 90.	
PT-CXJ	Learjet	24-176	SABRA-Servicios de Aero Taxi Brazil Ltda. Curitiba.	
PT-CXK	Learjet	24-122	W/o 4 May 73.	N461LJ
PT-DTY	HS 125/F400B	25243	Minas Maquinas S.A. Belo Horizonte.	G-AYOI/G-5-13
PT-DVL	Learjet	25B-077	W/o 12 Nov 76.	
PT-DZU	Learjet	24D-244	W/o 23 Aug 79.	
PT-FAT	Learjet	35A-361	Banco Central do Brasil S.A. Brasilia.	PT-LBS/N924GL
PT-GAP	Learjet	35A-589	Taxi Aereo Grendene Ltda. Porto Alegre.	/N8567K
PT-IBR	Learjet	25C-072	W/o 26 Sep 76.	N256GL
PT-IDW	HFB 320	1052	Uirapuru Taxi Aereo Ltda. Fortaleza.	D-CORI
PT-IIQ	Learjet	25C-089	Taxi Aereo Marilia S.A. Sao Paulo.	
PT-ILJ	Citation	500-0057	Brasil Warrant, Admin. de Bens e Empresas Ltda. Rio.	N557CC
PT-IOB	HFB 320	1053	Industria Villares, Sao Paulo.	D-CORO
PT-IQL	Citation	500-0069	Banorte Leasing SA.	N569CC
PT-ISN	Learjet	25C-113	W/o 4 Nov 89.	
PT-ISO	Learjet	25C-115	Consorcio Bonfiglioli, Sao Paulo.	
PT-JBQ	Learjet	25B-119	W/o 4 Sep 82.	N3810G
PT-JDX	Learjet	25C-131	W/o 26 Dec 78.	N3803G
PT-JGU	Learjet	24D-276	TAM/Bradesco Financiadora S.A. Sao Paulo.	
PT-JKQ	Learjet	24D-284	Taxi Aereo Marilia S.A. Sao Paulo.	

Registration	Type	c/n	Owner / Operator	Previous identity
PT-JKR	Learjet	24D-278	Lider Taxi Aereo S.A. Belo Horizonte.	
PT-JMJ	Citation	500-0134	TAMIG/Construction Mendes Jr. S.A. Belo Horizonte.	N134CC
PT-JMJ	Sabre-40A	282-118	Taxi Aereo Marilia SA. Sao Paulo.	N8339N
PT-JXS	Citation	500-0162	W/o 16 Mar 75.	
PT-KAP	Learjet	25C-156	Bandeirantes Participacoes Admin. Sao Paulo.	
PT-KBC	Learjet	25C-165	Construtora Andre Gutierrez, Belo Horizonte.	
PT-KBD	Learjet	25B-166	Taxi Aereo Grendene Ltda. Farroupilha.	
PT-KBR	Citation	500-0156	DM Constructora de Obras Ltda.	
PT-KIR	Citation	500-0103	Morro Vermelho Taxi Aereo, Sao Paulo.	N103CC/(N603CC)
PT-KIU	Citation	500-0172	W/o 12 Nov 76.	N172CC
PT-KKV	Learjet	25C-172	W/o 20 Feb 88. (rebuilt ?)	
PT-KOT	Sabre-60	306-80	Bradesco Seguros S.A. Sao Paulo.	N65756
PT-KPA	Citation	500-0181	Weston Taxi Aereo S.A. Recife.	N181CC
PT-KPB	Citation	500-0188	Manufacturers Hanover Brazil SA.	N5223J
PT-KPE	Learjet	24D-315	Cimento Portland Caue S.A. Belo Horizonte.	
PT-KQT	Learjet	36-011	Banco Real S.A. Sao Paulo.	
PT-KTO	Falcon 10	63	Participacoes Morre Vermelho Ltda. Sao Paulo.	N147FJ/F-WLCX
PT-KTU	Learjet	36A-018	Hidroservice-Eng. Projetos Ltda. Sao Paulo.	
PT-KYR	Learjet	25D-266	Fenix Taxi Aereo Ltda. Sao Paulo.	
PT-KZR	Learjet	35A-252	Carbonifera Metropolitana,	/N28CR
PT-KZY	Learjet	25B-204	W/o 16 May 82.	N472J/N373SC/N376SC
PT-LAA	Learjet	35A-295	Soc. Taxi Aereo Weston Ltda. Recife.	/
PT-LAS	Learjet	35A-326	Constructora Cowan S.A. Belo Horizonte.	
PT-LAU	Learjet	24D-239	Gralha Azul Taxi Aereo Ltda. Curitiba.	N83MJ/F-GBLZ/D-ILHM/D-ILVW
PT-LAX	Citation	500-0194	Alfenas Taxi Aereo Ltda. Alfenas (MG).	N310U/OY-ASR//D-IMSM
PT-LBN	Citation	500-0079	Sersan Taxi Aereo Ltda. Brasilia.	N40JF/N31088/D-INHH/N579CC
PT-LBW	Learjet	25XR-056	Central de Polimeros de Bahia SA.	N780A
PT-LBY	Learjet	35A-411	Lojas Riachuelo SA.	
PT-LCC	Citation Eagle	500-0413	Bank of Commerce and Industry S.A. Sao Paulo.	(PT-LBZ)/N6783X
PT-LCD	Learjet	35A-103	Lider Taxi Aereo S.A. Belo Horizonte.	/N50MJ/N96RE
PT-LCN	Learjet	24D-287	W/o 4 Apr 84.	N92565/I-MABU/HB-VDN/EC-CJA
PT-LCO	Falcon 10	154	Helijet Aero Taxi Ltda. Rio de Janeiro.	N219FJ/F-WZGA
PT-LCR	Citation	550-0142	Veloz Taxi Aerea Ltda. Sao Paulo.	N2648Z
PT-LCV	Learjet	24D-254	Transamerica Taxi Aereo SA. Sao Paulo.	N13606/D-CCAT/D-ICAY
PT-LCW	Citation	550-0333	CYM Taxi Aereo Ltda. Campo Grande.	N67990
PT-LDH	Citation	500-0049	Boavista SA.	PT-FXB/PP-FXB/N549CC
PT-LDI	Citation	500-0335	CATA Taxi Aereo Ltda. Parana.	N2937L/ZP-PUP/ZP-PNB/N5335J
PT-LDM	Learjet	35A-494	Lider Taxi Aereo S.A. Belo Horizonte.	
PT-LDN	Learjet	35A-436	Bradesco=Banco Brasileiro de Descontos S.A. Sao Paulo.	/N37988
PT-LDR	Learjet	55B-134	Lider/Bank of Brazil, Brasilia.	/N7261D
PT-LDY	Westwind-1124	251	TAMIG/Construction Mendes Jr. S.A. Belo Horizonte.	CX-CMJ/N6MJ/4X-CMW
PT-LEA	Learjet	25B-155	Jet Service Taxi Aereo Ltda. Brasilia.	N24TA
PT-LEB	Learjet	35A-474	Soc. de Taxi Aereo Weston Ltda. Recife.	/N37975/N39413
PT-LEL	Learjet	55-013	Lider Taxi Aereo S.A. Belo Horizonte.	/N3238K/OE-GNK/(D-CCHS)
PT-LEM	Learjet	24D-270	Lider Taxi Aereo S.A. Belo Horizonte.	N3979P/XA-BUY/XB-NAG
PT-LEN	Learjet	25B-093	Taxi Aereo Marilia S.A. Sao Paulo.	N33NM/N33HM
PT-LET	Learjet	55-080	Banco Real S.A. Sao Paulo.	/N85632
PT-LFS	Learjet	35-008	Lider Taxi Aereo S.A. Belo Horizonte.	/N673M
PT-LFT	Learjet	35A-473	Taxi Aereo Flamingo S.A. Sao Paulo.	//N3796P
PT-LGD	Diamond 1A	A072SA	Orion Taxi Aereo Ltda. Joinville.	N372DM
PT-LGF	Learjet	35-019	Lider Taxi Aereo S.A. Sao Paulo.	/N959AT
PT-LGI	Citation	S550-0024	Transar Taxi Aereo S.A. Sao Paulo.	(N12593)
PT-LGJ	Citation	S550-0025	W/o 6 Sep 88.	(N12596)
PT-LGM	Citation	550-0116	Sersan Taxi Aereo Ltda. Brasilia.	HZ-AAI/HZ-AAA/N2745M
PT-LGR	Learjet	35-009	Lider/Industrias Reunidas Sao Jorge S.A. Sao Paulo.	/N263GL/N275J/N14EL N44EL
PT-LGS	Learjet	35A-299	Lider/Governo do Estado Minas Gerais, Belo Horizonte.	/N244FC
PT-LGT	Citation	650-0081	Sharp Industries, Sao Paulo.	/(N1316N)
PT-LGW	Learjet	35A-598	Lider Taxi Aereo S.A. Belo Horizonte.	/N8567T
PT-LGZ	Citation	650-0088	Bradesco Seguros S.A. Rio de Janeiro.	/(N13170)
PT-LHA	Citation	650-0059	TAMIG/Mendes Jr. International Co. Belo Horizonte.	/N1313G
PT-LHB	BAe 125/800B	8031	CESP=Cia Energetica de Sao Paulo.	/PT-ZAA/G-5-15
PT-LHC	Citation	650-0086	Indaia Taxi Aereo Ltda. Recife.	/(N1317X)

Registration	Type	c/n	Owner / Operator	Previous identity
PT-LHD	Citation	S550-0059	Transar Taxi Aereo S.A. Sao Paulo.	(N1271N)
PT-LHK	HS 125/400B	25197	Minas Maquinas S.A. Belo Horizonte.	PP-EEM/G-5-11
PT-LHO	Citation	...		
PT-LHR	Learjet	55-044	Wanair Taxi Aereo S.A. Belo Horizonte.	/N3797C
PT-LHT	Learjet	35A-479	Lider/Constructora Norberto Odebrecht,	/N30SA/N31WT/N8565J
PT-LHU	Learjet	25C-099	CRASA Taxi Aereo Ltda. Curitiba.	PT-FAF/PT-IKR
PT-LHW	Citation	...		
PT-LHX	Learjet	35A-464	Angra Taxi Aereo S.A. Porto Alegre.	/(N75PK)/N1DC
PT-LHY	Citation	550-0427	Taxi Aereo Flamingo, Belo Horizonte.	N923RL/N1218K
PT-LIG	Learjet	55-111	Lider Taxi Aereo Ltda. Belo Horizonte.	/N7260G
PT-LIH	Learjet	35A-433	Lider Taxi Aereo S.A. Belo Horizonte.	/(N93RC)/N95AC/N26583/HB-VCZ/D-CARG
PT-LII	Learjet	35A-499	Lider Taxi Aereo S.A. Belo Horizonte.	/N84AD/N85645
PT-LIV	Citation	550-0499	Valle Taxi Aereo Ltda. Barretos (SP).	N550PT/(N1255G)
PT-LIX	Citation	500-0171	Taxi Aereo Marilia, Sao Paulo.	N728US/YV-370CP//N171CC
PT-LIY	Citation	500-0219	Taxi Aereo Xavante Ltda. Sao Carlos (SP).	N408CA/(N161KK)/N101KK/N25CS N219CC
PT-LIZ	Citation	501-0234	Misame Comercio e Industria/TAM, Sao Paulo.	N711RP/N61PR/N2617B
PT-LJC	Citation	650-0115	LINCE Taxi Aereo Ltda. Sao Paulo.	N1321K
PT-LJF	Citation	551-0289	Taxi Aereo Marilia SA. Sao Paulo. (was 550-0244).	N551BW/N666JT//N98GC N6860C
PT-LJI	Falcon 50	173	Construcciones Comercio Camargo, Sao Paulo.	N172FJ/F-WZHL
PT-LJJ	Citation	550-0247	Cx PT- /90 to ?	N928DS/(N18DD)/N6860T
PT-LJK	Learjet	35A-372	Lider Taxi Aereo S.A. Belo Horizonte.	N372AS/HB-VGX
PT-LJL	Citation	S550-0084	Tratex Taxi Aereo Ltda. Lagos Santa (MG).	N1274N
PT-LJQ	Citation	S550-0113	Taxi Aereo Sinuelo Ltda. Porto Alegre.	N553CC/(N12911)
PT-LJT	Citation	550-0318	Concordia Taxi Aereo Ltda. Concordia.	N642BB/N6889Y
PT-LKD	Learjet	24F-356	Lider Taxi Aereo S.A. Belo Horizonte.	N113JS/N677SW
PT-LKQ	Learjet	23-038	Polux Taxi Aereo Ltda. Pernambuco.	N175BA/N300TA/N100JZ/N100TA/N433JB N433J/9Q-CHB/9Q-CGM/N1002B/LN-NPE/VR-BCF/N812LJ
PT-LKR	Citation	550-0344	Alfenas Taxi Aerea Ltda. Alfenas (MG).	N532M/N6806X
PT-LKS	Citation	S550-0114	Taxi Aereo Marilia S.A. Sao Paulo.	N1292A
PT-LKT	Citation	S550-0117	Taxi Aereo Marilia S.A. Sao Paulo.	N1292N
PT-LLF	Learjet	35A-644	Araucaria Aero Taxi Ltda. Sao Jose dos Pinhais.	/N1043B
PT-LLK	Learjet	31-010	Lider Taxi Aereo Ltda. Belo Horizonte.	N446/N31LJ
PT-LLL	Learjet	25D-258	Conesul Taxi Aereo Ltda. Pelotas, RS.	N258MD/N333CD/N888GC/N54TA/(N54888) N144FC
PT-LLN	Learjet	25C-176	Belair Taxi Aereo, Belo Horizonte.	N28KV/N25KV/N50PE/N55VL
PT-LLQ	Citation	550-0495	Mouran Taxi Aereo Ltda. Sao Paulo.	/N505GL/JA8495/N495CC/(N1254Y)
PT-LLS	Learjet	35A-303	Lider/ALCOA Aluminio S.A.	/N771A
PT-LLT	Citation	550-0327	Turbo Taxi Aereo Ltda. Rio de Janeiro.	/N74JN/N74JA/N5474G
PT-LLU	Citation	550-0132	Turbo Taxi Aereo Ltda. Rio de Janeiro.	/(N330MG)/N500VB/N13627/G-CJHH N2633Y
PT-LMA	Learjet	24F-353	W/o 24 Feb 88.	/N63BW/N411MM/N711PD/N740GL
PT-LME	Citation	551-0023	TAM/Aerotaxi Paulista Ltda. Sao Paulo.	N34DL/N155TA/N98599
PT-LMF	Learjet	24-120	Rico Taxi Aereo Ltda. Manaus.	N44NJ/N44AJ/N633NJ/N633J/N457LJ
PT-LML	Citation	550-0013	TAM/Aerotaxi Paulista Ltda. Sao Paulo.	/N21SV/N21SW/N3952B/YV-151CP/N3216M
PT-LMM	Learjet	25D-323	Jet Service Taxi Aereo Ltda. Brasilia.	N6YY/N70SE/N323EJ
PT-LMO	Falcon 10	49	Flysul Aerotaxi Ltda. Porto Alegre.	N700TT/N26EN/N449A/N49AS/(N490A) N136FJ/F-WLCV
PT-LMS	Learjet	24D-296	Transamerica Taxi Aereo SA. Congonhas.	N500DJ/N500RK/N222BN/XA-FIW
PT-LMT	Learjet	....		
PT-LMV	Learjet	....		
PT-LMY	Learjet	35A-627	Lider Taxi Aereo Ltda.	N7260T
PT-LNC	Citation	550-0222	Chapeco Taxi Aereo Ltda.	N17RG/N6800Z
PT-LND	Citation	550-0227	Veloz Taxi Aereo Ltda. Sao Paulo.	N254CC/(N71CG)/N68027
PT-LNE	Learjet	24-114	Belair Taxi Aereo Ltda. Pernambuco.	/N99DM/N999M/N443LJ
PT-LNK	Learjet	24D-294	Unisa Taxi Aereo Ltda. Belo Horizonte.	N4F
PT-LNN	Diamond 1A	A048SA	Marilia Taxi Aereo SA. Sao Paulo.	N335DM/VH-JEP/N335DM
PT-LNV	Citation	501-0168	Taxi Aereo Franco, Golania.	N39LL/(N6777X)
PT-LOC	Citation	550-0550	Taxi Aereo Marilia SA. Sao Paulo.	N1299N
PT-LOE	Learjet	35A-393	SOTAN-Soc. de Taxi Aereo Nordeste Ltda. Rio Largo.	N700WJ/N666RB/N932GL
PT-LOF	Learjet	55-028	Lider Taxi Aereo Ltda. Rio de Janeiro.	N3794C/PT-LDR/N3794C

Registration	Type	c/n	Owner / Operator	Previous identity
PT-LOG	Citation	500-0284	TAM/Aerotaxi Paulista Ltda. Sao Paulo..	/N37DW/N8508Z/YV-43CP/N284CC (N5284J)
PT-LOJ	Learjet	24D-303	Seival Taxi Aereo, Rio de Janeiro.	N303EJ
PT-LOS	Citation	500-0239	Heliservice Taxi Aereo Ltda. Sao Paulo.	/N6034F/N239CC/(N5239J)
PT-LOT	Learjet	35A-093	Transamerica Taxi Aereo SA. Sao Paulo.	/N44PT/N5474G/C-GFRK/N804CC
PT-LPF	Citation	500-0249	Ilion Taxi Aereo, Videira, SC.	/N411DR/N27PA/N5249J
PT-LPH	Learjet	24D-275	Lider Taxi Aereo SA. Belo Horizonte.	/N216HB/N24TC/XB-NUR
PT-LPK	Citation	550-0010	TAM/Aerotaxi Paulista Ltda. Sao Paulo.	///N806C/N550PL/OE-GEP/N98858
PT-LPN	Citation	550-0294	CBM Taxi Aereo Ltda.	N323CJ/PH-HET/N68872
PT-LPP	Citation	550-0218	Taxi Aereo Marilia SA. Sao Paulo.	/N45EP/N98436
PT-LPT	Learjet	25-051	Progresso Taxi Aereo Ltda. Belo Horizonte.	//N70MP/N973GA
PT-LPV	Westwind-Two	441	Helijet Aero Taxi Ltda. Rio de Janeiro.	4X-CUP
PT-LPZ	Citation	500-0015	Taxi Aereo Marilia SA. Sao Paulo.	//N14JL/N979EE////N58CC/N5867/N515CC
PT-LQF	Learjet	35A-616	Lider Taxi Aereo Ltda. Belo Horizonte.	/N85680
PT-LQG	Citation	500-0271	Yapo Aerotaxi Ltda. Curitiba.	N53FB/N4403/N168RL/N5271J
PT-LQI	Citation	S550-0154	Taxi Aereo Marilia SA. Sao Paulo.	N26379
PT-LQJ	Citation	550-0578	Indaia Taxi Aereo Ltda. Recife.	N1300N
PT-LQK	Learjet	24E-333	Transamerica Taxi Aereo SA. Congonhas.	/N75GR/N75GP/N32WT/N76TR
PT-LQP	BAe 125/800B	8116	Metro Taxi Aereo Ltda. Sao Paulo.	G-5-592
PT-LQQ	Citation	501-0129	Veloz Taxi Aereo Ltda. Sao Paulo.	N70WP/(N50WP)/(N26499)
PT-LQR	Citation	500-0246	Klink Taxi Aereo Ltda. Soracaba.	N227VG//N50WM/N246CC
PT-LQW	Citation	550-0143	Futura Taxi Aereo Ltda. Sao Paulo.	/N550TT/N100VV/N2649D
PT-LSD	Learjet	25D-243	IPE Taxi Aereo Ltda. Uberlandia.	/N711JT
PT-LSF	Citation	500-0328	Nome Taxi Aereo Ltda.	(N571K)/N328CC/(N5328J)
PT-LSJ	Learjet	35A-181	Empresa de Aerotaxi e Manutenacao Pampulha Ltda B.H.	/N5114G/N35PD/N35PR N35LJ
PT-LSN	Citation	650-0049		/PJ-MAR/C-FJOE/(N1311A)
PT-LSR	Citation	550-0600	Indaia Taxi Aereo Ltda. Recife.	N1303H
PT-LSW	Learjet	35A-286	Wanair Taxi Aereo/Constructora Cowan S.A. Belo Horizonte.	/N200SX/(N333XX) N333X
PT-LTB	Citation	650-0166	Taxi Aereo Marilia SA. Sao Paulo.	N1313J
PT-LTI	Citation	500-0226	Aerotaxi Paulista, Sao Paulo.	/N100AD/JA8418/N5226J
PT-LTJ	Citation	550-0225	Aerotaxi Paulista, Sao Paulo.	/N258CC/(N34SS)/(N6803Y)
PT-LTL	Citation	550-0608	Taxi Aereo Marilia SA. Sao Paulo.	N12419
PT-LUA	Citation	500-0346	Universal Taxi Aereo Ltda. Varzea Grande.	N56DV/N82SE/(N99WB)/N4234K D-IJON/N5346J
PT-LUE	Citation	650-0091	Taxi Aereo Marilia SA. Sao Paulo.	N58HC/N68HC/N1318E
PT-LUG	Learjet	35A-356	LUG Taxi Aereo Ltda. Maceio.	/N800WJ/N54YP/N54YR
PT-LUK	Learjet	55-086	Taxi Aereo Weston, Recife.	N8227P/D-CACP
PT-LUO	Citation	650-0129	Taxi Aerea Marilia Ltda. Sao Paulo.	/(N309TA)/N61BE/(N1323N)
PT-LUZ	Learjet	25D-335	Unisa Taxi Aereo Ltda. Belo Horizonte.	N27KG
PT-LVB	Citation	501-0205	Jabur Taxi Aereo Ltda. Londrina.	/N6784T
PT-LVD	Falcon 100	223	Araruba Taxi Aereo Ltda. Sao Paulo.	N126FJ/F-WZGG
PT-LVF	Citation	650-0171	Taxi Aereo Marilia S.A. Sao Paulo.	N1354G
PT-LVO	Learjet	31-002	Lider Taxi Aereo Ltda. Belo Horizonte.	/N7262Y
PT-LVR	Learjet	31-013	Lojas Americanos SA.	
PT-LXG	Citation	550-0618	Eliane Taxi Aereo Ltda. Urussanga.	N1254C
PT-LXH	Citation	500-0133	Taxi Aereo Roma Ltda.	N1270K/N2070K/OO-SEL/F-BUYL/N133CC
PT-LXJ	Falcon 100	225	Aruba Taxi Aereo Ltda.	N127FJ/F-WZGI
PT-LXO	Learjet	55C-135	Lider Taxi Aereo, Belo Horizonte.	/N1055C
PT-LXS	Learjet	25B-111	Belair Taxi Aereo Ltda. Belo Horizonte.	N55ES/N30TP
PT-LXW	Challenger 600S	1063	Lider Taxi Aereo SA. Sao Paulo.	/N102ML/N31240/C-GLWX
PT-LXX	Learjet	31-007		N3819G
PT-LYA	Citation	550-0620	Copasoja Taxi Aereo Ltda. Campo Grande.	N1254G
PT-LYE	Learjet	24F-354	Taxi Aereo Feijo Tarauaca, Rio Branco.	/N678SP
PT-LYF	Learjet	35A-650	Vega Taxi Aereo Ltda. Brasilia.	N1022G
PT-LYL	Learjet	24D-291	Lumar Taxi Aereo, Belem.	N24PJ/N148J/N45862/ZS-GLD
PT-LYN	Citation	550-0625	Taxi Aereo Marilia SA. Sao Paulo.	(N12554)
PT-LYS	Citation	550-0624	Seguranca Taxi Aereo Ltda. S J Rio Preto.	N1255Y
PT-LZO	Citation	550-0249	CAVOK Taxi Aereo Ltda. (was 551-0236).	N201U/(N401U)/N829JM//N88718
PT-LZP	Learjet	35A-339	Aerotaxi Pampulha, Belo Horizonte.	/N1500//N15CC/N24CK/N24JK
PT-LZQ	Citation V	560-0045	Chapeco Taxi Aereo Ltda.	N2665Y
PT-LZS	Learjet	55C-139	Lider Taxi Aereo Ltda.	N1039L

Registration	Type	c/n	Owner / Operator	Previous identity
PT-MBZ	Astra-1125	022	Serv-Jet Servicios, Sao Paulo.	4X-CUT
PT-MMO	Citation	551-0455	Antares Servicios de Taxi Aero Ltda. Rio de Janeiro.	N90SF/(YV-04CP)
PT-OAA	Citation	550-0635		N1250B N1258H
PT-OAC	Citation	550-0613	Equip Taxi Aereo Ltda.	N1250P
PT-OAF	Citation	550-0326	Aerotaxi Paulista Ltda. Sao Paulo.	///N12FC/N6802T
PT-OAG	Citation	550-0357	Aerotaxi Paulista Ltda. Sao Paulo.	N29FA/HB-VJA/N29G/N632SC/N6808C
PT-OAK	Citation	650-0186		N2616L
PT-OBD	Learjet	24B-228	Angra Taxi Aereo Ltda. Porto Alegre.	/N150AB/N777SA/D-IIPD/(D-IIDD)/N7DL N4292G/N245GL
PT-OBR	Learjet	55-037	Lider Taxi Aereo Ltda.	/N86AJ/N41CP
PT-OBT	BAe 125/800B	8112	Caparao Taxi Aereo Ltda. Belo Horizonte.	G-5-664/OK1/G-5-583
PT-OBX	Citation	650-0181	Banco Bradesco SA. Osasco, SP.	N181CC/N2131A
PT-OCA	Learjet	55C-140	Araucaria Aerotaxi Ltda. Sao Jose dos Pinhais. 'Marcia Jose'	/N72616
PT-ODL	Citation	550-0640		N1308V
PT-ODZ	Citation	...		
PT-OJC	BAe 125/800B	8177	Frota Oceanica Brasileira,	G-5-668
PT-OSW	BAe 125/800B	8184	Wanair Taxi Aereo Ltda. Belo Horizonte.	G-5-678
PT-POK	Learjet	35A-619	Lider Taxi Aereo S.A. Belo Horizonte.	/N8568V
PT-SMO	Learjet	35A-414	Taxi Aereo Antares Ltda. Rio de Janeiro.	/(N135AB)/N39MW
PT-WAN	Falcon 50	188	Wanair Taxi Aereo Ltda. Belo Horizonte.	PT-LJK/N50FJ/N280FJ/F-WWHA

Philippines

Registration	Type	c/n	Owner / Operator	Previous identity
RP-C1177	F 28-3000	11153	Central Bank of Philippines, Manila.	PH-ZBV/PH-EXV
RP-C1747	Learjet	24XR-264	Menzi Agricultural Corp. Manila.	PI-C1747
RP-C1964	Citation	500-0242	Acme Plywood & Veneer Co Inc. Manila.	N5242J
RP-C1980	Falcon 20F	400	Butuan Logs Inc.	F-WRQR
RP-C235	HS 125/700B	7130	Filipino National Bank, Manila.	G-RJRI/N700FR/(G-5-588)/G-BNVU/G-CCAA G-DBBI
RP-C400	Learjet	25D-289	S.M. Inc & Louis Cason, Manila.	RP-C6610/N1087T
RP-C57	Learjet	35A-244	Philippines National Oil Co. Manila.	RP-57/N1451B
RP-C610	Learjet	35A-338	Odin Corp/United Coconut Planters Bank, Manila.	N610GE/RP-C7272/N1473B
RP-C653	Citation	550-0181	Tagum Agricultural Development Co. Manila.	N88826
RP-C689	Citation	550-0144	Philippine Overseas Telecom Corp. Manila.	/N2649E
RP-C911	B 707-321	17606	Wfu 10/82. Located at Manila as 'Club 707' restaurant.	N728PA/N99WT/N11RV N728PA

Sao Tome

Registration	Type	c/n	Owner / Operator	Previous identity
S9-NAD	JetStar-6	5065	Transafrik, Sao Tome.	/N1966G/N9229R
S9-NAE	JetStar-6	5085	Transafrik, Sao Tome.	//N5861/N586/N9241R
S9-TAE	BAC 1-11/211AH	084	(exec status ?).	A6-RAK/VR-CBX/D-ABHH/N504T

Sweden

Registration	Type	c/n	Owner / Operator	Previous identity
SE-...	Citation V	560-0078		/N2746B
SE-DCY	Jet Commander	136	W/o 4 Dec 69.	N5044E
SE-DDF	Falcon 10	27	Euroflight Sweden AB/Volvo AB. Goteborg.	F-WLCX
SE-DDG	Learjet	35A-172	Nordflyg AB. Eskiltuna.	N748GL
SE-DDX	Citation Eagle	500-0292	West Jet AB. Hagfors.	/N18BG/C-FSUN//N255LJ/N10FM/N5292J
SE-DEA	Learjet	35-051	Svensk Flygtjanst AB/Basair, Vasteras.	
SE-DEE	Corvette	34	Sadko Oil Service AB. Helsingborg.	OY-ARB/SE-DEE/OY-ARB/F-BYCR/F-WNGS
SE-DEF	Citation	550-0422	Falcon Executive AB. Save.	OO-RJE/N421CJ/N1217V
SE-DEG	Citation	500-0276	Volvo Flygmotor AB/Falcon Executive AB. Save.	N473LR/N473LP/N100CM/N276CC (N5276J)
SE-DEK	Falcon 10	156	SAAB-Scania AB. Linkoping.	N618S/N221FJ/F-WZGE
SE-DEL	Falcon 10	14	SAAB-Scania AB. Linkoping.	F-WJMK
SE-DEM	Learjet	35A-317	Wilh Becker AB/Interair AB. Malmo-Sturup.	/N10871
SE-DES	Citation	500-0405	Scanjet AB. Karlskoga.	(N6782T)
SE-DET	Citation	500-0406	Velox AB. Trelleborg.	N67829
SE-DEY	Citation	500-0370	Inter Air AB. Malmo-Sturup.	N36897
SE-DEZ	Citation	500-0371	Finans Skandia Luxembourg S.A./Kungsair AB. Norkoping.	N36919

Registration	Type	c/n	Owner / Operator	Previous identity
SE-DHH	HS 125/3A-RA	NA707	Crea Nord Business Air AB. Solna.	N627CR/N873G/N873D/N350NC/G-AWKH/G-5-15
SE-DHL	Citation	650-0030	Stora Kopparbergs Berlags AB. Falun.	/N650SC
SE-DHO	Learjet	35A-195	Nyge-Aero AB. Nykoping.	/N555JE/D-CONY/N1471B
SE-DHP	Learjet	35A-075	Nyge Aero AB. Nykoping.	N30FN/N48RW/(N117DA)/N3503F/JY-AFE/HB-VEV/N3503F
SE-DKA	Falcon 20F	308	Kungsair/SAAB-Scania AB. Linkoping.	37RM/N668S/N668P/N4447F/F-WMKF
SE-DKB	Falcon 10	132	Fairair AB/Scanjet Aviation AB. Norkopping.	N580GS/N500GS/N198FJ/F-WZGD
SE-DKC	Falcon 10	123	Velox AB. Trelleborg.	N25FF/N50TK/N312AN/N312AM/N312AT/N23ES/N194FJ F-WPUX
SE-DKI	Citation	S550-0008	Stralfors AB/Pa-Flyg AB. Ryssby.	N40PL/(N1256T)
SE-DLB	Falcon 100	183	Svenska Cellulosa AB. Sundsvall.	N183SR/N82CR/N249FJ/F-WZGO
SE-DLI	Citation V	...		
SE-DLY	Citation	550-0286	Ahlsell Control AB/Scanjet, Stockholm.	N306SC/N68631
SE-DLZ	Citation	500-0411	Investment AB Handlaren, Goteborg.	G-NCMT/G-BIZZ/N6784Y
SE-DPG	Citation V	560-0086		(N2748V)

Sudan

ST-DRS	B 707-368C	21104	Sudan Air/The Democratic Republic of the Sudan, Khartoum.	HZ-ACH
ST-PRS	Falcon 20F	372	Government of Sudan, Khartoum.	F-WRQV
ST-PSR	Falcon 50	114	Government of Sudan, Khartoum.	F-WPXM

Egypt

SU-AXJ	B 707-366C	20919	Government of Egypt, Cairo. (r/c Egyptian 01)	
SU-AXN	Falcon 20E	294	Government of Egypt, Cairo.	F-BVPM/F-WRQT
SU-AYD	Falcon 20F	361	Government/Air Force, Cairo.	F-WMKF
SU-AZJ	Falcon 20F	358	Government of Egypt, Cairo.	F-WRQY/SU-AZJ/F-WRQS
SU-DAF	JetStar-6	5025	ZAS Airlines/Zarkani Aviation Services, Cairo.	11+01/CA+101/(62-12166)
SU-DAG	JetStar-8	5121	ZAS Airlines/Zarkani Aviation Services, Cairo. 'Nadia'.	11+02/N7966S
SU-DAH	JetStar-6	5071	ZAS Airlines/Zarkani Aviation Services, Cairo. 'Shereen'	11+03/CA+103 (62-12845)

Greece

SX-ASO	Learjet	25B-074	W/o 18 Feb 72.	N251GL

Turkey

TC-ANA	Gulfstream 4	1043	Government of Turkey, Istanbul.	N1761B
TC-FMB	Citation	550-0323	Sancak Air, Istanbul.	TC-FAL/OE-GCP/(N5703C)
TC-FNS	HFB 320	1026	Nesu Air System, Istanbul.	/N71DL/N71CW/N890HJ/D-CARY
TC-GAP	Gulfstream 4	1027	Government of Turkey, Istanbul.	N416GA
TC-GEM	Learjet	35A-185	MARM/Wings Air Transport,	/(N900EM)/N99VA//N10BF/N99VA/N99ME
TC-KHE	HFB 320	1042	Nesu Air System, Istanbul.	16+02/D-CIRE
TC-LEY	HFB 320	1043	Nesu Air System, Istanbul.	16+03/D-CIRI
TC-MEK	Learjet	55C-138	Cukurova Adcus, Istanbul.	N4291G
TC-NSU	HFB 320	1046	Nesu Air System, Istanbul.	16+04/D-CISA
TC-OMR	HFB 320	1047	Nesu Air System, Istanbul.	16+05/D-CISE

Guatamala

TG-JAY	Learjet	35A-225	Distribuidora Textil S.A.	N225MC
TG-KIT	Citation	501-0225	Aviateca Aerolineas de Guatamala S.A. Guatamala City.	TG-MIL/N49BL/N2614C
TG-LAR	Diamond 1A	A062SA		N426DA/3D-AFH//N362MD/G-JMSO/N349DM
TG-RIF	Citation	501-0216	Trans RIF S.A.	N57TW/(N65T)/N57MJ/N1758E
TG-VOC	Learjet	25D-251	Fabrica de Jabon Valdes, Guatamala City.	N25FA/N290/N78SD/N752GL
TG-VWA	Jet Commander	109		N1MW/N379TH/N9DC/N350X

Cameroun

TJ-AAM	B 727-2R1	21636	Government of Cameroun, Yaounde.	
TJ-AAW	Gulfstream 3	486	Government of Cameroun, Yaounde.	N316GA
TJ-AHR	Corvette	12	Air Affaires Afrique, Douala.	TR-LYM/F-BVPC

Registration	Type	c/n	Owner / Operator Page 124	Previous identity

Central African Republic

Registration	Type	c/n	Owner / Operator	Previous identity
TL-AAI	Caravelle 3	10	Wfu. Broken up at Paris-Orly 2/83.	F-BNGE/XV-NJA/PP-VJC/F-WJAP
TL-AJK	Falcon 20C	32	Government of Central African Republic, Bangui.	5B-CGB/N218S/N418S/N805F F-WNGL
TL-FCA	Caravelle 3	42	Government of Central African Republic. (wfu ?).	TL-KAB/F-BLKF/F-BJAO N420GE/F-WJAM

Congo Republic

TN-ADB	Corvette	22	w/o 30 Mar 79.	F-ODFE/F-BTTU/N617AC/F-WNGT
TN-ADI	Corvette	9	Government of Congo Republic, Brazzaville.	F-OCRN/F-BTTR/N612AC/F-BRQK F-WRQK
TN-AEB	B 727-2M7	21655	Government of Congo Republic, Brazzaville.	N726RW

Gabon

TR-KHB	Gulfstream 2	127	W/o 6 Feb 80.	N17581
TR-KHC	Gulfstream 3	326	Government of Gabon, Libreville.	N17582
TR-LAU	HS 125/600B	6052	Ste. Crossair, Zurich/Air Affaires, Libreville.	G-BKBH/G-BDJE/G-5-11
TR-LCJ	Falcon 900	7	Government of Gabon, Libreville. 'Masuku II'	F-WWFG
TR-LDB	BAe 125/800B	8192	Ste. Crossair, Zurich/Air Affaires, Libreville.	G-5-6..
TR-LTR	F 28-1000	11104	Government of Gabon, Libreville.	PH-EXU
TR-LTZ	DC 8-73CF	46053	Government of Gabon, Libreville.	N8638
TR-LZI	Learjet	35A-313	Ste Crossair, Zurich/Air Affaires, Libreville.	(F-GCLT)/N39413

Tunisia

TS-IRS	Falcon 20C	117	Tunisavia, Tunis, Tunisia.	N421ZC/N171PF/N995F/F-WMKH

Tchad

TT-AAM	Caravelle 6R	100	Wfu 31 Dec 81. Located N'Djamena-Tchad.	(TT-AAD)/PH-TRS/N1015U

Benin

TY-BBK	Corvette	29	W/o 16 Nov 81.	F-OBZP/F-BVPJ/F-OBZP/F-BVPJ/F-WNGY
TY-BBR	B 707-336B	20457	W/o 13 Jun 85.	9G-ADB/G-AXXZ
TY-BBW	B 707-321	18084	Republique Populaire du Benin, Cotonou.	TY-AAM/N707HD/N433MA/C6-BDG/VP-BDG G-AYRZ/N758PA

Namibia

V5-KJY	Learjet	24-165	C J Schutte, Windhoek, Namibia.	ZS-KJY/N469J/N844GA

Brunei

V8-...	Gulfstream 4	1109	Government of Brunei.	N1761D
V8-...	Gulfstream 4	1150	Government of Brunei,	N443GA
V8-BG1	B 727-2U5	22362	Government of Brunei,	V8-HM2/VR-CCA/V8-HM1/(V8-UBT)/JY-HNH
V8-BG2	B 727-30	18371	Government of Brunei.	V8-BG1/V8-UHM/N727CH/VS-UHM/VR-UHM/VR-BHP/N727CH D-ABIQ
V8-HB1	B 757-2M6	23454	Government of Brunei,	
V8-OO7	Gulfstream 3	436	Amadeo Corp, Brunei.	V8-A11/V8-AL1/V8-HB3/N346GA
V8-SR1	Gulfstream 4	1059	Government of Brunei,	V8-AL1/V8-RB1/N459GA/N17581

Australia

VH-...	Citation Eagle	500-0123	Aeromil P/L. Sydney.	N947CC////N123CX/RP-C102/RP-C7777/(PI-C7777)/N123CC N523CC
VH-...	Citation	500-0279	Neilsen & Moller, Bankstown.	N70454//SE-DEX/OY-AJV/D-IMEN/(N5279J)
VH-AJJ	Westwind-1124	248	Pel-Air Aviation Pty Ltd. Sydney.	N25RE/4X-CMT
VH-AJK	Westwind-1124	256	Pel Air Aviation P/L. Sydney.	4X-CNB

Registration	Type	c/n	Owner / Operator	Previous identity
VH-AJP	Westwind-1124	238	Australia Post-Ansett Air Freight/Pel Air Aviation, Sydney.	4X-CMJ
VH-AJQ	Westwind-1124	281	TNT/Pel-Air Aviation Pty Ltd. Sydney.	4X-CQA
VH-AJS	Westwind-1124	221	Skywest Aviation, Perth. (N969EG)/N969KC/N969PW/N108GM/4X-CLS	
VH-AJV	Westwind-1124	282	Pel-Air Aviation P/L. Sydney.	/N186G/N711MB/4X-CQB
VH-ANQ	Citation Eagle	500-0283	W/o 11 May 90.	/N18AF//N10UC/N5283J
VH-ASG	Gulfstream 2B	95	Mines Transportation/Associated Airlines P/L. Melbourne.	/N887GA
VH-ASM	Challenger 601-3A	5033	Associated Airlines P/L. Melbourne.	/C-G...
VH-ASR	Westwind-1124	316	Associated Airlines/CRA Services Ltd. Melbourne.	4X-CRJ
VH-BCL	Westwind-Two	315	BCL Services/Bougainville Copper Mines, Brisbane.	N400YM/N371H/4X-CRI
VH-BGV	Falcon 900	32	Bond Corp. Perth. (F-GJBT)/VH-BGV/N423FJ/F-WWFG	
VH-BIB	Learjet	36A-035	Lloyd Aviation/RANAS, Nowra, NSW.	N266BS/VH-BIB/N3807G
VH-BNK	Citation	501-0171	North Broken Hill Ltd. Broken Hill, NSW.	N67780
VH-BRG	Challenger 601-3A	5064	Grollo Brothers, Melbourne.	C-FIOB/C-GLXW
VH-BSJ	Learjet	24D-266	Sundowner Investments P/L-Shortstop Aviation, Melbourne.	N266BS
VH-CAO	HS 125/3B	25015	Arondu P/L. Sydney.	(9M-AYI)
VH-ECE	HS 125/3B	25062	Wfu 1982. Located Camden Airport Museum, NSW.	
VH-ELC	Learjet	35A-428	Utah Development Corp. Brisbane.	
VH-EMO	Citation	S550-0063	ESSO Exploration & Production, Sale, Victoria.	
VH-EMP	Learjet	35A-345	ESSO Australia Ltd. Sydney.	N10RE/N3818G
VH-FOX	Learjet	35A-427	Fleet Support P/L.	//N1087Z
VH-FSA	Citation	500-0237	W/o 20 Feb 84.	N14TT/(N5237J)
VH-FWO	Falcon 20C	110	wfu as Cx VH- 21 Feb 89,	C-FWRA/F-WMKG/N989F
VH-HFJ	Falcon 20E	306	Australian Jet Charter, Sydney.	D-CGSO/(HB-VDO)/(HB-VDY)/F-WRQS
VH-HKX	Citation Eagle	500-0050	Pacific Rim Aviation, Brisbane.	/N333PP/N471HH/N471MH/N471MM/N550CC
VH-HSP	HS 125/700B	7215	Coles Myer Ltd. Melbourne.	
VH-HSS	HS 125/700B	7169	Shell Australia Ltd. Melbourne.	(VH-SOA)/G-5-21
VH-HVM	Citation	500-0349	Yulgibar Holdings P/L. Melbourne.	N888GZ/(N988AC)/N888AC/(N5349J)
VH-ICN	Citation	500-0024	Icena Aviation, Bankstown.	///N33TH//N524CA/N524CC
VH-ICX	Citation	500-0051	Icena Aviation, Bankstown.	/N4646S/N61BR/N61BP/N51BR/N51BP/N551CC
VH-III	BAe 125/800B	8002	Australia & New Zealand Bank, Melbourne. 'Kimberly Alice' (VH-CCC)/G-DCCC (G-5-16)	
VH-ING	Citation	550-0141	Inghams Enterprises Pty. Ltd. Sydney.	N26461
VH-IWJ	Westwind-1124	371	W/o 10 Oct 85.	4X-CUH
VH-IXL	BAe 125/800B	8040	Elders IXL Co/Carlton United Breweries, Melbourne.	/G-5-15
VH-JFT	HS 125/700B	7064	Civil Aviation Authority, Melbourne.	/G-5-519/G-BMOS/HZ-OFC/HZ-NAD
VH-JPG	Citation	550-0102	Balesteady P/L-International Business Jets, Sydney.	VH-JCG/VH-WNP/N2664Y
VH-JPK	Citation	550-0272	Begles Holdings/Australian Jet Charter, Sydney.	9M-WAN/N68633
VH-JPW	Westwind-1124	317	Lloyd Aviation, Adelaide.	(VH-NIJ)/VH-JPW/P2-BCM/VH-AYI/4X-CRK
VH-JSZ	Falcon 20C	90	Hawker Pacific P/L. Sydney. (status ?)	A11-090/F-WNGL
VH-JVS	Citation	550-0419	Johnston Village Services/Jennings Industries, Sydney.	G-JETD/N1217N
VH-KNS	Westwind-1124	323	Wards Express/Pel-Air Aviation P/L. Sydney.	N816H/4X-CRQ
VH-KTI	Citation	650-0144	Australian Jet Charter, Sydney.	N644CC/N1325Y
VH-KTK	Citation	550-0339	Dick Smith/Australian Geographic, Sydney.	N6802Y
VH-LAR	F 28-4000	11212	Santos/Lloyd Aviation, Adelaide.	PH-EXZ
VH-LCL	Citation	501-0145	W/o 22 Apr 90,	//(ZS-KGF)/N2652Z
VH-LEQ	Learjet	35A-239	Australia Jet Charter/Land Equity Group, Sydney.	/VH-KTI/(HB-VGC)/N847GL
VH-LGL	Citation	500-0206	Aeromil P/L. Sydney.	N946CC///N33NH
VH-LJK	Citation	550-0168	Lloyd Aviation Jet Charter, Adelaide.	N785CA/VH-LJK//VH-TNP/(VH-ICT) N88740
VH-LMP	HS 125/700B	7178	Jet Systems P/L-Santos Ltd. Adelaide.	//G-5-570/G-BMYX/G-5-530/4W-ACM G-5-14
VH-LOF	Westwind-1124	366	Mount Newman Mines, Perth.	VH-SQH/4X-CUT
VH-MXX	Challenger 600S	1061	Multiplex Constructions P/L. Perth, WA.	/N600JW/C-GLYO
VH-NEW	Citation	500-0268	Melbourne Net Centre, Essendon.	3D-ACR/ZS-JKR/N5268J
VH-NGA	Westwind-Two	387	Qwestair/Pelair, Perth.	N97AL/4X-CUJ
VH-NGF	Falcon 200	505	Goodman Fielder Wattie Ltd. Sydney.	/ZK-MAY/N221FJ/F-WZZA
VH-NJA	HS 125/600B	6037	National Jet Charter, Melbourne.	YN-BPR/AN-BPR
VH-NKS	Challenger 600S	1073	Kerry Stokes/Australian Capital Equity P/L. Perth, WA.	N888KS/N661JB (N331WT)//N31WT/N234MW/N234RG/C-GLXY
VH-NTH	Citation V	560-0041	North Broken Hill P/L. Melbourne. (still N26643 12/90).	N26643
VH-OIL	Citation	500-0225	Corpair/Westwind Air Charter, Perth.	VH-FSQ/D-IDFD/OO-GPN/PH-SAW/N5B (N5225J)

Registration	Type	c/n	Owner / Operator	Previous identity
VH-ORE	Citation	550-0219	Trans Media Aviation, Sydney. (was 551-0008).	N108WG/N4457A/HB-VGK/N108WG (N3261M)
VH-OVS	Learjet	25B-120	Shortstop Aviation P/L. Essendon. 'Persist'	N10BU/N10BD/(N278LE)/N744MC N111AF
VH-PAB	HS 125/731	NA766	Pacific Aviation, Sydney,	/N125MD//N200CC/N300LD/N711YR/N711YP/N63BH
VH-RRC	Falcon 20F	325	Rene Rivkin/Pacific Aviation, Sydney.	(N700GN)/(N400GX)/N400GN/N100GN N4457F/F-WMKG
VH-SGY	BAe 125/800B	8019	Queensland State Government, Brisbane.	(VH-SGJ)/G-5-12
VH-SLJ	Learjet	35-046	Fleet Support P/L.	//
VH-TFQ	Citation	550-0145	Lessbrook P/L-Transair, Brisbane.	N444JJ//N2635R
VH-TPR	Learjet	35A-400	New World Properties/Australian Jet Charter, Sydney.	VH-CPQ/VH-CPH
VH-ULT	Learjet	35A-463	Fleet Support P/L.	/
VH-WFE	Learjet	35A-221	Fleet Support P/L.	/N845GL
VH-WFJ	Learjet	35A-242	Fleet Support P/L.	/N846GL
VH-WGJ	Citation	550-0054	Lloyd Aviation Jet Charter Pty. Ltd. Adelaide.	/N501AA/(N3301M)
VH-WNZ	Citation	550-0057	Queensland Police Department, Brisbane.	//(N2661N)
VH-XDD	Citation	550-0076	Don Hodge Motors, Forbes, NSW.	/VH-TFY/VH-LSW/LN-HOT/(N2663X)

Bermuda

Registration	Type	c/n	Owner / Operator	Previous identity
VR-BGT	Gulfstream 2	211	Ditco Air Ltd/Sheikh El Khereiji, Saudi Arabia.	N17581
VR-BGW	B 727-30	18366	Sigair Ltd/Sheikh El Khereiji, Saudi Arabia.	(N44RQ)/N44R/N9233Z/D-ABIK
VR-BHF	JetStar-731	12/5062	Louis Luyt Group/Lanchem International, Braamfontein, RSA.	/N111G/RP-57 N2200M/N679RW
VR-BHM	DC 8-62	46111	Brisair/Sheikh El Khereiji, Saudi Arabia.	N8975U
VR-BHN	B 727-30	18370	H R H Al Muburak Al Sabah-Kuwait/Brithin Co. Ltd. Hamilton.	N26565/D-ABIP
VR-BHW	HS 125/700B	7209	Pacific Fruit Co/Pan American Trading Corp.	/(VR-BPF)/G-5-20
VR-BHX	Falcon 50	140	Olympic Maritime/Somers Navigation Ltd, Atens.	(F-GJTR)/VR-BHX/F-WPXH
VR-BJB	Falcon 20F	244	W/o 15 Jan 88.	(OE-GCS)/N61LL/N226G/N11LB/N20FJ/N4410F/F-WMKI
VR-BJD	Gulfstream 4	1134	Transworld Oil America Inc. Newark, NJ.	N445GA
VR-BJE	Gulfstream 3	347	Transworld Oil America Inc. Newark, NJ.	N17583
VR-BJI	JetStar-731	11/5149	Dennis Vanguard International (Switchgear) Ltd. Coventry.	N110MZ/N110MT N110MN/N524AC/N157JF/N711Z/N5513L
VR-BJN	Citation	501-0141	Pasair Ltd.	N166CB/N26510
VR-BJR	DC 8-72	46067	Bruce J Rappaport, Geneva.	N8966U
VR-BJT	Gulfstream 2	137	Ormond Ltd/USAL Inc. Wilmington, De.	N2711M/N1875P/N875GA
VR-BJV	Gulfstream 2	186	Uniexpress Jet Services Ltd.	/(D-AAMD)/5N-AML/D-AFKG/(D-ACVG)/N17582
VR-BJZ	Gulfstream 4	1005	Caxton Ltd/Sheikh Oteiba, UAE.	N17582
VR-BKC	B 727-1H2	20533	USAL Ltd.	HZ-122/N228G/N320HG
VR-BKG	Falcon 50	147	Sioux Co Ltd.	F-WPXG/HB-IED/F-WPXG
VR-BKI	Gulfstream 4	1029	Picton Ltd/Quetzal Inc. Wilmington, De.	/N429GA
VR-BKJ	Challenger 600S	1016	Trimjet Ltd/Oasis International Group, Madrid.	/EI-GPA/C-GWRT
VR-BKK	HS 125/731	25238	Air Man/Air 125/Business Real Estate Corp. NYC.	N808V/N125GC/G-TOPF/G-AYER 9K-ACR/G-AYER
VR-BKO	B 737-2S9	21957	Maritime Investment & Shipping/Niarchos.	VR-BEG/N57008
VR-BKP	Citation	501-0175	Star Aviation Ltd.	EI-BJN/N2072A
VR-BKS	Gulfstream 3	390	JABJ/Jameel SAM, Monte Carlo.	/N200SF
VR-BKT	Gulfstream 4	1074	JABJ/Natascha Estab. Vaduz.	N17587
VR-BKU	Gulfstream 4	1046	Interaviation Holdings Ltd/Petrolair Systems, Athens.	N1761D
VR-BKY	HS 125/F3A	25150	Corporate Jet/Bay Investments Ltd.	/N511BX/G-AWMS/G-5-13
VR-BKZ	HS 125/700A	NA0340	Dennis Vanguard International (Switchgear Ltd), Coventry-UK.	N702W/N710BW G-5-12
VR-BLA	Challenger 601	3013	Sol Kerzner/Sun International Hotels, Beverly Hills, Ca.	//N601TG/C-G...
VR-BLB	Falcon 900	49	Maritime Investment & Shipping/Niarchos,	F-WWFD
VR-BLC	Gulfstream 4	1093	Petrolair Systems SA. Geneva.	
VR-BLD	Challenger 600S	1035	Swift Aviation Ltd-Bermuda/Scorpio Aviation, London.	(EI-BYO)/C-FEAQ/N64FC N122WF/N122TY/C-GLYA
VR-BLF	Citation	501-0679		N2611Y/N679CC/N200GF/N2611Y
VR-BLJ	Gulfstream 2	40	Trand Aviation Services/NAMCO, Nigeria.	/N1039/(N5040)/N1040
VR-BLM	Falcon 900	72	Globus Travel/Aileron/Sen Montegazza, Lugano.	F-WWFF
VR-BLN	Gulfstream 3	402	Pegasus Aviation Ltd. Hamilton.	N3338//N303HB/N301GA
VR-BLP	BAe 125/800A	NA0426	BP International Inc. Farnborough-UK.	(VR-BPA)/N125BA/N580BA/G-5-612
VR-BLQ	BAe 125/800A	NA0446	BP International Inc. Farnborough-UK.	(VR-BPB)/N598BA/G-5-650

Registration	Type	c/n	Owner / Operator	Previous identity
VR-BLR	Gulfstream 4	1127	BP International Inc. Farnborough-UK.	N427GA
VR-BLT	Falcon 900	88	Triair (Bermuda) Ltd. UK-based.	F-WWFH
VR-BLU	Learjet	35A-389	Contship Ltd. Stansted-UK.	N31WE/N31WT/N377C/N59MJ
VR-BLW	Citation	...		
VR-BMA	Challenger 601	3012	Green Goose Ltd. Switzerland.	/C-GMII/N226G/N226GL/C-G...
VR-BMB	HS 125/400B	25240	Speedflight Ltd.	VR-BKN/I-GJBO/G-AYLI/G-5-11
VR-BMD	HS 125/700B	7200	D Manios Shipping, Athens, Greece.	/G-MSFY/G-5-14/(G-5-17)
VR-BME	Astra-1125	041	Technallum Inc.	N96AR/4X-C..
VR-BMF	Falcon 50	206	Glaxo (UK), London.	F-WWHB
VR-BMK	Challenger 601-3A	5029	Schorghuber Group/Bavaria Flug GmbH. Munich.	//N602CC/C-FDAT/C-G...
VR-BOB	Gulfstream 4	1120	Robert Maxwell, Farnborough-UK.	N410GA
VR-BPG	BAe 125/800B	8165	General Union Mining Corp. RSA.	G-5-657
VR-BRF	Gulfstream 4	1015	Rashid Engineering, Riyadh/Eiger Jet Ltd. Basle.	N17583
VR-BRJ	Falcon 20E	275	Frank Basil, Athens.	N9FB/VR-BRJ/N9FB/N661JB/N4434F/F-WMKH
VR-BRM	Gulfstream 2	194	VIP Aviation (Bermuda) Ltd/R Maxwell, Heathrow.	C6-BFE/C6-BEJ/HB-IMW N17584
VR-BRS	HS 125/600A	6004	Speedflight Ltd/Candie, Guernsey, C.I.	/N19HE/N19HH/N94BB/N94BD/N81BH
VR-BTQ	Citation	500-0340	Starway Co Ltd/Tarquin Yachts, Hurn-UK. (to RSA ?).	HB-VIV/N505AM/(N2610) N2630/(N5340J)
VR-BTT	Falcon 50	32	Jaguar Aviation/Inter Insurance. 'Terojet One'	F-WZHJ
VR-BUB	Citation	500-0345	Starway Co Ltd/Mid Air, London.	/N410N/N410NA/N23ND/(N5345J)
VR-BVI	HS 125/F400A	NA771	Corporate Jet/Bremen Ltd. Hamilton.	/N731H/C-FAOS/N68BH

Cayman Islands

Registration	Type	c/n	Owner / Operator	Previous identity
VR-C..	Citation	550-0409	TAG, Paris-Le Bourget.	N7153X/HI-496SP/HI-496/N22T/N1216J
VR-CAN	B 707-138B	18067	noted Marana 2/85,	9Y-TDC/VH-EBH/N93134
VR-CAR	Falcon 20F	440	TAG/McClaren Motor Racing, London.	(N768V)/N768J/N5152/N452F/F-WRQQ
VR-CBE	B 727-46	19282	Resebury Corp. Panama.	N4245S/D-AHLQ/JA8325
VR-CBQ	B 727-212	21460	Mezel Air, Jersey, C.I.	HZ-DA5/9V-SGF
VR-CBV	B 727-193	19620	Pinecroft Ltd. Jersey, C.I.	HZ-AMH/VR-CBG/G-BEGZ/XY-ADR/N878PC
VR-CBW	Gulfstream 4	1096	Rolls Royce PLC. Filton, UK.	N17582
VR-CBY	BAC 1-11/212AR	183	ARAVCO, London.	HZ-AMH/VR-CBY/N503T
VR-CCA	B 727-2L4	21010	Pinecroft Ltd/Trans Oceanic Aviation, Paris.	V8-HB1/VS-IHB/N111AK
VR-CCB	B 727-76	20228	MRH Aviation-London/Bell Resources, Perth, W Australia.	N727RE/HZ-GRP HZ-GP2/N8043E/VH-TJE
VR-CCC	JetStar-731	40/5006	Aerospace Finance Leasing Inc. London-UK.	N6NE/N222Y/N222Y/N731JS/N227K N12R/N9280R
VR-CCE	Citation	550-0441	Aeroleasing SA/Pilot Promotional Services,	N56PC/N50LM/N1220J
VR-CCG	BAC 1-11/401AK	081	ATM Aviation, Jeddah, Saudi Arabia.	VR-CTM/HZ-HR1/HZ-RH1/N5039
VR-CCH	Learjet	25B-091	(N816JA)/N2138T/C-FDAC/N96MJ/D-CBPD/N500MJ/N500CD/N500CA	
VR-CCJ	BAC 1-11/422EQ	126	ARAVCO Ltd. Cayman Islands.	A6-RKT/N111GS/N341TC/(N80GM)/N18813/PP-SRU
VR-CCL	Falcon 200	482	Aerowest Hannover/Herr Opermann, Hannover.	F-WGDZ/SE-DDZ/F-GDSB/F-WDSB F-WPUZ
VR-CCN	Gulfstream 3	345	K Jet Ltd. London-Heathrow.	G-BSAN/N17585
VR-CCP	Citation	500-0083	Aerospace Finance Ltd. London.	N50602/CP-2131/N50602/CP-2131/N800KC/N10UQ N10UC/N583CC
VR-CDI	Learjet	35A-264	ARAVCO Ltd. London.	N3056R/N40DK/N35GX/XA-ATA
VR-CKO	DC 9-15	47151	Adnan Khashoggi/Handlingair-MacDac Ltd.	VR-CKE/N112AK/N228Z
VR-CMF	Gulfstream 3	374	Mohammed Fakhry/M S F Aviation, Luton-UK.	N122DJ/N339GA
VR-CMM	B 727-30	18368	MME Farms Maintenance Corp. Warrenton, Va. 'Amel'	N841MM/N728JE/N72700 N9234Z/D-ABIM
VR-COJ	Challenger 601-3A	5043	TAG Aeronautics, Paris.	N779YY/C-G...
VR-CSF	BAe 125/800A	...		
VR-CTA	Falcon 900	16	ARAVCO, Nice.	N187H/(N187HG)/N412FJ/F-WWFN
VR-CYM	Gulfstream 4	1090	Jet Fly Corp. London.	N466GA

India

Registration	Type	c/n	Owner / Operator	Previous identity
VT-...	Learjet	29-004	Aviation Research Centre/Government of India Agency, Delhi.	N294CA
VT-EIH	Learjet	29-003	Aviation Research Centre/Government of India Agency, Delhi.	N289CA
VT-EQZ	HS 125/3B	25133	Surinder Gill, London. 'Raja'	G-ILLS//G-AVRF

Mexico

Registration	Type	c/n	Owner / Operator	Previous identity
XA-...	Learjet	25D-325		N1411S/N523SA/N123NC
XA-...	JetStar-8	5154	TAESA. Mexico City.	N766/N756/N3031/N5518L
XA-...	HS 125/600A	6065		N59JR/N73JA/XA-MAH/G-BJCB/G-5-16
XA-...	Learjet	24E-329	Transportes Aereos Monterrey SA.	N22MJ/N21AG/N102GL
XA-...	Sabre-60	306-57	Aviorrenta SA. Mexico City.	N465JH/N701FW/N122EH/N22EH/N53G/N7NR/N937R N7577N
XA-...	Sabre-40A	282-129		/(N99FF)/N75MD/N75WA/N75W
XA-...	Sabre-60	306-110	Aero Util SA. Cuauhtemoc.	N13SL/HZ-MA1/N60RS/N2103J
XA-...	Sabre-40	282-11	Aero Transportes Barlovento, Mexico City.	N10SL/N73PC/N167G/N167H/N6365C
XA-...	Learjet	24-141		N141PJ///N43AJ/N348BJ/N348VL
XA-...	JetStar-731	49/5083		N27FW/C-GAZU/N257HA/N257H/N161LM/N141LM/N208L
XA-...	Sabre-40	282-26	Flotapetroera Mexicana/Aurel Inc. Mexico City.	N300CH/N153G/N737E/N6087 N60Y/N6380C
XA-...	Learjet	35A-255	Rosa Maria Velaga Ruiz, Chula Vista, Ca.	/N616HC/N610HC/N44ET/N44EL
XA-...	Learjet	24E-331		//N12MJ
XA-...	Jet Commander	115	Aero Center Inc. Laredo, Tx.	//N500VF/N3252J/C-FWEC
XA-...	Learjet	24D-307		N307BJ/N307EJ
XA-...	Sabre-60	306-89	Chilacatazo Corp. Mexico City.	N86RM/N23DS/N65770
XA-...	Learjet	23-066		///N66MW/N72MK/N216RG
XA-...	Learjet	24D-290		//N24TK/N627ER/N87AP/N934H/N23JC/N462B
XA-ABB	Learjet	24D-299	Intervuelo S.A. Mexico City.	N299EJ
XA-ACC	JetStar 2	5212	Aero Servicio Trans-Mexico	N167G/N5030/N3030/N5538L
XA-ADC	Sabre-	...		
XA-AGA	Citation	501-0095	Puerto Vallarta Taxi Aereo SA. Puerto Vallarta.	N612DS/N3172M
XA-APD	Sabre-40A	282-123	Industrias Unidas SA. Mexico City.	/N8350N
XA-ARE	Sabre-60	306-146	Aviones ARE SA. Mexico City.	N360CH/N301MG/N301MC
XA-AVE	Westwind-1123	160	Aviatec SA. Nuevo Laredo.	XA-MUI//XA-AVE/N221RJ/N221MJ/N1123W/4X-CJJ USCG-160/4X-CJJ
XA-AVR	Gulfstream 2	200	Aerotaxi Mexicana/K2 del Aire SA. Mexico City.	N99VA/N135CP/N1806P/N826GA
XA-BAL	Gulfstream 2B	237	Aerovics SA. Mexico City.	/XA-MIX/N25BH/N816GA
XA-BOA	Citation	501-0202	Taxi Aereo del Nordeste SA. Sonora.	N607CJ/N520RP/N6783V
XA-BQA	Westwind-1124	276	Cia Mexicana de Taxis Aereos SA. Mexico City.	VR-CAD/4X-CNV
XA-BRE	Gulfstream 2	185	TAESA. Mexico City.	N511WP/N3EU/N3E/N372GM/N372CM/N862GA
XA-BUX	Learjet	35A-176	Aerotaxi Mexicana SA. Mexico City.	(N67GA)/N176JE/XA-ACC/N317MR
XA-CAF	Sabre-60	306-12	Aviorrenta S.A. Mexico City.	N900P/N18N/N9QN/N90N/N4722N
XA-CEN	Sabre-60	306-26	Copilco/Chilacatazo Corp. Mexico City.	(N377EM)//N31CJ/N71CD/N323R/N644X N4736N
XA-CHA	Sabre-75A	380-58	Chilchota Taxi Aereo, San Antonio, Tx.	N380T/N75RS/N2148J
XA-CHP	Sabre-60	306-22	Seguros Chapultepec SA.	(N450CE)/N743UP/N746UP/N4732N
XA-CHR	Gulfstream 2B	98	TAESA=Transportes Aereos Ejecutivos S.A. Mexico City.	N17MX/N925DS/N988DS N988H/N955H/N93M/N850GA
XA-CMN	Sabre-60	306-56	Aero Norte SA. Acalpulco.	///N19U/N19M/N14M/N935R/N7576N
XA-COL	HS 125/1A	25086	W/o 12 Oct 73.	N3699T/CF-DSC
XA-CPQ	Sabre-40R	282-48	Heliserv SA/Aviorrenta SA. Mexico City.	N4469M/XA-JUE/N153G/N90GM/N747R N6555C
XA-CUR	Sabre-60	306-127	Peninter Aerea SA de CV	N60DD/N5NE/N2142J
XA-CUZ	HS 125/400A	NA772	W/o 26 Dec 80.	N69BH/G-5-12
XA-DAK	Learjet	25B-190	TAESA. Mexico City.	
XA-DAZ	Learjet	25D-309	Transportes La DAZ S.A.	XB-DKS/XA-GRB
XA-DCO	Sabre-	...		
XA-DET	Learjet	24F-337	AEMSA/Gutsa Construcciones SA. Mexico City.	/XA-GEO
XA-DIJ	Learjet	24D-269	Jet Rent S.A. Mexico City.	
XA-ECM	Sabre-60	.....		
XA-EEU	Sabre-40	282-54	W/o 1980.	N256CT/N255CT/N7504V
XA-EQR	Sabre-40	282-82	Sistemas y Projectos Daval,	/N366DA/N19M//(N777ST)/N713MR/N736R/N574R
XA-ESQ	Learjet	25D-234	Procurad General de la Republica, Mexico City.	/N234KK/(N28CC)/(N234EJ) (N27GW)/N3815G
XA-ESS	Learjet	23-037	Aero Servicios Ejecutivos, Sinaloa.	N50AJ/N13LJ/N41AJ/N65LJ/N51AJ/N988SA N266JP
XA-FHS	JetStar 2	5215	Aero Santos SA. Monterrey.	/N329MD/VR-BJH/(N215HZ)//N5541L
XA-FIU	Falcon 10	83	Aeropersonal SA. Mexico City.	N5GD/N163FJ/F-WPXG

Registration	Type	c/n	Owner / Operator	Previous identity
XA-FLM	Falcon 20F	364	Aero Ejecutivo SA. Monterrey.	N285U/OE-GCS/N285U/N235U/N1013F/F-WMKI
XA-FOU	Gulfstream 3	449	Aviones Televisa/Jet Ejecutivos S.A. Mexico City.	N310GA
XA-FTC	Falcon 50	80	Leo Air Taxi,	/XB-OEM/N87FJ/F-WZHN
XA-FTN	Sabre-40	282-80	Aerotaxi Mexicano SA. Mexico City.	/N40WH/N40JF/N360E/N36050/N2249B
XA-FVK	Sabre-65	465-27	Aerolineas Ejecutivas SA. Mexico City.	/XA-AVR/XA-ARE
XA-GAC	Gulfstream 2B	155	Commander Mexicana SA. Mexico City.	/N308A
XA-GAP	Sabre-65	465-8	El Heraldo de Mexico SA. Mexico City.	N10581
XA-GBP	B 727-25	18252	Aero Ejecutivos SA. Mexico City.	XB-GBP/N8101N
XA-GCH	Sabre-40A	282-115	Comercial Area SA. Chihuahua.	XA-MNA/N376RP/N376DD/N376D/N8333N
XA-GDO	Learjet	35A-449	Guja SA. Mexico City.	/N449QS/N777LF/N37947
XA-GEO	Challenger 601-3A	5059	Transporte Ejecutivo/El Universal SA. Mexico City.	C-GLWV
XA-GMD	Learjet	31-005	TAESA. Mexico City.	N39415
XA-GZA	JetStar-731	41/5100	Avemex SA. Mexico City.	/N35JJ/XA-FIU/N207L/N9256R
XA-HEI	Sabre-	...		
XA-HEW	Falcon 20F	250	Commercial Aerea S.A. Chihuahua.	N111AM/N4422F/F-WMKF
XA-HNY	JetStar-8	5162	TAESA, Mexico City.	/N10JJ/N10CX/N5526L
XA-HOK	Sabre-40	282-17	Travel Air SA. Mexico City.	N900CS/N392F/N382RF/N911Q/N6371C
XA-HOS	Learjet	35A-341	Aerolineas Ejecutivas SA. Mexico City.	D-CARE/N3802G
XA-HRM	Learjet	31-026	TAESA. Mexico City.	N91164
XA-ICK	Sabre-60	306-86	Servicios Aereos del Centro SA. Mexico City.	/N60TG/N60SL/N65765
XA-ILV	Gulfstream 2	195	ASESA-Aerolineas Especializados SA. Monterrey.	N71TP/N212K
XA-JAX	Learjet	25B-104	Lineas Aereas Ejecutivos de Durango SA.	XA-RIN/N392T/N101JR/N1JR
XA-JCG	JetStar-8	5140	TAESA, Mexico City.	/N5504L
XA-JEX	Citation	500-0395	Aerotaxi Villa Rica SA. Veracruz.	/N2651S
XA-JEZ	Citation	550-0103	Arrendamiento de Aviones Jets, Naucalpan.	/N2747U
XA-JHR	JetStar-731	46/5066	TAESA, Mexico City.	XA-HRM//N7782/N228Y/N9230R
XA-JIQ	Learjet	24D-317	Servicios Especiales del Pacifico Jalisco S.A. Leon, Gto.	N45AJ/ZS-JJO N133GL
XA-JJA	Beechjet 400	RJ-33	Aero Lider SA. Mexico City.	(N233BJ)/N31733
XA-JJS	JetStar-731	15/5101	TAESA=Transportes Aereos Ejecutivos S.A.	N760DE/N760DL/N7008J/N7008/N9208R
XA-JMD	Sabre-60	306-119	Arrendadora Havre SA. Mexico City.	//N110MH/N167H/N2123J
XA-JMN	JetStar-731	50/5134	Servicios Aereos del Centro SA. Mexico City.	N136MA/N72HT/N50PS/N500S N295AR/N7979S
XA-JOC	Learjet	25D-303	Jet Rent S.A. Mexico City.	
XA-JRF	Citation	550-0642		N1309K
XA-JSC	Learjet	24-123	Aero Ejecutivo de Baja California SA. Tijuana.	//N700C/(N700ET)/N262HA
XA-JUA	Citation	500-0247	Aviones SA. Mexico City.	/N9065J/N4110S/(N5247J)
XA-KAC	HS 125/700A	NA0271	SARSA=Servicios Aereos Regiomontanos, Monterrey.	G-5-15
XA-KAJ	Learjet	28-004	Provedora de Servicios SA.	N225MS/XA-KAJ/HB-VGB/N125NE/N39394
XA-KCM	Learjet	35A-418	Kimberly Clark/Taxi Aereo de Mexico SA. Mexico City.	
XA-KEW	HS 125/700A	NA0276	W/o 2 May 81.	G-5-14
XA-KOF	HS 125/1A	25065	Astro Q SA. Mexico City.	N1YE/N631SQ/N631SC/G-ATKL
XA-KUT	HS 125/600A	6028	W/o 18 Jan 88.	C-GDHW/C6-BDH/VP-BDH/G-5-12
XA-LAN	Learjet	35A-267	AVEMEX/Empresas Lanzagorta, Mexico City.	N39418
XA-LAP	Learjet	25D-336	Taxi Aereo de Vera Cruz S.A. Jalapa.	
XA-LET	Learjet	25D-244	TAESA. Mexico City.	N7LA
XA-LFU	HS 125/3A	25112	Aviacion Corporativo SA. Mexico City.	/N252V/N2525/G-ATYI
XA-LIJ	Westwind-1124	285	Aerolineas Marcos SA. Mexico City.	/VR-CBK/XA-LIJ/VR-CAC/4X-CQE
XA-LIO	Falcon 10	40	Aero Ejecutivo/ASESA, Monterrey.	/N15SJ/N10XX/N128FJ/F-WJMN
XA-LIX	Sabre-40A	282-128	Harry Mazal/Travel Air S.A. Mexico City.	N99AP
XA-LMC	HS 125/	...		
XA-LML	Learjet	35A-296	Servicios Aereos Corporativos S.A. Mexico City.	/N296BS
XA-LOK	Falcon 10	175	Aeropersonal SA. Mexico City.	N241FJ/F-WZGF
XA-LOQ	Sabre-60	306-145	Aero Campeche S.A. Campeche.	N730CA/N60SL
XA-LOT	Citation	550-0211	AVEMEX/Aeropyc SA. Mexico City.	N6801T
XA-LOV	HS 125/403A	NA776	Aero Servicios, Mexico City.	G-BACI/N73BH
XA-LRA	Sabre-60	306-63	Aviorrenta SA. Mexico City.	XA-ABC/XA-CIS/XB-BIP/N978R
XA-LTH	Citation	550-0462	Servicios Ejecutivos Nortenos, Monterrey.	N67JW/N509TC/N12508
XA-LUC	Sabre-65	465-55	Transportes Aereos Terrestres SA.	//N2574E
XA-LUV	Citation	500-0412	Aerotaxis del Centro SA. Aguascalientes.	/N6782F
XA-LYM	Jet Commander-B	133		N122JB/N161X/N22976/N666JM/N133JC/N56AZ/N56AG/N1172Z/N5041E
XA-MAK	Westwind-Two	342	Cia Mexicana de Taxis Aereos SA. Mexico City.	4X-CTJ

| Regis-
tration | Type | c/n | Owner / Operator
Page   130 | Previous
identity |

Registration	Type	c/n	Owner / Operator	Previous identity
XA-MAL	Learjet	25D-274	Aerolineas Ejecutivas SA. Mexico City.	N274LJ/N110FP/N602N/N602NC/N3131G D-CEPD/N600CD
XA-MEY	Gulfstream 3	252	Manuel Espinosa Yglesias/Aviones ARE SA. Mexico City.	(N301GA)/N17582 (N777SL)
XA-MHA	Learjet	25XR-222	Constructora Midas/Aerolineas Ejecutivas SA. Mexico City.	/XA-KEY/N4MR N726GL/N1476B
XA-MIC	Gulfstream 3	323	Aviones Televisa/Jet Ejecutivos SA. Mexico City.	
XA-MIR	HS 125/1A-522	25068	Union National Bank of Laredo, Laredo, Tx. (maybe XB-SBC?).	XB-VUI/XA-BEM XA-BEA
XA-MMO	Learjet	25G-352	Avesen SA. Mexico City.	N7035C/RP-C1261/N3794P
XA-MUL	Sabre-60A	306-50	Aeroservicios Technicos Admin/Aeroventas SA. Monterrey.	/XA-VIT/N100Y N948R/N7529N
XA-MVF	Sabre-40A	282-134	Aceros San Luis SA. San Luis Potosi.	/N66CD/N60RC/N4ONR
XA-MVT	Sabre-75A	380-42	Aerotaxi Mexicano S.A. Mexico City.	N75AG/D-CHIC/N75RS/N2114J
XA-NAY	Falcon 20F	269	Aerolineas Ejecutivas SA. Mexico City.	N501F/N1902W/N4430F/F-WPUX
XA-NOG	Learjet	25D-349	TAESA. Mexico City.	N20GT/N349EJ/N40146
XA-OAF	Sabre-75A	380-55	Corporacion Aerea Cencor SA de CV. Chihuahua.	N120KC/HZ-CA1/N33KA/N2139J
XA-OVR	Falcon 50	88	Sr. Olegario Vasquez Rana, Mexico City. 'Angeles'	N92FJ/F-WZHU
XA-PAX	Sabre-60	306-123	Corporacion Aerea Cencor S.A. Chihuahua.	N28VM/N128VM/N2627M/N710MR/N2132J
XA-PAZ	Learjet	....		
XA-PEK	Sabre-60	306-38	Aero Taxi Corporativo/Jose Ortiz-Avila, Tampico.	N230A/N229LS/N251MA N253MZ/N4751N
XA-PGO	JetStar-731	20/5069		//N918MM///N910M
XA-PIH	Sabre-40A	282-102	Jet Rent SA. Mexico City.	(N157AT)//N74MJ/N74MG/N800DC/N2WR/N7597N
XA-PIJ	Citation	550-0077	David Garza, Monterrey/Servicio Aereo Gadel SA.	/N578W/N582CC/(N2662A)
XA-PIL	Learjet	55-014	Aeroventas SA. Monterrey.	N55KC/N90BS
XA-PIM	Learjet	25D-368	Cia Impulsora Deportiva de la Choya SA. Guadalajara.	N8567J
XA-PIN	Learjet	35A-201	Aerolineas del Oeste SA. Guadalajara.	///N35RF/N35RT/N79MJ/N39415
XA-PIP	Citation	650-0146	AVEMEX/Aeropyc SA. Mexico City.	N646CC/N13256
XA-PIU	Learjet	25D-293	Aerolineas Ejecutivas SA. Mexico City.	/N97JP/N999TH
XA-POG	Learjet	25B-080	TAESA-Transportes Aereos Ejecutivos S.A. Mexico City.	N30AP/(N90DH)/N1978L N1976L
XA-POI	Learjet	25XR-152	TAESA-Transportes Ejecutivos S.A. Mexico City.	N425ET/N515SC/N50L
XA-POJ	Westwind-1123	161	Aerolineas Marcos SA. Mexico City.	/N33WD/N185G/(N653J)/D-CGLS/4X-CJK
XA-PON	Sabre-75A	380-39	Transportes Aereos de Monterrey, Monterrey.	N40WP/(N60WP)/N38JM/N88JM N102MJ/N7NR/N2110J
XA-POO	JetStar-8	5158	AMSA=Aero Taxi Mexicano SA. Mexico City.	N1DT/C-GTCP/N516DM/N5522L
XA-POP	Learjet	25D-324	Aerolineas Ejecutivas SA. Mexico City.	/N711BF
XA-POQ	Learjet	25D-351	Aerolineas Ejecutivas SA. Mexico City. 'Bronco'	N878ME
XA-POR	Sabre-60	306-49	Aeronautica Interspacial,	N645CC/N29SX/N29S/N7522N
XA-POS	Learjet	24D-249	Aviorrenta SA. Mexico City.	N998M//N999M/N27MJ/9J-ADF
XA-POU	JetStar-731	2/5053	VETSA=Vuelos Ejecutivos de Toluca SA de CV. Toluca.	N14WJ//N69CN/N121CN N12R/N9219R
XA-PRL	Sabre-	...		
XA-PRO	Learjet	25D-216	Aero Zano SA. Monterrey.	/(N87MW)/N80RP/N80RE/(N345FJ)/N2426/N3556F
XA-PSD	JetStar-731	57/5132	TAESA=Transportes Aereos Ejecutivos de Mexico,	N989JN/N1JN/N801/N100GL N1620N/N1620/N7977S
XA-PUD	Sabre-60	...	now on King Air 300 FA-169,	
XA-PUE	Falcon 20F	393	Aerolineas Muri SA. Chihuahua.	N809F/N76TA/N21NL/N176F/F-WLCT
XA-PUF	Westwind-1123	153	Aerolineas Marcos SA. Mexico City.	N223WW////N200WC/N773EJ/4X-CJB
XA-PUL	JetStar-8	5151	TAESA. Mexico City.	N45K/N46KJ/N711Z/N5515L
XA-PUR	Sabre-60	306-2	Aero-Fe SA.	/N666BR/N2710T/N277CT/N22MA/N968R/N307NA
XA-PUV	Gulfstream 4	1079	Jet Ejecutivos SA. Mexico City.	N17603
XA-PVR	Sabre-65	465-12	Sr. Olegario Vasquez Rana/Aerotaxi Mexicano, Mexico City.	XA-OVR
XA-RAN	Learjet	....		
XA-RAP	Sabre-60	306-88	Taxi Aereo Nova SA. Mexico City.	/N22CG//N992/N65769
XA-RAQ	Learjet	...		
XA-RAR	Beechjet 400	RJ-32	Servicios Aereos Interstatales SA.	/N31432
XA-RAV	Learjet	35A-290	Aerora SA. Morelia.	N2022L
XA-RAX	Learjet	25D-218	Constantino Canelos, Sinalao/TAPSA. Culiacan.	N155AU/N18MJ
XA-REA	Learjet	....		
XA-REE	Learjet	25D-314	Aerolineas Muri SA. Chihuahua.	XA-LUZ/N40AD/N30AD/N38328/HB-VHM/I-DEAN N1466B

Registration	Type	c/n	Owner / Operator	Previous identity
XA-REI	Sabre-60	306-20	Servicios Aereos Alfa, Mexico City.	N155EC/XA-PEI//N155EC/N55BP/N78JP N44SB/N22JW/N330US/N938R/N4730N
XA-REK	Learjet	24XR-285	Aeroservicios 2000 SA.	XC-AZU
XA-REN	Citation	550-0243	Taxi Aereo del Valle de Toluca SA. Naucalpan.	N1333Z/VR-BHG/TI-APZ/N6860L
XA-REO	Jet Commander-B	124	Agente de Seguros SA.	//N300M/N1300M
XA-RET	Westwind-Two	409	Aeroservicios Ejecutivos Corporativos SA. Mexico City.	/N409WW/130/4X-CUM/ VH-JJA/4X-CUM
XA-REY	Falcon 20C	127	Aero Ejecutivo SA. Monterrey.	XA-EFB/N50AD//N4345F/F-WNGN
XA-RFB	Sabre-60	306-87	Aero Quimmco SA.	/N200CE/N400CE/N100MA/N60RS/N100CE/N65767
XA-RGB	JetStar-731	33/5079	TAESA, Mexico City.	//N9238R
XA-RGC	Sabre-40R	282-39	Transportes Ejecutivos SA de CV, Mexico City.	XA-BAF/(N4492V)/N333B/N947R N442A/N6394C
XA-RGS	Citation	650-0189	Vitro Corporativo SA. Monterrey.	N26174
XA-RIA	Learjet	36A-050	Servicios Aereos Ejecutivos Publanos SA. Colonia La Paz.	/N3456L
XA-RIH	Sabre-75A	380-46	Procurad General de la Republica, Mexico City.	N90C/(N50K)/N2125J
XA-RIL	HS 125/400A	NA761	Taxi Aereos de Guadalajara, Guadalajara.	N580MA/N500MA//N1924L/N125BH N56BH
XA-RIN	Learjet	....		
XA-RIR	Sabre-60	306-36	Intergalaxia SA.	N436CC/N9OR/N18N/N918R/N4749N
XA-RIW	Jet Commander	86		//N116MC/N13TV/N2JW/N1100M
XA-RLE	Citation	...		
XA-RLI	Learjet	25D-353	Aero Taxi Calzada SA. Coatzacoalcos.	XA-RQP/(N50MT)/N800DR/N353EJ
XA-RLL	Sabre-60	306-83	Hidrogenadora Nacional SA.	N99FF/N300YM/N411MD/N14CQ/N14CG
XA-RLP	Sabre-	...		
XA-RLR	Sabre-60	306-100		N60SE//N5379W/N81HP/N881MC/N65790
XA-RLS	Sabre-	...		
XA-RLX	Falcon 100	226	Banamex/Aero Personal SA. Mexico City. 'Achtli'	N130FJ/F-WZGJ
XA-RMA	Falcon 20	...		
XA-RMD	JetStar 2	5228	Aeroastra SA. Monterrey.	N372H/N4034M
XA-RMN	HS 125/	...		
XA-RMY	Citation	650-0179		/N679CC/(N1959E)
XA-RNB	Falcon 20C-5	142	Aerolineas Ejecutivas SA. Mexico City.	(N205FJ)/N220RT//N43SM/N511TA/N511T N777WJ/N298W/N1BF/N100S/N4355F/F-WJMM
XA-RNE	Beechjet 400	RJ-61		N1561B
XA-ROC	Learjet	25D-357	Servicios Aereos del Centro SA. Mexico City.	/N812MM/N148JW/N3797U
XA-ROD	Sabre-80A	380-50	Procurad General de la Republica, Mexico City.	N179S/N5PG/N5EQ/N5PG/N2129J
XA-ROF	JetStar-8	5133	TAESA, Mexico City. (maybe XA-ROK).	/HZ-WBT/VR-CAW/C-GPGD/N322K/N329K N7978S
XA-ROI	Gulfstream 2	10	TAESA-Transportes Aereos Ejecutivos SA. Mexico City.	N888CF/N343N/N343K
XA-ROJ	HS 125/400A	NA735		N11SQ/N400AG/N125AJ/VP-BDH/G-AXPX
XA-ROK	JetStar-8	5148	TAESA. Mexico City. (maybe XA-ROF).	/N900SA/HZ-SH4/N21SH/N964M/N5512L
XA-ROO	Learjet	...		
XA-ROZ	Learjet	25D-286	Aero Transportes Internationales de Torreon SA.	N28MJ
XA-RPS	Sabre-40	282-56	Aviorrenta SA. Mexico City.	N85DA/N204TM/(N722ED)/N722FD/N722ST/N10CC N322CS/N7506V
XA-RPT	HS 125/3A-RA	NA708	Aeroservicios Sipse SA. Merida, Yucatan.	N75GN/N756N/N9149/G-AWKI
XA-RPV	Learjet	25D-210	Aerolineas Ejecutivas SA. Mexico City.	/XA-JIN/N133MR
XA-RQI	Learjet	25-032	Transportes Aereos Pegaso SA de CV. Mixcoac.	XA-ZYZ/N357HC//N712DC/N711DB N373M
XA-RQP	Learjet	24-179		XC-GII/N717DB/N412PD/N410PB/N410PD/N111RE/N111RA/N300CC/N920FF
XA-RQT	Westwind	...		
XA-RRA	B 727-14	19427	DHL/TAESA, Mexico City.	XC-FAC/XA-SEM
XA-RRB	B 727-14	18911	TAESA, Mexico City.	XC-FAA/XA-SEA
XA-RRC	Learjet	24D-259	Aero Rey SA/Aero-Santos SA. Monterrey.	/N22MH/I-EJIA/N22ML/(N24EA)/N22MH N200JR
XA-RTH	Sabre-60	306-39	Servicios Aereos El Tapatio, Guadalajara. (maybe XA-ECM).	N745UP/N747UP N507TF/N888MC/N10PF/N4752N
XA-RUY	Learjet	35A-373	Aerolineas Ejecutivas SA. Mexico City.	XA-BRE/SE-DER
XA-RYJ	Sabre-75	370-5	Servicios Aereos Corporativos SA. Mexico City.	//N250BC/N58KS/N55KZ/N55KS N23G/N75NR/N7588N
XA-SAI	HS 125/600A	6016	Omnirent Aviones S.A. de C.V. Mexico City.	N99SC/N27BH
XA-SAM	Citation	500-0255	Servicio Aereos Moritani SA.	N885CA/N877BP//N37643/D-INCI/N5255J
XA-SAR	Falcon 10	125	Aerocer S.A. Monterrey.	/N100CK/N400SP/N195FJ/F-WNGD

Page 132

Registration	Type	c/n	Owner / Operator	Previous identity
XA-SEN	Sabre-40	282-7	Aviorrenta SA. Mexico City.	N122RP/N43NR/N101US/N42NR/N1102D/N576R/N360J N6361C
XA-SIN	Sabre-60	306-143	Aerolineas Mexicanas SA. Pedregal.	/N741RC/N741R/N80QM/N800M
XA-TAB	Falcon 100	204	Aerovics SA. Mexico City.	F-WGTG/N101EU/N268FJ/F-WZGK
XA-TAM	Learjet	25D-341	Tubes de Acero de Mexico SA. Mexico City.	N101DL//N341FW
XA-TEL	Citation	550-0254	Telefonos de Mexico SA. Mexico City.	N171CB/N6860S
XA-TIP	Learjet	24D-293	Aerovics SA. Mexico City,	/
XA-UMA	Learjet	35A-646	TAESA. Mexico City.	
XA-VIO	Sabre-60	306-34	Aviorrenta SA. Mexico City.	N747RC/N3533/N4746N
XA-VIT	Citation	650-0020	Vitro Corporitivo SA. Monterrey.	/N1307G
XA-VYF	Citation	500-0265	Ruben Velez/Corp Aerea Executiva S.A.	N504GP/N5265J
XA-ZAP	Learjet	35A-129	AVEMEX SA. Mexico City.	/N229X/N22BX
XA-ZTH	Learjet	31-004	Servicios Especiales del Pacifico Jalisco SA. Leon.	
XA-ZUM	Sabre-65	465-15	Axel Rent SA/Farmaceuticos Lakeside SA. Mexico City.	N2513E
XA-ZYZ	Learjet	25D-287	Transportes Aereos Pegaso SA de CV. Mixcoac.	N287MF/N63KH/RP-C4121/N39416
XB-AKW	HS 125/1A	25102	Casa Guajardo S.A. Monterrey.	N756M/N756/G-ATUU
XB-ALO	Falcon 20E	287	Aero Ejecutivo S.A. Monterrey.	YV-38CP/YV-TAVA/N4438F/F-WMKF
XB-AMO	Citation	500-0152	Fabricas Orion SA. Monterrey.	N2782D/XB-AMO/N152CC/N53J/I-FERN/(N194AT) N152CC
XB-AXP	HS 125/400A	NA755	Fabricas del Calzado Canada SA. Guadalajara.	N5MW/N755GW/N711SD/N50BH
XB-BBL	Sabre-40A	282-116	Sidermex International Inc. San Antonio, Tx.	/N4PH
XB-CCO	Citation	500-0175	Siderurgica Lazaro Cardenas SA. Mexico City..	/(XA-HOO)/N175CC
XB-CUX	HS 125/400A	NA764	Cementos de Chihuahua SA. Chihuahua.	N59BH
XB-CXZ	HS 125/1A-522	25060	Ceramica Regiomontana SA. Monterrey.	XA-HOU/XA-BOJ/XB-EAL/XB-FIS/N22DE N22DL/N2728/N26011/N2601/G-ATIM
XB-DBS	JetStar-8	5159	Sindicato Petrolero Mexicano, Mexico City.	/N520M/N5523L
XB-DNY	Westwind-1123	183	Exportadora de Sal SA.	HR-001/FAH318/4X-CKG
XB-DSQ	HS 125/400A	NA720	Cinsa S.A. y Copropietarios, (maybe XA-GUB).	XA-GUB/N7LG/N4PN/N14OC/G-AWXE
XB-DUH	JetStar-8	5157	Industrial Minera Mexico, Mexico City.	N29WP/N9WP/N5521L
XB-DUS	Sabre-40A	282-106	Coca Cola de Mexico/Soc Industrial S.A. Tampico, Tamaulipas.	N7595N
XB-DVF	Citation	500-0408	AESA/Construcciones Protexa, Monterrey.	XA-LUD/N67805
XB-DVP	Sabre-75A	380-53	Comision Federal de Electricidad, Mexico City.	XC-FIA/N75HZ/N8526A/HZ-THZ JY-AFN/N75NR/N2137J
XB-DVS	Sabre-	...		
XB-DYF	Citation Eagle	500-0313	SAI-Servicios Aereos Integrados SA. Mexico City.	XA-KUJ/N76GT/(N5313J)
XB-DZD	Learjet	24F-349	Comercial Mexicana de Pinturas SA. Mexico City.	XA-CAP/N349BS/VH-FLJ
XB-DZN	HS 125/700A	7158	Gustavo Ramero & Olga Macias Bringas, Tehuacan.	/N45KK/G-BJWB/G-5-14
XB-DZQ	Learjet	25D-332	PRI, Mexico City.	XC-FIF
XB-DZR	Learjet	24D-273	Sindicato Nacional de Trabaja Education,	XC-DOP/N51AJ/5Y-GEO/N118J/OH-GLA
XB-EBI	Gulfstream	96	Vitro Corporacion SA. Monterrey.	/XC-MEX/N75SR/N75WC/N100WC/N100KS/N888GA
XB-ECR	Falcon 200	513	Cementos Mexicanos, Guadalajara.	N225FJ/F-WPUV
XB-EDU	Falcon 20C	39	Aviorrenta SA. Mexico City.	/XA-LOB/N910U/N50MM/N6565A//N5555U/N843F F-WNGM
XB-EFR	Citation	500-0090	Tracto Partes y Equipos SA. Monterrey.	N590RB/N590CC
XB-EGP	Learjet	25B-194	Periodico el Diario de Monterrey, Monterrey.	XA-COC
XB-ELU	Citation	500-0402	El Universal Periodico Nacional, Mexico City. 'Aguila 1'	XA-JFE/(G-BHIW) (N1779E)
XB-EPM	Sabre-75A	380-19	Dinamica SA. Nuevo Leon.	N100RS//N500TF/D-CLUB/N65771
XB-EPN	Citation	500-0241	Calpan SA de CV. Mexico City.	/N9060Y/XA-DAJ/(N5241J)
XB-ERN	HS 125/3A-R	25148	NECO International, Mexico City.	(N100TT)/N450JD/N8125J/G-AVRI/G-5-13
XB-ERU	Sabre-75A	370-7	Comision Federal de Electricidad,	/N75DE/N60PT/N60PM/N75NR/N7590N
XB-ERX	Citation	501-0082	Productos Agro Pecurios,	(N386DA)/N6RF/C-GEVF/N84CF/N460CC/N3150M
XB-ESX	Sabre-60A	306-47	Servicios Aereos del Centro SA. Mexico City.	/XA-ZOM/XA-ZUM/XB-ZUM/N927R N4765N
XB-ETE	Citation	500-0274	Daniel Monraz Rodriguez, Guadalajara.	N111TH/XA-IIX/(N140H)/N111TH (N5274J)
XB-ETV	Sabre-60	306-96	Aceros San Luis SA. San Luis Potosi.	N315JM/N48HC/N68HC/N65784
XB-EWF	Corvette	36		XB-CYA/F-OCDE/PH-JSD/F-BTTS
XB-EWQ	Citation	500-0141	Aerorent SA de CV. Mexico City.	XA-PIC/N141CC
XB-FDH	Beechjet 400	RJ-54	Aceites Grasas y Derivado,	N1554R
XB-FDN	Citation	500-0068	Kaliroy Produce Co.	/N92FA/N53MJ/(PT-LAY)/N568CM/N568CC
XB-FFB	HS 125/	...		
XB-GSN	Gulfstream 2	.....		

Page 133

Registration	Type	c/n	Owner / Operator	Previous identity
XB-HHF	Sabre-40	282-6	Corporativo Grupo Tampico SA.	/N600R
XB-HHR	Sabre-60	306-6	Graciela G de Gonzalez,	N311RM/N662F/N662P/N4712N
XB-JFE	JetStar-8	5145	El Universal Periodico Nacional, Mexico City.	XB-DBJ/N46K/N5509L
XB-JHE	Beechjet 400	RJ-48	Industrial Patrona S.A. de CV. Cordova.	N1548D
XB-JMM	Sabre-60	306-130	Partido Revolucionario Institucional/TAF, Mexico City.	XA-JIK/XA-OVR N2145J
XB-JMR	Sabre-60	306-35	Cia J M Romo S.A. Aguascalientes.	N3456B/N4748N
XB-JOY	Learjet	24D-263	W/o 29 Jun 76.	N3812G
XB-MBM	HS 125/1A	25030	Commercial Todo Facility, Chihuahua.	/(N97VM)/N123VM/N413GH/G-ATBA
XB-NIB	Sabre-40A	282-125	Vitro Corporacion SA. Monterrey.	N8356N
XB-OBE	Citation	500-0273	Drogueria Benavides SA. Monerrey, NL.	N273RC/N5273J
XB-OEM	Gulfstream 4	1055	Organization Editorial Mexicana, Mexico City.	XB-EXJ/VR-BKV/N1761P
XB-PUE	HS 125/3A-RA	25158	Latex Occidental, Guadalajara.	G-AVZK
XB-RGS	Sabre-40A	282-114	Vitro Corporativo SA. Monterrey. (N7SL)/XA-ATC/XC-SUB/XA-ATC/N64MG/N64MC	
XB-SII	Falcon 10	4	Cementos Mexicanos S.A. Monterrey.	N101FJ/F-WJMK
XB-ZRB	Falcon 10	107	Zeferino Romero Bringas, Tehuacan, Puebla.	N182FJ/F-WPUY
XC-...	Learjet	35A-435	State Government of Chiapas.	/N435N
XC-...	Jet Commander-B	135	State Government of Colima.	N1121N/N721GB//N1KT/N2DB/N700HB/N5043E
XC-...	Sabre-75A	380-61	Secretaria de Finanzas, Mexico City.	N727US/9L-LAW/JY-AFO/N2522E
XC-AOF	Sabre	...		
XC-ASA	Citation	500-0061	TAF-Transporte Aereo Federal, Mexico City.	XC-GAD/N561CC
XC-ASB	Citation	500-0251	TAF-Transporte Aereo Federal, Mexico City.	XC-QRO/N500LP/(HB-VGI)/I-COKE N5251J
XC-BEN	Citation	500-0243	PEMEX, Mexico City.	XC-GOY/N5243J
XC-BEZ	Citation	500-0072	TAF-Transporte Aereo Federal, Mexico City.	N491/N49R/N572CC
XC-BIN	Falcon 20D	198	PEMEX, Mexico City.	N74196/FEC14/VR-BDK/F-WNGO
XC-BOC	Citation	500-0169	Comision Federal de Electricidad, Mexico City.	XC-CON/N19CM/N20FL
XC-BUR	Citation	500-0245	FERTIMEX SA. Mexico City.	TI-AHH/(TI-AHE)/N5245J
XC-CFM	Learjet	25D-284	Comision de Fomento Minero, Mexico City.	
XC-CUZ	Learjet	35A-213	Director General de Geografica, Mexico City.	(N935NA)/N800RD
XC-DAD	Learjet	25D-223	TAF-Transporte Aereo Federal, Mexico City.	N23AM
XC-DGA	Citation	500-0010	TAF-Transporte Aereo Federal, Mexico City.	XC-FIT/N510CC
XC-DIP	Falcon 20E	282	Banco Nacional de Credito Rural, Mexico City.	N282C/N282JJ/N131JA/N4436F F-WMKG
XC-DOK	Citation	550-0198	PEMEX, Mexico City.	N67980
XC-DUF	Citation	550-0206	PEMEX, Mexico City.	N679CC
XC-ERX	Citation	...		
XC-FEZ	Citation	500-0409	SCT/Dept de Verificaciones Aereo, Mexico City.	N67815
XC-FIU	Citation	500-0012	SCT/Dept de Verificaciones Aereo, Mexico City. (status ?).	N512CC/N6563C
XC-FIV	Citation	500-0013	SCT/Dept de Verificaciones Aereo, Mexico City.	N513CC
XC-GAW	Citation	500-0410	State Government of Tamaulipas, Victoria.	N6780Z
XC-GNL	Learjet	25D-329	State Government of Nuevo Leon, Apodaca.	N3799B
XC-GOV	Citation	500-0189	Comision Federal de Electricidad, Mexico City.	
XC-GOW	Citation	500-0193	PEMEX, Mexico City.	
XC-GOX	Citation	500-0197	PEMEX, Mexico City.	
XC-GTO	Citation	500-0396	Aviorrenta SA. Mexico City.	/(XA-JEW)/N26514
XC-GUB	Learjet	25D-306	Ministry of Agriculture, Mexico City.	XA-DUB
XC-GUH	Citation	500-0221	Comision Federal de Electricidad, Mexico City.	N221CC
XC-GUO	Citation	500-0201	TAF-Transporte Aereo Federal, Mexico City.	
XC-HAD	Jet Commander	85	Bank of Mexico, Mexico City.	N201S/N4554E
XC-HEP	Citation	550-0464	PEMEX, Mexico City.	N1251D
XC-HEQ	Citation	550-0257	PEMEX, Mexico City.	N68609
XC-HIE	Learjet	29-002	Director General of Security, Mexico City.	XC-DFS/N723LL
XC-HIS	Learjet	25D-312	State Government of Chiapas, Tuxtla Gut.	N94MJ
XC-HIX	Falcon 20E	248	Government of Sinalao, Guliacan. XB-VRM/XB-OEM/XB-AQU/N37JJ/OH-FFV/F-WRQV	
XC-IPP	Learjet	35-028	Productores Pesqueros Isla de Cedros, Ensenada.	/N20BG/N135CC
XC-IST	Learjet	29-001	Avemex SA/Institute of Security and Social Services.	N929GL/HB-VFY
XC-OAH	Sabre-40R	282-1	State Government of Coahuila.	N766R/N177A/N7820C
XC-PET	Gulfstream 2TT	173	PEMEX, Mexico City.	/N801GA
XC-PGE	Sabre-	...		
XC-PGN	Citation	650-0165		XA-FCP/N1312X
XC-PGR	Learjet	35A-460	Procurad General de la Republica, Mexico City.	
XC-PMX	Citation	500-0376	PEMEX, Mexico City.	N36949

Regis-tration	Type	c/n	Owner / Operator	Previous identity
XC-ROO	Citation	550-0598	State Government of Quintana Roo, Chetumal.	N13028
XC-RPP	Learjet	25D-236	Director General de Geografica, Mexico City.	N1466B
XC-SAG	Learjet	24D-255	TAF/Secretariat of Agriculture, Mexico City.	
XC-SCT	Citation	550-0138	SCT/Transporte Federal Aereo. 'Mexico es Primero'.	N2646X
XC-SEY	Falcon 20C	169	TAF/Secretriat of Public Education, Mexico City.	N4370F/F-WNGN
XC-SUP	Learjet	24XR-319	CONASUPO, Mexico City.	
XC-TIJ	HFB 320	1049	State Government of Baja California.	XC-DGA/D-CISO
XC-VSA	Learjet	28-002	State Government of Tabasco, Villahermosa.	N511DB/N39404

Burkina Faso

XT-BBE	B 727-14	18990	Government of Burkina Faso,	N21UC/N2741A/D-AHLP/N975PS

Iraq

YI-...	Falcon 20E	320	Government/Iraqi Airways, Baghdad.	EP-FIF/EP-AHV/F-WRQS
YI-AHH	Falcon 20F	337	Government/Iraqi Airways, Baghdad. (photo-recce).	F-WRQR
YI-AHJ	Falcon 20F	343	Government/Iraqi Airways, Baghdad. (photo recce).	F-WRQR
YI-AKA	JetStar 2	5233	Government/Iraqi Airways, Baghdad.	N4048M
YI-AKB	JetStar 2	5235	Government/Iraqi Airways, Baghdad.	N4055M
YI-AKC	JetStar 2	5237	Government/Iraqi Airways, Baghdad.	N4058M
YI-AKD	JetStar 2	5238	Government/Iraqi Airways, Baghdad.	N4062M
YI-AKE	JetStar 2	5239	Government/Iraqi Airways, Baghdad.	N4063M
YI-AKF	JetStar 2	5240	Government/Iraqi Airways, Baghdad.	N4065M
YI-ALC	Falcon 50	101	Government/Iraqi Airways, Baghdad.	F-WPXH
YI-ALD	Falcon 50	120	Government/Iraqi Airways, Baghdad.	F-WPXJ
YI-ALE	Falcon 50	122	Government/Iraqi Airways, Baghdad.	F-WZHG

Yugoslavia

YU-BIH	Learjet	24D-320	Government of Slovenia, Ljubljana.	N3802G
YU-BJG	Learjet	25B-187	Government of Yugoslavia, Belgrade.	
YU-BJH	Learjet	25B-186	W/o 18 Jan 77.	
YU-BKJ	Learjet	25B-205	Government of Macedonia, Skopje.	N1468B
YU-BKR	Learjet	25D-221	Government of Yugoslavia, Belgrade.	N3819G
YU-BKZ	Citation	500-0373	Govt of Bosnia & Herzogovina/Air Service Sarajevo.	N98449
YU-BLY	Sabre-75A	380-65	Government of Croatia, Zagreb.	
YU-BME	HS 125/600B	6048	INA-Yugoslav Oil Corp. Belgrade.	G-BHIE/HB-VDS
YU-BML	Citation	500-0399	Sour Fero-Elektro.	N2069A
YU-BNA	Falcon 50	43	Government of Yugoslavia, Belgrade.	72102/F-WZHO
YU-BOE	Citation	S550-0045	Energoinvest, Sarajevo.	N1269Y
YU-BOL	Learjet	35A-618	Adria Airways, Ljubljana.	
YU-BPL	Citation	550-0480		N72U/N72K/N12522
YU-BPU	Citation	550-0128	Government of Croatia.	/N220LA/N536M/N2631V

Venezuela

YV-....	Falcon 50	136	Bariven Corp. Houston, Tx.	N...../VR-BLL/N50HC/N204HC/N126FJ/F-W...
YV-03CP	JetStar-731	9/5106	Servicios Aerofacility SA. Caracas.	/N1329K/N8SC/CF-GWI/N288U/N238U
YV-100CP	Learjet	35A-083	Contivato C.A.	N121CL/N500CD/(N45SL)/(N400MJ)/N400CC/(N600CC)
YV-119P	Westwind-1123	184		/N866JM/N666JM/N1123T/4X-CKH
YV-123CP	Jet Commander	16	Bermudez Motors C.A. Caracas.	N177A/N217PM/N96B
YV-125CP	Learjet	55-126	Transportes La Mona S.A. Caracas.	N7260J
YV-12CP	Learjet	55-031	Aero Servicios ALAS C.A. Caracas.	
YV-132CP	Learjet	25C-071	Aero Ejecutivos S.A. Caracas.	YV-130P/YV-T-DTT
YV-147CP	Citation	551-0020	Banco Mercantil/Inversiones Menil S.A. Chua, Caracas.	YV-1478P/YV-147CP N26638
YV-160CP	Westwind-1124	211	Transpolar, Caracas.	4X-CLI
YV-162CP	Citation	550-0300	Aero Servicios ALAS C.A.	N68881
YV-169CP	Citation	551-0007	Pavimentadora Life C.A. Chua, Caracas.	N3223M
YV-17CP	Falcon 10	100	Banco de la Construccion y de Oriente C.A. Caracas.	N10FJ/N177FJ/F-WPXI
YV-190CP	Westwind-1124	219	Transpolar, Caracas.	4X-CLQ
YV-19CP	Citation	551-0004	Servicios Aereos Rigres C.A.	N553CJ/N98784

Registration	Type	c/n	Owner / Operator	Previous identity
YV-200C	Falcon 20D	200	DHL/MRI South America Inc. Caracas.	N38CC/N48CC/N44CC/N44MC/N550MC/N4389F F-WMKJ
YV-203CP	Learjet	25C-061	Tranarg C.A. Caracas.	N9CN/PT-DUO/N251GL
YV-210CP	Westwind-Two	308	Maraven S.A. Maquetia.	4X-CRB
YV-213CP	Citation	551-0015	Inversiones Gotan, Caracas.	(N26613)
YV-21CP	Citation	500-0115	Transportes Inland, Caracas.	YV-TAFA/N115CC
YV-2267P	Citation	500-0052	Aero Club Barquisimeto.	N52FP/N52MA/N552CC
YV-253C	Citation	501-0053	Tecnofly C.A.	N59PC/N98528
YV-276CP	Citation	550-0405	Consolid-Air S.A.	
YV-300CP	Citation	551-0032	Aero Charter Aviation C.A/Inversiones 05 C.A.	(N98715)
YV-301P	Citation	501-0131		//N490WC/N2650X
YV-309P	Diamond 1A	A049SA	Ireol CA. Caracas.	N300LA/N336DM
YV-327CP	Learjet	35A-344	Oficina Central Asesoria y Ayuda Tencia C.A. Caracas.	/N40149
YV-332CP	Westwind-Two	330	Transporte 330/Cia Tamesis SA. Caracas.	N723K/N52GW/4X-CRX
YV-376CP	Citation	550-0637		N1258U
YV-388CP	HFB 320	1057		VR-CYR/(N107TW)/D-COSE
YV-393CP	Westwind-1124	262	Venezuela TV Corp. Caracas.	N40DG/N262WW/4X-CNH
YV-432CP	Learjet	35A-437	Transporte Transilac S.A. Maracaibo.	N3803G
YV-451CP	Westwind-Two	343	Maraven S.A. Maquetia.	4X-CTK
YV-452CP	Falcon 50	4	Maraven SA. Caracas.	N5OFJ/N110FJ/F-WZHA
YV-52CP	Citation	500-0367	Construcciones CADE.	N36906
YV-55CP	Citation	500-0215	SABENPE, Caracas.	YV-T-000/N215CC
YV-572CP	Corvette	17	Hydrowell S.A. Caracas.	F-ODTM/F-BTTM/N614AC/F-WNGQ
YV-601CP	Falcon 10	73	TECNO Trading/Tecnoravia SA. Caracas.	N130FJ/C-GDCO/N88AT/N155FJ/F-WNGL
YV-65CP	Learjet	5A-161	C A de Edificaciones - Resid D Paulo.	N39415
YV-70CP	Falcon 10	66	Monumental Jet, Caracas.	/N5ORL/N150FJ/F-WJMN
YV-962P	Westwind	...		
YV-999P	HFB 320	1037		N555JM/N6ML/N6MK/N5ZA/N892HJ/D-CESE
YV-O-CVG 2	Citation	551-0006	Corpo Venezolana de Guyana,	YV-06CP/N3227A
YV-O-MAC-1	Citation	500-0336	W/o Jun 79.	N336CC
YV-O-MRI-1	Learjet	35A-270	Ministry of Interior Relations, Caracas.	N10871

Zimbabwe

Registration	Type	c/n	Owner / Operator	Previous identity
Z-TBX	HS 125/1B	25067	TABEX, Harare.	9J-EPK/9J-SAS/ZS-MAN/9J-RAN
Z-VEC	HS 125/403B	25215	Cone Textiles, Harare.	G-BHFT/9M-SSB/G-BHFT/HB-VBZ
Z-WPD	BAe 146 Statesman	E2065	Air Zimbabwe/Government of Zimbabwe,	G-5-065

New Zealand

Registration	Type	c/n	Owner / Operator	Previous identity
ZK-RJI	BAe 125/800B	8082	Robert Jones Investments Ltd. Wellington.	/G-5-548
ZK-WNL	Falcon 10	50	Wilson Neill Ltd. Dunedin.	VH-MEI/F-WLCS

Paraguay

Registration	Type	c/n	Owner / Operator	Previous identity
ZP-...	Citation	500-0008		////N11QC/(N38EP)/N11TC/N502CC/HB-VCX/N508CC
ZP-AGD	Westwind-1123	151		N88WP/N1123E/4X-CJD

South Africa

Registration	Type	c/n	Owner / Operator	Previous identity
ZS-...	Citation	500-0296	Comair, Johannesburg.	N882CA//N98DM/(N5296J)
ZS-CAL	HS 125/F3B-RA	25172	Directorate of Civil Aviation, Johannesburg.	(G-5-506)/G-AXEG/ZS-CAL G-AXEG
ZS-CAQ	Falcon 50	133	Department of Transport Services, Pretoria.	/HB-IEA/HZ-AKI/HB-IEA/F-WPXH
ZS-CAR	Citation	S550-0078	Director General of Transport, Jan Smuts.	N1273X
ZS-CAS	Falcon 50	91	Department of Transport Services, Pretoria.	ZS-BMB/F-WZHY
ZS-IDC	Citation	S550-0148	Aircraft Distributors of South Africa P/L. Rand.	N1296Z
ZS-JBA	HS 125/400B	25259	Sagel & Read, Pretoria.	SAAF05/G-AZEK
ZS-JIH	HS 125/400B	25260	Sagel & Read, Pretoria.	SAAF06/G-AZEL
ZS-JWC	Learjet	23-030	Wonderair P/L. Pretoria.	N431CA/ZS-JWC/N431CA/N431EJ
ZS-KPA	Citation	501-0183	Grinaker Holdings P/L.	N6777V
ZS-LDK	Citation	550-0274	African Explosives & Chemical Industries, Lanseria.	N6864C
ZS-LDO	Citation	501-0245	Dorbyl Air Ltd.	N26263

Registration	Type	c/n	Owner / Operator	Previous identity
ZS-LDV	Citation	500-0418	Industrial Development Corp. Johannesburg.	N2628B
ZS-LEE	Citation	550-0347	Kangra Coal Corp. Johannesburg.	N6826U
ZS-LHU	Citation	550-0165	H Hirsch/Helair Aviation, Lanseria.	3D-ACQ/N98871
ZS-LHW	Citation	550-0417	Mmabatho Air Services/Boputhatswana Government, Mafikeng.	N1217D
ZS-LIG	Citation	550-0474	Aviation Management Group P/L.	N12514
ZS-LME	HS 125/403B	25242	Sagel & Read, Pretoria.	3D-ABZ/G-BDKF/VH-TOM/G-5-20
ZS-LNP	Citation	550-0560	Aircraft Distributors of South Africa P/L. Rand.	N1298J
ZS-LWU	Learjet	24B-209	Executive Aerospace P/L. Durban.	/N14BC/N16MT/N970GA
ZS-LXH	Learjet	25D-206	Gordon Andrews Partnership, Lanseria.	/N206EQ/N206EC
ZS-LXT	Citation	501-0215		//N50MM/N1354G
ZS-LYB	Citation	500-0278	P Goch/National Airways Corp. Lanseria.	(N278SR)/N278SP/N278CC/(N5278J)
ZS-MBR	Learjet	23-064	Million Air, Lanseria.	3D-AFJ/ZS-MBR//N66AM/N73JT/N401RB/N400RB/N200G N365EJ
ZS-MBX	Citation	550-0587	Corporate Charter Services,	N1301S
ZS-MCP	Citation Eagle	500-0130	Professional Aviation Services,	N130G/N4LG/OY-ARW/(N9MH)/N4LG//VH-CRM
ZS-MCU	Citation	500-0137	Management Properties Co. Lanseria.	/N12ME/N12MB/N137CC
ZS-MDN	Learjet	23-081	Speed Air P/L. Lanseria.	N418LJ/(N81LJ)/XC-JOA/N437LJ/N369EJ
ZS-MGH	Citation Eagle	500-0299	Domberg Aviation, Lanseria.	N55AK/N66TR///N3JJ/HB-VEO/N5299J
ZS-MGJ	Learjet	24XR-207	Highveld Aviation/J Heyneke, Lanseria.	/N457JA/N878W/N851JH
ZS-MGK	Learjet	35A-357		(N100L)/(N289GA)//N1001L/N3797S
ZS-MGL	Citation	501-0021	Sandgate Consultants,	N203LH/N121SJ/XA-IEM/YV-166CP/(YV-135CP)/N36883
ZS-MHN	Beechjet 400	RJ-59		N1559U
ZS-MLN	Citation	551-0285	Comair P/L. (was 550-0240).	N551SR//(N550RL)/N6804S
ZS-MLS	Citation	550-0621		N12543
ZS-MPI	Citation	500-0334		(N527TA)//N44RD/N500DD/N5334J
ZS-MPN	Citation	501-0275	Rand Air,	N31AJ/YV-159CP/N36893
ZS-MVV	Citation V	560-0062		N2716G
ZS-MVZ	Citation V	560-0064		N2717X
ZS-MWW	Learjet	35A-157		N157DJ/N57FP/N57FF/YV-01CP/N746GL
ZS-PMC	Citation	551-0171	Rio Tinto Aviation Services,	/(9V-PUW)/N26178
ZS-RCC	Citation	500-0106	Inter Air P/L-Schwartz Diamonds, Johannesburg.	N606CC
ZS-RCS	Citation	550-0065	Red Cross Society, Cape Town.	/N55SX/N4191G

The following is a list of military 'Executive Jets' operating throughout the world. Each aircraft is listed by registration, type, serial/constructors number, owner/operator and previous identity.

Military operated

Israel

Registration	Type	c/n	Owner / Operator	Previous identity
4X-JYJ	Westwind-1124N	185	027, IDFAF, Tel Aviv.	N1123U/4X-CKI
4X-JYO	Westwind-1124N	186	031, IDFAF, Tel Aviv.	4X-CKJ
4X-JYR	Westwind-1124N	152	035, IDFAF, Tel Aviv.	4X-CJC/029-4X-JYF/4X-CJC

Niger

Registration	Type	c/n	Owner / Operator	Previous identity
5U-BAG	B 737-2N9C	21499	Government of Niger Republic, Niamey. 'Monts Baghezan'	(5U-MAF)

Togo

Registration	Type	c/n	Owner / Operator	Previous identity
5V-MAB	F 28-1000	11079	Government of Togo, Lome.	5V-TAB/PH-ZBK/PH-EXB
5V-MBG	Falcon 10	167	Government of Togo, Lome.	5V-TAE/N39K/N233FJ/F-WZGT

Malawi

Registration	Type	c/n	Owner / Operator	Previous identity
MAAW-J1	BAe 125/800B	8064	Government of Malawi, Zomba.	G-5-514

Algeria

Registration	Type	c/n	Owner / Operator	Previous identity
7T-VPA	Falcon 900	81	Ministry of Defence, Boufarik.	F-WWFL
7T-VPB	Falcon 900	82	Ministry of Defence, Boufarik.	F-WWFM
7T-VRB	Gulfstream 3	368	Ministry of Defence, Boufarik.	N17589
7T-VRC	Gulfstream 3	396	Ministry of Defence, Boufarik.	N1761S
7T-VRD	Gulfstream 3	399	Ministry of Defence, Boufarik.	N17581

Ghana

Registration	Type	c/n	Owner / Operator	Previous identity
G-530	F 28-3000	11125	Government/Ghana Air Force, Accra.	PH-ZBP/PH-EXP

Kuwait

Registration	Type	c/n	Owner / Operator	Previous identity
KAF 320	DC 9-32	47691	Government/Kuwait Air Force.	160749
KAF 321	DC 9-32	47690	Government/Kuwait Air Force.	160750

Malaysia

Registration	Type	c/n	Owner / Operator	Previous identity
M24-01	HS 125/400B	25189	9M-EDA, TUDM, 2 Bayan Squadron, Kuala Lumpur.	FM1801/FM1200/(G-AXFY) G-5-20
M24-02	HS 125/400B	25209	9M-EDC, TUDM, 2 Bayan Squadron, Kuala Lumpur.	FM1802/FM1201
M28-01	F 28-1000	11088	9M-EB., TUDM, 2 Bayan Squadron, Kuala Lumpur.	FM2101/PH-EXI
M28-02	F 28-1000	11089	9M-EB., TUDM, 2 Bayan Squadron, Kuala Lumpur.	FM2102/PH-EXL
M37-01	Falcon 900	64	9M-...., TUDM, 2 Bayan Squadron, Kuala Lumpur.	N446FJ/F-WWFH

Zaire

Registration	Type	c/n	Owner / Operator	Previous identity
9T-MSS	B 707-382B	19969	Government of Zaire, Kinshasa. 'Mount Hoyo'	CS-TBD

Botswana

Registration	Type	c/n	Owner / Operator	Previous identity
OK1	BAe 125/800B	8164	Government/Botswana Defence Force, Z1 Squadron.	G-5-654

Pakistan

Registration	Type	c/n	Owner / Operator	Previous identity
68-19635	B 707-351C	19635	Pakistan Air Force,	AP-BAA/N379US
68-19866	B 707-340C	19866	Pakistan Air Force,	YU-AGD/AP-AWY/AP-AVL
J 468	Falcon 20	468	Pakistan Air Force,	F-WMKG

Regis-tration	Type	c/n	Owner / Operator	Previous identity
J 469	Falcon 20	469	Pakistan Air Force,	F-WMKI
J 753	Falcon 20E	277	Pakistan Air Force, 12 Squadron, Karachi.	F-WPXD

Taiwan-Formosa

18351	B 720-051B	18351	Government of Republic of China-Taiwan,	N721US
2721	B 727-109	19399	Taiwan Air Force,	B-1818
2722	B 727-109	19520	Taiwan Air Force,	B-1820
2723	B 727-109C	20111	Taiwan Air Force,	B-1822
2724	B 727-121C	19818	Taiwan Air Force,	B-188/XV-NJB/N388PA

Canada

117503	Falcon 20C	92	British Columbia Institute of Technology, Vancouver.	///20503/F-WJMM
13701	B 707-347C	20315	CC137, 437 Squadron, Trenton.	(N1506W)
13702	B 707-347C	20316	CC137, 437 Squadron, Trenton.	N1785B/(N1507W)
13703	B 707-347C	20317	CC137, 437 Squadron, Trenton.	(N1508W)
13704	B 707-347C	20318	CC137, 437 Squadron, Trenton.	(N1509W)
13705	B 707-347C	20319	CC137, 437 Squadron, Trenton.	(N1510W)
144601	Challenger 600S	1040	CC144, DND, 412 (Transport) Squadron, Uplands.	C-GLYM
144602	Challenger 600S	1065	CC144, DND, 412 (Transport) Squadron, Uplands.	C-GBVE/C-G...
144603	Challenger 600S	1006	CE144A, DND, 414 Squadron, North Bay.	C-GCSN/HZ-AO4/N110KS/C=GCSN
144604	Challenger 600S	1007	CC144, DND, 412 (Transport) Squadron, Uplands.	/C-GBKC/HZ-TAG/C-GBKC
144605	Challenger 600S	1008	CC144, DND, 412 (Transport) Squadron, Uplands.	C-GBEY/(D-BBAD)
144606	Challenger 600S	1009	CC144, DND, 412 (Transport) Squadron, Uplands.	C-GCVQ/N606CL/C-GBFY
144607	Challenger 600S	1014	CE144A, DND, 414 Squadron, North Bay.	C-GBLL/HZ-TAG/N97941/C-GBLL-X
144608	Challenger 600S	1015	CC144, DND, 412 (Transport) Squadron, Uplands.	C-GBLN/N604CL/N37LB/C-GBLN
144609	Challenger 600S	1017	CC144, DND, 412 (Transport) Squadron, Uplands.	C-GBPX/N777XX/N4247C/C-GBPX
144610	Challenger 600S	1022	CC144, DND, 412 (Transport) Squadron, Uplands.	/C-GOGO/C-GLWZ
144611	Challenger 600S	1030	CE144A, DND, 414 Squadron, North Bay.	C-GCZU/N604CL/N1622/C-GLXQ
144612	Challenger 600S	1002	CC144, DND, AETE, Cold Lake, Alberta.	/C-GCGS-X/C-GCGS/C-GCGS-X
144613	Challenger 601	3035	CC144, DND, 412 (Transport) Squadron, Uplands.	C-GCUN/C-GLXW
144614	Challenger 601	3036	CC144, DND, 412 (Transport) Squadron, Uplands.	C-GCUP/C-GLXY
144615	Challenger 601	3037	CC144, DND, 412 (Transport) Squadron, Uplands.	C-GCUR/C-GLXB
144616	Challenger 601	3038	CC144, DND, 412 (Transport) Squadron, Uplands.	C-GCUT/C-GLYA

Chile

301	Falcon 200	401	VP-1, Chilean Navy, Santiago.	F-GEXF/VR-BJJ/F-GATF/VR-BJJ/F-GATF/N207FJ N200FJ/F-GATF/F-WZAH
302	Falcon 200	496	VP-2, Chilean Navy, Santiago.	F-WGSR/F-OGSR/(F-GGAR)/I-LXOT/F-GFAY/VR-BHY F-WZZC
351	Learjet	35-050	Fuerza Aerea de Chile,	CC-ECO
352	Learjet	35-066	Fuerza Aerea de Chile,	CC-ECP
902	B 707-351C	19443	Fuerza Aerea de Chile,	CC-CCK/N374US
903	B 707-330B	18926	Fuerza Aerea de Chile,	CC-CEA/D-ABUC

Morocco

CN-ANL	Gulfstream 2TT	182	Government of Morocco, Rabat.	N17589
CN-ANM	Falcon 20ECM	165	Ministry of Defence, Kenitra.	CN-MBH/F-WJMJ
CN-ANN	Falcon 20ECM	152	Ministry of Defence, Kenitra.	CN-MBG/F-WJMJ
CN-ANO	Falcon 50	12	Government of Morocco, Rabat.	F-WZHC
CN-ANR	B 707-3W6C	21956	Government of Morocco, Rabat.	N707QT
CN-ANS	B 707-138B	18334	Government of Morocco, Rabat. 'Africa Crown'	N58937/9Y-TDB/VH-EBK
CN-ANU	Gulfstream 3	365	Government of Morocco, Rabat.	/HZ-AFO/N1761J

Bolivia

FAB 001	Sabre-60	306-115	President of Bolivia, La Paz.	(XA-LEI)/N2118J
FAB 008	Learjet	25B-192	Fuerza Aerea Boliviana, photographic survey, La Paz.	
FAB 010	Learjet	25D-211	Fuerza Aerea Boliviana, photographic survey, La Paz.	

Portugal

7401	Falcon 50	195	Portuguese Air Force, Esc 504, Montijo, Lisbon.	F-WWHK
7402	Falcon 50	198	Portuguese Air Force, Esc 504, Montijo, Lisbon.	F-WWHC
8101	Falcon 20D	211	Portuguese Air Force, Esc 504, Montijo, Lisbon.	N30FE/N4398F/F-WJMK
8102	Falcon 20D	215	Portuguese Air Force, Esc 504, Montijo, Lisbon.	N34FE/N4401F/F-WLCS
8103	Falcon 20D	217	Portuguese Air Force, Esc 504, Montijo, Lisbon.	N35FE/N4403F/F-WLCY

Federal Republic of Germany

10+01	B 707-307C	19997	Luftwaffe, FBS, Koln-Wahn.	(68-11071)
10+02	B 707-307C	19998	Luftwaffe, FBS, Koln-Wahn.	(68-11072)
10+03	B 707-307C	19999	Luftwaffe, FBS, Koln-Wahn.	(68-11073)
10+04	B 707-307C	20000	Luftwaffe, FBS, Koln-Wahn.	(68-11074)
12+01	Challenger 601	3031	Luftwaffe, FBS, Koln-Wahn.	C-GTCB/N607CL/C-GTCB/C-G...
12+02	Challenger 601	3040	Luftwaffe, FBS, Koln-Wahn.	N608CL/C-GLYN
12+03	Challenger 601	3043	Luftwaffe, FBS, Koln-Wahn.	N609CL/C-GLWZ
12+04	Challenger 601	3049	Luftwaffe, FBS, Koln-Wahn.	C-FQYT/N610CL/C-GLXQ
12+05	Challenger 601	3053	Luftwaffe, FBS, Koln-Wahn.	N604CL/C-G...
12+06	Challenger 601	3056	Luftwaffe, FBS, Koln-Wahn.	N612CL/C-G...
12+07	Challenger 601	3059	Luftwaffe, FBS, Koln-Wahn.	N614CL/C-G...
16+06	HFB 320	1048	Wehrtechnisches Museum, Hamburg.	D-CISI
16+08	HFB 320	1025	Luftwaffe, Erprobungstelle 61, Manching.	D-9537/(YA+112)/(CA+112)/D-CARU
16+21	HFB 320ECM	1058	Luftwaffe, JbG-32, Lechfeld.	D-COSI
16+22	HFB 320	1059	W/o 27 Nov 76, Schwabmuenchen, West Germany.	D-COSO
16+23	HFB 320ECM	1060	Luftwaffe, JbG-32, Lechfeld.	D-COSU
16+24	HFB 320ECM	1061	Luftwaffe, JbG-32, Lechfeld.	D-CANI
16+25	HFB 320ECM	1062	Luftwaffe, JbG-32, Lechfeld.	D-CANO
16+26	HFB 320ECM	1063	Luftwaffe, JbG-32, Lechfeld.	D-CANU
16+27	HFB 320ECM	1064	Luftwaffe, JbG-32, Lechfeld.	D-CAMA
16+28	HFB 320ECM	1065	Luftwaffe, JbG-32, Lechfeld.	D-CAME
17+01	VFW 614	G14	Luftwaffe, FBS, Koln-Wahn.	
17+02	VFW 614	G18	Luftwaffe, FBS, Koln-Wahn.	
17+03	VFW 614	G19	Luftwaffe, FBS, Koln-Wahn.	
CA+102	JetStar-6	5035	W/o 16 Jan 68, Bremen, West Germany.	/(62-12167)

Spain

T 11-1	Falcon 20E	253	EC-ZCJ, 45-02, Ed1A/45 Grupo, Madrid. (prev code 401-02).	EC-BZV/F-WRQS
T 11-5	Falcon 20	475	EC-ZCN, 45-05, Ed1A/45 Grupo, Madrid.	F-WJML
T 15-1	DC 8-52	45814	EC-ZCI, 401-30, Ed1A/45 Grupo, Madrid. (prev code 401-01).	EC-BAV/N45814 EC-BAV
T 16-1	Falcon 50	84	EC-ZCP, 45-20, Ed1A/45 Grupo, Madrid. (prev code 45-09).	(N2711B)/F-WZHK
T 17-1	B 707-331B	20060	EC-Z.., 45-10, Ed1A/45 Grupo, Madrid.	N256B/N708A/N8731
T 17-2	B 707-331C	18757	EC-Z.., 45-11, Ed1A/45 Grupo, Madrid.	N792TW
T 17-3	B 707-368C	21367	EC-Z.., 45-12, Ed1A/45 Grupo, Madrid.	HZ-HM6/HZ-ACJ
T 18-.	Falcon 900	90	EC-ZC.., 45-..., Ed1A/45 Grupo, Madrid.	F-W...
T 18-1	Falcon 900	38	EC-ZC.., 45-40, Ed1A/45 Grupo, Madrid.	F-WWFE
TM 11-2	Falcon 20D	222	EC-ZCK, 45-03, Ed1A/45 Grupo, Madrid. (prev code 401-03).	EC-BXV/F-WNGL
TM 11-3	Falcon 20D	219	EC-ZCL, 45-04, Ed1A/45 Grupo, Madrid. (prev code 401-04).	EC-BVV/F-WPXH
TM 11-4	Falcon 20E	332	EC-ZCM. 45-01, Ed1A/45 Grupo, Madrid. (prev codes 401-01/05)	EC-CTV/F-WRQP
U 20-1	Citation	550-0425	01-405, Armada, Esc 004, Rota.	(LN-FOX)/N1218A
U 20-2	Citation	550-0446	01-406, Armada, Esc 004, Rota.	N1248N
U 20-3	Citation	550-0592	01-407, Armada, Esc 004, Rota.	N1302N

Ireland

236	HS 125/F600B	25256	W/o 27 Nov 79, Casement-Dublin, Ireland.	G-AYBH/G-5-13/RP-C111/G-AYBH
238	HS 125/700B	7082	Irish Air Corps. Casement-Dublin.	
249	Gulfstream 3	413	Irish Air Corps. Casement-Dublin.	N8226M/N1/N778SW/N77SW/N357GA

Registration	Type	c/n	Owner / Operator	Previous identity

Iran

Registration	Type	c/n	Owner / Operator	Previous identity
1001	B 707-386C	21396	Government of Iran, Tehran.	EP-HIM
1003	JetStar-8	5137	Government of Iran, Tehran.	EP-VRP/N5501L
1004	JetStar 2	5203	Government of Iran, Tehran.	EP-VLP/N5529L
5-2801	Falcon 20E	333	Ministry of Sepah L.D. D.A.L. Tehran.	F-WNGL
5-2802	Falcon 20E	336	Iranian Navy, Mehrabad.	F-WRQP
5-2803	Falcon 20E	340	Iranian Navy, Mehrabad.	F-WRQX
5-2804	Falcon 20E	346	Iranian Navy, Mehrabad.	F-WRQP
5-3020	Falcon 20E	348	Iranian Air Army, Mehrabad.	5-4039/F-WRQR
5-3021	Falcon 20E	350	Iranian Air Army, Mehrabad.	5-4040/F-WRQS
5-9001	Falcon 20F	351	Iranian Air Force, 1st Transport Base, Mehrabad.	F-WMKJ
5-9002	Falcon 20F	353	Iranian Air Force, 1st Transport Base, Mehrabad.	F-WRQP
5-9003	Falcon 20F	354	Iranian Air Force, 1st Transport Base, Mehrabad.	F-WRQR

France

Registration	Type	c/n	Owner / Operator	Previous identity
101	Falcon 10MER	101	Marine Nationale, 57S, Landivisiau.	F-WPXJ
129	Falcon 10MER	129	Marine Nationale, 57S, Landivisiau.	F-WZGA
133	Falcon 10MER	133	Marine Nationale, 57S, Landivisiau.	F-ZGTI/F-WZGE
141	Caravelle 3	141	Wfu 28 Mar 80, for preservation at Musee de l'Air-Le Bourget	F-BJTK
143	Falcon 10MER	143	Marine Nationale, 3S, Hyeres.	F-WZGO
154	Falcon 20C	154	W/o 22 Jan 76, Rambouillet, France.	F-WLCV
185	Falcon 10MER	185	Marine Nationale, 3S, Hyeres.	F-WZGQ
32	Falcon 10MER	32	Marine Nationale, 57S, Landivisiau.	
39	Falcon 10MER	39	W/o 30 Jan 80, Toul-Rosieres, France.	F-WPUX
48	Gardian	448	Marine Nationale, 12S, Papeete-Tahiti.	F-ZWVF
65	Gardian	465	Marine Nationale, 9S, Noumea-New Caledonia.	F-ZJTS
72	Gardian	472	Marine Nationale, 12S, Papeete-Tahiti.	
77	Gardian	477	Marine Nationale, 9S, Noumea-New Caledonia.	
80	Gardian	480	Marine Nationale, 12S, Papeete-Tahiti.	F-ZJSA
F-RAE.	Falcon 20C	167	A de l'Air, ET 1/65, Villacoublay.	F-RAFL/F-WMKG
F-RAE.	Falcon 20E	268	A de l'Air, ET 1/65, Villacoublay.	F-RAEB/F-WNGN
F-RAEA	Falcon 20E	260	A de l'Air, ET 1/65, Villacoublay.	F-WMKJ
F-RAF.	Falcon 50	27	A de l'Air, ET 1/60, Villacoublay.	F-WGTG/HB-IEB/F-WZHN
F-RAF.	Falcon 50	34	A de l'Air, ET 1/60, Villacoublay.	F-WEFS//HB-IEV/F-WZHH
F-RAFC	DC 8F-55F	45819	A de l'Air, ET 3/60, Roissy.	F-BNLD/TU-TXK/F-RCFA/TU-TXG/F-BNLD
F-RAFD	DC 8-72CF	46043	A de l'Air, ET 3/60, Roissy.	OH-LFV/OH-LFS
F-RAFE	DC 8-53	45570	A de l'Air, EE-51, Evreaux/Fauville.	F-ZARK/F-BIUZ
F-RAFF	DC 8-72CF	46130	A de l'Air, ET 3/60, Roissy.	OH-LFY
F-RAFG	DC 8-72CF	46013	A de l'Air, ET 3/60, Roissy.	OH-LFT
F-RAFH	Caravelle 10B	201	A de l'Air, ET 1/60, Villacoublay.	F-BNRA/TU-TXQ/F-BNRA
F-RAFI	Falcon 50	5	A de l'Air, ET 1/60, Villacoublay.	F-WZHB
F-RAFJ	Falcon 50	78	A de l'Air, ET 1/60, Villacoublay.	F-GEOY/TR-LAI/F-ODEO/F-WPXF
F-RAFM	Falcon 20C	238	A de l'Air, ET 1/60, Villacoublay.	F-WRQP
F-RAFN	Falcon 20C	93	A de l'Air, ET 1/60, Villacoublay.	F-RBQA/F-RAFN/F-WMKF
F-RAFO	Falcon 20F	342	A de l'Air, ET 1/65, Villacoublay.	F-RAEC/J2-KAC/YI-AHI/F-WRQP
F-RAFP	Falcon 900	2	A de l'Air, ET 1/60, Villacoublay.	F-GFJC/F-WFJC
F-RAFQ	Falcon 900	4	A de l'Air, ET 1/60, Villacoublay.	F-WWFA/VR-BJX/F-WWFC
F-RCAL	Falcon 20F	422	A de l'Air, ET 3/65, Villacoublay.	F-ZJTJ/F-WRQU
F-RCAP	Falcon 20E	291	A de l'Air, ET 3/65, Villacoublay.	F-RAEC/F-WRQT
F-SEBI	Falcon 20E-5	315	C.N.E.T., Lannion.	/F-GDLO/OO-VPQ/F-BVPQ/F-WRQP
F-TEOA	Falcon 20	49	A de l'Air, SIET 98/120, Cazaux.	F-RAFJ/F-WNGN
F-UGWL	Falcon 20SNA	115	A de l'Air, 339-WL, CITAC-339, Luxeuil.	F-WJML
F-UGWM/463	Falcon 20SNA	186	A de l'Air, 339-WM, CITAC-339, Luxeuil.	F-WPXL
F-UGWN	Falcon 20SNA	451	A de l'Air, 339-WN, CITAC-339, Luxeuil. 'Fil d'Ariane'	F-ZJTS/F-WRQP
F-UGWO	Falcon 20F	483	A de l'Air, 339-WO, CITAC-339, Luxeuil.	F-WRQQ
F-UGWP	Falcon 20E	309	A de l'Air, 339-WP, CITAC-339, Luxeuil. 'L'Etoile du Berger'	F-RAFU/TR-LUW
F-UKJA	Falcon 20C	182	A de l'Air, CIFAS-328, Bordeaux-Merignac.	F-BVFV/F-WVFV/I-ROBM/F-WTDJ HB-VCB/F-WNGN
F-Z...	Corvette	2	CEV,	F-BNRZ/F-WRNZ
F-Z...	Corvette	1	CEV,	F-BUAS/F-WUAS/F-BUAS/F-WUAS

Registration	Type	c/n	Owner / Operator	Previous identity
F-ZACB	Falcon 20C	96	CEV,	F-GERT/N89SC/N5RT/N511S/N981F/F-WNGM
F-ZACB	Falcon 10	02	CEV, Bretigny. Larzac test bed. (wfu ?).	F-ZJTA/F-WTAL
F-ZACC	Falcon 20C	124	CEV, Bretigny.	F-WJMJ
F-ZACD	Falcon 20C	131	CEV, Bretigny.	F-WJMK
F-ZACG	Falcon 20C	86	CEV, Cazaux. F-WRGQ/HB-VDW/G-BBEK/F-BUYI/(G-BBEK)/N622R/N808F/N976F/F-WMKI	
F-ZACR	Falcon 20C	138	CEV, Cazaux.	F-BUIC/(G-BAOA)/D-CGJH/D-CALL/F-WLCS
F-ZACS	Falcon 20C	22	CEV, Istres.	F-BMKK/F-WMKK
F-ZACT	Falcon 20C	79	CEV, Bretigny.	F-BNRH/F-WMKH
F-ZACU	Falcon 20C	145	CEV, Bretigny.	F-GCGY/OO=PJB/F-BPJB/F-WNGN
F-ZACV	Falcon 20E	288	CEV,	F-BUYE/F-WRQZ
F-ZACW	Falcon 20C	104	CEV, Bretigny.	F-BOXV/(OT-JFA)/F-WJMK
F-ZACX	Falcon 20C	188	CEV, Melun-Villaroche.	F-BRPK/F-WJMK
F-ZACY	Falcon 20E	263	CEV,	/F-BSBU/HB-VCR/F-WMKJ
F-ZACZ	Falcon 20F	375	CEV,	F-GBMD/F-WRQR

Great Britain

Registration	Type	c/n	Owner / Operator	Previous identity
XS709/M	Dominie T1	25011	RAF, 6 FTS, Finningley.	
XS710/O	Dominie T1	25012	RAF, 6 FTS, Finningley.	
XS711/L	Dominie T1	25024	RAF, 6 FTS, Finningley.	
XS712/A	Dominie T1	25040	RAF, 6 FTS, Finningley.	
XS713/C	Dominie T1	25041	RAF, 6 FTS, Finningley.	
XS714/P	Dominie T1	25054	RAF, 6 FTS, Finningley.	
XS726/T	Dominie T1	25044	RAF, 6 FTS, Finningley.	
XS727/D	Dominie T1	25045	RAF, 6 FTS, Finningley.	
XS728/E	Dominie T1	25048	RAF, 6 FTS, Finningley.	
XS729/G	Dominie T1	25049	RAF, 6 FTS, Finningley.	
XS730/H	Dominie T1	25050	RAF, 6 FTS, Finningley.	
XS731/J	Dominie T1	25055	RAF, 6 FTS, Finningley.	
XS732/B	Dominie T1	25056	RAF, 6 FTS, Finningley.	
XS733/Q	Dominie T1	25059	RAF, 6 FTS, Finningley.	
XS734/N	Dominie T1	25061	RAF, 6 FTS, Finningley.	
XS735/R	Dominie T1	25071	RAF, 6 FTS, Finningley.	
XS736/S	Dominie T1	25072	RAF, 6 FTS, Finningley.	
XS737/K	Dominie T1	25076	RAF, 6 FTS, Finningley.	
XS738/U	Dominie T1	25077	RAF, 6 FTS, Finningley.	
XS739/F	Dominie T1	25081	RAF, 6 FTS, Finningley.	
XW788	HS 125/CC1	25255	RAF, 32 Squadron, Northolt.	
XW789	HS 125/CC1	25264	RAF, 32 Squadron, Northolt.	
XW790	HS 125/CC1	25266	RAF, 32 Squadron, Northolt.	
XW791	HS 125/CC1	25268	RAF, 32 Squadron, Northolt.	
XW930	HS 125/1	25009	Royal Aerospace Establishment, Bedford.	G-ATPC
XX507	HS 125/CC2	6006	RAF, 32 Squadron, Northolt.	
XX508	HS 125/CC2	6008	RAF, 32 Squadron, Northolt.	
ZD620	BAe 125/CC3	7181	RAF, 32 Squadron, Northolt.	/G-5-16
ZD621	BAe 125/CC3	7190	RAF, 32 Squadron, Northolt.	
ZD703	BAe 125/CC3	7183	RAF, 32 Squadron, Northolt.	/G-5-20/N710BD/G-5-20
ZD704	BAe 125/CC3	7194	RAF, 32 Squadron, Northolt.	
ZE395	BAe 125/CC3	7205	RAF, 32 Squadron, Northolt.	/G-5-19
ZE396	BAe 125/CC3	7211	RAF, 32 Squadron, Northolt.	
ZE700	BAe 146 Statesman	E1021	RAF, Queen's Flight, Benson.	G-5-507/G-5-02
ZE701	BAe 146 Statesman	E1029	RAF, Queen's Flight, Benson.	G-5-03
ZE702	BAe 146 Statesman	E1124	RAF, Queen's Flight, Benson.	G-6-124/G-5-124
ZF130	HS 125/600B	6059	MODPE/BAe, Dunsfold. (had Royal Navy titles /89).	(9M-DMF)/G-BLUW/HZ-SJP HZ-DAC/G-5-19

Ecuador

Registration	Type	c/n	Owner / Operator	Previous identity
AEE-402	Sabreliner	...		
ANE-201	Citation	500-0389	Aviacion Naval Ecuatoriana, Guayaquil.	N3202M
FAC-001A	Sabre-60	306-117	Aviacion del Ejercito,	N22MY/N2120J
FAE-034	Sabre-75A	380-34	Ministry of National Defence,	N382MC/(N112KH)/N6LG/N2104J
FAE-043	Sabre-40R	282-43	Ministry of National Defence,	/N4469F/XA-JUD/N730R/N6398C

FAE-045	Sabre-75A	380-45	Ministry of National Defence. (status ?).	N753TW/N218UB/N218US/D-CCVW N2117J
FAE-068	Sabre-40R	282-68	W/o 3 Jun 88.	/N4469N/XA-LEL/N60RB/N22MV/N22MY/N801NC/N788R/N2235B
IGM-401	Learjet	24D-312	Instituto Geographico Militar, Ejercito-army photo survey.	

Colombia

FAC-001	F 28-1000	11992	SATENA/Fuerza Aerea Colombiana-Presidential, Bogota.	PH-EXA/PH-ZAU
FAC-1201	B 707-373C	19716	Fuerza Aerea Colombiana, Bogota.	HL7425/N368WA/AP-AWD/N368WA
FAC-1211	Citation	550-0582	Fuerza Aerea Colombiana,	(N1301A)

South Korea

85101	B 737-3Z8	23152	Government of South Korea, Seoul.	

Honduras

HR-002	Westwind-1124	333	FAH=Fuerza Aerea Honduras, Tegucigalpa.	4X-CTA

Thailand

22-222	B 737-2Z6	23059	Royal Thai Air Force, Bangkok.	N45733
33-333	B 737-3Z6	24480	HS-TGQ, Royal Thai Air Force, Bangkok.	
60109	DC 8-62AF	46150	Royal Thai Air Force,	HS-TGS/LN-MOC
60112	DC 8-62CF	45922	Royal Thai Air Force,	HS-TGQ/OY-KTE
60504	Learjet	35A-623	Royal Thai Air Force,	/N7260Q
60505	Learjet	35A-635	Royal Thai Air Force,	N1471B

China

090	Citation	550-0305	Flight Test Research Institute, Xian.	N67999
091/B-4103	Citation	550-0301	Flight Test Research Institute, Xian.	N6799T
092	Citation	550-0297	Flight Test Research Institute, Xian.	N68003

Saudi Arabia

101	JetStar-8	5129	RSAF, 1 Squadron, Riyadh.	N7974S
102	JetStar-8	5130	RSAF, 1 Squadron, Riyadh.	103/N7975S
HZ-103	Gulfstream 3	453	Royal Saudi Air Force, Riyadh.	103/N332GA
HZ-104	BAe 125/800B	8115	Royal Saudi Air Force, Riyadh.	G-5-665/HZ-104/(G-BPGR)/G-5-599
HZ-105	BAe 125/800B	8118	Royal Saudi Air Force, Riyadh.	/(G-BPGS)/G-5-605
HZ-106	Learjet	35A-374	Royal Saudi Air Force, Riyadh.	
HZ-107	Learjet	35A-375	Royal Saudi Air Force, Riyadh.	
HZ-108	Gulfstream 3	353	RESA=Royal Embassy of Saudi Arabia, Riyadh.	HZ-BSA/N26619
HZ-109	BAe 125/800B	8146	Royal Saudi Air Force, Riyadh.	/(G-BPYD)/G-5-629
HZ-110	BAe 125/800B	8148	Royal Saudi Air Force, Riyadh.	/(G-BPYE)/G-5-630
HZ-123	B 707-138B	17696	RESA=Royal Embassy of Saudi Arabia, Riyadh.	N138MJ//N220AM/N138TA/C-FPWV VH-EBA/N31239

Italy

MM577	PD 808-TA	501	AMI, RS-38, RSV=Reparto Sperimentale Volo, Pratica di Mare.
MM578	PD 808-TA	502	AMI, RS-5, RSV=Reparto Sperimentale Volo, Pratica di Mare.
MM61948	PD 808-VIP	506	AMI, 31 Stormo, Roma-Ciampino. (ex 31-48).
MM61949	PD 808-VIP	507	AMI, 31 Stormo, Roma-Ciampino. (ex 31-49).
MM61950	PD 808-VIP	508	AMI, 31 Stormo, Roma-Ciampino. (ex 31-50).
MM61951	PD 808-VIP	509	AMI, 31 Stormo, Roma-Ciampino. (ex 31-51).
MM61952	PD 808-TA	510	AMI, 14-.., 14 Stormo-71 Gruppo, Pratica di Mare. (ex 31-52)
MM61953	PD 808-TA	511	AMI, 31 Stormo, Roma-Ciampino. (ex 31-53).
MM61954	PD 808-TA	512	AMI, 14-52, 14 Stormo-8 Gruppo, Pratica di Mare. (ex 31-54).
MM61955	PD 808-TA	513	AMI, 14-.., 14 Stormo-71 Gruppo, Pratica di Mare. (ex 31-55)
MM61956	PD 808-TA	514	AMI, 31 Stormo, Roma-Ciampino. (ex 31-56).
MM61957	PD 808-TA	515	AMI, 31 Stormo, Roma-Ciampino. (ex 31-57).

Regis-tration	Type	c/n	Owner / Operator	Previous identity

MM61958	PD 808-ECM	505	AMI, 14-.., 14 Stormo-71 Gruppo, Pratica di Mare.	
MM61959	PD 808-ECM	516	AMI, 14-.., 14 Stormo-71 Gruppo, Pratica di Mare.	
MM61960	PD 808-ECM	517	AMI, 14-.., 14 Stormo-71 Gruppo, Pratica di Mare.	
MM61961	PD 808-ECM	518	AMI, 14-.., 14 Stormo-71 Gruppo, Pratica di Mare.	
MM61962	PD 808-ECM	519	AMI, 14-.., 14 Stormo-71 Gruppo, Pratica di Mare.	
MM61963	PD 808-ECM	520	AMI, 14-.., 14 Stormo-71 Gruppo, Pratica di Mare.	
MM620..	Falcon 50	211	AMI, 31 Stormo, Roma-Ciampino.	F-W...
MM62012	DC 9-32	47595	AMI, 31 Stormo, Roma-Ciampino. (ex 31-12).	N54635
MM62013	DC 9-32	47600	AMI, 31 Stormo, Roma-Ciampino. (ex 31-13).	
MM62014	PD 808-RM	521	AMI, 14-53, 14 Stormo-8 Gruppo, Pratica di Mare.	
MM62015	PD 808-RM	522	AMI, 14-54, 14 Stormo-8 Gruppo, Pratica di Mare.	I-PIAY
MM62016	PD 808-RM	523	AMI, 14-55, 14 Stormo-8 Gruppo, Pratica di Mare.	
MM62017	PD 808-RM	524	AMI, 14-56, 14 Stormo-8 Gruppo, Pratica di Mare.	
MM62020	Falcon 50	151	AMI, 31 Stormo, Roma-Ciampino.	F-WPXD
MM62021	Falcon 50	155	AMI, 31 Stormo, Roma-Ciampino.	F-WPXH
MM62022	Gulfstream 3	451	AMI, 31 Stormo, Roma-Ciampino.	N330GA
MM62025	Gulfstream 3	479	AMI, 31 Stormo, Roma-Ciampino.	N319GA
MM62026	Falcon 50	193	AMI, 31 Stormo, Roma-Ciampino.	F-WWHH

Japan

9201	Learjet U36A	36A-054	JMSDF=Japanese Maritime Self Defence Force,	N1087Z/(N54GL)
9202	Learjet U36A	36A-056	JMSDF=Japanese Maritime Self Defence Force,	N3802G
9203	Learjet U36A	36A-058	JMSDF=Japanese Maritime Self Defence Force.	N4290J
9204	Learjet U36A	36A-059	JMSDF=Japanese Maritime Self Defence Force.	N1087Z
9205	Learjet U36A	36A-060	JMSDF=Japanese Maritime Self Defence Force.	N1088A
9206	Learjet U36A	36A-061	JMSDF=Japanese Maritime Self Defence Force.	

Jordan

JY-HAH	Gulfstream 3	467	Government of Jordan, Amman.	N341GA
JY-HZH	Gulfstream 3	469	Government of Jordan, Amman.	N343GA

Norway

0125	Falcon 20C	125	RNAF, 335 Squadron, Gardemoen-Oslo.	LN-FOE/N812PA/N6810J/N4344F/F-WJMN
041	Falcon 20ECM	41	RNAF, 335 Squadron, Gardemoen-Oslo.	LN-FOI/F-BOED/SAAF431/F-WNGL
053	Falcon 20ECM	53	RNAF, 335 Squadron, Gardemoen-Oslo.	LN-FOD/F-BNRE/F-WNGO

Argentina

5-T-10-0740	F 28-3000M	11147	Armada-Argentina, Buenos Aires. 'Stella Maris'	PH-EXW
5-T-20-0741	F 28-3000C	11145	Armada-Argentina, Buenos Aires. 'Canal de Beagle'	PH-EXV
5-T-21-0742	F 28-3000M	11150	Armada-Argentina, Buenos Aires. 'Islas Malvinas'	PH-EXX
AE-175	Sabre-75A	380-13	Ejercito/Comision Especial do Adquisiciones, Buenos Aires.	N65761
AE-185	Citation	500-0356	Ejercito/Instituto Geografico Militar.	N36848/N5366J
T-01	F 28-1000	11028	FAA=Fuerza Aerea Argentina, Presidential.	T-02/T-01/PH-EXA
T-03	F 28-1000	11048	FAA=Fuerza Aerea Argentina.	LV-LZN/PH-ZBM/TG-CAO/N280FH/PH-EXF
T-10	Sabre-75A	380-3	FAA=Fuerza Aerea Argentina.	N8467N
T-21	Learjet	35A-115	Grupo 1 de Aerofotografico, II Brigada Aerea, Parana.	
T-22	Learjet	35A-136	Grupo 1 de Aerofotografico, II Brigada Aerea, Parana.	
T-23	Learjet	35A-319	Grupo 1 de Aerofotografico, II Brigada Aerea, Parana.	
T-24	Learjet	35A-333	W/o 7 Jun 82, Pebble Island, Falklands, South Atlantic.	
VR-17	Learjet	35A-369	Escuadron Verificacion Radio Ayudos, Moron.	
VR-18	Learjet	35A-484	Escuadron Verificacion Radio Ayudos, Moron.	

United States of America

01	Gulfstream 2	23	VC-11A, United States Coast Guard, Washington, DC.	N863GA
150542	Sabreliner T-39D	277-1	U. S. Navy. (stored).	
150543	Sabreliner T-39D	277-2	U. S. Navy, NAS Pensacola Base Flight, Fl.	
150544	Sabreliner T-39D	277-3	U. S. Navy/to AMARC 3/85 as 7T-006. Tt 5872.	
150545	Sabreliner T-39D	277-4	U. S. Navy.	

Regis-tration	Type	c/n	Owner / Operator	Previous identity

Registration	Type	c/n	Owner / Operator	Previous identity
150546	Sabreliner T-39D	277-5	U. S. Navy/to AMARC 7/85 as 7T-014. Tt 9124.	
150547	Sabreliner T-39D	277-6	U. S. Navy/to AMARC 1/86 as 7T-021. Tt 9561.	
150548	Sabreliner T-39D	277-7	U. S. Navy/to AMARC 3/85 as 7T-008. Tt 8127.	
150549	Sabreliner T-39D	277-8	U. S. Navy/to AMARC 3/85 as 7T-011. Tt 7886.	
150550	Sabreliner T-39D	277-9	U. S. Navy.	
150551	Sabreliner T-39D	277-10	U. S. Marine Corp/to AMARC 10/81 as 7T-002.	
150969	Sabreliner T-39D	285-1	U. S. Navy, NAS Pensacola Base Flight, Fl.	
150970	Sabreliner T-39D	285-2	U. S. Navy.	
150971	Sabreliner T-39D	285-3	U. S. Navy.	
150972	Sabreliner T-39D	285-4	U. S. Navy.	
150973	Sabreliner T-39D	285-5	U. S. Navy/to AMARC 4/85 as 7T-013. Tt 7155.	
150974	Sabreliner T-39D	285-6	U. S. Navy/to AMARC 7/85 as 7T-015. Tt 8737.	
150975	Sabreliner T-39D	285-7	U. S. Navy/to AMARC 3/85 as 7T-007. Tt 9524.	
150976	Sabreliner T-39D	285-8	U. S. Navy/to AMARC 7/85 as 7T-016. Tt 7943.	
150977	Sabreliner T-39D	285-9	U. S. Navy.	
150978	Sabreliner T-39D	285-10	U. S. Navy/to AMARC 3/85 as 7T-009. Tt 7576.	
150979	Sabreliner T-39D	285-11	U. S. Navy/to AMARC 7/85 as 7T-017. Tt 8631.	
150980	Sabreliner T-39D	285-12	U. S. Navy/to AMARC 3/85 as 7T-004.	
150981	Sabreliner T-39D	285-13	U. S. Navy/to AMARC 3/85 as 7T-012. Tt 8184.	
150982	Sabreliner T-39D	285-14	U. S. Navy/to AMARC 2/86 as 7T-022. Tt 8188.	
150983	Sabreliner T-39D	285-15	U. S. Navy/to AMARC 2/86 as 7T-023. Tt 9833.	
150984	Sabreliner T-39D	285-16	U. S. Navy/to AMARC 3/85 as 7T-010. Tt 8552.	
150985	Sabreliner T-39D	285-17	U. S. Navy, NAS Pensacola Base Flight, Fl.	
150986	Sabreliner T-39D	285-18	U. S. Navy/preserved Robins AFB. Ga.	
150987	Sabreliner T-39D	285-19	U. S. Navy/McDonnell-Douglas. (stored).	
150988	Sabreliner T-39D	285-20	U. S. Navy/to AMARC 3/85 as 7T-005. Tt 9208.	
150989	Sabreliner T-39D	285-21	U. S. Navy. (stored).	
150990	Sabreliner T-39D	285-22	U. S. Navy/to AMARC 2/86 as 7T-024. Tt 9804.	
150991	Sabreliner T-39D	285-23	U. S. Navy/to AMARC 7/84 as 7T-003. Tt 8677.	
150992	Sabreliner T-39D	285-24	U. S. Navy, Naval Weapons Center, China Lake, Ca.	
151336	Sabreliner T-39D	285-25	U. S. Navy/to AMARC 2/86 as 7T-025. Tt 9822.	
151337	Sabreliner T-39D	285-26	U. S. Navy.	
151338	Sabreliner T-39D	285-27	U. S. Navy.	
151339	Sabreliner T-39D	285-28	U. S. Navy/preserved NAS Pensacola, Fl.	
151340	Sabreliner T-39D	285-29	U. S. Navy/to AMARC 1/86 as 7T-018. Tt 8563.	
151341	Sabreliner T-39D	285-30	U. S. Navy/to AMARC 1/86 as 7T-019. Tt 10118.	
151342	Sabreliner T-39D	285-31	U. S. Navy/to AMARC 1/86 as 7T-020. Tt 8146.	
151343	Sabreliner T-39D	285-32	U. S. Navy.	
157352	Sabreliner CT-39E	282-46	W/o 21 Dec 75, Alameda AFB. Ca. USA.	N339NA/N6553C
157353	Sabreliner CT-39E	282-84	U. S. Navy, Code RG, VRC-50, Cubi Point, Phillipines.	N2254B
157354	Sabreliner CT-39E	282-85	U. S. Navy, Code RW, VRC-30, North Island NAS, Ca.	N2255B
158380	Sabreliner CT-39E	282-95	U. S. Navy, Code RW, VRC-30, North Island NAS, Ca.	N4704N
158381	Sabreliner CT-39E	282-93	U. S. Navy, VRC-50, Cubi Point, Phillipines.	N4701N
158382	Sabreliner CT-39E	282-92	U. S. Navy, Code JK, VRC-40, Norfolk NAS, Va.	N2676B
158383	Sabreliner CT-39E	282-96	U. S. Navy, Code JK, VRC-40, Norfolk NAS, Va. (status ?).	N4705N
158843	Sabreliner CT-39G	306-52	U. S. Navy, Code JK, VRC-40, Norfolk NAS, Va.	N955R/N7571N
158844	Sabreliner CT-39G	306-55	U. S. Navy, Department of the Navy, Andrews AFB. Md.	N5419/N908R/N7575N
159361	Sabreliner CT-39G	306-65	U. S. Navy, Code 30, VR-24, NAF Sigonella, Italy.	N8364N
159362	Sabreliner CT-39G	306-66	U. S. Navy, Code 31, VR-24, NAF Sigonella, Italy.	N8365N
159363	Sabreliner CT-39G	306-67	U. S. Navy, Code 32, VR-24, NAF Sigonella, Italy.	
159364	Sabreliner CT-39G	306-69	U. S. Marine Corps, Iwakuni MCAS, Japan.	
159365	Sabreliner CT-39G	306-70	U. S. Marine Corps, El Toro MCAS, Ca.	
160053	Sabreliner CT-39G	306-104	Commander Naval Reserve Forces, New Orleans NAS, La.	N65795
160054	Sabreliner CT-39G	306-105	Station Operations & Engineering Sqn. Cherry Point MCAS, NC.	N65796
160055	Sabreliner CT-39G	306-106	Station Operations & Engineering Sqn. Cherry Point MCAS, NC.	N65797
160056	Sabreliner CT-39G	306-107	Station Operations & Engineering Sqn. Cherry Point MCAS, NC.	N65798
160057	Sabreliner CT-39G	306-108	Commander Naval Reserve Forces, New Orleans NAS, La.	N65799
163691	Gulfstream 3	480	C-20D, USN, CFSLW, Andrews AFB. Md.	N302GA
163692	Gulfstream 3	481	C-20D, USMC/USN, CFSLW, Andrews AFB. Md.	N304GA
2101	Guardian HU-25B	374	USCG, Cape Cod, Ma. (noted 6/89).	N1045F/F-WRQP
2102	Guardian HU-25A	386	USCG, Mobile, Al. (noted 4/88).	N149F/F-WJMK
2103	Guardian HU-25A	394	USCG, Cape Cod, Ma. (noted 6/89).	N178F/F-WMKF
2104	Guardian HU-25C	390	USCG, Miami, Fl. (noted 4/89).	N173F/F-WJMN

Registration	Type	c/n	Owner / Operator	Previous identity
2105	Guardian HU-25B	398	USCG, Mobile, Al. (noted 10/88).	N183F/F-WMKF
2106	Guardian HU-25A	402	USCG, San Diego, Ca. (noted 4/89).	N187F/F-WJMJ
2107	Guardian HU-25A	409	USCG, Miami, Fl. (noted 11/90).	N407F/F-WMKJ
2108	Guardian HU-25A	405	USCG, Corpus Christi, Tx. (noted 9/87).	N405F/F-WMKI
2109	Guardian HU-25A	407	USCG, Miami, Fl. (noted 3/89).	N406F/F-WJMJ
2110	Guardian HU-25A	411	USCG, Elizabeth City, NC. (noted 5/89),	N408F/F-WMKG
2111	Guardian HU-25B	413	USCG, Cape Cod, Ma. (noted 6/89).	N410F/F-WJME
2112	Guardian HU-25C	415	USCG, Miami, Fl. (noted 11/90).	N413F/F-WLCW
2113	Guardian HU-25A	417	USCG, Corpus Christi, Tx. (noted 10/88).	N416FJ/N416F/F-WJMM
2114	Guardian HU-25B	418	USCG, Mobile, Al. (noted 10/88).	N417F/F-WJMI
2115	Guardian HU-25A	419	USCG, San Diego, Ca. (noted 5/89).	N419F/F-WMKJ
2116	Guardian HU-25A	420	USCG, Cape Cod, Ma. (noted 3/89).	N420F/F-WMKG
2117	Guardian HU-25A	421	USCG, Cape Cod, Ma. (noted 6/89).	N422F/F-WMKI
2118	Guardian HU-25B	423	USCG, Miami, Fl. (noted 10/88).	N423F/F-WJMJ
2119	Guardian HU-25A	424	USCG, Cape Cod, Ma. (noted 6/89).	N424F/F-WMKF
2120	Guardian HU-25A	425	USCG, Sacramento, Ca. (noted 3/89).	N425F/F-WMKC
2121	Guardian HU-25A	431	USCG, Cape Cod, Ma. (noted 6/89).	N429F/F-WMKJ
2122	Guardian HU-25B	433	USCG, Miami, Fl. (noted 10/88).	N432F/F-WJML
2123	Guardian HU-25A	435	USCG, Corpus Christi, Tx. (noted 11/88).	N433F/F-WJMM
2124	Guardian HU-25A	437	USCG, Corpus Christi, Tx. (noted 10/88).	N435F/F-WMKG
2125	Guardian HU-25B	439	USCG, Miami, Fl. (noted 4/89).	N443F/F-WMKJ
2126	Guardian HU-25A	441	USCG, Miami, Fl. (noted 11/90).	N445F/F-WJMK
2127	Guardian HU-25A	443	USCG, Sacramento, Ca. (noted 6/88).	N447F/F-WMKG
2128	Guardian HU-25A	445	USCG, San Diego, Ca. (noted 4/89).	N449F/F-WJMM
2129	Guardian HU-25A	447	USCG, Mobile, Al. (noted 3/89).	N455F/F-WLCS
2130	Guardian HU-25A	450	USCG, Cape Cod, Ma. (noted 6/89).	N458F/F-WMKG
2131	Guardian HU-25A	452	USCG, Miami, Fl. (noted 11/90).	N459F/F-WMKI
2132	Guardian HU-25A	454	USCG, Miami, Fl. (noted 11/90).	N461F/F-WJML
2133	Guardian HU-25A	456	USCG, Elizabeth City, NC.	N462F/F-WJMJ
2134	Guardian HU-25B	458	USCG, Miami, Fl. (noted 11/90).	N465F/F-WJMN
2135	Guardian HU-25A	459	USCG, Miami, Fl. (noted 3/89).	N466F/F-WMKJ
2136	Guardian HU-25B	460	USCG, Miami, Fl. (noted 11/90).	N467F/F-WJML
2137	Guardian HU-25A	462	USCG, Astoria, Or. (noted 8/88).	N470F/F-WMKI
2138	Guardian HU-25A	464	USCG, Astoria, Or.	N472F/F-WJMK
2139	Guardian HU-25C	466	USCG, Miami, Fl. (noted 11/90).	N473F/F-WJML
2140	Guardian HU-25C	467	USCG, Miami, Fl. (noted 4/89).	N474F/F-WJMM
2141	Guardian HU-25C	371	USCG, Miami, Fl. (noted 11/90).	N1039F/F-WMKJ
40063	Learjet C-21A	35A-509	USAF, 1375 FTS, Scott AFB. Il.	N7263C
40064	Learjet C-21A	35A-510	USAF, 1400 MAS, Det 4, Kirtland AFB. NM.	N7263D
40065	Learjet C-21A	35A-511	USAF, 1375 FTS, Scott AFB. Il.	N7263E
40066	Learjet C-21A	35A-512	USAF, 1375 FTS, Scott AFB. Il.	N7263F
40067	Learjet C-21A	35A-513	USAF, 1401 MAS, Scott AFB. Il.	N7263H
40068	Learjet C-21A	35A-514	USAF, 1401 MAS, Scott AFB. Il.	N7263K
40069	Learjet C-21A	35A-515	USAF, 1401 MAS, Scott AFB. Il.	N7263L
40070	Learjet C-21A	35A-516	USAF, 1401 MAS, Scott AFB. Il.	N7263N
40071	Learjet C-21A	35A-517	USAF, 1401 MAS, Scott AFB. Il.	N7263R
40072	Learjet C-21A	35A-518	USAF, 1401 MAS, Scott AFB. Il.	N7263X
40073	Learjet C-21A	35A-519	USAF, 1402 MAS, Andrews AFB. Md.	N400AD
40074	Learjet C-21A	35A-520	USAF, 1402 MAS, Andrews AFB. Md.	N400AK
40075	Learjet C-21A	35A-521	USAF, 1402 MAS, Andrews AFB. Md.	N400AN
40076	Learjet C-21A	35A-522	USAF, 1402 MAS, Andrews AFB. Md.	N400AP
40077	Learjet C-21A	35A-523	USAF, 1402 MAS, Andrews AFB. Md.	N400AQ
40078	Learjet C-21A	35A-524	USAF, 1402 MAS, Andrews AFB. Md.	N400AS
40079	Learjet C-21A	35A-525	USAF, 1402 MAS, Andrews AFB. Md.	N400AT
40080	Learjet C-21A	35A-526	USAF, 1401 MAS, Det 2, Wright-Patterson AFB. Oh.	N400AU
40081	Learjet C-21A	35A-527	USAF, HQ USEUCOM, Stuttgart, West Germany.	N400AX
40082	Learjet C-21A	35A-528	USAF, HQ USEUCOM, Stuttgart, West Germany.	N400AY
40083	Learjet C-21A	35A-529	USAF, HQ USEUCOM, Stuttgart, West Germany.	N400AZ
40084	Learjet C-21A	35A-530	USAF, 58 MAS, Ramstein AB. West Germany.	N400BA
40085	Learjet C-21A	35A-531	USAF, 58 MAS, Ramstein AB. West Germany.	N400FY
40086	Learjet C-21A	35A-532	USAF, 58 MAS, Ramstein AB. West Germany.	N400BN
40087	Learjet C-21A	35A-533	USAF, 1401 MAS, Det 1, Offutt AFB. Nb.	N400BQ
40088	Learjet C-21A	35A-534	USAF, 1401 MAS, Det 1, Offutt AFB. Nb.	N400BU

Regis-tration	Type	c/n	Owner / Operator	Previous identity
40089	Learjet C-21A	35A-535	USAF, 1401 MAS, Det 1, Offutt AFB. Nb.	N400BY
40090	Learjet C-21A	35A-536	USAF, 1401 MAS, Det 1, Offutt AFB. Nb.	N400BZ
40091	Learjet C-21A	35A-537	USAF, 1401 MAS, Det 1, Offutt AFB. Nb.	N400CD
40092	Learjet C-21A	35A-538	USAF, 1401 MAS, Det 1, Offutt AFB. Nb.	N400CG
40093	Learjet C-21A	35A-539	USAF, 1401 MAS, Det 1, Offutt AFB. Nb.	N400CJ
40094	Learjet C-21A	35A-540	USAF, 1401 MAS, Det 1, Offutt AFB. Nb.	N400CK
40095	Learjet C-21A	35A-541	USAF, 1401 MAS, Det 1, Offutt AFB. Nb.	N400CQ
40096	Learjet C-21A	35A-542	USAF, 1401 MAS, Det 2, Wright-Patterson AFB. Oh.	N400CR
40097	Learjet C-21A	35A-543	USAF, 1401 MAS, Det 2, Wright-Patterson AFB. Oh.	N400CU
40098	Learjet C-21A	35A-544	USAF, 4950 TW/AFSC, Andrews AFB. Md. (Trout 98).	N400CV
40099	Learjet C-21A	35A-545	USAF, 1401 MAS, Det 2, Wright-Patterson AFB. Oh.	N400CX
40100	Learjet C-21A	35A-546	USAF, 1401 MAS, Det 2, Wright-Patterson AFB. Oh.	N400CY
40101	Learjet C-21A	35A-547	USAF, 1403 MAS, Yokota AB. Japan.	N400CZ
40102	Learjet C-21A	35A-548	USAF, 1403 MAS, Yokota AB. Japan.	N400DD
40103	Learjet C-21A	35A-549	USAF, 1401 MAS, Det 4, Peterson AFB. Co.	N400DJ
40104	Learjet C-21A	35A-550	USAF, 1401 MAS, Det 4, Peterson AFB. Co.	N400DL
40105	Learjet C-21A	35A-551	USAF, 1401 MAS, Det 4, Peterson AFB. Co.	N400DN
40106	Learjet C-21A	35A-552	USAF, 1401 MAS, Det 4, Peterson AFB. Co.	N400DQ
40107	Learjet C-21A	35A-553	USAF, 1401 MAS, Det 4, Peterson AFB. Co.	N400DR
40108	Learjet C-21A	35A-554	USAF, 1401 MAS, Det 3, Barksdale AFB. La.	N400DU
40109	Learjet C-21A	35A-555	USAF, 1401 MAS, Det 3, Barksdale AFB. La.	N400DV
40110	Learjet C-21A	35A-556	USAF, 1401 MAS, Det 3, Barksdale AFB. La.	N400DX
40111	Learjet C-21A	35A-557	USAF, 1401 MAS, Det 3, Barksdale AFB. La.	N400DY
40112	Learjet C-21A	35A-558	USAF, 1401 MAS, Det 3, Barksdale AFB. La.	N400DZ
40113	Learjet C-21A	35A-559	USAF, 1402 MAS, Det 1, Langley AFB. Va.	N400EC
40114	Learjet C-21A	35A-560	USAF, 1402 MAS, Det 1, Langley AFB. Va.	N400EE
40115	Learjet C-21A	35A-561	USAF, 1402 MAS, Det 1, Langley AFB. Va.	N400EF
40116	Learjet C-21A	35A-562	USAF, 1402 MAS, Det 1, Langley AFB. Va.	N400EG
40117	Learjet C-21A	35A-563	USAF, 1402 MAS, Det 1, Langley AFB. Va.	N400EJ
40118	Learjet C-21A	35A-564	USAF, 1402 MAS, Det 2, Eglin AFB. Fl.	N400EK
40119	Learjet C-21A	35A-565	USAF, 1402 MAS, Det 2, Eglin AFB. Fl.	N400EL
40120	Learjet C-21A	35A-566	USAF, 1402 MAS, Eglin AFB. Fl.	N400EM
40121	Learjet C-21A	35A-567	W/o 15 Jan 87. Alabama, USA.	N400EN
40122	Learjet C-21A	35A-568	USAF, 1402 MAS, Det 3, Maxwell AFB. Al.	N400EQ
40123	Learjet C-21A	35A-569	USAF, 1402 MAS, Det 3, Maxwell AFB. Al.	N400ER
40124	Learjet C-21A	35A-570	USAF, 1402 MAS, Maxwell AFB. Al.	N400ES
40125	Learjet C-21A	35A-571	USAF, 1402 MAS, Maxwell AFB. Al.	N400ET
40126	Learjet C-21A	35A-572	USAF, 1400 MAS, Norton AFB. Ca.	N400EU
40127	Learjet C-21A	35A-573	USAF, 1400 MAS, Norton AFB. Ca.	N400EV
40128	Learjet C-21A	35A-574	USAF, 1400 MAS, Norton AFB. Ca.	N400EX
40129	Learjet C-21A	35A-575	USAF, 1400 MAS, Norton AFB. Ca.	N400EY
40130	Learjet C-21A	35A-576	USAF, 1400 MAS, Det 1, McClellan AFB. Ca.	N400EZ
40131	Learjet C-21A	35A-577	USAF, 1400 MAS, Det 1, McClellan AFB. Ca.	N400FE
40132	Learjet C-21A	35A-578	USAF, 1400 MAS, Det 1, McClellan AFB. Ca.	N400FG
40133	Learjet C-21A	35A-579	USAF, 1400 MAS, Det 1, McClellan AFB. Ca.	N400FH
40134	Learjet C-21A	35A-580	USAF, 1400 MAS, Det 2, Randolph AFB. Tx.	N400FK
40135	Learjet C-21A	35A-581	USAF, 1400 MAS, Det 2, Randolph AFB. Tx.	N400FM
40136	Learjet C-21A	35A-582	USAF, 1400 MAS, Det 2, Randolph AFB. Tx.	N400FN
40137	Learjet C-21A	35A-583	USAF, 1400 MAS, Det 2, Randolph AFB. Tx.	N400FP
40138	Learjet C-21A	35A-584	USAF, 1400 MAS, Det 2, Randolph AFB. Tx.	N400FQ
40139	Learjet C-21A	35A-585	USAF, 1400 MAS, Det 4, Kirtland AFB. NM.	N400FR
40140	Learjet C-21A	35A-586	USAF, 1400 MAS, Det 4, Kirtland AFB. NM.	N400FT
40141	Learjet C-21A	35A-587	USAF, 1400 MAS, Det 4, Kirtland AFB. NM.	N400FU
40142	Learjet C-21A	35A-588	USAF,	N400FV
58-6970	C-137B	17925	USAF, SAM, 1st MAS/89th MAW, Andrews AFB. Md.	
58-6971	C-137B	17926	USAF, SAM, 1st MAS/89th MAW, Andrews AFB. Md.	
58-6972	C-137B	17927	USAF, SAM, 1st MAS/89th MAW, Andrews AFB. Md.	
59-2868	Sabreliner CT-39A	265-1	USAF, (for Air Force Museum ?).	(N2259V)/USAF59-2868
59-2869	Sabreliner CT-39A	265-2	USAF/to AMARC 10/84 as TG033. Tt 10744.	(N4999G)/USAF59-2869
59-2870	Sabreliner NT-39A	265-3	USAF/4950th Test Wing-ASD, Wright-Patterson AFB. Oh.	
59-2871	Sabreliner T-39A	265-4	W/o	
59-2872	Sabreliner CT-39A	265-5	USAF/to AMARC 6/84 as TG015. Tt 12728.	(N2296C)/USAF59-2872
59-2873	Sabreliner CT-39B	270-1	USAF/4950th Test Wing-ASD, Wright-Patterson AFB. Oh.	

Registration	Type	c/n	Owner / Operator	Previous identity
59-2874	Sabreliner NT-39B	270-2	USAF/4950th Test Wing-ASD, Wright-Patterson AFB. Oh.	
59-5958	JetStar-6	5010	C-140A, USAF, 375th Aeromedical Airlift Wing, Scott AFB. Il.	
59-5959	JetStar-6	5026	C-140A, USAF, 375th Aeromedical Airlift Wing, Scott AFB. Il.	
59-5960	JetStar-6	5028	C-140A, USAF, 375th Aeromedical Airlift Wing, Scott AFB. Il.	
59-5961	JetStar-6	5030	W/o 7 Nov 62, Robins AFB. Ga. USA.	
59-5962	JetStar-6	5032	C-140A, USAF, 375th Aeromedical Airlift Wing, Scott AFB. Il.	
60-0376	C-135E	18151	USAF, 55th SRW, Offutt AFB. Nb.	
60-0377	C-135A	18152	USAF, 4950 TW/ASD, Wright-Patterson AFB. Oh.	
60-0378	C-135E	18153	USAF, 55th SRW, Offutt AFB. Nb.	
60-3474	Sabreliner CT-39B	270-3	USAF/4950th Test Wing-ASD, Wright-Patterson AFB. Oh.	
60-3475	Sabreliner CT-39B	270-4	USAF/4950th Test Wing-ASD, Wright-Patterson AFB. Oh.	
60-3476	Sabreliner NT-39B	270-5	USAF/4950th Test Wing-ASD, Wright-Patterson AFB. Oh.	
60-3477	Sabreliner CT-39B	270-6	USAF/4950th Test Wing-ASD, Wright-Patterson AFB. Oh.	
60-3478	Sabreliner CT-39B	265-6	USAF/4950th Test Wing-ASD, Wright-Patterson AFB. Oh.	
60-3479	Sabreliner CT-39A	265-7	USAF/to AMARC 8/85 as TG082. Tt 22494.	
60-3480	Sabreliner CT-39A	265-8	USAF/to AMARC 6/84 as TG013.	
60-3481	Sabreliner CT-39A	265-9	USAF/to AMARC 9/85 as TG085. Tt 9870.	
60-3482	Sabreliner CT-39A	265-10	USAF/to AMARC 7/84 as TG016. Tt 19194.	
60-3483	Sabreliner CT-39A	265-11	USAF/preserved at Travis AFB. Ca.	
60-3484	Sabreliner CT-39A	265-12	USAF/to AMARC 9/84 as TG024. Tt 17097.	
60-3485	Sabreliner CT-39A	265-13	USAF/to AMARC 11/83 as TG003. Tt 17269.	
60-3486	Sabreliner CT-39A	265-14	USAF/to AMARC 4/84 as TG008. Tt 16846.	
60-3487	Sabreliner CT-39A	265-15	USAF/to AMARC 8/84 as TG021. Tt 20175.	
60-3488	Sabreliner CT-39A	265-16	USAF/to AMARC 10/85. (status ?).	N431NA/USAF60-3488
60-3489	Sabreliner CT-39A	265-17	USAF/to AMARC 3/85 as TG058. Tt 18158.	
60-3490	Sabreliner CT-39A	265-18	USAF/to AMARC 3/85 as TG062. Tt 19182.	
60-3491	Sabreliner CT-39A	265-19	USAF/to AMARC 5/84 as TG009. Tt 20372.	
60-3492	Sabreliner CT-39A	265-20	USAF/to AMARC 2/84 as TG007. Tt 17313.	
60-3493	Sabreliner CT-39A	265-21	USAF/to AMARC 2/85 as TG057. Tt 19313.	
60-3494	Sabreliner CT-39A	265-22	USAF/to AMARC 12/85 as TG094. Tt 18375.	
60-3495	Sabreliner CT-39A	265-23	USAF/preserved at Scott AFB. Il.	
60-3496	Sabreliner CT-39A	265-24	USAF/to AMARC 5/85 as TG072. Tt 19957.	
60-3497	Sabreliner CT-39A	265-25	USAF/to AMARC 3/85 as TG066. Tt 20311.	
60-3498	Sabreliner CT-39A	265-26	USAF/to AMARC 6/85 as TG077. Tt 17832.	
60-3499	Sabreliner CT-39A	265-27	USAF/to AMARC 10/84 as TG037. Tt 20506.	
60-3500	Sabreliner CT-39A	265-28	USAF/to AMARC 10/84 as TG030. Tt 19305.	
60-3501	Sabreliner CT-39A	265-29	USAF/to AMARC 12/85 as TG093. Tt 15817.	
60-3502	Sabreliner CT-39A	265-30	USAF/to AMARC 12/85 as TG095. Tt 21770.	
60-3503	Sabreliner GCT-39A	265-31	USAF/Chanute TTC. Oh. (ground instruction).	
60-3505	Sabreliner CT-39A	265-33	USAF/preserved at Edwards Flight Test Museum, Ca.	
60-3506	Sabreliner T-39A	265-34	W/o 9 Feb 74, Colorado Springs, Co. USA.	
60-3507	Sabreliner CT-39A	265-35	USAF/to AMARC 3/85 as TG-061. Tt 19733.	
60-3508	Sabreliner CT-39A	265-36	USAF/to AMARC 12/84 as TG042. Tt 22378.	
61-0634	Sabreliner CT-39A	265-37	USAF/preserved at Dyess AFB. Tx.	
61-0635	Sabreliner CT-39A	265-38	USAF/to AMARC 1/85 as TG054. Tt 20828.	
61-0636	Sabreliner CT-39A	265-39	USAF/to AMARC 9/85 as TG-089. Tt 19841.	
61-0637	Sabreliner CT-39A	265-40	USAF/to AMARC 10/84 as TG035. Tt 21729.	
61-0638	Sabreliner CT-39A	265-41	USAF/to AMARC 9/85 as TG086.	
61-0640	Sabreliner T-39A	265-43	W/o	
61-0641	Sabreliner CT-39A	265-44	USAF/to AMARC 10/84 as TG036. Tt 21184.	
61-0642	Sabreliner CT-39A	265-45	USAF/to AMARC 12/84 as TG045. Tt 17270.	
61-0643	Sabreliner CT-39A	265-46	USAF/to AMARC 9/84 as TG022. Tt 20288.	
61-0644	Sabreliner T-39A	265-47	W/o	
61-0645	Sabreliner CT-39A	265-48	USAF/to AMARC 10/85 as TG-091. Tt 22183.	
61-0646	Sabreliner T-39A	265-49	USAF. (reported w/o 1978 ?).	
61-0647	Sabreliner CT-39A	265-50	USAF/to AMARC 6/85 as TG078. Tt 19781.	
61-0648	Sabreliner CT-39A	265-51	USAF/to AMARC 8/84 as TG017. Tt 20923.	
61-0649	Sabreliner T-39A	265-52	USAF/to AMARC 12/84 as TG047. Tt 5390.	(N1064)/USAF61-0649
61-0650	Sabreliner CT-39A	265-53	USAF/to AMARC 12/84 as TG043. Tt 22915.	
61-0651	Sabreliner CT-39A	265-54	USAF/to AMARC 12/84 as TG040. Tt 17587.	
61-0652	Sabreliner CT-39A	265-55	USAF/to AMARC 9/85 as TG087. Tt 16815.	(N4999H)/USAF61-0652
61-0653	Sabreliner CT-39A	265-56	USAF/to AMARC 5/85 as TG071. Tt 17913.	
61-0654	Sabreliner CT-39A	265-57	USAF/to AMARC 12/84 as TG044. Tt 17770.	

Registration	Type	c/n	Owner / Operator	Previous identity
61-0655	Sabreliner CT-39A	265-58	USAF/to AMARC 12/83 as TG005. Tt 19975.	
61-0656	Sabreliner CT-39A	265-59	USAF/to AMARC 5/84 as TG010. Tt 21617.	
61-0657	Sabreliner CT-39A	265-60	USAF/to AMARC 9/84 as TG023.	
61-0658	Sabreliner CT-39A	265-61	USAF/to AMARC 10/84 as TG034. Tt 18138.	
61-0659	Sabreliner CT-39A	265-62	USAF/to AMARC 9/84 as TG026. Tt 19525.	
61-0660	Sabreliner CT-39A	265-63	USAF/preserved at McClellan AFB. Ca.	
61-0661	Sabreliner T-39A	265-64	USAF. (reported w/o 9 Feb 69 ?).	
61-0662	Sabreliner CT-39A	265-65	USAF/to AMARC 10/84 as TG032. Tt 21305.	
61-0663	Sabreliner CT-39A	265-66	USAF/to AMARC 4/85 as TG067. Tt 21139.	
61-0664	Sabreliner CT-39A	265-67	USAF/to AMARC 3/85 as TG063. Tt 20916.	
61-0665	Sabreliner CT-39A	265-68	USAF/to AMARC 10/84 as TG028. Tt 19423.	
61-0666	Sabreliner CT-39A	265-69	USAF/to AMARC 6/84 as TG014. Tt 20336.	
61-0667	Sabreliner CT-39A	265-70	USAF/to AMARC 9/85 as TG088. Tt 19933.	
61-0668	Sabreliner CT-39A	265-71	USAF/to AMARC 1/85 as TG051. Tt 21795.	
61-0669	Sabreliner CT-39A	265-72	USAF/to AMARC 5/85 as TG-075. Tt 22303.	
61-0670	Sabreliner T-39A	265-73	USAF. (status ?).	
61-0671	Sabreliner CT-39A	265-74	USAF/to AMARC 9/85 as TG090. Tt 22000.	
61-0672	Sabreliner T-39A	265-75	W/o 13 Mar 79, Kunsong, Korea.	
61-0673	Sabreliner CT-39A	265-76	USAF/to AMARC 11/84 as TG038. Tt 20181.	
61-0674	Sabreliner CT-39A	265-77	USAF/preserved Norton AFB. Ca.	
61-0675	Sabreliner T-39A	265-78	USAF/preserved as 10475 - 475th ABW. Yokota AB. Japan.	
61-0676	Sabreliner CT-39A	265-79	USAF/to AMARC 12/84 as TG049. Tt 21692.	
61-0678	Sabreliner CT-39A	265-81	USAF/to AMARC 5/84 as TG012. Tt 14666.	
61-0679	Sabreliner CT-39A	265-82	USAF/to AMARC 4/85 as TG-069. Tt 16901.	
61-0680	Sabreliner CT-39A	265-83	USAF/to AMARC 11/84 as TG039. Tt 19721.	
61-0681	Sabreliner CT-39A	265-84	USAF/located at Willow Run-Detroit Museum.	
61-0682	Sabreliner CT-39A	265-85	USAF/to AMARC 10/84 as TG031. Tt 19741.	
61-0683	Sabreliner CT-39A	265-86	USAF/to AMARC 9/84 as TG025.	
61-0684	Sabreliner T-39A	265-87	USAF. (status ?).	
61-0685	Sabreliner CT-39A	265-88	preserved U S Army Aviation Museum, Fort Rucker, Al.	
61-2488	JetStar-6	5017	VC-140B, USAF/preserved Robins AFB. Ga.	/N9286R
61-2489	JetStar-6	5022	VC-140B, USAF/AMARC as CL006. Tt 15637. Sub to Pima Museum.	/
61-2490	JetStar-6	5024	VC-140B, USAF/to AMARC 4/87 as CL004. Tt 17701.	/
61-2491	JetStar-6	5027	VC-140B, USAF, battle damage repair training Rhein-Main, FRG	/
61-2492	JetStar-6	5031	VC-140B, USAF, SAM, Andrews AFB. Md.	
61-2493	JetStar-6	5034	VC-140B, USAF/to AMARC 2/84 as CL003. Tt 11732.	
62-4125	C-135B	18465	USAF, 58th MAS, Ramstein AB. West Germany.	
62-4126	C-135B	18466	USAF, 89th MAW, Andrews AFB. Md.	
62-4127	C-135B	18467	USAF, 89th MAW, Andrews AFB. Md.	
62-4129	C-135B	18469	USAF, 89th MAW, Andrews AFB. Md.	
62-4130	C-135B	18470	USAF, 89th MAW, Andrews AFB. Md.	
62-4197	JetStar-6	5041	C-140B, USAF/to AMARC 7/87 as CL007. Tt 13646.	
62-4198	JetStar-6	5042	C-140B, USAF. (BDR training RAF Mildenhall, UK.).	/
62-4199	JetStar-6	5043	C-140B, USAF/to AMARC 2/84 as CL002. Tt 13462.	
62-4200	JetStar-6	5044	C-140B, USAF/to AMARC 6/87 as CL005. Tt 14082.	/
62-4201	JetStar-6	5045	C-140B, USAF, (noted McConnell AFB 11/88).	/
62-4448	Sabreliner T-39A	276-1	W/o 28 Jan 64, Erfurt, East Germany.	
62-4449	Sabreliner CT-39A	276-2	USAF/preserved at Pima County Museum, Az.	
62-4450	Sabreliner CT-39A	276-3	USAF/to AMARC 1/84 as TG006. Tt 18151.	
62-4451	Sabreliner CT-39A	276-4	USAF/to AMARC 3/85 as TG060. Tt 19863.	
62-4452	Sabreliner CT-39A	276-5	USAF/preserved at Travis AFB. Ca.	
62-4453	Sabreliner T-39A	276-6	USAF/375th Aeromedical Airlift Wing (USAFE det).	
62-4454	Sabreliner CT-39A	276-7	USAF/to AMARC 8/84 as TG018. Tt 20878.	
62-4455	Sabreliner CT-39A	276-8	USAF/to AMARC 3/85 as TG065. Tt 20973.	
62-4456	Sabreliner CT-39A	276-9	USAF/to AMARC 2/85 as TG056. Tt 21007.	
62-4457	Sabreliner CT-39A	276-10	USAF/to AMARC 11/83 as TG002. Tt 19944.	
62-4458	Sabreliner T-39A	276-11	W/o 25 Mar 65, Clark AFB. Philippines.	
62-4459	Sabreliner CT-39A	276-12	USAF/to AMARC 12/84 as TG041. Tt 19376.	
62-4460	Sabreliner T-39A	276-13	W/o 28 Feb 70, Torrejon, Spain.	
62-4461	Sabreliner CT-39A	276-14	USAF/preserved Robins AFB. Ga.	
62-4462	Sabreliner CT-39A	276-15	USAF/to AMARC 12/84 as TG046. Tt 16167.	
62-4463	Sabreliner CT-39A	276-16	USAF/4950th Test Wing-ASD, Wright Patterson AFB. Oh.	
62-4464	Sabreliner CT-39A	276-17	USAF/to AMARC 12/83 as TG004. Tt 20825.	

Registration	Type	c/n	Owner / Operator	Previous identity
62-4465	Sabreliner T-39A	276-18	USAF/preserved March AFB. Ca.	
62-4466	Sabreliner CT-39A	276-19	USAF/to AMARC 8/84 as TG019. Tt 20689.	
62-4467	Sabreliner CT-39A	276-20	USAF/to AMARC 8/85 as TG083. Tt 20004.	
62-4468	Sabreliner CT-39A	276-21	USAF/to AMARC 8/84 as TG020. Tt 20689.	
62-4469	Sabreliner CT-39A	276-22	USAF/to AMARC 3/85 as TG064. Tt 20011.	
62-4470	Sabreliner T-39A	276-23	USAF. (status ?).	
62-4471	Sabreliner CT-39A	276-24	USAF/preserved Ramstein AB. West Germany.	
62-4472	Sabreliner CT-39A	276-25	USAF/to AMARC 10/84 as TG011. Tt 20375.	
62-4473	Sabreliner CT-39A	276-26	USAF/to AMARC 10/84 as TG029. Tt 19320.	
62-4474	Sabreliner CT-39A	276-27	USAF/to AMARC 10/84 as TG027. Tt 15967.	
62-4475	Sabreliner CT-39A	276-28	USAF/to AMARC 8/85 as TG084. Tt 20844.	
62-4476	Sabreliner T-39A	276-29	USAF/375th Aeromedical Airlift Wing (PACAF det).	
62-4477	Sabreliner CT-39A	276-30	USAF/to AMARC 12/84 as TG048. Tt 18763.	
62-4478	Sabreliner T-39A	276-31	USAF/preserved at Wright Patterson Museum, Oh.	
62-4479	Sabreliner CT-39A	276-32	USAF/to AMARC 1/85 as TG052. Tt 20011. (to N988MT ?).	
62-4480	Sabreliner CT-39A	276-33	USAF/to AMARC 4/85 as TG068. Tt 19761.	
62-4482	Sabreliner T-39A	276-35	USAF/preserved at Lackland AFB. Tx.	
62-4483	Sabreliner CT-39A	276-36	USAF/to AMARC 1/85 as TG055. Tt 19812.	
62-4484	Sabreliner T-39A	276-37	USAF/preserved Kadena AB. Okinawa, Japan.	
62-4485	Sabreliner T-39A	276-38	USAF/fire dump Yokota AB. Japan.	
62-4486	Sabreliner CT-39A	276-39	USAF/to AMARC 12/84 as TG050. Tt 20801.	
62-4487	Sabreliner T-39A	276-40	USAF/preserved Offutt AFB. Ne.	
62-4488	Sabreliner CT-39A	276-41	USAF. (status ?).	
62-4489	Sabreliner CT-39A	276-42	USAF/to AMARC 5/85 as TG074. Tt 21204.	
62-4490	Sabreliner CT-39A	276-43	USAF/to AMARC 6/85 as TG079. Tt 22319.	
62-4491	Sabreliner CT-39A	276-44	USAF/to AMARC 7/85 as TG081. Tt 21072.	
62-4492	Sabreliner CT-39A	276-45	USAF. (for Air Force Museum ?).	
62-4493	Sabreliner CT-39A	276-46	USAF/to AMARC 6/85 as TG076. Tt 20759.	
62-4494	Sabreliner CT-39A	276-47	USAF/preserved Chanute AFB. Il.	
62-4495	Sabreliner CT-39A	276-48	Pittsburgh Institute of Aeronautics,	
62-4496	Sabreliner T-39A	276-49	W/o 20 April 85, Scranton, Pa. USA.	
62-4497	Sabreliner CT-39A	276-50	USAF/to AMARC 1/85 as TG053. Tt 21247.	
62-4498	Sabreliner CT-39A	276-51	USAF/to AMARC 7/85 as TG080. Tt 20714.	
62-4499	Sabreliner T-39A	276-52	USAF. (status ?).	
62-4500	Sabreliner CT-39A	276-53	USAF/to AMARC 5/85 as TG070. Tt 21264.	
62-4501	Sabreliner CT-39A	276-54	USAF/to AMARC 5/85 as TG073. Tt 18175.	
62-4502	Sabreliner T-39A	276-55	USAF. (status ?).	
62-6000	C-137C	18461	Presidential Aircraft, 1st MAS/89th MAW, Andrews AFB. Md.	
71-0874	C-9A	47467	USAF, 374 TAW, Clark AB. Phillipines.	
71-0876	C-9A	47475	USAF, 435 TAW, SHAPE, Chievres, Belgium.	
71-0878	C-9A	47536	USAF, 435 TAW, Rhein-Main AB. West Germany.	
71-0882	C-9A	47541	USAF, 435 TAW, Rhein-Main AB. West Germany.	
72-0283	B 737-253	20690	USAF, T-43A, 58th MAS, Ramstein AB. West Germany.	
72-7000	C-137C	20630	Presidential Aircraft, 1st MAS/89th MAW, Andrews AFB. Md.	N8459
73-1681	C-9C	47668	USAF, SAM, 1st MAS/89th MAW, Andrews AFB. Md.	
73-1682	C-9C	47670	USAF, SAM, 1st MAS/89th MAW, Andrews AFB. Md.	
73-1683	C-9C	47671	USAF, SAM, 1st MAS/89th MAW, Andrews AFB. Md.	
83-0500	Gulfstream 3	382	C-20A, USAF, 58 MAS, Ramstein AB. West Germany.	N305GA
83-0501	Gulfstream 3	383	C-20A, USAF, 58 MAS, Ramstein AB. West Germany.	N308GA
83-0502	Gulfstream 3	389	C-20A, USAF, 58 MAS, Ramstein AB. West Germany.	N310GA
84-0193	B 727-30	18362	C-22A, USAF, 310th MAS, Howard AFB. Panama.	N78/N90558/D-ABID
85-0049	Gulfstream 3	456	C-20C, U. S. Army, 89th MAW, Andrews AFB. Md.	N336GA
85-0050	Gulfstream 3	458	C-20C, U.S. Army, 89th MAW, Andrews AFB. Md.	N338GA
86-0200	Gulfstream 3	465	USAF, C-20B, 89th MAW, Andrews AFB. Md.	N17582
86-0201	Gulfstream 3	470	USAF, C-20B, 89th MAW, Andrews AFB. Md.	N344GA
86-0202	Gulfstream 3	468	USAF, C-20B, 89th MAW, Andrews AFB. Md.	N342GA
86-0203	Gulfstream 3	475	USAF, C-20B, 89th MAW, Andrews AFB. Md.	N312GA
86-0204	Gulfstream 3	476	USAF, C-20B, 89th MAW, Andrews AFB. Md.	N314GA
86-0205	Gulfstream 3	477	USAF, C-20B, 89th MAW, Andrews AFB. Md.	N317GA
86-0206	Gulfstream 3	478	USAF, C-20B, 59th MAW, Andrews AFB. Md.	N318GA
86-0374	Learjet C-21A	35A-624	USAF/Air National Guard HQ.	
86-0375	Learjet C-21A	35A-625	USAF/Air National Guard HQ.	
86-0376	Learjet C-21A	35A-628	USAF/Air National Guard HQ.	N3801G

86-0377	Learjet C-21A	35A-629	USAF/Air National Guard HQ.	
86-0403	Gulfstream 3	473	USAF, C-20D, 89th MAW, Andrews AFB. Md.	N326GA
87-0026	Learjet	35A-280	U S Army AVSCOM Facility.	YN-BVO/HP-912/N80MJ
87-0139	Gulfstream 3	497	C-20E, United States Army,	N373GA
87-0140	Gulfstream 3	498	C-20E, United States Army,	N374GA
88-0269	BAe 125/800A	8129	C-29A, USAF, Scott AFB. Il.	N269X/G-5-622
88-0270	BAe 125/800A	8134	C-29A, USAF, Scott AFB. Il.	N271X/N270X/G-5-634
88-0271	BAe 125/800A	8131	C-29A, USAF, Scott AFB. Il.	N270X/(N271X)/G-5-611
88-0272	BAe 125/800A	8154	C-29A, USAF, Scott AFB. Il.	N272X/G-5-655
88-0273	BAe 125/800A	8156	C-29A, USAF, Scott AFB. Il.	N273X/G-5-661
88-0274	BAe 125/800A	8158	C-29A, USAF, Scott AFB. Il.	N274X/G-5-667
89-0266	Gulfstream 2	45	Corps of Engineers/Department of the Army, Baltimore, Md.	/N4OCE/N115GA
				VR-BHA/N215RL/N152RG/PK-PJG/N711R/N815GA
N413GA	Gulfstream 4	1034	EC-20, Fleet EWS Group,	
N12058	Citation T-47A	552-0004	USN, Code 04, TAW-6, Pensacola NAS, Fl.	(162758)/N12058
N12065	Citation T-47A	552-0011	USN, Code 11, TAW-6, Pensacola NAS, Fl.	(162765)/N12065
N12269	Citation T-47A	552-0015	USN, Code 15, TAW-6, Pensacola NAS, Fl.	(162769)/N12269
N12557	Citation T-47A	552-0003	USN, Code 03, TAW-6, Pensacola NAS, Fl.	(162757)/N12557
N12564	Citation T-47A	552-0010	USN, Code 10, TAW-6, Pensacola NAS, Fl.	(162764)/N12564
N12566	Citation T-47A	552-0012	USN, Code 12, TAW-6, Pensacola NAS, Fl.	(162766)/N12566
N12568	Citation T-47A	552-0014	USN, Code 14, TAW-6, Pensacola NAS, Fl.	(162768)/N12568
N12660	Citation T-47A	552-0006	USN, Code 06, TAW-6, Pensacola NAS, Fl.	(162760)/N12660
N12756	Citation T-47A	552-0002	USN, Code 02, TAW-6, Pensacola NAS, Fl.	(162756)/N12756
N12761	Citation T-47A	552-0007	USN, Code 07, TAW-6, Pensacola NAS, Fl.	(162761)/N12761
N12762	Citation T-47A	552-0008	USN, Code 08, TAW-6, Pensacola NAS, Fl.	(162762)/N12762
N12763	Citation T-47A	552-0009	USN, Code 09, TAW-6, Pensacola NAS, Fl.	(162763)/N12763
N12855	Citation T-47A	552-0001	USN, Code 01, TAW-6, Pensacola NAS, Fl.	(167255)/N552CC/N12855
N12859	Citation T-47A	552-0005	USN, Code 05, TAW-6, Pensacola NAS, Fl.	(162759)/N12859
N12967	Citation T-47A	552-0013	USN, Code 13, TAW-6, Pensacola NAS, Fl.	(162767)/N12967

Peru

FAP 300	Falcon 20F	434	Government of Peru, Lima.	F-WRQP
FAP 390	F 28-1000	11100	Government of Peru, Lima.	PH-EXY
FAP 400	B 727-44C	18894	Government of Peru, Lima.	N727CR/ZS-SBC/ZS-DYO
FAP 522	Learjet	25B-159	Fuerza Aerea del Peru, Las Palmas-Lima. (aero-photo).	
FAP 523	Learjet	25B-164	Fuerza Aerea del Peru, Las Palmas-Lima. (aero-photo)	
FAP 524	Learjet	36A-051	Fuerza Aerea del Peru, Las Palmas-Lima. (aero-photo).	N4290J
FAP 525	Learjet	36A-052	Fuerza Aerea del Peru, Las Palmas-Lima. (aero-photo).	N4291K

Finland

LJ-1	Learjet	35A-430	Finnish Air Force.	N10870
LJ-2	Learjet	35A-451	Finnish Air Force.	N1462B
LJ-3	Learjet	35A-470	Finnish Air Force.	N3810G

Belgium

CB-01	B 727-29C	19402	BAF 21, Belgian Air Force, 21 Sqn. Melsbroek, Brussels.	OO-STB
CB-02	B 727-29C	19403	BAF 22, Belgian Air Force, 21 Sqn. Melsbroek, Brussels.	OO-STD
CM-01	Falcon 20E	276	BAF 31, Belgian Air Force, 21 Sqn. Melsbroek, Brussels.	F-WNGL
CM-02	Falcon 20E	278	BAF 32, Belgian Air Force, 21 Sqn. Melsbroek, Brussels.	F-WNGM

Denmark

F-249	Gulfstream 3	249	RDAF, 721 Squadron, Vaerlose-Copenhagen.	N901GA/N300GA
F-313	Gulfstream 3	313	RDAF, 721 Squadron, Vaerlose-Copenhagen.	
F-330	Gulfstream 3	330	RDAF, 721 Squadron, Vaerlose-Copenhagen.	

Indonesia

A-2801	F 28-1000	11042	TNI-AU/Indonesian Government, Jakarta.	PK-PJT/(PK-PJX)
AI-7301	B 737-2X9	22777	TNI-AU maritime patrol.	

Regis-tration	Type	c/n	Owner / Operator	Previous identity

Page 151

Registration	Type	c/n	Owner / Operator	Previous identity
AI-7302	B 737-2X9	22778	TNI-AU maritime patrol.	N8288V
AI-7303	B 737-2X9	22779	TNI-AU maritime patrol.	
T-1645	JetStar-6	5059	TNI-AU = Tentara Nasional Indonesia Angkatan Udura.	/
T-9446	JetStar-6	5046	TNI-AU = Tentara Nasional Indonesia Angkatan Udura.	//N9282R

Brazil

Registration	Type	c/n	Owner / Operator	Previous identity
2401	B 707-345C	19840	FAB=Forca Aerea Brasileira.	N7321S/PP-VJY
2710	Learjet	35A-631	Brazilian Air Force,	N3818G
2711	Learjet	35A-632	Brazilian Air Force,	N1461B
2712	Learjet	35A-633	Brazilian Air Force,	N39416
2713	Learjet	35A-636	Brazilian Air Force,	
2714	Learjet	35A-638	Brazilian Air Force,	
2715	Learjet	35A-639	Brazilian Air Force,	
2716	Learjet	35A-640	Brazilian Air Force.	N8568Y
2717	Learjet	35A-641	Brazilian Air Force,	N7261H
2718	Learjet	35A-642	Brazilian Air Force,	N7262X
EC93-2125	HS 125/3B-RC	25164	FAB=Forca Aerea Brasileira. Flight inspection.	
EU93-2119	HS 125/403B	25274	FAB, G.E.I.V., Rio-Santos Dumont. (flight calibration).	G-5-20
EU93-2121	HS 125/3B-RC	25165	FAB, G.E.I.V., Rio-Santos Dumont. (flight calibration).	VC93-2121
FAB6000	Learjet	35A-613	FAB=Forca Aerea Brasileira.	N4289X
FAB6001	Learjet	35A-615	FAB=Forca Aerea Brasileira.	/N7260E
FAB6002	Learjet	35A-617	FAB=Forca Aerea Brasileira.	N4289Z
VC93-2120	HS 125/3B-RC	25162	FAB, GTE=Grupo do Transporte Especiale, Brasilia.	
VC93-2122	HS 125/3B-RC	25166	W/o 18 Jun 79, Brasilia, Brazil.	
VC93-2123	HS 125/3B-RC	25167	FAB, GTE=Grupo do Transporte Especiale, Brasilia.	
VC93-2124	HS 125/3B-RC	25168	FAB, GTE=Grupo do Transporte Especiale, Brasilia.	
VC96-2115	B 737-2N3	21165	FAB, GTE=Grupo do Transporte Especiale, Brasilia.	
VC96-2116	B 737-2N5	21166	FAB, GTE=Grupo do Transporte Especiale, Brasilia.	
VU93-2116	HS 125/400A	NA740	FAB, GTE=Grupo do Transporte Especiale, Brasilia.	N702P/G-AXTS
VU93-2117	HS 125/400A	NA738	FAB, GTE=Grupo do Transporte Especiale, Brasilia	N702D/G-AXOF
VU93-2118	HS 125/400A	NA729	FAB, GTE=Grupo do Transporte Especiale, Brasilia.	N702SS/N1C/N702S/G-AXJE
VU93-2126	HS 125/403B	25277	FAB, GTE=Grupo do Transporte Especiale, Brasilia.	
VU93-2127	HS 125/403B	25288	FAB, GTE=Grupo do Transporte Especiale, Brasilia.	
VU93-2128	HS 125/403B	25289	FAB, GTE=Grupo do Transporte Especiale, Brasilia.	G-5-16
VU93-2129	HS 125/403B	25290	W/o 9 Sep 87, Carajas, Brazil.	

Seychelles

Registration	Type	c/n	Owner / Operator	Previous identity
SY-001	Citation V	560-0003	Government of Seychelles, Mahe.	S7-AAP/N563CV

Sweden

Registration	Type	c/n	Owner / Operator	Previous identity
86001	Sabre-40/Tp 86	282-49	Defense Material Administration, Linkoping.	N905KB/N905K/N757R/N6556C
86002	Sabre-40/Tp 86	282-91	Defence Material Administration, Linkoping.	N40NR/N66ES/N5511Z/N5511A N9500B

Egypt

Registration	Type	c/n	Owner / Operator	Previous identity
SU-BGM	Gulfstream 4	1048	Egyptian Air Force/Arab Republic of Egypt, Cairo.	N448GA/(VR-BKL)/N1761K
SU-BGU	Gulfstream 3	439	Egpytian Air Force/Arab Republic of Egypt, Cairo.	N17586
SU-BGV	Gulfstream 3	442	Egyptian Air Force/Arab Republic of Egypt, Cairo.	N17587

Turkey

Registration	Type	c/n	Owner / Operator	Previous identity
12-001	Citation	550-0502	Turkish Air Force, 224 Filo, Etimesgut. (flight calibration)	N1255D
12-002	Citation	550-0503	Turkish Air Force, 224 Filo, Etimesgut. (flight calibration)	N1255G

Ivory Coast

Registration	Type	c/n	Owner / Operator	Previous identity
TU-VAA	Fokker 100	11245	Government of Ivory Coast, Abidjan.	
TU-VAB	F 28-1000C	11099	Force Aerienne de Cote d'Ivoire, GATL, Abidjan.	PH-EXL
TU-VAD	Gulfstream 4	1019	Government of Ivory Coast, Abidjan.	N17584

Registration	Type	c/n	Owner / Operator	Previous identity

Registration	Type	c/n	Owner / Operator	Previous identity
TU-VAF	Gulfstream 3	462	Government of Ivory Coast, Abidjan.	/N303GA/N324GA
TU-VAJ	F 28-4000VIP	11124	Government of Ivory Coast, Abidjan.	TU-VAZ/PH-EXY

Australia

Registration	Type	c/n	Owner / Operator	Previous identity
A20-103	B 707-368C	21103	RAAF, 33 Squadron, Richmond, NSW.	HZ-ACG
A20-261	B 707-368C	21261	RAAF, 33 Squadron, Richmond, NSW.	HZ-ACI
A20-623	B 707-338C	19623	RAAF, 33 Squadron, Richmond, NSW.	C-GRYN/VH-EAC/G-BDKE/VH-EAC
A20-624	B 707-338C	19624	RAAF, 33 Squadron, Richmond, NSW.	VH-EAD
A20-627	B 707-338C	19627	RAAF, 33 Squadron, Richmond, NSW. 'Windsor Town'	VH-EAG
A20-629	B 707-338C	19629	RAAF, 33 Squadron, Richmond, NSW.	C-GGAB/G-BDLM/VH-EAI
A26-070	Falcon 900	70	RAAF, 34 Squadron, Fairbairn, Canberra.	N450FJ/F-WWFN
A26-073	Falcon 900	73	RAAF, 34 Squadron, Fairbairn, Canberra.	N452FJ/F-WWFA
A26-074	Falcon 900	74	RAAF, 34 Squadron, Fairbairn, Canberra.	N453FJ/F-WWFF
A26-076	Falcon 900	76	RAAF, 34 Squadron, Fairbairn, Canberra.	N454FJ/F-WWFE
A26-077	Falcon 900	77	RAAF, 34 Squadron, Fairbairn, Canberra.	N455FJ/F-WWFG

India

Registration	Type	c/n	Owner / Operator	Previous identity
K2412	B 737-2A8	23036	Indian Air Force, Delhi.	VT-EHW
K2413	B 737-2A8	23037	Indian Air Force, Delhi.	VT-EHX
K2980	Gulfstream SRA-1	420	Indian Air Force, (used VT-ENR 9/87).	/N47449/N333GA

Mexico

Registration	Type	c/n	Owner / Operator	Previous identity
B-12001	B 737-247	20127	TP-03, Government of Mexico, Mexico City.	N4523W
ETE-1329	Citation	...		
JS 10201	JetStar-8	5144	DN-01, Ministry of Defence, Mexico City.	N5508L
MTX-01	Learjet	24D-313	Mexican Navy, Mexico City.	
XC-FAD	B 727-64	18912	10501, FAM, Mexico City.	XA-SEP
XC-FAY	B 727-14	18908	10503, FAM, Mexico City.	XA-SER
XC-FAZ	B 727-14	18909	10504, FAM, Mexico City.	XA-SEU
XC-UJA	B 727-51	19123	TP-05, Government of Mexico. 'Presidente Carranza'.	XC-UJA/TP-01/N477US
XC-UJB	B 727-51	19121	TP-02, Government of Mexico.	N475US
XC-UJC	Sabre-75A	380-67	W/o 26 Oct 89.	TP-103/N2528E
XC-UJD	Sabre-75A	380-68	TP-102, CGATP, Mexico City.	TP-104/N2538E
XC-UJE	Sabre-60	306-139	TP-103, CGATP, Mexico City.	TP-105
XC-UJF	Sabre-60	306-144	TP-104, TAF, Mexico City.	TP-106/N2519E
XC-UJH	Sabre-40A	282-117	TP-..., TAF, Mexico City.	N1WZ/I-MORA/(HB-VCZ)/N8338N
XC-UJI	Sabre-40A	282-130	TP-105, TAF, Mexico City.	XC-HEY/TP105/XC-UJG/TP-107/XC-SRA/N44NR/N33LB
XC-UJJ	B 737-112	19772	TP-03, Government of Mexico. 'Presidente Cardinas'	TP-04/XB-LCR/N48AF 9V-BFF/9M-AOW
XC-UJK	Gulfstream 2	161	TP-04, Government of Mexico, Mexico City.	XC-CFE/XC-FEZ/XA-ABC/N17589
XC-UJM	B 757-225	22690	TP-01, Government of Mexico. 'Presidente Juarez'	XC-CBD
XC-UJN	Gulfstream 3	352	TP-06, Government of Mexico, Mexico City.	/HB-ITM/N17586
XC-UJO	Gulfstream 3	386	TP-07, Government of Mexico, Mexico City.	N902KB/N902K/N316GA

Burma

Registration	Type	c/n	Owner / Operator	Previous identity
4400	Citation	550-0358	MoD/Burmese Air Force, Rangoon.	N6801Q

Syria

Registration	Type	c/n	Owner / Operator	Previous identity
YK-ASA	Falcon 20F	328	Government of Syria, Damascus.	N4459F/F-WMKJ
YK-ASB	Falcon 20F	331	Government of Syria, Damascus.	F-WRQS

Yugoslavia

Registration	Type	c/n	Owner / Operator	Previous identity
70401	Learjet	25B-202	Government of Yugoslavia, Belgrade.	10401/N3807G
70402	Learjet	25B-203	Government of Yugoslavia, Belgrade.	10402/N3811G
72101	Falcon 50	25	Government of Yugoslavia, Belgrade.	F-WZHI

Venezuela

Registration	Type	c/n	Owner / Operator	Previous identity
0001	B 737-2N1	21167	Government of Venezuela, Caracas.	
0002	Citation	550-0011	FAV, MoD, Caracas.	(N98876)
0003	DC 9-15	47000	FAV, MoD, Caracas.	YV-03C/YV-C-ANP/HZ-AEA
0004	Gulfstream 2	124	FAV, MoD, Caracas.	N203GA/VR-BGO/(VR-BGL)/HB-IEW/N834GA
0005	Gulfstream 3	400	FAV, MoD, Caracas.	N17585
0006	Learjet	24D-250	FAV, MoD, Caracas.	N85CD/N85CA/N1U/N2U/N122CG/D-IMAR/N112C
0222	Citation	500-0092	FAV, MoD, Caracas.	N592CC
2222	Citation	550-0224	FAV, MoD, Caracas.	YV-O-MTC-20/YV-O-MTC/N6802Y
442	Falcon 20D	235	FAV,	(N442)/N20FE/N4415F/F-WPXJ
5761	Falcon 20C	23	FAV,	(N582G)/N256MA/(N256M)/N256EN/N15CC/N424JX/N844F/F-BNKX/F-WNGL
5840	Falcon 20D	216	FAV,	N9FE/N4402F/F-WLCT
F-WJMM	Falcon 20	476	FAV,	
YV-2338P	Citation	550-0449	FAV, MoD, Caracas.	(FAV1107)/YV-2338P/N1249H

New Zealand

Registration	Type	c/n	Owner / Operator	Previous identity
NZ7271	B 727-22C	19892	RNZAF, 40 Squadron, Whenuapai.	N7435U
NZ7272	B 727-22C	19895	RNZAF, 40 Squadron, Whenuapai.	N7438U
NZ7273	B 727-22C	19893	RNZAF, for spares only.	N7436U

South Africa

Registration	Type	c/n	Owner / Operator	Previous identity
SAAF01	HS 125/400B	25177	W/o 26 May 71, Devil's Peak, South Africa.	G-AWXN
SAAF02	HS 125/400B	25181	W/o 26 May 71, Devil's Peak, South Africa.	G-AXLU/(G-5-13)
SAAF03	HS 125/400B	25182	W/o 26 May 71, Devil's Peak, South Africa.	G-AXLV
ZS-LPE	HS 125/400B	25184	S.A.A.F. VIP Unit, 21 Sqn. Waterkloof, Pretoria.	SAAF04/G-AXLW
ZS-LPF	HS 125/400B	25269	S.A.A.F. VIP Unit, 21 Sqn. Waterkloof, Pretoria.	SAAF07/G-AZEM

Production List

Appended below are production lists in brief format. Dates quoted are generally from official sources. However, these sources are not uniform in their choice of date, and may select the registration, bill of sale, customer acceptance, delivery completion date as their reference point. To specify each date is outside the scope of this publication, but the variance should be no more than a few months from the dates given.

The abbreviations FJC, GAC, BAe and GLC have been used for Falcon Jet Corp., Gulfstream Aerospace Corp, British Aerospace and Gates Learjet Corp. respectively. Others are standard and should be familiar to most readers.

Gulfstream 2/3/4

..... XB-GSN
1   1966. N801GA Ff 2 Oct 66, Grumman Corp demo, N55RG R W Galvin/Motorola Inc 9/70, N55RG R W Galvin/Motorola Inc. Wheeling, Il.
2   1967. N802GA Ff 2 Jan 67. Grumman Corp /67, N802GA to G-3 357, 1/88, GAC 4/88, Wesaire Inc 8/88, N369CS 3/89, N369CS Wesaire Inc. Morristown, NJ.
3   1967. N831GA Grumman Corp /67, N214GP Gillette Products 6/68,J&H Investment Aircraft 10/87, N214GP J&H Investment Aircraft Inc. Mason City, Ia.
4   1967. N832GA Grumman Corp /67, N680RW Coca Cola Co 6/68, N680RZ 12/76, 9K-ACY Gulf International Group 1/77, VR-CAS Petromin/Mobil Oil-Saudi Arabia 12/79, HZ-MPM Petromin/Ministry for Mineral Resources 7/80, No 8 2B cvtd 29 Nov 82, N8490P Petersen Publishing Co 6/88, N8490P Petersen Publishing Co. Van Nuys, Ca.
5   1967. N100P National Distillers & Chemical Co 1/68, N100PJ GenStar Corp 5/79, N65ST 6/80, Petersen Publishing Co 12/86, N65ST Petersen Publishing Co. Los Angeles, Ca.
6   1967. N834GA Grumman Corp /67, N430R Dow Jones & Co Inc 2/68, N122DJ 3/68, N122DJ to G-3 374, N122DU 6/83, Pincervale/Jet Services Corp 7/84, N122DU Jet Services Corp. Houston, Tx.
7   1967. CF-HOG Home Oil Co 2/68, N9300 Omni 8/72, Crown Cork & Seal 9/72, N9300 to G-4 1020, GAC 8/90, N93QQ 9/90, N93QQ Gulfstream Aerospace Corp. Savannah, Ga.
8   1967. N833GA Grumman Engineering Corp 9/67, Pulitzer Publishing Co 12/67, N18N A D Davis/G-11 International 12/72, Seward Johnson 12/73, N400SJ 1/74, rpo SA-226T T-209, N400SA 4/75, cx USA 7/75, HB-IMV ATES, Vaduz-Liechstenstein 5/75, cx HB- 5/77, (N820GA) Grumman American Aviation Corp 6/77,N400SA Salta Aviation SA-Panama 7/77, Gavilan Corp 7/77, N777GG 11/77, cx USA 9/79, PJ-ARI Growth's Aircraft Inc-Netherland Antilles 9/79 cx PJ- 1/80, N504TF Omni International Jet Trading Floor 1/80, N5UD (U Dantata-Nigeria) /80, Circus Circus Hotels Inc 7/80, N225CC 10/80, UFCW International-Washington 5/86, N11UF 1/87, N11UF UFCW International, Washington, DC.
9   1967. C-FSBR S B Roman/Denison Mines Ltd 6/68, N320FE FEDEX 12/81, (N115RS) 2/82, GAC 10/82, N209GA 11/82, Reese Aircraft 6/83, Silicon Valley Express 1/85, Eastman Kodak Co 9/85, No 33 2B cvtd 30 Apr 85, N343K 1/86, Orchard Funding Inc 6/90, N343K Eastman Kodak Co. Rochester, NY.
10 1968. N343K Eastman Kodak Co 2/68, N343K to G-2 9, N343N 12/85, Clark Financial/C & F Aviation 8/86, N888CF 9/86, Mercer Air Inc 7/89, XA-ROI TAESA 10/89, XA-ROI TAESA-Transportes Aereos Ejecutivos SA. Mexico City.
11 1968. N835GA Grumman Corp /68, N902 Owens Illinois 4/68, Owens-Illinois General Inc 8/87, N902 Owens-Illinois General Inc. Toledo, Oh.
12 1968. N500R Superior Oil Co 4/68, N11UM /70, N154X Quintana Petroleum Corp 8/74, McMoRan Properties Inc 9/84, N115MR 2/85, EAF 5/86, Aspen Jet Sales Inc 6/86, EAF 8/87, N121EA PHH Avn Sales/Financial Services 4/88, Washington Corp 2/89, N160WC Dixie Aire-OKC 7/89, N160WC Dixie Aire/Washington Corp. Missoula, Mt.
13 1968. N678RW Coca Cola Co 5/68, N678RZ Omni 2/77, N98AM NAMCO-Nigeria 5/77, 5N-AMN 12/77,N2GP Washington Jet 5/79, Paul Heim 5/79, UNO Charter /80, N373LP Louisiana Pacific Corp 7/80, N373LB 8/90, Austin Jet Corp 9/90, N373LB Austin Jet Corp. Austin, Tx.
14 1968. N663P Phillips Petroleum Co 5/68, N663B 10/82, Flight International/J Dominelli 8/83,N217JD 11/83, Albertino Parravano-Ca 3/85, N369AP 4/85, Bank of America/Orion Aircraft Sales 8/88, Mar Flite 12/88, N369AP Mar Flite Ltd Corp. Portland, Or.
15 1968. N375PK Seagram's Whiskey 7/68, N77SW 6/75, N77SW to G-3 413, N416SH 4/83, GAC 1/84, USAA Special Services Co 2/84, GAC 7/84, Turkish Govt 4/86 thru /88, Jack Kent Cooke Inc 8/88, N125JJ 4/89, N125JJ Jack Kent Cooke Inc. Middleburg, Va.
16 1968. N890A ALCOA 5/68, N697A 9/81, Southland Corp 2/82, N711MT 9/82, No 13 2B cvtd 9 May 83, N711MT to F100-207, Hill Air Corp 2/87, N38GL 4/87, N38GL Hill Air Corp. Dallas, Tx.
17 1968. N119K Kaiser Industries Inc 5/68, N819GA Grumman Corp 1/77, N456AS ITEL Corp 5/77, Firemans Fund Insurance Co 8/79, AMEX 5/85, N91AE 6/85, Ltd Enterprises Inc 4/88, N305F 6/88, Jet Air Inc 11/88, N917R 1/89, N917R Wildenstein/Jet Air Inc. NYC.
18 1968. N838GA Grumman Corp 5/68, N205M Richard Mellon 2/69, Constance Burrell /71, Rockwell International Corp 5/81, N43R 8/81, N43R Rockwell International Corp. Pittsburgh, Pa.
19 1968. N839GA Grumman Corp /68, N1929Y Paul Mellon 12/68, Rokeby Farms /86, N1929Y Rokeby Farms, Washington, DC.

20	1968. N2PG Procter & Gamble Co 11/68, N755S Shell Aviation Corp 2/80, Western Aircraft Inc 5/83, Cedar Group/Scimitair 12/83, Beneficial Finance Lsg 10/84, N4SP Saral Publications 2/85, N4SP Saral Publications Inc. Opa Locka, Fl.
21	1968. N4PG Procter & Gamble Co 11/68, N3PG /69, N7ZX 6/81, N8PG 2/82, Canadair Challenger Inc 10/89 N8PQ 6/90, O Gara Aviation Co 8/90, N8PQ O Gara Aviation Co. Las Vegas, Nv.
22	1968. N862GA Grumman Corp /68, N5152 CBS Inc 7/68, N145ST SW Toyota/Car Crafts Inc 1/81,USAL Inc/Kalair USA Corp 2/84, Consolidated Airways Inc 2/86, N22 Corp/Frank Sinatra 4/86, N22FS Universal Jet Sales 8/86, N22FS to F20-339, Freeport-McMoran Inc 12/87, N683FM 3/88, N206MD Mike Donahoe Aviation Co 9/90, N206MD Mike Donahoe Aviation Co. Phoenix, Az.
23	1968. N863GA Grumman Corp /68, 01 United States Coast Guard 7/68, 01 VC-11A, United States Coast Guard, Washington, DC.
24	1968. N536CS Campbell Soup Co 8/68, N4S Weyerhaeuser Co 5/74, (N98G) 2/82, N26WP 9/85,N26WP Weyerhaeuser Co. Seattle, Wa.
25	1968. N327K Ford Motor Co 9/68, N327K to F900-3, N527C 2/86, Polo Fashions Inc 3/86, N711RL 10/86,N711RL Polo Fashions Inc. Carlstadt, NJ.
26	1968. N328K Ford Motor Co 10/68, GAC 5/81, N202GA 9/81, PK-PJZ Pelita Air Services/Pertamina Oil-Jakarta 5/83, PK-PJZ Pertamina Oil, Jakarta.
27	1968. N1807Z Union Producing Co 9/68, Pennzoil Co /69, Richland Development 3/87, Joseph D Jamail/Liamaj Avn 10/88, N121JJ 12/88, N121JJ Liamaj Aviation Inc/Joseph D Jamail, Houston, Tx.
28	1968. N695ST Minneapolis Star & Tribune 9/68, N700ST /69, N7004T Coastal States Gas 12/75, C-GCFB Canadian MoT/Transport Canada Flight Inspection 11/76, N120EA EAF 6/87,Equitable Bancorporation-Md 8/87, N85EQ 2/88, N85EQ Equitable Bancorporation, Baltimore, Md.
29	1968. N869GA Grumman Corp /68, N930BS Bethlehem Steel Corp 11/68, N919G Western Electric International-Saudi Arabia 1/78, AT&T International Inc 7/86, GAC 8/87, Yorke Air Co 1/90, N41RC 3/90, N41RC Yorke Air Co. Jacksonville, Fl.
30	1968. N870GA Grumman Corp /68, N788S Signal Companies /69, N2601 Mobil Oil Corp 1/71, N2607 10/81, No 4 2B cvtd 6 Aug 82, FSB-Ut 2/90,GECC-Danbury 3/90, N333AX 10/90, N333AX GECC, Danbury, Ct.
31	1968. N1621 Texaco Inc 11/68, 685TA Corp/American Home Products 5/85, N685TA 6/85, N789FF 4/88, Southwestern Aircraft Holding Co 4/89, N200CC 11/89, National Aircraft Sales Inc 3/90, N200CC National Aircraft Sales Inc. Eagle, Co.
32	1968. N7602 Union Oil Co of Ca 12/68, No 2 2B cvtd 2 Apr 82, Sixty Eight Scarteen Corp-NYC 5/87, Unocal 7/87, N7602 Unocal, Burbank, Ca.
33	1968. N1624 Texaco Inc 12/68, EAF Aircraft Sales Inc 5/86, N1324 9/86, Thomas H Lee Co 5/88,N217TL 7/88, N217TL Thomas H Lee Co. Boston, Ma.
34	1968. N230E American Can Co 10/68, N130A /69, N11SX Saxon Oil/G-34 Corp 10/80, VR-CBM ARAVCO 9/82,N500JR Sun Jet Inc/Jackie Hinson-Tx 10/84, Air Waves Corp 5/88, N204RC 6/88, N204RC Air Waves Corp. Wilmington, De.
35	1968. N1004T Time Inc 12/68, N830TL Time Life Inc 1/69, N830TL to G-2 49, N30PR Rutherford Oil Co 2/84, N30PR Rutherford Oil Co. Houston, Tx.
36	1968. N26L Square D Co 12/68, N26LA Omni 1/77, Oster Corp 4/77, N5400G 5/77, Sunbeam Corp 5/79, No 3 2B cvtd 13 Aug 82, GAC 8/82, (N211GA) 1/83, Westinghouse Electric Corp 4/83, N901K 1/87,Aviation Assets Inc 2/90, N74A 6/90, N901KB 4/89, Aviation Assets Inc 1/90, N74A Aviation Assets Inc. Portland, Or.
37	1968. N179AR ARCO-Burbank 3/69, N179AP 5/90, Wichita Air Services Inc 6/90, N994JD 8/90, N994JD Wichita Air Services Inc. Wichita, Ks.
38	1968. N80A U S Steel Corp 1/69, Chrysler Corp 7/83, N880A 9/83, U S Steel Corp 1/85, Marathon Oil Co 6/85, River Intl Trading Co 2/87,Brant Allen Gulfstream Assoc7/87,Chrysler Pentastar Aviation Inc 11/90, N880A Chrysler Pentastar Aviation Inc. Ypsilanti, Mi.
39	1968. N80Q U S Steel Corp 1/69, N8000 Northrop Corp 8/78, N401HR International Harvester/Harco Leasing Inc 11/79, (N124BN) Burlington Northern Inc 10/82, N425A 11/82, (N12BN) 4/83, Burlington Northern RR 2/86, BN Leasing Inc 1/89, N425A Meridian Oil Inc. Houston, Tx.
40	1968. N1040 Cox Enterprises/Dayton Newspapers Inc 1/69, (N5040) Omni 8/80, N1039 9/80, Dantata-Nigeria 7/81, NAMCO/Trand Avn Services 9/83, VR-BLJ 1/90, VR-BLJ Trand Aviation Services/NAMCO, Nigeria.
41	1968. N38N Union Carbide Corp 1/69, GAC 12/89, N38N Gulfstream Aerospace Corp. Savannah, Ga.
42	1968. N8000J Northrop Corp 1/69, No 12 2B cvtd 5 May 83, U S West Inc 3/87, N937M 6/87, G-11B Leasing Corp 1/90, Baudovin C Terlinden-Ca 3/90, N937M Baudovin C Terlinden, Beverly Hills, Ca.
43	1969. N17583 Grumman Corp /69, F-BRUY HRH Prince Aga Khan-Paris 1/69, N84X Page Avjet Corp 7/82, McGraw Edison Transit Corp 9/82, N33ME 1/83, EAF Aircraft Sales Inc 5/86,Wham Leasing Corp-Fl 7/86,N691RC 9/86, N691RC Wham Leasing Corp. West Palm Beach, Fl.
44	1969. N814GA Grumman Corp /69, N830G CONOCO Inc 2/69, E I Dupont de Nemours Co 8/87, N585A 2/83, CONOCO Inc 5/86, E I Dupont de Nemours Inc 2/88, N585A E I Dupont de Nemours Inc. New Castle, De.
45	1969. N815GA Grumman Corp /69, N711R E Cockrell Jr 2/69, Estate of E Cockrell Jr 8/72, PK-PJG Pertamina Oil/Robin Air-Singapore 1/73, N152RG Robin Loh-Singapore /75, N215RL Robin Loh/Ednasa Air Inc 1/77, VR-BHA 2/80, N115GA GAC 10/80, N40CE Corps of Engineers/Department of the Army 4/81,Cx 89-0266 11/89, 89-0266 Corps of Engineers/Department of the Army, Baltimore, Md.

46	1969.	N806CC Chrysler Corp 2/69, N4OCC Carrier Corp 8/73, Union Pacific Railroad 6/74, N111RF Robert Fisher 5/75, C-GSLK Kaiser Resources Ltd-Vancouver 11/75, N9272K Caesars World Inc 9/81, N721CP 2/82,GAC 11/86, Boston Group Services Inc 1/88, N9BF 3/88, N9BF Boston Group Services Inc. Hanscom Field, Ma.
47	1969.	N803GA Grumman Corp demo /69, N35JM Johns-Manville Corp /71, N553MD Mike Davis/Tiger Oil Co 5/77, N809GA GAC 4/79, N809LS Lear Siegler Inc 9/79, N800FL 1/88, Robert E Torray & Co 3/90, N800RT 6/90, N800RT Robert E Torray & Co. Bethesda, Md.
48	1969.	N109G Gulf Oil Corp 4/69, N4411 Texas Eastern Transmission Corp 8/68,No 29 2B cvtd 2 Nov 84,N711MC 10/90, N711MC N & MD Investment Corp. Wilmington, De.
49	1969.	N871GA Grumman Corp /69, National Gypsum Co 11/69, N747G 1/70, N747G G-3 381, Consolidated Airways Inc 1/85, N74JK 2/85, Time Aviation Inc 4/85, N830TL 5/85, N830TE 5/87, Arepo Corp 7/87, Time Inc 8/88, N830TL 10/88, (N830TE) rsvd 14 Nov 89, Time Warner /90, Canadair Challenger 12/90, N830TL Canadair Challenger Inc. Windsor, Ct.
50	1969.	N39N Union Carbide Corp 5/69, N39N to G-3 403, N39NX 7/84, Consolidated Airways 6/85,PHH Financial Svcs 7/85, N767FL 8/85, Lear Siegler Management Corp 5/90, N767FL to G-4 1141, N800FL 10/90, N800FL Lear Siegler Management Corp. Livingston, NJ.
51	1969.	N2013M Monsanto Chemical Co 4/69, N2013M Monsanto Co. St. Louis, Mo.
52	1969.	C-FFNM Falconbridge Nickel Mines Ltd 10/69, N69SF Sky Flite Inc 2/83, N38KM 3/83, Jernigan Bros Holding Co 12/83, N5SJ 2/84, EAF Aircraft Sales 2/85, World Jet/Pleasure Air 7/85, Northeast Jet 6/88, (N52NE) rsvd 10 Jul 88, Personal Way Aviation Inc 9/89, N5SJ Personal Way Aviation Inc. Dallas, Tx.
53	1969.	N107A ARAMCO Saudi Arabia 4/69, EAF Aircraft Sales Inc 5/86, N167A 1/88, Thomas H Lee-Ma 4/88, Tinicum Aviation Inc 5/88, N167A Tinicum Aviation Inc. New York, NY.
54	1969.	N123H Hilton Hotels 5/69, C-FNOR Noranda Mines & Bank of Nova Scotia 9/73, No 36 2B cvtd 5 Jul 85, N955CC ANR Pipeline Co 6/87, N955CC ANR Pipeline Co. Detroit City Airport, Mi.
55	1969.	N875GA Grumman Corp /69, N225SF Standard Oil Co 6/69, Chevron Corp 8/84, N225SF to G-3 423, N225SE 5/90, N225SE Chevron Corp. San Francisco, Ca.
56	1969.	N1OXY Oxy Petroleum Inc 5/69, N2OXY 7/80, N105Y 11/80, N105Y Oxy Petroleum Inc. Bakersfield, Ca.
57	1969.	N876GA Grumman Corp /69, N770AC American Cyanamid Co 7/69, Auxiliary Carrier Inc 1/79, N300DK Ultimate/TDK Leasing Inc 12/84, N300DK to B-727 18998, N300DL 8/86, Solar Sportsytems Inc 2/87, N300DL Solar Sportsystems Inc. Buffalo, NY.
58	1969.	N878GA Grumman Corp /69, N720Q IBM Corp 10/69, N720Q W/O W/o 24 Jun 74. 24/JUN/74
59	1969.	N879GA Grumman Corp /69, N1823D Champion Spark Plug Co 8/69, Dwight L Stuart-Ca 6/87, N1823D National Jet Charter/Dwight L Stuart, Beverly Hills, Ca.
60	1969.	N892GA Grumman Corp /69, N500J Johnson & Johnson 8/69, N500J W/O W/o 26 Sep 76. 26/SEP/76
61	1969.	N18N A D Davis/Winn Dixie Stores 7/69, N711MM McLean Securities Inc 7/69, Barron Thomas Aviation 2/87, Jones Aviation Inc 9/87, N497TJ 2/88, Tyler Jet Aircraft Sales Inc 11/88, N800MC 1/89,Personal Way Aviation Inc 7/89, N800MC Personal Way Aviation Inc. Dallas, Tx.
62	1969.	N834GA Grumman Corp /69, N372CM Cordelia Scaife May 12/69, N372GM /76, Procter & Gamble Co 1/77, N1PG 2/77, N3ZQ 4/81, Kohlman Systems Research/Procter & Gamble 9/83, N7PG 12/81,Canadair Challenger Inc 11/89, N7PQ 6/90, O Gara Aviation Co 7/90, N7PQ O Gara Aviation Co. Las Vegas, Nv.
63	1969.	N835GA Grumman Corp /69, N238U Combustion Engineering Inc 8/69, N239P 5/82, Jarrett E Woods Jr 5/84, N149JW 9/84, EAF Sales 11/86, PHH Sales 5/88, James Morse/Jetaway Air 1/89, N17ND 9/90,N17ND James A Morse/Jetaway Air, Muskegon, Mi.
64	1969.	N836GA Grumman Corp /69, N940BS Bethlehem Steel Corp /69, N950BS 1/76, N341NS National Steel 6/76, No 27 2B cvtd 28 Sep 84, N95SV Silicon Valley Express Inc 9/84, Eastman Kodak Co 12/84, N620K 9/85, Orchard Funding Inc-NYC 6/90, N620K Eastman Kodak Co. NYC.
65	1969.	N837GA Grumman Corp /69, N720E IBM Corp 9/69, GAC 12/84, N1JG Pepsi Cola Bottling Co 1/85, Pepsico Inc 1/88, N500PC 3/88, Richmor Aviation Inc 4/89, N58JF 7/89, N58JF Sterling Jet/Richmor Aviation Inc. Hudson, NY.
66	1969.	N838GA Grumman Corp /69, N720F IBM Corp 9/69, GAC 1/85, Norden Systems Inc 1/88, N720F Norden Systems Inc. Norwalk, Ct.
67	1969.	N839GA Grumman Corp /69, N711S Cal-Jet/Frank Sinatra 9/69, Connex Press 1/73, Omni 12/73, EL-WRT Government of Liberia-Monrovia 1/74, N1OHR Omni 11/75, N400JD John Deere & Co 12/75,Rental Fleet Leasing Inc 12/88, N67PR 1/89, N67PR Rental Fleet Leasing Inc. Montgomery, Al.
68	1969.	N308EL Eli Lilly & Co 9/69, N308EL Eli Lilly & Co. Indianapolis, In.
69	1969.	N69NG NGC Amusement Corp 9/69, N25JM Johns Manville Corp 1/71, N33CR C Rittenberry/Deutsch Co /74, N45JM Johns Manville Corp 9/76, N45Y 2/81, Manville Service Corp 1/82, N45Y to BAe 125-8009, N45YP Jim Bath & Associates 10/86, Hooker Aviation Corp 6/87, VH-HKR Hooker Corp P/L-Sydney 3/88, N21066 Circus Circus Enterprises Inc 10/89, N123CC 2/90, N123CC Circus Circus Enterprises Inc. Las Vegas, Nv.
70	1969.	N711SC Helena Avn/Southland Corp 10/69, No 1 2B cvtd 17 Sep 81, N711SB PRL Avn 8/86, K Packer/Consolidated Press-Sydney /87, N711SB Kerry Packer/Consolidated Press Holdings, Sydney,Australia.
71	1969.	N4CP Chas Pfizer & Co 10/69, N4CQ Golden Nugget Inc 7/78, N711SW /80, N907SW 4/82, Joe Brown Ents 6/83, Consolidated Airways Inc 7/85, N48JK 8/85, Burlington Northern 11/85,N47A 1/86, B R Leasing 6/89, N47A B R Leasing Inc. Seattle, Wa.
72	1969.	N397F Faberge Inc 10/69, N397F W/O W/o 22 Feb 76. 22/FEB/76

73		1969. N116K Bank of America/Kaiser Industries 11/69, N555CS 11/73, No 9 2B cvtd 15 Dec 82, Andorra Aviation 9/85, N555CS Kaiser Air/Andorra Aviation, Oakland, Ca.
74		1969. N845GA Grumman Corp /69, N111AC Ambassador College/Worldwide Church 11/69,N111AC to G-3 417,N311AC 2/84, GAC 4/84, cx USA 11/84, (3X-GBD) Government of Guinea 12/84, restored to USA register 6/85, Ugone Corp 12/85, N204GA Ugone Corp. Houston, Tx.
75		1969. N823GA Grumman Corp /69, N1000 Swiflite/Cities Service Oil 7/70, N100AC Luqa Inc/Charter Oil Co 8/72, N100CC 9/72, N600CS Coastal States Gas 12/76, Union Oil Co of Ca 4/77, No 7 2B cvtd 16 Nov 82, N760U Unocal, Burbank, Ca.
76		1969. N711LS Lear Siegler Inc 12/69, N227G PHH Leasing/W R Grace & Co 10/71, N227GL Mobil-Saudi Arabia 6/82, W R Grace & Co /83, N227GX 8/84, N227G 10/84, EAF Aircraft Sales 6/87,PHH Aviation Sales Inc 5/88, N227GA 10/88, TWA Aviation Inc 1/89, N227GA Flight Services Group/TWA Aviation Inc. Mt Kisco, NY.
77		1969. N824GA Grumman Corp /69, N100WK Rockefeller/Wayfarer Ketch 1/70, N40CH Chase Manhattan Bank 4/79, N40CH to G-3 377, N140CH 12/82, Macflight Inc/R H Macy Co 4/83, N34MZ 8/83, N84MZ 12/85, Jimmy Swaggert Ministries 1/86, N777JS 3/86, N385M 6/88, Tyler Jet Aircraft Sales Inc 11/88, N7TJ 1/89, Powerhouse Corp 6/89, N707SH 7/90, N707SH Powerhouse Corp. Wilmington, De.
78		1969. N17585 Grumman Corp /69, PH-FJP F J Philips of Eindhoven 7/70, C-FIOT Imperial Oil Ltd-Toronto 7/72, N90HH Canadair Challenger Inc 10/89, O Gara Avn Co 2/90, N90HH O Gara Aviation Co. Las Vegas, Wa.
79		1970. N826GA Grumman Corp /70, N719GA Humble Oil & Refining Co 1/70, Exxon Corp 10/72, N204A 8/85, Midcoast Aviation Inc 6/89, Ibister Inc 7/89, N204A Ibister Inc. San Diego, Ca.
80		1970. N827GA Grumman Corp /70, Pittsburgh Plate Glass Inds 5/70, N827GA PPG Industries Inc. Pittsburgh
81		1970. N777SW Seagram's Whiskey 2/70, N44MD Mike Davis Oil Co 2/76, N44MD to G-3 427, GAC 9/84, N281GA 10/84, Walt Disney Productions 10/85, N283MM 2/86, Corrao Construction/N & MD Investment 4/88, N688MC 6/88, Delta Bravo Inc 3/90, N688MC Delta Bravo Inc. Dayton, Oh.
82		1970. N711DP AFLC/Mid Western Airlines 2/70, N1OLB Lindner Brothers 1/71, N9040 Intl Brotherhood of Teamsters 3/72, N600B 10/72, N600B to G-3 459, N600BT 12/85, N728T 8/86, N728T International Brotherhood of Teamsters, Washington, DC.
83		1970. N404M Martin Marietta Corp 2/70, N409M 8/79, N409MA Mutual Savings Life Insurance Co 5/84, (N48MS) 7/84, Louie J Russel III-La 8/85, N409MA Victory Management Group/Louie J Russell III, Metairie, La.
84		1970. N5101 General Motors Corp 3/70, N5101T 1/86, Wiley C Sanders Jr 4/86, N27SL 6/86, N27SL Wiley Sanders Truck Lines Inc. Troy, Al.
85		1970. N5102 General Motors Corp 3/70, lease Royal Danish AF 2/81-8/81, N510G 1/86, GAC 2/86, James Lenane-NH 6/86, N86SK 7/86, N86SK James Lenane, Livermore, Ca.
86		1970. N880GA Grumman Corp /70, Texas Eastern Transmission Corp 9/70, N179T 10/70,No 16 2B cvtd 9 Aug 83, N179T Texas Eastern Transmission Corp. Houston, Tx.
88		1970. N881GA Grumman Corp /70, N2600 Mobil Oil Corp 5/70, N2637M 8/81,HB-IMZ Nataścha Estab-Vaduz 10/81, No 21 2B cvtd 18 Feb 84, ABCO Aviation Trust Estab-Vaduz 4/89, N901AS FSB-Ut 9/90, I A S Inc-Shannon 11/90, N901AS I A S Inc. Shannon, Ireland.
89		1970. N882GA Grumman Corp /70, N100A Esso Air Inc 7/70, Exxon Corp 10/72, N100A to G-3 370, N203A 6/83, Midcoast Aviation Inc 4/89, N203A Midcoast Aviation Inc. St Louis, Mo.
90		1970. N883GA Grumman Corp /70, N7789 Dresser Industries Inc 7/70, N7789 Dresser Industries Inc. Dallas
91		1970. N17586 Grumman Corp /70, G-AYMI Rio Tinto Zinc Ltd 7/70, VH-ASM Associated Airlines P/L 4/72, N219GA GAC 3/84, G-OVIP Harry Goodman 3 Apr 85, Robert Maxwell/Mirror Holdings 7/86, VIP Marine & Aviation Ltd 16 Nov 87, Cx G- 13 Feb 89, VR-BRM 3/89, VR-BRM to G-2 194, N291GA GAC 1/90, lease Occidental International 1990, N291GA Gulfstream Aerospace Corp. Savannah, Ga.
92		1970. N884GA Grumman Corp /70, N300L Triangle Publications Inc 7/70, N300L to G-3 318, N300U GAC 2/81, Southern Natural Service Co 7/81, N114HC 10/81, Residence Inn-Hotel Corp 6/84, N994JD 9/84, Hotel Corp 12/88, USAA-United Svcs Auto Assoc 6/89, N430SA 7/89, N430SA USAA-United Services Auto Association, San Antonio, Tx.
93		1970. N885GA Grumman /70, N8785R 7/70, TJ-AAK Government of Cameroun 10/70, N215GA GAC 7/86, Terminix Intl Inc 8/86, Cook Intl Inc 1/87, N62K 3/87, N62K Cook International Inc. Palm Beach, Fl.
94		1970. N886GA Grumman Corp /70, N200A Esso Air Inc 7/70, Exxon Corp 5/73, N200A to G-3 372, N202A 5/83, Midcoast Aviation Inc 3/89,Montgomery Ward & Co 12/89, N623MW 9/90,N623MW Montgomery Ward & Co. Chicago, Il.
95		1970. N887GA Grumman /70, VH-ASG Associated Airlines P/L 4/71, No 39 2B cvtd Mar 86, VH-ASG Mines Transportation/Associated Airlines P/L. Melbourne.
96		1970. N888GA Grumman Corp /70, N100KS Kinney Services/General Transportation Co 6/71, N100WC Warner Communications 10/71, N75WC 6/77, N75SR 8/77, XC-MEX Bank of Mexico 9/77, XB-EBI Vitro Corporativo SA-Monterrey 10/87, XB-EBI Vitro Corporacion SA. Monterrey.
97		1971. N889GA Grumman Corp /70, I-SMEG Soc VIP Air-Milan 9/71, N66TF Omni's Trading Floor 3/78, N11AL Allegheny Ludlum 4/78, Emra Corp 3/82, F&G Assocs 9/87, Philadelphia Eagles Football Club 5/90,N930SD rsvd 8 Jun 90, N930SD Philadelphia Eagles Football Club, Philadelphia, Pa.
98		1971. N850GA Grumman Corp /70, N93M W L McKnight/3M Co 3/71, N955H Honeywell Inc 6/75, N955H to G-3 378, N988H 12/82, David Shakarian 10/83, N988DS 1/84, Diamond Shamrock/Harbor Land Co 1/85, N925DS 3/85, 2B conversion 1986, N17MX Maxus Energy Corp 7/87, XA-CHR TAESA 11/88, XA-CHR TAESA=Transportes Aereos

c/n   Page 158

Ejecutivos S.A. Mexico City.
99   1971. N851GA Grumman Corp /71, N99GA Greyhound Armour & Co 8/71, Conagra Inc 2/84, N822CA 4/84,Skyharbor Air Svc 2/90, DSC Transportation Inc 3/90, N900VL 5/90, N900VL DSC Transportation Inc. Cupertino, Ca.
100 1970. N852GA Grumman Corp /71, N4000X Xerox Corp 11/71, N4000X to CL600-1058, N400CX 1/82, Skybird Aviation Inc 2/82, N234DB 4/82, N911DB 5/88, N911DB Skybird Aviation Inc. Van Nuys, Ca.
101 1971. N853GA Grumman Corp /71, N1159K R Kroc/McDonald's Hamburgers 8/71, WOTAN America Inc 11/80, (N237LM) 1/82, Canadair Challenger 1/89, Hillbrook Building Co 4/89, N1159K Hillbrook Building Co. Moreland Hills, Oh.
102 1971. N854GA Grumman Corp /71, N88AE National Express Co 2/72, N88AE to G-3 398, GAC 7/83, N210GA 9/83, Wilmar Ltd 3/84, N119CC 10/84,Coalinga Corp 2/85,N400CC 3/85,No 32 2B cvtd 7 Mar 85, Marie Keck 1/88, Wells Fargo & Co 3/90, N400CC Wells Fargo & Co/Kaiserair, Van Nuys, Ca.
103 1971. N855GA Grumman Corp /71, N801GA Grumman demo 3/72, G-BDMF Rolls Royce (1971) Ltd 12/75, N833GA GAC 5/80, P2-PNF Government of Papua New Guinea 1/81, P2-PNG 3/81, stored Copenhagen 5/83-6/84, N833GA Robey Smith Co 8/84, HZ-MS4 Saudi Armed Medical Svcs 1/85, HZ-MS4 Saudi Armed Forces Medical Services, Riyadh.
104 1971. N856GA Grumman Corp /71, N856W Travelers Corp 1/72,N856W to G-3 484,No 10 2B cvtd 9 Feb 83, N858W 5/89, C-FHPM American Barrick Resources Corp 30 Oct 89, no longer 2B fm 12/89, wings transferred to N303GA s/n 303, C-FHPM American Barrick Resources Corp. Mississauga, Ontario.
105 1971. N807GA Grumman Corp /71, N23M 3M Co 1/72, N5997K 1/88, GAC 3/89, N5997K Gulfstream Aerospace Corp. Savannah, Ga.
106 1971. N808GA Grumman Corp /71, N33M 3M Co 1/72, N397LE 5/88, GAC 6/88, GECC-Charlotte 8/88, N226GA 3/90, lease Occidental International 1990, N226GA Gulfstream Aerospace Corp. Savannah, Ga.
107 1971. N809GA Grumman Corp /71, N5113H Amerada Hess Corp 2/72, H K Porter Co 3/83, N10123 3/86, Thermoid Inc 6/88, HBD Industries Inc 10/88, N10123 HBD Industries Inc. Bellefontaine, Oh.
108 1971. N810GA Grumman Corp /71, N11UC Superior Oil Co 2/72, N60GG 9/76, Alexander Dawson Inc 3/81, D H Braman 7/81, Beckwith Machinery 8/81, Mary Braman 4/82, N600MB 6/82, Flo-Sun Land Corp 4/89, N700FS 10/89, Flo-Sun Aircraft Inc 1/90, N700FS Flo-Sun Aircraft Inc. High Point, NC.
109 1972. N811GA Grumman Corp /72, N679RW Coca Cola Co 3/72, L R French Jr 11/83, N882W 1/84, Coca Cola Enterprises Inc 11/86, N86CE 12/86, N86CE Coca Cola Enterprises Inc. Atlanta, Ga. 'The Enterprise'
110 1972. N814GA Grumman Corp /72, N5000G Gannett Newspapers Inc 3/72, N200GN 3/77, N200PB Page Inc 11/80, Airmark Corp 12/80, N21AM 1/81, Hughes Aircraft 11/84, RTS Aircraft Services Corp 5/85,Charles Buggy-NYC 11/85, Joseph Dupont-Az 9/87, N21AM 1/81, N21AM Hughes Aircraft Co/Joseph A Dupont, Phoenix, Az.
111 1972. N815GA Grumman Corp /72, N10LB Lindner Brothers 4/72, N13LB /76, ARAMCO 6/76, N765A 7/76, ARAMCO Assoc Co 12/81, Banner Aircraft Resales 3/87, N900BR 8/87, Fly Inc 3/90, Highland Air Inc 7/90, N900BR Highland Air/Air Group Inc. Van Nuys, Ca.
112 1972. N816GA Grumman Corp /72, N102ML American Intl Avn/C V Starr 6/72, Hensley Schmidt Intl 7/82,N102HS 10/82, cx USA 12/84, VR-BJG AIC Avn/Afro-International Consultants Ltd 'Mina' 12/84, N36JK Consolidated Airways 3/87,Louisiana Land & Exploration 12/87 N909L 3/88, N909L Louisiana Land & Exploration Co. New Orleans, La.
113 1972. N817GA Grumman Corp /72, N3ORP RCA Corp 7/72, N34RP Continental Telephone Co 3/82, N6OCT 7/82, GAC 5/85, N203GA 6/85, Trousdale Inc 1/87, N2S 2/87, Harleyville Corp 8/87, N32HC 2/89, N2S 5/89,GECC-Dallas 10/90, N216HE Fairways Corp 11/90, N216HE Fairways Corp. Washington, DC.
114 1972. N818GA Grumman Corp /72, N100PM Philip Morris Inc 8/72, Ben Fortson Oil 1/85, N25BF 2/85, N25BF Fortson Oil Co. Fort Worth, Tx.
115 1972. N819GA Grumman Corp /72, N677S Sentry Insurance Co/SENCO Inc 8/72, N457SW 11/82, Sentry Corp 1/84, Consolidated Airways Inc 6/86, N47JK 10/86, Robert J Pond/Advance Machine Co 12/86, N200BP 10/87, Robert J Pond-Mn 2/89, N200BP Robert J Pond/Planes of Fame, Plymouth, Mn.
116 1972. N821GA Grumman Corp /72, 9M-ARR Government of Sabah-East Malaysia 10/72,N20XY Occidental Petroleum Co 5/77, N23W Hooker Chemicals 4/78, EAF 9/86, PHH Aircraft Sales 5/88, Conair Travel Corp 1/89,(N410LR) rsvd 4 Feb 89, N23W Conair Travel Corp. Stamford, Ct.
117 1972. N822GA Grumman Corp /72, N580RA Rapid American/View Top Corp 9/72, N888SW /75, Crown Controls Corp 9/84, N75CC 11/84, N75CC Crown Controls Corp. New Bremen, Oh.
118 1972. N823GA Grumman Corp /72, N399CB Citibank-NYC 10/72, Film Properties Inc 2/81, (N301FP) /81, N399FP 2/85, Lockheed Corp 5/86, N650PF 2/89, (Alison 501-M78 prop-fan engine on port wing), (N651NA) rsvd for NASA-Cleveland 25 Feb 89, N650PF NASA, Cleveland, Oh. (NASA 650).
119 1972. N824GA Grumman Corp /72, TU-VAF Govt of Ivory Coast-Abidjan 11/72, N825GA GAC 3/80,C-FHBX Hudson's Bay Oil & Gas 1/81, N2991Q Sheraton Inns Inc 5/82, N60HJ 10/82, No 22 2B cvtd 27 Mar 84, ITT Europe Inc 7/84, (N875E) 10/84, N720G 1/85, Louisiana Pacific Corp 10/86, N73LP 5/88, N73LP Louisiana Pacific Corp. Hillsboro, Or.
120 1972. N825GA Grumman Corp /72, N901BM Bristol-Myers Co 1/73, Sunbelt Service Corp 4/85, N777V 6/85, Mar Flite Ltd Corp 2/87, N677V 6/87, Twentieth Century Fox Film Co 11/88, N20FX 2/89,N20FX Twentieth Century Fox Film Co. Los Angeles, Ca.
121 1972. N200P National Distillers & Chemical Corp 1/73, Teterboro Aircraft Service Inc 1/87,EAF Aircraft Sales 4/87, N90EA 9/87, PHH Aviation Sales 5/88, United Jet Center 7/89, N507JC 12/89, N507JC United Jet Center Inc. Warren, Pa.

122	1973. N832GA Grumman Corp /72, N429JX PHH Keystone Leasing Inc/Dana Corp 4/73, N4290X GAC 8/81, HCS Leasing Corp/Smith International Inc 1/82, N61SM 6/82, BN Leasing Inc 10/85, N84A 2/86, Burlington Northern Railroad 1/89, N84A Burlington Northern Railroad, Fort Worth, Tx.
123	1973. N805CC Chrysler Corp 3/73, Allen & Co/G 11 Corp 8/81, N345CP 711 Avn/Columbia Pictures 10/81,No 25 2B cvtd 11 Jun 84, 711 Fifth Avenue Corp 8/88, 711 Air Corp 1/90, N345AA 7/90, N345AA 711 Air Corp. Teterboro, NJ.
124	1973. N834GA Grumman Corp /73, HB-IEW Aztec S.A. 8/73, (VR-BGL) /77, VR-BGO Sioux Corp/Livanos 5/77, N203GA GAC 5/81, 0004 FAV-MoD-Caracas 6/81, 0004 FAV, MoD, Caracas.
125	1973. N870GA Grumman Corp /73, N367G General Electric Co 4/73, No 26 2B cvtd 11 Jul 84, N364G 4/84,N364G to G-4 1091, N3643 9/89, Leucadia Aviation Inc 4/90, N92LA 5/90, N92LA Leucadia Aviation Inc. Salt Lake City, Ut.
126	1973. N43M 3M Co 5 Apr 73, N581WD 10 May 88, GAC 31 May 88, Importwood Ltd-Switzerland 4/89, Cx 4/89 never HB- regd. N578DF San Antonio Air Inc 8/89, N578DF San Antonio Air Inc. DC. 'Antonio Sandrita - Wings of Man'
127	1973. N17581 Grumman Corp /73, TR-KHB Government of Gabon 4/73, TR-KHB W/O W/o 6 Feb 80. 06/FEB/80
128	1973. N73M 3M Co 6/73, N367EG GAC 5/88, N367EG Gulfstream Aerospace Corp. Savannah, Ga.
129	1973. N871GA Grumman Corp /73, N1H Harrahs Club 6/73, Evergreen Intl Avn/Delford Smith 12/87, N711DS 1/88, N711DS Delford Smith/Evergreen International Avn, McMinnville, Or.
130	1973. N872GA Grumman Corp /73, N127V El Paso Natural Gas Co 7/73, El Paso Co 4/89,El Paso Natural Gas Co 8/90, N127V El Paso Natural Gas Co. El Paso, Tx.
131	1973. N17582 Grumman Corp /73, 9M-ATT Government of Sabah-East Malaysia 2/74, N759A ARAMCO Associated Co 6/76, No 23 2B cvtd 25 Apr 84, Budget Jet Inc 6/89, N2JR 8/89, N2JR Budget Jet Inc. Oneida, Tn.
132	1973. N873GA Grumman Corp /73, N400M Fluor Corp 8/73, Integrated Aircraft Corp 8/85, Eckert Cold Storage Co 12/85, N400M Eckert Cold Storage Co. Manteca, Ca.
133	1973. N17583 Grumman Corp /73, N88906 Page Gulfstream Corp 8/73, 5X-UPF Government of Uganda 3/74,5X-UPF Government of Uganda, Entebbe.
134	1973. N806CC Chrysler Corp 8/73, C-FROC Ranger Oil (Canada) Ltd 3 Dec 80, C-FROC Ranger Oil (Canada) Ltd. Calgary.
135	1973. N83M 3M Co 10/73, GAC 2/88, Air Transport Inc 6/88, N113EV 7/88, N113EV Air Transport Inc. NYC.
136	1973. N874GA Grumman Corp /73, N65M Motorola Corp 10/73, ZS-JIS Anglo American Corp 2/75, 3D-AAC Swaziland Iron Ore Dvlpment 6/75, Peak Timber Sales P/L /81, N207GA GAC 5/83,6V-AFL Mbaye Djilly-Dakar 7 May 84, 6V-AFL Monair S.A. Celigny, Switzerland/Mbaye Djilly, Dakar.
137	1973. N875GA Grumman Corp /73, N1875P Prudential Insurance Co 11/73, N2711M 10/84, USAL Inc 1/85, VR-BJT 12/86, VR-BJT Ormond Ltd/USAL Inc. Wilmington, De.
138	1973. N6JW Jim Walter Corp 12/73, Walter Industries Inc 2/88, N6JW Walter Industries Inc. Tampa, Fl.
139	1973. N440GA Grumman Corp /73, N18N A D Davis/Winn Dixie Stores/G-II International 12/73, HZ-PET Mobil Oil/Petromin-Jeddah 5/80, No 11 2B cvtd 15 Mar 83, HB-ITV Allway Estab-Geneva 4/88, HB-ITV Allway Estab. Geneva.
140	1974. N881GA Grumman /73, C-GTWO International Nickel/INCO & ALCAN Ltd 6/74, N2667M AMCA Resources Inc 11/82, (N101AR) 3/83, N104AR 11/83, N104AR to G-3 461, GAC 8/85, N212GA 3/86, VR-BJQ Glen Intl PLC/Northeast Jet Co 3/86, No 40 2B cvtd Jun 86, N189TC Pleasure Air Inc 5/88, N730TK 7/88, N730TK Pleasure Air Inc. Wilmington, De.
141	1974. N17584 Grumman Corp /74, JA8431 JCAB-Tokyo 6/74, JA8431 JCAB=Japanese Civil Aviation Board, Tokyo.
142	1974. N882GA Grumman Corp /74, N6OCC Carrier Corp 8/74, N5RD RDC Marine Inc 2/81, N5RD RDC Marine Inc. Houston, Tx.
143	1974. N883GA Grumman Corp /74, N334 John W Galbreath 8/74, N204C CONOCO Inc 10/80, E I Dupont de Nemours & Co 2/89, N204C E I Dupont de Nemours & Co. New Castle, De.
144	1974. N17585 Grumman Corp /74, HB-ITR Tiny Rowland/Lonrho Ltd/Lonair SA 8/74, N944NA NASA-Houston 5/83, N944NA NASA Johnson Space Center, Houston, Tx.
145	1974. N894GA Grumman Corp /74, N871D Diamond International Corp 5/74, N871E IT&T Corp 1/78, Halliburton Co 9/84, N339H 10/84, N339H Halliburton Industries Corp. Duncan, Ok.
146	1974. N897GA Grumman Corp /74, N946NA NASA Shuttle Trainer 5/74, N946NA NASA Johnson Space Center, Houston, Tx.
147	1974. N898GA Grumman Corp /74, N947NA NASA Shuttle Trainer 6/74, N947NA NASA Johnson Space Center, Houston, Tx.
148	1974. N710MR MARCOR 6/74, N710MP 2/77, N2615 Mobil Saudi Arabia Inc 3/78, No 5 2B cvtd 18 Aug 82, N2615 Mobil Saudi Arabia Inc. Jeddah.
149	1974. N896GA Grumman Corp /74, N17586 7/84, 5V-TAA Government of Togo-Lome 11/74, 5V-TAA W/O W/o 26 Dec 74. 26/DEC/74
150	1974. N803GA Grumman Corp /74, N966H Prulease Inc/Honeywell Inc 2/75, General Nutrition Inc 3/84, N988H N988H 4/84, ROP Aviation Inc 7/84, N636MF 10/84, N636MF to G-4 1012, N638MF 7/87, CK Aviation Inc-NYC 4/88, (N631CK) rsvd 7 May 88, N613CK 7/88, N613CK CK Aviation Inc. New York, NY.
151	1974. N804GA Grumman Corp /74, N979RA Ogden American Corp 10/74, No 24 2B cvtd 4 Jun 84, N979RA Ogden Management Services Inc. White Plains, NY.

152	1974. N17587 Grumman Corp /74, XA-FOU Aviones Televisa SA-Mexico City 10/74, N202GA GAC 6/85, Finevest Svcs Leasing/Mid Atlantic Airways 8/85, N62WB 12/85, Ultrajets Inc 3/90, Little Caesar Enterprises 6/90, N559LC 11/90, N559LC Little Ceasar Enterprises Inc. Detroit, Mi.
153	1974. N881GA Grumman Corp /74, N23A Superior Oil Co 11/74, Howard Keck Jr-LAX 12/84, Sam Hashman Resources/Mar-Flite Ltd Corp 2/87, (N602CM) rsvd for Maguire Cushman Aviation 17 Feb 88, N23A Maguire Cushman Aviation, Van Nuys, Ca.
154	1974. N1625 Texaco Inc 12/74, No 28 2B cvtd 15 Oct 84, Nicklaus/Air Bear Inc 5/88, N1JN 6/88, N1JN Jack Nicklaus/Air Bear Inc. N Palm Beach, Fl.
155	1974. N308A ARAMCO-Dhahran 12/74, No 14 2B cvtd 22 Jun 83, XA-GAC Commander Mexicana SA 11/88, XA-GAC Commander Mexicana SA. Mexico City.
156	1975. N806GA Grumman Corp /74, N400SJ Seward Johnson 1/75, N7000G Ashland Oil Inc 10/79, Castor Trading Co 3/82, N16NK 5/82, No 31 2B cvtd 19 Feb 85, Suncoast Aviation Services 3/85, lease CA Distribuidora-Alimentos 85,Castor Trading Co 11/85, N16NK Castor Trading Co. Coral Gables, Fl.
157	1975. N805GA Grumman Corp /75, N914BS Bethlehem Steel Corp 7/75, Flight Dept liquidation 12/85, N940BS Consolidated Airways Inc 4/86, Prince Corp 1/87, N74JK 6/86, Prince Corp 1/87, N658PC 8/87,N658PC Prince Corp/Wingspan Leasing Inc. Holland, Mi.
158	1975. N76CS CSX Beckett/Chessie Services Inc 3/75, Fluor Corp 5/89, N76QS 9/88, Fluor Corp 5/89, N401M BLC Corp 7/89, N401M BLC Corp. San Mateo, Ca.
159	1975. N345UP Union Pacific Corp 3/75, Personal Way Avn 6/89, N800DM 7/89, N800DM Personal Way Aviation Inc. Dallas, Tx.
160	1975. N80J U S Steel Corp 4/75, N801 7/84, GAC 10/84, N214GA 3/85, Sutom NV Ltd-NYC 5/86, Aero Dienst USA-Van Nuys 6/86, N900TP 7/86, FSB-SLC 3/89, N919TG 12/89, N919TG Federal Aviation Services Corp. Dallas, Tx.
161	1975. N17589 Grumman Corp /75, XA-ABC Aviones Banco Comercio 8/75, XC-FEZ Comision Federal de Electricidad 12/80, XC-CFE 8/81, XC-UJK/TP-04 Government of Mexico 6/86, XC-UJK TP-04, Government of Mexico, Mexico City.
162	1975. (C-GANE) Grumman Corp /75, N530SW Studebaker Worthington 1/76, N74RV Tripco Inc 3/78, C-GTCB Trans Canada Pipelines 5/80, N74RV Midcoast Aviation Inc 9/88, N666JT Janus Transair Corp 1/89, N666JT Janus Transair Corp. Bedford, NY.
163	1975. N17581 Grumman Corp /75, (YV-60CP) CEDICA-Caracas 12/75, PJ-ABA Cia Aerea del Caribe/CEDICA 2/76, N117JJ Gavilan Corp/CEDICA 3/78, N117JJ to G-3 448, N117JA 4/85, N117JJ 6/87,N117JJ Gavilan Corp. Miami, Fl. 'El Condor'
164	1975. N17582 Grumman Corp /75, 9K-ACX Sheikh Zayed-UAE 12/75, A6-HHZ /76, N93LA AIC Leasing Services Inc 11/89, N93LA AIC Leasing Services Inc. Norwalk, Ct.
165	1975. N810GA Grumman Corp /75, N7000C Cargill Inc 7/75, N7000C to G-3 344, N788C 8/82, Jet Aviation of America Inc 10/82, VR-BHR Abdul Latif Jameel Estab 11/82, No 37 2B cvtd Dec 85, Pegasus Avn-Hamilton to JTF to Cathay Holdings Inc 12/90, N26L JTF to ABCO Aviation Inc 12/90, N26L ABCO Aviation Inc. Wilmington, De.
166	1975. N811GA Grumman Corp /75, Kirby Leasing Inc 10/75, N515KA Alghanim-Kuwait/Star Jet 11/75,Allegheny International 8/81, N66AL 2/82, (N84AL) /83, No 15 2B cvtd 14 Jul 83, PPG Industries Inc 6/86, N826GA 11/86, N826GA PPG Industries Inc. Pittsburgh, Pa.
167	1975. N17583 Grumman Corp /75, 5V-TAC Government of Togo-Lome 1/76, VR-CBC Continental Dynamics 11/81, N204GA GAC 12/81, Santa Fe Air Transport Inc 2/82, N900SF 5/82, Bell Leasing-Mi 12/85, N430DP Domino's Pizza 2/86, IMCO Svcs/McMoRan Properties Inc 7/86, N681FM 8/86, (N82204) rsvd 30 Jun 89, N682FM 7/89, N682FM to G-3 305, N683FM 11/90, N683FM McMoRan Properties Inc. New Orleans, La.
168	1975. N812GA Grumman Corp /75, N1OLB Great American Insurance Co-Oh 8/75, N1OLB to G-4 1008, N26LB 6/87, Circle K Corp 9/87, AEAC Inc 3/89, N193CK 12/87, Avery Intl Corp 4/88, N635AV 5/88, AEAC Inc 3/89,N635AV AEAC Inc. Van Nuys, Ca.
169	1975. N17584 Grumman Corp /75, HB-IEX Interjet AG/Helmut Horten /75, Seestern Spedition AG/Private Jet Svcs 3/76, Jetex AG 6/83, N39JK Consolidated Airways Inc 4/87, Plateau Aircraft Inc 1/88, N31SY Slender You Inc 3/88, Crossland Industries Inc 1/89, N710JL Lonimar Stables Inc 8/90,N710JL Lonimar Stables Inc. Phoenix, Az.
170	1975. N991GA Grumman Corp /75, N14PC Pepsico Inc 11/75, N502PC 4/87, N502PC Pepsico Inc. Purchase, NY.
171	1975. N17586 Grumman Corp /75,HZ-AFH Saudia Special Flight Services 5/76, HZ-AFH Saudia Special Flight Services, Jeddah.
172	1975. N804GA Grumman Corp /75, N903G Owens-Illinois Inc 11/75, Owens-Illinois General Inc 8/87, N903G Owens-Illinois General Inc. Toledo, Oh.
173	1975. N801GA Grumman Corp /75, tip-tank development aircraft, XC-PET PEMEX /79,XC-PET PEMEX,Mexico City.
174	1975. N805GA Grumman Corp /75, N401M Fluor Corp 12/75, FSB of Utah 10/85, Cloud Dancer Co 12/87, N144ST 4/88, Ellis Smith-NY 8/89, Capital Cities ABC Inc 9/89, N7766Z 9/90, N7766Z Capital Cities ABC Inc. Westchester County Airport, NY.
175	1975. N17585 Grumman Corp /75, HZ-AFG Saudia Special Flight Services 8/76, 5T-UPR Government of Mauretania 11/85, 5T-UPR Government of Islamic Republic of Mauretania, Nouakchott.

c/n

c/n	
176	1976. N806GA Grumman Corp /76, Pittston Corp 1/76, N176P 2/76, Atlantic Land Improvement Co 5/84, N176SB CSX/Seaboard System Railroad Co 3/85, The United Co 1/88, N15UC 5/88, N15UC The United Co. Blountville
177	1976. N17587 Grumman Corp /76, 5N-AGV Government of Nigeria 11/76, 5N-AGV Federal Military Government, Lagos.
178	1976. N819GA Grumman Corp /76, Faberge Inc 4/76, N390F 5/76, View Top Corp 7/85, American Continental Corp 5/86, N104ME 6/86, Cameron Aviation Corp 8/89, (N128AD) rsvd for Arlie Group 18 Jan 90, Loral Properties Inc 3/90, N42LC 5/90, N42LC Loral Properties Inc. NYC.
179	1976. N17588 Grumman Corp /76, HZ-CAD Saudi Civil Aviation Directorate 12/76, HZ-PCA /78, HZ-PCA Presidency of Civil Aviation, Jeddah.
180	1976. N859GA Grumman Corp /76, Cooper Airmotive Inc 4/76, N329K Ford Motor Co 1/77, N359K 4/87, Consolidated Airways Inc 6/87, WACO Services Inc 5/88, N37WH 7/88, N37WH Huizenga Holdings/WACO Services Inc. Fort Lauderdale, Fl.
181	1976. N860GA Grumman Corp /76, N24DS Diamond Shamrock Corp 11/76, N924DS 10/82, Centex Service Co 5/86, N48CC 12/86, N48CC Centex Service Co. Dallas, Tx.
182	1976. N17589 Grumman Corp /76, CN-ANL Government of Morocco 4/77, CN-ANL Government of Morocco, Rabat.
183	1976. N17581 Grumman Corp /76, A40-AA Government of Oman 11/76,A40-AA Sultan H.M. Qaboos bin Said, Seeb. (r/c Oman 3).
184	1976. N861GA Grumman Corp /76, N80E United States Steel Corp 12/76, GAC 9/84, N220GA 10/84, Aviation Venture Inc 7/85, N254CR 8/85, N254CR Aviation Venture Inc. Cleveland, Oh.
185	1976. N862GA Grumman Corp /76, N372CM Cordelia Scaife May 7/76, N372CM to G-3 338, N372GM 10/81, Cameron Iron Works Inc 8/82, N3E 11/82, N3EU 7/84, EAF/West Point Pepperell Inc 8/84, N511WP 10/84, Abiron Inc 7/89, XA-BRE TAESA 10/89, XA-BRE TAESA. Mexico City.
186	1976. N17582 Grumman Corp /76, (D-ACVG) Friedrich Flick GmbH 8/76, D-AFKG 8/76, 5N-AML Al Hadji Deribe-Nigeria 1/82, (D-AAMD) H Stelling & Ptnrs-Hamburg (D- file closed 26 Jul 84), VR-BJV Uniexpress Jet Services Ltd-Bermuda 2/87, VR-BJV Uniexpress Jet Services Ltd.
187	1976. N17583 Grumman /76, N804GA 8/76, HZ-ADC Raytheon Middle East Systems/Air Defence Command 9/77, HZ-ADC HRH Khaled bin Sultan bin Abdoulah to G-4 1037, N202GA GAC 7/88, Chrysler Corp 3/89, N802CC 4/89, CIT Leasing Corp 8/90, N802CC Chrysler Corp. Detroit, Mi.
188	1976. N823GA Grumman Corp /76, N862G General Dynamics Corp 9/76, N662G 11/81, Mar Flite Ltd 9/86, McWane Inc 12/86, N662G McWane Inc. Birmingham, Al.
189	1976. N333AR ARCO-Dallas 10/76, ARCO-Anchorage 1/82, No 42 2B cvtd Jul 87, N333AR ARCO, Burbank, Ca.
190	1976. N130K American Can Co 10/76,Private Business Air Service Inc 1/82, N159B Carter Hawley Hale Stores 8/82, N169B 1/83, Rosecrans of Delaware Inc 5/86, WRH Investment/Red River Inc 6/86, N900WJ 9/86,William N Pennington Trustee-Reno 4/88, N1WP 7/88, N7WQ 10/88, Dame Greenbrook Leasing 1/89, N59CD 7/89, J B & A Aviation Inc 3/90, Fightertown Inc 4/90, N59JR 5/90, N59JR Fightertown Inc. Houston, Tx.
191	1976. N810GA Grumman Corp /76, N680RW Coca-Cola Co 10/76, N679RW 7/84, N677RW 3/90, N677RW Coca Cola Co. Atlanta, Ga.
192	1976. N811GA Grumman Corp /76, N678RW Coca Cola Co 11/76, N677RW 5/88,HB-ITW Minute Maid SA-Zurich 9/88, HB-ITW Minute Maid SA. Zurich.
193	1976. N808GA Grumman Corp /76, N26L Square D Co 12/76, N26L to G-3 387, N26LT 1/83, Wm Grainger/Doerr Electric Corp 6/83, N54J 7/83, Wm Grainger Inc 2/86, W W Grainger Inc 1/88, N54J W W Grainger Inc. Wheeling, Il.
194	1976. N17584 Grumman Corp /76, HB-IMW ATES/Count Agusta 12/76, C6-BEJ Chartair/Count Agusta 12/81,C6-BFE Aircor-Nassau /87, VR-BRM VIP Avn (Bermuda)/R Maxwell 12/89,VR-BRM VIP Aviation (Bermuda) Ltd/R Maxwell, Heathrow.
195	1976. N212K 195 Broadway Corp 12/76, N71TP Tesoro Petroleum Corp 11/80, XA-ILV ASESA-Monterrey 5/88, XA-ILV ASESA-Aerolineas Especializados SA. Monterrey.
196	1976. N400J Johnson & Johnson 1/77, Beatrice Foods Co 4/83, N200BE 5/83, Mar Flite Ltd Corp 5/86, May Dept Stores Co 7/86, N61OMC 9/86, N61OMC May Department Stores Co. St. Louis, Mo.
197	1977. N800GA Grumman Corp /77, N5117H Amerada Hess Corp 1/77, N5117H Amerada Hess Corp. Woodbridge, NJ.
198	1977. N825GA Grumman Corp /77, N365G General Electric Co 2/77, No 35 2B cvtd 7 May 85, N3652 AIC Leasing Services Inc 1/90, N91LA Leucadia Avn Inc 3/90, N91LA Leucadia Aviation Inc. Salt Lake City, Ut.
199	1977. N829GA Grumman Corp /77, N75WC Warner Communications/General Transportation Corp 3/77, N75RP 8/78, N75RP to G-3 328, N74RP 9/81, No 19 2B cvtd 4 Jan 84, N74RP to G-4 1040, N71RP 8/88, N71RP General Transportation Corp. NYC.
200	1977. N826GA Grumman Corp /77, N1806P Colgate Palmolive Co 11/77, N135CP 2/81, Magnum Land/George Ablah-Ks 11/83, N99VA 3/84, XA-AVR Aerotaxi Mexicana/K2 del Aire SA 11/88, XA-AVR Aerotaxi Mexicana/K2 del Aire SA. Mexico City.
201	1977. N17585 Grumman Corp /77,HZ-AFI Saudia Special Flight Svcs 12/77, HZ-AFI Saudia Special Flight Services, Jeddah.
202	1977. N17586 Grumman Corp /77, A9C-BG Government of Bahrain 2/78, A9C-BG Government of Bahrain. (r/c Bahraini Two).
203	1977. N17587 Grumman Corp /77,HZ-AFJ Saudia Special Flight Svcs 12/77, HZ-AFJ Saudia Special Flight Services, Jeddah.

204	1977.	N17588 Grumman Corp /77, G-CXMF Gulfstream Investments (CI) Ltd 8/78, N806CC Chrysler Corp 5/84, N937US U S West Corp 8/86, Prince Corp 1/89, N659PC 8/89, N659WL 10/89, N659WL Wingspan Leasing/Prince Corp. Holland, Mi.
205	1977.	N25UG United Gas Pipeline Co 8/77, Swiflite/Cities Svc Oil 6/86, N1000 7/86, N1000 Swiflite Aircraft Corp/Oxy USA Inc. Tulsa, Ok.
206	1977.	N2PK Scientific Design Co 9/77, Halcon SD Group Inc 8/81,Listowel Inc 9/82,N2PK Listowel Inc. NYC.
207	1977.	N700PM Philip Morris Inc 9/77, No 34 2B cvtd 2 May 85, N700PM Philip Morris Management Corp. Teterboro, NJ.
208	1977.	N808GA Grumman Corp /77, N62CB Cotton Belt/St Louis Southwestern Railway 9/77,C-FNCG Norcan Energy 1/86, Sugra Ltd 7 Jul 87, C-FNCG Sugra Ltd/Norcan Energy, Toronto.
209	1977.	N806GA Grumman Corp /77, N277T Trunkline Gas Co 8/77, N277T Trunkline Gas Co. Houston, Tx.
210	1977.	HB-IEY Petrolair Systems-Athens 5/78, G-IIRR Rolls Royce PLC 7/86, ALN Ltd-IOM 1/90,8P-LAD Augusto Lopez/Avianca-Colombia 3/90, 8P-LAD Augusto Lopez/Avianca, Bogota, Colombia.
211	1977.	N17581 Grumman Corp /77, VR-BGT Ditco Air/Sheikh El Khereiji 5/78, VR-BGT Ditco Air Ltd/Sheikh El Khereiji, Saudi Arabia.
212	1977.	N807GA Grumman Corp /77, N551MD Tiger Oil Co-Mike Davis 7/78, Chrysler Corp 1/85, N807CC 10/85,CIT Leasing Corp 8/90, N807CC Chrysler Corp. Ypsilanti, Mi.
213	1977.	N1707Z Pennzoil Co 2/78, Richland Development Corp 3/87,N1707Z Richland Development Corp. Houston, Tx.
214	1978.	N17582 Grumman Corp /78, G-BSAL Shell Aircraft Ltd 7/78, A4O-HA Government of Oman 4/84, A4O-HA Sultan H.M. Qaboos bin Said, Seeb. (r/c Oman 4).
215	1978.	N816GA Grumman Corp /78, N748MN Merle Norman Cosmetics Inc 1/78,N748MN Merle Norman Cosmetics Inc. Los Angeles, Ca.
216	1978.	HB-IEZ Sit Set AG/Aeroleasing/Intermaritime Service /78, N63SD Luna Films 6/78, Pan Eastern Corp 11/78, N200RG Reliance Group Inc 4/79, HZ-ND1 NADCO 11/82,HZ-ND1 NADCO=National Development Co. Dhahran.
217	1978.	N88GA Armour & Co 2/78, N88GA to G-4 1085,Guardian Inds Corp 5/89,N81728 6/89, N880WD 8/89, N880WD Guardian Industries Corp. Northville, Mi.
218	1978.	TU-VAC Government of Ivory Coast-Abidjan 8/78, N218GA GAC 12/87, Travel 17325 Inc 2/88, N187PH 5/88, N187PH Travel 17325 Inc. Wilmington, De.
219	1978.	N84V El Paso Natural Gas Co 11/78, VR-BJD Transworld Oil/Joc Oil 8/79, No 20 2B cvtd 17 Feb 84, N307AF Limited Enterprises 5 Jun 88, Marion Laboratories Inc 3/89, N923ML 5/89, N923ML Marion Laboratories Inc. Kansas City, Mo.
220	1978.	N805GA Grumman Corp /78, N404M Martin Marietta Corp 5/79, N404M to G-3 404, N307M 10/83, N405MM 2/87, N405MM Martin Marietta Corp. Bethesda, Md.
221	1978.	N575SF Standard Oil Co 5/78, Chevron Corp 8/84, N575SF Chevron Corp. San Francisco, Ca.
222	1978.	N817GA Grumman Corp /78, N5253A CBS Inc 6/78, Kiluna Avn Inc 1/86, N5253A Kiluna Aviation/CBS Inc. NYC.
223	1978.	N510US U S Gypsum Corp 6/78, USG Corp 5/85, The Windsong Corp 11/88, N510US The Windsong Corp. Mt Kisco, NY.
224	1978.	N17584 Grumman Corp /78, N810GA /78, Stauffer Chemical Co 10/78, N631SC 11/85, N90CP Chesebrough Ponds Inc/Hudson Finance Inc 8/85, N90CP Chesebrough Ponds Inc/Hudson Finance Inc. NYC.
225	1978.	N17585 Grumman Corp /78, G-BGLT The Marconi Co 5/79, N55922 Crawford Fitting Co 2/80, N289K 3/80, N289K Crawford Fitting Co. Cleveland, Oh.
226	1978.	N1902P J C Penney Co 8/78, N1902P J C Penney Co. Dallas, Tx.
227	1978.	N818GA Grumman Corp /78, N1841D Dun & Bradstreet Corp 8/78, N1841D to G-3 438, N1841L 4/85, GAC 7/85, N1BX Baxter/Delaware Bay Transport Inc 8/85, N1BX Baxter/Delaware Bay Transport Inc 8/85, Travenol Laboratories Inc 7/86, Baxter Healthcare Corp 6/88, N18XX Limited Stores/Northern Holding Corp 8/89, N200LS 9/89, N200LS Limited Stores/Northern Holding Corp. Columbus, Oh.
228	1978.	N819GA United Brands/Air Services Transportation Co 11/78, (N700CQ) /79, (N30B) rsvd 23 Sep 79, United Brands/Air Services Transportation Co. NYC.
229	1978.	N821GA Grumman Corp /78, N702H Sears Roebuck 2/79, N117FJ First Jersey Securities Inc 3/85, CIT Group/Equip Financing-NJ 2/87, CIT Leasing-NYC 12/89, PAB Aviation Inc-NYC 6/90, N117FJ PAB Aviation/First Jersey Securities Inc. NYC.
230	1978.	N17586 Grumman Corp /78, 7T-VHB MoD/Government of Algeria 7/79, 7T-VHB W/O W/o 3 May 82. 03/MAY/82
231	1978.	N808GA Grumman Corp /78, N1102 Gould Inc /79, VR-CAG 231 Gulfstream Ltd/NOGA 10/80,VR-BHD Nimex Co Ltd 7/81, N18RN NOGA/Chemco International Leasing 7/81, Unilease No 6 11/81, Ken Looney-HOU Trustee 9/83,Marflite Ltd 11/87, GAC 2/88, N205K Eastman Kodak Co 8/88, Orchard Funding Inc 6/90, N47EC Eastman Chemical Co rsvd 14 Nov 90, N47EC Eastman Chemical Co. Kingsport, Tn.
232	1978.	N806GA Grumman Corp /78, C-GDPB Dome Petroleum Ltd /79, N71WS Western Preferred Service Corp 1/84, EFA Leasing Co 6/84, N508T Tenneco Inc 10/85, Tennessee Gas Pipeline Co 7/88, N508T Tennessee Gas Pipeline Co. Houston, Tx.
233	1978.	N807GA Grumman Corp /78, Security Pacific National Bank 11/78, N320TR Triangle Industries 7/85, Trian Holdings Inc 9/88, Triangle Aircraft Svcs 2/89, Straight Arrow Publishers 8/89, N233RS 8/90,N233RS Straight Arrow Publishers Inc. NYC.

c/n	
234	1978. N808GA Grumman Corp /78, N910S Standard Oil Realty Co 12/78, AMOCO Properties Inc 4/85, AMOCO Corp 4/89, N910S AMOCO Corp. Chicago, Il.
235	1979. N17581 Grumman Corp /79, G-HADI Arab Express Aviation Ltd/Al Tajit Bank 7/79, N5519C Aircraft Services Corp-Il 12/85, Forum Group 5/86, N16FG 6/86, MAPCO Inc 7/89, N256M 10/89, N256M MAPCO Inc. Tulsa, Ok.
236	1979. N812GA Grumman Corp /79, N2998 General Foods Corp 1/79, Philip Morris Management Corp 7/87, N630PM 10/87, N630PM Philip Morris Management Corp. Richmond, Va.
237	1979. N816GA Grumman Corp /79, N25BH Riley Stoker Corp 7/79, U S Filter Corp 12/81, XA-MIX Aerolineas Ejecutivas 2/82, No 43 2B cvtd Oct 87, XA-BAL 1/88, Aerovics SA /90, XA-BAL Aerovics SA. Mexico City.
238	1979. N831GA Grumman Corp /79, N335H Halliburton Services 7/79, N335H Halliburton Co. Dallas, Tx.
239	1979. N17582 Grumman Corp /79, HZ-AFK Saudia Special Flight Svcs 1/80, HZ-AFK Saudia Special Flight Services, Jeddah.
240	1979. 5A-DDR Government of Libya-Tripoli 12/79, 5A-DDR Government of Libya, Tripoli.
241	1979. N830GA Grumman Corp /79, (N60TA) TigerAir Inc /79, (N801GA) Grumman Corp /80,N90MD J Ray McDermott & Co 1/80, McDermott Inc 1/83, N90MD McDermott Inc. New Orleans, La.
242	1979. 5A-DDS Government of Libya-Tripoli 1/80, 5A-DDS Government of Libya, Tripoli.
243	1979. N119R R J Reynolds Tobacco Co 12/79, RJR NABISCO Inc 10/86, N119RC 2/89, Eastman Kodak Co 4/89, N46TE 5/89, Cx USA 6/90, N46TE W/O w/o 19 Jan 90. 19/JAN/90 landing in fog, 5 pax, 2 crew k.
244	1979. N17584 Grumman Corp /79, 9K-AEB Government of Kuwait 1/80, N500T Tenneco Inc 5/85, N509T 10/85, Tennessee Gas Pipeline Co 7/88, N509T Tennessee Gas Pipeline Co. Houston, Tx.
245	1979. N829GA Grumman Corp /79, James Bath & Assoc 8/79, Emirates Air Service-UAE 2/80,Gulf States Toyota Inc 10/83, N141GS 2/84, No 30 2B cvtd 10 Jan 85, Diamond Interantional 11/86, N871D 1/87, N871D Diamond International Aviation Corp. Ronkonkoma, NY.
246	1979. N17587 Grumman Corp /79, HB-IEZ Sit Set AG-Geneva 11/79, N14LT Max Power 5/86,Lorimar-Telepictures Charter 6/86, SME Aircraft Leasing Co 11/88, N14LT SME Aircraft Leasing Co. Raleigh, NC.
247	1979. N828GA Grumman Corp /79, N888MC View Top Corp 8/79, C-GTEP Tele Direct & Bell Canada Intl/Ashbon Assoc-Saudi 9/81, N73MG MG75 Inc 6/89, N75MG 11/89, N75MG MG-75 Inc. Troy, Mi.
248	1979. N17589 Grumman Corp /79, 9K-AEC Government of Kuwait 3/80, N501T Tenneco Inc 5/85,N510T 10/85,Tennessee Gas Pipeline Co 7/88, N510T Tennessee Gas Pipeline Co. Houston, Tx.
249	1979. N300 GAC G-3 conversion roll out 21 Sep 79, N901GA Ff 2 Dec 79, F-249 Royal Danish Air Force 4/82, F-249 RDAF, 721 Squadron, Vaerlose-Copenhagen.
250	1979. N821GA Grumman Corp /79, N309EL Eli Lilly International Corp 11/79, N309EL Eli Lilly & Co. Indianapolis, In.
251	1979. N944H Honeywell Inc 10/79, N944H to 650-0083, Procter & Gamble Co 3/86, N9PG 4/86, N9PG Procter & Gamble Co. Hangar 4, Lunken Airport, Oh.
252	1979. (N777SL) GAC 11/80, N17582 11/80, (N301GA) /81, XA-MEY Aviones ARE SA /81, XA-MEY Manuel Espinosa Yglesias/Aviones ARE SA. Mexico City.
253	1979. N15TG Texas Gas Transmission 11/79, CONOCO Inc 2/86, N154C 5/86,N154C CONOCO Inc. Allegheny County Airport, Pa.
254	1979. N254AR ARCO-Dallas 12/79, ARCO-Anchorage 1/82, No 41 2B cvtd Sep 86, N254AR ARCO, Dallas, Tx.
255	1979. N442A ARMCO Steel Inc 1/80, No 18 2B cvtd 9 Nov 83, Rockwell International Corp 2/84, N4NR 3/84, N4NR Rockwell International Corp. Pittsburgh, Pa.
256	1979. N17581 Grumman Corp /79, HZ-MSD Saudi Armed Forces Medical Services 9/80,HZ-MSD Saudi Armed Forces Medical Services, Riyadh.
257	1979. N822GA Grumman Corp /79, IT&T Corp 1/80, N872E 6/81, No 17 2B cvtd 17 Oct 83, Wrigley Enterprises Inc 1/88, N411WW 6/88, Zeno Air Inc 9/88, N411WW Zeno Air Inc/Wrigley Enterprises Inc. Chicago, Il.
258	1979. N823GA Grumman Corp /79, N301EC Household Finance Corp 1/80, N301EC Household International, Wheeling, Il.
300	1980. N300GA Alexander Dawson Inc 3/81, Bristol-Myers Co 4/82, GAC 4/89, N300GA Gulfstream Aerospace Corp. Savannah, Ga.
301	1980. N100P National Distillers Corp 10/80, Shearson-Lehman Bros 11/86, N21NY GFI Air/World Jet Corp 4/87, (N100P) rsvd 13 Aug 87, Banner Aircraft Resales 7/89, N110BR 10/89, N110BR Banner Aircraft Resales Inc. Cleveland, Oh.
302	1980. N302GA GAC /80, N62GG Superior Oil Co 6/80, N2610 MASCO 2/85, Newsflight Inc via Jack Prewitt 8/85,N56L 11/85, N56L Newsflight Inc. NYC.
303	1980. N303GA GAC /80, N303GA 6/80, TU-VAF Government of Ivory Coast /81, accident Dakar-Senegal 1/88, N1761W GAC 25 Mar 88, wings of G2B s/n 104 used in repair, N303GA 11/89, Airbourne Charter Inc 3/90, N303GA Airbourne Charter Inc. Burbank, Ca.

Page 164

c/n	
304	1980. N17583 GAC /80, HZ-NR2 Rashid Engineering-Riyadh 6/81, N600YY Page Avjet Corp 9/87, Aircraft Financial Services Inc 12/87, N768J 3/88, N768J Aircraft Financial Services Inc. Miami, Fl.
305	1980. N305GA GAC /80, N235U Combustion Engineering Co 8/80, Mike Donahoe Avn Co 7/90, N305MD 10/90, N682FM Freeport McMoRan Inc 11/90, N682FM Freeport McMoRan Inc. New Orleans, La.
306	1980. N306GA GAC /80, N777SW Seagram's Whiskey 8/80, N777SW to G-4 1014, N72RK Reebok Aviation Inc 4/87, Reebok Intl Inc 5/90, N72RK Reebok International Inc. Stoughton, Ma.
307	1980. N17584 GAC /80, C-GSBR Denison Mines Ltd 7/81, 750423 Ontario Inc 10 Mar 88, C-GSBR Steven Roman/Denison Mines Ltd. Toronto.
308	1980. N717A ARAMCO 10/80, Cloud Dancer Co 6/89, N606PT 9/89, Mar Flite Ltd Corp 9/90, N606PT Mar Flite Ltd Corp. Portland, Or.
309	1980. N18LB ACSC/Lindner Bros/United Dairy Farmers Lsg 10/80, GAC 12/88, Chrysler Asset Management Corp 1/89, NASA-Washington 10/89, N1NA 1/90, N1NA NASA, Washington, DC.
310	1980. N719A ARAMCO 10/80, ARAMCO Associated Co 12/81, C-FYAG Execaire Aviation-Montreal 1/90, N6513X J Prewitt-Tx 9/90, Louisiana Pacific Corp 9/90,N373LP 10/90,N373LP Louisiana Pacific Corp. Hillsboro, Or.
311	1980. N17585 GAC /80, HZ-AFL Saudia Special Flight Services 5/81,HZ-AFL Saudia Special Flight Services, Jeddah.
312	1980. N304GA GAC /80, Gannett Inc 12/80, N100GN 4/81, N100GN to G-4 1007, N200GN 7/87, N200GN Gannett Inc. Arlington, Va.
313	1980. F-313 Royal Danish Air Force 4/82, F-313 RDAF, 721 Squadron, Vaerlose-Copenhagen.
314	1980. N1040 Cox Enterprises Inc 1/81, N1540 5/88, Windareen Corp 2/89, Cox Aviation Inc 12/89,N1540 Cox Aviation Inc. Honolulu, Hi.
315	1980. N315GA GAC /80, Mobil Corp-NYC 1/81, N2600 11/81, N2600 Mobil Corp. Washington, DC.
316	1980. N316GA GAC /80, Mobil Corp 1/81, N2601 2/82, N2601 Mobil Corp. Washington, DC.
317	1980. C-GKRL Kaiser Resources Ltd 9/81, N344GA GAC 7/82, A6-CKZ Government of UAE-Dubai 10/82, A6-CKZ Government of Dubai, UAE.
318	1980. N308GA GAC /80, Triangle Publications Inc 1/81, N300L 7/81, GAC 8/87, N300L to G-4 1018, (N300LF) rsvd 19 Sep 87, (XA-...) sale to Mexico ntu 1/88, N70050 Unitex Electronics Inc 6/88, Glaxo Inc 1/89, N150GX 2/89, Glaxo Aviation Inc 9/90, GAC 12/90, N150GX Gulfstream Aerospace Corp. Savannah, Ga.
319	1980. N319Z Dana Corp 8/81, Swanton Air One Inc 1/90, N319Z Dana Corp. Toledo, Oh.
320	1981. N873E IT&T Corp 4/81, Interfly Inc 3/88, N69FF 11/88, Lease Plan USA Inc 2/89,N69FF Lease Plan USA Inc. Atlanta, Ga.
321	1981. N3ORP RCA/CIT Corp 4/81, RCA/Wilmington Trust Co 2/82, Grabill Corp/Park Kenilworth Industries 6/87, N94GC 9/87, GAC 1/89, N321GA 3/89, Glaxo Inc 4/89, N100GX 6/89,N100GX Glaxo Aviation Inc. Raleigh, NC.
322	1981. N130A American Can Co 5/81, Primerica Inc 8/87, AREPO Corp 8/88, N110LE 3/89, N110EE rsvd 29 Oct 90, N110EE Time Inc/AREPO Corp. Westchester County Airport, NY.
323	1981. XA-MIC Aviones Televisa/Jet Ejecutivos S.A. /81, XA-MIC Aviones Televisa/Jet Ejecutivos SA. Mexico City.
324	1981. HZ-AFM Saudia Special Flight Services 10/81, HZ-AFM Saudia Special Flight Services, Jeddah.
325	1981. N890A ALCOA-Pittsburgh 3/82, N890A to BAe 125 8071, N890A 1/87, GAC 4/87, N393U Unisys Corp 5/87, GECC-Plymouth Meeting-Pa 1/90, N393U Unisys Corp. Mercer County Airport, Trenton, NJ.
326	1981. N17582 GAC /81, TR-KHC Government of Gabon 2/82, TR-KHC Government of Gabon, Libreville.
327	1981. N70PS American International Aviation Co 9/81, (N72PS) rsvd 6 Jul 87,Security Pacific Eurofinance 3/88, N57BJ 7/88, N57BJ TEA Executive Jet Services, Melsbroek, Belgium.
328	1981. N309GA GAC /81, General Transportation Corp 8/81, N75RP 2/82, N75RP to G-4 1073, N78RP 7/88, N78RP General Transportation Corp. NYC.
329	1981. N301GA GAC 8/81, General Dynamics Co 11/81, N862G 3/82, N862G General Dynamics Corp. St.Louis, Mo.
330	1981. F-330 Royal Danish Air Force 4/82, F-330 RDAF, 721 Squadron, Vaerlose-Copenhagen.
331	1981. N307GA GAC /81, Great American Insurance Co 10/81, N17LB 11/81, HZ-RC3 Royal Commission for Jubail & Yanbu 8/82, HZ-RC3 Royal Commission for Jubail & Yanbu, Riyadh.
332	1981. N310GA GAC /81, Texasgulf Aviation Inc 11/81, N77TG 3/82, Beatrice Worldwide Inc 6/84,N300BE 7/84, N65BE 9/86, Beatrice Companies Inc 10/86,RIM Air 2/89,N121JM 4/89, N121JM RIM Air, San Francisco, Ca.
333	1981. N600PM Philip Morris Inc 11/81, N600PM Philip Morris Management Corp. White Plains, NY.
334	1981. N1PG Procter & Gamble Co 11/81, N1PG Procter & Gamble Co. Cincinnati, Oh.
335	1981. HB-IMX Bruce Rappaport/Sit Set AG/Jet Aviation-Geneva 5/82, Bright Star Establishment-Vaduz 13 Sep 89, HB-IMX JABJ/Bright Star Estab. Vaduz.
336	1981. N3PG Procter & Gamble Co 11/81, N3PG Procter & Gamble Co. Cincinnati, Oh.
337	1981. N456SW Sentry Corp 11/81, Sentry Insurance-A Mutual Co 1/89, N456SW Sentry Insurance-A Mutual Co. Stevens Point, Wi.
338	1981. N862GA GAC /81, N372CM Cordelia Scaife May 8/82, N372CM to G-4 1049, N372GM 5/88, Hewlett Packard Co 2/89, N87HP 3/89, N87HP Hewlett Packard Co. San Jose, Ca.
339	1981. N302GA GAC /81, Bank of America 7/82, N522SB 10/82, N339A 6/90, N339A Bank of America, Oakland
340	1982. (F-WDHK) pre-delivery registration /81, F-GDHK HRH Prince Karim Aga Khan-Paris 23 Jul 82,N99WJ GAC 1/89, JP Aviation Inc 3/89,N99WJ to G-4 1139,N90WJ 7/90, N90WJ JP Aviation Inc. Charlotte, NC.

341	1981. N263C CONOCO Inc 12/81, E I Dupont de Nemours & Co 2/89,N263C E I Dupont de Nemours & Co. Houston, Tx.
342	1981. N441A ARMCO Steel Inc 2/82, Omni 12/84, B-N Leasing 1/85, N91LJ 8/86, Republic Airfinance 11/85, AMF Inc 12/85, Prudential Insurance Co of America 9/87, N82A 5/88, N82A Prudential Insurance Co of America, Newark, NJ.
343	1981. N305GA GAC /81, Phillips Petroleum Co 3/82, N664P 7/82, rpo F20-95, N664S 4/86, Abbott Aircraft 8/86, N400AL 11/86, Mardenaire/Admerex Inc 11/89, N221CM rsvd 15 Nov 89, N221CM Admerex Inc/Mardenaire Inc. NYC.
344	1981. N306GA GAC /81, Cargill Inc 4/82, N7000C 10/82, N7000C Cargill Inc. Minneapolis, Mn.
345	1982. N17585 GAC /82, G-BSAN Shell Aviation Ltd 12/82, VR-CCN Smith-Kline-Beecham 4/90,VR-CCN K Jet Ltd. London-Heathrow.
346	1982. N17581 GAC /82, HZ-RH2 Saudi Oger Ltd 9/82, HZ-HR2 /? HZ-HR2 Saudi Oger Ltd. Riyadh.
347	1982. N17583 GAC /82, VR-BJE Transworld Oil 1/83, VR-BJE Transworld Oil America Inc. Newark, NJ.
348	1982. N756S Shell Aviation Corp 6/82, N756S Shell Aviation Corp. Houston, Tx.
349	1982. N89AE National Express Co 7/82, N89AB Nike Inc 10/90, N89AB Nike Inc. Beaverton, Or.
350	1982. N317GA GAC /82, Amerada Hess Corp 7/82, N1454H 11/82, N1454H Amerada Hess Corp. NYC.
351	1982. N888MC View Top Corp 'Pia's Jet/Here Comes Pia' 9/82, Ltd Enterprises Inc 7/88, N308AF 2/89, Ropa Two Corp 3/89, N836MF 5/89,Waverly Avn Ltd 10/90, N836MF 5/89, Waverly Aviation Ltd 10/90, N18TM rsvd 8 Nov 90, N18TM Waverly Aviation Ltd. Teterboro, NJ.
352	1982. N17586 GAC /82, HB-ITM Lonrho/Lonair SA-Lausanna 1/83, XC-UJN/TP-06 Government of Mexico 4/90, XC-UJN TP-06, Government of Mexico, Mexico City.
353	1982. N26619 Noranda Exploration Inc 12/82, HZ-BSA Prince Bandar-Saudi Arabia 1/83, HZ-108 12/83, HZ-108 RESA=Royal Embassy of Saudi Arabia, Riyadh.
354	1982. 3D-AAC Anglo American Co/Peak Timber Sales P/L 5/83,3D-AAC Peak Timber Sales (Pty)Ltd. Piggs Peak.
355	1982. N318GA GAC /82, N676RW Coca Cola Co 8/82, N676RW Coca Cola Co. Atlanta, Ga.
356	1982. A6-HEH Government of UAE 6/83, A6-HEH Government of Dubai, UAE.
357	1982. N303GA GAC 11/82, National Intergroup Inc/FSB of Utah 2/83, N340 6/85, Grumman Corp 1/88, N802GA 3/88, G 3 Charter Corp 3/90, N802GA G 3 Charter Corp. Burbank, Ca.
358	1982. N1761B GAC /82, HZ-DA1 Dallah AVCO 3/83, N9711N Dunavant Enterprises Inc 10/86, N200DE 2/87,N200DE Dunavant Enterprises Inc. Memphis, Tn.
359	1982. N800J Johnson & Johnson 7/82, N800J Johnson & Johnson, West Trenton, NJ.
360	1982. N341GA GAC /82, Potomac Leasing Co/Lockheed-California Co 2/83, N9OLC 5/83, Dana Commercial Credit 10/87,CCD Air Fifteen Inc 1/90, N9OLC Lockheed-California Co. Burbank, Ca.
361	1982. (N875E) /82, N874RA I T & T Corp 8/82,Anadarko Petroleum Corp 10/89, N874RA Anadarko Petroleum Corp. Houston, Tx.
362	1982. N408M Fluor Corp 8/82, Riggs National Bank 6/85, N800AR 9/85, N800AR Riggs National Bank, Washington National, DC.
363	1982. N83AL Allegheny International Inc 12/82,The Henley Group Inc 6/86, Henley Mfg Holding Corp 2/88, FAK Services Inc 6/88, N77FK 8/88, K Services Inc 9/90, N77FK K Services Inc. NYC.
364	1982. N1761D GAC /82, HZ-AFN Saudia Special Flight Services 4/83, HZ-AFN Saudia Special Flight Services, Jeddah.
365	1982. N1761J GAC /82, HZ-AFO Saudia Special Flight Services 4/83, CN-ANU Government of Morocco 1/89, CN-ANU Government of Morocco, Rabat.
366	1982. N2SP Southern Pacific Co 7/83, N9OSF 1/90, SFP Properties 2/90, N9OSF SFP Properties Inc. Chicago, Il.
367	1982. (N910A) Standard Oil Realty Corp /82, re-allocated to s/n 369, N17588 GAC /83, HB-ITN/Interjet AG/Private Jet Services 4/83, HB-ITN Helmut Horten/Interjet AG/Private Jet Services, Basle.
368	1983. N17589 GAC /83, 7T-VRB MoD/Government of Algeria 19 Jul 83, 7T-VRB Ministry of Defence, Boufarik.
369	1982. N910A Standard Oil Realty Corp 1/83, AMOCO Properties Inc 4/85, AMOCO Corp 4/89, N910A AMOCO Corp. Chicago, Il.
370	1982. N319GA GAC /82, Exxon Corp 12/82, N100A 7/83, N100A to G-4 1072, N200A 1/89, N400K 10/90, N400K Exxon Corp. Dallas, Tx.
371	1983. HZ-NR3 Rashid Engineering 7/83, N680FM Freeport McMoRan Inc 6/89, (N8220F) rsvd 30 Jun 89, N681FM 7/89, N681FM Freeport McMoRan Inc. New Orleans, La.
372	1982. N320GA GAC /82, Exxon Corp 11/82, N200A 6/83, N200A to G-3 370, N500E 12/88, N500E Exxon Corp. Dallas, Tx.
373	1983. N340GA GAC /83, G 1 Aviation Inc 2/83, N232HC 6/83, N232HC G 1 Aviation Inc. Tampa, Fl.
374	1983. N339GA GAC /83, Dow Jones & Co 3/83, N122DJ 12/83,VR-CMF Mohammed Fakhry/M S F Aviation 13 Jun 88, VR-CMF Mohammed Fakhry/M S F Aviation, Luton-UK.
375	1983. N955CP Colgate Palmolive Co 3/83, VR-BOB Robert Maxwell/VIP Avn (Bermuda) 10/88, VR-BOB to G-4 1120, N375NM GAC 3/90, Arizona Executive Air Service 5/90,N375NM Arizona Executive Air Service, Burbank, Ca.
376	1983. N17582 GAC /83, A6-HHS Government of Abu Dhabi 10/83, A6-HHS Government of Abu Dhabi, UAE.

c/n	
377	1983. N342GA GAC /83, Chase Manhattan Bank 3/83, N4OCH 11/83, N4OCH Wayfarer Ketch/Chase Manhattan Bank, NYC.
378	1983. N343GA GAC /83, Honeywell Inc 3/83, N955H 6/83, Hardesty Co/United States Avn Co 5/87,N378HC 7/88, N378HC Hardesty Co/United States Aviation Co. Tulsa, Ok.
379	1983. N17586 GAC /83, HZ-MAL Dallah AVCO/Marawid Ltd/Saudi Intl Trading 10/83,HZ-MAL Dallah AVCO/Mawarid Ltd/Saudi International Trading Estab.
380	1983. N345GA GAC /83, N159B Carter Hawley Hale Stores 8/83, Merrill Lynch Leasing Inc 10/83, ILI Leasing Aircraft 12/86, N159B Carter Hawley Hale Stores, Los Angeles, Ca.
381	1983. N304GA GAC /83, Norton Simon Properties Inc 4/83, N277NS 7/83, rpo BAC 1-11 057,National Gypsum Co 1/85, N747G 4/85, Ingersoll-Rand Services Co 4/89, N1871R 7/89, N1871R Ingersoll-Rand Services Co. Woodcliff Lake, NJ.
382	1983. N305GA GAC /83, 83-0500 USAF Andrews AFB 9/83, USAF Ramstein 5/87, 83-0500 C-20A, USAF, 58 MAS, Ramstein AB. West Germany.
383	1983. N308GA GAC /83, 83-0501 USAF Andrews AFB 9/83, USAF Ramstein 5/87, 83-0501 C-20A, USAF, 58 MAS, Ramstein AB. West Germany.
384	1983. N1982C GAC /83, EAF/Citiflight Inc 6/83, N399WW 1/89, Canadair Challenger Inc 12/90, N399WW Canadair Challenger inc. Windsor, Ct.
385	1983. N1761K GAC /83, HZ-MS3 Saudi Armed Forces Medical Services 7/84, HZ-MS3 Saudi Armed Forces Medical Services, Riyadh.
386	1983. N316GA GAC /83, Westinghouse Transport Leasing Co 6/83, N902K 9/83, N902KB 1/90, XC-UJO/TP-07 Government of Mexico 7/90, XC-UJO TP-07, Government of Mexico, Mexico City.
387	1983. N26L Square D Co 4/83, Airstar Corp 3/90, N621JH 4/90, N621JH Airstar Corp. Salt Lake City, Ut.
388	1983. N309GA GAC /83, Sears Roebuck & Co 11/83, N902C 1/84, N1C 1/89, N1C Sears Roebuck & Co. Chicago
389	N310GA GAC /83, 83-0502 USAF Andrews AFB 9/83, USAF Ramstein 5/87, 83-0502 C-20A, USAF, 58 MAS, Ramstein AB. West Germany.
390	1983. N200SF Santa Fe Air Transport 8/83,Bancorp Leasing&Financial 12/83, VR-BKS JABJ/Jameel SAM-Monte Carlo 10/88, VR-BKS JABJ/Jameel SAM, Monte Carlo.
391	1983. N349GA GAC /83, Sun Refining & Marketing Co 7/83, N29S Sun Co Inc 9/83, N1S 9/87, N1S Sun Co Inc. Dallas, Tx.
392	1983. N30AH American Aviation Inc 5/83, American Hospital Supply 7/83, Baxter Travenol Avn 11/87, N6BX Baxter Healthcare Corp 2/88, N6BX Baxter Healthcare Corp. Waukegan, Il.
393	1983. N17587 GAC /83, A9C-BB Government of Bahrain 12/83, A9C-BB Government of Bahrain.
394	1983. N1761P GAC /83, N311GA 9/83, N379XX Nexxus Products Co 12/83, N379XX Nexxus Products Inc. Santa Barbara, Ca. 'Jheri Reading'
395	1983. N1761Q GAC /83, PK-PJA Pertamina Oil-Jakarta /83, N30GL EDS Administration 1/88, N30GL E D S Administration Corp. Dallas, Tx.
396	1983. N1761S GAC /83, 7T-VRC MoD/Government of Algeria 19 Aug 84, 7T-VRC Ministry of Defence, Boufarik.
397	1983. N351GA GAC /83, RTS Helicopter Service Corp 9/83,N59HA Hughes Aircraft Co/Top Spin Data Corp 1/84, N978FL 10/89, N978FL Hughes Aircraft Co/Top Spin Data Corp. NYC.
398	1983. N315GA GAC /83, American Express Co 10/83, N88AE 1/84,lease PPG Industries Inc 11/90-12/90, N88AE American Express Co. Stewart International Airport, NY.
399	1983. N17581 GAC /83, 7T-VRD MoD/Government of Algeria 19 Aug 84, 7T-VRD Ministry of Defence, Boufarik.
400	1983. N17585 GAC /83, O005 MoD/Government of Venezuela /84, O005 FAV, MoD, Caracas.
401	1983. N352GA GAC /83, Allied Stores Corp 11/83, N717 3/84, GECC-Oak Brook 11/90, De Luxe Flight Operations 11/90, N400LH rsvd 16 Nov 90, N400LH De Luxe Flight Operations, Minneapolis, Mn.
402	1983. N301GA GAC /83, Govt of Brunei/MPH Associates 3/84, N303HB 10/84, Arthur Ortenburg/Malt Aire Inc 8/87, Bucephalus Enterprises Inc 2/88, N3338 5/88, JTF 12/90, VR-BLN Pegasus Aviation Ltd 12/90, VR-BLN Pegasus Aviation Ltd. Hamilton.
403	1983. N347GA GAC /83, E F Gulf Inc 11/83, N39NA 2/84, Union Carbide Corp 3/84, N39N 7/84, N39N Union Carbide Corp. NYC.
404	1983. N355GA GAC /83, Martin Marietta Corp 12/83, N404M 4/84, rpo G-2 220, N404MM 12/85, N404MM Martin Marietta Corp. Bethesda, Md.
405	1983. N348GA GAC /83, E F Gulf Inc 12/83, N40NB 2/84, Union Carbide Corp 5/84, N40N 10/84,N91CH ICH Corp 3/87, Facilities Management Installation 5/90, N91CR rsvd 28 Aug 90, N91CR Facilities Management Installation, Louisville, Ky.
406	1983. N356GA GAC /83, U.S. Steel Corp 12/83, N8OL 3/84, USX Corp 6/87, N8OL USX Corp. Pittsburgh, Pa.
407	1984. N17603 GAC /83, G-XMAF Fayair (Jersey) Ltd 11/84, G-XMAF Fayair (Jersey) Ltd. C.I.
408	1983. 9K-AEG Kuwait Airways/Government of Kuwait 6/84, 9K-AEG Kuwait Airways Corp.
409	1983. N353GA GAC /83, N300BK Sunkist Services Co 8/84, GAC 5/85, N320GA 6/85, Warner-Lambert Co 5/86, N1526M 6/86, N1526R 4/90, Stevens Express Leasing Inc 10/90, N1526R Stevens Express Leasing Inc. Washington, DC.
410	1983. N350GA GAC /83, Jim Bath-Tx 1/84, HZ-AFR Saudia Special Flight Services-Jeddah 7/84, HZ-AFR Saudia Special Flight Services, Jeddah.

411	1983. N314GA GAC /83, Honeywell Inc 2/84, N966H 6/84, Deeside Trading Co 2/90, N461GT rsvd 9 Feb 90, N461GT Airmont Ltd. Sparks, Nv.
412	1983. N354GA GAC /83, Occidental Exploration & Producing Co 1/84, N2OXY 3/84,Occidental Intl Exploration 2/85,N2OXY to G-4 1080, N5OXY 5/89, N5OXY Occidental International Exploration, Bakersfield, Ca.
413	1983. N357GA GAC /83, Joseph E Seagram & Sons Inc 1/84, N77SW 2/84, N77SW to G-4 1023, N778SW 12/87, N1 FAA 8/88, GAC 10/88, Metlife Capital Credit 11/88, N8226M GAC 5/89, 249 Irish Air Corp 4 Jan 90, 249 Irish Air Corps. Casement-Dublin.
414	1983. N358GA GAC /83, Southeast Toyota Distributors 3/84, N165ST 4/84, GAC 8/88, Himont Strategic Services Inc 12/88, N165G 2/89, N165G Himont Strategic Services Inc. Wilmington, De.
415	1984. N17582 GAC /84, Saudi Oger Ltd 12/84, HZ-HR4 6/85, HZ-HR4 Saudi Oger Ltd. Riyadh.
416	1984. N312GA GAC /84, AL Transportation Inc 5/84, N500AL 2/85, Abbott Laboratories 4/85, N500AL Abbott Laboratories, Abbott Park, Il.
417	1984. N317GA GAC /84, Ambassador College/Worldwide Church of God 4/84, N111AC 8/84, N111AC to BAC 1-11 111, N1119C GAC 1/89, N300M Jet Fly Corp 2/89,Transair Leasing Inc 8/90, N300M Transair Leasing Inc. Dover, De.
418	1984. N17583 GAC /84, JY-ABL Arab Bank Ltd/Alia/Government of Jordan 9/85, JY-AMN 10/85, N717TR Triangle Aircraft Services 12/86, N717TR Triangle Aircraft Services Co. NYC.
419	1984. 9K-AEH Kuwait Airways/Government of Kuwait 7/84, 9K-AEH Kuwait Airways Corp.
420	1984. N333GA GAC SRA-1 ff 14 Aug 84, N47449 Farnborough demo 9/84, used 40420 for USAF/GAC PR photos, K2980/VT-ENR Indian Air Force 9/87, K2980 Indian Air Force, (used VT-ENR 9/87),
421	1984. N318GA GAC /84, N99GA Greyhound Armour & Co 3/84, B A Leasing & Capital Corp-SFO 11/89, N99GA Greyhound Armour & Co. Phoenix, Az.
422	1984. N319GA GAC /84, American Cyanamid/Auxiliary Carrier Inc 4/84, N750AC 8/84, N750AC Auxiliary Carrier/American Cyanamid, Teterboro, NJ.
423	1984. N1761D GAC /84, HZ-MIC Mouawad S.A. 11/84, Cx HZ- 3/90, N7134E Chevron Corp 3/90, N225SF 7/90, N225SF Chevron Corp. San Francisco, Ca.
424	1984. N320GA GAC /84, Bendix Corp 5/84, N6OAC Allied Corp 12/84, N228G W R Grace & Co 7/87, N228G W R Grace & Co. Stewart International Airport, NY.
425	1984. N344GA GAC /84, QRZX Leasing Co 5/84, Security Pacific NB 9/84, N425SP 10/84, Citicorp Nevada Credit Inc 9/88, Security Pacific NB 10/89, N425SP Security Pacific National Bank, Los Angeles, Ca.
426	1984. N321GA GAC /84, R H Macy & Co 6/84, N151MZ 11/84, N151MZ R H Macy & Co/Macflight, White Plains 'The Rachel Anne'
427	1984. N327GA GAC /84, N44MD Mike Davis Oil Co 10/84, N44MD to B-727 19318, N42MD 5/88, Casden Co 7/88, N87AC 12/88, N87AC Casden Co. Burbank, Ca.
428	1984. N322GA GAC /84, N760A IBM Corp 12/84, N760A IBM Credit Corp. Dutchess County Airport, NY.
429	1984. N323GA GAC /84, USAA Special Services Co 7/84, N429SA 10/84, N429SA United Services Automobile Association, San Antonio, Tx.
430	1984. N324GA GAC /84, N760C IBM Corp 1/85, N760C IBM Credit Corp. Dutchess County Airport, NY.
431	1984. N25SB U S Tobacco Co 7/84, GAC 3/89, (N259B) rsvd 16 Sep 88, GAC 3/89, Don Love Aircraft Sales 11/89, PK-... Mindo Petroleum Co 8/90, PK-... Indonesia Air Transport/Mindo Petroleum Co. Jakarta.
432	1984. N333GA Gulfstream Aerospace Corp 1/85, N333GA Gulfstream Aerospace Corp. Savannah, Ga.
433	1984. N325GA GAC /84, EAF/Citiflight Inc 8/84, N399CB 3/85, N399CB Citiflight Inc. NYC.
434	1984. N326GA GAC /84, Joan B Kroc/MacDonalds' 10/84, N811JK JBK Co/MacDonalds'12/84, N311JK 5/88, N311JK J Kroc/MacDonalds', Chicago, Il.
435	1985. N17581 GAC /85, HB-ITS Petrolair Systems SA-Athens 14 Feb 85, N435U United Technologies Cortran 5/89, N435U United Technologies Cortran Inc. East Hartford, Ct.
436	1985. N346GA GAC /85, V8-HB3 Government of Brunei 7/85, V8-AL1 4/89, V8-A11 8/89, V8-007 9/89, V8-007 Amadeo Corp, Brunei.
437	1984. N380TT Litton Industries Inc 10/84, N380TT Litton Industries Inc. Beverly Hills, Ca.
438	1984. N302GA GAC /84, Dun & Bradstreet Corp 10/84, N1841D 5/85, N1841D Dun & Bradstreet Corp. NYC.
439	1985. N17586 GAC /85, SU-BGU Government of Egypt del via LBG 10 Apr 85, SU-BGU Egpytian Air Force/Arab Republic of Egypt, Cairo.
440	1984. N304GA GAC /84, General Motors Corp 11/84, N5103 4/85, N5103 General Motors Corp. Detroit, Mi.
441	1984. N306GA GAC /84, U S Steel Corp 11/84, N8OJ 3/85, USX Corp 6/87, N8OJ USX Corp. Pittsburgh, Pa.
442	1985. N17587 GAC /85, SU-BGV Government of Egypt 17 Apr 85, SU-BGV Egyptian Air Force/Arab Republic of Egypt, Cairo.
443	1984. N315GA GAC /84, General Motors Corp 11/84, N5104 5/85, N5104 General Motors Corp. Detroit, Mi.
444	1984. N328GA GAC /84, MTI Aviation Inc 12/84, N110MT 2/85, N110MT MTI Aviation/Morton Thiokol Inc. Wheeling, Il.
445	1984. N316GA GAC /84, (N5103) General Motors Corp 12/84, N5105 4/85, N5105 General Motors Corp. Detroit, Mi.
446	1985. N309GA GAC /85, Unitech Corp 1/85, N446U 5/85, N446U United Technologies Corp. E. Hartford, Ct.
447	1985. N186DS Digi Corp/DSC Communications 22 Jan 85, MDFC Equip Leasing 1/87, Randolph Wright-Mi Trustee 12/87, N186DS DSC Comms/Randolph Wright Trustee, Troy, Mi.

c/n		
448	1984.	N339GA GAC /85, Gavilan Corp/EMC Corp 1/85, N117JJ rsvd 22 May 85, rpo G-2 163, N255SB 4/86,Silvio Berlusconi/Daclama Co Ltd 5/86, I-MADU Soc Alba-Milan 12/86, I-MADU Daclama Co Ltd/Silvio Berlusconi/Soc. Alba, Milan.
449	1985.	N310GA GAC /85, XA-FOU Aviones Televisa/Jet Ejecutivos SA 10/85, XA-FOU Aviones Televisa/Jet Ejecutivos S.A. Mexico City.
450	1985.	N329GA GAC /85, still at SAV 2/89, HZ-AFS Saudia Special Flight Services /89, N329GA GAC 8/90, Gulfstream Aerospace Corp. Savannah, Ga.
451	1985.	N330GA GAC /85, MM62022 Government of Italy del 19 Sep 85, MM62022 AMI, 31 Stormo, Roma-Ciampino.
452	1985.	N331GA GAC /85, RJR-NABISCO Inc 12/86, N27R 3/87, Aviation Methods/Pacent Funding Inc-NYC 6/89, N663P 7/89, N633P Aviation Methods, San Francisco, Ca.
453	1985.	N332GA GAC /85, 103 103 Royal Saudi Air Force BOS 2/85, del 1/86, HZ-103 9/87, HZ-103 Royal Saudi Air Force, Riyadh.
454	1985.	N334GA GAC /85, Continental Telephone 4/85, N6OCT 9/85, Contel Management Co 9/89, N6OCT Continental Telephone, Atlanta, Ga.
455	1985.	N335GA GAC /85, Samuel Fly/Gulf States Toyota Inc 4/85, N1SF 9/85, Transpacific Enterprises Inc 1/89, N103GC 4/89, Ansett Industries Leasing Inc 4/89, N103GC Ansett Industries Leasing Inc. Sun Valley, Id.
456	1985.	N336GA GAC /85, 85-0049 U S Army Andrews AFB /86, 85-0049 C-20C, U. S. Army, 89th MAW,Andrews AFB. Md.
457	1985.	N337GA GAC /85, N457H H J Heinz & Co 25 Apr 85, N457H H J Heinz & Co. Pittsburgh, Pa.
458	1985.	N338GA GAC /85, 85-0050 U S Army Andrews AFB /86, 85-0050 C-20C, U.S. Army, 89th MAW, Andrews AFB. Md.
459	1985.	N321GA GAC /85, Intl Brotherhood of Teamsters 8/85, N600B 12/85,N600B International Brotherhood of Teamsters, Washington, DC.
460	1985.	N322GA GAC /85, Limited Stores/Western Holding Corp 6/85, N500LS 1/86, Aircraft Services Corp-Fl 4/86, N500LS to G-4 1009, N500VS 4/87, Walt Disney Productions 1/88, N500MM 2/88, N500MN rsvd 9 Nov 90, N500MN Walt Disney Productions, Los Angeles, Ca.
461	1985.	N323GA GAC /85, AMCA/Tower Resources Inc 8/85, N104AR 4/86, Pitney Bowes Credit Corp-Ct 5/86, N104AR AMCA/Tower Resources Inc. Louisville, Ky.
462	1985.	N324GA GAC 11/85, N303GA 12/85, PLM Transport Inc 12/85, PLM International Inc 2/88, TU-VAF Government of Ivory Coast 4/88, TU-VAF Government of Ivory Coast, Abidjan.
463	1985.	N327GA GAC /85, Taubman Air Inc 7/85, N8OAT 3/86, N8OAT to G-4 1151, GAC 9/90, N808T rsvd 30 Oct 90, N808T Gulfstream Aerospace Corp. Savannah, Ga.
464	1985.	N340GA GAC /85, Polaris Investment Management Corp 11/85, FSB-Utah 12/85, N535CS Campbell Soup Inc 5/86, N535CS Campbell Soup Inc. New Castle, De.
465	1985.	N17582 GAC /85, 86-0200 USAF Andrews AFB /87, 86-0200 USAF, C-20B, 89th MAW, Andrews AFB. Md.
466	1985.	N325GA GAC /85, N37HE Hercules Engineering Inc 5/86, N37HE Hercules Inc. Wilmington, De.
467	1985.	N341GA GAC /85, JY-HAH Government of Jordan del 23 Dec 86, JY-HAH Government of Jordan, Amman.
468	1985.	N342GA GAC /85, 86-0202 USAF Andrews AFB /87, 86-0202 USAF, C-20B, 89th MAW, Andrews AFB. Md.
469	1985.	N343GA /85, JY-HZH Government of Jordan 2/87, JY-HZH Government of Jordan, Amman.
470	1985.	N344GA /85, 86-0201 USAF Andrews AFB 5/87, 86-0201 USAF, C-20B, 89th MAW, Andrews AFB. Md.
471	1985.	N347GA GAC /85, Wang Laboratories/First NH Resources Inc 11/85, N888WL 1/86, First NH Banks Inc 2/86, E I Dupont de Nemours 1/90, N583D 2/90, N583D E I DuPont de Nemours & Co. New Castle, De.
472	1985.	N348GA GAC /85, Olin Corp/Ct NB 12/85, Chrysler Corp 7/86, N800CC 8/86, Farnborough demo 9/86, N806CC 12/86, N800CC 3/87, N808CC 12/88, N357H H J Heinz & Co 9/89, Chrysler Asset Management 1/90,N357H H J Heinz & Co. Pittsburgh, Pa.
473	1985.	N326GA GAC /85, 86-0403 USAF Andrews AFB /87, 86-0403 USAF, C-20D, 89th MAW, Andrews AFB. Md.
474	1985.	N311GA GAC /85, D2-ECB Govt of Angola/Lineas Aereas de Angola 4/87, D2-ECB LAA/Government of Angola, Luanda.
475	1985.	N312GA GAC /85, 86-0203 USAF Andrews AFB /87, 86-0203 USAF, C-20B, 89th MAW, Andrews AFB. Md.
476	1985.	N314GA GAC /85, 86-0204 USAF Andrews AFB /87, 86-0204 USAF, C-20B, 89th MAW, Andrews AFB. Md.
477	1985.	N317GA GAC /85, 86-0205 USAF Andrews AFB /87, 86-0205 USAF, C-20B, 89th MAW, Andrews AFB. Md.
478	1985.	N318GA GAC /85, 86-0206 USAF Andrews AFB /87, 86-0206 USAF, C-20B, 59th MAW, Andrews AFB. Md.
479	1986.	N319GA GAC /86, MM62025 Government of Italy 12/86, MM62025 AMI, 31 Stormo, Roma-Ciampino.
480	1986.	N302GA GAC /86, 163691 USMC/USN Andrews AFB 5/87, 163691 C-20D, USN, CFSLW, Andrews AFB. Md.
481	1986.	N304GA GAC /86, 163692 USMC/USN Andrews AFB 6/87, 163692 C-20D, USMC/USN, CFSLW, Andrews AFB. Md.
482	1986.	N306GA GAC /86, N333HK 8/86, N600BL Bausch & Lomb 5/88, N600BL Bausch & Lomb. Rochester. NY.
483	1986.	N309GA GAC /86, D-Aire Inc/Duchossois Enterprises 5/86, N66DD 2/87, N66DD Duchossois Enterprises/D-Aire Inc. Advance, NC.
484	1986.	N310GA GAC /86, Upjohn Co 6/86, N4UP 11/86, N4UP to G-4 1088, GAC 3/89, Travelers Corp 5/89, N856W 6/89, N856W Travelers Corp. Windsor Locks, Ct.
485	1986.	N315GA GAC /86, N721CW Caesars World Inc 8/86, N721CW Caesars World Inc. Las Vegas, Nv.
486	1986.	N316GA GAC /86, TJ-AAW Government of Cameroun 7/87, TJ-AAW Government of Cameroun, Yaounde.

c/n	
487	1986. N324GA GAC /86, TC-GAP Government of Turkey 5/87, N377GA GAC 9/87, GECC-Atlanta 10/87,Siebe PLC-UK 11/87, N90005 12/87, N90005 to G-4 1103, Stockwood V Inc 12/89, N488SB 2/90, N488SB Stockwood V Inc. Morristown, NJ.
488	1986. N325GA GAC /86, The Copley Press Inc 11/86, N700CN 7/87, N700CN to G-4 1133, GAC 5/90, (N100BG) rsvd 19 Jun 90, N800BG 9/90, National Medical Enterprises Inc 11/90, N800BG National Medical Enterprises Inc. Santa Monica, Ca.
489	1986. N328GA GAC /86, John Jefferson Smurfit Group-Dublin 28 Jan 87, Pitney Bowes Credit Corp 2/87, N272JS del 26 Jun 87, Harlow Aircraft Inc-Ct 12/88, N272JS John Jefferson Smurfit Group, Dublin.
490	1986. N332GA GAC /86, RJR-NABISCO Inc 10/86, N28R 8/87, Reynolds Air Svcs Inc 12/89,R J Reynolds Tobacco Co 8/90, N28R R J Reynolds Tobacco Co. Winston Salem, NC.
491	1986. N337GA GAC 1/86, General Transportation Corp 11/86, N73RP 2/87, N73RP General Transportation Corp. NYC.
492	1986. N339GA GAC /86, A T & T Resources Management 10/87, N121AT 11/87, N212AT A T & T Resources Management, Morristown, NJ.
493	1986. N322GA GAC /86, N400J Johnson & Johnson 10/87, N400J Johnson & Johnson, West Trenton, NJ.
494	1986. N370GA GAC 12/86, Indian Air Force /90, N370GA Gulfstream Aerospace Corp. Savannah, Ga.
495	1986. N371GA GAC 12/86, Indian Air Force /90, N371GA Gulfstream Aerospace Corp. Savannah, Ga.
496	1986. N372GA GAC /86, N310SL Shearson Lehman Hutton 11/89, N310SL to G-4 1087, N21NY 1/90, National Express Co Inc 4/90, N89AE rsvd 8 Nov 90, N89AE National Express Co Inc. Newburgh, NY.
497	1986. N373GA GAC /86, 87-0139 U S Army Andrews AFB 7/88, 87-0139 C-20E, United States Army.
498	1986. N374GA GAC /86, 87-0140 U S Army Andrews AFB 9/88, 87-0140 C-20E, United States Army.
775	1969. N804GA Grumman Corp demo /69, N13GW Gulf & Western Industries Inc 3/72, No 6 2B cvtd 19 Sep 82, N723J 4/84, N6PC Paramount Pictures Corp 10/89, N6PC Paramount Communications Inc. Van Nuys, Ca.
875	1981. N333GA GAC /81, Gulf United Corp 3/82, N333GU 10/82, Omni Intl 2/86, Del Rayo Racing Stables/City NB 9/86, N210GK 1/87, N290GA GAC 10/90, N290GA Gulfstream Aerospace Corp. Savannah, Ga.
1000	1985. N404GA GAC roll out 11 Sep 85, ff 19 Sep 85, Skybird Avn 12/85, N234DB 7/88, N234DB Skybird Aviation, Van Nuys, Ca.
1001	1986. N17581 GAC 7/86, N441GA Chrysler Financial Corp/Bill Cosby 12/86, Ct NB Trust 6/87, N400GA 2/90, N400GA Chrysler Financial Corp/Bill Cosby, Teterboro, NJ.
1002	1986. N440GA GAC /86, Connecticut National Bank 12/86, N440GA Connecticut National Bank, Hartford, Ct.
1003	1986. N403GA GAC /86, N986AH American Home Products 10/87, G IV Corp 1/88, N685TA 10/88, N685TA G IV Corp/American Home Products,
1004	1986. N424GA GAC /86, Digital Equipment Corp 29 Sep 86, N424GA Digital Equipment Corp. Maynard, Ma.
1005	1986. N17582 GAC /86, VR-BJZ Caxton Ltd/Goverment of UAE 7/87, VR-BJZ Caxton Ltd/Sheikh Oteiba, UAE.
1006	1986. N99GM GAC /86, ACBGGC/Golden Goose-G Miller 3 Nov 86, JTF 12/90, Bucephalus Enterprises Inc 12/90, N99GM Bucephalus Enterprises Inc. Saltaire Fire Isl. NY.
1007	1986. N420GA GAC /86, Gannett Inc 12/86, N100GN 9/87, N100GN Gannett Inc. Arlington, Va.
1008	1986. N26LB GAC /86, N10LQ 2/87, Great American Insurance Co 7/87, N10LB 9/87, N10LB Great American Insurance Co. Cincinnati, Oh.
1009	1986. N423GA GAC /86, Limited Stores/Central Holding Corp 1/87, N500LS 10/87, N500VS 7/90,N700LS rsvd 26 Nov 90, N700LS Limited Stores/Central Holding Corp. Wilmington, De.
1010	1986. N426GA GAC /86, Northrop Corp 1/87, N444TJ 9/87, ConAgra Inc 1/90,N824CA 2/90,Pitney Bowes Credit 6/90, N824CA ConAgra Inc. Omaha, Ne.
1011	1987. N17581 GAC /87, A6-HHH Government of Dubai-UAE 12/87, A6-HHH Government of Dubai, UAE.
1012	1987. N445GA GAC /87, Ropa Two Corp 4/87, N636MF 8/87, N636MF Ropa Two Corp. Teterboro, NJ.
1013	1987. N446GA GAC /87, American Can Co 5/87, Primerica Inc 7/87, N130B 11/87, Primerica Holdings 3/89, Verochris Corp 3/90, Thomas W May Sr-WV 4/90, N130B Thomas W May Sr. Fairmont, WV.
1014	1987. N447GA GAC /87, Joseph E Seagram & Sons Inc-NYC 6/87, N777SW 11/87, N779SW rsvd 20 Sep 90, N779SW Joseph E Seagram & Sons Inc. NYC.
1015	1987. N17583 GAC /87, Rashid Engineering 11/87, VR-BRF 3/88, VR-BRF Rashid Engineering, Riyadh/Eiger Jet Ltd. Basle.
1016	1987. N427GA GAC /87, National Express Co 6/87, N95AE 10/87, N29GY 2/89, GAC 7/89, Guardian Industries Corp 8/89, N880GC 11/89, N880GC Guardian Industries Corp. Northville, Mi.
1017	1987. N405GA GAC /87, Coca Cola Co 3/88, N678RW 7/88, N678RW Coca Cola Co. Atlanta, Ga.
1018	1987. N407GA GAC /87, Triangle Publications 8/87, N300L 2/88, Provident National Leasing 11/88, Walter Annenberg-Pa 10/90, N300L Triangle Publications, Radnor, Pa.
1019	1987. N17584 GAC /87, TU-VAD Government of Ivory Coast, Abidjan.
1020	1987. N408GA GAC /87, Airplane Hangar Partnership 7/87, Liberty Service Corp 1/88, N600CS 3/88,DWC & B V Trustees 12/89, AHP Holdings Inc 3/90, GAC 4/90, Foreign Manufacturers Finance 8/90, N9300 Crown Cork & Seal 10/90, N9300 Crown Cork & Seal, Philadelphia, Pa.
1021	1987. N412GA GAC /87, N3M 4/87, 3M Co 5 Jan 88, N3M 3M Co. St Paul, Mn. (r/c Mining One).
1022	1987. (N63M) GAC /87, N23M 2/88, 3M Co 15 Apr 88, N23M 3M Co. St Paul, Mn.

1023	1987. N415GA GAC /87, Joseph E Seagram & Sons Inc 8/87, N77SW 2/88, N778W rsvd 10 Sep 90, N778W Joseph E Seagram & Sons Inc. NYC.
1024	1987. N130B GAC /87, American Can Co 5/87, N412GA GAC 6/87, National Express Co 8/87, N96AE 1/88, N96AE National Express Co. NYC.
1025	1987. N419GA GAC /87, N5BK W B Keck Jr 8/87, Galway Bay Corp 12/90, N5BK Howard Keck Sr/Galway Bay Corp. Van Nuys, Ca.
1026	1987. N151A GAC /87, I T & T Co 13 Oct 87, N151A International Telephone & Telegraph Co. Allentown, Pa.
1027	1987. N416GA GAC /87, TC-GAP Government of Turkey /87, TC-GAP Government of Turkey, Istanbul.
1028	1987. N428GA GAC /87, Bill Cosby 'Camille' 12/87, N712CW 6/88, N721CC 2/90, N712CC Bill Cosby,'Camille'.
1029	1987. N429GA GAC /87, Quetzal Inc 28 Oct 87, VR-BKI Picton Ltd 7/88, Cx USA 4/89, VR-BKI Picton Ltd/Quetzal Inc. Wilmington, De.
1030	1987. N430GA GAC /87, (N811JK) Joan B Kroc 1/88, WNP Aviation Inc 10/88, N1WP 1/89, N1WP Wm Pennington/WNP Aviation Inc. Wilmington, De.
1031	1987. N434GA GAC /87, arr UK 2/88 for outfitting, Aerospace Trading 1/89, HZ-AFU Saudia Special Flight Services 7/90, HZ-AFU Saudia Special Flight Services, Jeddah.
1032	1987. N17585 GAC /87, C-FSBR Steven Roman/Denison Mines Ltd 11/87, N315MC Management Corp of America 10/89, N315MC Management Corp of America/MCA Inc. Universal City, Ca.
1033	1988. (HB-IMY) GAC /88, N69GP Interfly Inc 6/88, N69GP Interfly Inc. Los Angeles, Ca.
1034	1988. N413GA GAC /88, Fleet EWS Group demo 88-90, N413GA EC-20, Fleet EWS Group.
1035	1987. N435GA GAC /87, arr UK 2/88 for outfitting, Aerospace Trading 1/89, HZ-AFV Saudia Special Flight Services 10/89, HZ-AFV Saudia Special Flight Services, Jeddah.
1036	1987. N152A GAC /87, ITT Corp 3 Feb 88, N152A ITT Corp. Wilmington, De.
1037	1988. N17588 GAC /88, VR-BKE Raytheon Middle East Systems-Jeddah 7/88, HZ-ADC 9/88, HZ-ADC Raytheon Middle East Systems, Jeddah.
1038	1988. N17603 GAC /88, arr UK 3/88 for outfitting, N438GA Aerospace Trading Co-Reno 1/89, HZ-AF. Saudia Special Flight Services /90, HZ-AF. Saudia Special Flight Services, Jeddah.
1039	1988. N431GA GAC /87, N1901M Monsanto Co 11/88, N1901M Monsanto Co. St Louis, Mo.
1040	1988. N423GA GAC /87, General Transportation Corp 25 Feb 88, N74RP 12/88, N74RP General Transportation Corp. Dover, De.
1041	1988. N433GA GAC /87, Figgie International 2/88, Bancboston Leasing 8/88, N366F 12/88, N366F Figgie International, Richmond, Va.
1042	1988. N17608 GAC /88, N400GA Round the world record 26/27 Feb 88- 36hrs 8 mins 34secs, 'Pursuit of Perfection', Allen Leasing & Financial 11/88, N22 7/89, N22 Gulfstream Aerospace Corp. Savannah, Ga.
1043	1988. N1761B GAC /88, TC-ANA Government of Turkey 23 Aug 88, TC-ANA Government of Turkey, Istanbul.
1044	1988. N423GA GAC /88, N1040 8/88, Cox Enterprises Inc 10/88, N1040 Cox Enterprises Inc. Atlanta, Ga.
1045	1988. N420GA GAC /88, W R Grace & Co 3/88, N227G 10/88,N227G W R Grace & Co. Westchester County Airport, NY.
1046	1988. N1761D GAC /88, Petrolair Systems 12/88, VR-BKU 2/89, VR-BKU Interaviation Holdings Ltd/Petrolair Systems, Athens.
1047	1988. N461GA GAC /88, Sally Beauty Co Inc/Alberto Culver 16 Nov 88, N23AC 6/89, N23AC Alberto Culver/Sally Beauty Co Inc. Wilmington, De.
1048	1988. N1761K GAC NBAA demo 10/88, (VR-BKL) Niarchos/Maritime Shipping 10/88, N448GA 10/88, SU-BGM Government of Egypt 6/89, SU-BGM Egyptian Air Force/Arab Republic of Egypt, Cairo.
1049	1988. N402GA GAC /88, N372CM Cordelia Scaife May 8/88, N372CM Cordelia Scaife May, Pittsburgh, Pa.
1050	1987. N153RA GAC /87, ITT Corp 7 Apr 88, N153RA ITT Corp. Wilmington, De.
1051	1988. N403GA GAC /88, Citiflight Inc 6/88, N399CC 12/88, N399CC Citiflight Inc. New Castle, De.
1052	1988. N419GA GAC 3/88, N800CC 7/89, Chrysler Corp 8/89, N800CC Chrysler Corp. Ypsilanti, Mi.
1053	1988. N47SL GAC /88, BOS Shearson Lehman Hutton 6 May 88, N26SL 12/88, National Express Co Inc 12/89, N91AE 5/90, N91AE National Express Co Inc. NYC.
1054	1988. N426GA GAC /88, Union Pacific Aviation Co 25 May 88, N400UP 1/89,N400UP Union Pacific Aviation Co. Allentown, Pa.
1055	1988. N1761P GAC /88, VR-BKV Interaviation Holdings/Petrolair Systems 2/89,XB-EXJ Organization Editorial Mexicana 12/89, XB-OEM 5/90, XB-OEM Organization Editorial Mexicana, Mexico City.
1056	1988. N436GA GAC /88, 3M Co 7 Jun 88, N33M 7/88, N33M 3M Co. St Paul, Mn.
1057	1988. N437GA GAC /88, 3M Co 13 Jun 88, N43M 10/88, N43M 3M Co. St Paul, Mn.
1058	1988. N458GA GAC /88, American International Avn 20 Jun 88, N70PS 11/88, N70PS American International Aviation, Wilmington, De.
1059	1988. N17581 GAC /88, N459GA /88, V8-RB1 Government of Brunei 4/89, V8-AL1 9/89, V8-SR1 6/90, V8-SR1 Government of Brunei.
1060	1988. N427GA GAC /88, Gulf States Toyota Inc 17 Nov 88, N1SF 6/89, N1SF Samuel Fly/Gulf States Toyota Inc. Houston, Tx.
1061	1988. N457GA GAC /88, Aircraft Promotion Svcs Inc-NYC 7/88, F-GPAK H R H Prince Karim Aga Khan 3 Feb 89, F-GPAK H R H Prince Karim Aga Khan, Paris.

c/n   Page 171

c/n	
1062	1988. N17583 GAC /88, BOS Henley Manufacturing Holding Co 17 Nov 88, N462GA 12/88, Newco Henley Holdings 7/89, N688H 8/89, New henley Holdings Inc 12/89, N688H Henley Group Inc. Manchester, NH.
1063	1988. N17584 GAC /88, N54SB United States Tobacco Co 15 Dec 88, U S Tobacco Sales & Management 12/89, N54SB United States Tobacco Co. White Plains, NY.
1064	1988. N439GA GAC /88, CSX Corp 7/88, HB-ITT Compagnie NOGA SA 1/89, HB-ITT Compagnie NOGA SA. Geneva.
1065	1988. N442GA GAC /88, N584D 5/88, CONOCO Inc 9/88, E I Dupont de Nemours & Co 1/89, N584D E I Dupont de Nemours & Co. New Castle, De.
1066	1988. N443GA GAC /88, Reynolds Air Services Inc 9/88, N118R 2/89, R J Reynolds Tobacco Co 8/90,N118R R J Reynolds Tobacco Co. Winston Salem, NC.
1067	1988. N446GA GAC /88, N145ST 7/88, Southeast Toyota Distributors 9/88, N145ST Southeast Toyota Distributors, Fort Lauderdale, Fl.
1068	1989. N17585 GAC /89, N95AE National Express Co 11/89, N90AE 12/89, N90AE National Express Co. NYC.
1069	1988. N459GA GAC /88, ARAMCO Associated Co 9/88, N765A 3/89, N765A ARAMCO Associated Co. Houston, Tx.
1070	1988. N407GA GAC /88, ARAMCO Associated Co 9/88, N107A 3/89, N107A ARAMCO Associated Co. Houston, Tx.
1071	1989. N410GA GAC 1/89, N1 FAA 6/89, N1 FAA, Washington, DC.
1072	1989. N100A Exxon Corp 6/89, N100A Exxon Corp. Dallas, Tx.
1073	1988. N75RP GAC /88, General Transportation Co 10/88, N75RP General Transportation Co. Dover, De.
1074	1989. N17587 GAC /89, VR-BKT JABJ/Natascha Estab-Vaduz /89, VR-BKT JABJ/Natascha Estab. Vaduz.
1075	1988. N412GA GAC /88, Westinghouse/Gateway Fleet Corp 10/88, N901K 4/89, N901K Westinghouse Electric Corp. Pittsburgh, Pa.
1076	1989. N17586 GAC /89, HZ-MNC Mouawad SA 11/89, HZ-MNC Mouawad S.A.
1077	1988. N445GA GAC /88, Reynolds Air Services Inc 4 Nov 88, N119R 4/89, McCaw Flight Operations 7/89, N119RC 9/89, Jack Prewitt-Tx 10/90, N119RC Jack Prewitt & Assocs Inc. Bedford, Tx.
1078	1989. N17589 GAC /89, G-DNVT Shell Aircraft Ltd 8/89, G-DNVT Shell Aircraft Ltd. London.
1079	1989. N17603 GAC /89, XA-PUV Jet Ejecutivos SA 9/89, XA-PUV Jet Ejecutivos SA. Mexico City.
1080	1988. N447GA GAC /88, Occidental Petroleum Corp 1 Dec 88, N2OXY 7/89, N2OXY Occidental Petroleum Corp. Bakersfield, Ca.
1081	1988. N955H GAC /88, Honeywell Inc 2 Dec 88, N955H Honeywell Inc. Minneapolis, Mn.
1082	1988. N1082A GAC /88, BN Leasing Inc 21 Dec 88, B R Leasing 6/89, N1082A B R Leasing Inc. Seattle, Wa.
1083	1989. N1761Q GAC /89, HB-ITZ Lonrho Ltd /89, HB-ITZ Lonrho Ltd/Lonair SA. Zug.
1084	1989. N1761S GAC /89, (N448GA) 1/89, HB-IMY Sit Set AG /89, HB-IMY Sit Set AG. Geneva.
1085	1988. N449GA GAC /88, Armour & Co/Greyhound Corp 6/89, N88GA 8/89, N88GA Armour & Co/Greyhound Corp. Phoenix, Az.
1086	1988. N460GA GAC /88, View Top Corp 'Kady' 'Kristofer' 29 Dec 88, N888MC 6/89, Bar International Operating Leasing Inc 7/90, N23SY rsvd 7 Sep 90, N23SY Daikyo (North Queensland) P/L. Cairns.
1087	1989. N463GA GAC /89, Shearson Lehman Hutton Holdings-NYC 24 Feb 89, (N94SL) rsvd 23 Mar 89,N310SL 2/90, Toyota Motor Credit Corp 4/90, N1TM 6/90, N1TM Toyota Motor Credit Corp. Torrance, Ca.
1088	1989. N464GA GAC /89, Upjohn Co 24 Feb 89, N4UP 7/89, N4UP Upjohn Co. Kalamazoo, Mi.
1089	1989. N465GA GAC /89, 3M Co 9 Mar 89, N53M 7/89, N53M 3M Co. St Paul, Mn.
1090	1989. N466GA GAC /88, VR-CYM Jet Fly Corp 3/90, VR-CYM Jet Fly Corp. London.
1091	1989. N467GA GAC 12/88, General Electric Co 27 Mar 89, N364G 9/89, N364G General Electric Co. NYC.
1092	1989. N468GA GAC /89, U S West Inc 31 Mar 89, N937US 10/89, N937US U S West Business Resources Inc. Englewood, Co.
1093	1989. VR-BLC Petrolair Systems SA 2/90, VR-BLC Petrolair Systems SA. Geneva.
1094	1989. N2610 GAC /89, Mobil Oil Corp 17 Apr 89, N2610 Mobil Oil Corp. NYC.
1095	1989. N469GA GAC /89, Eli Lilly & Co 28 Apr 89, N311EL 10/89, N311EL Eli Lilly & Co. Indianapolis, In.
1096	1989. N17582 GAC /89, VR-CBW Rolls Royce PLC 10 Jan 90, VR-CBW Rolls Royce PLC. Filton, UK.
1097	1989. N402GA GAC /89, ABT Flight Inc 5/89, N900AL 11/89, N900AL Abbott Laboratories/ABT Flight Inc. Waukegan, Il.
1098	1989. N403GA GAC 4/89, Keck Partners-LAX 8/89, N404CC Wilmar Ltd 10/89, N404CC Wilmar Ltd. Oakland, Ca.
1099	1989. N489H GAC /89, Fisher Air Corp-NYC 10/89, N299FB Fisher 299FB Corp 7/90, N299FB Fisher 299 Fox Bravo Corp. NYC.
1100	1989. N100AR GAC /89, ARCO 8/89, N100AR ARCO-Atlantic Richfield Co. Burbank, Ca.
1101	1989. N404GA GAC 4/89, General Electric Corp 8/89, N365G 2/90, N365G General Electric Co. White Plains
1102	1989. N405GA GAC 4/89, N910B AMOCO Corp 8/89, N910B AMOCO Corp. Chicago, Il.
1103	1989. N433GA GAC /89, GECC-Charlotte/Siebe PLC-UK 8/89, N90005 3/90, N90005 Siebe PLC. London.
1104	1989. N600ML GAC 4/89, DWC & BV Trustee/Liberty Service Corp 2/90, N700GD AHP Holdings Inc 3/90, N700GD AHP Holdings Inc. Van Nuys, Ca.
1105	1989. N408GA GAC 4/89, Eli Lilly & Co 8/89, N312EL 12/89, N312EL Eli Lilly & Co. Indianapolis, In.
1106	1989. N17608 GAC /90, 9M- Sultan of Johore /90, 9M-... Government of Johore. (maybe 9M-ISJ)
1107	1989. N17581 GAC 8/89, (JA8366) Kyoto Co /90, N101MU Century Industries Inc 2/90, N101MU Century Industries Inc. Honolulu, Hi.
1108	1989. N17584 GAC /89, N410GA 10/89, N114AN Asil Nadir/Anstar Corp 4/90, N11AN GECC rsvd 16 Nov 90, N11AN GECC, Atlanta, Ga.

1109	1990. N1761D GAC /90, V8- Government of Brunei /90, V8- Government of Brunei.
1110	1989. N415GA GAC /89, Bristol-Myers Co 9/89, N404M 11/89, Bristol Myers Squibb Co 12/89, N404M Bristol Myers Squibb Co. NYC.
1111	1989. N416GA GAC /89, James P Lennane-Fl 10/89, N111JL 5/90, N111JL James P Lennane, Naples, Fl.
1112	1989. N417GA GAC /89, N12UT United Technologies Cortran Inc 11/89, N12U 4/90, United Technologies Corp 8/90, N12U United Technologies Corp. Hartford, Ct.
1113	1989. N423GA GAC /89, Westinghouse Electric Corp 11/89, N902K 3/90, Gateway Fleet Corp 5/90, N902K Gateway Fleet/Westinghouse Electric Corp. West Mifflin, Pa.
1114	1989. N428GA GAC /89, N444LT Trousdale Enterprises/Wm Lyon Co 5/90, N555WL 9/90, N555WL Trousdale Enterprises/Wm Lyon Co. San Jose, Ca.
1115	1989. N430GA GAC 11/89, N410M Bristol Myers Squibb Co 1/90, N410M Bristol Myers Squibb Co. NYC.
1116	1989. N431GA International Lease Finance Corp 1/90, N971L Interlease Trading 7/90, Interlease Aviation 10/90, N971L Interlease Aviation Corp. Beverly Hills, Ca.
1117	1989. N1761J N1761J GAC /90,
1118	1989. N439GA GAC /89, Warner Lambert Co 1/90, N1526M 5/90, N1526M Warner Lambert Co. Morris Plains, NJ.
1119	1989. N407GA Uniden Jet Aviation Corp 12/89, N614HF 2/90, N614HF Uniden Jet Aviation Corp. Wilmington
1120	1990. N410GA GAC /90, VR-BOB Robert Maxwell 7/90, VR-BOB Robert Maxwell, Farnborough-UK.
1121	1989. N412GA GAC /89, Dresser Industries Inc 12/89, N7776 4/90, N7776 Dresser Industries Inc. Dallas
1122	1989. N4ON GAC /90, Union Carbide Corp 1/90, N4ON Union Carbide Corp. Wilmington, De.
1123	1990. N457GA GAC /90, I-LUBI Soc Alba-Milan 12/90, I-LUBI Silvio Berlusconi/Soc. Alba, Milan.
1124	1990. N420GA GAC /90, Whirlpool Corp 10/90, N1900W 11/90, N1900W Whirlpool Corp. Benton Harbor, Mi.
1125	1989. N432GA GAC 1/90, Eastern Aviation Inc 6/90, N415SH 8/90,N415SH Eastern Aviation Inc. Honolulu, Hi.
1126	1990. N426GA GAC 2/90, 5N-FGP Federal Government of Nigeria 12/90, 5N-FGP Federal Government of Nigeria, Lagos.
1127	1990. N427GA GAC /90, VR-BLR BP International Inc 10/90, VR-BLR BP International Inc. Farnborough-UK.
1128	1990. N429GA GAC /90, N429GA
1129	1990. N17585 GAC /90, EI-CAH Ardelis/Arklow P/L-Johannesburg 10/90, EI-CAH Ardelis/Arklow P/L. Johannesburg-RSA.
1130	1990. N436GA GAC /90, Martin Marietta Corp 4/90, N401MM 7/90, N401MM Martin Marietta Corp. Brthesda, Md.
1131	1990. N437GA /90, Coca Cola Co 5/90, N437GA Coca Cola Co. Atlanta, Ga.
1132	1990. N442GA GAC /90, Jetstar Enterprises (USA) Inc 4/90, N442GA Jetstar Enterprises (USA) Inc. Wilmington, De.
1133	1990. N443GA GAC 10/90, N700CN Copley Press Inc 11/90, N700CN Copley Press Inc. La Jolla, Ca.
1134	1990. N445GA GAC /90, VR-BJD Transworld Oil America Inc 11/90,VR-BJD Transworld Oil America Inc. Newark, NJ.
1135	1990. N435GA GAC /90, Earth Star Inc/Walt Disney Co 5 Dec 90, N435GA Earth Star Inc/Walt Disney Co. Burbank, Ca.
1136	1990. N401GA GAC /90, N27CD 9/90, Schering Plough Corp 30 Nov 90, N27CD Schering Plough Corp. Madison
1137	1990. N402GA GAC 6/90, Dun & Bradstreet Corp 6/90, N299DB 10/90, N299DB Dun & Bradstreet Corp. NYC.
1138	1990. N403GA GAC /90, N200A rsvd for Exxon Corp 18 Oct 90, N200A Exxon Corp. Dallas, Tx.
1139	1990. N404GA GAC /90, N99WJ rsvd 13 Nov 90, N99WJ JP Aviation Inc. Charlotte, NC.
1140	1990. N405GA GAC 5/90, N811JK MacDonald's Hamburgers 6/90, N811JK Joan Kroc/MacDonald's Hamburgers, Chicago, Il.
1141	1990. N407GA GAC /90, CIT Leasing Corp 8/90, N767FL rsvd 23 Oct 90, N767FL Lear Siegler Management Corp. Livingstone, NJ.
1142	1990. N408GA GAC /90, N408GA
1143	1990. N410GA GAC /90, N410GA
1144	1990. N415GA GAC 9/90, Philip Morris Management Corp 10/90, N100PM 3/91, N100PM Philip Morris Management Corp. Teterboro, NJ.
1145	1990. N102MU GAC /90, N102MU
1146	1990. N417GA GAC /90, N417GA
1147	1990. N419GA GAC /90, Taubman Air Inc 10/90, GAC 10/90, Philip Morris Mangement Corp 12 Dec 90, N200PM 5/91, N200PM Philip Morris Management Corp. NYC.
1148	1990. N427GA GAC /90, N427GA
1150	1990. N443GA GAC /90, V8-... Government of Brunei,
1151	1990. N375GA /90, Taubman Air Inc 31 Oct 90, N80AT /90, N80AT Taubman Air Inc. Bloomfield Hills, Mi.
1152	1990. N446GA GAC 11/90, 3M Co 26 Nov 90, N446GA 3M Co. St Paul, Mn.
1153	1990. N448GA GAC /90, AREPO Corp 17 Dec 90, N448GA AREPO Corp. Westchester County Airport, NY.
1154	1990. N1761D GAC /90, Glaxo Aviation Inc 18 Dec 90, N1761D Glaxo Aviation Inc. Raleigh, NC.

Falcon 50

1	1976. F-WAMD Ff 7 Nov 76, prototype, F-BAMD AMD-BA 6/77, F-BNDB 4/80, F-WNDB AMD-BA., Istres-Le Tube.
2	1978. F-WINR AMD-BA /78, F-BINR 22 Jun 78, Europe Falcon Service 2/81, F-RAFJ French AF whilst s/n 5 on mtx 2/85-4/85, F-BINR EFS 2 Apr 85, F-BINR Regourd/Europe Falcon Service, Le Bourget.
3	1979. F-WFJC AMD-BA /78, F-GBIZ 9/78, N5OFJ FJC 7/79, N5OEJ 11/79, N880F Anheuser Busch Cos 7/80, N8805 6/87, AA & MM Co Inc 1/88, N8805 AA & MM Co Inc. Youngstown, Oh.
4	1979. F-WZHA AMD-BA /79, N110FJ FJC 3/79, N5OFJ 9/80, YV-452CP Maraven SA 10/81, YV-452CP Maraven SA. Caracas.
5	1979. F-WZHB AMD-BA /79, F-RAFI French Air Force /79, F-RAFI A de l'Air, ET 1/60, Villacoublay.
6	1979. F-WZHB AMD-BA /79, N5OFB FJC 7/79, N1871R Ingersoll Rand Service Co 10/80, N1871R to G-3 381, N815CA Continental Aviation Inc 5/89, 9XR-NN Govt of Rwanda 5/90, 9XR-NN Government of Rwanda, Kigali.
7	1979. F-WZHA AMD-BA /79, HZ-AKI TAG-Paris 2/80, HZ-AO3 3/80, N8516Z RELCO/Thriftway/Great American Life Insurance 2/81, N26LB 6/81, N5DL 10/84, Regal Quad Inc 8/88, N5DL Regal Quad Inc. Cincinnati, Oh.
8	1979. F-WZHC AMD-BA /79, N5OFE FJC 9/79, N5OPG Amax Inc 11/80, Ed J DeBartolo Corp 5/83, N409ER 12/85, N409ER Ed J DeBartolo Corp. Youngstown, Oh.
9	1979. F-WZHD AMD-BA /79, I-SAFP Soc Fiat-Turin 10/80, XA-LOH Aero Personal SA-Mexico City 'Mixtli' 4/81, VR-CBR Parragrane S.A-Toronto 8/85, (N100WJ) photo taken at TEB 5/88,F-GGCP Ste Sporto/Aero France 7/88, F-GGCP Ste Sporto/Aero France, Paris-Le Bourget.
10	1979. F-WZHD AMD-BA /79, N5OFG FJC 12/79, N65B Borden Inc 2/81, N65B Borden Inc. Morristown, NJ.
11	1980. F-WZHE AMD-BA /80, N5OFH FJC 4/80, N5O1NC Internorth Inc later ENRON 1/81, N5739 4/86, Ed J DeBartolo Corp 8/87, F-GGVB Leadair 13 Mar 90, F-GGVB SLIBAIL/Leadair Unijet, Paris-Le Bourget.
12	1980. F-WZHC AMD-BA /80, CN-ANO Government of Morocco 5/80, CN-ANO Government of Morocco, Rabat.
13	1980. F-WZHF AMD-BA /80, N5OFK FJC 2/80, GELCO Corp 3/80, N150BG 6/81, National Medical Enterprises 11/84, N150BG National Medical Enterprises Inc. Los Angeles, Ca.
14	1980. F-WZHG AMD-BA /80, N5OFL FJC 3/80, N233U Combustion Engineering Inc 3/80, N283U 7/86, NYNEX Corp 8/86, N9X 12/86, N9X NYNEX Corp. White Plains, NY.
15	1980. F-WZHM AMD-BA /80, PH-ILR N V Philips 20 Nov 80, PH-ILR N V Philips, Eindhoven.
16	1980. F-WZHH AMD-BA /80, (N5OFM) FJC /80, D-BIRD Dornier Reparaturwerft GmbH 7/80, D-BFAR 3/87, D-BFAR Dornier Reparaturwerft GmbH. Munich.
17	1980. F-WZHI AMD-BA /80, 5A-DGI Government of Libya 8/80, TY-BBM Government of Benin 10/82, HB-IEB ALG Aeroleasing SA 10/83, N4679T CC Flight Services Inc 1/84, N3456F 3/84, Midwest Aviation Inc 11/85, N349K 3/86, N349K Midwest Aviation Inc/Kiewit Engineering Co. Omaha, Nb.
18	1980. F-WZHJ AMD-BA /80, N5OFN FJC 4/80, N187S Sperry Corp 5/81,Levelor Lorentzen Inc 4/83, N720M 12/83, Avon/MI Holdings Inc 9/86, N1102A 2/87, Rich Products Inc 7/88,N82RP 9/88, N82RP Rich Products Inc. Lake Worth, Fl.
19	1980. F-WZHB AMD-BA /80, N5OFC FJC 5/80, N63A Superior Oil Co 5/81, NL Industries Inc 8/82, N253L 10/82, NL Petroleum Svcs Corp 5/87,Valhi Inc 2/88,Contran Corp 1/89, N253L Contran Corp. Dallas, Tx.
20	1980. F-WZHK AMD-BA /80, N5OFR FJC 5/80, C6-BER Petroclor Services Inc-NYC 6/81, inscribed 'LPPNW 1985 Nobel Peace Prize' noted 12/85, C6-BER Petroclor Services Inc. New York.
21	1980. F-WZHN AMD-BA /80, (9K-ACQ) Mubarak Al Hassawi-Kuwait 9/80, 9K-AEE 10/80, N299W Wheelabrator-Frye/Signal Corp 1/81, Omni Assoc-Md 8/86, AOKI Avn Co 11/87, Randolph Wright 4/88, N299W Randolph Wright, Birmingham, Mi.
22	1980. F-WZHF AMD-BA /80, N5OFS FJC 6/80, N203BT Big Three Industries Inc 2/81, Federal Paper Board Co 9/86, N866FP 1/87, FJC 7/89, N866FP Falcon Jet Corp. Teterboro, NJ.
23	1980. F-WZHG AMD-BA /80, (D-BBAD) W Korf GmbH 7/80, D-BBWK 8/80, PH-ILD N V Philips 25 Jul 83, PH-ILD NV Philips, Eindhoven.
24	1980. F-WZHL AMD-BA /80, N51FJ FJC 7/80, N817M Standard Oil Co 1/81, B P America Inc 2/88, N817M BP America Inc. Cleveland, Oh.
25	1980. F-WZHI AMDBA /80, 72101 Governmemt of Yugoslavia 11/80, 72101 Government of Yugoslavia, Belgrade.
26	1980. F-WZHI AMD-BA /80, N52FJ FJC 7/80, MASCO Corp 8/80, N190MC 6/83, N190MC MASCO Corp. Taylor, Mi.
27	1980. F-WZHN AMD-BA /80, HB-IEB Gatair SA 2/81, Nome Air SA/ALG Aeroleasing 12 Dec 86, F-WGTG Dassault/EFS 10/90, F-RAF. French Air Force 12/90, F-RAF. A de l'Air, ET 1/60, Villacoublay.
28	1980. F-WZHD AMD-BA /80, N53FJ FJC 11/80, IBM World Trade Asia Corp 12/81, N131WT 1/81, IBM Credit Corp 7/85, PH-LEM KLM Helicopters BV 2/90, PH-LEM KLM Helicopters BV. Amsterdam.
29	1980. F-WZHB AMD-BA /80, I-SAFR Soc Fiat Aviazione 6 Mar 81, I-SAFR Soc. Fiat Aviazione, Turin.
30	1980. F-WZHD AMD-BA /80, I-SNAC Soc SNAM-Milan 9 Mar 81, I-SNAC Soc. Naz. Metanodotti, Milan.
31	1980. F-WZHC AMD-BA /80, (N54FJ) FJC /80, I-KIDO Soc Gitanair 2/81, N211CN Norman Hoffman 6/84, C N Ray 8/84, Evergreen Avn Inc 2/85, N211CN to F10-173, N145W Wetterau/Bi-Go Markets Inc 5/86,N145W to F900-40, N145WF Orioles Aviation Inc 9/90, N105EJ 11/90, N105EJ Eli Jacobs/Orioles Aviation Inc. Baltimore, Md
32	1980. F-WZHJ AMD-BA /80, VR-BTT Inter Insurance-Bermuda 4/81, VR-BTT Jaguar Aviation/Inter Insurance. 'Terojet One'
33	1980. F-WZHA AMD-BA /80, N56FJ FJC 12/80, Caribbean Falcon Inc 2/81, FJC 8/82, N8100E Emerson Electric 6/83, N8100E to F900-34, N8300E 5/88, N8300E Emerson Electric Co. St. Louis, Mo.

c/n	
34	1980. F-WZHH AMD-BA /80, HB-IEV Abaz Gokal/Aerogulf SA 3/81, Ilair/EJA 1/82, Industrie Leasing/Aerogulf SA 11 Jun 85 F-WEFS Dassault/EFS 10/90, F-RAF. French Air Force 12/90, F-RAF. A de l'Air, ET 1/60, Villacoublay.
35	1980. F-WZHF AMD-BA /80, N57FJ FJC 12/80, N800BD Becton & Dickinson Co 2/82, Bristol Myers 9/84, N907M 12/88, Bristol-Myers Sqibb Co 11/89, N907M Bristol-Myers Squibb Co. NYC.
36	1980. F-WZHJ AMD-BA /80, N54FJ FJC 12/80, Bristol-Myers Co 10/81, N345PA 2/82, Bristol Myers Squibb Co 11/89, N345PA Bristol-Myers Squibb Co. NYC.
37	1980. F-WZHM AMD-BA /80, (I-CAIK) /81, I-SAME Soc CAI-Rome 16 Apr 81, I-SAME Soc. CAI, Rome.
38	1980. F-WZHK AMD-BA /80, N58FJ FJC 1/81, Reynolds Metals Co 11/81, N993 2/82, N993 Reynolds Metals Co. Richmond, Va.
39	1981. F-WZHL AMD-BA /81, N59FJ FJC 1/81, N754S Shell Aviation Corp 9/81, N754S Shell Aviation Corp. Houston, Tx.
40	1981. F-WZHG AMD-BA /81, 9K-AEF Muburak Al Hassawi/Gulf International Group 5/81, N90005 Astrojet/Robertshaw Controls Co 12/86, N50GF GAC 11/87, Paragon Ranch Inc 1/88, N1PR 3/88, N1PR Astrojet/Paragon Ranch Inc. Broomfield, Co.
41	1981. F-WZHI AMD-BA /81, N60FJ FJC 2/81, N546EX Bristol-Myers Co 3/82, Bristol Myers Squibb Co 11/89, N546EX Bristol-Myers Squibb Co. NYC.
42	1981. F-WZHE AMD-BA /81, N61FJ FJC 2/81, N82MP Mesa Petroleum Co 9/81, Cx USA 2/83, D-BDWO DAIWO-Korea/Wolfgang Storm-Business Avn ManagementGmbH 5/84, OE-HCS Tyrolean Jet Service GmbH 3/86, OO-LFT Abelag Aviation 1/89, OO-LFT Abelag Aviation, Brussels.
43	1981. F-WZHO AMD-BA /81, 72102 Government of Yugoslavia 5/81, YU-BNA 8/81, YU-BNA Government of Yugoslavia, Belgrade.
44	1981. F-WZHA AMD-BA /81, N62FJ FJC 3/81, Wrather Corp 6/82, N150JP 9/82, Trousdale Enterprises 4/85, Falcon 50 Ptnrship 8/85, N50LT 11/85, GAC 10/89, Morrison Knudsen Co 5/90, N44MK 6/90, N44MK Morrison Knudsen Co. Boise, Id.
45	1981. F-WZHE AMD-BA /81, N63FJ FJC 2/81, Garrett Corp 5/81,N731F First Republic Credit Corp-Pa 5/87,Omni International 11/87, BAX Inc/Baxter Travenol Aviation Inc 12/87, N9BX Baxter Healthcare Corp 7/88, N9BX Baxter Healthcare Corp. Waukegan, Il.
46	1981. F-WZHK AMD-BA /81, N64FJ FJC 3/81, N908EF REFCO/Ray Friedman/R&T Partnership 10/81, N911RF 10/87, N911RF Mid Central Air/R & T Partnership, Wheeling, Il.
47	1981. F-WZHP AMD-BA /81, N65FJ FJC 4/81, N150WC 11/81, Western Co of N America 3/82, N23AC Alberto Culver/Sally Beauty Co 2/86, GAC 12/88, N23AQ 3/89, Wilmington Services Inc 8/89,Baxter Healthcare 9/89, N1BX Baxter Healthcare Corp. McGaw Park, Il.
48	1981. F-WZHK AMD-BA /81, HB-IET El Azem Co SARL-Geneva 7/81, Biz-Jet SA 4/86, I-ERDN Soc Eridania Zuccherifici Nazionali SpA 4/86, I-ERDN Soc. Eridania Zuccherifici Nazionali S.p.a.
49	1981. F-WZHL AMD-BA /81, N66FJ FJC 4/81, N43ES Esmark Inc 2/82, Beatrice Companies /85, Beatrice/Georgetown Interstate Aviation 7/86, N43BE 6/89, N43BE Beatrice Companies, Chicago, Il.
50	1981. F-WZHQ AMD-BA /81, N67FJ FJC 4/81, N747 10/81, FMC Corp 12/81, N747Y 12/84, N747Y FMC Corp. Wheeling, Il.
51	1981. F-WZHR AMD-BA /81, N70FJ FJC 5/81, Dow Chemical 11/81, N52DC Hartford NB & Trust Co 2/82, Connecticut NB 1/83, N52DC Dow Chemical, Freeland, Mi.
52	1981. F-WZHV AMD-BA /81, F-BMER 6/81, JY-HAH Government of Jordan 9/81, N18G Jack Prewitt 5/86, Air Ketchum/Helen Dow Whiting 6/86, N86AK 12/86, MDFC Equipment Leasing 7/87, N86AK Air Ketchum/Helen Dow Whiting, Sun Valley, Id.
53	1981. F-WZHS AMD-BA /81, N150JT FJC 8/81, Joseph Seagram & Sons Inc 5/82, (N77SW) rsvd 9/83, Sid Richardson Carbon & Gasoline 1/85, N45SJ 7/85, N45SJ to F900-37, (N50SJ) rsvd 10 Mar 88, N22T TAB Services Inc 5/88, N22T TAB Services Inc. Fort Worth, Tx.
54	1981. F-WZHT AMD-BA /81, N71FJ FJC 5/81, N450X Rose Associates Inc of Miami 3/82, (N50EF) rsvd 12/83, N204DD Dondi Group/Vernon Savings & Loan 3/84, N202DD 11/84, Unisys Corp 2/87, N392U 7/87, Verochris/Primerica 2/90, N130A 5/90, N130A Verochris Corp/Primerica, White Plains, NY.
55	1981. F-WZHU AMD-BA /81, N73FJ FJC 5/81, N839F 11/81,Clark Rental System Inc/Commercial Union 12/81, S W Jack Drilling 1/84, N1CN 10/84, MCI Telecommunications 5/86, N332MC 7/86, N332MQ 1/89, Crane Co 9/89, N652CR 2/90, N625CR Crane Co. NYC.
56	1981. F-WZHR AMD-BA /81, F-GDFE 11/81, F-WDFE 6/83, N112FJ FJC 7/83, Hewlett Packard Co 9/83, N84HP 11/83, N84HP Hewlett-Packard Co. San Jose, Ca.
57	1981. F-WZHC AMD-BA /81, HB-IER Giesecke und Devrient 6/81, HB-IER Socavia AG/Giesecke und Devrient, Munich.
58	1981. F-WZHA AMD-BA /81, N72FJ FJC 6/81, Lindy Aviation/Pillsbury 11/82, N744X 6/83, Shamrock Aviation/Pillsbury 1/89, N744X Shamrock Aviation/Pillsbury Co. Minneapolis, Mn.
59	1981. F-WZHB AMD-BA /81, N75FJ FJC 6/81, David Murdoch/Pacific Holding Corp 2/82, N31DM 3/82, Sec Pac Leasing 4/82, Anheuser-Busch Companies 5/89, N31V 2/90, N31V Anheuser Busch Companies Inc. St Louis, Mo.
60	1981. F-WZHD AMD-BA /81, JY-HZH Government of Jordan /81, N900W BFI Aviation Inc 27 May 86, N900W BFI=Browning Ferris Industries Aviation Inc. Houston, Tx.
61	1981. F-WZHI AMD-BA /81, HB-IES Logarcheo Anstalt Vaduz /81, HB-IES Logarcheo Anstalt Vaduz, Geneva.

c/n	
62	1981. F-WZHE AMD-BA /81, N77FJ FJC 7/81, N292BC 2/82, Boise Cascade Corp 6/82,N292BC Boise Cascade Corp. Boise, Id.
63	1981. F-WZHF AMD-BA /81, N78FJ FJC 7/81, Commercial Union 9/81, N841F 2/82, Bancorp Leasing & Financial 5/82, Aircraft at your Call 9/84, EBM Group Inc 8/88, HB-IAL Lubis SA 9/89, Gofir SA 11/89, HB-IAL Lubis SA-Lugano/Gofir SA. Agno.
64	1981. F-WZHH AMD-BA /81, N79FJ FJC 8/81, N418S Oilfield Avn/Schlumberger 3/82, Provident Natl Leasing 3/86, N300A 6/86, ICI Americas Inc 1/89, N300A ICI Americas Inc. New Castle, De.
65	1981. F-WZHT AMD-BA /81, Falcon International SA /81, N50FJ FJC 2/82, N50FJ to F50-85, N90FJ 4/83, Henry I Siegel Co 9/83, rpo F50-85, N65HS 11/83, Morgan Guarantee Trust Co 8/84,D-BFFB F & F Burda GmbH 16 May 88, D- CoA 30 Sep 89, D-BFFB F & F Burda GmbH. Baden Baden.
66	1981. F-WZHF AMD-BA /81, (PH-SDL) Film Air 5/82, N500BL Brunner & Lay Inc 12/82, N500BL Brunner & Lay Inc. Asheville, NC.
67	1981. F-WZHG AMD-BA /81, N76FJ FJC 9/81, Ashland Oil/Ayre Inc 10/82, HB-IEP Ilair/ALG 1/83, Ilair/Industrie Leasing SA 7/85, Koci SA 5/87, ALG Aeroleasing SA 1/88, HB-IEP ALG Aeroleasing SA/Koci S.A. Geneva.
68	1981. F-WZHQ AMD-BA /81, 5A-DCM LAAF/Government of Libya 9/81, 5A-DCM Government of Libya, Tripoli.
69	1981. F-WZHJ AMD-BA /81, N80FJ FJC 9/81, N650X Amax Inc 5/82, N650X Amax Inc. NYC.
70	1981. F-WZHL AMD-BA /81, N81FJ FJC 9/81, N230S 4/82, Norton Simon Properties 9/82, American Can Co 9/83, N130K 12/83,Primerica Corp 8/87,R Chambers/Stockwood III Inc 4/88, (N651SB) rsvd 16 May 88, PSI Funding Inc-NYC 9/90, N130K PSI Funding Inc. NYC.
71	1981. F-WZHF AMD-BA /81, YI-ALB Government/Iraqi Airways 3/82, J2-KBA Government of Djibouti 12/87, J2-KBA Government of Djibouti,
72	1981. F-WZHM AMD-BA /81, N82FJ FJC 10/81, N1181G Getty Refining & Marketing Inc 4/82, Texaco Refining & Marketing Inc 6/85, Cx USA 12/85, N1181G W/O W/o 12 May 85. 12/MAY/85
73	1981. F-WPXE AMD-BA /81, HZ-SAB SABIC 12/82, HZ-SAB SABIC=Saudi Arabian Basic Industries Corp. Riyadh.
74	1981. F-WZHA AMD-BA /81, N83FJ FJC 11/81, Anheuser-Busch Inc 8/82, N83FJ Anheuser-Busch Inc. St. Louis
75	1981. F-WZHH AMD-BA /81, N95FJ FJC 2/82, N45ES 9/82, MSE Aviation Inc 12/82, Esmark Inc 9/83, Georgetown Interstate Avn/Beatrice Cos 7/86, N45BE 4/89, N45BE Georgetown Interstate Aviation/Beatrice Co. Ontario, Ca.
76	1981. F-WZHB AMD-BA /81, N84FJ FJC 11/81, N85MD 4/82, McDermott Inc 11/82, Wm Wrigley Jr Co 3/86, N410WW 4/86, Zeno Air Inc 9/88, N410WW Zeno Air Inc/Wm Wrigley Jr Co. Chicago, Il.
77	1981. F-WZHC AMD-BA /81, N85FJ FJC 12/81, N366F 4/82, Figgie International Inc 9/82, Jack Prewitt-Tx 3/88, N992 Reynolds Metals Co 5/88, N992 Reynolds Metals Co. Richmond, Va.
78	1981. F-WPXF AMD-BA /81, F-ODEO Ministry of Co-operation-Gabon 3/82, TR-LAI Government of Gabon 'Masuku' 4/82, F-GEOY AMD-BA 4/87, F-RAFJ French Air Force 27 Oct 87, F-RAFJ A de l'Air, ET 1/60, Villacoublay.
79	1981. F-WZHE AMD-BA /81, N86FJ FJC 12/81, N60CN Champion International Corp 6/82, N60CN Champion International Corp. Stamford, Ct.
80	1981. F-WZHN AMD-BA /81, N87FJ FJC 12/81, XB-OEM Organization Editorial Mexicana 5/82, XA-FTC Leo Air Taxi 4/90, XA-FTC Leo Air Taxi,
81	1981. F-WZHA AMD-BA /81, N89FJ FJC 1/82, Alan Rosefielde-Fl Trustee 10/82, N718DW Colleen Corp 1/83, N718DW Colleen Corp. Philadelphia, Pa.
82	1981. F-WZHG AMD-BA /81, N88FJ FJC 1/82, N293BC Boise Cascade Corp 3/82, RP-C754 United Coconut Planters Bank 12/82, (N767W) 4/89, N40F Walter Fuller Aircraft Sales 10/89, N40F Walter Fuller Aircraft Sales, Addison, Tx.
83	1982. F-WZHJ AMD-BA /82, N88U FJC 5/82, International Paper Co 9/82, N881M 11/82, N881M International Paper Co. NYC.
84	1982. F-WZHK AMD-BA /82, (N2711B) Zhobi Corp 4/82,T 16-1 Government of Spain 2/83, T 16-1 EC-ZCP, 45-20, Ed1A/45 Grupo, Madrid. (prev code 401-09).
85	1982. F-WZHO AMD-BA /82, N90FJ FJC 1/82, N90FJ to F50-65, N50FJ 4/83, rpo F50-65, N40TH Sony Aviation 9/84, N40TH Sony Aviation Inc. Teterboro, NJ.
86	1982. F-WPXD AMD-BA /82, N94FJ FJC 1/82, Combustion Engineering Inc 5/82, N238U 9/82, F-GKDR Regourd Aviation 9/90, F-GKDR FIBIVIAT/Elf Acquitane/Regourd Aviation, Paris-Le Bourget.
87	1982. F-WZHS AMD-BA /82, N91FJ FJC 1/82, Kellogg Co 11/82, N283K 3/83, Northern Telecom Inc 4/90, N55NT 5/90, N55NT Northern Telecom Inc. Nashville, Tn.
88	1982. F-WZHU AMD-BA /82, N92FJ FJC 2/82, XA-OVR Olegario Vasquez Rana 6/83, XA-OVR Sr. Olegario Vasquez Rana, Mexico City. 'Angeles'
89	1982. F-WZHV AMD-BA /82, N93FJ FJC 2/82, 195 Broadway Corp 12/82, N212K 1/83, AT&T Resource Management Corp 4/84, N212K A T & T Resource Management Corp. NYC.
90	1982. F-WZHX AMD-BA /82, N290W FJC 7/82, Kellogg Rust Inc 11/82, N298W 12/82, Signal Corp/M W Kellogg Co 3/83, Allied Signal Inc 8/86, N600AS 12/86, N600AS Allied Signal Inc. Los Angeles, Ca.
91	1982. F-WZHY AMD-BA /82, ZS-BMB Government of South Africa 10/82, ZS-CAS 12/82, ZS-CAS Department of Transport Services, Pretoria.
92	1982. F-WZHZ AMD-BA /82, N97FJ FJC 2/82, N85A Burlington Industries Inc 11/82, Champion Intl Corp 11/87, N40CN 5/88, N40CN Champion International Corp. Stamford, Ct.

c/n	
93	1982. F-WZHB AMD-BA /82, N98FJ FJC 3/82, Pillsbury/Shamrock Aviation Inc 12/83, N844X 3/85, N844X Pillsbury/Shamrock Aviation, Cincinnati, Oh.
94	1982. F-WZHC AMD-BA /82, N99FJ FJC 4/82, N82NC 12/82, Natomas Energy Co 7/83, A T & T 8/83,N212JP 12/83, N212JP A T & T Resource Management Corp. Morristown, NJ.
95	1982. F-WPXD AMD-BA /82, VR-CBL ARAVCO-London 8/82, N3950N MCI Telecommunications Corp 6/83, MCI/Finalco Inc 8/83, N331MC 9/83, FSB-Ut 1/84, MDFC Equipment Leasing 9/89, N331MC MCI Telecommunications/Finalco Inc. McClean, Va.
96	1982. F-WZHE AMD-BA /82, N4AC FJC 9/82, AMCA Intl 3/83, N4AC to F10-184, C-FMFL McCain Foods Ltd 11/86, C-FMFL McCain Foods Ltd. Florenceville, N.B.
97	1982. F-WZHL AMD-BA /82, (N101FJ) FJC 3/82, re-allocated to F50-108, C-FSCL Seagrams/Execaire Avn 5/82, N33GG George Gund III-Ca 6/89, N33GG George Gund III, San Francisco, Ca.
98	1982. F-WPXF AMD-BA /82, VR-CBO ARAVCO-London 11/82, N39461 Omni Intl Corp 5/83, Morrison Knudsen Co 7/83, N50MK 10/83, N50MK Morrison Knudsen Co. Boise, Id.
99	1982. F-WZHM AMD-BA /82, (N96FJ) FJC 4/82, re-allocated to F50-106, Cx USA 5/82, C-FMYB Bank of Montreal/Execaire 5/82, N816M BP America Inc 6/90, N816M BP America Inc. Cleveland, Oh.
100	1982. F-WZHN AMD-BA /82, N102FJ FJC 3/82, N14CG Beta Aircraft/Continental Grain 1/83, Conticarriers & Terminals Inc 7/88, Beta Aircraft Corp 6/89, N14CG Beta Aircraft Corp. NYC.
101	1982. F-WPXH AMD-BA Ff 9 Sep 82,YI-ALC Government of Iraq 11/82,YI-ALC Government/Iraqi Airways, Baghdad
102	1982. F-WZHO AMD-BA Ff 13 Apr 82, N103FJ FJC 4/82, Bendix Corp 3/83, N50BX 5/83, (N50WB) rsvd for Wagner & Brown 1/85, N350WB 2/85, N350WB Wagner & Brown 11, Midland, Tx.
103	1982. F-WZHQ AMD-BA Ff 22 Apr 82, N104FJ FJC 4/82,N83MP Mesa Petroleum Co 4/83, Boone T Pickens 5/87, N83MP Boone T Pickens Jr/Mesa Petroleum Co. Amarillo, Tx.
104	1982. F-WZHR AMD-BA Ff 30 Apr 82, N105FJ FJC 4/82, Shearson Loeb Rhoades Inc 1/83, N90AE 3/83, American Express Co 2/84, Shearson Express Inc 10/84, F-GFGQ AMD-BA 3/88, F-WWHK 1/89, N50VG Volvo AB/VFNA Jet Leasing Inc 2/89, N50VG Volvo AB/VFNA Jet Leasing Inc. Washington, DC.
105	1982. F-WZHS AMD-BA Ff 6 May 82, N106FJ FJC 4/82, Champion International Corp 8/82, N80CN 1/83, N80CN Champion International Corp. Stamford, Ct.
106	1982. F-WZHT AMD-BA Ff 12 May 82, N96FJ FJC 5/82, Thoroughbred Management Svcs/Firestone Group 8/82, N50BF 4/83, Canadair Challenger Inc 4/90, N50BF Canadair Challenger Inc. Windsor, Ct.
107	1982. F-WPXK AMD-BA Ff 11 Oct 82, ZS-LJM Rembrandt Tobacco-Capetown 11/82, LX-RVR 12/82, LX-RVR Rupint Aviation/Rembrandt Tobacco, Capetown, RSA.
108	1982. F-WZHU AMD-BA Ff 27 May 82, N101FJ FJC 5/82, AMAX Inc 3/83, N350X 7/83, Koch Industries Inc 11/85, N150K 1/86, N150K Koch Industries Inc. Wichita, Ks.
109	1982. F-WZHV AMD-BA Ff 3 Jun 82, N109FJ FJC 5/82, N280BC Liberty Mutual Insurance Co 1/83, N280BC Jet Aviation/Liberty Mutual Insurance Co. Boston, Ma.
110	1982. F-WPXG AMD-BA Ff 11 Jun 82, 5N-ARE I Rabiu-Nigeria 2/83, VR-BJA Faljet Holdings Ltd 11/84, N77TE Jet Avn of America 11/84, Temple Eastex 12/84, Temple Inland Forest Products 11/88, N77TE Temple Inland Forest Products, Diboll, Tx.
111	1982. F-WZHZ AMD-BA Ff 16 Jun 82, N297W FJC 1/83, MPB Corp 4/83, Henley Investments Inc 1/87, Newco Henley Holdings Inc 1/89, Wheelabrator Group 8/89, FJC 11/90, F-GKTV Euralair 12/90, F-GKTV Euralair/Elf Acquitaine, Paris-Le Bourget.
112	1982. F-WZHA AMD-BA Ff 22 Jun 82, N107FJ FJC 6/82, N114AD Archer Daniels Midland Co 8/83, N144AD Archer Daniels Midland Co. Wilmington, De.
113	1982. F-WZHB AMD-BA Ff 1 Jul 82, N108FJ FJC 6/82, N186S 6/83, Sperry Corp 8/83, Unisys Corp 11/87, N394U 12/88, MDFC Equipment Leasing 1/90, N394U Unisys Corp. Mercer County Airport, Trenton, NJ.
114	1982. F-WPXM AMD-BA Ff 25 Nov 82, ST-PSR Government of Sudan 7/83, ST-PSR Government of Sudan, Khartoum.
115	1982. F-WZHC AMD-BA Ff 27 Jul 82, N111FJ FJC 8/82, N777MJ 10/83, ACM Aviation Inc 12/83, O Sullivan Industries 10/88, N50TC 11/88, N50TC O Sullivan Industries Inc. Lamar, Mo.
116	1982. F-WZHD AMD-BA Ff 2 Sep 82, N112FJ FJC 8/82, N781B 6/83, NABISCO Inc 9/83, N69R 9/88, F-GIDC DB Aviation 23 Nov 89, F-GIDC DB Aviation/Air Entreprise, Paris-Le Bourget.
117	1983. F-WPXI AMD-BA Ff 2 Mar 83, HB-ITH Jet Flug AG/Baron Thyssen 3/83,N50TG Tulsa Aircraft Charter Corp 3/90, N50TG Tulsa Aircraft Charter Corp. Charlotte, NC.
118	1982. F-WZHF AMD-BA Ff 13 Sep 82, N113FJ FJC 9/82, N784B NABISCO 7/83, (N183B) rsvd 8/83, Cx USA 4/86, N784B W/O w/o 10 Nov 85. 10/NOV/85
119	1982. F-WZHN AMD-BA Ff 14 Sep 82, N114FJ FJC 9/82,N83FC Fleming Companies 2/84,NEMLC Leasing Corp 11/88, N57DC 6/90, N57DC NEMLC Leasing Corp. Boston, Ma.
120	1983. F-WPXJ AMD-BA Ff 5 Jan 83, YI-ALD Government of Iraq /83, YI-ALD Government/Iraqi Airways, Baghdad
121	1982. F-WZHO AMD-BA Ff 28 Sep 82, N115FJ FJC 9/82, N9311 11/83, Sears Roebuck & Co 1/84, N824R 7/89, N824R Sears Roebuck & Co. Chicago, Il.
122	1983. F-WZHG AMD-BA Ff 9 Feb 83, YI-ALE Government of Iraq 4/83,YI-ALE Government/Iraqi Airways, Baghdad
123	1983. F-WZHH AMD-BA Ff 2 May 83, (F-GDSC) rsvd for Paris demo 6/83, VH-SFJ Griffin Holdings Ltd/Skywest Airlines 3/84, N211EF Interjet Inc 5/87, Evergreen Avn Inc/Ray Industries 7/87,F-GPSA Ste Gefco & Cie 10 Feb 88, F-GPSA Ste Gefco & Cie/Air Gefco, Paris.

c/n	
124	1982. F-WZHA AMD-BA /82, N116FJ FJC 10/82, The Southland Corp 3/83, N711TU 6/83, B A Leasing Co 2/84, N6666R Burnett Aviation Co 8/88, N6666R Burnett Aviation Co. Fort Worth, Tx.
125	1982. F-WZHB AMD-BA /82, N118FJ FJC 10/82, The Southland Corp 4/83, N711KT 6/83, B A Leasing Corp 2/84,I-DENR Soc Norfin SpA 26 Jan 89, I-DENR Soc. Norfin S.p.A/De Nora, Ciampino.
126	1982. F-WZHI AMD-BA /82, N119FJ FJC 10/82, N9312 11/83, Sears Roebuck & Co 1/84, N931G 6/88, N931G Sears Roebuck & Co. Chicago, Il.
127	1982. F-WZHD AMD-BA /82, N121FJ FJC 11/82, N1896T New York Times Co 11/83,N1896T AFM Corp/New York Times Co. NYC.
128	1982. F-WZHF AMD-BA /82, N122FJ FJC 11/82, N9313 11/83, Sears Roebuck & Co 12/83,N733E 1/89, N733E Sears Roebuck & Co. Chicago, Il.
129	1982. F-WZHQ AMD-BA /82, N123FJ FJC 11/82, N1903W Whirlpool Corp 12/83, Appliance Buyers Credit 2/84, Whirlpool Acceptance Corp 11/85, Whirlpool Financial Corp 6/89,N1903W Whirlpool Corp. Benton Harbor, Mi.
130	1982. F-WZHR AMD-BA /82, N124FJ FJC 11/82, N9314 2/84, Sears Roebuck & Co 3/84, N630L 4/89, N630L Sears Roebuck & Co. Chicago, Il.
131	1982. F-WPXD AMD-BA /82, HZ-BB2 BETA Co/Abdul Aziz Zaidan & Partners 6/83, I-ADAG Soc Fiat 6/85, I-ADAG Soc. Fiat, Turin.
132	1983. F-WPXF AMD-BA /83, I-EDIK Soc Pirelli Industrie SpA 7 Nov 85,Soc Orion SpA /88, I-EDIK Soc. Orion S.p.A. Milan.
133	1983. F-WPXH AMD-BA /83, HB-IEA TAG Aeronautics 8/83, HZ-AKI 10/83, HZ-AKI to CL601 3032,HB-IEA Transair (Suisse) SA-Geneva 12/85, ZS-CAQ Department of Transport Services 3/86, ZS-CAQ Department of Transport Services, Pretoria.
134	1984. F-WPXK AMD-BA Ff 12 Jan 84, HB-IEC ALG Aeroleasing SA 6/84, HB-IEC ALG Aeroleasing S.A. Geneva.
135	1983. F-WZHA AMD-BA /83, N125FJ FJC 1/83, N293BC Boise Cascade Corp 4/84, N293BC Boise Cascade Corp. Boise, Id.
136	1983. F-W... AMD-BA /83, N126FJ FJC 1/83, N204HC 6/84, SONAT Svc Co 7/84, Group Holdings Inc 6/86, N5OHC 6/87, GECC-Charlotte 11/89, VR-BLL Glaxo (Bermuda) Ltd-London 1/90, N..... FJC 11/90, YV- Bariven Corp 11/90, YV-.... Bariven Corp. Houston, Tx.
137	1983. F-WZHC AMD-BA /83, N127FJ FJC 6/83, N5OFJ 10/84, (N119FJ) rsvd 17 May 85, C-GTPL Trans Canada Pipelines 7/85, C-GTPL Trans Canada Pipelines, Toronto.
138	1983. F-WPXD AMD-BA /83, N75G FJC 5/84, ANR Pipeline Co 7/84, N941CC 1/87, I-CAFB Soc Fiat 24 Jun 87, I-CAFB Soc. Fiat, Turin.
139	1983. F-WZHD AMD-BA /83, N128FJ FJC 6/83, N96CE U S F & G Co 7/84, Whirlpool Leasing 10/84, Whirlpool Financial Corp 6/89, N96CE United States Fidelity & Guarantee Co. Baltimore, Md.
140	1983. F-WPXH AMD-BA /83, VR-BHX Olympic Maritime/Somers Navigation Ltd-Athens 7/84, (F-GJTR) Uni-Air International rsvd 18 Jan 90, VR-BHX Olympic Maritime/Somers Navigation Ltd, Atens.
141	1983. F-W... AMD-BA /83, N129FJ FJC 1/84, N16R R J Reynolds Industries Inc 9/84, RJR NABISCO Inc 10/86, Reynolds Air Services 12/89, R J Reynolds Tobacco Co 8/90, N16R R J Reynolds Tobacco Co. Winston Salem
142	1984. F-WZHK AMD-BA /84, N132FJ FJC 3/84, N4350M Mead Corp 10/84, N4350M Mead Corp. Dayton, Oh.
143	1984. F-WZHI N130FJ FJC 1/84, N77CP 6/84, Pfizer Inc 10/84, N77CP Pfizer Inc. Trenton, NJ.
144	1984. F-WZHL AMD-BA /84, N133FJ FJC 3/84, N70FL Flight Levels Corp 12/84,lease LASCA-Argentina 'Southern Star' 87-90, FJC 11/90, N70FL Falcon Jet Corp. Teterboro, NJ.
145	1984. F-WPXE AMD-BA /84, F-GEXE AMD-BA 11/85, A6-ZKM Sheik Mohammed bin Zaid Al Nahyan-Abu Dhabi 11/85, I-CAFC Soc SEGEST 20 Dec 87, I-CAFC Soc. Fiat/Soc. Servizi Gestionali-SEGEST, Turin.
146	1984. F-WZHA AMD-BA /84, N131FJ FJC 3/84, N747 1/85, FMC Corp 10/85, N747 FMC Corp. Wheeling, Il.
147	1984. F-WPXG AMD-BA /84, HB-IED Aeroleasing/Pan Ocean Energy Resources 1/86, F-WPXG AMD-BA 21 Apr 86, VR-BKG Sioux Co/Livanos 13 May 86, VR-BKG Sioux Co Ltd.
148	1984. F-WZHB AMD-BA /84, N134FJ FJC 6/84, N81R BOS R J Reynolds Industries 23 Apr 85, RJR NABISCO Inc 10/86, Reynolds Air Services Inc 12/89, R J Reynolds Tobacco Co 8/90, N81R R J Reynolds Tobacco Co. Winston Salem, NC.
149	1984. F-WZHJ AMD-BA /84, N135FJ BOS FJC 29 Oct 84, Whirlpool Corp 5 Apr 85, N1904W 5/85, F-GHAQ Regourd Aviation 17 Jul 90, F-GHAQ FIBIVIAT/Elf Acqitaine/Regourd Aviation, Paris-Le Bourget.
150	1984. F-WZHC AMD-BA /84, N136FJ FJC del 16 Jan 85, HB-IAE IBM-Switzerland 18 Jul 85, HB-IAE IBM (Schweiz), Zurich.
151	1984. F-WPXD AMD-BA /84, MM62020 Government of Italy 11/85, MM62020 AMI, 31 Stormo, Roma-Ciampino.
152	1984. F-WZHD AMD-BA /84, N137FJ FJC 11/84, Dun & Bradstreet Corp 12/84, N1841F 9/85, Meridian Leasing Corp 1/90, N75W Consumers Power Co 5/90, Fleet Credit Corp 7/90, N75W Consumers Power Co. Jackson, Mi.
153	1985. F-WZHE AMD-BA /85, N138FJ FJC del 28 Mar 85, N5OFJ FJC demonstrator 8/85, Pfizer Inc 1/86, N16CP 9/86, N16CP Pfizer Inc. W Trenton, NJ.
154	1985. F-WZHA AMD-BA /85, N139FJ FJC 5/85, Ford Motor Co 6/85, N320K 12/85, N920K 12/88, Bellsouth Services Inc 8/89, N404R 10/89, N404R Bellsouth Services Inc. Atlanta, Ga.
155	1985. F-WPXH AMD-BA /85, MM62021 Government of Italy 12/85, MM62021 AMI, 31 Stormo, Roma-Ciampino.
156	1985. F-WZHF AMD-BA /85, N140FJ FJC del 13 Jun 85, N7533 HNG Internorth Inc 11/85, Internorth Inc later Enron Corp 12/85,Citicorp Leasing 7/86, N5733 Enron Corp. Houston, Tx.

#	Entry
157	1985. F-WZHG AMD-BA /85, N141FJ FJC 5/85, N312A Ameritech Information Technologies 11/85, N312A American Information Technologies, Chicago, Il.
158	1985. F-WZHH AMD-BA /85, N142FJ FJC 9/85, Phifer Wire Products Inc 12/85, N54YR 1/86, N54YR Phifer Wire Products Inc. Tuscaloosa, Al.
159	1985. F-WZHC AMD-BA 10/85, LX-NUR Mr Jaffer-Sri Lanka/Kingson Investments-Luxembourg 7/86, I-LXAG Soc Luxottica SpA 28 Dec 87, I-LXAG Soc. Luxottica S.p.a. Tessera-Venezia.
160	1985. F-WZHI AMD-BA /85, N143FJ FJC del 11 Dec 85, N48R RJR Industries Inc 5/86, RJR NABISCO Inc 10/86, Reynolds Air Services Inc 1/90, R J Reynolds Tobacco Co 8/90, N48R R J Reynolds Tobacco Co. Winston Salem, NC.
161	1985. F-WZHA AMD-BA /85, N144FJ FJC del 17 Dec 85, Becton-Dickinson 12/85, N863BD 6/86, N863BD Becton-Dickinson/Heleasco Twenty-Four Inc. Wilmington, De.
162	1985. F-WZHB AMD-BA /85, N145FJ FJC 1/86, RJR NABISCO Inc 2/86, N9OR 5/86, C-GYPJ Petro Canada Inc 7 Feb 90, C-GYPJ Petro Canada Inc. Calgary.
163	1985. F-WZHA AMD-BA /85, N146FJ FJC del 27 Feb 86, N5OFJ 10/86, N185FJ VF Corp 8/87, N5VF 11/87, N5VF Vanity Fair/VF Corp. Wyomissing, Pa.
164	1986. F-WZHD AMD-BA /86, N164FJ FJC del 9 Apr 86, HB-IAM IBM Switzerland 25 Aug 86, HB-IAM IBM (Schweiz), Zurich.
165	1986. F-WZHF AMD-BA /86, HZ-SM3 Sheikh Mustafa M A Edrees 12/86, HZ-SM3 M M A Edrees/Saudi Arabian Monetary Agency/ARABASCO, Riyadh.
166	1986. F-WZHE AMD-BA /86, N165FJ 4/86, American Family Corp 9/86, N5OOAF 10/86, N5OOAF American Family Corp. Columbus, Ga.
167	1986. F-WZHG AMD-BA /86, N166FJ 6/86, N186HG Henley Group Inc 11/86, Newco Henley Holdings Inc 1/89, New Henley Holdings 12/89, N186HG New Henley Holdings Inc. Hampton, NH.
168	1986. F-WZHH AMD-BA /86, N167FJ FJC 6/86, N711SC Southland Corp 12/86, DRP Inc 8/90, N48GL 9/90, Hunter Air Corp 10/90, N48GL Hunter Air Corp. Dallas, Tx.
169	1986. F-WPXD AMD-BA /86, I-SNAB Soc SNAM 5/87, I-SNAB Soc. Naz. Metanodotti, Milan.
170	1986. F-WZHI AMD-BA /86, N169FJ FJC del 25 Sep 86, N293K Kellogg Co 2/87, N293K Kellogg Co. Battle Creek, Mi.
171	1986. F-WZHJ AMD-BA /86, N171FJ FJC del 22 Oct 86, N4OAS Allied Signal Inc 8 Apr 87, N4OAS Allied-Signal Inc. Morristown, NJ.
172	1986. F-WZHK AMD-BA /86, N170FJ FJC 11/86, N98R 6/87 RJR NABISCO Inc 6/87, Ashland Oil 7/89, N9OOOF 9/89, N9OOOF Ashland Oil Inc. Worthington, Ky.
173	1986. F-WZHL AMD-BA /86, N172FJ FJC 12/86, PT-LJI Construcciones Comercio Camargo 6/87, PT-LJI Construcciones Comercio Camargo, Sao Paulo.
174	1987. F-WPXE AMD-BA /87, HB-IAG ALG Aeroleasing SA 20 Sep 88, HB-IAG ALG Aeroleasing S.A. Geneva.
175	1987. F-WZHM AMD-BA /87, N177FJ FJC 2/87, N5OFJ FJC 8/87, N334MC MCI Communications Corp 7/88, N330MC 10/88, MCI Transcom Corp 1/90, N330MC MCI Transcom Corp. Washington, DC.
176	1987. F-WZHN AMD-BA /87, N178FJ FJC del 6 May 87, VH-PDJ Ariadne Australia P/L 9/87, M Gore/Bezwada Investments 4/88, N157SP Opex Aviation Inc 5/88, Jack Prewitt-Tx 7/88, Southern Pacific/Chandler Enterprises Inc 10/88, N95GC Wallingford Industries Inc 1/89, Business Aircraft Lsg 3/89, I-DEGF Soc Sirio SRL 5/89, I-DEGF Soc. Sirio SRL/Star, Monza.
177	1987. F-WPXF AMD-BA /87, 9Q-CGK ALG Aeroleasing/Gecamines-Zaire 8/88, 9Q-CGK ALG Aeroleasing/Gecamines, Kinshasa.
178	1987. F-WZHO AMD-BA /87, N179FJ FJC 4/87, N239K Kraft Inc 11/87, N59PM Philip Morris Management Corp 5/89, N59PM Philip Morris Management Corp. Teterboro, NJ.
179	1987. F-WZHP AMD-BA /87, N180FJ FJC del 9 Jul 87, HL7386 Korean Airlines 1/88, HL7386 Korean Airlines, Seoul.
180	1988. F-WWHC AMD-BA Ff 13 Oct 88, I-POLE Soc Gitanair 14 Nov 88, I-POLE Soc. Gitanair, Milan.
181	1987. F-WWHA AMD-BA Ff 21 Aug 87, N181FJ FJC 8/87, N345AP Air Products & Chemicals 10 Mar 88, N345AP Air Products & Chemicals Inc. Allentown, Pa.
182	1987. F-WWHB AMD-BA Ff 16 Oct 87, N182FJ FJC del 8 Nov 87, N250AS Albertsons Inc 21 Apr 88, N250AS Albertsons Inc. Boise, Id.
183	1988. F-WWHF AMD-BA Ff 19 Dec 88, I-CAFD Soc Fiat 21 Jan 89, I-CAFD Soc. Fiat, Turin.
184	1987. F-WWHD AMD-BA Ff 30 Nov 87, N183FJ FJC 11/87, N5OFJ 7/88, N89FC Fleming Companies Inc 12/88, N89FC Fleming Companies Inc. Oklahoma City, Ok.
185	1988. F-WWHE AMD-BA Ff 4 Jan 88, N184FJ FJC del 28 Apr 88, C-GDCO Gart Drabinsky-Cineplex Odeon 5/88, N23SY Bar International Operating Co 4/90, N238Y Peregrine International Inc 8/90, F-GKBZ GIE Air BG 2 Oct 90, F-GKBZ GIE Air BG, Paris-Le Bourget.
186	1988. F-WWHH AMD-BA Ff 8 Feb 88, N278FJ FJC del 9 Jun 88, N450K Kimball Intl Transit 25 Nov 88, N450K Kimball International Transit Inc. Jasper, In.
187	1988. F-WWHG AMD-BA Ff 14 Mar 88, N279FJ FJC BOS 19 Feb 88, N4CP Pfizer Inc 11/88, N4CP Pfizer Inc. Trenton, NJ.
188	1988. F-WWHA AMD-BA Ff 2 May 88, N280FJ FJC 24 May 88, N5OFJ 2/89, N5OFJ 2/89, PT-LJK Wanair Taxi Aereo Ltda-Belo Horizonte 12/89, PT-WAN 1/90, PT-WAN Wanair Taxi Aereo Ltda. Belo Horizonte.

c/n	
189	1988. F-WWHB AMD-BA Ff 31 Aug 88, N281FJ FJC 15 Jul 88, N50WG Gilliam & Co Inc 16 Feb 89, N55SN Sonat Services Inc 8/90, N55SN Sonat Services Inc. Birmingham, Al.
190	1989. F-WHHG AMD-BA Ff 6 Feb 89, I-CAFE Soc Fiat 1 Mar 89, I-CAFE Soc. Fiat, Turin.
191	1988. F-WWHD AMD-BA /88, N282FJ FJC del 9 Dec 88, N950F Russell Stover Candies Inc 5/89, N950F Russell Stover Candies Inc. Kansas City, Mo.
192	1989. F-WWHE AMD-BA /89, N283FJ FJC 2/89, N212T 6/89, A T & T Resource Management Corp 8/89, N212T A T & T Resource Management Corp. Morristown, NJ.
193	1989. F-WWHA AMD-BA Ff 30 Aug 89,MM62026 Government of Italy 12/89,MM62026 AMI, 31 Stormo, Roma-Ciampino
194	1989. F-WWHM AMD-BA /89, N284FJ FJC 4/89, Quaker Oats Co 6/89, N1OAT 9/89, N1OAT Quaker Oats Co. Wheeling, Il.
195	1989. F-WWHK AMD-BA Ff 20 Nov 89, 7401 Government of Portugal /90, 7401 Portuguese Air Force, Esc 504, Montijo, Lisbon.
196	1989. F-WWHD AMD-BA Ff 5 Jun 89, N285FJ FJC 6/89, N8575J Sony Aviation Leasing Corp 12/89, JA8575 Sony Corp 2/90, JA8575 Sony Corp. Tokyo.
197	1989. F-WWHA AMD-BA Ff 27 Jun 89, N286FJ FJC 6/89, N50FJ 1/90, N50FJ Falcon Jet Corp. Teterboro, NJ.
198	1989. F-WWHC AMD-BA Ff 11 Dec 89, 7402 Government of Portugal /90, 7402 Portuguese Air Force, Esc 504, Montijo, Lisbon.
199	1989. F-WWHB AMD-BA Ff 11 Sep 89, N287FJ FJC regd 28 Aug 89, Boise Cascade Corp 10/89, N291BC 1/90, N291BC Boise Cascade Corp. Boise, Id.
200	1989. F-WWHE AMD-BA Ff 13 Nov 89, N288FJ FJC 10/89, N664P Phillips Petroleum Corp 3/90, N664P Phillips Petroleum Corp. Bartlesville, Ok.
201	1989. F-WWHA AMD-BA Ff 7 Dec 89, N289FJ FJC via SNN 21 Dec 89, N41TH Sony Corp 4/90, N41TH Sony Corp. Teterboro, NJ.
202	1990. F-WWHB AMD-BA Ff 10 Jan 90, N290FJ FJC del via SNN 24 Jan 90, N212N AT&T Resource Management Corp 6/90, N212N AT&T Resource Management Corp. Morristown, NJ.
203	1990. F-WWHA AMD-BA /90, I-CSGA Soc CSG 18 Jul 90, I-CSGA Soc. Ferruzzi-Consorzio Servizi di Gruppo, Forli-Ravenna.
204	1990. F-WWHD AMD-BA /90, F-GKAR Lyon Air 23 Jul 90, F-GKAR Lyon Air, Lyon-Bron.
205	1990. F-WWHD AMD-BA /90, N291FJ FJC del via SNN 10 Apr 90, N57EL Enterprise Leasing Co 9/90, N57EL Enterprise Leasing Co. Charleston, SC.
206	1990. F-WWHB AMD-BA 10/90, VR-BMF Glaxo (UK) 10/90, VR-BMF Glaxo (UK), London.
207	1990. F-WWHC AMD-BA /90, N292FJ FJC 5/90, N55BP 9/90, 800 BP Corp 11/90,N55BP 800 BP Corp. Portland, Or.
208	1990. F-WWHP AMD-BA 10/90, I-CSGB Soc CSG 11/90, I-CSGB Soc. Ferruzzi-Consorzio Servizi di Gruppo, Forli-Ravenna.
209	1990. F-WWHE AMD-BA /90, N293FJ FJC del 6 Jul 90, N59CF Compass Foods Inc 27 Nov 90, N59CF Compass Foods Inc. Montvale, NJ.
210	1990. F-W... AMD-BA /90, F-GICN Cie Generale d'Electricite 29 Nov 90, F-GICN CGE=Compagnie Generale d'Electricite, Paris-Le Bourget.
211	1990. AMD-BA /90, MM620.. Government of Italy /91, MM620.. AMI, 31 Stormo, Roma-Ciampino.
212	1990. F-WWHH AMD-BA /90, N294FJ FJC del 19 Oct 90, N294FJ
213	1990. F-WWHW AMD-BA /90, N295FJ FJC del 7 Dec 90, N295FJ
214	1990. F-WWHX Dassault Aviation /90, N296FJ FJC 10/90, N296FJ
215	1990. F-W... Dassault Aviation /90, N297FJ FJC 17 Dec 90, N297FJ
216	1990. Dassault Aviation /90, N298FJ FJC 3 Dec 90, N298FJ

Falcon 900

c/n	
1	1984. F-WIDE AMD-BA Ff 21 Sep 84, F-GIDE 17 Sep 85 'Spirit of Lafayette' DGAC & FAA certification 13 Mar & 21 Mar 86 resp, EFS 10/87, F-GIDE Europe Falcon Service, Paris-Le Bourget.
2	1985. F-WFJC AMD-BA Ff 30 Aug 85, F-GFJC 9/85, F-RAFP French Air Force 11 Nov 87, F-RAFP A de l'Air, ET 1/60, Villacoublay.
3	1986. F-WWFA AMD-BA Ff 14 Apr 86, N403FJ FJC del 8 Jun 86, N327K Ford Motor Co 11/86, N327K Ford Motor Co. Dearborn, Mi.
4	1986. F-WWFC AMD-BA Ff 3 Dec 86, VR-BJX Triair (Bermuda)/Silver Sand Air Svcs/Mr Gordon-RSA 1/87, AMD 2-3/90, F-RAFQ French Air Force 3/90, F-RAFQ A de l'Air, ET 1/60, Villacoublay.
5	1986. F-WWFB AMD-BA Ff 6 Oct 86, N404FJ FJC 9/86, VH-BGF Bond Corp del 11 Apr 87,F-GGRH DB Aviation /90, F-GGRH Natiolocation/DB Aviation/Air Enterprise, Paris-Le Bourget.
6	1986. F-WWFD AMD-BA Ff 23 Oct 86, N405FJ FJC del 20 Nov 86,Anheuser-Busch Companies Inc 1/87, N80F 5/87, N80F Anheuser-Busch Companies Inc. Wilmington, De.
7	1987. F-WWFG AMD-BA Ff 11 Feb 87, TR-LCJ Government of Gabon 8/87, TR-LCJ Government of Gabon, Libreville. 'Masuku II'
8	1986. F-WWFE AMD-BA Ff 1 Dec 86, N406FJ FJC 12/86, N5731 Enron Corp 6/87, Citicorp Industrial Credit Inc-ATL 8/87, Citicorp North America Inc 12/87, N5731 Enron Corp. Houston, Tx.
9	1987. F-WWFJ AMD-BA Ff 9 Apr 87, (PH-ILC) Philips NV-Eindhoven /87, HB-IAB GFTA Trendanalyse 5/87, HB-IAB GFTA Trendanalysen, Basle.
10	1987. F-WWFF AMD-BA Ff 20 Jan 87, N407FJ FJC 1/87, N900FJ 4/87,Paris demo 6/87,3 World climb records at TEB 21 Feb 87, (N910FJ) rsvd 5 Nov 87, Great American Isurance Co 11/87, N26LB 2/88, PCC N26LB Inc 4/88, N96LB 2/89, Ed J DeBartolo 4/89, N96LB Edward J DeBartolo Corp. Youngstown, Oh.
11	1987. F-WWFK AMD-BA Ff 12 Jun 87, LX-AER Tabamark SA 6/87, LX-AER Tabamark S.A. Luxembourg.
12	1987. F-WWFH AMD-BA Ff 10 Mar 87, N408FJ FJC Bod-Little Rock 4748nm in 11.07hrs on 28 Mar 87, N991AS Allied-Signal Inc 8/87, N991AS Allied-Signal Inc. Morristown, NJ.
13	1987. F-WWFI AMD-BA Ff 19 Mar 87, N409FJ FJC 3/87, N328K Ford Motor Co 9/87, N328K Ford Motor Co. Detroit, Mi.
14	1987. F-WWFL AMD-BA Ff 27 Mar 87, N410FJ FJC 3/87, N900SB Southwestern Bell 8/87, N900SB Southwestern Bell, Chesterfield, Mo.
15	1987. F-WWFM AMD-BA Ff 29 Jun 87, HB-IAK Gatair SA 7/87, MBC Investment SA 5/89, Sofijet SA 19 Jun 89, HB-IAK Sofijet SA-Fribourg/Gatair S.A. Geneva.
16	1987. F-WWFN AMD-BA Ff 24 Apr 87, N412FJ FJC del 28 May 87, (N187HG) rsvd for Henley Group 19 Aug 87, N187H Henley Group Inc 1/88, VR-CTA ARAVCO-Nice 5/89, VR-CTA ARAVCO, Nice.
17	1987. F-WWFO AMD-BA Ff 28 Apr 87, N411FJ FJC 3/87, N944AD Archer Daniels Midland Co 8 Dec 87, N944AD Archer Daniels Midland Co. Wilmington, De.
18	1987. F-WWFA AMD-BA Ff 14 May 87, N413FJ FJC 4/87, American Intl Aviation Corp 11/87, N72PS 1/88, N72PS American International Aviation Corp. Teterboro, NJ.
19	1987. F-WWFB AMD-BA Ff 25 May 87, N414FJ FJC del 19 Jun 87, N900SJ Sid R Bass Holdings Inc 4 Nov 87, N900SJ Sid R Bass Inc. Fort Worth, Tx.
20	1987. F-WWFC AMD-BA Ff 11 Jun 87, N415FJ FJC 4/87, (N711T) rsvd 15 Jul 87 for Southland Corp N999PM Pacific Marine Leasing Inc 28 Dec 87, N999PM Pacific Marine Leasing Inc. Arlington, Wa.
21	1987. F-WWFJ FJC 10/87, (HZ-R4A) Saudia Special Flight Services 10/87, HZ-AFT 11/87, HZ-AFT Saudia Special Flight Services, Jeddah.
22	1987. F-WWFD AMD-BA /87, N416FJ FJC 6/87, N54DC Dow Chemical Co 18 Nov 87, N54DC Dow Chemical Co. Freeland, Mi.
23	1987. F-WWFK AMD-BA /87, I-BEAU Soc SARAS 4 Dec 87, I-BEAU Soc. SARAS, Milan.
24	1987. F-WWFE AMD-BA /87, N417FJ FJC 6/87, N901B Bristol Myers Co 1/88, GAC 4/89, Finevest Svcs Leasing 3/90, N67WB 5/90, N67WB Finevest Services Leasing Corp. White Plains, NY.
25	1987. F-WWFA AMD-BA /87, N418FJ FJC del 16 Sep 87, N70EW East West Air Inc 12/87, N70EW East West Air Inc. Teterboro, NJ.
26	1987. F-WWFM AMD-BA /87, HB-IAC ALG Aeroleasing SA 12/87, HB-IAC ALG Aeroleasing S.A. Geneva.
27	1987. F-WWFH AMD-BA /87, N419FJ FJC 7/87, N90EW East West Air Inc 12/87,N90EW East West Air Inc/Aviation Methods, San Francisco, Ca.
28	1987. F-WWFI AMD-BA /87, N420FJ FJC 7/87, N85D Castle Aviation Inc 23 Mar 88, N85D Castle Aviation Inc. Van Nuys, Ca.
29	1987. F-WWFL AMD-BA /87, N421FJ FJC del 30 Oct 87, C-GTCP Trans Canada Pipelines 3/88, C-GTCP Trans Canada Pipelines, Toronto.
30	1987. F-WWFL AMD-BA /87, HB-IAF ALG Aeroleasing SA 8 Jul 88,HB-IAF Pan Ocean Oil Co/ALG Aeroleasing S.A. Geneva.
31	1987. F-WWFB AMD-BA /87, N422FJ FJC 11/87, N900FJ 3/88, N910JW S C Johnson & Son Inc 19 Jul 88, N910JW S C Johnson & Son Inc/Johnson's Wax, Racine, Wi.
32	1987. F-WWFG AMD-BA/87, N423FJ FJC 11/87, VH-BGV Bond Corp 5/88, (F-GJBT) rsvd B T Aviation 24 Jul 90, VH-BGV Bond Corp. Perth.

c/n	
33	1987. F-WWFC AMD-BA /87, N424FJ FJC 9/87, N298W Henley Group Inc 31 May 88, Henley Mfg Holding 6/88, F-GHEA Regourd Aviation to FIBIVIAT/Elf Acquitaine 11/89, F-GHEA Natio Location/FIBAVIAT/Elf Acquitaine, Paris-Le Bourget.
34	1987. F-WWFD AMD-BA /87, N425FJ FJC 9/87, N8100E Emerson Electric Co 21 Apr 88, N8100E Emerson Electric Co. St Louis, Mo.
35	1987. F-WWFC AMD-BA /87, HB-IAD ALG Aeroleasing SA 4 Mar 88,HB-IAD ALG Aeroleasing S.A/Industrie Leasing Zurich S.A. Lausanne.
36	1987. F-WWFE AMD-BA /87, N426FJ FJC 10/87, N96PM U S F & G Finance Co 25 Apr 88, N96PM U S F & G Finance Co. Baltimore, Md.
37	1987. F-WWFN AMD-BA /87, N427FJ FJC 10/87, N45SJ Sid Richardson Carbon & Gasoline 8/88, N45SJ Sid Richardson Carbon & Gasoline, Fort Worth, Tx.
38	1987. F-WWFE AMD-BA /87, T 18-1 Government of Spain 4/88, T 18-1 EC-ZC., 45-40, Ed1A/45 Grupo, Madrid.
39	1988. F-WWFF AMD-BA /88, N428FJ FJC 1/88, (N900BF) rsvd 19 Oct 88, Stephens Group Inc 2/89, N1818S 6/89, N1818S Stephens Group Inc. Little Rock, Ar.
40	1988. F-WWFC AMD-BA /88, N429FJ FJC 1/88, N904M Bristol Myers Co 8/88, GAC 4/89, Midcoast Aviation Inc 8/90, N145W Wetterau/Bi-Go Markets Inc 9/90, N145W Wetterau/Bi-GO Markets Inc. Keene, NH.
41	1988. F-WWFI AMD-BA /88, N430FJ FJC 1/88, N404F WCF Corp 19 Jul 88, N404F WCF Corp. Detroit, Mi.
42	1988. F-WWFJ AMD-BA /88, N431FJ FJC del 25 Feb 88, N900FJ 10/88, N42FJ Brierly Investments/IEPL Aviation Inc 3/89, N42FJ Brierly Investments, Wellington, New Zealand.
43	1988. F-WWFF AMD-BA /88, I-MTDE Feruzzi/Soc Immobiliare Genova 4 May 88, I-MTDE Feruzzi/Soc. Immobiliare Genova, Forli-Ravenna.
44	1988. F-WWFA AMD-BA /88, N432FJ FJC del 3 Mar 88, N914J Metromedia Aircraft Co 30 Aug 88, N914J Metromedia Aircraft Co. Teterboro, NJ.
45	1988. F-WWFB AMD-BA /88, N433FJ FJC 1/88, N64BE FRC Holding Inc V/Beatrice Cos 24 Aug 88, N64BE Beatrice Companies, Chicago, Il.
46	1988. F-WWFD AMD-BA /88, N434FJ FJC del 8 Apr 88, N329K Ford Motor Co 22 Sep 88, N329K Ford Motor Co. Detroit, Mi.
47	1988. F-WWFA AMD-BA /88, A6-ZKM Government of Abu Dhabi 1/89, A6-ZKM Government of Abu Dhabi.
48	1988. F-WWFG AMD-BA /88, N435FJ FJC 16 Mar 88, N900MJ ACM Aviation/Apple Computers 9/88, N900MJ ACM Aviation/Apple Computers, San Jose, Ca.
49	1988. F-WWFD AMD-BA Paris demo 6/89,VR-BLB Niarchos 7/89,VR-BLB Maritime Investment & Shipping/Niarchos,
50	1988. F-WWFH AMD-BA /88, N436FJ FJC 3/88, Ford Motor Co 8/88, N330K 9/88, N330K Ford Motor Co. Dearborn, Mi.
51	1988. F-WWFM AMD-BA /88, N437FJ FJC del 14 Jun 88, N59LB 12/88, FJ 900 Inc/26LB Associates 2/89, N26LB 4/89, N26LB 26LB Associates, Cincinnati, Oh.
52	1988. F-WWFC AMD-BA /88, 5N-FGO Government of Nigeria 9/88, 5N-FGO Federal Government of Nigeria, Lagos.
53	1988. F-WWFN AMD-BA /88, N438FJ FJC 5/88, Sony Corp of America 4/89, JA8570 JMSA 16 Jun 89, JA8570 Japanese Maritime Safety Agency,
54	1988. F-WWFC AMD-BA /88, I-FICV Soc CAI 24 Jan 89, I-FICV Soc. CAI, Rome.
55	1988. F-WWFO AMD-BA /88, N439FJ FJC 5/88, C-FJES Execaire/J E Seagram 10 Mar 89, C-FJES Execaire/J E Seagram, Montreal.
56	1988. F-WWFB AMD-BA 5/88, N440FJ 5/88, Sony Aviation Inc 4/89, JA8571 JMSA 12 Jul 89, JA8571 Japanese Maritime Safety Agency,
57	1988. F-WWFK AMD-BA /88, N441FJ FJC del 7 Jul 88, N900WK Kellogg Co 14 Dec 88, N900WK Kellogg Co. Battle Creek, Mi.
58	1988. F-WWFE AMD-BA /88, OE-ILS Tyrolean Airways 11/88, OE-ILS Tyrolean Airways, Innsbruck.
59	1988. F-WWFD AMD-BA /88, N442FJ FJC 6/88, N32B Black & Decker Corp 4 Jan 89, N32B Black & Decker Corp. Baltimore, Md.
60	1988. F-WWFC AMD-BA /88, N443FJ FJC del 20 Oct 88, N900FJ 4/89, N91TH Sony Aviation Leasing Corp 12/89, N91TH Sony Aviation Leasing Corp. Teterboro, NJ.
61	1989. F-WWFB AMD-BA 9/89, VR-CSA Sheikh Abdul Aziz Ibrahim 2/90, HZ-AB2 10/90, HZ-AB2 Sheikh Abdul Aziz Ibrahim/Al Anwae Aviation,
62	1988. F-WWFJ 1000th Falcon constructed ff 17 Jun 88, F-GIVR 2/90, Natio Location/DB Aviation 3/90,F-GIVR Natio Location/DB Aviation, Paris-Le Bourget.
63	1988. F-WWFF AMD-BA /88, N445FJ FJC del 1 Dec 88, N90TH Sony Corp 4/89, N90TH Sony Corp. NYC.
64	1988. F-WWFH AMD-BA /88, N446FJ FJC 9/88, Royal Malaysian Air Force 5/89, M37-01 9/89, M37-01 9M-..., TUDM, 2 Bayan Squadron, Kuala Lumpur.
65	1988. F-WWFA AMD-BA /88, N447FJ FJC 12/88, Federal Paper Board Co 22 Dec 88, N216FP 6/89, N216FP Federal Paper Board Co Inc. Montvale, NJ.
66	1989. F-WWFE AMD /90, F-GJPM Ste Michelin 20 Mar 90, F-GJPM BFCE BAIL/Michelin, Clermont Ferrand.
67	1988. F-WWFD AMD-BA /88, N448FJ FJC 12/88, FJ 900 Inc 18 Jan 89, Danaher Inc 3/89, N900MA 6/89, GECC-Wilton 9/89, N900MA Danaher Inc.
68	1988. F-WWFL AMD-BA /88, N449FJ FJC 12/88, N900HC Group Holdings E G Inc 5/89, R Bass 9/89,N900HC Robert M Bass/Group Holdings E G Inc. Salem, Or.

c/n	
69	1989. F-WWFD AMD-BA 12/89, I-SNAX Soc Naz Metanodotti 15 Dec 89, I-SNAX Soc. Naz. Metanodotti, Milan.
70	1988. F-WWFN AMD-BA /88, N450FJ FJC del 13 Apr 89, A26-070 RAAF 9/89, A26-070 RAAF, 34 Squadron, Fairbairn, Canberra.
71	1989. F-WWFB AMD-BA /89, N451FJ FJC del 1 Jun 89, (N900BF) rsvd 8 Sep 89, Michael W Gibson-Jakarta 6/90, PK-TRP Indonesian Air Transport 11/90, PK-TRP Indonesian Air Transport, Jakarta.
72	1990. F-WWFF AMD Ff 24 Feb 90, VR-BLM Monarch General Aviation Ltd 3/90,VR-BLM Globus Travel/Aileron/Sen Montegazza, Lugano.
73	1989. F-WWFA AMD-BA /89, N452FJ FJC del 27 Apr 89, A26-073 RAAF /89, A26-073 RAAF, 34 Squadron, Fairbairn, Canberra.
74	1989. F-WWFF AMD-BA /89, N453FJ FJC 3/89, A26-074 RAAF /89,A26-074 RAAF,34 Squadron, Fairbairn, Canberra
75	1989. F-WWFC AMD /89, N458FJ FJC regd 22 Sep 89, C-FWSC Windlass Corp 11 Apr 90, C-FWSC Windlass Corp. Boston, Ma.
76	1989. F-WWFE AMD-BA /89, N454FJ FJC del 22 Jun 89, A26-076 RAAF 11/89, A26-076 RAAF, 34 Squadron, Fairbairn, Canberra.
77	1989. F-WWFG AMD-BA /89, N455FJ FJC /89, A26-077 RAAF /89,A26-077 RAAF,34 Squadron, Fairbairn, Canberra
78	1989. F-WWFH N456FJ FJC 7/89, N332MC MCI Transcon Corp 2/90, N332MC MCI Transcon Corp. Washington, DC.
79	1989. F-WWFM N457FJ FJC 28 Aug 89, N900FJ 2/90, N900FJ Falcon Jet Corp. Teterboro, NJ.
80	1989. F-WWFA N459FJ FJC 11/89, N914BD Dillard Department Stores Inc 5/90, N914BD Dillard Department Stores Inc. Little Rock, Ar.
81	1990. F-WWFL AMD /89, 7T-VPA Government of Algeria 3/90, 7T-VPA Ministry of Defence, Boufarik.
82	1990. F-WWFM AMD /90, 7T-VPB Government of Algeria 6/90, 7T-VPB Ministry of Defence, Boufarik.
83	1989. F-WWFG AMD-BA Ff 17 Jan 90, N460FJ FJC 5/90, N900WG Gilliam & Co 7/90, N900WG Gilliam & Co Inc. Charleston, SC.
84	1990. F-WWFD AMD-BA /90, A6-... Government of UAE 12/90, A6-... Government of UAE.
85	1990. F-WWFC AMD-BA /90, N461FJ FJC 3/90, N74FS 8/90, FS Air Inc 10/90, N74FS F S Air Inc. Houston, Tx.
86	1990. F-W... AMD-BA /90, A6-... Government of UAE 12/90, A6-... Government of UAE.
87	1990. F-WWFA AMD-BA /90, N462FJ FJC 6/90, Deerport Aviation Corp 12/90, N462FJ Deerport Aviation Corp. Dover, De.
88	1990. F-WWFH AMD-BA /90, VR-BLT Triair (Bermuda) Ltd 9/90, VR-BLT Triair (Bermuda) Ltd. UK-based.
89	1990. F-W... AMD-BA /90, I-.... Soc CAI /91, I-.... Soc. CAI, Rome.
90	1990. AMD-BA /90, T 18-. Government of Spain /91, T 18-. EC-ZC., 45-.., ED1A/45 Grupo, Madrid.
91	1990. AMD-BA /90, A7-... Government of Qatar /91, A7-... Qatari Government, Doha.
92	1990. F-WWFL AMD-BA /90, N463FJ FJC 19 Jul 90, PT-... Lince Taxi Aerea Ltda 12 Dec 90, PT-... Lince Taxi Aereo Ltda. Sao Paulo.
93	1990. F-W... AMD-BA /90, EC-... Bank of Santander /91, EC-... Bank of Santander,
94	1990. AMD-BA /90, A7-... Government of Qatar /91, A7-... Qatari Government, Doha.
95	1990. F-WWFO AMD-BA /90, N464FJ FJC 18 Sep 90, N464FJ
96	1990. F-WWFF AMD-BA /90, F-GHTD Dassault Aviation 10/90, F-GHTD Dassault Aviation, Paris-Le Bourget.
97	1990. F-W... AMD-BA /90, EC-... /91, EC-...
98	1990. F-WWFM /90, N465FJ FJC 10/90, N465FJ
101	1990. F-W... AMD /90, N466FJ FJC 3 Dec 90, N466FJ

Challenger 600/601/601-3A

c/n	
1001	1978. Ff 8 Nov 78. C-GCGR-X W/O W/o 3 Apr 80. 03/APR/80
1002	1979. C-GCGS-X Canadair Ltd Ff 17 Mar 79, C-GCGS 1980-86 test aircraft, C-GCGS-X noted Montreal in low vis camouflage 6/86, Cx C- 3/88, 144612 DND /? 144612 CC144, DND, AETE, Cold Lake, Alberta.
1004	1979. C-GXKQ-X Ff 21 May 79, C-GXKQ 1980-2, N2677S AVCO Corp 1/83, Zhobi Corporation Number Two 4/84, N227CC 8/84, Great Western Financial Corp 2/86, N227CC Great Western Financial Corp. Salinas, Ca.
1005	1980. C-GBDH-X Ff 13 Apr 80, N600CL Canadair Inc 5/80, ICOS Construction Corp 5/81, Canadair Challenger Inc 1/87, C-GBCC Canadair Ltd 4/88, B C Government Air Svcs 13 Oct 88,C-GBCC B C Government Air Services Branch, Sidney, BC.
1006	1980. C-GCSN Ff 1 Jun 80, N110KS Kalair USA Corp 7/81, cx USA 1/84, HZ-A04 TAG International 2/84,C-GCSN Canadair Ltd 8/84, 144603 DND /? 144603 CE144A, DND, 414 Squadron, North Bay.
1007	1980. C-GBKC Ff 13 Mar 80, Canadair Ltd 4/80, HZ-TAG TAG International 6/81, C-GBKC Canadair Inc 10/81, Canadian MoT 2/82, cx C- 1/86, 144604 DND 6/86, 144604 CC144, DND, 412 (Transport) Squadron, Uplands.
1008	1980. (D-BBAD) Ff 29 Jun 80, C-GBEY Canadian MOT 8 Nov 81, Cx C- 4/86, 144605 DND 6/86, 144605 CC144, DND, 412 (Transport) Squadron, Uplands.
1009	1980. C-GBFY Ff 31 Jul 80, N606CL Canadair Inc 9/80, Michael O'Connell 6/83, C-GCVQ Canadair Ltd 5/85, DND 9/85, 144606 CC144, DND, 412 (Transport) Squadron, Uplands.
1010	1980. C-GCIB Ff 3 Sep 80, Imperial Bank of Commerce 7/81, C-GCIB to 8048, N909MG Merv Griffin Records 9/86, Huntrip Inc 2/89, N909MG Huntrip Inc. Chesterfield, Mo. (status ?)
1011	1981. C-GBHS Ff 21 Jan 81, N42137 Film Properties Inc 2/81, N510PC 3/82, SSC No 1 Corp 8/85, N510PS Clarendon Group Svcs-NYC 'Positive Spread' 5/86, N601JR Executive Air Consulting 6/88, Kansas Skyview Corp 1/89, N678ML 3/89, Executive Aircraft Consulting 4/89, Berkshire Hathaway Inc 9/89,N678ML Berkshire Hathaway Inc. Omaha, Ne.
1012	1981. C-GBKE Ff 5 Mar 81, N600KC K C Aviation 4/81, Kimberly Clark Corp 9/82, (N78499) rsvd for Canadair Challenger Inc 23 Mar 88, N750PM Pet Inc 5/88, N750PM Pet Inc. St Louis, Mo.
1013	1981. C-GBHZ Ff 12 Dec 80, Owens Corning Fiberglas Corp 7/81, N2428 8/81, FSB-Ut 1/82, Summit Aviation Corp 1/90, N601SA 3/90, N601SA Summit Aviation Corp. E Farmingdale, NY.
1014	1980. C-GBLL-X Ff 19 Nov 80, N97941 Canadair Inc 8/81, TAG-Paris 9/81, HZ-TAG 11/81, C-GBLL Canadair Ltd 6/84, Cx C- /85, 144607 DND /85, 144607 CE144A, DND, 414 Squadron, North Bay.
1015	1980. C-GBLN Ff 15 Dec 80, N37LB American Financial Corp 11/81, TAG Flight Ltd 4/82, N604CL Canadair Inc 6/83, C-GBLN Canadair Ltd 4/84, 144608 DND 6/85, 144608 CC144, DND, 412 (Transport) Squadron, Uplands.
1016	1981. C-GWRT Ff 21 Mar 81, Sugra Ltd-Toronto 6/81, EI-GPA Air Tara Ltd/Guinness Peat Aviation 25 Jul 87, VR-BKJ Trimjet Ltd/Oasis International Group 2/89, VR-BKJ Trimjet Ltd/Oasis International Group, Madrid.
1017	1981. C-GBPX Ff 10 Apr 81, N4247C Canadair Inc 5/81, TAG Aviation Ltd 1/82, N777XX 4/82, C-GBPX Canadair Ltd 2/84, 114609 DND 9/85, 144609 CC144, DND, 412 (Transport) Squadron, Uplands.
1018	1981. C-GLWR Ff 22 Apr 81, N1812C EAF/Citiflight Inc 6/81, Canadair Challenger Inc 3/88, N198CC 6/88, Bombardier Credit Inc 11/88, J E Seagram & Sons 10/89,N375PK 1/90,N375PK Seagrams Distillers, London-UK.
1019	1981. C-GLWT Ff 7 May 81, N9071M HC Airlease Inc/Hyatt Corp 8/81, N603CL 4/83, Freelander Inc 1/85, N600FF 4/86, Mar Flite Ltd 1/88, Dover Leasing Co 10/88, N600FF Dover Leasing Co. Los Angeles, Ca.
1020	1981. C-GLWV Ff 27 May 81, N36LB ACSC Inc 8/81, First Security Bank of Utah 12/82, N602CL 2/83, N600MG Canadair/Ingersoll Publications 9/87, Price Productions Inc 10/90,N600MG Price Productions Inc. Trenton, NJ.
1021	1981. C-GLWX Ff 10 Jun 81, N914X Xerox Corp 8/81, Capital Associates International 1/87, N914X Xerox Corp. NYC.
1022	1981. C-GLWZ Ff 4 Jul 81, C-GOGO Ministry of Natural Resources-Toronto 1/82,Canadair Ltd /83, 144610 DND 5/85, 144610 CC144, DND, 412 (Transport) Squadron, Uplands.
1023	1981. C-GLXB Ff 28 Jul 81, N630M Olin Corp 9/81, Canadair Challenger Inc 2/90, N680M 4/90, N90UC Union Camp Corp 8/90, N90UC Union Camp Corp. Morristown, NJ.
1024	1981. C-GLXD Ff 14 Aug 81, N637ML EAF/Merrill Lynch 10/81,(637=tel code),Dacion Corp 2/82,N567L Canadair Challenger Inc 7/88, Bombardier Credit Inc 11/88, N326MM Metro Mobile Transport Inc 4/89, N326MM Metro Mobile Transport Inc. NYC.
1025	1981. C-GLXF Ff 2 Sep 81, N2636N GTE Service Corp 1/82, N111G 3/82, N111J Omni 9/88, HB-ILH C Hirschman/Jet Aviation Inc 11/88, HB-ILH C Hirshman/Jet Aviation, Zurich.
1026	1981. C-GLXH Ff 12 Sep 81, N507CC Celanese Corp 11/81, Hoechst Celanese Corp 6/87,N507HC 8/87, N507HC Hoechst Celanese Corp. Douglas Municipal Airport, NC.
1027	1981. C-GLXK Ff 25 Sep 81, N420L AVCO Financial Services Leasing Co 11/81, Textron Inc 3/86,N420TX 3/87, N420TX Textron Inc. Providence, RI.
1028	1981. C-GLXM Ff 7 Oct 81, HB-VHC Interjet AG/Kontinair AG-Zug 12/82, tt as of 10/88 52 hours, N600ST Seatankers USA Corp 4/89, 5B-CHX 11/90, 5B-CHX Seatankers USA Corp. Limassol.
1029	1981. C-GLX. Ff 19 Oct 81, HB-VGA Air Charter AG-Zug 11/81,HB-VGA Air Charter AG/Kraus & Naimer, Vienna.
1030	1981. C-GLXQ Ff 12 Nov 81, N1622 Texaco Inc 12/81, Canadair Inc 8/84, N604CL 2/85, C-GCZU Canadair Ltd 9/85, 144611 DND /86, 144611 CE144A, DND, 414 Squadron, North Bay.

c/n	
1031	1981. C-GLXS Ff 14 Nov 81, N620S Texasgulf Inc/Emery 12/81, Arlington Integrated Aircraft 2/83, Merkin Sandford 8/83, N620S Texasgulf Inc/Emery Air Charter, Rockford. Il.
1032	1981. C-GLXU Ff 28 Oct 81, N455SR St Regis Paper Co 12/81, Drum Financial/St Regis 10/82, N200CN 4/85, Champion International/MDFC Equipment Leasing 7/85, N11AZ 5/86, Geo J Priester Aviation Service Inc /87, N11AZ Priester Aviation Inc. Chicago, Il.
1033	1981. C-GLXW Ff 10 Dec 81, N2642F Canadair Inc 1/82, TAG Aviation Ltd 9/82, VR-CKK Adnan Khashoggi/Handlingair-Challenger 11/82, Cx VR- 3/86, N600YY Mar-Flite Ltd 8/85, Charles E Smith Management Inc 12/85, N101SK 3/86, EJA 1/90, N101ST 5/90, N101ST EJA, Columbus, Oh.
1034	1981. C-GLXY Ff 30 Nov 81, N2634Y Southern Railway Co 12/81, N153SR 3/82, Norfolk Southern Corp 2/83, N151SR rsvd 16 Mar 90, N151SR Norfolk Southern Corp. Norfolk, Va.
1035	1981. C-GLYA Ff 13 Dec 81, N122TY Tyco Laboratories Inc 1/82, Farley Metals Inc 1/84, N122WF 3/84, N64FC 11/88, Canadair Challenger Inc 12/88, Cx USA 4/89, C-FEAQ Bombardier Ltee 4/89,(EI-BYO) noted under wing 7/89, VR-BLD Swift Avn/Scorpio/BSM 9/89, VR-BLD Swift Aviation Ltd-Bermuda/Scorpio Aviation, London.
1036	1981. C-GLYC Ff 18 Dec 81, C-GBOQ Canadair Ltd 2/82, N80AT Taubman Air Inc 3/82, N80AT to G-3 463, N88AT 3/86, N66MF Maxair Inc/Wells Fargo Leasing 8/86, LB 1 Aircraft Inc-SFO 1/90, N66MF Maxair Inc. Pontiac
1037	1981. C-GLYE Ff 19 Dec 81, N805C A E Staley Manufacturing Co 2/82, Cx USA 9/83, N805C W/O W/o 3 Jan 83. 03/JAN/83
1038	1982. C-GLYH Ff 21 Jan 82, N8010X Xerox Corp 2/82, N1045X 2/84, Capital Associates Intl 1/87, N1045X Xerox Corp. NYC.
1039	1982. C-GLYK Ff 29 Jan 82, N26640 Metropolitan Life Insurance Co 2/82, N1868M 6/83, N1868S 8/89, N1868S Metropolitan Life Insurance Co. NYC.
1040	1982. C-GLYM Ff 4 Feb 82, 144601 DND 10/83, 144601 CC144, DND, 412 (Transport) Squadron, Uplands.
1041	1982. C-GLYO Ff 10 Feb 82, N733K HAC-Humana Inc 3/82, C R Bard Inc 8/87, N733CF 1/88, N733CF C R Bard Inc. Murray Hill, NJ.
1042	1982. C-GLWY Ff 20 Feb 82, Valley Line & Equipment 3/82, N770CA 4/82, CIGNA/American Fletcher Leasing Corp 2/83, Executive Aircraft Consulting 1/90, N999SR 4/90, U S Bancorp Leasing & Financial 10/90,N999SR U S Bancorp Leasing & Financial, Portland, Or.
1043	1982. C-GLWX Ff 28 Feb 82, N229GC W R Grace & Co 3/82, Cx USA 12/87, C-GJPC Jim Pattison Industries Inc 13 Jul 88, C-GJPG Jim Pattison Industries Ltd. Richmond, BC.
1044	1982. C-GLWZ Ff 3 Mar 82, N541MM Bowater North America Corp 4/82, Metromedia Inc 4/83, N205MM 5/83, Metromedia Aircraft Co 1/87, AAR Corp 4/87,N55AR 1/88, N55AR AAR Corp. Chicago, Il.
1045	1982. C-GLXB Ff 18 Mar 82, Geosurvey International Inc 4/82, N55PG Geosurvey Intl Inc 4/82, First City Texas Trans Inc 8/89, N900FC 9/89, N900FC First City Texas Trans Inc. Houston, Tx.
1046	1982. C-GLXD Ff 18 Mar 82, C-GTXV Petro-Canada Inc 28 May 82, C-GTXV Petro-Canada Inc. Calgary.
1047	1982. C-GLXH Ff 25 Mar 82, N2741Q Whitewind Company Ltd 6/82, N601WW 10/82, N601WW Whitewind Co Ltd. White Plains, NY.
1048	1982. C-GLXK Ff 6 Apr 82, N29687 Clinton Aviation Group Inc 4/82, N600TT 11/82,Retail Leasing Corp 7/83, N500LS 9/83 rpo NA0320, MORCO 11/83, N500LS to G-3 460, N600LS 11/85, N601LS 9/88, C-FSIP Intera Technologies Ltd 22 Dec 88, C-FSIP Intera Technologies Ltd. Calgary.
1049	1982. C-GLXM Ff 14 Apr 82, N2720B Sandor Kvassay-Ks 5/82, HB-VFW Swiss Air Ambulance 1/83, HB-VFW Swiss Air Ambulance, Zurich. 'Fritz Buhler'
1050	1982. C-GLXO Ff 21 Apr 82, N600MK Morrison Knudsen Co 5/82, AAFT/Telerate Systems 8/83,EJA 4/90,Airtrade Intl Inc 6/90, N600MK Airtrade International Inc. Fairfield, Ct.
1051	1982. C-GLXO Ff 6 May 82, N27341 Clorox Co 'Bleachcraft' 6/82, N20CX 12/82,Flight Services International 1/88, N601SR 4/88, Executive Aircraft Consulting 5/88, Emery Air Charter/MKDG Inc 8/88, Executive Aircraft Consulting 11/90, N601SR Executive Aircraft Consulting Inc. Newton, Ks.
1052	1982. C-GLXS Ff 5 Jul 82, N3330M Olan Mills Inc 9/82, N3330L 8/83, N110M 7/84, N110M Olan Mills Inc. Chattanooga, Tn.
1053	1983. C-GLYA Ff 30 Jul 82, HB-VHO Hamax SA 4/83, N4424P Bel Air Racing Stables 8/83, Trading & Transport Co-NYC /85, Brunswick Corp 1/86, N32BC 3/86, N32BC Brunswick Corp. Skokie, Il.
1054	1982. C-GLYC Ff 17 Sep 82, N80TF Omni International 6/83, B F Goodrich Co 9/83, N7008 3/84, N7008 B F Goodrich Co. N. Canton, Oh.
1055	1982. C-GLYE Ff 28 Oct 82, N2707T Credival Lease Service Inc 12/82, FEDEX 8/85, N1FE 2/86, N1FE Federal Express Corp. Memphis, Tn.
1056	1982. C-GLYH Ff 12 Nov 82, N26895 Canadair Inc 12/82,N600CC Charter Security Life Insurance 3/83,Bank of the South 8/83, N Central Aviation Inc 1/85, N600TE 4/85, GECC-Dallas 10/90, N600TE Jet East/North Central Aviation Inc. Dallas, Tx.
1057	1982. C-GLXU Ff 26 Apr 82, C-GBTK Canadair Ltd 5/82, N605CL Canadair Inc 9/82, (VH-OZZ) Bond Corp 12/83, Celanese Corp 1/85, N508CC 2/85, Hoechst Celanese Corp 6/87, N508HC 8/87, N508HC Hoechst Celanese Corp. Charlotte, NC.
1058	1982. C-GLXW Ff 30 Apr 82, N4000X Xerox Corp 5/82, Capital Associates International 1/87, N4000X Xerox Corp. NYC.
1059	1982. C-GLXY Ff 12 May 82, N227G W R Grace & Co 6/82, N227GL 9/84, N227GL 9/84,Bank of America-SFO 2/90, FCH 1560 Broadway Corp 8/90, N3HB Hamilton Brothers/Delaware Airjet 11/90,N3HB Hamilton Oil, Denver, CO

c/n	
1060	1982. C-GLYK Ff 20 May 82, N29984 Canadair Inc 6/82, Saber Aeronautique Inc 9/83, Rainier Leasing 8/85, MDFC Equipment Leasing 4/86, N22AZ 12/89, Josephine Abercrombie Interests 7/90, N74JA 9/90, N74JA Josephine Abercrombie Interests, Houston, Tx.
1061	1982. C-GLYO Ff 29 May 82, N60OJW Johnson's Wax 6/82, J Roth-Ks 11/88, Multiplex Inc USA 3/89, VH-MXX Multiplex Constructions P/L 8/89, VH-MXX Multiplex Constructions P/L. Perth, WA.
1062	1982. C-GLWV Ff 7 Jun 82, C-GBTT Canadair Ltd 6/82, M31-01 Royal Malaysian Air Force-Kuala Lumpur 6/84, N4FE FEDEX 8/89, Brooke Aviation Inc 11/89, N62BL 4/90, N62BL Brooke Aviation Inc. Greensboro, NC.
1063	1982. C-GLWX Ff 12 Jun 82, N31240 American International Group/Mid Atlantic Avn Corp 7/82, N102ML 9/83, Canadair Inc 7/88, Airsupport Services Corp 9/89, PT-LXW Lider Taxi Aereo SA 4/90, PT-LXW Lider Taxi Aereo SA. Sao Paulo.
1064	1982. C-G... Ff 23 Jun 82, C-GBUB Canadair Ltd 7/82, RMAF 6/84, M31-02 Royal Malaysian Air Force-Kuala Lumpur 6/84, N14FE FEDEX 8/89, Brooke Aviation Inc 12/89, N64GL 2/90, N64GL Brooke Aviation Inc. Greensboro, NC.
1065	1982. C-G... Ff 7 Jul 82, C-GBVE Canadair Ltd 8/82, 144602 DND 5/83, 144602 CC144, DND, 412 (Transport) Squadron, Uplands.
1066	1982. C-GLXD Ff 9 Jul 82, N67B Federated Dept Stores Inc 8/82,Golden Nugget Aviation 12/88, N721SW 4/89, Canadair Challenger Inc 8/89, N701QS 2/90, CIT Group 4/90, N701QS Stone Aviation, Chicago, Il.
1067	1982. C-GLXH Ff 21 Jul 82, C-GBZE Canadair Ltd 8/82, N50928 Allen Bradley Controls Inc 5/84, N800AB 10/84, Allen Bradley Co 4/86, N800AB Allen Bradley Co. Milwaukee, Wi.
1068	1982. C-GLXK Ff 13 Aug 82, N215RL Citadel Air Inc 10/82, Transwestern Pipeline Co 1/85, Harvard Industries 12/85, N938WH 4/86, N938WH Harvard Industries, Farmingdale, NJ.
1069	1982. C-GLXM Ff 24 Aug 82, N203G Grace Natural Resources Corp 9/82, Axial Basin Coal Co 3/83, Cactus Enterprises Inc 11/86, N816PD 2/87, Canadair Inc 2/88, Rocky Mountain Blue Corp-NYC 9/88, I-LPHZ SIBA Aviation-Milan 12/88, Filippo Fochi SpA /90, I-LPHZ Filippo Fochi SpA. Bologna.
1070	1982. C-GLXO Ff 3 Sep 82, N3237S TAG Flight Ltd 10/82, HZ-MF1 Prince Mohammed bin Faisal-Jeddah 5/83, N70DJ DuncanNe 10/87, N24JK Prudential Assurance Co 10/88, N24JK Central Investment/Prudential Insurance Co, Newark, NJ.
1071	1982. C-GLXQ Ff 24 Sep 82, N607CL Burroughs Corp 10/82, N523B 3/83, Rose Associates Inc 5/87, Trans UCU Inc 3/88, N588UC 8/88, N121DF Cintas Corp 9/89, N121DF Cintas Corp. Cincinnati, Oh.
1072	1982. C-GLXW Ff 14 Oct 72, N82A Prudential Insurance Co 1/84, Florida Progress Corp 11/87, (N137FP) rsvd 10 Dec 87, N331FP 3/88, N331FP Florida Progress Corp. St Petersburg, Fl.
1073	1982. C-GLXY Ff 21 Oct 82, N234RG Bristol Myers Co 1/83, N234MW Suncoast Aviation Services 4/84, Gemini Aviation Inc 7/84, N31WT 11/84, Wm Theisen-Godfather's Pizza 5/85, Fuqua Industries 7/86, N31WT to 35A-389, (N331WT) rsvd 8 Aug 86, N661JB 10/86, Australia Zephyr Corp 11/87, N888KS 2/88, VH-NKS Kerry Stokes-Perth 20 Sep 88, VH-NKS Kerry Stokes/Australian Capital Equity P/L. Perth, WA.
1074	1982. C-GLYK Ff 7 Nov 82, N317FE FEDEX 12/82, N1FE 3/85, N1OFE 1/86, HZ-SAA Arab Wings 11/89,HZ-SAA Arab Wings, Riyadh.
1075	1982. C-GLXO Ff 2 Dec 82, N60OCP J V Persand & Co 12/82, FEDEX 8/85, N2FE 2/86, N2FE Federal Express Corp. Memphis, Tn.
1076	1982. C-GLXK Ff 3 Dec 82, N8000 Northrop Corp 12/82, Sol Price Aviation Corp 7/85, N7SP 8/85, Canadair Challenger Inc 1/87,Third Ave Avn Corp 12/87, I-BLSM Soc Italnoli-Milan 9/88, I-BLSM Soc. ITALNOLI Spa. Milan.
1077	1982. C-GLXM Ff 4 Dec 82, N994TA TAG Flight Ltd 2/83, (N778XX) 7/83, cx USA 1/84, C-GBZK Canadair Ltd 2/84, N152SM Service Merchandise Inc 6/85,Multifoods Transportation 8/87, N71M 5/88, Sundstrand Corp 8/90, N71M Sundstrand Corp. Rockford, Il.
1078	1983. C-GLYO Ff 4 Feb 83, N600DL Dan Lasater-DC 3/83, Calumet Farm Inc 1/85, N60OCF 3/85,C-F Aircraft 8/85, Mar-Flite 8/86, Natl Can Corp 11/86, Triangle Aircraft Services Co 4/87, AeroSmith Penny 3/89, I-MRDV Soc Delta Aerotaxi SRL 5/89, I-MRDV Soc. Delta Aerotaxi SRL. Milan.
1079	1983. C-GLWV Ff 18 Jan 83, N46ES DRE Interstate Avn Inc 2/83, Natural Gas Pipeline Co 11/83,N125N 12/83, MRDC/Bernie Eccleston 7/88, N601Z 9/88, N601Z Bernie Eccleston/Motor Racing Development Corp. UK.
1080	1983. C-GLWX Ff 26 Jan 83, N80OCC Chrysler Corp 2/83, Great Western Coca Cola Bottling 12/84, N3JL 3/85, John Lupton-Tn 11/86, N3JL John Lupton/Great Western Coca Cola Bottling, Chattanooga.
1081	1983. C-GLWZ Ff 8 Feb 83, N19HF Hershey Foods Corp 3/83, N19HF Hershey Foods Corp. Hershey, Pa.
1082	1983. C-GLXT Ff 3 Mar 83, N3854B T W Oil (Houston) Inc 3/83, Continental Training Svcs 1/86,N600ST 6/86, I-PTCT Eli-Air SRL 24 Feb 89, I-PTCT Eli-Air SRL. Reggio Emilia.
1083	1983. C-GLXD Ff 17 Mar 83, N47ES Georgetown Interstate Avn Inc 4/83, Scott Paper Co 1/84, N471SP 4/84, N471SP Scott Paper Co. Philadelphia, Pa.
1084	1983. C-GLXH Ff 28 Apr 83, N730TL Time Inc 6/83, (N1OMZ) rsvd MacFlight Inc 11 Feb 85, N175ST Southeast Toyota Distributors 4/85, N175ST Southeast Toyota Distributors, Deerfield Beach, Fl.
1085	1983. C-GLXQ Ff 26 May 83, N20G Goodyear Tire & Rubber Co 6/83, N20G Goodyear Tire & Rubber Co. Akron
3001	1982. C-GBUU Ff 17 Sep 82, N601CL KRS Assocates/Rashid Pepsico 10/82,Canadair Challenger 12/85 The Spectrum Group Inc 12/87, N601AG 5/88, N601AG Exide Corp/The Spectrum Group Inc. Los Angeles, Ca.
3002	1983. C-GBXH Ff 23 Feb 83, (N509PC) Pepsico 6/83, re-allocated to s/n 3004,N4449F GTE Service Corp 9/83, N273G 4/84, Connecticut NB 8/84, N273G GTE Services Corp. Stamford, Ct.

c/n	
3003	1983. C-GLXU Ff 6 Apr 83, N500PC Pepsico Inc/Purchase Leasing Corp 12/83, N500TB Taco Bell Corp 9/87, N500TB Taco Bell Corp. Santa Ana, Ca.
3004	1983. C-GLXK Ff 3 Jun 83, N509PC Pepsico/Collin Leasing Corp 12/83, N967L Frito-Lay Inc 6/84, N967L to 3021, N501PC Pepsico Inc 7/85, N501PC Pepsico Inc. White Plains, NY.
3005	1983. C-G... Ff 21 Apr 83, C-FAAL Aluminium Co of Canada 5/83, ALCAN Aluminium Ltd 11 Aug 87, C-FAAL ALCAN Aluminium Ltd. Montreal.
3006	1983. C-GLXY Ff 20 May 83, N372G General Electric Co 6/83, N372G General Electric Co. NYC.
3007	1983. C-GLYE Ff 18 Jun 83, N711SR The Southland Corp 9/83, SLC Funding Inc 5/85, Wilmington Trust Co 7/90, N711SX Randland Cobey Holdings 10/90, N711SX Randland Cobey Holdings, Oklahoma City, Ok.
3008	1983. C-GLYA Ff 28 Jun 83, N733A HAC-Humana Inc 7/83, N733A HAC-Humana Inc. Louisville, Ky.
3009	1983. C-GLYO Ff 15 Jul 83, N373G General Electric Co 8/83, N373G General Electric Co. Cincinnati, Oh.
3010	1983. C-GLWV Ff 16 Aug 83, C-GBLX Canadair Ltd 9/83, N80CS Coastal Corp 10/83, Omni Intl 11/84, K-C Aviation Inc 7/85, N601UT Sharon Aviation/United Telecom 1/86, N601UT United Telecom/Sharon Aviation Kansas City, Mo.
3011	1983. C-GLWX Ff 29 Aug 83, C-GBYC Canadair Ltd 9/83, N601AG A G Spanos Construction Inc 10/83,Citiflight Inc 3/84, N399WW 7/84, Canadair Challenger Inc 4/88, Kapor Ents Inc 5/88, N899WW 6/88, N700MK 6/89, N700MK Kapor Enterprises Inc. Londonderry, NH.
3012	1983. C-G... Ff 8 Sep 83, N226GL W R Grace & Co 10/83, N226G 4/84, C-GMII Magna International 12/87, Transma Aviation Inc 8/88, VR-BMA Green Goose Ltd 7/90, VR-BMA Green Goose Ltd. Switzerland.
3013	1983. C-G... Ff 23 Sep 83, N601TG TAG Flight Ltd 1/84, TAG Aviation Ltd 12/84, TAG Group USA Inc 3/85, Sunair Corp 2/86, VR-BLA Sol Kerzner/Granaway Ltd/Sun Intl Hotels 3/89, VR-BLA Sol Kerzner/Sun International Hotels, Beverly Hills, Ca.
3014	1983. C-G... Ff 17 Oct 83, N14PN Pneumo Corp 11/83, Golden West Baseball Co 2/89,N292GA 5/89, N292GA Golden West Baseball Co. Anaheim, Ca.
3015	1983. C-G Ff 8 Nov 83, N374G General Electric Co 12/83, N374G General Electric Co. NYC.
3016	1983. C-G... Ff 22 Nov 83, N4562Q Pennzoil Co 12/83, N1107Z 8/84, Richland Development 3/87, N1107Z Richland Development Corp. Houston, Tx.
3017	1983. C-G... Ff 3 Dec 83, C-GBPX Canadair Ltd 1/84, N778XX TAG Aviation Ltd 2/84,TAG Group USA Inc 3/85, N778XX to 5003, HZ-SFS Saudia-Jeddah 1/87, TAG Aeronautics (Saudi Arabia) Ltd /90, N778YY TAG Aviation Inc 11/90, N778YY TAG Aviation Inc. Wilmington, De.
3018	1983. C-G... Ff 13 Jan 84, C-GBXW Canadair Ltd 2/84, N779XX TAG Aviation Ltd 3/84, TAG Group USA Inc 2/85, N779XX W/O W/o 7 Feb 85. 07/FEB/85
3019	1984. Ff 31 Jan 84, N375G General Electric Co 3/84, N375G General Electric Co. NYC.
3020	1984. C-G... Ff 27 Feb 84, C-GCFI Canadian MoT 6/84, Transport Canada /86, Govt of Canada DoT 22 Aug 89, C-GCFI Govt of Canada, DoT Aircraft Services Directorate, Ottawa.
3021	1984. C-G... Ff 15 Mar 84, N5069P Southland Corp/Florida Co 5/84, N711SJ 2/85, Somers Leasing Corp 6/85, N967L 8/85, N967L Frito-Lay Inc. Dallas, Tx.
3022	1984. C-G... Ff 4 Apr 84, C-GCFG Canadian MoT 6/84, Transport Canada /86, Govt of Canada DoT Aircraft Services Directorate 22 Aug 89, C-GCFG Govt of Canada, DoT Aircraft Services Directorate, Ottawa.
3023	1984. C-G... Ff 19 Apr 84, N778YY TAG Aviation Ltd/TAG Group USA 5/84, SBSMV Corp 12/85, N100WC Wickes Companies Inc 6/86, Frito-Lay Inc 3/89, N100WC Frito-Lay Inc. Dallas, Tx.
3024	1984. C-GLYA Ff 8 May 84, N711ST Southland Corp 6/84,SLC Funding 5/85,Jetflight Avn Inc 6/88, N711SD 1/89, HB-ILM Vad Air-Lugano 15 Mar 89, HB-ILM Vad Air, Mezzovico-Lugano.
3025	1984. C-GLWV Ff 26 May 84, N1620 Texaco Inc 6/84, N1620 Texaco Inc. NYC.
3026	1984. C-GLWX Ff 12 Jun 84, N5373U Penn Central Corp 7/84, N927A 11/84, L Aviation Inc 1/88, N601GL 3/88, Brook Avn Inc 9/88, Canadair Challenger Inc 10/89, FEDEX 3/90, N601GL Federal Express Corp. Memphis, Tn.
3027	1984. C-GLWZ Ff 29 Jun 84, N5402X Consolidated Natural Gas/CNG Transmission 7/84, N17CN 8/84, N17CN CNG Transmission Corp. Bridgeport, WV.
3028	1984. C-GLXB Ff 13 Jul 84, C-FBEL Execaire/Bell Canada Ents 9 Nov 84, C-FBEL Execaire/Bell Canada Enterprises, Montreal, PQ.
3029	1984. C-GLXD Ff 30 Aug 84, N5491V Chemgraphics Systems Inc 9/84, N1824T 4/85,N1824T Chemgraphics Systems Inc. Secaucus, NJ.
3030	1984. C-GLXX Ff 18 Sep 84, N611CL Canadair Challenger Inc 1/85, Schering Realty Corp 12/85, N34CD 4/86, N34CD Schering Realty Corp. Morristown, NJ.
3031	1984. C-G... Ff 12 Oct 84, C-GTCB Canadair Ltd 11/84, N607CL Canadair Challenger Inc 1/85, C-GTCB Canadair Ltd 3/86, 12+01 Luftwaffe 5/86, 12+01 Luftwaffe, FBS, Koln-Wahn.
3032	1984. C-GLXM Ff 22 Oct 84, N779YY TAG Group USA Inc 2/85, HZ-AKI TAG Aeronautics Ltd 3/86,(N601KR) 1/88, N601KR to 5015, N7011H TAG Aviation Inc 7/88, GTE Service Corp 8/88, N111G 12/88,N111G GTE Service Corp. Beverly, Ma.
3033	1984. C-GLXQ Ff 9 Nov 84, N601TJ Northrop Corp 11/84, HB-ILK Trimjet Ltd/Impala Air 1 Jul 88, HB-ILK Impala Air/Trimjet Ltd. Zurich.
3034	1984. C-GLXU Ff 26 Nov 84, N374BC Berwind Aviation Corp 12/84, N372BC /85, N372BG 8/86, N372BG Berwind Aviation Corp. Philadelphia, Pa.

c/n	
3035	1984. C-GLXW Ff 4 Dec 84, C-GCUN Canadair Ltd 1/85, 144613 DND /86, 144613 CC144, DND, 412 (Transport) Squadron, Uplands.
3036	1985. C-GLXY Ff 10 Jan 85, C-GCUP Canadair Ltd 2/85, 144614 DND 11/86, 144614 CC144,DND, 412 (Transport) Squadron, Uplands.
3037	1985. C-GLXB Ff 23 Jan 85, C-GCUR Canadair Ltd 2/85, 144615 DND 11/86, 144615 CC144,DND, 412 (Transport) Squadron, Uplands.
3038	1985. C-GLYA Ff 20 Feb 85, C-GCUT Canadair Ltd 3/85, 144616 DND /86, 144616 CC144, DND, 412 (Transport) Squadron, Uplands.
3039	1985. C-GLYH Ff 7 Mar 85, C-GPGD Power Corp 8/85, Power Corp of Canada 15 Sep 89, C-GPGD P G Desmarais/Power Corp of Canada, Montreal.
3040	1985. C-GLYK Ff 11 Apr 85, N608CL Canadair Challenger Inc 18 May 85, 12+02 Luftwaffe 6/86, 12+02 Luftwaffe, FBS, Koln-Wahn.
3041	1985. C-GLWV Ff 21 Apr 85, C-GRBC Royal Bank of Canada 18 Oct 85, C-GRBC Royal Bank of Canada, Mississauga, Ontario.
3042	1985. C-GLWX Ff 3 Jun 85, N613CL CIGNA Corp 9/85, N900CC 4/86, N900CC CIGNA Corp. Windsor Locks, Ct.
3043	1985. C-GLWZ Ff 14 Jun 85, N609CL Canadair Challenger Inc 7/85, 12+03 Luftwaffe 7/86, 12+03 Luftwaffe, FBS, Koln-Wahn.
3044	1985. C-GLXD Ff 12 Sep 85, N921K Aircraft Services Corp 10/85, N125N Natural Gas/Midcon 1/89, N125N Natural Gas/Midcon Corp. Chicago, Il.
3045	1985. C-GLXH Ff 27 Aug 85, N914BD Dillard Department Stores Inc 9/85, N914BB 10/88, Interstar Inc 11/88, N601RP 12/88, lease Welded Tube-Brisbane 2/89, OE-HCL Polsterer Jets-Vienna 10/89,OE-HCL Polsterer Jets, Vienna.
3046	1985. C-GLXH Ff 17 Sep 85, C-GDBX Canadair Ltd 11/85, B-4005 Government of China 8/86, B-4005 Government of People's Republic of China, Beijing.
3047	1985. C-GLXM C-GBZQ Canadair Ltd 11/85, B-4006 Government of China 11/86, B-4006 Government of People's Republic of China, Beijing.
3048	1985. C-GLXO /85, N35FP Crown American Corp 12/85, N35FP Crown American Corp. Johnstown, Pa.
3049	1985. C-GLXQ N610CL Canadair Challenger Inc 12/85, Cx USA 9/86, C-FQYT Canadair Ltd 1/87,12+04 Luftwaffe /87, 12+04 Luftwaffe, FBS, Koln-Wahn.
3050	1985. C-GLXS N9680Z Canadair Inc 1/86, (N9680N) as per USCAR 1/86,Melvin Simon/WellsFargo Leasing 12/85, N62MS 10/86, Melvin Simon/LB Aircraft II Inc 12/89, N62MS Melvin Simon & Assocs Inc. Indianapolis, In.
3051	1986. C-G... N445AC CIT Group/Mfrs Hanover 3/86, Melvin Simon & Assoc 9/86,N60MS 11/86, Melvin Simon/CIT Group 12/89, N6OMS Melvin Simon & Assocs Inc. Indianapolis, In.
3052	1986. C-GDCQ Canadair Ltd 3/86, B-4007 Government of China /86,B-4007 Government of People's Republic of China, Beijing.
3053	1986. C-G... N604CL Canadair Challenger Inc 3/86, 12+05 Luftwaffe 2/87, 12+05 Luftwaffe, FBS, Koln-Wahn.
3054	1986. C-G... N605CL Canadair Challenger Inc 4/86, VH-MZL Westfield Holdings Ltd 10/86,N54PR ChisAir Intl 10/90, Quantum Inc 10/90, N54PR Quantum Inc. Carson City, Nv.
3055	1986. C-G... N100HG Home Flite Corp 28 May 86, Great Eastern Financial Corp 3/89, Management Financial Services Inc 7/90, N100HG Management Financial Services Inc. Duluth, Ga.
3056	1986. C-G... N612CL Canadair Challenger Inc 6/86, 12+06 Luftwaffe 4/87, 12+06 Luftwaffe, FBS, Koln-Wahn.
3057	1986. C-G... N19J Meridien Aviation Services/Mines Air Service-Lusaka 9/86, 9J-RON Roan Air-Lusaka 7/90, 9J-RON Roan Air/Mines Air Services, Lusaka.
3058	1986. C-G... /87, N125PS Don W Callender Trustee 8/86, Omni Restaurant Consulting Co 1/87, N125PS Omni Restaurant Consulting Co. Newport Beach, Ca.
3059	1986. C-G... N614CL Canadair Challenger Inc 8/86, 12+07 Luftwaffe 6/87, 12+07 Luftwaffe, FBS, Koln-Wahn.
3060	1986. C-GLXY Ff 23 Aug 86, N601S Air Shamrock Inc 10 Sep 86, N601S Air Shamrock Inc. Burbank, Ma.
3061	1986. C-GLYO Ff 7 Oct 86, N9708N James River Corp/MDFC 11/86, N999JR 7/87, N999JR James River Corp. Sandston, Va.
3062	1986. C-GLYK Ff 29 Oct 86, N601HP Price Aviation Corp 14 Nov 86, N601HP Price Aviation Corp. La Jolla
3063	1986. C-GLYH Ff 22 Nov 86, C-FURG Government of Quebec 10 Dec 87, C-FURG Government of Quebec, Quebec City. (Air Ambulance).
3064	1986. C-GLYC Ff 4 Dec 86, N566N Nordstrom/Pitney Bowes Credit Corp 12/86, N356N 4/87, N224N 1/89, N224N Nordstrom Inc. Seattle, Wa.
3065	1986. C-GLYA Ff 13 Dec 86, N602CC Canadair Challenger Inc 10/87, N1623 Texaco Inc 4/88, N1623 Texaco NYC.
3066	1986. C-GLXQ N609CL Federal Avn Svcs/Syntex Comms Inc 5/87, N144SX 10/87, N144SX Federal Aviation/Syntex Communications Inc. Palo Alto, Ca.
3991	1979. Ff 14 Jul 79 as s/n 1003, to s/n 3991 for 601 development, Bombardier Inc 11/88, C-GCGT Bombardier Inc. Montreal. (-X suffix for test flights).
5001	1986. C-GDDP Canadair Ltd r/o 18 Jul 86, Ff 28 Sep 86, N245TT WOTAN America Inc 14 Dec 88, N245TT WOTAN America Inc. Fort Lauderdale, Fl.

c/n   Page   188

5002	1987. C-GDEQ N611CL Canadair Challenger Inc 2/87, C-GDEQ Canadair Ltd 10/87, N611CL Canadair Challenger Inc 11/87, GECC-I1 1/88, Commonwealth Plan/Trans UCU Inc-Utilicorp 8/89,N585UC 10/89, N585UC Utilicorp/Trans UCU Inc. Kansas City, Mo.
5003	1987. C-G... C-GDHP Canadair Ltd 3/87, N778XX TAG Aviation Inc 5/87, HB-IKT Belugair SA/Ortigest SA-Neuchatel 16 Feb 90, HB-IKT Belugair SA/Ortigest SA. Neuchatel.
5004	1987. C-GDKO Canadair Ltd 4/87, N100KT TNS Mills Inc 19 May 87, N180KT 10/90, Canadair Challenger Inc 12/90, N180KT Canadair Challenger Inc. Windsor, Ct.
5005	1987. C-G... N613CL Kalikow Real Estate Corp 6/87, N101PK 1/88, N101PK Kalikow Real Estate Corp. Teterboro, NJ.
5006	1987. /87, C-FLPC Canadian Pacific Ltd 3 Aug 87, C-FLPC Canadian Pacific Ltd. Montreal.
5007	1987. C-G... /87, N60GG Canadair Challenger 6/87, GECC Henley Group/Gillette Group 12/87, N60GG Henley Group, Manchester, NH.
5008	1987. C-G... /87, N601CC Canadair Challenger Inc 8/87, South Seas Helicopter Co 1/89, N601EG 4/89,N601EG South Seas Helicopter Co Inc. Carlsbad, Ca.
5009	1987. /87, N399SW Citiflight Inc 9/87, N399SW Citiflight Inc. Teterboro, NJ.
5010	1987. C-GLXB /87, N57HA Citiflight Inc 9/87, (N57HK) rsvd 1 Mar 88, N1812C 12/88, N1812C Citiflight Inc. Teterboro, NJ.
5011	1987. C-GLXD N603CC C Itoh Aviation Inc 11/87, JA8283 Imperial Wing/Kwoya Research-Nagoya 5/88, N611MH C Itoh Avn Inc 10/90, Canadair Challenger Inc 10/90, N611MH Canadair Challenger Inc. Windsor, Ct.
5012	1987. C-GLXU American Intl/Mid Atlantic Aviation Corp 11/87, N107TB 12/87, Metropolitan Life Insurance 5/89, N1868M 12/89, N1868M Metropolitan Life Insurance Co. NYC.
5013	1987. C-GLXW /87, N711PD Sonic Enterprises Inc 1/88, Paul L Deutz Jr/Totem Enterprises Inc 1/89, N711PD Paul L Deutz Jr/Totem Enterprises Inc. Palomar, Ca.
5014	1987. C-GLXY /87, N21CX IC Aviation Inc 12/87, N31WH 4/89, Whitman Corp 3/90, N31WH Whitman Corp. Chicago, Il.
5015	1987. C-GLXH /87, N601KR Rainin Investments 1/88, Rainin Instrument Co 3/89, N601KR Rainin Instrument Inc. Oakland, Ca.
5016	1987. C-GLXQ /87, N604CC Canadair Challenger Inc 12/87, N49UR Kingson Corp 31 May 88,N49UR Kingson Corp. Longmont, Co.
5017	1988. C-GLWX /88, N700KC K C Aviation Inc 9 Mar 88, Kimberly-Clark Corp 8/88,N700KC Kimberly-Clark Corp. Dallas, Tx.
5018	1988. C-GLWV N606CC BOS Canadair Challenger Inc 23 Feb 88, C-FBHX Canadair Inc 4/88, Cx C- 9/88, 9Q-CBS SCIBE-Kinshasa/Citoyen Bemba Saolona 9/88, 9Q-CBS to 5061, C-FBHX Bombardier Inc 6/90-7/90, N601HH Canadair Challenger 7/90, N601HH Canadair Challenger Inc. Windsor, Ct.
5019	1988. C-GLWT /88, N915BD Dillard Department Stores Inc 22 Mar 88, N915BB Orange County-Sunbird Avn 6/90, N247GA rsvd 31 Aug 90, N247GA Orange County/Sunbird Aviation, Costa Mesa, Ca.
5020	1988. C-GLYA /88, C-FBKR Canadair Ltd 4/88, I-BEWW Soc Benetton SpA 10/88, I-BEWW Soc. Benetton S.p.A. Veneto-Treviso.
5021	1988. C-GLYC /88, N64F Farley Inc 5/88, Pitney Bowes Credit 7/88, N122WF 12/88, N122WF Farley Inc. Chicago, Il.
5022	1988. C-GLYK /88, N449ML Merril Lynch/WFC Air Inc 6/88, N449ML WFC Air Inc. NYC.
5023	1988. C-GLYO /88, N608CC Canadair Challenger Inc 6/88, EI-LJG Larry Goodman/Hamilton Leasing Ltd 15 Nov 88, EI-LJG Larry Goodman/Ven Air, Dublin.
5024	1988. C-GLYH /88, C-FCDF Bombardier Inc 11/88, B-4010 Government of China 12/88, B-4010 Government of Peoples Republic of China, Beijing.
5025	1988. C-GLWR /88, C-FCGS Bombardier Inc 7/88, B-4011 Government of China /89, B-4011 Government of Peoples Republic of China, Beijing.
5026	1988. C-G... /88, N601WM Waste Management Inc 8/88, N601WM Waste Management Inc. Chiacgo, Il.
5027	1988. C-G... /88, Laguna Miguel Properties 9/88, N244BH 10/88, N64BH 4/90, N64BH Laguna Niguel Properties, Orange County, Ca.
5028	1988. C-G... /88, N601TL Canadair Challenger Inc 9/88, N601RL R Lewis/TLC Corp 1/89, GECC-Lincolnshire 4/89, N601RL Reginald Lewis/T L C Corp. Teterboro, NJ.
5029	1988. C-G... /88, C-FDAT Bombardier Inc 11/88, N602CC Canadair Challenger 2 Dec 88, C Itoh Aviation 19 Dec 88, Blue Jay Ltd-NYC 3/90, FSB-Ut 7/90, VR-BMK Schorghuber Group/Bavaria Flug GmbH 12/90, VR-BMK Schorghuber Group/Bavaria Flug GmbH. Munich.
5030	1988. /88, N312CT Centel Corp 10/88, N312CT Centel Corp. Sugar Grove, Il.
5031	1988. C-G... /88, N900CL Canadair Challenger Inc 14 Nov 88, GECC/CIGNA Corp 4/89, N900CL CIGNA Corp. Windsor Locks, Ct.
5032	1988. C-G... /88, N604CC Canadair Challenger 2 Dec 88, 801 Seventh Avenue 22 Dec 88, N667LC Loews Corp/Clinton Court Corp 3/89, N667LC Loews Corp/Clinton Court Corp. Teterboro, NJ.
5033	1989. C-G... /89, VH-ASM Associated Airlines P/L 2/89, VH-ASM Associated Airlines P/L. Melbourne.
5034	1989. /88, Bombardier Inc 16 Dec 88,C-GIOH Imperial Oil 10 Jan 89, C-GIOH Imperial Oil Ltd. Mississauga, Ontario.

5035 1988. C-G... /88, N606CC Canadair Challenger Inc 12/88, Merv Griffin/Griffco Avn Inc 22 Dec 88, N333MG 6/89, N333MG Merv Griffin/Griffco Aviation Inc. Burbank, Ca.
5036 1989. /89, N225N Nordstrom/Metlife Capital Corp 10 Feb 89, N225N Nordstrom Inc. Seattle, Wa.
5037 1989. C-G... /89, N608CC C Itoh Aviation Inc 10 Feb 89, (JA8360) Unden Cellular 'Phones /89,GAC 10/89, GGS Leasing (NV) 1/90, N707GG 4/90, GGS Leasing Inc 9/90, N707GG Avjet/GGS Leasing Inc. Burbank, Ca.
5038 1989. C-G... /89, C-GBJA Bombardier Inc 3 Mar 89, (N602CN) 5/89, N1271A Time Warner Inc 12/90, N1271A Time Warner Inc. White Plains, NY.
5039 1989. /89, N811BB Barnett Banks Inc 3/89, N811BB Barnett Banks Inc. Jacksonville, Fl.
5040 1989. C-G... /89, N652CN Conseco Inc 4/89, Pitney Bowes Credit Corp 7/89, CIT Leasing Corp-NYC 12/89, N652CN Conseco Inc. Indianapolis, In.
5041 1989. C-G... /89, C-FETZ Bombardier Inc 19 Apr 89, in UK 8/89 for CAA certification, G-FBMB Challenger Aviation Ltd/M Bouyghes 3/90, G-FBMB Challenger Aviation Ltd/M Bouyghes, Paris.
5042 1989. C-G... /89, C-FEUV Bombardier Inc 5/89, HB-IKS Kraus & Naimer del 22 Jun 89, HB-IKS Air Charter AG/Kraus & Naimer, Vienna.
5043 1989. C-G... /89, N779YY TAG Aviation Inc 5/89, VR-COJ 4/90, VR-COJ TAG Aeronautics, Paris.
5044 1989. C-G... /89, C-FBBY Bombardier Inc 5/89, I-NNUS SIBA Avn-Milan del 13 Dec 89, I-NNUS SIBA Aviation, Milan.
5045 1989. C-G... /89, C-FFSO Bombardier Inc 6 Jul 89, N616CC Canadair Challenger 7/89, N500GS General Signal Corp 1/90, N500GS General Signal Corp. White Plains, NY.
5046 1989. /89, N6SG HM Industries Inc 7/89, N6SG HM Industries Inc. Newark, NJ.
5047 1989. /89, N140CH Chase Manhattan Bank/Wayfarer Ketch 7/89, N140CH Wayfarer Ketch, White Plains, NY.
5048 1989. /89, N2004G Readers Digest Sales & Service 7/89, N716RD 12/89,N716RD Readers Digest Sales & Service, White Plains, NY.
5049 1989. C-G... /89, N721EW Golden Nugget Inc 16 Aug 89, N721SW 3/90, Golden Nugget Aviation Corp 9/90, N721SW Golden Nugget Aviation Corp. Las Vegas, Nv.
5050 1989. /89, N826JP Portland Glove Co/Marmon Aviation 12 Sep 89, N826JP Portland Glove Co/Marmon Aviation, Chicago, Il.
5051 1989. /89, N1903G Gaylord Broadcasting Co 21 Sep 89, N1903G Gaylord Broadcasting Co. Oklahoma City, Ok.
5052 1989. /89, 200th Challenger, N4PG Procter & Gamble Co 20 Oct 89, N4PG Procter & Gamble Co. Cincinnati
5053 1989. /89, N5PG Procter & Gamble Co 31 Oct 89, N5PG Procter & Gamble Co. Cincinnati, Oh.
5054 1989. C-G... /89, N619FE FEDEX 11/89, N3FE 4/90, N3FE Federal Express Corp. Memphis, Tn.
5055 1989. /89, N601HC Hunt Oil Co 11/89, N46F 4/90, N46F Hunt Oil Co. Dallas, Tx.
5056 1989. C-G... /89, N614CC Canadair Challenger Inc 12/89, Norfolk Southern/NW Equipment Corp 2/90, N153NS 7/90, N153NS Norfolk Southern/NW Equipment Corp. Norfolk, Va.
5057 1990. C-GLWR /90, N900NM Emery Air Charter 3/90, N900NM Emery Air Charter, Rockford, Il.
5058 1990. C-G... /90, N404SK Charles E Smith Management Inc 1/90, N101SK 6/90, N101SK Charles E Smith Management Inc. Washington, DC.
5059 1990. C-GLWV /90, XA-GEO Transporte Ejecutivo/El Universal /90, XA-GEO Transporte Ejecutivo/El Universal SA. Mexico City.
5060 1990. C-G... /90, N5060H Olin Corp 1/90, N630M 5/90, N630M Olin Corp. White Plains, NY.
5061 1990. C-G... /90, C-FHHD Bombardier Inc 2/90, 9Q-CBS SCIBE Airlift-Kinshasa 8/90, 9Q-CBS SCIBE Airlift, Kinshasa.
5062 1990. /90, N6OFC First National Bank of Chicago 1/90, N6OFC Emery/First National Bank of Chicago, Chicago, Il.
5063 1990. C-GLXS N612CC Canadair Challenger Inc 4/90, sale-Pa 5/90, Canadair Challenger Inc 9/90, N79AD 10/90, N79AD Arthur DeMoss Foundation, Philadelphia, Pa.
5064 1990. C-GLXW /90, C-FIOB Bombardier Inc 7/90, VH-BRG Grollo Brothers 12/90, VH-BRG Grollo Brothers, Melbourne.
5065 1990. C-G... /90, N601BF CIRC Service Systems Inc 4/90, N601BF CIRC Service Systems Inc. Washington, DC.
5066 1990. C-G... /90, N506TN TNS Mills Inc 4/90, N100KT 10/90, N100KT TNS Mills Inc. Blacksburg, SC.
5067 1990. /90, N603CC Canadair Challenger Inc 4/90, Blue Jay Ltd 5/90, N603CC Blue Jay Ltd/Itoh Aviation, NYC.
5068 1990. C-G... /90, N609CC C Itoh Aviation Inc 5/90, N88WG Kwoya (Hawaii) Inc 10/90, N88WG Kwoya (Hawaii) Inc. Honolulu, Hi.
5069 1990. C-G... C-FIGR Bombardier Inc 5/90, I-FIPP Soc Fimair SpA del 9 Nov 90, I-FIPP Soc. Fimair S.p.A. Milan.
5070 1990. /90, N980HC U S Health Aviation Corp 6/90, N980HC U S Health Aviation Corp. Blue Bell, Pa.
5071 1990. /90, N500PC Pepsico Inc 6/90, N500PC Pepsico Inc. Westchester County Airport, NY.
5072 1990. C-G... /90, N609K C Itoh Aviation Inc 6/90, N88HA rsvd 16 Nov 90, N88HA C Itoh Aviation Inc. El Segundo, Ca.
5073 1990. C-G... /90, N60KR Canadair Challenger Inc 7/90, PK-... Gatari Hutama Air Services, Jakarta.
5074 1990. /90, N23SB U S Tobacco Co 8/90, N23SB U S Tobacco Co. Greenwich, Ct.
5075 1990. C-G... /90, N810D Airsupport Services Corp 31 Oct 90, PT-... Lider Taxi Aereo Ltda.
5076 1990. /90, N5TM Toyota Motor Credit Corp 9/90, N5TM Toyota Motor Credit Corp. Torrance, Ca.
5077 1990. /90, N1622 Texaco Inc 9/90, N1622 Texaco Inc. Westchester County Airport, NY.

5078	1990. /90, N601MG C Itoh Aviation Inc 10/90, N601MG C Itoh Aviation Inc. El Segundo, Ca.
5079	1990. C-GLWV /90, HZ-...
5083	1990. C-G... /90, N189K Crawford Fitting Co 7/90, N189K Crawford Fitting Co. Solon, Oh.
5084	1990. Bombardier Inc /90, N399CF Citiflight Inc 18 Dec 90, N399CF Citiflight Inc. New Castle, De.

BAe 125 Series 700

c/n	
7001	1976. G-BEFZ HSA demo 11/76, McAlpine Aviation Ltd 1/79, VR-HIM McAlpine Aviation (Asia) Ltd /79, G-BEFZ McAlpine Aviation Ltd 1/81, (N4555E) Silicon Valley Express Inc 12/83, N700SV 5/84, N101SK Charles E Smith Management Inc 6/84, N101SK to CL600-1033, N101XS Page Avjet Inc 1/86, Laurence R Smith Inc-Ct 3/86, N80KA Keystone Avn Service Inc 6/86, Polestar Corp 8/89, N80KA Polestar Corp. Rowayton, Ct.
7007	1977. HB-VFA Ff 30 Sep 77. Chartag-Zurich/Knorrbremse AG-Munich 11/77, D-CADA Air Flight GmbH 29 Apr 85, German Wings GmbH /87, Aero-Dienst GmbH 6/90, D-CADA Aero-Dienst GmbH. Nuremberg.
7010	1977. (G-5-16) Ff 14 Oct 77. HZ-MMM Sheikh M Al Midani/Al Tass Heel Litijara 11/77, LX-MJM 12/85, N700WH Wayne Hilmer-Jet Trading Floor 5/89, PSI Funding Inc-NYC 10/89, Great Planes Sales Inc 9/90,N700WH Great Planes Sales Inc. Tulsa, Ok.
7013	1977. G-CBBI Ff 9 Nov 77, Barclays Bank International/McAlpine Avn 11/77, Series A conversion 8/81, N219JA Storage Technology 9/81, GenStar Financial Services 10/84, N75ST 9/85, N101HF Hardees Food System Inc 2/87, N101HF Hardees Food System Inc. Rocky Mount, NC.
7020	1978. (G-BFTP) re-allocated to SD 3-30 /78, (G-BFVN) Finamet Ltd-Heathrow /78, G-EFPT MAM/Save Energy Svcs Ltd/Castolin Eutectic Institute 6/78, VR-BHE Air Hanson/Air St George Ltd-Bermuda 3/81, (N2634B) 1/82, N125HM HM Holdings Inc 11/85, HM Industries Inc 2/88, ITT Automotive Inc 7/89, N818 11/89,N818 ITT Automotive Inc. Pontiac, Mi.
7022	1978. (G-5-11) Ff 1 Mar 78, F-GASL Ste Schlumberger-Paris 3/78, G-5-17 BAe 2/85, N34RE Raleigh Enterprises 12 Mar 85, Raleigh Jet Ents 4/89, N34RE Raleigh Jet Enterprises, Los Angeles, Ca.
7025	1978. (G-5-12) Ff 4 Apr 78, G-BFPI McAlpine Aviation Ltd 4/78, VR-HIN McAlpine Aviation (Asia) Ltd/Neptunia Corp-Hong Kong /79, G-BFPI McAlpine Aviation 1/81, N93TC Aircraft Trading Center 2/84, Dresser Industries Inc 8/84, N7782 2/85, N7782 Dresser Industries, Dallas, Tx.
7028	1978. G-BFSO Ff 4 May 78, Dravidian/De Beers International Air Svcs 5/78, Brown & Root (UK) Ltd 3/85, G-5-534 BAe 11/86, N700TL Thomas Lee-Ma 11/86, PHH Aviation Sales Inc 4/88, Bancboston Leasing Inc 7/88, Goody Products 11/88, N603GY 12/88, RTS Helicopter Services Corp 8/89, N603GY Goody Products, Teterboro, NJ.
7031	1978. G-BFSP De Beers/Dravidian Air Svcs Ltd 6/78, G-PRMC Ready Mixed Concrete Group Services Ltd 16 Apr 85, G-PRMC RMC Group Services Ltd. Biggin Hill.
7034	1978. G-5-14 G-BFXT Coca Cola Export Corp 'Meli Ya Hewa=Windship' 10/78, N7007X Coca Cola Export 7/88, ATC Inc 8/88,Tessler Avn 5/89, N7007X Tessler Aviation Leasing Corp. NYC.
7037	1978. G-5-18 G-BFVI MAM International/Bristow Helicopters Ltd 8/78,G-BFVI Marine & Avn Mgmt Intl/Bristow Helicopters Ltd. Redhill.
7040	1978. HZ-RC1 Saudi Parsons/Royal Commission-Riyadh 11/78, G-OWEB Magec Aviation/Rapid 3451 Ltd/Andrew Lloyd Weber 9/87, EC-375 Gestair/Services de Aerotransportes Especiales SA 12/89, EC-ETI /90, EC-ETI Gestair/Services de Aerotransportes Especiales SA. Madrid.
7046	1978. 4W-ACE Shaher Traders-Cairo 12/78, G-BKJV BAe 12/82, VH-JCC Pacific Avn P/L 2/84, VH-LRH Hancock Prospecting P/L 1/86, VH-LRH Hancock Prospecting P/L 1/86, N..... Continental Aviation Sales 12/90, N..... Continental Aviation Sales, Rolling Meadows, Il.
7054	1979. C6-BET Norwest Aviation-Bahamas 6/79, C6-BET Norwest Aviation, Nassau.
7055	1979. G-5-16 HZ-RC2 Saudi Parsons/Royal Commission-Riyadh 5/79, N876JC Jetcraft Corp 3/88,G-BOXI Tiphook Associated Finance Ltd 6/88, Tiphook PLC 3/89, F-WZIG Ste Transair 8/90, F-GGHG 10/90, Locafrance/COGIA 11/90, F-GHHG Locafrance Equipment/COGIA, Paris-Le Bourget.
7061	1979. G-5-19 G-BGGS BAe 5/79, G-OJOY Harry Goodman 10/81, N700SS Valley Acceptance Corp 1/84, Southwest Forest Inds 4/84, N700SF 12/86, GAP Inc 2/89, N810GS 7/89, N810GS GAP Inc. San Bruno, Ca.
7062	1979. G-5-15 HB-VGF Scintilla/Robert Bosch-Stuttgart 9/79, HB-VGF Scintilla/Robert Bosch, Stuttgart.
7064	1979. HZ-NAD NADCO-SAudi Arabia 6/79, HZ-OFC Olayan Finance Co 4/83, HZ-OFC to 8050,G-BMOS BAe PLC 4/86, cx UK 5 Jun 86, G-5-519 7/86, VH-JFT Pacific Aviatiion 7/86, DoT & Comms-Melbourne 10/87, VH-JFT Civil Aviation Authority, Melbourne.
7067	1979. HZ-DA1 Dallah-AVCO 12/79, N9113J Atlantic Aviation Corp 10/81, (N115RS) Federal Express Corp 9/82, Ottaway Newspapers Inc 8/83, N360N 1/84, Dow Jones & Co-NYC 2/86, N144DJ 5/87,N144DJ Dow Jones & Co. New York.
7070	1979. HB-VGG Scintilla/Robert Bosch-Stuttgart 9/79, HB-VGG Scintilla/Robert Bosch, Stuttgart.
7073	1979. G-5-12 G-BGTD Rank Xerox (UK) Ltd 11/79, N7788 Dresser Industries 3/85, N7788 Dresser Industries, Dallas, Tx.
7076	1979. G-5-17 7Q-YJI Government of Malawi 12/79, MAAW-J1 Malawi Army Air Wing-Blantyre 1/80, MAAW-J1 to 8064, G-5-524 BAe PLC 7/86, G-BMWW 8/86, G-5-571 9/87, XA-LML SACSA-Mexico 11/87,N111ZN Zenith Insurance Co 7/88, N111ZN Zenith Insurance Co. Woodland Hills, Ca.
7082	1980. 238 Irish Air Corp/Government-Dublin 2/80, 238 Irish Air Corps. Casement-Dublin.
7085	1980. G-5-15 G-BHIO McAlpine Aviation (Asia) Ltd 2/80, RP-C1714 San Miguel Corp-Manila 3/80, N10TN Coca Cola Bottling of Western Carolinas 1/88, N10TN Coca Cola Bottling of Western Carolinas, Asheville, NC.
7088	1980. HZ-DA2 Dallah AVCO 3/80, G-5-531 BAe PLC 10/86, N29RP Jack Prewitt-Tx 11/86, Aviation Enterprises Inc 1/87, Omni 4/87, Jimbar Inc 11/87, N29RP Jimbar Inc. Fort Lauderdale, Fl.

c/n	Entry
7091	1980. G-BHLF Ff 26 Mar 80, GEC-Marconi/Magec Aviation Ltd 4/80, G-BHLF GEC-Marconi/Magec Aviation Ltd. Luton.
7094	1980. G-OBAE BAe PLC demo 5/80, HB-VEK Aero & Road Club of Switzerland 9/83, G-5-16 BAe PLC 3/84, N49566 Page Avjet Corp 4/84, ADI Aerodynamics/K Mart Corp 9/84, N80KM 4/85, N713KM 11/90, N713KM K Mart Corp. Pontiac, Mi.
7097	1980. (G-BHTJ) Trust House Forte Airport Services Ltd 6/80, G-HHOI 7/80, G-BRDI Aravia (CI) Ltd 11/87, G-BHTJ BAe (Commercial Aircraft) Ltd 8/90, BAe PLC 9/90, G-BHTJ British Aerospace PLC. Hatfield.
7100	1980. (G-5-19) Ff 1 Jul 80, D-CLVW Volswagenwerk AG 8/80, G-5-549 BAe PLC 2/87, G-BNFW British Aerospace PLC 3 Mar 87, G-BNFW British Aerospace PLC. Filton.
7103	1980. G-5-12 G-BHSU Shell Aircraft Ltd-London 9/80, G-BHSU Shell Aircraft Ltd. London.
7107	1980. G-BHSV Shell Aircraft Ltd-London 10/80, G-BHSV Shell Aircraft Ltd. London.
7109	1980. G-BHSW Shell Aircraft Ltd-London 10/80, G-BHSW Shell Aircraft Ltd. London.
7112	1980. D-CMVW Volkswagenwerk AG 12 Nov 80, G-5-536 BAe PLC 11/86, G-BNBO 11/86, G-5-553 3/87, (9M-SSS) Malaysian Helicopter Services 5/87, 9M-SSL 6/87, 9M-SSL Malaysian Helicopter Services, Kuala Lumpur.
7115	1980. HZ-DA3 Dallah AVCO 12/80, (G-5-502) BAe PLC /85, G-BMIH Jaguar Aviation Ltd/RCN-Nigeria 1/86, 5N-AMX 2/86, 5N-AMX Jaguar Aviation/RCN, Lagos.
7118	1980. (G-BIHZ) BAe PLC 1980, 5N-AVJ Nigerian National Petroleum Co-Lagos 3/81,S I O Properties Ltd-Lagos /90, 5N-AVJ Aero Contractors/S I O Properties Ltd. Ikoyi, Lagos.
7124	1981. HZ-DA4 Dallah AVCO 3/81, HZ-DA4 Dallah AVCO.
7127	1981. G-TJCB J C Bamford (Excavators) Ltd 3/81, OY-MPA Maerskair/A P Moller 12/85, OY-MPA Maerskair/A P Moller, Copenhagen.
7130	1981. G-DBBI Barclays Bank International PLC 4/81, G-CCAA Civil Aviation Authority 12/82,G-BNVU McAlpine Aviation Ltd 8/87, (G-5-588) BAe PLC 3/88, N700FR James R Wickert & Associates Inc 3/88, G-RJRI R J Reynolds Inds 9/88, RP-C235 Filipino National Bank 6/90, RP-C235 Filipino National Bank, Manila.
7133	1981. G-5-14 LV-PMM YPF-State Oil Co-Buenos Aires 6/81, LV-ALW 7/81, LV-ALW W/O W/o 11 Apr 85. 11/APR/85 cr into mountains, 7k. (AL222-P8)
7136	1981. G-BIRU H Goodman/Barclay Mercantile/MAM 6/81, Yeates of Leics 5/86, G-5-545 BAe PLC 9/86, OH-JET Jetflite OY 1/87, OH-JET Jetflite OY. Helsinki.
7139	1981. G-5-18 (G-GAIL) 1981, G-BKAA Saudi Catering & Contracting 9/81, British American Tobacco/Abbey Investments (CI) Ltd 1/85, G-MHIH Queens Moat Houses PLC 9/88, G-MHIH Queens Moat Houses PLC. Southend.
7142	1981. G-5-12 G-BJDJ C C (UK Services) Ltd 7/81, C C International 8/86, G-BJDJ Consolidated Contractors International, London.
7151	1981. G-5-12 N161MM EAF/Aircraft Assoc/Berkshire Inn Inc 12/81, N161MM to 8061, N161G 11/86, May Department Stores Co 2/87, N613MC 4/87, N613MC May Department Stores Co. St Louis, Mo.
7158	1981. G-5-14 G-BJWB Opencity Ltd/McAlpine Aviation/Artoc 2/82,Rogers Aviation/Artoc/Makki Al Juma-Kuwait 'Raeda' 8/83, N45KK Sage Energy Co 12/85, N45KK to 35A-592, XB-DZN Gustavo Ramero & Olga Macias Bringas 4/87, XB-DZN Gustavo Ramero & Olga Macias Bringas, Tehuacan.
7160	1982. G-5-19 5N-AVK Federal Ministry of Aviation (CAFU) 19 Jan 83, 5N-AVK Federal Ministry of Aviation (CAFU), Lagos.
7163	1982. G-5-12 7T-VCW ENEMA-Algiers (met research) 24 May 82,7T-VCW E.N. pour l'Exploitation Meteorlogique et Aeronautique.
7166	1982. G-5-18 F-BYFB Ste Bouyghes-Paris 23 Jun 82, F-BYFB Ste. Bouyghes/Groupement International de Commerce, Paris.
7169	1982. G-5-21 (VH-SOA) Shell Australia Ltd 6/82, VH-HSS 6/82, VH-HSS Shell Australia Ltd. Melbourne.
7172	1982. 5H-SMZ Government of Zanzibar 6/82, G-BKFS ferry registration 7/82, 5H-SMZ Government of Zanzibar 8/82, G-5-568 BAe PLC 10/87, 5H-SMZ Government of Zanzibar 12/87, Government of Zanzibar.
7175	1982. (C9-TTA) Empresa Nacional de TTA 7/82, C9-TAC 7/82, C9-TAC Empresa Nacional de Transporte e Trabalho Aereo, Maputo.
7178	1982. G-5-14 4W-ACM Shaher Traders-Sana'a 'Anisa 111' 9/82, G-5-530 BAe PLC 10/86,G-BMYX 11/86, Cx UK 28 Aug 87, G-5-570 10/87, VH-LMP Pacific Aviation P/L-Sydney 10/87, Santos Ltd /88, Jet Systems/Santos Ltd /90, VH-LMP Jet Systems P/L-Santos Ltd. Adelaide.
7184	1982. G-5-12 9K-AGA Kuwait Airways Corp 11/82, 9K-AGA Kuwait Airways Corp.
7187	1982. G-5-14 9K-AGB Kuwait Airways Corp 11/82, 9K-AGB Kuwait Airways Corp.
7189	1982. G-BKHK BAe PLC 8/82, (G-OBSM) 10/82, G-OSAM Scorpio Aviation & Marine 12/82,BSM Holdings Ltd 1/83, N700BA CSX Beckett Aviation Inc 1/85, Interlake Steel Inc 2/85, N94B 4/85,Horsehead Industries Inc 2/90, N81HH Pitney Bowes Credit Corp 5/90, N81HH Horsehead Industries Inc. NYC.
7196	1983. G-5-11 5N-AXO Government of Nigeria del 30 Jul 85, 5N-AXO Government of Nigeria, Lagos.
7197	1983. G-5-12 N790Z Zestmo Ltd 7/83, Pacificorp Trans Inc 9/84, G-5-17 BAe PLC 9/84, N207PC 10/84, N207PC Pacificorp Trans Inc. Portland, Or.
7200	1983. (G-5-17) G-5-14 G-MSFY ARAVCO Ltd/Mohammed Fakhry 8/83, VR-BMD D Manios Shipping/Airman Ltd 7/89, VR-BMD D Manios Shipping, Athens, Greece.
7203	1983. G-5-14 5N-AXP Government of Nigeria 7/84, 5N-AXP W/O W/o 31 Dec 85. 31/DEC/85 4 military prisoners attempted escape - 8k

7208	1983. (N710BR) (S/n NA0346). BAe Inc 10/83, cx USA 5/84 as not imported, (G-BLMJ) Dravidian Air Services Ltd & cvtd Srs B 6/84, G-5-19 BAe PLC 2/85, G-BLSM Dravidian Air Services del 13 Feb 85,G-BLSM Dravidian Air Services Ltd. London.
7209	1983. G-5-20 (VR-BPF) Pacific Fruit Co/Pan American Trading Corp 12/83, VR-BHW 12/83, VR-BHW Pacific Fruit Co/Pan American Trading Corp.
7210	1983. (N710BQ) (S/n NA0347). BAe Inc 10/83, cx USA 5/84 as not imported, (G-BLMK) Dravidian Air Services Ltd & cvtd Srs B 6/84, G-5-18 BAe PLC 2/85, G-BLTP Dravidian Air Services del 20 Mar 85,G-BLTP Dravidian Air Services Ltd. London.
7212	1984. G-5-12 G-RACL Racal Avionics Ltd 4/84, N81CH ICH Corp 8/86, Jet East Intl Sales 3/87, N81CH to 55-036, N81CN 6/87, G-IJET One Jet/Yeates of Leicester/MAM Aviation Ltd /87, Twinjet Aircraft Sales Ltd 3/90, G-5-659 BAe PLC 3/90, OH-BAP Airwings/Planmeca OY 4/90, OH-BAP Airwings/Planmeca OY-Kone Air OY. Helsinki.
7213	1984. G-5-16 G-BLEK Southampton Airport Ltd 4/84, N213C Vulcan Materials Co 6/84, N213C Vulcan Materials Co. Birmingham, Al.
7214	1984. G-5-17 HZ-SJP Jouanou & Parskevaides Saudi Arabia Ltd /85, HZ-SJP to 8068, G-UKCA Magec Aviation/Civil Aviation Authority 8/87, G-UKCA Magec Aviation/Civil Aviation Authority, London.
7215	1984. VH-HSP Westfield Ltd-Sydney 18 Nov 84, Coles Myer Ltd 6/86, VH-HSP Coles Myer Ltd. Melbourne.
NA0201	1977. G-5-20 S/n 7002. N700HS Business Jet Aviation Co 6/77, BAe Inc 2/78, N40WB Warner Bros/General Transportation Corp 4/78, N40GT 12/78, Nassau Air Ventures 11/84, N700NY World Jet Charter Corp 1/85, Comcar Services Inc 10/86, N866GB 11/86,Owners Jet Services 12/88,Flightcraft Inc 4/89,B & S Investments Inc 12/89, N886GB B & S Investments Inc. Lake Oswego, Or.
NA0202	1977. G-5-19 S/n 7003. G-BERP HSA 4/77, N64688 Morgan Equipment/Pacific Systems Inc 'Lady J' 6/77,N333ME 1/78, Bankamerilease Capital Corp 6/83, M J Avn 2/87, N333ME M J Aviation, San Francisco, Ca.
NA0203	1977. G-BERV S/n 7005. HSA 4/77, N620M Olin Corp 6/77, N620M Olin Corp. Stamford, Ct.
NA0204	1977. G-5-18 S/n 7006. G-BERX HSA 4/77, N724B Blount Corp 7/77, Cessna Aircraft Co 10/90, N724B Cessna Aircraft Co. Wichita, Ks.
NA0205	1977. G-5-11 S/n 7008. Ff 17 Jun 77, (G-BEWV) HSA 7/77, C-GYYZ Gulf Oil 7/77,Alberta Gas Trunkline 9/78, Nova Corp of Alberta 20 Jun 88, N333PC U S Aircraft Turbine Sales to POLCO Inc 10/90, N333PC POLCO Inc. Landover, Md.
NA0206	1977. G-5-12 S/n 7009. G-BEYC HSA 7/77, N813H Hughes Aircraft Co 8/77,Global Truck & Equipment Inc 3/86, (N20GT) rsvd 16 Jul 86, United Services Life Insurance-DC 11/86, N986M 5/87, United Security Travel Service 1/88, J H Snyder Co 1/90, N986H J H Snyder Co. Los Angeles, Ca.
NA0207	1977. G-5-13 S/n 7011. G-BFAJ HSA 8/77, N255CT Caterpillar Tractor Co 10/77, (N255QT) rsvd 20 Dec 84, N255TT 1/86, Caterpillar Inc 11/86, First City Texas Trans Inc 6/89, N500FC 2/90,N500FC First City Texas Trans Inc. Houston, Tx.
NA0208	1977. G-5-14 S/n 7012. G-BFBI HSA 9/77, N125HS HSA Inc/Business Jet Aviation Co 10/77, N700HS BAe Inc 2/78, N162A AMF Inc 11/78, Omni 12/85, Flo-Sun Land Corp 2/86, N700FS 12/86, The Home Depot Inc 5/89, N622AB 7/89, Home Depot USA Inc 11/89, N622AB Home Depot USA Inc. Atlanta, Ga.
NA0209	1977. G-5-17 S/n 7014. Ff 7 Oct 77, G-BFDW HSA 10/77, N46901 GATX Third Aircraft Corp-SFO 11/77, N120GA 8/78, Melvin Simon/M S Aircraft Inc 11/78, N60MS /79, N60MS to CL601 3051, N453EP James River Inc 9/86, N586JR 2/87, Borden Inc 9/90, N74B 11/90, N74B Borden Inc. Columbus, Oh.
NA0210	1977. G-5-18 S/n 7015. Ff 14 Nov 77, G-BFFL HSA 11/77, N37P Nationwide Transport Inc 11/77, Nationwide Mutual Insurance Co 9/86, Bae Inc 4/90, N37P British Aerospace Inc. Washington, DC.
NA0211	1977. G-5-19 S/n 7017. Ff 18 Nov 77, G-BFFU HSA 11/77, N62MS Melvin Simon/M S Aircraft Inc 12/77, N62MS to CL601 3050, N454EP 9/86, Canadair Challenger Inc 1/87, Flightcraft Inc 9/87, McCormick & Co Inc 4/88, N757M 9/88, N757M McCormick & Co Inc. Hunt Valley, Md.
NA0212	1977. G-BFGU HSA 11/77, N733H HAC Inc 12/77, Humana Inc 10/78, Fuqua Industries Inc 5/84, N662JB 10/84, Citizens Southern Georgia Co 12/85, N125CS 1/86, N125CS Citizens Southern Georgia Corp. Dekalb Peachtree Airport, Ga
NA0213	1977. (G-BFGV) S/n 7019. HSA 11/77, Ff as N370M 16 Dec 77, N370M Murphy Oil USA Corp 5/84, Super Food Service Inc 9/86, B A Leasing & Capital Corp 6/90, N370RR 7/90, N370RR Reynolds & Reynolds/Super Food Service Inc. Dayton, Oh.
NA0214	1978. N34CH S/n 7021.Ff 30 Jan 78,Cutler Hammer 2/78, Eaton Corp 6/79, N900KC Kimberly-Clark Corp 3/80, Metropolitan Life Insurance 9/81, N1868M 5/82, N1868M to CL600 1039, N1868S 3/83, EAF/Hawker Associates 12/86, N926ZT 2/87, PHH Group Inc 7/88, N926ZT PHH/Hawker Associates, Hunt Valley, Md.
NA0215	1978. G-BFLF S/n 7023. Ff 18 Feb 78, BAe 2/78, N54555 The Garrett Corp-Los Angeles 3/78, N125GP /78,Intl Sales & Leasing 12/87, Gantt Aviation Inc 2/88, N6JB Fuqua Industries Inc 7/88,Fuqua National Corp 2/89, N6UB rsvd 22 Aug 90, N6UB Fuqua National Corp. Atlanta, Ga.
NA0216	1977. G-BFFH S/n 7016. Ff 30 Nov 77, N72505 Western Leasing Co-Van Nuys 12/77, PennCorp-LAX 3/78, N800CB 11/78, United States Tobacco Co 2/87, N23SB 7/87, U S Tobacco Sales & Marketing 1/90, N23SB to CL601-3A 5074, Canadair Challenger Inc 7/90, N23SK 8/90, N23SK Canadair Challenger Inc. Windsor, Ct.

c/n	
NA0217	1978. G-BFLG S/n 7024. Ff 4 Mar 78, BAe 3/78, N94BD Dillard Department Stores Inc 3/78, N94BD to 8004, N94BE 7/84, B F Goodrich Co 11/84, N7005 12/84, N7005 B F Goodrich Co. N. Canton, Oh.
NA0218	1977. G-5-15 S/n 7004. Ff 16 Aug 77, G-BGDM Wavertree Ltd/BSR Ltd 8/77 (GDM=G D MacDonald Chairman BSR), G-5-15 for 'A' conversion and re-serial to NA0218 9/77, N37975 9/77, N222RB Reading-Bates Offshore Drilling 11/77,American Standard 4/86 N700RJ 7/86, Baldwin Builders 4/88, N546BC 6/88, N746BC 12/88, N746BC Baldwin Builders, Driggs, Id.
NA0219	1978. G-BFMO S/n 7026. Ff 17 Mar 78, BAe 3/78, N1230A Uni Royal Inc 3/78, N372BC Berwind Corp 9/80, N372BD 8/85, Freeport Minerals/Freeport-McMoRan Inc 11/85, N685FM 5/86, James Stone-La 4/88,N685EM 9/89, Jettech Inc 10/89, Brass Aviation Inc 6/90, N685EM Brass Aviation Inc. Fairfield, NJ.
NA0220	1978. G-BFMP S/n 7027. Ff 11 Apr 78, BAe 4/78, C-GPPS Pacific Petroleum 4/78,E M Lawson/B C Teamsters Union 12/83, N705CC Central Conference of Teamsters 8/88, N725CC 9/90, N725CC Central Conference of Teamsters, Chicago, Il.
NA0221	1978. N465R S/n 7029. Ff 26 Apr 78, Gulf Resorces & Chemical Corp 5/78, N700PD Cactus Enterprises Inc 2/84, John H Harland Co-NC 11/86, (N248JH) rsvd 8 Apr 87, N700PD John H Harland Co. Greensboro, NC.
NA0222	1978. G-BFSI S/n 7030. Ff 12 May 78, BAe PLC 5/78, C-GSCL Shell Canada Resources Ltd 5/78, Shell Canada Ltd 20 Nov 84, C-GSCL Shell Canada Ltd. Calgary.
NA0223	1978. G-5-14 S/n 7032. G-BFUE HSA 5/78, N700BA BAe Inc demo 6/78, N353WC The Williams Companies 6/79, N853WC 12/88, Flightcraft Inc 1/89, J R Simplot Co 2/89, N154JS 9/89, N154JS J R Simplot Co. Boise, Id.
NA0224	1978. N50JM S/n 7033. Johns Manville Corp 7/78, N50TN 12/80, Manville Svc Corp 10/81, Manville Sales 12/86, BAe Inc 6/89, RTS Helicopter Services Corp 7/89, Glaxo Inc 10/89, N200GX 7/90, N200GX Glaxo Inc. Raleigh, NC.
NA0225	1978. G-5-16 S/n 7035. Nationwide Mutual Insurance Co 7/78, N36NP 8/78, BAe Inc 4/90,Tracey Leasing Corp 10/90, N36NP Tracey Leasing Corp. Herndon, Va.
NA0226	1978. G-5-17 S/n 7036. N60JM Johns Manville Corp 7/78, N60TN 12/80, Manville Service Corp 10/81, Holiday Inns Inc 10/85, N600HC 11/85, Rubbermaid Inc 4/87, N902RM 10/87, N902RM Rubbermaid Inc. Wooster, Oh.
NA0227	1978. G-5-19 S/n 7038. N10CZ Congoleum Corp 7/78, N&R Ents Inc 9/86, Crusader Avn 2/87, N81KA 9/87,N81KA Crusader Aviation/Keystone Aviation Service Inc. Oxford, Ct.
NA0228	1978. G-5-11 S/n 7039. N555CB Cleveland Brothers Equipment Co 8/78, N555CB Cleveland Brothers Equipment Co. Wilmington, De.
NA0229	1978. G-5-12 S/n 7041. N700BB BAe Inc 7/78, N400NW Northwest Industries Inc. 10/78, N400NU 12/84, Union Underwear Co 3/85, (N601UU) rsvd 19 Mar 85, Jet Exchange Corp 6/85, N700LS Lone Star Steel Co 8/85, Valley NB-Des Moines 3/86, Cooper Tire & Rubber Co 6/89, N825CT 9/89, N825CT Cooper Tire & Rubber Co. Findlay, Oh.
NA0230	1978. G-5-13 S/n 7042. N360X Panhandle Eastern Pipeline Co 9/78, N360X Panhandle Eastern Pipeline Co. Kansas City, Mo.
NA0231	1978. G-BFYH S/n 7044. BAe 8/78, N35D Continental Resources Co/Florida Gas Transmission Co 10/78, N5735 HNG Internorth 10/85, O Gara Aviation Co 4/88, American TV & Comms Corp 7/88, N5735 American TV & Comm Corp. White Plains, NY.
NA0232	1978. (G-5-15) S/n 7043. G-BFYV BAe 9/78, N900CC Luqa Inc 11/78, (N300LD) Lendee Co 9/82, RR Investments Inc 5/84, HNG Corp 10/84, N500ZB 2/85, Great Planes Sales Inc to Hahn Lease Corp 5/86, N22EH 9/86, N22KH 2/90, Carlsbad Aviation Inc 6/90, N22KH Carlsbad Aviation Inc. Carlsbad, Ca.
NA0233	1978. G-BFZI S/n 7047. BAe PLC 9/78, C-GABX Execaire/Nova an Alberta Corp 11/78, C-GABX Execaire/Nova an Alberta Corp. Calgary.
NA0234	1978. G-5-16 S/n 7048. Yellow Pages/L M Berry & Co 11/78, N711YP 12/78, Bellsouth Services Inc 1/90, N205BS 3/90, N205BS Bellsouth Services Inc. Birmingham, Al.
NA0235	1978. G-5-18 S/n 7050. N700GB BAe Inc 12/78, Dennis O Connor-Tx 5/79,N10C Dennis O'Connor, Victoria, Tx.
NA0236	1979. G-5-11 S/n 7051. N700UK BAe 1/79, N14JA J A Jones Construction Co 5/79, Hawkaire/Jones Group 3/86, N64HA 1/87, BDB Aircraft Charter Co Inc 10/87, N236BN 8/88,N236BN Barnes Noble Corp/BDB Aircraft Charter Co Inc. Teterboro.
NA0237	1978. G-5-19 S/n 7052. G-BGBJ BAe 10/78, N737X John T Dorrance 12/78, Great Planes Sales 7/89, Nekoosa Packaging Corp 9/89, N697NP 10/89, N511GP Georgia Pacific Corp 5/90, N511GP Georgia Pacific Corp. Atlanta, Ga.
NA0238	1978. G-5-20 S/n 7053. N700AR BAe Inc 1/79, N33CP Colonial Penn Group 3/79, PIR Transportation Inc 8/87, M A Hanna Co 11/88, N130MH 1/89, N130MH M A Hanna Co. Cleveland, Oh.
NA0239	1978. G-5-17 S/n 7049. G-BGBL BAe 10/78, N33BK B K Johnson/Chaparrosa Aircraft Inc 11/78, KSC Leasing Co-San Antonio 9/86, C-GKPM American Barrick Resources 7/87, C-GKPM American Barrick Resources, Toronto.
NA0240	1978. G-BFZJ S/n 7045. BAe 11/78, N130BA BAe Inc 2/79, N700HH Hilton Hotels Corp 6/79, N700HH Hilton Hotels Corp. Las Vegas, Nv.
NA0241	1979. N700NT S/n 7056. BAe Inc 1/79, N492CB Crocker National Bank 2/79, Summit Aviation Inc 5/83, N6VC 6/83, Robert Thornquist-Mo 8/84, (N64SA) rsvd 27 Sep 88, Flightcraft Inc 12/88, Bancorp Leasing & Financial 1/89,Morrison-Knudsen Corp 2/89, N25MK 3/89, Tanara Inc 8/90, N300BS rsvd 6 Nov 90, N300BS Tanara Inc. Wilmington, De.
NA0242	1979. G-5-14 S/n 7057. N700UR BAe Inc 2/79, N60HJ Sheraton Inns Inc 7/79, C-GPCC Pancanadian Petroleum Ltd 7/82, N125BW Bill Walker & Assocs Inc 9/89,N125BW Bill Walker & Associates Inc. McKinnon Airport, GA

NA0243   1979. G-5-17 S/n 7059. N130BH BAe Inc 3/79, N20S Storer Comms Inc 3/79, N20S to 8042,GECC-Dunwoody 1/85, N20SK 7/85, PNC Financial Corp 2/86, BAe Inc 4/90, N702BA 9/90, NBAA 700-2 demo 10/90, N702BA British Aerospace Inc. Washington, DC.
NA0244   1979. G-5-18 S/n 7060. N130BG BAe Inc 3/79, N1103 Gould Financial Inc 6/79, N1183 9/84, Bell Leasing/Domino's Pizza 1/85, N230DP 4/85, Fisher Group Inc 7/90, N414RF 8/90, N414RF Fisher Group Inc. Wilmington, De.
NA0245   1979. G-5-15 S/n 7058. N125HS BAe Inc 2/79, N700BA 8/79, N354WC The Williams Companies 3/80, N354WC to NA0436, N854WC 9/89, Norrell Corp 11/89, N750GM rsvd 28 Nov 89, N750GM Norrell Corp. Atlanta, Ga.
NA0246   1979. G-5-20 S/n 7063. N130BB BAe Inc 4/79, N79HC Harsco Corp 6/79, N79HC Harsco Corp. Camp Hill, Pa.
NA0247   1979. G-5-11 S/n 7065. N130BC BAe Inc 5/79, N30PR P R Rutherford Oil 6/79, Wayfarer Ketch-NYC 12/83, N530TL Time Life Inc 1/84, (N530TE) rsvd 18 Feb 87,Spectrum/Air Inc 6/87,N87AG Andy Galef 2/88, Spectrum Group Inc 2/89, Beneto Inc 5/90, N87AG Beneto Inc. W Sacramento, Ca.
NA0248   1979. G-5-17 S/n 7066. G-BGSR BAe PLC /79, C-GKCI Irving Oil Transport Ltd 12/79, C-GKCI Irving Oil Transport Ltd. Saint John.
NA0249   1979. G-5-14 S/n 7068. N130BD BAe Inc 7/79, N31LG Landis Tool Co 7/79,Salvatore Air Transportation 9/87, N799SC 11/87, PSI Funding Inc 2/89, N799SC Service Corp Intl/Salvatore Air Transportation, Houston, Tx.
NA0250   1979. G-5-15 S/n 7069. N130BE BAe Inc /79, N29GP Genuine Parts Co /79, N29GP Genuine Parts Co. Atlanta
NA0251   1979. G-5-17 S/n 7071. N130BF BAe Inc 7/79, N514B Burroughs Corp 8/79, Unisys Corp 10/87, N396U 12/87, Chemed Corp/U.S. Shoe Corp 4/88, N810CR 11/88, N810CR United States Shoe Corp/Chemed Corp. Cincinnati
NA0252   1979. G-5-18 S/n 7072. N700HS BAe Inc demo 8/79, N900MR Moore McCormack Resources 10/80, BAe Inc 2/88, Great Northern Nekoosa Corp 5/88, N401GN 11/88, N513GP 9/90,N513GP Great Northern Nekoosa Corp. Atlanta, Ga.
NA0253   1979. G-5-19 S/n 7074. N422X Fieldcrest Mills Inc 10/79, Great Lakes Holdings Inc 5/85, Marmon Holdings/Aviation Inc 6/86, (N831CJ) rsvd for Great Lakes Corp 2 Jul 86/10 Feb 88/4 Apr 88, Portland Glove Co 4/88, Canadair Challenger Inc 9/89, JWP Aircraft Inc 3/90,N422X JWP Aircraft Inc. Purchase, NY.
NA0254   1980. G-5-13 S/n 7075. (G-BHKF) BAe 1/80, N125AM BAe Inc 4/80, N125TR NBAA-KCI with Thrust Reversers 9/80, N124AR ARCO 3/81, N124AR ARCO, Dallas, Tx.
NA0255   1979. G-5-14 S/n 7077. N125AJ BAe Inc 11/79, N540B Jucamcyn Theaters Corp 12/79, N540B Virginia Binger/Jucamcyn Theaters Corp. Minneapolis, Mn.
NA0256   1979. G-5-15 S/n 7078. Ff 19 Nov 79, N125AK BAe Inc 12/79, N571CH W R Grace & Co 12/79, N571CH W R Grace & Co. Chemed Division, Cincinnati, Oh.
NA0257   1979. G-5-18 S/n 7080. N125HS BAe Inc 12/79, N611MC May Department Stores Co 1/80, N611MC May Department Stores Co. St. Louis, Mo.
NA0258   1979. G-5-19 S/n 7081. (N125AM) BAe Inc /79, N711CU Carborundum Co 12/79, N809M 6/83, Kennecott Corp 7/84,Standard Oil 6/87,B P America /88, N812M 5/89,N812M B P America Inc. Cleveland-Hopkins Airport, Oh.
NA0259   1980. G-5-12 S/n 7083. N125AH BAe Inc 1/80, N100Y Purolator Inc 3/80, Purolator Courier 11/84, Mar Flite Ltd 11/85, CIT Corp 3/86, Stone Container 12/89, N128CS Citizens & Southern Georgia Corp rsvd 19 Sep 90, N128CS Citizens & Southern Georgia Corp. Chamblee, Ga.
NA0260   1980. G-5-14 S/n 7084. N130BK BAe Inc 1/80, N202CH Crouse-Hinds 2/80,Cooper Industries Inc 6/83,N965JC 4/84, N965JC Cooper Industries Inc. Houston, Tx.
NA0261   1980. G-5-17 S/n 7086. N125AL BAe Inc 3/80, N277CT Caterpillar Tractor 5/80, Caterpillar Inc 11/86, N277CT Caterpillar Inc. Peoria, Il.
NA0262   1980. G-5-16 S/n 7087. (N130BL) BAe Inc 1/80, C-GKRS Kaiser Resources Inc 2/80, British Columbia Coal 1/81, N3234S Comair Inc 10/82, N404CB 4/84, Scientific Packaging 2/86, Comair Inc 1/89, N404CB Comair Inc. West Chester, Pa.
NA0263   1980. G-5-18 S/n 7089. N130BL BAe Inc 2/80, N151AE Aetna Life & Casualty Co 3/80, FSB-Ut 2/85, N151AE Aetna Life & Casualty Co. Hartford, Ct.
NA0264   1980. G-5-19 S/n 7090. N299CT Caterpillar Tractor Inc 3/80, Caterpillar Inc 11/86, N299CT Caterpillar Inc. Peoria, Il.
NA0265   1980. G-5-20 S/n 7092. N733M HAC-Humana Inc 3/80, N733M HAC-Humana Inc. Louisville, Ky.
NA0266   1980. G-5-11 S/n 7093. G-BHMP BAe PLC 2/80, C-GBRM Gulf Canada Ltd 11/80, Petro Canada Exploration Ltd /86, C-GBRM Gulf Canada Resources/Petro Canada Exploration Ltd. Calgary.
NA0267   1980. G-5-12 S/n 7095. N125L BAe Inc 4/80, N215G W R Grace Resources Corp 6/80, Grace Petroleum Co 2/83, Williams Companies 5/85, N352WC 2/86, N852WC rsvd 22 May 90, N852WC Northwest Pipeline/Williams Companies, Tulsa, Ok.
NA0268   1979. G-5-16 S/n 7079. Ff 16 Nov 79, XA-JIX SARSA 12/79, Hibbard Aviation 12/83, N74JA J S Abercrombie Mineral Co 2/84,J S Abercrombie Realty 1/85, Josephine Abercrombie 12/85, 74JA Inc 9/86, (N74JE) rsvd 12 Feb 90, Josephine Abercrombie Interests 4/90, N501MM Earth Star Inc 7/90,N501MM Earth Star Inc. Burbank, Ca.
NA0269   1980. G-5-15 S/n 7098. N125Y BAe Inc 5/80, N89PP Pogo Producing Co 7/80, Johnston Coca Cola Bottling 12/86, N70SK 4/87, N70SK to 8006, N50HS 8/87, N50HS Johnston Coca Cola Bottling, Chatanooga, Tn.
NA0270   1980. G-5-16 S/n 7099. Ff 15 May 80, G-BHSK BAe PLC 6/80, C-GDAO Daon Development Co 11/80,Noranda Mines & Bank of NS /? N621JH Airstar Corp 6/88, N621JH to G-3 387, N621JA 3/90,Aviation Enterprises Inc 12/90, N621JA Aviation Enterprises Inc. Wilmington, De.

NA0271	1980. G-5-15 S/n 7110. XA-KAC SARSA-Mexico 10/80, XA-KAC SARSA=Servicios Aereos Regiomontanos, Monterrey
NA0272	1980. G-5-17 S/n 7101. N89PP BAe Inc 6/80, N109JM JMAC/Worthington Industries 7/80, John H McConnell 1/89, N109JM John H McConnell, Worthington, Oh.
NA0273	1980. G-5-20 S/n 7104. N1OPW Pennwalt Corp 8/80,Keystone Foods Corp 1/89,N1OPW Keystone Foods Corp. Bryn Mawr, Pa.
NA0274	1980. G-5-11 S/n 7105. (N125AB) BAe Inc 7/80, N125BA 7/80, TigerAir Inc 1/82, N125TA 5/82, AMI Aviation of Delaware Inc 4/83, N44BB 9/83, Pace Industries/Avn Methods 2/88, Horn & Hardart 4/88, Dunavant Enterprises Inc 1/89, N700DE 4/89, N700DE Dunavant Enterprises Inc. Fresno, Ca.
NA0275	1980. G-5-13 S/n 7106. N125V BAe Inc 8/80, McDonough Power Equip/Fuqua Industries 11/80, N661JB 6/81, N664JB 9/86, Bell South Corp 1/87, N404CE 7/87, Bellsouth Services Inc 2/90, N404CE Bellsouth Services Inc. Atlanta, Ga.
NA0276	1980. G-5-14 S/n 7096. XA-KEW SARSA-Mexico 5/80, XA-KEW W/O W/o 2 May 81. O2/MAY/81
NA0277	1980. G-5-16 S/n 7111. N125AF BAe Inc 9/80, N324K Ford Motor Co 11/80, N824K 10/88, Indianapolis Motor Speedway Corp 2/89, N500 11/89, N500 Indianapolis Motor Speedway Corp. Indianapolis, In.
NA0278	1980. G-5-14 S/n 7108. XA-KON SARSA=Servicios Aereos Regiomontanos S.A. 8/80, N45500 Hibbard Aviation 9/83, Dondi Group 10/83, ATC Inc 12/83, Geo Gillette Broadcasting Inc 1/84, N6GG 3/84, N6GG to 8030,N6GQ 6/85, Wickes Companies Inc 11/85, N86WC 2/87, Federated Investors Inc 8/87, N700FE 5/88,N700FE Federated Investors Inc. Pittsburgh, Pa.
NA0279	1980. G-5-17 S/n 7113. N125AD BAe Inc 10/80, N204R Raytheon Corp 2/81,N204R Raytheon Corp. Lexington, MA
NA0280	1980. G-5-18 S/n 7102. XA-KIS SARSA-Mexico City 6/80, N700CN Hibbard Aviation 5/84, Copley Newspapaers Inc 5/84, Prospector Publishing Inc 6/84, The Copley Press Inc 12/84, N700CN to G-3 488, N700K 5/87, Standard Oil Co 7/87, N810M 9/87, N810M B P Exploration (Alaska), Anchorage, Ak.
NA0281	1980. G-5-18 S/n 7114. N125AN BAe Inc 10/80, N533 Marion Corp 2/81, Mar-Flite Ltd 2/83, C-GXYN Dome Petroleum Ltd 12/83,AMOCO Canada Petroleum 1/89, C-GXYN AMOCO Canada Petroleum Co Ltd. Calgary.
NA0282	1980. G-5-19 S/n 7116. N125AP BAe Inc 11/80, N1982G Ethyl Corp 2/81, BAe Inc 8/90, Bemis Co Inc 9/90, N120YB 11/90, N120YB Bemis Co Inc. Minneapolis, Mn.
NA0283	1980. G-5-20 S/n 7117. N125AS BAe Inc 11/80, N90B Midland Ross Corp 1/81, Manufacturers Hanover Leasing 4/84, (N90BN) rsvd 29 Nov 84, CIT Group/Equipment Financing 2/87, N220FL 3/88,FL Industries/Lear Siegler Inc 4/89, Lear Siegler Management 9/90,Corporate Airsearch Intl 11/90, BDA/U S Services Ltd 11/90, N93CR rsvd 30 Nov 90, N93CR BDA/U S Services Ltd. Wilmington, De.
NA0284	1980. G-5-11 S/n 7119. N125AE BAe Inc 12/80, N326K Ford Motor Co 3/81, N826K 10/87,N125AR ARCO-Anchorage 12/87, N125AR ARCO, Anchorage, Ak.
NA0285	1980. G-5-14 S/n 7120. N125AT BAe Inc 12/80, N40CN Champion International Corp 3/81, N40CN to F50 92, (N14WJ) World Jet Inc rsvd 24 Mar 87, N130YB Curwood Inc 11/87, N130YB Curwood Inc. Appleton, Wi.
NA0286	1980. G-5-14 S/n 7121. N125AU BAe Inc 12/80, Twentieth Century Fox Film Co 1/81, N20FX 10/81, Air Bunky Inc 11/88, N700SB 1/89, N700SB Steven Bochco/Air Bunky Inc. Los Angeles, Ca.
NA0287	1981. G-5-15 S/n 7122. N125U BAe Inc 1/81, Langham Petroleum Inc 3/81, N77LP 6/81, Fisher Brothers Financial Co 8/82, N299FB 11/82, Houston Industries Inc 6/85, N3444H 9/85,N3444H Houston Industries Inc. Houston, Tx.
NA0288	1981. G-5-16 S/n 7123. N125AH BAe Inc 1/81, Borg Warner Leasing 4/81, N700BW 4/82,Borg Warner Corp 3/87, N700BW Borg Warner Corp. Chicago, Il.
NA0289	1981. G-5-17 S/n 7125. N125AJ BAe Inc 2/81, Utility Leasing/Columbia Gas Systems 5/81, N125CG 6/81, WACO Services Inc 10/87, N62WH 12/87, Consolidated Airways Inc 5/88, N62WL Flightcraft Inc 6/88, GECC-Danbury 9/88, N62WL Flightcraft Inc. Portland, Or.
NA0290	1981. G-5-18 S/n 7127. N700AC Perpetual Corp 3/81, N700AC Lazy Lane Farms/Perpetual Corp. Houston, Tx.
NA0291	1981. G-5-19 S/n 7128. N125BC BAe Inc 3/81, N126AR ARCO 6/81, N126AR ARCO, Dallas, Tx.
NA0292	1981. G-5-20 S/n 7129. N125AK BAe Inc 2/81, MAPCO Inc 4/81, N256EN 9/81, SOHIO Petroleum Co 10/82, (N256MA) 11/81, N805M 12/82, N805M BP Explorations, Houston, Tx.
NA0293	1981. G-5-11 S/n 7131. N700BA BAe Inc 2/81, U S Steel Corp 3/82, N80G 6/82, Marathon Oil 8/85, N520M 3/86, Lone Star Industries Inc 1/88, N52LC 1/89, N52LC Lone Star Industries Inc. Stamford, Ct.
NA0294	1981. G-BIMY S/n 7132. Bae PLC /81, C-FIPG Interprovincial Pipeline 8/81, C-FIPG Interhome Energy Inc. Edmonton.
NA0295	1981. G-5-13 S/n 7134. N871D BAe Inc 4/81, Diamond Intl Corp 8/81, N871D to G-2 245, N371D 11/86, View Top Corp-NYC 12/86, N888SW 3/87, N888SW Rapid American/View Top Corp. NYC.
NA0296	1981. G-5-15 S/n 7135. N490MP BAe Inc 3/81, HBO & Co 6/81, American Standard Inc 2/85, N31AS 4/85, Genuine Parts Co 8/87, N28GP 9/87, N28GP Genuine Parts Co. Atlanta, Ga.
NA0297	1981. G-5-16 S/n 7137. N125BD BAe Inc 3/81, Chessie Service Inc 7/81, N78CS 10/81, (N78QS) rsvd 22 Dec 88, Trans UCU Inc 3/89, N589UC Commonwealth Plan Inc 6/89, N589UC Trans UCU Inc. Kansas City, Ks.
NA0298	1981. G-5-17 S/n 7138. N125G BAe Inc 6/81, U S Steel Corp 10/81,N80K 1/82, USX Corp 6/87, N80K USX Corp. Pittsburgh, Pa.
NA0299	1981. G-5-19 S/n 7140. N125BE BAe Inc 5/81, VR-BHH Caroana-Bermuda 10/81, N125BE Reading & Bates Corp 10/83, N555RB 1/84, Savanace Corp 9/86, Mar Flite Ltd 12/88, NMC Leasing Inc 2/89, N555RB National Medical Care/NMC Leasing Inc. Waltham, Ma.

c/n	
NA0300	1981. G-5-20 S/n 7141. N7OPM BAe Inc 6/81, Philip Morris Inc 8/81, N8OPM 11/81, N8OPM Philip Morris Management Corp. Milwaukee, Wi.
NA0301	1981. G-5-13 S/n 7146. N700HB BAe Inc 8/81,(sale to SARSA-Mexico ntu),Polo Wings Inc 8/82, N711RL 2/83, Polo Fashions Inc 6/83, EAF Aircraft Sales Inc 3/86, N711RL to G-2 25, N713RL 8/86, WNC Corp 10/86, N744DC Turbine Air Management 2/87, Eagle USA/Flt Service Inc 6/87, N421SZ 11/87, N421SZ Eagle USA Inc/Flight Service Inc. Westport, Ct.
NA0302	1981. G-5-19 S/n 7149. N700AA BAe Inc 8/81, (sale to SARSA-Mexico ntu), Hibbard Aviation 12/82, Holiday Inns Inc 3/83, N700HA 4/84, Embassy Suites Inc 2/90, N700HA Embassy Suites Inc. Memphis, Tn.
NA0303	1981. G-5-14 S/n 7147. N125P BAe Inc 8/81, Philip Morris Inc 11/81, (N8OPM) 1/82, N7OPM 4/82, N7OPM Philip Morris Management Corp. Milwaukee, Wi.
NA0304	1981. G-5-17 S/n 7148. N700BB BAe Inc 8/81, (sale to Caroana-Bermuda ntu), Vance Aircraft Brokers 12/82, Digi Corp 12/83, N707DS 3/84, C-GTDN Execaire/Tele Direct Ltee 8/85, C-GTDN Execaire/Tele-Direct Ltee. Montreal.
NA0305	1981. G-5-11 S/n 7150. N700HS BAe Inc 9/81, Sears & Roebuck 7/83, Brown & Root Inc 2/84, N73G 3/84, Halliburton Co 11/86, N730H 1/87, N730H Halliburton Co. Dallas, Tx.
NA0306	1981. (G-5-13) S/n 7152. G-5-17 BAe PLC /81, N700DD BAe Inc 10/81, Manufacturers Hanover Corp 11/81, N270MH 2/82, C-FEXB Execaire Inc 9/86, C-FEXB Execaire Inc. Montreal.
NA0307	1981. G-5-18 S/n 7154. N700GG BAe Inc 10/81, N270MC Manufacturers Hanover Corp 1/82, Park Aviation Corp 2/88, N270MC Parke Aviation Corp. NYC.
NA0308	1981. G-5-19 S/n 7155. N700KK BAe Inc 10/81, Texaco Inc 1/82, N1620 3/82, C-GYPH Petro Canada Explorations 3/84, N1843S Imperial Holly Corp/B A Leasing & Capital Corp 4/88, N1843S Imperial Holly Corp/B A Leasing & Capital Corp. SFO.
NA0309	1981. G-5-17 S/n 7156. N15AG BAe Inc 10/81, Amstar/Liggett Group 3/82, Grandmet USA 7/83, Kapor Enterprises Inc 2/87, N700MK Trust Investments Inc 8/88, N529DM 1/89, Trust Aviation Inc 11/89, N529DM Trust Aviation Inc. Salem, NH.
NA0310	1981. G-5-20 S/n 7157. N700LL BAe Inc 11/81, Superior Oil Co 2/82, N64GG 5/82, N2640 2/85, MASCO 11/85, N2640 Mobil Administrative Services=MASCO, Washington, DC.
NA0311	1981. G-5-15 S/n 7159. N91Y BAe Inc 12/81, Island Creek Coal Co 4/82, N5OJR Occidental Chemical Corp 4/85, (N620CC) rsvd 19 Sep 88, N5OJR Occidental Chemical Corp. Dallas, Tx.
NA0312	1982. G-5-18 S/n 7162. N700NN BAe Inc 1/82, The New York Times Co 3/82, N1896T 6/82, N1896T to F50-127, N1896F 9/83, Valley International Properties Inc 1/84,N176RS 10/87, N176RS Carling Switch/Valley Intl Properties Inc. Wolfboro, NH.
NA0313	1981. G-5-14 S/n 7153. G-BJOW BAe PLC 10/81, XB-CXK Novedades Editores SA 11/81, N18G Jack Prewitt & Assocs 2/90, PK-... Mindo Petroleum Co 8/90, PK-... Mindo Petroleum Co. Jakarta.
NA0314	1982. G-5-11 S/n 7164. N152AE BAe Inc 1/82,Aetna Life & Casualty 6/82,FSB-Ut 12/84, N152AE Aetna Life & Casualty Co. Hartford, Ct.
NA0315	1982. G-5-14 S/n 7165. N869KM BAe Inc 3/82, Colleen Corp 4/82,G D Searle & Co 1/87, N869KM G D Searle & Co. Skokie, Il.
NA0316	1982. G-5-15 S/n 7167. N700PP BAe Inc 3/82, N125BA 8/82, General Foods Corp 9/83, N2989 3/84, Philip Morris Management Corp 8/87, N640PM 1/88, N640PM Philip Morris Management Corp. Madison, Wi.
NA0317	1982. G-5-20 S/n 7168. N700SS BAe Inc 3/82, Vance A/c Brokers 12/82, May Dept Stores 8/83, N611MC 11/83, N612MC May Department Stores Co. St. Louis, Mo.
NA0318	1982. G-5-14 S/n 7170. N819M BAe Inc 4/82,Standard Oil Co 7/82,B P America Inc /88, N819M B P America Inc. Cleveland-Hopkins Airport. Oh.
NA0319	1982. G-5-15 S/n 7171. N700BP BAe Inc 3/82, Mid Atlantic Despatch 12/82, Lanair Inc 8/88, (N168H) Hanna Mining Co 10/83, N120MH 6/86, N120MH Hanna Mining Co. Cleveland, Oh.
NA0320	1982. G-5-17 S/n 7173. N710BN BAe Inc 4/82, Retail Leasing/Limited Stores 8/82, N500LS 6/83, N500LS to CL600 1048, N300LS 7/83, G Heileman Brewing Co 11/83, N300HB 11/83, G Heileman Brewing Co 3/84, Lars Aviation Inc 10/89, N100LR 4/90, N100LR Lars Aviation Inc. Cleveland, Oh.
NA0321	1982. G-5-18 S/n 7174. N710BL BAe Inc 4/82, James River Corp/Daniel Davis 9/82, N469JR 10/82, N469JR Daniel Davis/James River Corp. NYC.
NA0322	1982. G-5-20 S/n 7176. N109G BAe Inc 6/82, Gulf Oil Corp 9/82, Chevron Corp 7/85,N109G Chevron Corp. San Francisco, Ca.
NA0323	1982. G-5-17 S/n 7161. N700RR BAe Inc 2/82, C-GZZX Canadian Superior Oil 7/82, N700RR Mobil Administrative Services-NYC 12/86, N2630 9/87, N2630 Mobil Administrative Services, Washington, DC.
NA0324	1982. G-5-11 S/n 7177. N710BJ BAe Inc 5/82, AKI Finance Corp 7/82, JB&A Aircraft 9/82, The Philips Co 10/83, J Sloan/Thompson Cos 12/83, N711TG 5/84, MDFC Equipment Leasing 10/90, N711TG John Sloan/Thompson Companies, Dallas, Tx.
NA0325	1981. G-5-20 S/n 7143. N700HA BAe Inc 7/81, Halliburton Co 8/81, N26H 6/82, N26H Halliburton Co. Dallas, Tx.
NA0326	1981. G-5-11 S/n 7144. N522M Bae Inc 7/81, Marathon Oil Co 9/81,Maryland Natl Leasing Corp 1/87,Aristech Chemical Corp 2/89, N70AR 5/89, Alan B McPherson 3/90, Aristech Chemical 4/90, N70AR Aristech Chemical Corp. Pittsburgh, Pa.

NA0327	1982. G-5-15 S/n 7179. N810SC BAe Inc 6/82, Southern California Gas Inc 8/82,Aviationn Methods Inc 8/90, Southern Aircraft Services 9/90, N810SC Southern Aircraft Services Inc. Fort Lauderdale, Fl.
NA0328	1982. G-5-16 S/n 7180. N710BG BAe Inc 6/82, Helmerich & Payne Inc 10/82, N2HP 1/83, N2HP Helmerich & Payne Inc. Tulsa, Ok.
NA0329	1982. G-5-17 S/n 7182. N710BF BAe Inc 8/82, Chemgraphics Systems Inc 11/82, (N277CB) 12/82, N1824T 1/83, N1824T to CL601 3029, N18243 4/85, Nekoosa Papers Inc 5/88, N756N 9/88,N512GP Georgia Pacific Corp 6/90, N512GP Georgia Pacific Corp. Atlanta, Ga.
NA0331	1982. G-5-12 S/n 7185. N700BA BAe Inc 8/82, Bausch & Lomb/American Finance Group Inc 6/84, N900BL 11/84, Citizens & Southern National Bank 1/85, N900BL Bausch & Lomb/American Finance Group, Boston, Ma.
NA0332	1982. G-5-11 S/n 7186. N710BC BAe Inc 9/82, Chase Manhattan Bank 12/82, N400CH 9/83, Weber-Stephen Products Co 5/89, N400QH 6/89, N16GS 11/89, N16GS Weber-Stephen Products Co. Palatine, Il.
NA0333	1982. G-5-15 S/n 7188. N523M BAe Inc 10/82, Marathon Oil Co 12/82, Maryland National Leasing Corp 1/87, N523M Marathon Oil Co. Findlay, Oh.
NA0334	1983. G-5-18 S/n 7195. N710BY BAe Inc 3/83, Sears Roebuck & Co 12/83, N702M 2/84, Wallingford Industries/Wm J Stoecker-Il 7/86, N93GC 8/86, Weldbend Corp 4/89, N46WC 5/89, N46WC Weldbend Corp. Chicago, Il.
NA0335	1983. G-5-18 S/n 7198. N710BX BAe Inc 3/83, Sears Roebuck & Co 2/84, N702E 3/84,C-GJBJ Innotech Avn Ltd 7/86, Sears Canada Inc /87, C-GJBJ Sears Canada Inc. Toronto.
NA0336	1982. G-5-15 S/n 7191. N710BA BAe Inc 10/82, Coca Cola Co 2/83, N677RW 8/83, Consolidated Airways Inc 12/86, (N477RW) rsvd 11 Dec 86, Aircraft Operations Inc/NTS Corp 2/87, N11TS 11/87, N11TS Aircraft Operations Inc/NTS Corp. Louisville, Ky.
NA0337	1982. G-5-14 S/n 7192. N125MT BAe Inc 11/82, Monsanto Co 6/83, N2015M 10/83, N2015M Monsanto Co. Chesterfield, Mo.
NA0338	1982. G-5-15 S/n 7193. N710BZ BAe Inc 10/82, Limited Stores/Retail Leasing Corp 3/83, Clinton Aviation Group 5/83, Gulf States & Resources 7/83, Knickerbocker/American General Corp 9/83,GECC-Menlo Park 1/84, N710AG 4/84, GECC-Emeryville 1/88, N710AG American General Corp. Houston, Tx.
NA0339	1981. G-5-18 S/n 7145. N70FC Bae Inc 10/81, First National Chicago Assoc 1/82,N70FC Emery/First National Chicago Association, Il.
NA0340	1983. G-5-12 S/n 7199. N710BW BAe Inc 7/83, Sears Roebuck & Co 12/83, N702W 2/84, VR-BKZ Dennis Vanguard Intl (Switchgear) Ltd 4/89, VR-BKZ Dennis Vanguard International (Switchgear Ltd), Coventry-UK.
NA0341	1983. G-5-19 S/n 7201. N710BV BAe Inc 7/83, Kellwood/Tri W Corp 11/83, N2KW 2/84, N2KW Kellwood Co/Tri W Corp. St. Louis, Mo.
NA0342	1983. G-5-17 S/n 7202. N710BU BAe Inc 7/83, Oilfield Aviation Corp 9/83, N518S 1/84, Liebert Corp 3/86, (N67LC) rsvd 16 Apr 86, N65LC 9/86, N65LC Liebert Corp. Columbus, Oh.
NA0343	1983. G-5-15 S/n 7204. N524M BAe Inc 8/83, Marathon Oil 11/83,Cargill Leasing 5/84, N524M Marathon Oil/Cargill Leasing Corp. Minnetonka, Mn.
NA0344	1983. G-5-16 S/n 7206. N710BT BAe Inc 7/83, Sears Roebuck & Co 2/84, N1C 3/84, N502S 10/88, Westcoast Energy Inc 4/89, C-FWCE Westcoast Energy Inc. Vancouver, BC.
NA0345	1983. G-5-18 S/n 7207. N710BS BAe Inc 10/83, GFI=General Felt Industries Air Corp 4/84, N774GF 3/85, N686SG 6/87, Kihi Avn Corp 11/87, N686FG 4/89, 21 Avn Corp 10/90, N686FG General Felt Industries/21 Aviation Corp. NYC.

BAe 125/CC2

7181	1982. G-5-16 ZD 620 Royal Air Force 2/83, ZD620 RAF, 32 Squadron, Northolt.
7183	1982. G-5-20 (NA0330). N710BD BAe Inc 7/82, Cx USA as not exported for S Jernigan 8/82, G-5-20 BAe PLC 9/82, ZD703 Royal Air Force 2/83, ZD703 RAF, 32 Squadron, Northolt.
7190	1982. ZD621 Royal Air Force 3/83, ZD621 RAF, 32 Squadron, Northolt.
7194	1982. ZD704 Royal Air Force 3/83, ZD704 RAF, 32 Squadron, Northolt.
7205	1983. G-5-19 ZE395 Royal Air Force /83, ZE395 RAF, 32 Squadron, Northolt.
7211	1984. ZE396 Royal Air Force /85, ZE396 RAF, 32 Squadron, Northolt.

BAe 125 Series 800

8001	1983. G-5-11 Ff 26 May 83, N800BA BAe Inc 5/83, G-BKTF British Aerospace PLC /83, G-5-522 8/86, G-UWWB 'Up Where We Belong'=BAe motto, digital avionics demo 8/86, G-5-557 6/87, ZK-TCB Wilson Neill Ltd/C F Herbert-Dunedin, New Zealand 27 Jun 87, N785CA Continental Aviation Inc 5/89, OH-JOT Jet Flite OY 4/90, OH-JOT Jet Flite OY-Progressor OY. Helsinki.
8002	1984. (G-5-16) G-DCCC British Aerospace Aircraft Group /84, (VH-CCC) /86,VH-III arr Perth 7/86,Australia & New Zealand Bank 7/87, VH-III Australia & New Zealand Bank, Melbourne. 'Kimberly Alice'
8003	1984. G-5-20 G-BKUW BAe PLC /84, N800BA BAe Inc 6/84, Manufacturers Hanover/Navistar Intl 1/86, N800N 3/86,CIT Group Equip Financing 2/87,CIT Leasing 12/89, N800N Navistar International Corp. Chicago, Il.

c/n	
8004	1984. G-5-15 G-BLGZ BAe PLC /84, N800EE BAe Inc 6/84, Dillard Department Stores Inc 8/84, N94BD 10/84, (N98DD) rsvd 18 Nov 85, N98DD re-allocated to 650-0048 1/86, N94BD Dillard Department Stores Inc. Little Rock, Ar.
8005	1984. G-5-15 G-BLJC BAe PLC 8 May 84, N800GG BAe Inc 6/84, Storage Technology Corp 8/84. N601UU Union Underwear Co 7/85, N601UU Union Underwear Company. Bowling Green, Ky.
8006	1984. G-5-17 N800WW BAe Inc 6/84, Scovill Inc 7/84, N800S 12/84, FSB-SLC 1/85, Johnston Coca Cola Bottling Co 7/87, N70SK 10/87, N70SK Johnston Coca-Cola Bottling Co. Chattanooga, Tn.
8007	1983. G-GAEL Heron Management Services Ltd 17 Nov 83, G-5-20 BAe PLC /85, G-GAEL 2/85, lease ARPAC International-NZ 8/86-9/86, G-5-554 4/87, C-GKRL Kaiser Resources Ltd 4/87,C-GYPH Petro Canada Inc 8/88, Power Financial Corp 20 Jun 90, C-GYPH Power Financial Corp. Montreal.
8008	1984. G-5-11 N722CC BAe Inc 6/84, GECC/Crown Central Petroleum 9/84, N722CC Crown Central Petroleum, Baltimore, Md.
8009	1984. (G-5-12) G-5-15 N400AL BAe Inc 7/84,Abbott Laboratories Inc 9/84,N400AL to G-3 343, N408AL 8/86, Manville Sales Corp 10/86, N45Y 11/86, N45Y to NA0427, N48Y 5/89, N48Y Manville Sales Corp. Denver, Co.
8010	1984. (G-5-14) G-5-19 (G-BLKS) BAe PLC /84, (G-OVIP) Harry Goodman /84, N84A Page Avjet Corp 9/84, Basil Georges/Belchase Air Inc 2/85, N810BG 6/85, Belchase Air Inc 7/85,N810BG Basil Georges/Belchase Air Inc. Dallas, Tx.
8011	1984. (G-5-18) G-5-20 N800VV BAe Inc 7/84, Brown Group Inc 8/84, N1BG 12/84, FSB-Ut 2/85, N1BG Brown Group Inc. Chesterfield, Mo.
8012	1984. G-5-18 N800TT BAe Inc 8/84, NWT Aircraft Co 10/84, N400NW 1/85, N400NW Farley Industries/NWT Aircraft Co. Chicago, Il.
8013	1984. G-5-14 G-OCCC Consolidated Contractors (UK Svcs) Ltd 18 Sep 84, Consolidated Contractors International 8 Aug 86, G-OCCC Consolidated Contractors International. (based Athens).
8014	1984. G-5-15 N800MM BAe Inc 9/84, N294W MPB Corp 10/84, Henley Investments 1/87, Fisher Scientific Group 1/89, Airtrade International 11/89, US Bancorp Leasing & Financial 1/90, N294W Airtrade International Inc. Fairfield, Ct.
8015	1984. G-5-17 G-BLPC BAe Inc 10/84, C-FTLA Husky Oil-Calgary 4/85, C-FTLA Husky Oil Operations-Nova Alberta Corp. Calgary.
8016	1984. G-5-18 F-GESL Ste Air Transports Schlumberger 12/84, N415PT Pacific Telesis Group 2 Feb 87, N415PT Pacific Telesis Group, Oakland, Ca.
8017	1984. G-5-16 N800LL BAe Inc 9/84, Garrett Corp 9 Nov 84, N801G 8/85, Allied Signal Inc 7/89,N801G Allied Signal Inc. Los Angeles, Ca.
8018	1984. G-5-12 N800PP BAe Inc 10/84, CSX Beckett Avn Inc 12/84, Texas Gas Transmission Corp 11 Dec 84, N818TG 3/85, N818TG Texas Gas Transmission Corp. Owensboro, Ky.
8019	1984. G-5-12 (VH-SGJ) /84, VH-SGY Queensland State Government 13 Dec 84, VH-SGY Queensland State Government, Brisbane.
8020	1984. G-5-14 N800ZZ Bae Inc 10/84, Manufacturers Hanover Corp 27 Dec 84, N270HC 5/85, N270HC Manufacturers Hanover Corp. Hangar A, Westchester, NY.
8021	1985. G-GEIL Heron Management Services Ltd 31 Jan 85, G-GEIL Heron Management Services Ltd. Luton.
8022	1985. G-5-16 G-JJCB J C Bamford (Excavators) Ltd 'Exporter VIII' 1/85, G-5-569 BAe PLC 9/87, HZ-KSA Prince Karim Saudi Arabia 11/87, EC-193 Alfa Jet Charter SA 10/88, EC-ELK 12/88, EC-ELK Alfa Jet Charter SA. Madrid.
8023	1984. G-5-15 N810AA BAe Inc 27 Nov 84, Hallmark Cards Inc 11 Jan 85,N1910H 4/85, N1910H Hallmark Cards Inc. Kansas City, Mo.
8024	1984. G-5-18 N811AA BAe Inc 12/84, D L Paul/Centrust Savings Bank 2/85, N800DP 8/85,Westinghouse Credit 1/86,Air Traffic Service Corp 4/90, N802DC rsvd 19 Apr 90, N802DC Air Traffic Service Corp. Little Rock, Ar.
8025	1984. 3D-AVL Anglovaal Group /84, 3D-AVL Anglovaal Group, Lanseria, RSA.
8026	1985. G-5-18 N800HS BAe Inc 1/85, Globe Life-Accident Insurance 1/86, N6TM 6/86, N6TM Torchmark/Globe Life-Accident Insurance, Oklahoma City, Ok.
8027	1985. G-5-12 N812AA BOS BAe 4 Feb 85, Philip Morris Management Corp 6 Mar 85, N800PM 7/85, N800PM Philip Morris Management Corp. White Plains, NY.
8028	1985. G-5-12 G-TSAM BSM Holdings Ltd 28 Mar 85, BAe (CA) Ltd 24 Jan 89, BAe PLC 9/90, G-TSAM British Aerospace PLC. Hatfield.
8029	1985. G-5-16 (N600TH) BAe Inc /85, (originally to be 600th HS125), N813AA BAe Inc 20 Mar 85, Liberty Service Corp 12 Apr 85, N600HS 8/85, Genesee Management Inc 8/89, N600HS Genesee Management Inc. Rochester, NY.
8030	1985. G-5-14 N600TH BAe Inc 4/85, 600th HS-125, Gillette Broadcasting 4/85, N6GG 9/85, Rough Creek Aviation Co 10/89, N1OWF 1/90, N1OWF Rough Creek Aviation Co. Portland, Or.
8031	1985. G-5-15 PT-ZAA del reg for CESP-Cia Energetica de Sao Paulo 6/85, PT-LHB 9/85, PT-LHB CESP=Cia Energetica de Sao Paulo.
8032	1985. G-5-11 N815AA BAe Inc 2 Apr 85, Marathon Oil Co 2 May 85, N526M 7/85, Maryland National Leasing Corp 1/87, GECC-Danbury 12/90, N526M Marathon Oil Co. Findlay, Oh.

c/n	
8033	1985. G-5-19 N157H BAe Inc 24 Apr 85, H J Heinz & Co 4 May 85, Ore Ida Foods Inc 11/89, N57FF 2/90,N57FF Ore Ida Foods Inc. Boise, Id.
8034	1985. G-5-12 G-HYGA Hygena Kitchens-York Avn Ltd/Mills Pride-USA 11/85, Helpfactor Ltd 27 Apr 90, G-HYGA Helpfactor Ltd. London.
8035	1985. G-5-20 N816AA BAe Inc 5/85, Firestone Tire & Rubber 6/85, N30F 9/85, N30F Firestone Tire & Rubber, Akron, Oh.
8036	1985. G-5-18 N817AA BAe Inc 6/85, Firestone Tire & Rubber 6/85, N31F 9/85, N31F Firestone Tire & Rubber, Akron, Oh.
8037	1985. G-5-15 BAe PLC 7/85, G-5-501 3/86, 4W-ACN Shaher Traders-Sana'a del 20 Aug 86, 70-ADC 1/91, 70-ADC Shaher Traders, Sana'a. 'Anisa IV'.
8038	1985. G-5-20 N800TR BAe Inc 18 Jun 85,Pacificorp Trans Inc 6/87, N800TR to 8087, N206PC 10/87, Nerco Inc 1/88, N206PC Pacific Corp Trans/Nerco Inc. Portland, Or.
8039	1985. G-5-19 N818AA BAe Inc 7/85, Kakap Inc 7/85, N400TB Taco Bell Corp 11/85, N200KF Kentucky Fried Chicken 8/87, N200KF Kentucky Fried Chicken/KFC Natl Managemant Co. Louisville.
8040	1985. G-5-15 VH-IXL Elders IXL Co/Carlton United Breweries 10/85, VH-IXL Elders IXL Co/Carlton United Breweries, Melbourne.
8041	1985. G-5-18 N819AA BAe Inc 8/85, Nationwide Insurance Co 9/85, N71NP 11/85, N71NP Nationwide Mutual Insurance Co. Columbus, Oh.
8042	1985. G-5-11 N820AA BAe Inc 8/85, Storer Communications Inc 9/85, N20S 11/85, Kaiserair Inc 3/88, N112K 8/88,Wells Frago & Co 9/90, N112K Wells Fargo Co/Kaiserair Inc. Oakland, Ca.
8043	1985. G-5-12 (D-CAZH) Allianz AG Munich 5/85, N319AT Allianz Technical Service Inc 7 Nov 85, N319AT Allianz Technical Service Inc. Dallas, Tx.
8044	1985. G-5-12 N821AA BAe Inc 8/85, Nationwide Insurance Co 9/85, N72NP 11/85, N72NP Nationwide Mutual Insurance Co. Columbus, Oh.
8045	1985. G-5-16 N822AA BAe Inc 8/85, Tyson Foods Inc 10/85, N800TF 12/85, N800TF Tyson Foods Inc. Fayetteville, Ar.
8046	1985. G-5-20 N823AA BAe Inc 9/85, N800BA 5/86, McClatchy Newspapers Inc 11/87, N125SB 3/88, N125SB McClatchy Newspapers Inc. Sacramento, Ca.
8047	1985. G-5-11 N824AA BAe Inc 9/85, Tri Continental Leasing/Bell Atlantic 1/86, N84BA 3/86, N84BA Bell Atlantic/Tri-Continental Leasing Corp. Paramus, NJ.
8048	1985. G-5-16 G-BMMO British Aerospace PLC digital avionics demo 2/86, (N125BA) rsvd Mar 86, C-GCIB Canadian Imperial Bank 12 Sep 86, C-GCIB Canadian Imperial Bank of Commerce, Toronto.
8049	1985. G-5-19 N825AA BAe Inc 11/85, EX-CELL-O Corp 1/86, N800EX 2/86, United States Tobacco Co 11/87, N24SB 6/89, U S Tobacco Sales & Management 1/90, N24SB UST Corp/United States Tobacco Co. Greenwich, Ct.
8050	1986. G-5-503 HZ-OFC Olayan Finance Co 4/86, HZ-OFC Olayan Finance Co. Al Khobar.
8051	1986. G-5-18 N826AA BAe Inc 12/85, AFG Industries Inc 1/86, N889DH 6/86, Jaguar Investments Inc 11/88, N889DH Jaguar Investments Inc. Wilmington, De.
8052	1985. G-5-20 N360BA BAe Inc 12/85, Ethyl Corp 27 Jun 86, N87EC 11/86, N87EC Ethyl Corp. Richmond, Va.
8053	1985. G-5-11 N361BA BAe Inc 1/86, Diversitech General Inc 3/86,Gencorp Inc 7/86, N5G 8/86, N5G Gencorp/Diversitech General Inc. Akron, Oh.
8054	1986. G-5-15 BAe Inc 1/86, N527M Marathon Oil Co 28 Jan 86, Fifth Third Leasing Co-Cincinnati 9/86,N527M Marathon Oil Co. Findlay, Oh.
8055	1986. G-5-504 BAe Inc 1/86, N528M Marathon Oil Co del 11 Feb 86, Provident Commercial Group 10/86, N528M Provident Commercial Group/Marathon Oil Co. Findlay, Oh.
8056	1986. G-5-509 G-JETI Yeates of Leicester del 2 Sep 86,G-JETI Jet One/Yeates of Leicester/Magec Aviation, Luton.
8057	1986. G-5-508 2/86, N362BA BAe Inc del 21 May 86, Gannett Co Inc 6/86, N300GN 2/87, N300GN Gannett Co Inc. Arlington, Va.
8058	1986. G-5-510 6/86, ZK-EUI Bosphorus Intl 12/86, Euro National Corp-Auckland 4/87, VH-NMR NSCA/N M Rothchilds Bank P/L-Sydney 2 Nov 88, N125JW James Wikert & Assoc 6/89, Express One Intl 6/89, DPF Airlease Inc V 11/89, DPF Airlease Inc III 12/89, N125JW DPF Airlease Inc III, Woodcliff Lake, NJ.
8059	1986. G-5-506 N363BA BAe Inc 3/86, Gannett Co Inc 6/86, N400GN 2/87, N400GN Gannett Co Inc. Arlington
8060	1986. G-5-511 4/86, N364BA BAe Inc 6/86, Calfed Inc 6/86, N686CF 9/86, Texas Eastern Transmission Co 4/90, N330X 5/90, N330X Texas Eastern Transmission Co. Houston, Tx.
8061	1986. G-5-515 6/86, N365BA BAe Inc 5/86, Aircraft Assoc/Berkshire Inn Inc 7/86, N161MM 4/87, N161MM Aircraft Associates/Goodman Realty Corp. Teterboro, NJ.
8062	1986. G-5-516 6/86, N366BA BAe Inc 6/86, Cooper Industries Inc 7/86, N961JC 2/87, N961JC Cooper Industries Inc. Houston, Tx.
8063	1986. G-5-517 7/86, N367BA BAe Inc del 8 Sep 86, E I Dupont de Nemours 10/86, N684C 12/86, N684C E I Dupont de Nemours, Wilmington, De.
8064	1986. G-5-514 BAe PLC /86, MAAW-J1 Govt of Malawi del 22 Aug 86, MAAW-J1 Government of Malawi, Zomba.
8065	1986. G-5-520 7/86, N368BA BAe Inc del 16 Sep 86, CSX Corp 10/86, N77CS 3/87,Metlife Capital Credit Corp 4/87, N77CS CSX Corp. Richmond, Va.

c/n	Entry
8066	1986. G-5-521 7/86, N369BA BAe Inc del 23 Sep 86, CSX Corp 10/86, N75CS 3/87,Metlife Capital Credit Corp 4/87, N75CS CSX Corp. Richmond, Va.
8067	1986. G-5-525 8/86, D-CEVW Volkswagenwerk AG del 5 Nov 86, D-CEVW Volkswagenwerk AG. Braunschweig.
8068	1986. G-5-539 Bae PLC 11/86, HZ-SJP Jouanou & Parskevaides Saudi Arabia Ltd 15 Sep 87, G-5-653 BAe PLC 2/90, HZ-SJP Jouanou & Parskevaides Saudi Arabia Ltd. Riyadh.
8069	1986. G-5-526 8/86, N519BA BAe Inc 9/86, Union Pacific Railroad Co 12/86, N746UP 6/87, N746UP Union Pacific Railroad Co. Omaha, Ne.
8070	1986. G-5-527 8/86, N520BA BAe Inc 10/86, Amway Corp 10/86, N528AC 2/87, N528AC Amway Corp. Ada, Mi.
8071	1986. G-5-528 N521BA BAe Inc 10/86, ALCOA 10/86, N890A 5/87, N890A Aluminium Co of America, Allegheny County Airport. Pa.
8072	1986. G-5-529 9/86, N522BA BAe Inc 11/86, Union Pacific Railroad Co 12/86, N747UP 6/87, N747UP Union Pacific Railroad Co. Omaha, Ne.
8073	1986. G-5-532 10/86, D-CFVW Volkswagenwerk AG del 19 Dec 86, D-CFVW Volkswagenwerk AG. Braunschweig.
8074	1986. G-5-541 12/86, ZK-MRM Bosphorus Intl 4 Mar 87, Chase Corp 28 Apr 87, G-5-640 BAe PLC 8/89, N800MD Jet East 8/89, MNC Financial Corp 9/89, N800MN 12/89, N800MN American Flite Inc/MNC Financial Corp. Baltimore, Md.
8075	1986. G-5-533 10/86, N518BA BAe Inc 11/86, Private Business Air Service Inc 12/86, N189B 8/87, Pacent Funding Inc 8/90, N533P 10/90, N533P Pacent Funding Inc. NYC.
8076	1986. G-5-535 /86, D-CGVW Volkswagenwerk AG 12/86, D-CGVW Volkswagenwerk AG. Braunschweig.
8077	1986. G-5-538 11/86, N523BA Georgia Pacific Corp 12/86, N509GP 8/87, N509GP Georgia Pacific Corp. Atlanta, Ga.
8078	1987. G-5-544 G-BNEH BAe PLC 4 Feb 87, Osprey Aviation del 19 Oct 87, High Speed Flight Ltd 3/90, G-BNEH High Speed Flight Ltd.
8079	1986. G-5-542 1/87, G-GJCB J C Bamford (Excavators) Ltd del 1 Apr 87, G-GJCB J C Bamford (Excavators) Ltd. East Midlands. 'Exporter 9'
8080	1986. G-5-540 N524BA BAe Inc 12/86, Peter Bedford-Ca 1/87, N800BP 800BP Corp 8/87, N800BP Bedford Properties/800BP Corp. Portland, Or.
8081	1987. G-5-543 N525BA BAe Inc 1/87,Philip Morris Management Corp 2/87,N650PM 6/87, N650PM Philip Morris Inc. White Plains, NY.
8082	1987. G-5-548 /87, ZK-RJI Cory Wright & Salmon 10 Jun 87, Robert Jones Investments del 15 Oct 87, ZK-RJI Robert Jones Investments Ltd. Wellington.
8083	1987. G-5-546 N526BA BAe Inc 1/87, (N800HS) rsvd 29 Jan 87, Union Pacific/Champlin Petroleum Co 6/87,N5C 8/87, N5C Union Pacific Resources, Fort Worth, Tx.
8084	1987. G-5-547 N527BA Bae Inc 1/87, ALCOA 2/87, N780A 8/87, N780A ALCOA, Pittsburgh, Pa.
8085	1987. G-5-551 BAe 3/87, G-WBPR THF Airport Services Ltd del 16 Nov 87, G-WBPR Trust House Forte Airport Services Ltd. London.
8086	1987. G-5-550 N528BA BAe Inc 3/87, N125BA 9/87, N523WC Inc 11/88, N523WC 2/89, N523WC The Cafaro Co/N523WC Inc. Youngstown, Oh.
8087	1987. G-5-552 N529BA BAe Inc 5/87, N800TR 11/87, C-GAWH C W McCleod Fisheries Inc 12/87, IMASCO Ltd 23 Aug 89, C-GAWH IMASCO Ltd. Montreal.
8088	1987. G-5-563 BAe 8/87, (ZK-RHP) Cory, Wright & Salmon-Auckland /88, G-BOOA British Aerospace PLC 5/88, Hanover demo 6/88, G-BTAB ARAVCO/Abbey Investment Co 7/88, G-BTAB Abbey Investment Co. London.
8089	1987. G-5-555 N530BA BAe Inc 5/87, L M Berry Aircraft Inc 7/87, N125JB 2/88, N125JB Berry Investments Inc. Dayton, Oh..
8090	1987. G-5-556 N531BA BAe Inc 5/87, HM Holdings Inc 6/87, N2SG 9/87, HM Industries Inc 2/88, N2SG Hanson Industries/HM Holdings Inc. Newark, De.
8091	1987. G-5-560 8/87, HB-VIK Swiss Air Ambulance 16 Sep 87, HB-VIK Swiss Air Ambulance, Zurich.
8092	1987. G-5-558 N532BA BAe Inc 2/87, Media General Inc 7/87, N2MG 1/88, N2MG Media General Inc. Richmond
8093	1987. G-5-559 N533BA BAe Inc 7/87, ISC Group Inc 8/87, N331SC 9/88, Tracey Leasing Corp 3/89,N800S 4/89, LPL Air Inc 2/90, N358LL 4/90, N358LL LPL Air Inc. Greenville, De.
8094	1987. G-5-576 /87, D-CFAN Haeger & Schmidt GmbH del 19 Dec 87, D-CFAN Haeger & Schmidt GmbH/Thyssen, Dusseldorf.
8095	1987. G-5-561 N534BA BAe Inc 6/87, Limited Stores/Northern Holding Corp 8/87, N200LS 11/87,N200LS to G-2 227, (N500LL) rsvd 20 Jun 89, C-FPCP Pancanadian Petroleum Ltd 7/89, C-FPCP Pancanadian Petroleum Ltd. Calgary.
8096	1987. G-5-562 N535BA BAe Inc 8/87, Union Pacific Corp 8/87, N800UP 1/88, N800UP Union Pacific Aviation Co. Allentown, Pa.
8097	1987. G-5-567 /87, HB-VIL Swiss Air Ambulance del 19 Dec 87, HB-VIL Swiss Air Ambulance, Zurich.
8098	1987. G-5-564 N536BA BAe Inc 10/87, Southern Holding Corp/Limited Stores 11/87, N300LS 7/88, N300LS Limited Stores/Southern Holding Corp. Wilmington, De.
8099	1987. G-5-565 N537BA BAe Inc 9/87, C-FAAU ALCAN Aluminium Ltd 19 Feb 88, C-FAAU ALCAN Aluminium Ltd. Montreal.
8106	1988. G-5-580 /88, PK-WSJ East Indonesia Air Charter /88, PK-WSJ East Indonesia Air Charter, Jakarta.
8109	1988. G-5-581 /88, 5N-NPC Nigerian Petroleum 4/88, 5N-NPC Aero Contractors/Nigerian Petroleum Co. Lagos

c/n	
8110	1988. G-5-584 /88, D-CMIR Miro Flug KG /88, D-CMIR Miro Flug KG/Aero Dienst GmbH. Nuremberg.
8112	1988. G-5-583 Government/Botswana Defence Force del 15 Jun 88, OK1 Government/Botswana Defence Force (Z1 fin code) 15 Jun 88, G-5-664 BAe PLC /90, PT-OBT Caparao Taxi Aereo Ltda 7/90, PT-OBT Caparao Taxi Aereo Ltda. Belo Horizonte.
8115	1988. G-5-599 (G-BPGR) BAe PLC (Military Aircraft Division) 11/88, HZ-104 RSAF del 29 Nov 88, G-5-665 test flight following modification 5/90, HZ-104 6/90, HZ-104 Royal Saudi Air Force, Riyadh.
8116	1988. G-5-592 /88, PT-LQP Banco Real SA 7/88, Metro Taxi Aereo /89, PT-LQP Metro Taxi Aereo Ltda. Sao Paulo.
8118	1988. G-5-605 (G-BPGS) Bae PLC (Military Aircraft Division) 11/88, HZ-105 RSAF 12/88, HZ-105 Royal Saudi Air Force, Riyadh.
8120	1988. G-5-606 /88, G-POSN P & O Containers (Assets) Ltd 10/88, G-POSN P & O Containers (Assets) Ltd. Hatfield.
8129	1989. G-5-622 N269X LTV Aerospace & Defence del 15 Jun 89, 88-0269 USAF 5/90, 88-0269 C-29A, USAF, Scott AFB. Il.
8130	1988. G-5-620 BAe PLC 12/88, G-FDSL Ferranti Defence Systems Ltd 1/89, G-TPHK Tiphook PLC 2/90, G-TPHK Tiphook PLC. London.
8131	1989. G-5-611 (N271X) LTV Aerospace & Defense Co 4/89, N270X 4/89, 88-0271 USAF /90, 88-0271 C-29A,USAF, Scott AFB. Il.
8133	1988. G-5-616 G-GSAM Scorpio Commodities/BSM Holdings 11/88, Tiger Avn 2/89, G-5-642 Bae PLC 9/89,N800FK Intl Jet Inc/Keeley Granite-RSA 9/89, N800FK Keeley Granite, Lanseria, RSA.
8134	1989. G-5-634 N270X painted as such, N271X LTV Aerospace & Defense Co 4/89, 88-0270 USAF 5/90, 88-0270 C-29A, USAF, Scott AFB. Il.
8143	1989. G-5-656 5N-NPF Nigerian Police Force 'Mogambo' 7/90, 5N-AGZ Central Bank-Lagos 19 Sep 90, 5N-AGZ Central Bank, Lagos.
8146	1989. G-5-629 (G-BPYD) Bae PLC (Military Aircraft Division) 17 May 89, HZ-109 RSAF /89, HZ-109 Royal Saudi Air Force, Riyadh.
8148	1989. G-5-630 (G-BPYE) BAe PLC (Military Aircraft Division) 17 May 89, HZ-110 RSAF /89, HZ-110 Royal Saudi Air Force, Riyadh.
8149	1989. G-5-635 /89, G-FASL Fisons PLC /89, G-FASL Fisons PLC. East Midlands.
8151	1990. G-EXLR BAe (CA) Ltd Ff 16 Jun 90, Bae PLC 9/90, G-EXLR British Aerospace PLC. Hatfield.
8152	1989. G-5-626 /89, HB-VHU Rabbit-Air AG (outfitted in USA) 27 Apr 89, HB-VHU Rabbit-Air AG. Zurich.
8153	1989. G-5-627 /89, HB-VHV Rabbit-Air AG (outfitted in USA) 16 May 89, HB-VHV Rabbit-Air AG. Zurich.
8154	1989. G-5-655 N272X LTV Aerospace & Defense Co 4/89, 88-0272 USAF /90, 88-0272 C-29A, USAF, Scott AFB
8155	1989. G-5-628 N800BM BMW of North America Inc del 22 Jun 89,D-CBMW BMW GmbH 6/90, D-CBMW BMW GmbH Munich
8156	1989. G-5-661 N273X LTV Aerospace & Defense Co del 25 May 90, 88-0273 USAF /90, 88-0273 C-29A, USAF, Scott AFB. Il.
8158	1989. G-5-667 N274X LTV Aerospace & Defense Co del 17 Jul 90, 88-0274 USAF /90, 88-0274 C-29A, USAF, Scott AFB. Il.
8159	1990. G-OPFC BAe PLC Ff 26 Nov 90, G-OPFC British Aerospace PLC. Hatfield.
8164	1989. G-5-654 /90, OK1 Government of Botswana 4/90, OK1 Government/Botswana Defence Force, Z1 Squadron.
8165	1989. G-5-657 /90, VR-BPG GUMC-RSA/Atavar Holdings (Guernsey) Inc 5/90,VR-BPG General Union Mining Corp. RSA.
8167	1990. G-5-662 /90, N125AS Aarton Senna/Cavalier Air Corp 7/90, N125AS Aarton Senna/Cavalier Air Corp. Wilmington, De.
8169	1989. G-5-644 /89, N47CG Tigervest Leasing Inc 12/89, N47CG Tigervest Leasing Inc. Miami, Fl.
8176	1989. G-5-652 /90, HB-VJY Tricom Inc 19 Jan 90, HB-VJY JABJ/Tricom Inc. Lugano.
8177	1990. G-5-668 /90, PT-OJC Frota Oceanica Brasileira 10/90, PT-OJC Frota Oceanica Brasileira,
8180	1990. G-5-675 /90, G-XRMC RMC Group Services Ltd 3 Jul 90, G-XRMC RMC Group Services Ltd. Biggin Hill.
8182	1990. G-5-676 /90, G-PBWH Freedom Trust SA/Lynton Aviation Ltd 8/80, G-PBWH Freedom Trust SA/Lynton Aviation Ltd.
8184	1990. G-5-678 /90, PT-OSW Wanair Taxi Aereo Ltda del 16 Nov 90, PT-OSW Wanair Taxi Aereo Ltda. Belo Horizonte.
8186	1990. G-5-683 BAe PLC /90, G-BSUL 9/90, G-BSUL British Aerospace PLC. Hatfield.
8190	1990. G-5-684 /91, G-BTAE BAe PLC 12/90, PT-... Mesbla
8192	1990. G-5-6.. /90, TR-LDB Ste Crossair/Air Affaires 12/90, TR-LDB Ste. Crossair, Zurich/Air Affaires, Libreville.
8194	1990. /91, PT-...
8198	1990. /91, PT-...
9003	1990. G-ELRA British Aerospace PLC. Hatfield.
NA0401	1987. G-5-566 S/n 8100. N538BA BAe Inc 9/87, NBD Transportation Co 10/87, N108CF 1/88, N815CC 12/88, N815CC Chrysler Corp/NBD Transportation Co. Detroit, Mi.
NA0402	1987. G-5-572 S/n 8101. N539BA BAe Inc 9/87, National Intergroup Inc 12/87, N1125 5/88, N1125 National Intergroup Inc. Pittsburgh, Pa.

NA0403	1987.	G-5-573 S/n 8102. N540BA BAe Inc 9/87, Crawford Fitting Co 12/87, N89K 5/88, N89K Crawford Fitting Co. Cleveland, Oh.
NA0404	1987.	G-5-574 S/n 8103. N541BA BAe Inc 9/87, Pacific Telesis Group 4/88, N916PT 3/89, N916PT Pacific Telesis Group. Oakland, Ca.
NA0405	1987.	G-5-575 S/n 8104. N542BA BAe Inc 9/87, Amway Corp 3/88, N527AC 9/88, N527AC Amway Corp. Ada, Mi.
NA0406	1987.	G-5-577 S/n 8105. G-BNZW BAe PLC 11/87, C-GKLB Nova, an Alberta Corp 12 Apr 88, Nova Corp of Alberta 20 Jun 88, C-GKLB Nova Corp of Alberta, Calgary.
NA0407	1987.	G-5-578 S/n 8107. N552BA BAe Inc 11/87, Banc One Corp 12/87, N7ONE 6/88, N7ONE Banc One Corp. Columbus, Oh.
NA0408	1987.	G-5-579 S/n 8108. N553BA BAe Inc 11/87, Contel Credit Corp 12/87, N61CT 6/88, Contel Management Co 9/89, N61CT Contel Management Co. Atlanta, Ga.
NA0409	1987.	G-5-582 S/n 8111. N554BA BAe Inc del USA 23 Mar 88, N800TR /88, N375SC Steelcase Inc 10/88, N375SC Steelcase Inc. Grand Rapids, Mi.
NA0410	1987.	G-5-587 S/n 8113. N555BA BAe Inc 3/88, CONOCO Inc 3/88, N683E 7/88, E I Dupont de Nemours & Co 11/88, N683E E I Dupont de Nemours & Co. New Castle, De.
NA0411	1987.	G-5-586 S/n 8114. N556BA BAe Inc 11/87, Eastern Holding Corp 4/88, N600LS 11/88, N600LS Limited Stores/Eastern Holding Corp. Wilmington, De.
NA0412	1988.	G-5-589 S/n 8117. N557BA BAe Inc 3/88, Union Pacific Corp 4/88,N825PS Pluess-Stauffer/Omy Aviation Inc 8/88, Cobblestone Corp 9/88, First Fidelity Bank-Newark 9/88, N825PS Pleuss-Stauffer/Omy Avn Inc/Cobblestone Corp. Boston, Ma.
NA0413	1988.	G-5-591 S/n 8119. N558BA BAe Inc regd 3/88, Raytheon Corp 6/88, N203R 11/88, N203R Raytheon Corp. Lexington, Ma.
NA0414	1988.	G-5-593 S/n 8121. N559BA BAe Inc 3/88, G-BOTX BAe PLC 17 Jun-30 Jun 88, C-FRPP Execaire/Repap Enterprises Corp 23 Jan 89, C-FRPP Execaire/Repap Enterprises Corp. Montreal.
NA0415	1988.	G-5-594 S/n 8122. N560BA Crescent Investment Co 7 Jul 88, N800VC 1/89, Matthew H Day Trustee 2/89, N800VC Oakmont/Crescent Investment Co. Bend, Or.
NA0416	1988.	G-5-600 S/n 8123. N561BA BAe Inc del 5 Jul 88, Williams Companies Inc 17 Aug 88, N353WC 12/88, N353WC Williams Companies Inc. Tulsa, Ok.
NA0417	1988.	G-5-596 S/n 8124. N562BA BAe Inc 7/88, N800BA 10/88, N376SC Steelcase Inc 1/89, N376SC Steelcase Inc. Grand Rapids, Mi.
NA0418	1988.	G-5-601 S/n 8125. N563BA BAe Inc del 23 Aug 88, Exxon Corp 24 Aug 88, N802X 12/88, N802X Exxon Corp. Houston, Tx.
NA0419	1988.	G-5-597 S/n 8126. N564BA Sheikh bin Laden 28 Jul 88, HZ-BL2 Bin Laden Organization 5/89,HZ-BL2 Bin Laden Organization.
NA0420	1988.	G-5-602 S/n 8127. N565BA BAe Inc regd 7/88, Exxon Corp 19 Sep 88, N803X 1/89, N803X Exxon Corp. Hangar 12, Newark, NJ.
NA0421	1988.	G-5-603 S/n 8128. N566BA BAe Inc del 27 Sep 88, Exxon Corp 28 Sep 88, N804X 1/89,N804X Exxon Corp. Hangar 12, Newark, NJ.
NA0422	1988.	G-5-607 S/n 8132. N567BA BAe Inc regd 7/88, N125TR 2/89, N222MS Stavola Aviation Inc 9/89, N222MS Stavola Aviation Inc. Anthony, Fl.
NA0423	1988.	G-5-608 S/n 8135. N568BA BAe Inc del 20 Oct 88, Alexander & Baldwin 24 Oct 88, N801AB 4/89, N801AB Alexander&Baldwin, Concord, Ca. 'Manukapu' (Treasured Bird).
NA0424	1988.	G-5-609 S/n 8136. N569BA BAe Inc del USA 31 Oct 88, Service Merchandise 28 Feb 89, N452SM 6/89, N452SM Service Merchandise/SMC Aviation Inc. Salem, NH.
NA0425	1988.	G-5-610 S/n 8137. N570BA BAe Inc 9/88, HAC Inc 21 Dec 88, N733K 7/89, N733K HAC Inc. Louisville
NA0426	1988.	G-5-612 S/n 8139. N580BA BAe Inc /88, N125BA 4/89, (VR-BPA) 12/89, VR-BLP BP International Inc 3/90, VR-BLP BP International Inc. Farnborough-UK.
NA0427	1988.	G-5-613 S/n 8140. N581BA BAe Inc del 6 Dec 88, Manville Sales Corp 7 Dec 88, N45Y 6/89, N45Y Manville Sales Corp. Denver, Co.
NA0428	1988.	G-5-614 S/n 8138. N582BA BAe Inc 10/88, Worthington Inds/JMAC Inc 14 Dec 88, N244JM 1/89, N244JM Worthington Industries/JMAC Inc. Worthington, Oh.
NA0429	1988.	G-5-615 S/n 8141. N583BA BAe Inc 10/88, Key Bank NA 13 Dec 88, Key Corp 3/89, N72K 3/90, N72K Key Bank NA/Key Corp. Scotia, NY.
NA0430	1988.	G-5-617 S/n 8142. N584BA BAe Inc 10/88, J C Penney Co Inc 23 Dec 88, N1903P 3/90,N1903P J C Penney Co Inc. Dallas, Tx.
NA0431	1989.	G-5-618 S/n 8144. N585BA BAe Inc 1/89, N682B E I Dupont de Nemours & Co 5/89, N682B E I Dupont de Nemours & Co. New Castle, De.
NA0432	1989.	G-5-619 S/n 8145. N586BA BAe Inc del 8 Feb 89, CONOCO Inc 2/89, N540M 5/89,E I DuPont de Nemours & Co 3/90, N540M E I DuPont de Nemours & Co. Houston, Tx.
NA0433	1989.	G-5-621 S/n 8147. N587BA BAe Inc 1/89, CONOCO Inc 5/89, N919P 6/89, E I DuPont de Nemours & Co 3/90, N919P E I DuPont de Nemours & Co. Houston, Tx.
NA0434	1989.	G-5-625 S/n 8150. N588BA BAe Inc 4/89, AMP Inc 5/89, N77W 7/89, N77W AMP Inc. Harrisburg, Pa.
NA0435	1989.	G-5-632 S/n 8157. N589BA BAe Inc 1/89, N800BA 12/89, C-GMTR Alberta Energy Co Ltd 19 Oct 90,C-GMTR Alberta Energy Co Ltd.

c/n	
NA0436	1989. G-5-633 S/n 8160. N590BA BAe Inc del 6 Jul 89, Williams Companies Inc 7/89, N354WC 12/89, N354WC Williams Companies Inc. Tulsa, Ok.
NA0437	1989. G-5-636 S/n 8161. G-BPXW Bae PLC 17 May 89, del USA 14 Jul 89, C-FFTM Execaire/Canadian Pacific Forest Products 1 Dec 89, C-FFTM Execaire/Canadian Pacific Forest Products, Montreal.
NA0438	1989. G-5-638 S/n 8162. N591BA BAe Inc del 21 Jul 89, Grumman Corp/First NH Resources 7/89, N753G 10/89, SecPac Leasing 1/90, N753G Grumman Corp. Bethpage, NY.
NA0439	1989. G-5-641 S/n 8166. N592BA BAe Inc del 26 Sep 89, PNC Financial Corp 9/89, N74PC 4/90, N74PC PNC Financial Corp. Pittsburgh, Pa.
NA0440	1989. G-5-643 S/n 8168. N593BA BAe Inc del 9 Oct 89, Nationwide Mutual Insurance Co 10/89, N74NP 2/90, N74NP Nationwide Mutual Insurance Co. Columbus, Oh.
NA0441	1989. G-5-645 S/n 8170. N594BA BAe Inc del 27 Oct 89, Nationwide Mutual Insurance Co 10/89, N75NP 3/90, N75NP Nationwide Mutual Insurance Co. Columbus, Oh.
NA0442	1989. G-5-646 S/n 8171. N595BA BAe Inc del 21 Nov 89, Grumman/First NH Resources 12/89, N754G Bancireland/First Financial I2/90,SecPac Leasing 5/90, N754G Grumman Corp. Bethpage, NY.
NA0443	1989. G-5-639 S/n 8163. G-BRCZ British Aerospace (CA) Ltd del 29 Aug 89, C-GMOL 169084 Canada Ltd/Molson Companies 9/89, C-GMOL Molson Companies Ltd. Toronto.
NA0444	1989. G-5-647 S/n 8172. N596BA BAe Inc /89, Ethyl Corp 12/89, N290EC 4/90, N290EC Ethyl Corp. Richmond
NA0445	1989. G-5-649 S/n 8174. N597BA BAe Inc del 19 Dec 89, Bank of America 1/90, N174A 5/90, N174A Bank of America NT&SA. San Francisco, Ca.
NA0446	1989. G-5-650 S/n 8175. N598BA BAe Inc regd 9/89, (VR-BPB) 12/89, VR-BLQ BP International Inc 7/90, VR-BLQ BP International Inc. Farnborough-UK.
NA0447	1989. G-5-648 S/n 8173. N599BA BAe Inc del 15 Dec 89,Shearson Lehman Hutton Holdings 12/89, N95AE IDS Aircraft Services Corp 9/90, N95AE IDS Aircraft Services Corp. Minneapolis, Mn.
NA0448	1989. G-5-660 S/n 8179. N610BA BAe Inc del 16 May 90, N125BA 8/90, N125BA British Aerospace Inc. Washington, DC.
NA0449	1990. G-5-658 S/n 8178. N611BA BAe Inc 4/90,JF Aircraft Corp 5/90,N611BA JF Aircraft Corp. Dearborn, Mi.
NA0450	1990. G-5-663 S/n 8181. N612BA BAe Inc del 30 May 90, N355WC Northwest Pipeline Corp 8/90, N355WC Northwest Pipeline Corp. Salt Lake City, Ut.
NA0451	1990. G-5-666 S/n 8183. N613BA BAe Inc del 23 Jun 90, Philip Morris Inc /90, N50PM /91, N50PM Philip Morris Inc. Richmond, Va.
NA0452	1990. G-5-669 S/n 8185. N614BA BAe Inc del 17 Jul 90, PacifiCorp Trans Inc 7/90, N614BA PacifiCorp Trans Inc. Portland, Or.
NA0453	1990. G-5-670 S/n 8187. N615BA BAe Inc del 8 Aug 90, Philip Morris Inc /90, N60PM /91, N60PM Philip Morris Inc. Richmond, Va.
NA0454	1990. G-5-671 S/n 8188. N616BA BAe Inc del 29 Aug 90, Hallmark Cards Inc 9/90, N1910A rsvd 6 Sep 90, N1910A Hallmark Cards Inc. Kansas City, Mo.
NA0455	1990. G-5-673 S/n 8189. N617BA Bae Inc del 12 Sep 90, Fuqua National Corp 9/90, N617BA Fuqua National Corp. Atlanta, Ga.
NA0456	1990. G-5-674 S/n 8191. N618BA BAe Inc del 27 Sep 90, NW Equipment Corp 10/90, N618BA Norfolk Southern Corp. Norfolk, Va.
NA0457	1990. G-5-675 S/n 8193. N619BA BAe Inc 6/90, Philip Morris Management Corp 10/90, N619BA Philip Morris Inc. Teterboro, NJ. (prob N300PM).
NA0458	1990. G-5-679 S/n 8195. N630BA BAe Inc del 18 Oct 90, N800BA rsvd 14 Nov 90, N800BA British Aerospace Inc. Washington, DC.
NA0459	1990. G-5-680 S/n 8196. N631BA BAe Inc del 31 Oct 90, N631BA
NA0460	1990. G-5-681 S/n 8199. N632BA BAe Inc 9/90, General Mills Restaurants Inc /90, N632BA General Mills Restaurants Inc. Orlando, Fl.
NA0461	1990. G-5-682 S/n 8200. N633BA BAe Inc del 7 Dec 90, N633BA
NA0462	1990. G-5-685 S/n 8202. N634BA BAe Inc /90, N634BA
NA0463	1990. G-5-686 S/n 8203. N635BA BAe Inc del 21 Dec 90, N635BA
NA0464	1990. G-5-687 S/n 8204. N636BA

Learjet 35/35A

c/n	
35-001	1973. N731GA GLC/Garrett Corp ff 22 Aug 73, winglets 4/87, modified to Model 31 /87, Learjet Corp 4/88, N351GL 1/89, Learjet Inc 9/90, N351GL Learjet Inc. Wichita, Ks. (experimental).
35-002	1974. N352GL GLC /74, N35SC Superior Continental Corp /75, C-GVVA Von Van Aviation 3/76,Sulaero Ltd /79, Echo Bay Mines Ltd 3 Sep 86, C-GVVA Echo Bay Mines Ltd. Edmonton.
35-003	1974. N731GA GLC/Garrett Corp /74, N931BA GLC 5/77, N263GL 5/79, N370EC AMI Corp 9/80, R T Thompson-NC 9/81, N4RT 12/82, AMR Combs Florida Inc 4/90,N960AA 5/90,Kebra Co 8/90,N960AA Kebra Co Inc. Westwood, NJ
35-004	1974. N74MP Mesa Petroleum Co 11/74, N74MB 10/78, N74MJ MJI 11/78,C-GIRE Northgate Exploration Ltd 3/79, Central Trust Co 11/81, Air Niagara Express 1/88, Somerset Aero Corp 8/88, 536031 Ontario Ltd (Air One) 9/88, C-GIRE 536031 Ontario Ltd (Air One), Toronto.
35-005	1974. EC-CLS Activades Aereas Aragonesas S.A. /74, TR-LXP Air Affaires-Gabon 4/77, EC-CLS Activades Aereas Aragonesas S.A. 8/77, N175J Combs-Gates Denver 7/78, N178CP Coral Petroleum Inc 11/78, Chase Manhattan Svc Corp 10/83, Epps Air Service Inc 10/83, N178CP Epps Air Service Inc. Atlanta, Ga.
35-006	1974. N356P Potlatch Corp 12/74, N39DM Flight International Inc 4/87, N39FN rsvd 17 Aug 90, N39FN Flight International Inc. Newport News, Va.
35-007	1975. D-CONI Contact Air/G Eheim 3/75, N75DH Dee Howard Aircraft Sales 3/81, John Roberts Jr-Tx 8/82, N47JR 10/82, Mercury Properties Corp 9/83, J R Aircraft-HOU 12/83, Flight International Inc 3/88,(N65FN) rsvd 14 Jun 88, N47JR Flight International Inc. Jacksonville, Fl.
35-008	1975. N673M Omaha Indemnity Co 2/75,GLC 4/84, Airsupport Svcs Corp 7/84, PT-LFS Lider Taxi Aereo SA 21 Nov 84, PT-LFS Lider Taxi Aereo S.A. Belo Horizonte.
35-009	1974. N44EL Management Services Inc 12/74, N14EL U.S. Epperson Underwriting Co 9/78, N275J Combs Gates Denver Inc 1/80, N263GL GLC 10/80, Airsupport Services Corp 2/85, PT-LGR Lider Taxi Aereo SA 4/85,PT-LGR Lider/Industrias Reunidas Sao Jorge S.A. Sao Paulo.
35-010	1975. N888DH R D Hubbard/Alpha Investments 3/75, AFG Industries/UNO Investment Partnership 1/87, N888DH AFG Industries Inc. Fort Worth, Tx.
35-011	1975. N3816G GLC /75, N400RB Rogers Badgett Mine Stripping Corp 8/75, N400RB Badgett Rogers Sr. Madisonville, Ky.
35-012	1975. N711 W K Carpenter 4/75, N71LA Combs Gates Denver Inc 12/78, C-GVCB Business Flights Ltd 3/79, N2242P Sunaire/88TC Inc 1/83, N95SC 7/83, Alpha Aviation Inc 11/88, N975AA 12/88, Duncan-Ne 4/89, N975AD 5/89, N975AD Duncan Aviation Inc. Lincoln, Ne.
35-013	1975. N1DA Donald Anderson-NM 4/75, Tyler Jet Aircraft Sales Inc 4/88, N7TJ 5/88, Ltd Ents Inc 8/88, N304AF Reagan Charter Inc 12/88, Duncan-Ne 4/89, Apache Corp 6/89, N304AF Apache Corp. Denver, Co.
35-014	1975. N71TP Tesoro Petroleum Corp 4/75, N73TP 4/77, (N72TB) 2/82, George Ablah/Ryan Aviation 3/83, N98VA 4/83, Martin Aviation Inc 6/85, Hannes Tulving Jr-Ca 12/85, Powerplant Specialists Inc 3/90, N69PS 5/90, N69PS Powerplant Specialists Inc. Costa Mesa, Ca.
35-015	1975. N291BC Boise Cascade Corp 5/75, Ore Ida Foods Inc 4/82, N57FF 7/82, N57FF to 35A-157, N58FF GLC 3/85, Martin Avn Inc 7/85, Consolidated Allied Cos 2/86, Worthington Ford Inc 4/87, N58CW 12/87, N58CW Worthington Ford Inc. Anchorage, Ak.
35-016	1975. N136GL GLC /75, N5867 Bendix Corp 5/75, N9CN S Carolina State Dvlpment Board 2/80, N9CN State Development Board, Columbia, SC.
35-017	1975. N119GS Slab Fork Coal Co 5/75, Ramada Inns 5/79, N551CC Combs-Gates 5/80, Intercontinental Consolidated Corp 7/80, Milam Properties Inc 8/83, L J Aircraft Corp 12/83, N456MS 6/84, TIPS Aerospace Inc 8/88, N600DT 10/88, BAC Inc 11/89, N600DT B.A.C. Inc. Ketchum, Id.
35-018	1975. D-CORA Holstenflug GmbH 5/75, F-GBMB Uni Air 11 Dec 78, F-GBMB P Fabre/Cie Interagra/Uni-Air, Toulouse-Blagnac.
35-019	1975. N959AT Peoples NB-Seattle 5/75, Barron Thomas Aviation Inc 5/84, Airsupport Services Corp 10/84, PT-LGF Lider Taxi 17 Jun 85, PT-LGF Lider Taxi Aereo S.A. Sao Paulo.
35-020	1975. XA-BUK Assessoria Empresas/Aerotaxis de Mexico /75, N95TC Aircraft Trading Center Inc 4/84, Jet East Inc 7/84, Cx USA 10/88, N95TC W/O W/o 20 Dec 84. 20/DEC/84
35-022	1975. OY-BLG Grundfos A/S 6/75, Alkair Flight Operations 1/90, OY-BLG Alkair Flight Operations, Naerum.
35-023	1975. N986WC Western Conference of Teamsters 8/75, N886WC 3/82, Comm Scope Co 6/83, N886CS 8/89, N886CS Comm Scope Co. Catawba, NC.
35-024	1975. N316 Oman Construction Inc 7/75, Aircorp Inc 1/84, Gantt Aviation Inc 8/88, N24GA 10/88,McCall Air Inc 11/88, Gantt Aviation Inc 3/90, Wolf Financial Group Inc 6/90, N582JD 7/90, N582JD Tap Marina Inc/Wolf Financial Group Inc. NYC.
35-025	1975. 9K-ACT Alghanim & Sons 7/75, Muburak Hassawi 4/76, Sid Nasser 7/76, N40TF Omni 12/76, N135TX Texas International Co 7/77, N510LJ 8/82, SBA Corp 8/83, N185BA 11/83, Air Ambulance Assoc 1/90, Intl Jet Marketing Inc 4/90, James Markel & Assocs 6/90, N185BA James Markel & Assocs Inc. San Rafael, Ca.
35-026	1975. D-CDHS Bomin & Bochumer Mineraloges mbH 8/75, D-CBRK German Red Cross 8/77, N54754 Dodson Aviation Inc 9/84, ATC Inc 10/84, N89TC 12/84, N A Degerstrom Inc 12/85, N89TC N A Degerstrom Inc. Spokane, Wa.
35-027	1975. N31WS Windstar Co 7/75, Denveraire Inc 1/86, N31WS Denveraire Inc. Weston, Ct.
35-028	1975. N135GL GLC /75, N20BG Bandag Inc /75, TigerAir Inc 7/79, XC-IPP Productores Pesqueros Isla de Cedros 9/81, XC-IPP Productores Pesqueros Isla de Cedros, Ensenada.

c/n	
35-029	1975. Hydroplanes Inc/Transcontinental Log & Export Corp 7/75, Bahri Aviation Inc-Athens 7/77,N711AF W/O W/o 11 Aug 79. 11/AUG/79
35-030	1975. N816M SOHIO-Cleveland 4/78, N16FN Flight International Inc 10/87, N16FN Flight International Inc. Jacksonville, Fl.
35-031	1975. N77FC Omni /75, GLC 9/75, N77U /75, N77TE Temple Industries 4/76,American TV & Communications Co 2/80, N160AT 12/82, GLC 1/85, N233CC CCI Corp 6/85, N233CC CCI Corp. Tulsa, Ok.
35-032	1975. N711CH Carborundum Co 9/75, (N711QH) Kennecott Corp 10/82, Comm Scope Co 3/83, N711MA 4/83, N711MA Comm Scope Co. Catawba, NC.
35-033	1975. N7KA Interedec-Jeddah 10/75, HZ-KA1 Sheikh Kamal Adham 1/76, N2297B SABR Aeronautics 9/78, Combs-Gates Denver Inc 9/79,GLC 1/80, Bowlen Holdings (Oregon) Inc 4/85, Flight Intl Inc 11/87, N31FN 1/89, N31FN Flight International, Jacksonville, Fl.
35-034	1975. LPC Leasing/Thunderbird Airways /75, Norman Johnson 11/80, J&N Assocs 12/81,Keplinger Transportation 9/82,RLO Avn 1/84, N37TA RLO Aviation Inc. Peoria, Il.
35-035	1975. N711R ECEE Inc/Cockrell Corp 10/75, N711R ECEE Inc/Cockrell Corp. Houston, Tx.
35-036	1975. N134GL GLC /75, N76GL Bi-Centennial colour scheme 1976, N76GP Gerber Products Co 4/76, Learjet Inc 11/90, N9OAH AWH Corp 12/90, N9OAH AWH Corp. Winston Salem, NC.
35-037	1975. N1462B GLC /75, N100GL CSE Aviation Ltd-UK 10/75, MJI 4/76, N58M Mutual of Omaha 7/76, GLC 12/83, N58M to 55-077, N35GQ 1/84, John Kettle-NM 2/84, N600WT 3/84, Glen Ivy Financial Group Inc 3/85, Universal Jet Inc 10/86, N600WT Universal Jet Inc. Corona, Ca.
35-038	1975. (VH-UDC) Utah Development Corp /75, VH-ELJ 11/75, C-FBFP Business Flights Ltd 2/82, Westair Resources Ltd /86, Appeal Enterprises Ltd/Canada Jet Charters Ltd 13 Aug 86, C-FBFP Appeal Enterprises/Canada Jet Charters Ltd. Richmond.
35-039	1975. N1HP Helmerich & Payne Inc 11/75, N1HP Helmerich & Payne Inc. Tulsa, Ok.
35-040	1975. C-GGYV Canada Learjet Ltd 12/75, Business Flights Ltd 8/77, N39DM Flight International 2/84,Cx USA 5/86, N39DM W/O W/o 5 Mar 86. 05/MAR/86
35-041	1975. N202BT Big Three Industries Inc 12/75, N202BT to 35A-483, GLC 6/83, N202BD 8/83, Martin Sprocket & Gear Inc 9/83, Combs Gates 6/87, N711BH Hilton Hotels Corp 12/87, Northeast Jet Co 4/90, N41PJ 5/90, N41PJ Northeast Jet Co Inc. Allentown, Pa.
35-042	1975. N221UE United Engineers & Constructors Inc 12/75, N221UE United Engineers & Constructors Inc. Philadelphia, Pa.
35-043	1976. C-GVCA Business Flights Ltd 3/76, Westair Resources Ltd /86, Business Flights/414660 Alberta Ltd 5 Apr 90, C-GVCA 414660 Alberta Ltd/Business Flights, Edmonton.
35-044	1975. N38TA Air Ketchum/Helen Dow Whiting 4/76, N44MW /77, Westwind Partners/Carlton Financial 8/87, (N44VW) rsvd 27 Aug 87, N44MW Westwind Partners/Carlton Financial Inc. Las Vegas, Nv.
35-045	1976. N1461B GLC /76, HB-VEN Transair SA /76, N35HB MJI 2/76, N99786 /76, N999M Capitol Pipe & Steel 4/76, XA-HOS Aerotaxis de Mexico /78, N45MJ MJI 5/81, Charles Hall-Mt 2/82, 117CH Partners 5/82, N117CH 8/82,King Lear 11 Ltd 11/82,F Conner/Seagate Technology 9/83 American Transair/Betaco Inc 6/86, N304TZ 11/86, N304AT 1/89, N304AT American Transair/Betaco Inc. Indianapolis, In.
35-046	1976. VH-SLJ Bib Stillwell 2/76, Wards Express /79, lsd RAAF /82, CSR Ltd 4/84, Pacific Aviation /85, Lloyd Avn/RANAS 7/86, Fleet Support P/L /90, VH-SLJ Fleet Support P/L.
35-048	1976. N233R Dart Industries 5/76, Continental Aviation Svc Inc 10/83, N64MH 1/84, Eagle Aviation Inc 1/88. Alpha Aviation Inc 2/88, General Aviation Services 5/88, F-GHMP Michel Pinseau 7/88, F-GHMP Concorde Equipement/Michel Pinseau, Paris-Le Bourget.
35-049	1976. JY-AEV Arab Wings-Amman 5/76, N3759C GLC 3/80, C-GBWL Brooker-Wheaton Avn 5/80,Soundair Corp /86, Brooker Wheaton Aviation Ltd 5 Sep 89, C-GBWL Brooker Wheaton Aviation Ltd. Edmonton.
35-050	1976. CC-ECO Corporacion de Fomento /76, 351 Chilean Air Force /83, 351 Fuerza Aerea de Chile,
35-051	1976. SE-DEA Allamanna Svenska Electriska AB 3/76, Basair AB 9/80, SE-DEA Svensk Flygtjanst AB/Basair, Vasteras.
35-052	1976. JY-AEW Arab Wings-Amman 5/76, JY-AEW W/O W/o 28 Apr 77. 28/APR/77
35-053	1976. N1976L Coad Inc 3/76, Lowell Anderson-Ut 8/83, Flight International Inc 5/88, N53FN 7/88, N53FN Flight International Inc. Jacksonville, Fl.
35-054	1976. VR-BFX Olympic Maritime/Somers Navigation-Athens 4/76, N53650 Great Planes Sales Inc 6/84, N54PR 8/84, Guaranty Service Corp 10/84, Smith's Management Corp 12/88, N109MC 12/88,N109MC Smith's Management Corp. Salt Lake City, Ut.
35-055	1976. D-CONO Contact Air/G Eheim 8/76,N70WW Jack Prewitt-Tx 3/84,Arizona Jet 7/84,John Stiteler-Az 7/85, Eagle Aviation Inc 8/88, EBM Group-NYC 10/88, I-NIKJ Soc Desio & Brianza Leasing/EBM Group 23 Feb 89, I-NIKJ EBM Group, Roma-Urbe.
35-056	1976. (JY-AEX) Arab Wings-Amman /76,N106GL GLC 5/76, N645G Gates Rubber Co 6/76, Gates Corp 10/82, N645G Gates Corp. Denver, Co.
35-057	1976. N551MD Mike Davis Oil /76, N57GL Combs-Gates 8/77, Hobaugh Aviation Inc 11/77, C-GHOO Home Oil Co Ltd 12/83, C-GHOO to 650-0014, N57GL Cirrus Marketing Inc 3/84, Maralo Inc 7/84, N35MR 8/84, sale-Fl 11/87, Eagle Aviation Inc 2/88, Erie Airways 3/88, N35MR Erie Airways Inc. Erie, Pa.
35-058	1976. C-GPUN Canada Learjet Ltd 4/76, Worldways Airlines /? Canada Jet Charters Ltd 9 Aug 85, C-GPUN Canada Jet Charters Ltd. Vancouver.

35-059   1976. N221Z Zurn Industries Inc 4/76, AeroSmith/Penny Inc 4/84, Stan Collins-Ut 8/84, Flight Intl Inc 5/88, N51FN 4/89, N51FN Flight International Inc. Jacksonville, Fl. (status ?).
35-060   1976. N64MP Mesa Petroleum Co 4/76, N64MR 9/82, Brunswick Hospital Center 1/85, N47BA 3/85, Breed Equipment Corp 1/90, N47BA Breed Equipment Corp. Wilmington, De.
35-061   1976. N424DN Dana Corp 4/76, N4246N 7/76, Eagle Aviation Inc 3/88, Robinson Conner Inc 5/88, N238RC 10/88, Eagle Aviation Inc 10/89, N238RC Eagle Aviation Inc. W Columbia, SC.
35-062   1976. N217CS Charles Suhr-RSA /76, U S Aircraft Sales /78, ZS-LII Egineering Design & Construction Co 4/78, TL-ABD registration for use outside S Afruica 1978-81, N701US U S Aircraft Sales Inc 4/81,Somerset Distributors Inc 5/81, N310BA 11/81, Consolidated Airways 3/86, IDP Inc 4/86, N31DP 6/86, N31DP Innovation Data Processing Inc. Little Falls, NJ.
35-063   1976. N828M Ken Davis Industries Intl 5/76, Amason Holding Inc 10/83, Continental Avn Co 5/84, N663CA 10/84, Continental Air Transport Co 3/85, Air Transport International 8/88, Continental Air Transport Co 10/88, N663CA Continental Air Transport Co. Tulsa, Ok.
35-064   1976. N290BC Boise Cascade Corp 5/76, N290BC to 35A-380, N291BC 4/83, O Gara Aviation Co 12/84, Geo J Priester Avn 1/85,N100GP 2/85, Pal Waukee Aviation Inc 6/88,N100GP Pal Waukee Aviation Inc. Wheeling, IL
35-065   1976. N425DN Dana Corp 5/76, N4358N 7/76, New Creations Inc 1/87, N4358N New Creations Inc. Pontiac, Mi.
35-066   1976. CC-ECP Corporacion de Fomento /76, 352 Chilean Air Force /83, 352 Fuerza Aerea de Chile,

35A-021 1975. N101GP Interedec/Oceanic Air Inc 8/75, MJI 5/77, cvtd 35A 9/77, N91CH ICH Corp 9/78, American Consolidated 6/83, ICH Corp 9/84, N33TS Aircraft Operations/NTS Developemnt 4/85,Thornton Oil 3/89, N442JT 9/89, N442JT Thornton Oil Corp. Louisville, Ky.
35A-047 1976. XA-ALE Mexican customer not delivered /76, N13MJ MJI /76, N701AS AID Corp 8/76, New Creations Inc 10/86, N701AS New Creations Inc. Pontiac, Mi.
35A-067 1976. N118K Ford Motor Credit Co 9/76, Kaiser Steel Corp 1/82, Delta Jet Inc 9/84, Flight International Inc 2/88, N888DJ Flight International Inc 2/88, (N66FN) rsvd 24 Apr 89, N32FN 8/89, Air Stewart Inc 10/90, N32FN Air Stewart Inc. Sarasota, Fl.
35A-068 1976. HB-VEM Swiss Air Ambulance 'Albert Schweitzer' /76, Swiss Air Force 5/88, HB-VEM Swiss Air Force, Dubendorf.
35A-069 1976. N103GL GLC /76, N591D Dixico 10/76, Walston Airbusiness 5/81, Sky Flite Inc 8/81, Coin Acceptors Inc 10/83, N1CA 10/84, N10AQ C A Leasing 3/90, Jet East Inc 5/90, HPH Aviation Inc 8/90, N10AQ HPH Aviation Inc. Englewood, Co.
35A-070 1976. D-CITA Holstenflug GmbH 7/76, ACV GmbH 6/78, Phoenix/EAV AG 9/82, N3GL Cartair Inc 1/85, N503RP 9/87, Flight International Inc 3/88, N50FN 4/88, N50FN Flight International Inc. Jacksonville, Fl.
35A-071 1976. JY-AFD Arab Wings-Amman 7/76, F-WDCP /80, F-GDCP Uni-Air 28 Aug 80, Ste Sporto 12/87, Uni Air International 24 Aug 90, F-GDCP BNP Bail/Uni Air International, Toulouse.
35A-072 1976. N2015M Monsanto Co 8/76, N2015M to NA0337, N4415M JBC Avn Inc 9/83, N4415M JBC Aviation Inc. Wichita, Ks.
35A-073 1976. N108GL GLC /76, N163A AMF Inc 12/76,Lasma Air Inc 1/83,Superior Savings Assoc 4/85 Alpha Aviation Management Svc 6/88, (N64FN) rsvd for Flight International Inc 13 Oct 88,N163A Flight International Inc. Jacksonville, Fl.
35A-074 1976. N5000B Ashland Oil Co 12/76, N530J Omni/Combs-Gates 8/80, N666JR Mercury Oil Co 10/80,Flying X Inc 8/86, N Central Avn 11/87, Tyler Corp 2/88, N100T 3/88, TCC Inc 6/88, N100T TCC Inc. Dallas, Tx.
35A-075 1976. N3503F GLC /76, HB-VEV Transair SA /76, JY-AFE EJA/Arab Wings-Amman 12/76, N3503F Duncan Aviation Inc-Ne 1/87, (N117DA) rsvd 28 Jan 87, N48RW Consul Inc 7/87, Flight International Inc 11/87, N30FN 1/88, SE-DHP Nyge Aero AB 11 Dec 89, SE-DHP Nyge Aero AB. Nykoping.
35A-076 1976. N959SA Omni/Intl Teamsters /76, Omni 9/82-1/83, FRCC 1/88, James Wickert & Assoc 2/88, Martin Avn 4/88, Eagle Avn 6/88, N959SA Eagle Aviation Inc. West Columbia, SC.
35A-077 1976. N814M Standard Oil Co 9/76, Jet East Inc 4/90, N819JE 7/90, N819JE Jet East Inc. Dallas, Tx.
35A-078 1976. N95BA Burlington Industries /76, N95BH Omni 3/77, N711SW Golden Nugget Inc 5/77, N711SD 9/78, N440JB Blocker Energy Corp 2/79, N121EL GECC/Standard Brands 1/80, ATC Inc 6/88, A M Transport Inc 9/88, N45AW 5/89, N45AW A/M Transport Inc. Cincinnati, Oh.
35A-079 1976. N6000J Ashland Oil Co 12/76, N660CJ Omni 6/81, WTCR Associates-DC 9/81, N560KC Kenneth Copeland Ministries 2/87, Maxfly Aviation-Fl 3/88, N7777B Bergstrom Pioneer Auto & Truck Leasing 7/88, N7777B Bergstrom Pioneer Auto & Truck Leasing, Neenah, Wi.
35A-080 1976. N109GL GLC /76, N23HB Hamilton Brothers Petroleum /76, N10AZ Anschutz Corp 4/79, N10AZ Anschutz Corp. Denver, Co.
35A-081 1976. N3523F GLC /76, JY-AFF EJA/Arab Wings-Amman 12/76, N3523F Duncan-Ne 1/87, N118DA 4/87, New Creations Inc 5/87, N118DA New Creations Inc. Pontiac, Mi.
35A-082 1976. N235HR Hoffmann LaRoche Inc 11/76, N235HR to 55-094, N285HR 11/83, GLC 2/84, Boca Investors & Realty Inc 6/84, N700GB 6/85,SJA Corp 1/87,N700SJ 3/87, Palumbo Aircraft Sales 6/90, N700SJ Palumbo Aircraft Sales Inc. Uniontown, Oh.

c/n	
35A-083	1976. (N600CC) Luqa Inc/Charter Oil /76, N400CC /76, (N400MJ) MJI /79,(N45SL) Sutherland Lumber Co 9/79, N500CD Lear Leasing 4/80, HDR Inc 10/80, Clay Lacy Avn Inc 12/85, N121CL 10/86, YV-100CP Contivato CA 10/88, YV-100CP Contivato C.A.
35A-084	1976. N111GL Gulf Life Insurance Co 11/76, Million Air 9/84, Quorum Sales 6/85, Kay Mary Ash 12/85, GECC-Brea-Ca 4/89, N111GL Kay Mary Ash, Dallas, Tx.
35A-085	1976. N15WH F&D Enterprises Inc 1/77, U S Aircraft Sales Inc 2/88, N Central Aviation 4/88, Jet East Inc 10/88, Consignment Aircraft Sales HQ 8/89, River City Invs 4/90, N15WH River City Investments Inc. San Antonio, Tx.
35A-086	1976. N435M Motorola Inc 12/76, Owners Jet Services 1/85, Duncan-Fl 1/85 N26DA 5/85, WNC Corp 2/88, Mike Donahoe Aviation Co 6/88, N98MD Valkyrie Helicopter Corp 10/88,N98MD Valkyrie Helicopter Corp. Bellevue, Wa.
35A-087	1976. N720GL GLC /76, Presidential Airways 4/77, Combs-Gates 2/79,N835GA Parker Drilling Co 9/79, N835GA Parker Drilling Co. Tulsa, Ok.
35A-088	1977. N3545F GLC /77, HB-VEW Jet Air Services AG 1/77, N35GE GLC 10/83, OE-GBR Jet Air/Fa Durst 3/84, Airtaxi mbH 8/90, OE-GBR Airtaxi Bedarfsluftverkehrsges mbH. Vienna.
35A-089	1976. N3547F GLC /76, D-CCHB Bauhaus GmbH 12/76, D-CCHB Bauhaus GmbH. Mannheim.
35A-090	1976. HB-VEY Ste de Leasing Aerea SA/Sub Alpina-Milan 3/77, I-FIMI Soc Air Fimi 4/77, Soc Air Nardi /87, Soc Recordati Industria Chimica e Farmacia 1/88,I-FIMI Soc Recordati Industria Chimica e Farmacia, Milan
35A-091	1976. VH-TLJ Bib Stillwell 3/77, Cold Storage Transport Co 9/77, C-GBLF Mannix Construction/Loram Intl 1/80, Innotech Avn Ltd /86, N8GA Gantt Aviation Inc 9/88, D-CIRS MTM Aviation GmbH 28 Dec 88, D-CIRS Aviation Leasing KG/MTM Aviation GmbH. Munich.
35A-092	1977. N722GL Jet Sales & Management Corp /77, N424JR Randall Invs 10/77, MJ1 10/77, Glovers Mills Co 11/77, C-GPFC Pocklington Financial Corp 7/81, N46931 IJA Inc 2/84, N92NE 3/84,Northeast Jet 7/87,Lehigh Valley Lear Inc 6/88, Duncan-Ne 10/88, Martin Aviation Inc 2/89,N92NE Martin Aviation Inc. Santa Ana, CA
35A-093	1977. N804CC Chrysler Corp 6/78, (700th Learjet), C-GFRK Execaire Aviation Ltd 6/81, Innotech Aviation Ltd /83, N5474G Omni 10/84, Templair Corp 10/84, N44PT 1/85, Duncan-Ne 8/87, Global Airways Inc 11/87, PT-LOT Transamerica Taxi Aereo SA 3/88, PT-LOT Transamerica Taxi Aereo SA. Sao Paulo.
35A-094	1977. N506C Celanese Corp 5/77, 35 Management Corp 6/85, N935BD Brown Distributing Co 8/85,35 Management Corp /90, Aircraft Management Service Corp 11/90, N935BD Aircraft Management Service Corp. Roper, NC.
35A-095	1977. N971H Harris Corp 4/77, N971H Harris Corp. Melbourne, Fl.
35A-096	1977. N214LS Dynamic Development Corp /77, Hart & Associates 2/79, Universal Health Care Inc 8/80, MJI 4/81, (N11JV) 10/81, Asplundh Tree Expert Co 2/82, N87AT 1/83, Midlantic Aircraft Sales 7/89, FSB-Ut 11/89, N87AT Midlantic Aircraft Sales, King of Prussia, Pa.
35A-097	1977. N135J Dana Corp 3/77, Swanton Air Two Inc /90, N135J Dana Corp. Toledo, Oh.
35A-098	1977. N20CR NCR Corp 5/77, Cirrus Marketing Inc 10/84, N21GL 12/84, Universal Equipment Co 8/85, N44UC 12/85, (N998DJ) rsvd for Duncan Aviation Inc-Ne 19 Aug 87, N72DA 11/87, N72DA Duncan Aviation Inc. Lincoln, Nb.
35A-099	1977. N40146 GLC /77, HB-VFC Transair SA 5/77, I-MCSA Maniglia Construzioni 5/77, I-MCSA W/O W/o 22 Feb 78. 22/FEB/78
35A-100	1977. N550E Taft Broadcasting Co 4/77, Consolidated Airways Inc 9/81, N558E 2/82, Keith Wood Agency Inc 11/88, N558E Keith Wood Agency Inc. Fort Worth, Tx.
35A-101	1977. N40149 GLC /77, N109JR Ruan Cab Co 7/77, N109JR Ruan Cab Co. Des Moines, Ia.
35A-102	1977. N1451B GLC /77, N232R Dart Industries 5/77, Premark Financial 2/89, Global Airways Inc 10/90,N232R Global Airways Inc. Maimi, Fl.
35A-103	1977. N96RE Reliance Electric Co 4/77, N50MJ MJI 5/80, Airsupport Services Corp 2/81, PT-LCD Lider Taxi Aereo SA 11/81, PT-LCD Lider Taxi Aereo S.A. Belo Horizonte.
35A-104	1977. N87W El Paso Products Co 5/77, Louisiana Pacific Corp 7/83, N873LP 1/84, N873LP to 35A-220, Cx USA 3/86, N873LP W/O W/o 22 Sep 85. 22/SEP/85 collision with microlight, 2k & 5 injured
35A-105	1977. (N720GH) Allstate Insurance Co 5/77, N102GH 5/77, N102GP 6/82, K Aviation Inc 7/83, N612KC 9/83, ATC Inc 6/87,Flight International Inc 8/87,N18FN 1/88, N18FN Flight International Inc. Jacksonville, Fl.
35A-106	1977. N101BG Barnes Group Inc 6/77, Thomas Pumpelly/NTW Inc 8/82, N15TW 1/83, Corporate Air 3/84, Cx USA 3/86, N15TW W/O W/o 8 Dec 85. 08/DEC/85 missed approach, 3k.
35A-107	1977. N723GL Presidential Jet 9/77, General Telephone SW 7/79, Cx USA 3/89, N723GL W/O W/o 12 Dec 85. 12/DEC/85 on take off, 2k.
35A-108	1977. D-COCO Holstenflug GmbH 7/77, F-GCLE Ste Regourd-Paris 7/79, Cx F- to Combs Gates 3/82, N86PC Pepsi-Cola Bottling Co 3/82, GAC 1/85,S Primack/PC Air 3/85, (N86PQ) rsvd /85, P C Air Charter Inc 7/90, N86PC Samuel Primack/PC Air Charter Inc. Englewood, Co.
35A-109	1977. N506GP Georgia Pacific Co 9/77, AMR Combs-Co 9/90, N506GP AMR Combs, Englewood, Co.
35A-110	1977. (N12EP) GLC /77, N4J Interstate Constructors Inc 6/77, Interstate Couriers Inc 8/87, McCrae Aviation Services 2/89, N4J McCrae Aviation Services Inc. Wilmington, De.
35A-111	1977. N3815G GLC /77, (HB-VFE) Fraissinet /77, (I-SIDU) Siderurgica Duina /77, OE-GMA Alp-Air 8/77, Air Charter-Austria /80, I-LIAD Soc ALI 14 Apr 81, I-LIAD Soc. ALI=Aero Leasing Italiana, Rome.
35A-112	1977. 3810G GLC /77, D-CCAY Gustav Schickendanz/Quelle-Flug GmbH 7/77,D-CCAY Quelle-Flug GmbH. Nuremberg

c/n		
35A-113	1977.	N763GL MJI 9/77, Collier Cobb & Assoc 9/77, T C Services Inc 10/77, N35CL 12/82, N35RN 1/83, Marno Air Inc 6/86, Mathis Bros Furniture Co 12/87, N14M Kelly A McCombs-Ca 1/88, Mike Donahoe Aviation Co 9/88, Anderson Management Corp 3/89, N684LA 2/90, N684LA Anderson Management Corp. New Canaan, Ct.
35A-114	1977.	N3807G GLC /77, D-CONA Contact Air/G Eheim 8/77, N18G Jack Prewitt 3/85, International Lease Finance Corp 9/85, N851L 10/85, Prewitt Leasing Inc 9/89, Flying A Ltd 3/90, D-CATY Aviation Leasing KG 4/90, D-CATY Aviation Leasing KG. Dusseldorf.
35A-115	1977.	T-21 Argentine Air Force 10/77, T-21 Grupo 1 de Aerofotografico, II Brigada Aerea, Parana.
35A-116	1977.	I-MMAE Soc Estramed SpA 8/77, Soc Sicilsud Leasing SpA 4/89, Soc Fortune Aviation SRL /89, I-MMAE Soc. Fortune Aviation SRL. Rome.
35A-117	1977.	N3155B Budd Leasing 8/77, Mitel Inc 5/83, Grain Valley Farms 1/84, N78MC 9/84, Aircraft Services Corp 9/86, Gerard Aircraft Sales & Leasing 10/90, N78MC Gerard Aircraft Sales & Leasing, Wilmington, De.
35A-118	1977.	N39391 GLC /77, HB-VFK Transair SA 10/77, John von Neumann-Geneva /77,Koci SA 8/82, N118MA McMoy & Assocs Inc 12/89,Automotive Management Service 2/90, N5OMT 5/90, N5OMT Automotive Management Service, Daytona Beach, Fl.
35A-119	1977.	HB-VFG Transair SA 8/77, D-CHER Holstenflug GmbH 11/77, N93MJ MJI 3/80, OY-ASO Kali A/S 9/82,N93MJ 12/85, Corporate Air Inc 2/84, Flight International 10/87, N36FN 1/88, (N64DH) rsvd 18 Aug 89, N36FN Flight International Inc. Jacksonville, Fl.
35A-120	1977.	N400JE Public Service Co of NM 8/77, (N400RV) Ronald Roderick-Or 4/83, Robert Woolley-Az 11/84, White Tank Aviation 4/86, Jet Trading Floor Inc 7/89, Gantt Aviation Inc 8/89, Robert F Barber-Tn 10/89, Robert F Barber, Murfreesboro, Tn.
35A-121	1977.	N43EL Universal Underwriters Inc 8/77, (D-CFVG) Aero-Dienst GmbH 1/85, James Haldan-Nv Netair International Corp 2/89, Gantt Aviation Inc 9/89, George Shinn Sports Inc 1/90, George Shinn Sports Inc. Charlotte, NC.
35A-122	1977.	N3810G GLC /77, D-CCHS Bochumer Mineral GmbH 8/77, OE-GMP Air Charter Austria /80, N27TT Thomas Tureen-Me 1/83, N27TT United Executive Jet/Thomas Tureen, Portland, Me.
35A-123	1977.	N3802G GLC /77, N900JE Jack Eckerd Corp 9/77, N900JE Jack Eckerd Corp. Clearwater, Fl.
35A-124	1977.	N1500E Bucyrus-Erie Co 8/77, Western Gear Corp 7/87, N35WG 8/87, Lucas Western Inc 3/89,N8LA 8/89, N8LA Lucas Aerospace, Jamestown, ND.
35A-125	1977.	N3803G GLC /77, N777MC Meredith Corp 9/77, N777MC to 55-081, N777NQ 6/83, Majestic Air/Miller & Zupnik Equipment Corp 9/83, N111MZ 3/84, Gantt Aviation Inc 2/89, N125GA 3/89, U S Bancorp Leasing & Finance 9/89, N351EF 8/90, N351EF Executive Flight Inc. Pangborn Memorial Airport, Wa.
35A-126	1977.	N744GL GLC /77, N15EH Sinclair Marketing Inc 7/78, N15EH Sinclair Marketing Inc. Sinclair, Wy.
35A-127	1977.	N727GL Anheuser-Busch Companiess /77, Gantt Aviation 2/88, Reinholtz Aviation Inc 4/88, N727GL Reinholtz Aviation Inc. Madison, Wi.
35A-128	1977.	N231R Dart Industries Inc 10/77,Premark Financial Corp 1/89,N231R Dart Industries Inc. Orlando, FL
35A-129	1977.	N22BX Bendix Corp 10/77, N229X 9/78, XA-ZAP Aerotaxis de Mexico 3/79,Aerolineas Ejecutivas SA /83, AVEMEX SA /84, XA-ZAP AVEMEX SA. Mexico City.
35A-130	1977.	N230R Dart Industries Inc 1/78, Premark Financial Corp 1/89, N230R Dart Industries Inc. West Bend, Wi.
35A-131	1977.	N3812G GLC /77, N26GB HIBOS Co 10/77,Fayez Sarofin & Co 3/89,N26GB Fayez Sarofin & Co. Houston, TX
35A-132	1977.	N431M Motorola Inc 11/77, Owners Jet Services Ltd 2/85, Maxfly Avn Inc 7/88, Refreshment Svcs Inc 2/89, N420PC 3/89, N420PC Refreshment Services Inc. Springfield, Il.
35A-133	1977.	N728GL GLC /77, N35NB Braman Cadillac 8/78, Tulsa Aircraft Charter Corp 8/80, Martin Avn Inc 6/84,Robert Woolley-Tx 9/84, N58RW 4/85, Martin Avn /87, Gantt Avn Inc 2/89, EBM Group 5/89, I-ALPM Soc Ithifly SpA 21 Jun 89, I-ALPM Soc. Ithifly S.p.A. Venezia.
35A-134	1977.	N1473B GLC /77, Great Western Management & Realty Corp 10/77, N88EP El Paso NB 3/79, DHL Airways Inc 3/83, N235DH 5/83, N235DH DHL Airways Inc. San Francisco, Ca.
35A-135	1977.	(OO-LFX) Abelag-Brussels 10/77, N22MJ MJI /77, D-CDAX Blendax Werke GmbH 1/78, N719US U S Aircraft Sales 12/82, Jetaway Inc 1/83, N11AK 5/83, rpo 25B-082, I-ZOOM Soc I F P Immobiliaria SRL 12/85, Soc Priv Air SRL /? Soc Perini Fabio-Pisa /88, I-ZOOM Soc. Perini Fabio, Pisa.
35A-136	1977.	T-22 Argentine Air Force 1/78, T-22 Grupo 1 de Aerofotografico, II Brigada Aerea, Parana.
35A-137	1977.	N3819G GLC /77, HB-VFL Transair SA 1/78, EC-DEB Gestair-Madrid 'Virgen de Lluck' 9/78, Balboa de Aviacion y Transportes S.A. /86, N41FN Flight International Inc 11/87, N41FN Flight International Inc. Jacksonville, Fl.
35A-138	1977.	N7735A GTE Services Corp 10/77, N31FB Rumike Corp 8/79, NCRA Sales & Service Inc 11/81,N3RA 10/82, National Co-operative Refinery 8/89, N3RA National Co-operative Refinery, McPherson, Ks.
35A-139	1977.	N15SC Sea Containers Associates 12/77, Learjet Corp 7/89, D-CGFD Aero Dienst GmbH 6 Oct 89, D-CGFD Gesellschaft fuer Flugzieldarstellung mbh. Hohn AFB.
35A-140	1977.	N742GL GLC /77, N888BL Bayliner Marine Corp 4/78, Tesoro Petroleum Corp 12/79, N72TP 1/80,N72TP to 55-032, A R Dillard Jr via J Prewitt 11/84, N40BD 2/85, Newcastle Corp 5/88, N40BD Newcastle Corp. Wichita Falls, Tx.
35A-141	1978.	N743GL GLC /78, Waste Management Inc 3/78, N66WM 4/78, New Century Freight Traffic Association 4/90, N553M 6/90, Portland Glove Co 8/90, N553M Portland Glove Co. Carlton, Or.
35A-142	1977.	Amerock Corp 12/77,J L Clark Mfg Co 7/87,Clarcor Inc 11/87, N815A Clarcor Inc. Rockford, Il.

35A-143 1978. N301SC Sabine Corp 1/78, Combs-Gates Denver Inc 9/81, M P Appleby-Mt 10/81, Air Traffic Service Corp 8/83, Learjet Inc 10/90, Aviation Consultants Inc 11/90, OE- Airtaxi-Vienna 11/90, OE-... Airtaxi Bedarfsluftverkehrsges mbH. Vienna.
35A-144 1977. N39398 GLC /77, D-CCAP Aero-Dienst GmbH 12/77, N705US U S A/c Sales 9/81,Marathon Air 11/81,St Lucie Skyways 3/82, N35KC Marathon Air Inc 7/82, Bizjet Inc-Fl 5/84, Duncan-Ne 8/87, (N84DJ) rsvd 1 Jul 88, OY-CCT Basair/Alkair Flight Operations 9/88, N118MA McMoy & Assoc 3/90,Enterprise Aviation Inc 6/90, N118MA Enterprise Aviation Inc. Houston, Tx.
35A-145 1978. N39394 GLC /78, HB-VFB Swiss Air Ambulance 1/78, Swiss AF 5/88, HB-VFB Swiss Air Force, Dubendorf
35A-146 1978. N55AS Albertsons Inc 2/78, N55AS to 55-072, N351AS 2/87, N351AS Albertsons Inc. Boise, Id.
35A-147 1978. N717W John Hanson/Winnebago Industries 1/78, MJI 2/78, HZ-KTC Al Khodair Trading & Contracting Co 3/78, N499G Walston Airbusiness 10/81,Jason Fox Drilling & Rykoff 11/81, N717W 2/82, Ford Motor Credit 9/82, N55F 11/82,New Creations 6/89, N55F New Creations Inc. Columbus, Oh.
35A-148 1978. N103GH Allstate Insurance Co 8/78, N103GP 6/82, Leroy Pesch Industries Ltd 1/83, N333RP 5/83, Duncan Aviation-Nb 8/87,Robwal International Ltd 9/87, N500RW 1/88, Air SRV Inc 2/88, Cx USA 3/89,N500RW W/O W/o 24 May 88. 24/MAY/88 shortly after t.o. 4 aboard all k
35A-149 1978. OO-KJG Abelag-Brussels 2/78, operated in Lebanon, HB-VGN Total (Suisse) SA 1/80,N85351 Combs Gates Denver Inc 1/81, N273MC Meredith Corp 5/81, N273MC to 55-119, N273MG ATC Inc 3/86, N Central Avn Inc 2/88, Huntrip Inc 8/88, Lands End Direct Merchants 1/89,N600LE 6/89,N600LE Lands End Inc. Dodgeville, WI
35A-150 1978. N100EP Avion Inc 3/78, GLC 3/84, Mountain Fuel Resources 4/84,Eagle Jet Inc 1/87,Cx USA 4/90, N100EP W/O W/o 11 May 87. 11/MAY/87 cr and burnt out after take off, 2 crew killed.
35A-151 1978. N39399 GLC /78, N711L Carborundum Co 3/78, SOHIO/Kennecott Corp 10/82,N813M 11/82, N813M Old Ben Coal Co/stolen ex Wichita 13 Apr 84, cx USA 6/86.
35A-152 1978. N101HB First Hawaiian Bank 4/78, Jefclay/Clay Lacy 4/83, N964CL 8/83, with Bolivian Air Force /90, N964CL Clay Lacy, Van Nuys, Ca. (confiscated in Bolivia-status ?).
35A-153 1978. C-GZVV Perimeter Aviation Ltd 2/78, N573LP Louisiana Pacific Corp 3/83, N573LR 4/90, N573LR Louisiana Pacific Corp. Hillsboro, Or.
35A-154 1977. N650NL National Life & Accident Inc 3/78, Million Air 8/84, Gillman Air Inc 10/84, N117RB 11/84, Ramsbar Inc 11/87, N117RB Ramsbar Inc. Houston, Tx.
35A-155 1978. N760LP Penley Associates 5/78, N760DL 11/83, Garff Ents Inc 2/84, N110KG 10/84, sale-Al 7/88, Jet East Inc 11/88, N1001L 2/90, N1001L Jet East Inc. Dallas, Tx.
35A-156 1978. N170L Dana Corp 4/78, DRS Aviation Inc 7/89, N190EB 9/89, Davisair Inc 12/89, N190EB Corporate Wings/Davisair Inc. Pittsburgh, Pa.
35A-157 1978. N746GL GLC /78, YV-O1CP Dr Albert Finol/Transporte Transilac SA 3/78, Cx YV- 3/85, N57FF Ore-Ida Foods Inc 3/85, N57FF to BAe 125-8033, N57FP 1/90, Duncan-Ne 2/90, N157DJ 3/90, ZS-MWW 6/90, ZS-MWW
35A-158 1978. N835AC Allis Chalmers Corp-Leasing Svcs 4/78, MJI 4/85, N158MJ 5/85, IJA/Northeast Jet 9/85,N158NE 10/85, Barron Thomas Aviation 2/88,Pal Waukee Aviation 8/88, N800GP 8/90,N800GP Pal Waukee Aviation Inc. Wheeling, Il.
35A-159 1978. N93C Greyhound Leasing & Financing-Phoenix 4/78, N93CK 1/84, Combined Aviation Co 6/84, (N135CK) rsvd 9 Oct 84, Flying A Ltd Inc 11/89, D-CAPO Phoenix Air GmbH 11/89, D-CAPO Phoenix Air GmbH. Munich.
35A-160 1978. D-CCCA Maschinenfabrik E Mollers GmbH 3/78, (800th Learjet), D-CCCA Maschinenfabrik E Mollers GmbH Paderborn.
35A-161 1978. N39415 GLC /78, YV-65CP C A de Edificaciones - Resid D Paulo 4/78, YV-65CP C A de Edificaciones - Resid D Paulo.
35A-162 1978. N751GL GLC /78, (HB-VFO) originally for Oman 4/78, N711HH Hilton Hotels Corp 6/78, N1978L Coad Inc 9/79, Shamrock Investment Co 9/83, N222SL 8/85, Jet East Inc 3/89, Flying Best Air Inc 9/90, N222SL Flying Best Air Inc. Wilmington, De.
35A-163 1978. YV-173CP Terrenaca C.A. 4/78, N27BL B L Jet Sales Inc 2/79, Anheuser-Busch Cos Inc 1/84, New Creations Inc 5/89, N27BL New Creations Inc. Columbus, Oh.
35A-164 1978. N1473B GLC /78, N248HM Herman Miller Inc 6/78, Falcon Aircraft Conversions 8/87, N50MJ 1/88, N50MJ Falcon Aircraft Conversions Inc. San Antonio, Tx.
35A-165 1978. N40144 GLC /78, A40-CA Omani Inspector General of Police 4/78, VH-HOF Lloyd Aviation Jet Charter-Adelaide 7/88,N16BJ AMR Combs Floriad Inc 10/90,N16BJ AMR Combs Florida Inc. Fort Lauderdale, FL
35A-166 1978. N2CJ GLC /78, Great Lakes Corp 10/82, Anheuser-Busch Cos 5/85,N831J 7/85, Huntrip Inc 5/89, Jet Cap Inc 5/90, N831J Jet Cap Inc. Chesterfield, Mo.
35A-167 1978. N725P Butler Manufacturing Co 6/78, N831AS Allan Stillman-Fl 8/85, A Stillman Management 2/87, Airtrade Intl Inc 11/89, RKM Leasing Co 2/90, N813AS RKM Leasing Co. Dover, De.
35A-168 1978. N22SF State Farm Mutual Auto Insurance Co 5/78, N22SF State Farm Mutual Auto Insurance Co. Bloomington, Il.
35A-169 1978. N135ST Southeast Toyota Distributors 6/78,N135ST Southeast Toyota Distributors, Pompano Beach, Ca.
35A-170 1978. N100K Fred Shaulis-Pa 5/78, N100K Fred Shaulis, Friedens, Pa.
35A-171 1978. N747GL GLC /78, C-GNSA Nabors Drilling Ltd 11/78, N823J Combs-Gates Denver 6/81, Associated Inns & Restaurants 4/82, N1968A 11/82, N1968T 8/85, Terry Jet Inc 11/85, N196DT 2/86, James Wickert & Assoc 2/88, RPM Aviation Inc 5/88, N455RM 9/88, Duncan-Ne 4/89, Corporate Jets Inc 11/89, (N48DK) rsvd 26 Mar 90, N40DK 6/90, N40DK Corporate Jets Inc. Pittsburgh, Pa.

c/n	
35A-172	1978. N748GL GLC /78, SE-DDG Swedair AB 3/79, Nordflyg AB /90, SE-DDG Nordflyg AB. Eskiltuna.
35A-173	1978. N750GL GLC /78, HZ-MIB Sheikh Mohammed Imran Bamieh 12/78, N750GL NCI Aviation Inc 2/79, (HZ-NCI) /79, N100GU GECC/Grand Union 4/80, N116EL GECC-Ct 8/82, Flight International Inc 9/82, (N83DM) 2/83, United Executive Jet 3/86, Duncan-Ne 6/90, N116EL Duncan Aviation Inc. Lincoln, Ne.
35A-174	1978. TR-LYC Air Affaires-Gabon/Business Flyers 4/78, N65DH Dee Howard-Tx 11/80,D-CAVI Avia Luftreederei GmbH/Air Traffic GmbH 8/81, (F-GGRG) Transair-Le Bourget rsvd 27 Jan 88, Deutsche Rettungsflugwacht 'Bjorn Steiger' 6/88, N130TA Templehof Airways USA Inc 9/89, N130TA Templehof Airways USA Inc. Miami, FL
35A-175	1978. D-CDWN Diehl Werke KG 10 JUl 78, D-CDWN Diehl Werke KG/Aero Dienst GmbH. Nuremberg.
35A-176	1978. N317MR MJI 9/78, Blue River Alloys/Corprojet 3/79, Proform 4/80, XA-ACC Intervuelo SA 9/82, Aero Servicio Trans-Mexico SA /? N176JE Jet East Inc 15 Nov 88, Gantt Aviation Inc 12/88, (N67GA) rsvd 3 Jan 89, XA-BUX 4/89, XA-BUX Aerotaxi Mexicana SA. Mexico City.
35A-177	1978. N1461B GLC /78, N77CP Pfizer Inc 7/78, N77CQ 2/84, Parc Aviation Inc 2/84, N174CP 7/84, Imperial Avn Inc 2/86, Duncan-Ne 2/88, Cx USA 1/89, Huntrip Inc 3/88, Great Circle Aviation Inc 9/88, D-CITY Helmut Idzkowiak 1/89, D-CITY Helmut Idzkowiak, Ahlen.
35A-178	1978. N40146 GLC /78, N22CP Pfizer Inc 8/78, N22CQ 3/84, George Gund 111 5/84, N35GG 8/84, Conaero Inc 9/89, Jet Charter International Inc 11/89, N900JC 3/90,N900JC Jet Charter International Inc. Hayward, CA
35A-179	1978. N39412 GLC /78, D-CCAR Aero-Dienst GmbH demo 7/78, D-CAPD Peter Dreidoppel 7/78, N718SW Memphis Aero Intl Sales 5/81, Scotland Oil 8/82, NC Transportaion 1/84, Dolphin Avn 8/88,N718SW Dolphin Aviation Inc. Sarasota, Fl.
35A-180	1978. N3819G GLC /88, N222BE Chesapeake Leasing Co 6/78, N222BE to 35A-489, N222BK 8/82, GLC 10/82,N35CX 9/83,Conax Corp 10/83,Kane Aircraft Corp 6/86, HSG Avn 3/89, N44HG 3/90, N44HG H S Geneen/HSG Aviation Inc. NYC.
35A-181	1978. N35LJ McTan Corp 9/78, N35PR 12/82, Lear Flite Inc 9/84, N35PD 10/84, N5114G 3/88, Combs-Gates Denver Inc 4/88, Shepherd Inc 6/88, PT-LSJ Empresa de Aerotaxi e Manutenacao Pampulha 1/89, PT-LSJ Empresa de Aerotaxi e Manutenacao Pampulha Ltda. B.H.
35A-182	1978. N1450B GLC /78, N33HB Hamilton Brothers Oil/Delaware Airjet Inc 8/78, N3HB GLC 9/82, N3HA 12/82, A Rothman-Pa 2/83, N221SG Intl Signal & Control 9/83, Combs-Gates 2/88, Learjet Corp 3/89, Path Corp 4/89, N221SG Path Corp. Rehoboth Beach, De.
35A-183	1978. N3802G GLC /78, N720M Levolor Lorentzen Inc 8/78, N720M to F50-18, N72JM 12/81, AeroSmith Penny 11/87, N106XX Conaero Inc 1/88, Bomar Leasing Inc 2/88, IAL Leasing Inc 5/89, N106XX IAL Leasing Inc. Hialeah, Fl.
35A-184	1978. N1462B GLC /78,HB-VFO Transair SA 8/78, Citicorp Intl Finance 2/82, HB-VFO W/O W/o 6 Dec 82. 06/DEC/82
35A-185	1978. N99ME H C Price Co /78, Ryan Avn/Magnum Land Corp 4/79, N99VA Geo Ablah 6/79, Abko Properties Inc 11/79, N99VA to G-2 200, N10BF 1/84, Emira Inc 3/84, Thomas Jets Inc 12/85, American Diversified Real Estate 5/88, N99VA 5/89, Gantt Aviation Inc 10/89, Wings USA Inc 5/90, (N900EM) 6/90, TC-GEM MARM/Wings Air Transport 6/90, TC-GEM MARM/Wings Air Transport,
35A-186	1978. N753GL GLC /78, N590 Prestige Jet/Braman Aviation Inc 1/79, N96DM J David Co 8/82, (N317JD) 1/84, N96DM Flight International Inc 8/82, N96FN rsvd 17 Aug 90, N96FN Flight International Inc. Newport News, Va.
35A-187	1978. N755GL GLC /78,N32HM Southeastern Jet-NC 1/79,Dal-Title Corp 10/86, Dal Briar Corp 1/90, Southaire Inc 4/90, N32HM Southaire Inc. Memphis, Tn.
35A-188	1978. VH-AJS Bib Stillwell 6/78, Australian Jet Charter /79, N39293 Refrigerated Transport/Richard Beauchamp-Ga 7/83, N2ORT 12/83, ATC Inc/Ray Henderson-Fl 1/86, (N38FN) rsvd 24 Sep 87 for Flight International, N3MJ 3/88, GPM Transport Inc 4/88, N343MG 7/88, Aqua Air Aviation Corp 4/90, N135AC 6/90, N135AC Aqua Air Aviation Corp/Aviation Consultants, Aspen, Co.
35A-189	1978. N3811G GLC /78, VH-AJV Bib Stillwell /78, Australian Jet Charter /79, N39292 ATC Inc 8/83,(N189TC) Personal Jet Management Leasing 9/83, ATC Inc 2/85, N32TC 5/85, Savvy Jets II Inc-FTL 1/86,Flight International 10/87, N32FN 4/88, N35KC 8/88, (N32FN) rsvd 5 Jun 89,Gantt Avn Inc 10/89, Executive Fliteways 8/90, N32KC Executive Fliteways Inc. Ronkonkoma, NY.
35A-190	1978. N32BA Centurion Investment 9/78, Coronado Air/Vernon Savings 3/84, N202VS 8/84, Dumont Associates Inc 3/87, N202WR 1/89, N202WR Dumont Associates Inc. Morristown, NJ.
35A-191	1978. N3810G GLC /78, (YV-15CP) /78, HB-VFX Latisair/Petrolair Systems SA 10/78, N75TF Omni 3/84,Heitman Holdings Ltd 6/85, N35NP 6/85, N35NP to 35A-492, N35SE 3/87, N35SE Heitman Holdings Ltd. Dover, De.
35A-192	1978. N4995A Circo Resorts Inc /78, N225CC Circus Circus Hotels Inc 9/78, N225QC 9/80, Pum Air Corp/Puma Engineering Co 6/81, N49PE 10/81, N49PE to 55-045, N49BE 8/87, GLC 9/87, CWW Inc 10/87, N49BE CWW Inc. Denver, Co.
35A-193	1978. N1465B GLC /78, (YV-131CP) /78, VH-SBJ Swan Brewery Co 10/78, N620J Combs Gates Denver 3/81,VH-SBJ Westfield Holdings Ltd 5/81, N2743T UCO Aviation Inc 9/82, James Haldan-Nv 6/84, Duncan-Ne 8/89, N9EE 10/89, E & E Partnership 12/89, N9EE E & E Partnership, Bellevue, Wa.
35A-194	1978. N91W Island Creek Coal 10/78, Liberty Exploration 7/82, N86BL C&J Co/Bruce Leven 2/86, Burbank Jet Ltd 3/88, N86BE 12/88, N86BE Burbank Jet Ltd. Chelmsford, Ma.
35A-195	1978. N1471B GLC /78, D-CONY G Eheim/Contactair-Stuttgart 1/79, Cx D- /89, N555JE Jet East Inc 7/88, Flight International Inc 8/88, SE-DHO Nyge Aero AB 5/89, SE-DHO Nyge-Aero AB. Nykoping.

c/n	
35A-196	1978. HB-VFU Transair SA 10/78, EC-DFA Spantax SA 2/79, EC-DFA W/O W/o 13 Aug 80. 13/AUG/80
35A-197	1978. N754GL GLC /78,Braman Avn 12/78, Armored Transport Inc 7/81, Ameriflight Inc 10/87, N754GL Ameriflight Inc. Burbank, Ca.
35A-198	1978. N25FS Gt Western Management & Realty 11/78, General Avn Svcs 6/87, I-ALPT Ithifly SpA 7 Aug 87, I-ALPT Ithifly S.p.a/ALPI Eagles, Thiene (VI).
35A-199	1978. N40144 GLC /78, N9HM DHL/Holt Machinery Co-San Antonio 11/78,Dee Howard Co 11/86,(N9HV) rsvd 5 Aug 86, N30DH 2/87, Lindsey Leasing Inc 9/89, N34TC 11/89, N34TC Lindsey Leasing Inc. St Joseph, Mi.
35A-200	1978. N3818G GLC /78, D-CCAR Aero Dienst GmbH 11/78, OO-LFY Abelag Aviation 12/79, OO-LFY Locabel Fininvest SA/Abelag Aviation, Brussels.
35A-201	1978. N39415 GLC /78, N79MJ MJI 9/78, N35RT Townsend Engineering Co 11/78, N35RT to 35A-420, N35RF Georges A Rolfes Co 2/82, Consolidated Airways Inc 5/84, Intl Jet Leasing Co-In 2/85, Wimbledon Aviation Inc 1/86, Jet East Inc 8/87, Eagle Aviation Inc 11/87, XA-PIN Aerolineas de Oeste SA 12/87, XA-PIN Aerolineas del Oeste SA. Guadalajara.
35A-202	1978. VH-MIQ Mount Isa Mines Ltd 12/78, N499G Walston Airbusiness 4/82, Caruth C Byrd Enterprises 11/82, Jet Associates 3/85, Cycare Systems Inc 3/87, C-CGPD Peter Dreidoppel 11/87, D-CGPD Peter Dreidoppel/Air Traffic GmbH. Dusseldorf.
35A-203	1978. N744E Eaton Corp 12/78, N744E Eaton Corp. Cleveland, Oh.
35A-204	1978. N1466B GLC /78, D-COSY Holstenflug GmbH 1/79, N87MJ MJI 1/80, N99ME Moran Energy Inc 3/80, Perlman Ents Inc 1/83, N7PE 5/83, GLC 12/83, Anne Hora Zobel 12/84, Garrett Corp 9/85, Flight Systems Inc 11/85, Tracor Flight Systems Inc 11/88, (N277AM) rsvd for Aircraft Marketing Inc 1 Feb 90, D-CFTG FTG Air Service KG 3/90, D-CFTG FTG Air Service KG. Cologne-Bonn.
35A-205	1978. N39418 GLC /78, N80SM GLC Special Missions aircraft /79, Flight Intl Inc 11/81, N59DM FNB-Dallas 2/82, Interfirst Bank-Dallas/Lucas-Flt Intl 1/84, N59FN rsvd 30 Jul 90, N59FN Flight International Inc. Newport News, Va.
35A-206	1978. N760GL GLC demo /78, (N66HM) Southeastern Jet Corp 2/79, HB-VGH EJA-Geneva 7/79, Air Leman Ecole les Ailes-Heli Ski 9/81, Inwelco SA 10/82, Palepo AG 7/83, N189TC ATC Inc 8/84,Circus Circus Enterprises Inc 2/85, N123CC 4/85, Palace Air Inc 1/86, N123CC to Falcon 200 488, N38PS 2/86, Palace Station Inc 12/87, N38PS Palace Station Inc. Las Vegas, Nv.
35A-207	1978. N40146 GLC /78, N711 Wm K Carpenter-Fl 1/79, Jet Charter Inc 1/88, N3PW 2/88, M-S Air Inc 2/89, N620JM 5/89, N620JM M-S Air Inc. Indianapolis, In.
35A-208	1978. N40149 GLC /78, N40TA Bandag Inc 1/79,Jet East 1/83,All American AssuranceCo 2/83, (N691NS) rsvd for National Saving Corp 29 Jun 83, U S Jet Inc 6/83, Eagle Air Corp 9/86, RR Investors Inc 6/88, Duncan-Ne 7/88, David Kenenash-NJ 8/88, N39DK 1/89, (N39DJ) rsvd 11 May 89,Palumbo Aircraft Sales 11/89, N67PA 12/89, Aircraft Trading Center Inc 3/90, JP Foodservice Inc 4/90, PHH Financial Services Inc 8/90, N67PA JP Foodservice Inc. Hanover, Md.
35A-209	1978. N399W Williams Research Corp 1/79, N399W to 650-0098, N339W Cessna 11/85, Duncan Avn-Nb 6/86, Evergreen Intl Avn 7/86, N711DS 9/86, N711DS to G-2 129, N22MS 12/87, N22MS Evergreen International Aviation, McMinnville, Or.
35A-210	1978. N840GL Southeastern Jet Corp 1/79, (N35HM) /79, N42HM 1/83, Conaero Inc 7/90, N721CM 9/90, N721CM Conaero Inc. Wilmington, De.
35A-211	1978. N1461B GLC /78, D-CATY Holstenflug GmbH /78, N15MJ MJI 12/79, N600LC Lincoln National Corp 1/80,Lincoln Natl Life Insurance 2/84, N500KK 11/90, N500KK Lincoln National Life Insurance Co. Fort Wayne, In.
35A-212	1978. N3803G GLC /78, N180MC Hughes International Finance Corp 5/79, International Jet Inc 5/82, N180MC International Jet Inc. Minneapolis, Mn.
35A-213	1979. N800RD Procurement & Contracts Office 6/79, (N935NA) /81, XC-CUZ Procurad General /81, Dir Gen de Geografica /89, XC-CUZ Director General de Geografica, Mexico City.
35A-214	1979. N279DM Domar Jet Charter 2/79, Monterey Airplane Co 3/84, N279DM Monterey Airplane Co. Pebble Beach, Ca.
35A-215	1979. VH-UPB Narich P/L /79, Stillwell/Publishing & Broadcasting P/L /81, N2951P Omni 4/82, Baron Leasing/North Carolina Leasing Co 7/82, N80CD 11/82, N80GD 10/85, HDR Corporate Services Inc 11/85,E H Derby & Co 2/87, N35ED 4/87, N35ED E H Darby & Co. Sheffield, Al.
35A-216	1978. D-CATE Holstenflug GmbH 5/79, N24MJ MJI 12/79, N39MB Richard Black-Wy 1/80, N39MB Richard Black, Moose, Wy.
35A-217	1979. N111RF R C Fisher-Fl 3/79, N111RF R C Fisher, West Palm Beach, Fl.
35A-218	1979. N256TW Tidewater Realty 7/79, McMoRan Properties Inc 10/84, N481FM 4/85, Thompson Helicopters Inc 11/85, Lyle B McGinnis 8/89, sale-De 9/90, N481FM sale, Dover, De.
35A-219	1979. N39416 GLC /79, VH-BJQ Barclay Jet Charter 3/79, N502G Walston Airbusiness Inc 2/82, Barton & Barton Co 3/82, N350JF 6/82, Interglobal Products Inc 9/84, CFS Flight Systems Inc 9/90, N350JF CFS Flight Systems Inc. Coral Springs, Fl.
35A-220	1979. N79BH AWECO Inc 3/79, N333RB Reading & Bates 11/80, Green Holdings Inc 10/84, N220GH 1/85, Louisiana Pacific Corp 12/85, N873LP 6/86, N873LR 6/90, N373LP rsvd 17 Oct 90, N373LP Louisiana Pacific Corp. Hillsboro, Or.

c/n		
35A-221	1979.	N845GL GLC /79, VH-WFE WardsExpress 11/79, Norfolk Jet Avn /87, Fleet Support P/L /90,VH-WFE Fleet Support P/L.
35A-222	1979.	HB-VFZ EJA-Geneva 3/79, I-EJID Soc Executive Jet Italia SRL 8/89, I-EJID Soc. Executive Jet Italiana SRL. Milan.
35A-223	1979.	N215JW James Wilson Jr-Al 4/79, N215JW James Wilson Jr. Montgomery, Al.
35A-224	1979.	N96AC Wabash Enterprises Inc 4/79, Oxmill Inc 5/82, Caravelle Corp 11/82, Colpay Inc 1/83, N96AC Colpay Inc. White Plains, NY.
35A-225	1979.	N225MC J N O McCall Coal Co 5/79,TG-JAY Distribuidora Textil 8/87,TG-JAY Distribuidora Textil S.A.
35A-226	1979.	N1127M Miles Laboratories Inc 6/79, N1127M Miles Laboratories Inc. Elkhart, In.
35A-227	1979.	N211BY Institute of Basic Youth Conflicts Inc 6/79, N25RF Combs-Gates 11/80,General Svc Operations 3/85, N88NE 5/85, N88NE General Service Operations Inc. Cleveland, Oh.
35A-228	1979.	N101PG Geo Survey Intl inc 5/79, Omni 2/84, Forest Hills Corp 4/84, Barrington Aviation Inc 1/86, Gene O Bicknell-Ks 5/90, N4GB 8/90, N4GB Gene O Bicknell/National Pizza Co. Pittsburgh, Ks.
35A-229	1979.	N8MA ARO Corp 5/79, World Jet Inc 2/90, Laurel Avn Ents Inc 4/90, N717JB 9/90, N717JB Laurel Aviation Enterprises Inc. St James, NY.
35A-230	1979.	N714K Gulf States Utilities/Beaumont Car Leasing 6/79, BLC Corp 1/81,N714K BLC Corp. San Mateo, CA
35A-231	1979.	(N10AB) GLC 1/79, (N712DM) 3/79, N911DB Skybird Aviation Inc 6/79, Donald Kroll-Ca 3/87, N62DK 9/87, N62DK Donald Koll Co-Trustee, Newport Beach, Ca.
35A-232	1979.	N8281 McDonnell-Douglas Corp 5/79, (900th Learjet), N8281 McDonnell-Douglas Corp. St. Louis, Mo.
35A-233	1979.	N35SL Southland Life Insurance 6/79, Aircraft Charter Inc 3/84, Quorum Sales Inc 3/85, Arkansas Wings Inc 5/85, N35AW 9/87, N35AW Arkansas Wings Inc. Wilmington, De.
35A-234	1979.	N35WR Rollins Inc 5/79, LOR Inc 6/87, N35WR LOR Inc/Rollins Inc. Atlanta, Ga.
35A-235	1979.	N841GL GLC /79, N600CN Coca Cola Bottling Co 7/79,Navarre Co 10/83, MAPCO Inc 3/85, N256MA 4/85, N256MA MAPCO Inc. Tulsa, Ok.
35A-236	1979.	G-ZOOM Falmer International Ltd 8/79,N8537B Lisle Aircraft Inc 1/81,Waukesha Pearce Industries Inc 4/81, N9OLP 8/81, Brae Transportation 2/84,Jack Silberberg-NJ 6/85, N4XL Jack Silberberg-NJ 6/85, N900EC 3/88, N900EC Jack Silberberg, Maplewood, NJ.
35A-237	1979.	N843GL GLC /79, Morris Newspaper Corp 10/79,N78MN 11/79, I-KUSS Soc Gitanair SpA 7/89, I-KUSS Soc. Gitanair S.p.a. Bologna.
35A-238	1979.	N844GL GLC /79, N8OHK Ford Development Corp 8/79, ZS-INS Aaron Searl-RSA 6/80, 3D-ACZ Swaziland Government 11/91, ZS-INS Aaron Searl-RSA /82, extensively damaged 27 Aug 85, N248DA Dodson Avn Inc 1/86, CRG Productions/Telecom Svcs Inc 1/87, N500CG 3/87, LJ Investments Inc 8/88, N500HG 2/90, N500HG L J Investments Inc. Wilmington, De.
35A-239	1979.	N847GL GLC /79, (HB-VGC) Transair SA /79, VH-KTI Katies Fashions 6/79, RAAF/Australian Jet Charter /86, VH-KTI to 650-0144. VH-LEQ Land Equity Group 7/88, VH-LEQ Australia Jet Charter/Land Equity Group, Sydney.
35A-240	1979.	N240B FSB/Budd Co 6/79, N240B FSB/Budd Co. Troy, Mi.
35A-241	1979.	N42FE Fritz Egger 1/80, WAK Air Ltd 1/84, Jane Air Inc-Ca 4/85, N500GP Geo J Priester Aviation Inc 7/86, N500FD Red Force Inc 11/88, Owners Jet Svcs Ltd 3/90, N240JS 5/90, N240JS Owners Jet Services Ltd. Las Vegas, Nv.
35A-242	1979.	N846GL GLC /79, VH-WFJ Wards Express 6/79, Norfolk Jet Avn /87, Fleet Support P/L /90,VH-WFJ Fleet Support P/L.
35A-243	1979.	N3812G GLC /79, HZ-ABM Sheikh Ali bin Hussein Al Musallam 7/79, N81863 Learjet Corp 6/89, I-AGEB Soc Eurojet Italia 10/89, I-AGEB Soc. Eurojet Italia, Milan.
35A-244	1979.	N1451B GLC /79, RP-57 Philippines National Oil Co /79, RP-C57 5/88,RP-C57 Philippines National Oil Co. Manila.
35A-245	1979.	N2WL Cardinal Associates 8/79, Warner Lambert Co 1/87, N1526L 2/87, Palumbo Aircraft Sales Inc 11/89, N30PA 1/90, World Jet Inc 7/90, N30PA World Jet Inc. Fort Lauderdale, Fl.
35A-246	1979.	N50PH Regional Transportation Service 9/79, N50PH to 35A-497, N50PL 4/84, N555GB 7/84, Gene Branscome-Tx 9/84, Dye Aircraft Inc 3/86, Ark Air Flight Inc 8/87, N1DC 9/89,N1DC Dallas Cowboys/Ark Air Flight Inc. Little Rock, Ar.
35A-247	1979.	YV-265CP Palcosa Co /79, N110JD Omni 10/83, Garff Leasing Co 2/84,Flight International 1/88, N38FN 5/88, N38FN Flight International Inc. Jacksonville, Fl.
35A-248	1979.	N3811G GLC /79, C-GBFA Business Flights Ltd 8/79, Westair Resources /86, N128CA Jack Wall Aircraft Sales 9/86, Ameriflight Inc 1/88, N128CA Ameriflight Inc. Burbank, Ca.
35A-249	1979.	N107JM HLM Enterprises 8/79, I-KALI Soc Gitanair del 25 Jun 86, I-KALI Soc. Gitanair, Bologna.
35A-250	1979.	N3250 Vulcan Materials Co 8/79, GLC 2/83, Air Travel Inc 8/83, (N87RS) Redifussion Simulation Inc 2/84, SPM Inc 5/84, Redifussion Simulation Inc 2/84, SPM Inc 3/84, Land's End Yacht Stores Inc 2/86, N63LE 5/86, N63LE Land's End Yacht Stores Inc. Dodgeville, Wi.
35A-251	1979.	N27NB Nolan Bushnell 'The Danieli' 10/79, GLC 7/85, S&B Properties Inc 11/85,Arcadia Avn Ltd 7/87, N27HF 7/88, N27HF Arcadia Aviation Ltd. Asheville, NC.
35A-252	1979.	N28CR GLC 7/79, PT-KZR Lider Taxi Aereo /79, Banco Bamerindus /81, Carbonifera Metropolitana /85, PT-KZR Carbonifera Metropolitana.
35A-253	1979.	N40144 GLC /79,N211DH Hagadone Newspapers Co 8/79,N211DH Hagadone Newspapers Co. Coeur d'Alene, ID

International Inc. Jacksonville, Fl.
35A-255 1979. N44EL U.S. Epperson Underwriting Co 12/79, N44EL to 55-123, N44ET 8/85, GLC 1/86,B D Holt Co 2/86, H C Aviation Co 6/86, N61OHC 1/87, N616HC 2/89, Conaero Inc 5/89, Rosa Maria Velaga Ruiz 10/90, XA-11/90, XA-... Rosa Maria Velaga Ruiz, Chula Vista, Ca.
35A-256 1979. N712L Eagle-Picher Industries Inc 11/79, George Gillette-Tn 3/83, N6GG 4/83, N50DD 2/84, Gaylord Leasing Partners-Il 1/86, R Dupree-Il 3/86, Firstlear Leasing Inc 4/88, N911ML 5/88, N911ML Firstlear Leasing Inc. Wilmington, De.
35A-257 1979. F-GCMS Pamys/Air Affaires Intl/Chargeurs SA/Korreda/Euralair 79-87, N275DJ Duncan-Ne 4/87, Public Service Transit Inc 7/87, Duncan-Ne 6/89, N257DJ Duncan Aviation Inc. Lincoln, Ne.
35A-258 1979. (N1700) GLC 5/79, N28BG Konfara Co 7/79, GLC 1/85, N35MH Marriott Corp 6/87, N35MH Marriott Corp. Washington, DC.
35A-259 1979. N39413 GLC /79, HB-VGC Fidinam Fiduciara-Lugano 10/79, accident Lugano 14 Jan 87, N9113F Dodson Investments Inc 8/87, Hill Aircraft & Leasing 7/88, N259HA 10/88, Huntrip Inc 2/89, Jet Cap Inc 4/90, N259HA Jet Cap Inc. Chesterfield, Mo.
35A-260 1979. N40PK Porta Kamp Manufacturing Co 10/79, N40PK Porta Kamp Manufacturing Co. Inc. Houston, Tx.
35A-261 1979. N900RD GLC 7/79, XA-ELU AVEMEX SA 11/79, N35SJ Stacis Jet Center/Corporate Air 2/84, Flight Intl Inc 10/87, N35FN 8/88, N63DH 10/89, Malecki Music Inc 3/90, N58MM rsvd 25 Apr 90, N58MM Malecki Music Inc, Grand Rapids, Mi.
35A-262 1979. N237GA G Argyros-Ca 1/80,Jack Wall Sales 1/87,Ameriflight Inc 1/88, N237AF 11/90, N237AF Ameriflight Inc. Burbank, Ca.
35A-263 1979. D-CCAD Minitrans GmbH 10/79, Air Traffic GmbH 7/83, N4577Q MJI 12/83, Corporate Air Inc 1/84, Flight Intl Inc 10/87, N37FN 5/88, N37FN Flight International Inc. Patrick Henry Airport, Va.
35A-264 1979. XA-ATA Minera Autlan SA de CV 11/79, N35GX GLC 10/83, Fred Shaulis-Pa 1/84, N4ODK 2/84, Jack Piatt-Pa 10/86, Bryant Jet Services 7/89, N3056R Gantt Aviation Inc 4/90, VR-CDI ARAVCO 7/90, VR-CDI ARAVCO Ltd. London.
35A-265 1979. N1462B GLC /79, (G-ZEST) /79, G-LEAR CSE Aviation 5/79, Northern Executive Avn 12/79, G-LEAR Northern Executive Aviation Ltd. Manchester.
35A-266 1979. N39404 GLC /79, SE-DDI Joint Trawlers AB 10/79, N922GL 35A-266 Ltd Partnership 12/79, N35GC G C Services Corp 7/80, DLS Enterprises Inc 7/89, N35GC DLS Enterprises Inc. Houston, Tx.
35A-267 1979. N39418 GLC /79, XA-LAN AVEMEX SA /79, XA-LAN AVEMEX/Empresas Lanzagorta, Mexico City.
35A-268 1979. N10870 GLC /79, YV-286CP J V Persand & Co 11/79, (N286CP) /83, N3857N 5/83, Valley Jet Corp 1/84, N510SG 7/84, N510SG Valley Jet Corp. Portland, Or.
35A-269 1979. N881W L R French-Tx 1/80, N881W L R French, Midland, Tx.
35A-270 1979. N10871 GLC /79, YV-O-MRI-1 Ministry of Interior Relations 11/79, YV-O-MRI-1 Ministry of Interior Relations, Caracas.
35A-271 1979. N1088A GLC /79, LV-OAS Ledesma 11/79, LV-OAS Ledesma, Buenos Aires.
35A-272 1979. N39398 GLC /79, N272HS Lanair Inc 7/80, Omni International 9/83, Nevis Enterprises Inc 1/84,Martin Chevrolet-Buick 11/84, Fittipaldi USA Inc 4/90, N500EF 6/90, N500EF Fittipaldi USA Inc. Miami, Fl.
35A-273 1979. N35FH GLC /79, N103C Adolph Coors Co 5/80, N103CL 4/84, N103CL Adolph Coors Co. Vero Beach, Ca.
35A-274 1979. N1087Y GLC /79, N274JS Bill Hodges Truck Co 1/80, N274JH 4/80, GLC 10/83, N83CP Capital Holding Corp 12/83, N83CP Capital Holding Corp. Louisville, Ky.
35A-275 1979. N10872 GLC /79, G-ZEAL Fairflight Charter/Jointair 2/80, N43FE Hop a Jet Inc 5/83, N43FE Hop a Jet Inc. Fort Lauderdale, Fl.
35A-276 1979. N44LJ C W Culpepper 1/80, James Lyon 2/83, RR Investments 10/84, N613RR Quorum Sales Inc 3/85, Benanti Inc 9/85, N69BH 7/86, Dorothy Josephs-Ca 3/88, N69BH Dorothy Josephs, Hayward, Ca.
35A-277 1979. N925GL GLC 2/80, N723LL Gary Levitz-Dallas 2/80, Cole National Corp 6/81, N7OCN 8/81, Delta Helicopter Service Inc 3/87, N127HC 8/87,Delta Jet Ltd 10/87,GLC 2/88, Aero Executive Intl 5/88, XA-PUI Aeroservicios Ejecutivos Sinaloenses SA 10/88, N350MD Mike Donahoe Aviation 7/89, N350MD Mike Donahoe Aviation Co. Phoenix, Az.
35A-278 1979. N1476B GLC /79, HB-VGL Transair SA 1/80, ECT-028 Gestair SA-Madrid 2/80, EC-DJC 4/80, N300ES E D S Administration Corp 3/83, N17GL 4/83, Ingles Market Inc 12/89, N12RP Stevens Aviation 2/90,N12RP Stevens Aviation Inc. Greer, SC.
35A-279 1979. Hillair Inc 3/80, Jetero Management Co 10/82, Sanders Intl Leasing-HOU 2/85, Orion Aircraft Sales 11/86, N19LH Orion Aircraft Sales Inc. Burbank, Ca.
35A-280 1979. N80MJ MJI 9/79, HP-912 Leybda CA-Panama 2/80, YN-BVO Aero Ejecutivo SA-Managua 4/80, 87-0026 U S Army 5/90, 87-0026 U S Army AVSCOM Facility.
35A-281 1980. N80WG US Fidelity & Guaranty Co 3/80, GLC 1/85, GEICO Corp 9/85, N425M 10/85, N425M GEICO Corp. Washington, DC.
35A-282 1980. N504Y Valley Acceptance Corp/Southwest Forest Inds 5/80, Baron Leasing Inc 8/85, N80CD N Carolina Leasing Co 1/86, Margaret Mead Ents Inc 8/89, N80GD 11/89, Great Planes Sales 1/90, Hurd Distributing Co 10/90, N9CH rsvd 26 Nov 90, N9CH Hurd Distributing Co. El Paso, Tx.
35A-283 1980. N920C Sky City Stores 3/80, GLC 2/84, Rexnord Inc 8/84, GLC 3/87, Invemed Aviation Services-NC 4/87, N205EL 12/87, N205EL Invemed Aviation Services Inc. Winston Salem, NC.

c/n

c/n	
35A-284	1980. (D-CEFL) GLC /80, D-CCAX Aero Dienst GmbH 3/80, Joachim Bohl /80, OO-GBL Abelag Aviation 8/83, OO-GBL Bank Lambert/GBL-Air, Brussels.
35A-285	1980. N777RA Ramada Airways Inc 4/80, Aerosmith Penny Inc 9/85, Knape & Vogt Manufacturing Co 12/85, N75KV 5/86, Conaero Inc 9/90, N75KV Conaero Inc. Wilmington, De.
35A-286	1980. N333X The Augsbury Organization Inc 3/80, Mitel Inc 12/81, (N333XX) /81, N200SX 8/82, GLC 9/84,Air Support Services Corp 10/84, PT-LSW Wanair Taxi Aereo 25 Jun 85, PT-LSW Wanair Taxi Aereo/Constructora Cowan S.A. Belo Horizonte.
35A-287	1980. N17EM Intermedics Inc 4/80, Hi-Stat Manufacturing 2/86,N71HS 3/86, N71HS Hi-Stat Manufacturing Co. Lexington, Oh.
35A-288	1979. N1476B GLC /80, HB-VGM Transair SA 3/80, Minitair SS-Geneva /80, N43DD Minitair Co 2/87, Jaindl Aviation Inc 4/87, N288NE Northeast Jet 8/87, Jet East Inc 2/89, N288JE 7/89, N288JE Jet East Inc. Dallas, Tx.
35A-289	1980. N3JL JTL Corp 4/80, J Guy Beatty Jr 10/80, Denver Coca Cola Bottling Co 5/84, N802CC Chrysler Corp 12/84, MJI 1/85, N289MJ 4/85, Northeast Jet/IJA Inc 5/85, N289NE 7/85, Martin Aviation Inc 2/89, N289NE Martin Aviation Inc. Santa Ana, Ca.
35A-290	1980. N2022L Rexnord Inc 4/80, XA-RAV Aerora SA 12/86, XA-RAV Aerora SA. Morelia.
35A-291	1980. N7US EAF/United States Underwriters-NYC 4/80, N7US to 55B-128, N535PC Seanaire Inc 2/87, N535PC Seanaire Inc. Midland Park, NJ.
35A-292	1980. N634H Hillenbrand Industries Inc 4/80, N634H Hillenbrand Industries Inc. Batesville, In.
35A-293	1980. N182K Koch Industries Inc 4/80, N182K Koch Industries Inc. Wichita, Ks.
35A-294	1980. N745E Eaton Corp 4/80, N745E Eaton Corp. Salt Lake City, Ut.
35A-295	1980. PT-LAA Cimento Nassau/Lider Nordeste Taxi 11/80, Taxi Aereo Weston 7/85, PT-LAA Soc. Taxi Aereo Weston Ltda. Recife.
35A-296	1980. N296BS Gemini Avn Inc 5/80, Berlin Regional 2/88, Aval Inc 3/88, XA-LML Servicios Aereo Corporativos SA 1/89, XA-LML Servicios Aereos Corporativos S.A. Mexico City.
35A-297	1980. N746E Eaton Corp 5/80, N746E Eaton Corp. Milwaukee, Wi.
35A-298	1980. I-FLYC Eurofly Service del 6 May 80, I-FLYC Eurofly Service S.p.a. Turin/Olivetti Leasing, Turin
35A-299	1980. N244FC Fru Con Corp 7/80, Ammest Services Inc 10/82, Air Support Services Corp 11/84, PT-LGS Lider/State Government of Minas Gerais 23 Jun 85, PT-LGS Lider/Governo do Estado Minas Gerais, Belo Horizonte.
35A-300	1980. N365N Nielson Ents Inc 5/80, FNB-Boston 1/85, Santa Barbara Jet Charter 4/85, ATC Air Inc 10/87, N365N ATC Air Inc. Lincoln, Ne.
35A-301	1980. N301TP Thomas Petroleum Products Inc 6/80, N999RB Reading & Bates Corp 2/81, ATC/Ray Henderson-Fl 11/85, N102ST 10/86, N102BT Gantt Avn 3/88, Executive Express 8/88, Eagle Aviation 5/89, Valero Management Co 9/89, N190VE 2/90, N190VE Valero Management Co. San Antonio, Tx.
35A-302	1980. N717DS ALCOA 7/80, N780A 3/83, N780A to 8084, N78QA EJA 8/87, Sterling Inc 3/88, N41ST 5/88, Executive Aviation Inc 3/90, N631CW 6/90, LAICO Inc 7/90, N51LC rsvd 10 Aug 90,N51LC LAICO Inc/Corporate Wings, Cleveland, Oh.
35A-303	1980. N771A ALCOA 6/80, ALCOA Alumnio SA 8/86, PT-LLS 2/88, Cx USA 4/89,PT-LLS Lider/ALCOA Aluminio S.A.
35A-304	1980. N464HA Holiday Inns Inc 10/80, Jack Prewitt & Assoc 10/85, N112PG 1/86, Hillenbrand Investment Advisors 4/87, N534H 12/87, N534H Hillenbrand Investment Advisors, Wilmington, De.
35A-305	1980. N3VG V A Deverian-Id 6/80, Flight International Inc 7/89, N3VG Flight International Inc. Jacksonville, Fl.
35A-306	1980. N926GL GLC /80, LLM Aircraft Co 2/81, N66LM 6/81, Lincoln Aircraft Co 2/85,MCorp Management-Dallas 4/85, N601MC 6/86, L&N Equities-Dallas 1/87, N77LN 5/87, Lomas Bankers Management Corp 7/89, First USA Management Inc 12/89, N111US 2/90, N111US First USA Management Inc. Dallas, Tx.
35A-307	1980. N120MB Milton Bradley Co 6/80, (N119HB) rsvd 23 Sep 85, Milton Bradley Co. East Longmeadow, RI.
35A-308	1980. N99MJ MJI 3/80, N747GM Glen Martin/Laredo NB 6/80, (N7LA) rsvd 27 Jun 81,Aero Center Inc/Laredo NB 7/81, N747GM Aero Center Inc. Laredo, Tx.
35A-309	1980. HB-VGT Skyjet AG-Zurich 6/80, OE-GAR Jet-Air Bedarfsluft Gmbh-Graz 11/84, N8216Z Conaero Inc 1/89, Flight International Sales 2/89, MNC Financial-Baltimore 5/89, N100MN 10/89, JCJ Wings Corp 4/90, D-CHPD Peter Dreidoppel 6/90, D-CHPD Peter Dreidoppel/Air Traffic GmbH. Dusseldorf.
35A-310	1980. N97JL System Integrators 9/80,Delaware Airjet/Hamilton Bros 11/81, N13HB 3/82, (N13HQ) McDonnell-Douglas Corp 8/82, N8280 1/83, N8280 McDonnell-Douglas Corp. St. Louis, Mo.
35A-311	1980. D-CDHS Bochumer Mineralol GmbH 6/80, Aero Dienst GmbH 7/82, N723US U S Aircraft Sales Inc 9/83, Shelby Financial Corp 11/83, N35BG Bruce Gillis-Ca 11/85, Flightcraft Corp 10/87, OE-GPN Alpenair GmbH del 14 May 89, OE-GPN Alpenair GmbH. Vienna.
35A-312	1980. LV-PHX /80, LV-OFV Estab Modelo Terrabusi SACI /80, LV-OFV Estab. Modelo Terrabusi SACI, Buenos Aires.
35A-313	1980. N39413 GLC /80, (F-GCLT) Air Affaires-Le Bourget /80, TR-LZI Air Affaires-Gabon 9/80, TR-LZI Ste Crossair, Zurich/Air Affaires, Libreville.
35A-314	1980. N35AK Fort Howard Paper Co 7/80, Griffith Management Inc 2/86,(N118GM) Imperial Air Travel rsvd 19 Dec 88, Paul Sutton Aircraft Sales to World Jet Inc 12/90, World Jet inc. Fort Lauderdale, Fl.

c/n	
35A-315	1980. N927GL GLC 4/80, N662AA Central States Investment/Adams Energy 7/80, FNB-Tulsa 3/85, D-CCAA German Red Cross-Stuttgart 3/85, D-CCAA Deutsche Rettungsflugwacht, Stuttgart.
35A-316	1980. N39398 GLC /80, N1503 Continental Group 8/80, CGI Mnagement Corp 10/84, MJI 12/84, N1507 1/85, Atlas Hotels Inc 5/85, N35AH 11/85, N35AH Atlas Hotels Inc. San Diego, Ca.
35A-317	1980. N10871 GLC /80, SE-DEM Joint Trawlers 8/80, Basair AB 2/82, Interair AB /89, SE-DEM Wilh Becker AB/Interair AB. Malmo-Sturup.
35A-318	1980. N444WB Bauer Development Co 8/80, Macomb Aviation Associates 7/83,N108CF 8/83, Eagle Jet Inc 7/87, N103CF Eagle Jet Inc. Allegheny County Airport, Pa.
35A-319	1980. T-23 Argentine Air Force 10/80, T-23 Grupo 1 de Aerofotografico, II Brigada Aerea, Parana.
35A-320	1980. N905LC Air Treks Inc 8/80, N905LD MJI Inc 12/83, FSL Inc 4/84, N35FS 7/84, Lyle B McGinnis Jr-WV 10/85, N320M 7/86, Huntrip Inc 4/89, Chesterfield Aircraft Co 11/89, N320M Chesterfield Aircraft Co. Chesterfield, Mo.
35A-321	1980. N14TX Fidelity Union Life Insurance Co 9/80, (N19LM) 5/83, N77LP 11/83, Lincoln Aircraft Company Inc 10/87, Jet East Inc 7/90, N77LP Jet East Inc. Dallas, Tx.
35A-322	1980. N305SC Sigmor Corp 8/80, Jetstream Corp via J Prewitt 4/85, Jetstream Transportation Corp 3/90, N305SC Jetstream Transportation Corp. Wilmington, NC.
35A-323	1980. N735A ALCOA 8/80, EJA 8/87, Eagle Aviation Inc 1/88, National Collegiate Athletic Assoc 7/88,N735A National Collegiate Athletic Assoc. Mission, Ks.
35A-324	1980. G-JJSG John Jefferson Smurfit Group 8/80, Container Corp-USA 7/87, G-JJSG John Jefferson Smurfit Group, St Louis, Mo-USA.
35A-325	1980. D-CARO M Roth/Aero Dienst GmbH/RZV GmbH 8/80, I-FFLY Soc Frifly 23 Feb 88, I-FFLY Soc. Frifly, Ronchi dei Legionari.
35A-326	1980. PT-LAS Lider Taxi Aereo 8/80, Constructora Cowan SA 7/85, PT-LAS Constructora Cowan S.A. Belo Horizonte.
35A-327	1980. N3797N GLC /80, United Telecom 9/80, N135UT Sharon Aviation 2/81, GLC 4/84, Crane Homes Inc 6/84, Barbara Fasken-Ca 8/86, N327F 9/88, N327F Barbara Fasken, Oakland, Ca.
35A-328	1980. N3807G GLC /80, N1502 Continental Group Inc 10/80, Greenwich Aviation Co 8/82, N35NY World Jet Charter 11/82, The Continental Group Inc 10/83, N35NX 3/84, Amerada Hess Corp 6/85, N35NX Amerada Hess Corp. Wilmington, De.
35A-329	1980. N39412 GLC /80, N53DM Del Monte Banana Co 2/81, Park Companies-Cleveland 5/86, N261PC 7/87, N261PC Park Companies, Cleveland, Oh.
35A-330	1980. N930GL Airplane Svcs 10/80, Africair/Boscovic-Kenya 11/80, O Hara & Kendall Avn 11/85, Air Pacific NC Inc-Miami 2/86, U S Jet Sales 8/89, stolen fm Florida but returned shortly after Panama invasion with bullet holes 12/89, Performance Aircraft Co 9/90,N930GL Performance Aircraft Co. FLE.(Noriega's aircraft - status ?)
35A-331	1980. N10870 GLC /80, HB-VGU John von Neumann-Geneva 9/80, I-EJIB Soc Executive Jet Italiana SRL 3 Jan 87, I-EJIB Soc. Executive Jet Italiana SRL. Milan.
35A-332	1980. N600LN Lincoln National Corp 10/80, Lincoln National Life Insurance Co 2/84, N600LN Lincoln National Life Insurance Co. Fort Wayne, In.
35A-333	1980. T-24 Argentine Air Force 12/80, T-24 W/O W/o 7 Jun 82, Pebble Island, Falklands, South Atlantic. 07/JUN/82
35A-334	1980. N2815 Texas Eastern Transmission 10/80, GLC 1/84, Rainier NB 4/84, N350RB 8/84, N334SP SecPac Corp 10/88, Rainier Companies Inc 5/90, N334SP Rainier Companies Inc. Seattle, Wa.
35A-335	1981. N25MJ MJI 10/80, N155TD SAJ Inc 12/80, Hal Dickson-Tx 11/84, Dulles Equities 8/86, N8YY 9/86, N15Y 2/88, N335DJ Duncan Aviation Inc-Ne 5/88, Northeast Jet Co 6/88, N335NE 8/88, Executive Express Inc 10/88, N335EE 5/89, Vested Flight Inc 7/89, Cardal Inc 6/90, N335EE Cardal Inc. Dublin, Oh.
35A-336	1980. HB-VGW FFA Leasing Altenrhein AG/Repair AG 9/80, N590J Combs Gates Denver Inc 5/81, Intravia Inc 8/81, N166RM 11/81, Riverside Inc 7/84, FSB-Ut 1/85, N782JR James River Corp. Richmond, Va.
35A-337	1980. N80ED C E Miller Corp 1/81, R E Job Cement Contractor Inc 6/81, N337WC 8/82, Talon Inc 11/85, N710AT 1/86, N710AT Talon Inc. Roseville, Mi.
35A-338	1980. N1473B GLC /80, RP-C7272 Learjet Philippine Inc 9/80, N610GE Odin Corp 1/81,RP-C610 United Coconut Planters Bank 7/84, RP-C610 Odin Corp/United Coconut Planters Bank, Manila.
35A-339	1980. N24JK MDFC 11/80, N24CK 8/85, GLC 10/85, N15CC Hudson International Inc 12/86, N Central Aviation Inc 4/88, N15CC to 465-42, N1500 5/88, Action Trading Corp 7/88, Shepherd Inc 1/90, PT-LZP Empresa Brasileira Taxi 2/90, Aerotaxi Pampulha /90, PT-LZP Aerotaxi Pampulha, Belo Horizonte.
35A-340	1980. N11AM International Association of Machinists 11/80,N11AM International Association of Machinists, Washington, DC.
35A-341	1980. N3802G GLC /80, D-CARE Aero Dienst GmbH 11/80,XA-HOS Aerolineas Ejecutivas 6/81, XA-HOS Aerolineas Ejecutivas SA. Mexico City.
35A-342	1980. N1088D GLC /80, N37931 9/80,VH-SDN Sydney Doctors Nominees 11/80, Hancock Prospecting 7/85, VH-LGH 8/85, Australian Jet Charter /85,Lloyd Avn Jet Charter /89, N678S AMR Combs Florida Inc 11/90, N678S AMR Combs Florida Inc. Fort Lauderdale, Fl.
35A-343	1980. N135MB Oregon MB-35 Corp 12/80, GLC 1/85, N80BT Northrop Corp 5/85, N80BT Northrop Corp. Los Angeles, Ca.

c/n	
35A-344	1980. N40149 GLC /80, YV-327CP Officina Central Asesoria y Ayuda Tencia CA 10/80, YV-327CP Oficina Central Asesoria y Ayuda Tencia C.A. Caracas.
35A-345	1980. N3818G GLC /80, N1ORE Reliance Electric Co 12/80, VH-EMP ESSO Australia Ltd 9/83, VH-EMP ESSO Australia Ltd. Sydney.
35A-346	1980. N3803G GLC /80, C-GMGA Sefel & Assoc 2/81, Jim Pattison Industries-Vancouver 10/84, N35AJ Willhead Aviation Inc 11/87, N35AJ to 35A-626, I-DLON Soc NAUTA SRL 5 Feb 88, I-DLON Soc. Nauta SRL. Venezia.
35A-347	1980. OE-GNP Air Charter Austria 11/80, Viennair Luftfahrt Gmbh 6/81, N85SV Silicon Valley Express Inc 10/85, N85SV Silicon Valley Express Inc. San Jose, Ca.
35A-348	1980. (N17ND) GLC /80, N3798B Blocker Energy Corp 1/81, N600BE 11/81, N500MJ 4/83, Thomas Lee 10/84, N35TL 12/84, Cameron-Henkind Corp 3/87, N35DL Panoramic Flight Service 12/87, N35DL Panoramic Flight Svc/Cameron-Henkind Corp. Scarsdale, NY.
35A-349	1980. N272T Sorenson Development Inc 11/80, Gantt Aviation Inc 1/90, The Flying Ws Inc 3/90, N272T The Flying Ws Inc. Houston, Tx.
35A-350	1980. (N88NE) /80, N35WB NESCO 10/80, Stoltz Wagner & Brown 3/81, Wagner & Brown 10/89, N35WB Wagner & Brown, Midland, Tx.
35A-351	1980. N500RP Penske Jet Inc 1/81, N500RP to 55-053, N500DD Detroit Diesel 1/88, Uno Leasing Corp 12/90, N500DD Uno Leasing Corp. Joliet, Il.
35A-352	1980. YV-326CP Servicios Aero Facility 1/81, N30GD GLC 8/83,Chathree Investors/Chase National Inc 10/83, N600G 9/85, N71A Aeromet Inc rsvd 23 Jul 90, N71A Aeromet Inc. Tulsa, Ok.
35A-353	1980. N3819G GLC /80, C-GDJH Canada Learjet Ltd 12/80, Canada Jet Charters Ltd 9 Aug 85, C-GDJH Canada Jet Charters Ltd. Vancouver.
35A-354	1980. N1450B GLC /80, D-CART Bavaria Flug KG 23 Dec 80, D-CART Bavaria Flug KG. Munich.
35A-355	1980. N1468B GLC /80, LV-PJZ /80, LV-ONN Dahm Automotores S.A.C.I.I.F 12/80, LV-ONN Dahm Automotores S.A.C.I.I.F. Buenos Aires.
35A-356	1980. N54YR Phifer Wire Products Inc 2/81, N54YR to F50-158, N54YP 12/85, Prestige Jet/The Coronado Co 1/86, N800WJ Prestige Jet 4/86, Coronado Co Inc 8/86, Jet East Inc 8/87, PT-LUG LUG Taxi Aereo Ltda 11/88, PT-LUG LUG Taxi Aereo Ltda. Maceio.
35A-357	1980. N3797S GLC /80, N1001L Triton Oil & Gas Corp 1/81, N Central Aviation Inc 4/83, Jet East 6/88, Specialised Aircraft Services 11/88, (N289GA) rsvd 19 Dec 88, (N100L) rsvd 21 Aug 89, ZS-MGK 9/89,ZS-MGK
35A-358	1980. N524HC Harbert Construction 12/80, Harbert Intl Inc 9/81, N524HC Harbert International Inc. Birmingham, Al.
35A-359	1980. (N127RM) GLC /80, HB-VHB Glorenade Anstalt-Vaduz 5/81, N136JP GLC 6/87, Dape Corp 7/87, James Petropoulos 2/88, N136JP James Petropoulos/Dape Corp. Columbus, Oh.
35A-360	1980. N185FP Federal Paper Board Co 12/80, Arthur Goldberg-NYC 6/81, SP Statebank Leasing/Miles Laboratories 4/87, N1129M 6/87, N1129M Miles Laboratories/SP Statebank Leasing, San Francisco, Ca.
35A-361	1980. N924GL GLC 12/80, PT-LBS Taxi Aereo Lider Ltda /81,PT-FAT Banco Central Brasil 10/81, PT-FAT Banco Central do Brasil S.A. Brasilia.
35A-362	1980. N3794M GLC 12/80, REC Aircraft Inc Trustee-NYC 2/81, N888MV 8/81, Duncan-Ne 10/87, Federal Data Corp 11/87, Alabama River Pulp Co 6/88, N399KL 9/88, N399KL Alabama River Pulp Co. Perdue Hill, Al.
35A-363	1981. N52MJ MJI 11/81, Mataagordo Drilling/J Imparato 8/81, Johnson Controls Inc 9/87, N183JC 10/83, N183JC Johnson Controls Inc. Milwaukee, Wi.
35A-364	1981. N3794Z Howard Hughes 4/81, (N65TA) TigerAir /81, N981TH 10/82, Duncan-Ne 8/87, N950CS 9/87, Executive Flights Inc 10/87,Duncan-Ne 1/88, BASF 3/88, N490BC 11/88, N490BC BASF Corp. Williamsburg, Va.
35A-365	1981. G-ZONE Jointair Ltd 2/81, (N4564S) /83, Yewlands Executive Transports Ltd 12/83, G-ZIPS RMC Group 5/84, Rialto Aviation (Hertford) Ltd /84, G-SEBE Siebe PLC 9/85, G-CJET Manx Helicopters 7/87, Interflight (CI) Ltd 12/87, G-CJET Interflight (CI) Ltd. Gatwick.
35A-366	1981. N411LC Calabras of NC Inc 3/81, GLC 10/83, Alltel Corp 3/84, N49AT 1/85, Jetcraft Corp 3/89, Alpha Avn Inc 4/89, N49AT 1/85, Jetcraft Corp 3/89, Alpha Aviation Inc 4/89, (N94AA) rsvd 2 Oct 89, N119CP Florence Wings Inc 4/90, N119CP Florence Wings Inc. Houston, Tx.
35A-367	1981. N714S Prufunding Inc 3/81, General Telephone Co of SW 8/82, N714S General Telephone Co of Southwest, San Angelo, Tx.
35A-368	1981. N35FM First Mississippi Corp 4/81, Combs Gates 11/87, SE-DHE T Johansson/Transwede-Stockholm 2/88, Cx SE- 8/89, N368BG Bruce Gillis/MPH Inc 8/89, Eastern Executive Leasing Inc 12/89, N368BG Eastern Executive Leasing Inc. High Point, NC.
35A-369	1981. VR-17 Argentine Air Force 5/81, VR-17 Escuadron Verificacion Radio Ayudos, Moron.
35A-370	1981. HB-VGY Transair SA 3/81, Sonco Hotel /81, Sonco/Alair AG 5/82,N11MY Marshall R Young Oil Co 10/83, N1MY 9/85, Guaranty Service Corp 10/86, (N56PR) rsvd 1 Dec 86,VR-BKB Galen Ltd 10 Aug 87, N8216Q Conaero Inc 2/89, R J Gallaher Co 10/89, N8216Q R J Gallaher Co. Houston, Tx.
35A-371	1981. LV-P.. /81, LV-ALF Cia Loma Negra SA 6/81, LV-ALF Cia Loma Negra S.A.
35A-372	1981. HB-VGX Transair SA 3/81, Zakair S.A-Fribourg 7/81, N372AS Airsupport Services Corp 8/86, PT-LJK Lider Taxi Aereo 1/87, PT-LJK Lider Taxi Aereo S.A. Belo Horizonte.
35A-373	1981. SE-DER Joint Trawlers 5/81, XA-BRE Aerolineas Ejecutivas SA /81, XA-RUY 4/90, XA-RUY Aerolineas Ejecutivas SA. Mexico City.
35A-374	1981. HZ-106 RSAF 8/81, HZ-106 Royal Saudi Air Force, Riyadh.

35A-375 1981. HZ-107 RSAF 5/81, HZ-107 Royal Saudi Air Force, Riyadh.
35A-376 1981. N458JA ERA Helicopters /81, Ryan Aviation 5/81,K Services Inc 6/81, N77FK 11/81, Finevest Services Leasing Corp 6/84, N33WB 7/84, Ultrajets Inc 1/90,National Guardian Security Services 2/90, N33WB National Guardian Security Services, Greenwich, Ct.
35A-377 1981. (N711EV) GLC /81, N933GL 5/81, Wm Fuller-Tx 6/81, N1OWF 10/81, N18WE Natl Aircraft Sales 10/89, Bandag Inc 12/89, N18WE Bandag Inc. Muscatine, Ia.
35A-378 1981. T-500/CX-BOI TAMU-Transporte Aereo Militar Uruguayo /81, N354ME Duncan-Ne 11/88, Bean Ball Co 11/88, N354ME Bean Ball Co. Seattle, Wa.
35A-379 1981. N23VG Deverian/F B N Ltd 9/81, Flight International 7/89, N23VG Flight International Inc. Jacksonville, Fl.
35A-380 1981. N82JL James Lennane-Or 6/81, Boise Cascade Corp 12/84, N291BX 1/85, N291BC 4/85, N281BC 7/89, Jet East Inc 5/90, N281BC Jet East Inc. Dallas, Tx.
35A-381 1981. D-CORA MEXPO Flugzeug/P Malinowski 5/81, N65DH Dee Howard Sales 2/82,CMI Corp 5/82, GECC-Oak Brook 7/82, (N40TM) rsvd 24 Sep 85, N300CM 6/86, Koch Industries Inc 10/88, N335K 7/89, N335K Koch Industries Inc. Wichita, Ks.
35A-382 1981. N382BL BLC Corp 5/81, Peter Bedford-Or 1/86, N382BP 9/86, OE-GAF Alpenair GmbH 11/87, Aerzteflugambulanz 12/89, OE-GAF Aerzteflugambulanz GmbH. Vienna.
35A-383 1981. N66FE MJI 3/81, A J Perenchio 6/81, PLY Aircraft Co 7/82, Tandem Aircraft Co 1/84, Clay Lacy Aviation Inc 7/90, N66FE Clay Lacy Aviation Inc. Van Nuys, Ca.
35A-384 1981. N37984 TigerAir Inc 5/81,Four Winds Air Inc 1/82,Jane Air Inc 4/85,Martin Avn 4/86, Robert Volk-Ca 9/86, Martin Avn Inc 2/88, Eagle Aviation Inc 11/88, Flynn Financial Corp 1/89, N811DF Willowbrook Air Assocs 10/89, N811DF Willowbrook Air Assocs. Willowbrook, Il.
35A-385 1981. N535MC Mississippi Chemical Corp 8/81, N350EF Duncan-Ne 3/88, Executive Flight Inc 5/88, N350EF Executive Flight Inc. Wenatchie, Wa.
35A-386 1981. N13VG V A Deverian 5/81, Flight International Inc 7/89, Corporate Aviation Services Inc 10/89, N13VG Corporate Aviation Services Inc. Tulsa, Ok.
35A-387 1981. D-CARL Aero Dienst GmbH 5/81, Industrieflug Ott GmbH 9/84, RZV/Aero Dienst GmbH /86, Aero Dienst GmbH 3/88, D-CARL Aero Dienst GmbH. Nuremberg.
35A-388 1981. N1929S Standard Brands Inc 6/81, NABISCO Inc 7/84, Cape Aviation Inc 8/87, N1929S Cape Aviation Inc. Wilmington, De.
35A-389 1981. N59MJ MJI 3/81, N377C Commonwealth Aviation Partners 8/81, N31WT Wm Theisen/Godfathers Pizza 9/86, Duncan-Ne 7/89, N31WE 9/89, VR-BLU Contship Ltd-UK 4/90, VR-BLU Contship Ltd. Stansted-UK.
35A-390 1981. N500PP Patrick Petroleum Co 6/81, Patrick Energy Corp 2/83, Potomac Leasing 11/83, N508P Dana Corp 1/84, Dana Commercial Credit Corp 10/87, CCD Air Ten Inc 1/90, N508P Dana Corp. Swanton, Oh.
35A-391 1981. N3793D GLC /81, N444BF Ben Forston Oil 12/81, R R Investments Inc 5/83, N813RR 7/83, Asplundh Tree Expert Co 8/85, N89AT 11/85, I-RYVA Soc ICIPA 10 Jan 90, I-RYVA Soc. ICIPA, Milan-Malpensa.
35A-392 1981. N931GL GLC 6/81, Edward J DeBartolo Corp 9/81, N1ED 1/82,N1ED Edward J DeBartolo Corp. Youngstown, Oh.
35A-393 1981. N932GL GLC 6/81, GECC-Dallas 12/81, N666RB 8/82, Quorum Sales 8/85, Academic Way Inc 9/85, N700WJ 11/85, Jet East Inc 8/87, PT-LOE Belair 8/88, SOTAN /89, PT-LOE SOTAN-Soc. de Taxi Aereo Nordeste Ltda. Rio Largo.
35A-394 1981. N1466K Knoell Bros Construction 3/81, Omni 4/81,J Imparato-Tx 9/81, N816JA 8/82, MJI 4/83, N94MJ 5/83, Koll Co 9/83, N60DK 4/84, Scott Bros Avn Corp 1/87,N60DK Scott Brothers Aviation Corp. Wilmington, De.
35A-395 1981. HB-VHD Transair (Suisse) SA 6/81, N3261L E D S Administration Corp 11/82, N30GL 12/82, Duncan-Ne 6/90, Tri City Beverages Inc 7/90, N246CM 9/90, N246CM Tri City Beverages Inc. Abilene, Tx.
35A-396 1981. N2000M Brunner & Lay Inc 7/81, N938GL 10/83, David L Paul 1/84, N5139W 7/84, cx USA 12/85, VR-CBU Skybird Holding/Bristow Helicopters-UK 12/85, N5FF Circle F Inc 9/88, Orea Corp 2/90, N74JL 4/90, N74JL Orea Corp. NYC.
35A-397 1981. N33PT Pel-Tex Oil Co 7/81,D-CLAN Private Jet Charter del 1 Feb 86, D-CLAN Private Jet Charter KG. Dusseldorf.
35A-398 1981. N3797A GLC /81, AGH/U S Financial Corp 7/81, N1AH 12/84, N1AH AGH Aviation/U.S. Financial Corp. Dallas, Tx.
35A-399 1981. N37965 GLC /81, PIP Capital Inc-Los Angeles 8/81, N540HP 7/82, Duncan-Ne 9/89,(N399DJ) rsvd 25 Sep 89,N399AZ International Airlines Holdings 12/89,N399AZ A Zanatti/International Airlines Holdings, Dover, De.
35A-400 1981. VH-CPH Stillwell Aviation /81, Consolidated Press Holdings 4/81,VH-CPQ 6/87, VH-TPR Australian Jet Charter /87, VH-TPR New World Properties/Australian Jet Charter, Sydney.
35A-401 1981. N66LJ C W Culpepper-OKC 7/81, Defense Research Inc 12/82, Carrier Research Inc 5/90, N66LJ Carrier Research Inc. Naples, Fl.
35A-402 1981. N3402 Vulcan Materials Co 8/81, GLC 8/84, N610JR Metallic Braden Building 3/85, N7AB American Buildings Co 5/85, N35BG Bruce S Gillis-LAX 4/90, Louise Gund-Ca 12/90,N35BG Louise L Gund, Berkeley, CA
35A-403 1981. N37966 GLC /81, Centel Communications Co 8/81, N312CT Central Telephone-Utilities 2/82, N312CF 8/88, JEM Investments Inc 2/89, KLW Aircraft Inc 6/90, N312CF KLW Aircraft Inc. Columbia, Mo.

c/n	
35A-404	1981. N500JS Jet South Inc 8/81, Bruce D Brooks 1/84, N404BB 7/84, N404BB Bruce Brooks, Sacramento, Ca.
35A-405	1981. N41MJ MJI 5/81, Dharma Aircraft Ltd 11/81, (N181GL) rsvd 20 Aug 83, Capair Corp 9/83, Alvin Siteman-Co 1/87, N35AS 1/87, ASCO Inc 10/87, Huntrip Inc 3/89, N35FS 12/89, Jetcap Inc 2/90,CVG Aviation Inc 4/90, N442DM rsvd 20 Jun 90, N442DM CVG Aviation Inc. Cincinnati, Oh.
35A-406	1981. N764G IBM Corp 9/81, GLC 4/84, N35Q Ed Wachs 7/84, Midwest Jet Lsg 1/86, GLC 2/88, I-KELM Soc Kelemata SpA 26 May 88, I-KELM Soc. Kelemata S.p.a. Turin.
35A-407	1981. N3793P GLC /81. Public Service Co-Albuquerque 8/81, N234DT 2/89, Thompson Machinery Commerce Co 10/90, N234DT Thompson Machinery Commerce Co. Lavergne, Tn.
35A-408	1981. (N33VG) GLC /81, N3798P 6/81, USAF titles 10/83, LV-POG Learjet Consult SA 10/85,LV-AIT DCA 11/85, LV-AIT Direccion de Aeronautica, Tierra del Fuego.
35A-409	1981. N50PD Cactus Ents Inc 9/81, Teachers Management-Investment 2/85, N858TM 9/85, Summit Jet Corp 12/87, N123LC 3/88, Bank South Corp-Atlanta 9/88, N888BS 10/88, N888BS Bank South Corp. Atlanta, Ga.
35A-410	1981. N12109 M H Whittier Corp 12/81, N1210M 2/83, Epson America Inc 4/83, GLC 9/87, Combs Gates 11/87, C-FHDM Hayes-Dana Inc 18 Jan 88, C-FHDM Hayes-Dana Inc. St. Catherines, Ont.
35A-411	1981. PT-LBY Confeccoes Guararapes SA /81, Lojas Riachuelo SA /89, PT-LBY Lojas Riachuelo SA.
35A-412	1981. N37980 GLC /81, Burnett Aviation Co Inc 9/81, N6666R 11/81, GLC 6/84, N412GL 7/84, Copperweld Corp 8/84, (N31LM) /84, N314C 5/85, Carter Wallace Inc 6/87, N314C Carter Wallace Inc. NYC.
35A-413	1981. HB-VHE Transair (Suisse) SA 7/81, N2637Z Global/Citicorp Leasing Intl-Geneva 2/82, F-GHAE Raymond Gillion 7/88, Air Entreprise 10 Nov 88, F-GHAE Air Entreprise, Troyes.
35A-414	1981. N39MW Jet East 4/81, (N135AB) rsvd 11 Feb 82, Robert Bass 3/82, PT-SMO Taxi Aereo Antares Ltda 1/89, PT-SMO Taxi Aereo Antares Ltda. Rio de Janeiro.
35A-415	1981. N125AX Amerex Corp 4/81, E D S Administration Corp 8/83, N19GL 2/84, Duncan-Ne 7/90, N415DJ 9/90, D-C... 10/90, D-C...
35A-416	1981. N306M Martin Marietta Corp 7/81, Duncan-Ne 8/86, N35MV Movats Inc 4/87, Duncan-Ne 8/88, GECC-Aurora-Co 10/88, N35MV Duncan Aviation Inc. Lincoln, Ne.
35A-417	1981. N934GL GLC 8/81, N117FJ First Jersey Securities Inc 2/82, (N117RJ) 2/85, D-CONO Gunther Eheim/Contactair Flugdienst KG 3/85, N97D Jack Prewitt 9/88, Doskovil Companies Inc 1/89, San Diego Jet Center Inc 7/90, Midwest Avn Corp 10/90, Sacramento Aviation Inc 11/90, N97D Sacramento Aviation Inc. Sacramento, Ca.
35A-418	1981. XA-KCM Kimberly Clark de Mexico /81, XA-KCM Kimberly Clark/Taxi Aereo de Mexico SA. Mexico City.
35A-419	1981. N935GL GLC /81, Xerox Credit Corp 2/82, Enterprise Leasing 5/82, N25EL 9/82, John McConnell-Oh 4/87, N53JM 8/87, Learjet Corp 1/89, State of Mississippi 6/89, N35SM 9/89, N35SM State of Mississippi, Jackson, Ms.
35A-420	1981. N35RT MJI 10/81, Townsend Engineering Co 2/82, rpo 35A-201, N35PT MJI 3/84, Kohler Co 11/84,N100KK 1/85, N100KK Kohler Co. Kohler, Wi.
35A-421	1981. N44MJ Aircraft Marketing Inc 11/81, MHC Inc 12/81, N85CA ConAgra Inc 5/82, N85CA ConAgra Inc. Omaha, Ne.
35A-422	1981. YV-434CP TAECA /81, P Lovera/Ingeniera Electronica /86, N86BL Bruce Leven-Wa 3/89, N86BL Bruce Leven, Redmond, Wa.
35A-423	1981. N369XL L J Ltd-Ft Lauderdale 3/82, Southeast Air Assoc Inc 1/87, N200TC 9/87, Gantt Aviation Inc 2/88, (N335GA) rsvd 21 Mar 88, D-CAVE AVIA Luftreederei GmbH 15 Jun 88,D-CAVE AVIA Luftreederei GmbH/Air Traffic GmbH. Dusseldorf.
35A-424	1981. N2844 Texas Eastern Transmission 10/81, GLC-Georgia Pacific 9/84, N508GP 11/84, N508GP Georgia Pacific Corp. Atlanta, Ga.
35A-425	1981. N111KK Kohler Co 11/81, N111KK Kohler Co. Kohler, Wi.
35A-426	1981. D-CARD Aero Dienst GmbH 9/81, N43W H L Brown Jr-Tx 1/84, N43W N43W 2/84, N43H Specialised Aircraft Services 5/89, Wingspan Inc 9/90, N43H Wingspan Inc. Wichita, Ks.
35A-427	1981. N1087Z GLC /81, VH-FOX Stillwell/Adelaide Holdings Ltd 25 Sep 81, Pacific Aviation /? Avtex Air Services P/L /88, Fleet Support P/L /90, VH-FOX Fleet Support P/L.
35A-428	1981. VH-ELC Utah Developemnt Corp 25 Sep 81, VH-ELC Utah Development Corp. Brisbane.
35A-429	1981. G-ZING CSE Aviation 11/81, G-GAYL Heron Aviation 9/82, AA Travel Services Ltd /84, AA Developmnets Ltd 3/87, Northern Executive Aviation Ltd 8/90, G-GAYL Northern Executive Aviation Ltd. Manchester.
35A-430	1981. N10870 GLC /81, LJ-1 Finnish Air Force 9/82, LJ-1 Finnish Air Force.
35A-431	1981. N1088A GLC /81, YV-433CP Finequipos-Caracas 'ElCorrecaminos-The Roadrunner' /81, N34FD Executive Avn Inc 1/89, N431CW 5/89, Akron Avn Inc 7/89, High Energy Inc 11/90,N431CW High Energy Inc. Camden, DE
35A-432	1981. F-GDCN Transair SA 10/81, Uni-Air 12/81, Avimart Intl 6/83, N4445Y Avimart-US 9/83, J E R Chilton 111-Tx 2/86, N330BC 5/86, N330BC J E R Chilton 111, Vail, Co.
35A-433	1981. D-CARG Aero Dienst GmbH 11/81, HB-VCZ ALG Aeroleasing SA 7/82,N26583 Amstar Financial Corp 1/83, N95AC 5/83, Summit Savings 1/85, Robert Callaway Corp 6/85, (N93RC) rsvd 1 Jul 85, Air Support Services Corp 4/86, PT-LIH Lider Taxi Aereo SA 16 Jul 86, PT-LIH Lider Taxi Aereo S.A. Belo Horizonte.
35A-434	1981. N4401 Red Lobster Inns 10/81, General Mills Restaurant Group 12/81,N4401 General Mills/Red Lobster Inns of America, Orlando, Fl.
35A-435	1981. N435N Norfolk & Western Railway 12/81, Norfolk Southern Corp 2/83, Airflite Inc 8/90,Cx USA 10/90, XC-... State Government of Chiapas.

c/n	
35A-436	1981. N37988 GLC 9/81, Airsupport Services Corp 1/82, PT-LDN Bradesco 8 Dec 82, PT-LDN Bradesco-Banco Brasileiro de Descontos S.A. Sao Paulo.
35A-437	1981. N3803G GLC /81, YV-432CP Transporte Transilac SA /81, YV-432CP Transporte Transilac S.A. Maracaibo
35A-438	1981. N17ND James Morse/Jetaway Air Service 1/82, (N8JA) rsvd 20 Dec 88, N600LL Lincoln National Life Insurance 1/89, N600LL Lincoln National Life Insurance Co. Fort Wayne, In.
35A-439	1981. N439ME Mammoth Exploration Co 12/81, HK-3121X Arbrom International Distributors 3/84, Astral Ltd 4/84, HK-3121 10/85, HK-3121 Astral Ltd. Bogota.
35A-440	1981. N101HK H J Kalikow Development Co 2/82, N101PK 3/84, Hytrol Conveyor Co 10/84, N903HC 2/85, N903HC Hydrol Conveyor Co. Jonesboro, Ar.
35A-441	1981. N551WC Westchase Corp 12/81, Combs Gates Denver 6/87, TC-MEK Cukurova Ithalat Ve Ihracat TAS, Istanbul 8/87, N441PC Learjet Corp 11/88, Allmetal Inc 1/89, N441PC Allmetal Inc. Itasca, Il.
35A-442	1981. N40149 GLC /81, N3799C 10/81, Jet Airways Inc 2/82, N35BK 11/82, Resource Savings Assoc 10/85, Northeast Jet Co 4/87, N442NE 8/87, Cx USA 9/88, N442NE W/o 26 Jul 88.
35A-443	1981. N135RJ Kanair Inc 3/82, Learjet Corp 3/90, N258G 258G Corp 4/90, N258G 258G Corp. Dover, De.
35A-444	1981. N3818G GLC /81, D-CARH Aero Dienst GmbH 12/81, N44695 MJI/Standard Register Co 10/83,N444MJ 11/83, Bancboston Leasing 3/85, N144WB Wright Brothers IAero Sales 5/85, N144WB Wright Bros/Standard Register Co. Vandalia, Oh.
35A-445	1981. N3802G GLC /81, HB-VHG Transair (Suisse) SA 2/82, Ajhoury Investment Svcs SA 5/83, Golden Jet Aviation 4/84, I-MOCO Soc LOCAT/EAS 22 Aug 87, I-MOCO E A S-Executive Aviation Services, Vicenza.
35A-446	1981. N37962 GLC 9/81, Toreson Industries Inc 11/83, XEBEC Inc 7/85, Jack Prewitt 6/87, A Senna/Cavalier Air Corp 8/87, N80AS 7/88, UCLA Medical Center 4/90, N80AS UCLA Medical Center, Los Angeles, Ca.
35A-447	1981. N127K Kamyr Inc 3/82, Industrial Investment Corp 9/88, N127K Industrial Investment Corp. Providence, RI.
35A-448	1981. N48MJ GLC /81, MJI 1/82, Jervis Webb Co 4/84, N48MJ Jervis Webb Co. Farmington Hills, Mi.
35A-449	1981. N37947 GLC /81, Levitz Furniture Co 2/82, N777LF 3/82, N449QS 11/87, RTS Aircraft Svcs 12/87,Gantt Avn 1/88, XA-GDO Guja SA 8/88, XA-GDO Guja SA. Mexico City.
35A-450	1981. N450KK EJA 12/81, K K Associates 2/82, N450KK K K Associates, Columbus, Oh.
35A-451	1982. N1462B GLC /82, LJ-2 Finnish Air Force 9/82, LJ-2 Finnish Air Force.
35A-452	1981. N25MJ MJI 2/82, Southwestern Public Service Co 7/82, N279SP 10/82, Bancboston Leasing Inc 6/89, N279SP Southwestern Public Service Co. Amarillo, Tx.
35A-453	1982. N124MC Air Charter Funding 7/82, Newport Aviation Inc 10/86, Jeld-Wen Inc 1/87, N802JW 7/89,N802JW Jeld-Wen Inc. Klamath Falls, Or.
35A-454	1981. N3794W GLC 11/81, Bindley Western Industries Inc 3/83, (N379BW) rsvd 8 Oct 83, Bindley Western Industries Inc. Charlotte, NC.
35A-455	1981. N3794U GLC 11/81, Miles Galin-NYC 3/83, N455NE 11/84, N988QC 12/88,Flight Services Group Inc 1/89, R D Scinto Aircraft Corp 7/89, N988QC R D Scinto Aircraft/Flight Services Group, Fairfield, Ct.
35A-456	1981. N711CD Condor 12/81, Denison Jet Sales 6/88, Duncan-Ne 9/88, Richards Group Inc 2/89, N711CD Richards Group Inc. Dallas, Tx.
35A-457	1981. N900P Pickands Mather & Co 3/82, rpo 25-049, Great Planes 1/86, N974JD Residence Inns Inc 3/86, Wichita Air Services Inc 2/88, N874JD 9/89, Superior Industries International 11/89, N113LB 7/90, N113LB Superior Industries International Inc. Van Nuys, Ca.
35A-458	1982. Mariner Equipment Inc 2/82, PBR Offshore Marine Corp 7/84, Avn Investors-Or 1/85, Key Financial Svcs 9/86, J Park 1/87, James Park-Mi 1/87, Fowler & Creech Investments 7/90, N276JS Fowler & Creech Investments, Jonesboro, Ar.
35A-459	1982. VH-MIE Mount Isa Mines 3/82, cx VH- 2 Jan 85, N306SP Opex Avn Inc 1/85, AeroSmith Penny 2/85, Brunner & Lay 9/85, N80BL 10/86, Sky Harbor Air Service Inc 8/90, Montford/Pitney Bowes Credit 9/90, N969MT 11/90, N969MT Montford of Colorado Inc. Greeley, Co.
35A-460	1982. XC-PGR Procurad General 3/82, DETENAL /85, XC-PGR Procurad General de la Republica, Mexico City.
35A-461	1982. N64CF CF Industries Inc 4/82, N64CF CF Industries Inc. Chicago, Il.
35A-462	1982. N8562W GLC /82, Richmor Aviation/Kamyr Inc 9/82, N147K 11/82, Business Jet Inc 9/88, N801K 10/88, N7117 11/88, N7117 Business Jet Inc. Riverside, Ct.
35A-463	1982. VH-ULT Stillwell/Trak Investment P/L 4 Mar 82, Fleet Support P/L /90, VH-ULT Fleet Support P/L.
35A-464	1982. N1DC Doyle Cotton Petroleum Corp 8/82, (N75PK) /?, Air Support Services Corp 2/86, PT-LHX Angra Taxi Aerea SA 6 Jan 86, PT-LHX Angra Taxi Aereo S.A. Porto Alegre.
35A-465	1982. N465NW Norfolk & Western Railway 5/82, Norfolk Southern Corp 2/83, N465NW Norfolk Southern Corp. Norfolk, Va.
35A-466	1982. VH-WFP Westfield Holdings 3/82, N39SA Suncoast Aviation Services Inc 10/84, Academic Way Inc 8/85, (N700WJ) rsvd 12 Sep 85, re-allocated to 35A-393 11 Oct 85, N600WJ 12/85,Blanco River Corp 6/87,Jet East 8/87, Gantt Avn 3/88, D-COCO Phoenix Air GmbH 6/88, DS Flugdienst KG 7/89, D-COCO DS Flugdienst KG. Nuremberg.
35A-467	1982. N3796Q GLC 2/82, HZ-MS1 Saudi Armed Forces Medical Services 4/82,HZ-MS1 Saudi Armed Forces Medical Services, Riyadh.
35A-468	1982. VH-ANI Australian National Industries 24 Mar 82, Cx VH- 7/89, N486LM Orion Aircraft Sales 7/89, OY-CCJ Alkair Flight Ops 9/89, OY-CCJ Alkair Flight Operations, Copenhagen. 'Skydreamer'

35A-469 1982. N660SA Safeway Stores Inc 10/82, AJS Leasing Co 5/87, N444TG 8/87, N444TG Adrian J Scribante=AJS Leasing Co. Laurel, Mt.
35A-470 1982. N3810G GLC /82, LJ-3 Finnish Air Force 9/82, LJ-3 Finnish Air Force.
35A-471 1982. VH-BQR Stillwell Avn/Pacific Aviation/Rivkin & Co-Sydney 3/82, N95AP Aero/Smith Penny 12/86, Great Western Leasing 5/87, Jet East Inc 10/88, Eagle Aviation Inc 6/89, Tarkenton Investments Inc 1/90, N95AP Tarkenton Investments Inc. Atlanta, Ga.
35A-472 1982. N448GC Westmoreland Coal Co 6/82, Mlease Corp-Dallas 9/85, N448WC 9/86, Chester County Avn Inc 6/89, N448WG 7/89, CBC Sales Inc 3/90, N448WG CBC Sales Inc. Savoy, Il.
35A-473 1982. N3796P GLC 2/82, West Shoreline Cable Corp/Omni 12/83, GLC 3/84, Airsupport Services Corp 8/84, PT-LBT Taxi Aereo Flamingo SA 17 Jul 85, PT-LFT Taxi Aereo Flamingo S.A. Sao Paulo.
35A-474 1982. N39413 GLC /82, N37975 Airsupport Services Corp 9/82, PT-LEB Lider Taxi Aereo Ltda 2/84,Taxi Aereo Weston 7/85, PT-LEB Soc. de Taxi Aereo Weston Ltda. Recife.
35A-475 1982. N10873 GLC /82, N3797K 4/82, Aircraft Facilities Ltd 8/82, 3D-ADC Lonrho-RSA 1/83, 3D-ADC Lonrho, Rand, Johannesburg, RSA.
35A-476 1982. N476VC Corporate Funding Inc 7/82, N476VC Corporate Funding Inc. Grand Rapids, Mi.
35A-477 1982. N3797B GLC /82, Curtiss Inc/Stanley Averch 3/83, N82GL 5/83, GFN Aviation Services 8/85, Mar Flite Ltd 3/89, Baron Leasing Inc Trustee 8/89, N80CD 4/90, N80CD Baron Leasing Inc Trustee, Charlotte, NC.
35A-478 1982. N3815G GLC /82, LV-TDF Province of Tierra del Fuego 9/82, LV-TDF W/O w/o 15 May 84. 15/MAY/84
35A-479 1982. N8565J GLC /82, William Thiesen-Gemini Aviation 3/83, N31WT 6/83, Sun Coast Avn Svcs Inc 7/84, N31WT to CL600 1073, N30SA 9/84, Airsupport Services Corp 12/85, PT-LHT Lider Taxi Aereo SA 6 Jun 86, PT-LHT Lider/Constructora Norberto Odebrecht,
35A-480 1982. N3819G GLC /82, (VH-ALH) Lang Hancock /82, N8563A GLC 9/82, Fort Howard Paper Co 4/84, N35CK 7/84, (N484) rsvd 3 Sep 87, AMR Aircraft Sales 9/89, David Kemenash 2/90, N39DK 4/90, N39DK David Kemenash, Milmay, NJ.
35A-481 1982. N6666K Burnett Aviation Co 8/82, N666KK GLC 1/85, Robin Investments Inc 2/85,N728MP 5/85, McMurrey Oil & Gas 6/85, N729HS High Sky Aviation 3/86, HK-3122X Astral Ltd-Bogota 4/86, HK-3122 /86, N729HS AMR Combs Marketing 4/89, Ballaman Aviation Inc 8/89, N27NR Nigel Mansell Racing-IOM 9/89, OO-LFV Abelag Aviation 7/90, OO-LFV Abelag Aviation, Brussels.
35A-482 1982. N482U Upali (USA) Inc 8/82, N482U W/O W/o 14 Feb 83. 14/FEB/83
35A-483 1982. N8562Y GLC /82, Big Three Industries Inc 6/83, N202BT 9/83, N202BT Big Three Industries Inc. Houston, Tx.
35A-484 1982. VR-18 Argentine Air Force 10/82, VR-18 Escuadron Verificacion Radio Ayudos, Moron.
35A-485 1982. N485S Kenneth Scholz Aviation Inc 3/83, N485S Kenneth Scholz Aviation Inc. Lubbock, Tx.
35A-486 1982. N821PC GECC-Dallas 9/82, N117EL 11/89, Pratt Air 7/90, Chrysler Corp 9/90, CIT Leasing Corp 11/90, N117EL Chrysler/CIT Leasing Corp. Park Ridge, Il.
35A-487 1982. N206FC Arlington Integrated Holding 8/82, Hartford-CT NB 10/82, N206EC 3/83, N206EC Connecticut National Bank, Hartford, Ct.
35A-488 1982. N8563G GLC /82, N848GL Thomas Worrel Jr 1/83, N3OW 4/83, N3OW Thomas Worrell Jr Newspapers, Charlottesville, Va.
35A-489 1982. N222BE Southland Cork/Chesapeake Leasing Co 10/82, N222BE Southland Cork/Cheaspeake Leasing Co. Norfolk, Va.
35A-490 1982. N64MP Mesa Petroleum Co 11/82, Boone T Pickens Jr 5/87,N64MP Boone T Pickens Jr/Mesa Petroleum Co. Amarillo, Tx.
35A-491 1982. N8563N GLC /82, N491HS 8/82, Columbia Savings & Loan/Liberty Svc Corp 12/83,N241AG Aerojet General Co 8/85, Fort Howard Paper Co 6/87, N485 11/87, I-AGEN Soc Eurojet Italia 23 Jan 89, I-AGEN Soc. Eurojet Italia, Milan.
35A-492 1982. N8566B GLC /82, R T Vanderbilt Co 12/83, Combs-Gates 10/86,Heitman Holdings Ltd 12/86, N35NP 9/87, N35NP Heitman Holdings Ltd. Dover, De.
35A-493 1983. N8564M GLC 2/83, Richard Snyder-NC 12/83, N482SG 2/84, N482SG Snyder Leasing Co. Wilmington, NC.
35A-494 1982. PT-LDM Lider Taxi Aereo SA 10/82, PT-LDM Lider Taxi Aereo S.A. Belo Horizonte.
35A-495 1983. N440MC McClane Co 2/83, N440MC McClane Company Inc. Temple, Tx.
35A-496 1983. N8564K GLC 5/83, Twigg Corp 3/84, N856RR 7/84, Southwire Corp 2/89, N496SW 1/90, N496SW Southwire Corp. Carrollton, Ga.
35A-497 1983. N8565N GLC 5/83, Regional Transportation Service 4/84, N5OPH Pace Setter Corp 6/84, N5OPH Pace Setter Corp. Omaha, Nb.
35A-498 1983. N8564P GLC 6/83, Equitable Life Leasing Corp 3/84, I-FLYH Eurofly Service Spa del 28 Jul 88,I-FLYH Eurofly Service S.p.a. Turin.
35A-499 1983. N8564S GLC 9/83, Dulaney Land & Cattle Co 1/85, N84AD 4/85, Air Support Services Corp 3/86, PT-LII Lider Taxi Aereo SA 16 Jul 86, PT-LII Lider Taxi Aereo S.A. Belo Horizonte.
35A-500 1983. N8566X GLC 12/83, Lincoln Aircraft Co 1/85, N66LN L & N Equities Inc 4/85, N66LN L & N Equities Inc. Dallas, Tx.
35A-501 1983. HB-VHR Jet Air Service AG 12/83, HB-VHR Jet Air Service AG. Zurich.
35A-502 1983. N8565X GLC 10/83, VIP Air Charter Ltd 2/84, Bretford Manufacturing Inc 4/89, N747CP 7/89, N747CP Bretford Manufacturing Inc. Schiller Park, Il.

c/n	Details
35A-503	1983. N8567A GLC 12/83, R L Evans-Tx 9/84, Jack Prewitt 11/86, HB-VII Fidinam Fudiciara SA 3/87, HB-VII Fidinam Fudiciara S.A. Lugano.
35A-504	1983. N8568B GLC 12/83, G-RAFF Graff Aviation Ltd 7/84, G-RAFF Graff Aviation Ltd. London.
35A-505	1983. N7259J 12/83, N505EE 3/84, NOS Corp 7/84, Commercial Plastics 4/88, N505EE Commercial Plastics Co. Mundelein, Il.
35A-506	1983. N317BG Kon Fara Co 12/83, Daniels Holdings Inc 8/88, N10BD 12/88, N10BD Daniels Holdings Inc. Denver, Co.
35A-507	1983. N35GJ GLC /83, Heinz Prechter 2/84, N35HP 3/84, N42HP 1/85, Aero Service Co 3/85, N42HP Aero Service Co. Southgate, Mi.
35A-508	1983. N741E Eaton Corp 1/84, N741E Eaton Corp. Cleveland, Oh.
35A-509	1984. N7263C GLC 6/84, Security Pacific Equipment Leasing 7/84, 40063 USAF, 1375 FTS, Scott AFB. Il.
35A-510	1984. N7263D GLC 6/84, Security Pacific Equipment Leasing 7/84, 40064 USAF, 1400 MAS, Det 4, Kirtland AFB. NM.
35A-511	1984. N7263E GLC 6/84, Security Pacific Equipment Leasing 7/84, 40065 USAF, 1375 FTS, Scott AFB. Il.
35A-512	1984. N7263F GLC 6/84, Security Pacific Equipment Leasing 7/84, 40066 USAF, 1375 FTS, Scott AFB. Il.
35A-513	1984. N7263H GLC 6/84, Security Pacific Equipment Leasing 7/84, 40067 USAF, 1401 MAS, Scott AFB. Il.
35A-514	1984. N7263K GLC 6/84, Security Pacific Equipment Leasing 7/84, 40068 USAF, 1401 MAS, Scott AFB. Il.
35A-515	1984. N7263L GLC 6/84, Security Pacific Equipment Leasing 7/84, 40069 USAF, 1401 MAS, Scott AFB. Il.
35A-516	1984. N7263N GLC 6/84, Security Pacific Equipment Leasing 7/84, 40070 USAF, 1401 MAS, Scott AFB. Il.
35A-517	1984. N7263R GLC 6/84, Security Pacific Equipment Leasing 7/84, 40071 USAF, 1401 MAS, Scott AFB. Il.
35A-518	1984. N7263X GLC 6/84, Security Pacific Equipment Leasing 7/84, 40072 USAF, 1401 MAS, Scott AFB. Il.
35A-519	1984. N400AD QRZX Leasing Co 8/84, 40073 USAF, 1402 MAS, Andrews AFB. Md.
35A-520	1984. N400AK QRZX Leasing Co 8/84, 40074 USAF, 1402 MAS, Andrews AFB. Md.
35A-521	1984. N400AN QRZX Leasing Co 8/84, 40075 USAF, 1402 MAS, Andrews AFB. Md.
35A-522	1984. N400AP QRZX Leasing Co 8/84, 40076 USAF, 1402 MAS, Andrews AFB. Md.
35A-523	1984. N400AQ QRZX Leasing Co 8/84, 40077 USAF, 1402 MAS, Andrews AFB. Md.
35A-524	1984. N400AS QRZX Leasing Co 8/84, 40078 USAF, 1402 MAS, Andrews AFB. Md.
35A-525	1984. N400AT QRZX Leasing Co 8/84, 40079 USAF, 1402 MAS, Andrews AFB. Md.
35A-526	1984. N400AU QRZX Leasing Co 8/84, 40080 USAF, 1401 MAS, Det 2, Wright-Patterson AFB. Oh.
35A-527	1984. N400AX QRZX Leasing Co 8/84, 40081 USAF, HQ USEUCOM, Stuttgart, West Germany.
35A-528	1984. N400AY QRZX Leasing Co 8/84, 40082 USAF, HQ USEUCOM, Stuttgart, West Germany.
35A-529	1984. N400AZ GLC 7/85, 40083 USAF, HQ USEUCOM, Stuttgart, West Germany.
35A-530	1984. N400BA GLC 7/85, 40084 USAF, 58 MAS, Ramstein AB. West Germany.
35A-531	1984. N400FY GLC 7/85, 40085 USAF, 58 MAS, Ramstein AB. West Germany.
35A-532	1984. N400BN GLC 7/85, 40086 USAF, 58 MAS, Ramstein AB. West Germany.
35A-533	1984. N400BQ Westinghouse Credit Corp 11/84, 40087 USAF, 1401 MAS, Det 1, Offutt AFB. Nb.
35A-534	1984. N400BU Westinghouse Credit Corp 11/84, 40088 USAF, 1401 MAS, Det 1, Offutt AFB. Nb.
35A-535	1984. N400BY Westinghouse Credit Corp 11/84, 40089 USAF, 1401 MAS, Det 1, Offutt AFB. Nb.
35A-536	1984. N400BZ Westinghouse Credit Corp 11/84, 40090 USAF, 1401 MAS, Det 1, Offutt AFB. Nb.
35A-537	1984. N400CD Westinghouse Credit Corp 11/84, 40091 USAF, 1401 MAS, Det 1, Offutt AFB. Nb.
35A-538	1985. N400CG GLC 7/85, 40092 USAF, 1401 MAS, Det 1, Offutt AFB. Nb.
35A-539	1985. N400CJ GLC 7/85, 40093 USAF, 1401 MAS, Det 1, Offutt AFB. Nb.
35A-540	1985. N400CK GLC 7/85, 40094 USAF, 1401 MAS, Det 1, Offutt AFB. Nb.
35A-541	1985. N400CQ GLC 7/85, 40095 USAF, 1401 MAS, Det 1, Offutt AFB. Nb.
35A-542	1985. N400CR GLC 7/85, 40096 USAF, 1401 MAS, Det 2, Wright-Patterson AFB. Oh.
35A-543	1985. N400CU GLC 7/85, 40097 USAF, 1401 MAS, Det 2, Wright-Patterson AFB. Oh.
35A-544	1985. N400CV GLC 7/85, 40098 USAF, 4950 TW/AFSC, Andrews AFB. Md. (Trout 98).
35A-545	1985. N400CX GLC 7/85, 40099 USAF, 1401 MAS, Det 2, Wright-Patterson AFB. Oh.
35A-546	1985. N400CY GLC 7/85, 40100 USAF, 1401 MAS, Det 2, Wright-Patterson AFB. Oh.
35A-547	1985. N400CZ GLC 7/85, 40101 USAF, 1403 MAS, Yokota AB. Japan.
35A-548	1985. N400DD GLC 7/85, 40102 USAF, 1403 MAS, Yokota AB. Japan.
35A-549	1985. N400DJ GLC 7/85, 40103 USAF, 1401 MAS, Det 4, Peterson AFB. Co.
35A-550	1985. N400DL GLC 7/85, 40104 USAF, 1401 MAS, Det 4, Peterson AFB. Co.
35A-551	1985. N400DN GLC 7/85, 40105 USAF, 1401 MAS, Det 4, Peterson AFB. Co.
35A-552	1985. N400DQ GLC 7/85, 40106 USAF, 1401 MAS, Det 4, Peterson AFB. Co.
35A-553	1985. N400DR GLC 7/85, 40107 USAF, 1401 MAS, Det 4, Peterson AFB. Co.
35A-554	1985. N400DU GLC 7/85, 40108 USAF, 1401 MAS, Det 3, Barksdale AFB. La.
35A-555	1985. N400DV GLC 7/85, 40109 USAF, 1401 MAS, Det 3, Barksdale AFB. La.
35A-556	1985. N400DX GLC 7/85, 40110 USAF, 1401 MAS, Det 3, Barksdale AFB. La.
35A-557	1985. N400DY GLC 7/85, 40111 USAF, 1401 MAS, Det 3, Barksdale AFB. La.
35A-558	1985. N400DZ GLC 7/85, 40112 USAF, 1401 MAS, Det 3, Barksdale AFB. La.
35A-559	1985. N400EC GLC 7/85, 40113 USAF, 1402 MAS, Det 1, Langley AFB. Va.
35A-560	1985. N400EE GLC 7/85, 40114 USAF, 1402 MAS, Det 1, Langley AFB. Va.
35A-561	1985. N400EF GLC 7/85, 40115 USAF, 1402 MAS, Det 1, Langley AFB. Va.

c/n	Details
35A-562	1985. N400EG GLC 7/85, 40116 USAF, 1402 MAS, Det 1, Langley AFB. Va.
35A-563	1985. N400EJ GLC 7/85, 40117 USAF, 1402 MAS, Det 1, Langley AFB. Va.
35A-564	1985. N400EK GLC 7/85, 40118 USAF, 1402 MAS, Det 2, Eglin AFB. Fl.
35A-565	1985. N400EL GLC 7/85, 40119 USAF, 1402 MAS, Det 2, Eglin AFB. Fl.
35A-566	1985. N400EM GLC 7/85, 40120 USAF, 1402 MAS, Eglin AFB. Fl.
35A-567	1985. N400EN GLC 7/85, 40121 W/O W/o 15 Jan 87. Alabama, USA. 15/JAN/87
35A-568	1985. N400EQ GLC 7/85, 40122 USAF, 1402 MAS, Det 3, Maxwell AFB. Al.
35A-569	1985. N400ER GLC 7/85, 40123 USAF, 1402 MAS, Det 3, Maxwell AFB. Al.
35A-570	1985. N400ES GLC 7/85, 40124 USAF, 1402 MAS, Maxwell AFB. Al.
35A-571	1985. N400ET GLC 7/85, 40125 USAF, 1402 MAS, Maxwell AFB. Al.
35A-572	1985. N400EU GLC 7/85, 40126 USAF, 1400 MAS, Norton AFB. Ca.
35A-573	1985. N400EV GLC 7/85, 40127 USAF, 1400 MAS, Norton AFB. Ca.
35A-574	1985. N400EX GLC 7/85, 40128 USAF, 1400 MAS, Norton AFB. Ca.
35A-575	1985. N400EY GLC 7/85, 40129 USAF, 1400 MAS, Norton AFB. Ca.
35A-576	1985. N400EZ GLC 7/85, 40130 USAF, 1400 MAS, Det 1, McClellan AFB. Ca.
35A-577	1985. N400FE GLC 7/85, 40131 USAF, 1400 MAS, Det 1, McClellan AFB. Ca.
35A-578	1985. N400FG GLC 7/85, 40132 USAF, 1400 MAS, Det 1, McClellan AFB. Ca.
35A-579	1985. N400FH GLC 7/85, 40133 USAF, 1400 MAS, Det 1, McClellan AFB. Ca.
35A-580	1985. N400FK GLC 7/85, 40134 USAF, 1400 MAS, Det 2, Randolph AFB. Tx.
35A-581	1985. N400FM GLC 7/85, 40135 USAF, 1400 MAS, Det 2, Randolph AFB. Tx.
35A-582	1985. N400FN GLC 7/85, 40136 USAF, 1400 MAS, Det 2, Randolph AFB. Tx.
35A-583	1985. N400FP GLC 7/85, 40137 USAF, 1400 MAS, Det 2, Randolph AFB. Tx.
35A-584	1985. N400FQ GLC 7/85, 40138 USAF, 1400 MAS, Det 2, Randolph AFB. Tx.
35A-585	1985. N400FR GLC 7/85, 40139 USAF, 1400 MAS, Det 4, Kirtland AFB. NM.
35A-586	1985. N400FT GLC 7/85, 40140 USAF, 1400 MAS, Det 4, Kirtland AFB. NM.
35A-587	1985. N400FU GLC 7/85, 40141 USAF, 1400 MAS, Det 4, Kirtland AFB. NM.
35A-588	1985. N400FV GLC 7/85, 40142 USAF,
35A-589	1984. N8567K GLC 7/84, U S Aircraft Sales Inc 11/84, PT-GAP Taxi Aereo Grendene Ltda 10 Jan 85, PT-GAP Taxi Aereo Grendene Ltda. Porto Alegre.
35A-590	1984. N35GA MNC Leasing Corp 1/85, K T Developments One Inc 3/90, N35KT 7/90, N35KT K T Developments One Inc. Biggin Hill-UK.
35A-591	1984. N72626 GLC 3/85, Electrolux/PHH-CFC Leasing Inc 9/85, N500EX 10/85, Duncan-Ne 6/87,Ansonia Air Inc 12/87, Sky Harbor Air Service /90, Pitney Bowes Credit 12/90, N500EX ConAgra Inc. Omaha, Ne.
35A-592	1984. N925GL GLC 6/85, Sheller Globe Corp 1/86, Sage Energy Co 4/87, N45KK 5/87, K K Amini 1/90, N45KK K K Amini, San Antonio, Tx.
35A-593	1984. N32B Black & Decker (US) Inc 12/84, I-FLYG Eurofly Service Spa 8/87, I-FLYG Eurofly Service S.p.a. Turin.
35A-594	1984. N72596 GLC /84, N7007V Mimosa Film Corp 22 Mar 85, N7007V Mimosa Film Corp. Eugene, Or.
35A-595	1984. N85PM Fidelity & Guarantee Life Insurance Co 1/85, Del Mar Co 10/87, Green Bay Packaging Inc 2/88, N85PM Green Bay Packaging Inc. Green Bay, Wi.
35A-596	1985. N72612 GLC /85, N62WM Waste Management Inc 24 Mar 86, N62WM Waste Management Inc. Wilmington, De.
35A-597	1985. N8567R GLC /85, Electronic Data Systems 2/85, N54GL 6/85, N54GL Electronic Data Systems, Bethesda, Md.
35A-598	1985. N8567T GLC /85, Airsupport Services Corp 2/85, PT-LGW Lider Taxi Aereo SA 5 Jun 85, PT-LGW Lider Taxi Aereo S.A. Belo Horizonte.
35A-599	1985. N40144 GLC /85, N58GL Electronic Data Systems 7 May 85, Hill Acquiring Corp 3/87, Hill Air Corp 6/90, N58GL Hill Air Corp. Dallas, Tx.
35A-600	1985. N823CA ConAgra Inc 1/85, N823CA ConAgra Inc. Omaha, Nb.
35A-601	1985. HY-986 Government of China /86, HY-986 Poly Technologies Inc.
35A-602	1985. HY-987 Government of China /86, HY-987 Poly Technologies Inc.
35A-603	1985. HY-988 Government of China /86, HY-988 Poly Technologies Inc.
35A-604	1985. N59GL GLC /85, Electronic Data Systems 17 Dec 85, N59GL Electronic Data Systems, Heathrow-UK.
35A-605	1985. N185HA Health America Inc 10/85, Air SRV 8/88, ASCO Inc 3/89, N35AS 8/90, N35AS ASCO Inc. Englewood, Co.
35A-606	1985. N1735J GLC 10/85, Valley National Corp 12/85, GLC 3/88, N35PD Lear Flite Inc 6/88,N35PD Lear Flite Inc. Portland, Or.
35A-607	1986. N72614 GLC 1/86, Airsupport Services Corp 12 Jun 86, PT-LIJ Lider Taxi Aereo 18 Jul 86, N68MJ Airsupport Services Corp 8/88, Jervis B Webb Co 10/88, N68MJ Jervis B Webb Co. Farmington Hills, Mi.
35A-608	1985. N8567Z GLC /85, Michigan Sugar Co 12/85, N111SF 3/87, N111SF Michigan Sugar Co. Saginaw, Mi.
35A-609	1985. N36NW GLC /85, Mid Ohio Aircraft Inc /86, N788QC 4/89, N788QC Mid Ohio Aircraft Inc. Columbus, Oh.
35A-610	1986. N101AR AMCA/Aircraft Services Corp 8/86, N101AR AMCA/Aircraft Services Corp. Dunwoody, Ga.
35A-611	1986. N622WG Mountain Aviation Inc 5/86, Zarego Inc 2/88, N622WG Zarego Inc. Mesquite, NM.
35A-612	1986. N8568D GLC /86, Motor Racing Development Corp-UK 2 May 86, N2FU 8/86, N501TW Tom Walkinshaw Racing Inc 11/89, TWR Inc 10/90, N501TW Tom Walkinshaw Racing Inc. Oxford-UK.

c/n	Year	Details
35A-613	1987.	N4289X GLC /87, FAB6000 Brazilian Air Force 8/87, FAB6000 FAB=Forca Aerea Brasileira.
35A-614	1986.	N3815G GLC demo 1986, G-PJET Corporate Aviation, Ramsey. IOM (Barlow Clowes) /87, Svenska Finans (UK) Ltd 8/88, HB-VJC ALG Aeroleasing SA 3 Oct 88, G-SOVN Sovereign Svcs/Air Ambulance Services (UK) Ltd 3/89, G-VIPS MDFC Industrial Leasing/Executive Air Chrtr 5/90, G-VIPS Executive Air Charter, Biggin Hill
35A-615	1986.	N7260E GLC 7/86, Peer International Inc 9/86, GLC 2/87, FAB 6001 Brazilian Air Force 8/87, FAB6001 FAB=Forca Aerea Brasileira.
35A-616	1986.	N8568Q GLC 8/86, Airsupport Services Corp 1/88, PT-LQF Lider Taxi Aereo Ltda 1/88, PT-LQF Lider Taxi Aereo Ltda. Belo Horizonte.
35A-617	1987.	N4289Z GLC /87, FAB6002 Brazilian Air Force 8/87, FAB6002 FAB=Forca Aerea Brasileira.
35A-618	1986.	YU-BOL Inex Adria Airways del 26 Sep 86, YU-BOL Adria Airways, Ljubljana.
35A-619	1986.	N8568V GLC /86, Airsupport Services Corp 19 Sep 86, PT-POK Lider Taxi Aereo SA 14 Apr 87, PT-POK Lider Taxi Aereo S.A. Belo Horizonte.
35A-620	1986.	I-KODM Soc Locafit 8/86, I-KODM Codemi/Soc. Locafit, Rome.
35A-621	1986.	N999TH Journal Publishing Co 20 Oct 86, N999TH to F200-512, N999TN 7/89, Duncan-Ne 8/89, Solair Leasing of America 9/89, PT-...
35A-622	1986.	N7260H GLC /86,Enserco Inc 12/86,N610R 6/87,Iowa Power&Light 11/88, N610R Iowa Power & Light Co. Des Moines, Ia.
35A-623	1987.	N7260Q GLC 11/87, Natwest USA Credit Corp 12/87, 60504 Royal Thai Air Force 3/88, 60504 Royal Thai Air Force.
35A-624	1987.	86-0374 USAF 8/87, 86-0374 USAF/Air National Guard HQ.
35A-625	1987.	86-0375 USAF 8/87, 86-0375 USAF/Air National Guard HQ.
35A-626	1987.	N39398 GLC /87, N7261R Natwest USA Credit Corp 12/87, Willhead Aviation Inc 2/88, N35AJ Williams Engineering-UK 5/88, Neil Group Management 10/88, N711NF 11/88,C-GNPT Northwood Pulp & Timber Ltd 27 Jul 89, C-GNPT Northwood Pulp & Timber Ltd. Prince George, BC.
35A-627	1987.	N7260T GLC /87, PT-LMY Lider Taxi Aereo Ltda 12/87, PT-LMY Lider Taxi Aereo Ltda.
35A-628	1987.	N3801G GLC /87, 86-0376 USAF 10/87, 86-0376 USAF/Air National Guard HQ.
35A-629	1987.	86-0377 USAF 10/87, 86-0377 USAF/Air National Guard HQ.
35A-630	1987.	N42905 GLC /87, Natwest USA Credit Corp 12/87, N72630 GLC 1/88, Learjet Corp 4/88,N742E Eaton Corp 6/88, N742E Eaton Corp. Cleveland, Oh.
35A-631	1987.	N3818G GLC /87, 2710 Brazilian Air Force 11/87, 2710 Brazilian Air Force.
35A-632	1987.	N1461B GLC /87, 2711 Brazilian Air Force 11/87, 2711 Brazilian Air Force.
35A-633	1987.	N39416 GLC /87, 2712 Brazilian Air Force 11/87, 2712 Brazilian Air Force.
35A-634	1988.	I-EAMM Soc Estramed S.p.A. 2/88, Soc Dragomar SpA /90, I-EAMM Soc. Dragomar S.p.a. Rome.
35A-635	1988.	N1471B GLC /88, 60505 Royal Thai Air Force /88, 60505 Royal Thai Air Force.
35A-636	1988.	2713 Brazilian Air Force 4/88, 2713 Brazilian Air Force.
35A-638	1988.	2714 Brazilian Air Force 5/88, 2714 Brazilian Air Force.
35A-639	1988.	2715 Brazilian Air Force 5/88, 2715 Brazilian Air Force.
35A-640	1988.	N8568Y Learjet Corp 5/88, 2716 Brazilian Air Force 5/89, 2716 Brazilian Air Force.
35A-641	1988.	N7261H Learjet Corp 5/88, 2717 Brazilian Air Force 5/89, 2717 Brazilian Air Force.
35A-642	1988.	N7262X Learjet Corp 5/88, 2718 Brazilian Air Force 5/89, 2718 Brazilian Air Force.
35A-643	1988.	N39418 Learjet Corp 10/88, G-LJET Atlantic Learjet Sales 25 Feb 89, Tiger Aviation Ltd 9/89,G-LJET Tiger Aviation Ltd. Woking.
35A-644	1988.	N1043B Learjet Corp 1/89, Bartertrade Intl Inc 30 Jan 89, PT-LLF Araucaria Aero Taxi Ltda 1/90, PT-LLF Araucaria Aero Taxi Ltda. Sao Jose dos Pinhais.
35A-645	1988.	N43TR Learjet Corp /88, Three Rivers Aluminum Co 23 Dec 88, N43TR Three Rivers Aluminum Co.
35A-646	1988.	XA-UMA Taxi Aerea Lerma SA 1/89, XA-UMA TAESA. Mexico City.
35A-647	1989.	N410RD SMI Inc 20 Mar 89, N410RD SMI Inc. Norfolk, Va.
35A-648	1989.	N1045J Learjet Corp 7/89, Wichita Air Services 8/89, N974JD 10/89,N974JD Wichita Air Services Inc. Wichita, Ks.
35A-649	1989.	N10870 Learjet Corp /89, HB-VJJ EJA SA 15 Sep 89, HB-VJJ Executive Jet Aviation SA. Geneva.
35A-650	1989.	N1022G Learjet Corp 9/89, PT-LYF Vega Taxi Aereo Ltda 11/89, PT-LYF Vega Taxi Aereo Ltda. Brasilia
35A-651	1989.	HB-VJK Aeroleasing SA 8/89, HB-VJK ALG Aeroleasing SA. Geneva.
35A-652	1989.	N6307H Learjet Corp 10/89, N99FN Flight International Inc 12/89, N99FN Flight International Inc. Jacksonville, Fl.
35A-653	1989.	HB-VJL ALG Aeroleasing SA 24 Nov 89, HB-VJL ALG Aeroleasing SA. Geneva.
35A-654	1989.	N633WW Life Jet Services Inc 1/90, N633WW Life Jet Services Inc. Bloomington, Il.
35A-655	1990.	N16FG Airsupport Services Corp 4/90, PT-... 10/90, PT-...
35A-656	1990.	N3810G LJC 1/90, G-JETL Atlantic Learjet Sales del 30 Apr 90, Cameron Hall Developments Ltd 18 Jul 90, G-JETL Cameron Hall Developments Ltd. Hatfield.
35A-657	1990.	N1CA C A Leasing 4/90, N1CA C A Leasing, St Louis, Mo.
35A-658	1990.	N4290Y Learjet Corp /90, N573LP Louisiana Pacific Corp 14 May 90, N573LP Louisiana Pacific Corp. Hillsboro, Or.
35A-659	1990.	N873LP Louisiana Pacific Corp 12 Jun 90, N873LP Louisiana Pacific Corp. Hillsboro, Or.
35A-660	1990.	N1087Z Learjet Inc 7/90, N1087Z

35A-661 1990. N1268G Learjet Inc 30 Jul 90, Unicorn Intl (USA) Inc 9/90, N1268G Unicorn International (USA) Inc. Richland, Wa.
35A-662 1990. G-NEVL Atlantic Learjet Sales Ltd 10/90, G-NEVL Atlantic Learjet Sales Ltd. Cranfield.
35A-663 1990. N91480 Learjet Inc 11/90, N91480 Learjet Inc. Wichita, Ks.
35A-664 1990. N9130F Learjet Inc 12/90, N9130F Learjet Inc. Wichita, Ks.

Learjet 55/55B/55C

55-003 1981. N553GP The Garrett Corp 12/81, Arnel Interiors 7/86, N162GA 9/86, Orange County/Sunbird Aviation 1/87, Duncan-Ne 6/90, N553DJ 5/90, N553DJ Duncan Aviation Inc. Lincoln, Ne.
55-004 1981. N90E TRANSCO 6/81, N50L 8/84, GLC 4/85, N24JK 10/85, Prudential Interfunding Corp 11/85, N24CK 9/88, Dunacn-Ne 10/88, Combined Aviation Co 1/89, N24CK Combined Aviation Co. Phoenix, Az.
55-005 1981. N40ES Esmark Inc 6/81, EAF Aircraft Sales Inc 4/85, Consolidated Airways Inc 3/86, Milburn Investments Inc 8/86, N128VM 9/86, Gulfstream Flights Services Inc 3/90, N550CS 7/90, N550CS Gulfstream Flights Services Inc. Boca Raton, Fl.
55-006 1981. N113EL /81, N212JP GECC-Wilton 9/81, N126EL 8/83, Alamo Jet Inc 6/89, N355DB 1/90,N355DB Alamo Jet Inc. Fort Myers, Fl.
55-007 1981. N41ES Esmark Inc 9/81, EAF Aircraft Sales Inc 6/85, I-KILO Soc Gitanair del 12 Jun 86, I-KILO Soc. Gitanair, Bologna.
55-008 1981. N551SC Sabine Corp 10/81, Hal E Dickson 6/85, N551SC Hal E Dickson, San Angelo, Tx.
55-009 1981. N42ES Esmark Inc 10/81, Jernigan Production Co 2/85, N55SJ 5/85, Glenfield Financial Corp 12/85, HB-VIB Green Hawk SA/EJA 19 Mar 86, Argos Jet Estab 12/89, HB-VIB Argos Jet Estab. Geneva.
55-010 1981. N57TA Gates Learjet Corp /81, N57TA W/O W/o 13 Nov 81. 13/NOV/81
55-011 1981. (N57TA) GLC /81, N57TA re-allocated to 55-010, N37951 GLC 9/81, J&N Associates 3/82, GLC 5/83, N411GL 4/85, Worthington Industries Inc 8/85, N574W 10/85,N574W Worthington Industries Inc. Columbus, OH
55-012 1981. N55GH Sears Roebuck 1/82, Goodyear Tire & Rubber 6/84, N23G 7/84, N23G Goodyear Tire & Rubber Co. Akron, Oh.
55-013 1981. (D-CCHS) /81, OE-GNK Air Charter-Austria /81, N3238K Airsupport Services Corp 11/82, PT-LEL Lider Taxi Aereo SA 8/84, PT-LEL Lider Taxi Aereo S.A. Belo Horizonte.
55-014 1981. N90BS Kickerillo Co 1/82, N55KC 7/82, Allied Bank-Houston 4/87, XA-PIL Aeroventas SA 11/87, XA-PIL Aeroventas SA. Monterrey.
55-015 1981. HB-VGV ALG Aeroleasing SA /81, N515DJ Duncan-Ne 9/89, N550LJ LAS Aviation Corp 11/89, N550LJ LAS Aviation Corp. Cupertino, Ca.
55-016 1982. N646G Gates Rubber Co 2/82, Gates Corp 10/82, N646G Gates Corp. Denver, Co.
55-017 1982. N760AC American Cyanamid/Auxiliary Carrier Inc 2/82, N760AC Auxiliary Carrier Inc. Hasbrouck Heights, NJ.
55-018 1982. N39E TRANSCO 2/82, N39E TRANSCO, Houston, Tx.
55-019 1982. YV-41CP Construcciones-CADE-Caracas /82, N141SM Kad Air Corp 10/85, N141SM Kad Air Corp. Wilmington, De.
55-020 1982. N720M Levolor Lorentzen Inc 2/82, Spencer Blaine Jr-Tx 4/83, N20DL Faulkner Point Learjet 7/83, N20DL to 35A-479, N57B General Telephone Co of SW 6/84, N57B General Telephone Co of SW, San Angelo, TX
55-021 1982. N3794B GLC /82, Jim Bath 5/82, Emilio Bravo 10/83, TG Assoc 4/84, N700TG 10/84, Transatlantic Petroleum lease 8/85, EI-BSA S M McDaniel/Sanclare Aviation Services 11/85, I-LOOK Soc SNA 28 Mar 86, I-LOOK Soc. SNA-Navigazione Area, Florence.
55-022 1982. N64WM Waste Management Inc 3/82, N64WM Waste Management Inc. Wilmington, De.
55-023 1982. N3796B GLC 2/82, Daniel Urschel 8/82, Dresser Industries Inc 11/83, N7784 1/84, Xerox Corp 3/85, International Jet Leasing 2/87, Addington Inc 4/87, N7784 Addington Inc. Ashland, Ky.
55-024 1982. HB-VGZ Aeroleasing SA-Geneva 2/82, N224DJ Duncan-Ne 2/89, HB-VGZ R Schwarz Beteiligungen AG 11 Dec 89, R Schwarz Beteiligungen AG. Hilterfingen.
55-025 1982. N236R Dart Industries Inc 6/82, Duracell Inc 12/86,Kraft Inc 7/88, (N58PM) rsvd 10 Feb 89, N57PM 9/89, N57PM Philip Morris Management Corp. Teterboro, NJ.
55-026 1982. N8565H GLC /82, Howard Aviation Inc 4/82, N55HD 8/82, Howard Intl Corp 6/87,Great Planes Sales Inc 1/88, J Prewitt & Assoc 4/88, V B Aviation Inc 6/88, N21VB 10/88, N21VB V B Aviation Inc. Englewood, Co.
55-027 1982. N3796X GLC /82, OE-GKN Air Charter Austria 5/82, Transair-Vienna 8/85, N3796X Learjet Corp 8/88, N123LC Summit Jet Corp 12/88, N123LC Summit Jet Corp. Valhalla, NY.
55-028 1982. N3794C GLC /82, PT-LDR Lider/Bank of Brazil-Brasilia 9/83, PT-LDR to 55B-134, N3794C Learjet Corp 1/88, PT-LOF Lider Taxi Aereo Ltda 1/89, PT-LOF Lider Taxi Aereo Ltda. Rio de Janeiro.
55-029 1982. N4CP Pfizer Inc 5/82, N4CP to F50-187, D-CLIP Helmut Gartner/FVH GmbH 5/88, N10CP Miami Leasing Aviation Co 10/89, N10CP Miami Leasing Aviation Co. Miami, Fl.
55-030 1982. N986WC Western Conference of Teamsters 6/82, N959WC 7/84, N117WC 5/85,N117WC Western Conference of Teamsters, Hillsboro, Or.
55-031 1982. YV-12CP Aero Servicios ALAS C.A. /82, YV-12CP Aero Servicios ALAS C.A. Caracas.

c/n	
55-032	1982. N75TP Tesoro Petroleum Corp 9/82, (N72TP) rsvd 27 Feb 85, N71TP 7/89, N71TP Tesoro Petroleum Corp. San Antonio, Tx.
55-033	1982. N96CE United States Fidelity & Guarantee 6/82, N96CE to F50-139, N96OE 4/84, Epson America Inc 6/84, N917S 2/85, Omni 9/87, Fisher Group Inc 1/88, N414RF 4/88, N155CS Central States Joint Board 4/90, N155CS Central States Joint Board, Chicago, Il.
55-034	1982. N3795Y GLC /82, cx USA 6/82, D-CARX Bohl Airflight KG/Aero Dienst GmbH. Nuremberg 8/82, N84DJ Duncan Aviation-Ne 10/88, D-CLUB Ratioflug GmbH 4/89, D-CLUB Ratioflug GmbH. Frankfurt.
55-035	1982. N115EL Aircraft Services Corp 7/82, (N100GU) /?, N1968A ASC/AIRCOA=Assoc Inns & Restaurant Co of America 11/85, N127EL 5/90, N127EL Aircraft Services Corp/AIRCOA, Denver, Co.
55-036	1982. N3803G GLC /82, N555GL /82, N81CH ICH Corp 9/83, N81CH to 7212, N76AW 6/86, Jet East Intl Sales & Leasing 9/86, I C H Corp 3/87, N81CH 8/87, Facilities Management Installation 5/90, N81CH Facilities Management Installation, Louisville, Ky.
55-037	1982. N41CP Pfizer Inc 8/82, James R Wickert & Assoc 8/88, N86AJ 12/88, Airsupport Services Corp 6/89, PT-OBR Lider Taxi Aereo Ltda 12/89, PT-OBR Lider Taxi Aereo Ltda.
55-038	1982. N551HB First Hawaiian Bank 8/82, N551HB First Hawaiian Bank, Honolulu, Hi.
55-039	1982. N39418 GLC /82, N770JM M Air Inc 8/82, Harvey Wagner-Nv 1/83, GTC of SW 5/86, N97J 6/86, N97J General Telephone Co of SW, San Angelo, Tx.
55-040	1982. N3802G /82, HZ-AMII AMC Aviation/National Commercial Bank, Jeddah /82, HZ-AM2 /? HZ-AM2 to 55-127, N426EM GLC 7/86, Emhart Corp 8/86, Learjet Corp 8/89, N55HK Specialised Aircraft Services 1/90,Hekro Air Inc 9/90, N55HK Hekro Air Inc. Wichita, Ks.
55-041	1982. N401JE Public Service Co of New Mexico 8/82, Flighcraft Corp 4/89, N155PJ 5/89, High Flight Inc 2/90, N155PJ High Flight Inc. Waco, Tx.
55-042	1982. N3796U GLC /82, Omni 8/82, GLC 3/84, American TV & Comms Corp 2/85, N160TL 2/85 American TV & Communications Corp 2/85, D-CMTM MTM Aviation GmbH 1/88, D-CMTM Aviation Leasing KG/MTM Aviation GmbH. Munich.
55-043	1982. N5543G Universal Equipment Gathering Co/Omni 8/82, GLC 3/84, N785B NABISCO Brands Inc 12/85, PHD Penske Corp 11/87,N500JW 4/90, N500JW Golden State Foods/PHD Penske Corp. San Diego, Ca.
55-044	1982. N3797C GLC 4/82, Nutri System Inc 12/82, Airsupport Svcs Corp 1/86, PT-LHR Lider Taxi Aereo Ltda 5/86, Wanair Taxi Aereo /89, PT-LHR Wanair Taxi Aereo S.A. Belo Horizonte.
55-045	1982. HB-VHK Transair (Suisse) 7/82, EC-DSI Gestair-Madrid /82, VR-BHV /83, EC-DSI Gestair-Madrid 3/84, N90583 Combs Gates Denver Inc 6/87, Pum Air Corp 8/87, N49PE Pum Air/Power Engineering 8/87,Learjet Corp 10/89, (N49PD) rsvd 8 Dec 89, I-AGER Soc Eurojet Italia SpA 3 Apr 90, I-AGER Soc. Eurojet Italia S.p.A. Milan.
55-046	1982. N23HB Hamilton Bros/Delaware Airjet Inc 8/82, (N13HB) /83, N3HB 4/83, San Francisco Aviation Co 8/90, N55HL 10/90, N55HL San Francisco Aviation Co. Salinas, Ca.
55-047	1982. N600C HIBOS/35-55 Partnership 2/83, Fayez Sarofim & Co 3/89, N600C Fayez Sarofim & Co. Houston, TX
55-048	1982. N3796Z GLC /82, (N734) /82, VH-LGH Lang Hancock Prospecting 7/82, N73TP General Avn Svcs 10/84, Tesoro Petroleum Corp 12/84, United Suites Inc 12/85, N67RW 3/86, Robert Woolley-Tx 1/87, Rew Air Inc 7/87, Airsupport Services Corp 6/89, PT-... 1/90, PT-...
55-049	1982. N3796C GLC /82, D-CCHS Bomin International Handel GmbH 8/82, N150MS Combs Gates 3/87, Martin Sprocket & Gear 7/87, N150MS Martin Sprocket & Gear Inc. Arlington, Tx.
55-050	1983. D-CARP Aero Dienst GmbH 1/83, Kiliani Flug GmbH 7/89, Aero Dienst GmbH 1/90, D-CARP Aero Dienst GmbH. Nuremberg.
55-051	1983. N734 Goodyear Tire & Rubber Co 7/83, N22G 8/83, N22GH 6/85, Kelly-Springfield Tire Co 7/85, N55KS 8/85, N55KS Kelly-Springfield Tire Co. Cumberland, Md.
55-052	1983. YV-292CP /83, N55GF GLC 4/83, N551DB Skybird Aviation Inc 11/83, N551DB Skybird Aviation Inc. Van Nuys, Ca.
55-053	1983. N85653 GLC /82, YV-374CP Transportes La Mona S.A. 10/82, N1450B GLC 9/87,N500RP Hertz Penske Truck Leasing 2/88, N500RP Hertz Penske Truck Leasing Inc. Red Bank, NJ.
55-054	1982. HB-VHL Transair (Suisse) SA /82, HB-VHL Transair (Suisse) S.A. Geneva.
55-055	1982. N155LP L B P Trading 11/82, Harris Corp 5/85, N970H 3/86, N970H Harris Corp. Melbourne, Fl.
55-056	1983. N8563E GLC 8/82, Westinghouse Credit Corp 2/83, (N854GA) /83, N946FP Frank Pasquerilla/Crown American 8/83, First Fidelity Leasing Group 1/90,N946FP Frank Pasquerilla/Crown American, Cambria County Apt. Pa.
55-057	1982. N10CR National Cash Register Corp 10/82, N10CR National Cash Register Corp. Dayton, Oh.
55-058	1982. (N55BE) Bucyrus Erie Corp /82, N500BE 10/82, name change Becor Western Inc 9/85,PCI Transportation Inc 8/87, N200PC 8/88, Consolidated Airways Inc 9/88, N200PC Consolidated Airways Inc. Fort Wayne, In.
55-059	1982. (N211BY) GLC /82, D-CAEP Aero Dienst GmbH /82, FG Flugzeugleasing GmbH 5/83, Ratioflug GmbH /88, D-CAEP Flugzeugleasing GmbH/Ratioflug GmbH. Frankfurt. (now 55C ?).
55-060	1983. N60MJ MJI 11/82, Denver Coca Cola Bottling Co 2/83,N53JL 8/83,Great Western Coca-Cola Bottling/JTL Corp/D Randy 10/83 Consolidated Airways Inc 11/86, Omni 3/87, WSE Inc 4/87, N86AJ 9/87, Dulles Equities Inc 1/88, N8YY 4/88, Airsupport Services Corp 9/90, N60LT rsvd 24 Sep 90,N60LT Airsupport Services Corp. Miami, Fl.

c/n	
55-061	1982. N117EL GECC/Jetwinds Avn Corp 11/82, McCaw Communications 6/86, N222MC McCaw Communications 6/86, N132EL GECC-Wilton 7/90, N132EL GECC, Wilton, Ct.
55-062	1983. N62GL Goodyear Tire & Rubber Co 7/83, N24G 1/84, N24G Goodyear Tire & Rubber Co. Akron, Oh.
55-063	1982. N8563P GLC /82, FSB-Ut/Triangle Inds Inc 12/82, Parc Avn Inc 11/85, N1744P 12/85, Aviation Sales Co-Miami 7/87, N74RY 10/87, N74RY Aviation Sales Co. Miami, Fl.
55-064	1982. N255ST Southeast Toyota Distributors Inc 11/82,N255ST Southeast Toyota Distributors Inc. Deerfield Beach, Fl.
55-065	1982. N8565K GLC /82, N555GL 6/83, Coopervision Inc 4/85, Cooper Companies Inc 11/87, Technicon Instruments Inc 6/89, N1125M Miles Laboratories Inc 12/89, N1125M Miles Laboratories Inc. Elkmart, In.
55-066	1983. N237R Dart Industries 1/83, Duracell Inc 12/86, (N550DD) rsvd 23 Mar 88, Gaylord Leasing Partners 2/88, Meridian Trust Co/Deerpath Group 8/88, N50DD 9/88, N50DD The Deerpath Group, Wheeling, Il.
55-067	1983. N120EL GECC/195 Broadway Corp 2/83, Express One Intl Inc 6/89, N127GT 9/89, 127 GT Corp 10/89, N127GT 127 GT Corp. Dover, De.
55-068	1982. N38D Black & Decker (US) Inc 12/82, Mar Flite Ltd Corp 5/90, N38D Mar Flite Ltd Corp. Portland, OR
55-069	1983. N551UT United Telecoms Inc 1/83,Westinghouse Communities Inc 12/87, N102ST 5/88, N102ST Westinghouse Communities Inc. Coral Springs, Fl.
55-070	1982. F-GDHR Transair/Aero France 30 Dec 82, F-GDHR W/O W/o 5 Feb 87. 05/FEB/87 9k, last reported flying at 39000ft.
55-071	1982. (N155UT) N155JC GLC /82, Johnny Carson/St Cloud Corp 1/83, Cole National Corp 11/86, N155JC Cole National Corp. Cleveland, Oh.
55-072	1983. N58AS Boise Cascade/Albertsons Inc 1/83, N55AS 3/87, N55AS Boise Cascade/Albertsons Inc. Portland, Or.
55-073	1983. HB-VHN Transair (Suisse) SA /83, I-VIKY Soc SICEL 5/85, I-VIKY Perini/Soc Romaleasing, Rome.
55-074	1983. N5574 Vulcan Materials Co 2/83,N74GL Electronic Data Systems 3/88, N74GL Electronic Data Systems Corp. Dallas, Tx.
55-075	1983. N8563Z GLC /83, Alpine Panorama Corp 3/83,Dubai Service Corp 1/84, GLC 3/84, Mutual of Omaha 6/84, N675M 8/84, Learjet Corp 3/89, N55GM Western Aviation Corp 4/89, N55GH rsvd 26 Nov 90, N55GH Western Aviation Corp. Miami, Fl.
55-076	1983. (N155JC) GLC /83, N2855 Texas Eastern Transmission Corp 2/83, EDS Corp 6/90,N30GL 10/90, N30GL E D S Corp. Dallas, Tx.
55-077	1983. N3812G GLC /83, N8563M United Omaha Insurance Co 2/84, N58M 4/84, N58M United Omaha Life Insurance Co. Omaha, Nb.
55-078	1983. (N55GJ) GLC /83, N55GV Tulsa Aircraft Charter Corp 6/83, N56TG 10/83,I-ALPR Soc ALPI Eagles 31 Jul 90, I-ALPR Soc. ALPI Eagles, Thiene (VI).
55-079	1983. (N2855) GLC /83, N1983Y ARA Services Inc 6/83, N1983Y ARA Services Inc. Philadelphia, Pa.
55-080	1983. N85632 GLC 2/83, Airsupport Services Corp 4/83, PT-LET Banco Real SA 3 Sep 84, PT-LET Banco Real S.A. Sao Paulo.
55-081	1983. N85631 GLC 2/83, N777MC Meredith Corp 8/83, N777MC Meredith Corp. Des Moines, Ia.
55-082	1983. N1075X Xerox Corp 9/83, Electronic Data Systems 6/89, N33GL 11/89, N33GL Electronic Data Systems, Dallas, Tx.
55-083	1983. N55GZ Thomas Watson Jr 12/83, N6789 /84, N6789 Thomas Watson Jr. Stowe, Vt.
55-084	1983. N85643 GLC 6/83,Alpine Panorama Corp 9/83, Dubai Service Corp 1/84, GLC 12/84, Auxiliary Carrier Inc 1/85, N740AC 3/85, N740AC Auxiliary Carrier Inc. Hasbrouck Heights, NJ.
55-085	1983. N238R Dart Industries Inc 9/83,Duracell Inc 12/86, Kraft Inc 8/88, N58PM 3/90, N58PM Kraft Inc. Glenview, Il.
55-086	1983. D-CACP Aero Dienst GmbH 3 Aug 83, N8227P Learjet Corp 8/89, N8227P Learjet Corp 8/89, PT-LUK Taxi Aereo Weston 11/89, PT-LUK Taxi Aereo Weston, Recife.
55-087	1983. N8564Z GLC 8/83, N103C Adolph Coors Co 3/84, N103C Adolph Coors Co. Golden, Co.
55-088	1983. N55GJ Sky City Stores Inc 2/84, Cathay Holdings Inc 9/89, Express One International Inc 11/89, N55GJ Express One International Inc. Dallas, Tx.
55-089	1983. N8564X GLC /83, GATX Leasing/Valero Energy Corp 2/84, N170VE 4/84, N170VE Valero Energy Corp. San Antonio, Tx.
55-090	1984. N723H IBM Corp 3/84, N723H IBM Corp. NYC.
55-091	1983. N8566F GLC /83, ICH Corp 1/85, N91CH 7/85, N91CH to G-3 405, N991CH 7/86, Qantum Inc 3/87, N91PR 11/87, Bruce Gillis-Ca 10/90, N69B rsvd 1 Nov 90, N62B Bruce S Gillis, Los Angeles, Ca.
55-092	1984. N724J IBM Corp 2/84, N724J IBM Corp. NYC.
55-093	1984. N725K IBM Corp 3/84, N725K IBM Corp. NYC.
55-094	1984. N235HR Hoffman La Roche Inc 2/84, N235HR Hoffman La Roche Inc. Nutley, NJ.
55-095	1984. N8565Z GLC /83, N55RT Townsend Engineering Co 3/84, N55RT Townsend Engineering Co. Des Moines, IA
55-096	1984. (N1045X) GLC /84, N8010X Xerox Corp 3/84, N8010X Xerox Corp. NYC.
55-097	1983. N8566Q GLC /83, NCR Corp 2/84, N4OCR 4/84, N20CR 6/85, N20CR NCR Corp. Dayton, Oh.
55-098	1984. N726L IBM Corp 5/84, N726L IBM Corp. NYC.
55-099	1984. (N5599) GLC /84, Texas Eastern Transmission Corp 5/84, N2992 6/84, E D S Corp 6/90, N17GL 7/90, N17GL E D S Corp. Dallas, Tx.

c/n	Details
55-100	1984. N552UT United Telecom 5/84, N552UT United Telecom, Hood River, Or.
55-101	1984. N101HK PSK Development Co 7/84, H J Kalikow & Co 7/85, N101PK 10/86, N101PK to Challenger 5005, N101HK 8/87, Evergreen Aviation Inc 2/88, N211EF 8/88, N211EF Evergreen Aviation Inc. Salem, Or.
55-102	1984. N55DG Richmor/Associated Dry Goods 7/84, Enterprise Leasing Co 3/87, FSB-Ut 10/90,N55DG Enterprise Leasing Co. Charlotte, NC.
55-103	1984. N921FP EAF/Federal Paper Board 7/84, Cx USA 9/87, N921FP W/O 6 Aug 86. ran off runway following aborted take off
55-104	1984. N18CG Corning Enterprises Inc 7/84, N18CG Corning Enterprises Inc. NYC.
55-105	1984. N55GK Goodyear Tire & Rubber Co 14 May 85, N22G 8/85, N22G Goodyear Tire & Rubber Co. Akron, Oh.
55-106	1984. N60E TRANSCO 8/84, N60E TRANSCO, Houston, Tx.
55-107	1984. N760G IBM Corp 10/84, N760G IBM Corp. NYC.
55-108	1984. (N888FK) F Klingenstein/K Services Inc /84, N77FK 10/84, N78FK 7/88, McCaw Communications 3/89, N222MC rsvd 30 Jul 90, N222MC McCaw Communications, Seattle, Wa.
55-109	1984. N348HM Herman Miller Inc 9/84, N348HM Herman Miller Inc. Zeeland, Mi.
55-110	1985. N55GY E P Enterprises 23 Jul 85, Huber Hunt & Nichols 10/88, N55GY Huber Hunt & Nichols Inc. Indianapolis, In.
55-111	1985. N7260G GLC Paris 6/85 demo, Airsupport Services Corp 6/86, PT-LIG Lider Taxi Aereo Ltda 16 Jul 86, PT-LIG Lider Taxi Aereo Ltda. Belo Horizonte.
55-112	1985. YV-325CP /85, N325CP Bricair Inc 1/85, N325CP Bricair Inc. Fort Lauderdale, Fl.
55-113	1985. N7262M GLC /85, Mutual of Omaha Insurance Co 3/85, N713M 5/85, N713M Mutual of Omaha Insurance Co. Nb.
55-114	1984. N72608 GLC /84, Konfara Co 12/84, N34GB 4/85, N34GB Konfara Co. Ann Arbor, Mi.
55-115	1985. N6666R Burnett Aviation Co 1/85, N6666K 5/88, Xidex Corp 10/88, N633AC 10/89, N633AC Xidex Corp. Santa Clara, Ca.
55-116	1985. N85GL GLC 6/85, N116DA Aries Realty 1/86,TAC Holdings Inc-Tx 8/87, N116DA T A C Holdings Inc. Bryan, Tx.
55-117	1985. N8567X GLC /85, Oregon MB-35 Corp 8 Jan 85, N255MB 6/85, N255MB Oregon MB-35 Corp. Portland, Or.
55-118	1985. C-FCLJ Canada Jet Charters Ltd 22 May 85, C-FCLJ Canada Jet Charters Ltd. Vancouver, BC.
55-119	1985. N72613 GLC /85, Meredith Corp 11/85, N273MC 3/86, N273MC Meredith Corp. Des Moines, Ia.
55-120	1985. N72629 GLC /85, Fort Howard Paper Co 11/85, N55LK 4/86, (N486) rsvd 3 Sep 87, N55LK Fort Howard Paper Co. Green Bay, Wi.
55-121	1986. N8568J GLC /86, Bielfeldt Lauritsen & Hagemeyer 3/86, N65Y 7/86, N65Y Bielfeldt Lauritsen & Hagemeyer, Peoria, Il.
55-122	1985. N8568P Philip Crosby/Sun Bank National Assoc 24 Dec 85, N18ZD 5/86, N18ZD Philip Crosby/Sun Bank National Assoc. Orlando, Fl.
55-123	1985. N44EL Lynn Insurance/U S Epperson Underwriting Co 24 Dec 85, N44EL Lynn Insurance/U S Epperson Underwriting Co. Boca Raton, Fl.
55-124	1986. N58CG Corning Enterprises Inc 28 Oct 86, N58CG Corning Enterprises Inc. Corning, NY.
55-125	1986. N610JR Tele/Com Air Inc 8/86, N610JR Tele/Com Air Inc. Oak Brook, Il.
55-126	1986. N7260J GLC NBAA demo 10/86, YV-125CP Transportes La Mona SA 1/88,YV-125CP Transportes La Mona S.A. Caracas.
55B-127	1986. HZ-AM2 AMC Aviation/National Commercial Bank 9/86, N73GP Gerber Products Co 31 Jul 90,N73GP Gerber Products Co. Fremont, Mi.
55B-128	1986. N1087T GLC /86, N255BL U S Aviation Underwriters Inc 12/86, N7US 3/87, N7US U S Aviation Underwriters Inc. NYC.
55B-129	1986. N75GP Gerber Products Inc 3 DEc 86, Whirlpool Leasing 2/87, Whirlpool Financial Corp 6/89, N75GP Gerber Products Co. Fremont, Mi.
55B-130	1986. N55VC R T Vanderbilt Co 24 Dec 86, N55VC R T Vanderbilt Co. Norwalk, Ct.
55B-131	1987. N7260K GLC /87, Coyne Textiles/Textron Financial 3/87, N52CT 8/87, N52CT Coyne Textiles/Textron Financial Corp. Fort Worth, Tx.
55B-132	1987. N67WM Waste Management Inc 10 Jul 87, N67WM Waste Management Inc. Wilmington, De.
55B-133	1987. N155PL Electronic Engineering Co 8 Feb 88, N155PL Electronic Engineering Co. Miami, Fl.
55B-134	1988. N7261D GLC 2/88, Airsupport Services Corp 27 Apr 88, PT-LDR Lider Taxi Aereo Ltda /88, PT-LDR Lider/Bank of Brazil, Brasilia.
55C-001	1987. N551GL GLC s/n 55-001 cvtd to 55C-001 1987, Learjet Corp 6/89, Learjet Inc 9/90,N551DF Learjet 55C prototype cvtd from 55-001
55C-135	1988. N1055C Learjet Corp 6/88, Farnboro demo 9/88, Airsupport Svcs 4/89, PT-LXO Lider Taxi Aereo /90, PT-LXO Lider Taxi Aereo, Belo Horizonte.
55C-136	1988. N767AZ Learjet Corp 1/89, N767NY 2/89,General Instrument Corp 4/89,N767NY General Instrument Corp. Hickory, NC.
55C-137	1989. N39413 LJC 5/89, N95SC Sea Containers Assoc Inc 6/89, N95SC Sea Containers Assoc Inc. NYC. (based UK).

c/n		
55C-138	1989.	N4291G LJC 4/89, TC-MEK Cukurova Adcus del 12 Jul 89, TC-MEK Cukurova Adcus, Istanbul.
55C-139	1989.	N1039L Learjet Corp 9/89, PT-LZS Lider Taxi Aereo Ltda 2/90, PT-LZS Lider Taxi Aereo Ltda.
55C-140	1989.	N72616 Learjet Corp 1/90, Airsupport Service Corp 27 Apr 90, PT-OCA Aracaria Aerotaxi Ltda 5/90, PT-OCA Araucaria Aerotaxi Ltda. Sao Jose dos Pinhais. 'Marcia Jose'
55C-141	1990.	N155DB Dal Briar 4/90, N155DB Dal Briar, Dallas, Tx.
55C-142	1989.	N555MX Pacific Flight Services Inc 12/89, N555MX Pacific Flight Services Inc. Lake Oswego, Or.
55C-143	1990.	N10871 Learjet Inc 3/90, D-CMAD Aero Dienst GmbH 5/90, Gustav und Grete Schickedanz KG 12 Jun 90, D-CMAD Gustav und Grete Schickedanz KG. Fuerth.
55C-144	1990.	N144LT Learjet Inc 22 Jun 90, Airsupport Services Corp 9/90, N144LT Airsupport Services Corp. Miami, Fl.
55C-145	1990.	N66WM Learjet Inc 9/90, Waste Management Inc 11/90, N66WM Waste Management Inc. Oak Brook, Il.
55C-146	1990.	N9125M Learjet Inc 11/90, N9125M

Citation III

c/n	
650-0001	1982. N651CC Cessna CoA 10/82, Arnold Palmer 4/83, N1AP 8/83, N1AP to 650-0082, (N651AP) rsvd 2 Apr 85 N654CC Cessna Aircraft Co 7/85, Attwood Enterprises Inc 8/86, N651CC 9/87, Larken Inc 5/88, Larken Inc. Cedar Rapids, Ia.
650-0002	1983. N652CC Cessna CoA 2/83, N5000C Cargill Inc 6/83, N5000C Cargill Inc. Minneapolis, Mn.
650-0003	1983. N653CC Cessna CoA 4/83,HZ-AAA Arabian International Services Co-Jeddah /83,N187CP Omni Intl 3/85, Monumental Jets Inc 4/85,Leucadia Avn 10/86, N92LA 1/87, AIC Leasing Inc 1/90,OY-CCG Alkair Flight Ops 2/90, Grundfos A/S /90, OY-CCG Grundfos A/S. Bjerringbro.
650-0004	1983. (N654AR) Cessna CoA 6/83, N654GC Garrett Corp 11/83, Allied Signal Inc 12/88, Executive Aircraft Consulting 6/90, N654GC Executive Aircraft Consulting, Newton, Ks.
650-0005	1983. N137S Cessna CoA 7/83, Sperry Flight Systems 9/83, Sperry Aerospace Marine 4/86, Honeywell Inc 8/87,N439H 6/88, N439H Honeywell Inc. Phoenix, Az.
650-0006	1983. N656CC Cessna CoA 7/83, Flight Pro Leasing Inc 10/83,N44HS 4/84,Dixie Equipment Leasing Inc 6/87, EJA 2/89, (N306QS) rsvd 2 Mar 89, REW Air Inc 9/89, N58RW 10/89, N58RW REW Air Inc. Irving, Tx.
650-0007	1983. (N13047) Cessna CoA 8/83, (N3Q) /83, N657CC Harbor Land Co/Diamond Shamrock 10/83, N929DS 11/83,C-FLTL Laidlaw Transport/Air Niagara Express20 Jun 85, Transma Aviation /89, Odessey Aviation Ltd 21 Jun 90, C-FLTL Odessey Aviation Ltd. Mississauga.
650-0008	1983. (N13049) Cessna CoA 8/83, N618CC /83, N10TC Overnight Transportation Co 3/84, N10TC Overnight Transportation Co. Richmond, Va.
650-0009	1983. (N1305C) Cessna CoA 9/83, N933DB Shaw Industries Inc 12/83, N933SH 12/84, N933SH Shaw Industries Inc. Dalton, Ga.
650-0010	1983. (N1305N) Cessna CoA 9/83, N2UP The Upjohn Co 1/84, N2UP The Upjohn Co. Kalamazoo, Mi.
650-0011	1983. N1305U Cessna CoA 9/83, First Security Leasing Co 12/83, (C-GWPA) Oxford Properties /84, Daon Developments Ltd /86, Leucadia Aviation Inc 7/86, (N9OLA) rsvd 23 Sep 86, N91LA 6/87,Turner Enterprises Inc 11/89, N17TE 2/90, N17TE Turner Enterprises Inc. Atlanta, Ga.
650-0012	1983. N1305V Cessna CoA 10/83, N15VF H D Lee Co 4/84, N15VF H D Lee Co. Shawnee Mission, Ks.
650-0013	1983. (N13052) N119EL GECC-Wilton/Winston Network Inc 1/84, (N13QS) rsvd 10 Jul 87, N313QS 3/90, N313QS EJA/Winston Network Inc. NYC.
650-0014	1983. (N1306B) Cessna CoA 10/83, N650CJ /83, C-GHOO Home Oil Co Ltd /84, HWR Aircraft Co Ltd 11/87, OE-GCN Polsterer Jets GmbH 12/87, OE-GCN Dr. L Polsterer/Viennair Luftfahrt GmbH. Vienna.
650-0015	1983. (N1306F) Cessna CoA 10/83, N83CT Contel Service Corp 4/84, Ladd Petroleum Co 7/84, N369G General Electric Co 9/84, N15QS 7/87, RTS Aviation Sales Inc 8/87, III Corp-NY 3/89, N15QS EJA/III Corp. Port Jefferson, NY.
650-0016	1983. N1306V Cessna CoA 10/83, N720ML Northwestern Mutual Life Insurance Co 1/84, N720ML Northwestern Mutual Life Insurance Co. Milwaukee, Wi.
650-0017	1983. N1307A Cessna CoA 11/83, C-GHLM Hudson's Bay Co-Calgary 1/84, N900CM Cargill Leasing Corp 20 Mar 85, N900CM Excel Corp/Cargill Leasing Corp. Minneapolis, Mn.
650-0018	1983. (N1307C) Cessna CoA 11/83, N715BC Citation Assoc/Winston Network-NYC 9/84,N275WN 10/84, Stockwood Inc 6/87, N650SB 8/87, N650SB Stockwood Inc. Morristown, NJ.
650-0019	1983. (N1307D) Cessna CoA 12/83, (N44BH) /83, N30CJ Sylva Equip Corp 3/84,Printacolor Corp 9/85, Russ Lyon 3/86, N333RL 6/86, N333RL Russ Lyon Jr/Westcor Aviation, Scottsdale, Az.
650-0020	1983. N1307G Cessna CoA 12/83, Consolidated Bank/Tigervest Leasing 2/84, sale-Tx 3/90, XA-VIT 7/90, XA-VIT Vitro Corporitivo SA. Monterrey
650-0021	1983. N2624M Cessna CoA 1/84, Mobil Oil Corp 2/84, N2604 4/84, Mobil Corp 8/89, N2604 Mobil Corp. Fairfax, Va.
650-0022	1983. N650J Cessna CoA 1/84, Gerald D Hines Interests Inc 3/84, Hines Florida Corp 1/89, N650J Hines Florida Corp. Houston, Tx.
650-0023	1984. Cessna CoA 1/84, N889G General Dynamics Corp 3/84, N889G General Dynamics Corp. Ontario, Ca.
650-0024	1984. N1UP Cessna CoA 2/84, The Upjohn Co 4/84, N1UP The Upjohn Co. Kalamazoo, Mi.
650-0025	1984. N1OPX Cessna CoA 2/84, CMI Aircraft 4/84, Torray Clark & Co 7/84, N200RT 10/84, Proflights Inc-PR 7/86, (N376HW) rsvd 14 Nov 86, (N277HG) rsvd 14 Sep 88, National Underwriting Services Co 5/90, N700RR 7/90, N700RR National Underwriting Services Corp. Wilmington, De.
650-0026	1984. N626CC Damaged on production line 1984, now test airframe.
650-0027	1984. N375SC Cessna CoA 2/84, Steelcase Inc 5/84, N875SC 11/88, Owners Jet Services Ltd 3/89, N650NY 4/90, Trans Marine Management Corp 5/90, N650NY Trans Marine Management Corp. Tampa, Fl.
650-0028	1984. N148C Cessna CoA 2/84, CONOCO Inc 6/84, EJA 8/89, N328QS 2/90, N328QS Executive Jet Sales, Columbus, Oh.
650-0029	1984. (N30CJ) Cessna CoA 3/83, N600GH General Host Corp 6/84, N600GH General Host Corp. Westchester Airport Hangar D-1, NY.
650-0030	1984. N650SC Cessna CoA 4/84, Sundstrand Corp 5/84,SE-DHL Stora Kopparbergs Berlags AB 22 Mar 88,SE-DHL Stora Kopparbergs Berlags AB. Falun.
650-0031	1984. N631CC Cessna CoA 5/84, H B Zachary Co 6/84, N1ZC 9/85, Bexar Equipment Co 2/89, N1ZC Bexar Equipment Co. San Antonio, Tx.

c/n	
650-0032	1984. N54WC Cessna CoA 4/84, Paccar/Weyerhaeuser Co 6/84,N38WP 10/85,N38WP Weyerhaeuser Co. Seattle, WA
650-0033	1984. (N1309A) Cessna CoA 3/84, CC-ECE CORFO /84, CC-ECE CORFO=Corporacion de Fomento, Santiago.
650-0034	1984. N80CC Circus Circus Ents 7/84, Cessna 8/84, F&A Marketing 9/84, N34QS 10/87,N777LF 12/87,N777LF F & A Marketing Corp. Dallas, Tx.
650-0035	1984. N650MD Cessna CoA 4/84, Continental Protection System 5/84, Deere & Co 2/89, N400JD 3/89, N400JD Deere & Co. Moline, Il.
650-0036	1984. N700CS Cessna CoA 5/84, Roger Dean/Executive Car & Trucking 12/84, (N700RD) rsvd 8 Jan 85, N20RD 5/86, N36CD 5/88, Cessna 8/88, Town & Country Food Markets Inc 10/88, N43TC 1/89, N43TC Town & Country Food Markets Inc. Wichita, Ks.
650-0037	1984. N411BB Cessna CoA 5/84, Barnett Operations Co 6/84, Barnett Banks Inc 1/88, Cessna Aircraft Co 3/90, N37CD 4/90, N37CD Cessna Finance Corp. Wichita, Ks.
650-0038	1984. N366G Cessna CoA 5/84, General Electric Co 7/84, N366G General Electric Co. Hangar E, Westchester Airport, NY.
650-0039	1984. N81TC Cessna CoA 5/84, Trane Co 8/84,Weyerhaeuser/Paccar Inc 2/85, N39WP 9/85, N39WP Weyerhaeuser Inc. Seattle, Wa.
650-0040	1984. N82TC Cessna CoA 5/84, Trane Co 7/84, VR-BJY Scanair Ltd 5/87, HB-VIY Execair SA 27 Oct 88,HB-VIY Industrie Leasing AG-Zurich/Execair SA. Lugano.
650-0041	1984. N55BH Cessna CoA 5/84, Gilbert Imported Hardwoods Inc 6/84, N55BH Gilbert Imported Hardwoods Inc. Gilbert, WV.
650-0042	1984. N142AB Cessna CoA 2/85, Allied Bendix Corp 3/85, N342QS EJA 4/90, N342QS Executive Jet Sales Inc. Columbus, Oh.
650-0043	1984. (N1310B) Cessna CoA 6/84, OY-GKL Lego Systems 8/84, OY-GKL Kirkbi A/S-Lego Systems, Billund.
650-0044	1984. (N234HM) Cessna CoA 6/84, N650M Masuco Inc 10/84, Mann GmbH 6/85, N650M Moebel-Mann GmbH. Baden-Baden.
650-0045	1984. N84G Burlington Industries Inc 8/84, Jetcraft Corp 5/88, Caribbean Overseas Investment 2/89, EJA 4/90, N84G Executive Jet Sales Inc. Columbus, Oh.
650-0046	1984. N658CC Cessna CoA 6/84, Boeing Equipment Holding 26 Apr 85, N658CC Boeing Equipment Holding Co. Wichita, Ks.
650-0047	1984. N1102 Cessna CoA 6/84, Gould Inc 8/84, (N1109) rsvd 18 Aug 86, Conseco Inc 2/87, N650CN 5/87, Brunswick Bowling & Billiards 10/90, N33BC 11/90, N33BC Brunswick Bowling & Billiards, Muskegon, Mi.
650-0048	1984. N98BD Cessna CoA 8/84, Dillard Department Stores Inc 9/84, N98DD 3/86, cx USA 4/86, restored to Canadair Inc 6/86, Cessna 9/86, Aircraft Services Corp-Ga 9/86, N986M 12/86, N986M Michelin Tire Corp. Greenville, SC.
650-0049	1984. (N1311A) Cessna CoA 7/84, C-FJOE Bradley Air & Taggart Services-Montreal 10/84, PJ-MAR Servicios Technicos Maracaibo CA-Caracas 3/86, PT-LSN /90, PT-LSN
650-0050	1984. (N1311K) Cessna CoA 9/84, N44M Corporate Jets/A W Mathieson 10/84, N44M Corporate Jets/A W Mathieson-Mellon Bank, Pittsburgh, Pa.
650-0051	1984. (N1311P) Cessna CoA 7/84, N910F Standard Oil Realty Corp 10/84, AMOCO Properties Inc 12/84, AMOCO Corp 4/89, N910F AMOCO Corp. Chicago, Il.
650-0052	1984. N20MW Cessna CoA 8/84, Mountain Air Inc 10/84, Highland Aviation Inc 8/85, N20MW Hidro Gas Juarez S.A/Highland Aviation Inc. El Paso, Tx.
650-0053	1984. N367G Cessna CoA 7/84, General Electric Co 9/84, N367G General Electric Co. Hangar E, Westchester Airport, NY.
650-0054	1984. (N1312D) Cessna CoA 9/84, N1103 Gould Inc 10/84, N1183 2/86, Combined International Corp 5/86, (N26RG) Ryan Group Avn rsvd 24 Jun 86, CIC Aviation Inc 1/87, AON Aviation Inc 11/87, N17AN 1/88, N17AN AON Aviation Inc. Chicago, Il.
650-0055	1984. N173LP Cessna CoA 8/84, Louisiana-Pacific Corp 10/84,Jack Prewitt-Tx 9/90,N173LR Vicon Flight Inc 10/90, N515VC 11/90, N515VC Vicon Flight Inc. Livonia, Mi.
650-0056	1984. N273LP Cessna CoA 8/84, Louisiana Pacific Corp 10/84, (N273LB) rsvd 16 Mar 90, J Prewitt /90, Wuliger Corp 10/90, N760EW rsvd 8 Nov 90, N760EW Corporate Wings/Wuliger Corp. Cleveland, Oh.
650-0057	1984. N368G Cessna CoA 8/84, General Electric Co 10/84,N368G General Electric Co. Hangar E, Westchester Airport, NY.
650-0058	1984. N88DD Cessna CoA 9/84,BA Leasing Corp/Duchossois Inds 10/84, DD66 Corp 9/88, N88DD DD66 Corp. Elmhurst, Il.
650-0059	1984. N1313G Cessna CoA 9/84, Mendes Jr Intl Co 17 Oct 84,PT-LHA TAMIG 3 Jul 85,PT-LHA TAMIG/Mendes Jr. International Co. Belo Horizonte.
650-0060	1984. N1313J Cessna CoA 9/84, HB-VHW Sky Jet AG 9/84, HB-VHW Sky Jet AG. Zurich.
650-0061	1984. (N1313T) Cessna CoA 10/84, N137M Motorola Inc 11/84, (N129TC) rsvd for ATC Inc 5 Nov 87, N137X 7/88, Cessna 12/88,N650TP Ray-O-Vac 1/89,N650TP Ray-O-Vac/Banc One Equipment Finance Inc. Indianapolis, In.
650-0062	1984. N626CC Cessna CoA 9/84, C-GHGK 559300 Ontario Inc/Magna International Ltd 1/85, N388DA Owners Jet Services Ltd 11/88, San Quintin Corp 2/89, N19FR 1/90, Southeastern Jet Corp 7/90, N342HM 9/90, N342HM Southeastern Jet Corp. Fort Lauderdale, Fl.

c/n	Details
650-0063	1984. N13138 Cessna CoA 10/84, Suncoast Aviation Services Inc 11/84, Premier Aircraft Sales Inc 4/85, sale-De 3/90, Sterling Inc 4/90, N14ST 8/90, N41ST Sterling Inc. Akron, Oh.
650-0064	1984. (N1314H) Cessna CoA 10/84, N801CC Chrysler Corp 11/84,GAC 3/89,Central Trust Co 4/89,N650TC City of Dayton Partnership 8/89, N650TC City of Dayton Partnership, Vandalia, Oh.
650-0065	1984. (N1314T) Cessna CoA 11/84, N500E Exxon Corp 11/84, C-FIMO Imperial Oil Ltd 7/87, C-FIMO Imperial Oil Ltd. Toronto.
650-0066	1984. (N1314V) Cessna CoA 11/84, N138M Motorola Inc 11/84, N138V 7/88, Cessna 1/89, N650CD Russell Corp 2/89, N650CD Russell Corp. Alexander City, Al.
650-0067	1984. (N1314X) Cessna CoA 12/84, N210F Flint Industries Inc 12/84, Flint Aviation Inc 1/87, N210F Flint Aviation Inc. Tulsa, Ok.
650-0068	1985. (N1314X) Cessna CoA 1/85, N273W M W Kellogg/Signal Holdings Inc 6/85,RTS Avn Sales Inc 5/85, Aircraft Services Corp 7/87, N985M Michelin Tire Corp 10/87, N985M Michelin Tire Corp. Greenville, SC.
650-0069	1984. (N13142) Cessna CoA 12/84, N910M Standard Oil Realty Corp 14 Jan 85, AMOCO Properties Inc 3/85, AMOCO Corp 4/89, N910M AMOCO Corp. Chicago, Il.
650-0070	1984. (N1315A) Cessna CoA 12/84, CONOCO Inc 1/85, N149C RTS Helicopter Services Inc 7/89, N370QS EJA/Comdisco Aviation Inc 11/89, N370TG 4/90, N370TG Comdisco Aviation Inc. Rosemont, Il.
650-0071	1985. (N1315B) Cessna CoA 2/85, N334H Hillenbrand Industries Inc 27 Mar 85,N334H Hillenbrand Industries Inc. Batesville, In.
650-0072	1985. (N1315C) Cessna CoA 2/85,N277W Wheelabrator-Frye/Signal Corp 2/85,Conseco Inc 10/87, N651CN 2/88, GECC-Oak Brook-Il 1/89, N651CN Conseco Inc. Carmel, In.
650-0073	1985. (N1315D) Cessna CoA 1/85, N650JA J A Albertson Enterprises 21 Feb 85, N650JA J A Albertson Enterprises, Boise, Id.
650-0074	1985. (N1315G) Cessna CoA 2/85, (N555EW) /85, N234YP GTE Directories Corp 1 Mar 85, N234YP Yellow Pages/GTE Directories Corp. Dallas, Tx.
650-0075	1984. N1315T Cessna CoA 12/84, AJT Aviation Inc 1/85, N16AJ 4/85, Frank Williams Engineering/Willhead Aviation Inc 11/88, Concorde Jet Service Inc 12/89, N16AJ Concord Jet Service Inc. Troutdale, Or.
650-0076	1985. N1315V Cessna CoA 1/85, Steelcase Inc 2/85, N376SC 7/85, N876SC 9/88, N876SC 9/88, Owners Jet Services Ltd 3/89, HB-VJT Jetag AG 11/89, HB-VJT Jetag AG. Zurich.
650-0077	1985. (N1315Y) Cessna CoA 3/85, N677CC /85, Allied Mutual Insurance Co 8/86, N701AG Allied Group 2/87, N701AG ASC/Allied Group, Des Moines, Ia.
650-0078	1985. (N13150) Cessna CoA 6/85, N652CC 6/85, Asian Aviation Services Inc 8/86, PK-TRJ Indonesian Air Transport 8/86, PK-TRJ Indonesian Air Transport, Jakarta.
650-0079	1985. (N1316A) Cessna CoA 3/85, N66ME Cooper Industries/Met Co 4/85, N290SC Coleman Co 6/87, N290SC to 650-0140, N288CC Dame Construction Co 2/88, N59CD 4/88, Raymond J Rutter-Ca 5/89, N217RR 6/89, N217RR Raymond J Rutter, Irvine, Ca.
650-0080	1985. N1316E Cessna CoA 4/85, Britt Aviation 5/85, McKee Baking Co 6/86, N69LD 9/86, N69LD McKee Baking Co. Collegedale, Tn.
650-0081	1985. (N1316N) Cessna CoA 5/85, PT-LGT Banco Brasileiro de Descontos 6/85, Sharp Industries 4/86,PT-LGT Sharp Industries, Sao Paulo.
650-0082	1985. (N13162) Cessna CoA 6/85, N651AP Arnold Palmer 7/85, N1AP 9/85, N1AP Arnold Palmer, Charlotte, NC
650-0083	1985. N13166 Cessna CoA 6/85,Britt Aviation Inc 7/85, Honeywell Inc 4/86, N944H 6/86, N944H Honeywell Inc. Minneapolis, Mn.
650-0084	1985. N13168 Cessna CoA 6/85, N85AW A L Williams & Assoc 7/85, Management Financial Services 2/90,N85AW Management Financial Services, Duluth, Ga.
650-0085	1985. N1317G Cessna CoA 7/85, JA8249 Nozaki & Co Ltd 10/85, N650DA Philko Aviation 12/85, Peer International I2/86, I-CIST Soc CISET SpA 14 Jul 86, I-CIST Soc. CISET-Cia Italiana Servizi Tecnici S.p.a. Brescia.
650-0086	1985. (N1317X) Cessna /85,PT-LHC Indaia Taxi Aereo Ltda 12 Nov 85,PT-LHC Indaia Taxi Aereo Ltda. Recife
650-0087	1985. (N1317Y) Cessna /85, N988H Honeywell Inc 8/85, N988H Honeywell Inc. Minneapolis, Mn.
650-0088	1985. (N13170) Cessna /85, PT-LGZ Bradesco Seguros SA 30 Sep 85, PT-LGZ Bradesco Seguros S.A. Rio de Janeiro.
650-0089	1985. (N13175) Cessna /85, N653CC N650JC Jepson Corp/EQK Aviation Corp 1/86, R Jepson-Il 9/89, Jepson Associates Inc 1/90, N650JC Jepson Assocs Inc. W Chicago, Il.
650-0090	1985. (N1318A) Cessna /85, N694CC 6/85, N1823S Champion Aircraft Spark Plug Co 1/86, Great Planes Sales 5/89, Charter Oak Fed Savings Bank 6/89, N651TC 10/89, N651TC CTC of Dayton Partnership, Vandalia, Oh.
650-0091	1985. N1318E Cessna /85, N68HC Hospital Corp of America 2/86,First Aero Services Corp 5/89, N58HC 7/89, PT-LUE Taxi Aerea Marilia SA /89, PT-LUE Taxi Aereo Marilia SA. Sao Paulo.
650-0092	1985. (N1318L) Cessna /85, N692CC /85, Boeing Equipment Holding Co 9/87,N692CC Boeing Equipment Holding Co. Wichita, Ks.
650-0093	1985. (N1318M) Cessna /85, N693CC /86, N773M Marshall & Ilsley Bank 4/86, N773M Marshall & Ilsley Bank, Milwaukee, Wi.
650-0094	1985. (N1318P) Cessna /85, N5114 General Motors Corp 17 Jan 86, N5114 General Motors Corp. Detroit, Mi.
650-0095	1985. (N1318Q) Cessna /85, N5115 General Motors Corp 3 Jan 86, N5115 General Motors Corp. Detroit, Mi.
650-0096	1985. (N1318X) Cessna /85, N5116 General Motors Corp 17 Jan 86, N5116 General Motors Corp. Detroit, Mi.

650-0097 1985. (N1318Y) Cessna /85, N697MC Manor Care Aviation Inc 9 Jan 86, N697MC Manor Care Aviation Inc. Silver Springs, Md.
650-0098 1985. (N13189) Cessna /85,N399W Williams Research Corp 10 Dec 85,N399W Williams Research Corp. Pontiac, Mi.
650-0099 1985. N1319B Cessna /85, (N555EW) Wausau Service Corp /85, N26SD SD Aviation Inc 24 Jan 86, N26SD SD Aviation Inc/Square D Co. Palatine, Il.
650-0100 1985. (N1319D) Cessna /85, N200LH De Luxe Check Printers 12 Jan 86, N200LH De Luxe Check Printers Inc. St. Paul, Mn.
650-0101 1985. N1319M Cessna /85,National Gypsum Co 31 Dec 85,N847G 4/86,N847G National Gypsum Co. Charlotte, NC
650-0102 1985. (N1319X) Cessna /85, (N406M) 6/85, N406MM 11/85, Martin Marietta Corp 21 Mar 86, N406MM Martin Marietta Corp. Bethesda, Md.
650-0103 1985. (N13194) Cessna /85, (N407M) 6/85, N407MM 11/85, Martin Marietta Corp 11 Apr 86, N407MM Martin Marietta Corp. Bethesda, Md.
650-0104 1986. N13195 Cessna /86, I-BETV Soc Benetton 9Sep86,Soc Olimpias SpA /87, I-BETV Soc. Olimpias S.p.a. Milan.
650-0105 1986. (N1320B) Cessna /86, N655CC /86, N15TT Cleo J Thompson-Tx 5/87, N48TT 9/90,N48TT Cleo J Thompson, Ozona, Tx.
650-0106 1986. (N1320K) Cessna /86, N106CC 1/86, IEPL Aviation Inc-New Zealand 27 Oct 86, GFN Aviation Services Inc 8/89, N106CC GFN Aviation Services Inc. NYC.
650-0107 1986. (N1302P) Cessna /86, N8000U 3/86, Ash Property Inc 6 Jun 86, N8000U Ash Property Inc. Dublin, Oh.
650-0108 1986. (N1302U) Cessna /86, N650Z Dana Commercial Credit Corp 7/86, CCD Air 13 Inc 1/90, N650Z Dana Commercial Credit Corp. Maumee, Oh.
650-0109 1986. (N1320V) Cessna /86, N650AT Quaker Oats Co 10/86, N2OAT /87, N134M Motorola Inc 3/90, N134M Motorola Inc. Schaumburg, Il.
650-0110 1986. (N1320X) Cessna /86, N76D Dayton Hudson Corp 6 Nov 86, N76D Dayton Hudson Corp. Minneapolis, Mn.
650-0111 1986. (N13204) Cessna /86, N500CM Cargill Inc 28 Jul 86, N500CM Cargill Inc. Minneapolis, Mn.
650-0112 1986. N1321A Cessna /86, N60BE Beatrice Foods/FRC Holding Inc III 12/86, N93DK 6/89, N93DK Beatrice Foods/FRC Holding Inc III, oak Brook, Il.
650-0113 1986. N1321C Cessna /86, Comdisco 1/87, N10ST System Services Inc 10/88,N10ST System Services Inc. New Orleans, La.
650-0114 1986. (N1321J) Cessna /86, N7000G Ash Property Inc 15 Oct 86, N7000G Ash Property Inc. Dublin, Oh.
650-0115 1986. N1321K Cessna /86, PT-LJC Transar Taxi Aereo 10/86, LINCE Taxi /89,PT-LJC LINCE Taxi Aereo Ltda. Sao Paulo.
650-0116 1986. (N1321L) Cessna /86, N78D Dayton Hudson Corp 31 Oct 86, N78D Dayton Hudson Corp. Minneapolis, Mn.
650-0117 1986. N1321N Cessna /86, F-GGAL Ste Euralair del 12 Dec 86, F-GGAL Euralair/S.P.F.D. Holding, Paris-Le Bourget,
650-0118 1986. (N13210) Cessna /86, Ash Property Inc 9 Dec 86, N6000J 9/86, Cessna 11/89, N118CD Westair/GPA Group-Shannon 1/90, Cessna 9/90, N118CD Cessna Aircraft Co. Wichita, Ks.
650-0119 1986. (N13217) Cessna /86, VR-BJS Flight Line Ltd 10/86, HB-VIN Aileron Anstalt-Vaduz 1/88, N100WH Willhead Aviation Inc/Frank Williams Engineering-UK 5/89, EC-EQX Gestair 9/89, EC-EQX Gestair, Madrid.
650-0120 1986. N13218 Cessna /86, N143AB 12/86, Allied Bendix Co 3/87, Jackson National Life Insurance Co 10/88, (N818TP) rsvd 11 Mar 89, Cathay Holdings Inc 5/90, N143AB Cathay Holdings Inc. Wilmington, De.
650-0121 1986. (N1322D) Cessna 11/86, D-CATP 5/87, N1322D 4/87, N121AG Cableair Inc 8/87, N121AG Cablevision Industries Corp. Liberty, NY.
650-0122 1986. (N1322K) Cessna /86, EC-EAS Gestair del 17 Jan 87, EC-EAS Gestair, Madrid.
650-0123 1986. (N1322Y) Cessna /86, N624CC 4/86, Hillenbrand Investment Advisors 12/86, N434H 2/87, N434H Hillenbrand Investment Advisors, Wilmington, De.
650-0124 1986. (N1322X) Cessna /86, N95CC 9/86, N7HV CPAC Properties Inc 3/87, Hoover Co 9/87, Chicago Pacific Corp 5/88, Terrible Herbst Inc 5/89, N650HC Collin Bros 9/89, N650HC Collins Bros/Terrible Herbst Inc. Las Vegas, Nv.
650-0125 1986. N13222 Cessna /86, EC-EAP Gestair 1/87, EC-EAP Gestair, Madrid.
650-0126 1986. (N1323A) Cessna /86, N55HF James T Hudson 1/87, N55HF James T Hudson, Rogers, Ar.
650-0127 1986. N1323D Cessna /86, N723BH Bell Helicopter Textron Inc 10 Mar 87, N723BH Bell Helicopter Textron Inc. Fort Worth, Tx.
650-0128 1986. (N1323K) Cessna /86, N628CC 12/86,N125Q Milliken & Co 27 Feb 87,N125Q Milliken & Co. Spartanburg, SC.
650-0129 1986. (N1323N) Cessna /86, N61BE Beatrice Companies 3/87, Jetcraft Corp 9/88, (N309TA) rsvd 2 Nov 88, First Aero Services Corp 5/89,PT-LUO Taxi Aerea Marilia SA 9/89,PT-LUO Taxi Aerea Marilia SA. Sao Paulo
650-0130 1986. (N1323Q) Cessna /86, N227LA 12/86, Unicharter Inc 6/87, N227BA 10/88, Shea Aviation Inc 5/89, N543SC 9/89, Motorola Inc 3/90, N159M 4/90, N159M Motorola Inc. Schaumburg, Il.
650-0131 1987. (N1323R) Cessna /87, CC-ECL CORFO 5/87, CC-ECL CORFO-Corporacion de Fomento, Santiago.
650-0132 1987. N1323V Cessna /87, N24KT Jostens Inc 16 Apr 87, MDFC Equipment Leasing 5/87, Randolph Wright Trustee 12/87, N24KT Jostens Inc. Minneapolis, Mn.

c/n	Entry
650-0133	1987. N1323X Cessna /87, N633CC 2/87,N133LE Industrial Equity/Brierly Investments Ltd 11/87, Wilmington Trust Co 12/89, N133LE Industrial Equity/Brierly Investments Ltd. Sydney.
650-0134	1986. (N1323Y) Cessna /87, N75RD Air Operations Co 5 Jun 87, N75RD Air Operations Co. Wilmington, De.
650-0135	1986. (N1324B) Cessna /87, N5109 General Mills Inc 3 Jun 87, N5109 General Mills Inc. Minneapolis, Mn.
650-0136	1986. (N1324D) Cessna /87, N841G General Dynamics Corp 1 Jul 87,N841G General Dynamics Corp. Clayton, MO
650-0137	1986. (N1324G) Cessna /87,N874G General Dynamics Corp 9 Jun 87,N874G General Dynamics Corp. Fort Worth, Tx.
650-0138	1986. (N1324R) Cessna /87,N828G General Dynamics Corp 9 Jun 87, N828G General Dynamics Corp. San Diego, Ca.
650-0139	1987. (N13242) Cessna /87, N4EG Edward S Gordon Co 17 Jun 87, N4EG Edward S Gordon Co. NYC.
650-0140	1987. (N1325D) Cessna /87, N95CC 5/87, Coleman Co 1/88, N290SC 3/88,N220CC 7/89,Sacramento Aviation Inc 10/90, N220CC Sacramento Aviation inc. Sacramento, Ca.
650-0141	1987. N1325E Cessna /87, N110TM Toyota Motor Sales USA Inc 11/87, N110TM Toyota Motor Sales USA Inc. Torrance, Ca.
650-0142	1987. N1325L Cessna /87, N142CC 1/87,Executive Car & Trucking Leasing 25 Feb 88, N20RD 12/88, N20RD Executive Car & Trucking Leasing, West Palm Beach, Fl.
650-0143	1987. N1325X Cessna /87, N143WR IEPL Avn/Wellesley Resources-New Zealand 11/87, N11NZ 5/89, N11NZ IEPL Aviation Inc/Wellesley Resources Ltd. Wellington, NZ.
650-0144	1987. N1325Y Cessna /87, N644CC 4/87, VH-KTI Australian Jet Charter 8/88,VH-KTI Australian Jet Charter, Sydney.
650-0145	1987. N1325Z Cessna /87, C-GCFP Canadian Forest Products Ltd 27 Nov 87, C-GCFP Canadian Forest Products Ltd. Vancouver, BC.
650-0146	1987. N13256 Cessna /87, N646CC 8/87, XA-PIP Aeropyc SA 3/88, XA-PIP AVEMEX/Aeropyc SA. Mexico City.
650-0147	1987. N13259 Cessna /87, OE-GNK Transair Bedarfsflugunternehmen 8/88, OE-GNK Transair Bedarfsflugunternehmen 8/88, PSK Leasing 12/90,N148N Motorola Inc 12/90,N148N Motorola Inc. Schaumberg, Il.
650-0148	1987. (N1326A) Cessna /87, N55SC Scharbauer Cattle Co 12/87, N55SC Scharbauer Cattle Co. Midland, Tx.
650-0149	1987. N1326B Cessna /87, N649CC 10/87, Cessna Citation 5/88, N139M Brunswick Bowling & Billiards 14 Jul 88, N139M Brunswick Bowling & Billiards, Muskegon, Mi.
650-0150	1987. (N1326D) Cessna /87, N150F Dana Corp 11/87, CCD Air 11 Inc 1/90, N150F Dana Corp. Toledo, Oh.
650-0151	1987. N1326G Cessna /87, G-MLEE Paramount/Mountleigh Air Services Ltd 3/88, N91D Jack Prewitt-Tx 3/90, N91D Jack Prewitt & Assocs. Bedford, Tx.
650-0152	1987. N4EG Cessna /87, N4EG to 650-0139, N1326H 4/87, N650AE 10/87, Atwood Enterprises Inc 5 Apr 88, N650AE Atwood Enterprises Inc. Rockford, Il.
650-0153	1988. N1326K Cessna /88, N95CC 5/88, N653CC 8/88, Carolina Mills Inc 10/88, N47CM 1/89, N47CM Carolina Mills Inc. Maiden, NC.
650-0154	1988. (N1326P) Cessna 1/88, N154CC 1/88, Henry Crown & Co 11/88, N696HC 10/89, N696HC Henry Crown & Co. Wheeling, Il.
650-0155	1988. N13264 Cessna /88, NCNB Corp 10/88, N788NB 12/88, N788NB NCNB Corp. Charlotte, NC.
650-0156	1988. N13267 Cessna /88, Safety-Kleen/SK-K Transportation Co 6/89, N68SK 9/89, N68SK Safety-Kleen/S-K Transportation Co. Wilmington, De.
650-0157	1988. N1327A Cessna /88, N657CC 8/88, Community Psychiatric Centers 18 Jan 89, N657CC Community Psychiatric Centers, Laguna Hills, Ca.
650-0158	1988. N1327B Cessna /88, N658CJ 7/88, N121AT Alltel Corp 17 Feb 89, N121AT Alltel Corp. Little Rock, AR
650-0159	1988. N13113 Cessna /88, Meridian Bancorp Inc 11/88, N683MB 1/89, N683MB Meridian Bancorp Inc. Reading
650-0160	1988. N1312D Cessna /88, N95CC 9/88, N24UM Plastene Supply Co 21 Feb 89, N831CB 7/89, N831CB Plastene Supply Co. Portageville, Mo.
650-0161	1988. (N1312K) Cessna /88, N161CC 3/89, I-ATSA Aerotaxi Sud SpA 14 Jul 89, I-ATSA Aerotaxi Sud S.p.A. Naples.
650-0162	1988. N1312Q Cessna /88, Jones Chemicals Inc 10 Nov 88, N202RB 3/89,N202RB Jones Chemicals Inc. Le Roy, NY.
650-0163	1988. N1312T Cessna /88, N137M Motorola Inc 25 Nov 88, N137M Motorola Inc. Schaumberg, Il.
650-0164	1988. N1312V Cessna /88, N138M Motorola Inc 12 Dec 88, N138M Motorola Inc. Schaumberg, Il.
650-0165	1989. N1312X Cessna /88, XA-FCP Aviacion Ejecutivo Condor SA 1/89, XC-PGN 2/90, XC-PGN
650-0166	1989. N1313J Cessna /89, PT-LTB Taxi Aereo Marilia SA 3/89, PT-LTB Taxi Aereo Marilia SA. Sao Paulo.
650-0167	1989. N667CC Cessna 3/89, Charlotte Pipe & Foundry Co 8/89,N532CC 10/89,N532CC Charlotte Pipe & Foundry Co. Charlotte, NC.
650-0168	1989. N1314H Cessna /89, N175J Dana Commercial Credit Corp 5/89, CCD Air 12 Inc 1/90, N175J Dana Commercial Credit Corp. Maumee, Oh.
650-0169	1988. N169CC Cessna 12/88, N88JJ Agri-Empire 18 Oct 89, N88JJ Agri-Empire, San Jacinto, Ca.
650-0170	1989. N1414V Cessna /89, N95CC Paris demo 6/89,N170CC 9/89,N32JJ ADM Milling Co 1/90,N32JJ ADM Milling Co. Wilmington, De..
650-0171	1989. N1354G Cessna /89, PT-LVF Taxi Aereo Marilia SA 4/89, PT-LVF Taxi Aereo Marilia S.A. Sao Paulo.

650-0172 1989. (N1772E) N672CC Cessna /89, Hillenbrand Industries Inc 6/89, N934H 7/89, N934H Hillenbrand Industries Inc. Batesville, In.
650-0173 1989. (N1779E) Cessna /89,N843G General Dynamics Corp 5 Oct 89,N843G General Dynamics Corp. Clayton, MO
650-0174 1989. (N1782E) Cessna /89, N674CC 4/89, D-CLUE EFS Flug-Service KG /90, D-CLUE EFS Flug-Service KG. Dusseldorf.
650-0175 1988. (N175J) Cessna regd 7/88, re-allocated to 650-0168, N1820E 9/89, N235KK Kenneth Kirschman 12/89, N235KK Kenneth Kirchman, Altamonte Springs, Fl.
650-0176 1988. N1874E Cessna 5/89, N176L 12/89, N1874E Warner Lambert Co 1/90, N1526L 3/90,N1526L Warner Lambert Co. Morris Plains, NJ.
650-0177 1989. N1930E Cessna 12/89, JA8367 Kozeni Housing 2/90, JA8367 Kozeni Housing, Hanamaki.
650-0178 1989. N1958E Cessna /89, N95CC 3/90, N178CC 5/90, JA8378 Nozaki Sanyo 18 Jun 90, JA8378 Nozaki Sanyo, Kikai.
650-0179 1989. (N1959E) Cessna /89, N679CC 12/89, XA-RMY 8/90, XA-RMY
650-0180 1990. (N2089A) Cessna /90, N768NB NCNB Corp 5/90, N768NB NCNB Corp. Charlotte, NC.
650-0181 1989. N2131A Cessna 12/89, N181CC /90,PT-OBX Banco Bradesco SA 6/90, PT-OBX Banco Bradesco, Osasco, SP
650-0182 1989. N26105 Cessna /89, N682CC 12/89, N491JB rsvd 24 Oct 90, N491JB Cessna Aircraft Corp. Wichita, KS
650-0183 1990. N2614Y Cessna 2/90, EI-SNN GPA Group 9/90, EI-SNN Westair/GPA Group, Shannon.
650-0184 1990. N2615D Cessna 3/90, N95CC 9/90, N1128B 10/90, Florida Light & Power Co 11/90,N1128B Florida Light & Power Co.
650-0185 1990. N2615L Cessna 3/90, N708CT Centel Corp 9/90, N708CT Centel Corp. Chicago, Il.
650-0186 1990. N2616L Cessna 3/90, PT-OAK 5/90, PT-OAK
650-0187 1990. N2617K Cessna /90, N187CM 9/90, N187CM Cessna Aircraft Co. Wichita, Ks.
650-0188 1990. N2617P Cessna /90,N587S Diamond Shamrock Leasing Inc 9/90,N587S Diamond Shamrock Leasing Inc. San Antonio, Tx.
650-0189 1990. N26174 Cessna 7/90, XA-RGS 9/90, XA-RGS Vitro Corporativo SA. Monterrey.
650-0190 1990. N142B Blount Inc 1 Nov 90, N142B Blount Inc. Montgomery, Al.
650-0191 1990. N191CM Cessna 12/90, N191CM Cessna Aircraft Co. Wichita, Ks.
650-0192 1990. N2622C Cessna 9/90, N15TT Cleo J Thompson-Tx 11/90, N15TT Cleo J Thompson, Ozona, Tx.
650-0193 1990. N2622Z Cessna 9/90, N95CC 11/90, N95CC Cessna Aircraft Co. Wichita, Ks.
650-0194 1990. N26228 Cessna 9/90, N111VW CIT Leasing/Volkswagen of America 12/90, N111VW Volkswagen of America Inc. Troy, Mi.
650-0195 1990. N26233 Cessna 9/90, N411MB /90, N411MB
650-0196 1990. (N2624L) Cessna /90, N196CM 5/90, N196CM
650-0198 1990. N650GA Cessna 8/90, N650GA
650-0199 1990. N900JD Cessna 5/90, N900JD
650-0200 1990. N650CM Cessna /90, N650CM
650-0201 1990. N40PH Cessna 8/90, N40PH

PREMIER 55

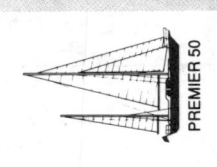

PREMIER 45

PREMIER 50

THE PREMIER COLLECTION

"The Premier range represents our ideas on a traditional approach to modern design concepts in performance cruising yachts. They reflect the traditional virtues of stability, comfort and control, while utilising modern methods of steel construction, coatings, rig design, interior space utilisation and deck arrangements, for short handed sailing. This combination of features will produce, we believe, a range of yachts exhibiting a timeless quality."
says Bill Dixon, designer of the Premier range.

Complementing the design skills of Bill Dixon, the Premier range is built to the highest standards of boatbuilding craftsmanship, while allowing the owner a free hand in the interior layout.
No wonder Premier Yachts are the first choice in blue water cruisers.
For full details of any of the highly specified and superbly built boats in our range, contact:

P · R · E · M · I · E · R
YACHTS

PREMIER YACHTS LIMITED · 30 CLOVELLY ROAD · SOUTHBOURNE · NR. EMSWORTH · HAMPSHIRE · PO10 8PD
TEL: 0243 374560 · FAX: 0243 376771

THE BIG DIFFERENCE

☐ Have you ever needed to know the owner of an aircraft and all you know is the N-Number of the aircraft? How about finding out if that same owner has more than one aircraft.

☐ Perhaps you are trying to locate a King Air C-90 and you only have a serial number. How could you locate all the C-90 owners in Iowa?

☐ Would you like to know how many King Air C-90's have changed hands in the last 30 days?

☐ IATS MICROFICHE LIBRARY can answer all these questions and more.

AVIATION MICROFICHE LIBRARY

The most cost efficient aircraft registry information available for compiling prospect lists, locating aircraft and researching aircraft ownership and activity.

DIRECTORIES:
- N-NUMBER
- ALPHABETICAL BY REGISTRANT
- MANUFACTURER, MAKE, MODEL AND SERIES
- TYPE - ZIP
- STATE - ZIP - ALPHA

SPECIAL REPORTS:
- MONTHLY ACTIVITY
- CHANGE OF POSSESSION
- RESERVED N-NUMBER
- AIRMEN

ADVANTAGES TO OUR LIBRARY

☐ Complete information on each aircraft on all directories.
☐ Make and model is clearly indicated - no confusing codes to decifer.
☐ Aircraft manufactured by more than one company are listed under the most popular manufacturer, i.e., Aerostar appear under Piper; Aero Commanders are all listed as Rockwell. Cross-references appear to aid the user.
☐ Special reports available only through IATS - Change of Possession.
☐ We have over 25 years of Aviation experience and, because we are located in Oklahoma City at the FAA Aeronautical Center, we obtain information faster than any other microfiche source.
☐ Toll Free number to call for assistance.

CALL TODAY FOR
AFFORDABLE SUBSCRIPTION RATE
INFORMATION

TENA STUDDARD
Marketing Director
& Research Consultant

I A T S Insured Aircraft Title Service Inc.
P.O. BOX 19527   OKLAHOMA CITY, OK 73144

1-800-654-4882
1-405-681-6663

TELECOPIER
405-681-9299

In 1989 we abstracted and issued title insurance policies on aircraft valued over $5,000,000,000.00

We now serve over 5,600 financial institutions around the world with title and lien status clearance, title insurance policies and bonded escrow services.

Your highly profitable aircraft financing activities can now have IATS protection extended to most countries throughout the world. Call us toll free today.

Insured Aircraft Title Service Inc.

358 LOMBARD STREET
SAN FRANCISCO, CALIFORNIA 94133
(415) 362-0544

WILL ROGERS WORLD AIRPORT
P.O. BOX 19527
OKLAHOMA CITY, OKLAHOMA 73144
(800) 654-4882

CUSTOM ENGINEERED AIRBORNE ENTERTAINMENT

- Custom engineered video and audio systems
- FAA/CAA approved
- Fully compatible with aircraft electrics and avionics
- O/E or retrofit
- Systems for VIP, corporate, government, and commercial aircraft

- Single/multi-monitor systems
- Fixed/removable systems
- New sophisticated control and switching system
- Proven worldwide capability and support
- Individual video 8 player and combined LCD colour monitor

JET-SETS FROM

Curtis & Green Ltd.
Arundel Road,
Uxbridge, Middlesex,
UB8 2RR. England.
Tel: 0895 31777
Telex: 8950051
Telefax: 0895 53267

Curtis & Green Ltd

Curtis & Green Systems Inc.
Arlington Airport,
18810 59th Ave. N.E.,
Arlington, WA98223, USA.
Tel: (206) 455 5426
Telex: 292969 UR
Telefax: (206) 435 3705

Falcon Jet Centre Ltd. Representatives for The Avions Marcel Dassault range of executive jets.

WE ARE BROKERS FOR ALL TYPES OF EXECUTIVE JETS & TURBOPROPS.

Contact MIKE CAPPUCCITTI or GRAHAM REITH
Falcon Jet Centre Ltd, Fairoaks Airport, Chobham, Surrey, GU24 8HU.
England. Tel: Chobham (09905) 7777. Telex: 858492 AMSALE G.

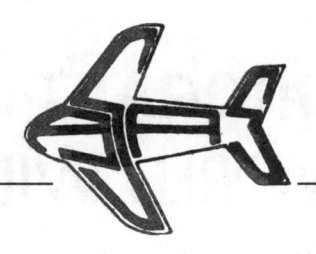

AIRCRAFT SUPPORT & SERVICES LTD

24 hour spares support with AOG service
7 days a week
at Stansted Airport
for all corporate owners
who need to have no delays
we can arrange all your requirements
from Flight Support together with TOTAL spares coverage

PARTS COVERAGE ON

Boeing 707	BAC1-11	Learjet	DC 8
Boeing 727	Gulfstream I,II,III,IV	Falcon	DC 10
Boeing 737	HS125	Jetstar	Airbus

Contact: SALES DEPT

Aircraft Support & Services

U.K. Office

Room 29, Building 56D
Stansted Airport
Stansted, Essex CM24 8QH

Tel: 0279 680411
Fax: 0279 680292
Tlx: 818355/ASAS-G

USA Office

1746 Stafford Drive
Orlando
Florida 32809

Tel: 407 8551758
Fax: 407 8590821
Tlx: 9102506496

CAN WE HELP YOU

JET AIRCRAFT SALES
WORLD WIDE

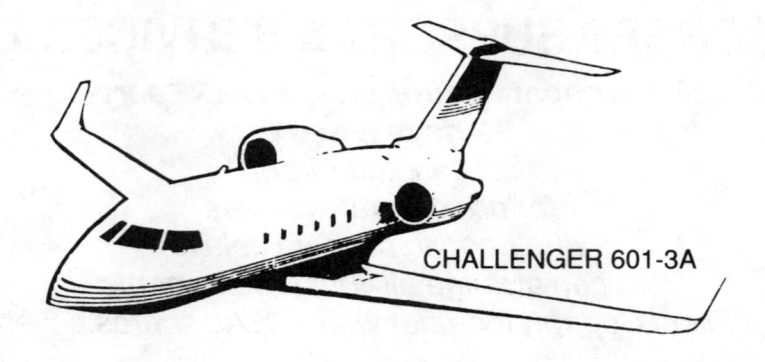

CHALLENGER 601-3A

Contact

GENE KINSELLA

P.O. BOX 548
PALM BEACH, FLORIDA 33480
PHONE 407/655-8259 TELEX 803446
FAX: 407 575 2591

BIZ-JET

DO YOU HAVE A REQUIREMENT FOR FREQUENT AND UP TO DATE INFORMATION?

Extensive data covering the period 1963–91 is available from my data base, and can be reproduced in varying formats:

- By type, country, region or state
- Production listings, current and historical
- Mailing lists
- Statistical analysis

ADDITIONALLY **BIZ JET NEWSLETTER**

outlines monthly changes in The Business Jet Fleet at £30.00 (UK), £40.00 (Europe), $70.00 (USA) per annum.

Enquiries & Quotations from:
Brian Gates
BG Business Aviation Services
17 Pine Croft Road, Wokingham, Berks RG11 4AL
Tel: 0734-776189   Fax: 0734-894387

---

jp airline-fleets international 91/92

25th edition

of the World's famous fleetlist-reference-yearbook. 38 000 aircraft operated by 4500 airlines with full details each, 90 postcard-sized colour photos. Abbreviation-lists etc.

BUCHairDATABASE and BUCHairDATA – the data (with or without software) of the **jp airline-fleets** int'l and/or **jp Biz-Jet** on electronic media, with the possibilities of up to monthly updates.

ASK FOR MORE DETAILS

BUCHair (U.K.) Ltd
P.O. Box 89
Reigate, Surrey RH2 7FG
Great Britain
Phone: +44 (0737) 76 28 30
Fax: +44 (0737) 76 28 73

Bucher Publications
P.O. Box 44
CH-8058 **Zurich-Airport**
Switzerland
Phone: +41 (01) 810 03 11
Fax: +41 (01) 810 85 45

Contents

Acknowledgments	=	II
Introduction by author	=	III
Foreword by publishers	=	IV
Civil operated (3A- to LX-)	=	5
United States of America (N)	=	29
Civil operated (OB- to ZS-)	=	116
Military operated	=	138
Production Lists	=	155

Country Index

Algeria (Civil)	=	6	Greece (Civil)	=	124	Pakistan (Military)	=	138
Algeria (Military)	=	138	Great Britain (Civil)	=	19	Paraguay (Civil)	=	136
Angola (Civil)	=	13	Great Britain (Military)	=	142	Peru (Civil)	=	116
Argentina (Civil)	=	29	Guatemala (Civil)	=	124	Peru (Military)	=	151
Argentina (Military)	=	144	Honduras (Civil)	=	23	Philippines (Civil)	=	123
Australia (Civil)	=	125	Honduras (Military)	=	143	Portugal (Civil)	=	12
Australia (Military)	=	153	India (Civil)	=	128	Portugal (Military)	=	140
Austria (Civil)	=	116	India (Military)	=	153	Qatar (Civil)	=	8
Bahamas (Civil)	=	11	Indonesia (Civil)	=	118	Rwanda (Civil)	=	7
Bahrain (Civil)	=	8	Indonesia (Military)	=	151	Sao Tome (Civil)	=	123
Barbados (Civil)	=	7	Iran (Civil)	=	14	Saudi Arabia (Civil)	=	23
Belgium (Civil)	=	117	Iran (Military)	=	141	Saudi Arabia (Military)	=	143
Belgium (Military)	=	151	Iraq (Civil)	=	135	Seychelles (Military)	=	152
Benin (Civil)	=	125	Ireland (Civil)	=	14	South Africa (Civil)	=	136
Bermuda (Civil)	=	127	Ireland (Military)	=	140	South Africa (Military)	=	154
Bolivia (Military)	=	139	Israel (Civil)	=	5	South Korea (Civil)	=	23
Botswana (Civil)	=	7	Israel (Military)	=	138	South Korea (Military)	=	143
Botswana (Military)	=	138	Italy (Civil)	=	25	Spain (Civil)	=	13
Brazil (Civil)	=	119	Italy (Military)	=	143	Spain (Military)	=	140
Brazil (Military)	=	152	Ivory Coast (Military)	=	152	Sudan (Civil)	=	124
Brunei (Civil)	=	125	Japan (Civil)	=	28	Swaziland (Civil)	=	5
Burkina Faso (Civil)	=	135	Japan (Military)	=	144	Sweden (Civil)	=	123
Burma (Military)	=	153	Jordan (Civil)	=	28	Sweden (Military)	=	152
Cameroun (Civil)	=	124	Jordan (Military)	=	144	Switzerland and		
Canada (Civil)	=	8	Kuwait (Civil)	=	7	Liechtenstein (Civil)	=	21
Canada (Military)	=	139	Kuwait (Military)	=	138	Syria (Military)	=	153
Cayman Islands (Civil)	=	128	Lebanon (Civil)	=	116	Taiwan Formosa (Military)	=	139
Central African Rep (Civil)	=	125	Liberia (Civil)	=	14	Tanzania (Civil)	=	5
Chile (Civil)	=	11	Libya (Civil)	=	5	Tchad (Civil)	=	125
Chile (Military)	=	139	Luxembourg (Civil)	=	29	Thailand (Military)	=	143
China (Civil)	=	23	Malawi (Civil)	=	6	Togo (Civil)	=	6
China (Military)	=	143	Malawi (Military)	=	138	Togo (Military)	=	138
Colombia (Civil)	=	23	Malaysia (Civil)	=	7	Tunisia (Civil)	=	125
Colombia (Military)	=	143	Malaysia (Military)	=	138	Turkey (Civil)	=	124
Congo Republic (Civil)	=	125	Malta (Civil)	=	7	Turkey (Military)	=	152
Cyprus (Civil)	=	5	Mauritania (Civil)	=	6	Uganda (Civil)	=	6
Denmark (Civil)	=	118	Mexico (Civil)	=	129	United Arab Emirates (Civil)	=	7
Denmark (Military)	=	151	Mexico (Military)	=	153	United States of America		
Djibouti (Civil)	=	28	Monaco (Civil)	=	5	(Civil)	=	29
Dominican Republic (Civil)	=	23	Morocco (Civil)	=	11	United States of America		
Ecuador (Military)	=	142	Morocco (Military)	=	139	(Military)	=	144
Egypt (Civil)	=	124	Mozambique (Civil)	=	11	Venezuela (Civil)	=	135
Egypt (Military)	=	152	Namibia (Civil)	=	125	Venezuela (Military)	=	154
Finland (Civil)	=	117	Netherlands (Civil)	=	118	Yemen (Civil)	=	8
Finland (Military)	=	151	New Zealand (Civil)	=	136	Yugoslavia (Civil)	=	135
France (Civil)	=	15	New Zealand (Military)	=	154	Yugoslavia (Military)	=	153
France (Military)	=	141	Niger (Military)	=	138	Zaire (Civil)	=	7
Gabon (Civil)	=	125	Nigeria (Civil)	=	5	Zaire (Military)	=	138
Germany Fed. Rep. (Civil)	=	12	Norway (Civil)	=	28	Zambia (Civil)	=	7
Germany Fed. Rep. (Military)	=	140	Norway (Military)	=	144	Zimbabwe (Civil)	=	136
Ghana (Military)	=	138	Oman (Civil)	=	7			